D1212698

The Common Cause

Published for the

Omohundro Institute of

Early American History and Culture,

Williamsburg, Virginia, by the

University of North Carolina Press,

Chapel Hill

The Common Cause

Creating Race and Nation in the
American Revolution

ROBERT G. PARKINSON

*The Omohundro Institute of
Early American History and Culture
is sponsored by the
College of William and Mary.
On November 15, 1996,
the Institute adopted the present name
in honor of a bequest from
Malvern H. Omohundro, Jr.*

Cover image: Johannes Adam Oertel,
Pulling Down the Statue of King George III, 1848, oil on canvas,
32¾ x 42⅛ inches, negative #6278, object #1925.6,
New-York Historical Society

Library of Congress Cataloging-in-Publication Data
Names: Parkinson, Robert G., author.
Title: The common cause : creating race and nation in the
American Revolution / by Robert G. Parkinson.
Description: Chapel Hill : Published for the Omohundro Institute of Early
American History and Culture, Williamsburg, Virginia, by the University of North
Carolina Press, [2016] | Includes bibliographical references and index.
Identifiers: LCCN 2016000574| ISBN 9781469626635 (cloth : alk. paper) |
ISBN 9781469626925 (ebook)
Subjects: LCSH: United States—History—Revolution, 1775–1783—
Propaganda. | United States—History—Revolution, 1775–1783—
Social aspects. | Racism—United States—History—18th century.
Classification: LCC E209 .P34 2016 | DDC 973.3/1—dc23
LC record available at http://lccn.loc.gov/2016000574

*This publication was supported by a donation
from the Dean's Office of Harpur College of Arts and Sciences,
Binghamton University.*

For Abby and Carly

ACKNOWLEDGMENTS

This book is about the consequences of setting thoughts down in type, a process that can have terrible power. Some people in this book used that power to motivate other people through print, at the tragic expense of still others. Those words, set into type, come down to us as artifacts too easily drained of the emotions and intentions that surrounded their original composition. Now this book, too, is an artifact, another collection of types conveying an argument. When I look at this relic, however, I will be pleasantly reminded of all of the emotions and intentions of the good people whose support was essential in the decade it took to make it a tangible object. Years from now, it gives me great pleasure, this object will be a capsule on my shelf containing the memory of all the intangible love that is interwoven into the skeins of wood pulp that comprise each page.

First, there is Peter Onuf. For a decade and a half, ever since he asked me to come along on a very memorable walk in Knoxville, Peter has been a model in just about every way: as a mentor, a scholar, a teacher, and a person. It has been my great, great fortune to be counted among his students. He knew when to push and when to let me be. He listened and offered consistently excellent advice on all topics about the present and the past. I know he wished to have seen this artifact several years ago, but I wanted to get it right, in no small part as a testament to the scholarship he taught and practiced. My gratitude to him is boundless. Thank you so much, Peter.

Other teachers in Charlottesville—the late Steve Innis, John Stagg, Brian Balogh, and Ed Russell—continue to shape my views of the American past. At the head of this list is Edward Ayers. Though this book is not about his war, Ed's influence is manifest throughout. He is another model for how historians should write, teach, and engage the American public. Thank you, Ed, not only for your moving and infectious engagement with the past, but also your taking a fellow University of Tennessee alum under your wing.

Before Charlottesville, my mentor in Knoxville was the indomitable Bruce Wheeler. This book would not exist if it hadn't been for Bruce and his writing partner, the late Susan Becker, taking a special interest in a naïve undergraduate and channeling their excitement for the past into professional avenues. Wheeler's particular skill to weave stories about the American past inspired countless students. I, certainly, can attest to being among them. Thank you, Professors Wheeler and Becker.

At various stages this project has received institutional support in the form of research and writing fellowships from the International Center for Jefferson Studies, the David Library of the American Revolution, the Colonial Williamsburg Foundation, the Clements Library at the University of Michigan, and the Library Company of Philadelphia. My thanks go to Andrew O'Shaughnessy of the ICJS, Meg McSweeney at the DLAR, James Horn, now of the Jamestown Rediscovery Foundation, John Dann of the Clements Library, and James Green at the LCP for their support and assistance.

I owe Jim Green of the Library Company my great thanks for putting me up in the Cassatt House next to Brad Jones in September 2004. He said he thought it would be good if I got to know Brad, then over from Scotland working on similar issues regarding Revolutionary mobilization. He couldn't have been more right. That coincidence turned into one of my most important friendships. Although he scarcely knew it, a few timely phone conversations with Brad repeatedly saved this project from collapse. His hospitality, encouragement, collegiality, and support are present throughout these pages. Thank you, Brad and Flo.

My further thanks to some pretty great friends (and pretty great historians) who have been in my corner over the years: Jan Lewis, Brian Murphy, Johann Neem, James Lewis, Charlene Boyer Lewis, Honor Sachs, Ben Carp, Carrie Janney, Molly Warsh, and Leonard Sadosky.

Jim Horn has been very important to this study in several capacities, but perhaps the most important was his arranging of fellows at the Rockefeller Library to give informal talks to interested folk in Williamsburg. When it came time for mine, Ron Hoffman, Chris Grasso, and Fredrika Teute slipped into the back row of the room. The conversation that afternoon didn't go as I would have liked, so those three very busy pillars of the Omohundro Institute invited me for coffee the next morning to iron out some of my project's wrinkles. That was way over and above, the first of many examples of their generosity and encouragement of young scholars.

From 2007 to 2009 I had the great fortune to continue those conversations as a National Endowment of the Humanities Post-Doctoral fellow at the Omohundro Institute of Early American History and Culture. The NEH and the Institute gave me the gift of time to mull the questions and concepts

Acknowledgments

at the heart of this book. The decision I made early on in Williamsburg to rewrite the entire work was only possible because of this incredible opportunity. Ron, Chris, and, especially, Fredrika have continued to be great believers in this project and its author. Their confidence in me has been a sustaining force over many years, and I am deeply grateful for their investment. Ron's guidance and community building, Chris's critical eye and sage advice, and Fredrika's vision and impeccable standards were central in the creation of this book. It is an honor to be a part of the Institute series.

My thanks to Institute staff up and down the hall—Ginny, Kathy, Gil, Beverly, Ron, and Sally—for making my time there so pleasant. Special thanks to Kim Foley for all her help with everything technological, especially when my hard drive started clicking. Very special thanks to Mendy Gladden for her friendship, letting me accompany her on dog walks at the end of long writing days. Others in Williamsburg listened and lent much-needed support, especially my fellow fellows Mark Hanna and Joe Cullon, as well as W&M faculty Brett Rushforth, Paul Mapp, and Jim Allegro.

My two years in Williamsburg came in the middle of my tenure at Shepherd University in Shepherdstown, West Virginia. Thanks to the support and creative leadership of Dow Benedict, I was able to take advantage of this opportunity. I couldn't have asked for more from my colleagues in the history department at Shepherd since 2005. Their friendship for nearly a decade means a great deal to me. Thank you to Anders Henriksson, David Gordon, and, especially, Sally Brasher and Julia Sandy. I would not have seen this to completion without Sally's friendship and support through hard times. Julia patiently read and listened to page after page, draft after draft, with much-appreciated affection. Thanks, you two, for everything. My thanks also to the generosity of Ray and Madeline Johnston and the Shepherd University Foundation for bestowing upon me the Johnston Chair in American History. Further, the West Virginia Humanities Council also offered monetary support to aid in the completion of this book. Although the manuscript was finished when I arrived at Binghamton University last fall, the support of my new department deserves its own mention. Thanks to my new colleagues, especially Howard Brown, who offered expertise right at the finish line, and the unrivaled generosity and humor of Diane Miller Sommerville. My express thanks to Anne McCall and the Dean's Office of Harpur College of Arts and Sciences at Binghamton University for financially supporting this book's publication.

Edward Countryman, Alan Taylor, and David Waldstreicher all read this manuscript at different stages, offering criticism and encouragement.

David's advice was especially influential to my revisions; this book is far superior thanks to his penetrating analysis and substantive suggestions.

The staffs at several archives helped me track down newspapers and other documents crucial to this study. Thank you to the archivists in the manuscript divisions of New York Public Library, New-York Historical Society, Boston Public Library, Earl Gregg Swem Library, Massachusetts Historical Society, South Carolina Historical Society, Perkins Library, Wilson Library, Carnegie Library of Pittsburgh, Virginia Historical Society, and American Antiquarian Society. The bulk of the research for this book took place in front of the microfilm readers at a place I dearly cherish, Alderman Library at the University of Virginia. My great thanks to all the staff at Alderman for their help in locating stray microfilm reels and unjamming printers.

Nadine Zimmerli read the entire manuscript, offered superb advice, and was an overall indispensable fount of encouragement and cheer, taking great care of me at late stages of a long game. Kathy Burdette copy-edited this tome, smoothed out lots of rough edges, saved me from several errors, and identified my latent Pittsburgh writing tendencies, all without damaging our friendship. Several apprenti—Katherine Cartwright, Justin Clement, Amanda Gibson, Casey Schmitt, and Stephen Vickory—checked the footnotes (poor souls), Gerry Krieg drew the maps, and Rebecca Wrenn, the graph. Thank you Nadine, Kathy, Gerry, Rebecca, and the apprenti for your help.

Portions of chapters 3 and 9 appeared previously in John Craig Hammond and Matthew Mason, eds., *Contesting Slavery: The Politics of Bondage and Freedom in the New American Nation* (Charlottesville, Va., 2011), 49–68; Francis D. Cogliano, ed., *A Companion to Thomas Jefferson* (Malden, Mass., 2012), 44–59; and Rachel Hammersley, ed., *Revolutionary Moments: Reading Revolutionary Texts* (London, 2015), 53–60.

By happenstance, my parents, Jane and Jerry Parkinson, retired to Williamsburg even before I went to Charlottesville. They were gracious enough to welcome me back home during my two years there, a very small portion of the tangible and intangible support they have given through the years. They nurtured and developed their son's connection to the past from a very young age. Sharon Parkinson and Susan Parkinson Carter were proud of me, even if that manifested itself in exasperation of how long this process was taking. The family paragraph in acknowledgments is usually pretty standard fare: couldn't have done it without you. But in this case I mean it.

Finally, I wish I could echo a favorite line from the acknowledgments of one of my favorite historians, Jan Lewis, who expressed happiness about her son's "cheerful obliviousness" to the writing of her first book. My daughters, the dedicatees, can't say the same. They were quite aware of the demands of this one. Abigail was born the week I proposed the dissertation, which this book now only vaguely resembles. She's in high school now; it's grown up with her and her sister, Caroline. My hopes are that watching their father write and write and write for a decade has taught them lessons about perseverance (occasionally cheerful). And that someday, eventually, projects do finish, and it is time for new pages. Thank you, Abby and Carly, for your love, support, and genuine enthusiasm.

CONTENTS

ILLUSTRATIONS

PLATES

MAPS

GRAPH

ABBREVIATIONS

BOOKS AND PERIODICALS

4 *Am. Archives*

    M. St. Clair Clarke and Peter Force, eds., *American Archives*, 4th
Ser., *Containing a Documentary History of the English Colonies in North
America . . .* , 6 vols. (Washington, D.C., 1837–1846).

5 *Am. Archives*

    Peter Force, ed., *American Archives*, 5th Ser., *Consisting of a Collection
of Authentick Records, State Papers, Debates, and Letters and Other Notices of
Publick Affairs . . .* , 3 vols. (Washington, D.C., 1848–1853).

DHFFC

    Linda Grant De Pauw et al., eds., *Documentary History of the First Federal
Congress of the United States of America, March 4, 1789–March 3, 1791*
(Baltimore, 1972–).

Early American Imprints

    Charles Evans, ed., *Early American Imprints, Series I: Evans, 1639–1800*
(1903–1959; rpt., New York, [1983?]–).

JAH

    Journal of American History

JCC

    Worthington C. Ford et al., eds., *Journals of the Continental Congress,
1774–1789*, 34 vols. (Washington, D.C., 1904–1937).

JER

    Journal of the Early Republic

LDC

    Paul H. Smith et al., eds., *Letters of Delegates to Congress, 1774–1789*,
26 vols. (Washington, D.C., 1976–2000).

PBF

    Leonard W. Labaree et al., eds., *The Papers of Benjamin Franklin* (New
Haven, Conn., 1959–).

PGW: RW

W. W. Abbot et al., eds., *The Papers of George Washington: Revolutionary War Series* (Charlottesville, Va., 1985–).

PHL

Philip M. Hamer et al., eds., *The Papers of Henry Laurens,* 16 vols. (Columbia, S.C., 1968–2003).

PJA

Robert J. Taylor et al., eds., *The Papers of John Adams* (Cambridge, Mass., 1977–).

PJM

William T. Hutchinson et al., eds., *The Papers of James Madison,* 17 vols. (Chicago, 1962–1991).

PMHB

Pennsylvania Magazine of History and Biography

PNG

Richard K. Showman et al., eds., *The Papers of General Nathanael Greene,* 13 vols. (Chapel Hill, N.C., 1976–2005).

PTJ

Julian P. Boyd et al., eds., *The Papers of Thomas Jefferson* (Princeton, N.J., 1950–)

Rev. Va.

Robert L. Scribner et al., eds., *Revolutionary Virginia: The Road to Independence; A Documentary Record,* 7 vols. (Charlottesville, Va., 1973–1983).

VMHB

Virginia Magazine of History and Biography

WMQ

William and Mary Quarterly

ARCHIVES

AAS

American Antiquarian Society, Worcester, Massachusetts

BPL

Boston Public Library, Massachusetts

CL

William L. Clements Library, The University of Michigan

HSP

Historical Society of Pennsylvania, Philadelphia

LoC
  Library of Congress, Washington, D.C.
MDHS
  Maryland Historical Society, Baltimore
NYPL
  Manuscripts and Archives Division, New York Public Library
SCHS
  South Carolina Historical Society, Charleston
Swem
  Special Collections Research Center, Earl Gregg Swem Library,
  College of William and Mary, Williamsburg, Virginia
VHS
  Virginia Historical Society, Richmond

NEWSPAPERS

American Gazette
  The American Gazette: or, the Constitutional Journal (Salem, Mass.)
American Journal
  The American Journal and General Advertiser (Providence, R.I.)
Boston Evening-Post
  The Boston Evening-Post: and the General Advertiser (Powars)
Boston Evening Post (White & Adams)
  The Evening Post; and the General Advertiser (White & Adams)
Boston Gazette
  The Boston Gazette, and Country Journal
Boston News-Letter
  The Massachusetts Gazette; and the Boston Weekly News-Letter
Boston Post-Boy
  The Massachusetts Gazette, and the Boston Post-Boy and Advertiser
Cape-Fear Mercury
  The Cape-Fear Mercury (Wilmington, N.C.)
Connecticut Courant
  The Connecticut Courant (Hartford)
Connecticut Gazette
  The Connecticut Gazette and the Universal Intelligencer (New London)
Connecticut Journal
  The Connecticut Journal (New Haven)
Constitutional Gazette
  The Constitutional Gazette (New York)

Continental Journal
    The Continental Journal, and Weekly Advertiser (Boston)
Dresden Mercury
    The Dresden Mercury, and the Universal Intelligencer (Hanover, N.H.)
Dunlap's Maryland Gazette
    Dunlap's Maryland Gazette; or, the Baltimore General Advertiser
Essex Gazette
    The Essex Gazette (Salem, Mass.)
Essex Journal
    The Essex Journal and the Massachusetts and New-Hampshire General Advertiser
    (Newburyport, Mass.)
Exeter Journal
    The Exeter Journal, or, New Hampshire Gazette
Freeman's Journal (Philadelphia)
    The Freeman's Journal: or, the North-American Intelligencer (Philadelphia)
Freeman's Journal (Portsmouth)
    The Freeman's Journal, or New-Hampshire Gazette (Portsmouth)
Gazette, of the State of South-Carolina
    The Gazette, of the State of South-Carolina (Charleston)
Georgia Gazette
    The Georgia Gazette (Savannah)
Independent Chronicle
    The Independent Chronicle (Boston)
Independent Gazetteer
    The Independent Gazetteer; or, the Chronicle of Freedom (Philadelphia)
Independent Ledger
    The Independent Ledger, and American Advertiser (Boston)
Maryland Gazette
    The Maryland Gazette (Annapolis)
Maryland Journal
    The Maryland Journal, and the Baltimore Advertiser
Massachusetts Gazette
    The Massachusetts Gazette, or the Springfield and Northampton Weekly
    Advertiser
Massachusetts Spy
    The Massachusetts Spy (Boston)
New-England Chronicle
    The New-England Chronicle: or, the Essex Gazette (Cambridge)

New-Hampshire Gazette
    The New-Hampshire Gazette, and Historical Chronicle (Portsmouth)
New Hampshire Gazette (Exeter)
    The New Hampshire Gazette, or Exeter Morning Chronicle
New-Jersey Gazette
    The New-Jersey Gazette (Trenton)
New-Jersey Journal
    The New-Jersey Journal (Chatham)
Newport Gazette
    The Newport Gazette (Rhode Island)
Newport Mercury
    The Newport Mercury (Rhode Island)
New-York Gazette
    The New-York Gazette; and the Weekly Mercury
New-York Gazetteer
    New-York Gazetteer, or, Northern Intelligence (Albany)
New-York Journal
    The New-York Journal, and the General Advertiser
New-York Mercury
    The New-York Mercury
New York Packet
    The New York Packet
New-York Weekly Journal
    The New-York Weekly Journal
North-Carolina Gazette
    The North-Carolina Gazette (Newbern)
Norwich Packet
    The Norwich Packet (Connecticut)
Pennsylvania Chronicle
    The Pennsylvania Chronicle, and Universal Advertiser (Philadelphia)
Pennsylvania Evening Post
    The Pennsylvania Evening Post (Philadelphia)
Pennsylvania Gazette
    The Pennsylvania Gazette (Philadelphia)
Pennsylvania Journal
    The Pennsylvania Journal; and the Weekly Advertiser (Philadelphia)
Pennsylvania Ledger
    *The Pennsylvania Ledger: or the Virginia, Maryland, Pennsylvania,
    & New-Jersey Weekly Advertiser* (Philadelphia)

Pennsylvania Mercury
    Story & Humphreys's Pennsylvania Mercury, and Universal Advertiser
    (Philadelphia)
Pennsylvania Packet
    The Pennsylvania Packet, or the General Advertiser (Philadelphia)
Providence Gazette
    The Providence Gazette; and Country Journal (Rhode Island)
Rivington's New-York Gazetteer
    Rivington's New-York Gazetteer; or the Connecticut, New-Jersey, Hudson's River,
    and Quebec Weekly Advertiser
Royal American Gazette
    The Royal American Gazette (New York)
Royal Gazette (Charleston)
    The Royal Gazette (Charleston, S.C.)
Royal Gazette (New York)
    The Royal Gazette (New York)
Royal Georgia Gazette
    The Royal Georgia Gazette (Savannah)
Royal Pennsylvania Gazette
    The Royal Pennsylvania Gazette (Philadelphia)
Royal South-Carolina Gazette
    The Royal South-Carolina Gazette (Charleston)
Salem Gazette
    The Salem Gazette, and General Advertiser (Salem, Mass.)
South-Carolina and American General Gazette
    The South-Carolina and American General Gazette (Charleston)
South-Carolina Gazette
    The South-Carolina Gazette (Charleston)
South-Carolina Gazette; And Country Journal
    The South-Carolina Gazette; And Country Journal (Charleston)
Vermont Gazette
    The Vermont Gazette, or Freeman's Depository (Bennington)
Virginia Gazette (Clarkson & Davis)
    The Virginia Gazette (Williamsburg; Clarkson & Davis)
Virginia Gazette (Dixon & Hunter)
    The Virginia Gazette (Williamsburg; Dixon & Hunter)
Virginia Gazette (Dixon & Nicolson)
    The Virginia Gazette (Richmond; Dixon & Nicolson)

Virginia Gazette (Hayes)

    The Virginia Gazette, or, the American Advertiser (Richmond; Hayes)

Virginia Gazette (Nicolson & Prentis)

    The Virginia Gazette, or Weekly Advertiser (Richmond; Nicolson & Prentis)

Virginia Gazette (Pinkney)

    The Virginia Gazette (Williamsburg; Pinkney)

Virginia Gazette (Purdie)

    The Virginia Gazette (Williamsburg; Purdie)

Virginia Gazette (Purdie & Dixon)

    The Virginia Gazette (Williamsburg; Purdie & Dixon)

Virginia Gazette (Rind)

    The Virginia Gazette (Williamsburg; Rind)

Virginia Gazette, or the Norfolk Intelligencer

    The Virginia Gazette, or the Norfolk Intelligencer (Holt)

The Common Cause

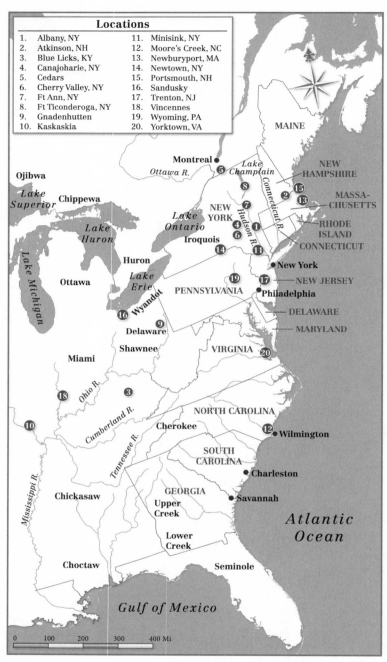

Locations

1. Albany, NY	11. Minisink, NY
2. Atkinson, NH	12. Moore's Creek, NC
3. Blue Licks, KY	13. Newburyport, MA
4. Canajoharie, NY	14. Newtown, NY
5. Cedars	15. Portsmouth, NH
6. Cherry Valley, NY	16. Sandusky
7. Ft Ann, NY	17. Trenton, NJ
8. Ft Ticonderoga, NY	18. Vincennes
9. Gnadenhutten	19. Wyoming, PA
10. Kaskaskia	20. Yorktown, VA

Map 1. *British North America during the American Revolution.*

Drawn by Gerry Krieg

INTRODUCTION

The first order of business was to clear the galleries. After all spectators had been escorted out of the chamber late in the afternoon of March 14, 1774—a "day of such importance"—the House of Commons opened debate on how to punish Boston for destroying nearly 100,000 pounds of the East India Company's tea leaves. A week before, the king had informed Parliament of the "violent and outrageous Proceedings" that had taken place in Boston Harbor the past December and sought legislation "for better securing the Execution of the Laws, and the just Dependence of the Colonies upon the Crown and Parliament of *Great Britain.*" For the remainder of March, Parliament debated the Boston Port Bill, the first of what would later be known as the set of punitive measures called the Coercive Acts. The sticking point was whether Boston should be singled out. Lord North insisted that Boston was the "ringleader in all riots" and therefore "ought to be the principal object of our attention for punishment."[1]

Focusing their wrath on Massachusetts made sense. Despite the myriad things they did not recognize about the colonial complaints, the North ministry was certain that American unity was impossible. The prevailing wisdom in Britain, continually reinforced by colonial correspondents, imperial officials, military officers, returning travelers, and Atlantic merchants, was that the resistance movement in America was anything but universal. The mainland American colonies, they were sure—and reassured—could never sustain a united front. The thirteen colonies simply could not get along with one another. Since Boston could not count on any steady friends, there was no need for a general interdiction. Or, as another member of Parliament

---

1. R. C. Simmons and P. D. G. Thomas, eds., *Proceedings and Debates of the British Parliaments respecting North America, 1754–1783* (White Plains, N.Y., 1982–), IV, 31, 55–82 (Mar. 14, 1774, debate), esp. 55, 79. See also [William Cobbett], ed., *The Parliamentary History of England: From the Earliest Period to the Year 1803....* (London, 1806–1820), XVII, 1159, 1163–1184.

suggested, it "appears to be wise, first, to single out Boston as the principal ringleader of the whole disturbance, and begin this punishment there, in order to see what effect the proceedings will have." Few anticipated how widespread, how continental, those effects would be.[2]

Parliament and the North ministry were right to foresee American disunity. As the son of one Boston patriot put it fifty years after the Revolution, "The real cause of wonder is, that a harmony so perfect, and a union . . . so general, should have been effected at such an early period." The odds against sustained, effective political cohesion were indeed long. From the benches of the House of Commons in the spring of 1774, they seemed incredible.[3]

After all, the catalog of forces acting against American unity was impressive. Previous attempts at colonial union had been abortive, most famously at Albany in 1754. Long-standing provincialism and jealousies, running simultaneously along both north-south and east-west axes, abided. Accusations that backcountry settlers were even more "savage" than Indians redounded from Atlantic settlements while frontiersmen countered that they, in fact, were the true representations of masculine courage and pure liberty. Internal conflicts surfaced throughout the continent. Clashes over land rights, political access, religious toleration, and good government flared up during the 1760s and 1770s in New York, New Jersey, Virginia, and the Carolinas. Disadvantaged men and women in Philadelphia, Boston, and New York City demanded economic and political reforms. Border controversies and jurisdictional tensions sometimes devolved into violence and threatened relations between Pennsylvania and Virginia, New York and New Hampshire, and Connecticut and Pennsylvania. And agitation against the institution of slavery was rising to unprecedented levels in the early 1770s.[4]

2. [Cobbett], ed., *Parliamentary History of England*, XVII, 1181. British notions of American disunity and subsequent effects on imperial policy are explored in Julie Flavell, "British Perceptions of New England and the Decision for a Coercive Colonial Policy, 1774–1775," in Flavell and Stephen Conway, eds., *Britain and America Go to War: The Impact of War and Warfare in Anglo-America, 1754–1815* (Gainesville, Fla., 2004), 95–115.

3. Josiah Quincy, *Memoir of the Life of Josiah Quincy Jun. of Massachusetts* (Boston, 1825), 117.

4. For background on the Albany Congress, see Fred Anderson, *Crucible of War: The Seven Years' War and the Fate of Empire in British North America, 1754–1766* (New York, 2000), 77–85; Timothy J. Shannon, *Indians and Colonists at the Crossroads of Empire: The*

Many on both sides of the Atlantic surely concurred with the vicar of Greenwich, England, Andrew Burnaby: "Fire and water are not more heterogeneous than the different colonies in North America." Burnaby's pronouncements, published in 1775, contained a dark codicil. "In short," he prophesied, "such is the difference of character, of manners, of religion, of interest, of the different colonies, that I think . . . were they left to them-

Albany Congress of 1754 (Ithaca, N.Y., 2000). For colonial provincialism, see Jack P. Greene, "A Fortuitous Convergence: Culture, Circumstance, and Contingency in the Emergence of the New American Nation," in Greene, *Imperatives, Behaviors, and Identities: Essays in Early American Cultural History* (Charlottesville, Va., 1992), 290–309; Merrill Jensen, "The Sovereign States: Their Antagonisms and Rivalries and Some Consequences," in Ronald Hoffman and Peter J. Albert, eds., *Sovereign States in an Age of Uncertainty* (Charlottesville, Va., 1981), 226–250. For white savagery, see Peter Silver, *Our Savage Neighbors: How Indian War Transformed Early America* (New York, 2008); Jane T. Merritt, *At the Crossroads: Indians and Empires on a Mid-Atlantic Frontier, 1700–1763* (Chapel Hill, N.C., 2003), 285–292; Patrick Griffin, *American Leviathan: Empire, Nation, and Revolutionary Frontier* (New York, 2007).

New York: Sung Bok Kim, *Landlord and Tenant in Colonial New York: Manorial Society, 1664–1775* (Chapel Hill, N.C., 1978); Edward Countryman, *A People in Revolution: The American Revolution and Political Society in New York, 1760–1790* (Baltimore, 1981). New Jersey: Brendan McConville, *These Daring Disturbers of the Public Peace: The Struggle for Property and Power in Early New Jersey* (Ithaca, N.Y., 1999), 239–245. Virginia: Rhys Isaac, *The Transformation of Virginia, 1740–1790* (Chapel Hill, N.C., 1982), 161–177. North Carolina: Marjoleine Kars, *Breaking Loose Together: The Regulator Rebellion in Pre-Revolutionary North Carolina* (Chapel Hill, N.C., 2002); Wayne E. Lee, *Crowds and Soldiers in Revolutionary North Carolina: The Culture of Violence in Riot and War* (Gainesville, Fla., 2001). South Carolina: Rachel N. Klein, *Unification of a Slave State: The Rise of the Planter Class in the South Carolina Backcountry, 1760–1808* (Chapel Hill, N.C., 1990); Richard Maxwell Brown, *The South Carolina Regulators* (Cambridge, Mass., 1963). For growing urban discontent, see Gary B. Nash, *The Urban Crucible: The Northern Seaports and the Origins of the American Revolution* (Cambridge, Mass., 1979); Paul A. Gilje, *The Road to Mobocracy: Popular Disorder in New York City, 1763–1834* (Chapel Hill, N.C., 1987), 37–68; Benjamin L. Carp, *Rebels Rising: Cities and the American Revolution* (New York, 2007). For more on intercolonial border conflicts, see David C. Hendrickson, *Peace Pact: The Lost World of the American Founding* (Lawrence, Kans., 2003); Peter S. Onuf, *The Origins of the Federal Republic: Jurisdictional Controversies in the United States, 1775–1787* (Philadelphia, 1983). For abolitionism in the eighteenth-century British Atlantic, see Christopher Leslie Brown, *Moral Capital: Foundations of British Abolitionism* (Chapel Hill, N.C., 2006).

selves there would soon be a civil war, from one end of the continent to the other; while the Indians and Negroes would, with better reason, impatiently watch the opportunity of exterminating them all together."[5]

* * *

Although many of these controversies, conflicts, and fissures had ties to the burgeoning crisis over Britain's efforts to reform the empire in the 1760s and 1770s, they were not directly about that particular problem. That problem—the imperial relationship—invited a new host of divisions, most notably thousands of colonists who believed that Parliament was within its constitutional rights to make some reforms to their empire or that the ancient liberty of Englishmen meant respecting representative government and order as defined by the crown.

Those who opposed imperial reform devised a capacious campaign to prove that their definition of opaque words such as "liberty," "rights," "obligation," "consent," and "allegiance" were the correct ones. At bottom, what would become known as the American Revolution was a massive argument over the meaning of those words, whom they applied to, and who were the most legitimate, responsible guardians of those ideals; success, then, meant convincing enough of the colonial public that the people who called themselves "whigs" or "patriots" were those guardians. The leaders of that movement had to craft an appeal that simultaneously overcame some of those inherited fault lines and jealousies, neutralized their opponents' claims, and made them the only true protectors of freedom. They needed to make what they called "the cause" common.

The phrase "common cause" was well established long before the 1770s. In the seventeenth century, it appeared as a vague call to Protestants to join forces against their religious foes, whether Catholics or Muslims. The subtitle of William Chillingworth's 1638 defense of English Protestantism, *The Religion of Protestants a Safe Way to Salvation,* referred to the "common cause of Protestants." The "Solemn League and Covenant" reached in 1643 between Scots Presbyterians and English Parliamentarians during the English Civil War—a document well known to patriot leaders in New England— referred to the "common cause of Religion, Liberty, and Peace of the King-

5. Andrew Burnaby, *Travels through the Middle Settlements in North America in the Years 1759 and 1760: With Observations upon the State of the Colonies* ([1775]; rpt. Ithaca, N.Y., 1960), 113–114.

Introduction

doms." This spiritual clarion appealed to individuals; it was a personal call for moral action.[6]

In the early eighteenth century, the "common cause" began to develop a second valence. Throughout the first half of the 1700s, European heads of state began to refer to the "common cause" as their side of the balance of power alliances on the Continent. The annual speeches of George I and George II, widely republished in colonial American prints, consistently referred to the "common cause" with Prussia or Austria, whereas Louis XV suggested France make "common cause" with Spain in order to maintain diplomatic equilibrium. During the Seven Years' War, colonial papers used the phrase in stories about the military exploits of Prussian and British soldiers on the Continent, but at the same time, they also featured it in relation to friends and enemies on the American side of the Atlantic. "We doubt not," a New York paper effused in 1756, "the wise and prudent Behaviour of the British Officers will gain the Affections of the Americans, and greatly promote the common Cause." When the Cherokees attacked the southern backcountry in 1760, news spread throughout North America that "several large parties of the Six Nations . . . [and] both Virginia and North Carolina are raising men for the common cause" against the Indians. And, when the war was won, the *New-Hampshire Gazette* celebrated how the "spirited *Englishman,* the mountainous *Welchman,* the brave *Scotchman,* and *Irishman,* and the loyal *American*" had come together "as *British Brothers,* in defending the Common Cause."[7]

6. John Patrick, ed., *Mr. Chillingworth's Book Called "The Religion of Protestants a Safe Way to Salvation"* . . . ([1638]; rpt. London, 1687); *A Solemn League and Covenant, for Reformation, and Defence of Religion, the Honour and Happinesse of the King, and the Peace and Safety of the Three Kingdoms of England, Scotland, and Ireland* (London, 1643), 6. For examples in eighteenth-century colonial print culture of this older Christian trope of making "common cause" against the Turks, see *Boston News-Letter,* Jan. 26, 1719; *Boston Evening-Post,* Nov. 21, 1737; *New-York Weekly Journal,* Feb. 25, 1739.

7. *New-York Mercury,* Aug. 2, 1756 ("We doubt not"); *Boston News-Letter,* May 7, 1761 (Cherokees); *New-Hampshire Gazette,* July 13, 1764 ("British Brothers"). For colonial prints publishing George I's and George II's speeches that invoked "common cause" to refer to the European balance of power, see *Boston Gazette,* Apr. 3, 1727; *New-England Weekly Journal* (Boston), Apr. 5, 1731; *Boston News-Letter,* Jan. 29, 1741; *American Weekly Mercury* (Philadelphia), July 25, 1745. On Louis XV's doing the same, see *New-England Weekly Journal,* June 30, 1735. For official statements from Parliament using "common cause" to talk about foreign alliances, see *New-York Weekly Jour-*

During the imperial crisis, then, when the patriots turned to the language of the common cause, that rhetoric signified action at several levels: individuals enacting Providence's plan by sympathizing with the plight of fellow Protestants and coming to their aid, armed groups of neighbors acting in concert against shared enemies, provincial political leaders seeing their interests aligned with others at that level, disparate parts of the British Empire coming together. This multivalent fuzziness worked to the patriots' advantage. Because it was so malleable and useful, the rhetoric of "common cause" became almost hegemonic by 1774, a fact utterly lost on the members of Parliament. By then, the appeal was shorthand for getting as many colonists as possible to believe that an assault on one colony was an attack on everyone throughout the mainland and that good, liberty-loving patriots would not only instantly recognize this conspiracy but also feel compelled to take action to defeat it. In the early 1770s, patriot writers promulgated the appeal in the language of both reason and passion. Patriot political leaders formed "committees of correspondence" to broadcast their messages, calling on colonists throughout North America to use their heads: when Parliament and the crown encroached on representative government in New York and Massachusetts, patriot leaders reasoned this a precedent whereby New Jersey and North Carolina could be next. At the same time, they appealed to hearts: fellow colonists in Boston were suffering for their beliefs and deserved continental sympathy. A mixture of equal parts affection and logic, the patriots' entreaties in 1774 stressed both "common" and "cause." They were proving Lord North, Andrew Burnaby, and all the prognosticators of colonial discord wrong.

From the perspective of the fall of 1774, it is hard to discount that colonial discourses of reason or emotion or shared experiences of the marketplace animated the mobilization of political support. These were the halcyon days of the American Revolution and the bundled ideas about rights, consent, and representation. The Continental Association, a comprehensive boycott drafted by the First Continental Congress that fall, encapsulated all these themes, especially its nonconsumption provisions encouraging colonists to be frugal and virtuous by rejecting extravagant entertainments or luxury goods. The Association was the zenith of the American Revolution, from

---

nal, June 22, 1741; *Boston Post-Boy,* Feb. 22, 1742. For others invoking the phrase to describe their own military or diplomatic efforts, see *Boston News-Letter,* Apr. 23, 1705 (duke of Wirtenburg); *Boston Evening-Post,* Apr. 24, 1738 (Dutch States General); *Boston Post-Boy,* Sept. 28, 1741 (Massachusetts governor William Shirley).

Introduction

this point of view. At this heady moment, Benjamin Rush was almost over-come. He was so sanguine that the rhetoric of liberty would sweep away all obstacles ahead of it that he rejoiced to a correspondent in Britain, "I ven-ture to predict there will be not a Negro slave in North America in 40 years." Just nine days after his friends in Congress included Africans in the non-importation provisions of the Association, he effused to Granville Sharp, "I now feel a *new* attachment to my native country, and I look forward with *new* pleasure to her future importance and grandeur." The noble qualities that patriots insisted comprised the common cause appeal as it had devel-oped since the Stamp Act protests carried the day. That appeal could even encompass abolition, according to Rush. Or Thomas Jefferson, who had recently written in his widely circulated tract *A Summary View of the Rights of British Americans,* "The abolition of domestic slavery is *the great object of desire* in those colonies where it was unhappily introduced in their infant state." Patriot leaders argued that the common cause, so framed, would lead to a rebirth of human freedom for all. Who could challenge that?[8]

* * *

But a drastic change occurred when the American Revolution became the Revolutionary War. For patriot writers who had warned of conspiracy, Lexington and Concord sealed the verdict. The actions of April 19, though, did more than simply clinch the case that Britain was plotting to enslave them. The war thoroughly changed the dynamics of the argument that would be necessary to sustain the common cause appeal. It placed addi-tional demands on each level of the public (local, provincial, continental, global) to respond with more than economic boycotts. It offered new op-portunities for those publics to clash with one another. Most of all, war would mean tremendous new tensions for the infant bonds of intercolonial unity. Combat shifted the patriots' mobilization campaign into a whole new channel.

8. Benjamin Rush to Granville Sharp, Nov. 1, 1774, in John A. Woods, ed., "The Correspondence of Benjamin Rush and Granville Sharp, 1773–1809," *Journal of American Studies,* I (1967), 13–14; *PTJ,* I, 121–137, esp. 130 (emphasis added); David Ammerman, *In the Common Cause: American Responses to the Coercive Acts of 1774* (Char-lottesville, Va., 1974). For Congress and the Continental Association, see Jack N. Rakove, *The Beginnings of National Politics: An Interpretative History of the Continental Con-gress* (New York, 1979); Jerrilyn Greene Marston, *King and Congress: The Transfer of Political Legitimacy, 1774–1776* (Princeton, N.J., 1987).

For too long, a single letter John Adams wrote late in his life has enthralled some students of the Revolution. "What do We Mean by the Revolution?" Adams queried Thomas Jefferson in 1815. "The war? That was no part of the Revolution. It was only an effect and consequence of it. The Revolution was in the Minds of the People, and this was effected, from 1760 to 1775." This sentiment framed one landmark study, but it has led interpreters astray. Although there is no disputing a sea change in the attitudes of many colonists toward Britain and the empire, this was hardly a completed project before 1775. Indeed, with Lexington, the rebellion entered a different, desperate phase, and consumer goods alone—no matter how loaded with political meaning—were not sufficient to animate military resistance. Now the imperative for action became critical; for the "cause" to survive against British forces, thousands of people had to recognize that if they took up arms against their king, they were doing it for a legitimate purpose. The patriots needed a new script to animate a new kind of resistance. They needed war stories. Adams continued to lecture Jefferson that future historians should consult the "records of the thirteen Legislatures, the Pamp[h]lets, [and] Newspapers in all the colonies" during those fifteen years "to ascertain the Steps by which the public Opinion was enlightened." Perhaps. But what Adams's pupils would discover there before 1775 hardly matched what they would find after the shooting started—and he knew so.[9]

Wars put societies under great pressure. They awaken latent tendencies, force people to choose sides, produce emotive events that stir action, and shake up political systems, legal systems, and value systems. War's inherent ability to shock requires explanation; it needs narratives to justify actions, soothe consciences, and galvanize participants for future campaigns. But words and stories are hardly distinct from bullets and bayonets. They are potentially just as destructive. Wars are equal parts "injuries and . . . interpretations." The party that inflicts the most casualties often gains the opportunity to decide names, label events, and adjudicate ethics. As soon as the shooting started, a supply of narrative became as critical to secure as stores

9. JA to TJ, Aug. 24, 1815, in Lester J. Cappon, ed., *The Adams-Jefferson Letters: The Complete Correspondence between Thomas Jefferson and Abigail and John Adams* (Chapel Hill, N.C., 1959), II, 454–456, esp. 455. Adams repeated and deepened his opinion a few years later in a letter to Hezekiah Niles, Feb. 13, 1818, in Charles Francis Adams, ed., *The Works of John Adams, Second President of the United States . . .* (Boston, 1856), X, 282–289. Bernard Bailyn chose Adams's sentiment as the leading epigraph in *The Ideological Origins of the American Revolution* (Cambridge, 1967), 1.

Introduction

of gunpowder. Totems, tropes, images: patriot publicists had to discover and disseminate stories with clear, compelling heroes and villains if they wanted the rebellion to have broad, popular support.[10]

The "common cause" rested on the concept of representation. Of course, the Revolution was about representation in the political sense: the colonial rejection of British theories of virtual representation, the embrace of binding instructions, annual elections, and popular sovereignty, the vestiges of virtuality remaining to justify denying suffrage for propertyless men and nearly all women. "No taxation without representation" is, after all, the Revolution's unofficial motto, and it was "the representatives of the united States of America" who declared independence "in the Name and by the Authority of the good people of these colonies."[11]

"Representation," though, meant far more to the patriots than simply who would sit in the assembly houses and vote on taxes. The other suprapolitical definitions of "representation" were just as instrumental to the success or failure of the patriot argument. Whether in the notion of outward performance, projection of ideas, or image production, the cultural valances of "one who stands in for another" were an important part of the contest to win the definitions of other key words, like "liberty" and "freedom," once the war began. Both the political and cultural connotations of "representation" involve focusing many into few, but if the ends were securing consent and the principle of actual representation, cultural or rhetorical representations were the means of achieving that goal.[12]

10. Jill Lepore, *The Name of War: King Philip's War and the Origins of American Identity* (New York, 1998), x. For a brilliant exposition of the power of narrative in eighteenth-century America, see Joshua Piker, *The Four Deaths of Acorn Whistler: Telling Stories in Colonial America* (Cambridge, Mass., 2013).

11. J. R. Pole, *Political Representation in England and the Origins of the American Republic* (London, 1966); Bailyn, *Ideological Origins*, 161–175; Gordon S. Wood, *The Creation of the American Republic, 1776–1787* (Chapel Hill, N.C., 1969),162–196; Willi Paul Adams, *The First American Constitutions: Republican Ideology and the Making of the State Constitutions in the Revolutionary Era,* trans. Rita Kimber and Robert Kimber (Chapel Hill, N.C., 1980), 228–253; Marc W. Kruman, *Between Authority and Liberty: State Constitution Making in Revolutionary America* (Chapel Hill, N.C., 1997); Wood, *Representation in the American Revolution*, rev. ed. (Charlottesville, Va., 2008).

12. The *Oxford English Dictionary* provides eight definitions for "representation"; only the seventh and eighth concern the political process (s.v. "representation"). For more on how politics and language intersected for the Revolutionary genera-

In other words, the common cause was about representation and was itself a representation. Gaining acceptance among jealous provincials meant that the patriots had to be better than their opponents at concentrating many values or issues into one durable, lucid, projectable image. This had consistently been part of the patriots' challenge during the imperial crisis through the end of 1774.

But the American Revolution and the Revolutionary War were not the same thing. Now, as part of waging war against the crown, the demands to monitor information—to establish your own representations as well as undermine your opponents'—became essential. War stories, appearing as facts inside printed publications, offered the best medium to cordon off friends from enemies and cement union. Representations of British deception and heroic American volunteers rushing to defend liberty were the polestars of patriot narratives during the war; they were the proof that all colonists should recognize the common cause as the proper side to take. In this context of civil war and disunity, substantiating this appeal meant the difference between an abortive colonial uprising and revolution.

* * *

The most advanced method of communication of the age, newspapers were the best medium at hand to make the cause common. Ever since David Ramsay observed in his 1789 history of the Revolution, "In establishing American independence, the pen and press had merit equal to that of the sword," newspapers have been acknowledged as critical to the patriots' mobilization campaign. The colonial press had expanded greatly in the mid-eighteenth century, thanks in part to both the Great Awakening and the Seven Years' War. The number of prints published in English had doubled in the decade before the Stamp Act, and they would increase by more than 250 percent over the next ten years. The imperial controversy spurred the founding of more than a dozen new prints. The context of the 1760s and 1770s, moreover, shaped the public's expectations for printers. Freedom of the press was one of the essential rights patriots claimed they defended, but political partisanship—long rejected as bad professional form by printers—became not only acceptable but an imperative that threatened printers'

---

tion, see Robert A. Ferguson, *The American Enlightenment, 1750–1820* (Cambridge, Mass., 1997), 124–149; Ferguson, *Reading in the Early Republic* (Cambridge, Mass., 2004); John Howe, *Language and Political Meaning in Revolutionary America* (Amherst, Mass., 2004).

Introduction

neutrality. Some printers became highly vested in the patriot movement; others participated less directly but still opened their papers up to one side over the other. By 1775, the bundles of weekly sheets that emerged from those few dozen print shops were as powerful as any cannons the colonists might deploy against the British army.[13]

Benjamin Franklin, it should not surprise, grasped perfectly the power of newspapers in a civil war or "revolution." "By the press we can speak to Nations," the printer-turned-politician wrote a friend in 1782. Thanks to newspapers, Franklin concluded, political leaders could not only "strike while the Iron is hot" but also stoke fires by "continual Striking." Those bundles of newspapers—dropped off at crossroad inns and subscribers' rural estates in the countryside, distributed among urban taverns and gathering places in the cities, imported into the army camps—had the capacity to be potent instruments of mobilization.[14]

Six decades after independence, the narrator of Nathaniel Hawthorne's 1836 short story "Old News" discovered several stacks of "yellow and time-stained" New England papers and described the contents of these supposedly ephemeral documents, which he insisted "have proved more durable, as to their physical existence, than most of the timber, bricks, and stone, of the town where they were issued." "The first pages, of most of these old papers, are as soporific as a bed of poppies," Hawthorne's narrator opined about a volume from the mid-eighteenth century. "Here are literary essays, from the Gentleman's Magazine; and squibs against the Pretender, from the London newspapers." By the 1770s, those front pages featured politics as much as belles lettres. On the eve of the Revolution, printers often published a political essay or speech, or a transcript of legislative resolutions either from Parliament or the provincial assembly. Though they did not have the significance that they do today, the front pages have earned a great deal of scholarly attention for explaining what moved the people to resist.[15]

For historians who contend that ideas drove the Revolution, the lessons

13. David Ramsay, *The History of the American Revolution,* ed. Lester H. Cohen, 2 vols. ([1789]; Indianapolis, 1990), II, 633. For the growth of colonial prints, see David A. Copeland, *The Idea of a Free Press: The Enlightenment and Its Unruly Legacy* (Evanston, Ill., 2006); Copeland, *Colonial American Newspapers: Character and Content* (Newark, Del., 1997), 279.

14. BF to Richard Price, Passy, June 13, 1782, *PBF,* XXXVII, 472–473.

15. Nathaniel Hawthorne, "Old News," in [Roy Harvey Pearce, ed.], *Hawthorne: Tales and Sketches* (New York, 1982), 251–275, esp. 251–252.

elite colonists learned from their libraries and distilled onto those front pages was a serious business. They argue that the men who would become patriot leaders gleaned a political education from their voracious reading, and those examples from history shaped their notions about consent and representation, tyranny and freedom, virtue and corruption, interests and power. The result of all this reading, this interpretation posits, was a conviction that the British government was plotting to enslave the American colonies. More recently, scholars have suggested another vein of reading that inspired some colonial elites to resist imperial reform. They were also imbibing social instruction from new novels and moral philosophies, ranging from the sentimental novels of Richardson to the poetry of Pope to the sociability studies coming out of Scotland. These texts convinced colonial elites and middling folk that the Revolution was really an opportunity to remake body, mind, and society. It was not about home rule but self-rule. These interpretations, one focusing on political culture, the other on cultural politics, have drawn their evidence from the type of material that would have appeared on the front pages of newspapers—in Hawthorne's "bed of poppies." According to this view, reading and writing political pamphlets or serialized newspaper essays caused the Revolution.[16]

Others, dissatisfied with the explanatory power of intellectual history, have approached the opaque intersection between ideas and the everyday

16. Edmund S. Morgan and Helen M. Morgan reasserted the motivating power of ideas or principles for the Revolutionary movement in *The Stamp Act Crisis: Prologue to Revolution* (1953; rpt. Chapel Hill, N.C., 1995), followed by Edmund's *Birth of the Republic, 1763–1789* (Chicago, 1956). Clinton Rossiter's *Seedtime of the Republic: The Origin of the Tradition of American Political Liberty* (New York, 1953) also contributed to this revision. Several landmark studies followed, including Bailyn, *Ideological Origins;* Wood, *Creation of the American Republic;* Pauline Maier, *From Resistance to Revolution: Colonial Radicals and the Development of American Opposition to Britain, 1765–1776* (New York, 1972); J. G. A. Pocock, *The Machiavellian Moment: Florentine Political Thought and the Atlantic Republican Tradition* (Princeton, N.J., 1975). Two historiographical essays survey the ensuing debate over the source of these ideas: see Robert E. Shalhope, "Toward a Republican Synthesis: The Emergence of an Understanding of Republicanism in American Historiography," *WMQ,* 3d Ser., XXIX (1972), 49–80; Daniel T. Rodgers, "Republicanism: The Career of a Concept," *JAH,* LXXIX (1992), 11–38. Studies on the centrality of sensibility to the Revolutionary movement include Nicole Eustace, *Passion Is the Gale: Emotion, Power, and the Coming of the American Revolution* (Chapel Hill, N.C., 2008); Sarah Knott, *Sensibility and the American Revolution* (Chapel Hill, N.C., 2009).

Introduction

by analyzing the role consumer culture played in political mobilization, arguing that Parliament's politicization of goods gave patriot leaders the opportunity to use objects as a tangible site to ground concepts. The real Revolutionary movement, they argue, came from the energy exploding from the "empire of goods" displayed on the back page of the weekly paper. To this point, Hawthorne's enthralled reader, bored with the front page, was indeed impressed with the quantity of items listed on the back pages. "There are tokens," he put it, "of a style of luxury and magnificence, which we do not usually associate with our ideas of the times." Looking back from the distance of nearly a century, Hawthorne's narrator was taken with the "mercers and the milliners imported good store of fine broadcloths—especially scarlet, crimson, and sky-blue, silks, satins, lawns, and velvets, gold brocade, and gold and silver lace." But there were other advertisements on the back pages. "No advertisements are more frequent than those of 'a negro fellow, fit for almost any household work;' 'a negro woman, honest, healthy, and capable;' 'a young negro wench, of many desirable qualities;' 'a negro man, very fit for a taylor,'" Hawthorne's narrator observed with disdain, adding, "When the slaves of a family were inconveniently prolific, . . . notice was promulgated" on the paper's final page "of 'a negro child to be given away.'"[17]

Using these kinds of advertisements has led other historians to reject the argument that well-connected, well-educated, well-heeled whites in their libraries were the prime movers of the Revolutionary movement. The real engines were the people who pushed their way onto that back page, not the ones who submitted pseudonymous essays for publication under the masthead. For these scholars, the notices for escaped slaves and runaway servants or apprentices, the proclamations announcing thousands of acres of western land for sale, and the announcements of incoming ships carrying new arrivals to America—whether by their own choice from Europe or against their will

17. Hawthorne, "Old News," in [Pearce, ed.], *Tales and Sketches,* 266 ("These are tokens"), 266–267 ("mercers and milliners"), 267 ("notice was promulgated"). The phrase "empire of goods" comes from T. H. Breen, "An Empire of Goods: The Anglicization of Colonial America, 1690–1776," *Journal of British Studies,* XXV (1986), 467–499. Studies that feature the marketplace and consumerism as central to the Revolution include Breen, *Tobacco Culture: The Mentality of the Great Tidewater Planters on the Eve of Revolution* (Princeton, N.J., 1985); Breen, *The Marketplace of Revolution: How Consumer Politics Shaped American Independence* (New York, 2004); Bruce A. Ragsdale, *A Planters' Republic: The Search for Economic Independence in Revolutionary Virginia* (Madison, Wis., 1996).

from Africa—were all markers of a society in flux, full of people struggling to maximize their opportunities or resist prevailing political, economic, or social power structures. Just behind the screen of those terse advertisements were thousands of frustrated urban workers and sailors, resistant slaves, religious dissenters, encroached-upon Indians, and rural protestors: evidence of all the conflict that stalked the common cause appeal in the 1760s and 1770s and further convinced British officials that Americans were incapable of uniting in revolt. These groups put pressure on those who would become patriot leaders to accommodate some part of their efforts to improve their economic, political, or social standing in exchange for support against Parliament, often to their significant discomfort. Hardly the pawns of provincial elites, members of these groups used the opportunity of the imperial controversy to express their collective agency, according to these scholars. These were the dissatisfied men and women who shaped the Revolution. But historians who seek to advance such an interpretation of the Revolution, one that ignores or discounts elites—the back page without the front, as it were—wind up with just as incomplete an account of the ways in which colonists were mobilized to fight against their cultural cousins.[18]

* * *

The interior of the newspaper, where the bulk of the actual news appeared, deserves its own advocate. The succinct paragraphs, the extracted accounts, the mundane details: these items—largely hidden in plain sight from scholars thus far—were essential to political and, especially, military mobilization during the Revolutionary War. On these inner pages, most of the stories usually focused on the eastern side of the Atlantic even as late as the mid-1700s. Hawthorne's reader put it better: "Without any discredit to the colonial press, these [papers] might have been, and probably were, spread out on the tables of the British coffee-house, in King street for the perusal of the throng of officers who then drank their wine at that celebrated establishment." "To interest these military gentlemen," he continued, "there were bulletins of the war between Prussia and Austria; between England

18. For a few examples of this approach, see Woody Holton, *Forced Founders: Indians, Debtors, Slaves, and the Making of the American Revolution in Virginia* (Chapel Hill, N.C., 1999); Peter Linebaugh and Marcus Rediker, *The Many-Headed Hydra: Sailors, Slaves, Commoners, and the Hidden History of the Revolutionary Atlantic* (Boston, 2000); Gary B. Nash, *The Unknown American Revolution: The Unruly Birth of Democracy and the Struggle to Create America* (New York, 2005).

and France, . . . and in our own trackless woods, where white men never trod until they came to fight there." Hawthorne's narrator was right; before the 1770s, news from mainland North America did get precious little space in these six weekly columns. But on the eve of war, patriot political leaders managed to dominate the interior of the newspapers. With that closer management came the ability to promulgate singular representations.[19]

The methods by which printers assembled these interior pages made them crucial to mobilizing support for the common cause after 1775. One of the primary professional rules governing printing in the eighteenth century was that editors would send free copies of their weekly paper to colleagues outside their city for the purposes of "exchanging" stories. Through the common practice of "exchanges"—the clipping of pieces from other papers to insert into your own—colonists across colony and region learned much of the same information and read many of the same stories. The printers' exchanges had an effect akin to modern newswires; once a story entered into one newspaper, it very likely would be picked up and, over the next several weeks, be reprinted in faraway papers. The role this commonplace practice of "exchanges" played in Revolutionary mobilization was essential, but it has received little notice.[20]

Those who were emerging as patriot leaders certainly understood the power of the middle pages, the exchange system, and its potential to cement unity. An illuminating episode involving one of those men, John Adams, indicates the patriots' recognition of the potential impact of the press and their subsequent management of it to their advantage.

19. Hawthorne, "Old News," in [Pearce, ed.], *Tales and Sketches,* 259. For more on the European content of colonial newspapers in the early to mid-eighteenth century, see Charles E. Clark, *The Public Prints: The Newspaper in Anglo-American Culture, 1665–1740* (New York, 1994); Copeland, *Colonial American Newspapers.*

20. Philip Davidson, *Propaganda and the American Revolution, 1763–1783* (Chapel Hill, N.C., 1941), 245. In studying the effects of the exchanges, my thinking is influenced by theories of the role print played in the social construction of nations and nationalism, especially Benedict Anderson, *Imagined Communities: Reflections on the Origin and Spread of Nationalism,* rev. ed. (1983; London, 1991); Ernest Gellner, *Nations and Nationalism* (Ithaca, N.Y., 1983); Eric Hobsbawm and Terence Ranger, eds., *The Invention of Tradition* (Cambridge, 1983); Edmund S. Morgan, *Inventing the People: The Rise of Popular Sovereignty in England and America* (New York, 1988); E. J. Hobsbawm, *Nations and Nationalism since 1780: Programme, Myth, Reality* (Cambridge, 1990); David Waldstreicher, *In the Midst of Perpetual Fetes: The Making of American Nationalism, 1776–1820* (Chapel Hill, N.C., 1997).

On Sunday, September 3, 1769, Adams wrote in his diary that he was in the company of his cousin Sam, James Otis, and *Boston Gazette* printers Benjamin Edes and John Gill. "The evening [was] spent in preparing for the Next Days Newspaper," he noted, "a curious Employment. Cooking up Paragraphs, Articles, Occurrences etc.—working the political Engine!" What, exactly, did Adams, Otis, and the printers "cook up?" Not a front-page political essay, and much more than a bed of poppies.[21]

The front page of the September 4 issue of the *Boston Gazette* did not feature an extended essay on natural rights or sociability but rather petitions and excerpts of English newspapers. The back page, true to form, contained notices of runaway servants and apprentices as well as advertisements of items for sale, including Madeira wine, spermaceti candles, choice choco-late, lost pieces of gold, houses to let, and a "Likely Negro Girl," for which interested buyers should "Inquire of Edes and Gill." Neither side of the ex-terior sheet, it seems, was what Adams referred to by "cooking up" or "work-ing the political engine." Inside the *Gazette* was a different matter. There, readers found an assortment of private letters, closely crafted "news" about Lieutenant Governor Thomas Hutchinson's recent importation of tea, and pseudonymous poems attacking Governor Francis Bernard. All of these items showed evidence that this was the fare the patriots scrupulously pre-pared. Focusing on the exterior pages of the weekly papers, historians have overlooked the Bostonians' labor. Adams, Otis, and the *Gazette* printers spent their time and attention on items scholars have largely ignored ever since. Not only have interpreters downplayed the importance of these items, but they also have missed the effect of the "exchanges." Adams and his friends knew their "cooking" would reach readers far outside Boston. Because of the exchange system, over the next few weeks, fourteen other newspapers—half of active colonial prints from New York and Philadelphia to Williamsburg and Savannah—included some parts of their handicraft. The political com-mentary Bostonians fashioned in the waning daylight on the *Gazette*'s type tables found its way to hundreds of other tables, in public and private houses across New England, New York, Pennsylvania, Virginia, and Georgia.[22]

21. Entry for Sept. 3, 1769, in L. H. Butterfield, ed., *Diary and Autobiography of John Adams*, series 1 of *The Adams Papers* (Cambridge, Mass., 1961), I, 343.

22. *Boston Gazette*, Sept. 4, 1769; *Boston Chronicle*, Sept. 11, 1769; *Essex Gazette*, Sept. 12, 1769; *Boston News-Letter*, Sept. 14, 1769; *Connecticut Gazette*, Sept. 15, 1769; *Connecticut Journal*, Sept. 15, 1769; *New-Hampshire Gazette*, Sept. 15, 22, 1769; *Provi-dence Gazette*, Sept. 16, 1769; *New-York Gazette*, Sept. 18, 1769; *Newport Mercury*, Sept.

The word most often enlisted to describe this kind of effort to manipulate information is "propaganda." "Propaganda," though, is problematic for several reasons, not least because it was a word unknown to late-eighteenth-century colonists. Also, because it recalls totalitarian systems, mass media, corporatism, and disinformation campaigns, "propaganda" fits awkwardly with the American Revolution. To match that word to the late eighteenth century, it has to be stripped of two key elements: the mass delivery systems that can saturate images and the centralized clearinghouses that operate those systems. Only the husk remains.[23]

18, 1769; *Pennsylvania Chronicle,* Sept. 18, 1769; *Pennsylvania Journal,* Sept. 21, 1769; *New-York Journal,* Sept. 21, 1769; *Georgia Gazette,* Sept. 27, 1769; *Virginia Gazette* (Purdie & Dixon), Sept. 28, 1769.

23. For generations, historians have grappled with the role of propaganda in the American Revolution. Progressive historians in the early twentieth century (themselves influenced by the propaganda campaigns of World War I) were the first to argue that the Revolutionaries, especially Samuel Adams, Paul Revere, and Benjamin Franklin, were master propagandists who used false arts to manipulate the American public into embracing radical political positions against their best interests—a claim that echoed contemporary loyalist critiques. But totalitarian techniques of mass propaganda, especially Joseph Goebbels's black disinformation campaigns, in part discredited this interpretation, especially the Progressives' insinuation that the populace was deceived. See John C. Miller, *Sam Adams: Pioneer in Propaganda* (Boston, 1936); Davidson, *Propaganda and the American Revolution.* When historians at midcentury emphasized ideas or ideology as the engines driving the Revolution, they argued that there was no false consciousness; patriot writers and their readers believed in the arguments about rights and representation they espoused.

Modern theoretical studies of propaganda, influenced especially by Noam Chomsky, focus on the world wars, the Cold War, the "War on Terror," and current corporate advertising campaigns. Their reliance on contemporary examples loads this work with too much cultural baggage. As one of the most important scholars of modern propaganda, Jacques Ellul, put it, before the twentieth century, propaganda "did not appear as a specific phenomenon that needed to be defined and considered in itself" (Ellul, *Propaganda: The Formation of Men's Attitudes* [1962; rpt. New York, 1973], 5). In the eighteenth century, he argues, there was no recognition of propaganda. For an overview on theories of propaganda, see Garth S. Jowett and Victoria O'Donnell, *Propaganda and Persuasion,* 3d ed. (Thousand Oaks, Calif., 1999). For the philosophical underpinnings of propaganda, see Stanley B. Cunningham, *The Idea of Propaganda: A Reconstruction* (Westport, Conn., 2002). Chomsky's critiques of modern propaganda techniques by corporations and the state are in his *Letters from Lexington: Reflections on Propaganda,* rev. ed. (Boulder, Co., 2004); Chom-

"Propagate," or "propagation," is a far superior descriptor. This endorsement of a return to the Latin root, however, is much more than a shift of suffixes. "Propagation"—with its organic connotations to agriculture, nature, breeding, and disease—is a term contemporaries would have recognized as a central part of their lives. No matter where one lived in North America, everyone did his or her best to propagate: increase crop yields, breed animals, extend families, build estates for posterity. Or, in the case of smallpox or dysentery, one tried to limit propagation. For three generations, colonists throughout the Atlantic had become familiar with Anglican missionaries from the Society for the Propagation of the Gospel who sought to convert Catholics, lapsed Christians, and "heathen" Indians or Africans. Less charged than "propaganda," "propagation" better describes what the patriots were trying to do with the common cause—that is, grow more patriots.[24]

This move away from propaganda does not mean that the common cause was not a "conscious, systemic effort on the part of certain colonial leaders to gain public support for their ideas." It certainly was, but it was simultaneously more and less than that. More, in that patriot political leaders and newspaper printers worked together to shape the news even more than they had in previous years: nearly all the anonymous stories that appeared in weekly papers whose editors were sympathetic to the rebellion originated from people highly vested in the patriot movement, be they local members of committees of safety, county militia officers, representatives to provincial assemblies or conventions, Continental army generals, or delegates to the Continental Congress. Less, in that the majority of those reports supplied details (rumored or real) of actual events. There were some instances of blatant "black propaganda" (hoaxes intentionally meant to deceive and agitate), most of which originated from Benjamin Franklin, but, though important, these were rare. What marked the common cause—especially after war began—and made it at first glance seem much less than "a conscious, systemic effort" was that the patriots accused their enemies of real phenomena. Andrew Burnaby was not wholly wrong, as it turned out; his

sky, *Media Control: The Spectacular Achievements of Propaganda,* 2d ed. (New York, 2002); Edward S. Herman and Chomsky, *Manufacturing Consent: The Political Economy of the Mass Media* (New York, 1988).

24. For a modern defense of the patriots as effective propagandists, especially in print, see Russ Castronovo, *Propaganda 1776: Secrets, Leaks, and Revolutionary Communications in Early America* (New York, 2014); William B. Warner, *Protocols of Liberty: Communication Innovation and the American Revolution* (Chicago, 2013).

Introduction

observation that impatient African Americans and Indians would play a significant role if war broke out in North America was prescient.[25]

* * *

The Revolutionary War, we know now, involved wide swaths of the population of the mainland North American colonies. Thanks to an efflorescence of historical works about the participation of African Americans and Indians, particularly, our understanding of the experience of that war is deeper and more nuanced than ever. Thousands of African Americans, free and enslaved, saw war with Britain as an opportunity to challenge legal, social, or economic obstacles circumscribing their lives, by linking their future to one of the armies marching through North America. Indians across the trans-Appalachian backcountry greeted the conflict between Britain and the colonies in a similar fashion, often by playing the two sides off one another in a complex diplomatic game. Both American and British officials at several levels understood that the loyalty of both African Americans and Indians would be essential to projecting power and civil order in the colonies, and they worked assiduously to attain influence over them. But our discovery of all this activity is really a rediscovery of phenomena with which colonists were already well acquainted. Or at least they were with half the story.[26]

25. Davidson, *Propaganda and the American Revolution*, xiv.

26. For an excellent overview of this scholarship, see the collection of essays edited by John Resch and Walter Sargent, *War and Society in the American Revolution: Mobilization and Home Fronts* (Dekalb, Ill., 2007). Also see Charles Patrick Neimeyer, *America Goes to War: A Social History of the Continental Army* (New York, 1996); and Nash, *Unknown American Revolution*. Major studies of the experience of African Americans during the Revolution include Benjamin Quarles, *The Negro in the American Revolution* (Chapel Hill, N.C., 1961); Ira Berlin and Ronald Hoffman, eds., *Slavery and Freedom in the Age of the American Revolution* (Charlottesville, Va., 1983); Sidney Kaplan and Emma Nogrady Kaplan, *The Black Presence in the Era of the American Revolution*, rev. ed. (Amherst, Mass., 1989); Holton, *Forced Founders;* Cassandra Pybus, *Epic Journeys of Freedom: Runaway Slaves of the American Revolution and Their Global Quest for Liberty* (Boston, 2006); Simon Schama, *Rough Crossings: Britain, the Slaves, and the American Revolution* (New York, 2006); Douglas R. Egerton, *Death or Liberty: African Americans and Revolutionary America* (New York, 2009); Gerald Horne, *The Counter-Revolution of 1776: Slave Resistance and the Origins of the United States of America* (New York, 2014). For histories of Indians and the Revolution, see Barbara Graymont, *The Iroquois in the American Revolution* (Syracuse, N.Y., 1972); James H. O'Donnell, *Southern Indians in the American Revolution* (Knoxville, Tenn., 1973); Richard White, *The Middle Ground:*

Especially in the war's early years, British officials in America—royal governors, Indian agents, army commanders, naval captains—did their best to suppress the rebellion as quickly and cheaply as possible, and they saw Indians and African Americans as viable weapons at their disposal. Without waiting the endless months it might take for military backup or political permission, several officials enacted plans to encourage slave resistance across southern plantations and sent emissaries into the backcountry to negotiate for Indian military aid.

This presented the patriots with an excellent opportunity to adapt the wartime appeal of the common cause. These understandable efforts on the part of British officials held great potential for patriots to turn their actions against them. Stories about blacks, Indians, and, starting in 1776, foreign mercenaries joining forces with Britain opened a golden door for the patriots. These war stories, in part based on actual events, accomplished a great deal of political work. If enough people believed that British agents sponsored these groups, the patriots could malign their enemies and demarcate their cultural cousins as aliens by associating them with resistant slaves, hostile Indians, and rapacious foreign mercenaries. At the same time, narratives highlighting the participation of these groups allowed patriots to deflect and redefine terms like "rebel," "insurrectionist," or "traitor."

It was a perfect convergence. Stories of slave "insurrections," Indian "massacres," and Hessian "atrocities" became as much a part of the news of the Revolutionary War as the battles of Saratoga and Yorktown. They were a key component of the common cause appeal, as it evolved with the war. If newspapers were the medium by which patriot leaders believed they could best propagate the common cause, then the messages that most colonial readers learned inside the columns of those weekly issues revolved around stories of British officials' "instigating" slave rebellions or "tampering with" Indians on the frontier. Given the nature of the eighteenth-century newspaper business, these particular images' appearance on an almost consistent basis in patriot papers was not accidental. Someone had to give the news to the newspapers. In the hopes of shoring up an unstable political

Indians, Empires, and Republics in the Great Lakes Region, 1650–1815 (Cambridge, 1991); Gregory Evans Dowd, _A Spirited Resistance: The North American Indian Struggle for Unity, 1745–1815_ (Baltimore, 1992); Colin G. Calloway, _The American Revolution in Indian Country: Crisis and Diversity in Native American Communities_ (Cambridge, 1995); Alan Taylor, _The Divided Ground: Indians, Settlers, and the Northern Borderlands of the American Revolution_ (New York, 2006); and Griffin, _American Leviathan_.

union and out of military desperation, patriot political leaders delivered into the hands of sympathetic printers any evidence of British "instigation" that might appear in their private correspondence.

* * *

The Common Cause is about how patriot leaders mobilized political authority and military resistance to defeat their cultural cousins. This study examines the overall shape of mobilization, how a discourse evolved delineating friends and enemies in the hopes of garnering support. It focuses on how, through print, patriot leaders propagated certain representations they thought would resonate with a wide colonial audience. Because they had to make the familiar alien, those depictions centered on conflating representations of the British with other dangerous populations within colonial society.

Those stories were based, at some level, on real events but heightened for effect precisely because the patriots' political and military situation was tenuous at the start and grew more desperate as the conflict deepened. Intercolonial unity was fragile at best leading into the war. A significant percentage of the population was reticent to commit to one side or another; another not-insignificant segment of the public was as committed to defeating the rebellion as the patriots were in continuing it. At nearly every engagement, their military forces were underfunded, undersupplied, and undermanned. These micro problems were exacerbated by the macro: they were conducting the first large-scale colonial rebellion in history. Worse, they had to make this appeal to the least taxed, most socially mobile, highest landowning, arguably most prosperous people in the western world. Survival depended on convincing enough people they were right.

To survive, the patriots had to destroy as much of the public's affection for their ancestors as they could. The political and cultural models they had revered, as well as the communities many of them came from, suddenly had to appear completely foreign. Patriot leaders had to convince enough colonists to see common-ness in one another. The best way to foster trust and mutual reference in each another was to demonstrate that the British were strangers. Suspicious foreigners. To accomplish this vital, difficult task, they embraced the most powerful weapons in the colonial cultural arsenal: stereotypes, prejudices, expectations, and fears about violent Indians and Africans.

When the war began, the common cause appeal, which had first been promulgated as celebrating masculine, virtuous, selfless action and denigrating passivity and conspiratorial treachery, developed a second, darker aspect. It became as much about fear and outrage as the defense of inalienable rights. For decades, colonists had viewed slaves as passive and Indians as treacherous. In shaping the wartime common cause appeal, patriot publicists embraced another notion of "representation," the proxy, to disassociate patriots from enemies who did not wear red coats. African Americans, Indians, and foreign mercenaries served as proxies for King George. Their actions were especially dangerous and untrustworthy. A true patriot was not simply anti-British but anti-slave, anti-savage, and anti-mercenary, as well. Patriots defended "the cause" against these proxies. Yet war stories *not* told mattered as much as those that patriot publicists widely amplified. Not all the proxies suffered from deep cultural prejudice produced by generations of colonial experience. Stories about those groups did not gain the same traction and, in the case of the German mercenaries, disappeared. The thousands of Indians and African Americans who served with Washington, moreover, stood in such contrast to this construction of the "King's proxies" that they had to go unheralded. "Good" blacks and Indians were all but invisible in patriot newspapers throughout the conflict. Rather, they were lumped together, as Jefferson would in the Declaration, as "domestic insurrectionists" and "merciless savages." The totality of these printed stories created a convincing interpretation: these groups opposed the nation, and they were not eligible for any of the benefits of American independence.

The consequences of this founding narrative cannot be overestimated. Of course, this sharpening of ideas of difference had happened before in the American past, but this was not just any colonial episode of violence. The Revolutionary War created the United States of America. When patriot leaders roundly rejected monarchy and instead chose republican forms of government, they also rejected the theory of subjecthood in favor of citizenship. These political choices are what makes the Revolution different. They were not part of the experience of the Seven Years' War or King Philip's War, for example. The nation-making, constitution-making side of the Revolution cannot be overlooked in our histories of the race-making in the eighteenth century.[27]

27. For studies that focus on other episodes of violence as the origins of ideas of racial difference in colonial America, see Alden T. Vaughan, "'Expulsion of the Salvages': English Policy and the Virginia Massacre of 1622," *WMQ*, 3d Ser., XXXV (1978), 57–84; Francis Jennings, *The Invasion of America: Indians, Colonialism, and the Cant of Conquest* (Chapel Hill, N.C., 1975); Edmund S. Morgan, *American Slavery,*

As Edward Coke ruled in *Calvin's Case* (1608), all subjects are theoretically equal under the aegis of the monarch; each offers allegiance to the sovereign, who, in turn, promises protection. Only the monarch can make distinctions between the statuses of his subjects. Citizenship, on the other hand, allows for people to decide who belongs to the community and who does not. Inclusion confers certain privileges, including participation in the political process, the ability to own and alienate property, and the mechanisms to seek justice. In short, citizenship is a club. Members can choose whom they let in and whom they exclude. The patriots based inclusion on what one scholar termed "volitional allegiance": "Every man had to have the right to decide whether to be a citizen or an alien." It would be naïve to think this choice would ever be free or universal. *The Common Cause* examines patriot leaders' efforts to develop a publicity campaign that would cement intercolonial unity, achieve military victory, and secure independence; they did this by telling war stories that, in turn, shaped who would be deemed a proper member of the club. Stories of violence on slave plantations or on the frontier were no longer tales from the colonial past. Instead, these were Revolution stories—founding stories—freighted with theories of self-government and the ongoing construction of a republican regime. Although they sprang from those old sources and retained much of the same, terrifying power that they held in 1676 or 1741, these founding stories of Indian massacres and slave insurrections would take on a permanence unlike those that came before.[28]

American Freedom: The Ordeal of Colonial Virginia (New York, 1975); Kathleen M. Brown, *Good Wives, Nasty Wenches, and Anxious Patriarchs: Gender, Race, and Power in Colonial Virginia* (Chapel Hill, N.C., 1996); Lepore, *Name of War;* and Silver, *Our Savage Neighbors.* As will become clear, this book shares several themes with Carroll Smith-Rosenberg's *This Violent Empire: The Birth of an American National Identity* (Chapel Hill, N.C., 2010). Although this study puts more emphasis than Smith-Rosenberg does on matters political and military rather than cultural, our conclusions about racial exclusion, fear, and the centrality of print at the founding are very much in agreement.

28. This analysis of subjecthood and citizenship is based on Christopher Vincenzi, *Crown Powers, Subjects, and Citizens* (London, 1998); Derek Heater, *What Is Citizenship?* (Cambridge, 1999); Ronald Beiner, *Liberalism, Nationalism, Citizenship: Essays on the Problem of Political Community* (Vancouver, B.C., 2003); Quentin Skinner and Bo Stråth, eds., *States and Citizens: History, Theory, Prospects* (Cambridge, 2003); Derek Heater, *Citizenship: The Civic Ideal in World History, Politics, and Education,* 3d ed. (Manchester, U.K., 2004); Andreas Fahrmeir, *Citizenship: The Rise and Fall of a Modern Con-*

Jefferson, Franklin, Adams, Washington, and scores of their colleagues made republican policies of exclusion possible by supplying patriotic ammunition for attacking Indians and expanding west. The common cause appeal would also provide rhetorical cover for those who sought to deepen and extend the slave system and opened a discursive avenue for proslavery advocates to counter abolitionist claims. With the war stories they would tell, refused to tell, or were ineffective in telling, the patriots would bury race deep in the political structure of the new republic. The wartime appeal they created would undermine the "great object of desire."

Our search to find compelling explanations for the blindness? hypocrisy? naïveté? cruelty? optimism? of these men—how they could promote such ideas of universal human equality, natural rights, and self-government while denying it to so many—is now centuries old. Generations, vexed by this conundrum, have turned over their letters, writings, and lives looking for answers to the founders' dualism. *The Common Cause* suggests that our quest to understand or come to terms with this disjuncture is a journey made treacherous by Adams, Jefferson, and Franklin themselves. It is understandable that scholars have been unable to solve this puzzle, the American founding mystery. The reason is that those patriot leaders, by crafting their own powerful interpretation, blinded us.

The histories of the Revolution, whether those that celebrate the founders' political ideals or those that chastise them for being unable to square the universal rights circle, are haunted by the narratives the patriots themselves created. When the eighty-year-old John Adams instructed us (via Jefferson, who hardly needed the signal) to ignore the newspapers after 1775 as unimportant afterthoughts to the real revolution, he was "cooking up" again: creating a diversion to draw our attention away from his involvement in shaping exclusionary narratives and toward ones based on natural rights. Adams was closer to the truth three years later when, in developing these themes, he said that the unification of the American people "was certainly a very difficult enterprise." "The complete accomplishment of it, in so short a time and by such simple means, was perhaps a singular example in the history of mankind. Thirteen clocks were made to strike together— a perfection of mechanism, which no artist had ever before effected." The particular ways in which Adams and his colleagues timed those clocks after 1775—by defining the common cause as an American story of both inclu-

cept (New Haven, Conn., 2007). "Volitional allegiance": James H. Kettner, *The Development of American Citizenship, 1608–1870* (Chapel Hill, N.C., 1978), 208–209.

sion and exclusion—was indeed an accomplishment. It framed not only the founding but how we have analyzed it ever since.[29]

In 1836, the same year fellow Concordian and friend Nathaniel Hawthorne published "Old News," Ralph Waldo Emerson broadened Adams's project, mythologizing the "embattled farmers" who stood at the Old North Bridge and "fired the shot heard round the world." Even though there had been several black and Indian minutemen standing at the "rude bridge," they were effaced, in part because they had been stripped of the "spirit, that made those heroes dare." That was not a new story; in fact, Emerson was simply bringing the sixty-year-old representation full circle. John Adams and other patriot political and communication leaders had begun telling that story in 1775 on the inside pages of their weekly newspapers. Those stacks of papers might have seemed archaic by Hawthorne and Emerson's time, but they were essential to understanding the founding of the United States, and, just as important, who belonged—and belongs—to the nation the Revolutionary War created.[30]

29. JA to Hezekiah Niles, Feb. 13, 1818, in Adams, ed., *Works of John Adams,* X, 283.

30. Ralph Waldo Emerson, "Hymn: Sung at the Completion of the Concord Monument," in [John Hollander, ed.], *American Poetry: The Nineteenth Century* (New York, 1993), I, 318–319.

## CHAPTER 1

"A Work of Difficulty"

COMMUNICATION NETWORKS, NEWSPAPERS,

AND THE COMMON CAUSE

To rouse and unite the inhabitants, and to persuade them to patience
for several years, under present sufferings, with the hope of obtaining remote
advantages for their posterity, was a work of difficulty: This was effected in a
great measure by the tongues and pens of the well informed citizens, and on it
depended the success of military operations.
David Ramsay, 1789

When the House of Commons, on the portentous day of March 14, 1774, isolated Boston for punishment, believing American unity impossible, the assembled, outraged body proceeded from a false assumption. By the spring of 1774, there was more linking colonists who opposed British imperial policy than most across the Atlantic imagined. Over the early 1770s, political leaders in most mainland colonies had built communication networks connecting like-minded patriots to one another. They paid significant attention to what urban and rural inhabitants thought about the imperial controversy and took steps to manage the information people received.[1]

Resistance leaders, such as Samuel Adams and Richard Henry Lee, focused on information flows in the early 1770s, including schemes to organize a postal service entirely separate from the royal post. Those efforts culminated by 1773 in intercolonial committees of correspondence, which connected men who deemed themselves patriots in colonial cities from Boston and Providence south to Annapolis, Williamsburg, and Charleston. At

---

1. David Ramsay, *The History of the American Revolution*, ed. Lester H. Cohen, 2 vols. ([1798]; rpt. Indianapolis, 1990), II, 633–634.

the same time, as men opposed to imperial reform attempted to take control of political information and regulate post riders, they also increasingly turned their attention to the other means of transmitting information in the colonies: the newspaper. For several decades, newspaper printers in America had prided themselves on stubborn neutrality, proclaiming their columns free from influence and open to all. What "free press" actually meant, however, was in flux as the imperial crisis deepened in the 1760s and 1770s. By the time the colonies heard about Parliament's Coercive Acts, the ability—or desire—of the three dozen printers operating between Boston and Charleston to maintain anything resembling neutrality in their weekly newspapers was largely a facade.

The bolstering of increasingly politicized information networks in the early 1770s helped mitigate the various pressures undermining American unity. Political leaders were in search of the slippery, abstract concept of trust among faraway colonists they neither knew nor particularly liked. The institutions they built or transformed constituted a quiet revolution, and a necessary one, in the months before the destruction of the tea in Boston Harbor. Given the fundamental nature of the American Revolution—a massive argument—the contours of information and knowledge at the outset of the conflict are vital to understanding why the colonies did not simply fly apart once shots rang out on Lexington Green. Ideas and interests were at the heart of the argument, but victory would go to whichever side could present the more convincing assessment of what "liberty" and "tyranny" meant. Print carried those ideas and interests, and the patriots worked relentlessly in the 1770s to propagate the notion that their definition of those terms was the only choice.

1: CORRESPONDENCE COMMITTEES
AND A NEW POSTAL SYSTEM

Under the guise of "Massachusettensis," loyalist writer Daniel Leonard castigated the Boston committee of correspondence as "the foulest, subtlest, and most venomous serpent ever issued from the eggs of sedition." Leonard's hyperbole was not unjustified. What the Boston Town Meeting authorized on November 2, 1772, was indeed, in Leonard's words, "a new and, till lately unheard of, mode of opposition." Spurred by distressing news that the crown had stripped the province of the right to set the governor's salary and expenses, on November 3, the twenty-one men elected to organize a "committee of correspondence" set to work. Led by Samuel Adams,

Joseph Warren, and Benjamin Church, they drafted a statement of rights and list of grievances and, within three weeks, had scattered them to the 260 Massachusetts towns and abroad to other provinces.[2]

Boston's consciousness-raising touched off meetings and debates throughout Massachusetts. Starting in December, over the next several months more than half the province's towns discussed the Boston committee's grievances and established their own correspondence committees to continue the dialogue. Within a few weeks of its establishment, Adams and his colleagues wrote to towns in western Massachusetts, like South Hadley, reassuring them that they should not despair as long as our *"righteous cause is so well understood and zealously espoused by our worthy fellow countrymen"*; or Brimfield, in central Massachusetts, lobbying them that "universal resentment which the People of this Province have discovered . . . have a natural tendency to form an *indissoluble union* among us. We are all brethren in one common cause, the good of which we are all aiming to promote." Of course, as the leaders of the Boston committee well knew, promoting concepts like "indissoluble union" and "righteous cause" did not make them so. Those underscored expressions were enormous sighs of relief, and they allowed both ends of this new correspondence to express their complaints in collective terms. Not only did the Boston committee's initial set of grievances employ a totalizing "we" (speaking for the entire town of Boston), which eliminated dissent and projected a uniform sense of outrage, but the towns were able to respond in a similar fashion. The Massachusetts committees of correspondence acted as a new type of town crier—with their shouts of unflagging support captured and preserved in written pledges tucked away in riders' bags. Each returning rider shored up Boston's confidence that it did not stand alone. This was precisely how Adams, Warren, and Church imagined their new "mode of opposition," and its success explains Daniel Leonard's exasperation.[3]

2. *Boston Post-Boy,* Jan. 2, 1775. For more on the Boston committee of correspondence (hereafter BCC), see Richard D. Brown, *Revolutionary Politics in Massachusetts: The Boston Committee of Correspondence and the Towns, 1772–1774* (Cambridge, Mass., 1970); William B. Warner, *Protocols of Liberty: Communication Innovation and the American Revolution* (Chicago, 2013), 31–74.

3. BCC to South Hadley, Feb. 3, 1773, in BCC records, NYPL, reel 2, 681, BCC to Brimfield, Feb. 9, 1773, reel 1, V, 380; William B. Warner, "The Invention of a Public Machine for Revolutionary Sentiment: The Boston Committee of Correspondence," *Eighteenth Century,* L (2009), 150–151.

"A Work of Difficulty"

But there was far more work to be done. Luckily for the Boston leaders, the idea of closing the communication gap between the disparate colonies was not limited to Massachusetts. Virginia leaders were, at that moment, becoming increasingly concerned about the attacks on the legal rights of Rhode Islanders accused of raiding the ship *Gaspée,* a Royal Navy schooner enforcing customs laws that had run aground near Providence in June 1772. Early in 1773, Richard Henry Lee met with several other prominent Virginians, including Patrick Henry and Thomas Jefferson, at the Raleigh Tavern in Williamsburg to discuss the *Gaspée* case — especially the crown's potentially precedent-setting move of trying the accused in Britain — and wanting to discuss the matter with colleagues in New England. The next week, these men found themselves at the center of a new standing intercolonial committee of correspondence, tasked by the House of Burgesses to write to the speakers of other colonial assemblies to discover "a full Account of the Principles and Authority" of the *Gaspée* investigation.[4]

Most other colonial assemblies followed the lead of Boston and Virginia's burgesses, forming committees of correspondence during 1773, with only Pennsylvania holding out until the following summer. The committees were crucial developments. Each one vested more people in the resistance movement. They were the foundation of a continental shadow government. These extralegal committees served as models for future bodies, particularly the committees of observation and inspection formed by the 1774 Continental Association and wartime committees of safety.

The committees of correspondence, moreover, were not simply clearinghouses for information. They channeled and amplified certain modes of political expression. Committee members in Williamsburg and Boston simultaneously broadcast arguments and received word of how (hopefully) like-minded colonists greeted those representations in other provincial capitals or throughout the small towns of New England. Both leading and following, they explored the limits of legitimate rhetoric. When Bostonians heard their words echo back from the towns, they knew they were on more stable ground. The inhabitants of Marlborough, Massachusetts, for instance, stated they, too, recognized they were "engaged in one Common

---

4. *Rev. Va.,* II, 17. The resolutions creating the standing committee of correspondence were printed in the *Virginia Gazette* (Purdie & Dixon), Mar. 18, 1773, and *Virginia Gazette* (Rind), Mar. 18, 1773. For more on the *Gaspée* incident, see Merrill Jensen, *The Founding of a Nation: A History of the American Revolution, 1763–1776* (New York, 1968), 425–430.

Cause" and anticipated that every town "assisting and Uniting Like a band of Brothers may Banish Tyranny from our Land." Those paper pledges were the first evidence that such notions existed west of Boston.[5]

When the news of the Coercive Acts—dubbed "Intolerable" by patriot publicists—reached America, then, this new communication infrastructure began to transport messages of fidelity and support for Boston from far outside New England. The correspondence committees went into a new phase of importance and activity in May 1774 as soon as colonists learned that Parliament had closed the port of Boston and revoked Massachusetts's charter. Providence informed the Boston committee of correspondence of its latest town meeting, whereby it reassured its neighbors, "The inhabitants of this town will firmly adhere to them and will be ready to testify their zeal in support of their Rights as Englishmen in every other way that shall be thought serviceable to the cause." New Haven sent word that the people had also convened "in large numbers" and "testified their disapprobation." Correspondence committees in Philadelphia, New York City, and Baltimore sent pledges of support, and the Bostonians reveled in the "harmony of sentiment . . . which generally prevails throughout the Continent." Boston leaders made sure to maximize the effect of these encomiums. "The early exertions of our brethren in the town of Providence," they wrote in response to the effusive encouragement from the Rhode Island city, "discover at once their sympathy, generosity and sense of the common danger. We have held up your worthy example to the Southern Colonies, and have reason to expect great advantages from so disinterested a Spirit." Indeed, as they had hoped, assurances redounded up and down the Atlantic coast, as the records of the Maryland committee of correspondence in Annapolis attest. Extant in their files are circular letters passing rapidly in late May between committees in Virginia (Alexandria, Norfolk, Portsmouth, Williamsburg), Maryland (Baltimore, Annapolis), South Carolina (Charleston), and Pennsylvania (Philadelphia, Chester), each raising awareness of Boston's plight and vowing not to abandon the beleaguered city. Riders on the roads throughout America that spring had bags filled with papers containing the phrases "agreeable prospect of unanimity," "an attack on all," "cause of all America," and, simply, the "common cause."[6]

---

5. Marlborough, Mass., to BCC, Jan. 7, 1773, quoted in Brown, *Revolutionary Politics in Massachusetts*, 106.

6. Providence to BCC, May 17, 1774, BCC records, reel 1, VIII, 702, New Haven to BCC, May 25, 1774, 714, BCC to Philadelphia, June 17, 1774, X, 815, BCC to

"A Work of Difficulty"

New Haven's promise to Boston, however, contained an adverb that pointed toward problems that might yet threaten this outpouring of sympathy. "As soon as the Sentiments of our Sister Towns can be had, we shall carefully transmit them to you," the New Haven committee wrote on May 25. What could they have meant by *"carefully* transmit them?" That they would take extra pains or expense in forwarding them quickly? Or perhaps did "carefully" reveal something more troublesome? Two months before, the Boston committee had expressed concerns that the British would not stand idly by while colonial leaders openly resisted Parliament. "When we consider the importance of the Post, by which not only private letters of friendship and commerce but *public intelligence* is sent from Colony to Colony," they felt pressured to bring it under American control,

> more especially when we further consider that the British Administration and their Agents have taken every step in their power to prevent an Union of the Colonies, which is so necessary for our making a successful opposition to their Arbitrary Designs, and which depends upon a free communication of the Circumstances and sentiments of each to the other and their mutual Councils.

If the Boston committee was right, this was grounds for careful transmission; if royal officials decided to interdict the post roads leading to Boston as they did the sea lanes, then not only would the sentiments of unity be blocked but incriminating evidence of a larger resistance movement far outside Massachusetts would have been impossible to deny. The written pledges of support—with many featuring individual signatures—could be proof of sedition as much as sympathy. There was, in short, risk all around in May 1774: Bostonians put their faith in the rest of the continent, betting with little collateral that they did not stand alone, while more colonists across North America inched closer to committing themselves to treasonous acts, at least on paper and by association. The entire enterprise of a common

NYC, June 16, 1774, 818, BCC to Baltimore, June 16, 1774, 818; quotes from letters to Philadelphia, ibid., reel 1, X, 815, and to Providence, May 21, 1774, 796. The records of the Annapolis committee of correspondence are in Robert Purviance Papers, 1766–1849, MS 1394, MDHS. "Agreeable prospect of unanimity": Baltimore CC to Philadelphia CC, June 13, 1774. "An attack on all": Norfolk CC to Charleston CC, May 30, 1774. "Cause of all America": Alexandria CC to Baltimore CC, May 27, 1774. "Common cause": Baltimore CC to Boston CC, June 4, 1774, Annapolis CC to Virginia CC, May 25, 1774, Boston CC to Chester CC, June 23, 1774.

cause depended on words trumping the structural weaknesses of intersectional discord, territorial disputes, and social differences enervating the project at this fragile juncture. It was a dangerous gamble.[7]

✳ ✳ ✳

Some colonists developed schemes to ensure there was more than rhetoric underscoring the resistance movement. One notable project was the brainchild of a somewhat nomadic printer named William Goddard. The purpose of the Boston committee's letter in which they warned of British interception of the mail was to recommend Goddard's plan to create a Constitutional Post Office.

The idea of an independent postal system came from Goddard's professional frustration. For a decade after the Seven Years' War, Goddard had struggled to sustain a viable newspaper, first in Providence and later in Philadelphia. He believed much of his trouble in Philadelphia stemmed from his idea that because a competitor, *Pennsylvania Journal* printer William Bradford, also served as the city's postmaster, he cornered the market on fresh news. So in 1773 Goddard left for Baltimore to start a new paper. But the problem of communication flows remained. Baltimore was not part of the established system of post riders, so he would have to pay private carriers to transport newspapers to his subscribers. Annoyed by this exclusion, the political and communications entrepreneur began to devise an alternative. Goddard asked his sister Mary Katherine to manage his Baltimore paper, and, at winter's end, he traveled northward to lobby the committees of correspondence for a subsidy in support of his plan for a postal service outside British control.[8]

Goddard revealed his business acumen by taking advantage of the political implications of his proposal. From February to June 1774, Goddard

7. BCC to Marblehead and three other towns, Mar. 24, 1774, BCC records, reel 1, IX, 734–735. Royal officials did not attempt to disrupt the committees of correspondence. For efforts to discover American sedition in letters to England after war began, see Julie M. Flavell, "Government Interception of Letters from America and the Quest for Colonial Opinion in 1775," *WMQ*, 3d Ser., LVIII (2001), 403–430.

8. Goddard's effort to establish the Constitutional Post Office is covered in Ward L. Miner, *William Goddard, Newspaperman* (Durham, N.C., 1962), 111–136; Arthur M. Schlesinger, *Prelude to Independence: The Newspaper War on Britain, 1764–1776* (New York, 1957), 192–195; T. H. Breen, *American Insurgents, American Patriots: The Revolution of the People* (New York, 2010), 105–110; Konstantin Dierks, *In My Power: Letter Writing and Communications in Early America* (Philadelphia, 2009), 189–206.

"A Work of Difficulty"

attended committee of correspondence meetings from New York through all the postal stations in New England. In these sessions, he argued for his postal service in terms of the imperial controversy. Eventually, he would publish these reasons in a broadside. Though Goddard clearly had ulterior motives, he put his case in terms of the dangers to American liberty. The royal post, he warned, centralized into a few "Hands all the social, commercial, and political Intelligence of the Continent"; it opened the possibility that "our Letters . . . are liable to be stopt and opened by a Ministerial Mandate"; and worse, "our News-Papers, those necessary and important Alarms in Time of public Danger, may be rendered of little Consequence for want of Circulation." Goddard's promotional tour, highly publicized (and sometimes criticized) in colonial newspapers, was an instant success. What he proposed—creating new committees in each colony that would appoint postmasters, hire riders, and regulate postage by subscription—began to operate before he even returned to Baltimore in June.[9]

Several elements buoyed Goddard's scheme. First, he had impeccable timing. The newly established committees of correspondence outside Massachusetts were in search of an issue to correspond about in the months between the destruction of the tea in Boston and Parliament's response. A proposal for a new post office met that need. Second, an independent post offered security, an imperative that became a priority when letters began to fly between cities and towns just a few weeks later with the news of the Coercive Acts. Finally, and most important, Goddard framed his plan as a way to underscore the union. Samuel Adams recognized the proposal as essential: Goddard was "engaged in this attempt, not only with a View of serving himself as a Printer, but equally from the more generous motive of serving the Common Cause of America," he wrote in recommendation to a Marblehead committee of correspondence. Although not convincing everyone (especially Ben Franklin's friends who had benefited from his postal position), Goddard's claims of disinterest and patriotism matched the mood of the spring of 1774. As Benjamin Edes and John Gill put it in their *Boston Gazette,* "How cheerfully will every well wisher to his country lay hold of an opportunity to risque [wrest] the channel of public and private intelligence out of the hands of a power openly inimical to its Rights and Liberties." How, indeed.[10]

9. William Goddard, *The Plan for Establishing a New American Post-Office* (Boston, 1774), *Early American Imprints,* 42609.

10. Samuel Adams to Marblehead Committee of Correspondence, in Henry Alonzo Cushing, ed., *The Writings of Samuel Adams* (1907; rpt. Middlesex, Mass,

Another factor in Goddard's success was the poor condition of the royal post by the mid-1770s. At the same time that colonial cities and towns held meetings to create new committees of correspondence in 1773 and 1774, Hugh Finlay began to undertake the task the crown had given him: to inspect all the post offices in America. Finlay was a faithful believer in royal authority and bureaucratic efficiency, so what he found appalled him. The meticulous journal he kept on his inspection tour, was a cataract of disappointment and frustration.

As Finlay made his way through the sixty-four postal stations from September 1773 to June 1774, he encountered lots of American operators cutting corners, avoiding crown regulations, and making "private bargain[s] . . . for their own emolument." Every rider who pocketed postage that was meant to go to England violated the Revenue Act—and these transgressions were epidemic. Things were especially bad in the southern colonies. There, Finlay learned of drunk riders, dead postal officers, unruly children, negligent records, and hostile ship captains compounding problems of swampy lands, washed-out or unattended ferries, and lonely, dangerous roads preventing letters from reaching their destinations. From Finlay's perspective, it was a miracle that any information changed hands at all. In New England, the situation was better. Most of the post officers he found there were sober and careful, keeping tidy offices and precise account books. But Finlay was a stickler for order, a man better suited for the efficiency of an industrialized age than eighteenth-century America. He expressed despair at the condition of riders' unlocked, sometimes exposed, bags. During his visit to the New Haven office, he noted the pitiful condition of the arriving rider from Hartford: "His Portmanteau was not lock'd, it was stuff'd with bundles of different kinds, and crammed with newspapers: . . . the rider had saddle bags quite full besides, so that his horse (a poor looking beast) was loaded too

---

2006), III, 70–71. Opponents of American resistance also criticized Goddard's plan as another hostile patriot attempt to seize power and funds from the crown. See *Boston Post-Boy*, Mar. 24, 1774. Since Goddard's plan would have been financially, politically, and socially detrimental to Benjamin Franklin—the postmaster for America since 1753—news of Franklin's being stripped of that position as a result of his involvement in the publication of Thomas Hutchinson's private letters would also have been an impetus for Goddard's launching of his independent post plan. Franklin's friends sent letters informing of Goddard and his plan, planting seeds that would bear bitter fruit the following year, when the two competed over who would head the new postal system. See Miner, *William Goddard, Newspaperman,* 129. "How cheerfully": *Boston Gazette*, Mar. 21, 1774.

"A Work of Difficulty"

much to make the necessary speed." Although Finlay would have recoiled at the politics that underpinned it, if Goddard's constitutional system could improve on these deficiencies, so much the better.[11]

Finlay's journal also relates the hunger for information throughout America in the mid-1770s. In Falmouth, in the Maine district, the postal officer had to bear constant interruption, for "every person who looks for a letter or a news paper freely enters his house, be it post day or not." In New London, Connecticut, the inhabitants had "free access at all times to the office," a bad "custom" the officer tried to break. Georgians, too, begged for more infrastructure, promising significant revenues if a regular post could be established. Perhaps this was a function of the imperial crisis: Finlay related in Salem, Massachusetts, that any informer interfering in the post "wou'd get tar'd and feather'd," and "no jury wou'd find the fact." "It is deem'd necessary to hinder all acts of Parliament from taking effect in

11. Frank H. Norton, ed., *The Hugh Finlay Journal: Colonial Postal History, 1773–1774* (1867; rpt. Washington, D.C., 1975), 43, 55. This could have been the problem of a few bad Connecticut riders. The same New Haven post officer also complained to Finlay, "The Portmanteaus seldom come locked: the consequence is that the riders stuff them with bundles of shoes, stockings, canisters, money or anything they get to carry, which tears the Portmanteaus, and rubs the letters to pieces" (41). But this is taking Finlay's journal as the final authority on the status of the post in the mid-1770s. Although there were definite problems with the royal post in 1774, Finlay had good things to say about a lot of the system. He had few complaints about post officers in the northern colonies—only about riders and coach operators seeking side business. Finlay's journal has indeed been interpreted as evidence of an inefficient, disordered information network calling out for reform on the eve of the Revolution. In her revisionist interpretation of the material breadth of print in Revolutionary America, literary scholar Trish Loughran adopted Finlay's critical attitude as proof that incompetency governed the transmission of information in the 1770s. Before the age of steam, Loughran sides wholly with Finlay: it was simply unreliable. But, like Finlay's complaints (which are mostly found in the South), her perspective needs counterbalance. Yes, ship captains and post riders were often negligent in their care of other people's letters, but the expectations that they treated their portmanteaus as sacred trusts is anachronistically applying a value of the nineteenth-century liberal, industrial age back onto the colonial past. Anecdotes like the singular examples of Connecticut riders not locking their bags or one Georgia rider delivering mail while drunk should not condemn the entire information network as incapable or as evidence that it was impossible for colonists to share common texts or print phenomena before the Industrial Revolution. See Loughran, *The Republic in Print: Print Culture in the Age of U.S. Nation Building, 1770–1870* (New York, 2007), 6–9.

America. They are they say to be governed by laws of their own framing and no other." As they would just two months later with the Tea Act on Griffin's Wharf, colonists in Salem and elsewhere did, indeed, view the Revenue Act—as William Goddard and Samuel Adams hoped they would—as one of those laws to be disregarded in defense of American rights.[12]

2: CHANGES IN THE PRESS

Or else. Finlay understood the menace that underpinned the calls for a common cause. Edes and Gill's reference to "every well wisher" was a not-so-veiled threat for dissenters to either change their minds or risk having them changed by force. It is fitting that such "cheerful" sentiment would come from a newspaper. Newspaper printers were among the earliest to comprehend this political polarization—and threat of retribution.[13]

"Printers are educated in the Belief, that when Men differ in Opinion, both Sides ought equally to have the Advantage of being heard by the Publick," Benjamin Franklin had written forty years earlier in his "Apology for Printers." "It is unreasonable to imagine Printers approve of every thing they print, and to censure them on any particular thing accordingly; since in the way of their Business they print such great variety of things opposite and contradictory." This, the ideal of a free and open press, was increasingly a valued goal for Anglo-American printers and the public at large over the eighteenth century. By the mid-1700s, many Britons saw press freedom as a cherished legacy of the Glorious Revolution; at the same time, they began to see leaders in London embrace print as a unique way of managing, magnifying, and manipulating an emerging element of political culture: public opinion.[14]

12. Norton, ed., *Finlay Journal*, 16 ("freely enters his house"), 23–24 ("tar'd and feather'd"), 35 ("free access"), 57–59 ("hinder all acts of Parliament").

13. For a startling interpretation of the "American terror"—the threat of violence and social intimidation that lay behind patriot speech, behavior, and writing starting in 1773–1774—see Brendan McConville, *The King's Three Faces: The Rise and Fall of Royal America, 1688–1776* (Chapel Hill, N.C., 2006), 286–300.

14. *Pennsylvania Gazette,* June 10, 1731. For more on the eighteenth-century British press, see Charles E. Clark, *The Public Prints: The Newspaper in Anglo-American Culture, 1665–1740* (New York, 1994); Hannah Barker, *Newspapers, Politics, and English Society, 1695–1855* (New York, 2000), 22–23; Jeremy Black, *The English Press, 1621–1861* (Phoenix Mill, U.K., 2001), 127; Ann C. Dean, *The Talk of the Town: Figurative Publics in Eighteenth-Century Britain* (Lewisburg, Pa., 2007); Troy Bickham, *Making Headlines: The American Revolution as Seen through the British Press* (Dekalb, Ill., 2009).

"A Work of Difficulty"

Still, since printing was always precarious, especially in the colonies, neutrality made good business sense. The public had the liberty to use the press to announce their side of the story; no customers need be excluded. Even in the three major American cities of Philadelphia, New York, and Boston, printers could rarely sustain themselves on newspaper subscriptions alone. They had to diversify to survive. Most supplemented their income by producing blank legal forms, broadside advertisements, almanacs, and perhaps a few tracts. Many doubled as postmasters. Goddard's nemesis in Philadelphia, William Bradford, branched the furthest out, opening the London Coffee House and, later, insuring ships. As Franklin himself learned, the only surefire way to financial security was to win lucrative government contracts for the right to print the colony's money or laws. Printers could hardly risk alienating large swaths of potential subscribers. Moreover, with ink-stained, callused hands, they were not gentlemen—even though much of their information came from those ranks. They depended on the circles of elites but were not welcome in them. Gifted writers like Franklin bristled at the notion that a colonial printer was "not generally expected to possess a mind of his own." By at least midcentury, even master printers were considered machine operators—not learned men capable of nuanced argument and biting satire or connoisseurs of graceful rhetoric and style.[15]

15. Stephen Botein, "'Meer Mechanics' and an Open Press: The Business and Political Strategies of Colonial American Printers," *Perspectives in American History*, IX (1975), 158; *Pennsylvania Gazette*, June 10, 1731. The historiography of a "free press" is dominated by Leonard W. Levy, *Legacy of Suppression: Freedom of Speech and Press in Early American History* (Cambridge, Mass., 1960), revised and updated as *Emergence of a Free Press* (New York, 1985). Also see Richard Buel, Jr., "Freedom of the Press in Revolutionary America: The Evolution of Libertarianism, 1760–1820," in Bernard Bailyn and John B. Hench, eds., *The Press and the American Revolution* (Worcester, Mass., 1980), 59–98; and Jeffrey A. Smith, *Printers and Press Freedom: The Ideology of Early American Journalism* (New York, 1988); Robert W. T. Martin, *The Free and Open Press: The Founding of American Democratic Press Liberty, 1640–1800* (New York, 2001). For what printers did to supplement their incomes, see also Botein, "'Meer Mechanics,'" *Perspectives in American History*, IX (1975), 127–225; Rollo G. Silver, "Aprons Instead of Uniforms: The Practice of Printing, 1776–1787," *Proceedings of the American Antiquarian Society*, N.S., LXXXVII (1977), 111–194; Carol Sue Humphrey, *"This Popular Engine": New England Newspapers during the American Revolution, 1775–1789* (Newark, Del., 1992), 40–43; and Rosalind Remer, *Printers and Men of Capital: Philadelphia Book Publishers in the New Republic* (Philadelphia, 1996), 11–27. For Bradford's coffeehouse, see Peter Thompson, *Rum Punch and Revolution: Taverngoing and Pub-*

With the Stamp Act of 1765, however, this ideal of a neutral, open press began to change entirely. The Stamp Act politicized paper, and with it began a transformation of the meaning of "free press." Early on in the imperial crisis, several newspaper printers shrugged off any pretense to professional detachment and joined the opposition. A few printers in Boston (Benjamin Edes and Samuel Hall), Providence (William Goddard), and Philadelphia (William Bradford) were known members of their local Sons of Liberty. In 1766, when debts forced the *New-York Gazette; or, the Weekly Post-Boy* printer John Holt to relinquish his lease of James Parker's shop, the New York Sons helped the reliably pro-patriot Holt secure new equipment and start a new paper, the *New-York Journal.*[16]

Growing polarization and politicization also put pressure on editors to protect their contributors. Anonymity had long been a key feature of eighteenth-century print culture, even more so as it became politicized. Contributors to the newspapers shielded themselves with pseudonyms, often judiciously employed to cast themselves as public defenders ("Populus," "Salus Populi," "Rusticus") or guardians of ancient liberty and virtue ("Mucius Scaevola," "Cato," "Nestor," "Neoptolemus"). Printers were the keepers of these secrets; they alone knew who had submitted a manuscript for publication. As pressure increased in the 1760s and 1770s, the impulse to throw off these veils could be very strong. Throughout the Revolution, printers on both sides of the imperial question found themselves or their property at risk when they refused to bow to angry demands that they name names.[17]

The highly charged content of those publications also fueled partisan-

lic Life in Eighteenth-Century Philadelphia (Philadelphia, 1999), 106–107. Despite his success as the publisher of "Poor Richard's Almanack" and the popular *Pennsylvania Gazette,* it was not until he earned the right to print Pennsylvania's laws that Benjamin Franklin became affluent and able to retire from the mechanic's trade of printing. See Gordon S. Wood, *The Americanization of Benjamin Franklin* (New York, 2004), 26–27. The lure of the government contract was the reason why Virginia had three separate papers all with the confounding title of *Virginia Gazette.* Since the law stated that the contract would be given to "the Virginia Gazette," each printer had to give his or her publication that title in order to be eligible.

16. Schlesinger, *Prelude to Independence,* 83; Clarence S. Brigham, *History and Bibliography of American Newspapers, 1690–1820* (Worcester, Mass., 1947), I, 635–636.

17. Eran Shalev, *Rome Reborn on Western Shores: Historical Imagination and the Creation of the American Republic* (Charlottesville, Va., 2009), 157–162.

ship. The imperial crisis witnessed what one scholar has called the advent of the "exposé" in America. As printers increasingly gave space to contributors who claimed they were unmasking corruption or conspiracy, they aided in the disintegration of established concepts of what kept a press "free." The most impassioned publications of the 1760s and 1770s, from John Dickinson's *Letters from a Farmer in Pennsylvania* to Massachusetts governor Thomas Hutchinson's private letters, centered on revealing or dramatizing the government's true aims of stripping American colonists of their liberties. There were not two sides to "truth." Behind pseudonyms or not, the patriot writers or artists who brought these plots to light claimed they were heroic servants of the people, informants seeking to protect an unwitting public from tyranny's stealthy advance. At the same time, the appearance of each of these "exposés" also represented a choice by the printers themselves. By giving space to the "truth"—and, by extension, to the protection of the people's rights—they took a side that changed the older values of press freedom. If the press were truly free or open, would that necessitate, in the face of this interpretation, allowing deceivers equal space to jeopardize the public good?[18]

By the eve of the Revolution, whether they embraced this change or not, colonial printers found the values that underpinned their craft shifting beneath their feet. Neutrality, previously their lodestar, was increasingly a chimera. Either personal or professional affiliation to one political side or the other was becoming the sine qua non of American printing. What was left of that middle ground vanished with the news of casualties on Lexington Green.

* * *

When General Gage ordered his regulars to Lexington, there were thirty-six active newspapers in nearly every English colony on mainland North America. The printers of many of these papers had ties to one another. Sometimes these connections were family based. Members of the Green family, one the most venerable clans in the American printing trade throughout the eighteenth century, published nearly all of the newspapers in Connecticut in 1775 as well as the sole newspaper in Annapolis, Maryland. Marriage connected *New-York Journal* printer John Holt to Williamsburg printer

18. Thomas C. Leonard, "News for a Revolution: The Exposé in America, 1768–1773," *JAH*, LXVII (1980), 26–40.

William Hunter, and his nephew, John Hunter Holt, supervised the *Virginia Gazette, or the Norfolk Intelligencer* in 1775. The printers of the *South-Carolina Gazette* and *South-Carolina Gazette; And Country Journal* were brothers-in-law.[19]

More often, the relationships between printers were of a professional nature. Publishers, especially Benjamin Franklin, saw their apprentices and journeymen establish organs in other American cities. Before he took over the *Providence Gazette* in 1769, John Carter was an apprentice in Franklin's *Pennsylvania Gazette* shop. Samuel Hall was, too, before he started the *Essex Gazette* in Salem, Massachusetts. Peter Timothy's father was a journeyman in that same shop before assuming command of the *South-Carolina Gazette* in 1735. Benjamin Towne of the *Pennsylvania Evening Post* was William Goddard's journeyman, whereas Goddard, in turn, had learned his craft from John Holt when he was caretaker of the *Post-Boy*, owned by James Parker, also a Franklin associate. As a Green and former Franklin apprentice, *Maryland Gazette* printer Jonas Green sat at the center of this Venn diagram of professional and personal connections.[20]

Less frequently, printers combined forces or shared equipment. In Boston, two papers shared the same types and even partial name. In the early 1770s, on Thursdays, while riders carried copies of the latest issue of Richard Draper's *Massachusetts Gazette; and the Boston Weekly News-Letter* throughout the colony, his types and other equipment were hauled a few blocks away to School Street, where John Green, Joseph Russell, and their workmen would labor through the weekend to bring out the *Massachusetts Gazette, and the Boston Post-Boy and Advertiser* by Monday. Shortly before the Revolution, *Massachusetts Spy* printer Isaiah Thomas also branched out, becoming partner in a Newburyport paper, the *Essex Journal*.[21]

With the burgeoning imperial crisis, however, politics became another imperative that fostered a competing sense of community. Political identification—whether through personal participation in or against the resistance movement or simply by making columns more available to one side or the other—constituted a new network. Older ties did not disappear, but they did change, especially after the war began. The Holts, for instance,

19. Isaiah Thomas, *The History of Printing in America: With a Biography of Printers and an Account of Newspapers,* ed. Marcus A. McCorison (1810; rpt. New York, 1970), 571.

20. Ralph Frasca, *Benjamin Franklin's Printing Network: Disseminating Virtue in Early America* (Columbia, Mo., 2006); David C. Skaggs, "Editorial Policies of the *Maryland Gazette,* 1765–1783," *Maryland Historical Magazine,* LIX (1964), 341.

21. Thomas, *History of Printing,* 229–230, 262–263.

"A Work of Difficulty"

would see family ties and politics converge in 1775 when Virginia governor Lord Dunmore raided the Norfolk offices of John Hunter Holt's *Virginia Gazette*. All his uncle could do to help was print scathing condemnations of the attack in his *New-York Journal*. On the other hand, when British troops occupied Philadelphia late in 1777, James Humphreys, Jr., formerly an apprentice of staunch patriot printer William Bradford, returned to resume publication of his *Pennsylvania Ledger* a year after having been driven from the city under suspicion of being a loyalist.

These personal and professional ties connected printers to one another across space, offering alternate webs by which they could obtain supplies, personnel, and information. They were the sinews of colonial print trade, the everyday understanding of what it meant to be a colonial newspaper printer in 1775.[22]

During the war, these thirty-seven presses sent out newspaper sheets various days of each week. The epicenter was, of course, in New England, with nearly half of the print shops (four in Connecticut, eight in Massachusetts, one in New Hampshire, and three in Rhode Island). Another quarter were in New York City (three) and Philadelphia (six). The Chesapeake had six more (two in Maryland and four in Virginia). Finally, there were six in the South (two in North Carolina, three in South Carolina, and one in Georgia). Female family members often stepped up to the type cases when their husbands or brothers could not.

Throughout the 1760s and 1770s, these men and women had grown divergent in outlook—or, at least, their productions had. Their print shops were the most important nodes of information in their home cities, receiving, organizing, digesting, and presenting news from far away longitudes (across the Atlantic Ocean) and, increasingly, from more proximate but still strange latitudes (across the Atlantic seaboard). Though on a puny scale hardly imaginable to modern readers deluged with information platforms and outlets, their meager twelve columns of print were essential in connecting people across vast expanses. As one classic account has theorized, they created "imagined linkages" and fostered a sense of sameness, simultaneity, and belonging that stretched far across local boundaries. The ability of print to challenge those limited, parochial horizons was a critical component of forming intercolonial unity and making the cause common. Patriot political and communications leaders understood print's unique power early on

22. For more background on the personal history, geography, and publishing careers of printers on the eve of the Revolution, see Appendix A, below.

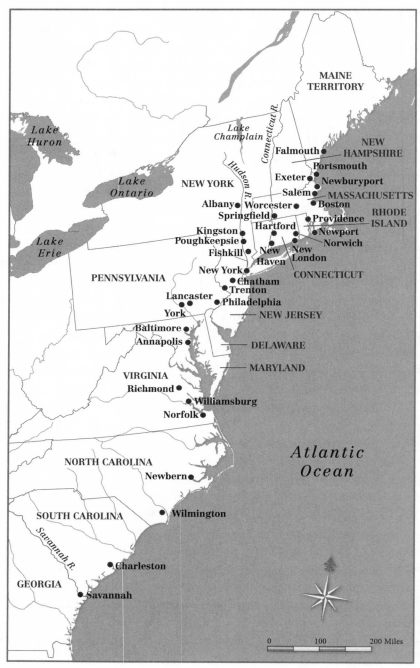

Map 2. *Locations of newspaper publication, 1775–1783.*
Drawn by Gerry Krieg

to put forward their own selective arguments for resisting British authority, whereas loyalists did not—at least, until it was nearly too late.[23]

In the 1770s, these three dozen newspapers created three dozen intricate communication webs emanating from American seaports. Colonists did more than just imagine themselves as part of a larger interest group, association, or, indeed, community. When they wrote to the printer asking to take their newspaper, they were also joining a real network. What were the material entities of shared information created by subscribing to a specific newspaper? Many people in New York City, Boston, Philadelphia, and Charleston sat down in private homes and public houses and read one, perhaps several, newspapers. But newspapers—not just their readers' imaginations—traveled. The full title of James Rivington's *New-York Gazetteer; or, the Connecticut, Hudson's River, New-Jersey, and Quebec Weekly Advertiser* reflected the scope of a network that stretched far outside Manhattan.

How far? If Rivington was not exaggerating when he bragged of 3,600 subscribers (and counting!), then his *Gazetteer* was the most widely circulated paper in the colonies on the eve of war. Printers advertising to start new papers often claimed they needed upward of 700 reliable subscribers to make the enterprise economically feasible. This threshold was becoming less daunting as the intensity of the imperial crisis boosted subscriptions. More colonists took newspapers in the 1760s and 1770s, with the average run rising approximately to 2,500.[24]

Instead of relying on publishers' boasts or anecdotal evidence, however, thanks to the preservation of William Bradford's 1774 and 1775 subscription books for the *Pennsylvania Journal*, we may at least depend upon one printer's accurate and illuminating record of the communication skeins radiating out from colonial cities and towns at the start of war. Bradford's books shed light on exactly who took this paper, one of the most partisan patriot prints. These books laid bare the structure of Bradford's delivery system: the routes the riders took to carry the news, the places across the Atlantic world to which he sent the *Journal,* and the people who received them. They show not only the geographic reach of this sole Philadelphia paper but also its architecture. Together, these books reveal one print network, a single web. Although evidence remains for only Bradford's, there were three

23. Benedict Anderson, *Imagined Communities: Reflections on the Origin and Spread of Nationalism*, rev. ed. (1983; rpt. London, 1991), 33–36, 45–46, esp. 33.

24. See, for example, *Massachusetts Spy*, Feb. 10, 1775. Print run information in Schlesinger, *Prelude to Independence*, app. A, 303–304.

dozen similar webs of varying sizes and reach, spread throughout the main-land colonies. The war stories documented in the chapters that follow all traveled along and across these networks. They constitute the materiality of this study: how the stories patriot leaders sought to propagate throughout the colonial countryside actually found their way to people's ears and eyes.

3: THE ATLANTIC WORLD OF THE
PENNSYLVANIA JOURNAL, 1774–1776

The "List of Customers for Pennsylvania Journal Taken January 1774" is mistitled. Because the printer (or someone in his shop) notated the issue number in which they first opened their subscription, this book is more than just a survey of current customers. The book actually begins when Bradford took on his twenty-one-year-old son as a partner in September 1766, making it possible to track the flow of customers throughout the im-perial crisis. As of January 1774, Bradford and son had 1,703 subscribers' names on the rolls. Next to 286 of these (16.8 percent) were some sort of title suggesting elite status, whether a militia officer's rank (66), a physician's degree (45), a member of the clergy (47), or a gentleman (102). At least 24 women had their own *Journal* subscriptions. The Bradfords sent issues to the colonial governors of Virginia, New Hampshire, and New Jersey. One went to London to aid William Petty, the earl of Shelburne, in his opposition of the North administration. Also among the names were several prominent (or about to be) men. Thirteen men who took the Bradfords' paper would sign the Declaration of Independence, a document that then allowed three more subscribers to stand for election as governors of their now-sovereign states. Seven would become officers in the Continental army. Most lived far outside Philadelphia.[25]

Indeed, the Bradfords' 1774 subscription book illustrates the geographic coverage of the *Journal.* Of the approximately 1,700 issues their shop on Front and Market Street put out each Wednesday, nearly one-third of them (551, or 32.35 percent) stayed in the city, noted in the subscription book as headed "downtown," "uptown," left in the shop for pickup, or the result of "small rounds" through the outskirts of Philadelphia (see Appendix B, Table 1). The remaining two-thirds of the Bradfords' weekly output traveled outside the city, overland into the Pennsylvania interior, across Delaware River ferries to New Jersey, onto coastal boats headed into the Chesapeake

25. "List of Customers for Pennsylvania Journal Taken January 1774," Bradford Family Papers, Collection 1676, 2d Ser., box 9, folder 1, HSP.

"A Work of Difficulty"

Bay, or in more seaworthy vessels to New England, South Carolina, the English West Indies, Nova Scotia, Scotland, England, and Portugal.

According to the 1774 book, only 14.4 percent of the *Journal*'s subscribers lived in the Pennsylvania hinterland. This low number of 246 subscribers is perhaps a result of less-than-detailed accounting, for the next subscription book relates great detail on the rural Pennsylvania business. Most of the customers in the 1774 book, however, resided near the Maryland and Delaware border clustered around the village of Nottingham, in larger settlements in Lancaster and Reading, or up the Delaware River in Easton and Bristol. A full quarter of the Bradfords' rural Pennsylvania subscribers eschewed their delivery service entirely, opting to pick up their papers at the London Coffee House (see Appendix B, Table 2). Twice as many people in New Jersey and Delaware relied on the Bradfords' post riders as their counterparts in rural Pennsylvania. Nearly one-third of the weekly *Journals* either crossed the Delaware River against the current to central and northern New Jersey or plied it downstream to settlements in New Castle County, Delaware. Another 11 percent of the *Journal* went out into the Chesapeake, with more than eighty papers headed to Baltimore. Several other small towns in rural Maryland and Virginia took the Bradfords' paper (see Appendix B, Tables 3 and 4). Almost as many issues of the *Journal* as went weekly to the Chesapeake, where printers in Williamsburg and Annapolis could exchange news, went much farther out into the Atlantic. Nearly 9 percent of all the news sheets drying in the Bradfords' wharfside print shop would find space on vessels headed far from the Delaware Capes. Over the course of the decade, an increasing number of New Yorkers, perhaps unsatisfied with the news provided in their city by Rivington and Gaine, entered the Bradfords' customer lists. Another thirty-five went to New England. More went south, headed to printers, merchants, and more than a few political leaders in the Carolinas and Georgia. Thirty-two papers were cargo on ships headed farther south, scattering Philadelphia's news across the British and Dutch West Indies. And, according to the 1774 book, a few papers went to Nova Scotia, the British Isles, and Europe, mostly for printers' exchanges (see Appendix B, Table 5).

In other words, the *Pennsylvania Journal* enjoyed prosperity during the imperial controversy with England. Its registered readership almost tripled in the city; in the countryside, it more than doubled across the board. The Bradfords' reach into tidewater Maryland and Virginia increased even more substantially over the decade (see Appendix B, Table 4). The number of people in New Jersey taking the *Journal* also stands out from the 1774 book.

Situated between the two most important centers of print outside New England, New Jersey inhabitants interested in attaching themselves to a communications network had the greatest choice: in 1774, there were seven active papers within a few miles. About halfway between New York City and Philadelphia is Princeton, where a steadily growing number of people, including the leading patriots in town, wrote to the Bradfords asking for their paper. John Witherspoon did so in 1770, Richard Stockton in May 1773, and another future Continental Congressman, William Churchill Houston, subscribed just before Bostonians boarded the East India Company's tea ships. Even as the tea leaves still floated in Boston Harbor, those men and thirty-nine of their neighbors received the *Journal* in their home every week. But how many other neighbors' names were in similar books shelved in competitors' print shops? How many issues of the *New-York Journal, Pennsylvania Gazette, New-York Gazette; and the Weekly Mercury, Pennsylvania Evening Post,* or *Rivington's New-York Gazetteer* also arrived in Princeton during those anxious days? How many Princetonians were on multiple lists? We cannot know, but we should keep in mind that the expanding web the Bradfords cast into New Jersey, Virginia, and Maryland—and into the Atlantic Ocean—was only one of three dozen such overlapping networks on the eve of Revolution.

* * *

In fact, business had gotten so good that the number of people spread out over such an increasing distance necessitated a new method of accounting. The Bradfords' new subscription book, dated August 25, 1775, and numbering more than one hundred pages, is a complete reorganization and reorientation from its predecessor.

There are two striking omissions from the 1775 subscription book: the city of Philadelphia and the British Empire outside the mainland American colonies. Not having possession of the 1774 book would leave analysts wondering, Whither Philadelphia? Though there are notations for a few single papers left for Philadelphians to pick up in the shop, and mention of a handful of issues going to Germantown, the detailed city lists found in the previous book are not included. The most plausible explanation for this absence is that the printers used these two books simultaneously. Indeed, they managed the city lists in the old book after starting a new customer book, striking off people who stopped their subscriptions through the end of 1776. Though we cannot prove when people joined the city lists after January 1774 (for no dates or issue numbers from that period through the end of 1776 are provided), we can surmise that if those remaining cus-

"A Work of Difficulty"

tomers not struck out continued, then the *Journal* still had more than five hundred customers in Philadelphia through independence.

The second omission cannot be readily explained. All mention of newspapers leaving the mainland American colonies disappeared in the new book. Perhaps these continued, too, but this is impossible to substantiate. It is more plausible that the interruptions of war and the Royal Navy largely put an end to the *Pennsylvania Journal's* travel to Barbados, Jamaica, Halifax, or Edinburgh. Though it would be an overstatement to suggest that the *Journal* disappeared from the Atlantic wholesale — because it surely did not — the regular transmission of papers to faraway British colonies seems to have stopped by the summer of 1775.

On the other hand, what is in the 1775 book astounds. The level of description and organization denoting where the papers were going and how they were getting there is greatly magnified. In the old book, there was an eighteen-page-long entry for "Newtown" — really New Castle, Delaware. On these eighteen pages were smaller notations detailing where these papers were actually destined: down the Eastern Shore of Maryland to Chestertown, across the western side of the Chesapeake to Fredericktown and Georgetown. In 1774, the Bradfords had lumped people across Talbot, Kent, and Queen Anne's Counties in Maryland all into the "Newtown" column. No longer. Whether the result of a new account manager or increased expectations of developing commerce, the new book gave each of these places its own entry. Names of locales abound. The 1774 book listed 70 places they sent the *Journal* outside Philadelphia, including 14 outside the mainland American colonies. In the 1775 book, even without the Caribbean and British places, the different headings ballooned to 115.

The new book suggests an increased attention to geographic precision and rationalization. But even more important, it regrouped the places into apparent delivery routes and identified the key players in the distribution system. Thus the new, 1775 ledger sheds a very different — and even more penetrating — light on the construction and operation of the Bradfords' communication network throughout the mid-Atlantic and beyond.

Unlike its predecessor, the 1775 subscriber list faced forward, not backward. It is dated August 25, and the dates throughout suggest it was kept until the *Journal's* hiatus, when the British occupied Philadelphia in September 1777. The places are grouped very differently, the groups themselves not exactly keeping with a recognizable geographic plan.

It starts with central New Jersey, noting papers dropped off at "Mrs. Cunningham's" for a client in Gloucester and papers forwarded to Springfield

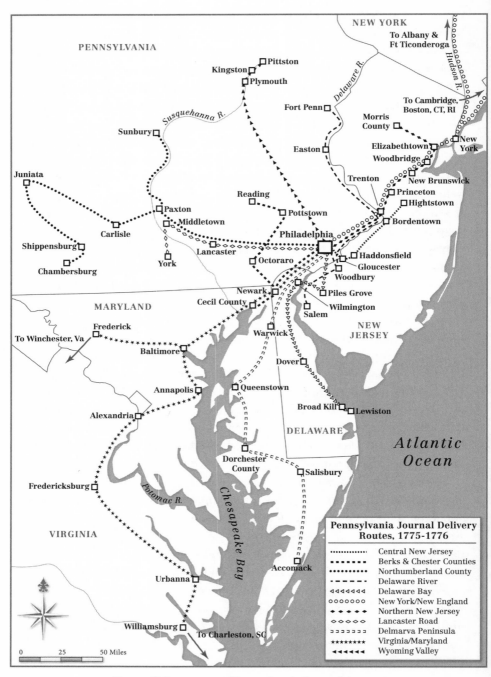

Map 3. *Delivery routes of* Pennsylvania Journal *in 1775.*

Drawn by Gerry Krieg

by way of the Burlington postmaster. Hightstown, New Jersey, customers received their papers via Bordentown, whereas the seven Haddonsfield customers had to rely on the *Pennsylvania Gazette* delivery rider to get their *Journal*. This customer segment increased only slightly over the first two years of war, with more than two dozen new subscribers added but nearly that many removed (see Appendix B, Table 7). The second section of the 1775 book was the only inclusion of people living in or close to the city. The Bradfords listed all the people getting their papers singly in the shop—fifty-one by the middle of 1777—and included the eleven papers going to Germantown, just a few miles to the northwest (see Appendix B, Table 8).[26]

From there, the book begins an extensive list of locations in Berks and Chester Counties. Starting up the Schuylkill in Pottstown and Reading and moving through southeastern Pennsylvania down to the Maryland border, riders dropped off handfuls of papers in small settlements like East Nottingham, Fogg's Manor, and New Garden. Just across the border near Norrisville, in Cecil County, Maryland, riders dropped ten papers at John Strawbridge's house, a number that had doubled since 1775. In all, the Bradfords' business in southeastern Pennsylvania had increased by one-third after the war began and almost doubled in 1776, with very few subtractions (see Appendix B, Table 9).[27]

Next, the subscription book documents the role of one particular subscriber in Reading, the single most important person for the Bradfords in Pennsylvania: Peter Withington. On September 28, 1776, the Pennsylvania Assembly gave Withington a captaincy in the Continental army's newly formed 12th Pennsylvania Regiment. His military service would be short. Just after mustering a large unit from Northampton County and traveling down the Susquehanna to serve in New Jersey, Withington took sick from camp fever and was a convalescent in Philadelphia in December 1776, just as William Bradford donned his militia colonel's uniform to defend the city. The ill captain soon returned home to Reading and died in May 1777. This brief service, however, does not encapsulate Withington's participation in the common cause, for several months before he was commissioned, his Reading house served as a distribution center for the *Journal,* one of the patriots' most important prints. That the recruiters were able to fill up the 12th Pennsylvania in Northampton County stemmed, in some part, from

26. List of subscribers, *Pennsylvania Journal,* 1775, 3, 5, Bradford Family Papers, box 9, folder 2.

27. Ibid., 13, 16, 17.

Withington's association with the Bradfords. When David Ramsay remembered in his 1789 history how "in establishing American independence . . . the press had merit equal to that of the sword," Withington was among those who had participated in both campaigns.[28]

The Bradfords sent 184 issues of the *Journal* up the Schuylkill to Withington's house each week, a large number nearly equal to the amount of papers the Bradfords had previously sent to the entire Chesapeake Bay region. Entrusted "to his care" were the thirteen papers for his Reading neighbors—eleven of whom started their subscriptions in the fall of 1776, around the time that Withington's military service began. Reading, apparently, was growing staunch in the cause. But there were many other bundles left to Withington's care. The subscription book notes there were a dozen other towns that depended on his protection to get their news. He held ten single issues for runners from Sunbury and Fort Augusta, on the Susquehanna, seventy miles to the northwest, to collect. He also directed a few more to a tavern in Northumberland County, called the Sign of the Garden of Eden.[29]

The other stacks sat waiting for William Carheart, a delivery rider who would come to Withington's house to take up the bundles and set off down the road west from Reading to the Paxton settlement, near what is now Harrisburg. Carheart was to drop off more than thirty papers for inhabitants in Paxton and Upper Paxton, then proceed farther north, where the Juniata River flows into the Susquehanna, to supply thirteen more customers. He probably returned downstream to the west side of the river, for he had seven papers to deliver at Tobias Hendrick's house, near Conestoga, where customers in East Pennsborough came to collect their papers. From there, he would have followed the road west.[30]

Then again, it is possible that Carheart wanted to lighten his load more quickly, left the mouth of the Juniata and then crossed Shoreman's Creek to find the road south through Stevenson's Gap to Carlisle; after all, lots of customers were waiting there. By late 1776, seventy-eight people depended on Carheart for their weekly news from Philadelphia—at least in the form of Bradford's *Journal*. The Bradfords had enjoyed success in Carlisle with the Revolution (and, surely, Carheart's service), bringing on forty-five new

28. Samuel Hazard et al., eds., *Pennsylvania Archives,* 2d Ser. (Harrisburg, Pa., 1896), X, 775, 777; Ramsay, *History of the American Revolution,* ed. Cohen, II, 633–634.

29. List of subscribers, *Pennsylvania Journal,* 1775, 9, 16, 20.

30. Ibid., 18–19.

customers in 1775 and thirty-seven more in 1776, losing only four along the way.[31]

Carheart had three more western deliveries to make before heading back to Withington's house to complete the circuit: Big Spring, a settlement a few miles up Conodoguinet Creek from Carlisle, then down the road to Shippensburg, and finally, Chamberstown (Chambersburg). Carheart dropped off thirteen in Big Spring (including ten new ones in 1776), seven in Shippensburg, and six in Chamberstown. From here, Carheart had a long, one hundred–mile ride loping back east to the Schuylkill, where Withington had another delivery ready (see Appendix B, Table 10).[32]

Peter Withington and William Carheart are not deemed founding fathers. They have no memorials or protected heritage sites. But the success of the American Revolution depended just the same on their efforts in small yet essential ways. They were the protectors and carriers of the news, which made them nurturers of the patriot movement. Patriot leaders claimed that their side of the dispute was an organic expression of an outraged populace. Though this was never truly the case, they needed men like Withington and Carheart to substantiate those claims. The Revolution relied upon them, too.

After detailing the Withington-Carheart route, the Bradfords' book then returned to New Jersey. Here, a few entries noted the importance of Hyder's Ferry, where a delivery person named George Johnson would cross the Delaware south of Philadelphia and carry three dozen papers to Woodberry and Salem. The following entries specified other agents carrying papers for the Bradfords. Matthew Knox, keeper of the Sign of Prince Henry, picked up nine papers when he came down from Bucks County to Philadelphia. Rider Jacob Abel had an arduous journey, delivering twenty-eight papers several miles up the east branch of the Delaware to Easton. Five papers were packed off for Stamper's Wharf, where someone was to carry them to Fort Penn, on the northern frontier in Northampton County (see Appendix B, Table 11).[33]

The next section of the 1775 book continues the theme of dropping off small bundles of papers for various people to carry them into the Delaware Bay: Joseph Rigby got five for Lewistown, Delaware; Captain Nathaniel Donnell carried six to nearby Broad Kill, Delaware; Daniel Mulford took a dozen to Bridgetown, Delaware, and then gave four more to John Hutton

31. Ibid., 20–22.
32. Ibid., 22, 24–25.
33. Ibid., 30, 37, 38.

for Piles Grove, New Jersey, across the river from Wilmington, where the Bradfords sent twenty-two more issues to the care of a man named Thomas Sulley (see Appendix B, Table 12).[34]

From the Delaware River region, the book shifts focus northward to New York City and New England. The Bradfords sent twenty-four papers to New York City at the start of 1775, which increased by another twelve until the British occupation. Six of those went to fellow printers, including Hugh Gaine, whose name carries the note "a slave to George the Tyrant," added ostensibly soon after the trimming *New-York Gazette; and Weekly Mercury* printer irrevocably cast his lot with the British late in 1776. At the very least, he was dead in the Bradfords' subscription book, for after this insult, his name was scratched out. The Bradfords would no longer extend the courtesy of a free paper to such a "slave." Seven papers went to Albany, including one to General Philip Schuyler. The number of papers sent to Newark, New Jersey, also increased after Manhattan fell to the British, from four before the war to fifteen by the middle of 1777. They sent five issues to printers in Connecticut and six more to other customers there; five to people in Rhode Island, including *Newport Mercury* printer Solomon Southwick. Entries for Massachusetts include Cambridge, Boston, and headquarters, where George Washington, Nathanael Greene, and several other leading army officers had subscriptions. For a brief period in 1776 (before its ignominious fall in 1777), they also arranged to send *Journals* to four men at Fort Ticonderoga, including a young Captain Aaron Burr (see Appendix B, Table 13).[35]

The customer list then returns to northern and central New Jersey, with entries for areas that would be significant theaters of war during the period this account book documents, including Elizabethtown (ten papers by 1777), New Brunswick (fifteen by 1777), and Trenton (fifty-four by 1777). Even before it became the neutral ground between two armies, central Jersey constituted a print front between Bradford and Rivington. Rivington's paper, unlike the less-committed Gaine's, was the boldest outlet supporting the crown since its first issue in 1772. Loyalist essayists knew their arguments would be well received at Rivington's shop and that he would publish sentiments such as these, sent in by a Long Island subscriber: "I fret, I storm, I spit, I spew / At Sound of YANKEE DOODLE DO." Patriot supporters in New Jersey knew it, too. Late in 1774, a committee in Elizabethtown called him

34. Ibid., 39, 40, 43–44, 65; for the New Castle, Del., entry, see 83.
35. Ibid., 45–47, 51–52 (Gaine's name scratched out on 45).

"A Work of Difficulty"

Laſt Thurſday was hung up by ſome of the lower claſs of Inhabitants, at New-Brunſwick, an effigy, repreſenting the perſon of Mr. Rivington, the printer at New-York, merely for acting conſiſtent with his profeſſion as a free printer.

To the P U B L I C.

THE Printer has been Informed, that a number of Bacchanalians, at Brunſwick, fluſhed with the loathſome draughts, not of the juice of the Vine, but of New-England Rum, have lately ſacrificed him to the Idol of Licentiouſneſs. Left this ſtate of heroiſm ſhould not be ſufficiently known, he is thought proper to exhibit a Repreſentation of the farce in which he was thus offered up a Victim, that the fame of the exploit may ſpread from Pole to Pole." From this publication too, theſe little, ſhabby, piddling politicians may know how much their vengeance is reſented: But while he conſigns theſe ſnarling tu s who, he is well Informed, were, and Indeed could be no other, than the very Dregs of the City, to the ſame in…

Figure 1. *James Rivington, hanged. From* Rivington's New-York Gazetteer, *April 20, 1775. On April 13, 1775, a crowd of patriots in New Brunswick, New Jersey, hanged an effigy of Rivington for publishing pro-British items in his* New-York Gazetteer. *Rivington responded to his mock murder the with this woodcut, complete with the caption: "The Printer has been informed that a number of Bacchanalians, at Brunswick, flushed with . . . New England Rum, have lately sacrificed him to the Idol of Licentiousness." Within a few months, growing patriot threats (and actual attacks) convinced Rivington to leave New York City.*

a *"vile ministerial hireling,* employed to disunite the colonies" and pledged "they will take no more of said Rivington's Gazettes." In New Brunswick, a crowd—perhaps including some of the fifteen *Journal* subscribers—hanged him in effigy just as the war began.[36]

But it was not a complete victory for the Bradfords in central New Jersey. War would take a toll on their business in Princeton. Whereas they had more than forty names listed in the old book, that number had dropped to twenty by the start of the war, declining further as Princeton saw heavy disruption in 1776 and 1777.

Following entries for these contested towns, the routes continue with a rider named Joseph Burwell carrying several papers to Hunterdon and Sussex Counties in northern New Jersey. He took them to Andover, where

36. Ibid., 48, 50–51; *Rivington's New-York Gazetteer,* Jan. 12, Mar. 2, 1775. Budding poet Philip Moreau Freneau published a broadside offering his literary take on the New Brunswick performance, *The Last Words, Dying Speech, and Confession of James Rivington* (New York, 1775), in which the devil receives him for the "lies I've framed against this happy land." Freneau announced,

That tree on which my body hang'd will be,
Which they once call'd by name of Liberty,
A growing monument will there remain,
Of my past, present, and my future shame.

others distributed them to Amwell, Kingswood, and other places in rural Jersey (see Appendix B, Table 14). Burwell's burden increased considerably after the war began, with the number of subscribers in central Jersey doubling from 111 to 208 by the end of 1776.[37]

The subsequent route laid out in the Bradfords' book turned west, following the road from Philadelphia to Lancaster. Eight manuscript pages detail the different houses along the Lancaster Road where riders were to deliver the *Journal*. At the White Horse, thirty papers were left in tavern keeper Samuel Henry's care. Subscribers living in East Caln, near the road in Chester County, were to proceed to William Clingan's house to collect their paper. Nearby, at the Mariner's Compass Inn on the road, a deliveryman dropped three more papers; another subscriber picked his up at Jonathan Thomas's store. Jacob Miller's tavern, the Sign of the Bull's Head, was a center for people from southern Lancaster County (such as Chestnut Level, Drummore, and Salisbury Township) to congregate and get their paper. A bundle of more than thirty papers went to the Bull's Head every week. The person in charge of this route next went through Lancaster, a town with thirty new subscribers in 1775 and 1776, and then to York, where another tavern keeper, Rudolph Spangler, distributed another fifty-seven papers. Spangler handled the final delivery of a few more papers, sending a set of six over the Monocacy Road southwest to Hanover. This route ended with one more stop, due north from York: Middletown, on the Susquehanna, where a contingency of thirty-five people subscribed in late June 1775, just a few weeks after the news of war broke, and twelve more neighbors joined a few weeks later. By the end of 1775, the Lancaster Road rider had to carry fifty-two issues to Middletown (see Appendix B, Table 15).[38]

Points south of Pennsylvania dominate most of the last third of the 1775 book. The next twenty manuscript pages intermingle many places in Maryland and Virginia but connote, nevertheless, a deeper familiarity with locales on the Delmarva Peninsula and in the lower Chesapeake Bay than the previous ledger. Two distinct routes emerge in the next phase of the 1775 book, one down each side of the bay. The Bradfords delineated papers delivered throughout the Eastern Shore, from Salisbury, Maryland (four in 1777), and throughout rural Somerset County, including one copy to a young schoolteacher named Hugh Henry Brackenridge. Either over land

37. List of subscribers, *Pennsylvania Journal*, 1775, 52–53.
38. Ibid., 54–56, 59–61.

"A Work of Difficulty"

or via coasting vessels, papers went down to Accomack and, late in the year, Northampton County, Virginia, on the southern tip of the Eastern Shore.[39]

It is worth pausing to examine the timing of when Northampton County, Virginia, became a separate entry in the *Journal* list. On November 7, 1775, their royal governor, Lord Dunmore, issued a proclamation offering freedom to all able-bodied male slaves and servants willing to fight for the crown, as will be discussed below. Three weeks later, the Northampton County committee drafted a letter to the Virginia committee of safety expressing their fear and feelings of vulnerability, being so far from aid if a slave rebellion engulfed the Eastern Shore. Worried about the "risk of our Boats being intercepted and our dispatches destroyed," they also sent an express to carry their concerns directly to the Continental Congress. It was this letter, arriving on December 2, that first informed the Continental Congress of Dunmore's proclamation. Delegate Francis Lightfoot Lee wrote immediately, "Fatal consequences may follow if an immediate stop is not put to that Devil's career," while his colleague from North Carolina vented, "Indians, Negroes, Russians, Hanoverians, and Hessians are talked of as the Instruments . . . [to] humble America."[40]

But the Bradfords' book reveals another detail. It seems the express sent from Northampton had a second task to accomplish while in the capital city. Six men, all of them prominent county leaders and most steady participants in patriot committees since 1774, entered the *Journal*'s subscription list the week of issue number 1722: December 6, 1775. The first *Journal* sent to Northampton County was published just five days after their rider delivered their plea to Congress. News, these local patriot leaders understood, was vital to the common cause. It needed, moreover, to be a two-way street, and, with Williamsburg an unreliable source for the unknown future, they tasked their harried express rider to make not one but two stops in Philadelphia: the State House and the Bradfords' print shop. In the Revolution, these were hardly distinct errands.[41]

39. Ibid.; 66, 68.

40. "Samuel Smith McCroskey on Behalf of Committee of Northampton County, Virginia, to the Honorable the President of the Congress at Philadelphia," Nov. 25, 1775, *Rev. Va.*, IV, 467; *JCC*, III, 395; Francis Lightfoot Lee to Robert Carter, Dec. 2, 1775, *LDC*, II, 425–426, William Hooper to Samuel Johnston, Dec. 2, 1775, 424–425.

41. List of subscribers, *Pennsylvania Journal*, 1775, 69. Four of the six served on

Northampton's sudden compulsion to subscribe, one of the many consequences of Dunmore's proclamation, was an unusual occurrence for the Bradfords' Eastern Shore market in the early years of the war. With the exception of an influx of customers in Queen's Town in Queen Anne's County, Maryland, most of this route stayed fairly static from 1775 to 1777. Business for the Bradfords on the Delmarva Peninsula did not enjoy the explosion seen elsewhere (see Appendix B, Table 16).

Despite the dislocations of war caused first by Dunmore in 1775 and 1776 and later by Howe's invasion of the Chesapeake in 1777, the *Journal* increased its registered readership on the western side of the bay. The Bradfords had privately condemned Lord Dunmore himself before Congress had, striking the name of "His Excellency and Right Honorable" Governor off the roll weeks before the news from Northampton arrived. The several *Virginia Gazette* printers in Williamsburg each received a copy, as did military officers sent there in mid-1776 to defend the capital, including Robert Howe and his commander, General Charles Lee. The entry for Charleston, South Carolina, intruding abruptly into the long list of Maryland and Virginia towns, features the kind of subscribers found in the Williamsburg entry. Amid the war, papers went mostly to printers (Timothy, Wells) and patriot military and political officials, with a few merchants besides. The *Journal*'s presence in the deep southern colonies had faded, however. Where they used to send twenty-five papers to readers in Wilmington, Savannah, and Charleston before the war, now only one-third of that number went, and then just to the South Carolina capital. It is difficult to account for this change in Savannah, but perhaps the Wilmington committee of safety's success in reviving the *Cape-Fear Mercury* early in 1775 lessened the demand for the Bradfords' paper in North Carolina.[42]

Returning to the Chesapeake tidewater, the ledger documents that the number of the Bradfords' papers going to Fredericksburg, Virginia, increased sharply with the war, with a few of those issues going thirty-five more miles overland to Culpeper by 1777. Richard Henry Lee had an entry all his own. Like his Northampton colleagues, Lee tied politics to newspaper subscriptions, for his *Journal* account started just as his service in the Continen-

---

patriot committees either in Northampton County or Norfolk in 1774–1776. See *Rev. Va.*, II, 194, III, 367, 372.

42. List of subscribers, *Pennsylvania Journal*, 1775, 71, 73; "Minutes of Wilmington Committee of Safety," Jan. 30, 1775, in William L. Saunders, ed., *The Colonial Records of North Carolina*, 10 vols. (Raleigh, N.C., 1886–1890), IX, 1118.

"A Work of Difficulty"

tal Congress ended in October 1774. Lee, too, went to the *Journal* office before leaving Philadelphia, seeing it as the best way to remain involved while back in Virginia.[43]

The war did not significantly affect the number of issues going to Baltimore and Annapolis. Entrepreneurial printers saw Baltimore as an emerging market in the 1770s, with Goddard and John Dunlap taking up business there that might have otherwise gone to the *Journal*. The Bradfords' readership grew slightly, as it did in Annapolis. A rider known just as Perkins carried seventy-one papers to Baltimore, with forty-nine (including issues for Goddard and Dunlap) staying in the city. Samuel Purvaince, one of Baltimore's most important patriot leaders, held the fourteen issues headed to Annapolis, which included customers Samuel Chase, William Paca, Charles Carroll, Sr., and *Maryland Gazette* printer Jonas Green. A different rider, Absolom Bonham, took the remaining eight papers left in Baltimore and carried them west to Frederick. Other than one subscriber in Hagerstown, Maryland, who picked his copy up when visiting Baltimore, the *Journal* had a slight presence in the Shenandoah Valley, with four subscribers in Winchester, Virginia, in 1775. That number expanded, especially in 1777, when the Bradfords left sixteen issues "at the Winchester Box" (see Appendix B, Table 17).[44]

The opacity of the reference to "the Winchester Box" reflects an increasing weariness to maintain such arduous detail by the end of the Bradfords' book. Although the modern reader wants more—where the "Winchester Box" actually was, who managed it, and how often—no assistance is forthcoming. Several pages toward the end of book signal surrender, with vague entries titled "papers left at the Red Lion," "papers left on the Road," "left at the Cross Roads," "papers left at William Stuart's," "papers left at Robinson's Tavern," and "papers left at John Rouse's" abounding by the book's end. They are, worse, just counts of total papers delivered, not offering any sense of who these subscribers were, when they started, or where such places were. But those raw numbers were rather significant—10 percent of the *Journal*'s weekly production—and they do serve as a reminder that all the previous pages document formal readership. The pages of names added and subtracted constituted people who contacted the Bradfords individu-

43. List of subscribers, *Pennsylvania Journal*, 1775, 72.

44. Ronald Hoffman, *A Spirit of Dissension: Economics, Politics, and the Revolution in Maryland* (Baltimore, 1973), 242–243; list of subscribers, *Pennsylvania Journal*, 1775, 87, 91–92.

ally or in small groups to ask for their own, personal copy of the paper. What those individuals did with that copy after perusing it, who else might have read their copy (to themselves or aloud) as it sat for days in a public house waiting for pickup, or how far it passed afterward are questions impossible to answer. Though likely a function of a fatigued bookkeeper, the Bradfords' simple references to bundles of papers scattered at crossroads, taverns, and houses reinforce the notion that there was an informal, communal element to eighteenth-century newspaper readership (see Appendix B, Table 18).[45]

45. List of subscribers, *Pennsylvania Journal*, 1775, 83–86. This analysis focuses on the men and women who had arranged with the Bradfords to subscribe to the *Pennsylvania Journal* in 1774 and 1775. How many colonists actually learned of the contents of the *Journal* each week is impossible to determine, owing to sharing of issues in public houses or among family members and neighbors, and paragraphs being read aloud either in private or public. Information conveyed orally or through other modes remained a force in the colonial countryside, as Rhys Isaac has argued in "Dramatizing the Ideology of Revolution: Popular Mobilization in Virginia, 1774 to 1776," *WMQ*, 3d Ser., XXXIII (1976), 357–385. For the seminal accounts that argue the late eighteenth century was a crucial time of transition from orality to print, see especially Michael Warner, *The Letters of the Republic: Publication and the Public Sphere in Eighteenth Century America* (Cambridge, Mass., 1990); Larzer Ziff, *Writing in the New Nation: Prose, Print, and Politics in the Early United States* (New Haven, Conn., 1991); Jay Fliegelman, *Declaring Independence: Jefferson, Natural Language, and the Culture of Performance* (Stanford, Calif., 1993); Christopher Looby, *Voicing America: Language, Literary Form, and the Origins of the United States* (Chicago, 1996); David Waldstreicher, *In the Midst of Perpetual Fetes: The Making of American Nationalism, 1776–1820* (Chapel Hill, N.C., 1997); Sandra M. Gustafson, *Eloquence Is Power: Oratory and Performance in Early America* (Chapel Hill, N.C., 2000). David D. Hall argues the there had long been two cultures of reading in America, one intellectual and the other popular. This is more than just conflating print with a modern, metropolitan, intellectual culture and orality with premodern, local, popular culture, however. In early New England, for example, the idea of "publication" meant reading texts aloud to gatherings of townspeople. The Revolution, he argues, saw a convergence between these two traditions. See his *Cultures of Print: Essays in the History of the Book* (Amherst, Mass., 1996), 16; and Hall, *Worlds of Wonder, Days of Judgment: Popular Religious Belief in Early New England* (New York, 1989), 45. Most germane to this study is Charles C. Clark's argument that newspapers brought Hall's two spheres together by supporting and extending oral culture and allowing those who were only semiliterate to participate, thus closing the "information gap between the privileged and the merely competent." See especially Clark, "The Newspapers of Provincial America," *Proceedings of the American Antiquarian Society*, N.S., C (1990), 367–389, esp. 387. For a similar argument in England,

Details make a welcome return for the final pages of the 1775 book. In two clusters of villages, late in 1776, a few dozen people asked to add their names to the Bradfords' list, expanding the *Journal*'s territory. The first was in the Wyoming Valley, an area of civil discord that would witness much worse in the near future. In the small settlements of Kingston, Pittstown, and Plymouth, all on the east branch of the Susquehanna, forty-four people sent their names to the Bradfords to take the *Journal,* most of them doing so between May 1 and July 17, 1776. In fact, the mean start date for the forty-four Wyoming inhabitants works out to issue number 1752, or July 3, 1776 (see Appendix B, Table 19).[46]

The final page of the new book offers another glimpse into how everyday

---

see Dean, *Talk of the Town.* For public houses as a vector for information networks in colonial America, see Carl Bridenbaugh, *Cities in Revolt: Urban Life in America, 1743–1776* (New York, 1955); David W. Conroy, *In Public Houses: Drink and the Revolution of Authority in Colonial Massachusetts* (Chapel Hill, N.C., 1995); Thompson, *Rum Punch and Revolution;* Benjamin L. Carp, *Rebels Rising: Cities and the American Revolution* (New York, 2007). On the issue of literacy rates, E. Jennifer Monaghan compiled figures from several studies of literacy rates for men and women in the Atlantic world from 1650 to 1810. In 1775, men and women showed an extremely high level of literacy, as revealed in the signing of their name (rather than "X") to wills, deeds, and other legal documents, a rate across the board higher than in England.

Men	
Vermont will signers	95%
Virginia legal document signers	87%
New England urban signers	86%
New England rural signers	83%
Pennsylvania will signers (Chester County)	77%
Pennsylvania will signers (Lancaster County)	63%
England	60%
Women	
Connecticut deed signers	83%
Massachusetts widow signers	67%
Virginia legal document signers	56%
New England rural signers	40%
England	38%

See appendix 1 of Monaghan's *Learning to Read and Write in Colonial America* (Amherst, Mass., 2005), 384–385.

46. List of subscribers, *Pennsylvania Journal,* 1775, 96–97.

people interacted with the news of the Revolution, often as they witnessed it firsthand. On the hundredth page is an intriguing entry for Morris County, New Jersey, in that it is forty pages removed from the last reference to a place in Jersey. Something unusual had occurred in Morris County.

In late November 1776, twenty-two people in Hanover, Morristown, Troy, and Boontown, New Jersey, wrote en masse to the Bradfords to start subscriptions. Six started with issue 1772 (November 20), seventeen more with issue 1773 (November 27). A resident of Hanover, Alexander Carmichael, handled distribution. They did this, as we will see, just as Washington stood on the Palisades—twenty miles due east of them—and watched the British army take the patriots' last stronghold in Manhattan, an action that prompted the Continental army's flight across Jersey at a time soon to be known by the name Thomas Paine gave it: the "American crisis."[47]

This was quite a moment to send for the paper. Ultimately, these new subscribers would be disappointed, because the "crisis" would force the *Journal* into a two-month suspension. We can only speculate why this community acted as it did, but, like the men of Northampton County, Virginia, at their own dark moment, the issue of newspaper subscription was evidently significant for these Jersey men. After all, just as the Bradfords added the men from the Morristown area to the book's final page, the sick from Washington's defeated army—likely including the ailing Captain Peter Withington—trudged through their very streets. The war had come to Morris County, and, with New York City gone, they needed, more than ever, to maintain communication with the greater cause.[48]

* * *

Together, the two subscription books kept by William Bradford and his son offer a remarkable glimpse into the inner workings of the newspaper business over the most important decade for colonial printers. Public expectations about the meaning of "freedom of the press" were changing from 1765 to 1775, and so were the business practices for the Bradfords and their colleagues throughout the mainland colonies. It is valuable to remember two things about these particular artifacts. First, no matter how many details the Bradfords' ledgers provide, they render only one of the three dozen webs of customers who sustained colonial newspapers on the eve of the American

47. Ibid., 100–101. To keep with geographic cohesion, the Morris County group is part of Table 14 for northern and central New Jersey.

48. David Hackett Fischer, *Washington's Crossing* (New York, 2004), 129.

"A Work of Difficulty"

Revolution. If subscription books survived for the *Massachusetts Spy, Connecticut Courant, Virginia Gazette, South-Carolina Gazette,* and others, they would illustrate the networks as they really were: overlapping, extensive, and thick, with multiple strands crisscrossing the same towns and often the same residences. Thirty-five other such ledgers are needed for a full accounting of the real colonial newspaper webs in 1775. Second, these other (sadly theoretical) books would still show only what the Bradfords' records show: subscribers. Those lists would include only those people who signed up for and (ostensibly) paid for a newspaper—not the sum total of all the people who read its columns or heard its contents. If those informal, second- and third-hand networks could also be mapped, then we would truly grasp the actual effect of print's diffusion.

Unfortunately, only the Bradfords' books survive. However, thanks to them—though not without some inevitable speculation—we can track closely bundles of papers being stuffed into riders' portmanteaus and imagine them making their way over a myriad of country roads fanning out in all directions: into the Pennsylvania hinterland, down the Delmarva Peninsula, along the Delaware River, and across central New Jersey. In picturing these carriers, we may recall Hugh Finlay's dyspeptic comments about the carelessness some may have used in handling their cargo, and, indeed, there is little in the Bradfords' books to undermine his observation that those riders' bags were quite "crammed with newspapers." The Bradfords' books also suggest that the *Journal* traveled extensively via watercraft, tied up below decks on ships headed for places far from Philadelphia. With destinations across the southern mainland colonies, the Caribbean, Nova Scotia, England, Scotland, and Portugal, the Bradfords had to pay attention to outbound ship schedules as well as monitor the progress of their riders crossing Delaware River ferries or catching local water traffic to nearby places in Delaware or southern Jersey. Some papers going to various places in the Chesapeake likely traveled over both land and water to get to Fredericksburg, Annapolis, and Williamsburg.[49]

No matter how the papers moved, their destinations multiplied over the period chronicled in the two subscription books. After the Stamp Act controversy, with William Bradford playing a key role in Philadelphia, the number of names of people asking for the *Journal* grew steadily, as did the number of places in which these colonists lived. Like many of their peers, the Bradfords enjoyed a robust growth in subscribers as a result of the imperial

49. Norton, ed., *Finlay Journal*, 43.

controversy. So much so that, by the middle of 1775, the geographic expanse of their customer base necessitated a new system of accounting, one centered much more closely on making sense of delivery routes and on those men who made an enlarged delivery area possible. The Bradfords' ledgers exhibit just how saturated the mid-Atlantic was in weekly newspapers. Of course, having five hundred city customers and another thousand outside was nothing like it would be, but for the 1770s, these were unprecedented numbers of registered readers who promised to pay for a copy of the *Journal*. The actual number of people who read or heard information from the *Journal*'s twelve weekly columns was surely far more than 2,000. This was, certainly, before steam power revolutionized communications in the early nineteenth century; all sorts of troubles from supply problems to inclement weather to negligent employees could beset this rather fragile system. Nonetheless, the Bradfords' books show an ambitious reach across the mainland colonies.

The 1775 book, however, holds even more analytical importance. Close study reveals the difference the war made. Partisanship in assembly houses and print shops reached new levels when war broke out in Massachusetts, something a few of the Bradfords' colleagues would experience through violence to their property and person. At some point during 1775, William and his son must have contemplated what war might mean for their business. As it turned out, until General William Howe and his British regulars strode into the city in September 1777, the *Journal* fared better than many of its competitors. According to the 1775 book, the Bradfords gained a total of 436 new subscribers in 1775 and scarcely lost any. In 1776, they gained a net total of 391, and the following year, in the eight months before the occupation, they picked up more than 80 more. As far as can be ascertained, the war had brought the Bradfords a 35 percent increase in registered readers as of the summer of 1777. Then, of course, things would take an unfortunate turn, as Philadelphia's patriot printers joined their dispersed colleagues in Boston, Norfolk, Newport, and New York City as fellow victims of British arms. Until then, however, the Bradfords had a good run. Whether or not they acknowledged it, that success was not just the product of their own business acumen or the energy of the politically charged moment; it was also the result of substantial aid from actors far outside Philadelphia, especially Peter Withington, William Carheart, and many other post riders, tavern keepers, and ship captains who delivered the hundreds of copies of their *Journal* each week. These men, too, were critical to everyday communication throughout the mainland colonies. Lots of people handled these

"A Work of Difficulty"

papers. The patriots' ability to propagate the images and stories they needed to sustain the cause depended on all kinds of sailors and riders. Since they were the actual carriers of ideas, our understanding of the Revolution has to account for them.

Of course, on one level, the Bradfords' prosperity in the first years of war hardly surprises, for the political allegiances of self-selected new subscribers to the *Journal* clearly leaned toward the patriots. When the news of the Boston Tea Party reached Philadelphia on December 24, 1773, the gleeful Bradfords published the news in a broadside with the bold title *Christmas-Box for the Customers of the Pennsylvania Journal.* Of all the names in the 1775 book, the Bradfords made bitter political comments next to those of just three subscribers: two were perhaps the Revolution's most notorious loyalists, William Franklin and Hugh Gaine, and the third, Dr. John Davenport of Fogg's Manor, Pennsylvania, they labeled "a Devil of a Tory." There were many more people on those lists who harbored private doubts about independence or considered themselves disaffected to the common cause. Others who looked favorably on the patriot cause did not consider that attachment as automatic or everlasting. Even the warmest friends of the cause—many of whom were customers of the *Journal*—needed constant reassurance that the political values and military objectives of the common cause matched their own. That the Bradfords did not lose hundreds of customers over the essays they printed and the news items they exchanged from 1775 to 1777 was not a coincidence (see Appendix B, Table 20).[50]

In other words, what was in the weekly issues of the *Pennsylvania Journal* mattered as much as the ability to hold the material object in one's hand. Withington, Carheart, and their fellow distributors were vital to maintaining the Bradfords' (and, by extension, the patriots') communication web, but it was the information that traveled along that network—or did not—that was essential. What was in those newspapers traveling over roads and ferries in 1775, in a macro sense? How were they constructed? Where did the information come from? What, exactly, did all those subscribers encounter when they went to the taverns to get their paper?

4: THE WORLD IN THE *PENNSYLVANIA JOURNAL*, 1775
William Bradford's London Coffee House faced the wharves lining the Delaware riverfront on the southwest corner of Front and Market Streets. In

50. *Christmas-Box for the Customers of the Pennsylvania Journal* (Philadelphia, 1773), *Early American Imprints*, 42425; list of subscribers, *Pennsylvania Journal*, 1775, 13.

1754, Bradford purchased the building, already fifty years old, measuring twenty-five by one hundred feet and rising more than three stories from the street. On the first floor, he put in a large public room for Philadelphians to find refreshment, socialize, and gather information. Inside, they could buy tickets for an evening's entertainment; outside, they could purchase a human to provide extra labor. If a group needed more discrete or private space, they could gather in one of the several meeting rooms on the two upstairs floors. Christopher Marshall, a minor player in the city's patriot leadership, frequently wrote in his diary about attending meetings in Bradford's "committee room" in 1775 and 1776, with business ranging from dealing with loyalists to planning a ball for Martha Washington to helping protect vessels traveling between the colonies. Philadelphia's committee of safety drafted resolutions in those upstairs rooms and sometimes sent copies of them the five blocks up Market Street to the Continental Congress. Other times, the direction of political traffic was reversed. In any case, the London Coffee House was one of Philadelphia's most important nodes for communication, socialization, and political participation.[51]

Because Bradford's printing office and bookshop were adjacent to this nucleus, it was not difficult for the publisher to procure news for the *Journal*. Assuming the shop had an adequate supply of paper, the type compositors (often journeymen) would probably begin assembling the sticks of type immediately after Wednesday's paper went out into the American countryside, correcting grammar all the while. Some parts of the back page would not need resetting, since advertisements for land auctions, runaway servants, or lost items might run over several consecutive weeks. Each new issue of the *Journal* began with compositors either setting type for the remainder of the advertisements on the back page or composing the two thousand words for the front page, which often featured an essay submitted by

51. John William Wallace, *An Old Philadelphian, Colonel William Bradford, the Patriot Printer of 1776, Sketches of His Life* (Philadelphia, 1884), 48–50; Robert Earle Graham, "The Taverns of Colonial Philadelphia," *Transactions of the American Philosophical Society*, XLIII (1953), 318–325, esp. 320–321; Gary B. Nash, *First City: Philadelphia and the Forging of Historical Memory* (Philadelphia, 2002), 50; Edwin B. Bronner, "Village into Town, 1701–1746," in Russell F. Weigley, ed., *Philadelphia: A 300-Year History* (New York, 1982), 33–67, esp. 57–58; William Duane, ed., *Extracts from the Diary of Christopher Marshall, 1774–1781* (1877; rpt. New York, 1969), 39, 40–41, 42, 43, 44, 48, 53. See also Benjamin H. Irvin, *Clothed in Robes of Sovereignty: The Continental Congress and the People out of Doors* (New York, 2011), 23–24.

Figure 2. *Sketch of the* London Coffee House. *By William L. Breton. 1830. Breton's rendering recalled the colonial past of Bradford's building, where slave auctions occurred just outside the doors on Front Street. Courtesy of the Library Company of Philadelphia.*

a local interested party or a literary piece taken from another periodical. This was tedious work, as each letter and space had to be set in reverse, a process that took a long, full day to complete, with the master occasionally interjecting tiny details concerning typefaces and italics. Unlike their peers in other eighteenth-century workshops, printers' journeymen could not rely on spirits to ease the tedium of standing for hours in front of the type cases.[52]

William and Thomas would then supervise and participate in the physical production of each week's *Journal*. With the sticks of type for the outer page prepared and locked into place on the press, two men—a puller and a beater, often apprentices—would begin making copies. Both tasks demanded much of the printers' bodies. While the beater pounded the type with two animal skin–covered balls soaked in ink (a combination of lampblack and varnish), the puller attached a blank page to the wood frame, ma-

52. Thomas, *History of Printing*, 21–24, 38–39; Patrick Erben, "William Rittenhouse," in Marianne S. Wokeck, ed., *Immigrant Entrepreneurship: German-American Business Biographies, 1720 to the Present*, I, German Historical Institute, http://www.immigrantentrepreneurship.org/entry.php?rec=9, accessed Nov. 8, 2012.

neuvered it under the plate, and pulled the lever to turn the heavy worm screw and impress the types onto the paper. The process had not changed much since Gutenberg's day; it was still dirty, sweaty, boring work. Analysts of the early American press estimate a good team could produce more than two hundred sheets in an hour. As much as the hundreds of names the Bradfords added to their subscription books were good for them, all the extra people wanting the *Journal* in the 1770s translated into longer hours at the press for the shop's beaters and pullers. Once these unfortunates—had this been the *South-Carolina Gazette,* they would have been slaves—finished cranking out that week's run of outer pages and hung them to dry throughout the shop, Bradford's apprentices rested weary shoulders and elbows, waiting for their superiors to finish composing materials for the other side. Given the value of the machine itself, though, it is doubtful that the press sat idle for long, with other printing tasks—books, almanacs, broadsides, handbills, or other ephemera—to complete. That week's *Journal* was halfway finished.[53]

On those outer pages, the *Journal* apprentices had made copies of essays and advertisements. It is on this half of the workweek that historians have traditionally focused, holding up the political essay under the masthead or the material items for sale on the back page as the part of the colonial newspaper most worth our attention. What the *Journal*'s subscribers actually received does not quite match up to either interpretation.

On the first pages of the sixty-seven issues of the *Journal* the Bradfords sent out in 1775 (which included several two-page supplements, or "postscripts"), there were seventy-three separate items that could be considered opinion, most of them concerning politics (see Appendix C, Table 1). The Bradfords published nineteen essays written by colonists on the imperial crisis, including Thomas Jefferson's *Summary View of the Rights of British Americans.* "Antoninus," "Humanus," "An American Guesser," "Salus Populi," "A Citizen," "Neoptolemus," and a few others advised their fellow colonists in and out of leadership how to proceed. Oratory submitted by students graduating from Princeton or the ill-fated Dr. Joseph Warren also found space.[54]

---

53. Lawrence C. Wroth, *The Colonial Printer* (New York, 1931), 118–119; Rollo G. Silver, *The American Printer, 1787–1825* (Charlottesville, Va., 1967), 9–10. David A. Copeland, *Colonial American Newspapers: Character and Content* (Newark, Del., 1997), 17; Sidney Kobre, *The Development of the Colonial Newspaper* (Dubuque, Iowa, 1969), 49.

54. *Pennsylvania Journal* (supplement), Feb. 10, 1775 (*Summary View*), Oct. 11, 1775

"A Work of Difficulty"

But original American compositions made up only a part of the opinion forwarded by the *Journal*. Voices from Britain competed with colonial viewpoints on these pages. Extracts of pro-American pamphlets published in London appeared, as did petitions by West Indian assemblies and London merchants to Parliament, and selections from Scottish magazines. This British accent was especially prominent in the re-publication of speeches. Eminent British voices supporting American rights, especially Edmund Burke and London mayor George Johnstone, led the way. *Journal* readers in the public houses on the Lancaster Road or next to their fireplaces in rural New Jersey absorbed as many thoughts about the imperial crisis from the opposition across the Atlantic as from their fellow colonists. The Bradfords published a total of forty-seven opinion pieces on the political crisis: thirty-seven written by American (nineteen) or British (eighteen) authors in support of colonial resistance, and ten penned by loyalists in opposition. In all, less than a third of all the *Journal* issues in 1775 (28 percent) contained an ideological tract—written at a colonial desk—that some scholars have deemed as the precipitant for revolution.[55]

If the actual amount of American opinion was rather meager, the front page featured other public and private documents that were probably even more convincing than a speech or essay. They were "proof." Over several weeks in the summer and fall, the *Journal* continued to dedicate the front page's first two columns to publishing Governor Hutchinson's infamous letters in full, which the *Boston Gazette* had begun nearly two years before. Other letters exchanged between opposing generals on the conduct of war around Boston appeared, as well, usually by order of the Continental Congress. Statements issued by that body also commanded the front page throughout the year, as the Bradfords published the "Declaration of the Causes and Necessity of Taking up Arms," the regulations for a Continental army, and a proclamation to the inhabitants of Great Britain.[56]

("Antonius"), Oct. 18, 1775 ("Humanus"), Dec. 27, 1775 ("An American Guesser"), Dec. 27, 1775 ("Salus Populi"), Sept. 20, 1775 ("A Citizen"), Mar. 8, 1775 ("Neoptolemus"), Nov. 29, 1775, Apr. 14, 1775 (Princeton commencement).

55. Ibid., Jan. 4, 25, 1775 (London pamphlets), June 28, 1775 (West Indian petition), July 5, 1775 (London merchant petition), Feb. 1, 1775 ("Junius Brutus," from *Gentleman's Magazine*), Mar. 29, Apr. 5, 12, 1775 (Burke), Apr. 19, 1775 (Johnstone). Other speeches included Joseph Warren's "Massacre Oration" (Mar. 29, 1775), and a speech by New Jersey governor William Franklin (Nov. 22, 1775).

56. Ibid., July 26, Aug. 2, 9, 23, Sept. 6, 27, Oct. 25, 1775 (Hutchinson letters),

Two weeks before Lexington, the Bradfords dredged up Franklin's 1754 Albany Plan, and they were already apprising readers of how to make saltpeter, an essential ingredient in gunpowder, advice they would continue to give all year. Of the seventy-three front page items, fourteen were of these sort: documents submitted as evidence, official pronouncements, or items on political matters that were not essays. It was impossible to miss which side of the controversy the Bradfords were on, but the depth of the intellectual or ideological arguments in the *Journal* is lacking.[57]

No matter how slight, these pieces had a reputation—for both contemporaries and historians—as powerful tools in shaping public opinion. As one loyalist writer suggested, however, perhaps this had as much to do with the men operating the press as those wielding the pen. "Every Essay that makes its appearance in a paper, which is confessedly under the influence of the Republican Party, and is copied into other papers of the same stamp," "M" wrote in a December 1774 issue of Rivington's paper, "I consider as containing the sentiments of that party: it is their general way of broaching a new doctrine, to try how it will be relished by the palates of the people." As much as the arguments made in those essays themselves, "M" seethed, it was the "Republican" printers like the Bradfords and their exchanges that actually changed people's minds.[58]

Analyzing the back page is a different type of exercise but vital in getting a global picture of what *Journal* subscribers encountered during 1775. Over the sixty-seven *Journal* issues that year, the Bradfords ran 900 separate notices, or, with several advertisements repeated over a few weeks, an average of about 15 per number (see Appendix C, Table 2). These advertisements provide another opportunity to discover people interacting with their newspaper. The 163 ads for runaway servants, for example, came into the Bradfords' shop from all over their circulation area: the Maryland Eastern Shore, rural Pennsylvania, the northern frontier, southern New Jersey. Speculators advertised land for sale in Bedford and Loudoun Counties in

---

Oct. 4, 1775, Aug. 9, 1775 (Lee-Burgoyne), July 12, 1775 (Necessity of Taking up Arms), Nov. 20, 1775 (army regulations), July 19, 1775 (proclamation to inhabitants of Great Britain). For more on the printing of Hutchinson's letters, see Bernard Bailyn, *The Ordeal of Thomas Hutchinson* (Cambridge, Mass., 1974), 243–244; Schlesinger, *Prelude to Independence*, 151–152.

57. *Pennsylvania Journal*, Apr. 5, 1775 (Albany), Jan. 25, Feb. 1, July 26, Nov. 22, Dec. 6, 1775 (saltpeter).

58. *Rivington's New-York Gazetteer*, Dec. 1, 1774.

"A Work of Difficulty"

Virginia, in Carlisle, Pennsylvania, in Chestertown, Maryland. Others asked for a partner in the Andover Iron Works in New Jersey, for a keeper of a Baltimore tavern, or to take over the Lebanon Forge in Harford County, Maryland.

Other advertisements in the *Journal* suggest an understanding that readership had little to do with Philadelphia at all. People all over the mid-Atlantic expected that advertising in the Bradfords' paper might lead to the recovery of their stolen horses. Descriptions of horses taken in Hagerstown, Maryland, Northumberland County, Pennsylvania, Christiana Bridge, Delaware, and even Fredericksburg, a village on the Hudson in Dutchess County, New York—more than 150 miles away—appeared throughout 1775. The twenty-eight advertisements for ships departing the city also suggest Philadelphia's mercantile and information connection into the Atlantic, with three headed to Northern Ireland, ten to England, six to Ireland, three to Jamaica, and six bound for the Carolinas.[59]

The back page depicts colonists in motion. It offers an understanding of their horizons, showing them at their most optimistic (returning a stolen pocketbook, beginning a new business venture, forwarding a sense of civic pride) and most calculating (purchasing humans, tracking them down when they ran away, breaking into homes, encroaching on Indian land). Rarely, however, would any of the outer sheet of the weekly paper qualify as news. Though many readers might have been invested in the essays or advertisements that the *Journal* workers put together at the beginning of the work cycle, it was inside the fold that one found the most current events.

While the apprentices worked the press throughout Thursday and Friday afternoon, master and journeymen culled, edited, and prepared to print the news, foreign and domestic. They were passive receivers. Lacking reporters, they depended on others to provide information. One imagines colonial printers casting a concerned eye toward the water, wondering if the packet boat was going to arrive, or anxiously looking up the street to see if someone in the city might be coming to contribute part of a private letter. Because they were "meer mechanics," when printers welcomed gentlemen (often merchants or lawyers) who came by their shop to volunteer either correspondence or an original composition, it was surely a satisfying ex-

59. *Pennsylvania Journal,* May 10, 1775 (Hagerstown, Md.), July 5, 1775 (Northumberland County, Pa.), Nov. 22, 1775 (Christiana Bridge, Del.), Oct. 25, 1775 (Fredericksburg, N.Y.).

perience, producing simultaneous feelings of social achievement and professional relief.

The Bradfords needed to gather six columns of news every week to complete an issue. Thanks to their prime location, this task was not as burdensome for them as it was for others. Foreign news often came from the docks across Front Street. Ship captains crossed the street to drop off mailbags and newspapers from England and Europe at the coffeehouse. Since Bradford was also the city's postmaster, this must have been a welcome convenience for thirsty mariners. In addition to their handing over parcels of public letters and private correspondence, the captains would also pass along any news gathered on the voyage, whether ships sighted from faraway or information gained from friendly vessels that pulled alongside.

Bradford's position as postmaster also helped ease the difficulty of acquiring domestic news. He wielded this advantage rather roughly, controlling the timing of news to aid his interests only, much to William Goddard's frustration. In the post, Bradford received newspapers from other colonial towns, which traveled without cost and weighed down riders' saddlebags, much to Hugh Finlay's frustration. Bradford and his colleagues exchanged news from one another concerning events in their locales, selecting a few paragraphs from other papers to fill up the columns.[60]

The Bradfords sent 863 pieces of news to subscribers in the sixty-seven issues of the *Journal* in 1775 (see Appendix C, Table 3). An average weekly issue had about thirteen separate news items. Fewer than 7 percent of these items directly documented the lives of Philadelphians, such as auction results, food prices, local crime, and, increasingly, committee resolutions or militia musters. More than 30 percent of the total (266) appeared under the dateline of "Philadelphia," and these might or might not have been about city affairs. They were stories, reports, rumors, letters, or documents that the Bradfords (or one of their competitors in town) introduced into the communication bloodstream of colonial America. Often dominating the *Journal*'s third page, they were not exchanged but rather "fresh intelligence"—what in modern news parlance might be called a "scoop." In all, one-third of the Bradfords' news started in Philadelphia; the rest were paragraphs clipped out of another newspaper they received from elsewhere.

By a slim margin, the largest percentage of news items the Bradfords exchanged over 1775 came from London. The London news was sporadic

60. Richard B. Kielbowicz, "Newsgathering by Printers' Exchanges before the Telegraph," *Journalism History,* IX, no. 2 (Summer 1982), 42–48.

and, on average, more than two months old. When incoming ships brought London newspapers to Bradford's coffeehouse, though, he often exchanged several items at a time. A little more than half of the *Journal* issues in 1775 had news from London (thirty-eight of sixty-seven), but when they did, they normally included many pieces. Of the thirty-eight *Journals* that had London news, fifteen only had one or two items, but occasionally the Bradfords would send out issues that featured upward of seven or nine items clipped from London (see Appendix C, Table 4). Often, these London papers themselves exchanged news from the Continent. One scholar's judgment about early-eighteenth-century American readers' "seeing Europe specifically through London eyes" still applied in 1775. William clipped London news about the Continent, but much less than he used to. Only forty-seven times throughout the year did items appear in the *Journal* about Europe, with most paragraphs from the Hague (nine), Warsaw (four), Madrid (four), and Rome (three), appearing in a third of the 1775 issues. In total, 20 percent of the news items (as separate from opinion-based oratory or essays) sent to the Bradfords' subscribers came from sources across the Atlantic, a number that continued a trend toward more colonial news since 1740.[61]

The remaining 40 percent of the news items the Bradfords exchanged in 1775 came from newspapers published in the colonies. The Bradfords relied heaviest on Manhattan's papers, with a total of 105 items (or 12.1 percent of the total) under a "New York City" dateline appearing in more than 80 percent of the papers that year. Items from Boston, not surprisingly, also appeared frequently, with at least 1 item in two-thirds of the issues. They exchanged 80 items from Boston, amounting to 9.3 percent of the total amount of news provided by the *Journal.* Unlike the larger number of selections the Bradfords would clip from London papers, when they exchanged news from New York and Boston, they often did so in smaller bits, 1 or 2 items per issue. They never took more than 5 items from Boston and only once took 6 from New York City (see Appendix C, Tables 5 and 6). The time lag for New York averaged just under five days, whereas Boston's average was ten and a half days.

So, a typical issue mainly featured exchanged news from London, New York, and Boston. The Bradfords did take items from other colonial sources, mostly from Williamsburg, Virginia, and Newport, Rhode Island. When sub-

61. Clark, *Public Prints,* 221 ("London eyes"); Charles E. Clark and Charles Wetherell, "The Measure of Maturity: The *Pennsylvania Gazette,* 1728–1765," *WMQ,* 3d Ser., LXVI (1989), 279–303; Copeland, *Colonial American Newspapers,* 264–272.

scribers saw a "Williamsburg" dateline, for example, there was usually one story underneath, and it was, on average, just over two weeks old (see Appendix C, Table 7). The *Virginia Gazette*s provided forty-eight news items (5.5 percent of the total), whereas the Bradfords clipped thirty-three stories from the *Newport Mercury* (3.8 percent of the total). These items appeared in about 40 percent of the 1775 issues.

Journal readers also found ninety-one items from papers in a variety of other colonial towns. Most often, they chose stories from one of the South Carolina papers, fifteen in all. They took ten items each from the *Providence Gazette* and *Massachusetts Spy*, after Isaiah Thomas relocated it to Worcester from Boston. They took a few paragraphs from still more papers over the course of 1775, including the *Georgia Gazette* (eight), *North-Carolina Gazette* (nine), and *Maryland Gazette* (six), and a total of fifteen from the four Connecticut papers combined (see Appendix C, Table 8).

Most of these items also appeared in small doses, with one or two per issue, on the *Journal*'s second page, mixed together with more regular datelines from Boston and New York (see Appendix C, Table 9). But a closer look at the context of those items reveals that the Bradfords began to include more pieces from a more varied selection of papers after the war began. Starting in midsummer, just as the war became a sustained conflict, the amount of news exchanged from colonial papers outside Boston and New York expanded. In the first half of 1775, the Bradfords exchanged twenty-seven pieces from other papers, especially the *Maryland Gazette* and *Georgia Gazette*. But after issue number 1701—the July 12 *Journal* that featured Congress's "Declaration of the Causes and Necessity of Taking up Arms"—the number of items exchanged from a wider array of sources more than doubled to sixty-four pieces. Of the forty-eight pieces exchanged from Williamsburg papers in 1775, thirty-two of them appeared after mid-July. Halfway through the year, the amount of news originating in London, New York, or Boston papers or introduced in Philadelphia was also almost exactly 50 percent. But during the second half of the year, *Journal* readers learned much more from other places in the colonies. The Bradfords included a greater overall number of stories from places outside Boston and New York starting that July, giving more space on the second and third pages of the *Journal* to news from the Canadian frontier and the Deep South. In other words, by year's end, supply and demand were reaching a point of convergence; just as more people outside Philadelphia began taking the *Journal*, like the small group of patriot leaders from Northampton County, Virginia, in December, that paper was becoming more about them (see Appendix C, Graph 1). As we will see below, what was in those paragraphs from Charleston and Hartford and Portsmouth—the news they related, the messages they contained, the images they forwarded—helps explain why the Bradfords felt compelled to give them an increasing place inside the *Pennsylvania Journal* starting with the summer of that unprecedented year.

Over most weeks in 1775, then, the Bradfords planned out the inner pages of the *Journal* by drawing on several communication networks. First, they perused incoming papers from London and clipped a few opinions and news items they thought their readers would enjoy or that were of greatest import. There was no rush with these items, already two months old, so they could be included over the next few weeks, sometimes given large space on the front page. They repeated the same process by examining incoming colonial papers, primarily from Boston and New York, which were often less than a week old. They would insert one or two stories from these places, often beginning on the middle of the second page and spilling over onto the third. As communication with Boston became problematic and other priorities impinged in the second half of the year, the Bradfords diversified the inner pages of the *Journal,* clipping more stories from places many subscribers probably had only a faint knowledge even existed. Finally, the Bradfords would complete the process of news gathering by excerpting letters that came to the London Coffee House, summarizing ship captains' reports, or including a few paragraphs of private correspondence turned over to them by interested parties (often patriot political and military leaders) who wanted the content to reach a wide audience. This "fresh" news appeared under the column marked "Philadelphia," was dated the same as the issue itself, and normally started at the top left corner of the third page, followed by local news that most concerned Philadelphians. As the reader's eyes (or ears) moved from the first column of the inner pages to the last, the news grew closer and closer in space and time to current events.

The Bradfords composed this type over the weekend, and, after the outer pages had dried, starting on Monday the apprentices returned to the task of inking and pressing the thousands of copies of that week's *Journal.* By Wednesday morning, the *Journal*—folded, stacked, and bundled—was ready to make the first leg of its myriad journeys: up the Schuylkill to Peter Withington's house, across Delaware River ferries to New Jersey, onto ships bound for the Chesapeake, and stuffed into riders' bags bound for taverns along the Lancaster Road.

On Monday mornings in 1775, there were similar riders ready to carry similar bundles of the *Connecticut Courant* over New England's roads. On Fridays, Alexander Purdie also tied up bundles of his *Virginia Gazette* and passed them along to riders and rowers who distributed them throughout the tidewater and beyond. On Thursdays, this same action happened at shops in Norwich, New York, Annapolis, Baltimore, Philadelphia, and Williamsburg. Each printer had his or her own Peter Withington and William Carheart; they all packed off papers to send in boats headed along the coasts and often farther. Each printer also kept his or her own subscription accounts, detailing who the customers were, how long they had been faithful consumers, and where they were to receive the paper. If those printers were as meticulous as the Bradfords, those now-lost books would also supply the names of rural taverns in Maryland, New Hampshire, and the Carolinas where colonists read and discussed the contents of their columns. The Bradfords spun a large web, among the most extensive in North America, but there were thirty-five others of varying size diffusing information deep into the countryside. Each day, people carried the folded sheets across American land and water, from shops to subscribers.

This is not to suggest that 1775 ushered in a golden age for American printers. The past few years had been flush for more than just the Bradfords, but there were lean times ahead. The above snapshot, captured just as the first shots rang out, documents the world newspaper printers inhabited before the exigencies of war caused most of them terrible hardship. For some of them, it was not new: the markings in the Bradfords' subscription book do not suggest which of the thousands of names had actually paid their bill. Not paying the amount due was something of a tradition in the eighteenth century, given how often and loudly printers complained of the offense. Weather still brought the whole system to a halt. In February 1780, Isaiah Thomas thanked the "Gentlemen in this, and a few of the neighbouring towns, who have continued to take his paper during the late tedious weather; as the roads in many parts of the County still remain impassable on horseback." And families still got ill. John Holt begged his customers' forgiveness "for not having any domestic news, as the Printer's family has been very sick, and have scarcely been able (tho' with much difficulty) to publish any at all." Winter still stalked hungry children. One February, Holt inserted a poem about the ramifications when people pinched pennies by canceling their subscription in the winter. When "Thomas" tells his neighbor that "living is hard, and provisions are dear," and so he has stopped his subscription, he is rebuked:

If times are so hard, as you do not deny
The Printer, unless he's supported must die.
Till summer or spring, he can never survive,
Unless thro' the winter you keep him alive.
And if you once starve him, it will be in vain,
To expect that he ever will serve you again.

This brings Thomas up short: "We did not none of us think / that Printers could feel, or could want meat or drink." Obviously sympathetic, both Bradford and Goddard exchanged this poem. Securing a government printing contract was still the only way to make it safely through the cold. Hugh Finlay's criticisms of careless riders, wet saddlebags, and corrupt schemers hampering the system were all still valid.[62]

The war would, to say the least, exacerbate these common problems. Boston printers were only the first to experience dislocation brought on by war. Printers in Newport, New York City, Philadelphia, Charleston, and Williamsburg all had to shut their operations and flee at some point during the conflict. John Holt would have much to complain of, relocating his *Journal* twice to avoid British arms, first to Kingston, then to Poughkeepsie, far off the regular path of news. In the war's later years, he struggled to get information. The conflict compounded his and most others' problems in securing material supplies, especially paper. Rampant inflation was also a consequence of war, and the price of subscriptions rose accordingly. In 1778, the much-suffering Holt decided to abandon the collapsing monetary system. A three-month subscription to the *New-York Journal* was now available in exchange for "12 pounds of beef, pork, veal or mutton, or 4 pounds of butter, or 7 pounds of cheese, or 18 pounds of fine flour."[63]

62. *Massachusetts Spy,* Feb. 17, 1780 ("late tedious weather"); *New-York Journal,* Sept. 14, 1778 (Holt illness), Feb. 28, 1780 ("living is hard"), rpt. in *Pennsylvania Journal,* Mar. 22, 1780; *Maryland Journal,* Mar. 28, 1780; *New-Jersey Journal,* Apr. 12, 1780.

63. Holt informed his readers on November 6, 1780, "A Disappointment in getting paper, which is not now to be obtained without great difficulty and expence, will, after this week, prevent our publication of any more news-papers, at least till we receive a supply of paper." His *New-York Journal* would be silent for eight months, returning on July 30, 1781. See *New-York Journal,* Nov. 6, 1780. For more, see Eugene Andruss Leonard, "Paper as a Critical Commodity during the American Revolu-

But in the spring of 1775, most of those hardships lay in the unknown future. What patriot leaders were beginning to perceive was that the three dozen communications webs that emanated from each of the printing shops were important tools for propagating ideas and interests. Ineffective as they would seem after the invention of the steam press and railroad, these networks were highly cultivated and innovative in 1775. Patriots knew friendly networks needed to be nourished and hostile ones needed to be neutralized. In the war's first autumn, Henry Laurens wrote his son to relate his pleasure with the "Cookery of your old Schoolfellow Jack Wells," printer of the *South-Carolina and American General Gazette,* for "he gives us once a Week an exceeding good collection—he is diligent, judicious and discreet." It was no accident that Wells's weekly "collection" met with the approval of the most important patriot leader in South Carolina. Partisans like Laurens, realizing the potential of these networks, took a particular and intense interest in the issues coming out of the Charleston offices of John Wells and Peter Timothy, just his colleagues did in cities throughout the mainland. British officials in London, crown agents in America, and leading loyalists all either ignored, downplayed, or missed this critical component of the imperial conflict, a symptom of the inability of all these groups to take the rebellion seriously.[64]

As soon as the shooting started, therefore, patriot leaders seized the colonial communication network. They established their own postal system, provided money or intelligence to sympathetic printers, and intimidated and silenced those who dissented. But simply monopolizing the means to propagate their notions of patriotic resistance did not mean that patriot political and communication leaders possessed a magic key, or that success was assured. It was, indeed, a work of difficulty.

Patriot leaders knew they had to involve themselves in the actual stories found inside those papers. They understood that although riders might have carried copies of the *Maryland Gazette, Connecticut Journal, Newport Mercury,* or *South-Carolina Gazette* in their saddlebags, those separate titles contained much of the same information in their columns. It was the content of the messages traveling inside those newspapers that galvanized support for the common cause. Dominating what people knew about friends and

---

tion," *PMHB,* LXXIV (1950), 488–499. On Holt's accepting barter, see *New-York Journal,* Aug. 17, 1778.

64. HL to John Laurens, Charles Town, Sept. 26, 1775, *PHL,* X, 425–430.

enemies only went so far. Dominating what they said about them mattered more.

Because of the exchange system, readers of newspapers from all across North America could read the same story. By the start of war, patriot leaders had already begun turning the weekly paper into an evolution of the committees of correspondence. Through the stories they featured (or forgot), the papers had the potential to defuse intercolonial conflicts and close the distance between faraway strangers—the things British leaders thought impossible in the American colonies. The exchanges promoted trust, the most crucial ingredient in making the cause not just common but self-evident.

Interlude

THE "SHOT HEARD 'ROUND THE WORLD" REVISITED

Eighty years after American independence, a local attorney compiled a history of the town of Natick, Massachusetts. He had an interesting story to chronicle. Despite its diverse history as one of John Eliot's original Algonquian "praying towns," Natick responded to the Lexington Alarm in the small hours of April 19, 1775, just like other shaken-awake towns throughout the Boston hinterland. "When the news came, early in the morning," he memorialized in the 1850s, "the people rapidly assembled on the common, provided themselves with ammunition, and marched, full of zeal, to attack the British." The historian and his source, a proud veteran, further cemented the mythology that had encased the events of that wild night. "Every man that morning was a minute-man," the witness claimed. But there was much more to the story. What he did not relate was the participation of several Natick Indians in that group of seventy-five minutemen who stood shoulder-to-shoulder with the "embattled farmers" to beat back the British advance.[1]

Nor did he say what happened back at home after those men mustered and marched the seventeen miles to Lexington. Apparently, it was a sleepless night for all in the Natick area. Another local chronicler told a different story in his 1887 history of Framingham, the next town over from Natick. Josiah Temple, whose ancestor would be later wounded in the shoulder on Lexington Green, stated that for a century, the local memory of the Lexington Alarm turned not on Thomas Gage or Paul Revere or John Hancock.

---

1. Oliver N. Bacon, *A History of Natick from Its Settlement in 1651 to the Present Time with Notices of the First White Families* . . . (Boston, 1856), 41.

The inhabitants of Framingham, Temple wrote, were more afraid of a slave rebellion. As soon as the minutemen left, a "strange panic" spread among those left behind: "The Negroes were coming to massacre them all!" After Framingham's militia started on the road to Lexington, some in the rest of the town allegedly "brought the axes and pitchforks and clubs into the house, and securely bolted doors, and passed the day and night in anxious suspense." This surprising recollection may seem hard to credit, even more so given that Framingham was the hometown of Crispus Attucks, the martyr of the Boston Massacre, and that one of those minutemen marching toward Lexington was Peter Salem, a free black man whose bravery two months later at Bunker Hill would be touted at that time and for long after. And, closer to Temple's time, it was a favorite spot for the Massachusetts Anti-Slavery Society to hold Independence Day rallies from the 1840s until emancipation, featuring illustrious speakers such as William Lloyd Garrison and Henry David Thoreau. Temple himself found the story dubious. He claimed, from the distance of 1887, that "all our own colored people were patriots" and that the scare was "probably a lingering memory of the earlier Indian alarms, which took this indefinite shape." But, on both counts, he was wrong. A series of newspaper articles published just a few weeks before Lexington corroborates Framingham's popular memory that a real rebellion instigated by free and enslaved blacks—and perhaps Indian partners— was indeed something to be feared in the spring of 1775.[2]

A month before, newspapers throughout the colonies printed stories about potential slave plots in the mid-Atlantic. The *New-York Journal* reported that in Esopus, a small town on the Hudson, two suspects "have been detected and confessed that their design was to convey ammunition to the Indians, and to set fire to Esopus, Marble-town and other places." Details of this plan further revealed that blacks from four different towns were involved, that they had collected a "large Quantity" of powder and ball, and that the number of Indians supporting them was rumored to have

2. J[osiah] H. Temple, *History of Framingham, Massachusetts, Early Known as Danforth's Farms, 1640–1880; with a Genealogical Register* (Framingham, Mass., 1887), 275; Elaine Brooks, "Massachusetts Anti-Slavery Society," *Journal of Negro History*, XXX (1945), 311–330; Eric J. Chaput, "Republicans and Abolitionists on the Road to 'Jubilee': Recent Scholarship and Primary Sources on the Destruction of American Slavery, 1861–1865," *Common-Place*, XIV (2014), https://web.archive.org/web/20150 426021823/http://common-place.org/vol-14/no-03/school/#.ViZRpRCrRE4, accessed Sept. 20, 2015.

reached as high as five to six hundred. Giving their deposition to the county magistrate, the accused slaves revealed their modus operandi in words that must have sent shivers up readers' spines: "When once begun, we must go through with it. We are to set Fire to the Houses, and stand by the Doors and Windows, to receive the People as they come out." At that same moment, two different plots downriver in Perth Amboy, New Jersey, and on Long Island were also discovered, facts that often appeared in the same columns of print alongside the Esopus event, heightening notions that rebels—slave rebels, that is—lurked in the days before what would be the Revolutionary War.[3]

But these events were too far away from Framingham to induce the "strange panic." A similar scene next door, however, would. On March 9, the same day that the *Boston Weekly News-Letter* printed news of the foiled plot in Esopus, the *Norwich Packet* reported that a free black man was arrested in Natick, just a handful of miles east of Framingham, under charges of conspiracy. "It appeared that said Fellow has for some Time past been employed in forming a Plot to destroy the white People; for that Purpose he had enlisted Numbers of his own Complexion, as Associates, and they only waited until some Disturbance should happen that might occasion the Militia to turn out, and in their Absence it was proposed to Murder the defenceless inhabitants." Not everyone in Natick was a minuteman, after all. The article in the *Packet* continued: "The same Gentleman also informs us, that, last Monday Evening, another African, in the Vicinity of Natick, was discovered to have been deeply concerned in the above-mentioned infernal Scheme; and that his Master had delivered him up to Justice." And where was that justice located? "After Examination," the suspect was "committed to the Concord G[ao]l." Strange as it may seem, it is possible that those left behind in Framingham were truly petrified that a very different sort of rebellion might

3. *New-York Journal*, Mar. 2, 1775; *Rivington's New-York Gazetteer*, Mar. 2, 1775; *Pennsylvania Evening Post*, Mar. 4, 1775; *New-York Gazette*, Mar. 6, 1775; *Connecticut Courant*, Mar. 6, 1775; *Connecticut Journal*, Mar. 8, 1775; *Pennsylvania Gazette*, Mar. 8, 1775; *Boston News-Letter*, Mar. 9, 1775; *Connecticut Gazette*, Mar. 10, 1775; *Providence Gazette*, Mar. 11, 1775; *Maryland Journal*, Mar. 13, 1775; *Virginia Gazette* (Pinkney), Mar. 16, 1775; *Virginia Gazette* (Purdie), Mar. 17, 1775; *Virginia Gazette* (Dixon & Hunter), Mar. 18, 1775. For Long Island, see *Rivington's New-York Gazetteer*, Feb. 9, 1775; *New-York Gazette*, Mar. 6, 1775; *Pennsylvania Gazette*, Mar. 8, 1775; *Virginia Gazette, or the Norfolk Intelligencer*, Mar. 9, 1775; *Maryland Journal*, Mar. 29, 1775. For Perth Amboy, see *Pennsylvania Evening Post*, Mar. 4, 1775; *New-York Gazette*, Mar. 6, 1775; *Pennsylvania Gazette*, Mar. 22, 1775; *Maryland Journal*, Mar. 29, 1775.

The "Shot Heard 'round the World" Revisited

break out in Massachusetts on April 19, 1775. In Massachusetts and outside, colonists interpreted the outbreak of combat in ways we might not suspect. This "Disturbance" was a difficult one to comprehend.[4]

The news of war sped down the Atlantic coast. Within a week, notices of Lexington and Concord had traveled nearly one thousand miles. The unprecedented speed at which this unprecedented news shuttled was a result of the energy the patriots had expended building communication networks (an independent postal system, the committees of correspondence) in the months before April 1775. As early as mid-morning on April 19—even before the fighting at Concord—the first postrider took up his mount armed with a report hastily drafted by Joseph Palmer of the Boston committee of safety. On Friday, two days after the battles, the first newspaper report appeared in the *New-Hampshire Gazette* under the heading "Bloody News." By Monday, printers in Connecticut, Rhode Island, and New York published various accounts taken from express riders, committee members, and witnesses. In order to establish legitimacy, these reports listed the full names of local patriot leaders who attested that they were to be trusted.[5]

4. *Norwich Packet*, Mar. 2–9, 1775. They were not the only ones who worried that one "Disturbance" might lead to another. A similar dread swept through other New England towns when the news of Lexington inspired militiamen to rush to Boston. According to a remembered account in Killingly, Connecticut, after Colonel Israel Putnam set off from neighboring Pomfret to join the gathering New England force — an event that future generations would valorize as America's Cincinnatus throwing down the plow in defense of his country—rumors that former slaves were already on their own march led some residents to post watches and boil pots of water and others to flee into the swamps. See Clifford K. Shipton, *Sibley's Harvard Graduates: Biographical Sketches of Those Who Attended Harvard College*, XI, *1741–1745* (Boston, 1960), 438.

5. Frank Luther Mott, "The Newspaper Coverage of Lexington and Concord," *New England Quarterly*, XVII (1944), 489–505; Richard D. Brown, *Knowledge Is Power: The Diffusion of Information in Early America, 1700–1865* (New York, 1989), 247–253; David Hackett Fischer, *Paul Revere's Ride* (New York, 1994), 269–275; "The Following Interesting Advices Were This Day Received Here, by Two Vessels from Newport, and by an Express by Land," New York, Apr. 23, 1775, *Early American Imprints*, 14337. For a representative example of this chain-letter approach to convince the populace the attack on Lexington was true, see the broadside published in Lancaster by Francis Bailey on Apr. 25, 1775. Bailey's sheet starts with Palmer's report and then lists all the local committees along the way to Pennsylvania that "Attested and forwarded" the news (*Philadelphia; Apr. 25th, 1775; An Express Arrived at Five o'Clock This Evening, by Which We Have the Following Advices* [Lancaster, (Pa.)], *Early American*

Once reports reached areas with denser slave populations, similar scenes of confusion and anxiety, remembered by some New England inhabitants, gripped the countryside from the Chesapeake to Carolina. Within hours of the announcement of the news in Annapolis, Maryland, Governor Robert Eden "was waited on by six gentlemen of respectable characters, requesting me, that as, in consequence of this news, they were under great apprehensions of some attempt being made by the servants or slaves for their liberty." Eden related to his brother in England that the gentlemen asked him to "commit the custody of the arms and ammunition to the freemen of the country for that otherwise they would not answer for consequences from an insurrection." Although less concerned than the planters, Eden relented, delivering four hundred stands of arms "to be employed to keep the servants and negroes in order."[6]

Hours after Governor Eden sat down in Annapolis to write to his brother about the "state of thorough confusion" brought on by the news, the wave reached Williamsburg. When it did, it capped what was already one of the most tumultuous weeks in the history of the Virginia capital. As Massachusetts drifted toward open conflict, rising tensions that spring were not limited to New England. Nor were they limited to the imperial crisis. The previous November, James Madison had written his college friend William Bradford, Jr., younger son of the *Pennsylvania Journal* printer, worried that "an Insurrection among the slaves may and will be promoted" if war broke out with Britain. "In one of our Counties lately a few of those unhappy wretches met together and chose a leader who was to conduct them when the English Troops should arrive." These "Intentions were soon discovered" and the "Infection" prevented, but, Madison cautioned, "It is prudent such attempts should be concealed as well as suppressed." A few months later, however, with similar schemes being discovered—and publicized—along the Hudson River, Virginia slaveholders like Madison could do neither.[7]

In the third week of April, slaves along the James River—in five counties

Imprints, 14026). "Bloody News": *New-Hampshire Gazette*, Apr. 21, 1775; *Salem Gazette*, Apr. 21, 1775; *Norwich Packet*, Apr. 22, 1775 (supplement); *Providence Gazette*, Apr. 22, 1775; *New-York Gazette*, Apr. 24, 1775.

6. Robert Eden to William Eden, Apr. 28, 1775, quoted in Ronald Hoffman, *A Spirit of Dissension: Economics, Politics, and the Revolution in Maryland* (Baltimore, 1973), 146–147.

7. James Madison to William Bradford, [Jr.], Virginia, Nov. 26, 1774, *PJM*, I, 129–131, esp. 130.

stretching over 150 miles—threatened insurrections. On April 15, Prince Edward County authorities charged a slave named Toney with insurrection and conspiracy to commit murder. Three days later, while Paul Revere watched the steeple at the Old North Church, the Chesterfield County slave patrol embodied itself to prevent rebellion. Then, on April 21, Norfolk, Surry County, and Williamsburg all reported slave disturbances. In Norfolk, two slaves, Emanuel and Emanuel de Antonio, were found guilty of conspiracy and sentenced to hang.[8]

The night of the Williamsburg scare, as the news of bloodshed galloped south, Virginia governor Lord Dunmore ordered the gunpowder stored in Williamsburg's public magazine removed to the nearby warship HMS *Magdalen*. His decision had nothing to do with the outbreak of violence in New England; Dunmore acted to prevent endemic conflict throughout Virginia. Local authorities in Williamsburg, also worried about a large-scale slave uprising, reacted angrily to what they interpreted as betrayal. The next day, the city government issued a strong public statement in the *Virginia Gazette*, arguing that the "magazine was erected at the public expence of the colony," whereby the munitions were kept "for the protection and security of the country, by arming thereout such of the militia as might be necessary in cases of invasions and insurrections"; the governor must therefore return the hijacked powder immediately. The news of Lexington would not arrive for another six days, so they were not yet concerned that Dunmore's action left them defenseless against a British government that had moved into open conflict with the colonies. Instead, they saw the removal as leaving them without the ability to counteract the "various reports at present prevailing in different parts of the country . . . that some wicked and designing persons have instilled the most diabolical notions into the minds of our slaves, and that therefore the utmost attention to our internal security is become the more necessary."[9]

For some Virginians, then, just as for many in New England, the opening of the Revolutionary War witnessed the actions of a restive slave popula-

8. Woody Holton, *Forced Founders: Indians, Debtors, Slaves, and the Making of the American Revolution in Virginia* (Chapel Hill, N.C., 1999), 140–148; Gerald W. Mullin, *Flight and Rebellion: Slave Resistance in Eighteenth-Century Virginia* (New York, 1972), 131; Philip Schwarz, *Twice Condemned: Slaves and the Criminal Laws of Virginia, 1705–1865* (Baton Rouge, La., 1988), 182–183; John E. Selby, *The Revolution in Virginia, 1775–1783* (Williamsburg, Va.,1988), 1–7.
9. *Virginia Gazette* (Dixon & Hunter), Apr. 22, 1775.

tion and a royal government that, at best, undermined the colonists' ability to maintain security. To make matters worse, Dunmore played his trump card. Through an intermediary, the governor sent a message to Burgesses Speaker Peyton Randolph that unless they acquiesced in his removal of the powder, he would "declare freedom to the slaves and reduce the City of Wmsburg to ashes." Sensing a far greater threat than the loss of fifteen barrels of gunpowder, city officials quietly resorted to doubling the number of nightly slave patrols. In part of his own volition, and also because of the independent actions of the slaves themselves, Governor Dunmore rattled a sword in late April that would prove to be a very powerful and intimidating weapon throughout the southern colonies. Although not a direct result of the outbreak of war in Massachusetts, the timing and connections made by the powder removal incident in Williamsburg illustrated for Virginians the potential destructiveness of a combined force of Britain and the enslaved.[10]

One week later, they began to learn about General Gage's attempt to seize gunpowder in Concord. Official reports forwarded by northern committees arrived in Fredericksburg on Sunday, April 30, and in Williamsburg two days later. But informal, oral reports had gotten ahead of the paper wave. John Harrower, an indentured servant living near Fredericksburg, noted in his journal that "an express from Boston" had arrived on Friday, April 28, with the bare news that the British "were repuls'd with loss, but no particulars as yet." Once this news arrived in Virginia, it threw Dunmore's action into a different light. Now, it seemed impossible that his order for British Marines to "secure" the public gunpowder on board the HMS *Magdalen* could be coincidental. The next day, six hundred "well armed and disciplined men, friends of constitutional liberty and America," gathered in a public space near Fredericksburg to decide whether they should discover the truth in Williamsburg. Although they decided not to march on that Saturday, other volunteers in Albemarle, Orange, and Hanover Counties did take to the roads almost as soon as they heard the news from Massachusetts; Dunmore called for reinforcements and issued a proclamation reminding Virginians not forget about the problems facing "this distracted country," which not only included "intestine insurgents" but also "the dangers . . . [of] a savage enemy . . . ready to renew their hostilities."[11]

10. "Deposition of Dr. William Pasteur, in regard to the Removal of Powder from the Williamsburg Magazine," 1775, *VMHB*, XIII (1905), 49. Pasteur was the intermediary between Dunmore and Randolph.

11. Apr. 28, 1775, in Edward Miles Riley, ed., *The Journal of John Harrower: An In-*

This was how Virginia's Revolution began: more agitated than it might have because of rising tensions from slave quarters throughout the colony. It was bad enough that Dunmore issued the same orders as Gage in Massachusetts—although unwittingly and for completely different reasons. That coincidence smacked of conspiracy. But Dunmore compounded that mistake by threatening Virginians with one of their greatest fears.

This same panic gripped Charleston, South Carolina, one week later. Again, a coincidence that went to the heart of Carolina's worst nightmare shaped how the capital received the news of Lexington. According to John Stuart, the British Superintendent for Indian Affairs, "Upon the news of the affair at Lexington . . . the people of [South] Carolina were thrown into a great Ferment." Edward Allen's ship, *Industry*, fresh from Salem with copies of the *Essex Gazette*, arrived in Charleston on Monday, May 8. But, as in Virginia, the "great Ferment" was not reserved strictly for the news of war. Allen's ship pulled up at the wharf alongside another vessel that had completed its trans-Atlantic voyage only a couple of days before. That ship had carried a letter from Arthur Lee, South Carolina's agent in London, addressed to the president of Charleston's committee of safety, Henry Laurens. Lee's advice was explosive. In the event of armed conflict with Britain, he wrote, the administration was exploring granting "freedom to such Slaves as should desert their Masters and join the King's troops." Such an event had already taken place, Carolinians learned instantly. As soon as they had those two pieces of information, Laurens and his patriot colleagues moved with requisite speed.[12]

---

dentured Servant in the Colony of Virginia, 1773–1776 (Williamsburg, Va., 1963), 94; *Virginia Gazette* (Pinkney), May 11, 1775; "Pledge of Readiness at a Moment's Warning," *Rev. Va.*, III, 70–72. On the question of conspiracy, Dunmore stated that his reasons for seizing the powder were "to anticipate the malevolent designs of the enemies of order and government or to prevent the attempts of any enterprizing Negroes." See Governor Dunmore to his council, Williamsburg, Va., May 2, 1775, in *Rev. Va.*, III, 77–78, esp. 77, also published in *Virginia Gazette* (Pinkney), May 4, 1775. "Intestine insurgents": *Virginia Gazette* (Pinkney), May 4, 1775.

12. John Richard Alden, "John Stuart Accuses William Bull," *WMQ*, 3d Ser., II (1945), 318; D. D. Wallace, "Gage's Threat—or Warning?" *South Carolina Historical and Genealogical Magazine*, XLVII (1946), 191; Alexander Innes to [Lord Dartmouth], May 16, 1775, in B. D. Barger, ed., "Charles Town Loyalism in 1775: The Secret Reports of Alexander Innes," *South Carolina Historical Magazine*, LXIII (1962), 125–136, esp. 128. Others have detailed these events in 1775 Charleston. See Sylvia R. Frey, *Water from the Rock: Black Resistance in a Revolutionary Age* (Princeton, N.J., 1991),

Wasting no time on that memorable Monday, the committee gathered to send word to the Second Continental Congress that was scheduled to convene two days hence. They forwarded Lee's letter to their delegates who had recently left for Philadelphia, where a similar letter from London carried the same gossip that "arms [are] to be given to all the Negroes to act against the Colonies." In both Carolina and Virginia, this was the charged atmosphere into which the newspaper notices of Lexington and Concord would be read, read aloud, posted, passed back and forth, and discussed.[13]

The fear that gripped Charleston that day would be amplified by one individual, a man named "Black David." David, an African American preacher who lived in George Whitefield's famous settlement in Bethesda, Georgia, had "shown some impudent airs" in Charleston—and, on a day like May 8, 1775, this was dangerous. "The Gentlemen of this Town are so possessed with an opinion that his Designs are bad," a man wrote from the Carolina capital, "that they are determined to pursue, and hang him if they can lay hold of him. . . . I wou'd indeed be very sorry that the poor fellow should lose his life." David's crime had been his exhortation, delivered to "several white people and Negroes, who had collected together to hear him," that God would "send Deliverance to the Negroes, from the power of their Masters, as He freed the Children of Israel from Egyptian Bondage." This was no time to discuss that topic; so, for his own protection, David's benefactors quietly ushered him onto a ship bound for England.[14]

55–67; Robert Olwell, *Masters, Slaves, and Subjects: The Culture of Power in the South Carolina Low Country, 1740–1790* (Ithaca, N.Y., 1998), 226–243, esp. 228; and Peter H. Wood, "'Taking Care of Business' in Revolutionary South Carolina: Republicanism and the Slave Society," in Jeffrey J. Crow and Larry E. Tise, eds., *The Southern Experience in the American Revolution* (Chapel Hill, N.C., 1978), 279–287.

13. James Kenny to Humphry Marshall, Philadelphia, Apr. 25, 1775, in Humphry and Moses Marshall Papers, CL.

14. James Habersham to Robert Keen, Savannah, May 11, 1775, *Collections of the Georgia Historical Society*, VI, *The Letters of Hon. James Habersham, 1756–1775* (Savannah, Ga., 1904), 243–244. It is clear that corroboration of the news of Lexington arrived sometime on May 10. That evening, the Charleston Committee of Intelligence forwarded a letter and newspaper "with momentous intelligence this instant arrived" to another unknown patriot committee. See "Miscellaneous Papers of the General Committee, Secret Committee and Provincial Congress, 1775," *South Carolina Historical Magazine*, VIII (1907), 138. Henry Laurens described the charged atmosphere in Carolina a few days later, telling a correspondent that a few patriots in Charleston had to work hard "to restrain the Zeal and ardour of the many from entering upon

The "Shot Heard 'round the World" Revisited

Although this quick action saved David's life, it did not calm the city's nerves. Four days later, the Charleston committee of safety issued a proclamation that again connected the two issues: "The actual Commencement of Hostilities against this Continent, the threats of arbitrary impositions from abroad, and the dread of instigated Insurrections at home, are causes sufficient to drive an oppressed People to the use of Arms . . . [and] we do solemnly promise that . . . we will go forth and be ready to sacrifice our Lives and fortunes in attempting to secure her Freedom and Safety." Neither rights nor principles were sufficient causes to take up arms, according to this proclamation. But "instigated Insurrections" (a phrase South Carolinians would become very familiar with before year's end) were. In mid-May, a Charleston merchant maintained, "our Province at present is in a ticklish Situation, on account of our numerous Domesticks, who have been unhappily deluded by some villainous Persons into the notion of being set free." From the first hours of the Revolution, patriots in Charleston framed the conflict in relation to the enslaved.[15]

David could well have been the first casualty of South Carolina's American Revolution. The "great Ferment" produced by a remarkable double front of news from Salem and London nearly cost David his life. As it was, his exile would be the first of thousands over the next eight years of conflict. Nor would David be the last person whose life would be changed by news—real or not—forwarded in personal correspondence or newspaper columns. Moreover, the immediate intervention by David's friends to escort him out of an unsettled Charleston reveals how the news of Lexington was received: in towns and capitals from New England to Carolina, many colonists were worried about their slaves during the opening hours of the Revolution. Imperial conflict was the new filter through which colonists interpreted social conflict that might have had little to do with the bloodshed in Massachusetts.

Take an encounter in Dorchester County, on Maryland's Eastern Shore, on Saturday, May 6. Less than a week after the news of Lexington induced

---

Acts which appear to us to be at present impolitic and inexpedient" (Laurens to William Manning, Charleston, S.C., May 22, 1775, *PHL,* X, 128).

15. Josiah Smith, Jr., to James Poyas, Charleston, May 18, 1775, and Smith to George Appleby, Charleston, June 16, 1775, both quoted in Jeffrey J. Crow, "Slave Rebelliousness and Social Conflict in North Carolina, 1775–1802," *WMQ,* 3d Ser., XXXVII (1980), 79–102, esp. 84n–85n. Laurens included the proclamation in his letter to his son, John Laurens (Charleston, May 15, 1775, *PHL,* X, 118–119).

nervous Maryland planters to beg Governor Eden for security, a passerby asked John Simmons, a Dorchester wheelwright, whether he was going to town on Monday to muster. Simmons returned, "Damn them (meaning the gentlemen), if I had a few more White People to join me I could get all the Negroes in the county to back us, and they would do more Good in the Night than the White people could in the day." Simmons, angry at his economic betters, swore that if he "had one of Colonel William Ennall's bags, I would put it to a better use than he does." But, when the local committee of inspection reported the incident a few weeks later, Simmons's venting of class frustrations was transformed into political demagoguery. The committee informed their colleagues in Baltimore that "the insolence of the Negroes in this county is come to such a Height that we are under a necessity of disarming them . . . the malicious and imprudent speeches of some of the lower class of Whites have induced them to believe that their Freedom depended on the success of the King's Troops; we cannot therefore be too vigilant nor too rigorous with those who promote and encourage this disposition in our slaves." Simmons was tarred and feathered, and—like Black David before him and many after—because of "his intimacy and connection with the negroes . . . we did not think it prudent to let him remain in the Province."[16]

The very instant the common cause reached a new, critical phase, then, patriot leaders and many of their supporters reacted to the news based upon the impact war might have on other potential enemies. Patriots in Massachusetts did their best to shape the story of the first battles in order to manage public opinion. That kind of campaign was necessary, for not only did many throughout the colonies receive the news with suspicion, but many others throughout the continent saw this as an opportunity to change the course of their lives. Slaves along the Hudson and James Rivers saw themselves connected to the burgeoning "disturbance" that spring, as did blacks in New England, the Chesapeake, and the Deep South. They were not alone.

* * *

Many years later, historian George Bancroft helped to fix the mythology of the Lexington Alarm. He rejoiced that "with one impulse the colonies sprung to arms" all across the continent, and that the news of war had

16. James Mullineaux, deposition, Dorchester County, Maryland Committee of Inspection to Baltimore Committee of Inspection, May 23, 1775, Robert Gilmor, Jr. Papers, 1774–1848, MS 387, III, MDHS.

The "Shot Heard 'round the World" Revisited

miraculous effects even deep into the American interior. The "voice" of Lexington "breathed its inspiring word to the first settlers of Kentucky; so that hunters who made their halt in that matchless valley of the Elkhorn, commemorated the nineteenth day of April by naming their encampment LEXINGTON." Writing from the safe distance of the mid-nineteenth century, Bancroft's crafting of a Lexington legend—complete with origin story for what would become the capital of Kentucky—masks the chaos that the "voice" produced.[17]

But what about the people who lived all around the Kentucky campsite of Bancroft's heroic hunters? Like free and enslaved African Americans, natives from Canada to the Gulf of Mexico paid attention to the new realities of war between Britain and its colonies; the "voice" inspired them, too. And, in turn, what critical role they might play was one of the most pressing issues facing both sides in the conflict's first days. The issue of what to do about Indians—how far to go in welcoming their support—was a particular and immediate problem for patriot authorities.

In March, Thomas Gage wrote to the new northern Superintendent for Indian Affairs, Guy Johnson, who had just replaced his revered father-in-law Sir William Johnson a few weeks earlier. Gage advised Johnson to tell the Six Nations that "they will never be molested by the King's troops, while they chuse to be his friends, but on the Contrary, that they may expect from him every assistance and Justice he can give them." Soon after Lexington, Gage considered activating this contingency. "I would have you immediately cultivate the friendship of the Indians as much as possible, have them ready to detach on the first notice, and in the mean time have scouts out to get what intelligence you can," he wrote to Fort Niagara on May 10. He sent messages to other outposts ordering them to "cultivate the Friendships of the Indians on All Occasions, as they may be wanted for His Majesty's Service."[18]

Gage justified his actions to supervisors in Britain by claiming that he was not the first to seek Indian assistance. "You may be tender of using Indians," he wrote back to Whitehall in mid-June, "but the Rebels have shewn us the Example, and brought all they could down upon us here." He was right: while Gage secretly ordered his officers to maintain Indian relations in the

17. George Bancroft, *History of the United States from the Discovery of the American Continent,* 4th ed. (Boston, 1860), VII, 312.

18. Thomas Gage to Guy Johnson, Boston, Mar. 10, 1775, Thomas Gage Papers, CXXVI, CL, Gage to Captain DePeyster, Boston, May 20, 1775, and Gage to Captain Lernoult, Boston, May 20, 1775, CXXIX.

weeks before the outbreak of violence, so, too, patriots across the northern frontier tried to convince neighboring Indians that Boston's cause was theirs, as well.[19]

On April 1, the Massachusetts Provincial Congress invited the Stockbridge Indians to join them in becoming minutemen. "This is a common cause," they proclaimed. "We are all brothers; and if the Parliament of *Great Britain* takes from us our property and our lands, without our consent, they will do the same by you." Three weeks later, almost as soon as the smoke cleared from Lexington Green, patriot leaders raced to get their message out, scattering letters and envoys across the frontier. Within a few days, it was increasingly apparent that these initial efforts to enlist nearby Indians to help them surround Gage in Boston were a great success. A correspondent in Pittsfield, Massachusetts, wrote a militia officer at Cambridge that Solomon, the "Indian King of Stockbridge," said "that the Mohawks had not only given liberty to the Stockbridge Indians to join us, but had sent them a belt, denoting that they would hold five hundred men in readiness to join us immediately on the first notice; and that the said *Solomons* holds an *Indian* post in actual readiness to run with the news as soon as they shall be wanted." "Those Indians would be of great service to you should the King's Troops march out of Boston," he added.[20]

Flush with their success with the Stockbridge, the Massachusetts Provincial Congress soon expanded its efforts to gain Indian support. On May 13, they adopted Goddard's scheme of a new "Constitutional Post." Two days later, they put that new system to use by sending those post riders out with a general address to the "Eastern Indians." Trying to convince Indians across New England that they were all in similar straits, the Massachusetts Congress explained, "What is for our good is for your good; and we, by standing together, shall make those wicked men afraid, and overcome them, and all be freemen." "We will do all for you we can," the speech concluded, "and [will] fight to save you any time, and hope none of your men, or the Indians in Canada, will join with our enemies." These attempts to make their case to the "Eastern Indians" did not deviate from the language patriots

19. Gage to Lord Barrington, Boston, June 12, 1775, in Clarence Edwin Carter, ed., *The Correspondence of General Thomas Gage with the Secretaries of State, 1763–1775*, 2 vols. (New Haven, Conn., 1931), II, 684.

20. "To Johoiakin Mothksin, and the Rest of Our Brethren, the Indians, Natives of Stockbridge," Apr. 1, 1775, 4 *Am. Archives*, I, 1347, "A Gentleman at Pittsfield, in Berkshire County, to an Officer in Cambridge," May 9, 1775, II, 546.

used to convince their fellow colonists to support the common cause. They extended the conspiracy argument to include Indians: just as Virginians would surely become enslaved after New Englanders, so, too, Seneca and Stockbridge Indians would suffer the same fate if they did not take action now. But the congress made these statements without any real authority. When local provincial bodies took up their own initiatives, they began to craft Indian policy even before the Continental Congress—whose lead they promised to follow—had a chance to reconvene, let alone decide what tack to take regarding Indian participation in the war.[21]

It was just this problem on the New York frontier that greeted the delegates when they gaveled the Second Continental Congress to order on May 10, 1775. When they agreed to reconvene the following spring, the delegates to the First Continental Congress anticipated they would need to do so in order to check on the effectiveness of the Continental Association. As it turned out, their mandate was one of organizing the colonies for a defensive war.

The delegates at Philadelphia had to deal with several pressing issues, especially what to do about the military force gathering in Cambridge, Massachusetts. But even before they could consider the central question of how to organize the New England militia, it began to dawn on the delegates that the most dangerous threat to the common cause might not be Gage and Boston but, instead, Guy Johnson and the New York frontier.

During the same days that Virginians traded threats with their royal governor and South Carolina patriots stepped up their slave patrols, and while New Englanders streamed into Cambridge, a storm from northern New York began to demand increasing attention. In the two months between Lexington and Bunker Hill, colonial printers spent much of their time assembling type about Albany, not Boston.

When Ethan Allen and the Green Mountain Boys snuck across Lake Champlain and surprised the commander at Fort Ticonderoga on the evening of May 9, allegedly claiming the fort "in the name of the great Jehovah, and the Continental Congress," they turned the northern frontier into the Revolutionary War's second theater. One hundred miles away, Guy Johnson had not yet heard the news of the fortress's capitulation, but he was worried nonetheless. The Indian Superintendent for the Northern Department was

21. "Proceedings of Massachusetts Provincial Congress," May 13–15, 1775, 4 *Am. Archives*, II, 802, 805, Letter [from Massachusetts Provincial Congress] to the Eastern Indians, May 15, 1775, 610–611.

hearing threatening whispers in his neighborhood. On May 18, he sent a letter to officials in nearby Schenectady denouncing the "gross and notorious falsehood, uttered by some worthless scoundrels, respecting my intentions." Two days later, Johnson sent another missive flatly denying "a ridiculous and malicious report that I intend to make the Indians destroy the inhabitants." But, like Dunmore that month, Johnson's second refutation concluded with a stern but impolitic warning: "But should I neglect myself, and be tamely made prisoner, it is clear to all who know anything of Indians, they will not sit still and see their Council fire extinguished, and Superintendent driven from his duty, but will come upon the frontiers, in revenge, with a power sufficient to commit horrid devastation." Johnson's written warnings that any attempts to dislodge him would be met with a "hot and disagreeable reception" only aggravated colonists already on the watch for any sign that the British and Indians were sweeping down against them. Soon, those reports would land on colonial printers' tables. On the same day Johnson sent his first letter to Schenectady, one such report began to appear in newspapers across the northern colonies.[22]

Benjamin Towne's *Pennsylvania Evening Post* reported a suspicious hunting trip conducted by a small group of Canadian officers and Caughnawaga Indians on May 18. Stopped along the way by some curious settlers who wanted to know their "real intention," the Caughnawagas admitted that they were reconnoitering the woods "to find a passage for an army to march to the assistance of the King's friends in Boston." Worse, the report went on to expose the identities of two suspicious officers, including one infamous name from the last war that surely raised the hairs on the necks of colonial readers: "The conductors of this grand expedition are to be Monsieur St. Luke le Corne, the villain who let loose the Indians on the prisoners at Fort William Henry." In case the point was still opaque, an editorial comment punctuated the end of the account: *"Oh George, what tools art thou obliged to make use of!"* Printers in cities up and down the continent exchanged both the story and its concluding remark. This would not be the last time in 1775

---

22. Ethan Allen, *A Narrative of Colonel Ethan Allen's Captivity: Containing His Voyages and Travels* (1799; rpt. Mineola, N.Y., 2013), 8; Colonel Guy Johnson to Committee of Schenectady, New-York, Guy Park, May 18, 1775, 4 *Am. Archives,* II, 638, Johnson to the Magistrates of Schenectady and Albany, Guy Park, May [20?], 1775, 661–662. For background on Allen's attack on Ticonderoga, see Michael A. Bellesiles, *Revolutionary Outlaws: Ethan Allen and the Struggle for Independence on the Early American Frontier* (Charlottesville, Va., 1993), 113–123.

The "Shot Heard 'round the World" Revisited

patriot newspaper raised the specter of La Corne—and the 1757 "massacre" at Fort William Henry.[23]

Reportage of this type of suspicious behavior did not ease tensions. Rumors had reached Johnson that a band of New England militia was in fact on its way to capture him, a report that disturbed the Six Nations. "He is our property," a contingent of Mohawks warned the Albany committee of safety on May 25, "and we shall not part with him." This was concerning: New England patriots calculated that attempts to kidnap Johnson might broaden the war. These worries continued to build throughout the month. In early June, the New York Provincial Congress requested the immediate intervention of the Continental Congress. Worried that "our publick peace is more endangered by the situation of the barbarians to the westward of us, than it can be by any inroads made upon the sea-coast," they asked their delegates in Philadelphia for help. "We do not presume to dictate any measure to you," they wrote, yet "at the same time we submit it to your consideration whether it is proper to leave the management of the numerous tribes of Indians entirely in the hands of persons appointed and paid by the Crown." In other words, no matter how close conflict might be to their door, these county committee members were not enthusiastic about moving against well-connected imperial officials.[24]

Luckily, delegates returning to reconstitute the Continental Congress were weighing what to do about the northern frontier, too. Not knowing that his colleagues in Massachusetts had made similar invitations just a week before, Richard Henry Lee wrote his brother on May 21, "We know the

23. The Caughnawaga Indians are also known as the "Seven Nations of Canada." They lived along the northern bank of the St. Lawrence in the vicinity of Montreal and Quebec and included the Mohawks of Caughnawaga, the Mohawks and Algonkins of Oka, the Hurons of Lorette, the Abenakis at Odanak, and the Cayugas and Onondagas at Oswegatchie. See Colin G. Calloway, *The American Revolution in Indian Country: Crisis and Diversity in Native American Communities* (Cambridge, 1995), 35. *"Oh George": Pennsylvania Evening Post*, May 18, 1775; *Pennsylvania Mercury*, May 19, 1775; *Pennsylvania Journal*, May 24, 1775; *Pennsylvania Gazette*, May 24, 1775; *New-York Gazette*, May 29, 1775; *Virginia Gazette* (Purdie), June 2, 1775; *New-England Chronicle*, June 8, 1775; *Essex Journal*, June 9, 1775; *Virginia Gazette, or the Norfolk Intelligencer*, June 21, 1775. All exchanges recopied the editorial comment.

24. "Answer of the Mohawks to the Speech of the Magistrates, etc. of Albany and Schenectady," Guy Park, May 25, 1775, 4 *Am. Archives*, II, 842–843, esp. 843, New York Provincial Congress to New York Delegates of Continental Congress, June 7, 1775, 1281.

plan of ministry is to bring Canadians and Indians down upon us." New Hampshire's delegates also wrote home from Philadelphia that Johnson had "really Endeavoured to persuade the Indians to Enter into a war with us and that many other Steps have been Taken by a Bloody Minded and Cruel Ministry to Induce those Hereditary Enemies of America to fall upon and Butcher its Inhabitants." And in his notes for a speech during those days, John Dickinson listed "the Danger of Insurrection by Negroes in Southern Colonies—Incursions of Canadians and Indians upon the Northern Colonies—Incidental Proposals to disunite Us—false Hopes [and] selfish designs" in his catalog of "Considerations that deserve the Attention of Gentlemen." But this was just hand wringing. Formulating a coherent plan was a more difficult prospect. Doing so in the chaotic days of mid-May, with various patriot authorities fumbling about, searching for legitimacy and coordination, was impossible.[25]

At that moment, another tumult swept through the capital of South Carolina that suggested Dickinson's worries were materializing. This one was attributable to a choice one Charleston printer made. Upon entering the house of an acquaintance, James Dealey boasted he had "good news" from England. One wonders whether or not he carried a copy of Peter Timothy's May 29 *South-Carolina Gazette* under his arm when he initiated what would be a near-fatal conversation. In that issue, Timothy published a letter from London that referenced "seventy-eight thousand guns, and bayonets, to be sent to America, to put into the hands of N[egroe]s, the Roman Catholics, the Indians and Canadians; and all the wicked means on earth used to subdue the Colonies." Timothy, a staunch patriot, surely did not intend readers to greet this as "good news." But Dealey did. Dealey's acquaintance later testified that when he asked Dealey about the report, the latter responded "that a number of arms was sent over to be distributed amongst the *Negroes, Roman Catholicks,* and *Indians.*" Dealey's happy receipt of this startling information, especially for Catholics, led to a heated exchange. The confrontation, complete with drawn swords, spilled outdoors, where Dealey and a

25. Richard Henry Lee to Francis Lightfoot Lee, Philadelphia, May 21, 1775, *LDC,* I, 367. Several paragraphs of this letter (but not the ones quoted above) appeared in the *Virginia Gazette* (Pinkney), June 1, 1775, under the vague—and misleading—description "Extract of Letter from Gentleman in Philadelphia to a Friend in Williamsburg." See New Hampshire Delegates to the Provincial Committee of New Hampshire, Philadelphia, May 22, 1775, *LDC,* I, 369–370, esp. 369, John Dickinson's Notes for a Speech in Congress, May 23–[25?], 1775, 371–383, esp. 377.

The "Shot Heard 'round the World" Revisited

friend, Laughlin Martin, threatened to chop off their opponent's head in the middle of King Street. After their potential victim begged for his life, they relented, ending the incident with raised glasses, toasting "damnation to the Committee and their proceedings." The committee, ignoring the malediction, ordered Dealey and Martin tarred, feathered, carted through the streets, and put aboard ship for England.[26]

The following day, Henry Laurens searched the minds of his brother's slaves in South Carolina for evidence as to whether they sympathized with Dealey or his friends. "I called in all your Negroes last Saturday Evening," Laurens wrote, "admonished them to behave with great circumspection in this dangerous times, [and] set before them the great risque of exposing themselves to the treachery of pretended friends and false witnesses." Laurens contented himself that his audience was "sensibly affected," but, after what had just happened on King Street and what had just appeared in the local paper, he could not really feel secure. In fact, that very day, Laurens

26. *South-Carolina Gazette,* May 29, 1775; Timothy had exchanged the Feb. 10, 1775, letter from a London correspondent in John Holt's *New-York Journal,* Apr. 27, 1775. Holt did not substitute "N*****s" for "negroes" as Timothy did for sensitive Charleston readers. A few months later, British surgeon Dr. George Millegan wrote, "Letters were likewise said to be received from England and New York to support th[e] assertion" that slaves were to be armed by the king. The first reference (to England) was obviously Arthur Lee's; the second (to a letter from New York) could only mean this exchanged report, corroborating the linkage between the *South-Carolina Gazette* article and Dealey's actions. See "Narrative by [Dr.] George Millegen of His Experiences in South Carolina," brig *"Eagle* at sea," Sept. 15, 1775, in K. G. Davies, ed., *Documents of the American Revolution, 1770–1783,* Colonial Office Series, XI, *Transcripts, 1775 July–December* (Dublin, 1976), 109–114, esp. 110.

The Dealey fight is reported in Petition of Michael Hubart to the Committee of Correspondence at Charlestown, [c. June 1775], 4 *Am. Archives,* II, 922–923. Dealey was exiled. Martin, after begging forgiveness, was eventually allowed to stay in Charleston. Martin's apology is in the *South-Carolina Gazette; And Country Journal,* June 9, 1775. Henry Laurens described these events in his June 8 letter to his son John (Charleston, June 8, 1775, *PHL,* X, 167). Laurens told John, "Members of the Congress preserved their dignity and proceeded to their House on business. Some of the lower people Set up a Judge and called Witnesses and in less than an Hour the Ceremony of Tarring and feathering passed upon Laughlin Martin and James Dealey," but the extant evidence belies this insistence of a reliance on legal procedure: "Secret—tar and feather him. Passed the Secret Committee and ordered to be put in execution." See Petition of Michael Hubart, [c. June 1775], 4 *Am. Archives,* II, 923.

had presided over an agreement that free South Carolina men would "associate as a band in [the colony's] defense" and hold themselves "ready to sacrifice our lives and fortunes to secure her freedom and safety." That this martial step was made necessary because of "the dread of instigated insurrections in the Colonies" must have further undermined Laurens's confidence, no matter what his slaves professed.[27]

What Laurens and his compatriots in South Carolina did not know when they helped establish an emerging patriot catchphrase—"instigated insurrections"—was that their neighbors in Williamsburg, Virginia, and Newbern, North Carolina, were dealing with the same issue. The latter sent out warnings during the last weekend in May that "there is much Reason to fear, in these Times of general Tumult and Confusion, that the Slaves may be instigated, encouraged by our inveterate Enemies to an Insurrection." Just as New Yorkers viewed Guy Johnson and St. Luc la Corne that spring, many southerners viewed men like James Dealey or Black David as even more dangerous to America than Thomas Gage.[28]

* * *

These were the real ripples of the "shot heard round the world." In the month that followed the news of Lexington, Thomas Gage and his troops in Boston dominated a surprisingly small part of patriots' attention. Colonists viewed the conflict in terms of who might aid the so-called "enemies to the country." Often, the first response to the news of bloodshed produced a changed vision; it necessitated a new way of seeing the people who lived on the frontiers or in slave quarters. But, as of the last spring days of 1775, for the most part those colonists did not know they shared analogous responses. An aerial perspective, high above the Atlantic littoral, would have been the only way for colonists to see how they reacted to the news in strikingly similar ways. To be sure, both patriots and loyalists noted with vigor the "Infection which is so generally diffused thro' the Continent" that May. But for how long? Given all the fractures, fissures, and suspicions that had

27. HL to James Laurens, Charleston, June 7, 1775, *PHL*, X, 162–163; Provincial Congress of South Carolina, "Association," June 3, 1775, 4 *Am. Archives*, II, 897.

28. "In the Committee at Newbern, May 31, 1775," in Adelaide L. Fries et al., eds., *Records of the Moravians in North Carolina*, 11 vols. (Raleigh, N.C., 1922–1969), II, 929. North Carolina patriots in Wilmington officially adopted the language of instigated insurrections when they copied South Carolina's "Association" verbatim on 20 June. See 4 *Am. Archives*, II, 1030.

divided the colonies for decades, that initial "astonishing" spirit of unity, which John Adams contended "arose all of a Sudden," might have subsided just as quickly. After all, Adams confessed later, "the continent is a vast, unwieldy machine. We cannot force events."[29]

It would take newspapers to make the cause common—and durable. As the summer started, so did the stories. Beginning in late June, patriot newspapers began to inform colonists of the activities of British officials throughout North America. Readers across the continent learned about negotiations with Indians on the frontier with Guy Johnson and Canadian governor Sir Guy Carleton in the north, and their colleagues John Stuart and Alexander Cameron in the southern backcountry. Stories flooded the colonies that Lord Dunmore was only one of several royal governors plotting to arm slaves. By season's end, rumors about the crown's hiring of Russian or German mercenaries to conquer America were appearing in print.

Patriot political leaders and publicists reinforced the foundations of American unity with fear. If all went well, they would not read those stories "wrong," as James Dealey did. By emphasizing the connections between the ministry, its supporters, and a host of terrifying proxies, patriots began to turn the British into foreigners by enlarging the notion of "enemy to the country" to include far more groups than just men in red coats. This was not a reflection or a memory fastened decades later; this was a purposeful campaign fashioned from colonial anxiety and amplified by patriot political leaders, by William Bradford and his fellow patriot printers, and delivered by Withington, Carheart, and their many peers throughout North America. And it began early in the summer of 1775.

29. William Hooper to Samuel Johnston, Philadelphia, May 23, 1775, *LDC*, I, 398–400, esp. 399, JA to James Warren, Philadelphia, May 2, 1775, 364, JA to Moses Gill, Philadelphia, June 10, 1775, 466.

## CHAPTER 2

"Britain Has Found Means to Unite Us"

1775

As soon as they opened their proceedings, the delegates to the Second Continental Congress, though shocked by the news from Massachusetts and suddenly overwhelmed with work, were buoyed by the impassioned expressions of patriotism that swirled about them. "All parties are now extinguish'd here," Benjamin Franklin wrote to a friend in England. "Britain has found means to unite us." Franklin's quip was true at that first blush of accord, but it did not mean that a lasting continental effort would be either automatic or inevitable. The events of war, combined with assiduous work on the part of Franklin and his myriad colleagues and efforts of British officials in the colonies to find new "means" barely imagined in mid-May, solidified those feelings throughout this singular year. For the remainder of 1775, the anxieties that gripped many in the wake of Lexington would continue to develop. Patriot leaders were quick to propagate those concerns with an eye toward mobilizing the populace for war.[1]

Five days before he ordered the assault on the patriot defenses on Breed's Hill, General Gage broke the news to his superiors: if the king wanted to end the rebellion now, certain tactics—justified yet unsavory—would be necessary. "You will have heard of the boldness of the Rebels, in Surprizing Ticonderoga; and making excursions to the Frontiers of Montreal," he wrote to Lord Barrington, the secretary at war,

> but I hope such Hostilities, will Justify Gen[eral] Carleton in raising all the Canadians and Indians in his power to Attack them in his turn, I have wrote to him to that Effect . . . Things are now come to that Crisis, that we must avail ourselves of every resource, even to raise

1. BF to Jonathan Shipley, Philadelphia, May 15, 1775, *LDC*, I, 350.

the Negroes, in our cause. . . . Nothing is to be neglected of which we can avail ourselves. Hanoverians, Hessians, perhaps Russians May be hired, let Foreigners Act here to the Eastward, particularly Germans, as they will find none of their Country in these parts to seduce them.

For the remainder of 1775 (and after), the ideas behind Gage's proposals would be the main story of the Revolutionary War. Colonial printing shops and assembly houses broadcast stories, whether real, rumored, or imagined, about British agents encouraging Indians, Africans, and other proxies to participate in the conflict. Lord Barrington did not turn Gage's suggestions into official military policy, but that mattered little. So many of the king's representatives in America were accused of "tampering," "instigating," "whispering," or "exciting," it certainly seemed to colonial audiences that they had explicit orders to do so.[2]

At the same time, many patriots weighed the merits of those very tactics. New York delegate to the Continental Congress James Duane confessed he did not approve of patriots' pursuing Indian allies. He wrote in early June, "I should abhor the Thought of employing them in our Service. Nothing could so effectually Shut the door of Accommodation as the inhuman policy of making, on either side, those treacherous Savages the Tools of Revenge." John Adams also admitted, that same June day, he did not know whether it was wise for the patriots to try to secure Indian allies. Adams was conflicted about whether Congress should pursue their services. He wrote to his patriot colleague James Warren, "The Indians are known to conduct their Wars, so entirely without Faith and Humanity, that it would bring eternal Infamy on the Ministry throughout all Europe, if they should excite these Savages to War." "To let loose these blood Hounds to scalp Men, and to butcher Women and Children is horrid," he opined, but then shrugged that it might come to this: "Still its such kind of Humanity and Policy as we have experienced, from the Ministry."[3]

Ironically, that same week, one Virginian thought John Adams should know his ideas for defeating the British in the South: the patriots should preemptively free and arm their slaves. An anonymous stranger from Fredericksburg offered Adams his "hints . . . with an Assurance, that your Re-

2. Thomas Gage to Lord Barrington, Boston, June 12, 1775, in Clarence Edwin Carter, ed., *Correspondence of General Thomas Gage with the Secretaries of State, and with the War Office and the Treasury, 1763–1775* (New Haven, Conn., 1933), II, 684.

3. James Duane to Robert Livingston, Philadelphia, June 7, 1775, *LDC*, I, 453–455, JA to James Warren, Philadelphia, June 7, 1775, 452.

gard for your Country, will improve upon them for the general Good of all America." "Palliative Measure[s] will be found ineffectual" to end the crisis. Only "bold, daring, and strenuous Exertions of Force in the Beginning of the Contest" would "effectually preserve [American] Liberty." What would be more daring than "to proclaim instant Freedom to all the Servants that will join in the Defence of America?" Since the crown would assuredly "engage these Servants to espouse [its] Interest," the emancipator from Fredericksburg suggested, "is it not incompatible with the glorious Struggle America is making for her own Liberty, to hold in absolute Slavery a Number of Wretches, who will be urged by Despair on one Side, and the most flattering Promises on the other, to become the most inveterate Enemies to their present Masters?" There was no arguing with his logic: slavery undermined patriot claims of liberty, not least for Europeans who sympathized with the American protest. But war made that conundrum vastly more difficult. Patriots desperately needed military assistance if they wanted to win the so-called "glorious struggle." Before that could come from other side of the ocean, it had to be secured in North America. The colonists needed to stay unified.[4]

Patriot leaders understood that even considering the encouragement of these groups was a thorny problem, but they had little control over the actions of thousands of African Americans and Indians who saw the outbreak of war as an opportunity to improve their situation. Leaders on both sides knew that whomever they decided to endorse or whichever actions they decided to ratify would alter the conflict. They masked any doubts with a projection of mastery. When officials on either side passed around reports, letters, and "hints" discussing whether or not they should "use" Indians or slaves to support their side, the subjects of these suggestions were objects. They wrote of them as machine switches, not actors. The verbs Gage, Duane, Adams, and his Fredericksburg correspondent chose connoted a need for activation; once so stimulated, the machines automatically produced horrific violence. The action implied in verbs such as "instigate," "employ," or "excite" flowed in one direction, from the prime mover down to the passive lever.

Of course, if they really believed this, colonists would not have been so frightened when express riders and ship captains first brought word of war. The business of employing proxies was dangerous at yet another level. The

4. Letter to JA, Fredericksburg, June 9, 1775, *PJA*, III, 18–20. What Adams thought of this idea is unknown; he did not reflect on the anonymous letter from Fredericksburg in subsequent letters.

British ran the risk of, as Adams stated in his letter to Warren, incurring public opprobrium at home and abroad: "The French disgraced themselves last War, by employing" Indians, let alone emancipating and arming people in one part of an extensive, slave-based empire. The patriots, however, faced an even more significant threat because proxies imperiled the already fragile notion of American unity. If the question of arming slaves might alienate the southern colonies from the cause, encouraging Indians to participate in the war could also estrange many settlers throughout the backcountry. And, if these efforts prevented the cause from being common, the rebellion would not survive long.[5]

For patriot leaders, with Adams at the forefront, a smarter tactic would be to publicize British efforts on the frontiers and plantations while obscuring their own. During the remainder of 1775, patriot political, military, and communications leaders broadcast as loudly as they could the reasons why people should rally behind them. Beginning in early summer, they called on the public to recognize the tyranny unfolding before their eyes and defend their rights from the grasping power of an unchecked empire. These leaders then set out to develop these two interrelated messages, one based on encouraging all liberty-loving people to take up arms, the other on making sure colonists understood the depths to which the king's corrupt agents were willing to descend. They used every avenue of communication available to make their case. In areas of lower literacy, like the Carolina backcountry, they used orality, dispatching political missionaries to expound messages to large gatherings. But the most popular and effective medium for convincing the public to support the rebellion was print, especially the weekly newspapers, the front page delivering official proclamations and the interior pages clinching their argument.

Starting in the summer of 1775, newspaper printers throughout the colonies began paying greater attention to places they had mostly ignored in earlier decades. Suddenly, domestic news crowded out notices from Europe. Nearly every week, printers began relating events happening throughout North America, from the Canadian frontier to the islands off the Georgia coast. The majority of these stories, too, were about the role African Americans and Indians might play in the burgeoning war. Most of these tiny incidents, like Ethan Allen's cousin Remember Baker shooting Indians in canoes on the Richelieu River, are lost to us. They do not figure in our retelling of the events of 1775. But they were widely reported in the inner pages of

5. JA to Warren, Philadelphia, June 7, 1775, *LDC*, I, 452.

those weekly newspapers. The ramifications of those seemingly trivial incidents were unknowable in the first days of revolution, yet we should return our attention to the small paragraphs inside the fold of Bradford's *Pennsylvania Journal*, Holt's *New-York Journal*, and Purdie's *Virginia Gazette*, as together they created and reinforced a continental portrait of oppression—aided by ready Indian and enslaved proxies. Those paragraphs were an archive in the making, a documentary record of British tyranny that deepened each week as new places and proxies featured in those interior bulletins.

The people who contributed those stories (normally men who were heavily invested in the patriot movement) set much store in their importance. Not only were local, provincial, and continental patriot leaders spending time and resources on things happening far away from the camp at Cambridge; they also spent a great deal of effort managing what people knew about those developments. The genesis of this wartime common cause argument was *the* story of 1775. Composed of hundreds of smaller messages, it had little to do with George Washington or the Continental army camp outside Boston. What war meant for thousands of people far removed from Massachusetts—free or enslaved, colonist or Indian, loyalist, patriot, or neither—and how the patriot leadership attempted to turn those experiences into a coherent narrative were critical to the success of the rebellion in its first days.

1: "INSTIGATED INSURRECTIONS" IN THE CAROLINAS

Soon after James Dealey nearly beheaded a man on King Street in Charleston, South Carolina patriots began to have trouble with John Stuart, the Indian Superintendent for the Southern Department. At the same time colonists began to learn that the Northern Indian Superintendent, Guy Johnson, and the governor of Canada, Guy Carleton, were meeting with Indians "1500 Miles back of [Quebec]" and had "made them great Offers to take Arms against the English Colonies," patriot leaders began to publicize rumors and reports that Stuart and his deputy, Alexander Cameron, were doing the same thing with the Cherokee and Creek Indians.[6]

6. *New-Hampshire Gazette*, July 11, 1775; *Pennsylvania Ledger* (Philadelphia), July 22, 1775; *Pennsylvania Packet*, July 24, 1775; *Pennsylvania Journal*, July 26, 1775; *Virginia Gazette, or the Norfolk Intelligencer*, Aug. 2, 1775; *Virginia Gazette* (Pinkney), Aug. 3, 1775; *Virginia Gazette* (Purdie), Aug. 4, 1775. Norfolk printer John Hunter Holt made a telling slip of the type when he recopied the story, mistakenly increasing the distance from 1,500 miles to a whopping 15,000. Other accusations that Johnson was

A few days before the battle on Bunker Hill, a group of Catawba Indians visiting Charleston made a public reference to Stuart's calling upon them and the Cherokees to take up arms against the province. Stuart had already left town after the "fury of a merciless and ungovernable Mob" had encouraged him to flee to Savannah in late May. The committee sent two representatives down to Georgia to question him. On June 15, they called on the ill superintendent, demanding that he "lay before us his letters with respect to Indian affairs." "Unluckily for Mr. Stuart he produce[d] a number of his letters to his deputy, Mr. [Alexander] Cameron," which ordered Cameron to "use his influence to dispose those people to act in defense of his Majesty and Government, if found necessary."[7]

The importance of Stuart's suspected negotiations with the Indians cannot be overstated. At the very moment that patriot leaders in Charleston learned of imminent danger from the backcountry, there was also turbulence in the South Carolina capital regarding slave rebellion's connection to war with Britain. Dealey and Martin were not the only two arrested after the June 8 fight that almost led to a beheading on King Street. Charleston authorities took that opportunity to round up other people they deemed suspicious.[8]

"suspected of endeavouring to stir up Indians against the Colonies" appeared in *New-York Journal*, June 22, 1775; *Connecticut Journal*, June 28, 1775; *New-England Chronicle*, June 22–29, 1775; *Essex Journal*, June 30, 1775; *New-Hampshire Gazette*, July 4, 1775.

7. J. Russell Snapp, *John Stuart and the Struggle for Empire on the Southern Frontier* (Baton Rouge, La., 1996), 160. Stuart sent Thomas Gage two packets of letters on July 9 and 20, 1775, which explained the episode in great detail, including his disappointment that "any set of Gentlemen of Probity would pay attention to a Drunken Catawba." See Thomas Gage Papers, CXXXI, XVVVII, CL.

8. These incidents are also discussed in two essays by Peter H. Wood. See "'Taking Care of Business' in Revolutionary South Carolina: Republicanism and the Slave Society," in Jeffrey J. Crow and Larry E. Tise, eds., *The Southern Experience in the American Revolution* (Chapel Hill, N.C., 1978), 268–293, esp. 284, and "'Liberty Is Sweet': African-American Freedom Struggles in the Years before White Independence," in Alfred F. Young, ed., *Beyond the American Revolution: Explorations in the History of American Radicalism* (DeKalb, Ill., 1993), 149–184. See also Robert Olwell, *Masters, Slaves, and Subjects: The Culture of Power in the South Carolina Low Country, 1740–1790* (Ithaca, N.Y., 1998), 234–235. The Jeremiah incident has been explored in J. William Harris, *The Hanging of Thomas Jeremiah: A Free Black Man's Encounter with Liberty* (New Haven, Conn., 2009); and William R. Ryan, *The World of Thomas Jeremiah: Charles Town on the Eve of the American Revolution* (New York, 2010).

On June 15, as patriots perused Stuart's letters in Savannah, the Charleston slave court tried a harbor pilot named Thomas Jeremiah and several other blacks on the charge of "plotting an Insurrection." The star witness for the prosecution, a slave named Sambo, testified that Jeremiah had asked him whether he knew "anything of the war that is coming." When Sambo answered no and asked what that would mean for the enslaved, Jeremiah reportedly answered, "Jump on shore, and join the [British] soldiers," for "the war was come to help the poor Negroes." Another slave relayed that Jeremiah had been spreading guns and ammunition to other slaves, that "he believed he had Powder enough already, but that he wanted more arms," and that he was trying to "get as many as he could." As a result of this testimony, Jeremiah was sentenced to hang in August, despite his adamant protestations of innocence.[9]

The Jeremiah case aggravated public opinion about the alleged connections between Britain and its potential proxies. Another victim of poor timing, South Carolina's newly appointed royal governor, Lord William Campbell, reached Charleston in the midst of this turmoil. Reporting for duty on June 17, Campbell sympathized with the doomed Jeremiah, but those feelings were politically risky in the tense Charleston atmosphere, where rumors of instigated insurrections were "universally believed." Reporting back to the earl of Dartmouth, Campbell wrote, "My blood ran cold when I read on what grounds they had doomed a fellow creature to death." The new governor decided to keep his compassion to himself, a move that was simultaneously wise and tragic.[10]

Not only did Carolinians believe that the British were attempting "to in-

9. Wood, "'Taking Care of Business,'" in Crow and Tise, eds., *Southern Experience,* 284.

10. Lord William Campbell sent this report on Aug. 31, 1775. See W. Noel Sainsbury, ed., *Records in the British Public Record Office Relating to South Carolina, 1663–1782* (Columbia, S.C., 1955), XXXV, 191. The phrase "instigated insurrections" was repeated again in the South Carolina Provincial Congress's "humble Address and Declaration" to the new governor on June 20. Echoing the reasons outlined in the association agreement, they told Campbell, "Alarmed and roused by a long succession of arbitrary proceedings by wicked Administrations; impressed with the greatest apprehensions of instigated insurrections, and deeply affected by the commencement of hostilities by the *British* Troops against this Continent, solely for the preservation and defence of our lives, liberties, and properties, we have been impelled to associate and take up arms" (South Carolina Provincial Congress to Lord William Campbell, June 20, 1775, 4 *Am. Archives,* II, 1043).

"Britain Has Found Means to Unite Us"

stigate, and encourage an insurrection of the Slaves," Campbell related, but they were also convinced that "the Ministry had in agitation . . . to bring down the Indians on the inhabitants of this Province." As quickly as they had moved against Black David, Dealey, and Jeremiah, patriot authorities initiated proceedings against Stuart. The committee of safety swore out a warrant to demand that he appear before them, restricted the activities of the superintendent's wife, and confiscated his estate as, in the words of Henry Laurens, "a Guarantee for the quiet and good conduct of the Savages." The circumstances surrounding Stuart, in the judgment of one historian, "were to the Revolution in the lower South what the Boston Tea Party was to the Revolution in New England." Coupled with the rumors of slave plots that washed over the Charleston region that summer, Stuart posed a dire threat to the Deep South if he and Alexander Cameron could, indeed, deliver the Cherokees and Creeks. Discontent about the potential scope of internecine war in South Carolina embroiled the province throughout the spring and summer of 1775.[11]

On July 4, the South Carolina committee of safety sent copies of Stuart's confiscated letters to their colleagues in Newbern, Savannah, and Philadelphia. When Adam Boyd—printer of the Wilmington, North Carolina, *Cape-Fear Mercury*—published the damning letters, he invoked the dual message of the day in his editorial comment: "Thus we see every engine is set to work and every tool of a corrupt ministry employed, to subjugate this once happy land. Forbid it Heaven, and rouse the old Roman virtue, found spontaneous in these regions, to repel the force of wicked tyrants, who would level the world with their own base principles."[12]

Near Boyd's Wilmington print shop, patriots in New Hanover County, North Carolina, signed an association pledging faith to the common cause, stating, "The Increase of Arbitrary Imposition from a Wicked and despotic Ministry and the dread of Instigated Insurrections in the Colonies are causes sufficient to drive an Oppress'd people to the Use of Arms." One of their first acts after signing was to disarm blacks and keep "the Negroes in order within the County of New Hanover." Appointing eight patrols, the residents of Wilmington also attempted to combat the "instigated insurrections" that had helped move them to rebellion against the crown. About seventy miles away, in Pitt County, just north of Newbern, nearly one hundred members

11. Sainsbury, ed., *Records Relating to S.C.*, XXXV, 192. "Revolution in the lower South": Snapp, *John Stuart and the Struggle for Empire*, 162.

12. *Cape-Fear Mercury*, Aug. 7, 1775.

of the committee of safety signed an association swearing they were "determined never to become slaves to any power upon earth." One of their next resolutions was to bolster surveillance and intimidation of people they actually enslaved: "If any Negro slave be found with any fire arms or ammunition," the patrollers were to seize it. Anxious about widespread rumors and the consequences of slaves' seeing British officers as beacons of freedom, localities did their best to stop the desultory effects of gossip. For North Carolinians, like their anxious neighbors in South Carolina, the outbreak of war translated into renewed fears of slave violence.[13]

According to Janet Schaw, a Scottish lady visiting the Wilmington area, rumors of slaves' taking advantage of war were as thick as Carolina's humidity that summer. The inhabitants of Wilmington believed the British were "ordering the tories to murder the whigs, and promising every Negro that would murder his Master and family that he should have his Master's plantation." This particular twist, Schaw thought, was a fabrication concocted by Carolina patriots to scare the populace into supporting their side. "This last artifice they may pay for," she observed, "as the Negroes have got it amongst them and believe it to be true. 'Tis ten to one they may try the experiment, and in that case friends and foes would be all one." Schaw worried that patriot fearmongering might just prove successful.[14]

Her prediction was not far off base. In early July, she again found Wilmington "in an uproar." "I found my short prophesy in regard to the Negroes was already fulfilled, and that an insurrection was hourly expected." Wilming-

13. Leora H. McEachern and Isabel M. Williams, eds., *Wilmington–New Hanover Safety Committee Minutes, 1774–1776* (Wilmington, N.C., 1974), 30–31; Minutes of Pitt County Committee of Safety, July 1, 1775, in William L. Saunders, ed., *The Colonial Records of North Carolina* (Raleigh, N.C., 1890), X, 61, 63.

14. [Janet Schaw], *Journal of a Lady of Quality: Being the Narrative of a Journey from Scotland to the West Indies, North Carolina, and Portugal, in the Years 1774 to 1776*, ed. Evangeline Walker Andrews and Charles McLean Andrews (1921; rpt. New Haven, Conn., 1923), 199. Gage's proclamation did not reference supporting slave rebellions (although the letter he wrote to Barrington that day did). The proclamation did, however, blame the patriot press for all the crown's troubles in Massachusetts: "The press, that distinguished appendage of publick liberty, and, when fairly and impartially employed, its best support, has been invariably prostituted to the most contrary purposes; the animated language of ancient and virtuous times, calculated to vindicate and promote the just rights and interests of mankind, have been applied to countenance the most abandoned violation of those sacred blessings." See 4 *Am. Archives*, II, 969.

ton's expectations stemmed from more than rampant rumors. "There had been a great number of [blacks] discovered in the adjoining woods the night before, most of them with arms, and a fellow belonging to Doctor [Thomas] Cobham was actually killed," Schaw reported. Committee leaders immediately dispatched patrols and searched blacks' houses, and all of Wilmington's free men who had arms carried them.[15]

The Wilmington scare was but one of several major, aborted insurrections in the Carolinas. On July 8, along the Pamlico River, slaves in Beaufort, Pitt, and Craven Counties were massing for rebellion. Word reached Captain Thomas Respess of an "intended insurrection of the negroes against the whole people which was to be put into execution that night" in Beaufort County. The county committee went into action, arresting and jailing forty black suspects. The next morning, the committee "proceeded to examine into the affair and [found] it a deep laid Horrid Tragick Plan laid for destroying the inhabitants of this province without respect of persons, age or sex."[16]

Local leaders, however, could hardly breathe easy. The following day, a new report arrived that 250 blacks were in arms and under pursuit "on the line of Craven and Pitt" Counties, about a dozen miles from Newbern. The situation in Pitt had reached the point that the county committee of safety had authorized the slave patrollers to "shoot one or any number of Negroes

15. [Schaw], *Journal of a Lady of Quality,* ed. Walker and Andrews, 199–200.

16. John Simpson to Richard Cogdell, July 15, 1775, in Saunders, ed., *Col. Records of N.C.,* X, 94–95. It is impossible to know exactly how many were punished for the first outbreak of rebellion in Beaufort County. Some historians have suggested the number is as low as five, but this is a misreading of the evidence. According to the Pitt County Committee chair John Simpson, relating the episode to his colleague in Craven County, five "were whipt" on Sunday, July 9. The following day, however, the committee ordered "several to be severely whipt and sentenced several to receive 80 lashes each to have both Ears cr[oppe]d which was executed in presence of the Committee and a great number of spectators." If five "were whipt" on Sunday, then they were again punished the next day in front of the "great number of spectators." Although we will never know an exact number—Jeffrey J. Crow's approximation of ten seems reasonable—the number of slaves arrested and punished seems to match the scope and extension of both the rebellion in Pitt County and its attention by the white population. See Sylvia R. Frey, *Water from the Rock: Black Resistance in a Revolutionary Age* (Princeton, N.J., 1991), 59; Crow, "Slave Rebelliousness and Social Conflict in North Carolina, 1775 to 1802," *WMQ,* 3d Ser., XXXVII (1980), 86; Wayne E. Lee, *Crowds and Soldiers in Revolutionary North Carolina: The Culture of Violence in Riot and War* (Gainesville, Fla., 2001), 142–144.

who are armed and doth not willingly surrender their arms, and that they have Discretionary Power, to shoot any Number of Negroes above four, who are off their Masters Plantations, and will not submit." On Tuesday, July 11, Pitt militia sent four companies to capture the runaway mob. Finding themselves in the middle of an extensive military operation, the local militia uncovered several plots as they kept "taking up, examining and scourging more or less every day." One of the reports implicated a black, female slave whose plan was to use the opportunity of the roving band of runaways to "kill her master and mistress and Lay it upon those negroes." Most of the arrested slaves, though,

> all confess nearly the same thing, . . . that they were one and all on the night of the 8th inst to fall on and destroy the family where they lived, then to proceed from House to House (Burning as they went) until they arrived in the Back Country where they were to be received with open arms by a number of Persons there appointed and *armed by Government for their Protection,* and as a further reward they were to be settled in a free government of their own.

The last part of this confession was the most distressing for North Carolina patriots. Revealing that the conclusion of their plans involved getting help from the British government, the slave testimonies confirmed what provincial whites had suspected for at least a month: the British administration was aiding and abetting slave insurrections.[17]

Just a few days before all this activity near the Pamlico, Governor Josiah Martin wrote London about the rumors that he was stirring poisonous pots. Explaining his retreat from Newbern to the safety of Fort Johnston, a coastal outpost on the point of Cape Fear, ten miles south of Wilmington, Martin worried he would soon be taken captive. A "most infamous report had lately been propagated among the People, that I had formed a design of Arming the Negroes, and proclaiming freedom to all such as should resort to the King's Standard," he related to his superiors. Martin vehemently denied this "infamous report" and its "insinuations [of] abominable designs with pretended apprehensions of intestine insurrections."[18]

Martin's mid-July retreat to Fort Johnston turned the colony upside down.

17. Minutes of Pitt County Committee of Safety, July 8, 1775, in Saunders, ed., *Col. Records of N.C.,* X, 87, Simpson to Cogdell, July 15, 1775, 94–95 (emphasis added).

18. Governor Martin to the Earl of Dartmouth, June 30, 1775, ibid., 43, "A Proclamation by Governor Martin," June 16, 1775, 17.

In the midst of slave revolts the week before, the Wilmington committee of safety wrote on July 13 to Samuel Johnston, their representative in the Provincial Congress, "Our situation here is truly alarming, the Governor collecting men, provisions, warlike stores of every kind, spiriting up the back counties, and perhaps the Slaves, finally strengthening the fort with new works, in such a manner as may make the Capture of it extremely difficult." The writers accused Captain John Collet, Fort Johnston's commander, of severe infractions; most serious was "his base encouragement of Slaves eloped from their Masters, feeding and employing them, and his atrocious and horrid declaration that he would excite them to an Insurrection." Not only had Martin and his superiors threatened slave insurrection—now Captain Collet was carrying out the plan. Although Martin returned a message to "the People" that "the charge of encouraging Negroes to elope from their Masters and of exciting them to insurrection, Captain Collet most solemnly and absolutely denies," for many anxious North Carolina patriots, it was too late.[19]

Martin received the people's letter at 9:00 the night of July 18 and returned his answer immediately, but to no avail. Within hours, Fort Johnston was ablaze. By threatening to incite the slaves and harboring runaways in the fort, Martin and Collet had crossed a line, and the militia responded with violence. The tensions of a harrowing couple of weeks had taken their toll on Carolina whites. Their revolution in the summer of 1775 had little to do with taxes and rights, or even Thomas Gage and redcoats. It was a war over slavery.[20]

19. "Letter from Safety Committee in Wilmington to Samuel Johnston, Esq.," July 13, 1775, ibid., 91. Samuel Johnston's mail, interestingly, was full of this kind of intelligence. His friend and delegate Joseph Hewes had written him a few days before from Philadelphia that the ministry "has endeavored to let loose the Indians on our Frontiers, to raise the Negroes against us." Hewes had no idea that slaves were plotting along the Pamlico during the very hour he sat down to write. He nevertheless thought this was vital information and was determined to get the news "that they have in contemplation a Scheme to set our Slaves free and arm them against us" to North Carolina, sending the same frightening message to another patriot, Judge James Iredell, that very day. See Hewes to Johnston, Philadelphia, July 8, 1775, *LDC*, I, 612–614, Hewes to James Iredell, Philadelphia, July 8, 1775, 611–612; "Letter from 'the People' to Governor Martin," July 16, 1775, in Saunders, ed., *Col. Records of N.C.*, X, 102–103, Martin's reply, 104.

20. Martin to Dartmouth, July 20, 1775, in Saunders, ed., *Col. Records of N.C.*, X, 108–109, "Depositions about the Burning of Fort Johnson," 130–133; Frey, *Water from the Rock*, 211.

Furthermore, because of the exchange system and the political need for unity, Carolina's problems with Martin, Collet, and a host of rebellious slaves were not solely their own. This news would have an impact far outside the Carolinas. Probably aided by North Carolina's delegation to the Continental Congress, a letter from North Carolina appeared in James Humphreys, Jr.'s *Pennsylvania Ledger* on July 15. "We are much alarmed here with the intentions of Administration," an anonymous Carolinian wrote just before the Pitt-Craven uprising, admitting, "Unless affairs take a turn in our favor very shortly, we shall expect the worst effort of its villainy—that of spiriting up an enemy among ourselves, from whose barbarity, if roused, the most dreadful consequences must follow." Colonists in New York, Connecticut, and Massachusetts also read this letter. In addition, printer Alexander Purdie thought this news had local import for Virginians. When he copied this extract in his *Virginia Gazette,* Purdie italicized "an enemy amongst ourselves" and punctuated the article with the biting comment, *"Lord Dunmore and Governor Martin have certainly compared notes."* Despite these dangers, the thrust of this article was not that British agents were conspiring with slaves all over the mainland; it was that northern readers should not imagine that Carolinians would abandon them. "Our brethren in the Colonies may be assured that we never shall be bribed, by the benefit of an exclusive trade, to desert the common cause," the writer concluded. This letter offered a two-pronged message: the conspiracy from the king's men was real, but North Carolina's dedication to resist was unbowed. Such a representation was essential. Soon it would be a stock part of the patriot script.[21]

When historians tell the story of the beginning of the Revolutionary War, their narratives often feature George Washington on his trip to Cambridge, Massachusetts, to take command of the new Continental army. Of course, Washington's assumption of the motley militia force on July 2 was critical; no one can deny his importance to the development of the Continental army, the Revolutionary War, or the larger American Revolution. But his journey, though celebrated, was not what many colonists were thinking and talking about at that moment. Given what had occurred during the days Washington accepted his appointment, bade farewell to Martha and Mount

21. *Pennsylvania Ledger,* July 15, 1775; *New-York Journal,* July 20, 1775; *Virginia Gazette* (Purdie), July 22, 1775; *Virginia Gazette, or the Norfolk Intelligencer,* July 26, 1775; *Connecticut Journal,* July 26, 1775; *Connecticut Gazette,* July 28, 1775; *Virginia Gazette* (Dixon & Hunter), July 29, 1775. Purdie's italicized comment is in the *Virginia Gazette* (Purdie), July 22, 1775.

"Britain Has Found Means to Unite Us"

Vernon, and began to ride north, the centrality of the role Indians, slaves, and their British sponsors would play in the conflict trumped his own.

By the time Washington reached Cambridge, the continent was electric. It was full of movement, with emissaries fanning out in all directions across the frontier, "enemies" leaving their homes under duress, and slave patrols keeping watch day and night. Washington also shared the road with dozens of express riders laden with letters and newspapers, galloping from station to station carrying news of all these developments. Small wonder this was the moment printer William Bradford began to crowd the inner columns of his *Pennsylvania Journal* with colonial news. *This* was the news! In the summer of 1775, the middle pages of his *Journal* and the three dozen other colonial prints featured an assortment of rumors of British involvement in slave and Indian hostilities. They drew readers' attention to another conspiracy in South Carolina, complete with frightening details that slaves "expected the King would send Troops here, on the Arrival of which they were to set the Town on fire, and fall on the Inhabitants" and that "the Insurrection was to have been general throughout the Province." They exchanged rumors that the "Cagnawaga Tribe have taken their Children from Dartmouth College, from which there is great Reason to fear some Attack upon our back Settlements will shortly be commenced." When a man was found murdered in a field not far from Iroquoia, some anxious inhabitants in the neighborhood leaped to the conclusion that it had been "perpetrated by the Oneida Indians, and that this was only a commencement of Hostilities."[22]

22. "Set the Town on fire": *Providence Gazette,* July 29, 1775; *Newport Mercury,* July 31, 1775; *New-York Gazette,* July 31, 1775; *Massachusetts Spy,* Aug. 9, 1775; *Essex Journal,* Aug. 11, 1775; *New-Hampshire Gazette,* Aug. 22, 1775. Dartmouth: *New-Hampshire Gazette,* July 11, 1775; *Pennsylvania Evening Post,* July 22, 1775; *Essex Journal,* July 22, 1775; *Pennsylvania Packet,* July 24, 1775; *Pennsylvania Journal,* July 26, 1775; *Maryland Gazette,* July 27, 1775; *Rivington's New-York Gazetteer,* July 27, 1775; *Virginia Gazette* (Pinkney), Aug. 3, 1775. "Only a commencement": *New-York Journal,* July 27, 1775; *New-York Gazette,* July 31, 1775; *Connecticut Journal,* Aug. 2, 1775; *Connecticut Gazette,* Aug. 4, 1775; *Norwich Packet,* Aug. 7, 1775; *Massachusetts Spy,* Aug. 16, 1775; *New-Hampshire Gazette,* Aug. 22, 1775. Josiah Johnson was murdered in Butternut, near Cherry Valley, New York (a place that would see terrible devastation in the coming years), on June 10. A few days later John McCormick, a neighbor's servant, was found with the victim's clothes. The snap judgment that it was an Indian attack—and that it was the first of a general war—reveals how nervous the New York backcountry was that June. The colonists were not the only ones who wanted to keep the peace. The Oneidas quickly called Samuel Kirkland to help them write a message to the

The broad distance and pervasive fears suggested by these reports—why did Williamsburg residents need to know about a meeting between Guy Carleton and Indians 1,500 miles back of Quebec?—expose how vital patriot political and communications leaders found these stories early on in the Revolutionary War. The images they forwarded needed to reach as wide an audience and be carried over as many American roads as possible. Yet, while these stories blared out of colonial print shops, leaders of many county committees also tried to limit communication and movement, enacting laws that slaves and loyalists had to obtain passes or locking suspects in jail. Only certain people and stories were to crowd the roads. Patriots framed these actions, too, in dualistic terms, either as moves to protect and defend the common cause or as positive expressions of its universality throughout the mainland. The danger of people acting on the crown's behalf and the need for words to stabilize the common cause (or not) was evident in South Carolina for the remainder of the summer.

After the discovery of Stuart's letter and Jeremiah's arrest, a significant movement of organized loyalism began to build in the backcountry. Its leaders were former South Carolina Regulators like Moses Kirkland, Robert Cunningham, James Robinson, and Thomas Fletchall. Some of these, like Fletchall, were prominent local officeholders and influential men. Because their power base, in the neighborhood of Ninety-Six, was nearer to the Cherokees than to Charleston, the threat posed by backcountry disaffection only added to worries about the influence of John Stuart and Alexander Cameron. If those groups both saw the imperial rebellion as a greater obstacle to their future than each other, that union of interests could be devastating to the patriot cause across the Deep South. The chances of such an alliance were not likely, but given the gale-force winds that patriot leaders had already withstood in the first few weeks of the Revolution, they could take no chances.[23]

Cherry Valley committee of safety expressing their condolences for the crime and to reassure them that they should "quiet [their] minds, and indulge no fears nor jealousies respecting our friendship; don't leave your plantations, continue where you are, and follow your work." Only two of the seven papers that printed news of the murder published the Oneida denial. See *New-York Journal,* Aug. 3, 1775; *Connecticut Journal,* Aug. 9, 1775. See also 4 *Am. Archives,* II, 1766.

23. Rachel N. Klein, *Unification of a Slave State: The Rise of the Planter Class in the South Carolina Backcountry, 1760–1808* (Chapel Hill, N.C., 1990), 84–89; Keith Krawczynski, *William Henry Drayton: South Carolina Revolutionary Patriot* (Baton Rouge, La., 2001),

Henry Laurens, then-president of the South Carolina Council of Safety, wrote an official letter to Fletchall in mid-July pleading for his support at this treacherous moment "when this Colony in particular is alarmed by threats of Invasions by the British Soldiery, of instigated Insurrections by our Negroes, of inroads by the Neighboring Tribes of Indians, and of what is far more to be dreaded the practices and insidious acts of false Brethren." Laurens and his colleagues relaxed a little when they learned that these shared threats of Indian and black unrest were the real stuff of common cause. The "Counter-Association" Robinson and Fletchall both passed around the Carolina frontier maintained that they, too, were "ready and willing at all times to assist in defending the Province, in order to oppose and suppress the incursions of Indians [and] insurrections of negroes." As comforting as that pledge was, it did not solve the crisis. Letters arrived in the capital from the backcountry, warning that not only were loyalist militias growing in strength, but despite Stuart's exile to Saint Augustine, a "good deal of Confusion" remained on the frontier "on account of the expected Danger from the Cherokees."[24]

Patriot leaders in Charleston knew they had to defuse the growing loyalist problem. The Revolution would not succeed against three opponents, whether those forces fought in concert or not. They had to take the offensive with rhetoric. On July 4, the Council of Safety received two emissaries from the Catawba Indians and sent them back the following day armed with a speech that forwarded the patriot argument with the "Great King over the Great Water" but also threatened, "If you do not mind what we say, you will be sorry for it by and by." Three weeks later, the council authorized pa-

153–159; Robert Stansbury Lambert, *South Carolina Loyalists in the American Revolution* (Columbia, S.C., 1987), 33–58; Rebecca Nathan Brannon, "Reconciling the Revolution: Resolving Conflict and Rebuilding Community in the Wake of Civil War in South Carolina, 1775–1860" (Ph.D. diss., University of Michigan, 2007), 17–21.

24. HL to Thomas Fletchall, Charleston, July 14, 1775, *PHL*, X, 214. "Ready and willing": Fletchall to Laurens, July 24, 1775, in Robert Wilson Gibbes, ed., *Documentary History of the American Revolution . . .* (New York, 1855), I, 123–124; Fletchall's resolution enclosed in William Thomson to Laurens, Granby, July 29, 1775, *PHL*, X, 253–256; Robinson's resolution in "Journal of the Council of Safety," South Carolina Historical Society, *Collections*, II (Charleston, S.C., 1858) 22–74, esp. 72. "Good deal of Confusion": James Mayson to William Thomson, Glasgow near Ninety-Six, July 18, 1775, "Papers of the First Council of Safety of the Revolutionary Party in South Carolina, June–November, 1775," *South Carolina Historical Magazine*, I (1900), 44–47; Andrew Williamson to Laurens, Long Canes, July 14, 1775, *PHL*, X, 222–223.

triot leader William Henry Drayton and two ministers, William Tennent and Oliver Hart, to undertake an evangelical mission deep into the backcountry, "explain[ing] to the people the causes of the present disputes between Great Britain and the American colonies."[25]

The missionaries were chosen with care. Dogma—whether religious or political—mattered. Patriots thought Tennent, grandson of the renowned New Light Presbyterian preacher, and Hart, a Baptist clergyman, would encounter sympathetic constituencies in the backcountry, whereas Judge Drayton was a fiery patriot who could best expound on the cause. On August 7, the three missionaries reached Congarees, 130 miles into the interior, where they immediately convened their first assembly. "During our discourses, the falling tears from the audience showed that their hearts were penetrated, and that we might hope for success," they wrote back to Charleston. Drayton was confident that "such a proceeding," which "tended to compose the people," would be effective in binding "their obedience to the measures of the Congress."[26]

Over the next few weeks, the three missionaries continued proselytizing the common cause. They tasted defeat far more often than victory. Drayton, Tennent, and Hart encountered not only debilitating gossip but also genuine disaffection and, worse, something new: enemy polemics. Two days after German settlers at Congarees allegedly wept with sympathy for the cause, Hart noted that a few miles up the Saluda River, another speech was greeted with shouts that, with any luck, "1000 Bostonians might be kill'd in Battle." To make matters worse, Robinson and Fletchall arranged their own

25. "Journal of the Council of Safety," July 4–5, 1775, SCHS, *Colls.*, II, 31–34. A few weeks later, word came back from the Catawba country that they were indeed "hearty" in the patriot interest and that it was hoped "forty or fifty of them will chearfully enter into the Service of the Colony" (Laurens to Kershaw, Charleston, July 25, 1775, *PHL*, X, 247). For more on the Catawbas' engagement in the American Revolution, see James H. Merrell, *The Indians' New World: Catawbas and Their Neighbors from European Contact through the Era of Removal* (Chapel Hill, N.C., 1989), 215–216. Mission to backcountry: South Carolina Council of Safety proceedings, July 23, 1775, 4 *Am. Archives*, II, 1715–1716.

26. Drayton wrote in his memoirs that he kept a pair of pistols on him for this journey, just in case his oratorical skills deserted him in this hostile country. See William Henry Drayton, *Memoirs of the American Revolution as Relating to the State of South Carolina* (1821; rpt. New York, 1969), I, 378n. "Tended to compose": Drayton to Council of Safety, Congarees, Aug. 9, 1775, *PHL*, X, 287.

public assembly the next day, whereby Robinson produced a pamphlet recently published in London that refuted each point the patriot emissaries might have made hours earlier. The publication, Sir John Dalrymple's *Address of the People of Great Britain to the Inhabitants of America*, argued that the designing lawyers and grasping politicians were leading America to economic, military, and political disaster. Dalrymple warned of the logical conclusion for Carolinians if civil war indeed broke out. The "Southern Provinces [are] composed of slaves ready to rebel against their masters, or run away from them on the appearance of an enemy," he stated. Was that what Carolina patriots wanted? Slaves to "become the masters; yourselves fled for protection from them to the woods"?[27]

Where had Robinson procured a copy of Dalrymple's pamphlet? The new governor, William Campbell, anticipating the need to win over hearts and minds in his agitated province, had packed his baggage with several copies of the address. Upon his arrival in mid-June, he sent those copies to loyalist leaders like Fletchall and Kirkland to counter patriot polemics. Unlike his peers, Campbell recognized that texts were strengthening the rebellion. He tried to curb patriot messages as soon as he arrived in Charleston, with promising results. Hart, for one, witnessed those results firsthand. After Robinson finished reading Dalrymple's "well calculated" address, the neighborhood was so overwhelmed with loyalist support that Hart began writing his diary in cipher for his own protection. Campbell's attention to texts

27. J. Glenwood Clayton and Loulie Latimer Owens, eds., "Oliver Hart's Diary of the Journey to the Back-Country," *Journal of the South Carolina Baptist Historical Society*, I (Greenville, S.C., 1975), 18–30, esp. 20; [Sir John Dalrymple], *The Address of the People of Great Britain to the Inhabitants of America* (London, 1775), 5–6. This pamphlet was published at public expense just before Campbell left for South Carolina. Dalrymple did advise British army officers to consider arming slaves at the outset of the war. In his 1775 paper, "A Project for Strengthening General Howe's Operations in the North by a Diversion in the South," Dalrymple suggested Dunmore should supplement his forces with "the bravest and most ingenious of the black slaves whom He may find all over the Bay of Chesapeake. People in England are apt to confound an African born Black in the West Indies with a Virginia or Maryland Black born in those Provinces. The first is the meanest of mankind, the others are full of Intelligence, Fidelity, and Courage as will be found upon Inquiry." Dalyrmple's paper, which was supported by a second, similar plan in 1775 that suggested Lord Cornwallis's diversion should be the Chesapeake, not the Carolinas, are found in George Sackville Germain Papers, IV, CL.

fought the patriots on their own turf, a maneuver they were unfamiliar with. And it was succeeding.[28]

Five days and several miles removed from the scene of Hart's difficulties, Drayton also witnessed Campbell's counterpropaganda campaign. Here the same scene replayed. Drayton called together another "pretty large gathering . . . and I gave a discourse which was generally satisfactory," until Robert Cunningham and another loyalist from Georgia, Thomas Brown, arrived. Brown, who had been tarred and feathered in Augusta the same day that Drayton had set off on his mission, pulled a copy of Dalrymple's address from his pocket and began to read it aloud. Drayton reported that Brown held forth for two hours reading Dalrymple to the multitude, no insignificant feat for a man whose skull had been fractured and his feet burned severely just two weeks earlier. Though Drayton claimed victory and insisted that "Cunningham is beat out of the field," this was not the case. Drayton's comrade confessed to his journal, "The pamphlet sent up by the Governor has done much damage here, it is at present their Gospel. It seems as though nothing could be done here, as they have industriously taught the people that no man from Charleston can speak the truth, and that all the papers are full of lies." Thanks to Campbell, Dalrymple continued to plague the patriot missionaries for the remainder of August. By then, support had disintegrated to the point that Drayton asked the Council of Safety for permission to start arresting prominent loyalist leaders, including Fletchall and Kirkland. The council was shocked to hear that conditions on the frontier had reached this dangerous threshold.[29]

They were dealing with their own security problems in Charleston. Thomas Jeremiah, after two months in the city workhouse awaiting sentencing, was scheduled for execution on August 18. Although he had the authority to pardon Jeremiah and sympathized with his plight, Campbell

28. Clayton and Owens, eds., "Hart's Diary," *Jour. S.C. Baptist Hist. Soc.*, I, 21; Krawczynski, *William Henry Drayton*, 172.

29. William Henry Drayton to Council of Safety, King's Creek near Enoree, Aug. 16, 1775, in Gibbes, ed., *Doc. Hist. of American Revolution*, I, 140–143, esp. 142; William Tennent diary, Aug. 14, 1775, 228; Krawczynski, *William Henry Drayton*, 173. For Brown's ordeal, see Edward J. Cashin, *The King's Ranger: Thomas Brown and the American Revolution on the Southern Frontier* (Athens, Ga., 1989), 27–29; for more of Brown's opinion of the patriot mission, see James H. O'Donnell, "A Loyalist View of the Drayton-Tennent-Hart Mission to the Upcountry," *South Carolina Historical Magazine*, LXVII (1966), 15–28.

"Britain Has Found Means to Unite Us"

decided to keep his compassion to himself. Even slight signals he sent out about staying the execution engendered vociferous criticism. "My attempting to interfere in the matter raised such a clamour amongst the people as is incredible," the governor wrote to London. "They openly and loudly declared if I granted the man a pardon they would hang him at my door." Henry Laurens warned that a pardon "would raise a flame all the water in the Cooper River would not extinguish." "In the Calamitous Situation of this Colony under the threats of Insurrections," he wrote on August 17, "strong proofs of which the people are possessed of, no wonder they are alarmed at the Sound of a Pardon to a Man circumstanced in all respects as [Jeremiah] is." Campbell's sympathies did not overtake these political exigencies. Thomas Jeremiah's life would indeed end during the afternoon of August 18.[30]

While Charleston patriots burned Jeremiah's corpse as a warning to any other potential insurrectionists, and while disaffection continued to plague Drayton's outreach efforts, concerns persisted that John Stuart and his deputy Alexander Cameron would convince the Cherokees to take up the hatchet. On August 21, Drayton interviewed a man who swore Cameron had told a gathering of four hundred Cherokees that "they should join his army against the people of America" and that he would "take care to supply them" with gunpowder and ammunition to complete the task. Drayton sent off a letter to the Cherokees informing them that his journey to the back-country "to explain to the People the Causes of the Quarrel" was a stunning success. He concluded with a bald-faced lie: "All except a few bad men are

30. William Campbell to Lord Dartmouth, Charleston, Aug. 19, 1775, in Sainsbury, ed., *Records Relating to S.C.*, XXXV, 184–190. The Jeremiah execution controversy is also detailed in Wood, "'Liberty Is Sweet,'" in Young, ed., *Beyond the American Revolution*, 166–167; Olwell, *Masters, Slaves, and Subjects*, 234–238; Harris, *Hanging of Jeremiah*, 136–150. For Laurens's comments, see his letter to William Campbell, Charleston, Aug. 17, 1775, *PHL*, X, 330. A few days later, Laurens wrote his son, "Uncommon pains taken to Save [Jeremiah's] Life had filled the minds of many people with great Jealousies against certain Crown Officers acting under direction" (HL to John Laurens, Charleston, Aug. 20, 1775, *PHL*, X, 321). In the backcountry at nearly that same moment, Fletchall made reference to Charleston's slave troubles as the real reason why patriots needed the support of the frontier. He explained that the "people below" simply wanted the backcountry militia "to go down and assist them against the Negroes." Only a "Fool . . . would go," Fletchall reasoned, boasting, "They will not get a man from here." See Clayton and Owens, eds., "Hart's Diary," *Jour. S.C. Baptist Hist. Soc.*, I, 22; Klein, *Unification of a Slave State*, 89.

satisfied with what I say." They must not listen to Cameron, who "has two tongues," or to false rumors that "we are getting our Warriors together . . . to make war upon you"; instead, he proclaimed, they should come down in twelve days to hear his side of the story.[31]

Six leaders of the Cherokees responded to Drayton's invitation. He explained further the imperial crisis and begged them again to disregard Cameron. Like several of his patriot colleagues in the Revolution's first months, Drayton extended the common cause to include the Cherokees: "If they use us, their own flesh and blood, in this unjust way, what must you expect; you who are red people . . . you who have fine lands? You see, by their treatment to us, that agreements, even under hand and seal, go as nothing with them. Think of these things, my friends, and reflect upon them day and night." The Cherokee leaders explained that they relied on Cameron and Stuart to supply them with gunpowder; if South Carolina patriots could provide that valuable commodity, they would adjust their loyalty accordingly. The Cherokee request for powder underscored the fragility of the peace Drayton had worked so arduously to secure over the past two months. Although he and other patriots applauded the mission as a success, that gunpowder could literally blow up the entire situation. If the council agreed to send the Indians ammunition, they would encounter a whipsaw problem whereby keeping Cherokees in arms would aggravate frontier fears, particularly among those who believed Dalrymple's warnings. As the autumn pro-

31. Cameron had recently sent a letter to Stuart lamenting the "aspersions which some malicious people have circulated" about both of them. He was sorry that some of his correspondence appeared in that infamous "white Calf Skin book where Copies of most of your letters were kep[t]," which led to the controversy and Stuart's exile. All was apparently not well with the Cherokees, either. Cameron wrote from Kiowa in late July that the "common report here says that I am to be killed here or taken prisoner out of the Nation and tormented with lighted torches," but as long as he kept friends with the key chiefs, "all of the threats of my neighbors give me very little uneasiness." See Alexander Cameron to John Stuart, Kiowa, July 21, 1775, enclosed in John Stuart to Lord Dartmouth, Jan. 8, 1776, in K. G. Davies, ed., *Documents of the American Revolution, 1770–1783*, Colonial Office Series, XI, *Transcripts, 1775 July–December* (Dublin, 1976), 176–178; "Affidavit of Jonathan Clark concerning Cameron and the Cherokee Indians," South Carolina–Ninety-Six District, Aug. 21, 1775, in Gibbes, ed., *Doc. Hist. of American Revolution*, I, 147–148, esp. 148, Drayton to Council of Safety, Aug. 21, 1775, 149–154; Drayton to Cherokees, Aug. 21, 1775, CO 5/77, 143–145, Kew, U.K.

"Britain Has Found Means to Unite Us"

gressed, Carolina patriots realized it was near impossible to keep all parties happy.[32]

These complicated issues—whether to support the Council of Safety or stay loyal to Governor Campbell and the British administration, whether to view the execution of Thomas Jeremiah as an act of justice or an act of murder, whether to listen to the Catawbas and their patriot friends or listen to Cameron and assist the king—were matters of import for inhabitants across the Deep South late that first summer of revolution. These kinds of struggles, of communities weighing sides, of emissaries making pitches, of "justice" being put under pressure, were not unique to the Carolinas. These issues occurred in backcountry New York, in western Pennsylvania, and in the Chesapeake. Each locality had its own political struggles that summer, with the war overlaying long-standing rivalries and factions jockeying for power.

What mattered was how Carolina patriots represented their efforts to shore up the cause. Charleston was a thousand miles from the Continental army camp in Cambridge, but the solidity of the cause in the Deep South was essential for patriot fortunes nonetheless. Political leaders and printers in the Carolinas and outside made sure many colonists knew what they were doing. Or knew at least some version of the truth.

In narrating for his superiors the "heartrending story" of Jeremiah's murder—"I can call it nothing else"—Campbell touched the key point when he concluded, "Such [is] the foundation on which they have the matchless assurance to publish to the world that His Majesty's ministers have instigated insurrections amongst their slaves and directed the Indians to fall upon the inhabitants . . . and by these arts the Committee and Council of Safety have got the government into their hands, which they exercise in the most arbitrary, cruel and wanton manner." Those "arts" were indeed the secret to success or failure. Whoever could gain an advantage in that publishing campaign would determine what was justice and what was murder or whether it was British or patriot leaders who were truly the authors of "dark Hellish plots." Campbell himself tried his hand at those "arts" by carrying with him

32. "A Talk from the Honourable William Henry Drayton, Esq., One of the Beloved Men of South Carolina, to the Beloved Men, Headmen, and Warriours of the Cherokee Nation, at the Congarees," Sept. 25, 1775, 4 *Am. Archives,* III, 790–794, esp. 791; James H. O'Donnell, *Southern Indians in the American Revolution* (Knoxville, Tenn., 1973), 25; Tom Hatley, *The Dividing Paths: Cherokees and South Carolinians through the Era of Revolution* (New York, 1995), 186–188.

copies of John Dalrymple's "Address" and then distributing them to loyalist leaders. The Drayton-Tennent-Hart mission "to explain" the imperial crisis was itself one of the most extensive, arduous expressions of those "arts." How Carolina patriots publicized to outsiders what had been going on in their busy colony was just as critical.[33]

In August, news underscoring the connection between slave uprisings and Carolina's support for the Revolution began to circulate throughout the northern colonies. A letter from Charleston, written a couple of days after Jeremiah's death, was published in a Philadelphia paper. This bland but still revealing letter began, "Every thing here is suspended but war-like preparations. . . . We are putting the town in a posture of defense, and are all determined to oppose whatever troops may come here. Yesterday a Negro was hanged and burnt, for intended sedition, and burning the town, etc." A few days later, another letter, dated September 12, began making its run through the papers. "We are not altogether without our fears from the Indian enemy," this correspondent wrote to the *Pennsylvania Packet,* "but our Negroes are quite quiet since the execution of one of the most sensible and daring of them, [Jeremiah], a free Negro, who was found guilty of having endeavored to cause an insurrection." The pedestrian style that largely governed eighteenth-century newspapers still informed readers of twelve colonial papers that Charleston supported the common cause with force.[34]

The matter-of-factness of the reports from Carolina is instructive. These brief notices connected Charleston with the rest of the American cities; that the South's major city had its business in order—in the backcountry and with their "domestics"—was vital information for northerners who did not prefer to face British arms alone. In the midst of a yet-uncertain war against the metropolis, security issues in Charleston were suddenly imperative to colonists throughout North America. Eventually, a significant amount of in-

33. Davies, ed., *Docs. of the Am. Rev.,* XI, 97.

34. *Pennsylvania Evening Post,* Aug. 31, 1775; *Pennsylvania Mercury,* Sept. 1, 1775; *Constitutional Gazette,* Sept. 2, 1775; *Pennsylvania Ledger,* Sept. 2, 1775; *Pennsylvania Packet,* Sept. 4, 1775; *Rivington's New-York Gazetteer,* Sept. 7, 1775; *Connecticut Courant,* Sept. 11, 1775; *Newport Mercury,* Sept. 11, 1775; *Connecticut Journal,* Sept. 13, 1775; *Virginia Gazette* (Purdie), Sept. 15, 1775; *New-Hampshire Gazette,* Sept. 19, 1775; *Essex Journal,* Sept. 22, 1775. This letter was dated Charleston, Sept. 12, 1775. See *Pennsylvania Packet,* Oct. 16, 1775; *New-York Journal,* Oct. 19, 1775; *New-York Gazette,* Oct. 23, 1775; *Connecticut Journal,* Oct. 25, 1775; *Maryland Gazette,* Oct. 26, 1775; *Massachusetts Spy,* Oct. 27, 1775; *Providence Gazette,* Oct. 28, 1775.

formation would flow through the print exchange networks about Charleston's battles with insurrectionary slaves, dangerous loyalists, threatening Indians, and treacherous British agents.

"We are informed from undoubted authority," John Anderson reported in early October in one of the first issues of his new paper, the New York *Constitutional Gazette*, "that Lord William Campbell, governor of South Carolina has fled with the utmost precipitation, on board the man of war in the harbour. The committee of Charlestown having very fortunately discovered that his Excellency had employed one Cameron . . . to engage the Indians in the ministerial service." To make matters worse, the article continued, this time the campaign was a success: the deputy superintendent "had actually inlisted 600 of them, and furnished them with every necessary in order to butcher the back inhabitants." That the patriots in Charleston had "very fortunately" uncovered this intelligence was no understatement. Anderson's article forwarded exactly how lucky they were. "This plan was discovered by a gentleman who seized the express on his way from said Cameron to the Governor. . . . The above gentleman disguised himself in a Drover's habit, and attended the express to the Governor's house, and heard the conversation between them, and then discovered the whole plot to the committee." Reprinted throughout the northern colonies, this hair-raising account provided two clear lessons to sympathetic readers: the British were still up to their by-now well-known tricks across the American frontier, and providence continued to smile down upon the Revolutionaries as they dodged yet another backcountry threat.[35]

Another report that provided extensive details about Charleston's progress in preparing the city for war appeared in Anderson's paper a few weeks later. This notice concluded with a summary that, in a few words, recounted all the turmoil of late summer: "The Regulators in the back country, who were under oath, have entered into a treaty to remain neuter [*sic*]; . . . The people are under no apprehensions from their Negroes. The Hon. William Henry Drayton, the worthy Judge of the Superior Court, has made

35. *Constitutional Gazette*, Oct. 7, 1775; *New-York Gazette*, Oct. 9, 1775; *Pennsylvania Evening Post*, Oct. 10, 1775; *Pennsylvania Gazette*, Oct. 11, 1775; *Pennsylvania Journal*, Oct. 11, 1775; *Connecticut Journal*, Oct. 11, 1775; *New-York Journal*, Oct. 12, 1775; *Pennsylvania Mercury*, Oct. 13, 1775; *Connecticut Gazette*, Oct. 13, 1775; *Newport Mercury*, Oct. 16, 1775; *Pennsylvania Packet*, Oct. 16, 1775; *Boston Gazette*, Oct. 16, 1775; *Maryland Gazette*, Oct. 19, 1775; *New-England Chronicle*, Oct. 12–19, 1775; *Massachusetts Spy*, Oct. 20, 1775; *Virginia Gazette* (Dixon & Hunter), Oct. 28, 1775.

a treaty with the Cherokees to assist the inhabitants in case of necessity." Since the last report would appear in a dozen papers, too, this was how many of Laurens and Drayton's fellow patriots gleaned a sanitized version of the turbulence that had threatened to overwhelm the Deep South over the past few months. No one mentioned the patriots' troubles with Dalrymple or Oliver Hart's having to encrypt his journal.[36]

That filter was hardly accidental. To be sure, these stories conflicted in both time and information. From week to week, readers in Connecticut or Pennsylvania might not know whether the Cherokees were hostile or satisfied, whether Cameron was effective or neutralized. For the most part, Carolina patriots projected only confidence and mastery: there was no need to worry about their ability to fight the British—even though there was quite a cause for concern. Whenever the situation seemed out of patriot control, though, it was not their fault; there was a fiend—Stuart or Campbell or Cameron—pulling the strings. The almost monotonous way South Carolina patriots represented to the rest of America all that had gone on in Charleston and the backcountry during the late summer and early fall was no trifling affair. No matter how unstable the political situation truly was on the ground in the Deep South, colonists far removed from the Carolina frontier knew very little about it. When crown officials recognized the need to win hearts and minds and engaged in propaganda activities, the situation changed significantly. Because Campbell had preemptively armed backcountry loyalist leaders with a London pamphlet that countered patriot narratives, it was more difficult to garner real support—concrete decisions like attaching their names to the association or volunteering to take up arms—for the common cause in those contested areas. Thanks to Campbell's recognition of the necessity to play the polemics game, Dalrymple stymied Drayton, at least for a time, in the backcountry. But because patriots had done an effective job of taking control of the communication networks throughout the continent—either by establishing their own avenues or by default, as the larger British administration did not see the need to fight for them—the effectiveness of Campbell's efforts remained localized.

36. *Constitutional Gazette*, Nov. 8, 1775; *Maryland Journal*, Nov. 8, 1775; *New-York Journal*, Nov. 9, 1775; *Rivington's New-York Gazetteer*, Nov. 9, 1775; *Pennsylvania Evening Post*, Nov. 9, 1775; *Connecticut Courant*, Nov. 13, 1775; *Connecticut Gazette*, Nov. 17, 1775; *Massachusetts Spy*, Nov. 17, 1775; *Boston Gazette*, Nov. 20, 1775; *Newport Mercury*, Nov. 20, 1775; *Connecticut Journal*, Nov. 22, 1775; *Essex Journal*, Nov. 24, 1775; *Boston News-Letter*, Dec. 14, 1775.

No one understood the need to propagate unity and martial resistance better than the Continental Congress. On July 5, while Drayton and Laurens battled British officials, loyalists, Indians, and slaves, John Adams and Benjamin Franklin each commented on that day's work in the Continental Congress. Adams wrote a friend, "This day has been spent in debating a manifesto setting forth the causes of our taking arms. There is some spunk in it. It is ordered to be printed, but will not be done soon enough to be enclosed in this letter." Franklin must have absorbed some of that attitude when he sat down that day to write one of his most famous letters. "Look upon your Hands!" he penned in a cathartic but unsent epistle. "They are stained with the Blood of your Relations! You and I were long friends: You are now my Enemy and I am, Yours, B Franklin." Franklin's irritation was stoked, as Adams said, by that day's debate over a document that would become the "Declaration of the Causes and Necessity for Taking up Arms."[37]

Thomas Jefferson had arrived in Philadelphia only five days before Congress added him and John Dickinson to a subcommittee to write "a declaration, to be published by General Washington, upon his arrival at the camp before Boston." The "Declaration of the Causes and Necessity of Taking up Arms" began in typical Enlightenment fashion. It invoked "a Reverence for our great Creator, Principles of Humanity, and the Dictates of Common Sense" that together justified colonists' use of force to resist Parliament's attempts "to effect their cruel and impolitic Purpose of enslaving these Colonies by violence." The bulk of the address, like Jefferson's more famous declaration the following year, focused on fresh grievances. And, like the Declaration of Independence, this first official justification of the conflict reached its climax with war crimes. Dickinson, who wrote much of the final copy after an earlier draft by Jefferson, protested the treatment of women and children in Boston, the way in which British regulars "have butchered our Countrymen," and the torching of Charleston, Massachusetts. Greater transgressions, though, were occurring far away from the New

---

37. JA to Joseph Palmer, Philadelphia, July 5, 1775, *LDC*, I, 584; BF to William Strahan, Philadelphia, July 5, 1775, *PBF*, XXII, 85. Although Franklin never sent this famous letter, it did eventually surface in American newspapers in 1778. See *Pennsylvania Packet*, Sept. 29, 1778; *Massachusetts Spy*, Oct. 15, 1778; *Boston Evening Post* (White & Adams), Oct. 17, 1778.

England coast. The final paragraphs of this declaration echoed many of the swirling newspaper reports early that first wartime summer: "We have received certain intelligence that General Carleton, the Governor of Canada, is instigating the People of that Province and the Indians to fall upon us; and we have but too much reason to apprehend, that Schemes have been formed to excite domestic Enemies against us." Although Dickinson chose the formulation "to excite domestic enemies" instead of "instigated insurrections," as his friends in Carolina did, it undoubtedly meant rebellious slaves. Attempting to employ Indians and blacks to help quell the rebellion: this was the crown's most serious crime. From the very first days of the fighting, patriot leaders coupled blacks and Indians with their British enemy; they were already in the process of crafting this into an official theme in the summer of 1775.[38]

Conversely, true patriots would not stand for this type of behavior. "Our cause is just. Our union is perfect," the declaration stated. "We will, in defiance of every Hazard, with unabating Firmness and Perseverance, employ for the preservation of our Liberties; being with one Mind resolved to die Freemen rather than to live Slaves." This construction of heroic, masculine, liberty-loving patriots locked in mortal combat with those who wanted to strip them of their freedom by any means necessary was difficult to miss. In another punctuative statement, Congress exposed the problem at the heart of the common cause, stating that colonists faced either "unconditional submission to tyranny of irritated ministers or resistance by force. The latter is our choice." Convincing enough people that the choice of fighting in a unified effort was the only one—this was the crux of the cause.[39]

When an embodiment of that choice appeared in front of the Pennsylvania State House that very afternoon, it was too great an opportunity to let pass. John Adams told his patriot allies back in Boston all about it. "We have Spent this whole Day in debating Paragraph by Paragraph, a Manifesto [with] Some Mercury in it," Adams wrote to William Tudor. At some point during the proceedings, he related in a second letter to James Warren, "a curious Phenomenon appeared at the Door of our Congress." It was "a German Hussar, a veteran in the Wars of Germany, in his Uniform, and on Horseback, a forlorn Cap upon his Head, with a Streamer waiving from

38. *JCC*, II, 105–108. For the full details of the "Declaration of the Causes and Necessity of Taking up Arms," see *PTJ*, I, 187–219, esp. 213, 217.

39. *PTJ*, I, 217. The ending sections of the declaration were Jefferson's; Dickinson did not amend the final four paragraphs from Jefferson's draft.

"Britain Has Found Means to Unite Us"

it half down to his Waistband, with a Deaths Head painted in Front . . . [i]n short the most warlike and formidable Figure, I ever saw." This impressive exhibition was exactly the kind of response the delegates were hoping their mercurial manifesto would produce, and the public needed to know about it. Adams recognized the potential of such a display and how the German soldier's spontaneous presentation might benefit the common cause. Adams concluded his letters with a suggestion that Warren and Tudor turn them over to patriot printers because it "would Set before our New England People, a fine Example for their Imitation: But what is of more Moment, it would engage the Affections of the Germans, of whom there are many in N[ew] York, Pennsylvania, Maryland, and other Colonies, more intensely in the Cause of America." Either Tudor, Warren, or both followed Adams's advice, for his words did indeed appear in Edes and Gill's *Boston Gazette* and four other subsequent papers under the heading from a "gentleman in Philadelphia to his Friend in this Town." Adams pulled back the curtain to reveal not only the strong connections between patriot political leaders and printers but also how they understood the centrality of public opinion and the necessity that all ethnic groups—especially the key demographic of Pennsylvania Germans—purchase the common cause.[40]

40. JA to William Tudor, Philadelphia, July 6, 1775, *LDC*, I, 586–588, JA to James Warren, Philadelphia, July 6, 1775, 590–591; *Boston Gazette*, July 24, 1775; *Essex Journal*, July 28, 1775; *Newport Mercury*, July 31, 1775; *Massachusetts Spy*, Aug. 2, 1775; *Connecticut Journal*, Aug. 2, 1775. The excerpt was nearly verbatim from what appears in the block quote above. What Edes, Gill, Tudor, Warren, and Adams did not want the public to know, of course, did not appear. That was the section of Adams's letter to Warren where he confessed that the union was not quite "perfect." "They have a Secret Fear," he wrote of the middle and southern provinces, "a Jealousy, that New England will soon be full of Veteran Soldiers, and at length conceive Designs unfavourable to the other Colonies. This may be justly thought whimsical. But others Say, that by engaging their own Gentlemen and Peasants and Germans [etc.] they shall rivet their People to the public Cause" (JA to Warren, July 6, 1775, *LDC*, I, 591).

With Adams's help, this story would be the second instance of patriot newspapers highlighting the passion Pennsylvania Germans exhibited for the cause in recent weeks. Back in June, Benjamin Towne and several others had run a singular story about how a group of aged former soldiers in the backcountry town of Reading had organized an "Old Man's Company." Its commander was "ninety-seven years of age, has been forty years in the regular service, and in seventeen pitched battles; and the drummer is eighty-four." "In lieu of cockade," the notice continued, "they wear in

Adams's twin epistles were an excellent example of how the patriots could manage the message and, hopefully, "engage the affections" of as many colonists as possible. They were a behind-the-scenes management that complemented the "Declaration of the Causes and Necessity." Benjamin Franklin's affections, however, needed no such lesson. His response to Dickinson's address illustrates how the news from the frontiers and slave quarters had smothered the last embers of his once-burning affection for Britain. The next day, Franklin wrote Jonathan Shipley, an Anglican bishop friendly to America. He angrily detailed all the conspiracies he had heard about over the last few weeks. Some people in Britain had "recommend[ed]" schemes to use the slaves and Indians against the colonists, and now these plans were coming to fruition. "Lord Dunmore and Governor Martin have already, we are told, taken some steps towards carrying one part of the Project into Execution, by exciting an Insurrection among the Blacks. And Governor Carleton, we have certain Accounts, has been very industrious in engaging the Indians to begin their horrid Work." Franklin fumed in disbelief, "This is making War like Nations who never had been Friends, and never wish to be such while the World stands." Franklin's letter—which he actually mailed—fleshed out the signal grievances in the previous day's declaration and shed light on what the Congress meant by "domestic enemies." It also reveals how central those stories were to the patriots' framing of the common cause. These accounts, loaded with dread of potential massacres, were the wedge by which Adams, Franklin, Jefferson, and even Dickinson divided the two sides of this conflict.[41]

The newspapers provided corroborating evidence to back up the patriot claim. If colonial readers needed proof that British agents were indeed encouraging Indians to attack the backcountry, all they needed to do was turn the page. During the same weeks in July that the "Declaration of the Causes

---

their hats a black crape, as expressive of their sorrow for the mournful events which have occasioned them, at their late time of life, to take arms against our brethren, in order to preserve that liberty which they left their native country to enjoy." Like Adams's parading German hussar, this story had symbolic value. It promoted the right kind of patriotism, and it came from a crucial demographic, Pennsylvania Germans, whose political and military support patriots needed. See *Pennsylvania Evening Post*, June 1, 1775; *Newport Mercury*, June 26, 1775; *Massachusetts Spy*, June 28, 1775; *Essex Gazette*, June 30, 1775; *Connecticut Courant*, July 3, 1775.

41. BF to Jonathan Shipley, Philadelphia, July 7, 1775, *LDC*, I, 604–608, esp. 607.

"Britain Has Found Means to Unite Us"

and Necessity" ran through the prints, the other stories that those issues often shared featured news of John Stuart, Josiah Martin, and Indian agents in the north Guy Johnson and Guy Carleton. John Stuart's confiscated letters arrived at the Pennsylvania State House a few days after the Congress sent the "Declaration of the Causes and Necessity" to the city's printers. They whisked this packet from Charleston to the corner of Front and Market Streets, into the waiting arms of Bradford and his *Pennsylvania Journal*. Bradford published the incriminating evidence, whereby Stuart instructed Cameron to "use your influence to dispose those people to act in defense of his Majesty," on July 12, the same issue that featured Congress's declaration across its front page. The middle pages were the proof, the affidavits that clinched the case made on the front. For the remainder of July, newspapers throughout New England and the mid-Atlantic exchanged the Stuart letters from the *Pennsylvania Journal*. A few papers in Connecticut and New York even split the report into two sections and ran them on consecutive weeks in order to flesh out details from the Deep South.[42]

42. Nearly every colonial paper published the "Declaration of the Causes and Necessity." The publication run was as follows: *Pennsylvania Packet*, July 10, 1775; *Pennsylvania Evening Post*, July 11, 1775; *Dunlap's Maryland Gazette*, July 11, 1775; *Pennsylvania Journal*, July 12, 1775; *Pennsylvania Gazette*, July 12, 1775; *Connecticut Journal*, July 12, 1775; *Maryland Journal*, July 12, 1775; *Rivington's New-York Gazetteer*, July 13, 1775; *Pennsylvania Mercury*, July 14, 1775; *Pennsylvania Ledger*, July 15, 1775; *New-York Gazette*, July 17, 1775; *Connecticut Courant*, July 17, 1775; *Virginia Gazette, or the Norfolk Intelligencer*, July 19, 1775; *Maryland Gazette*, July 20, 1775; *Virginia Gazette* (Pinkney), July 20, 1775; *Connecticut Gazette*, July 21, 1775; *Virginia Gazette* (Purdie), July 21, 1775; *Massachusetts Spy*, July 22, 1775; *South-Carolina Gazette; And Country Journal*, July 22, 1775; *Virginia Gazette* (Dixon & Hunter), July 22, 1775; *Boston Gazette*, July 24, 1775; *Norwich Packet*, July 24, 1775; *New-England Chronicle*, July 21–27, 1775; *Essex Journal*, July 28, 1775; *South-Carolina and American General Gazette*, July 28, 1775; *Providence Gazette*, July 29, 1775; *Georgia Gazette*, Aug. 2, 1775; *South-Carolina Gazette*, Sept. 19, 1775. Two papers, Solomon Southwick's *Newport Mercury* and John Holt's *New-York Journal*, are conspicuously absent. It seems more likely that these two staunch patriots printed the address in handbills or broadsides that have not survived rather than ignored it altogether. Or they might have done as Daniel Fowle did. Fowle advertised in the Aug. 1, 1775, issue of his *New-Hampshire Gazette* that he was selling the declaration in pamphlet form at his printing office. Stuart letters: *Pennsylvania Journal*, July 12, 1775; *Pennsylvania Packet*, July 17, 1775; *New-York Gazette*, July 17, 24, 1775; *Connecticut Journal*, July 19, 26, 1775; *New-York Journal*, July 20, 1775; *Connecticut Gazette*, July 21, 28, 1775; *Providence Gazette*, July 22, 1775; *Virginia Gazette* (Dixon

Stuart's letters were significant, but they hardly comprised the vast amount of incriminating evidence that occupied colonial newspapers during the same days that the declaration was received by the new regiments at Cambridge "with great Applause . . . [and] three Huzzas." Readers wanting relief from those summer days should not have turned to the papers to find it. The other news that competed for space in July and early August proved Congress's point repeatedly. The letter claiming North Carolina governor Josiah Martin and Captain John Collet were trying to "spirit up an enemy within ourselves" circulated through the networks at this time. Soon enough, a suspicious letter written by Martin and published by the Newbern committee of safety on August 2 appeared in northern papers. When Martin addressed the "false, malicious, and scandalous report" that he was inciting slave revolts, his half-denial gave patriots the opening they needed to destroy another royal official. "Nothing could ever justify the design, falsely imputed to me, of giving encouragement to the Negroes," he wrote in a private June 24 letter, "*but* the actual and declared rebellion of the King's subjects, and the failure of all other means to maintain the King's government." Since this was the case in Cape Fear, the Newbern committee contended Martin's letter was, "in plain English . . . a justification of the design of encouraging the slaves to revolt . . . and the publick avowal of a crime so horrid and truly black a complexion could only originate in a soul lost to every sense of the feelings of humanity and long hackneyed in the detestable and wicked purpose of subjugating these Colonies to the most abject slavery." Martin's letter was another smoking gun for the patriots. Twenty printers published this letter in conjunction with news of Captain Collet hiding runaway slaves in Fort Johnston and the burning of that outpost. Like Stuart's confiscated packet of dispatches, the letter and the committee's commentary were so important that several printers spread them over two issues to publish them in full.[43]

& Hunter), July 22, 1775; *Connecticut Courant,* July 24, 1775; *Newport Mercury,* July 24, 1775; *Norwich Packet,* July 24, 31, 1775; *Massachusetts Spy,* Aug. 2, 1775; *Cape-Fear Mercury,* Aug. 7, 1775. The *New-York Gazette, Connecticut Gazette, Connecticut Journal,* and *Norwich Packet* also published the declaration and Stuart's letters in the same issues. The *Essex Journal* and *New-England Chronicle* published it at the same time as Adams's letter on the German soldier at Congress.

43. *New-England Chronicle,* July 13–21, 1775; *Connecticut Courant,* July 24, 1775. General Nathanael Greene corroborated this celebration. On July 17, he wrote fellow Rhode Islander Nicholas Cooke, "Yesterday, a manifesto from the Continental

"Britain Has Found Means to Unite Us"

Rumors from London also surfaced that clinched, yet again, Dickinson's argument that creating "domestic enemies" was part of the plot to enslave America. Ten papers picked up on the "early hint," sent to *Cape-Fear Mercury* printer Adam Boyd from a correspondent in London, that it would be wise to "sell your slave estate" as fast as possible. Also that month, thirteen printers published a London story that "the ministerial tools are regretting, that 20,000 Swiss were not sent over to cut the throats of our fellow subjects

---

Congress was published at Cambridge, setting forth the accumulated grievances of all the Continent in general, the Massachusetts Bay in particular, and pronouncing this to be a just and necessary war. It was read with great solemnity, and followed by three cheers that made the heavens and earth ring with the approbation of the camp" (Nathanael Greene to Nicholas Cooke, Jamaica Plains, July 17, 1775, *PNG*, I, 101). One brief notice that ran through several papers starting in mid-July punctuates the collective threats facing the lower South. The following letter (written on June 29 and quoted in full) kept northern readers abreast of what was happening in Charleston:

> Our place has rather the appearance of a garrison town than a mart for trade; one company keeps guard all day, and two every night, in our situation we cannot be too watchful and may require much strength; for our Negroes have all high notions of their liberty, and we lately learnt by intercepted letters and other ways, that there has been endeavours to set the Indians on us. Mr. Stewart [Stuart], the superintendent of Indian affairs, is accused of being the person, who has forwarded this wicked design, and he is fled for safety.

See *Pennsylvania Packet*, July 17, 1775; *Pennsylvania Evening Post*, July 18, 1775; *New-York Gazette*, July 24, 1775; *Connecticut Journal*, July 26, 1775; *Connecticut Gazette*, July 28, 1775; *Norwich Packet*, July 31, 1775. For the committee of safety's comments, see "Proceedings of the Safety Committee at Newbern," Aug. 2, 1775, in Saunders, ed., *Col. Records of N.C.*, X, 138, 138a. Those comments then appeared in *North-Carolina Gazette*, Aug. 6, 1775; *South-Carolina and American General Gazette*, Aug. 11, 1775; *Maryland Journal*, Aug. 13, Sept. 8, 1775; *Virginia Gazette, or the Norfolk Intelligencer*, Aug. 16, 1775; *Pennsylvania Mercury*, Aug. 18, 25, 1775; *Constitutional Gazette*, Aug. 19, Sept. 2, 1775; *Pennsylvania Ledger*, Aug. 19, Sept. 2, 1775; *Pennsylvania Packet*, Aug. 21, 1775; *New-York Gazette*, Aug. 21, 1775; *Connecticut Journal*, Aug. 23, 1775; *Maryland Gazette*, Aug. 24, 1775; *Rivington's New-York Gazetteer*, Aug. 24, 1775; *Newport Mercury*, Aug. 28, 1775; *Norwich Packet*, Aug. 28, 1775; *Massachusetts Spy*, Aug. 30, 1775; *New-England Chronicle*, Aug. 31, Sept. 21–28, 1775; *Essex Gazette*, Sept. 5, Oct. 6, 1775; *New-Hampshire Gazette*, Sept. 5, Oct. 10, 1775; *Connecticut Gazette*, Sept. 8, 1775; *Providence Gazette*, Sept. 9, 1775. The August 6 issue of *North-Carolina Gazette* is no longer extant, but it is inferred since the print run of this story was headed by "Newbern, August 6."

in America, in conjunction with the Negroes, who were to be emancipated to slaughter their masters." "This scheme is imputed to Sir William Draper," the story noted, exposing to the public the name of another government advisor who, like Dalrymple, had proposed arming slaves. "That gallant officer ought to disclaim an imputation, which would only become a butcher not an English soldier."[44]

Patriot political leaders and publicists labored to forward an emerging narrative that the king's representatives, from Carolina to Canada, were attempting to use all means to slaughter their countrymen. Of course, these were far from the only complaints patriots lodged against the British government that summer. But these accusations were not abstract ones about representation or consent. They welled up from the darkest parts of the colonial imagination. Insurrectionist slaves and hostile Indians destroying houses and families were the most terrifying of colonists' fears. These nightmares seemed more likely to come true than ever in 1775 because African Americans and Indians all over North America were the spark that ignited these stories. Without the myriad attempts of slaves and Indians to improve their situation, none of these accusations would have held water. Thomas Jeremiah, hundreds of slaves along the Pamlico River, and leaders of the Caughnawaga and Cherokee Indians were each trying to discern the best ways of taking advantage of the conflict. Unintentionally, they presented patriots with a promising opportunity. If the British could be tied to those deep-seated fears, the problem of turning the colonists' cultural, political, and social models into bitter enemies might be resolved.

Connecting British agents to "schemes [that] have been formed to excite

44. *Cape-Fear Mercury*, June 16, 1775; *North-Carolina Gazette*, July 7, 1775; *South-Carolina Gazette; And Country Journal*, July 11, 1775; *New-York Journal*, July 27, 1775; *New-York Gazette*, July 31, 1775; *Connecticut Journal*, Aug. 2, 1775; *Massachusetts Spy*, Aug. 2, 1775; *Newport Mercury*, Aug. 7, 1775; *Providence Gazette*, Aug. 12, 1775; *Pennsylvania Ledger*, Aug. 19, 1775; *New-Hampshire Gazette*, Aug. 22, 1775. Aside from the threat about slaves, this article accusing Draper was one of the first to suggest the crown was contemplating sending foreign soldiers to America. That theme would gain great attention in the weeks to come. See *Pennsylvania Evening Post*, July 29, 1775; *Pennsylvania Packet*, July 31, 1775; *Maryland Gazette*, Aug. 3, 1775; *New-York Journal*, Aug. 3, 1775; *Norwich Packet*, Aug. 7, 1775; *Massachusetts Spy*, Aug. 9, 1775; *Connecticut Journal*, Aug. 9, 1775; *New-England Chronicle*, Aug. 3–10, 1775; *Essex Journal*, Aug. 11, 1775; *Connecticut Gazette*, Aug. 11, 1775; *Providence Gazette*, Aug. 12, 1775; *Newport Mercury*, Aug. 14, 1775; *Boston Gazette*, Aug. 14, 1775.

domestic enemies" and plots to "instigat[e] . . . the Indians to fall upon us" was becoming a theme that defined the common cause. It was increasingly how the patriots depicted the reasons why colonists should pick up arms and why outside observers should view the rebellion as legitimate and justified.

In addition to publishing the "Declaration of the Causes and Necessity" for domestic consumption, the delegates issued several other proclamations aimed at distant audiences. On July 8, they approved an address to the inhabitants of Great Britain begging them to understand their actions and intercede on their behalf. Fewer than two weeks later, on the same day Benjamin Franklin introduced a draft of the Articles of Confederation, they considered two more proclamations, these to the people of Ireland and the Jamaican Assembly. The address to Jamaica was particularly emotional, suggesting, "Ministerial insolence is lost in ministerial barbarity," which has "plunged us in all the horrors and calamities of civil war." The second address, to the Irish, was an act of preaching to the choir, in Congress's denouncing "barbarous" actions by British troops. Far more than in Dickinson's declaration, the Irish address laid the rhetoric of destruction thickly on: "When we perceive our friends and kinsmen massacred, our habitations plundered, our houses in flames, and their once happy inhabitants fed only by the hand of charity . . . Who can censure our repelling the attacks of such a barbarous band?" Worse, "the wild and barbarous savages of the wilderness have been solicited, by gifts, to take up the hatchet against us, and instigated to deluge our settlements with the blood of innocent and defenceless women and children." Hopeful that the general outcry against ministerial activities in America, including the use of Indians as proxy combatants, would provide enough pressure to restore balance in the empire, Congress broadcast this justification in all directions. Since a majority of colonial printers in America published the Irish address, it was not just for remote readers; it aimed to "engage the affections" of people living in New York or Baltimore as much as those in Dublin or Belfast.[45]

45. Address to Inhabitants of Britain: *JCC*, II, 158–162. The addresses to Ireland and Jamaica were first considered on July 21. The Jamaica address was completed on July 25, for which see "Address to the Assembly of Jamaica," *JCC*, II, 204–207, esp. 206; and the Irish declaration was completed on July 28, for which see "To the People of Ireland," *JCC*, II, 212–218, esp. 215–217. The Irish address printed in *Pennsylvania Mercury*, Aug. 4, 1775; *Pennsylvania Ledger*, Aug. 5, 1775; *Pennsylvania Evening Post*, Aug. 5, 1775; *Pennsylvania Packet*, Aug. 7, 1775; *Dunlap's Maryland Gazette*, Aug. 8,

Despite these prodigious efforts, it was not at all apparent that the patriot argument enjoyed overwhelming success in the conflict's early months, as Drayton, Tennent, and Hart learned when competing for backcountry affection in South Carolina. This was a serious problem. The success of the Revolution was dependent on the effectiveness of the common cause. Of course, war stories had an impact on policy; the relationship between polemics and the ways patriots organized their military defense or diplomacy was a powerful one that had real consequences for real people's lives. But, setting aside this critical component, if the majority of the colonial populace rejected the patriots' causes and necessities for taking up arms, then all would be lost. The case of James Dealey rejoicing in the "good news" of the king's arming of Indians, slaves, and Catholics was a distressing one. When Peter Timothy exchanged that letter in his *South-Carolina Gazette,* he surely did not think readers would relish such threats.

In case their statements did not resonate—or, worse, there were lots of potential Dealeys out there who read their messages the "wrong" way— patriot leaders took preemptive actions to proselytize to areas or communities that were riven with conflict going into the Revolutionary War. There were several spots throughout the colonies where clashes that had little to do with the imperial controversy could, in fact, breed disaffection for the common cause. Patriot leaders at both provincial and continental levels understood that they needed to shore up those areas where conflict reared its head in the years before Lexington: the Regulator movement in the piedmont region of North Carolina, the heated dispute over the Vermont territory, the Yankee-Pennamite violence in the contentious Wyoming Valley, the boundary controversy between Pennsylvania and Virginia over the Pittsburgh region. Some extra convincing was necessary to defuse threats from these quarters.[46]

1775; *Pennsylvania Gazette,* Aug. 9, 1775; *New-York Journal,* Aug. 10, 1775; *Connecticut Journal,* Aug. 16, 1775; *Massachusetts Spy,* Aug. 16, 1775; *Virginia Gazette* (Pinkney), Aug. 17, 1775; *Virginia Gazette* (Dixon & Hunter), Aug. 19, 1775; *Boston Gazette,* Aug. 21, 1775; *Connecticut Courant,* Aug. 21, 1775; *New-England Chronicle,* Aug. 17–24, 1775; *Essex Journal,* Aug. 25, 1775; *Virginia Gazette, or the Norfolk Intelligencer,* Aug. 30, 1775; *Massachusetts Gazette,* Aug. 31, 1775; *Connecticut Gazette,* Sept. 1, 1775.

46. For the North Carolina Regulators, see Marjoleine Kars, *Breaking Loose Together: The Regulator Rebellion in Pre-Revolutionary North Carolina* (Chapel Hill, N.C., 2002). For Vermont, see Michael A. Bellesiles, *Revolutionary Outlaws: Ethan Allen and the Struggle for Independence on the Early American Frontier* (Charlottesville, Va., 1993). There are surprisingly few secondary studies of the Wyoming controversy. Most

"Britain Has Found Means to Unite Us"

In early July, at the same time Dickinson and Jefferson worked on their declaration, the North Carolina delegates were worried about the loyalty of the former Regulators in the backcountry of their province. Concerns about whether those recent wounds would combine with the burgeoning slave unrest to destroy the patriot movement worsened when another intercepted letter from Gage to Martin arrived on July 3, whereby the commander ordered that a supply of gunpowder be sent to Newbern to arm loyalists. With slave patrols already on high alert, any possibilities of a second internal threat needed to be neutralized. One of North Carolina's delegates to Congress, Joseph Hewes, moved quickly to enlist a different type of soldier. On behalf of his delegation, he asked four of Philadelphia's Presbyterian ministers to "use their pastoral Influence to work a change in the disposition of the people" in North Carolina. The real "dupes to the designs of Administration," he explained to the Philadelphia preachers, were the "Inhabitants of the back parts of that Colony, a laborious hardy set of people who become formidable from that as well as their numbers, and should Gov[ernmen]t have influence enough to draw them into action, might endanger [the] liberties of North Carolina and go far to defeat the plan of Opposition devised by the Continental Congress." "Such a struggle would be productive of bloodshed and therefore loudly calls for the kind offices of the ministers of peace to prevent its baneful Consequences."[47]

The ministers responded with an appropriate sense of urgency, producing an eight-page pamphlet two days later. Chiding their flock for being "somehow led aside from the cause of freedom and liberty by men who have given you an unfair representation" of the imperial crisis, the four Philadelphia clergymen utilized the increasingly popular two-pronged rhetorical assault that patriots used at many levels. First, they appealed to the disaffected

---

analyses rely on the introductions from Julian P. Boyd's eleven volumes of *The Susquehanna Company Papers* (Wilkes-Barre, Pa., 1930). For the Virginia-Pennsylvania border dispute, see Richard White, *The Middle Ground: Indians, Empires, and Republics in the Great Lakes Region, 1650–1815* (New York, 1991), 351–365; Michael N. McConnell, *A Country Between: The Upper Ohio Valley and Its Peoples, 1727–1774* (Lincoln, Neb., 1992), 255–279; Patrick Griffin, *American Leviathan: Empire, Nation, and Revolutionary Frontier* (New York, 2007), 72–123; and Robert G. Parkinson, "From Indian Killer to Worthy Citizen: The Revolutionary Transformation of Michael Cresap," *WMQ*, 3d Ser., LXIII (2006), 97–122.

47. Gage to Martin, Boston, Apr. 12, 1775, 4 *Am. Archives*, II, 1323–1324; North Carolina Delegates to the Presbyterian Ministers of Philadelphia, July 3–[8?], 1775, *LDC*, I, 575–576, esp. 575.

former Regulators to recognize that "we must unite if possible, as one man, to maintain our just rights, not by fire and sword, or by shedding the blood of our fellow-subjects, unless we be driven to it in our own defence." If they did not listen, there would be trouble. "If you now desert the cause of liberty . . . if you will offer yourselves to voluntary slavery, and desert the loyal sons of liberty of all denominations, in this most honorable and important contest, we can have no fellowship with you." Suggesting that they would "not be able any longer to number you among our friends" if they aided Governor Martin, the clergymen extended the same veiled threat to potential disaffected whites that other patriot leaders did to the king's other possible proxies, Indians and slaves.[48]

At the outset, then, patriots employed similar rhetorical strategies to identify, ostracize, and, with luck, defuse all enemies to the common cause. They trusted, at this early state, that well-placed, well-argued, direct statements might win hearts and minds in crucial pockets of disaffection. If not, the near-universal trope of dreadful instigation might. In Rowan County, a Regulator stronghold on the North Carolina frontier, the local committee drafted its own address that tried to encourage militia enlistments by using the prevailing theme of the day: British officers sought to arm "one part of us . . . against the other

> by which cruel means each neighborhood would be engaged in bloody massacre with its adjacent, in that bitter scourge to humanity, a civil war. Brother against brother, and son against the father, letting loose upon our defenceless frontier a torrent of blood, by the savage rage of Indian barbarity; who are ordered a supply of arms and ammunition, by Lord North, immediately to attack us and resent the inhuman cruelties of the last war. Ripping infants from the wombs of their expiring mothers, roasting Christians to death by slow fire.

Far from Philadelphia or Newbern or Charleston, Rowan County patriots also saw the merits in framing their arguments in what one historian termed an "anti-Indian sublime" to inspire military ardor. Former Regulators might not like the men who had tried to kill them a few years earlier, but they

48. "An Address of the Presbyterian Ministers of the City of Philadelphia to the Ministers and Presbyterian Congregations in the County of [ ] in North Carolina" (Philadelphia, 1775), 7 ("we must unite"), 8 ("desert the cause"), *Early American Imprints,* 14411. The four ministers were Francis Alison, James Sprout, George Duffield, and Robert Davidson.

"Britain Has Found Means to Unite Us"

could find one consensual issue: protecting their families from British-instigated Indian roasts.[49]

If trust was the foundation of the common cause, public confidence was the essential ingredient to keeping the rebellion alive. Whenever they appealed to the public to end the controversy, British officials and loyalists alike consistently came back to the accusation that the patriots were demagogues subverting the British constitution and leading the colonies to utter destruction. The people, in short, were making a terrible mistake by putting their faith in the patriot leadership. If that faith could be shaken, the Revolution might collapse from within. The greatest threat to the common cause might be having one of the most visible members of the core patriot leadership turn out to be a secret British agent. On September 30, James Warren reported, "An Event has lately taken place" in the Cambridge camp "which makes much Noise." Patriot authorities had arrested Dr. Benjamin Church for carrying on a correspondence with one of Gage's officers across the lines in Boston.[50]

This was no trifling matter. Church was part of the "nucleus of the Massachusetts revolutionary movement" alongside Otis, Hancock, Quincy, Warren, and the Adams cousins. In the wake of the scandal, John Adams recited his patriot résumé: "a Man of Genius, of Learning, of Family, of Character, a Writer of Liberty Songs and good ones too, a Speaker of Liberty orations, a Member of the Boston Committee of Correspondence, a Member of the Massachusetts Congress, an Agent for that Congress to the Continental Congress, a Member of the House, a Director General of the Hospital and Surgeon General." Colonial readers outside New England, if they had paid attention during the past few years, were not unaware of these accomplishments. The arrest of this lofty a patriot was an unwelcome surprise. Adams summed it up better: "Good God!"[51]

49. Rowan County Committee of Safety Proceedings, July 18, 1775, in John H. Wheeler, ed., *Historical Sketches of North Carolina, from 1584 to 1851* (Philadelphia, 1851), II, 365–366. "Anti-Indian sublime": Peter Silver, *Our Savage Neighbors: How Indian War Transformed Early America* (New York, 2007), xx.

50. James Warren to JA, Watertown, Oct. 1, 1775, *PJA*, III, 177–180, esp. 177. For the problem of trust during the imperial crisis, see T. H. Breen, *The Marketplace of Revolution: How Consumer Politics Shaped American Independence* (New York, 2004), 7, 247–250.

51. Pauline Maier, *From Resistance to Revolution: Colonial Radicals and the Development of American Opposition to Britain, 1765–1776* (New York, 1972), 164. See also Richard D. Brown, *Revolutionary Politics in Massachusetts: The Boston Committee of Cor-

One of Church's letters, dated July 23 and in cipher, was the incriminating document. Written to one of Gage's brigade commanders, it provided information about colonial morale, numbers of cannon, and recent supplies of gunpowder Church had gleaned on his official trip to the Congress and other reconnaissance trips taken that summer. Church swore that he was no traitor; he claimed he was aiding the cause by giving Gage inflated numbers, and any other facts he related were things "I learned myself from the News Papers." The final line of his intercepted letter, however, did not exude innocence. "Make use of every precaution, or *I perish,*" he begged.[52]

respondence and the Towns, 1772–1774 (Cambridge, Mass., 1970); JA to Charles Lee, Philadelphia, Oct. 13, 1775, *PJA*, III, 202. Church's name appeared several times in colonial newspapers beginning in 1768. Just to take the *Virginia Gazettes* in Williamsburg, he was mentioned in the following instances: when elected to the Massachusetts Assembly ([Purdie & Dixon], June 8, 1769); when he gave a protest petition to Governor Thomas Hutchinson ([Rind], Dec. 3, 1772); when he helped form the Boston committee of correspondence ([Rind], Apr. 29, 1773); when he helped draft an address to Gage ([Purdie & Dixon], Oct. 6, 1774); and when he was elected to the Provincial Congress ([Purdie & Dixon], Oct. 13, 1774; [Pinkney], Oct. 13, 27, 1774). There are only two articles in the last half-century on the Church episode: David Kiracofe, "Dr. Benjamin Church and the Dilemma of Treason in Revolutionary Massachusetts," *New England Quarterly*, LXX (1997), 443–462; Tara Dirst and Allan Kulikoff, "Was Dr. Benjamin Church a Traitor? A New Way to Find Out," *Common-Place*, VI (2005), http://www.common-place.org/vol-06/no-01/tales, accessed January 13, 2015. For older accounts, see Allen French, *General Gage's Informers* (Ann Arbor, Mich., 1932), 147–197; Carl Van Doren, *Secret History of the American Revolution* (Garden City, N.Y., 1941), 18–23.

52. Benjamin Church to Major Kane, Cambridge, July 23, 1775, 4 *Am. Archives*, II, 1713–1714. Warren's initial letter to Adams gives some reasons for Church's possible motivations. Boston patriots assumed Church's downfall stemmed from his "Infamous Connection, with an Infamous Hussey," which led only "to the disgrace of his own reputation, and probable ruin of his Family" (Warren to JA, Oct. 1, 1775, *PJA*, III, 178). "I learned myself": Church to GW, Oct. 3, 1775, *PGW: RW*, II, 85–87. Samuel Adams, when he heard the deciphered letter read aloud, tended to believe Church's defense. "I do not recollect that it in any measure was calculated to expose the Weakness of our Army," he wrote to James Warren, "which a Traitor would gladly have seizd the opportunity of doing, especially as he might have done it at that time with great Truth. The Union of Individual Colonies and of the Continental Congress, and their firmness and Resolution are picturd in high Colours." Adams did admit that he had not "thoroughly examind" the letter but had only "heard it read" (Samuel Adams to James Warren, Philadelphia, Oct. 13, 1775, *LDC*, II, 179).

"Britain Has Found Means to Unite Us"

Washington convened a Council of War on October 3 and 4 to interrogate the army's chief surgeon. Lacking any legal provisions for treason charges, Washington and his generals decided to keep Church under close arrest and referred the entire matter to Congress. Soon, the news of Church's arrest began to gallop south to Philadelphia. But, for the most part, it did so in private letters tucked away in riders' portmanteaus. The day after the council's decision, Charles Lee, one of the generals that sat in judgment, wrote John Adams of the "astonishing and terrifying accusation or rather detection of Doctor Church." Lee grasped the threat Church posed to the common cause. His actions "will spread an universal diffidence and suspicion than which nothing can be more pernicious to Men embark'd in a cause like ours, the cornerstone of Which is laid not only on honour virtue and disinterestedness—but on the perswasion that the whole be actuated by the same divine principles." Washington's comment that "the Army and Country are exceedingly irritated" by the affair further verified Lee's interpretation. Abigail Adams also perceived the central problem. "Let not that man be trusted who can violate private faith," she wrote John, adding, "How is he to be bound whom neither honor nor conscience holds?" The patriots stood to lose the public's confidence. John Adams wrote home with exasperation: "What shall we say?"[53]

53. Council of War, Oct. 3–4, 1775, *PGW: RW*, II, 82–83, GW to President of Continental Congress, Cambridge, Oct. 5, 1775, 98–103. Congress received Washington's letter on October 13. See Charles Lee to JA, Cambridge, Oct. 5, 1775, *PJA*, III, 184–186, esp. 185; GW to President of Continental Congress, Cambridge, Oct. 5, 1775, *PGW: RW*, II, 98–103; Abigail Adams to JA, Braintree, Oct. 9, 1775, in L. H. Butterfield et al., eds., *Adams Family Correspondence*, 2d Ser. (Cambridge, Mass., 1963–), I, 298; JA to William Tudor, Philadelphia, Oct. 12, 1775, *LDC*, II, 169–170. Others in Congress also understood what the Church treachery might mean. Rhode Island delegate Samuel Ward wrote his brother, "The greatest that I am apprehensive of is that it may induce Suspicions and lessen that Confidence which is necessary to a cordial Union and our mutual Support, this ought carefully to be guarded against as fatal, and at the same Time the utmost Vigilance is necessary least we should be betrayed" (Samuel Ward to Henry Ward, Philadelphia, Oct. 11, 1775, *LDC*, II, 163–165, esp. 164). Mercy Otis Warren also wrote from Massachusetts that she feared the affair "will occasion many Invidious Reflections from the Enemies of the American Cause" (Warren to JA, Oct. 12, 1775, *PJA*, III, 199–201, esp. 200). John Adams wrote a second version of his rhetorical query to Charles Lee on Oct. 13: "What shall We say of American Patriots? or rather what will the World Say?" (JA to Lee, *PJA*, III, 203).

"Britain Has Found Means to Unite Us"

Perhaps they did not have to say anything. Guilty or not, Church's betrayal was monumental news. Yet the accusation of treason committed by one of the most important Massachusetts patriots and a high-ranking member of the Continental army left few traces in colonial newspapers. Church was kept under house arrest for three weeks, until his former colleagues in the Massachusetts House of Representatives decided to put him through a second examination. During that time, a great number of letters passed one another on the post road from Boston to Philadelphia. The Warrens and Adamses kept one another apprised of every development in the story. Army officers wrote to Congress, and the delegates answered. None of those letters appeared in the papers. This was unusual: recall Adams's letter to Warren about the German soldier outside the door of Congress several months earlier. Adams clearly instructed Warren to turn that letter over to the printers "to engage the Affections of the Germans." In this case, however, only the faintest sketches of what had occurred at Cambridge appeared.

Compared to the amount of ink spilled about Stuart or Martin or Carleton, in terms of either reportage or circulation, the Church affair was far less visible. The report that appeared most often in print consisted of three sentences. One was extracted out of a letter from Cambridge: "Dr. Church (Surgeon-General of the army, and Chairman of the Committee of Safety at Watertown) having been found guilty of traiterous practices, in corresponding with the enemy, is put under an arrest." This was followed by the lines: "We are informed that Dr. Church is confined in a house opposite to the head quarters, in Cambridge; his correspondence, it is said, was carried on in cyphers with a field officer in General Gage's army." The only paper that differed from this standard account was the *Pennsylvania Ledger*. Printer James Humphreys, Jr., related that Church was "under close confinement, on suspicion of holding a traitorous correspondence with General Gage. The particulars we have not been able to collect." Why did Humphreys have so much trouble getting details before the *Ledger*'s Saturday publication? Congress had received Washington's official report the day before; Samuel and John Adams had written home about it on Tuesday, Samuel Ward on Wednesday.[54]

54. *Rivington's New-York Gazetteer,* Oct. 12, 1775; *Pennsylvania Evening Post,* Oct. 14, 1775; *New-York Gazette,* Oct. 16, 1775; *Pennsylvania Packet,* Oct. 16, 1775; *Pennsylvania Journal,* Oct. 18, 1775; *Connecticut Journal,* Oct. 18, 1775; *Pennsylvania Gazette,* Oct. 18, 1775; *Pennsylvania Mercury,* Oct. 20, 1775; *Connecticut Gazette,* Oct. 20, 1775; *Virginia*

"Britain Has Found Means to Unite Us"

John Adams's reaction upon receipt of the news might offer one answer to why Humphreys was having such difficulty. Obviously shocked, John wrote Abigail that the news "has made me more cautious of Writing than ever. I must be excused from writing a Syllable of any Thing of any Moment. My Letters have been and will be nothing, but Trifles. I don't cho[o]se to trust the Post. I am afraid to trust private Travellers. They may peep. Accidents may happen, and I would avoid, if I could, even Ridicule, but especially Mischief." "Pray, bundle up every Paper not already hid," he instructed his wife, "and conceal them in impenetrable Darkness. Nobody knows what may occur." The threat to public confidence inherent in this story surely played a significant role in why its newspaper coverage was so meager and scattered. Even in late November, when Church was moved to a Connecticut jail, the news was conveyed in a one-sentence report that, admittedly, still packed a punch. The *New-England Chronicle* tried to save face by turning the tables, describing Church's crime as corresponding "with the ministerial rebels in Boston." Because of this offense, the "noted Dr. Church . . . was carried from this town, under a strong guard, and conducted to the interior part of the country." Ten papers exchanged this update, none south of Philadelphia.[55]

This is not to suggest that there was a conspiracy of censorship or even that no one knew or talked about Church. At the camp, a lieutenant from

---

Gazette (Pinkney), Oct. 26, 1775; *Virginia Gazette* (Purdie), Oct. 27, 1775; *Virginia Gazette* (Dixon & Hunter), Oct. 28, 1775. Dixon and Hunter omitted the Cambridge extract and only included the final paragraph (*Pennsylvania Ledger*, Oct. 14, 1775).

55. JA to Abigail Adams, Oct. 10, 1775, *LDC*, II, 157; *New-England Chronicle*, Nov. 23, 1775; *Boston Gazette*, Nov. 27, 1775; *Connecticut Courant*, Nov. 27, 1775; *New-Hampshire Gazette*, Nov. 28, 1775; *Norwich Packet*, Nov. 30, 1775; *New-York Journal*, Nov. 30, 1775; *Newport Mercury*, Dec. 4, 1775; *Pennsylvania Evening Post*, Dec. 5, 1775; *Pennsylvania Packet*, Dec. 11, 1775; *Constitutional Gazette*, Dec. 13, 1775. Another obstacle to getting information in Philadelphia about Church might have been that the city had experienced its own turmoil about secret loyalists—including a physician, no less—the week before. The Pennsylvania committee of safety had arrested Dr. John Kearsley, James Brooks, Leonard Snowden, and Christopher Carter for a similar crime, secretly conducting correspondence with British officials (in England, in this case). Upon inspection of packets of their papers, they, too, were jailed, in part to protect them from the Philadelphia crowd. See 4 *Am. Archives*, III, 1814–1829; *JCC*, III, 280; Caesar Rodney to Thomas Rodney, Philadelphia, Oct. 9, 1775, *LDC*, II, 151–153. See also Richard Alan Ryerson, *The Revolution Is Now Begun: The Radical Committees of Philadelphia, 1765–1776* (Philadelphia, 1978), 131–132.

Norwich wrote in his diary on October 7 that Church was the main topic of conversation over Saturday dinner. Three days later, one Massachusetts man wrote to delegate Robert Treat Paine, "Doctor Church's Affair is the only Topic of the Day." Lieutenant Jabez Fitch opined, "No man on the continent could be more perfectly acquainted with the doings of all the congresses, both continental and provincial, as well as all the other conventions wherein the common cause of liberty was concernd than he, so that it seems he was perfectly furnishd for a compleat traitor." Loyalist printer James Rivington, perhaps sensing public pressure building against him again, inserted a poem of sixty-four lines, which two of the staunchest patriot printers also ran, about "the late detection" of Church's correspondence. Benjamin Towne published a lengthy satire of the political spectrum, "Grand Political Race," which called Church "an infamous Judas like Tory jockey." Early in the new year, too, eight newspapers transcribed Church's "much-talked-of traitorous letter." It is possible that Church's treachery was indeed "much talked of." But it was not printed much, especially compared to John Stuart's letters or the news of Thomas Jeremiah's hanging. Details, such as eyewitness accounts of the military and civil interrogations—or even his side of the story—never surfaced in print. Nor does any evidence suggest the news ever made it south of Williamsburg.[56]

In fact, the bare-bones coverage is reminiscent of how newspapers before the Revolution treated slave rebellions. Patriot leaders and publicists before the war "sought to mute the news of slave insurrection lest the contagion of liberty be misinterpreted by bondsmen and women as having something to do with them." Starting almost immediately after Lexington, that "official silence" was broken. Now, slave insurrections—because they had an attributable, identifiable cause—were described in detail. The silence that surrounded the Church affair, on the other hand, suggests that those

56. David Cobb to Robert Treat Paine, Oct. 10, 1775, in Edward W. Hanson, ed., *Papers of Robert Treat Paine* (Charlottesville, Va., 2006), III, 95; entry for Oct. 7, 1775, in "Diary of Jabez Fitch, Jr.," Massachusetts Historical Society, *Proceedings*, 2d Ser., IX (Boston, 1894), 41–91, esp. 65. Poem: *Rivington's New-York Gazetteer*, Oct. 19, 1775; *Pennsylvania Packet*, Oct. 23, 1775; *Essex Journal*, Nov. 17, 1775. "Grand Political Race": *Pennsylvania Evening Post*, Nov. 21, 1775. Church letter: *New-England Chronicle*, Dec. 28–Jan. 4, 1776; *Pennsylvania Ledger*, Jan. 20, 1776; *Massachusetts Spy*, Jan. 12, 1776; *Pennsylvania Packet*, Jan. 15, 1776; *Norwich Packet*, Jan. 15, 1776; *Maryland Gazette*, Jan. 25, 1776; *Virginia Gazette* (Dixon & Hunter), Feb. 3, 1776; *Connecticut Courant*, Feb. 5, 1776.

filters were not cast aside, just repositioned. Because it posed such a threat to how fully the populace endorsed the common cause, betrayal by one of the highest-ranking patriots from New England had to be treated with the same care as slave insurrection had been.[57]

It is impossible to know where the breakdown occurred in the Church case. Maybe no patriot military or political leaders gave the press any information. Because printers were largely beholden to correspondents to turn over their private letters of their own volition, if they withheld those documents, there would be silence. The news did not reflect either side in a positive light, so it is not surprising that loyalist printers (what few of them were secure by the end of 1775) did not broadcast the story, either. That the plot was detected—like Stuart, Cameron, Johnson, and, soon, Dr. John Connolly—was one avenue patriots could have explored to turn the news to their benefit, but even this was only touched in verse. To adapt Adams's words, the Church story would without doubt disengage colonial affections toward the common cause. It is naïve to suggest that political calculations by patriot publicists and political leaders played no role in the hushed print response. Though their efforts seem collective or planned from a distance, these patriots did so by way of many individual choices.[58]

3: SNOWBALLS IN VIRGINIA: DUNMORE AND CONNOLLY
Few parts of mainland North America had escaped some experience with a narrative of proxies aiding or threatening to aid crown officials over this

57. Patricia Bradley, *Slavery, Propaganda, and the American Revolution* (Jackson, Miss., 1998), 133–134, esp. 133.

58. The poem Rivington and two others ran developed the theme of detection, and even ended by holding up John Hancock as the anti-Church:

That *Church,* on whom his country's hopes relied,
That *Church* has prov'd a lurking parricide;
In treason's dark recesses long hath stray'd,
And hostile schemes against fair freedom laid?
Abus'd the confidence which she repos'd,
And to her foes, each secret plan disclos'd! . . .
But some there are, from whom distrust refrains;
Whose patriot souls will ne'er admit the stains
Of trait'rous guilt; amid this glorious band,
Tow'ring, I see, the virtuous HANCOCK stand!

Rivington's New-York Gazetteer, Oct. 19, 1775.

unprecedented year. That Virginians faced many of the same challenges and threats as their southern neighbors only added to the sense that a general plot against American liberty was indeed afoot. On the same day that Drayton and Tennent set out from Charleston on their mission to the backcountry, and a day after the North Carolina Council ordered Governor Martin's incriminating letters published, a clergyman in Maryland recited the increasingly commonplace accusations to a friend in England. Beginning with older claims that "the ministerial agents are endeavouring to raise the Indians against us, and General Carleton is using every method to embody the Canadians to fall upon us, and has actually hanged several of them for refusing to obey his mandates," he added a new wrinkle:

> To complete the horrid scene, the Governor of Virginia, the Captains of the men-of-war, and mariners, have been tampering with our negroes; and have held nightly meetings with them; and all for the glorious purpose of enticing them to cut their master's throats while they are asleep. Gracious God! That men, noble by birth and fortune, should descend to such ignoble base servility!

Beginning late that summer, people throughout the Chesapeake would hear stories about the willingness of Virginia's governor, like the two Carolina royal executives, to use all available resources in quelling the rebellion.[59]

Only two days before that Maryland clergyman sat down to convey the news, the Norfolk Borough committee wrote to the Virginia Convention that Lord Dunmore, who had taken refuge on the HMS *Otter* since early June, welcomed a reinforcement of sixty troops from Saint Augustine. Such a development would have consequences, the committee contended. Even though "at present we are under no apprehensions from them, we find exceeding bad effects have arisen among the blacks from the neighborhood of the men of war, which we have great reason to believe will be very much increased by the arrival of these troops." Either local printer John Hunter Holt was privy to this meeting, was given a copy of the note, or was told about it two days later, for his *Virginia Gazette* reported—with anxious redactions—that "this town and neighborhood have been much disturbed lately by the elopement of their [negroes], owing to a mistaken notion which has unhappily spread amongst them, of finding shelter on board the men

---

59. "Letter from a Clergyman in Md. to His Friend in England, Aug. 2, 1775; Signed 'T.T.'," 4 *Am. Archives*, III, 9.

of war in this harbor." This intelligence, which fourteen other printers inserted in their own papers, was just the start of what would be a storm of news concerning runaway Virginia blacks being protected by Royal Navy officers and Dunmore. By the time Dunmore issued his emancipation proclamation, it would have been difficult for colonial readers all over North America to have missed the long-simmering controversy in the Chesapeake over British officials' harboring runaway slaves. The theater of operations shifted north from Wilmington to Hampton Roads, but the story remained constant: royal governors, aided by naval officers, were encouraging slaves to rebel against their masters. In June and July, it had been Josiah Martin and Captain John Collet; in August and September, it was Lord Dunmore and Captain Matthew Squire. The differences mattered little; the aggregate effect, however, was powerful.[60]

Over the next several weeks, tensions continued to build in the Chesapeake. They exploded when a hurricane swept over the mouths of the James and York Rivers on the afternoon of Saturday, September 2, a fierce storm that drove a tender attached to Captain Squire's Royal Navy squadron ashore near Hampton Roads. Local residents were increasingly angry at Squire's "most unfriendly disposition to the liberties of this continent, in promoting a disaffection among the slaves, and concealing some of them for

60. Norfolk Borough Committee to Peyton Randolph, Norfolk, July 31, 1775, *Rev. Va.*, III, 378. Concerns over a spike in black unrest were not limited to Norfolk. The following day, the officers of the independent militia companies in Williamsburg also wrote, "The Governor's cutter has carried off a number of Slaves belonging to private Gentlemen. We think it high [time] to establish the doctrine of reprisal and to take immediate possession (if possible of his person) at all events of his property." See *Rev. Va.*, III, 385. "Mistaken notion": *Virginia Gazette, or the Norfolk Intelligencer,* Aug. 2, 1775; *Virginia Gazette* (Purdie), Aug. 4, 1775; *Virginia Gazette* (Dixon & Hunter), Aug. 5, 1775; *Pennsylvania Evening Post,* Aug. 15, 1775; *Pennsylvania Journal,* Aug. 16, 1775; *Pennsylvania Gazette,* Aug. 16, 1775; *Rivington's New-York Gazetteer,* Aug. 17, 1775; *Pennsylvania Mercury,* Aug. 18, 1775; *New-York Gazette,* Aug. 21, 1775; *Pennsylvania Packet,* Aug. 21, 1775; *Dunlap's Maryland Gazette,* Aug. 22, 1775; *New-York Journal,* Aug. 24, 1775; *Norwich Packet,* Aug. 28, 1775; *South-Carolina and American General Gazette,* Sept. 8, 1775; *Newport Mercury,* Oct. 2, 1775. This first story of the "elopement" of Norfolk blacks appeared in four of the above papers in the same issue as August 6 reports from Newbern that Collet's hiding of slaves in Fort Johnston was the reason why North Carolina militia forces had to burn the outpost down. See *Pennsylvania Journal,* Aug. 16, 1775; *Pennsylvania Mercury,* Aug. 18, 1775; *Pennsylvania Packet,* Aug. 21, 1775; and *New-York Gazette,* Aug. 21, 1775.

a considerable time on board their vessels," as the Norfolk committee wrote on August 16. They were less than happy with the governor, too; one Williamsburg paper reported that Dunmore had fallen overboard in the hurricane and been "severely ducked" but, alas, survived, bringing its printer to invoke "the old saying, those who were born to be HANGED will never be DROWNED." The "gust" had provided an opportunity for tidewater Virginians to vent those frustrations. A group of nearby inhabitants set the foundered tender on fire early Sunday morning. This arson touched off a spiral of accusations—most of which were well reported in the patriot press—that built toward Dunmore's November decision to proclaim freedom for Virginia's slaves.[61]

On September 6, the printer of the *Virginia Gazette, or the Norfolk Intelligencer,* John Hunter Holt, published a short gloss on what had happened the previous Sunday morning at Hampton. That issue featured columns of other stories about British efforts to gain proxies, including an account of Canadian Indians' "not being persuaded by Governor Carleton," a letter from London that the ministry had given four men £40,000 each "for the barbarous purpose of hiring the Indians to . . . cut our throats," and a report of "atrocious FREE BOOTER" Captain Collet's being "dislodged" from Fort Johnston. Matthew Squire, though, took offense at Holt's observation on the third page about the crew of the *Otter:* "Is it not a melancholy reflection, that men, who affect on all occasions to stile themselves 'his Majesty's servants,' should think the service of their Sovereign consists in plundering his subjects, and in committing such pitiful acts of rapine as would entitle other people to the character of robbers?" Incensed, Squire fired off a warning to Holt that he had seen how the printer had "lately taken the freedom to mention MY NAME" in such a context, and if he ever did so again, "I will most assuredly seize your person, and take you on board the *Otter.*"[62]

61. For another notice about slaves being "concealed" aboard the *Otter,* see *Virginia Gazette, or the Norfolk Intelligencer,* Aug. 16, 1775; *Rev. Va.,* III, 452–453. Other accusations of Dunmore's men harboring slaves in *Virginia Gazette* (Pinkney), Sept. 14, 1775, which was then exchanged in *Pennsylvania Journal,* Sept. 27, 1775, and *Pennsylvania Ledger,* Sept. 30, 1775. "The gust": Wilson Miles Cary to Alexander Purdie, Hampton, Sept. 4, 1775, *Rev. Va.,* IV, 69. For more on the storm, see Tony Williams, *Hurricane of Independence: The Untold Story of the Deadly Storm at the Deciding Moment of the American Revolution* (Naperville, Ill., 2008).

62. *Virginia Gazette* (Purdie), Sept. 8, 1775. The £40,000 account received significant attention. It was reprinted in *New-York Journal,* Sept. 21, 1775; *Connecticut Courant,* Sept. 25, 1775; *Connecticut Journal,* Sept. 27, 1775; *New-England Chronicle,*

"Britain Has Found Means to Unite Us"

The charred tender and the exchange between Squire and Holt quickly became major news stories throughout the continent. A few papers in Pennsylvania and South Carolina simply reprinted Squire's threat. More copied Alexander Purdie's confirmation in the *Virginia Gazette* in Williamsburg that the crowd had indeed burned Squire's tender "in return for his harbouring gentlemen's negroes." Perhaps in defiance of Squire's attempt to intimidate his colleague, Purdie the following week condemned the captain in similar language to Holt's. "Squire," he sneered, "has seized three passage boats, with the Negroes in them, by way of reprisal" for the burnt tender, "which boats and Negroes, it is likely he intends taking into the *King's service*, to send out a pirating for hogs, fowls, etc—A very pretty occupation for the Captain of one of his Majesty's ships of war." Thirteen other papers exchanged this comment, as well.[63]

Sept. 21–28, 1775; *Maryland Gazette*, Sept. 28, 1775; *Connecticut Gazette*, Sept. 29, 1775; *Massachusetts Spy*, Sept. 29, 1775; *Newport Mercury*, Oct. 2, 1775; *New-Hampshire Gazette*, Oct. 10, 1775. "Melancholy reflection": *Virginia Gazette, or the Norfolk Intelligencer*, Sept. 6, 1775. This issue also informed readers, "Monday evening WILLIAM GODDARD, Esq., surveyor, etc. to the General American post-office, arrived here on a tour through the several united colonies, to establish offices in the principal towns and other commercial places, under the authority of BENJAMIN FRANKLIN, Esq., who is appointed postmaster-general by the Hon. the Continental Congress; and as soon as the officers are commissioned, and the routes fixed, the establishment will immediately take place. [The representatives of this borough and county and other principal gentlemen, having kindly recommended the Printer of this Paper as a proper person to act as Deputy Postmaster here, Mr. Goddard hath, in consequence, presented him a Commission, under the 'Authority of Congress,' authorizing him to hold that post; and he expects to open his Office about the first of next month.]" Of course, the day before that expected opening, Holt's office would be sacked by Squire. For Squire's threat, see *Virginia Gazette, or the Norfolk Intelligencer*, Sept. 13, 1775. Holt prefaced the publication of Squire's letter with a defense of the "open and liberal press," being that "he does not conceive that his press is to be under the direction of any one but himself, and while he has the sanction of the law, he shall always pride himself in the reflection that the liberty of the press is one of the grand bulwarks of the English constitution."

63. Squire/Holt exchanged in *Virginia Gazette* (Pinkney), Sept. 14, 1775; *Virginia Gazette* (Purdie), Sept. 15, 1775; *Pennsylvania Journal*, Sept. 27, 1775; *Pennsylvania Ledger*, Sept. 30, 1775; *Pennsylvania Packet*, Oct. 2, 1775; *South-Carolina Gazette*, Oct. 24, 1775. "In return for his harbouring": *Virginia Gazette* (Purdie), Sept. 8, 1775; *Virginia Gazette* (Dixon & Hunter), Sept. 9, 1775; *Pennsylvania Journal*, Sept. 20, 1775; *New-York Journal*, Sept. 21, 1775; *Pennsylvania Mercury*, Sept. 22, 1775; *New-York*

The charge of "instigating" slaves had powerful effects in 1775. Only ten months earlier, James Madison had suggested to William Bradford, Jr., that prudence dictated printers, like his father, keep details of slave insurrections out of the newspaper. No longer. The Revolutionary War had altered the context of black unrest—principally, that this terrible type of rebellion could be laid at the feet of their enemies—and patriot printers now went out of their way to feature such articles. John Hunter Holt found out how explosive the accusation of encouraging runaways could be. Holt tested the "commodore of the Virginia fleet" in the September 20 issue of his Norfolk paper. First calling him a plunderer and pirate, Holt then turned to the matter of Joseph Harris. Like Thomas Jeremiah in Charleston, Harris was a pilot, and therefore extremely valuable. Sometime in July, Harris had run to the HMS *Fowey,* and his master, Henry King, wanted him back. When Squire demanded that the people of Hampton who had burned the tender return the stores they had stolen off it, they responded they would do so when the captain returned Harris to King. Squire balked, and Holt jumped at this chance to attack "the honest captain." "After damning the IMPUDENCE of these people in demanding his Ethiopian director, swore he would make them no other reply than what his cannon could give them; according he has taken his station between the two bars to be more convenient for the business." Perhaps it was the intimation behind the phrase "his Ethiopian director"—that maybe Harris was more commander than pilot—which set the captain off, but something in that issue certainly did.[64]

Gazette, Sept. 25, 1775; *Pennsylvania Packet,* Sept. 25, 1775; *Connecticut Journal,* Sept. 27, 1775; *New-England Chronicle,* Sept. 28, 1775; *Essex Journal,* Sept. 29, 1775; *Connecticut Gazette,* Sept. 29, 1775; *Massachusetts Spy,* Sept. 29, 1775; *New-Hampshire Gazette,* Oct. 10, 1775. "A pirating": *Virginia Gazette* (Purdie), Sept. 15, 1775; *Virginia Gazette* (Dixon & Hunter), Sept. 16, 1775; *Pennsylvania Evening Post,* Sept. 26, 1775; *Pennsylvania Gazette,* Sept. 27, 1775; *Pennsylvania Journal,* Sept. 27, 1775; *Pennsylvania Mercury,* Sept. 29, 1775; *New-York Gazette,* Oct. 2, 1775; *Pennsylvania Packet,* Oct. 2, 1775; *Connecticut Journal,* Oct. 4, 1775; *Boston Gazette,* Oct. 9, 1775; *Norwich Packet,* Oct. 9, 1775; *Essex Journal,* Oct. 13, 1775; *Newport Mercury,* Oct. 16, 1775; *South-Carolina Gazette,* Oct. 24, 1775.

64. Patriots in mid-September published an intercepted July 20 letter from Captain George Montague, commander of the HMS *Fowey,* which discussed Harris. Montague told Squire at that time that since the *Fowey* would "soon leave the province, I think him too useful to his Majesty's service to take away," suggesting the pilot should be transferred to the HMS *Otter.* See *Virginia Gazette* (Purdie), Sept. 15, 1775;

"Britain Has Found Means to Unite Us"

Ten days later, with Dunmore's permission, Squire made good on his threat. On September 30—the same day Massachusetts patriots discovered Benjamin Church's traitorous correspondence—a squad of twelve marines from the *Otter* landed at Norfolk, broke into Holt's printing office, confiscated his press and types, took two apprentices hostage, gave "three huzzas, in which they were joined by a crowd of negroes," and left town without any resistance, all in front of two or three hundred surprised onlookers. Squire was allegedly "very angry that they did not get Mr. Holt," but that was not Dunmore's main concern. The governor approved of the raid, not to settle a score, but to get his hands on a printing press, and, presumably, a beater and a puller. "They say they want to print a few papers themselves," a Norfolk writer observed, "that they looked upon the press not to be free, and had a mind to publish something in vindication of their own characters." Word of the theft spread quickly throughout Virginia and beyond. A few days later, all three *Virginia Gazettes* in Williamsburg reported news of what had happened to Holt. From there, printers throughout the colonies took up the cause, and over the next few weeks, stories about the confiscation surfaced in a total of twenty-three of thirty-one active papers.[65]

Pennsylvania Evening Post, Sept. 26, 1775; *Pennsylvania Packet,* Oct. 2, 1775. For the Elizabeth City County committee's Sept. 16 resolution to Squire which made getting its top priority the "restitution of a certain Joseph Harris," see *Rev. Va.,* IV, 119–120. The resolutions were printed in *Virginia Gazette* (Purdie), Sept. 22, 1775; *Virginia Gazette* (Dixon & Hunter), Sept. 23, 1775; *Pennsylvania Evening Post,* Oct. 5, 1775; *Norwich Packet,* Oct. 23, 1775. "Ethiopian director": *Virginia Gazette, or the Norfolk Intelligencer,* Sept. 20, 1775. Also printed in *Pennsylvania Journal,* Oct. 4, 1775, and *Constitutional Gazette,* Oct. 11, 1775.

65. *Virginia Gazette* (Purdie), Oct. 6, 1775; "Extract of a Letter Received in Williamsburgh, Dated Norfolk, Virginia, October 1, 1775," 4 *Am. Archives,* III, 923. The letter appeared at least in *South-Carolina Gazette,* Nov. 14, 1775. Holt was apparently hidden in the printing house the entire time the soldiers were packing up his press. See also *Virginia Gazette* (Purdie), Oct. 6, 1775; *Virginia Gazette* (Pinkney), Oct. 7, 1775; *Virginia Gazette* (Dixon & Hunter), Oct. 7, 1775; *Pennsylvania Evening Post,* Oct. 17, 1775; *Pennsylvania Gazette,* Oct. 18, 1775; *Pennsylvania Journal,* Oct. 18, 1775; *Maryland Gazette,* Oct. 19, 1775; *Pennsylvania Mercury,* Oct. 20, 1775; *Pennsylvania Ledger,* Oct. 21, 1775; *Constitutional Gazette,* Oct. 21, 1775; *Pennsylvania Packet,* Oct. 23, 1775; *New-York Gazette,* Oct. 23, 1775; *Connecticut Journal,* Oct. 25, 1775; *New-York Journal,* Oct. 26, 1775; *Rivington's New-York Gazetteer,* Oct. 26, 1775; *Connecticut Gazette,* Oct. 27, 1775; *Connecticut Courant,* Oct. 30, 1775; *Norwich Packet,* Oct. 30, 1775; *Newport Mercury,* Oct. 30, 1775; *Essex Journal,* Nov. 3, 1775; *Massachusetts Spy,* Nov. 3, 1775;

The ideal of a free press was at stake, but for some printers, the attack was personal. John Hunter Holt was following in the family business: two patriot printers were uncles of the victim. When the news reached Manhattan, *New-York Journal* printer John Holt was especially incensed. Underneath the story of the assault on his nephew, he printed an ironic letter from Ireland on the consequences that arose when colonies lacked a free press: "The common people are industriously kept from the knowledge of public affairs. They know nothing but what the great people please to let them. . . . Keep your Presses free that the people may know all that concerns them, and all that is doing against them."[66]

Many outside Holt's family were just as disturbed by the attack on the *Norfolk Intelligencer*. For the patriots, Dunmore had crossed a serious line. Squire wanted revenge, but the governor wanted to control information. In the short term, he succeeded. He had silenced Holt's paper, which, he claimed, was "poisoning the minds of the people." One delegate to Congress wrote, "What have I read in the Virginia newspapers today! . . . Ah! why do we suffer them indeed! It would not be permitted in any other colony on the continent, I am convinced. But what are we to do?" Others were furious that no one in Norfolk had fought back. "You will, no doubt, have heard of the disgraceful conduct of our Norfolk, in suffering Lord Dunmore, with a few men to take away their printing press!" Richard Henry Lee exclaimed in a letter to Washington. On second thought, the reasons might not have been so obscure. "It happened when the good men of that place were all away, and none but Tories and Negroes remained behind," Lee then explained. "I expect, by every Post, to hear of the demolition of that infamous nest of Tories."[67]

The news of the confiscation was as yet in Williamsburg newspapers traveling north toward Philadelphia when the aggrieved Norfolk printer

New-Hampshire Gazette, Nov. 8, 1775; *South-Carolina and American General Gazette,* Dec. 8, 1775; *Pennsylvania Magazine,* I (1775), 485.

66. *New-York Journal,* Oct. 26, 1775.

67. Lord Dunmore, Address to the Borough of Norfolk, Oct. 3, 1775, in *Rev. Va.,* IV, 161–162, also published in *Virginia Gazette* (Purdie), Oct. 13, 1775; Letter from Virginia Delegate, Oct. 16, 1775, *LDC,* II, 193–195, Richard Henry Lee to GW, Philadelphia, Oct. 22, 1775, 229–230. When Dunmore told Dartmouth about the incident, he explained, "I am now going to have a press for the King on board one of the ships" (Dunmore to Dartmouth, HMS *William,* Oct. 5, 1775, in Davies, ed., *Docs. of the Am. Rev.,* XI, 137).

took out an advertisement swearing that he, for one, would not be cowed by Dunmore's "arbitrary power." Holt informed the public in tidewater Virginia that he was "procuring a new set of materials, which, if he should be so fortunate as to succeed in, will enable him once more to apprize his countrymen of the danger they may be in from the machinations and black designs of their common enemy." For more than two months, that public had been agitated by constant stories of slaves' "eloping," being "stolen" off plantations, or being instigated by sinister brokers. What they did not yet know was that Dunmore had other agents operating in other theaters, attempting to extinguish the common cause. On the same day Holt pledged his defiance to the Norfolk reading public, a servant—who, ironically, was also running away from his master—asked to speak with George Washington in Cambridge. His story revealed that, throughout the Squire controversy, Dunmore had also been approving plans to include Ohio Indians in the panoply of proxies to defeat the patriots in Virginia.[68]

About the same time Drayton, Tennent, and Hart traveled to the South Carolina frontier to "explain" the Revolution to Indians and backcountry settlers, militia captain James Wood was also trekking through the Ohio River valley, inviting representatives of the Shawnee, Delaware, Wyandot, and Mingo Indians to a meeting at Fort Pitt in early September. The Ohio Indians, Wood repeatedly noted, were aware of what had occurred in Boston a season earlier. They had their own communication networks. The Wyandots were "much surprised" to hear about war with Britain and about "several engagements at Boston in which a great number of men were killed on both sides." Far down the Ohio, Wood listened while Shawnee leaders informed him they knew all about Dunmore's flight to the Royal Navy for protection. And, he learned to his dismay, it did not take British officials like Cameron or Guy Johnson living among the Indians to spread information that undermined the common cause. Connections at Detroit had told the Delawares that "the people of Virginia were determined to drive us off and to take [their] lands." Worse, Wood noted, the gossip of local loyalists was leaving "bad impressions." He, too, did his best to combat this talk, sending

68. John Hunter Holt to the Public, Norfolk, Oct. 12, 1775, 4 *Am. Archives,* III, 1031; *Virginia Gazette* (Purdie), Oct. 13, 1775. Holt was not able to gain another press during the Revolution, especially after the city of Norfolk burned on January 1, 1776. He did publish the *Virginia Gazette and Independent Chronicle* in Richmond with John Dixon from 1783 to his death in 1787. See Clarence S. Brigham, *History and Bibliography of American Newspapers, 1690–1820* (Worcester, Mass., 1947), II, 1129, 1147.

word back about what he had learned in his travels. Three different reports found their way to printers in Baltimore, Philadelphia, and Williamsburg, and, from there, across North America.[69]

Chief among these whisperers was Dr. John Connolly. Connolly was Dunmore's agent in the border controversy between Pennsylvania and Virginia that sparked war with the Shawnees in 1774. When word reached Pittsburgh of war in Massachusetts, Connolly, ever the governor's man, began to hatch a plan for himself and the Ohio Indians. His vocal loyalism almost got him thrown in prison at several points during that tumultuous summer. For his own safety, Connolly fled to the Chesapeake while Wood was out courting Indians in the Ohio country. Reaching Dunmore in mid-August, Connolly pitched his idea to his benefactor: he would get the Ohio Indians "to act in concert with me against his Majesty's enemies . . . to penetrate through Virginia and join his Excellency, Lord Dunmore, at Alexandria early next

---

69. James Wood, journal, in Reuben Gold Thwaites and Louise Phelps Kellogg, eds., *Revolution on the Upper Ohio, 1775–1777* (Madison, Wis., 1908), 36, 47, 51, 57. Another take on loyalism at Fort Pitt is in Lincoln Macveagh, ed., *The Journal of Nicholas Cresswell, 1774–1777* (New York, 1924), 100. For more, see Randolph C. Downes, *Council Fires on the Upper Ohio* (Pittsburgh, 1940), 180–186; and Larry L. Nelson, *A Man of Distinction among Them: Alexander McKee and the Ohio Country Frontier, 1754–1799* (Kent, Ohio, 1999), 89–95. One report first ran in Dixon and Hunter's *Virginia Gazette*, stating that the Ohio Indians "appear to be friendly . . . but that many of the more western and southwestern tribes seem determined to take up the hatchet against us." See *Virginia Gazette* (Dixon & Hunter), Aug. 26, 1775; *Pennsylvania Journal*, Sept. 6, 1775; *Pennsylvania Gazette*, Sept. 6, 1775; *Rivington's New-York Gazetteer*, Sept. 7, 1775; *New-York Gazette*, Sept. 11, 1775; *Connecticut Journal*, Sept. 13, 1775; *Boston Gazette*, Sept. 18, 1775. A second, longer article originated from *Dunlap's Maryland Gazette*, Aug. 29, 1775. This one confessed that "diabolical artifices had been used by those tools of government, to instigate these savages to attack our frontiers" and was exchanged in fourteen papers. See *New-York Gazette*, Sept. 4, 1775; *Connecticut Journal*, Sept. 6, 1775; *New-York Journal*, Sept. 7, 1775; *Rivington's New-York Gazetteer*, Sept. 7, 1775; *Pennsylvania Mercury*, Sept. 8, 1775; *Pennsylvania Ledger*, Sept. 9, 1775; *Pennsylvania Packet*, Sept. 11, 1775; *New-England Chronicle*, Sept. 7–14, 1775; *Connecticut Gazette*, Sept. 15, 1775; *Virginia Gazette* (Dixon & Hunter), Sept. 16, 1775; *New-Hampshire Gazette*, Sept. 19, 1775; *Massachusetts Spy*, Sept. 20, 1775; *Essex Journal*, Sept. 22, 1775; *Providence Gazette*, Sept. 30, 1775. A third report, which took up an entire page, was Wood's Aug. 10 testimony to the Pittsburgh committee of safety on his return. See *Pennsylvania Evening Post*, Sept. 8, 1775; *Dunlap's Maryland Gazette*, Sept. 11, 1775; *New-York Gazette*, Sept. 18, 1775; *Boston Gazette*, Oct. 2, 1775. Several of these papers printed more than one article from Wood.

"Britain Has Found Means to Unite Us"

spring." Connolly's plot was bold—and frightening. If it was successful, an army of hostile Indians, aggrieved loyalists, emancipated slaves, and British regulars would link up on the Potomac and, in his own words, cut off "the communication between the southern and northern governments," giving "a favorable turn indisputably . . . to his Majesty's affairs in the southern Provinces." Dunmore liked the plan enough that he sent this "active, spirited officer" north to get permission from General Gage.[70]

Connolly had an audience with the commander while Squire's tender still smoldered at Hampton. Not having much military capital to lose by approving the plan, and having just written to Carleton that he should "strain every nerve to rouse both Canadians and Indians," Gage agreed. Turning the operation over to Dunmore, Gage wrote the Virginia governor that he would give "every aid in my power" toward putting Connolly's plan into action. Over the following three days, Gage spun off a series of notes to all interested British agents across the frontier, alerting them that Connolly was on his way with the commander's blessing. Even though letters flew out of Boston in all directions, Gage understood the proposal's combustibility. He concluded his letter to Dunmore with a prescient warning: "The greatest care ought to be taken, that the inclosed letters do not fall into the Rebels' hands."[71]

70. Connolly's biography can be gathered from Clarence M. Burton, "John Connolly: A Tory of the Revolution," *Proceedings of the American Antiquarian Society*, N.S., XX (1909), 70–105; and "A Narrative of the Transactions, Imprisonment, and Sufferings of John Connolly, an American Loyalist and Lieutenant Colonel in His Majesty's Service," republished in five parts in *PMHB*, XII (1888), 310–324, 407–420, XIII (1889), 61–70, 153–167, 281–291. For Connolly's plot, see John Connolly to John Gibson, Portsmouth, Va., Aug. 9, 1775, 4 *Am. Archives*, III, 72; this letter to the Indian trader Gibson also contained Lord Dunmore's letter to Delaware chief Captain White Eyes (72). See also Burton, "John Connolly," *Proceedings of the American Antiquarian Society*, N.S., XX (1909), 17–18; Connolly, "Narrative," *PMHB*, XII (1888), 411; Dunmore to Gage, August 1775, in Thomas Gage Papers, CXXXIV, CL.

Virginia printers made their readers aware of Connolly's meeting with Dunmore: "It is said CONNOLLY, who had so principal a share in the disturbances between some of our frontier inhabitants and the Pennsylvanians, came down last week to L[ord] D[unmore] with a belt from the Shawnese nation of Indians" (*Virginia Gazette, or the Norfolk Intelligencer*, Aug. 16, 1775; also in *Newport Mercury*, Oct. 2, 1775). Two weeks later, they also inserted notice that Connolly had departed for Boston. See *Virginia Gazette* (Dixon & Hunter), Aug. 26, 1775; *Virginia Gazette, or the Norfolk Intelligencer*, Aug. 30, 1775.

71. Gage to Carleton, Boston, Sept. 5, 1775, to Dunmore, Boston, Sept. 10, 1775,

Across the lines in Boston, Gage's opponents did find out about the Connolly plan, but not because a British courier was stopped and searched. William Cowley, Connolly's personal servant, began writing a letter to Washington on the same Saturday that Squire's men packed up Holt's printing office, but he could not find the means to get it to Cambridge. A few days later, when Connolly's southbound ship stopped at Newport, Cowley "left all my clothes and all that I had" and escaped. It would all be worthwhile if he "could be of any service to [his] country," he later affirmed. Cowley approached Washington's headquarters just as it was abuzz with the Church examinations. He explained to the sentries that he "could not be at rest until [he] had disclosed [a] matter" to the commander. He told Washington of Connolly's plans to meet Dunmore at Alexandria and "sweep all the country before him." "A person who has lately been a Servant to Major Connolly, a tool of Lord Dunmore's," Washington wrote to Congress, "has given an Account of a Scheme to distress the Southern Provinces, which appeared to me of sufficient Consequence to be immediately transmitted." Because of the proximity of the rendezvous point, Washington also that day forwarded Cowley's letter to his cousin and plantation manager Lund Washington at Mount Vernon to alert his neighbors.[72]

From these notices, the patriot leadership initiated what passed for an all points bulletin in 1775. Having received Washington's letter on Saturday, October 21, the Virginia delegates to Congress turned around on Monday and—despite a schedule burdened with the preparations for the funeral of colleague and president Peyton Randolph—drafted instructions to the Virginia committee of safety. Informing them of the plot, the delegates instructed the committee to forward a copy to their peers in North Carolina. For his part, Lund forwarded the letter to George Mason, who sent it to the Maryland committee of safety. Through both official and unofficial channels, news was getting out that Dr. Connolly was a dangerous enemy.[73]

---

to Captain Lernoult, Detroit, Sept. 10, 1775, to Carleton, Sept. 10, 1775, to Guy Johnson, Sept. 11, 1775, to Captain Hugh Lord, Illinois, Sept. 12, 1775, to Alexander McKee, Sept. 12, 1775, and to John Stuart, Sept. 12, 1775, all in Gage Papers, CXXXV, CL.

72. "Deposition of William Cowley," *Rev. Va.,* IV, 202–203, and 4 *Am. Archives,* III, 1047–1048; Cowley to GW, Sept. 30, 1775, *PGW: RW,* II, 67–69, GW to John Hancock, Cambridge, Oct. 12, 1775, 148.

73. Receipt of GW's letter at Congress on Oct. 21, 1775, *JCC,* III, 302; Virginia Delegates to Congress to Virginia Committee of Safety, Philadelphia, Oct. 23, 1775,

As Connolly made plans to head west and the news of his plot fanned out, Virginia militia forces began to ready themselves for a clash with his benefactor. When Dunmore learned of men and matériel gathering south of Great Bridge, he ordered Captain Samuel Leslie and about 130 men—including a significant number of slaves who had already joined him—to attack a force of Princess Anne militia at least twice their size near Kemp's Landing on November 14. Leslie's greatly outnumbered men still routed the Virginians, killing seven and capturing eighteen while suffering only a single flesh wound in return. Two of the captured men were colonels, including Joseph Hutchings, apprehended by his own slave who had escaped to the governor. This victory at Kemp's Landing buoyed Dunmore's expectations for success. The performance of runaway slaves also confirmed Dunmore's suspicions that slaves might make effective counter-revolutionary soldiers. A week before, Dunmore had already drafted and printed two proclamations. With the success at Kemp's Landing, he decided to distribute them far and wide. Together, they would send white Virginians, and then colonists throughout North America, reeling.[74]

Dunmore thought his fortunes were fair enough to send out word that he was "raising the king's standard," an action which officially proclaimed Virginia in a state of rebellion, and ordered all loyal subjects to assist in its suppression under penalty of law. But the governor had decided to make the king's standard a beacon for more than loyalists. Dunmore's newfound confidence encouraged him to unsheathe the sword he had rattled in Williamsburg the April before. As soon as word of Kemp's Landing reached him on board the *Fowey*, he issued the fateful declaration on November 14 with which Dunmore's name will forever be associated: "I do hereby declare all indented Servants, Negroes, or others (appertaining to Rebels) free that are able and willing to bear Arms, they joining His Majesty's Troops as soon as

Rev. Va., IV, 262; George Mason to Maryland Committee of Safety, in Robert Rutland, ed., *Papers of George Mason* (Chapel Hill, N.C., 1970), I, 258–259.

74. Michael A. McDonnell, *The Politics of War: Race, Class and Conflict in Revolutionary Virginia* (Chapel Hill, N.C., 2007), 131–132; John E. Selby, *The Revolution in Virginia, 1775–1783* (Williamsburg, Va., 1988), 64; Woody Holton, *Forced Founders: Indians, Debtors, Slaves, and the Making of the American Revolution in Virginia* (Chapel Hill, N.C., 1999), 155; Simon Schama, *Rough Crossings: Britain, the Slaves, and the American Revolution* (New York, 2006), 78–79. For the classic, pathbreaking account of Dunmore's 1775 campaign, see Benjamin Quarles, *The Negro in the American Revolution* (Chapel Hill, N.C., 1961), 19–32.

they may be, for the more speedy reducing this Colony to a proper Sense of their Duty, to his Majesty's Crown and Dignity." Hundreds, if not thousands, of blacks from Virginia, Maryland, and North Carolina would do their best to get to Norfolk.[75]

As word spread that Dunmore had followed through on his threat, Virginians did not suddenly realize that the rebellion was doomed and rally around the governor. From what the patriots have told us, they did just the opposite. For contemporaries then and historians since, alarm followed by backlash has been the standard interpretation that described Virginia's reaction to the proclamation. Traveling through the Shenandoah Valley in late November, Philip Vickers Fithian noted in his journal that Dunmore's "infernal Scheme . . . seems to quicken all in Revolution to overpower him however at every risk." Richard Henry Lee wrote from Philadelphia on November 29, "Lord Dunmore's unparallelled conduct in Virginia has, a few Scotch excepted, united every Man in that large Colony. If Administration had searched thro' the world for a person the best fitted to ruin their cause, and procure union and success for these Colonies, they could not have found a more complete Agent than Lord Dunmore." Jefferson wrote the same day that the governor's actions had "raised the country into a perfect phrensy." Fifteen years later, David Ramsey deepened the backlash thesis: "The injury done the royal cause by the bare proposal of the scheme, far outweighed any advantage that resulted from it. The colonists were struck with horror, and filled with detestation of a government which was exercised in loosening the bands of society." Modern historians have followed this lead, suggesting, "Whatever loyalty there was in Virginia pretty much flickered out with Dunmore's call." That backlash was not an accidental or organic reaction. Although the proclamation was indeed "every white Virginian's nightmare" that sent "shock waves throughout the colony," by the middle of November, it was hardly an innovation. To be sure, Dunmore had taken the unprecedented step of printing the words "free" and "Negroes" in the same sentence, but accusations that royal officials across the South had been whispering such notions to the slaves were months old by then.[76]

75. Dunmore's proclamation, *Rev. Va.*, IV, 334.

76. Entry for Nov. 28, 1775, in Robert Albion and Leonidas Dodson, eds., *Philip Vickers Fithian: Journal, 1775–1776; Written on the Virginia-Pennsylvania Frontier and in the Army around New York* (Princeton, N.J., 1934), 135; Richard Henry Lee to Catherine Macauley, Philadelphia, Nov. 29, 1775, *LDC*, II, 406; TJ to John Randolph, Nov. 29,

In other words, the backlash was managed. Dunmore's proclamation handed the patriots an interesting—if dangerous—opportunity to propagate the cause. For his part, Dunmore hoped the news would spread throughout the upper South. He ordered the proclamation printed on broadsides to disseminate all around the Chesapeake. But he also counted on the news crossing over from print-based information networks into the orally based slave quarter. The potential for the news to be carried across vast distances through these networks was great, as John Adams had recently learned from two Southern slaveowners. In September, Adams listened while two newly arrived delegates briefed him on the "melancholy account of the state of Georgia." "They say that if 1000 regular Troops should land in Georgia and their commander be provided with Arms and Cloaths enough and proclaim Freedom to all the Negroes who would join his Camp," he wrote in his diary, "20,000 Negroes would join it from the two Provinces in a fortnight. The Negroes have a wonderfull Art of communicating Intelligence among themselves. It will run severall hundreds of Miles in a Week or Fortnight." This was what Dunmore was counting on, especially after the military prowess displayed by runaway slaves at Kemp's Landing. Patriots across the upper South wanted to do their best to prevent this type of communication and response from their slaves, but they also wanted to broadcast the news of the "diabolical schemes," as Washington referred to Dunmore's actions—with their own explanation, of course.[77]

Patriot printers made Dunmore's proclamation and its aftermath infamous throughout North America. They amplified the address far more

---

1775, *PTJ*, I, 269; David Ramsey, *History of the American Revolution,* ed. Lester Cohen (1789; rpt. Indianapolis, 1990), I, 233; Robert Middlekauff, *The Glorious Cause: The American Revolution, 1763–1789,* rev. ed. (1982; rpt. New York, 2005), 322. Nightmare: Cassandra Pybus, *Epic Journeys of Freedom: Runaway Slaves of the American Revolution and Their Global Quest for Liberty* (Boston, 2006), 9. "Shock waves": McDonnell, *Politics of War,* 135. For a hyperbolic reading of the effects, see Schama, *Rough Crossings,* 76–77; a more measured analysis is offered in Holton, *Forced Founders,* 157–160.

77. John Adams, diary, Sept. 24, 1775, *LDC,* II, 49–51; GW to Richard Henry Lee, Cambridge, Dec. 26, 1775, *PGW: RW,* II, 611. According to another correspondent, the network that the southern delegates warned Adams about was indeed active and effective in Virginia. Dunmore, an anonymous writer from North Carolina noted in a late December letter to a friend in England, "seized a printing press at Norfolk, which he employs for his own purposes; and, by the means of Negroes, and others, continues to circulate his proclamations and intelligence through the country" (4 *Am. Archives,* IV, 476–477).

than the governor ever could have on his purloined press. The staunchest patriot papers—*Pennsylvania Journal, Massachusetts Spy, Boston Gazette, New-York Journal, Providence Gazette*—and even some of the less radical ones—*Pennsylvania Evening Post* and *Pennsylvania Mercury*—printed the proclamation in full. Others referred to it without publishing the text. In every instance of reprinting except one (*Pennsylvania Mercury*), however, the proclamation was encircled by patriot commentary. The patriots turned to literature to malign Dunmore properly. Alexander Purdie in Williamsburg foreworded his printing of the proclamation with an updated version of one of Shakespeare's invectives from *Macbeth:*

> ——*Not in the legions*
> *Of horrid hell, can a devil more damn'd*
> *In evils, to top D*****e.*

New-York Journal printer John Holt, still upset that the governor produced the order on his nephew's press, inserted a short paragraph signed by "Minos," the judge from Virgil's *Aeneid* and Dante's *Inferno.* Minos opined that since Dunmore was "guilty of at least seven capital crimes . . . it is hoped he will shortly be taken, publickly tried and hanged, as the most atrocious criminal that ever appeared in America."[78]

78. *Pennsylvania Packet,* Dec. 4, 1775; *Connecticut Journal,* Dec. 13, 1775; *New-England Chronicle,* Dec. 7–14, 1775; *Essex Journal,* Dec. 15, 1775; *Norwich Packet,* Dec. 18, 1775. The first two of these papers censored the mention of slaves, saying that Dunmore had called "upon indented servants etc. to join his Majesty's troops." The entire text of Dunmore's proclamation appeared in *Virginia Gazette* (Pinkney), Nov. 23, 1775; *Virginia Gazette* (Purdie), Nov. 24, 1775; *Virginia Gazette* (Dixon & Hunter), Nov. 25, 1775; *Pennsylvania Evening Post,* Dec. 5, 1775; *Pennsylvania Journal,* Dec. 6, 1775; *New-York Journal,* Dec. 7, 1775; *Pennsylvania Mercury,* Dec. 8, 1775; *Massachusetts Spy,* Dec. 15, 1775; *Providence Gazette,* Dec. 23, 1775; *Boston Gazette,* Dec. 25, 1775. "*Not in the legions*": *Virginia Gazette* (Purdie), Nov. 24, 1775. The lines are Macduff's from *Macbeth,* 4.3. Others who exchanged the *Macbeth* lines were *Pennsylvania Journal,* Dec. 6, 1775; *New-York Journal,* Dec. 7, 1775; *Massachusetts Spy,* Dec. 15, 1775; *Providence Gazette,* Dec. 23, 1775; *Boston Gazette,* Dec. 25, 1775.

"Minos" has a strange publishing history. Holt added it to the end of Purdie's version of the proclamation, and three other papers published the entire Holt/Purdie package: *Massachusetts Spy,* Dec. 15, 1775; *Providence Gazette,* Dec. 23, 1775; *Boston Gazette,* Dec. 25, 1775. Three New England papers published the "Minos" paragraph without the telling signature: *New-England Chronicle,* Dec. 7–14, 1775; *Essex Journal,* Dec. 15, 1775; *Norwich Packet,* Dec. 18, 1775. All three of those, however, state that

The most extraordinary editorial comment that was appended to the re-printing of Dunmore's proclamation appeared right away. When John Pink-ney printed the emancipation proclamation in his November 23 issue of the *Virginia Gazette,* it was followed by a singular counterstatement, unique not least because it directly addressed the slaves themselves. Slaves should not heed the call of Dunmore's "cruel declaration," the anonymous writer charged.

> But should there be any amongst the negroes *weak* enough to believe that Lord Dunmore intends to do them a kindness, and *wicked* enough to provoke the fury of the Americans against their defenceless fathers and mothers, their wives, their women and children, let them only consider the difficulty of effecting their escape, and what they must expect to suffer if they fall into the hands of the Americans.

Do not be weak and wicked: this was the striking admonition Virginia patri-ots gave to their slaves. Dropping the facade that slaves were mindless, de-pendent objects, this Virginian asked blacks to "consider." "Be not then, ye negroes, tempted by this proclamation to ruin yourselves. . . . I have con-sidered your welfare, as well of that of the country. Whether you will profit by my advice, I cannot tell; but this I know, that whether we suffer or not, if you desert us, you most certainly will." This remarkable piece laid bare the patriot argument. People who were "sincerely attached to the interest of their country," people who "stand forth in opposition to the arbitrary and oppressive acts of any man, or set of men," people who were "moved by compassion and actuated by sound policy": these were the true patriots, the real Americans. Those who rejected these lofty principles were subject to suffering. A few months later another Virginian would cordon off these "domestic insurrectionists" from "we" who held truths to be self-evident.[79]

"The public, no doubt, will be exceedingly incensed on finding Lord Dunmore has taken into his service, the *very scum* of the country to assist him in his diabolical schemes, against the good people of this government," one widely reprinted letter read. Blacks who wished to make good on Dun-

---

the "Minos" paragraph calling for Dunmore's execution was "taken from a late Wil-liamsburg paper." I cannot find that article originating in Williamsburg but instead in the *New-York Journal.*

79. *Virginia Gazette* (Pinkney), Nov. 23, 1775. The address ran in the other two papers over the next two days. See *Virginia Gazette* (Purdie), Nov. 24, 1775; *Virginia Gazette* (Dixon & Hunter), Nov. 25, 1775.

more's offer found the avenue treacherous, indeed. White Virginians immediately threw up an extensive dragnet to prevent as many slaves as they could from reaching the governor. Keeping watch over the countless rivers and creeks, whites attempted to curb the appeal of Dunmore's promise by vowing draconian punishment for all they captured. As if the dragnet were not difficult enough, runaways also had to contend with the problem of finding the governor.[80]

In a letter to Richard Henry Lee, Edmund Pendleton anxiously surveyed the slaves' reaction to Dunmore's proclamation. "Letters mention that slaves Flock to him in abundance," Pendleton wrote on November 27, "but I hope it is Magnified." Those who paid attention to patriot newspapers, however, learned that Pendleton's earnest wish was illusory. Most printed Dunmore's proclamation alongside a series of articles taken from the *Virginia Gazette* that added meaning to the November declaration. One often-reprinted (and italicized) selection reported, *"Since Lord Dunmore's proclamation made its appearance, it is said he has recruited his army . . . to the amount of about 2000 men, including his black regiment, which is thought to be a considerable part, with this inscription on their breasts:—Liberty to Slaves."* This information, including what looked at first glance like insignificant accounts of raiding parties and tiny boats of runaways on Chesapeake rivers, was far from trifling in the uncertain context of 1775. How blacks responded to Dunmore's proclamation was a development to which readers paid close attention—or, at least, patriot leaders hoped they would.[81]

80. Printers did their professional best to emphasize the words "very scum" for their readers. Some used italics, others all capital letters. See *Virginia Gazette* (Purdie), Nov. 17, 1775; *Pennsylvania Evening Post*, Nov. 28, 1775; *Maryland Journal*, Nov. 29, 1775; *New-York Journal*, Nov. 30, 1775; *Pennsylvania Mercury*, Dec. 1, 1775; *Connecticut Courant*, Dec. 4, 1775; *New-York Gazette*, Dec. 4, 1775; *Connecticut Journal*, Dec. 6, 1775; *Boston Gazette*, Dec. 11, 1775; *Maryland Journal*, Dec. 13, 1775; *New-England Chronicle*, Dec. 14, 1775.

81. Pendleton's letter appended to Richard Henry Lee's letter to GW, Dec. 6, 1775, *PGW: RW*, II, 500. *"Liberty to Slaves"* ran in 20 papers: *Virginia Gazette* (Dixon & Hunter), Dec. 2, 1775; *Pennsylvania Evening Post*, Dec. 12, 1775; *Pennsylvania Gazette*, Dec. 13, 1775; *Pennsylvania Journal*, Dec. 13, 1775; *Maryland Gazette*, Dec. 14, 1775; *Pennsylvania Mercury*, Dec. 15, 1775; *Pennsylvania Ledger*, Dec. 16, 1775; *Constitutional Gazette*, Dec. 16, 1775; *New-York Gazette*, Dec. 18, 1775; *Connecticut Journal*, Dec. 20, 1775; *New-York Journal*, Dec. 21, 1775; *North-Carolina Gazette*, Dec. 22, 1775; *Connecticut Gazette*, Dec. 22, 1775; *Providence Gazette*, Dec. 23, 1775; *Newport Mercury*, Dec. 25, 1775; *Norwich Packet*, Dec. 25, 1775; *New-England Chronicle*, Dec. 21–28, 1775;

"Britain Has Found Means to Unite Us"

Consider the language with which reporters from the scene (mostly militia officers) described the groups they encountered. When the militia from Virginia and North Carolina skirmished with Dunmore's troops, the groups were mostly classified by color—and blacks nearly always outnumbered whites. Witnesses categorized Dunmore's forces, never forgetting to mention the large number of blacks in his ranks, usually accompanied by a snide reference to his "Royal Regiment of Black Fusileers" or the "Queen's Own Black Regiment." "Last Tuesday night," Colonel Woodford related, "a party of men, *chiefly blacks,* from a tender came up to Mr. Benjamin Wells's . . . pillaged his house of everything valuable, such as bedding, wearing apparel, liquors, a watch, a stock of poultry, and carried off two Negro girls." Reportage of another clash used similar language. "Since my last, we have sent a party of 100 men . . . over the river, who fell in last night, about 12 o'clock with a guard of about thirty men, *chiefly Negroes.*" Casualty reports were also skewed toward giving the impression that surely exaggerated the number of fugitive slaves in Dunmore's ranks. The above skirmish ended with the comment, "We killed one, burnt another in the house, and took two prisoners (all blacks) with four exceeding fine muskets, and defeated the guard." "We have been well informed," Lt. Colonel Scott wrote in the *Pennsylvania Gazette,* "that we killed sixteen Negroes and five white men the first day we got to this place." Accounts of raiding parties throughout 1776 also carefully counted the number of black participants. With all the incidental references to "all black" raiding parties, skirmishes with groups that were "chiefly Negroes," and notices of open boats full of runaways, American readers probably took away from their newspapers a similar image that their commander in chief had privately expressed: the situation in Virginia was akin to a very dangerous rolling snowball.[82]

Essex Journal, Dec. 29, 1775; *New-Hampshire Gazette,* Jan. 2, 1776; *Massachusetts Gazette,* Jan. 4, 1776; *New York Packet,* Jan. 4, 1776.

82. *Virginia Gazette* (Pinkney), Dec. 9, 1775; *Pennsylvania Gazette,* Dec. 13, 20, 1775; *Maryland Gazette,* Dec. 14, 1775; *Pennsylvania Mercury,* Dec. 15, 1775; *New-York Gazette,* Dec. 18, 1775; *Pennsylvania Evening Post,* Dec. 19, 1775; *Connecticut Journal,* Dec. 20, 1775, Jan. 3, 1776; *North-Carolina Gazette,* Dec. 22, 1775; *Pennsylvania Packet,* Dec. 25, 1775; *Newport Mercury,* Dec. 25, 1775; *New-York Journal,* Dec. 28, 1775; *Norwich Packet,* Jan. 1, 1776; *Connecticut Gazette,* Jan. 5, 1776; *Massachusetts Spy,* Jan. 5, 1776; *New-Hampshire Gazette,* Jan. 9, 1776. Washington referred to Dunmore's actions as a "snow Ball in rolling" in a December 27 letter to Richard Henry Lee; see *PGW: RW,* II, 611. But the slaves were not to blame for this anarchy in tidewater Virginia. While patriot leaders paid close attention to the number and actions of run-

The first notices about Dunmore's proclamation began to appear in print in late November, right at the same time that Dr. John Connolly found himself surrounded by forewarned patriot militiamen in western Maryland. It had been a few weeks since Washington had dispatched riders to Congress armed with William Cowley's information that Connolly was plotting to lead an Indian force east from the Ohio Valley to meet up with Dunmore's (now mostly black) men in Alexandria.

As it turned out, Cowley's information proved ineffective in helping catch his former master. The servant thought Connolly was planning to get to Detroit by going to Saint Augustine and, from there, through the interior. Instead, Connolly resolved to take the "shortest way through Maryland." Traveling with Allen Cameron and Dr. John Smyth, two officers of his proposed Indian and tory regiment, Connolly set off from Virginia the day before the engagement at Kemp's Landing. A week later, as the group rested outside Hagerstown, Maryland, one man who had served under Connolly as a private in Pittsburgh recognized him. In the middle of the night on November 19, a group of Maryland militia broke into their rooms and, according to Smyth, "without the least provocation abused us perpetually with every opprobrious epithet language can afford."[83]

----

away blacks, they largely kept their accusatory eye on the "Virginia Negro Thief" himself. As they had done with Martin, Collet, Stuart, and Campbell, polemicists found much more political benefit in attacking Dunmore's character and reputation than in focusing on the runaway slaves. Often, they did so by conflating the two. For example, in mid-1776, several papers reported "a lusty likely *Negro Wench* was delivered of a male child, who, in memory of a certain notable *Negro Chief,* is named DUNMORE." Feeling sorry for the child, the report concluded that "tho' an act of justice to Dunmore," this was name was perhaps too cruel "to the innocent negro." A close reading of these items suggests African Americans were not themselves to blame, but they were still guilty by association. "Virginia Negro Thief": *New-York Journal,* Jan. 11, 1776; *Pennsylvania Ledger,* Jan. 20, 1776; *Constitutional Gazette,* Jan. 20, 1776; *Connecticut Journal,* Jan. 24, 1776; *Maryland Gazette,* Jan. 25, 1776; *New-England Chronicle,* Jan. 25–Feb. 1, 1776; *Virginia Gazette* (Purdie), Feb. 2, 1776; *Virginia Gazette* (Dixon & Hunter), Feb. 3, 1776. *"Negro Wench"*: *Connecticut Journal,* May 15, 1776; *Newport Mercury,* May 20, 1776; *New-York Journal,* May 23, 1776; *Virginia Gazette* (Purdie), May 24, 1776; *Massachusetts Spy,* May 24, 1776; *Virginia Gazette* (Dixon & Hunter), May 25, 1776; *New-England Chronicle,* May 23–30, 1776; *Freeman's Journal,* June 8, 1776.

83. Cowley deposition, *PGW: RW,* II, 67–68; Connolly, "Narrative," *PMHB,* XII (1888), 411; John Frederick Dalziel Smyth, *A Tour in the United States of America*

"Britain Has Found Means to Unite Us"

The captives were taken to Frederick to appear before the local committee. Even though Connolly had taken pains to hide his papers in his saddle, thorough searches turned up part of a piece of paper containing his proposal to Gage, a damning bit of evidence that bound them over for further incarceration. After a month in town, a grateful Congress wrote to the Frederick committee requesting they send the three prisoners to Philadelphia. Arriving on New Year's Day, 1776, Connolly observed that they were greeted in the city by a "drum beating the rogue's march." Chances are, had he entered any city in America that day, Connolly would have met with a similar reception.[84]

During the month Connolly, Cameron, and Smyth sat in the Frederick jail, news of their arrest in Hagerstown had spread across the continent. Not all the details were clear, but that did not stop patriots from publicizing the scheme. Williamsburg printer John Pinkney broke the story only three days after the fact. By the first days of December, all but one of the six Philadelphia papers had published it. Within a week, New York and Maryland prints

---

(London, 1784), II, 252–253. Allen Cameron has often been confused with the aforementioned Alexander Cameron, Stuart's deputy in the Carolina backcountry. People at the time confused them (George Mason) and historians since have also (Woody Holton). It is probable that Allen and Alexander were related. Connolly's "Narrative" does not help either, referring to Allen Cameron as "having acted as agent under the honorable John Stuart" (Connolly, "Narrative," *PMHB,* XII [1888], 412). See Mason ("Cameron I take to be the Deputy Indian agent to the Southward") to Maryland Committee of Safety, Nov. 29, 1775, *Rev. Va.,* IV, 491, and Holton, *Forced Founders,* 163.

84. Connolly's papers were secreted away in the "pillion sticks" of his saddle. At first, they eluded the Frederick committee. A loyal servant got rid of the pillion sticks and tried to hide the Gage proposal, which "had been wrapped round a stick of black ball by my servant, so soiled and besmearched." Unfortunately, Connolly said, the Frederick committee was "as industrious as they were suspicious" and found the manuscript. In Massachusetts, Cowley and another informant (one of the ship captains who had transported Connolly to Boston) told Washington about the hiding place, and the general exchanged several letters with Congress about the hidden papers. See Connolly, "Narrative," *PMHB,* XII (1888), 415, 418; Smyth, *Tour in the U.S.,* II, 254–256. For correspondence between Washington and Congress on the Connolly evidence, see Hancock to GW, Philadelphia, Dec. 2, 1775, *PGW: RW,* II, 469, Richard Henry Lee to GW, Philadelphia, Dec. 6, 1775, 500–501, GW to Hancock, Cambridge, Dec. 25, 1775, 601, GW to Lee, Cambridge, Dec. 26, 1775, 610–613, Hancock to GW, Philadelphia, Jan. 30, 31, 1776, III, 215–218.

had picked it up, followed by New England prints the next week. By the time Connolly was settling into his new accommodations in the Philadelphia jail, nearly two-thirds of active papers in nearly every American province had featured at least one account about Connolly, Dunmore, and the plot to involve the Ohio Indians.[85]

"Thus you see," the most widely reprinted account concluded, "a part of the diabolical scheme is defeated." Indeed, the timing of Connolly's capture only multiplied public outrage at Dunmore's "diabolical scheme," which was now known to have several remarkable facets. The news from western Maryland merged with that of the Chesapeake in December. It seemed that Dunmore and his superiors would stop at nothing to destroy colonial liberty; at least, that was the conclusion patriots wanted the public to reach. Some audiences were very receptive to this message. During the late fall, another round of runaway slave scares had encouraged patriots in South Carolina to take preemptive actions at the same time that Virginians were battling Dunmore.[86]

85. Many papers ran multiple reports about the story. One of Connolly's letters to the west—written to Indian trader John Gibson and laying the groundwork for the expedition—had already surfaced in a few papers before the Hagerstown arrest, one factor Connolly himself attributed to his eventual fate. See *Virginia Gazette,* Nov. 10, 1775; *Maryland Journal,* Nov. 22, 1775; *Pennsylvania Evening Post,* Nov. 25, 1775. Reports of the arrest: *Virginia Gazette* (Pinkney), Nov. 23, Dec. 16, 1775; *Virginia Gazette* (Purdie), Dec. 1, 1775; *Pennsylvania Mercury,* Dec. 1, 1775; *Pennsylvania Evening Post,* Dec. 2, 12, 23, 1775; *Pennsylvania Ledger,* Dec. 2, 1775; *Pennsylvania Packet,* Dec. 4, 25, 1775; *Pennsylvania Gazette,* Dec. 6, 27, 1775; *Constitutional Gazette,* Dec. 6, 30, 1775; *Maryland Gazette,* Dec. 7, 1775; *New-York Journal,* Dec. 14, 1775; *Essex Journal,* Dec. 15, 1775; *Massachusetts Spy,* Dec. 15, 1775; *Virginia Gazette* (Dixon & Hunter), Dec. 16, 1775; *Connecticut Journal,* Dec. 20, 1775; *Maryland Journal,* Dec. 20, 1775; *Newport Mercury,* Dec. 25, 1775; *Pennsylvania Journal,* Dec. 27, 1775; *New-York Gazette,* Jan. 1, 1776; *South-Carolina and American General Gazette,* Jan. 5, 1776; *Norwich Packet,* Jan. 8, 15, 1776; *Pennsylvania Magazine,* I (1775), 583–584. Missed details included Connolly's holding a "considerable sum in specie" when caught, and Cameron's name being "Campbell"—a tantalizing error that leads one to wonder whether the earlier October story that connected South Carolina governor William Campbell and Alexander Cameron had any influence.

86. By November, enough slaves had run to the British naval squadron off Charleston Harbor that it touched off a confrontation between Captain Edward Thornbrough, commander of the HMS *Tamar,* and the Charleston Council of Safety. In a replay of the confrontation in Hampton over the fate of pilot Joseph Harris, the Charleston council informed Captain Thornbrough on October 28 that they had "received information that a Negro Man named Shadwell, a Mariner by profes-

"Britain Has Found Means to Unite Us"

The military success that Dunmore thought his proclamation would bring did not materialize. Two weeks after Dunmore marched into Norfolk and fortified his position, a sizable patriot militia under the command of Colonel William Woodford gathered near Great Bridge on the Elizabeth River, twelve miles south of Norfolk. Woodford's troops, numbering 700, engaged Dunmore's men on December 9, killing 17 and wounding 49. Five days later, Woodford and his victorious force, now swelled to 1,275, marched unopposed into Norfolk. With Virginia troops taking the town, Dunmore quickly evacuated onto his gubernatorial sloop and, rather than allow the city and its resources to be available to his rebellious enemies, bombarded Norfolk on January 1, 1776. His loyalist base of operations lost, Dunmore's remaining eight months of tenure in Virginia would be mainly at sea. Accompanied by as many loyalists and emancipated slaves as he could fit on board, the governor's swollen fleet—known derisively as the "floating town"—stayed out on Chesapeake Bay for the first half of 1776. Dunmore's proclamation did not result in the military advantage its author imagined it would. Far from the Chesapeake, however, the military consequences of his proclamation were still being felt.[87]

* * *

By November, the men in the Cambridge camp were bored. Except for small skirmishes between pickets and scouts across the lines, there had been no fighting in Massachusetts since Bunker Hill six long months ago. One ob-

_____

sion, . . . is employed on board." "As the said Negro is a runaway," they commanded, "and as harbouring him is highly penal and the carrying such a one off the Colony Felony by the laws of this Country . . . we think it necessary to give you this intimation, in order that the Negro be delivered to his lawful owner." Not wishing for Thornbrough's immediate response to be cannon salvos, the committee softened their accusation, claiming they were not "insinuating that you Sir, give any encouragement for Slaves to leave their Masters." However, the suggestion that the captain was a felon was a serious charge. Thornbrough reacted accordingly. According to the messenger, the captain "appeared angry at the contents of the letter [and] declared his astonishment and concern that any Gentleman could Suspect that any runaway Negro could be on board his Sloop." Thornbrough threatened that if Charleston leaders did not treat him or his men fairly, he would shut the port. See Council of Safety to Edward Thornbrough, Oct. 28, 1775, *PHL*, X, 504–505. See also Ryan, *World of Thomas Jeremiah*, 98–99; Krawczynski, *William Henry Drayton*, 198–205.

87. Adele Hast, *Loyalism in Revolutionary Virginia: The Norfolk Area and the Eastern Shore* (Ann Arbor, Mich., 1982), 55.

server of the Continental army—"as dirty a set of mortals as ever disgraced the name of soldier"—concluded in early November, "The soldiers in general are most heartily sick of the service, and I believe it would be with the utmost difficulty that they could be prevailed upon to serve in another campaign." He was right: General Charles Lee pleaded with the Adams cousins in mid-November that it was "absolutely necessary" they

> should without delay repair to this Province, the affairs of which are really in a most alarming if not frightful situation. There seems to be a dearth or at least a total stagnation of all public virtue amongst your Countrymen. . . . If you therefore or some good Genius do not fly and anticipate the impending evil, God knows what may be the effects. I conjure You therefore. . . . You and your Friend Samuel have ever been their prime conductors—and unless they have from time to time a rub of their prime conductors no electrical fire can be struck out of 'em.

Making matters worse, enlistments were starting to run out. Washington saw this as the first significant opportunity to achieve his goal of establishing the army on a more professional footing. Washington sought to redistribute officers so they did not command units from their own colonies; he widened the social and economic distinctions between officers and enlisted men; and, convinced the men were paid well enough and that they were there because "the cause of liberty is undoubtedly the cause of all," he rejected the need for a reenlistment bounty.[88]

88. Benjamin Thompson, *Stopford-Sackville Manuscripts,* Great Britain Historical Manuscripts Commission, II, 15–18, quoted in Henry Steele Commager and Richard B. Morris, eds., *The Spirit of Seventy-Six: The Story of the American Revolution as Told by Its Participants* (New York, 1958), 153–154; Charles Lee to JA, Cambridge, Nov. 19, 1775, *PJA,* III, 311–312; Don Higginbotham, *The War of American Independence: Military Attitudes, Policies, and Practice, 1763–1789* (1971; rpt. Boston, 1983), 57–80; David Hackett Fischer, *Washington's Crossing* (New York, 2004), 12–29; James Kirby Martin and Mark Edward Lender, *A Respectable Army: The Military Origins of the Republic, 1763–1789* (Wheeling, Ill., 1982), 15–20, 40–48; "Address from the General Officers to the Soldiery of the Grand Continental Army," Nov. 24, 1775, 4 *Am. Archives,* III, 1666–1667. For more on conditions in the Cambridge camp and the problem of discipline, see Holly A. Mayer, *Belonging to the Army: Camp Followers and Community during the American Revolution* (Columbia, S.C., 1996), 30–84; Caroline Cox, *A Proper Sense of Honor: Service and Sacrifice in George Washington's Army* (Chapel Hill, N.C., 2004), 37–117; Charles Royster, *A Revolutionary People at War: The Continen-*

His intentions began to backfire almost immediately. Several thousand men from Connecticut regiments made plans to walk away from the Revolution when their enlistments ran out on December 1. They decided that they did not want to fight under officers from Rhode Island or Massachusetts, they were angry that they were going to be paid on a calendar schedule instead of a lunar one as they were accustomed (and thus be paid twelve times per year instead of thirteen), and they flatly stated they would not stay without a bounty. Washington and his staff were furious. The commander snarled about the "mercenary spirit [that] pervades the whole." "Could I have foreseen what I have experienced, and am likely to experience," he admitted, "no consideration upon earth should have induced me to accept this command." Washington reported to Congress of the "egregious want of publick spirit which reigns here. Instead of pressing to be engaged in the cause of their Country, which I vainly flattered myself would be the case, I find we are likely to be deserted at a most critical time."[89]

Congress, for its part, was busy dealing with its own pressing needs of union; the delegates were still laboring to get settlers from Connecticut and Pennsylvania to stop threatening to kill one another, and still so worried about the potential disaffection of backcountry North Carolina that they dedicated a small amount of their tiny budget to send two Presbyterian ministers south to appeal to the former Regulators in person. Washington's report reached Philadelphia around the same moment the express rider from Northampton County, Virginia, turned up to alert them to Dunmore's proclamation—and to file subscriptions for the *Pennsylvania Journal*. This rider was just one more sudden arrival that changed everything that season. After they had calmed down, the delegates promised to take up the Virginia question.[90]

tal Army and American Character, 1775–1783 (Chapel Hill, N.C., 1979), 58–63; Martin and Lender, *A Respectable Army*, 34–41.

89. Massachusetts General Court to Massachusetts Delegates at Congress, Watertown, Dec. 5, 1775, 4 *Am. Archives*, IV, 194–195; GW to Joseph Reed, Cambridge, Nov. 28, 1775, *PGW: RW*, II, 449, GW to John Hancock, Cambridge, Nov. 28, 1775, 446. On the centrality of the lunar cycle in colonial life, see John Demos, *Circles and Lines: The Shape of Life in Early America* (Cambridge, Mass., 2004), 1–24, esp. 8–9.

90. For Congress's dealing with the Wyoming dispute, see *JCC*, III, 376–377. Despite all their missives appealing to the Wyoming rivals to put their differences aside while there was war with Britain, the crisis was deepening in the last weeks of 1775. See Charles Stewart to Governor Penn, Ringwood, Dec. 13, 1775, 4 *Am. Archives*, IV,

In Cambridge, Washington and his officers did their best to keep Connecticut men in the ranks. According to General Nathanael Greene, all appeals to Yankee patriotism were failing. "Where is that Enthusiastic Love of Liberty that has ever been the distinguished Characteristic of a New Englandman?" he wrote to a fellow patriot leader in Rhode Island. "If neither the Love of Liberty nor dread of Slavery will rouse them from the present stupid state they are in, and they obstinately persist in quitting the Service, they will deserve the curses of the present and future Generations to the latest ages." This "infamous desertion" imperiled colonial unity and made New England appear a "laughing stock" to the world: "We shall receive the curses of all the Southern Governments, [and] New England will be held in detestation and Abhorrence in every part of the Globe. We that have boasted so loud of our private Virtue and public spirit, not to have the very Vital principles of liberty. We have been considered a brave and spirited people, but without a great alteration we shall be as contemptible as we ever were honorable." Essays in Samuel and Ebenezer Hall's *New-England Chronicle* made similar public calls for the soldiers to remember the cause. Those printers even inserted a letter from "a mother to her only son, a soldier in the Connecticut troops at Roxbury." This Connecticut "mother" shamed her son into putting "a quarrel about calendar months, lunar months, poll taxes, and I do not know what" ahead of "your country, when she stands most in need of your aid." "Your sister Lucy bids you stay, and I conjure you not to return; you will meet with nothing but scorn and ridicule if you attempt it," this Spartan mother — or, more likely, the Hall brothers — wrote. When these pleas fell short, one of the inundated enlisted men, Simeon Lyman, wrote in his journal that the officers were starting to lose their tempers. Charles Lee cursed and swore at them "and said that if we would not stay he would order us to go on Bunker Hill and if we would not go he would order the riflemen to fire at us." Despite Lee's threats, Lyman and about six

––––––
251–252, "Letter to the Governour [John Penn] from Northumberland," Dec. 30, 1775, IV, 1473. On December 18 and 20, New York delegate Richard Smith wrote in his diary that most of those two days were "spent on the Wyoming Dispute," which ended in a vote for Connecticut. "The Delegates of Penns[ylvania] were very angry and discontented with this Determination of Congress," he wrote (*LDC*, II, 494, 500–501, esp. 501); for the resolves, see *JCC*, III, 439–440. For November 28 resolutions concerning North Carolina, see *JCC*, III, 388. Rider carrying news of Dunmore's proclamation: Northampton County (Virginia) Committee to President of Congress, Nov. 25, 1775, *Rev. Va.*, IV, 467–469, esp. 468.

thousand of his fellow citizen soldiers did march home over the first ten days of December. It is remarkable that the British command did not find out about this turmoil and discover a way to exploit the substantial gaps in the line. The emergency was so great that Washington was forced to call out the Massachusetts minutemen again. They responded in enough numbers that by December 10, the crisis was averted.[91]

That several thousand men abandoned the common cause at such a moment suggests that the appeal the patriots had crafted in 1775 did not matter much to their calculus after all. Money—when it was to be given, how much, and by whom—not liberty, drove men's decisions about participating in the war, even at this early and perilous stage. It is difficult for the historian not to adopt the attitude of Greene, Lee, and Washington: given that Dunmore was "like a snow Ball in rolling" in the Chesapeake, how could they walk away?[92]

The problem was that they did not yet know about what was going on in the South. From their perspective, the war was going well, so well that Providence was surely on their side. So far, the frontiers and plantations had not been gruesome theaters of bloodshed. Patriots had foiled loyalist plots and exposed spies. Many of those who had been away from their Connecticut farms since late April probably would agree with one South Carolina patriot leader that the events of 1775 were a "great reason to bless God, for all his abundant mercies." Even with all the various British agents had tried—including "call[ing] in Savages to ravage our frontiers, to massacre our defenceless women and children, offer[ing] every incitement to our Slaves to rebel and murder their masters, ravage and burn our unfortified sea-coast"—not only did the rebellion survive, but the union flourished. "The people

91. Nathanael Greene to Nicholas Cooke, Prospect Hill, Massachusetts, Nov. 29, 1775, *PNG*, I, 154–155. For similar letters, see Lemuel Robinson to JA, Nov. 30, 1775, *PJA*, III, 330–332, Samuel Osgood, Jr., to JA, Roxbury, Nov. 30, 1775, 328–330, James Warren to JA, Watertown, Dec. 3, 1775, 345–349, esp. 346, Elbridge Gerry to JA, Watertown, Dec. 4, 1775, 349–351; *New-England Chronicle*, Dec. 7–14, 1775 (see also Nov. 30, 1775); "Journal of Simeon Lyman of Sharon, August 10 to December 28, 1775," Connecticut Historical Society, *Collections*, VII (Hartford, Conn., 1899), 111–133, esp. 129. For more on Greene's attitudes, see Terry Golway, *Washington's General: Nathanael Greene and the Triumph of the American Revolution* (New York, 2005).

92. For Washington's use of the snowball metaphor, see GW to Joseph Reed, Cambridge, Dec. 15, 1775, *PGW: RW*, II, 553, and a December 27 letter to Richard Henry Lee on 611.

so earnestly pressed to attack us, refusing every act, every force; our Indians keeping up peace, against all acts used to detach them from us, by lies, calumnies, and interest. Our Slaves remaining faithful—against the promise even of liberty, dearest-best-of all rewards. . . . Could our most sanguine hopes, have gone so far last spring?" The writer did not know what Dunmore had proclaimed five days earlier, and that might have curbed his zeal.[93]

It might have made a difference in Cambridge, too. Samuel Ward thought so. Ward, one of Rhode Island's delegates, wrote that the "news from Virginia . . . is alarming and if it had arrived before the Resolve against a Bounty would I think have helped us in that question." He meant that Dunmore's activities in the Chesapeake might have softened Washington's stance against a bounty. He was probably right. But the dire news might have had an even broader effect: numbers of New England troops might have reconsidered leaving the camp. Reports that verified Dunmore's proclamation reached Philadelphia at the height of the Connecticut controversy, but they had not yet traveled to Cambridge. The last accounts from points south that literate soldiers in the camp read about the conflict were that things were under control. A calming letter from Charleston—which concluded that Carolinians were under "no apprehensions from their negroes" and that the backcountry was stable—might have stoked their desires to go home. It would not be until the last days of December that the reports of significant numbers of slaves flocking to Dunmore were published in Massachusetts. If the enlistments were up a month later, on January 1, some might have reconsidered their flight. By then, the "dangerous Storm . . . gathering in the South" might have given some rank-and-file patriots pause. It certainly did for their leaders. The assurances that all was well, born out of anxiety, almost ended the Revolution. Their bravado nearly cost them everything.[94]

In the last weeks of 1775, the effects of Dunmore's proclamation, aided

93. Thomas Lynch to Ralph Izard, Philadelphia, Nov. 19, 1775, *LDC*, II, 363.

94. Samuel Ward to Henry Ward, Philadelphia, Dec. 2, 1775, *LDC*, II, 429. The extract of a letter from Charleston appeared in seven of the nine papers closest to the camp. See *Connecticut Courant*, Nov. 13, 1775; *Connecticut Gazette*, Nov. 17, 1775; *Massachusetts Spy*, Nov. 17, 1775; *Boston Gazette*, Nov. 20, 1775; *Newport Mercury*, Nov. 20, 1775; *Connecticut Journal*, Nov. 22, 1775; *Essex Journal*, Nov. 24, 1775. The last significant news from Williamsburg that reached New England by the end of November was the fight between Matthew Squire and the people of Hampton over Joseph Harris. "Dangerous Storm": Connecticut Delegates to Jonathan Trumbull, Sr., Philadelphia, Dec. 5, 1775, *LDC*, II, 440.

by patriot printers who broadcast it to impugn its author, were difficult to deny. Virginians at the highest level of patriot organizations wrung their hands from a distance. Washington received reports from the vulnerable Mount Vernon and read the Virginia papers, but there was little he could do from Massachusetts. Having already weathered several internal storms (but little gunfire) brought on by Benjamin Church, John Connolly, and a wholesale abandonment by the majority of his men, by the middle of December Washington was less than sanguine about the Revolution's future. "If the Virginians are wise," he wrote to Joseph Reed,

> that Arch Traitor to the Rights of Humanity, Lord Dunmore, should be instantly crushd, if it takes the force of the whole Colony to do it. Otherwise, like a snow Ball in rolling, his army will get size—some through Fear—some through promises—and some from Inclination joining his standard—But that which renders the measure indispensably necessary, is, the Negroes; for if he gets formidable, numbers of them will be tempted to join who will be afraid to do it without.

In the private letters and newspaper accounts that express riders carried over wet December roads at the end of that inimitable year, the phrase "slaves flock" to Dunmore recurred again and again. The widespread circulation of stories about slaves going to Dunmore in boats, taking part in raids, or being captured on their way magnified impressions of mass desertions. Uncertainty was also a factor. No one knew at that moment just how many slaves had reached Dunmore, how many were running to the king's standard, or how many more were planning to escape. Printed accounts suggested that scores were in motion. Lund Washington identified another reason why white colonists were worried. Sending word that one of George's slaves, a painter, had run to the governor, he allowed himself the ultimate confession: "Liberty is sweet." White Virginians did their best to stop Mount Vernon's painter and hundreds of others through persuasion and redoubled patrols, but the wave was strong.[95]

Local committees and provincial authorities far from Virginia witnessed its effects. On December 14, as the text of Dunmore's proclamation was

95. Lund Washington to GW, Mount Vernon, Dec. 3, 1775, *PGW: RW*, II, 479, Lund Washington to GW, Mount Vernon, Dec. 17, 1775, 570, GW to Joseph Reed, Cambridge, Dec. 15, 1775, 553; John Page to TJ, Williamsburg, Nov. 24, 1775, *PTJ*, I, 265, Robert Carter Nicholas to Virginia Delegates in Congress, Williamsburg, Nov. 25, 1775, 266.

making its way through patriot print networks, the Maryland Convention resolved to post a guard on the estate of a suspected Worcester County loyalist so as "to prevent the Negroes on the said Estate being carried out of this Province" and into the governor's ranks. On that same Thursday, the South Carolina committee of safety approved an attack on Sullivan's Island, a remote sandbar on the edge of Charleston Harbor. In previous years, captains of incoming slave ships would quarantine their cargo before bringing them into the city for sale, but it had become a "den for runaway slaves, who were encouraged and protected by the people belonging to the ships." Approximately sixty soldiers dressed up as Indians and attacked the maroon camp on Sullivan's, killing four blacks and capturing eleven, including three British sailors. The "Indian Rangers" burned down the remaining structures and dispersed the remaining population. The committee justified the attack on the "alarming evil" posed by the "villains," "banditti," and "wretches" on Sullivan's as the best way "to humble our Negroes in general and perhaps to mortify his Lordship [Campbell] not a little."[96]

At that same moment, David Owen, "a person suspected of inlisting Negroes," was sent to the workhouse after the Pennsylvania committee of safety found his explanations wanting. In New York, too, a Long Island man had just finished testifying before the Provincial Congress about the "disaffection of sundry people in Queen's County, and of a suspicion that they

96. 4 *Am. Archives,* IV, 717, "Extract of a Letter to a Gentleman in Philadelphia," dated Charleston, Feb. 7, 1776, 950; "Minutes of the South Carolina Council of Safety," Dec. 14, 1775, in William Bell Clark, ed., *Naval Documents of the American Revolution* (Washington, D.C., 1968–), III, 105; Josiah Smith, Jr., to James Poyas, Jan. 10, 1776, Josiah Smith Letter Book, no. 3018, Southern Historical Collection, The Wilson Library, University of North Carolina at Chapel Hill; "Council of Safety to Richard Richardson," Dec. 19, 1775, *PHL,* X, 576. Actually, the safety committee had tried the week before to send Colonel Moultrie and a militia company to Sullivan's, but they were stymied by a lack of transportation. A second eyewitness reported on Dec. 14 that a "number of slaves belonging to the inhabitants of this town on board some of the ships of war, and on shore upon Sullivan's Island, several of which he knew." The deponent, a schooner captain named Alexander Wylly, also indicted the British navy's complicity in the maroons on Sullivan: "A few days ago, when a report prevailed that they were to be attacked upon Sullivan's Island, they were taken off the shore in boats sent from the ships, and . . . he saw about twenty of them carried on board the schooner seized from him." This corroborating report initiated a second, this time successful, incursion against the maroons. See South Carolina Committee of Safety to Richard Richardson, Charleston, Dec. 19, 1775, *PHL,* X, 576.

"Britain Has Found Means to Unite Us"

had about inlisting Negroes." A dozen residences along the Narragansett Bay were still smoldering after another African American pilot had, earlier that week, "pointed out" to Royal Navy raiders—including two hundred "marines, sailors, and negroes"—which patriot "houses to burn." Finally, the most revealing episode of that singular moment occurred in Philadelphia. Benjamin Towne's issue of the *Pennsylvania Evening Post* from that same Thursday, December 14, reported an encounter between a white woman and a black man on a city street. When she reprimanded him for getting in her way, his impassioned reply laid bare the raw tension that was in the air across North America. "Stay, you damned white bitch, 'till Lord Dunmore and his black regiment come," he allegedly responded, "and then we will see who is to take the wall." It is impossible to know whether this exchange actually occurred or was invented by Towne or one of his contributors. It seemed plausible, given the anxious moment, but more important, it appeared in print—in Pennsylvania, Connecticut, and Virginia—as fact.[97]

The impact of Dunmore's proclamation was significant and immediate. People were paying attention. Leading New England minister Ezra Stiles, for example, closely followed Dunmore's actions from Newport, copying long summaries into his diary from the newspaper reports about blacks fighting with the governor. Observers drew their own conclusions about what the proclamation meant, moreover. Ripples from the war in Virginia, as the above confrontation in Philadelphia shows, shaped colonial attitudes.[98]

Samuel Hopkins, the Newport minister who had recently partnered with Stiles to send two black missionaries to Africa, saw Dunmore's campaign as a powerful opportunity for the patriots. "Does not the conduct of Lord Dunmore, and the ministerialists, in taking the advantage of the slavery practiced among us, and encouraging the slaves to join them, by promising their liberty," he wrote at year's end, "point out the best, if not the only way to defeat them in this, viz., granting freedom to them ourselves, so as

97. 4 *Am. Archives*, IV, 403, 498; Nathanael Greene to Samuel Ward, Sr., Prospect Hill, Dec. 17, 1775; *PNG*, I, 165; Dec. 11, 1775, in Franklin Bowditch Dexter, ed., *The Literary Diary of Ezra Stiles* (New York, 1901), I, 642. "Stay, you": *Pennsylvania Evening Post*, Dec. 14, 1775; *Norwich Packet*, Dec. 25, 1775; *Virginia Gazette* (Purdie), Dec. 29, 1775.

98. Dexter, ed., *Literary Diary of Ezra Stiles*, I, 644 (entry for Dec. 21, 23, 1775), 645 (Jan. 1, 1776), 648 (Jan. 23, 1776), 659 (Jan. 29, 1776). See also Jan. 2, 1776, entry of Robert Honyman Diary, 1776–1782, no. 8417, University of Virginia Library, Charlottesville, 3–5.

to no longer use our neighbor's service without wages, but give them for their labors what is equal and just?" As consistent as Hopkins's logic was, few others wished to follow it. Hopkins was out of step with the ways in which the ground had shifted over the past few months. In the early 1770s, pressure had been building against slavery, but that was before the shooting—and the stories of British instigation—started. A year earlier, Benjamin Rush had predicted that slavery would soon be extinct in North America. Now fears of slave insurrections were at their highest levels in colonial memory, and as that unprecedented year drew to a close, those fears were being realized all over North America. The stories about Lord Dunmore, Matthew Squire, John Collett, Josiah Martin, and Thomas Jeremiah, extensively publicized by patriot leaders, edged antislavery arguments, like those forwarded by Hopkins, to the margins of colonial opinion. In 1776, the Newport minister would write *A Dialogue concerning the Slavery of the Africans,* a pamphlet addressed to the Continental Congress and published in Norwich, but this treatise would be the only major publication about emancipating slaves produced during the war years.[99]

The stories detailing "liberty to slaves" shifted colonial attitudes toward Britain and each other. They galvanized opinion against the crown. As one exasperated Congressman wondered, Did the English people "really imagine . . . that after . . . our Liberties repeatedly invaded—our women and children, driven from their Habitations—our nearest Relatives sacrificed at the Altar of Tyranny, our Slaves emancipated for the express purpose of massacreing their Masters—can they . . . expect that we shall return to our former connection with a forgiving, and cordial Disposition[?]" As we have seen, the last of these, the threat of sponsored slave revolt, was the most terrifying because it had grounded, measurable effects. Patriot leaders had to

99. Samuel Hopkins to Thomas Cushing, Newport, Dec. 29, 1775, *PJA,* III, 389; Hopkins, *A Dialogue concerning the Slavery of the Africans* (Norwich, Conn., 1776), *Early American Imprints,* 14804. Hopkins's next pamphlet on slavery would not be published until 1784. For the mission, see Samuel Hopkins and Ezra Stiles, *To the Public: There Has Been a Design Formed . . . to Send the Gospel to Guinea* (Newport, R.I., 1776), *Early American Imprints,* 14803. For more on Hopkins's antislavery, see David Lovejoy, "Samuel Hopkins: Religion, Slavery, and the Revolution," *NEQ,* XL (1967), 227–243; Samuel Hopkins, "'Some Thoughts on the Subject of Freeing the Negro Slaves in the Colony of Connecticut, Humbly Offered to the Consideration of All Friends of Liberty and Justice,' by Levi Hart," ed. John Saillant, *New England Quarterly,* LXXV (2002), 107–128; Catherine A. Brekus, *Sarah Osborn's World: The Rise of Evangelical Christianity in Early America* (New Haven, Conn., 2013), 284–288, 309–315.

react to African Americans in their neighborhoods taking similar actions. And, at the Cambridge camp, again, the news from Virginia shaped Washington's construction of the Continental army.[100]

Throughout the several months since Washington had taken command, he had convened multiple conferences to determine the present and future makeup of the ranks. At every turn, Washington and his generals had voted unanimously to reject free and enslaved African Americans from the new Continental army. Some patriots were uncomfortable with the number of blacks already in the camp and did not wish to see them remain there, in spite of the courage they had shown, especially at Bunker Hill. When the dust settled after the Connecticut emergency in early December, Washington decided not to allow those black veterans, including some of the more renowned fighters in camp like Salem Poor and Framingham's Peter Salem, to continue fighting for the cause. Even though it was Peter Salem who killed Major Pitcairn at Bunker Hill, his cause could not be Washington's, too. But Dunmore changed the commander's mind. More precisely, the threat of seasoned black troops deserting his ranks to take up arms for the crown had changed it for him.[101]

100. Edward Rutledge to Ralph Izard, Philadelphia, Dec. 8, 1775, *LDC*, II, 462.

101. See "Instructions for the Officers of the Several Regiments of the Massachusetts Bay Forces," July 8, 1775, 4 *Am. Archives*, II, 1368; Committee of Conference proceedings, Oct. 18–24, 1775, *PGW: RW*, II, 199, General Orders, Oct. 31, 1775, 268, General Orders, Nov. 12, 1775, 354; Henry Wiencek, *An Imperfect God: George Washington, His Slaves, and the Creation of America* (New York, 2003), 190; Charles Neimeyer, *America Goes to War: A Social History of the Continental Army* (New York, 1996), 65–88. The July instructions also appeared in: *Connecticut Gazette*, July 26, 1775; *Pennsylvania Evening Post*, July 29, 1775; *Newport Mercury*, July 31, 1775; *Essex Journal*, Aug. 4, 1775; *Connecticut Gazette*, Aug. 4, 1775; *New-Hampshire Gazette*, Aug. 8, 1775; *Virginia Gazette* (Pinkney), Aug. 10, 1775. For more on Salem and Poor, see Quarles, *Negro in the American Revolution*, 13–18; Sidney Kaplan and Emmy Nogrady Kaplan, *The Black Presence in the Era of the American Revolution*, rev. ed. (1973; rpt. Amherst, Mass., 1989), 20–24. Whether recruiting officers were actually following orders and turning away blacks is a crucial question. One free African American testified much later that Washington's instructions were being ignored. Jacob Francis, a New Jersey slave who had earned his freedom on January 1, 1775, wrote in his 1836 pension application that he had enlisted in "the United States service" at Salem, Massachusetts, "about the last day of October" and was to serve through the end of 1776. See John C. Dann, ed., *The Revolution Remembered: Eyewitness Accounts of the War for Independence* (Chicago, 1980), 390–399, esp. 392.

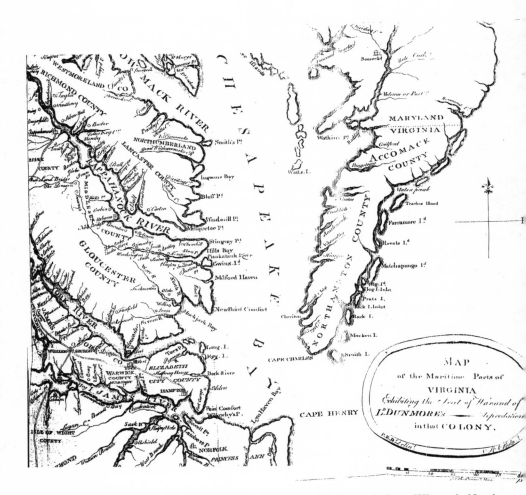

Figure 3. *"Map of the Maritime Parts of Virginia, Exhibiting the Seat of War and of Lord Dunmore's Depredations in That Colony."* From Pennsylvania Magazine *(April 1776), 184–185. By the spring of 1776, so many war stories had emanated out from the Chesapeake that Thomas Paine, editor of the* Pennsylvania Magazine, *inserted this map to help readers visualize all the inlets, islands, and creeks that had come to prominence over the past year.*

Washington again used his metaphor of a rolling snowball to describe to Richard Henry Lee what might happen "if some expedient cannot be hit upon to convince the slaves and servants of the impotency of his designs." But, as Washington was about to experience in his first New England winter, snowballs could form in places other than Virginia. Four days after writ-

"Britain Has Found Means to Unite Us"

ing to Lee, Washington suddenly amended his decision about excluding all blacks from army service, allowing reenlistments to those who had already served. The following day, he wrote Congress to explain why. Washington informed Hancock that a group of veteran free blacks had complained to his headquarters that they were "very much dissatisfied at being discarded." In an atmosphere charged with Dunmore's actions, the last thing Washington needed was for the British to benefit from the intelligence that could be gained from Peter Salem, Salem Poor, and other spurned veteran troops. "As it is to be apprehended *that they may seek employ in the ministerial Army* I have presumed to depart from the resolution respecting them, and have given license for their being enlisted." Though he had not budged on the question of recruiting slaves, Washington knew he had ventured an unauthorized policy shift: "If this is disapproved of by Congress, I will put a stop to it." Congress did support the decision, approving the reenlistment of those free blacks "who had served faithfully in the army at Cambridge . . . but no others." Without their threat of going over to the other side of the siege lines, it is unlikely that the free African American soldiers would have had enough leverage to change Washington's policy.[102]

Seventeen-seventy-five was quite a year for Peter Salem. When he marched out of Framingham in the middle of the night on April 19, his neighbors whispered that there was a slave revolt, not an imperial one, afoot in Middlesex County. Soon Salem was a hero, but not a welcome one. Many

102. GW to Richard Henry Lee, Dec. 26, 1775, *PGW: RW*, II, 611, Dec. 30, 1775, 620, GW to John Hancock, Dec. 31, 1775, 623. Both Frey and Wiencek quote Washington as finishing his December 26 letter to Richard Henry Lee with the statement that the war's outcome would depend "on which side can arm the Negroes the faster." Washington did not say this. Both quote the same page of Philip Foner's *Blacks in the American Revolution* (Westport, Conn., 1976), 46, where the error originated. See Frey, *Water From the Rock*, 78; Wiencek, *An Imperfect God*, 204. Washington would, however, make that statement more than three years later, after the British occupied Georgia; see GW to HL, Mar. 20, 1779, *PGW: RW*, XIX, 543. Congress's support of Washington came on Jan. 16, 1776, in *JCC*, IV, 60; *LDC*, III, 102. See also Dorothy Twohig, "'That Species of Property': Washington's Role in the Controversy over Slavery," in Don Higginbotham, ed., *George Washington Reconsidered* (Charlottesville, Va., 2001), 114–138. Benjamin Quarles, interestingly, failed to mention the influence of Dunmore on this decision, only citing the request by the black soldiers themselves as the cause for Washington's changed mind. See *Negro in the American Revolution*, 15.

patriot political and military leaders, from Washington on down, did not want Salem and scores of other free African Americans who manned the siege lines outside Boston that year as part of their Grand Continental army. Wave after wave of stories about the British rousing slaves throughout North America added to long-standing colonial prejudices to solidify suspicions of their loyalty and value. At the same time, however, Dunmore's emancipation proclamation gave Salem and other African American veterans just enough clout to force the patriots to accept them.

* * *

Printing presses were revolutionary weapons in 1775. Having one meant you could control the message—even the name—of the conflict. Newspapers provided a template for colonists to understand the issues they were dealing with, identify enemies they were trying to neutralize, and realize that the problems they encountered in their community were the same ones their fellow settlers in faraway regions faced. They were mortar, not the bricks themselves but the daub that reinforced the structure and kept it true. At the same time, they could act as disintegrative materials. Patriot publicists took their trade more seriously than their opponents did. By denying that same framework of understanding to their opponents and preventing them from imagining their cause as common, a minority of patriots could convince enough of the populace that they were right. Securing the types could mean the difference between revolution and rebellion, patriots and traitors.

Few of the ministry's representatives in America in 1775 understood this; it was a fatal flaw. Some did, though. Campbell's foresight in packing his trunks with Dalrymple's pamphlet was a great help to South Carolina loyalists. Dunmore also grasped this aspect of the burgeoning rebellion. He recognized that controlling the press was the best way to destabilize the patriot information network. Neither side had confiscated a press before he seized John Hunter Holt's late in September.

In late November, Isaac Sears led a band of seventy-five patriot partisans from Connecticut into New York City to get revenge. Sears was among the patriot vanguard in New York as one of the city's original Sons of Liberty, and his antipathy for loyalist printer James Rivington ran deep. By the final weeks of 1775, he was equally angry that his friends in New York had not taken sufficient action to aid the common cause. So, following Dunmore's lead, he took matters in his own hands. According to one newspaper account, on November 23, "with bayonets fixed [and] in the greatest regularity," Sears and his men, mounted on horseback, went down the main street and drew up in close order before the printing office of the infamous James Rivington. A small detachment entered it and [in] about three quarters of an hour, brought off the principal part of his types, *for which they offered to give an order on Lord Dunmore.* They then faced and wheeled to the left, and marched out of town to the tune of Yankee Doodle. The vast concourse of people assembled at the Coffee-House bridge, on their leaving the ground gave them three very hearty cheers.

They carried Rivington's press back to New Haven in triumph. Sears's performance mirrored the Norfolk attack almost perfectly.[103]

103. For a sample of their relationship, see Sears's angry threats to the printer and Rivington's brilliant and cutting lampoons of them in *Rivington's New-York Gazetteer,* Sept. 2, 8, 1774. For more on Sears, see Pauline Maier, *The Old Revolutionaries: Political Lives in the Age of Samuel Adams* (New York, 1980), 51–100, esp. 86–89. This was the account generated from New Haven; see *Connecticut Journal,* Nov. 29, 1775; *Pennsylvania Journal,* Dec. 6, 1775 (emphasis added). That article is also in 4 *Am. Archives,* III, 1707–1708. On November 29, the *Connecticut Journal* also reprinted a second, shorter account of the attack, taken from a New York paper (either Gaine or Anderson), which contained most of the same information except references to Dunmore and Yankee Doodle. See *Constitutional Gazette,* Nov. 25, 1775; *New-York Gazette,* Nov. 25, 1775; *Connecticut Journal,* Nov. 29, 1775; *New-York Journal,* Nov. 30, 1775; *New-England Chronicle,* Dec. 7, 1775; *Essex Journal,* Dec. 8, 1775; *Massachusetts Spy,* Dec. 8, 1775. See also I. N. Phelps Stokes, *The Iconography of Manhattan Island* (New York, 1922), IV, 906; Richard Ketchum, *Divided Loyalties: How the American Revolution Came to New York* (New York, 2003), 355–356; Arthur M. Schlesinger, *Prelude to Independence: The Newspaper War on Britain, 1764–1776* (New York, 1957), 240.

It is apparent that Virginians did not miss the point. On December 8, Alexander Purdie printed the word from New York that "a party of 100 armed men on horseback, from New England, surrounded the house of James Rivington, printer of the Gazetteer, and carried away the types, without offering any violence to his person. Some think that it was intended as a retaliation for Lord Dunmore's conduct, and others attribute it to an apprehension of his relapsing into his former iniquitous publications" (*Virginia Gazette* [Purdie], Dec. 12, 1775). Underneath the report, *Constitutional Gazette* editor John Anderson inserted an italicized paragraph entitled "intelligence extraordinary," which stated, "We hear, the Earl of Dunmore has composed a most elaborate and profound Treatise on the Art of Government, with which his Lordship intends soon to favour the public; and that is the true reason of the printing-press in Virginia being carried on shipboard" (Nov. 25, 1775). Many historians, however, have invariably missed the connection to Norfolk. Of the

Leading New York patriots were appalled at this behavior. Alexander Hamilton, just shy of his twenty-first birthday, wrote to John Jay to express his concerns about "the late incursion." Hamilton argued that, although it was a good idea to silence the "dangerous and pernicious" Rivington, "I cannot help disapproving and condemning the step." Hamilton was worried that if the patriot authorities did not repudiate this act, clearly an expression of "the passions of men . . . worked up to an uncommon pitch," the consequences might lead to a "disregard of all authority." Moreover, because the raid was conducted by "men coming from a neighboring province," embracing the act might lead people to "imagine the New Yorkers are totally, or a majority of them, disaffected to the American cause, which makes the interposal of their neighbors necessary." The New York City committee distanced themselves, proclaiming in their petition to the Provincial Congress that Sears had done this "without any authority" from them or the Continental Congress. They, too, worried that this kind of naked attack on private property threatened the "internal peace and harmony of the general union of the Continent." British officials in New York interpreted this as another example of the warped patriot definition of "free press." Sears was a dangerous but typical product of the patriot movement, royal governor William Tryon snorted, "a tool of the Continental Army."[104]

As much as the raid made some New York patriots uncomfortable, Sears

---

several Revolutionary press scholars who have discussed the attack on Rivington, only Arthur M. Schlesinger put the two together in *Prelude to Independence,* 240.

104. Alexander Hamilton to John Jay, New York, Nov. 26, 1775, in Harold C. Syrett, ed., *Papers of Alexander Hamilton* (New York, 1961), I, 176–178; Petition of the General Committee for the City and County of New York to the New York Provincial Congress, Dec. 5, 1775, 4 *Am. Archives,* IV, 185–186; William Tryon to Dartmouth, HMS *Duchess of Gordon,* Dec. 6, 1775, in Davies, ed., *Docs. of the Am. Rev.,* XI, 206. Jay agreed that this made New York appear to be lacking in spirit for the cause. He wrote to Alexander McDougall that "the late valorous Expedition against Rivington, gives me Pain. I feel for the Honor of the Colony, and most sincerely hope they will upon this occasion act a Part that may do some little Credit to their Spirit as well as Prudence" (Jay to McDougall, Philadelphia, Dec. 4, 1775, *LDC,* II, 437). Captain George Vandeput also thought that the raid was sparked because Rivington had "ventured to put several paragraphs from England in his papers against the rebels about three weeks ago" (Vandeput to Captain Hyde Parker, *Asia,* Dec. 18, 1775, in Davies, ed., *Docs. of the Am. Rev.,* XI, 212). For Sears's radical tendencies in New York City politics, see Gary B. Nash, *The Unknown American Revolution: The Unruly Birth of Democracy and the Struggle to Create America* (New York, 2005), 94–101.

performed a vital service to the common cause. He never faced punishment for destroying Rivington's livelihood. Silencing the leading loyalist newspaper did benefit the patriot movement in New York and throughout the mid-Atlantic. Maintaining control of the communications networks was essential to sustaining the rebellion, a fact not lost on Congress early on in the conflict. At the end of 1775, the patriots had as strong a grip on those networks as they would at any other time during the Revolution.[105]

But, even more than their control of information flows, the kinds of messages, images, and representations that those networks disseminated were critical to building and maintaining support for the cause. This, too, dominated patriot attention. The private correspondence of patriot political leaders revealed just how incensed they were at British officials' reaction to the news of war in Massachusetts. The letters Benjamin Franklin sent across the Atlantic in the fall of 1775 capture the patriots' exasperation, no matter how manufactured. "Your Nation must stop short, and change its Measures, or she will lose the Colonies forever," he wrote to an English friend. Specifically, "the exciting the Indians to fall on our innocent Back Settlers, and our Slaves to murder their Masters, are by no means Acts of a legitimate Government: they are of barbarous Tyranny and dissolve all Allegiance." "The Insolence of your Captains of Men of War is intolerable," he added, "but we suppose they know whom they are supposed to please." This was small fare compared to the language he used the next day in his response to the Bishop of St. Asaph, Jonathan Shipley. One wonders what Shipley, as someone sympathetic to the colonial cause, made of the list of grievances Franklin appended to his letter. Back in May, Franklin had written Shipley that "Britain has found means to unite us." By September, Franklin sounded unhinged:

The encouraging our Blacks to rise and murder their Masters. But above all,
The Exciting the Savages to fall upon our innocent Outsettlers, Farmers, (who have no Concern in, and from their Situation can scarce have any Knowledge in this Dispute) especially when it is considered that the Indian Manner of making War, is by surprising Families in the Night, and killing all, without Distinction of Age or Sex!*
These proceedings of Officers of the Crown, who it is presumed either act by Instruction, or know they shall please by such Conduct, give People here a horrid idea of the Spirit of your Government.

105. *JCC*, II, 209–211.

Franklin added one last comment to his list, a catalog that foreshadowed the Declaration of Independence. His asterisk at the end of "exciting the savages" offered a clarification. "What would be thought of it," he thundered, "if the Congress should hire an Italian Bravo to break into the House of one of your Ministers, and murder him in his Bed? All his Friends would open in full Cry against us as Assassins, Murders, and Villains, and the Walls of your Parliament House would resound with their Execrations! Of these two damnable Crimes which is the greatest?" Franklin's writing ability makes these letters singular in their expression, but not the content or emotions conveyed. Although they, too, considered how best to use Indians and African Americans in their armed forces, another task that preoccupied both Congress and the Continental army in 1775, patriot leaders like Franklin treated British use of proxies as a monstrous crime perpetrated by devious enemy agents.[106]

Franklin and his colleagues dedicated prodigious efforts to make sure as many people in America as possible agreed with them, and the issue of British agents' "exciting" and "encouraging" was the issue that could deliver results. Or so they thought.

That the patriots were quite conscious in sponsoring these messages to shape attitudes is evident in the genealogy of the final story of 1775. At the same time that colonial printers exchanged columns about groups of "chiefly negroes" wearing uniforms emblazoned with "liberty to slaves" and attacking whites in the Chesapeake, Congress directed the printers to insert another story from the New York frontier. On December 22, Congress re-

---

106. BF to David Hartley, Philadelphia, Sept. 12, 1775, *PBF*, XXII, 196–197, BF to Jonathan Shipley, Philadelphia, Sept. 13, 1775, 199–200. For example, a delegation of the St. François Indians toured Massachusetts and offered military assistance to the patriots, a visit that caused much consternation and attracted attention. See GW to Philip Schuyler, Cambridge, Aug. 20, 1775, *PGW: RW*, I, 332; 4 *Am. Archives*, III, 339, 348. See the newspaper coverage in *Boston Gazette*, Aug. 21, 1775; *New-England Chronicle*, Aug. 24, 1775; *Essex Journal*, Aug. 25, 1775; *Connecticut Gazette*, Aug. 25, 1775; *Norwich Packet*, Aug. 26, 1775; *Pennsylvania Evening Post*, Aug. 29, 1775; *Pennsylvania Journal*, Aug. 30, 1775; *Connecticut Journal*, Aug. 30, 1775; *Pennsylvania Gazette*, Aug. 30, 1775; *Rivington's New-York Gazetteer*, Aug. 31, 1775; *Pennsylvania Mercury*, Sept. 1, 1775; *Pennsylvania Ledger*, Sept. 2, 1775; *Pennsylvania Packet*, Sept. 3, 1775; *Newport Mercury*, Sept. 4, 1775; *Maryland Gazette*, Sept. 7, 1775; *Virginia Gazette, or the Norfolk Intelligencer*, Sept. 13, 1775; *Virginia Gazette* (Dixon & Hunter), Sept. 21, 1775; *South-Carolina Gazette*, Oct. 17, 1775; *South-Carolina and American General Gazette*, Oct. 20, 1775; *Pennsylvania Magazine*, I (1775), 391.

ceived two packets of intelligence that they wanted the public to be aware of. The first was the cache of letters found on John Connolly, along with his interrogation by patriot authorities in Maryland. The second was a startling letter from General Philip Schuyler in Albany. They wasted no time in ordering both sets published in the Philadelphia newspapers. But not all of the letters were for public consumption. For Schuyler's letter, the people only needed to learn about the second paragraph.[107]

The day after Christmas, *Pennsylvania Evening Post* printer Benjamin Towne obeyed orders. He had received Congress's resolution asking him to publish the key paragraph of Schuyler's letter "to perpetuate the *humanity* of the Ministers of George the Third and their Agents":

> The Indians delivered us a speech on the 12th, in which they related the substance of all the conferences Col. [Guy] Johnson had with them the last summer, concluding with that at Montreal, where he delivered to each of the Canadian tribes a war belt and a hatchet, who accepted it. After which they were invited to FEAST ON A BOSTONIAN AND DRINK HIS BLOOD.
>
> An ox being roasted for the purpose, and a pipe of wine given to drink, the war song was sung. One of the Chiefs of the Six Nations, that attended at the conference, accepted a very large black war belt with a hatchet depictured in it; but would neither eat nor drink, nor sing the war song. This famous belt they have delivered up, and we have now a full proof that the ministerial servants have attempted to engage the savages against us.

Over the next few weeks, seventeen other publications throughout the colonies followed Congress's request, many of which were published in parallel columns alongside Connolly's papers, which compounded the phrase "now we have a full proof."[108]

---

107. Philip Schuyler to President of Congress, Albany, Dec. 14, 1775, 4 *Am. Archives*, IV, 260–261. Congress ordered Connolly's letter published on December 22, Schuyler's letter on December 23. See Richard Smith's diary for Connolly, *LDC*, II, 513, and also that day's official journal, *JCC*, III, 443, 445. For Schuyler, see *JCC*, III, 456. Sam Adams also copied down the contents of Schuyler's letter for John Adams on December 22; see *LDC*, II, 507.

108. *Pennsylvania Evening Post*, Dec. 26, 1775. Schuyler's letter reprinted in the *Pennsylvania Gazette*, Dec. 27, 1775; *Pennsylvania Journal*, Dec. 27, 1775; *Pennsylvania Ledger*, Dec. 30, 1775; *Constitutional Gazette*, Dec. 30, 1775; *Pennsylvania Packet*, Jan. 1,

Schuyler and the Congress made sure that the information of purported cannibalism reached as wide an audience as possible. The ubiquity of these stories—and the role played by political leaders like Franklin, Adams, or Schuyler in their production—was a critical factor in solidifying the common cause. Both their pervasiveness and their importance has disappeared from our understanding of the Revolutionary experience. We need to recover their centrality. Reports that the ministry was "putting Arms into the Hands of all that would receive them, English, Scotch, Irish, Roman Catholics, Hessians, Hanoverians, etc."—not to mention blacks, Indians, and maybe even Russians, as one account guessed—were almost weekly affairs in colonial newspapers by the end of 1775. When printer Alexander Purdie published an essay by "An American" in his first *Virginia Gazette* of 1776, his audience would be hard-pressed to miss the references. "An American" summed up the shift in attitude that the pile of "instigation" stories had produced:

> How sunk is Britain! Could not Britons venture to wage war with America till they were told Americans were cowards, till they had disarmed them; or had, as they thought, put it out of their power to procure arms, nor even then without the assistance of Roman Catholicks and Indians, and endeavouring to raise amongst us a domestic enemy? Was this like a brave and generous nation! . . . Why make use of every base and inhuman stratagem, and wage a savage war unknown amongst civilized nations? Surely whoever has heard of Carleton's, Connelly's, and Dunmore's plots against us cannot but allow that they must have been authorized by a higher power, and whoever believes this cannot but wish to be instantly and for ever removed from

------

1776; *New-York Gazette,* Jan. 1, 1776; *Maryland Journal,* Jan. 3, 1776; *Maryland Gazette,* Jan. 4, 1776; *New-York Journal,* Jan. 4, 1776; *Virginia Gazette* (Purdie), Jan. 5, 1776; *Norwich Packet,* Jan. 8, 1776; *New-England Chronicle,* Jan. 11, 1776; *Massachusetts Spy,* Jan. 12, 1776; *Connecticut Gazette,* Jan. 12, 1776; *Providence Gazette,* Jan. 13, 1776; *Boston Gazette,* Jan. 15, 1776; *Pennsylvania Magazine,* I (1775), 581. Connolly's letters: *Pennsylvania Evening Post,* Dec. 23, 1775; *Pennsylvania Packet,* Dec. 25, 1775, Jan. 1, 1776; *Pennsylvania Journal,* Dec. 27, 1775; *Pennsylvania Gazette,* Dec. 27, 1775; *Maryland Journal,* Dec. 27, 1775; *Pennsylvania Ledger,* Dec. 30, 1775; *Constitutional Gazette,* Dec. 30, 1775; *New-York Gazette,* Jan. 1, 1776; *Maryland Gazette,* Jan. 4, 1776; *Norwich Packet,* Jan. 15, 1776. Four of these issues had the two stories on the same page (*New-York Gazette, Pennsylvania Journal, Maryland Gazette,* and *Constitutional Gazette*).

such a power, and to be guarded most effectually against it. Most freely would I *cut the Gordian knot.*

This essayist meant "higher power" as the sordid man in Britain who approved the plots, be it Lord Dartmouth or Lord North or even the king himself. But for many readers of this essay, which would be reproduced in five other colonies, the protection afforded Americans by the "higher power" in defusing these schemes was the other key component to the patriots' depiction of the common cause in 1775. Thanks to Providence or virtuous colonists, they had been saved thus far from destruction at the hands of Stuart's Cherokees, Carleton's Iroquois, or Dunmore's slaves.[109]

Even though they were shooting stars that captured the public's attention for only a brief moment, the panoply of Revolutionary celebrities in the war's first seasons was vast, far more so than traditional narratives of the Revolution reflect. Public outrage focused on the king's officers in North America, especially Guy Carleton, William Tryon, Josiah Martin, William Campbell, and, of course, Lord Dunmore. Names of lesser British agents were also renowned throughout the colonies: Matthew Squire, John Collett, Alexander Cameron, John Stuart, Guy Johnson, and John Connolly. For each, the wellspring of their infamy was their alleged connections with insurrectionist slaves and bloodthirsty Indians. Those groups were largely an amorphous mass of latent danger, but colonial newspaper readers knew some of their names, too, like Joseph Harris and Thomas Jeremiah.

Theirs were the stories that traveled every week along the communications networks William Bradford and his three dozen associates managed throughout the colonies. These were the images that Bradford's postrider, William Carheart, dropped off in bundles in Pennsylvania towns. Carheart's colleagues, from New Hampshire to South Carolina, delivered similar stacks of weekly papers that carried these stories all over colonial roads.

Each of these stars in the Revolutionary firmament shone in some respect because the patriots took hypothetical suggestions or actual efforts to re-

109. "Putting arms": *Providence Gazette,* Nov. 18, 1775; *New-York Journal,* Nov. 23, 1775; *Connecticut Gazette,* Nov. 24, 1775; *Newport Mercury,* Nov. 27, 1775; *Constitutional Gazette,* Nov. 29, 1775; *New-England Chronicle,* Nov. 30, 1775; *New-Hampshire Gazette,* Dec. 5, 1775; *Maryland Journal,* Dec. 13, 1775. "An American": *Virginia Gazette* (Purdie), Jan. 5, 1776; *Pennsylvania Journal,* Jan. 17, 1776; *Constitutional Gazette,* Jan. 24, 1776; *New-York Journal,* Jan. 25, 1776; *Norwich Packet,* Jan. 29, 1776; *New-England Chronicle,* Feb. 1, 1776; *Providence Gazette,* Feb. 10, 1776.

cruit slaves and Indians—whether real, threatened, or manufactured—and broadcast them as widely as possible, through official congressional proclamations, intentional political leaks, or the newspaper exchange system. That all this occurred in just six columns of print in a weekly newspaper underscores how prevalent these stories were throughout 1775. Few weeks went by that year without the local paper featuring some account of British attempts at "instigation." Often, multiple stories from multiple sources would collide in those columns, reinforcing the sense that this threat was universal. These accounts appeared, in large part, because they were excellent transmitters of political and cultural messages about the common cause. This is not to suggest that there was a patriot conspiracy, but, as the relative silence over Benjamin Church's betrayal shows, these stories and images did not randomly appear in print. They had sources and sponsors.

Amid all this commotion, colonists also read about one another as they never had before. When they were not marching or listening or talking about how the war might touch their lives and families, they read about others who were doing the same things. The months that followed Lexington and Concord offered little opportunity for somber reflection. There were few major essays published on abstract issues, whether the imperial controversy or the African slave trade. Rights were not what dominated discussions at colonial dinner tables or tavern bars in 1775. John Stuart knew what the public was really talking about. "The newspapers were full of Publications calculated to excite the fears of the People," the exiled Indian Superintendent reflected bitterly from the safety of Florida. "Massacres and Instigated Insurrections," he wrote, "were Words in the mouth of every Child." Those words—and how they got there—were a central story of 1775. The following year, that story would be a cornerstone for the new republic itself.[110]

110. John Richard Alden, "John Stuart Accuses William Bull," *WMQ*, 3d Ser., II (1945), 320.

## CHAPTER 3

Merciless Savages, Domestic Insurrectionists, and Foreign Mercenaries

INDEPENDENCE

In March 1776, Abigail Adams wrote to her husband asking for any insight on how the Virginians were fighting British tyranny. Like many other colonists, Abigail did not know much about them but had nagging suspicions. "Are not the Gent[ry] Lords and the common people vassals, are they not like the uncivilized Natives Brittain represents us to be?" she queried. "I hope their Riffle Men who have shewen themselves very savage and even Blood thirsty; are not a specimen of the Generality of the people." Abigail was concerned about the quality of the people who, if all went well, would soon be her fellow countrymen. Two paragraphs later, after prodding John to get Congress to declare independence, she made a simple request, on behalf of all the members of her sex, that would become famous. "In the new Code of Laws which I suppose it will be necessary for you to make," she wrote, "I desire you would Remember the Ladies, and be more generous and favourable to them than your ancestors."[1]

John's reaction was insulting. "As to your extraordinary Code of Laws," he joked, "I cannot but laugh." "We have been told that our Struggle has loosened the bands of Government everywhere," he began. "That Children and Apprentices were disobedient—that schools and Colledges had grown turbulent—that Indians slighted their Guardians and Negroes grew insolent to their Masters," and now, John teased, his own wife hinted that

1. Abigail Adams to JA, Braintree, Mar. 31, 1776, in L. H. Butterfield et al., eds., *The Book of Abigail and John: Selected Letters of the Adams Family, 1762–1784* (Cambridge, Mass., 1975), 120–121.

"another Tribe" was following suit. We may judge John's reticence to acknowledge Abigail's request as petty, especially his choice to call her "saucy" for suggesting that women should be included in new American concepts of political participation. But there is more to unpack about John's banter than patriarchy. Indeed, the frame into which he interpreted her request is revealing: John had just added colonial women to the list of America's enemies.[2]

John responded as if Abigail had made a veiled military threat. Writing just five days before the anniversary of Lexington and Concord, his extended reaction to Abigail's request reflected both the unsettling events that had engulfed the patriots throughout the first year of war and the recurring, near-reflexive terms in which they represented those events. That John poured women into the stream illustrates how deep the channel of patriot rhetoric about British proxies was by the spring of 1776. "I begin to think the Ministry as deep as they are wicked," he continued. "After stirring up Tories, Landjobbers, Trimmers, Bigots, Canadians, Indians, Negroes, Hanoverians, Hessians, Russians, Irish Roman Catholicks, Scotch Renegadoes, at last they have stimulated the [women] to demand new Priviledges and threaten to rebell." After a full year of hearing news that ranged from whispered gossip to eyewitness evidence that British authorities had recruited these assorted groups to assist in quelling the rebellion, it was only natural for John to joke that perhaps now they had turned their attention to "another Tribe more numerous and powerfull than all the rest." This renowned exchange of letters is about women's rights, but it is also about more than that. It is an arresting, illuminating conversation about unity, the common cause, and the people who might be included in a new, independent America. Though Abigail was worried about the problems of including "savage" Virginians and not virtuous colonial ladies, John understood her letter in terms of the undertaking that his colleagues faced throughout 1775–1776 in general and that spring in particular: cataloging, explaining, and dealing with all the Revolution's alleged enemies.[3]

Adams's list of proxy enemies was hardly a laughing matter, but it was

2. JA to Abigail Adams, Apr. 14, 1776, ibid., 122–123. For an account of Abigail's fury about John's response and how she vented this frustration to her friend Mercy Otis Warren, see Rosemarie Zagarri, *A Woman's Dilemma: Mercy Otis Warren and the American Revolution* (Wheeling, Ill., 1995), 91–92.

3. JA to Abigail Adams, Apr. 14, 1776, in Butterfield et al., eds., *Book of Abigail and John*, 121–123.

Merciless Savages, Domestic Insurrectionists, and Foreign Mercenaries

laughable. At the moment he sat down to reply to Abigail, most of those groups had never really threatened the common cause. For nearly an entire year, patriot publicists had featured accounts in their weekly papers accusing suspicious Indians of threatening to take up the king's hatchet or actually doing so. In truth, throughout the backcountry, Indians had done nothing of the kind. The patriots' behind-the-scenes negotiations on the frontier from Canada to the Carolinas had been successful: Indians had not really intended to "feast on a Bostonian." Though Adams and his colleagues had shouted down the British for trying to instigate them, Indians had rejected all entreaties thus far. Likewise, there was, as yet, no general rising of slaves against their masters, although many African Americans across the Atlantic seaboard had responded to the outbreak of war as a way to better their situation. Moreover, as a few newspapers reported in early 1776, there was also evidence of blacks' saying "God d—n the K—g, —— and the Governor too." As for the various foreigners John invoked, their entrance in the war was a hazy rumor.[4]

Nevertheless, the power of the images John cataloged remained vital, thanks in no small part to Adams himself and his patriot colleagues in assembly houses and print shops. By the first anniversary of the Revolutionary War, those images of America's enemies had crystallized into a compelling reason for declaring American independence.

The standard, heroic narrative of the run-up to independence is normally a hurried recitation that moves in a direct line from Thomas Paine to Thomas Jefferson, from Common Sense's emphasis on the abuse of monarchy and hereditary privilege in January to the Declaration's laying blame directly at King George's feet in July. This is, of course, perfect fodder for national founding myths. The lived experience of those significant six months was a bit different. Colonists would have millions of ways of telling their stories about 1776, mixing in the personal and the local. Though each person had his or her own narrative of American independence, John Adams and his peers in the patriot leadership had the version they wanted colonists to imbibe, believe, and act upon. For several months, they had been constructing the keystone of that narrative arch. Ever since the conflict began, patriot political leaders and publicists had labored to convince the colonists that they all shared a common cause, that their cultural cousins were

---

4. *Virginia Gazette* (Dixon & Hunter), Jan. 6, 1776; *Pennsylvania Ledger,* Jan. 20, 1776; *Connecticut Journal,* Jan. 24, 1776; *New-England Chronicle,* Feb. 8, 1776; *Essex Journal,* Feb. 9, 1776.

really their bitter enemies—not least because British officials were plotting with Indian, slave, and foreign proxies to destroy them. Patriot leaders had propagated scores of stories about imperial agents encouraging those groups to take part in the conflict and had published column after column of evidence.

This particular cache of war stories was ubiquitous in 1775, and not by accident. Stories about whether slaves or Indians would take up arms in defense of the king featured prominently in the war's first seasons. As supporters of the crown finally realized what the patriots had long understood—that newspapers were weapons as valuable as cannonballs—printers' shops became battle sites in 1775. But, for British officials, it was too late. As pressure increased on printers to subscribe to the patriot argument, literate colonists had less and less choice regarding the information they received about the conflict in other colonies. Whether they accepted, rejected, or were indifferent to it, this propagation campaign governed the limits of what most colonists knew about the larger Revolution, especially in 1776.

Two hundred years on, we have forgotten much of the information inside those knowledge boundaries. Instead, a handful of national, operatic episodes, telescoped into a triumphalist narrative, serve as the myth of American independence. Returning to the everyday experience of 1776, as colonists read or listened to details about remote events in their current newspaper, offers a better comprehension of how the patriots survived that crucial year and, more important, what was at stake. The first months of 1776 would turn out to be pivotal, of course, but not just because of Thomas Paine. There is more to the colonial reception to *Common Sense* than the language he used or the arguments he forwarded. Loyalists suspected that Paine's pamphlet was really the work of the Continental Congress, and they were not off base. Delegates helped manufacture and manage the reception of *Common Sense,* just as they did the other big news stories that dominated colonial newspapers in the spring of 1776: the battle at Moore's Creek Bridge in North Carolina, the crown's purchase of German auxiliaries to help kill Americans, and the debacle at the Cedars on the northern frontier. Though narrators of 1776 tend to focus on the "organic" response to Paine or George Washington's victory in the siege at Boston that spring, those were not the tales with which colonists were most familiar. News about North Carolina, German mercenaries, and the northern frontier—because they imparted significant information about the common cause—monopolized the inner pages of newspapers in early 1776. The first months of that year, in part because of these stories, were essential to turning public opinion in favor of independence. They would be especially so for real African Americans and Indians, people who were the subjects of the patriots' foundational common cause narrative dividing Americans from their proxy enemies.

1: *COMMON SENSE* AND MOORE'S CREEK

Common Sense appeared in Philadelphia on Tuesday, January 9. Although the degree to which the impact of *Common Sense* was indeed "astonishing"—as Eric Foner famously described it—has been challenged, Paine's pamphlet was perfectly timed, appearing at "precisely the moment when Americans were ready to accept [his] destruction of arguments favoring conciliation." A few days after its publication, one delegate to the Continental Congress commented that copies were being "greedily bought up and read by all ranks of people" throughout the city.[5]

Over the next several weeks, many prominent patriot political and military leaders discussed the pamphlet, writing each other about its influence. They sent multiple copies to family members and sympathetic friends at home, wondered aloud who the true author was, and generally celebrated colonial audiences for being so receptive to its "sound Doctrine, and unanswerable reasoning," as Washington put it. One writer from Charleston, South Carolina, was even more effusive, offering three short sentences to the *Pennsylvania Evening Post:* "Who is the author of COMMON SENSE? I can scarce refrain from adoring him. He deserves a statue of gold." This worship, in addition to Paine's own postwar braggadocio, grew into a "cult of *Common Sense.*" The unique nature of so many correspondents discussing the influence of a particular text has contributed to a hyperinflation of both the saturation and influence of *Common Sense.* That is not a dismissal; Paine's forty-six-page pamphlet was a remarkable political statement. Thousands read it, thousands more heard it read, and even more listened in on conversations about it in public and private places. According to one correspondent from Maryland, the pamphlet "has done wonders and miracles, made TORIES WHIGS, and washed Blackamores white." Paine's invocation of "common sense" was groundbreaking. His vernacular rhetoric, direct ar-

5. Eric Foner, *Tom Paine and Revolutionary America* (New York, 1976), 86; Josiah Bartlett to John Langdon, Philadelphia, Jan. 13, 1776, *LDC,* III, 88. For a vigorous challenge to the material impact of *Common Sense,* see Trish Loughran, *The Republic in Print: Print Culture in the Age of U.S. Nation Building, 1770–1870* (New York, 2007), 33–104.

guments, and use of the Bible to drive home his points were so singularly effective that lots of colonists were wondering who "Common Sense" was. Some colonists thought the author was John Adams. Others were convinced Common Sense was really Benjamin Franklin.[6]

Nonetheless—numbers aside—the commentary on *Common Sense* by patriot political and military leaders, especially their guesses that Franklin or even John Adams was the true author, illuminates something vital about the American Revolution. Many people believed that a delegate to the Continental Congress wrote *Common Sense.* That a political representative would advocate, in capital letters, "'TIS TIME TO PART" confirmed for many loyalists that this had been the patriots' thinly veiled plan all along. After fleeing Maryland for England, former Anglican rector and staunch tory Jonathan Boucher forwarded his thoughts about the "very extraordinary pamphlet" to a friend. "The real author [is], Dr. Franklin, the ostensible one, Mr. Payne,

6. GW to Joseph Reed, Salem, Mass., Jan. 31, 1776, *PGW: RW,* III, 228. The following patriot military and political leaders wrote letters from mid-January through February that mentioned *Common Sense* in some way: in Congress, John Hancock, Oliver Wolcott, Samuel Ward, Joseph Hewes, John Adams, Josiah Bartlett, Benjamin Franklin, Thomas Nelson; in the army, Horatio Gates, Charles Lee, and Washington. William Tudor kept John Adams informed about the pamphlet's reception in Massachusetts. In Newport, Ezra Stiles documented reading the pamphlet in his diary on Feb. 24, 1776, in Franklin Bowditch Dexter, ed., *The Literary Diary of Ezra Stiles, D.D., LL.D.: President of Yale College,* 3 vols. (New York, 1901), I, 662. "Who is the author": *Pennsylvania Evening Post,* Mar. 26, 1776; *Pennsylvania Journal,* Mar. 27, 1776; *Newport Mercury,* Apr. 8, 1776. "Cult": Loughran, *Republic in Print,* 37–44. "Has done wonders": *Pennsylvania Evening Post,* Feb. 13, 1776; *Constitutional Gazette,* Feb. 21, 1776. Adams as "Common Sense": The *Connecticut Gazette* exchanged a story from the *London Evening Post* from May 21, 1776, that noted, "This pamphlet, they say, has been ascribed to Mr. Adams, one of the Delegates in the Continental Congress." See *Connecticut Gazette,* Aug. 30, 1776; *Virginia Gazette* (Dixon & Hunter), Sept. 27, 1776. In the third installment of *The American Crisis,* Paine himself addressed the popular belief that Franklin, Samuel Adams, and John Adams were all "severally spoken of as the supposed Author" of *Common Sense.* See [Paine], *The American Crisis, Number III,* in Eric Foner, ed., *Thomas Paine: Collected Writings . . .* (New York, 1995), 132. For an excellent analysis of Paine's approach, see Sophia Rosenfeld, *Common Sense: A Political History* (Cambridge, Mass., 2011), 136–180. Franklin as "Common Sense": Horatio Gates to Charles Lee, Cambridge, Mass., Jan. 22, 1776, "The Lee Papers, Vol. I, 1754–1776," *Collections of the New-York Historical Society: For the Year 1871,* IV (New York, 1872), 252; Joseph Hewes to Samuel Johnston, Feb. 13, 1776, *LDC,* III, 247; William Tudor to JA, Cambridge, Mass., Feb. 29, 1776, *PJA,* IV, 41.

[a] member in Congress for New Hampshire," Boucher wrote in July. "Its object is to persuade the People of America at once to declare for Independency," he surmised, adding that it had been published by congressional authority because "they meant it preparatory to their own" declaration of independence. Boucher's mistake about Paine's rank in patriot political circles was hardly a function of seething anger. His error mirrored colonial confusion about not only who Common Sense was but also what role patriot authorities played in disseminating the pamphlet.[7]

Samuel Ward, an actual delegate from Rhode Island, was disappointed to learn that John Carter had not advertised it in his *Providence Gazette.* "That Pamphlet," he wrote his brother, "ought surely to be distributed throughout all the Colonies if it was even at the public Expence. It has done immense Service." One of Ward's colleagues—and one who thought Franklin wrote the celebrated text—took the idea of patriot politicians–as–publishing agents a step further. A day after Ward suggested using public monies to subsidize the pamphlet, Joseph Hewes wrote that he was arranging a shipment of pamphlets home to North Carolina. "The Council can Judge of the propriety of distributing them," he offered. Though they did not have a hand in its creation, patriot political leaders did participate in the dissemination of *Common Sense.* As with war stories, they were managing reactions. They helped propagate the "cult."[8]

The discussion over *Common Sense* induced Samuel Adams to blur the line further. He sent a lengthy essay to printer Benjamin Towne under the pseudonym "Candidus," which was published in the *Pennsylvania Evening Post* on February 3. Candidus underscored many of Paine's arguments. "By declaring independance, we place ourselves on a footing for an equal negociation," he stated. "Does not the most superficial politician know that while we profess ourselves the subjects of Great-Britain, and yet hold arms against her, they have a right to treat us as rebels, and that according to the laws of nature and nations no other state has a right to interfere in the dispute?" Ten days later, Adams again took up his pen, this time to elaborate on Candidus's statement that "all Europe knows the illegal and inhuman treatment we have received from Britons." On February 13, another impassioned Adams essay—this time under the name "Sincerus"—occupied

7. Jonathan Boucher to John James, Paddington, July 10, 1776, box I, folder 7, Jonathan Boucher Papers, Swem.

8. Samuel Ward to Henry Ward, Philadelphia, Feb. 19, 1776, *LDC,* III, 285–286, Joseph Hewes to Samuel Johnston, Philadelphia, Feb. 20, 1776, 289–290.

more than an entire page of Towne's *Evening Post*. Sincerus ridiculed those who held out for reconciliation with Britain by reminding colonists that although their enemies had tried their best, Americans had survived all the terrible conspiracies Britain had attempted throughout the first year of war. Like Paine, Adams asked, Why should the colonies go back now? Adams took a different tack from *Common Sense* in arguing for independence: he cited the king's proxies in detail. Sincerus reminded his readers that the "great hopes" of British officials to incite the Indians on the New York frontier had failed. "Dunmore, with all his wanton rage, has done little more than exasperate the Virginians," Adams argued, "and convinced that brave colony, that they can be formidable to savages on the east as well as west side of their dominion."[9]

Adams believed the well-established narrative of the king's conspiring "pensioners" and their proxies was an argument for American independence that complemented Paine's. A few colonial printers agreed. A week after Sincerus appeared in the *Pennsylvania Evening Post*, Paine's original publisher, Robert Bell, had already included it and Candidus in a new, enlarged edition of *Common Sense*. In New York, bookseller William Green also advertised in the Manhattan papers the same enlarged edition that included both Adams essays. The extra essays turned this new round of *Common Sense* into more of a patriot anthology. For those confused about who the real Common Sense was, this expanded edition featured Samuel Adams along with Thomas Paine; any line between elected officials advocating independence in the assembly houses and writers calling for it from the printing houses was obliterated. It was becoming more and more difficult to discern between patriot political or military officials and publicists, just as loyalists like Jonathan Boucher had protested all along. Though several printers had been deeply involved in patriot protests since the mid-1760s, once the war began, increasing numbers opened their columns to patriot leaders. By the time of Paine's "phenomenon," this was surely the case—a collaboration that undoubtedly contributed to the sales of *Common Sense*.[10]

9. *Pennsylvania Evening Post*, Feb. 3, 13, 1776; *Pennsylvania Packet*, Feb. 15, 1776, and *Constitutional Gazette*, Feb. 21, 1776; and see William V. Wells, *The Life and Public Services of Samuel Adams: Being a Narrative of His Acts and Opinions* . . . (Boston, 1865), II, 349–352, 360–363.

10. *Pennsylvania Evening Post*, Feb. 13, 1776; *Pennsylvania Evening Post*, Feb. 20, 1776; *Constitutional Gazette*, Mar. 6, 1776; *New-York Journal*, Mar. 14, 1776. Delegate Samuel Ward sent a copy of the enlarged edition home to Rhode Island on

The inclusion of Sincerus in the enlarged edition of *Common Sense,* with its catalog of British conspirators and would-be proxies, also illustrates that there were alternative pro-independence arguments to Paine's in the late winter and early spring of 1776. *Common Sense* made only one reference to the crown's 1775 attempts to gain the assistance of proxy forces. Near the conclusion of his "Thoughts on the Present State of American Affairs" section, Paine mentioned the now-infamous British "plots." He warned that any moves to block independence might precipitate terrible civil violence. "There are thousands, and tens of thousands, who would think it glorious to expel from the continent, that barbarous and hellish power, which hath stirred up the Indians and Negroes to destroy us," he counseled; "the cruelty hath a double guilt, it is dealing brutally by us, and treacherously by them." In the main, though, Paine focused on the potential of American commerce and republican government to justify why colonists should reject any call for reconciliation. Essays by Sincerus show that Paine's voice was not the only one; though growing prominent, the arguments of *Common Sense* should be interpreted as part of a larger chorus against reconciliation.[11]

Other publicists continued to attack Britain via Indians and slaves that season. "What stone have they left unmoved?" asked a so-called "honest, sensible, and spirited farmer" in a speech "addressed to an assembly of his neighbours, on his engaging in the continental service," which appeared in the *Pennsylvania Journal* in late February. "What device to ruin us, tho' never so mean, barbarous and bloody, such as no heart, but that of a Devil and a tyrant can refrain shuddering at, have they not pursued?"

Have they not attempted to spirit up the Indian savages to ravage our frontiers, and murder, after their inhuman manner, our defenceless

---

Mar. 4 with instructions that [*Providence Gazette* printer John] "Carter can print the Appendix separately to compleat the Work." See Ward to Henry Ward, Philadelphia, Mar. 4, 1776, *LDC,* III, 329–332. This new edition further instigated a publishing war in Philadelphia between Bell and *Pennsylvania Journal* printers William and Thomas Bradford, whom Paine went to after a disagreement with Bell over the size of the first edition's publishing run. The Bradfords' advertisement appeared next to Bell's in the Feb. 20 *Pennsylvania Evening Post* and warned consumers, "The Pamphlet advertised by Robert Bell intitled ADDITIONS to COMMON SENSE, or by any other Name he may hereafter call it, consist of Pieces taken out of News Papers, and not written by the Author of COMMON SENSE."

11. [Thomas Paine], *Common Sense: Addressed to the Inhabitants of America,* in Foner, ed., *Paine: Writings,* 20, 35.

wives and children? Have not our Negro slaves been enticed to rebel against their masters, and arms put into their hands to murder them? Have not the King of England's own slaves, the Hanoverians, been employed? And were not the poor Canadians made slaves, that they might be made fit instruments, with other slaves and savages, to make slaves and more wretched beings than savages of us?

All that was left, the "farmer" concluded, was to "fight or die." *Pennsylvania Packet* printer John Dunlap also joined in at the end of February. Dunlap published "A Dialogue between the Ghost of General Montgomery and a Delegate, in a Wood Near Philadelphia" on February 26. "Don't hesitate to declare independence," Montgomery's ghost lectured the waylaid Congressman in the *Pennsylvania Packet.* "Your friends (as you call them) are to [*sic*] few—too divided—and too interested to help you. And as for your enemies, they have done their worst. They have called upon Russians—Hanoverians—Hessians—Canadians—Savages—and Negroes to assist them in burning your towns—desolating your country—and in butchering your wives and children." Sending the Congressman scurrying off to the city, the apparition implored, "You have nothing further to fear from them. Go, then, and awaken the Congress to a sense of their importance; you have no time to lose." Although this sounds like Samuel Adams, in fact "A Dialogue" has been attributed to Common Sense himself, Thomas Paine.[12]

In short, although the vernacular language, reassuring arguments, and frontal assault on monarchy that Paine employed in *Common Sense* has dominated scholarly understandings of why colonial support for reconciliation flagged in early 1776, many patriots contended that America should declare independence simply because of British treachery. Whereas *Common Sense* laid out the positive reasons why colonists should embrace American independence, other writers, publishers, and political leaders remained focused on attacking the crown for embracing Indians, slaves, and foreign mercenaries and thereby pushing them toward "cutting the Gordian knot."

It is worth recalling that Robert Bell and the Bradfords first set the type for *Common Sense* right on the heels of some of the most widely circulated stories about alleged British conspiracy. Schuyler's letter about Indians'

12. Paine, "A Dialogue," in Philip S. Foner, ed., *The Complete Writings of Thomas Paine*, 2 vols. (New York, 1945), II, 88–93. "Honest farmer": *Pennsylvania Journal*, Feb. 28, 1776; *Boston Gazette*, Mar. 25, 1776; *Essex Gazette*, Apr. 5, 1776. "Dialogue": *Pennsylvania Packet*, Feb. 26, 1776; *Virginia Gazette* (Purdie), Mar. 8, 1776; *Continental Journal*, May 30, 1776.

being asked to "feast on a Bostonian," the news of John Connolly's arrest, Dunmore's proclamation, and reports of Virginia runaways wearing "Liberty to Slaves" emblazoned on their new uniforms—all of these stories made their run through colonial newspapers from late December through mid-January. Colonial readers were as familiar with the smallest of stories emerging from the Chesapeake as they were with Paine. Even the most mundane, trivial events involving Dunmore's runaway slaves found space in most colonial newspapers, such as the reportage of a raiding party that descended on "Mr. Narsworthy's" plantation in Isle of Wight County, which included one "Negro dressed in the uniform of the 14th regiment" but was luckily thwarted by the alarm of a "loyal" slave. Half of the newspapers in North America exchanged this story; lots of readers in February 1776 knew about the attack on Narsworthy's sheep by "the Governor's men," just as they knew about *Common Sense*.[13]

This was the context into which Paine's forty-six-page pamphlet appeared; it was not Paine alone who transformed American attitudes toward the king. *Common Sense* cannot be credited for solely creating an atmosphere whereby, as John Adams wrote, "Scarcely a Paper comes out, without a Speculation or two in open Vindication of opinions, which Five Months ago were Said to be unpopular." Paine's pamphlet was a phenomenon, but it flourished in well-nourished soil.[14]

* * *

Success on the battlefield could also make that propagation campaign easier. In addition to Canada, another region Congress was especially concerned about was the North Carolina piedmont. In late 1775, two Presbyterian ministers traveled there to act as patriot evangelists at Congress's expense. Those ministers left Philadelphia in mid-January only to find the province already in an uproar. In the first days of the new year, Governor Josiah Martin received permission to act on the multiple reports he had received from the interior that many North Carolinians still supported the king. On January 10, the day after Robert Bell brought out the first edition

13. *Virginia Gazette* (Dixon & Hunter), Feb. 3, 1776; *Dunlap's Maryland Gazette*, Feb. 20, 1776; *Maryland Gazette*, Feb. 22, 1776; *Pennsylvania Gazette*, Feb. 21, 1776; *New-York Gazette*, Feb. 26, 1776; *New-York Journal*, Feb. 29, 1776; *Connecticut Courant*, Mar. 4, 1776; *Connecticut Journal*, Mar. 6, 1776; *South-Carolina and American General Gazette*, Mar. 8, 1776; *Essex Journal*, Mar. 8, 1776.

14. JA to James Warren, Philadelphia, Feb. 14, 1776, *LDC*, III, 253–254, esp. 253.

of *Common Sense*, Martin issued a proclamation calling on all good Carolina subjects to resist this "most daring, horrid, and unnatural Rebellion" perpetrated "by the base and insidious artifice of certain traitorous, wicked, and designing men." Martin commanded "all His Majesty's faithful subjects" to prove their allegiance by reporting to the King's Standard, which he was to raise in Brunswick on February 15, or risk being labeled "Rebels and Traitors." Two days later, Martin elaborated in his report to the recently removed American secretary of state, Lord Dartmouth. "My Latest information from the interior parts of the Province," he wrote, "corresponds with my warmest wishes. The people called Regulators . . . to the number of between two and three thousand men have given me the strongest assurances of their joining the King's Standard whenever they shall be called upon." Even greater numbers of Scottish Highlanders who had recently settled in the piedmont, he added, would also rally to put down the rebellion. Appropriately, he appointed Donald MacDonald, a British veteran of Bunker Hill and, patriots were quick to indicate, Culloden, as brigadier general and sent him out to organize this gathering loyalist force.[15]

Martin's confidence would be misplaced. This force was troubled from the start. Although Martin had received various pieces of intelligence that the countryside was with him, rumors and misinformation had swept through the Carolina backcountry. Patriots had disrupted communication between Martin and those who would likely respond to the king's standard. The Moravians in the piedmont settlement of Salem related in December 1775, "A report has spread" that the Regulators' former nemesis William Tryon had landed in Carolina and was marching toward the backcountry, as he had done four years earlier to put down the Regulator protest—a campaign that climaxed in bloodshed at Alamance. Tryon was not in North Carolina this time, but several of his deputies who had commanded men at that 1771 battle were, including James Moore, Richard Caswell, and John Ashe. Moore, the man who had fired the opening cannon shot at Alamance,

---

15. Gov. Josiah Martin of North Carolina, "A Proclamation," Jan. 10, 1776, 4 *Am. Archives*, IV, 980–981; Josiah Martin to Earl of Dartmouth, HMS *Scorpion*, Jan. 12, 1776, in William L. Saunders, ed., *The Colonial Records of North Carolina*, 10 vols. (Raleigh, N.C., 1886–1890), X, 406–409, esp. 406. As they did with Dunmore's family, several patriot printers later pointed out that MacDonald, who was "in rebellion in the year 1745, against his lawful sovereign," had some nerve to fight against their cause. See *Pennsylvania Packet*, Mar. 25, 1776; *Constitutional Gazette*, Mar. 30, 1776; *Connecticut Courant*, Apr. 15, 1776; *Providence Gazette*, Apr. 20, 1776.

was now in charge of North Carolina's patriot militia. He, along with Caswell, Ashe, and Alexander Lillington, raised more than one thousand men to face MacDonald.[16]

On February 27, Moore's patriot militia dug in on the east side of Moore's Creek, about twenty miles northwest of Wilmington, pulled the planks up on the bridge, and waited for MacDonald's forces, which numbered nearly 1,500 Highlanders and about 200 former Regulators (far fewer than Martin boasted to his superiors), to attack. When they did, just a few instants decided the outcome. According to Colonel Caswell, in about three minutes, patriot troops had killed 50 Highlanders and 2 officers. In the subsequent chaos, Carolina patriots captured MacDonald and nearly half of the fleeing loyalists.[17]

The battle of Moore's Creek Bridge lasted just a few minutes, but, thanks to patriot publicists, political leaders, and the exchange networks, this short fight dominated colonial attention throughout the early spring. Because it was the first significant confrontation between patriots and tories on the battlefield, Moore's Creek Bridge elicited interpretation and comment that was far out of proportion to the encounter itself. Normally, narrators of the events of February and March 1776 focus on George Washington, on the Continental army's taking of Dorchester Heights, and on the cannon transported from Fort Ticonderoga through the snow and mountains to break the siege of Boston. Colonial attention, however, was not enthralled by the drama around Boston. Patriot publicists gave even more space to the civil conflict in North Carolina, in part because the definition of the fundamental term "rebel" was at stake.[18]

Battle reports from Caswell and Moore to Cornelius Harnett, president

16. "Diary of Salem Congregation, 1775," in Adelaide L. Fries, eds., *Records of the Moravians in North Carolina* (Raleigh, N.C., 1922–1969), II, 891; Jon F. Sensbach, *A Separate Canaan: The Making of an Afro-Moravian World in North Carolina, 1763–1840* (Chapel Hill, N.C., 1998), 91–92.

17. Wayne E. Lee, *Crowds and Soldiers in Revolutionary North Carolina: The Culture of Violence in Riot and War* (Gainesville, Fla., 2001), 152–156; Christopher Ward, *The War of the Revolution*, ed. John Richard Alden (New York, 1952), II, 662–664.

18. Hugh F. Rankin, *The North Carolina Continentals* (Chapel Hill, N.C., 1971), 53. Rankin notes that patriots exaggerated the victory at Moore's Creek "to an importance out of all perspective," especially in the northern colonies. I have previously explored the patriots' coverage of Moore's Creek in "'An *Astonishing Account* of CIVIL WAR in North Carolina': Rethinking the Newspaper Response to the Battle of Alamance," *Journalism History*, XXXII (2007), 223–230.

of the North Carolina Provincial Council, found their way into the hands of colonial printers, who published them with apparent relish. Caswell's letter, written two days after the engagement, forwarded the news that the tories were "totally put to the rout, and will certainly disperse." "Our officers and men," he concluded, "behaved with the spirit and intrepidity becoming freemen, contending for their dearest privileges." To ensure readers believed Caswell's words, printers prefaced his report with his credentials: "late a Delegate for the province of North-Carolina in the Continental Congress, and now Commander of a body of troops in that province." Though no issues from 1776 have survived, Caswell's report was probably first printed in James Davis's Newbern newspaper, the *North-Carolina Gazette,* in early March. By late March, it had spread throughout the continent. In all, more than half of the colonial printers exchanged Caswell's good news. Nearly as many included James Moore's longer report of March 2. In it, Moore detailed to Harnett that one officer had fallen at the bridge with "upwards of twenty balls through his body," that the enemy had lost about fifty men in the skirmish, but that the patriots had miraculously suffered only two casualties. His summary of this event, though, was the real news from North Carolina: "Thus, Sir, I have the pleasure to inform you, has happily terminated a very dangerous insurrection, and will I trust put an effectual check to Toryism in this country." If the sheer amount of print space is any indicator as to significance, Moore's summation was as important to the future of the patriot movement as the barrage that Washington's cannons rained down into Boston from the heights of Dorchester that same weekend.[19]

19. Because this report was printed in Williamsburg on March 22 and Philadelphia on March 23, it could not have been sent in a letter to North Carolina's delegates to Congress, who then turned it over to one of the Philadelphia printers, as was often the case. The publication of Caswell's report, therefore, had to have another source; the likeliest candidate is Davis's *North-Carolina Gazette.* Also, the fact that Alexander Purdie did not publish James Moore's report but did Caswell's, and Benjamin Towne printed both, suggests that some choice of exchange was at work instead of copying from manuscript letters or patriot dispatches. See Isaiah Thomas, *The History of Printing in America: With a Biography of Printers and an Account of Newspapers,* ed. Marcus A. McCorison, 2d ed. (1810; rpt. New York, 1970), 563–564; Clarence S. Brigham, *History and Bibliography of American Newspapers, 1690–1820,* 2 vols. (Worcester, Mass., 1947), II, 770; and Robert N. Elliott, Jr., "James Davis and the Beginning of the Newspaper in North Carolina," *North Carolina Historical Review,* XLII (1965), 1–20. Caswell letter: *Virginia Gazette* (Purdie), Mar. 22, 1776; *Pennsylvania Evening Post,* Mar. 23, 1776; *Pennsylvania Packet,* Mar. 25, 1776; *Mary-*

The battle at Moore's Creek Bridge gave the patriots a unique opportunity to call their enemies "rebels," "insurgents," and "insurrectionists." It was a perfect screen for patriots to project their own representations. For the first months of the conflict, when they had talked about loyalists in the newspapers, patriot publicists often had to damn the elusive tories by association, principally by conflating them with blacks and Indians. But at Moore's Creek, for the first time, they were able to counter the definition of what constituted a "traitor" and what one was rebelling against. This gave patriots an opportunity to give definition to the amorphous concept of "tory."[20]

---

land Journal, Mar. 27, 1776; *Pennsylvania Journal,* Mar. 27, 1776; *Constitutional Gazette,* Mar. 27, 1776; *Pennsylvania Gazette,* Mar. 27, 1776; *New-York Journal,* Mar. 28, 1776; *Connecticut Courant,* Apr. 1, 1776; *New-York Gazette,* Apr. 1, 1776; *Connecticut Journal,* Apr. 3, 1776; *Maryland Gazette,* Apr. 4, 1776; *Connecticut Gazette,* Apr. 5, 1776; *Providence Gazette,* Apr. 6, 1776; *Essex Journal,* Apr. 12, 1776; *Norwich Packet,* Apr. 22, 1776 (supplement). "Happily terminated": *Pennsylvania Evening Post,* Mar. 23, 1776; *Pennsylvania Packet,* Mar. 25, 1776; *Constitutional Gazette,* Mar. 27, 1776; *New York Packet,* Mar. 28, 1776; *New-York Journal,* Mar. 28, 1776; *New-York Gazette,* Apr. 1, 1776; *Norwich Packet,* Mar. 25–Apr. 1, 1776; *Connecticut Courant,* Apr. 1, 1776; *Connecticut Journal,* Apr. 3, 1776; *New-England Chronicle,* Apr. 4, 1776; *Maryland Gazette,* Apr. 4, 1776; *Connecticut Gazette,* Apr. 5, 1776; *Providence Gazette,* Apr. 6, 1776; *Essex Journal,* Apr. 12, 1776; *Massachusetts Spy,* Apr. 12, 1776.

20. Take the interpretation that grew out of the episode late in the summer of 1775 when loyalists cut down Boston's Liberty Tree, for example. The first mention, in the August 31 issue of the *New-England Chronicle,* simply recounted events, and most of the northern printers exchanged it as soon as they could find space for such a valuable partisan story. But in the hands of the twenty-three-year-old poet Philip Freneau, the description of the crowd was made explicit. A few weeks after the story appeared in the New York papers, Freneau sent a completed poem entitled "A Voyage to Boston" to the *Constitutional Gazette* in New York.

> In Boston's southern end there stands a tree,
> Long sacred held to darling Liberty,
> It's branching arms with verdant leaves were crown'd,
> Imparting shade and grateful coolness round:
> To its fam'd trunk, invisible as air,
> I from the sleepy council did repair,
> And at its root, fair Freedom's shrine, I paid
> My warmest vows, and blest the virtuous shade.
> Now shin'd the gay fac'd sun with morning light,
> All Nature joy'd exulting at the sight,

They did not waste such an opportunity. Harnett's Provincial Council in Newbern proclaimed that Governor Martin "has been too successful in exciting an insurrection of the banditti among the Highlanders and Regulators." Luckily, "a noble ardor appeared in every part of the country through all ranks of people" to defeat Martin's scheme. North Carolina patriots also arranged for the full publication of an exchange of letters that had passed between James Moore and Donald MacDonald a few days before the February 27 engagement. MacDonald had sent a message to Moore to offer him and his men one last chance to respond to Martin's proclamation and "repair to the King's royal standard." Moore returned a herald contending that Martin's proclamation was "incompatible with the freedom of Americans," but he was not ignorant to the "feelings of humanity" and would be certain his men showed "that civility to such of your people as may fall into our hands." Moore boasted that North Carolina's patriots were unanimous in "consider[ing] ourselves engaged in a cause the most glorious and honourable in the world, the defence of the liberties of mankind, in support of which we are determined to hazard everything dear and valuable." Moore countered MacDonald's opening gambit by declaring that if his "deluded" and "ungrateful" troops did not move away from the "dangerous and destructive precipice on which they stand," he would be forced to declare them "enemies to the constitutional liberties of America, and treat them accordingly." MacDonald, rhetorically outflanked, responded that he "con-

---

When swift as wind, to vent their base-born rage,
The Tory Williams and the Butcher Gage,
Rush'd to the tree, a nameless number near,
Tories and Negroes following in the rear—
Each, ax in hand, attack'd the honor'd tree,
Swearing eternal war with Liberty;
Nor ceas'd their strokes, 'till each repeated wound
Tumbled its honours headlong to the ground.

[Philip Freneau], "A Voyage to Boston: A Poem" (Philadelphia, 1775), 17–18, *Early American Imprints*, 14044. Freneau's "Voyage to Boston" cemented the pulling down of the Liberty Tree—an event loyalists probably celebrated—as another instance of British attacks on liberty. But, for Freneau, the "nameless number" who attacked the Tree consisted of "Tories and Negroes." Gage might have been in the lead, but it took proxy supporters to bring down the symbol of colonial resistance. Freneau recited the essential elements of the common cause: only with the help of such proxies could Gage wage "eternal war with Liberty."

tinue[d] in my present sentiments . . . embarked in a cause which must . . . extricate this country from anarchy and licentiousness." This dialogue between Moore and MacDonald was one of the best forums for patriots to display the differences between them and loyalists. For that reason, the Moore-MacDonald exchanges, despite the several columns of print they required, appeared in more than a dozen newspapers north of Moore's Creek.[21]

Several anonymous reports from North Carolina—which could well have been penned by Harnett, Caswell, or Moore just the same—overflowed in their praise for Carolina's devotion to the common cause. From the perspective of these missives from Carolina, it is puzzling that Thomas Paine believed Americans lacked confidence to separate from the crown. One self-congratulatory letter, dated March 6 and first printed in John Dunlap's *Pennsylvania Packet*, crowed, "It is altogether out of my power to describe the ardor that at this very hour prevails in this province, almost every man at an hour's warning is ready to turn out in his country's cause." "Since I was born I never have heard of so universal an ardour for fighting prevailing, and so perfect a union amongst all degrees of men," a different correspondent from Carolina observed a few days later. Now that the "rascally disturbers of government" had been defeated, "you will, my dear friend, rejoice with me in finding all the wicked machinations of our wicked Governor likely to be brought to naught. He has been most indefatigable in his endeavours to bring upon this province every species of calamity, by secretly spiriting up our internal foes, misrepresenting our weakness, and soliciting forces to destroy us." A third anonymous letter inferred that perhaps North Carolina had more "internal foes" than just Scots emigrants or former Regulators. Just before sounding the same note about Carolina's new "true patriotism"—"You never knew the like in your life"—this contributor

21. Brigadier General Donald MacDonald to Brigadier General Moore, Headquarters, Feb. 19, 1776, Moore's Answer, Camp at Rockfish, Feb. 19, 1776, Moore to MacDonald, Feb. 20, 1776, and MacDonald to Moore, Feb. 20, 1776, all in 4 *Am. Archives*, V, 63–65; *Pennsylvania Packet*, Mar. 25, 1776, and supplement; *Pennsylvania Gazette*, Mar. 27, 1776; *New-York Gazette*, Apr. 1, 1776; *New-York Journal*, Apr. 4, 1776; *Norwich Packet*, Apr. 1–8, 1776; *Providence Gazette*, Apr. 13, 1776. Moore/MacDonald: *Pennsylvania Packet*, Mar. 25, 1776, and supplement; *Constitutional Gazette*, Mar. 27, 1776; *Pennsylvania Journal*, Mar. 27, 1776; *New York Packet*, Mar. 28, 1776; *Connecticut Courant*, Apr. 1, 1776; *Norwich Packet*, Mar. 25–Apr. 1, 1776; *New-York Gazette*, Apr. 1, 1776; *Maryland Gazette*, Apr. 4, 1776; *Connecticut Gazette*, Apr. 5, 1776; *Virginia Gazette* (Dixon & Hunter), Apr. 13, 1776; *Providence Gazette*, Apr. 13, 20, 1776; *New-England Chronicle*, Apr. 25, 1776; *Massachusetts Spy*, May 3, 1776.

to the *Pennsylvania Evening Post* offered reassurances that "the Negroes at Cape Fear were never known to behave so well as they have lately." In several cases, notably the March 25 issue of Dunlap's *Pennsylvania Packet*, most, if not all, of these reports and letters were collected together onto one complete page of "Intelligence from North-Carolina." Though there were many authors writing from different places and times in Carolina after the engagement at Moore's Creek, two consistent themes emerged: the celebration of the universal patriotism of "all ranks" in North Carolina, and the castigation of dissenters as the true "rebels" of 1776.[22]

The military victory won by Moore and Caswell was not inconsequential: the capture of MacDonald and so many of his men prevented Martin from taking advantage of a reinforcement from General Henry Clinton, who was already en route to Cape Fear from Boston with ten thousand muskets. Had MacDonald beaten Moore north of Wilmington and then joined forces with Clinton, many more moderately disaffected Carolinians—and, surely, runaway slaves—might indeed have gravitated toward supporting Martin and the crown, and the future of the Revolution in the Deep South might have taken a different path.[23]

No matter what might have been, there was a more significant, dual legacy of the short fight at Moore's Creek. The overwhelming victory provided an unmatched opportunity for North Carolina patriots to display their patriotism to the rest of the continent. They argued now, on the heels of this impressive victory, that they were more dedicated to the common cause than ever before. John Penn, who had recently left Congress to return home to North Carolina, updated his former colleague John Adams on the status

---

22. "Out of my power": *Pennsylvania Packet*, Mar. 25, 1776; *New-York Gazette*, Apr. 1, 1776; *Connecticut Gazette*, Apr. 5, 1776; *Norwich Packet*, Apr. 1–8, 1776; *Providence Gazette*, Apr. 13, 1776; *Connecticut Courant*, Apr. 15, 1776. "Rascally disturbers": *Pennsylvania Packet*, Mar. 25, 1776; *New-York Gazette*, Apr. 1, 1776; *New-York Journal*, Apr. 4, 1776; *Connecticut Courant*, Apr. 1–8, 1776; *Norwich Packet*, Apr. 8, 1776; *Boston Gazette*, Apr. 15, 1776. "Negroes at Cape Fear": *Pennsylvania Evening Post*, Mar. 26, 1776; *Pennsylvania Gazette*, Mar. 27, 1776; *Providence Gazette*, Apr. 13, 1776. On March 28, Philadelphia diarist Christopher Marshall had read the previous day's *Pennsylvania Journal*, recording that "News brought of the defeat of the Ministerial party in North Carolina" (William Duane, ed., *Extracts from the Diary of Christopher Marshall, 1774–1781* [1877; rpt. New York, 1969], 64).

23. John Ferling, *Almost a Miracle: The American Victory in the War of Independence* (New York, 2007), 127.

of patriot opinion in the South after Moore's Creek. "From several letters I have received" from home, Penn wrote from Petersburg, Virginia, "I find they are for independence, as they either have, or intend to repeal the instructions that were given to their Delegates, and to leave them at liberty to vote . . . as they may think best." Penn's information was accurate: the same day he wrote Adams, the North Carolina Convention joined South Carolina as the second province to empower their representatives in Congress "to concur with the Delegates of the other Colonies in declaring Independency." North Carolinians, Penn concluded in his letter to Adams, "are quite spirited and unanimous; indeed, I hear nothing praised but Common Sense and Independence." They "say they are determined to die hard." Patriot political and military officials in North Carolina propagated an interpretation about the battle of February 27 that best exhibited their support for the Revolution. This province, which had been wracked by multiple scares of slave insurrections and the most significant loyalist military challenge, now claimed a place in the patriot pantheon right next to Massachusetts.[24]

At the same time, patriots many miles north of Newbern co-opted Carolina's promotional opportunity by turning both the province of North Carolina and its heroes, Colonels Moore, Caswell, and their colleagues, into a synecdoche for the entire common cause. The day after John Adams received Penn's letter about North Carolina's newfound enthusiasm for the common cause, there appeared in Benjamin Towne's *Pennsylvania Evening Post* a "letter from Petersburg, (Virginia) April 12." Adams, the erstwhile contributor of his personal correspondence, again did his best to push the patriot argument. Again it was successful: Penn's letter boasting of "Common Sense and independence" appeared in six other prints. A few days later, Adams received another letter from Penn, and this one he gave to the Bradfords. Penn informed Adams—and, subsequently, readers in Philadelphia, New York, New Haven, New London, and Portsmouth, New Hampshire, under the cover of a "gentleman of undoubted veracity"—that in addition to ongoing suspicions about the Highlanders and Regulators, "Governor Martin has coaxed a number of slaves to leave their masters in the lower parts;

24. JA to James Warren, Apr. 20, 1776, *LDC*, III, 558. N.C. vote on independence: "Extract of a Letter from Petersburgh, Virginia, Dated April 12, 1776," 4 *Am. Archives*, V, 859–860. That Penn found *Common Sense* popular in North Carolina was surely gratifying; he and his fellow Congress delegate Joseph Hewes had arranged to send copies there. See Joseph Hewes to Samuel Johnston, Philadelphia, Feb. 20, 1776, *LDC*, III, 289–290.

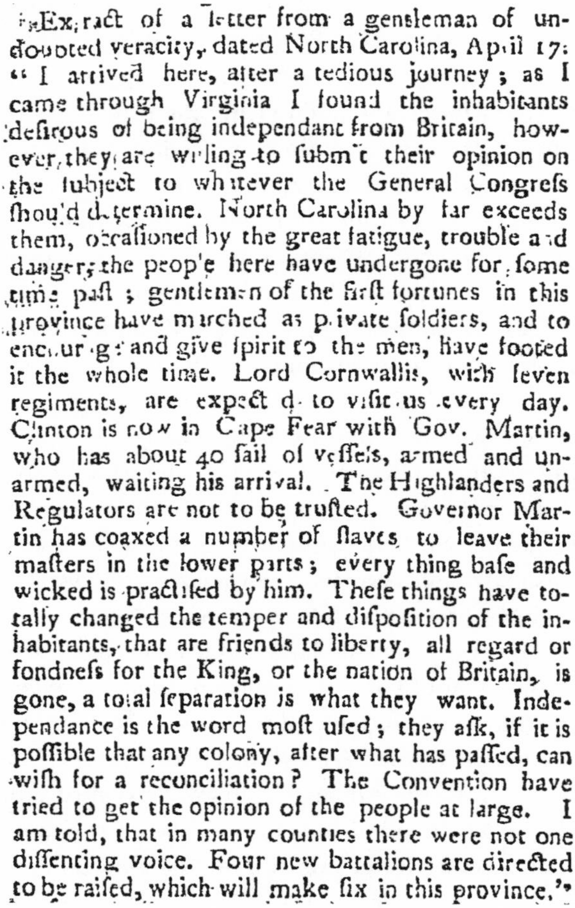

‡ﾗEx;ract of a letter from a gentleman of undoubted veracity, dated North Carolina, April 17:
" I arrived here, after a tedious journey ; as I
came through Virginia I found the inhabitants
desirous of being independant from Britain, however, they are willing to submit their opinion on
the subject to whatever the General Congress
should determine. North Carolina by far exceeds
them, occasioned by the great fatigue, trouble and
danger; the people here have undergone for some
time past ; gentlemen of the first fortunes in this
province have marched as private soldiers, and to
encourage and give spirit to the men, have footed
it the whole time. Lord Cornwallis, with seven
regiments, are expect d to visit us every day.
Clinton is now in Cape Fear with Gov. Martin,
who has about 40 sail of vessels, armed and unarmed, waiting his arrival. The Highlanders and
Regulators are not to be trusted. Governor Martin has coaxed a number of slaves to leave their
masters in the lower parts ; every thing base and
wicked is practised by him. These things have totally changed the temper and disposition of the inhabitants, that are friends to liberty, all regard or
fondness for the King, or the nation of Britain, is
gone, a total separation is what they want. Independance is the word most used ; they ask, if it is
possible that any colony, after what has passed, can
wish for a reconciliation? The Convention have
tried to get the opinion of the people at large. I
am told, that in many counties there were not one
dissenting voice. Four new battalions are directed
to be raised, which will make six in this province.'"

Figure 4. *"Letter from a
Gentleman of Undoubted
Veracity, North Carolina,
April 17, 1776." From*
New York Constitutional
Gazette, *May 8, 1776. This
was actually John Penn, one
of North Carolina's delegates
to the Continental Congress.
The cloak of anonymity,
however, kept readers from
knowing just how invested
its writer was in the public's
submission to congressional
authority. Adams hurried
this letter down to the
Bradfords, who published
it in the* Pennsylvania
Journal *on May 1, 1776.
From there, as Adams surely
knew, the exchange system put
Penn's letter before readers in
New York, Connecticut, and
New Hampshire within a few
weeks.*

every thing base and wicked is practiced by him." "These things have totally
changed the temper and disposition of the inhabitants," Penn rejoiced; "a
total separation is what they want. Independence is the word most used;
they ask, if it is possible that any colony, after what has passed, can wish for
a reconciliation?"[25]

25. John Penn to JA, Halifax, Apr. 17, 1776, *PJA*, IV, 128–129. Letter from Petersburg: *Pennsylvania Evening Post*, Apr. 20, 1776; *Pennsylvania Packet*, Apr. 22, 1776;
New York Packet, Apr. 25, 1776; *Maryland Gazette*, May 2, 1776; *Connecticut Journal*,
May 3, 1776; *Essex Journal*, May 10, 1776. "Extract of a Letter from a Gentleman
of Undoubted Veracity, Dated North Carolina, April 17, 1776": *Pennsylvania Journal*, May 1, 1776; *Constitutional Gazette*, May 8, 1776; *New-York Journal*, May 9, 1776;

Merciless Savages, Domestic Insurrectionists, and Foreign Mercenaries

Hundreds of miles away, in Newport, Ezra Stiles copied into his diary one sentence from an item that was circulating through the papers. Reading over an article in the April 5 issue of the *Connecticut Gazette* that boasted Carolinians, just like the heroes of Lexington Green, were ready to oppose the enemy at an "hour's warning," Stiles transcribed: "The Colonels Moore, Martin, Caswell, Polk, Thackston, Lillington, and Long, have great Merit: any one of these Gent[lemen] in this County would be an over match for a Howe, a Burgoyne, or a Clinton. . . . The whole Province in general consider Regulars in the woods an easy Conquest." Stiles documented the outward posture put forward by patriot publicists concerning loyalism in the South. Privately, they might have had much deeper concerns, as exemplified in Joseph Reed's anxious letter to Washington in mid-March. "We have every Thing to fear from the Southward," Reed wrote from Philadelphia, "a cursed Spirit of Disaffection has appeared in the back Parts of North and South Carolina," which he feared might "prove a most formidabl piece of Business especially when connected with the Hosts of Negroes in the lower Part of the Country." Reed was right to be worried, but none of those reservations found their way into the public discourse.[26]

The cumulative effect of all those stories about North Carolina's fulsome patriotic ardor and military spirit did more than reinforce the justice of the common cause in the minds of staunch patriots or diminish imperial officials in the minds of those less committed. It produced real action on the ground: a significant demonstration in the streets of New York City. To be more precise, the campaign to propagate the common cause actually influenced many New Yorkers to disturb the peace during the last few days of winter.

* * *

On Monday, March 18, George Washington entered Boston in triumph; the ten-month siege was finally over. Thanks to the three-week lag in communication, that same day, New Yorkers learned on the third page of Hugh Gaine's *New-York Gazette* that a clash was impending in Carolina, but that patriots there were confident they could "attack 10,000 tories and beat them too." On the adjoining column, Samuel Loudon, printer of the three-month-old *New York Packet,* advertised the publication of a pamphlet that

---

Connecticut Gazette, May 10, 1776; *Connecticut Journal,* May 15, 1776; *Freeman's Journal* (Portsmouth), May 25, 1776.

26. Stiles diary entry for Apr. 8, 1776, in Dexter, ed., *Literary Diary of Ezra Stiles,* II, 6–7; Joseph Reed to GW, Philadelphia, Mar. 15, 1776, *PGW: RW,* III, 474.

answered *Common Sense,* proclaiming, "The scheme of Independence is ruinous and delusive." That same Monday evening, the Mechanics Committee, a radical patriot group created in 1774 out of the Sons of Liberty, summoned Loudon to explain why he had agreed to publish *The Deceiver Unmasked* and to reveal the author's identity. Loudon refused to tell the committee that the Anglican rector of Trinity Church, Charles Inglis, had written the pamphlet, so six of them went to his shop and, in Loudon's words, "nailed and sealed up the printed sheets in boxes, except a few which were drying in an empty house, which they locked, and took the key with them." They warned Loudon to stop publishing the pamphlet or else his "personal safety might be endangered." Although he "promised to comply," this pledge "availed nothing for my security." Late the next night, forty men returned, broke into his office, grabbed all 1,500 copies of Inglis's pamphlet, "carried them to the commons, and there burned them."[27]

Loudon was still complaining to patriot authorities about what the "sturdy Sons" had done when, at noon on Thursday, March 21, "an EFFIGY was exhibited through the principal parts of this city, attended by a great concourse of the inhabitants, with the following labels":

> WILLIAM TRYON, late Governor of this province, but now is professed REBEL and TRAITOR to its dearest rights and privileges, as well as to his *native country;* who, in order to extinguish every spark of American Liberty, and recommend himself to the favour of a brutal Tyrant, and an insidious Court, did, illegally, unjustly, and cruelly, shed the blood of an innocent and worthy citizen, when he had the command in North-Carolina. For which, and his numberless traiterous practices against the liberties of this country, he is to suffer the just demerits of his atrocious villany, as a warning to all others.

27. Memorial of Samuel Loudon to the New-York Committee of Safety, Mar. 20, 1776, 4 *Am. Archives,* V, 439, 440. "Attack 10,000 tories": *New-York Gazette,* Mar. 18, 1776. Vague news about Martin's forces being "between two fires" appeared in the *Constitutional Gazette* on March 16. For the Mechanics Committee (New York), see Gary B. Nash, *The Urban Crucible: The Northern Seaports and the Origins of the American Revolution,* abr. ed. (1979; rpt. Cambridge, Mass., 1986), 237. The Loudon episode is covered in Arthur M. Schlesinger, *Prelude to Independence: The Newspaper War on Britain, 1764–1776* (New York, 1958), 257; Paul A. Gilje, *The Road to Mobocracy: Popular Disorder in New York City, 1763–1834* (Chapel Hill, N.C., 1987), 64; Joseph S. Tiedemann, *Reluctant Revolutionaries: New York City and the Road to Independence, 1763–1776* (Ithaca, N.Y., 1997), 246–247.

Calm thinking villains, whom no faith can fix,
Of crooked counsels, and dark politicks.

Secondly, *Behold the bloody Tool of a sanguinary Despot, who is using his utmost efforts to enslave you! — With how secure a brow, and specious form he gilds the secret Traitor!*

Thirdly, TORIES *take Care!!!*

This effigy, "after it had been sufficiently exposed," was hanged on a gallows, "where, after receiving the contempt of an oppressed, insulted, and incensed people, it was cut down and destroyed." As usual, New York *Constitutional Gazette* printer John Anderson was sure to point out that the crowd action was "conducted without any matter of injury to any person whatever."[28]

Governor Tryon had recently published a confident proclamation reassuring loyalists that they only had to wait "a very few months" for relief from their "present oppressed, injured, and insulted condition." This missive, historians have argued, is the reason why New York patriots, including "several Hundred of the lower Class," hanged him in effigy. Yet, the fact that the news from North Carolina occurred at that same moment (and that the effigy invoked his violent repression of the Regulators) suggests that the impending battle in Cape Fear also touched off the street action. "The utmost Pains were taken to shake the Confidence of the People" in Tryon, one loyalist opined. The placards suggest an even deeper motive: this was also the moment to show support for colleagues in the South and act out against Carolinians' former (and New Yorkers' current) tyrannical governor.[29]

28. "Sturdy Sons": Hugh Hughes to JA, New York City, Mar. 31, 1776, *PJA*, IV, 98–101, esp. 99. "TORIES take Care": *Constitutional Gazette*, Mar. 23, 1776; *Connecticut Journal*, Mar. 27, 1776; *Connecticut Gazette*, Mar. 29, 1776; *New-York Journal*, Apr. 4, 1776; *Boston Gazette*, Apr. 8, 1776. Effigy destroyed and "without any matter of injury": *Constitutional Gazette*, Mar. 23, 1776. New Yorkers were apparently on edge that week no matter how well conducted this demonstration was. Two days after the Tryon effigy, loyalist William Smith noted in his diary that there was "a new Alarm upon which the Inhabitants flew out of Town with the utmost Precipitation." See entry for Mar. 23, 1776, in William Smith, *Historical Memoirs from 16 March 1763 to 25 July 1778*, ed. William H. W. Sabine (1956; rpt. New York, 1969), I, 270.

29. Tryon proclamation: *Pennsylvania Evening Post*, Mar. 23, 1776; *New-England Chronicle*, Apr. 4, 1776; Smith diary, Mar. 21, 1776, *Historical Memoirs*, I, 269; Philip Davidson, *Propaganda and the American Revolution, 1763–1783* (Chapel Hill, N.C., 1941), 183; Paul David Nelson, *William Tryon and the Course of Empire: A Life in British Imperial Service* (Chapel Hill, N.C., 1990), 140–141.

But there was something upside down in this episode. To be sure, many colonial newspapers had excoriated Tryon for attacking the valiant Regulators at Alamance back in May 1771, especially Isaiah Thomas's *Massachusetts Spy*. As such, some argued his behavior was quite consistent over the 1770s; Tryon had shown himself to be America's enemy, then as now. But something was different about the argument offered by the placards pasted onto the governor's effigy on the first day of spring, 1776. The "bloody Tool of a sanguinary Despot" was also a rebel. This connotation fits with how patriots interpreted the emerging news from North Carolina: the men who turned out to support Martin (or Tryon or Dunmore) were the real traitors, the true disturbers of good government.

To make matters even stranger, Tryon's comrades in opposing the patriot movement were his former nemeses, the very men he vanquished at Alamance. The Revolution's friends in Carolina now were, not the Regulators, the darlings of the *Massachusetts Spy*, but James Moore and Richard Caswell. Back in 1771, the *Spy* had done more than just denounce Tryon. Isaiah Thomas and his contributors had also condemned the "extortioners, traitors, robbers and murderers" who supported the governor at Alamance. The Revolution's great southern heroes, including Colonels John Ashe and Richard Caswell, were among those "murderers." The celebrated James Moore had fired the first cannon on Tryon's behalf at Alamance. The *Spy* had so offended Tryon's colonial elite supporters that they ordered the newspaper ceremoniously burned by the hangman as a measure of their disgust. Now, five years on and several hundred miles to the north, there was another act of street theater involving Tryon and the North Carolinians, but this time the governor was the rebel, the Regulators were the banditti, and former traitors suddenly became ideal defenders of American liberty. The rhetorical demands of the present common cause instantly transformed that past. The interpretation of who was right and wrong at Alamance went through a Revolutionary revision. Although emotions had run high in 1771, all was forgotten in this new context. Now the overwhelming message was, "TORIES take Care!"[30]

30. Three of the leaders of the Boston resistance movement—Dr. Thomas Young, Joseph Greenleaf, and Isaiah Thomas—published a series of articles in the June 27, 1771, issue of the *Massachusetts Spy* excoriating Governor Tryon and his supporters in Newbern for making war on the Regulators at Alamance, people they sympathetically portrayed as fellow aggrieved colonists. Young called Tryon a bloodthirsty tyrant and indicted the militia force as a medieval "Posse Commita-

Merciless Savages, Domestic Insurrectionists, and Foreign Mercenaries

This frenetic week in New York City illustrates several important points about the patriot movement before independence. First, the fact that these two episodes can be traced back to items in the local newspaper again underscores the circular relationship between events and discourse. The events of March 18–21 are powerful examples of the ethereal concept of "reader response." Loudon and his staff had labored in his print shop for several days, producing more than one thousand copies of Charles Inglis's pamphlet, but it was only when he purchased an advertisement in Gaine's *New-York Gazette* that he became a problem for local patriot leaders. Moreover, the explicit reference to Tryon's past in North Carolina plastered across his effigy—and the stark warning for tories to "take Care"—cannot be explained fully without recognizing New Yorkers' knowledge of a looming, large-scale battle between patriots and loyalists in the governor's former province gleaned from the newspapers.

Second, these events reveal how seriously patriots took the promulgation of the common cause. New Yorkers especially favored street demonstrations as a means of putting their support for the Revolution on display so that as many as possible could see and participate. They often took to the streets to evangelize. At the same time, they showed a proclivity for vandalizing the shops of printers who deviated from that line. Samuel Loudon—who was himself a staunch patriot—experienced the same violation that drove James Rivington out of business in Manhattan. Though Loudon's shop was not dismantled, as Rivington's had been the previous November, this was still a significant financial loss for the newest printer in town. The actions of the third week in March, both constructive and destructive, should be viewed as a whole. It is quite possible that at least some of the forty men who

—————

tus." Greenleaf referred to Tryon's friends as a "banditti of robbers" and retorted, "What shall we in future think of the term Loyalist, should it continue any time to be exclusively applied to extortioners, traitors, robbers, and murderers?" (*Massachusetts Spy*, June 27, 1771). Naturally, supporters of the government—including future patriot leaders like Samuel Johnston, William Hooper and Robert Howe—were outraged when copies of the *Spy* reached Newbern. On July 29, in a public meeting at the King's Arms Tavern to in Newbern, they voted to indict Thomas, Greenleaf, and Young, and conduct a public "execution" of the Massachusetts printer. Issue number 17 of the *Spy* was then remanded to the county sheriff to be "publicly burnt under the gall[ow]s by the common hangman . . . as a testimony of the utter abhorrence and detestation in which that infamous production and its still more infamous authors are held by the people of this government" (*North-Carolina Gazette*, July 29, 1771). For more on this affair, see Schlesinger, *Prelude to Independence*, 158–160.

invaded Samuel Loudon's shop to seize the dangerous rebuttal to *Common Sense* also participated in the Tryon effigy just a few hours later. Propagating your arguments and silencing your opponents, patriot leaders in New York City understood, were two sides of the same coin.[31]

These actions, however, stemmed from weakness. New York patriots took these steps because they had to. A third point to be gathered from the disturbances was that, in truth, support for the common cause was not nearly as strong in New York City and its environs as in other urban areas at the start of spring 1776. "New York is still asleep or dead, in Politicks and War," John Adams would soon complain. During those same weeks, General Charles Lee claimed military necessity in dealing with the dangerous loyalist problem around New York. Without permission, he began enforcing a test oath and set about arresting suspected loyalists, a personal policy that earned him a rebuke from the Continental Congress. The Mechanics Committee was doing its own type of policing by making sure no rebuttal to Thomas Paine had the chance to galvanize support for Tryon and the crown in the city. That Inglis's pamphlet was deemed "unfit to be read at this time," as one loyalist commented, suggests the "sturdy Sons" who raided Loudon's shop acted out of concern rather than confidence. Patriot fortunes in Manhattan were better than in previous seasons, and the populace seemed to be tipping toward the common cause, but this was not at all assured. Charles Lee was not the only one who had significant doubts that rhetoric alone could solidify patriot support. Political leaders at the local, provincial, and continental levels continued to expend substantial effort — and ink — to broadcast their argument for resisting British tyranny.[32]

31. A notable example of New Yorkers' taking to the streets was the large funeral procession conducted for Maryland militia captain Michael Cresap, who died in the city in October 1775. See Robert G. Parkinson, "From Indian Killer to Worthy Citizen: The Revolutionary Transformation of Michael Cresap," *WMQ*, 3d Ser., LXIII (2006), 97–122. For other out-of-doors demonstrations, see Gilje, *Road to Mobocracy*, 58–68. Loudon began the *New York Packet* on Jan. 4, 1776; he had only published eleven issues when this occurred. He estimated his loss at £150. For Loudon's unsuccessful attempts to get redress for his losses, see New York Provincial Congress, May 30, June 4, 11, 1776, 4 *Am. Archives*, VI, 1348, 1363, 1393.

32. JA to William Tudor, Philadelphia, June 24, 1776, *PJA*, IV, 335–336, esp. 335; Letter from New York, Mar. 22, 1776, *The Remembrancer; or, Impartial Repository of Public Events,* part 2 (London, 1776), 85. For Charles Lee's antiloyalism activities, see John Shy, *A People Numerous and Armed: Reflections on the Military Struggle for American Independence*, rev. ed. (1976; rpt. Ann Arbor, Mich., 1990), 142–143.

In the case of both *Common Sense* and the coverage of Moore's Creek, these efforts did not involve invoking British proxies directly, although references to restive slaves did surface in Samuel Adams's appended essays and the news from Carolina. Yet the print phenomenon of Paine's pamphlet and the news of Moore's Creek in the spring of 1776 were still part of the same project: forwarding your own definition of legitimate resistance and rejecting all other claims (whether by rhetorical or physical force). Patriot political and military leaders were essential in providing this information, managing its promotion, and denying counterarguments any similar space. Yet this should not suggest that the proxies disappeared while the patriots broadcast news from North Carolina or helped disseminate *Common Sense.*

A defiant Samuel Loudon managed to produce a *New York Packet* just a few days after his shop had been pillaged. Inside the Thursday, March 21, issue, which appeared just as other New Yorkers constructed their effigy of Tryon, Loudon featured a catalog of British crimes that he, like six of his colleagues, exchanged from the *Pennsylvania Gazette.* "Americans! Remember," the article exclaimed, listing all the injuries the colonists had suffered. Toward the end of the list, as the offenses built toward a climax, readers were implored not to forget "their hiring Foreign Troops against you." "Remember their hiring Savages to murder your Farmers with their Families. Remember the Bribing Negroe Slaves to assassinate their Masters." In that same issue, Loudon also printed a more formal request from the Continental Congress ordering Americans to remember British sins. Congress had agreed to set aside a day for fasting and thanksgiving. New Jersey delegate William Livingston drafted the call for colonists to observe this holiday, which several of Loudon's peers also printed. "In times of impending calamity and distress; when the liberties of America are imminently endangered by the secret machinations and open assaults of an insidious and vindictive administration," the proclamation began, it was the colonies' "indispensable duty" to recognize God's sovereignty. Livingston then got to the details:

> The Congress, therefore, considering the warlike preparations of the British Ministry to subvert our invaluable rights and priviledges, and to reduce us by fire and sword, by the savages of the wilderness, and our own domestics, to the most abject and ignominious bondage . . . Do earnestly recommend, that Friday, the Seventeenth day of May next, be observed by the said colonies as a day of humiliation, fasting, and prayer; that we may, with united hearts, confess and bewail our manifold sins and transgressions.

The next week, Congress went to this well again, citing the ministry's practices of "not only urging savages to invade the country, but instigating negroes to murder their masters" as justification for allowing colonial privateers to place cannons on board their vessels.[33]

Months before Thomas Jefferson sat at his desk to write the Declaration of Independence, many writers, both within the Pennsylvania State House and without, honed their skills in justifying the common cause. They did so especially by making reference to British proxies, sometimes loyalists but more often resistant slaves and hostile Indians. These arguments, as much as Thomas Paine's, were the ones patriots forwarded to suggest America might be better off independent. "Is the King a legal Sovereign?" another writer asked "all the sound Heads and honest Hearts in America." Clearly not, this anonymous contributor to Bradford's *Pennsylvania Journal* opined (anticipating the Declaration rather strikingly), "when he endeavours to engage even savages to assassinate them and their wives and children in their dwellings" or when "he orders even slaves to be encouraged to rise and murder their masters, and furnishes them with arms for that purpose."[34]

There was a third reason why the Americans should break with the crown: "He hires foreign troops, to enable him the more effectually to destroy his people." As spring bloomed in North America and the first anniversary of war came and went, stories about another group of proxies, soldiers purchased from the German states, were about to sweep across the continent.[35]

33. "Remember": *Pennsylvania Gazette,* Mar. 13, 1776; *Maryland Journal,* Mar. 20, 1776; *Constitutional Gazette,* Mar. 20, 1776; *New York Packet,* Mar. 21, 1776; *Connecticut Gazette,* Apr. 5, 1776; *Newport Mercury,* Apr. 8, 1776; *Boston Gazette,* Apr. 8, 1776; *Massachusetts Spy,* Apr. 12, 1776. Livingston's call for thanksgiving: Mar. 16, 1776, *JCC,* IV, 208–209, published in *Pennsylvania Evening Post,* Mar. 19, 1776; *New York Packet,* Mar. 21, 1776; *New-York Gazette,* Mar. 25, 1776; *Connecticut Journal,* Mar. 27, 1776; *New-York Journal,* Apr. 4, 1776; *Virginia Gazette* (Purdie), Apr. 5, 1776; *Essex Journal,* Apr. 5, 1776; *Virginia Gazette* (Dixon & Hunter), May 11, 1776; *Providence Gazette,* May 11, 1776. Arming privateers: Mar. 23, 1776, *JCC,* IV, 229–230, published in *Pennsylvania Magazine,* II (1776), 150.

34. *Pennsylvania Journal,* Mar. 20, 1776; *Constitutional Gazette,* Mar. 30, 1776; *Connecticut Gazette,* Apr. 12, 1776; *Newport Mercury,* Apr. 29, 1776; *Virginia Gazette* (Dixon & Hunter), May 18, 1776.

35. *Pennsylvania Journal,* Mar. 20, 1776.

2: THE LAST NEWS STORY OF COLONIAL AMERICA:
GERMAN MERCENARIES

Gossip had consistently cropped up in colonial newspapers throughout 1775 about British efforts to employ Russian or German soldiers. British commanders inside besieged Boston initially fueled that fire. Back in August 1775, General Thomas Gage was allegedly warning Bostonians that they should stay in the city because "30,000 Hanoverians, 30,000 Hessians, and as many Russians, are shortly expected, when they shall destroy all the rebels at once." An intercepted message from one of his aides to General John Burgoyne, published in Philadelphia, New York, and New Haven, boasted the British would have "early next Spring 20,000 Russians."[36]

In early 1776, more accounts about Russians circulated through the colonial press. The House of Lords' debates on the propriety of George's request to Catherine the Great for 20,000 soldiers ran in a few northern newspapers. Another letter from a "gentleman in Virginia" informed readers in Providence, New York, Philadelphia, and New Haven that the Russians were, in fact, not coming. Russia's "apprehension entertained of American cruelties to their prisoners of war" lay behind Catherine's refusal of Britain's request—it was the Americans who were the real barbarians. But in April, seven newspapers informed their readers that Britain had asked Russia to reconsider. For months, while they worried about slaves rising from within and Indians sweeping down from Canada, a possible invasion of Russians also hung over patriot heads.[37]

As rumors of potential Russian involvement continued to spread in 1776, so did the passion of American rhetoric in the newspapers. Conspiracies began to take flight. In one Massachusetts print, a letter from London stated that "by way of compliment to the Empress of all the Russians, for their assis-

---

36. Gage: *Pennsylvania Gazette,* Aug. 23, 1775; *Maryland Journal,* Aug. 20, 1775. "20,000 Russians": *Pennsylvania Packet,* Nov. 27, 1775; *Pennsylvania Journal,* Nov. 29, 1775; *Pennsylvania Gazette,* Nov. 29, 1775; *Constitutional Gazette,* Dec. 2, 1775; *New-York Gazette,* Dec. 2, 1775; *Connecticut Courant,* Dec. 11, 1775.

37. House of Lords: *Boston Gazette,* Jan. 15, 1776; *Norwich Packet,* Jan. 15–22, 1776; *New-York Journal,* Jan. 25, 1776. "American cruelties": *Pennsylvania Journal,* Feb. 14, 1776; *Pennsylvania Mercury,* Feb. 19, 1776; *Constitutional Gazette,* Feb. 21, 1776; *Connecticut Journal,* Feb. 28, 1776; *Providence Gazette,* Mar. 2, 1776. British request to Russia: *Pennsylvania Journal,* Mar. 20, 1776; *New-England Chronicle,* Apr. 13, 1776; *Connecticut Gazette,* Apr. 19, 1776; *Connecticut Courant,* Apr. 22, 1776; *Newport Mercury,* Apr. 22, 1776; *Connecticut Journal,* Apr. 24, 1776; *Constitutional Gazette,* Apr. 24, 1776.

tance in reducing the American colonies, the Greek church will be established in such colonies as fast as they may be reduced, or *clumsily conquered*." Another writer in the *Virginia Gazette* wondered whether "Russia, in refusing the 20,000 she had promised to the king of Britain, is waiting only for an offer of a share in the dominion of the colonies, after they are subdued?" In March, papers in Providence and New York printed an oration delivered by a graduating student at Rhode Island College (later Brown University). The impassioned speech discussed the "inhuman horrid plans of the present British ministry," including gruesome detail about Britain's "contaminated hands" extending the *"butchering knife* to savages" on the frontier. "But it seems," the student explained, "though Britons' hearts recoil, and kindred blood doth chill and stagnate at the horrid deed, yet Hanoverians and Hessians are demanded, and even Russia's frozen and half settled regions must be dispeopled for the purpose."[38]

In reality, the crown had shifted its attention away from Russia long before the spring of 1776. They next called on the small German principalities of Hanover, Hesse-Cassel, Brunswick, and Waldeck for auxiliaries. Colonial understanding of British efforts to recruit German mercenaries followed a pattern similar to the Russian attempts: George III applied to a foreign state for military assistance, Americans heard a little about it, and—in the absence of substantive information—speculation ran wild. In the case of Germans, though, patriot leaders would realize at a very late date that these reports were indeed credible.[39]

The crown's effort to procure troops from the German states was always more likely to succeed than the Russian gambit. Britain had long experience with troops from Hesse and Brunswick. This familiarity, along with the

38. *"Clumsily conquered"*: *Essex Journal*, Mar. 1, 1776 (supplement). "Waiting for a share": *Virginia Gazette* (Purdie), May 10, 1776; *Virginia Gazette* (Dixon & Hunter), May 11, 1776. College oration: *Providence Gazette*, Mar. 9, 1776; *Constitutional Gazette*, Mar. 23, 1776.

39. Despite Britain's aid in Russia's recent war against the Ottoman Empire, Catherine feared sending troops to the American colonies might cause general war in Europe. For the refusal, see Nikolai N. Bolkhovitinov, *Russia and the American Revolution*, trans. and ed. C. Jay Smith (Tallahassee, Fla., 1976), 6–7; Catherine II to George III, Moscow, Sept. 23, [Oct. 4], 1775, in Nina N. Bashkina et al., eds., *The United States and Russia: The Beginning of Relations, 1765–1815* (Washington, D.C., 1980), 33–35. See also David M. Griffiths, "Catherine the Great, the British Opposition, and the American Revolution," in Lawrence S. Kaplan, ed., *The American Revolution and "A Candid World"* (Kent, Oh., 1977), 85–110.

king's direct connections with Hanover and the professional soldier market the German states had perfected in the eighteenth century, facilitated negotiations with individual provinces. In November 1775, William Faucitt, a colonel in the British army, was already drumming up recruits in Hanover and Hesse; by mid-December, the princes had drawn up a draft treaty and sent it to England for confirmation. They finalized an official agreement in February 1776.[40]

Although Britain had employed German mercenaries in several earlier wars, at first the crown was not convinced that soldiers from Germany should be sent across the Atlantic. Initial plans instead called for them to replace garrisons in Ireland, Gibraltar, Port Mahon, or Minorca. The combination of several factors—defeat in Massachusetts, Canada, and Virginia and the protests of the Irish Parliament—forced the British government to change its plans. Four principalities—Hesse-Cassel, Hanau, Waldeck, and Brunswick—signed treaties with Britain. Hesse-Cassel sent the largest contingent of troops, 12,000 infantrymen, while the other provinces sent various amounts: 3,964 infantry and cavalry from Brunswick, 668 soldiers from Hanau, and 500 from Waldeck. A fifth state, the Electorate of Hanover, also assisted, but because of the connection with George III, no treaty was necessary.[41]

According to the treaties, Britain was to be responsible for transporting, paying, and caring for the German soldiers, who were to receive the same wages as regular British troops. Forbidden from altering the mission of these mercenaries, the treaties stipulated that they were only to serve in North America. In return, each prince was to receive a levy of thirty crowns banco (four shillings, nine pence, three farthings) for every soldier enlisted, along with large bonuses paid annually for every year the troops were in America and double subsidies for two years after the conflict ended. The treaties demanded another fiscal responsibility of Britain: blood money. Although absent from the Hessian agreement, the contracts with Brunswick, Waldeck, and Hanau guaranteed that the crown would reimburse the princes for troops lost, stipulating that three wounded soldiers would equal

40. Rodney Atwood, *The Hessians: Mercenaries from Hessen-Kassel in the American Revolution* (Cambridge, 1980), 25; Charles W. Ingrao, *The Hessian Mercenary State: Ideas, Institutions, and Reform under Frederick II, 1760–1785* (Cambridge, 1987), 122–163.

41. Piers Mackesy, *The War for America, 1775–1783* (Cambridge, Mass., 1964), 61–62.

one dead man and thus thirty more crowns to the affected German state's treasury.[42]

As much as Americans would later criticize the treaties and their precise economic calculations of human life, by the practices of eighteenth-century warfare, the hiring of auxiliary troops was commonplace. Sanctioned by international law, all the European powers supplemented their forces with mercenaries, including Britain on several occasions in their recent wars on the Continent. A few years earlier, William Pitt boasted that he had conquered North America in Germany through his hiring and equipping ninety thousand German troops in the Seven Years' War. Dedicated to expanding its new naval supremacy, Britain increasingly left land warfare to the hired help.[43]

Word that Britain was negotiating with the princes of Germany rapidly reached America. Again, as in the case of Russia, verifiable information was difficult to come by; in the absence of hard facts, unconfirmed reports flourished. Hearsay about German mercenaries began as early as the fall of 1775, but the reports would not receive any corroboration until the following spring. Early on in 1776, then, stories about Germans coming over did not receive as much attention as patriot speculation about the possibility of thousands of Russians disembarking in Boston or New York City.

That all changed in the first few days of May.

Despite all the rumors about German troops coming to America, the news Captain John Lee had to relate upon landing in Massachusetts still came as a shock. Lee reached Newburyport after a month-long voyage from Bilboa, Spain. Along the way, he fell in with a convoy of sixty sail of transports carrying twenty-seven commissioners sent by Britain to negotiate a settlement with America—and, failing that, twelve thousand Hessian troops "to burn and destroy all in their power."[44]

42. Frances Gardiner Davenport and Charles Oscar Paullin, eds., *European Treaties Bearing on the History of the United States and Its Dependencies* (Washington, D.C., 1937), IV, 118–122.

43. Atwood, *Hessians*, 1–2, 22–24; Ingrao, *Hessian Mercenary State*, 136–137. For more on Pitt and Britain's experience with auxiliaries in the Seven Years' War, see Eliga H. Gould, *The Persistence of Empire: British Political Culture in the Age of the American Revolution* (Chapel Hill, N.C., 2000), 52; Richard Middleton, *The Bells of Victory: The Pitt-Newcastle Ministry and the Conduct of the Seven Years' War, 1757–1762* (Cambridge, 1985), 148; Sir Reginald Savory, *His Britannic Majesty's Army in Germany during the Seven Years War* (Oxford, 1966).

44. Thomas Cushing to John Hancock, [Watertown, Mass.], May 3, 1776, in

The speed with which Lee's information ascended the chains of command reflected patriot concerns about the mercenaries. Lee arrived in port just after noon on May 2. That same day, he briefed the Salem committee of safety about his encounter with the British fleet. The Salem committee immediately scribbled a letter to Thomas Cushing in the Massachusetts General Court. The following day, General Ward wrote to Washington, who was already in New York making plans to defend the city against that expected fleet, while Cushing also dashed off letters to Congress and other army commanders. Cushing's express arrived at Washington's headquarters first, after seven o'clock on the evening of May 7. With no time to lose, Washington composed his own letter to Congress that night. Ward's confirmation of this account arrived from Salem before Washington sealed the note; Washington added a discussion of it in a postscript. On May 10, just a week after the news reached shore in Newburyport, all the key patriot authorities—the Massachusetts provincial government, the Continental army in New York, and the Continental Congress in Philadelphia—had strong testimony that an invasion fleet was imminent.[45]

The remainder of the populace was informed with commensurate speed. Just as the political and military network had transmitted Lee's message to Washington in the span of a few days, so, too, the continental communication system spread the word. In fact, New England newspaper readers knew about the Hessian transports before the commanding general did.

John Carter's *Providence Gazette* was the first to publish Lee's testimony on May 4. This report came directly from the Salem committee to the Massachusetts governor and then immediately to the print shop. Unlike the spectrum of conflicting reports over the past few months, the Lee account was quite accurate. It informed of the commissioners and twelve thousand Germans, but it also relayed fresh news from the Continent, including the

---

William Bell Clark et al., eds., *Naval Documents of the American Revolution*, 12 vols. (Washington, D.C., 1964–), IV, 1390–1391; Cushing to GW, Watertown, Mass., May 3, 1776, *PGW: RW*, IV, 190–191; Richard Derby, Jr., to Gen. Artemas Ward, Ipswich, May 2, 1776, and Ward to GW, Boston, May 3, 1776, in 4 *Am. Archives*, V, 1183–1184.

45. GW to Hancock, New York, May 7, 1776, *PGW: RW*, IV, 226. This was not the only channel that provided information about the Lee account. Isaac Smith wrote to John Adams from Salem on May 4 with some of the Lee information (*PJA*, IV, 165–167). Portsmouth merchant Pierse Long also wrote to New Hampshire delegate to Congress Josiah Bartlett three days later relating the ship captain's sighting. See Frank C. Mevers, ed., *The Papers of Josiah Bartlett* (Hanover, N.H., 1979), 58.

settlement of disagreements between Britain and Prussia that made the deal with Hesse-Cassel possible and the intelligence that four thousand Hanoverians were soon to accompany General Burgoyne's expedition to Quebec. Most important, the committee's report ended with a chilling disclosure: if peace could not be achieved with the commissioners, then the mercenaries were to "lay waste the Country, if in their Power."[46]

The official Salem statement shot through American newspapers. Two days later—still before Washington knew about it—Norwich, Connecticut, learned of the Lee report. New York papers picked it up a couple of days after that, then Philadelphia and Williamsburg. In all, thirteen prints in the month of May copied the Salem statement. Part of the reason for the electric response to Lee's intelligence was that it came as a surprise. As far as colonial newspapers were concerned, all had been quiet on the European mercenary front. By May, Americans were largely aware that Britain's first efforts to convince Russia had failed, but little other information on this topic had been newsworthy for several months. Naturally, Americans were kept in the dark about Britain's military plans; the ink was dry on Britain's treaties with the German provinces before Americans learned of the provisions. So Lee's eyewitness testimony about the presence, quantity, and location of the Hessian transports came as a shock. But another reason the Lee account gained such attention throughout the Eastern Seaboard was that it was not the only news about the Hessians that broke in the first few days of May. Alongside the Salem statements were other articles about Britain and their hireling soldiers. In many cases, whole pages of the newspapers throughout May and June related news of the Germans.[47]

A second article, initially appearing in Dunlap's *Pennsylvania Packet,* copied information from an Irish print that almost doubled the number of German mercenaries. Twenty thousand Hessians, Brunswickers, Waldeckers, and Hanoverians were part of a total force of forty-five thousand soldiers making their way across the Atlantic, the Dublin paper reported. More than just troop statistics, this extract was also the first to put a dol-

46. *Providence Gazette,* May 4, 1776.

47. *Norwich Packet,* Apr. 29–May 6, 1776; *Constitutional Gazette,* May 8, 1776; *New-England Chronicle,* May 9, 1776; *New-York Gazette,* May 9, 1776; *Pennsylvania Evening Post,* May 9, 1776; *Connecticut Gazette,* May 10, 1776; *Connecticut Journal,* May 15, 1776; *Pennsylvania Gazette,* May 15, 1776; *Pennsylvania Journal,* May 15, 1776; *Pennsylvania Ledger,* May 18, 1776; *Maryland Gazette,* May 23, 1776; *Virginia Gazette* (Purdie), May 24, 31, 1776.

lar amount on the expedition, contending that the mercenary recruitment would cost an already indebted Britain £900,000 in soldiers' wages alone, adding £350,000 for transporting them over the ocean plus £300,000 more for ammunition and supplies. Dunlap's publishing of this account, which traveled north along the same roads that Captain Lee's account traversed coming south, did not pass without a sharp comment.[48]

Patriot leaders had expected Britain to send emissaries or ambassadors to investigate and perhaps settle the rebellion, and rumors about who would be among the envoys spread rapidly. Many believed respected veterans of the Seven Years' War, especially Sir Jeffrey Amherst, would be among the 1776 mission. But in the days before Captain Lee hailed the fleet of commissioners and their bodyguards, speculation still surrounded this delegation. The Dublin account's suggestion that the emissaries would not be British peace officials but, instead, foreign mercenaries sent to subdue them, was news. That thousands of mercenary troops would accompany the commissioners did not bode well for negotiations, and the hopes of many who looked to this peace initiative to end the war were dashed. Dunlap's terse but emotional comment reflects this feeling of betrayal, a sentence appended to nearly all the reprintings of the Dublin article: *"Oh* GEORGE! *Are these thy commissioners of peace and reconciliation? However, we fear them not — Their treachery, is all we have to fear."* The report appeared in twenty colonial newspapers from Virginia to Massachusetts, with its highest frequency coming in coastal cities that were the potential targets of this invasion force. Papers in Baltimore, Annapolis, Norwich, Portsmouth, and Providence each ran the story, along with impressive coverage in Boston, New York City, and Philadelphia.[49]

Together, the Dublin article (with Dunlap's exclamation) and Lee's eyewitness account confirmed that Britain was committed to continuing the

48. *Pennsylvania Packet,* May 6, 1776.

49. For the plans and preparations of the 1776 peace commission, see Ira D. Gruber, *The Howe Brothers and the American Revolution* (New York, 1972), 72–88. Dublin account, published Mar. 2, 1776 (emphasis added): *Pennsylvania Packet,* May 6, 1776 (supplement); *Pennsylvania Evening Post,* May 7, 1776; *Pennsylvania Journal,* May 8, 1776; *New-York Journal,* May 9, 1776; *New York Packet,* May 9, 1776; *Pennsylvania Ledger,* May 11, 1776; *Massachusetts Spy,* May 13, 1776; *Maryland Journal,* May 13, 1776; *Norwich Packet,* May 6–13, 1776; *Connecticut Courant,* May 13, 1776; *New-York Gazette,* May 13, 1776; *Constitutional Gazette,* May 15, 1776; *Maryland Gazette,* May 16, 1776; *New-England Chronicle,* May 16, 1776; *Connecticut Gazette,* May 16, 1776; *Virginia Gazette* (Purdie), May 17, 1776; *Providence Gazette,* May 18, 1776; *Newport Mercury,* May 20, 1776; *Boston Gazette,* May 20, 1776; *Freeman's Journal* (Portsmouth), May 25, 1776.

war with vigor. Often the stories ran in sequential issues, with Lee's report acting almost as proof that clinched Dunlap's point. But as the stories swept through the continent's communication networks, another account of the Hessian mercenaries also came to the attention of Congress and the Continental army, a third source that subsequently appeared in most colonial papers right alongside the first two. This third version also had concrete information of Britain's treaties with the German states: the texts themselves.[50]

The day after Washington's letter about Captain Lee and the fleet reached Congress in Philadelphia, news from another informant reached Continental army headquarters. On May 10, just three days after he had forwarded Captain Lee's report to President Hancock, New Hampshire patriot John Langdon sent General Washington information about George Merchant, an escaped prisoner of war making his way south with an exciting story and even more exciting documents. A rifleman in Captain Daniel Morgan's company, Merchant was captured in November while he stood guard in Quebec. The Virginia marksman and his hunting shirt fascinated his captors; they sent him across the Atlantic to London for interrogation, and he was later incarcerated in Bristol. According to one Congressman who later recounted the tale to his brother, in Bristol "a number [of] Gentn, procured [Merchant] a passage to Hallifax. . . . Tho[ugh] Searched at Hallifax two or three times, [he] brought undiscovered a Number of Letters and Newspapers to the Congress, by which we are possessed of all their plans for the destruction of America." Actually, the Virginia rifleman had presented himself and his papers to Langdon in New Hampshire. Among Merchant's papers, which he had hidden in the lining of his clothes, were copies he had made of the treaties between Britain and the German principalities and letters from colonial agent Arthur Lee that further detailed the imminent mercenary invasion force. Langdon took one look, dashed off a letter, and sent Merchant on to see Washington. The commander had the same reaction. He took no chances risking this momentous news to express riders and sent Horatio Gates to lay the treaties in front of Congress personally. Merchant went along, turning up in a Philadelphia coffeehouse (perhaps Bradford's) on the evening of May 20, where, ironically, he ran into Josiah

---

50. Ten papers printed both the Dublin and Lee stories: *Connecticut Gazette, Maryland Gazette, New-England Chronicle, Constitutional Gazette, New-York Gazette, Norwich Packet, Pennsylvania Evening Post, Pennsylvania Journal, Pennsylvania Ledger,* and *Virginia Gazette* (Purdie).

Merciless Savages, Domestic Insurrectionists, and Foreign Mercenaries

Bartlett, Langdon's friend and New Hampshire delegate, to whom he again recounted his story.[51]

Like the Salem statement, which was currently in the Philadelphia papers, Congress immediately sent Merchant's copies of the German treaties to the *Pennsylvania Journal* and *Pennsylvania Gazette*. Here, again, as with the re-copying of Dunlap's Irish report, Merchant's intelligence—especially the exact text of the treaties—quickly rippled out from Philadelphia: north-west to Peter Withington's house, west on the Lancaster Road, southwest to the "Winchester Box," on board coasting ships bound for the lower Chesa-peake, and beyond. Eventually, they appeared in more than half of all the colonial presses in operation at that time. Reprinting the lengthy text of the treaties required more than a small commitment; often, papers would dedicate two or even three straight weeks to getting the information to their readers. They were, after all, only following the orders of the Continental Congress.[52]

The May news stories acted not unlike turbulent weather fronts coming into contact with each other. One eye moved south from Massachusetts; the other two blew in all directions out from Pennsylvania. The news coverage

51. Don Higginbotham, *Daniel Morgan: Revolutionary Rifleman* (Chapel Hill, N.C., 1961), 38–39; John Langdon to Washington, Portsmouth, N.H., May 10, 1776, *PGW: RW*, IV, 255–257; Caesar Rodney to Thomas Rodney, Philadelphia, May 22, 1776, *LDC*, IV, 61–63, esp. 62. See also May 30, 1776, *JCC*, IV, 405; Josiah Bartlett to John Langdon, Philadelphia, May 21, [1776], *LDC*, IV, 55.

52. *Pennsylvania Gazette*, May 22, 1776; *Pennsylvania Journal*, May 22, 24, 1776; *Pennsylvania Packet*, May 27, 1776; *Constitutional Gazette*, May 29, June 1, 1776; *Connecticut Journal*, May 29, June 5, 1776; *New York Packet*, May 30, June 6, 1776; *Connecticut Gazette*, May 31, 1776; *New-York Gazette*, June 3, 1776; *Norwich Packet*, May 27–June 3, 3–10, and 10–17, 1776; *Newport Mercury*, June 3, 6, 1776; *Connecticut Courant*, June 3, 10, 17, 1776; *Maryland Gazette*, June 6, 1776; *New-England Chronicle*, June 13, 1776; *Freeman's Journal* (Portsmouth), June 15, 1776. Even this long list does not fully encapsulate what readers of colonial newspapers learned about foreign troops in May. Other accounts from Bordeaux and Hamburg also appeared, albeit with less frequency. Bordeaux reported the movement of 20,000 Germans, a report that six papers picked up; information out of Hamburg about Faucitt's activities ran in five more. The day after Merchant appeared before Congress, the delegates resolved to "extract and publish the treaties, and such parts of the intelligence as they think proper; also, to consider of an adequate reward for the person who brought the intelligence; and to prepare an address to the foreign mercenaries who are coming to invade America" (May 21, 1776, *JCC*, IV, 369).

that resulted from these storms, moreover, was extensive. Except for one print in Williamsburg, every colonial newspaper then in operation inserted at least one of the three major stories. In short, it would have been difficult not to have known that the Hessians were coming. Whether colonists read about them in their local prints, heard them being talked about in taverns and other social spaces, or learned of them from personal letters, Americans in May 1776 were well aware of the mercenary phenomenon. Indeed, the news of the Hessians would be the last big news event of America's colonial history.[53]

Learning almost simultaneously of the arrangement to bring German mercenaries into the conflict and their being sighted in the north Atlantic produced a panic and a dramatic surge of the rumor mill. Once it was established that the fight against Britain would include foreign proxies, colonists sought to discover more about these mercenaries. On the heels of the information that the commissioners and their auxiliaries were on the western side of the Atlantic came more information about the troops themselves. Specifically, printers inserted stories in late May and early June about who the Germans were, how excited they were to come to put down the rebellion, and the deal George III made to procure them. The final point was the most significant. Colonial printers provided as much factual information about these foreign hirelings as they could, but, at bottom, these reports were like the others that involved the proxies: their purpose was really to denigrate the British and make them seem just as foreign as Russians or Hessians. As Samuel Adams had written as "Sincerus" a few months earlier, "In case foreigners are to be procured to be poured in upon us, the greatest opposers of our total separation from Britain acknowledge they would then no longer defer a declaration of independency, and application to other powers for their protection." Adams suggested that Britain's sending "foreigners" would convince all Americans that their former parent was to be regarded as equally foreign. The flurry of news about the mercenary proxies worked to prove Sincerus right. Collectively, the stories sharpened

53. The only print that did not run one of the Lee, Dublin, or Merchant reports was Dixon and Hunter's *Virginia Gazette*. This is not to suggest that Virginia's capital was entirely in the dark. Edmund Pendleton, writing to Thomas Jefferson from Williamsburg on May 24, said, "We have heard much of the Arrival of Russians, Hessians, and Comm[issione]rs to the Eastward, but nothing we can rely on" (Pendleton to TJ, Williamsburg, May 24, 1776, *PTJ*, I, 297).

and broadened colonial hatred for Britain and the king while providing room and reason for the patriots to mobilize.[54]

One way patriot printers instructed their readers about the imminent mercenary force was to describe in great detail who was coming. Printers delineated how many battalions were recruited and who their German commanders were. They related how many infantrymen were aboard transports, the number of cavalry units that were enlisted, and information about their equipment. They published descriptions to help Americans tell the difference between Brunswickers and Waldeckers. Benjamin Edes lampooned their lack of horses in his *Boston Gazette,* stating that the Hessians were "to be supplied with reign deer from his Serene Highness the Landgrave of Hesse's repository of wild beasts, for carrying their tents, artillery, and baggage."[55]

An article about one distinct group of Hessian troops made the rounds. The British had purchased 1,000 "Jagers," elite troops with famous rifles and renowned ferocity, specifically to engage the American frontiersmen. According to one report, taken from a London paper, the Jagers were "brought up to the use of the rifle barrel guns in boar hunting." Boasting of their amazing expertise, the article explained, "Every petty prince, who hath forests keeps a number of them, and they are allowed to take apprentices, by which means they are a numerous body of people." Seeing them as an antidote to America's celebrated riflemen, the London article concluded that the British government "plume themselves much" in deploying the Jagers, whom they intended to send to America without delay.[56]

Expectations about how foreign mercenaries would act once they got to America varied widely, ranging from smug dismissal to worries that they would Europeanize America. But one reaction to the news that the king had sent an overwhelming force of British and German soldiers to quell the rebellion was consistent. In mid-May, the flurry of news about expected mercenaries served as a rallying point both for the common cause and hatred for the British. One letter from Philadelphia, which appeared in four news-

54. *Pennsylvania Evening Post,* Feb. 13, 1776. As mentioned above, Philadelphia printer Robert Bell included this essay in his enlarged edition of *Common Sense* in March, adding to its circulation.

55. *Boston Gazette,* July 8, 1776.

56. *Connecticut Journal,* May 15, 1776; *Maryland Gazette,* May 16, 1776; *Connecticut Gazette,* May 24, 1776; *Freeman's Journal* (Portsmouth), May 25, 1776; *Connecticut Courant,* May 27, 1776; *New-England Chronicle,* May 23, 1776.

papers in New York and Connecticut, underscores this point. Philadelphians, after learning that thousands of offshore foreign mercenaries were about to invade, quickly became of one mind about independence. "This," the correspondent related, "gives the *Coup de Grace* to the British and American connection. It has already wrought wonders in this city; conversions have been more rapid than ever happen'd under Mr. Whitfield." Virginia planter Landon Carter, no staunch supporter of the patriots, observed a similar development in his locale. After reading about fresh news of German mercenaries in northern papers, Carter insisted in his diary that the reports were baseless rumors concocted by patriot newspapers "to alarm the people to promote the precipitate declaration of Independence." "Indeed," he concluded, "it is a pure contrivance for weak minds to bring about Independency, and it has done it in Virginia, God help us all."[57]

Carter was more right than he knew. As he wrote those words on May 18, patriot leaders in the Continental Congress had already set in motion the severing of all imperial ties with Great Britain. Even though the consti-

57. In the fall of 1775, colonial papers widely exchanged one story from London about "the plan which will be put in execution for reducing America." According to "the plan," ten thousand Hanoverians were to be "taken into British pay, the expences to be defrayed out of duties laid by parliament, and levied in America." Not only would the rebellious colonists pay for the initial costs of this expeditionary force—a body "to be kept on foot in peace as well as war"—they would be a burden to the American local governments for decades to come. "Every Hanoverian soldier, who shall have served seven years with the approbation of his superior officer or officers shall have a portion of ground, not more than 50 nor less than 20 acres, rent free, *for ever*." In addition to having to provide their conquerors with free farms, the now-subjugated colonists would foot the bill for "the expence of raising a proper habitation, furnishing the same, purchasing implements of husbandry, etc." Establishing feudal clients, standing armies, state-subsidized manors, quasi-serfs, and redistributing up to a half a million acres of land, "the plan" horrified Americans from Massachusetts to South Carolina. See *Constitutional Gazette*, Sept. 30, 1775; *Pennsylvania Packet*, Oct. 2, 1775; *Pennsylvania Evening Post*, Oct. 3, 1775; *South-Carolina Gazette*, Oct. 3, 1775; *Connecticut Journal*, Oct. 11, 1775; *Massachusetts Spy*, Oct. 13, 1775; *Virginia Gazette* (Dixon & Hunter), Oct. 14, 1775; *Boston Gazette*, Oct. 16, 1775; *Boston News-Letter*, Oct. 19, 1775; *Essex Gazette* (Salem), Oct. 20, 1775. "Coup de Grace": *New-York Journal*, May 9, 1776; *New-York Gazette*, May 13, 1776; *Connecticut Journal*, May 15, 1776; *Connecticut Gazette*, May 16, 1776. For Carter's diary entry, see May 18, 1776, in Jack P. Greene, ed., *The Diary of Colonel Landon Carter of Sabine Hall, 1752–1778*, 2 vols. (Richmond, Va., 1987), II, 1041.

tutional procedure of American independence was hardly assured by that date, the debate over independence had begun. It was the news brought by Captain John Lee and George Merchant that signaled its beginning.

The influence of men in the Continental Congress who wanted to declare independence had been growing in 1776. Often identified as the "Adams-Lee junto," this group advocated for the colonies to cut ties with Britain so they could make alliances with France or Spain and perhaps secure much-needed military and economic aid. Over the first months of 1776, Congress took some small steps, each justified in terms of defending colonial liberty from the machinations of the British ministry and its proxies. During those same weeks, some patriot provincial authorities revised their instructions to allow for their delegates to Congress to vote in favor of independence. This, again, was far from radical. Georgia had not given explicit instructions to its representative, Lyman Hall, but instead asked that he never "lose sight" of Georgia's "peculiar situation," which included "the Indians both South and North-westardly upon our backs, the fortified Town of Saint Augustine made a continual Rendezvous for Soldiers in our very Neighbourhood, together with our blacks and tories within us. Let these weighty truths be the powerful Arguments for support." Rhode Island and the Carolinas had recently given their delegates liberty to vote *yea* on the question of separation, but none of them was allowed to introduce it on the floor of Congress. Only North Carolina's instructions even used the word "independence." In many regions of the continent, especially the cities, public opinion was moving away from reconciliation in the spring of 1776. But "patriots" in Congress were not a monolith. There remained a wide spectrum of opinion on how to proceed in resisting the crown. Independence, even in early May, was not inevitable.[58]

58. The influence of the "Adams-Lee junto" has been a subject of historical debate. Merrill Jensen first wrote that the Adams cousins and Richard Henry Lee were the irresistible, driving forces that, frankly, forced the colonies to embrace independence in his 1940 book *The Articles of Confederation: An Interpretation of the Social-Constitutional History of the American Revolution, 1774–1781* ([Madison, Wis.], 1940), 54–103, esp. 102. Jack N. Rakove rejected this thesis as too determinative and instead highlighted the contingent factors and context in which the Second Continental Congress reached their decisions. See his *Beginnings of National Politics: An Interpretive History of the Continental Congress* (New York, 1979), 101–110, esp. 102. See also Robert Middlekauff, *The Glorious Cause: The American Revolution, 1763–1789*, rev. ed. (1982; rpt. New York, 2005), 326. Hall on Georgia: May 20, 1776, *JCC*, IV,

Then John Lee's ship docked in Newburyport, and the captain quickly went to relate what he saw to the Salem committee of safety. Lee's eyewitness testimony provided patriot authorities with new evidence that the king was unwilling to compromise. This information made it to Philadelphia at the start of the second week in May. Benjamin Towne published Lee's statement in his *Pennsylvania Evening Post* on May 9; Dunlap had just brought out the intelligence from Dublin in the May 7 issue of his *Pennsylvania Packet*. This was the context into which the Congress passed the resolution instructing all colonies to "adopt such government as shall, in the opinion of the representatives of the people, best conduce to the happiness and safety of their constituents in particular, and America in general."[59] The news of foreign mercenaries and the British invasion fleet was not the only cause of this critical decision—as several historians have argued, some in the Congress were searching for a way to overturn moderate adherents to proprietary government in Pennsylvania and Maryland—but this development was, nonetheless, a catalyst for action.[60]

For all it entailed, the language of this resolution was practical and vague; it did not engender a great deal of controversy among the delegates. Congress nominated John Adams, Richard Henry Lee, and South Carolinian Edward Rutledge to write a preamble for this resolution. What they came up with three days later, however, touched off an acrimonious debate on the floor of the State House. Adams, the preamble's principal author, wrote a provocative summation that was "even more radical than the resolution it introduced." His preamble was unprecedented for two reasons. First, he personally blamed "his Britannic Majesty" for the troubles of the past year.

---

367. For North Carolina's instructions to delegates, see "Friday, April 12th, 1776," in Saunders, ed., *Col. Records of N.C.*, X, 510–513, esp. 512.

59. May 10, 1776, *JCC*, IV, 342. The same day they passed this well-known resolution, it should be noted that they also discussed how to apprehend Moses Kirkland, the loyalist leader from South Carolina who had recently escaped from the Philadelphia jail. They posted a reward and sent an express south warning patriots in the Carolinas that he might return to cause more civil unrest (346).

60. For the relationship between Congress, the Pennsylvania and Maryland Assemblies, and the May 10 resolution, see Merrill Jensen, *The Founding of a Nation: A History of the American Revolution, 1763–1776* (New York, 1968), 681–687; Richard Alan Ryerson, *The Revolution Is Now Begun: The Radical Committees of Philadelphia, 1765–1776* (Philadelphia, 1978), 208–216; Rakove, *Beginnings of National Politics*, 96; William Hogeland, *Declaration: The Nine Tumultuous Weeks When America Became Independent, May 1–July 4, 1776* (New York, 2010).

Merciless Savages, Domestic Insurrectionists, and Foreign Mercenaries

Also, he added the fresh news from the Atlantic to the list of the king's crimes, stating, "The whole force of that Kingdom aided by foreign Mercenaries is to be exerted for the destruction of the good People of these Colonies." In both of these innovations, Adams anticipated Jefferson's Declaration of Independence, which, incidentally, he believed he had just written.[61]

According to notes Adams made during the debate that raged from May 13–15, New York delegate James Duane asked, "Why all this Haste? Why this Urging? Why this driving?" Thomas McKean of Delaware gave the obvious response: "Dont doubt that foreign Mercenaries are coming to destroy Us. I do think We shall loose our Liberties, Properties and Lives too, if We do not take this Step." The news of more than ten thousand Germans did seem difficult to believe; Joseph Hewes fumed that it seemed the British had bought "near half of Germany." Even Adams himself wrote the next day, "The Story of Such formidable Numbers of foreign Mercenaries, I conjecture to be chiefly Puff, but yet there may be Some Truth in it." When George Merchant arrived in Congress five days later to present the German treaties, even Duane had to concede that McKean was right.[62]

By a slim margin, Congress passed the resolution with Adams's preamble on May 15. That same day, in Williamsburg, the Virginia Convention also thought that the time had come for the colonies to declare independence. At least some frontier Virginians believed so. On May 10, Alexander Purdie published the instructions sent by Charlotte County, out near Virginia's southwestern frontier. The Charlotte County committee had charged that because "the despotick plan adopted by the king, ministry, and parliament of Great Britain" had encouraged "by every means in their power, our savage neighbours, and our more savage domesticks, to spill the blood of our wives and children," all hopes for reconciliation "being now at an end." Intending their instructions to become part of the public discourse, the Charlotte County committee ordered the resolves printed in the *Virginia Gazette*. They were reprinted in Boston and Philadelphia.[63]

61. Pauline Maier, *American Scripture: Making the Declaration of Independence* (New York, 1997), 37; May 10, 15, 1776, *JCC*, IV, 342, 357–358; Adams diary entry, May 15, 1776, in L. H. Butterfield, ed., *Diary and Autobiography of John Adams*, III (Cambridge, Mass., 1961), 385–386.

62. John Adams's Notes on Debates, May 13–15, 1776, *LDC*, III, 668, 669, Joseph Hewes to James Iredell, Philadelphia, May 17, 1776, IV, 27, JA to Joseph Palmer, May 16, 1776, IV, 3.

63. "Charlotte County Committee to Delegates Paul Carrington and Thomas

Then, on May 14, Indian agent Captain John Gibson arrived in the Virginia capital straight from Fort Pitt with his own stunning news: there was a "great Probability" that some of the Ohio Indians, including the Wyandots and Ottawas, would be "Troublesome" on the frontiers "this Summer." The following day, as Adams saw passage of the "most important Resolution that ever was taken in America," the Virginia Convention took steps that pleased many patriots in Charlotte County. They first drafted a warning to Lord Dunmore that if he sent any more runaway slaves under a flag of truce to negotiate with patriot militia officers, they would be seized instantly. When one patriot, very probably a member of the convention itself, related this behavior in a letter to Philadelphia—which was naturally given to the *Pennsylvania Journal*—he wrote, "Dunmore lately had the unparalleled brutality to insult us with a flag, accompanied by stolen slaves." "Orders are now given, to acquaint that infernal monster, that if such an insult should be repeated, the slaves will be seized and secured." With that affront out of the way, they took up the business of proving Adams wrong about important resolutions dated May 15, 1776. The convention's 112 members passed a near-unanimous resolution instructing Virginia's delegation in Congress to bring forward a motion of independence. The convention also decided to begin drafting a declaration of rights and a new constitution, not waiting for Congress to give them authorization.[64]

Like the other May 15 resolution, Virginia's proclamation came with a lengthy preamble. In this, it should not surprise, the proxies featured prominently. The colonies had no choice, argued Edmund Pendleton, author of Virginia's resolution:

Read: A Public Letter of Instructions," Apr. 23, 1776, *Rev. Va.*, VI, 447–448, esp. 447. They were printed in *Virginia Gazette* (Purdie), May 10, 1776; *Pennsylvania Evening Post,* May 21, 1776; *Essex Journal,* June 14, 1776.

64. JA to James Warren, May 15, 1776, *LDC*, III, 676, 678–679; Fifth Virginia Convention, "Proceedings of Ninth Day of Session," May 15, 1776, *Rev. Va.*, VII, 141. Fort Pitt: Fifth Virginia Convention, "Proceedings of Eighth Day of Session," Charlestown, S.C., May 14, 1776, and Botetourt County Committee, "Patrick Lockhart to the Chairman of the Committee of Botetourt," Williamsburg, Va., May 14, 1776, ibid., 6–7, 124–125n, 135. The Virginia committee of safety responded to Gibson's intelligence by ordering 2,250 pounds of gunpowder to the frontier immediately ("Proceedings of the Committee," May 14, 1776, 132–134). "Unparalleled brutality": *Pennsylvania Journal,* May 29, 1776; *Constitutional Gazette,* June 1, 1776; *New-York Journal,* June 6, 1776; *Norwich Packet,* June 10, 1776. Virginia motion for independence: *PTJ,* I, 290. See also *Rev. Va.,* VII, 4–6.

Merciless Savages, Domestic Insurrectionists, and Foreign Mercenaries

Fleets and Armies are raised, and the aid of foreign troops engaged to assist these destructive purposes: The king's representative in this colony hath not only withheld all the powers of government from operating for our safety, but, having retired on board an armed ship, is carrying on a piratical and savage war against us, tempting our slaves, by every artifice, to resort to him, and training and employing them against their masters.

Claiming, "In this state of extreme danger we have no alternative left," the Virginia Assembly contended that only "a total separation from the crown and government of Great Britain" could "unit[e] and exer[t] the strength of all America."[65]

Pendleton and the Virginia Convention initiated the process that, in six weeks, would produce the Declaration of Independence. Although neither Lee's report nor Dunlap's article from Dublin had surfaced in either of Williamsburg's local papers yet (they would the following week), the news of foreign mercenaries was still at the core of patriots' justification for severing ties with Britain. The combination of thousands of German mercenaries, the long-standing ordeal Virginians had endured with Dunmore, and now perhaps Indian attacks across the frontier convinced them that they needed to separate. The time for reconciliation had passed: "We are driven from that inclination by . . . wicked councils, and the eternal laws of self-preservation."[66]

3: "NOW WE ARE A PEOPLE!"
THE CONTEXT FOR INDEPENDENCE AND THE DECLARATION

It took a week for Virginia's resolution to reach Congress. On Monday, May 27, their delegation introduced it, and thus began the movement toward independence. But an examination of the context for independence and the Declaration reveals what else was going on for the delegates to Congress. At that moment, they were thinking about the proxies quite a bit. On that Monday, Benjamin Franklin wrote with signature brevity, "The German Auxiliaries are certainly coming. It is our Business to prevent their Returning." Meanwhile, during those same hours, Dunmore landed his ships on a small island in the Chesapeake Bay to prevent the spread of smallpox through his black regiment. And, in the Philadelphia papers, stories

65. *PTJ*, I, 290–291.
66. Ibid.

had just been published relating Britain's true plans for the upcoming campaign. "Charles Town, South Carolina, is to be the first sacrifice, and then he is to go northward," an anonymous letter from London reported in the *Pennsylvania Journal*. "I withhold any comments on this scheme, or those of setting the Indians and slaves to murder defenceless women and children; but surely the God who presides over the universe, with justice and mercy will shower down destruction on the advisers as well as executors of such horrid deeds." With that information, the London correspondent concluded, "There is no alternative but an instant declaration of independence and a consequent negotiation, at least for naval assistance; or an humble submission to be slaves to Scotchmen." Not all Scotchman would be their overseers: the papers informed readers that Highlanders captured at Moore's Creek had arrived in Philadelphia that week to be incarcerated alongside John Connolly in the crowded Philadelphia jail. Finally, Dunlap's *Pennsylvania Packet* reported that one prominent loyalist had run to Dunmore, taking sixty or seventy slaves with him, "thereby marking himself a vile apostate, and *black* traitor."[67]

Some delegates might have had that fresh issue of the *Packet* with them as they opened business that Monday morning, May 27. Whether or not they had read about ongoing troubles with British proxies in that week's paper, the issue would be inescapable on that particular day, as it had been on many, many days over the previous twelve months. The morning's business began with a letter from George Morgan, Indian Superintendent for the Middle Department, stationed at Fort Pitt. Morgan, who had just arrived at that post, having been elected superintendent in April, corroborated patriot concerns that the situation with the Ohio Indians was as they had feared. The treaties of neutrality negotiated the previous autumn were beginning to fall apart. "This is a critical time, and unless the Commissioners can attend to their department, or I have full powers, you will hear of things going very wrong." To make matters worse, Morgan related, "Things are not right with the Northern Indians, particularly with the Senecas," and he feared that a combined British, loyalist, and Indian force from the Niagara area was planning to move against Pittsburgh. Neither Morgan nor Con-

---

67. BF to the Commissioners of Canada, New York, May 27, 1776, *LDC*, IV, 85; *Pennsylvania Journal*, May 24, 1776. Jail: *Pennsylvania Evening Post*, May 25, 1776. "Black traitor": *Pennsylvania Gazette*, May 22, 1776; *Pennsylvania Packet*, May 27, 1776 (supplement).

gress yet knew that Indians and patriot soldiers were at war on the St. Lawrence, just downriver from Montreal.[68]

The information contained in Morgan's letter surely influenced how the members of Congress interacted with representatives from those same "northern Indians" who had recently arrived in Philadelphia. General Philip Schuyler had arranged transportation for this twenty-one-person delegation from the Six Nations, which had arrived in Philadelphia on Saturday, May 25. Leaving the details to be worked out later, Congress issued orders to Morgan at Fort Pitt and Schuyler at Albany to "prevail upon" the Indians in their neighborhoods "to undertake the reduction" of British forts at Detroit and Niagara. This new strategy, which Congress deemed "highly expedient," was exactly what patriot publicists had been accusing their enemies of doing for an entire year. That they did this just as the delegation from the Six Nations arrived should not suggest that those deputies had traveled to Philadelphia to request patriot assistance, however. Washington had informed Congress that Indian relations on the northern frontier were "rather delicate," so patriot leaders decided to keep this development a secret. Instead, Congress chose to "give those savages some idea of our strength and importance," as one representative put it.[69]

At 9:00 on that Monday morning, before opening business on what would be a very eventful day, the delegates supervised a military review for the Iroquois, with, in the words of Richard Henry Lee, "between 2 and 3 thousand men parading on the Common," to the Indians' "great astonish-

68. Morgan was made superintendent on April 10, 1776 (*JCC*, IV, 266–270). See George Morgan to Lewis Morris, Pittsburgh, May 16, 1776, *4 Am. Archives*, VI, 474–475, read in Congress on May 27 (*JCC*, IV, 396). Also on that day, Virginia militia commander Andrew Lewis wrote to Charles Lee from Williamsburg, "We have most alarming Intelligence from the Cherokee Nation, many emissaries being amongst them with a very large quantity of powder, and their declared intention of acting against us." See Andrew Lewis to Charles Lee, Williamsburg, May 27, 1776, "The Lee Papers, Vol. II, 1776–1778," *Collections of the New-York Historical Society: For the Year 1872*, V (New York, 1873), 43.

69. May 25, 1776, *JCC*, IV, 394–395; GW to Major General Philip Schuyler, Amboy, N.J., May 22, 1776, *PGW: RW*, IV, 372–374, esp. 373; Joseph Hewes to Samuel Johnston, Philadelphia, May 26, 1776, *LDC*, IV, 78. For more background, see Barbara Graymont, *The Iroquois in the American Revolution* (Syracuse, N.Y., 1972), 100–101. For the expectations of these deputies of the Six Nations, see "Message from the Six Nations," *PGW: RW*, IV, 319–320.

ment and delight. We hope effectually to secure to the friendship of their people." Not willing to announce their change in policy, this display of military prowess was the pretense Congress relied on during the last days of May. On the New York frontier, Schuyler—who knew best just how "delicate" the situation was—suggested to Washington that, if the charade to impress the Six Nations collapsed, a more effective solution might be to detain them "as long as possible . . . that they might serve as a Kind of Hostages, for the peaceable Demeanor of the others." Perhaps once they learned about what had happened on the St. Lawrence, at a place called the Cedars, patriot leaders might have wished they had followed Schuyler's advice.[70]

It was a coincidence that Congress's military performance for the Six Nations occurred on the same day delegates entered three dispatches into the minutes. In addition to Morgan's letter, Joseph Hewes, currently the sole member of the North Carolina delegation, received the new instructions of April 5 freeing him to support independence. Also that day, the Virginia members presented Edmund Pendleton's resolution of May 15. Those disparate packets of intelligence had begun their journey toward Philadelphia from three different directions and over several different weeks. That, one, they collided together in a single day's session of Congress (the morning of which they happened to spend watching a parade thrown to impress proxy visitors), and two, they all referred in some way to a threat to the Revolution posed by people allied with the crown, occurred too often to be deemed a phenomenon. The war's first year witnessed many of these confluences. Worries that British officials might successfully prevail on blacks, Indians, or foreigners to destroy the common cause were a constant presence in the minutes of patriot organizations at all levels. Patriots tried to counteract events on the ground involving real or invented resistant slaves, hostile Indians, or conspiring tories by fashioning a narrative that explained such behavior as illegitimate and treacherous, and that discourse would shape policy outcomes in the future.

The circular relationship between event, discourse, and policy was evident in the delegates' hectic agenda on May 27. Faced with the possible problem of resistant Indians on the Pennsylvania frontier, they took two

70. Richard Henry Lee to Charles Lee, Philadelphia, May 27, 1776, *LDC*, IV, 87; Schuyler to GW, Fort George, May 26, 1776, *PGW: RW*, IV, 388–390, esp. 388. The Six Nations reciprocated with their own performance, putting on a "War-dance" on May 28. See Caesar Rodney to Thomas Rodney, Philadelphia, May 29, 1776, *LDC*, IV, 99.

Merciless Savages, Domestic Insurrectionists, and Foreign Mercenaries

interrelated steps to allay it. First, they put on a performance, a representation, to try to shape a second representation: how those twenty-one Iroquois described patriot power when they returned home. Second, they ordered hundreds of pounds of gunpowder west to ensure the Fort Pitt arsenal was well stocked in case theatricality failed. The resolutions from North Carolina and Virginia the delegates read to their colleagues that day only underscored the virtue of these political moves. Both colonies justified undertaking independence because the British government employed proxies: the crown protected "slaves who should imbrue their hands in the blood of their masters" (North Carolina) and engaged "foreign troops . . . to assist these destructive purposes" (Virginia). These were stock images and arguments by the end of May, but that did not diminish their power. They had become the reason patriots most readily invoked to validate leaving the British Empire. In fact, as the Continental Congress began to consider the question of independence—over the forty days between the arrival of Virginia's proposal and the approval of the Declaration—the problem of the king's proxies, heretofore a chronic hum in patriot ears, was becoming a loud roar.

* * *

After Horatio Gates laid George Merchant's well-traveled copies of the German treaties in front of Congress, the delegates ordered them extracted and printed, then formed a committee to "prepare an address to the foreign mercenaries who are coming to invade America." They might have been encouraged to take this step by similar suggestions that appeared throughout the newspaper scene at that time. On May 16, John Holt published a letter from a sympathetic English correspondent that opined, "If offers of settlement etc. are prepared to fling into the camp in German, when the Germans arrive, it must have a great effect." Seven other printers, including two Philadelphia ones, exchanged this suggestion. In late May, Dunlap's *Pennsylvania Packet* printed another message from London that also suggested, "If the Congress have proposals prepared in English and German to distribute among them when they land, which no precautions can prevent, multitudes will desert." Not to be outdone, another Philadelphia publisher offered a solution. William Bradford drafted a blueprint for an official "Declaration" straight from General Washington. His proposal laid out generous acreage to be given to officers (5,000–10,000) and enlisted soldiers (200–500) who left British ranks. Bradford, too, suggested that the offer should be "published in every news paper throughout the Colonies, and also in hand bills in the German and English languages." Holt's *New-York Journal* brought out one more idea for persuading mercenaries to desert, this one darker and less helpful. Holt excerpted a letter from Bristol recommending that, since foreign troops had "nothing to do in this quarrel," Congress should declare "every soul taken, should be put to death, officers and men, without distinction,—it would not be unreasonable but equitable." "They are invaders of the worst kind," the Bristol correspondent fumed, "and should be treated accordingly. . . . Desperate situations require desperate exertions." It is a comforting reflection that no other publisher picked up on this gruesome proposition.[71]

Congress's formation of a committee to draft an address to the foreign mercenaries, then, took place in the middle of an energetic conversation in the press. That committee would consist of Richard Henry Lee, William Livingston, John Adams, Roger Sherman, and Thomas Jefferson; the last three would also be tapped to draft the Declaration just over a fortnight later. The committee never completed this task, but another delegate from Virginia, George Wythe, did, most likely at the behest of his former law student, Jefferson.[72]

It is unclear when Wythe finished his draft address to the foreign mercenaries, since he left it undated, but it was surely before he returned to Virginia on June 13. In other words, during the same days and hours that patriots debated enlisting Indians to serve in Continental army units in Canada, and even as they puffed out their chests to show the Six Nations they were

71. Apr. 12, 1776, in Saunders, ed., *Col. Records of N.C.*, X, 510–513, esp. 512; Fifth Virginia Convention, "Proceedings," May 15, 1776, *Rev. Va.*, VII, 141–148, esp. 142–143. See also May 21, 1776, *JCC*, IV, 369. "Fling into camp": *Providence Gazette*, May 18, 1776; *Norwich Packet*, May 13–20, 1776; *Freeman's Journal* (Portsmouth), May 22, 1776; *Connecticut Journal*, May 22, 1776; *Pennsylvania Gazette*, May 22, 1776; *Pennsylvania Journal*, May 22, 1776; *New-York Journal*, May 23, 1776; *Pennsylvania Ledger*, May 25, 1776; *Virginia Gazette* (Purdie), June 14, 1776. "Multitudes will desert": *Pennsylvania Packet*, May 27, 1776; *New-York Journal*, May 30, 1776; *Connecticut Courant*, June 3, 1776; *Connecticut Journal*, June 5, 1776; *Providence Gazette*, June 15, 1776; *Virginia Gazette* (Purdie), June 21, 1776. Bradford plan: *Pennsylvania Journal*, June 19, 1776; *Norwich Packet*, June 17–24, 1776; *Massachusetts Spy*, July 10, 1776. "Invaders of the worst kind": *New-York Journal*, May 30, 1776.

72. Lyman H. Butterfield suggests Jefferson probably asked Wythe to write the draft address in "Psychological Warfare in 1776: The Jefferson-Franklin Plan to Cause Hessian Desertions," *Proceedings of the American Philosophical Society*, N.S., XCIV (1950), 233–241.

invincible and opened debate over whether America should be independent, Wythe was constructing his own plan to neutralize British proxies.

"It is no small pleasure, when in this first address we ever made to you
we must call you enemies, that we can affirm you to be unprovoked enemies," Wythe began, searching for a reason why the Germans agreed to
participate in the Revolution. "We have not," he continued, "invaded your
country, slaughtered wounded or captivated your parents children or kins-
folk, burned plundered or desolated your towns and villages, wasted your
farms and cottages, spoiled you of your goods, or annoyed your trade." Why,
then, he asked rhetorically, did they interfere? Was it because of principles
("Do you think the cause you are engaged in just on your side?"), monarchical oppression ("Were you compelled by your sovereigns to undertake
the bloody work of butchering your unoffending fellow-creatures?"), bloodlust ("Did lust of conquest prompt you?"), or perhaps opportunity ("Were
you tempted by the prospect of exchanging the land you left for happier
regions—for a land of plenty and abhorrent of despotism?") that the Hessians volunteered to "join in this quarrel with our foes . . . and at so great a
distance from both you and us?" "We wish," he confessed, that opportunity

> might be your motive; because we have the means, and want not in-
> clination, to gratify your desires, if they be not hostile, without loss to
> ourselves, perhaps with less expense, certainly with more honour and
> with more advantage to you than victory can promise. Numberless ger-
> mans and other foreigners settled in this country will testify this truth.

He then left space for Congress to append a resolution, perhaps an adoption of Bradford's idea to grant land to mercenaries who deserted the
British. Though taking land in exchange for not fighting was just as mercenary, Wythe consistently denigrated the Germans in the address for their
base opportunism. True patriots would never behave in such a manner, he
projected. In the end, Wythe's draft turned out to be a dead letter. Congress
never filled in the space left in the middle of his address. They would, however, again take up the issue of inciting Germans to desert over the summer.[73]

One explanation for why Congress did not fill in the blank space in
Wythe's address is that they had other, more pressing concerns to deal with
that June. A few weeks earlier, in mid-April, the smallpox-ridden Ameri-

73. "George Wythe's Draft Address to the Foreign Mercenaries," *LDC*, IV, 110–
112, esp. 110–111.

can army that had been laying siege to Quebec fell back across the St. Lawrence River. Benedict Arnold, commander at the temporarily occupied city of Montreal, worried about his vulnerability and dispatched 400 men under New Hampshire colonel Timothy Bedel to build an outpost about thirty-five miles west, at a place called the Cedars. Not long after construction began at the Cedars stockade, Bedel departed to negotiate with the Caughnawaga Indians, leaving Major Isaac Butterfield in command. Around the same time Virginians were drafting proposals for independence, rumors began to swirl across the Canadian border of an approaching force of Indians, numbering anywhere from 400 to a terrifying 1,300. British captain George Foster, who in reality did not have nearly that many, attacked on May 18 with a force of 36 regulars, 11 Canadian volunteers, and 160 Indians from the neighborhood of Detroit. According to one of the defenders, the Indians came "skipping and running out of the woods" with "nothing but a sort of wildgrass to secret or hide them from us." Unaware that reinforcement was imminent and fearful of what the enemy might do to his sickly men, Butterfield immediately surrendered the post. His relief, consisting of Major Henry Sherburne and 120 Continental soldiers, was also ambushed by Indians and surrendered after a short encounter. In all, nearly one-quarter of Arnold's force in Canada was captured in the debacle.[74]

What happened to those prisoners clinched, in many colonists' minds, the accusation that the Indians were indeed merciless savages—even though, to this point in the war, they could only be described as utterly merciful. Since the Americans had unconditionally surrendered to the Indians and not to Foster, they were under the Indians' control. The Indians, allegedly, "fell to work" on the prisoners and "stripped them stark naked" as they took the soldiers' clothing as spoils of victory. After they "dispatched the wounded by knocking them in the head," one impassioned account detailed, "the dead [were] stripped naked, and thrown by the side of the road, the remaining troops was drove like cattle by them, it was a horrible sight . . . to see the Indians brandishing their knives and tomahawks over their heads

---

74. John Greenwood journal, 33, CL; Zaphaniah Shepardson, "Journal," 7, quoted in Robert McConnell Hatch, *Thrust for Canada: The American Attempt on Quebec in 1775–1776* (Boston, 1979), 198. For the Cedars fiasco, see Elizabeth A. Fenn, *Pox Americana: The Great Smallpox Epidemic of 1775–82* (New York, 2001), 72–74; Hatch, *Thrust for Canada*, 197–208; Robert S. Allen, *His Majesty's Indian Allies: British Indian Policy in the Defence of Canada* (Toronto, 1992), 47–48.

and hollering and screaming and likewise dancing like so many mad men or devils."[75]

Knowing Arnold would come after him, Foster warned the American commander that if he attacked, Foster would allow the Indians to kill the prisoners. Foster did offer to exchange Butterfield and Sherburne's forces if they each pledged never again to take up arms against the king. Outraged, Arnold refused all offers and made plans to reach the captives, who were now being kept on an island in the St. Lawrence River, exposed to the Canadian elements. Foster convinced Butterfield and Sherburne to agree to the cartel, and, against his wishes, Arnold signed it; the prisoners were set free on May 27, the same Monday Philadelphians were doing their best to impress the Six Nations. The American leadership was incensed. Washington condemned the "Cowardly and disgraceful Behaviour" of Bedel and Butterfield (who were later court-martialed), and John Adams lamented that the Cedars was "the first Stain upon American Arms" and thought Butterfield deserved "the most infamous Death."[76]

News of this surrender and the Indians' rough treatment of American prisoners stormed through colonial newspapers. The first few months of 1776 had been quiet on the backcountry, compared to the intensity of the previous year's rumors. Still, rumblings about British plots persisted, reminding many colonial readers that the Indians were still a danger. Back in March, a few printers had picked up one story that the British commander at Detroit was offering anywhere from £10 to £50 for American scalps along the Ohio River.[77]

The story of the Cedars, however, was a different matter. Here was proof of Indians' acting on the king's behalf. The first report from the St. Lawrence had the situation exactly wrong. A militia captain stated in the New

75. John Greenwood journal, 34, 36, CL.

76. GW to Schuyler, New York, June 16, 1776, *PGW: RW*, V, 8; JA to John Sullivan, Philadelphia, June 23, 1776, *PJA*, IV, 330–331, esp. 330. See also Hatch, *Thrust for Canada*, 206. The May 26, 1776, Articles of Capitulation at the Cedars is in item 29, 251–256 in the *Papers of the Continental Congress, 1774–1789*, National Archives Microfilm Publication M247, roll 36.

77. *Pennsylvania Ledger*, Mar. 9, 1776; *Pennsylvania Packet*, Mar. 11, 1776; *Pennsylvania Gazette*, Mar. 13, 1776; *Connecticut Journal*, Mar. 20, 1776; *Connecticut Gazette*, Mar. 22, 1776; *Norwich Packet*, Mar. 18–25, 1776; *New-England Chronicle*, Mar. 28, 1776; *Essex Journal*, Mar. 29, 1776.

York papers that the "whole body of the enemy" had been attacked and "killed and taken prisoners." *Connecticut Courant* printer Ebenezer Watson related the accurate, terrible news on June 10, a few columns over from a London account that divulged British plans of "setting on the Indians and slaves to murder defenceless women and innocent children." Within a few days, other New England papers exchanged Watson's notice of the Cedars. The next week, John Holt's *New-York Journal* provided an "authentic account" from "an officer of the detachment it principally concerns." This report was nearly a column long and packed with images of savagery. Once the Americans surrendered, "then a scene of Savage barbarity ensued; and many of our people were sacrificed to their fury," the officer from Sherburne's unit related. These instances of "barbarity" were repeated as the prisoners were "again and again stripped of the small remainder of their clothes, till many of them had not sufficient to hide their nakedness." Most papers throughout the northern colonies exchanged this account throughout June.[78]

The earliest news of disaster at the Cedars reached Philadelphia by Sunday, June 2. New Hampshire delegate William Whipple wrote that day, "Here is a report" that Bedel "is cut off by a party of the 8th regt and Indians," but

---

78. *Constitutional Gazette*, June 8, 1776; *New-York Gazette*, June 10, 1776; *Connecticut Journal*, June 12, 1776; *Continental Journal*, June 13, 1776; *New-England Chronicle*, June 13, 1776; *Freeman's Journal* (Portsmouth), June 13, 1776; *Essex Journal*, June 14, 1776; *Pennsylvania Evening Post*, June 15, 1776; *Providence Gazette*, June 15, 1776; *American Gazette*, June 18, 1776; *Virginia Gazette* (Purdie), June 21, 1776; *Virginia Gazette* (Dixon & Hunter), June 22, 1776. Another report that originated in Philadelphia telling of Arnold's rush to reinforce Bedel appeared in *Pennsylvania Evening Post*, June 8, 1776; *Pennsylvania Ledger*, June 8, 1776; *Constitutional Gazette*, June 12, 1776; *Connecticut Journal*, June 12, 1776; *Providence Gazette*, June 15, 1776. British plans: *Connecticut Courant*, June 10, 1776. "Authentic Account": *Connecticut Journal*, June 12, 1776; *New-England Chronicle*, June 13, 1776; *Continental Journal*, June 13, 1776; *Essex Journal*, June 14, 1776; *Pennsylvania Evening Post*, June 15, 1776; *Boston Gazette*, June 17, 1776; *Newport Mercury*, June 20, 1776.

"Scene of Savage barbarity": *New-York Journal*, June 20, 1776; *Pennsylvania Evening Post*, June 22, 1776; *New-York Gazette*, June 24, 1776; *Pennsylvania Packet*, June 24, 1776; *Connecticut Courant*, June 24, 1776; *New-England Chronicle*, June 27, 1776; *Essex Journal*, June 28, 1776; *Newport Mercury*, July 1, 1776; *Norwich Packet*, June 24–July 1, 1776; *American Gazette*, July 2, 1776; *Maryland Gazette*, July 4, 1776; *Connecticut Gazette*, July 5, 1776; *Freeman's Journal* (Portsmouth), July 6, 1776; *Virginia Gazette* (Dixon & Hunter), July 6, 1776. For a different letter from Canada, see *Pennsylvania Magazine*, II (1776), 294.

he did not put much stock in it. "This story comes in so loose a way . . . that I do not credit it; however it may be true; we must expect to meet with some hard rubs." The next day, an express arrived from Albany bearing a letter from Ticonderoga confirming that patriot forces had indeed taken those rubs. Whipple's colleague Josiah Bartlett also hoped it would "not prove so bad as reported," but Congress took steps to improve security on the Canadian frontier just in case. Armed with the intelligence from the Albany express, Congress decided to provide details on the resolution passed the previous week allowing the recruitment of Indians into the Continental army. In addition to calling up nearly fourteen thousand militia to create a "flying camp" to protect New England from invasion, they resolved that Philip Schuyler "be empowered to employ in Canada a number of Indians, not exceeding two thousand." Samuel Adams, for one, fixed his hopes that, despite "displeasing" recent affairs in Canada, this step—which was exactly what they had loudly excoriated their enemies for attempting—would rescue patriot fortunes on the northern frontier. "Measures," he wrote to Massachusetts patriot James Warren, "have been adopted which I trust will repair Misfortunes and set Matters right in that Quarter." Those measures were sensitive, especially with the Six Nations delegation still in town, but deemed necessary to deal with collapsing patriot fortunes in Canada. The situation was indeed dire.[79]

Warren soon would receive another letter from Philadelphia, this time from Samuel's cousin. John, ever the pessimist, was in a panic. He believed the loss of Canada could mean the concession of all northern Indians to Britain, a probable fatal blow to the common cause. Not only would the British have control of the St. Lawrence and Great Lakes and uninterrupted communication between Niagara, Detroit, and Michilimackinac, but

> they will have a free Communication with all the numerous Tribes of Indians, extending along the Frontiers of all the Colonies, and by their Trinketts and Bribes will induce them to take up the Hatchett, and Spread Blood and Fire among the Inhabitants by which Means, all the Frontier Inhabitants will be driven in upon the middle settlements, at a Time when the Inhabitants of the Seaports and Coasts, will be driven back by the British Navy.

79. William Whipple to John Langdon, June 2, 1776, *LDC*, IV, 120, Josiah Bartlett to Langdon, Philadelphia, June 3, 1776, 126, Samuel Adams to James Warren, June 6, 1776, 150; June 3, 1776, *JCC*, IV, 412.

"Is this Picture too high coloured?" he asked, recovering his nerve. "Perhaps it is."[80]

Others in Congress were shaken by the news from Canada, too. On Tuesday, June 4, Congress issued a new round of proclamations in President Hancock's name, imploring patriot authorities from Maryland north to remain steadfast in the cause, despite the bad news.

This address, probably written by Jefferson, Edward Rutledge, George Wythe, and Samuel Adams, rehearsed several of the themes the Declaration would make famous just one month hence, though the tone was more one of pleading than of proclaiming. The "Tyrant of Britain and his Parliament" had such an "unrelenting Spirit," the writers said, "that they have left no Measure unessayed." Although the cause had survived thus far, British "measures" were beginning to bear fruit. In Canada, this proclamation related, "it appears, that our Affairs in that Quarter wear a melancholy Aspect. Should the Canadians and Indians take up Arms agt. us (which there is too much Reason to fear) we shall then have the whole Force of that Country to contend with, joined to that of Great Britain, and all her foreign auxiliaries." What now, Congress asked: "In this Situation what Steps must we pursue?" If the Revolution was to survive, only "superior Exertions" would decide whether colonists would "live Slaves, or die Freemen." Instructing the various provincial governing bodies to call up their militia forces, now was the time for men to "step forth in Defence of their Wives, their Children, their Liberty, and every Thing they hold dear." This June 4 address invoked the patriot "spirit" as the polar opposite of the king's tyrannical measures—despite the fact that they, too, had secretly called on proxies to take up arms the day before. "The Cause is certainly a most glorious one and I trust every Man [in the northern colonies] is determined to see it gloriously ended, or to perish in the Ruins of it. In short, on your Exertions at this Critical Period, together with those of the other Colonies, in the Common Cause, the Salvation of America now evidently depends." The first of what would be several calls for colonists to remain dedicated to the cause that year, Congress sent those beseeching messages with express riders galloping off in all directions and then opened an investigation to find out what had gone wrong in Canada.[81]

80. JA to James Warren, Philadelphia, June 16, 1776, *LDC*, IV, 228–229.

81. In the secret journals of Congress, the May 29, 1776, entry stipulates Congress's order for those four members to produce "an animated address . . . to impress the minds of the people with Necessity of now stepping forward to save their coun-

Merciless Savages, Domestic Insurrectionists, and Foreign Mercenaries

From the middle of May through the first days of June, in other words, foreign mercenaries or Indians, both in person and hundreds of miles away, dominated Congress's attention. This absorption matched the newspapers during those weeks: papers in many locales published accounts from the Cedars together with—or closely behind—the news of Hessians on their way, or the text of the German treaties themselves. During the weeks of 1776 in which Jefferson, Adams, Franklin, and their colleagues are now commonly depicted as weighing the question of independence, they were, in fact, doing other things: working arduously on addresses to convince the people to keep faith, meeting with Indians to impress upon them the power of unified patriot arms, quietly issuing orders to recruit northern Indians to defend New England, calling up an emergency militia force (again), and concocting plans to convince German mercenaries to desert as soon as they arrived in America. All this helps explain why Richard Henry Lee did not act on his instructions to propose independence for ten hectic days. Concerns about Indians threatening from the St. Lawrence or German troops sailing across the Atlantic prevailed.

Or, more likely, these were exactly the reasons Lee introduced a motion on the floor for Congress on Friday, June 7, to consider "that these United Colonies are, and of right ought to be, free and independent States, that they are absolved from all allegiance to the British Crown, and that all political connection between them and the State of Great Britain is, and ought to be, totally dissolved." Debate opened the next day, June 8, and continued the following Monday. The factions and arguments remained the same as had divided the Congress over Adams's preamble three weeks earlier. At the end of the second day of debate, the committee of the whole voted to postpone a decision on Lee's motion until the first of July. In the meantime, they appointed five members to draft a declaration of independence, a decision that lives on at the core of the founding mythology of the United States.[82]

The drafting committee, consisting of John Adams, Benjamin Franklin, Thomas Jefferson, Robert Livingston, and Roger Sherman, had eighteen days to craft a polished statement of purpose for the American Revolution

---

try, their freedom, and property." See "Secret Journals of Congress," May 29, 1776, in Charles Thomson Papers, case 76, MSS, HSP; "John Hancock to Certain Colonies," Philadelphia, June 4, 1776, *LDC,* IV, 136–137. Congress also sent a slightly modified version to the Pennsylvania Assembly on the same day, for which see John Hancock to the Pennsylvania Assembly, Philadelphia, June 4, 1776, *LDC,* IV, 138.

82. June 7, 1776, *JCC,* V, 425–426.

that would be seen as legitimate and acceptable for foreign and domestic audiences alike. Despite all the practice the delegates had had in justifying the rebellion, this was a difficult assignment. It did not help matters that they still had lots of business to attend to over those hectic days.

Given what occurred since, it would be easy to assume that this two-day debate was the most monumental discussion Congress had ever undertaken. It was—but what is most surprising about the debate over independence was that it only lasted two days. At the end of Monday's session the delegates decided that they had other pressing things to take care of and, famously, tabled further discussion until July 1 and in the meantime passed the task off to the five members of the drafting committee. American mythology lingers here, following the committee members as they filed out of the State House and listening in for Adams's insistence that Jefferson alone possessed the "peculiar felicity of expression" that made him the only suitable author. But, in reality, they had too much work to do to spend any more time on this question, significant as it was.[83]

Indian affairs overshadowed everything. The secret journals of Congress reveal that, on the same day Lee introduced the fateful motion, Congress enlarged Washington's orders to employ Indians "where he shall judge they will be most useful" and extended a bounty for any British soldiers captured by Indian allies. Just before the body named Adams, Franklin, Jefferson, Sherman, and Livingston to the Declaration drafting committee, they received the Six Nations representatives for a second time. By necessity, this time they were more forthcoming: they handed out presents and pledged a firm friendship that would "continue as long as the sun shall shine." Three days later, they wrote to Schuyler to solidify that relationship, authorizing him to call for a new conference with the Six Nations "to engage them in our interest upon the best terms that can be procured."[84]

Schuyler, for his part, had already started down this road. The commissioners of the Northern Indian department thought they were following orders when they held a meeting at Albany on June 13 to engage up to two thousand Indians for military service. But they made an error when they organized two companies of Stockbridge and Mohican Indians to be incorpo-

83. JA to Timothy Pickering, Aug. 6, 1822, in Charles Francis Adams, ed., *The Works of John Adams, Second President of the United States . . .* , 10 vols. (Boston, 1856), II, 512n–514n. See also Maier, *American Scripture*, 97–102.

84. June 7, 1776, "Secret Journals of Congress," Thomson Papers, case 76, HSP; June 11, 14, 17, 1776, *JCC*, V, 430, 442, 452.

rated into the Continental army then in New York. Disturbed that the commissioners had apparently misinterpreted orders—the original intention was to enlist Indians from Canada to use *only* in Canada—Washington asked Congress to deal swiftly with the mistake. The delegates agreed, instructing Washington to "have a Stop put to raising the Mohickan and Stockbridge Indians as soon as possible." That Schuyler and his fellow commissioners misconstrued the public intentions of Congress should not have surprised Washington; he too had spent much of the previous year wondering how to deal with friendly Indians.[85]

Frontier affairs continued to monopolize Congress's attention throughout June. On June 15, they took Jefferson away from the Declaration so he could act as secretary to investigate the Cedars prisoner debacle. The four-man committee on the Cedars cartel interviewed Major Henry Sherburne and presented a report—in Jefferson's hand—two days later, a paper containing language that invoked prisoners' being delivered into the "hands of the Savages," a "horrid act," "cruel and inhuman death," and a "gross and barbarous violation of the laws of nature and nations." News also circulated, during Jefferson's few remaining days to draft the Declaration, that the common cause might be as vulnerable in the southern backcountry as in the north. During the spring, Indian Superintendent John Stuart, still exiled in Saint Augustine and too conspicuous to make the offer himself, sent his brother Henry into Cherokee country to explore their willingness to fight for the king. Henry fared little better. As he truly followed in his brother's footsteps, Henry's efforts—again assisted by deputy Alexander Cameron—to engage the Cherokee and Creek Indians were discovered by patriot leaders. Henry's May 18 warning letter to frontier inhabitants across the south promised all who refused to join him would soon be at risk from "five hundred warriors" each from the Creeks, Chickasaws, and Cherokees, who were about to "take possession of the frontiers of North-Carolina and

85. Congress's apparent confusion over where they wanted Washington to deploy Indian allies reveals how explosive this decision was. The secret journals show Congress giving Washington a free hand; the published journals, however, restrict the Indians to be used in Canada only. It seems concern over public opinion won out, for they went back to the original restriction when this contradiction came to light. See "At a Meeting of the Commissioners for Transacting Indian Affairs for the Northern Department . . . ," 4 *Am. Archives*, VI, 914; GW to Hancock, New York, June 21, 1776, *PGW: RW*, V, 66–67, Hancock to GW, Philadelphia, July 25, 1776, 102–104, Schuyler to GW, New York, June 24, 1776, 87–90.

Virginia." This letter was intercepted, sent to Williamsburg, given to *Virginia Gazette* printer Alexander Purdie, and forwarded to Jefferson and his colleagues in Philadelphia, where it arrived by June 18. While Congress considered what to do about potential hostile Indians in the south, twelve more printers from Maryland north exchanged this fresh threat from the patriots' old nemesis in June and July.[86]

Stuart and Cameron were not the only villains from 1775 to surface in what would be the last few days of colonial America. Lord Dunmore had never vanished from colonial news. On May 2, in the same hours that Captain Lee was pulling into Newburyport, *New-York Journal* printer John Holt published news of an "odd event" in Monmouth County, New Jersey. The Jersey contributor remarked that since a woman in Connecticut had recently "honored" Thomas Gage by naming her newborn son after the general, "a lusty likely *Negro Wench* was delivered of a male child, who, in memory of a notable Negro Chief, is named DUNMORE." The correspondent, a *Journal* customer, then appended a verse:

Hail! doughty Ethiopian chief!
Thou ignominious Negro-Thief!
This BLACK shall prop thy sinking name,
And damn thee to perpetual Fame.

Holt felt sorry for the infant; "though an act of justice to Dunmore," burdening him with such an infamous moniker was perhaps too cruel "to the innocent Negro." Several printers in Boston, Newport, New Haven, Ports-

---

86. "Report of the Committee on the Cedars Cartel," June 17, 1776, *PTJ*, I, 400–404, esp. 401–402; Henry Stuart to John Stuart, Toquah, May 7, 1776, in K. G. Davies, ed., *Documents of the American Revolution, 1770–1783*, Colonial Office Series, XII, *Transcripts, 1776* (Dublin, 1976), 130–133; "Letter Addressed to the Frontier Inhabitants by Mr. [Henry] Stuart . . . ," May 18, 1776, 4 *Am. Archives*, VI, 497. Elbridge Gerry gave particulars of this letter, including his hopes that Stuart's "Vile Designs will be frustrated" in his June 18 letter to Joseph Trumbull, Philadelphia, June 18, 1776, *LDC*, IV, 263–264. Henry Stuart letter published in: *Virginia Gazette* (Purdie), June 7, 1776; *Maryland Journal*, June 17, 1776; *Dunlap's Maryland Gazette*, June 19, 1776; *Maryland Gazette*, June 20, 1776; *New-York Journal*, June 27, 1776; *New York Packet*, June 27, 1776; *Pennsylvania Ledger*, June 29, 1776; *Pennsylvania Packet*, July 1, 1776; *New-York Gazette*, July 1, 1776; *Norwich Packet*, July 1–8, 1776; *Connecticut Courant*, July 8, 1776; *Massachusetts Spy*, July 10, 1776; *Newport Mercury*, July 11, 1776.

mouth, and Williamsburg also enjoyed this laugh at the governor's expense over several weeks in May.[87]

On that portentous Monday of May 27, as Arnold was being forced to sign the Cedars cartel and Congress was busy in Philadelphia, Dunmore landed his fleet on Gwynn's Island, a move that sparked yet another round of newspaper reports. Just a few yards off the Virginia mainland, Gwynn's Island was a small sandbar in the Chesapeake between the mouths of the York and Rappahannock Rivers. As it would turn out, this was the last piece of solid ground in Virginia Dunmore would occupy for the king that year.

Dunmore unloaded his ships there in the hopes of stopping the smallpox that was tearing through the soldiers and loyalist refugees, black and white, on board the "floating town." According to one published letter, this raging epidemic cost Dunmore "nine or ten of his black regiment every day." Nevertheless, a Royal Navy captain estimated on June 10 that the governor still gained "Six or eight fresh Men every day" just the same. Even though many of these new recruits would die as soon as they reached the purported

---

87. This article left a complex trail in surviving colonial newspapers. Most printers attributed this news as coming from New York on April 4, but no Manhattan newspaper published this story from Monmouth County on that date. Holt did publish it on May 2, but, interestingly, the particular issue scanned by Readex for their online database has a redaction over this particular story (it appears as a white space) in the May 2, 1776, issue (page 3, far right column), so it is difficult to tell what text Holt actually published there. When they exchanged this story, some printers published Holt's "query" about whether naming the child Dunmore was too cruel, but others did not. Those who published the query were: *New-York Journal*, May 2, 1776; *Newport Mercury*, May 20, 1776; *Virginia Gazette* (Dixon & Hunter), May 25, 1776; *New-England Chronicle*, May 30, 1776; *Freeman's Journal* (Portsmouth), June 8, 1776. Two papers, *Connecticut Journal* and *Massachusetts Spy*, published the Monmouth story without Holt's query; see *Connecticut Journal*, May 15, 1776; *Massachusetts Spy*, May 24, 1776. Finally, Purdie's *Virginia Gazette* summarized the story without Holt's query or the verse, just giving the news of the baby's being named after the "notable Negro chief" (May 24, 1776). John Gill's *New-England Chronicle* offered more prefatory information about the Connecticut mother who named her baby after Gage, including how other women in Stratford reacted to it: "170 young ladies formed themselves into a battalion, and with solemn ceremony appointed a general, and the other officers to lead them on, then the petticoat army marched with the greatest good order to pay their compliments to THOMAS GAGE and present his mother with a suit of tar and feathers" (*New-England Chronicle*, May 30, 1776).

promised land, the sustained stream of runaways even in the face of small-pox testifies to the attraction of Dunmore's proclamation. Eight of Landon Carter's slaves thought the risk worthwhile. In late June, he noted in his diary that they had gone "to be sure, to Ld. Dunmore," taking guns, ammunition, silver buckles, and new sets of clothes with them. Dunmore quarantined most of the runaway slaves on the bay side of the island and dug fortifications nearest to the mainland to prepare for a patriot assault. *Virginia Gazette* printers John Dixon and William Hunter first published a report on June 15 that Dunmore had taken this opportunity to initiate a new stage of germ warfare. Employing the most vague, least corroborated method of introducing a story, they wrote, "We learn from Gloucester, that Lord Dunmore has erected hospitals upon Gwyn's-island . . . and that they are inoculating the blacks for the small-pox." "Two of those wretches," they continued, were "inoculated and sent ashore, in order to spread the infection, but it was happily prevented." Nine patriot newspapers would exchange this accusation, in some cases in the same column of Williamsburg news with Henry Stuart's proclamation about the southern Indian threat.[88]

Patriot leaders in Virginia, then, had to pay attention to threats from both east and west as they started drafting their first state constitution. Jefferson, despite being preoccupied with piles of congressional business in Philadelphia, was thinking about Dunmore, Stuart, and Virginia that June. At some point during the seven summer weeks when the governor was camped there, Jefferson sketched an intricate map of Gwynn's Island. Although it is not certain when he received the information incorporated into this map or even who supplied that intelligence, his detailed sketches of the besieging American fleet and surrounding breastworks suggest that Jefferson had more than a passing interest in the actions on Gwynn's Island—even as he

88. *Constitutional Gazette*, June 22, 1776; *Providence Gazette*, June 29, 1776; *South-Carolina and American General Gazette*, Aug. 2, 1776; "Narrative of Captain Andrew Snape Hamond," in Clark et al., eds., *Naval Documents*, V, 840; June 26, 1776, in Greene, ed., *Diary of Landon Carter*, II, 1051–1052, esp. 1051; *Virginia Gazette* (Dixon & Hunter), June 15, 1776. For more on the accusations that Dunmore purposely spread smallpox, see Fenn, *Pox Americana*, 58–61. "Sent ashore": *New-York Journal*, June 27, 1776; *New York Packet*, June 29, 1776; *Pennsylvania Ledger*, June 29, 1776; *New-York Gazette*, July 1, 1776; *Massachusetts Spy*, July 5, 1776; *Connecticut Courant*, July 8, 1776; *Boston Gazette*, July 8, 1776; *Freeman's Journal* (Portsmouth), July 13, 1776; *American Gazette*, July 16, 1776. Three papers (*New-York Journal*, *New-York Gazette*, and *Connecticut Courant*) published this alongside the Henry Stuart letter.

was helping George Wythe craft an address to the German mercenaries, investigating Indian attacks in Canada, and drafting the Declaration of Independence. Further, Jefferson sent several drafts of potential frames of government for the Virginia Convention to consider as they composed the first state constitution. These drafts contained a preamble that rehearsed the essential grievances against the king, which Jefferson was also assembling on Congress's behalf. These accusations reached their highest pitch with the following assertions: George III attempted a "detestable and insupportable tyranny . . ."

> by prompting our negroes to rise in arms among us; those very negroes whom [he hath from time to time] by an inhuman use of his negative he hath refused us permission to exclude by law;
> by endeavouring to bring on the inhabitants of our frontiers the merciless Indian savages, whose known rule of warfare is an undistinguished destruction of all ages, sexes, and conditions of existence;
> by transporting at this time a large army of foreign mercenaries to compleat the works of death, desolation, and tyranny already begun with circumstances of cruelty and perfidy so unworthy the head of a civilized nation.

When the Virginia Convention approved the constitution on June 29, they added only a couple of commas to these charges; with the exception of a final accusation that the king had answered "our repeated Petitions for Redress with a Repetition of injuries," the indictment of attempting to use proxy fighters was the most damning crime the crown had committed against Virginia.[89]

Jefferson was not the only person to argue that encouraging slaves, Indians, and foreigners to interfere in this civil dispute constituted a point of no

---

89. Even the famously thorough Julian Parks Boyd could not deduce when Jefferson drew this map (*PTJ*, I, 566). For more on the connections between Dunmore and the Declaration, see Sidney Kaplan, "The 'Domestic Insurrections' of the Declaration of Independence," *Journal of Negro History*, LXI (1976), 243–255. Jefferson sent three drafts of a potential state constitution to Williamsburg. For the first draft, he wrote out this preamble; for the second, he did not copy it but left only blank space for it; and for the third, he copied a large part of it, making some editorial changes. See "The Virginia Constitution," [June 1776], *PTJ*, I, 329–386, esp. 356–357. For the final text of the preamble as adopted, see "The Constitution as Adopted by the Convention," [June 29, 1776], *PTJ*, I, 378.

return. In fact, the grievances of slave instigation, Indian tampering, and foreign invaders were so well known by the public that many local and provincial proclamations of independence cited British plots as a main justification for nationhood. Termed "little declarations of independence" by one historian, these often overlooked statements by counties, towns, and provincial associations also reflected the centrality of British proxies in building a consensus for independence. Taken together, these documents reveal a general consensus about America, the king, independence, and the proxies forming early that summer.[90]

In New England, statements by provincial assemblies in Connecticut and New Hampshire as well as instructions from Boston and other Massachusetts towns, including Scituate and Wrentham, listed the incitement of proxies as a signal reason for independence. From Pennsylvania, groups at several levels, including militia groups in Chester County, the colonial assembly, and the Deputies of Philadelphia, also featured British proxies in their lists of grievances. Charles and Talbot Counties in Maryland drafted their own declarations, stating, "Slaves, savages, and foreign mercenaries, have been meanly hired to rob a people of their property, liberties, and lives." Some of these found space in colonial newspapers. The June 24 declaration by Philadelphia's city deputies was especially popular. Appearing in more than a dozen papers, this justification for independence concluded with "whereas [the king] hath paid no regard to any of our remonstrances and dutiful petitions for redress of our complicated grievances, but hath lately purchased foreign troops to assist in enslaving us, and hath excited the Savages of this country to carry on a war against us, as also the Negroes to embrue their hands in the blood of their masters, in a manner unpracticed by civilized nations."[91]

90. Maier, *American Scripture*, 69–75. These "little" declarations are found throughout 4 *Am. Archives*, VI. Consult appendix A of Maier's *American Scripture*, 217–223, for a full list.

91. Scituate town meeting, June 4: 4 *Am. Archives*, VI, 699. Wrentham town meeting, June 5: 699–700. Natick town meeting, June 20: 703. Connecticut Assembly, June 14: 867–868. New Hampshire Assembly: 1030. Elk Battalion, Chester County, June 10: 786. First Battalion, Chester County, June 6: 785. Pennsylvania Assembly instructions to Congress delegates, June 8: 755. Delegates of Charles County, Maryland: 1018. Talbot County, Maryland, June 21–22: 1019–1020. See also "A Declaration of the Delegates of Maryland," July 6, 1776, 1506. "Paid no regard": *Pennsylvania Gazette*, June 26, 1776; *Pennsylvania Ledger*, June 29, 1776; *Pennsylvania Packet*, July 1, 1776; *Maryland Journal*, July 2, 1776; *New-York Journal*, July 4, 1776; *New York*

The line between rhetoric and reality had been obliterated. Again, it should be remembered that precious little of this apocalypse had actually occurred. Nonetheless, blaming the king for undertaking these terrible acts was, by the eve of independence, an article of faith among patriots. The polemicists were winning. "Armatus," in an exchanged screed against George III, argued in late June that "the ____ of England delights in blood: yea, thirsteth for the blood of America. Hessians, Hanoverians, Brunswickers, Canadians, Indians, Negroes, Regulars and Tories are invited to the carnage. This is no fiction, but an awful reality, not the production of a delirium, but substantial matter of fact." The degree to which these parties would actually respond to those "invitations" was yet to be determined. However, because patriot organizations at all levels, from local to provincial to continental, had given this argument their imprimatur, it was now widely accepted as a "substantial matter of fact." Armatus, rather recklessly, invoked imagery of bloodthirsty cannibals feasting on Americans, but by the first days of July 1776, there was little separating Armatus from the Declaration of Independence.[92]

* * *

June, as it turned out, would be the time to codify grievances. Although Jefferson believed that the "most interesting" work of drafting new constitutions was "In truth . . . the whole object of the present controversy," he understood that this creative task was not feasible before he justified writing those new charters. A constitution's articles were essential for securing liberty in the future; that document's preamble was essential for making that future possible. If the people were going to recognize and abide by the provisions of a new constitution, first they had to accept the reasons those laws needed to exist.[93]

Congress's declaration of independence was meant as an extended preamble. Its purpose was to legitimize this decision, unprecedented in the

Packet, July 4, 1776; *Connecticut Gazette,* July 5, 1776; *Freeman's Journal* (Portsmouth), July 6, 1776; *Norwich Packet,* July 1–8, 1776; *Connecticut Courant,* July 8, 1776; *Continental Journal,* July 11, 1776; *Boston Gazette,* July 15, 1776; *Massachusetts Spy,* July 17, 1776.

92. *Connecticut Courant,* June 17, 1776; *Boston Gazette,* June 24, 1776; *Maryland Journal,* June 26, 1776; *Massachusetts Spy,* June 28, 1776; *Constitutional Gazette,* July 3, 1776; *Essex Journal,* July 5, 1776.

93. TJ to Thomas Nelson, May 16, 1776, *PTJ,* I, 292.

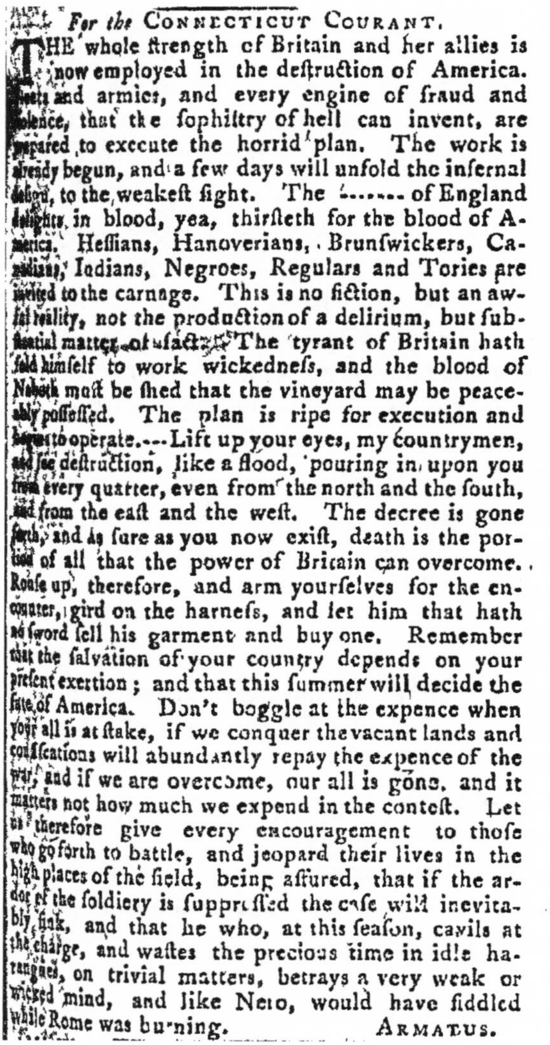

For the CONNECTICUT COURANT.

THE whole strength of Britain and her allies is now employed in the destruction of America. Her fleets and armies, and every engine of fraud and violence, that the sophistry of hell can invent, are prepared to execute the horrid plan. The work is already begun, and a few days will unfold the infernal labor, to the weakest sight. The ——— of England delights in blood, yea, thirsteth for the blood of America. Hessians, Hanoverians, Brunswickers, Canadians, Indians, Negroes, Regulars and Tories are invited to the carnage. This is no fiction, but an awful reality, not the production of a delirium, but substantial matter of fact. The tyrant of Britain hath sold himself to work wickedness, and the blood of Naboth must be shed that the vineyard may be peaceably possessed. The plan is ripe for execution and begins to operate.——Lift up your eyes, my countrymen, and see destruction, like a flood, pouring in upon you from every quarter, even from the north and the south, and from the east and the west. The decree is gone forth, and as sure as you now exist, death is the portion of all that the power of Britain can overcome. Rouse up, therefore, and arm yourselves for the encounter, gird on the harness, and let him that hath no sword sell his garment and buy one. Remember that the salvation of your country depends on your present exertion; and that this summer will decide the fate of America. Don't boggle at the expence when your all is at stake, if we conquer the vacant lands and confiscations will abundantly repay the expence of the war; and if we are overcome, our all is gone, and it matters not how much we expend in the contest. Let us therefore give every encouragement to those who go forth to battle, and jeopard their lives in the high places of the field, being assured, that if the ardor of the soldiery is suppressed the cause will inevitably sink, and that he who, at this season, cavils at the charge, and wastes the precious time in idle harangues, on trivial matters, betrays a very weak or wicked mind, and like Nero, would have fiddled while Rome was burning.   ARMATUS.

Figure 5. *Letter from "Armatus." From* Connecticut Courant, *June 17, 1776. "Armatus" implored readers of the* Connecticut Courant *to resist because of the king's proxies just as Thomas Jefferson drafted very nearly the same grievances in the Declaration of Independence. Armatus also reached audiences in Massachusetts, New York, and Maryland.*

history of New World colonies, and garner support from audiences foreign and domestic for the patriot cause. If the Continental Congress expected thousands of colonists to continue placing their lives at risk voluntarily, they had to craft a manifesto.[94]

94. For the argument that the Declaration was really just one of a "suite of documents," including the Model Treaty and the Articles of Confederation, that established the United States as equal and legitimate participants in the international

The grievances, then, were vital to the success of the document and, possibly, of the common cause. They had to be ironclad and compelling to contemporary readers or listeners. Long before generations would revere it as a sacred text, in its time, the Declaration of Independence was simply a political document with pressing work to accomplish: it had to clarify a very confusing conflict, distinguish "friends" from "enemies," inspire military resistance, and earn sympathy (and hopefully aid) from Europe. The pressure on the Declaration to rouse the people to a spirited defense increased exponentially on July 2, when the first scout ships carrying the largest invasion fleet ever known arrived in New York Harbor and began unloading the first of what would be thirty thousand British and German troops on Staten Island. John Adams called that Tuesday America's "Day of Deliverance" because it saw Congress vote unanimously for independence. Many loyalists hoped that what was beginning on Staten Island would be remembered as the first day of their salvation.

In Philadelphia, meanwhile, the nearly thirty charges that Jefferson leveled at George III were the core of the matter. They were not assembled at random. Instead of presenting the evidence chronologically, Jefferson grouped them for maximum effect. They began slowly and gained emotional speed. The first dozen detailed the king's abuses of executive power, the next ten protested "pretended legislation," and the final five documented acts of war and cruelty.[95]

The twelve grievances that began the Declaration's presentation of "facts [to] be submitted to a candid world" reached back a decade or more into the imperial crisis. They centered on perceived abuses of executive authority, accusing the king of a myriad of misdeeds, especially concerning the legitimacy of colonial assemblies and the authority of the laws they passed. But, again, Jefferson was starting softly, building to a dramatic crescendo. Many of these first charges—although they were broadly accepted in the colonies as violations of constitutional authority—in and of themselves were hardly inspiring enough to encourage farmers to rush to their muskets. Often, they

---

states system, see Leonard J. Sadosky, *Revolutionary Negotiations: Indians, Empires, and Diplomats in the Founding of America* (Charlottesville, Va., 2009), 82–89.

95. The Declaration lists twenty-seven grievances against the king. Jefferson originally provided twenty-nine, but during their editing sessions of July 2–3, Congress cut two. See Appendix C, "A Declaration by the Representatives of the United States of America in General Congress Assembled," in Maier, *American Scripture*, 236–241, esp. 238.

referred to disagreements certain provinces had with crown authorities, and although Congress wanted to include everyone's issues in this continental declaration, local controversies did not quite motivate. Further, the tone of the first dozen accusations is rather modest; the crown is indicted with mild verbs such as "obstructed," "refused," and "affected."

The second group of grievances focused on specific acts of Parliament and the king's willingness to enforce them, including each of the Coercive Acts, various mercantile regulations governing imperial trade, and the Quebec Act. To heighten the reader or listener's sense of these acts as an unceasing assault on American liberties, Jefferson abandoned his device of beginning each accusation with "he has," placing personal blame upon the king. Charges fourteen through twenty-two are, instead, a list separated by colons. Rhetorically, they act as one single sentence that dramatizes the sheer volume of oppression the colonies had endured over the decade.

The real drama was yet to come. The final five charges highlighted the past year's violence. The verbs in the last grievances are more evocative and stirring than the previous ones. In these indictments, George's crimes are deeper than moving the seat of government or discouraging immigration. In the concluding charges, Jefferson and Congress submitted accusations that the king had "plundered," "ravaged," "destroyed," forced Americans to become "executioners of their friends and brethren," and recruited foreign mercenaries "to complete the works of death, desolation, and tyranny, already begun with circumstances of cruelty and perfidy, scarcely paralleled in the most barbarous Ages, and totally unworthy the Head of a Civilized Nation." These charges carried a great deal of weight; their acceptance by the "candid world," both at home and abroad, could determine whether American independence was deemed righteous and defensible.

The delegates understood this. They tinkered with this last group of war accusations more than all the other grievances during their editing sessions on July 2–3. Other than a few touches to rearrange words or slice extraneous phrases, for the most part, Jefferson's first twenty grievances entered the final Declaration intact. But, as the stakes increased, so did Congress's attention, much to Jefferson's discomfort. Often, they deepened the king's crimes, inserting stirring phrases such as "waging war against us" and the stinging comment that his hiring of German troops was "scarcely paralleled in the most barbarous ages." They also struck out two of Jefferson's accusations almost entirely. The first charged George with inciting loyalists to fight for the promise of gaining confiscated patriot property. This was, on its face, a problematic charge, awkwardly condemning the king for encour-

Merciless Savages, Domestic Insurrectionists, and Foreign Mercenaries

aging his subjects to stay loyal. At the same time, it made practical political sense to leave the tories out of the Declaration: castigating and condemning the loyalists might engender antipathy toward the common cause among those on the fence and, worse, prove an obstacle for incorporating those people into the polity in the future. The second grievance Congress eliminated was Jefferson's long passage censuring the king for "wag[ing] cruel war against human nature itself" by promoting the slave trade, then doubly damning him for manipulating "those very people to rise in arms among us, and to purchase that liberty of which *he* has deprived them, by murdering the people upon whom *he* also obtruded them; thus paying off former crimes committed against the *liberties* of one people, with crimes which he urges them to commit against the *lives* of another." Blaming the king wholesale for the slave trade was too tenuous as the final accusation, so Congress eliminated nearly all of it. They removed the part that accused the king of foisting slavery upon the colonists, yet they retained the second half of that charge by inserting the words "excited domestic insurrections amongst us" in what would now be the twenty-seventh and final grievance against George III. They struck the antislavery part—the "great object of desire"— but retained Dunmore's proclamation, choosing the "Revolutionary War" of 1775 over the "American Revolution" of 1774. Whereas Jefferson had separated the proxies into four separate categories—Indians, loyalists, foreign mercenaries, and slaves—Congress removed the tories and combined the others to create a formidable last word: "He has excited domestic insurrections among us and has endeavoured to bring on the inhabitants of our frontiers the merciless Indian savages, whose known rule of warfare is an undistinguished destruction of all ages, sexes, and conditions." This is the ultimate deal breaker with the British. The language Congress put forward in this final accusation would have powerful consequences. Its inclusion at the heart of the founding document of the new American nation would cast a long shadow over the idea of who was a part of the new republic and who was not.[96]

96. For Declaration text, see: Appendix C, "A Declaration," in Maier, *American Scripture*, 237–239. "Great object of desire": Thomas Jefferson, *A Summary View of the Rights of British America* . . . (Williamsburg, Va., 1774), 29. For an exceptional discussion of Jefferson, the Declaration, and the slave trade clause, see Peter S. Onuf, *Jefferson's Empire: The Language of American Nationhood* (Charlottesville, Va., 2000), 154, 156, esp. 154. See also Garry Wills, *Inventing America: Jefferson's Declaration of Independence* (Garden City, N.Y., 1978), 66–67; Maier, *American Scripture*, 146–147. Steve

The most important two words in the Declaration are not about equality or happiness. They are actually among the shortest words in it: "he" and

---

Pincus's forthcoming book on the Declaration does not agree with this interpretation, suggesting that Congress did indeed retain Jefferson's strictures on the king's disallowance of the Virginia bill abolishing the slave trade with the first grievance: "He has refused his assent to laws the most wholesome and necessary for the public good." While this conflation is conceivable, there is no evidence that this was what the delegates had in mind or that they folded the slave trade disallowance in with the other laws the crown had vetoed over the imperial crisis. In his drafts of the Virginia constitution, on which the grievances were modeled, Jefferson's first charge referred to the king's use of his negative without direct reference to the slave trade bill. Pincus's view, that this is proof of the patriots' commitment to antislavery through independence, it should be clear, differs from mine. My thanks to Steve for generously sharing his draft chapter with me.

There is some scholarly debate over whom Congress meant by "domestics." Historian Sidney Kaplan believed that it strictly meant slaves, and Congress was explicitly referring to Dunmore's proclamation. See his "'Domestic Insurrections' of the Declaration of Independence," *Journal of Negro History*, LXI (1976), 243–255. Rhetoric scholar Stephen Lucas disagrees, contending that "domestics" was an umbrella term that included loyalists, servants, and slaves who were disaffected to the patriot cause. See his "Justifying America: The Declaration of Independence as a Rhetorical Document," in Thomas W. Benson, ed., *American Rhetoric: Context and Criticism* (Carbondale, Ill., 1989), 67–130, esp. 109. For one critic in 1776, this question was obvious. British pamphleteer John Lind, in his *Answer to the Declaration of the Congress,* wrote, "But how did his Majesty's Governors excite domestic insurrections? Did they set father against son, or son against father, or brother against brother? No—they offered *freedom* to the *slaves* of these assertors of liberty" (Lind, *An Answer to the Declaration of the American Congress* [London, 1776], 107). I believe that since slaveholders frequently referred to their slaves as their "domestics," this was whom Congress was referring to. It is possible they had servants in mind. Dunmore included them in his proclamation, after all. It is not plausible that the term included the tories; when they discussed slave revolts in other proclamations and statements, provincial committees and the Continental Congress consistently used the euphemism "domestics." They differentiated loyalists as a related, but separate group. A reading of North Carolina patriot James Iredell's February 1777 essay "To His Majesty George the Third" provides a simple and clear restatement of Jefferson's controversial clause that I believe settles the matter. Speaking of the "provocations" that led to independence, Iredell listed "the hire of foreign troops, the actual excitation of the Indian Savages to destroy us, and that Completion of all Villainy, the endeavour to raise our Domestics (Domestics you forced on us) to involve us in one indiscriminate Massacre." See "A British American" [James Iredell], "To His Majesty George the Third,

Merciless Savages, Domestic Insurrectionists, and Foreign Mercenaries

"we." The Declaration was an effort to draw a line between friends and enemies, between "us" and "them"—or, in this case, between "we" and "he." These pronouns are mighty weapons, rhetorically and conceptually. They are independence. The interpretation signified by "he" and "we" is the central premise of the Declaration. It is a formal announcement of the separation of one people ("we") from another ("he"). In this distinction lay the American assertion of self-determination, of casting off monarchical subjecthood and a claim of popular sovereignty. It contained the first assertion of an "American people."

As soon as Congress approved the Declaration's final text, they sent the edited manuscript to *Pennsylvania Packet* printer John Dunlap for publication as a broadside, even though the news was already spreading through the city. Dunlap completed his work over that Thursday night. The next day, copies of that broadside, featuring the actual names of only President John Hancock and Secretary Charles Thomson, were disseminated to assembly halls, brigade headquarters, and printing shops throughout North America. Twenty-nine English papers followed Congress's orders to print the text, starting with Benjamin Towne's *Pennsylvania Evening Post* on July 6 and ending with the *Boston Gazette* two weeks later. Patriot political organizations at the provincial and local level staged public readings over the next few July weeks. Army officers assembled their troops in formation to hear why they were fighting.[97]

King of Great Britain," in Don Higginbotham, ed., *Papers of James Iredell* (Raleigh, N.C., 1976), I, 427–443, esp. 441.

97. Massachusetts delegate Elbridge Gerry wrote on July 2 that, after the vote succeeded on independence, "the facts are as well known at the Coffee House of the City as in Congress" (Gerry to James Warren, Philadelphia, July 2, 1776, *LDC*, IV, 370). That rumor had spread to New York City's coffeehouse by the time Dunlap was setting the type for the Declaration broadside, according to another patriot (Ebenezer Hazard to Horatio Gates, New York City, July 5, 1776, 5 *Am. Archives*, I, 20). The first to publish notice of the Declaration was, interestingly, Henrich Miller, printer of the German language *Wöchentliche Pennsylvanischer Staatsbote*, on July 5. For the textual intricacies of the Declaration's publication, see *PTJ*, I, 413–432; Wilfred Ritz, "From the *Here* of Jefferson's Handwritten Rough Draft of the Declaration of Independence to the *There* of the Printed Dunlap Broadside," *PMHB*, CXVI (1992), 499–512; Thomas Starr, "Separated at Birth: Text and Context of the Declaration of Independence," *Proceedings of the American Antiquarian Society*, N.S., part 1, CX (2000), 153–199. A survey of the public readings is found in Maier, *American Scripture*, 155–160. For a list of the printings of the Declaration in the newspapers, see Clarence S.

One group listening to the Declaration grasped the document's performative aspects immediately. At the already war-weary Fort Ticonderoga, after Colonel Arthur St. Clair read the text to a cheering crowd, an observer commented, "It was remarkably pleasing to see the spirits of the soldiers so raised after all their calamities; the language of every man's countenance was, Now we are a people!" The packet of values attributed to that "free people" undoubtedly contributed to their collective happiness. If they had paid even cursory attention, the crowd at Ticonderoga and similar venues throughout the mainland would have been reminded of what comprised that abstract "we": "humble," "patient" sufferers who placed a "firm reliance on the protection of Divine Providence," displayed a "manly firmness," believed that everyone was "created equal," respected "the rights of the people," "the consent of the governed," and the "pursuit of happiness," and broadcast the "voice of justice and consaguinity" even when no one was listening. The king opposed these virtuous people and therefore was an enemy of freedom. The "long train of abuses"—especially the last few items on the list—only threw the Americans' heroic qualities into greater relief. The ecstatic garrison apparently grasped the point: without even having to say anything, they became Americans. It was written on their faces. But, as much as the patriot officers at Ticonderoga might have wanted this expression to be sufficient, it was more complicated than that. What did that phrase mean? Who, exactly, were "the American people"?[98]

The crucial division in the Declaration, denoted by "he" and "we," did provide some answers to this puzzle. Jefferson's Declaration cordoned off far more than just Americans from Britons, republicanism from monarchy. As is well documented, the transfer of blame from Parliament and the ministry to King George himself was an innovation of 1776, a shift usually ascribed to the influence of *Common Sense*. Jefferson addressed the king directly in the grievances; George was America's enemy. But, again, it was not that simple. Others fought on his behalf. When the Declaration connected

Brigham, *Journals and Journeymen* (Philadelphia, 1950), 58–59. For a bracing essay on Jefferson, the Declaration, and the issue of orality in the eighteenth century, see Jay Fliegelman, *Declaring Independence: Jefferson, Natural Language, and the Culture of Performance* (Palo Alto, Calif., 1993).

98. *Constitutional Gazette*, Aug. 12, 1776; *New York Packet*, Aug. 15, 1776; *Pennsylvania Evening Post*, Aug. 15, 1776; *New-York Gazette*, Aug. 19, 1776; *Connecticut Courant*, Aug. 19, 1776; *Pennsylvania Packet*, Aug. 20, 1776; *Continental Journal*, Aug. 22, 1776; *Providence Gazette*, Aug. 24, 1776; *New-Hampshire Gazette* (Exeter), Aug. 24, 1776.

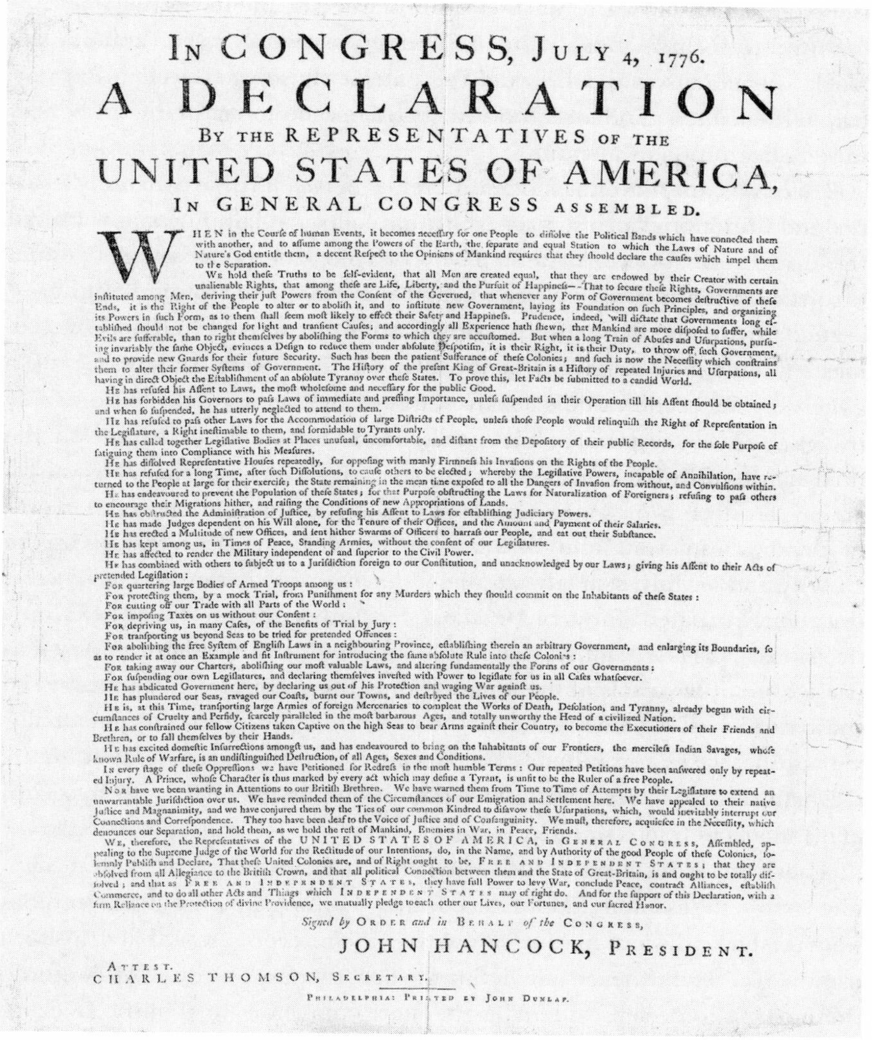

IN CONGRESS, JULY 4, 1776.

A DECLARATION

BY THE REPRESENTATIVES OF THE

UNITED STATES OF AMERICA,

IN GENERAL CONGRESS ASSEMBLED.

WHEN in the Course of human Events, it becomes necessary for one People to dissolve the Political Bands which have connected them with another, and to assume among the Powers of the Earth, the separate and equal Station to which the Laws of Nature and of Nature's God entitle them, a decent Respect to the Opinions of Mankind requires that they should declare the causes which impel them to the Separation.

WE hold these Truths to be self-evident, that all Men are created equal, that they are endowed by their Creator with certain unalienable Rights, that among these are Life, Liberty, and the Pursuit of Happiness—That to secure these Rights, Governments are instituted among Men, deriving their just Powers from the Consent of the Governed, that whenever any Form of Government becomes destructive of these Ends, it is the Right of the People to alter or to abolish it, and to institute new Government, laying its Foundation on such Principles, and organizing its Powers in such Form, as to them shall seem most likely to effect their Safety and Happiness. Prudence, indeed, will dictate that Governments long established should not be changed for light and transient Causes; and accordingly all Experience hath shewn, that Mankind are more disposed to suffer, while Evils are sufferable, than to right themselves by abolishing the Forms to which they are accustomed. But when a long Train of Abuses and Usurpations, pursuing invariably the same Object, evinces a Design to reduce them under absolute Despotism, it is their Right, it is their Duty, to throw off such Government, and to provide new Guards for their future Security. Such has been the patient Sufferance of these Colonies; and such is now the Necessity which constrains them to alter their former Systems of Government. The History of the present King of Great-Britain is a History of repeated Injuries and Usurpations, all having in direct Object the Establishment of an absolute Tyranny over these States. To prove this, let Facts be submitted to a candid World.

HE has refused his Assent to Laws, the most wholesome and necessary for the public Good.

HE has forbidden his Governors to pass Laws of immediate and pressing Importance, unless suspended in their Operation till his Assent should be obtained; and when so suspended, he has utterly neglected to attend to them.

HE has refused to pass other Laws for the Accommodation of large Districts of People, unless those People would relinquish the Right of Representation in the Legislature, a Right inestimable to them, and formidable to Tyrants only.

HE has called together Legislative Bodies at Places unusual, uncomfortable, and distant from the Depository of their public Records, for the sole Purpose of fatiguing them into Compliance with his Measures.

HE has dissolved Representative Houses repeatedly, for opposing with manly Firmness his Invasions on the Rights of the People.

HE has refused for a long Time, after such Dissolutions, to cause others to be elected; whereby the Legislative Powers, incapable of Annihilation, have returned to the People at large for their exercise; the State remaining in the mean time exposed to all the Dangers of Invasion from without, and Convulsions within.

HE has endeavoured to prevent the Population of these States; for that Purpose obstructing the Laws for Naturalization of Foreigners; refusing to pass others to encourage their Migrations hither, and raising the Conditions of new Appropriations of Lands.

HE has obstructed the Administration of Justice, by refusing his Assent to Laws for establishing Judiciary Powers.

HE has made Judges dependent on his Will alone, for the Tenure of their Offices, and the Amount and Payment of their Salaries.

HE has erected a Multitude of new Offices, and sent hither Swarms of Officers to harrass our People, and eat out their Substance.

HE has kept among us, in Times of Peace, Standing Armies, without the consent of our Legislatures.

HE has affected to render the Military independent of and superior to the Civil Power.

HE has combined with others to subject us to a Jurisdiction foreign to our Constitution, and unacknowledged by our Laws; giving his Assent to their Acts of pretended Legislation:

FOR quartering large Bodies of Armed Troops among us:

FOR protecting them, by a mock Trial, from Punishment for any Murders which they should commit on the Inhabitants of these States:

FOR cutting off our Trade with all Parts of the World:

FOR imposing Taxes on us without our Consent:

FOR depriving us, in many Cases, of the Benefits of Trial by Jury:

FOR transporting us beyond Seas to be tried for pretended Offences:

FOR abolishing the free System of English Laws in a neighbouring Province, establishing therein an arbitrary Government, and enlarging its Boundaries, so as to render it at once an Example and fit Instrument for introducing the same absolute Rule into these Colonies:

FOR taking away our Charters, abolishing our most valuable Laws, and altering fundamentally the Forms of our Governments:

FOR suspending our own Legislatures, and declaring themselves invested with Power to legislate for us in all Cases whatsoever.

HE has abdicated Government here, by declaring us out of his Protection and waging War against us.

HE has plundered our Seas, ravaged our Coasts, burnt our Towns, and destroyed the Lives of our People.

HE is, at this Time, transporting large Armies of foreign Mercenaries to compleat the Works of Death, Desolation, and Tyranny, already begun with circumstances of Cruelty and Perfidy, scarcely paralleled in the most barbarous Ages, and totally unworthy the Head of a civilized Nation.

HE has constrained our fellow Citizens taken Captive on the high Seas to bear Arms against their Country, to become the Executioners of their Friends and Brethren, or to fall themselves by their Hands.

HE has excited domestic Insurrections amongst us, and has endeavoured to bring on the Inhabitants of our Frontiers, the merciless Indian Savages, whose known Rule of Warfare, is an undistinguished Destruction, of all Ages, Sexes and Conditions.

IN every stage of these Oppressions we have Petitioned for Redress in the most humble Terms: Our repeated Petitions have been answered only by repeated Injury. A Prince, whose Character is thus marked by every act which may define a Tyrant, is unfit to be the Ruler of a free People.

NOR have we been wanting in Attentions to our British Brethren. We have warned them from Time to Time of Attempts by their Legislature to extend an unwarrantable Jurisdiction over us. We have reminded them of the Circumstances of our Emigration and Settlement here. We have appealed to their native Justice and Magnanimity, and we have conjured them by the Ties of our common Kindred to disavow these Usurpations, which, would inevitably interrupt our Connections and Correspondence. They too have been deaf to the Voice of Justice and of Consanguinity. We must, therefore, acquiesce in the Necessity, which denounces our Separation, and hold them, as we hold the rest of Mankind, Enemies in War, in Peace, Friends.

WE, therefore, the Representatives of the UNITED STATES OF AMERICA, in GENERAL CONGRESS, Assembled, appealing to the Supreme Judge of the World for the Rectitude of our Intentions, do, in the Name, and by Authority of the good People of these Colonies, solemnly Publish and Declare, That these United Colonies are, and of Right ought to be, FREE AND INDEPENDENT STATES; that they are absolved from all Allegiance to the British Crown, and that all political Connection between them and the State of Great-Britain, is and ought to be totally dissolved; and that as FREE AND INDEPENDENT STATES, they have full Power to levy War, conclude Peace, contract Alliances, establish Commerce, and to do all other Acts and Things which INDEPENDENT STATES may of right do. And for the support of this Declaration, with a firm Reliance on the Protection of divine Providence, we mutually pledge to each other our Lives, our Fortunes, and our sacred Honor.

Signed by ORDER *and in* BEHALF *of the* CONGRESS,

JOHN HANCOCK, PRESIDENT.

ATTEST.
CHARLES THOMSON, SECRETARY.

PHILADELPHIA: PRINTED BY JOHN DUNLAP.

Figure 6. *John Dunlap's broadside of the Declaration of Independence. Unlike the engrossed copy (with a single block of script lines) that has become the iconic image, the printed version of the Declaration features the list of twenty-seven grievances prominently. Americans in 1776 would have seen the Declaration exclusively in this broadside form or as printed in newspaper columns. Courtesy of the Library of Congress.*

these proxy fighters with "he," they also enlarged the definition of America's "enemy" to include those groups. Leaving no room for the thousands of blacks or Indians who supported the patriot cause, the Declaration portrayed them all as mindless, bloodthirsty barbarians too naïve to realize they were being duped by a tyrant.

There was, moreover, a subtle difference between these proxies listed at the end of the grievances, a tiny shift that helps explain how many viewed the distinctions between them. The so-called "merciless savages" would take the war into their own hands and devastate the frontiers, Congress argued. "Insurrections" also connoted a hostile activity initiated by "domestics." But the foreign mercenaries charge is messier. In fact, it pulls a switch on the reader. The grievance argues they were going to do deadly things once they stopped being "transported," but on closer inspection, the final clause turns back to the king for deciding to include them. His was an action "totally unworthy the Head of a civilized nation." It seems the "works of Death, Desolation, and Tyranny, already begun with circumstances of Cruelty and Perfidy, scarcely paralleled in the most barbarous Ages" were, not the anticipated works of Hessians, but rather the product of George's decisions. This is a brilliant sleight of hand: with the Hessians rendered as passive—empty vessels of the king standing on transport ships to carry out the tyrant's evil schemes—the blame did not center on them personally, very unlike slaves and Indians. The Declaration withholds judgment on the German troops, making a future redemption possible. African Americans and Indians were not so lucky.

These war grievances help clarify the problems inherent in drawing a line between "us" and "them." According to Congress, the king's proxies were unable to discern liberty from slavery, an interpretation that drips with irony. "We" would never fall victim to such crimes. The "we" of "we hold these truths to be self-evident" is the most important word in the Declaration. Who are "we"? The twenty-seventh grievance helps solve that puzzle: those patriotic, liberty-loving people who had the foresight and moral courage to resist the "repeated injuries and usurpations" of the "Present King of Great Britain." "We"—the American people—would not include "he" nor his helpers: the "merciless savages," "domestic insurrectionists," and—at least for now—"foreign mercenaries."

At the key founding moment, then, the definition of what it meant to be "an American" was a negative one: "not British." But the heated language of the Declaration's final grievance gave it other shapes: "not slave," "not savage," and "not mercenary." Those constructions reinforced the patriots' positive assessment of themselves as holding the moral, philosophical, and political high ground in this conflict. Because those tropes plugged into embedded colonial prejudices about Africans and Indians, however, they were about more than merely not behaving in manners that were slavish or savage. They had the effect of casting out real Indians and African Americans.[99]

For another group of New Yorkers gathering to listen to the Declaration, they were enemies just like the king. While soldiers at Fort Ticonderoga cheered, "Now we are a people," a crowd on Long Island's north shore celebrated the same announcement. In a less sanguine mood, this crowd "from all the distant quarters of the district" of Huntington showed their approval for independence by constructing a visual representation of the multiple enemies of the new United States of America. A newspaper report detailed the actions of that July afternoon: "An effigy of [George III] being hastily fabricated out of base materials, with its face black, like *Dunmore's* Virginia regiment, its head adorned with a wooden crown, and its head stuck full of feathers, like *Carleton* and *Johnson's* Savages, and its body wrapped in the Union [Jack], instead of a blanket or robe of state, and lined with *gun-powder,* which the original seems to be fond of." "The whole," the article concluded, "was hung on a gallows, exploded, and burnt to ashes." In essence, the crowd of Long Islanders gave their own performance of the Declaration, using fire instead of ink to kill the king and his various proxies. They defended "life, liberty, and the pursuit of happiness" by animating and then destroying both His Majesty and his proxies simultaneously. The New Yorkers consigned all their enemies—the king, the merciless savages, and the domestic insurrectionists—to the flames, leaving "Americans" to stand outside and watch the blaze.[100]

Although we do not have the luxury of a patriot observer to interpret the faces of the onlookers in this crowd, it is important to consider what might have been on their minds. At least a few of them greeted the news of independence, the Declaration's accusations, and the specific behavior it sparked with trepidation. Since this was Long Island, there were surely

99. I have explored these elements of the Declaration in "The Declaration of Independence," in Francis D. Cogliano, ed., *A Companion to Thomas Jefferson* (Oxford, 2012), 44–59; and "Exclusion at the Founding: The Declaration of Independence," in Rachel Hammersley, ed., *Revolutionary Moments: Reading Revolutionary Texts* (London, 2015), 53–60.

100. *New-York Journal,* Aug. 8, 1776.

some in the crowd who doubted whether independence was the best course. People in Huntington and Suffolk County showed much more support for the common cause than their western neighbors in King's or Queen's County—where the popular perception was that "Tories are 3 to 1 against the Whiggs"—but there were quite a few disaffected folk in the area. Considering the strong possibility that there were many in places like Long Island (and lots of other locales throughout the continent) who greeted the news with apprehension, it was wise of Congress not to indict them in the Declaration. The decision to omit Jefferson's loyalist grievance might have paid considerable dividends in a place like Huntington, which, in a matter of weeks, would be fewer than twenty miles away from the right flank of a massive British army. At the same time, since nearly one in ten residents of Suffolk County was African American, there was also a decent chance more than a few watched their neighbors spread black powder all over the effigy to prepare the king for execution. That fastening could only have raised doubts in the minds of African Americans in Huntington and elsewhere as to the patriots' true interest in making the cause common to everyone.[101]

From the patriot perspective, however, this exclusion could not be

101. William Tudor to JA, July 7, 1776, *PJA*, IV, 368. It was in Queen's County that Charles Lee initiated his own disarmament campaign without congressional approval earlier that spring. In reality, historians believe that the numbers were closer to two-to-one in favor of loyalists in Queen's County. See Joseph S. Tiedemann, "A Revolution Foiled: Queens County, New York, 1775–1776," *JAH*, LXXV (1988), 417–444. For Suffolk's political allegiances, see Edward Countryman, *A People in Revolution: The American Revolution and Political Society in New York, 1760–1790* (Baltimore, 1981), 103–104, 149. Four months later, after Long Island was under British army occupation, Suffolk County's committees dissolved themselves and refused to obey Congress. Huntington, like many of the towns, informed Governor Tryon that they were "thoroughly convinced of the injurious and criminal tendency of our former meetings and resolutions . . . do hereby dissolve this Committee . . . and disavow the orders and resolutions of all Committees and Congresses whatsoever." Though the pro forma nature of this confession raised doubts about its truthfulness even at the time, its existence suggests that staunch patriots did not completely populate the village. See Declarations of Committees of Suffolk County, New York, 5 *Am. Archives*, II, 1219–1221 (Huntington's disavowal is on 1219). A census taken in July 1776 listed 821 blacks and 7,523 whites in Suffolk County, or 9.8 percent of the population. See "Number of Inhabitants in the Several Towns of Suffolk County, New-York, July 1776," 4 *Am. Archives*, VI, 1236–1252. This return counted white and black populations in nine Suffolk locales, but Huntington was not among them.

helped, especially at this moment, with more ships from the British invasion fleet appearing on the horizon each day. Like the Declaration itself, the exploding proxy effigy in Huntington was a production that patriots believed would inspire political and military mobilization in a strategic area—but it was a production based in reality nonetheless. Its power derived from that foundation. If capitalizing on that rhetorical opportunity meant the sacrifice of "good" blacks or Indians who supported the Revolution, so be it. Once the historical moment passed—after the Long Islanders had dispersed and the king's ashes were cast to the winds—that powerful accusation casting out "domestics" and "merciless savages" would remain, indelible.[102]

More than four decades later, John Adams wrote that independence was "perhaps a singular example in the history of mankind." "Thirteen clocks were made to strike together," he remembered in 1818, "a perfection of mechanism, which no artist had ever before effected." Adams's turn of phrase is telling. Even from such a distance, Adams's memory was that a particular agent aligned the "distinct, unconnected, and independent" clocks of "so little resemblance" to chime together. On July 8, 1776, most Americans who gathered in places like Easton, Pennsylvania, and Trenton, New Jersey, to give "their hearty assent" to the Declaration's grievances "with three loud huzzas" would argue that the king was that artist. But Adams, his colleagues in Congress, and thousands of other patriots were just as responsible for the timing of American independence and the terms by which it was proclaimed. Adams himself recognized this: he encouraged "young men of letters in all the States" to investigate "all the records, pamphlets, newspapers, and even handbills, which in any way contributed to change the temper and views of the people, and compose them into an independent nation."[103]

102. This local anxiety was heightened by potential alliances between loyalists and African Americans. A militia officer from Huntington had reported to the New York Provincial Congress just a few months earlier that his neighbors worried about "the disaffection people of sundry people," including "a suspicion . . . about enlisting negroes." See *Journal of the Provincial Congress . . . of the State of New York, 1775–1777* (Albany, N.Y., 1842), I, 214–215.

103. JA to H[ezekiah] Niles, Quincy, [Mass.], Feb. 13, 1818, in Adams, ed., *Works of John Adams*, X, 282–289, esp. 283; Easton, Northampton County, and Trenton, [N.J.], Jul. 8, 1776, 5 *Am. Archives*, I, 119–120, quotes from the Easton event, I, 119. Adams did make a similar observation at the time. On August 2, 1776, he wrote to his brother-in-law Richard Cranch, "Is not the Change We have seen astonishing? Would any Man, two Years ago have believed it possible, to accomplish such

Independence, in other words, was not an organic upwelling of patriotic fervor, the natural result of the "rage militaire" of the war's first year. That "rage" was "composed"—in both senses of the term. It was focused by patriot polemicists and propagated by composers of type. They assisted in disseminating *Common Sense* and built upon Paine's arguments by developing that pamphlet into an enlarged patriot anthology. Moreover, they broadcast the news of Moore's Creek and carefully managed the story of German mercenaries in the spring of 1776. All of these activities were essential to preparing the American public for independence. Though Adams meant for America's "young men" to scour front-page essays in the years and months leading up to Lexington, the stories found inside the weekly newspapers after the shooting started cannot be ignored. They were what wound the mechanisms inside the thirteen colonial clocks. The list of enemies John assembled to respond to Abigail's call to "remember the ladies" was no joking matter. Perhaps he forgot after four decades, but in 1776, Adams grasped the importance of the proxies perfectly.[104]

It is impossible to know which parts of the Declaration colonists most agreed with or connected to when they read the text at home in their local newspapers, in taverns on broadsides scattered around, or in town squares as handbills pasted on poles. Neither is it clear which particular phrases earned the loudest acclamations when it was proclaimed from state house balconies, county courthouse steps, or platforms at the head of troop formations. Observers recorded only how various groups reacted to the fact of independence, most often with celebratory huzzas followed by violent attacks on royal iconography—a founding ritual that blended birth and funeral customs. Since 1776, the implicit answer to which parts were Americans' favorites involved the opening statements about equality, happiness,

---

an Alteration in the Prejudices, Passions, Sentiments, and Principles of these thirteen little States as to make every one of them completely republican, and to make them own it? Idolatry to Monarchs, and servility to Aristocratical Pride, was never so totally eradicated, from so many Minds in so short a Time" (JA to Richard Cranch, Aug. 2, 1776, in L. H. Butterfield et al., eds., *Adams Family Correspondence*, 2d Ser. [Cambridge, Mass., 1963–], II, 74).

104. "Rage militaire": Charles Royster, *A Revolutionary People at War: The Continental Army and American Character, 1775–1783* (Chapel Hill, N.C., 1979), 25. Royster borrowed this term from a Philadelphian who invoked it in a letter that was published in *Lloyd's Evening Post and British Chronicle*, June 28–30, 1775.

and inalienable truths. This reflected the perspective Adams wanted future generations to realize: that of front-page essays about political liberty.[105]

Those opening paragraphs do not explain the timing and final, necessary causes of independence, however. The ultimate grievances concerning foreign mercenaries, merciless savages, and domestic insurrectionists brought those clocks to strike in early July 1776. It was those stories that would alter the common cause from a movement that insisted the crown recognize colonists' proper rights as English subjects to one that convinced a majority of Americans that "all political connection between them and the State of Great Britain is, and ought to be, totally dissolved."

105. David Waldstreicher, *In the Midst of Perpetual Fetes: The Making of American Nationalism, 1776–1820* (Chapel Hill, N.C., 1997), 30–37; Brendan McConville, *The King's Three Faces: The Rise and Fall of British America, 1688–1776* (Chapel Hill, N.C., 2006), 306–311.

## CHAPTER 4

"By the American Revolution
You Are Now Free"

STICKING TOGETHER IN TRYING TIMES

On July 2, 1776, as Congress neared a final vote on independence, Washington issued general orders in which he reiterated the main tropes of the wartime common cause. He reminded his men, "The time is now near at hand which must probably determine, whether Americans are to be, Freemen, or Slaves." Upon the "Courage and Conduct" of American arms, "the fate of unborn Millions will now depend. . . . We have therefore to resolve to conquer or die: Our own Country's Honor, all call upon us for a vigorous and manly exertion, and if we now shamefully fail, we shall become infamous to the whole world." "Let us therefore rely upon the goodness of the Cause," Washington proclaimed, "and the aid of the supreme Being, in whose hands Victory is, to animate and encourage us to great and noble Actions . . . Let us . . . shew the whole world, that a Freeman contending for Liberty on his own ground is superior to any slavish mercenary on earth."[1]

This statement, even more than Jefferson's opening paragraphs of the Declaration, encapsulates all the qualities patriots wanted every American to grasp about the common cause on the eve of independence. True patriots "contended for Liberty" through "vigorous and manly exertion," whereas anyone who opposed these "great and noble Actions" was the opposite of the freemen, a "slavish mercenary." Beginning that summer, Washington's injunction would be put to more stringent tests. Whether enough of the public would rally around this interpretation of what constituted the duties of freemen remained to be seen. The abstract metaphors through which patriot polemicists had defined this conflict might not be sufficient to de-

1. General Orders, New York, July 2, 1776, *PGW: RW*, V, 179–182, esp. 180.

fend the now-independent United States of America. It helped the project of animating and encouraging each other that patriot leaders were also able to justify that defense against real slaves and mercenaries.

For the remainder of 1776, patriot publicists broadcast as much good news as they could, featuring stories about how "vigorous," "manly" "Freemen" turned back British incursions on both the Carolina coast and backcountry and how similar heroes in Virginia ousted Dunmore from his refuge in the Chesapeake Bay. Readers were, as ever, reminded that these British agents depended on proxies to achieve the "Tyranny meditated against them," as Washington put it. When the fearsome invasion force of British and German soldiers finally attacked at summer's end, however, there was little good news to report, especially after the fall of New York City. Patriot political leaders scrambled to blunt this force, renewing their efforts to encourage the Germans to desert and reconsidering their stances on arming Indians. But print remained the most effective weapon at their disposal; patriot publicists exchanged stories depicting the appalling behavior of the "slavish mercenaries" in America.

Then those stories stopped. With the capture of nearly a thousand Hessian soldiers in Washington's surprise Christmas raid on Trenton, newspaper reports that had previously described the Hessians as rapists, plunderers, murderers, and destroyers—"Men monsters," in the eyes of one contemporary—vanished. The frightening Hessians were suddenly transformed, a remarkable conversion that again underscores the power of print and the exchanges during the Revolution. But, even more than that, the Hessians' "redemption" illustrates how contrived the common cause truly was. It was a construction that selected certain materials and left others unused, notably the participation of "good" African Americans and Indians on the American side. Moreover, when their practicality waned, the common cause construction abandoned previously vital materials. It was more expedient to the patriots not to remind readers of the mercenaries' vileness.

All of this was a creative act. Patriot leaders understood this, but, as yet, few British or loyalists acknowledged the political power of the common cause argument. Late in 1776, one did. Ambrose Serle, the secretary of British army commander Lord William Howe, comprehended that newspapers were the epicenter of this creativity. They were the reason the patriots had survived all British military maneuvers thus far. Serle was one of the most astute British observers of the American rebellion. He recognized the source of patriot success—the power of the press and the stories of British proxies—and moved to counter their efforts. Luckily for the patriots, there were not many like him in 1776. Contrived though it may have been, by the summer of independence, the common cause was beginning to have real political consequences for a growing number of people in North America.

1: THE FIRST DAYS OF INDEPENDENCE IN THE SOUTH

By the time Congress had unanimously approved independence, patriot forces in South Carolina already had fought a significant conflict that was as much about real slavery as it was about abstract freedom. On June 28, the same day Jefferson delivered his rough draft six hundred miles to the north, British naval forces under the command of Sir Peter Parker opened fire on the outer defenses of Charleston.

Earlier in the year, Congress had sent General Charles Lee south to ready patriot fortifications in case of British attack. Upon arriving in Williamsburg, he fretted that Virginia's capital might indeed be an irresistible target for British strategists, not the least because "it would give an air of superiority and dignity to their arms, which in this Slave Country might be attended with important consequences by the impressions it would make in the minds of the Negroes." He next proceeded to Charleston. Even before arriving, he had not heard good things. In fact, the situation was just the same as in Williamsburg. If the British moved against Charleston, a patriot officer informed him, that attack "may instigate the Indian Tribes by the aid of their Deputy Superintendent (which some say is in agitation)—join to these Malcontents, and peradventure the domesticks." When he got to Charleston, Lee found the city vulnerable; he immediately labored to, in the words of one Charlestonian, put the city "into an exceeding good Posture of Defence."[2]

Lee promptly ordered the overhaul of a half-finished palmetto-log fort on Sullivan's Island. The island was a contested site of authority between not

2. Charles Lee to Edward Rutledge, Williamsburg, Apr. 3, 1776, in "The Lee Papers, Vol. I, 1754–1776," *Collections of the New-York Historical Society: For the Year 1871*, IV (New York, 1872), 372 (hereafter referred to as NYHS, *Colls.*); General John Armstrong to Charles Lee, Charleston, S.C., May 8, 1776, "Lee Papers, Vol. II, 1776–1778," NYHS, *Colls.*, V (New York, 1873), 11; Richard Hutson to Isaac Hayne, June 24, 1776, 68, Richard Hutson Letterbook, 1765–1777 (34/559), SCHS. Lee reiterated this opinion in another letter two days later to Richard Henry Lee, adding one crucial sentence: "Your dominion over the black is founded on opinion; if this opinion falls, your authority is lost" (Charles Lee to Richard Henry Lee, Williamsburg, Apr. 5, 1776, "Lee Papers, Vol. I, 1754–1776," 379).

only patriots and the British but also blacks and whites in 1775 and 1776. That a fort even existed on the ocean side of the four-mile-long barrier island was a result of the fact that Charleston militiamen had conducted a raid there in December 1775 to disperse gathering numbers of fugitive slaves who hoped to hail the Royal Navy. The militia, dressed as Indians, had killed and captured a number of slaves and burned down the "pest house," which, of late, had served as a shelter for runaways.[3]

The soon-to-be heralded Fort Sullivan would be constructed on top of the ashes of this pest house. Thanks to the combination of poor strategy and execution on the part of the British navy, the natural sponginess of palmetto trunks that allowed them to absorb British cannonballs, and accurate fire from Colonel William Moultrie's artillery, the small fort that guarded the harbor withstood Parker's assault and saved South Carolina's independence.

The repulse at Sullivan's Island was a significant opportunity to propagate the common cause, as Moore's Creek Bridge had been four months earlier. This "illustrious event in our history," as the South Carolina Assembly put it later, led to a whole new spate of legends and heroes, including Moultrie and a Sergeant William Jasper, who risked his life to raise Carolina's blue flag—emblazoned with the word "liberty"—after it had been struck down in a barrage. Soon enough, Jasper's "liberty" flag would be transmogrified and merged with a new symbol: the astounding palmetto logs themselves. South Carolinians made the logs that "saved" the Revolution in Charleston their new state emblem. But a closer look at what Carolinians celebrated when they put the palmetto tree at the center of their new state flag, took June 28 as their state holiday, and venerated the defenders of Fort Sullivan reveals the sharp edges of the common cause.[4]

Nearly the entire event at Sullivan's Island involved the removal of blacks from participation in the defense of Charleston—and from Jasper's idea of "liberty." The soon-to-be-sacred palmetto fort sat on the spot where captured Africans throughout the eighteenth century were quarantined before being transported across the harbor for sale in the city's slave markets (thus

3. John Shy, "American Strategy: Charles Lee and the Radical Alternative," in Shy, *A People Numerous and Armed: Reflections on the Military Struggle for American Independence* (1976; rpt. Ann Arbor, Mich., 1990), 133–162, esp. 144.

4. South Carolina Legislative Council, Sept. 19, 1776, 5 *Am. Archives*, II, 393–394. This also appeared in *Connecticut Gazette*, Oct. 4, 1776; *Pennsylvania Packet*, Oct. 29, 1776.

the existence of the "pest house"). Sullivan's "might well be viewed as the Ellis Island of black Americans." Yet patriot authorities violently removed blacks from that area when the danger of their running to the British grew too great; and when Charles Lee ordered construction on Fort Sullivan to be renewed, he forbade Charlestonians from volunteering their slaves to build it. Whites sawed, laid, and daubed the logs that became the stuff of Carolina myth. In order to attain patriot victory, therefore, blacks not only had to be physically removed from the original site but were prevented from constructing a symbol of the very founding of the state of South Carolina. According to patriot witnesses, the only black participant at the battle was a pilot who provided Parker with special information, just as Thomas Jeremiah surely would have, had he still been alive.[5]

When Carolinians celebrated victory, they championed a story about Sullivan's Island that was entirely different from all previous renderings of that place. Sullivan's became a place of white freedom, not black bondage. It was no longer a cordoned-off site for quarantining blacks but rather a place for heroes like William Jasper, a man who, to borrow from Washington,

---

5. Peter H. Wood, *Black Majority: Negroes in Colonial South Carolina from 1670 through the Stono Rebellion* (New York, 1974), xiv; Shy, "American Strategy," in Shy, *A People Numerous and Armed*, 144. See also Philip D. Morgan, *Slave Counterpoint: Black Culture in the Eighteenth-Century Chesapeake and Lowcountry* (Chapel Hill, N.C., 1998), 75, 79. One letter reprinted in three of the most staunch patriot newspapers celebrated Lee's rapid preparations but emphasized community cohesiveness instead of the general's order not to allow slave labor: "The people expressed the greatest alacrity in [preparing] immediately, OLD and YOUNG, HIGH and LOW, RICH and POOR, WHITE and BLACK, ONE WITH ANOTHER, set about the work." See *Pennsylvania Evening Post*, July 23, 1776; *New-York Journal*, Aug. 1, 1776; *Continental Journal*, Aug. 15, 1776. After the battle, Lee himself wanted to reverse this policy, asking the South Carolina council to employ a "Corps of Blacks" to repair the fort instead of soldiers. See Lee to Colonel [William] Moultrie, Lee to President Rutledge, Charleston, S.C., July 1, 1776, "Lee Papers, Vol. II, 1776–1778," NYHS, *Colls.*, V, 104, 106. In the narrative Charles Lee collected from five Americans who were on board Parker's fleet but escaped, one reported, "The negro pilot, (*Sampson,*) who is exceedingly caressed, was on board the *Commodore,* and put down with the Doctor, out of harm's way." See "Narrative, by Thomas Bennett, of Colonel Danielson's Massachusetts Regiment; Daniel Hawkins, of Boston; Robert Scott and Edmund Allston, of New-Hampshire . . . ," enclosed in "Extract of a Letter from General [Charles] Lee to President of Congress, Dated Charlestown, July 2, 1776," 4 *Am. Archives*, VI, 1205–1206, esp. 1206, published in *Pennsylvania Magazine*, II (1776), 340–341.

"By the American Revolution You Are Now Free"

patently showed "vigorous and manly exertion" to defend *his* liberty. According to the most widely republished account of the battle—Charles Lee's July 2 letter to Congress—Moultrie, Jasper, and the rest of the garrison were "brave soldiers and excellent citizens." Inside the fort, Lee reported with astonishment, even those who had "lost their limbs . . . did not lose their spirits; for they enthusiastically encouraged their comrades, never to abandon the standard of liberty and their country." Lee anticipated this would be hard to believe, adding that it was "not in the stile of gasconading romance . . . but literally a fact." "They acted like Romans in the third century," Lee wrote to Washington. After such a display of republican virtue and sacrifice, it was easy for patriot authorities in Carolina to substitute the palmetto symbol for the word "liberty." That behavior, complete with the requisite erasure of African Americans, reflected the essence of the common cause.[6]

But no sooner had white South Carolinians congratulated themselves for turning back British invaders from the sea when they learned that their western frontier was under attack. Many, including Henry Laurens, saw the timing as more than coincidental and were satisfied with the positive effects this perception might have on the public. As he stated, "After the attack upon Sullivant's Island seconded by the Ravages and Murders by the Cherokee Indians on our Western frontier who probably acted in a concerted Plan with the Ships and Troops, I believe there were few Men here who had not lost all inclination for renewing our former connexion with your King and his Ministers." One of Benjamin Franklin's correspondents wrote him from Savannah, Georgia, "It clearly appears a plan of the Vile Ministry" to attack the frontier "at the same time the Fleet etc. is on our Sea coast." Southerners that July might well have found the phrases "domestic insurrections" and "merciless savages" particularly apt as they read the Declaration in the midst of all this commotion.[7]

6. *Pennsylvania Evening Post*, July 20, 1776; *Pennsylvania Ledger*, July 20, 1776; *Pennsylvania Packet*, July 22, 1776; *Pennsylvania Journal*, July 24, 1776; *New-York Journal*, July 25, 1776; *New-York Gazette*, July 29, 1776; *American Gazette*, July 30, 1776; *Continental Journal*, Aug. 2, 1776; *Connecticut Gazette*, Aug. 2, 1776; *Essex Journal*, Aug. 2, 1776; *New Hampshire Gazette* (Exeter), Aug. 3, 1776; *Pennsylvania Magazine*, II (1776), 339–340; Lee to GW, Charleston, July 1, 1776, "Lee Papers, Vol. II, 1776–1778," NYHS, *Colls.*, V, 100–103, esp. 101.

7. HL to John Laurens, Charleston, Aug. 14, 1776, *PHL*, XI, 227–228; Noble Wimberly Jones to BF, Savannah, July 11, 1776, *PBF*, XXII, 510. In fact, the South Carolina Assembly explicitly used the term "merciless savages" in its September 19,

Since Lexington, relations between patriot authorities and the Cherokee Indians had been tense but peaceful as yet. In the spring, Tsi'yu Gunsi'ni, or Dragging Canoe, a militant Cherokee leader who saw the conflict as an opportunity to protect his people's interests, traveled to Mobile to meet with British Indian agent Henry Stuart. Dragging Canoe was angry with his father Atakullakulla (Little Carpenter) for ceding thousands of acres of prime Cherokee land to Carolina speculators. Pledging military support for the crown, Dragging Canoe returned home to Chota with ammunition. Contrary to what the patriots thought, Stuart and Alexander Cameron had begged Dragging Canoe to remain neutral; it was a delegation of Indians from the north, including the Shawnees, who produced a war belt and asked the Cherokees for support. Dragging Canoe saw this as an excellent chance to regain control over lost land and punish greedy southern frontiersmen.[8]

On June 26, two days before Parker's ships opened fire on Fort Sullivan, a party of Cherokees exchanged fire with patriot militiamen who were searching for the infamous Cameron. This skirmish touched off a series of raids behind the Blue Ridge, starting on July 1, that resulted in the burning of some farmhouses along the Holston and Watauga Rivers and the deaths of five dozen white settlers. The response sheds significant light on how seriously patriots viewed the participation of Indians in the war. Although this was not a major offensive that threatened many people in the southern backcountry, patriots across the South responded with a vengeance. Charles Lee, flush with recent victory, recommended Carolinians make an example of the Cherokees. Patriot leader William Henry Drayton seconded that notion: "For my part, I shall never give my voice for a peace with

---

1776, proclamation just before they discussed the Declaration itself as a "decree now worthy of America" (5 *Am. Archives,* II, 393).

8. Tom Hatley, *The Dividing Paths: Cherokees and South Carolinians through the Revolutionary Era* (New York, 1993), 217–218; Gary B. Nash, *The Unknown American Revolution: The Unruly Birth of Democracy and the Struggle to Create America* (New York, 2005), 257–258; Jim Piecuch, *Three Peoples, One King: Loyalists, Indians, and Slaves in the Revolutionary South, 1775–1782* (Columbia, S.C., 2008), 68–69. Two men passed along third-hand information from the Cherokee villages to North Carolina patriot authorities that Cameron asked the Indians not to take prisoners "but kill as they went." See "Letter from Charles Roberson and James about the Cherokees," Wataugah, July 13, 1776, in William L. Saunders, ed., *The Colonial Records of North Carolina,* 10 vols. (Raleigh, N.C., 1886–1890), X, 666.

the Cherokee Nation upon any other terms than their removal beyond the mountains."[9]

Once the news reached Philadelphia about unrest on the southern frontier, Jefferson agreed. He advised a full invasion to John Page, now lieutenant governor of Virginia: "Nothing will reduce those wretches so soon as pushing the war into the heart of their country. But I would not stop there. I would never cease pursuing them while one of them remained on this side [of] the Mississippi." The author of the Declaration called for a similar removal of persons deemed a threat to the cause, as Carolinians had accomplished on Sullivan's Island. He had already supervised the rhetorical removal of all friendly Indians in the Declaration by lumping them all together as merciless enemies. Now he, too, called for physical removal: "So unprovoked an attack and so treacherous one should never be forgiven while one of them remains near enough to do us injury."[10]

Jefferson hardly needed to worry that a strong statement would be made to the offending Cherokees. Beginning in late summer and throughout the harvest, three columns of men from Virginia and the Carolinas ripped through Cherokee country, taking revenge on their cornfields and towns. Virginia delegate Thomas Nelson also advised John Page to "give them no quarter, but drive them into the South Sea if it were possible." "The gross infernal breach of faith which they have been guilty of shuts them out from every pretension of mercy," urged the North Carolina delegation to Congress, "and it is surely the policy of the Southern Colonies (and justice to our fellow whites on our Frontiers not only will vindicate but loudly demands such a Conduct) to carry fire and Sword into the very bowels of their Country and sink them so low that they may never be able again to rise and disturb the peace of their Neighbours." The North Carolina delegates stood with Jefferson: they hoped their countrymen would "exercise that manly

9. John W. Gordon, *South Carolina in the American Revolution: A Battlefield History* (Columbia, S.C., 2002), 46–48; Wayne E. Lee, *Crowds and Soldiers in Revolutionary North Carolina: The Culture of Violence in Riot and War* (Gainesville, Fla., 2001), 158–162; William Henry Drayton to Francis Salvador, Charleston, July 24, 1776, in R. W. Gibbes, ed., *Documentary History of the American Revolution: Consisting of Letters and Papers Relating to the Contest for Liberty, Chiefly in South Carolina . . .* , II, *1776–1782* (New York, 1857), 29.

10. TJ to John Page, Philadelphia, Aug. 5, 1776, *PTJ*, I, 485–486. For native understandings of American demands for general extermination, see Jeffrey Ostler, "'To Extirpate the Indians': An Indigenous Consciousness of Genocide in the Ohio Valley and Lower Great Lakes, 1750s-1810," *WMQ*, 3d Ser., LXXII (2015), 587–622.

and generous method of pursuing them to destruction which our own Customs and the Law of nations will vindicate." Apparently, neither the North Carolinians nor Jefferson appreciated the irony of sanctioning a war against so-called "merciless savages" with the judgment that "mercy to their Warriors is cruelty to ourselves."[11]

Patriot leaders in Virginia and South Carolina agreed. By October, the force they sent into the mountains had destroyed thirty-six Cherokee towns and the provisions that were to carry them through the winter. The news of what the men under patriot commanders William Christian, Griffith Rutherford, and Andrew Williamson had done would become well documented in the press that autumn. From the patriot perspective, the destruction of the Cherokee Overhill towns was the only bright spot in a season that was otherwise a cascade of military setbacks in New York.[12]

The Cherokees had corroborated the Declaration of Independence's ultimate grievance, and patriot forces had responded in kind. In this case, it is hardly a stretch to connect events, policy, and discourse. To quote one letter from Carolina that appeared in eight newspapers, the Cherokees "have committed several outrages; which seems to be only a part of the capital and favourite plan laid down by his *most excellent* and *clement* majesty, George the Third, to lay waste the provinces, burn the habitations, and mix men, women, and children, in one common carnage, by the hands of those merciless savages." At the moment of independence, South Carolina patriots were acting on the same impulse as the crowd at Huntington, Long Island. What was ritual in New York was happening to real people in South Carolina.[13]

That letter, which appeared anonymously in local papers from Virginia to New England, was actually written by Charles Lee. Or most of it was. General Lee related the violence on the southern frontier to Virginia Convention president Edmund Pendleton, but he did not explicitly connect it to the king. Lee had written Pendleton about the "carnage by the hands of the *Indians* . . . as this part of the plan." When Pendleton had turned the let-

---

11. Thomas Nelson to John Page, Philadelphia, Aug. 13, 1776, *LDC*, IV, 676, North Carolina Delegates to the North Carolina Council of Safety, Philadelphia, Aug. 7, [8], 1776, 640, 641.

12. Lee, *Crowds and Soldiers*, 160–161.

13. *Virginia Gazette* (Purdie), July 26, 1776; *Maryland Journal*, Aug. 5, 1776; *Pennsylvania Gazette*, Aug. 7, 1776; *Pennsylvania Journal*, Aug. 7, 1776; *Dunlap's Maryland Gazette*, Aug. 12–13, 1776; *New-York Journal*, Aug. 15, 1776; *Providence Gazette*, Aug. 17, 1776; *Norwich Packet*, Aug. 12–19, 1776; *Boston Gazette*, Aug. 26, 1776.

"By the American Revolution You Are Now Free"

ter over to Alexander Purdie, the Williamsburg printer had, in the words of Samuel Adams, "improved on" Lee's language. Purdie — or his assistants — cannot be blamed for making this connection. After all, they had just set the type for those same words earlier in the week: the text of the Declaration appeared in the same July 26 issue, two pages before this anonymous account from Charleston. Purdie was only providing proof for his readers who might have questioned whether Indians really were either working for the king or "merciless." This intelligence was just one comment on independence that crowded that issue. It followed reports about the Declaration's being read to "loud acclamations" in Trenton and in front of the thrilled Continental army, a story about the proposed melting down of New York's George III statue into bullets "to assimilate with the brain of our infatuated adversaries," and, finally, a note about the firing of cannon and musketry in Williamsburg for the announcement of independence. Purdie's license with Lee's words was another way of expressing the meanings of the common cause at the founding. The crowd on Long Island did it through street theater, Purdie used type and text, and South Carolinians used forts and expeditions. All of these efforts were part of the same project.[14]

Over the next few months, from late August through October, publishers exchanged multiple reports of the progress of Virginia and Carolina columns as they laid waste to Cherokee country. Testimonies were the first stories to emerge from the frontier. Patriots placed great confidence in affidavits, crucial documents that could fix the narrative of innocence or guilt. After Lexington, patriot authorities claimed the moral high ground by sponsoring the widespread publication of sworn eyewitness testimony about British "atrocities" on the April 19 retreat back to Boston. A year later, they could be enough to justify invasion. Printers published notarized statements of attacks on innocents, in particular one by Fincastle County, Virginia, resident Jarrett Williams. Williams testified that six hundred Cherokees were planning a "general attack" aiming to "take away negroes, horses, etc. and . . . also to destroy all corn, burn houses, etc." Worse, they were not alone: Williams reported (accurately) that the Cherokees "had received the war belt from the Shawanese, Mingo, Taawah, and Delaware nations to

14. General Charles Lee to Edmund Pendleton, Charlestown, July 7, 1776, 5 *Am. Archives*, I, 95. Purdie had published a June 29 letter from Lee to Pendleton about the victory at Sullivan's Island the week before *with* the names of both author and recipient. See *Virginia Gazette* (Purdie), July 26, 1776. "To assimilate": *Virginia Gazette* (Purdie), July 26, 1776.

strike the white people." Williams's deposition, sworn by the Fincastle justice of the peace, was evidence enough for patriot leaders; nearly 60 percent of the twenty-seven active presses exchanged this story in August. Another four published an alternative set of depositions filed by a group of Fincastle "officers of rank." Two more exchanged a third round of sworn statements in September, making the *New-England Chronicle, New-York Journal, South-Carolina and American General Gazette,* and *Dunlap's Maryland Gazette* the only newspapers that—as far as can be ascertained—did not publish at least one set of affidavits from the southern frontier.[15]

Having established frontier farmers as innocent victims, patriot publicists looked for villains to reinforce the central theme of the common cause.

15. *Virginia Gazette* (Purdie), Aug. 2, 1776; *Virginia Gazette* (Dixon & Hunter), Aug. 3, 1776; *Pennsylvania Gazette,* Aug. 7, 1776; *Pennsylvania Packet,* Aug. 13, 1776; *Pennsylvania Journal,* Aug. 14, 1776; *New York Packet,* Aug. 15, 1776; *Pennsylvania Ledger,* Aug. 17, 1776; *New-York Gazette,* Aug. 19, 1776; *Connecticut Journal,* Aug. 21, 1776; *Connecticut Gazette,* Aug. 23, 1776; *Norwich Packet,* Aug. 19–26, 1776; *Massachusetts Spy,* Aug. 28, 1776; *Continental Journal,* Aug. 29, 1776; *Essex Journal,* Aug. 30, 1776; *Providence Gazette,* Aug. 31, 1776; *Freeman's Journal* (Portsmouth), Sept. 7, 1776. Four papers that published the letters from "officers of rank" in Fincastle, but not the Jarrett Williams deposition, were *Maryland Gazette,* Aug. 15, 1776; *Pennsylvania Evening Post,* Aug. 20, 1776; *Newport Mercury,* Sept. 2, 1776; *Boston Gazette,* Sept. 2, 1776. Eight more published both. For the Fincastle "officers'" extracts, see *Virginia Gazette* (Purdie), Aug. 9, 1776; *Virginia Gazette* (Dixon & Hunter), Aug. 10, 1776; *Pennsylvania Packet,* Aug. 13, 1776; *Pennsylvania Journal,* Aug. 21, 1776; *Pennsylvania Gazette,* Aug. 21, 1776; *Pennsylvania Ledger,* Aug. 24, 1776; *Connecticut Journal,* Aug. 28, 1776; *Massachusetts Spy,* Sept. 11, 1776. Three of these papers are missing issues in September. There is a gap in the *New-England Chronicle* from Sept. 19, 1776, to Jan. 2, 1777; the September 21 issue of Holt's *New-York Journal* is no longer extant; and there is a gap between Aug. 21 and Oct. 2 in the surviving run of the *South-Carolina and American General Gazette.* Again, given the proximity to the war for Charleston and the political stance of John Holt and *New-England Chronicle* printers Powars and Willis, it is quite likely one version of these depositions did appear in those lost issues. John Dunlap did publish this news in his *Pennsylvania Packet,* but not in his Baltimore paper. The two papers that published letters from four North Carolina farmers were *Maryland Journal,* Sept. 11, 1776, and *New Hampshire Gazette* (Exeter), Oct. 12, 1776. Others who included this third round included *Pennsylvania Evening Post,* Aug. 31, 1776; *Pennsylvania Gazette,* Sept. 4, 1776; *Pennsylvania Ledger,* Sept. 7, 1776; *New-York Gazette,* Sept. 9, 1776; *Maryland Gazette,* Sept. 12, 1776; *Providence Gazette,* Sept. 21, 1776; *Norwich Packet,* Sept. 16–23, 1776; *Connecticut Courant,* Sept. 23, 1776; *Massachusetts Spy,* Sept. 25, 1776; *Essex Journal,* Oct. 4, 1776.

"By the American Revolution You Are Now Free"

Williams testified that the Cherokees were not independent actors. They had been convinced by Alexander Cameron to "go to see if there were any king's men among the inhabitants, and . . . When this was done, they were to fall on the inhabitants, and kill and drive all they possibly could." Printers exchanged, with apparent relish, stories that featured the participation of Cameron and John Stuart's brother Henry with the Cherokees. A letter from Charleston explained, "That detestable villain Stewart [*sic*] has prevailed upon the Cherokees to take up the hatchet against our countrymen." But, the writer continued, this had the opposite effect for the common cause in Carolina: "Our people march forth against the savages, with all the alacrity and cheerfulness you can conceive, and with a full determined resolution to extirpate the whole tribe." First appearing in Dunlap's *Pennsylvania Packet*, the key messages contained in this letter—that Carolina was still with them, that British agents were still instigating proxy enemies, and that southerners were thrilled to carry the war to them—made it inviting for patriot printers. Eleven northern papers from Annapolis to Boston exchanged it. Far away, Ezra Stiles observed in his diary, "The greatest Assiduity has been used by our enemies to excite Indians, Negroes, etc. against us. They tho't the Indians numerous and formidable, I think them not so."[16]

By the middle of October, the six thousand southern militiamen had forced the Cherokees to sue for peace. Dragging Canoe's gambit had failed, but he was not willing to accept defeat. He and a group of other intransigent militants split off and moved southwest to Chickamauga Creek, where they continued to fight. Patriot troops from Virginia and the Carolinas conducted a scorched-earth attack that foreshadowed future campaigns against Indian communities. One participant remembered, decades later, that his militia colleagues had "burn[ed] their town, killed and destroyed as many

16. *Virginia Gazette* (Purdie), Aug. 2, 1776; Nov. 2, 1776, in Franklin Bowditch Dexter, ed., The *Literary Diary of Ezra Stiles, D.D., LL.D.: President of Yale College*, II, *March 14, 1776–December 31, 1781* (New York, 1901), 69. For one report that said the Cherokees "[have Alexander] Cameron at their head," see *Pennsylvania Journal*, Sept. 11, 1776; *Pennsylvania Packet*, Sept. 17, 1776; *Maryland Gazette*, Sept. 19, 1776; *New-York Gazette* (Newark), Sept. 21, 1776; *Virginia Gazette* (Dixon & Hunter), Sept. 27, 1776. Cameron letter: *Pennsylvania Packet*, Sept. 3, 1776; *Pennsylvania Gazette*, Sept. 4, 1776; *Pennsylvania Journal*, Sept. 4, 1776; *New-York Gazette* (Newark), Sept. 9, 1776; *Dunlap's Maryland Gazette*, Sept. 10, 1776; *Maryland Gazette*, Sept. 12, 1776; *Providence Gazette*, Sept. 14, 1776; *Newport Mercury*, Sept. 16, 1776; *Connecticut Journal*, Sept. 18, 1776; *Continental Journal*, Sept. 19, 1776; *Connecticut Courant*, Sept. 23, 1776; *Boston Gazette*, Sept. 23, 1776.

of the Indians as we could get hold of." Few expressed qualms about this behavior. The extensive print campaign neutralized any objections. The flood
of depositions, documents, and hearsay that inundated patriot newspapers
paved the way for a brutal military expedition against the Cherokees. It
closed off any other explanations for war, especially Dragging Canoe's argument that they were the injured party taking revenge against Carolina
speculators and their rapacious land grabs. The common cause had given
full sanction to a just war waged by innocent Americans against an Indian
enemy acting as a proxy for the king. This narrative had great explanatory
power. It supplied villains in Cameron and Stuart and illuminated conspiracy in the timing with Sullivan's Island. The discursive representations
of the Cherokees' actions contributed to the massive, bloody response. The
common cause argument that underlay all the excerpted letters in the newspapers reinforced patriots' determination, from the policy makers at the top
levels down to the executors of that policy, to "extirpate," "drive west," "kill
all." The Iroquois must know, like the Cherokees—or the Shawnees, or the
Delawares—if they decided to act "against us nationally," as Jefferson put
it, the United States would respond in kind. It was now the duty of the new
nation to make war on all "merciless savages."[17]

* * *

Back in midsummer, just after Congress declared independence, stories
about the other key British proxy—the domestic insurrectionists—
resurfaced yet again in patriot newspapers. In addition to passing along
"Glorious News in So. Carolina" about Sullivan's Island or initial reports
from the backcountry, Alexander Purdie and his fellow Williamsburg
printers had their own local victory to propagate: Gwynn's Island. Soon,
many of Purdie's peers would make that tiny island just south of the mouth
of the Rappahannock River famous throughout North America.[18]

17. TJ to John Page, Aug. 5, 1776, *PTJ*, I, 485–487, esp. 486; Piecuch, *Three
Peoples, One King*, 69–72, esp. 72; Nash, *Unknown American Revolution*, 258–259;
Edward J. Cashin, "But Brothers, It Is Our Land We Are Talking About: Winners
and Losers in the Georgia Backcountry," in Ronald Hoffman, Thad W. Tate, and
Peter J. Albert, eds., *An Uncivil War: The Southern Backcountry in the American Revolution* (Charlottesville, Va., 1985), 252–253. Pension record of Thomas Cook quoted
in William M. Sweeny, ed., *Captain Thomas Cook (1752–1841): A Soldier of the Revolution*
(n.p., [1909]), 4; Lee, *Crowds and Soldiers*, 160.

18. *Virginia Gazette* (Purdie), July 12, 1776 (supplement).

Early in the morning of July 9—a day that would end with the pulling down of the George III statue in lower Manhattan—patriot cannons began to fire on the governor's fleet anchored around Gwynn's Island, only two hundred yards off of the Virginia mainland. After only an hour's fighting, Dunmore hurried the remainder of his force onto the rest of the "floating town," including those runaway slaves who were still alive in the quarantined area on the eastern edge of the island.

After they evacuated, patriot militia investigated what Dunmore had left behind. The appalling conditions that observers found on the island— especially on the eastern side—were detailed in the Williamsburg papers. They described the scene in terms of an assault, not of war, but on their sensibilities. One officer wrote, "Many poor Negroes were found on the island dying of the putrid fever; others dead in the open fields; a child was found sucking at the breast of its dead mother." Another counted 150 graves and "12 dead negroes lying in the open air." A third was "struck with horrour at the number of dead bodies . . . others gasping for life; and some had crawled to the water's edge, who could only make known their distress by beckoning to us." "In short," this patriot added, "such a scene of misery, distress, and cruelty, my eyes never beheld; for which the authors, one may reasonably conclude, never can make atonement in this world." The first correspondent used the "shocking scene" to reiterate that this was what slaves deserved for trusting the governor: "Dunmore's neglect of those poor creatures, suffering numbers of them to perish for want of common necessaries and the least assistance, one would think enough to discourage others from joining him." Excusing their own responsibility again, the patriot officers who were so moved by what they saw on the bay side of Gwynn's Island nevertheless were reticent to grasp why those blacks risked their lives going to Dunmore. It was beyond their comprehension why these people would run *away* from the Declaration of Independence. That prickly question, though, was dismissed: Dunmore was the real cause of this suffering. Gwynn's Island reinforced the narrative that British agents were to blame for all America's troubles. American patriots would never initiate this trauma.[19]

19. *Virginia Gazette* (Dixon & Hunter), July 20, 1776; *Pennsylvania Packet,* July 22, 1776; *Virginia Gazette* (Purdie), July 19, 1776. "Many poor Negroes": *Virginia Gazette* (Dixon & Hunter), July 20, 1776. "12 dead negroes lying in the open air": *Virginia Gazette* (Dixon & Hunter), July 13, 1776; *Pennsylvania Packet,* July 22, 1776; *Pennsylvania Gazette,* July 24, 1776; *Constitutional Gazette,* July 24, 1776; *Pennsylvania Journal,* July 24, 1776; *New-York Journal,* July 25, 1776; *Connecticut Courant,* July 29, 1776;

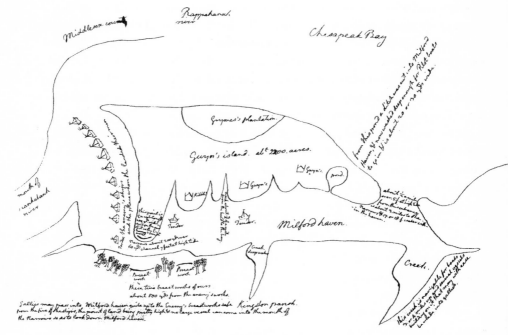

Figure 7. *Map of Gwynn's Island, Virginia. It is not known when Thomas Jefferson made this or who provided the information on which the map is based. It is revealing, however, that around the time that Jefferson put the accusation about the king's inciting of "domestic insurrectionists" at the climax of the Declaration, he also gathered these details about Dunmore's final battle with Virginia. Courtesy of the Library of Congress.*

The news of Gwynn's Island—and especially the fate of the runaways— became, along with the news from South Carolina, the first significant story of the new nation. The attack on Gwynn's garnered much attention. At least

Connecticut Journal, July 31, 1776; *Essex Journal,* Aug. 2, 1776; *Continental Journal,* Aug. 2, 1776; *New-England Chronicle,* Aug. 2, 1776; *Providence Gazette,* Aug. 3, 1776; *New-Hampshire Gazette* (Portsmouth), Aug. 3, 1776; *New Hampshire Gazette* (Exeter), Aug. 3, 1776; *Freeman's Journal* (Portsmouth), Aug. 3, 1776; *Boston Gazette,* Aug. 5, 1776. "Scene of misery, distress, and cruelty": *Virginia Gazette* (Purdie), July 19, 1776; *Pennsylvania Evening Post,* July 30, 1776; *Pennsylvania Gazette,* July 30, 1776; *Pennsylvania Journal,* July 31, 1776; *Maryland Gazette,* Aug. 1, 1776; *New-York Gazette,* Aug. 5, 1776; *Connecticut Courant,* Aug. 12, 1776; *Norwich Packet,* Aug. 5–12, 1776; *Continental Journal,* Aug. 15, 1776; *Connecticut Gazette,* Aug. 16, 1776; *Pennsylvania Magazine,* II (1776), 341–342.

one of the accounts by shocked patriot officers published in the Williamsburg papers was exchanged in nearly every American newspaper. At least two readers were paying enough attention to transcribe long passages about Gwynn's into their diaries.[20]

Further comment about Dunmore and his fleet ensued. After being ejected from Gwynn's, "our African Hero," as Richard Henry Lee styled him, moved up Chesapeake Bay and eventually into the Potomac River in early August, where he threatened Alexandria and Mount Vernon. News reports tracked his progress, usually by commenting on his "stinking black prisoners" or his "miscreants" being attacked by Maryland partisans. When Dunmore's "motly crew" finally left the Chesapeake on August 5, one report assessed the damages and decided the governor had "perpetrated crimes that would even have disgraced the noted pirate BLACK BEARD."[21]

Once observers spotted Dunmore and his "scrubby fleet" leaving the Capes of Virginia on their way to rendezvous at Staten Island, many patriots and printers took stock of the past six months of war. Boston's *New-England Chronicle* published a letter relating an estimate from one member of Virginia's congressional delegation that his province had "lost 1000 negroes already by Dunmore." The same day, Frederick Green reached a similar number in his *Maryland Gazette*. His math was more ghastly. Noting that a "great

20. The diarists both copied down the account of "150 graves and 12 dead negroes in the open air." Chaplain Benjamin Trumbull of the First Connecticut Regiment quoted it nearly verbatim in his July 23, 1776, journal entry. See microfilm reel 3 of American Revolution Collection, Connecticut Historical Society, Hartford. Ezra Stiles also copied down two paragraphs from the news article on Aug. 5, 1776 (Dexter, ed., *Literary Diary of Ezra Stiles*, II, 34–35).

21. Richard Henry Lee to TJ, Chantilly, July 21, 1776, *PTJ*, I, 471; John West to Maryland Council of Safety, Alexandria, July 18, 1776, 5 *Am. Archives*, I, 408. "Stinking black prisoners": *Virginia Gazette* (Purdie), July 26, 1776; *Virginia Gazette* (Dixon & Hunter), Aug. 7, 1776; *New-York Journal*, Aug. 15, 1776; *New-England Chronicle*, Aug. 15, 1776; *Connecticut Gazette*, Aug. 16, 1776; *New Hampshire Gazette* (Exeter), Aug. 17, 1776; *Freeman's Journal* (Portsmouth), Aug. 31, 1776. Dunmore's "miscreants": *Virginia Gazette* (Dixon & Hunter), July 29, 1776; *Pennsylvania Evening Post*, Aug. 6, 1776; *Connecticut Courant*, Aug. 12, 1776. "Motley crew, were entirely gone off": *Constitutional Gazette*, Aug. 12, 1776; *New-York Gazette*, Aug. 19, 1776; *Continental Journal*, Aug. 22, 1776; *Essex Journal*, Aug. 23, 1776; *New Hampshire Gazette* (Exeter), Aug. 24, 1776; *Providence Journal*, Aug. 24, 1776; *Boston Gazette*, Aug. 26, 1776. "BLACK BEARD": *Maryland Gazette*, Aug. 20, 1776; *New-York Journal*, Aug. 29, 1776; *Newport Mercury*, Sept. 2, 1776; *Massachusetts Spy*, Sept. 11, 1776.

number of dead bodies floated on shore" as a result of disease and warfare in the Chesapeake, the Annapolis printer wrote, "The most intelligent of the deserters say that upwards of one thousand Negroes have died within these six months." Even after Dunmore had left the Chesapeake and was no longer a threat to patriot plantations, his name and image remained transcendent. In the years to come, patriot polemicists would often invoke Dunmore as shorthand for condemning the British incitement of slave insurrections. A few months after Gwynn's Island, when the British captured William Alexander (a Continental army general also known as Lord Stirling), several papers reported a few pointed lines from a patriot officer who related a conversation Alexander was rumored to have had with the infamous governor. "Lord Dunmore told Lord Stirling he was sorry he kept such bad Company; — [Stirling] replied, My Lord, I have kept whiter company than your Lordship has of late." But perhaps the most curious story exchanged that summer reveals how Americans' strong feelings about Dunmore and his "Ethiopian Regiment" blurred the line between fact and fiction.[22]

In May 1776, John Leacock, a Philadelphia silversmith, artist, and associate of the Sons of Liberty, wrote a play about the political events of the past year, entitled *The Fall of British Tyranny*. The comedy, which jumped rapidly from London to Boston and to Canada, lingered over the Chesapeake Bay for nearly an entire act, lampooning the activities of "Lord Kidnapper." Leacock's Dunmore is a base, conniving fiend. As one of his crew comments, "The Kidnapper seems as fond of these black regulars (as you call 'em Jack) as he is of [a] brace of whores." Leacock introduced "Major Cudjo," a runaway-turned–uniformed officer of Kidnapper's regiment and

22. *Independent Chronicle*, Oct. 24, 1776; *Massachusetts Spy*, Oct. 30, 1776; *Connecticut Gazette*, Nov. 1, 1776; *Newport Mercury*, Nov. 4, 1776; *Pennsylvania Evening Post*, Nov. 7, 1776. Dunmore's "scrubby fleet" with a force of 150, including "about fifty fighting men, but with Negroes, tories, etc.," was listed in a tally of forces that Staten Island patriots compiled in August 1776. See *Pennsylvania Journal*, Aug. 21, 1776; *Pennsylvania Evening Post*, Aug. 22, 1776; *Pennsylvania Ledger*, Aug. 24, 1776; *Dunlap's Maryland Gazette*, Aug. 27, 1776; *Connecticut Journal*, Aug. 28, 1776; *Constitutional Gazette*, Aug. 28, 1776; *Massachusetts Spy*, Sept. 4, 1776; *Virginia Gazette* (Dixon & Hunter), Sept. 7, 1776; *Continental Journal*, Sept. 12, 1776. "Have lost 1000": *New-England Chronicle*, Aug. 8, 1776; *Essex Journal*, Aug. 9, 1776; *New Hampshire Gazette* (Exeter), Aug. 10, 1776. "Great number of dead bodies": *Maryland Gazette*, Aug. 8, 1776; *Pennsylvania Evening Post*, Aug. 13, 1776; *Pennsylvania Journal*, Aug. 14, 1776; *New-York Journal*, Aug. 15, 1776; *Pennsylvania Packet*, Aug. 20, 1776; *Connecticut Journal*, Aug. 21, 1776; *Essex Journal*, Aug. 23, 1776.

the first black character with dialogue written for the American stage by an American playwright. When Cudjo appears before Kidnapper "to [en]list" along with twenty-one other runaways from Hampton and Norfolk, Kidnapper "christens" him and makes him a major, with the promise, "If you behave well, I'll soon make you a greater man than your master."

> Kidnapper: To morrow you shall have guns like them white men—Can you shoot some of them rebels ashore, Major Cudjo?
> Cudjo: Eas, massa, me try.
> Kidnapper: Wou'd you shoot your old master, the Colonel, if you could see him?
> Cudjo: Eas, massa, you terra me, me shoot him down dead.
> Kidnapper: That's a brave fellow—damn 'em—down with them all—shoot all the damn'd rebels.

Kidnapper is then shown boasting to a chaplain that his black regiment is "no small acquisition"—they would "strengthen us vastly; the thoughts of emancipation will make 'em brave, and the encouragement given them by my proclamation, will greatly intimidate the rebels—internal enemies are worse than open foes."[23]

Leacock's message in *The Fall* fitted squarely with the overall patriot interpretation of the war's first year. In the Chesapeake scenes, Cudjo and his fellow runaways seem dupes of the evil governor. Blacks were not the engines of tyranny in these scenes, but their presence denoted inferiority just

---

23. [John Leacock], *The Fall of British Tyranny; or, American Liberty Triumphant: The First Campaign; A Tragi-Comedy of Five Acts* . . . (Philadelphia, 1776), rpt. in Norman Philbrick, ed., *Trumpets Sounding: Propaganda Plays of the American Revolution* (New York, 1972), 57–134, esp. 108, 111–113; Francis James Dallett, Jr., "John Leacock and the *Fall of British Tyranny*," *PMHB*, LVVVIII (1954), 456–475, esp. 468n. Dallet argues for the preeminence of Cudjo on the basis that "Ralpho," in Robert Munford's *The Candidates* (1770), was unknown until the play's publication in 1798. The 1820 edition of John Trumbull's popular 1776 epic poem *M'Fingal* mentions "Captain Cuff and Ensign Sambo," but they do not speak. See John Trumbull, *The Poetical Works of John Trumbull, LL.D; Containing M'Fingal, a Modern Epic Poem* . . . , 2 vols. (Hartford, Conn., 1820). See also Kenneth Silverman, *A Cultural History of the American Revolution: Painting, Music, Literature, and the Theatre in the Colonies and the United States from the Treaty of Paris to the Inauguration of George Washington, 1763–1789* (New York, 1976), 310–312; Jared Brown, *The Theatre in America during the Revolution* (Cambridge, 1995), 75–78; and Jason Shaffer, *Performing Patriotism: National Identity in the Colonial and Revolutionary American Theater* (Philadelphia, 2007), 138–152.

the same. As one of Kidnapper's cooks says, "I'll not disgrace my station, I'll throw up my commission, before I'll stand cook for a parcel of scape gallows, convict Tory dogs and run-away Negroes." This is how patriots had strived to portray resistant African Americans since the war began. They were dangerous but inert; terrible weapons but harmless without priming agents. Kidnapper had ignited that fuse and was surrounded by explosives. Leacock expresses this statement at the end of Kidnapper's exchange with Cudjo, where the governor encourages him to shoot his master. Whispering to a sergeant, Kidnapper expresses his concern in—for the patriot cause— a crucial aside: "Set a guard over them every night, and take their arms from them, for who knows but they may cut our throats."[24]

Although Leacock's biting satire was never performed, it was published in several northern cities beginning in early July. One of New Hampshire's delegates to Congress sent a copy home to Portsmouth. A number of newspapers gave the play enough advertising space to list the titles of all twenty-six scenes, including "a very black scene between Lord Kidnapper and Major Cudjo." The play and its characters were known well enough for patriot publishers to circle back and superimpose them onto reality.[25]

On August 28, *Constitutional Gazette* printer John Anderson brought out what would turn out to be his last issue. Anderson—the first in Manhattan to publish copies of Leacock's play—compiled a digest of reports detailing the earliest reports of losses suffered by American and British forces in the previous day's huge battle on Long Island. At the bottom of the list, Anderson noted that "Major Cudgjo, commander of Lord Dunmore's black regiment" had been captured. Even more strangely, two weeks later, the back page of the *New-England Chronicle* featured a nearly column-long advertisement for the play, and at the bottom of the middle column on the previous

24. [Leacock], *Fall of British Tyranny,* in Philbrick, ed., *Trumpets Sounding,* 109 ("disgrace my station"), 112 ("cut our throats").

25. William Whipple to John Langdon, Philadelphia, July 16, 1776, *LDC,* IV, 477. Advertisements for Leacock's play appeared in *Constitutional Gazette,* July 3, 6, 1776; *New-York Journal,* July 4, 1776; *New York Packet,* July 11, 1776; *Pennsylvania Evening Post,* July 16, Aug. 31, 1776; *Dunlap's Maryland Gazette,* July 30, 1776; *Continental Journal,* Sept. 5, Oct. 17, 1776; *New-England Chronicle,* Sept. 12, 1776; *Providence Gazette,* Sept. 14, 1776; *Boston Gazette,* Sept. 16, 1776. For Langdon's request to send a copy up, see Langdon to Whipple, Portsmouth, July 1, 1776, in William Bell Clark, ed., *Naval Documents of the American Revolution,* V, *American Theatre: May 9, 1776–July 31, 1776* (Washington, D.C., 1970), V, 847.

page, printers Powars and Willis wrote, "Among the Prisoners lately taken at Long Island, is Major Cudgjo, chief Ethiopian Commander of Lord Kidnapper [Dunmore's] Regiment of Blacks." This "Cudgjo" was a "real," newsworthy subject on the third page, and a fictional "Cudjo" appeared on the fourth page. Powars, Willis, and Anderson were playing with their readers, and their prestidigitation struck a chord. Five other patriot newspapers from New England to the Chesapeake reprinted the notice as news, and fiction morphed into fact.[26]

Patriot printers did not allow a representation as potent as Cudjo to fade. Cudjo—apparently free and still roaming about the edges of America—reappeared the following March to impugn loyalists again by association. Isaiah Thomas published a fictional "Dialogue" in his *Massachusetts Spy* that featured a group of unsavory tories asking Canadian governor and alleged Indian inciter Guy Carleton for a military assignment. Carleton attached the "ragged Jacobites to their fellow crew, (viz) Lord Kidnapper's fleet, under the command of Major Cudjo, as I cannot think of any fitter place for them." Neither Carleton nor "Jacobite" loyalists nor the elusive Cudjo and his master were welcome in the patriot cause.[27]

Cudjo had turned from Atlantic legend—referring to "Captain Cudjoe," who led a group of maroons to war against the British in 1730s Jamaica—into a ready synonym for resistant slaves and their British sponsors in the 1770s. Leacock's use of Cudjo and patriot publicists' dance across the line between fantasy and reality exposes the nerve Dunmore had touched with his emancipation proclamation and subsequent "Ethiopian Regiment." Landon Carter, for one, was disturbed. "A strange dream . . . about these runaway people" haunted the Virginia planter. Long after Washington's worries about Dunmore as a "snowball rolling" had dissipated, the explosive nature of Dunmore's antics continued to function as cultural dynamite, providing excellent materials for the common cause. When war and its potential consequences for slave rebellion returned to the Virginia tidewater in later years, the specter of Kidnapper and Cudjo would also rise again.[28]

26. *Constitutional Gazette*, Aug. 28, 1776. Advertisement: *New-England Chronicle*, Sept. 12, 1776. This is the exact quote; Powars and Willis supplied Dunmore's name in brackets in case anyone was unclear. See *Pennsylvania Ledger*, Aug. 31, 1776; *Maryland Gazette*, Sept. 5, 1776; *Essex Journal*, Sept. 13, 1776; *New Hampshire Gazette* (Exeter), Sept. 14, 1776; *Connecticut Gazette*, Sept. 20, 1776.

27. *Massachusetts Spy*, Mar. 13, 1777.

28. For more on maroon wars in Jamaica, see Michael Craton, *Testing the Chains:*

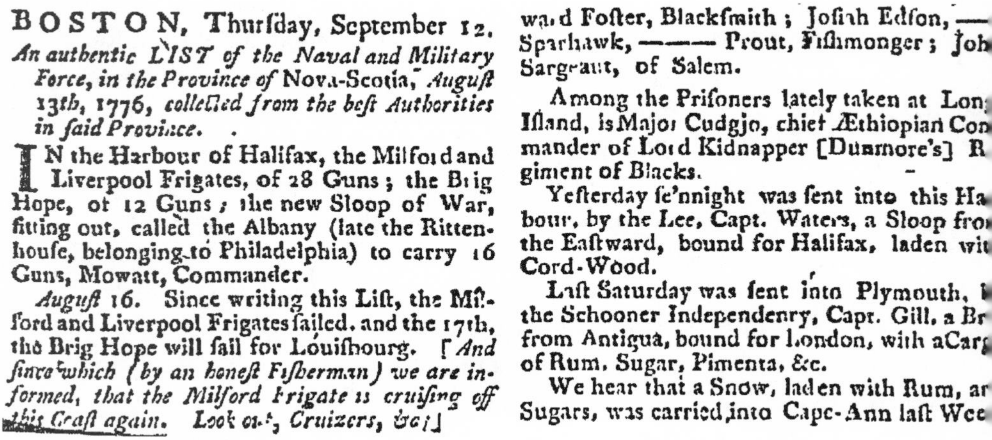

BOSTON, Thurſday, September 12.

An authentic LIST of the Naval and Military Force, in the Province of Nova-Scotia, *Auguſt 13th, 1776, collected from the beſt Authorities in ſaid Province.* .

IN the Harbour of Halifax, the Milford and Liverpool Frigates, of 28 Guns ; the Brig Hope, of 12 Guns ; the new Sloop of War, fitting out, called the Albany (late the Ritten-houſe, belonging to Philadelphia) to carry 16 Guns, Mowatt, Commander.

Auguſt 16. Since writing this Liſt, the Milford and Liverpool Frigates ſailed. and the 17th, the Brig Hope will ſail for Louiſbourg. [*And ſince which (by an honeſt Fiſherman) we are in-formed, that the Milford Frigate is cruiſing off this Coaſt again.* Look o—, *Cruizers, &c.*]

ward Foſter, Blackſmith ; Joſiah Edſon, —— Sparhawk, —— Prout, Fiſhmonger ; Joh Sargeant, of Salem.

Among the Priſoners lately taken at Long Iſland, is Major Cudgjo, chief Æthiopian Con mander of Lord Kidnapper [Dunmore's] R giment of Blacks.

Yeſterday ſe'nnight was ſent into this Ha bour, by the Lee, Capt. Waters, a Sloop from the Eaſtward, bound for Halifax, laden wit Cord-Wood.

Laſt Saturday was ſent into Plymouth, the Schooner Independenry, Capt. Gill, a Br from Antigua, bound for London, with a Carg of Rum, Sugar, Pimenta, &c.

We hear that a Snow, laden with Rum, ar Sugars, was carried into Cape-Ann laſt Wee

Figure 8. *News from Long Island and advertisement for* The Fall of British Tyranny. *From* New-England Chronicle, Sept. *12, 1776. It is difficult to separate fact from fiction in the September 12, 1776, issue of the* Chronicle. *An advertisement on the back page for John Leacock's play features "a very black scene between Lord Kidnapper and Major Cudgjo."*

But the news about Dunmore's final weeks in the Chesapeake that July was far more significant because it was an important backdrop for Congress's discussions about the place of slaves in the new nation. In the last days of July, Congress debated whether slaves counted as property for taxation pur-poses under the new Articles of Confederation. Samuel Chase, whose home state of Maryland Dunmore's fleet currently menaced, argued, "Negroes in fact should not be considered as members of the state more than cattle and that they have no more interest in it." Of course, this opinion was not born with Dunmore or his proclamation. But the common cause, with its insis-

---

Resistance to Slavery in the British West Indies (Ithaca, N.Y., 1982), 81–96. For representa-tions of Cudjoe and maroons, see Kathleen Wilson, "The Performance of Freedom: Maroons and the Colonial Order in Eighteenth-Century Jamaica and the Atlantic Sound," *WMQ*, 3d Ser., LXVI (2009), 45–86. Captain Cudjoe continued to sur-face in print during the Revolution, for which see below. For Carter, see entry for July 25, 1776, in Jack P. Greene, ed., *The Diary of Colonel Landon Carter of Sabine Hall, 1752–1778*, 2 vols. (Richmond, Va., 1987), II, 1064. For more on how the trauma of Dunmore had caused a "psychic disturbance" for Carter, see Rhys Isaac, *Landon Carter's Uneasy Kingdom: Revolution and Rebellion on a Virginia Plantation* (New York, 2004), 12–13, esp. 12.

Just Published, and to be fold by POWARS *and*
WILLIS, *in Queen-Street,*
(*Price Two Shillings*)

THE FALL OF
BRITISH TYRANNY,
OR,
AMERICAN LIBERTY TRIUMPHANT.
THE FIRST CAMPAIGN.

A TRAGI-COMEDY, *of Five Acts, containing
twenty-six Scenes, among which are the following, viz.*

A pleasing fcene between Roger *and* Dick,
two fhepherds near Lexington.

Clariffa, &c. *A very moving fcene on the
death of Doctor* Warren, *&c in a chamber near
Bofton, the morning after the battle at Bunker's-
Hill.*

*A humorous fcene between the Boatfwain and
a Sailor on board a man of war, near Norfolk in
Virginia.*

*Two very laughable fcenes between the Boatf-
wain, two Sailors, and the Cook, exhibiting fpeci-
mens of feafaring oratory, and peculiar eloquence
of thofe fons of Neptune, touching Tories, Convicts
and black Regulars; and between* Lord Kidnapper
and the Boatfwain.

A very black fcene between Lord Kidnapper
and Major Cudgjo.

A religious fcene between Lord Kidnapper,
Chaplain, and the Captain.

A fcene, the Lord Mayor, *&c. going to St.
James's with the Addrefs.*

A droll fcene, a council of war in Bofton, between
Lord Bofton, Admiral Tombftone, Elbow-Room,
Mr. Caper, General Clinton, *and* Earl Piercy.

A diverting fcene between a Whig *and a* Tory.

A fpirited fcene between General Prefcot, *and*
Colonel Allen.

A fhocking fcene, a dungeon, between Colonel
Allen *and an officer of the guard.*

Two affecting fcenes in Bofton, *after the flight
of the Regulars from* Lexington, *between* Lord
Bofton, *meffenger, and officers of the guard.*

A patriotic fcene in the camp at Cambridge,
between the Generals Wafhington, Lee, *and*
Putnam, *&c. &c.*

*With a dedication, preface, addrefs of the God-
defs of Liberty to the Congrefs, dramatis perfonæ,
prologue, epilogue, and a fong in praife of King
Tammany, the American Saint.*

*A truly dramatic performance, interfperfed
with wit, humour, burlefque, and ferious matter,
which cannot fail of affording abundant entertainment to readers of every difpofition.——*

*The whole comprifed in feventy-one pages
octavo, and a good type. Allowance to thofe who
buy a number.*

tence that runaway blacks were passive proxies of the king's ministers, gave this notion a fresh valence. After all, the delegates were, as John Witherspoon put it, "entering into a new compact and therefore stand on original ground." Their extended debate—which itself was as much about unity and the common-ness of the cause as it was about slavery at all—might have taken a different path had it not been for the delegates' nearly yearlong experience with stories of resistant slaves running away from the Revolution.[29]

Certainly they had convinced Benjamin Franklin, who had recently announced his own personal declaration of independence from the British Empire. On July 20, Franklin wrote to Admiral Lord Richard Howe:

> It is impossible we should think of Submission to a Government, that has with the most wanton Barbarity and Cruelty, burnt our defenceless Towns in the midst of Winter, excited the Savages to massacre our Farmers, and our Slaves to murder their Masters, and is even now bringing foreign Mercenaries to deluge our Settlements with Blood. These atrocious Injuries have extinguished every remaining Spark of Affection for that Parent Country we once held so dear.

As for Jefferson in the Declaration, these were the final straws for Franklin. "Long did I endeavour with unfeigned and unwearied Zeal, to preserve from breaking, that fine and noble China Vase the British Empire," but now with the crown's employment of proxies, that vessel was indeed broken, and "a perfect Re-Union of those Parts could scarce even be hoped for." Ten days after writing these words to Howe, Franklin added his thoughts in the Articles debate of whether blacks were people or property. No matter how much the patriots denied it, Lord Kidnapper—as well as Josiah Martin, Captain John Collet, Sir William Campbell, and others—had provided evidence that "slaves rather weaken than strengthen the State, and there is therefore some difference between them and Sheep. Sheep will never make any Insurrections."[30]

29. "Thomas Jefferson's Notes on Proceedings in Congress," [July 12–Aug. 1, 1776], *LDC*, IV, 439, 441.

30. BF to Lord [Richard] Howe, Philadelphia, July 20, 1776, *LDC*, IV, 499–500, "John Adams' Notes of Debate," July 30, 1776, 568.

"By the American Revolution You Are Now Free"

The summer of American independence had been a success, so far. "What must the King think now?" John Page wrote to Charles Lee after Gwynn's Island. "The whole Continent in arms against him, seven hundred and fifty of his favourite Highlanders in our possession, and his fleets repulsed and disgraced along our coasts for two thousand miles!" Indeed, all of the provinces south of Maryland had proved their commitment to the cause with martial ardor, and, for the time being, were safe from British threat. Attention turned fully to Staten Island and the overwhelming force of 30,000 British and German soldiers preparing there to bring the rebellion to a swift end. Colonel Joseph Trumbull, the Continental army's commissary general, had been watching those developments for some time. On July 4, he wrote home to a friend in Connecticut about the impending invasion. Trumbull had spent America's independence day anxiously awaiting the "arrival, of the Hessians Cossacks Tartars, etc. etc." He told Jeremiah Wadsworth, "possibly they will attack us sooner, [and] we should wish it."[31]

Back in Connecticut, Joseph's younger brother, the *Norwich Packet* printer John Trumbull, was setting type for an essay that the colonel might not have wanted to read. It sought to educate Americans about "what we are to expect from foreign mercenaries, if we do not now exert ourselves." The German troops, the essayist exclaimed, "will exhibit such a scene of cruelty, death and devastation, as will fill those of us who survive the carnage, with indignation and horror; attended with poverty and wretchedness — and make the ears of our posterity, the millions who are yet unborn, tingle, when they read the transaction in the pages of some future history." Taking up the entire front page and two columns of another, the essay buttressed its accusations with an atrocity story from 1758. The details of what hirelings would do were terrible. Property destroyed, whole cities burned, livestock slaughtered, and local officials whipped and stabbed to death only topped the list.

How many that tried to escape from the fire of their own houses, were by these cruel savages, driven into the flames of their neighbours dwellings. — Whilst the old and sick that were not able to escape, and children, which in the fright had been forgotten of their mothers, fell victims to the devouring flames. — Some of the inhabitants indeed

31. John Page, President of Virginia Council, to General [Charles] Lee, Williamsburg, July 12, 1776, 5 *Am. Archives*, I, 214; Joseph Trumbull to Jeremiah Wadsworth, New York, July 4, 1776, in Clark, ed., *Naval Documents*, V, 918.

escaped to moors, and marshy places; but even there the more than devilish desire for murder, induced those monsters to pursue them, where they trod on the childrens heads, forced their legs from their bodies, and dashed their tender foreheads in pieces against the stones.

Although some suggested a similar level of brutality might be appropriate against the Cherokees that summer, Trumbull inserted this artifact to shock: this was what lay in store for America. Naturally, the real blame for this, just as Jefferson would write in that week's Declaration, was the "Royal Tyrant, the Pharoah of Great Britain—together with his Ministry and Parliament," who sought to exert their "combined influence to involve this Continent in a scene of blood and ashes." It was the "influence and malice of the sceptered savage of Great-Britain" that "heightened and whetted" the "native ferosity" of the German troops and made possible the horrors of unbridled warfare.[32]

Patriot leaders shared the Trumbulls' concern. Neither Joseph nor John might have known it in early July, but their fellow political and military officials had already taken a few steps to blunt the possibilities of "cruelty, death and devastation" at the hands of those foreign troops. In May, Congress crafted an initial address to the foreign mercenaries. Although that declaration was lost in the hectic business of drafting and editing other declarations at that time, they would revisit the issue in August. Meanwhile, Washington had some ideas of his own about how to use the military to promote German defection. As soon as he had confirmation of the German auxiliaries, he asked Congress to consider whether the best way to convince the mercenaries to lay down their arms might be to have them encounter fellow Germans who could "testify to the truth" of American opportunity. Would it not be "advisable and good policy," Washington queried, "to raise some Companies of our Germans to send among [th]em when they arrive, for exciting a spirit of disaffection and desertion?" "If a few sensible, trusty fellows cou'd get with them, I should think they woud have great weight and influence with the common Soldiery, who certainly have no enmity towards us, having received no Injury, nor cause of Quarrel from us."[33]

Washington's vision for a German unit was more than just a way to get Hessians and Hanoverians to throw down their arms. His concern was also how the king's involvement of ten thousand Germans might affect the loy-

32. *Norwich Packet,* July 1–8, 1776.
33. GW to Hancock, New York, May 11, 1776, *PGW: RW,* IV, 279.

alty of the tens of thousands of German Americans whose support the common cause desperately needed. In Pennsylvania, western Maryland, and the Shenandoah Valley, German Americans became viable political actors in the imperial crisis, spurred by radical pietism, transplanted concepts of liberty, and a proliferation of German-language print. With war, many German Americans rallied to the patriot cause, but that backing could not be taken for granted. This was an essential demographic that would require cultivation.[34]

Congress approved Washington's suggestion on May 25 but then referred it to the delegations from New Jersey and Pennsylvania to work out how to go about organizing a German battalion. On June 27, they commissioned this unit of German Americans and recommended that the provincial governments of Maryland and Pennsylvania take the lead in appointing officers and fitting it out. This delegation led to significant delays; Washington's idea that fellow Germans would be the first men the Hessians and Hanoverians would meet on the battlefield did not come to pass. In September, Congress, exasperated, ordered the German battalion to be "forwarded to New York . . . with all possible expedition."[35]

Once the Howes' full naval and army outfit had arrived off Staten Island in the first days of August, that potential force began to frighten the patriot leadership. They began rethinking older policy decisions, including the question of recruiting Indians. Six weeks earlier, they had put a stop to enrolling Stockbridge and Mohican Indians from serving with the main body of the Continental army in New York. Now, facing thirty thousand enemy troops, they decided to waive their stipulations that those Indians should only serve on the northern frontier. On August 2, just after members began attaching their names to the new engrossed copy of the Declaration, they allowed Washington to use "as many of the Stockbridge Indians as he shall judge proper" wherever he needed them. Washington then wrote to one of Congress's Indian commissioners that "our Enemies are prosecuting the

34. Wolfgang M. Splitter, "'A Free People in the American Air': The Evolution of German Lutherans from British Subjects to Pennsylvania Citizens, 1740–1790" (Ph.D. diss., Johns Hopkins University, 1993); A. G. Roeber, *Palatines, Liberty, and Property: German Lutherans in Colonial America* (Baltimore, 1993); Aaron Spencer Fogleman, *Hopeful Journeys: German Immigration, Settlement, and Political Culture in Colonial America, 1717–1775* (Philadelphia, 1996), 149–153.

35. Feb. 9, June 17, 27, July 19, Aug. 29, Sept. 3–4, 1776, *JCC*, IV, 125, V, 454, 487–488, 590–591, 716, 734–735.

War with unexampled Severity and Industry, and that these Indians are anxious to take a part in our favour," so he should make all "friendly exertions upon this occasion . . . [to] Engage in the Service as great a number of them as you possibly can."[36]

The following week, Jonathan Dickinson Sergeant—a former member of Congress who had resigned to chair the framing committee for New Jersey's state constitution—sent a proposal to John Adams. Sergeant wondered why the patriots were not considering all options to defend against the Howes' invasion. Specifically, Sergeant had a "Scheme of a Negro Battalion" in mind. "I rather apprehend it to be heretical," he began, "if so commit it to the Flames, or deal with it in what other Manner You think best; only I except to *Tarring and Feathering,* for the poor thing is no Tory." Attached to his letter was a proposal Sergeant had written up for the newspaper under the pseudonym "Speculator." Since this was a military emergency, and since "Slaves left at home excite an Alarm for the Safety of their Families," Speculator questioned whether "a Method might not be devised for employing those Slaves as Soldiers in the public Service"? Citing the success of the Jamaica maroons (though not Captain Cudjoe), Sergeant suggested paying them and their masters and freeing them if they behaved well. He did not make this suggestion out of morality or a troubled conscience; even the patriots' ubiquitous natural rights discourse about liberty never entered his proposal. Furthermore, when discussing objections some might have to freeing large numbers of armed slaves, he suggested that they should be encouraged to "form a Settlement of Blacks if they will. There is Room enough on this Continent for them and us too." Adams indeed found this suggestion heretical—at least to the prospect of American unity. Four days later, he responded to Sergeant, "Your Negro Battallion will never do. S. Carolina would run out of their Wits at the least Hint of such a Measure." Recruiting Stockbridge Indians was one thing. Freeing and arming thousands of slaves was entirely another.[37]

Another option patriot political leaders considered was to embrace the power of rhetoric. On August 14, Congress again put its faith in argument and texts to save the Revolution. As the ten thousand mercenaries were

36. Aug. 2, 1776, ibid., V, 627; GW to Timothy Edwards, New York, Aug. 7, 1776, *PGW: RW,* V, 594–595. See also GW to Hancock, New York, Aug. 8[–9], 1776, 625–626.

37. Jonathan Dickinson Sergeant to JA, Princeton, Aug. 13, 1776, *PJA,* IV, 453–455; JA to Sergeant, Philadelphia, Aug. 17, 1776, *LDC,* V, 11.

"By the American Revolution You Are Now Free"

now on American soil, Congress reinvigorated its strategy to "devise a plan for encouraging the Hessians, and other foreigners, employed by the King of Great Britain, and sent to America for the purpose of subjugating these states, to quit that iniquitous service." Congressional delegates drafted a new proclamation for Hessian enlisted men, promising that those who deserted would be "protected in the free exercise of their respective religions, and be invested with the rights, privileges and immunities of natives, as established by the laws of these states," and would each receive fifty acres of free land. A few days later, Congress hastily assembled another committee to compose a second proposal for officers, increasing the reward to one thousand acres. Congress ordered the proclamations translated into German and secretly dispersed in the camp at Staten Island. Benjamin Franklin sent a few translated copies to Thomas McKean in New Jersey, informing him, "Some of the Papers have Tobacco Marks on the Back . . . that if a little Tobacco were put up in each as the Tobacconists use to do, and a Quantity made to fall into the Hands of that Soldiery . . . it would be divided among them as Plunder before the Officers could know the Contents of the Paper and prevent it." Washington happily wrote Congress the day before the battle at Long Island that the "papers designed for the Foreign troops have been put into several Channels . . . [and] I have reason to beleive [*sic*] many have fallen into their Hands."[38]

Washington's optimism would be short-lived. Hours after he wrote this letter, British and Hessian columns took up assault positions along the Jamaica and Flatbush Passes. The next morning, the battle for Long Island began. Soon, many of the questions that had been building for nearly a year about foreign mercenaries' role in the Revolutionary War would finally be answered. On the cusp of that campaign, with potential disaster in the offing, patriot leaders explored creative options for weakening the impressive

38. Aug. 9, 14, 1776, *JCC*, V, 640, 653–655; Lyman H. Butterfield, "Psychological Warfare in 1776: The Jefferson-Franklin Plan to Cause Hessian Desertion," *Proceedings of the American Philosophical Society*, N.S., XCIV (1950), 233–241; BF to Thomas McKean, Philadelphia, Aug. 24, 1776, *PBF*, XXII, 578–579; GW to John Hancock, New York, Aug. 26, 1776, *PGW: RW*, VI, 130. Many of the proclamations that did make it to Staten Island were intercepted. One Hessian officer "seized many hundred printed German papers sent over with a design of dispersing them," a British official wrote. See Sir George Osborn to Lord George Germain, Oct. 29, 1776, in K. G. Davies, ed., *Documents of the American Revolution, 1770–1783*, Colonial Office Series, XII, *Transcripts, 1776* (Dublin, 1976), 242.

force that was arrayed against them in New York. Faced with onslaught, they hurriedly reexamined policy decisions that they had been loathe to accept, from the embrace of Indians as part of Washington's command to the automatic naturalization of Europeans who were being paid to kill them. Some options, however, remained out of bounds. For fear of imperiling the common cause, patriot leaders were unwilling to consider including large numbers of African Americans as part of their fight for liberty.

The battle that parties on both sides of the Atlantic had been waiting for all summer began early in the morning of August 27. It was over by noon. Lord Stirling, who would soon be dining with Dunmore, commanded on the American right. His men fought courageously though foolishly, as they were drawn out into open fields just as the professional British troops wanted. Meanwhile, the center and left flank collapsed in the face of charging British and German bayonets. The rout was on. In the words of one historian, "Through the woods, down the slopes, across the fields, singly, in groups, in companies, they fled."[39] It is difficult to believe that these demoralized American soldiers were able to capture Major Cudjo in this precipitous flight. They ran past General John Sullivan, who would also be captured. Even though most made it back to the safety of Washington's prepared defenses at Brooklyn Heights, the most significant casualty of the debacle at Long Island was the myth that had grown since Bunker Hill: that virtuous American citizen-soldiers could best any British troops. The thousand casualties Howe had inflicted on them in one morning only reinforced Washington's conviction that military success depended on his ability to turn the Continental army into a professional fighting force.[40]

If that vision were ever to be realized, however, he had to get his 9,500 men off Long Island. Surrounded, his position in Brooklyn was instantly untenable after the August 27 collapse. Thick fog saved the Revolution, as Washington was able, miraculously, to get his men into boats and ferried across to Manhattan in nine hours. A regiment from Marblehead, Massachusetts, fishermen and sailors under the command of Colonel John Glover, carried them to safety. Glover's unit contained a "number of negroes," men

39. Christopher Ward, *The War of the Revolution,* ed. John Richard Alden (New York, 1952), I, 223.

40. For more on the battle, see Ward, *War of the Revolution,* I, 216–230; John Ferling, *Almost a Miracle: The American Victory in the War of Independence* (New York, 2007), 129–136; Don Higginbotham, *The War of American Independence: Military Attitudes, Policies, and Practice, 1763–1789* (1971; Boston, 1983), 152–159.

"By the American Revolution You Are Now Free"

like Salem Poor and Peter Salem who had served the patriot cause well but whom Washington did not want around. Here were more examples of African Americans supporting the Revolution, men whose presence—let alone their participation and sacrifice—found little space in the common cause narrative. Thanks to Glover's black and white fishermen, the Continental army survived.[41]

By September 15, the British began what would be a seven-year occupation of New York City, and six days later, a massive conflagration ripped through the lower sections of the city. Redcoats and fire scattered New York's printers. In a repeat of the scurry to sneak presses out of Boston just hours before Lexington, most New York printers tried to get their equipment out of town. Samuel Loudon took his types up the Hudson to Fishkill, New York, where he restarted his *New York Packet* in December. John Holt's *New-York Journal* would have a longer hiatus. He also fled up the Hudson to Kingston, New York (also known as Esopus), reviving his paper in July 1777. John Anderson decided not to risk the hardship of relocating, instead choosing to end his *Constitutional Gazette*. Always a lukewarm patriot, Hugh Gaine published his *New-York Gazette; and the Weekly Mercury* in Newark for a few weeks that autumn. While he was in New Jersey, Governor Tryon commissioned one of Howe's aides to start a crown newspaper. Gaine, who had been printing a paper in New York since 1752, quickly decided that the British market would better serve his financial interests, and he returned to the city by early November to restart his paper as a British concern. In his first issue, he made this decision manifest by denouncing the "Absurdities and Falsehoods, with which the Leaders of the present Rebellion endeavour to keep up the Spirits and Opposition of their deluded Followers."

41. George H. Moore, *Historical Notes on the Employment of Negroes in the American Army of the Revolution* (New York, 1862), 16, reprinted in Philip S. Foner, *Blacks in the American Revolution* (Westport, Conn., 1975), 186. Alexander Graydon wrote in his memoirs that there were "a number of negroes" in Glover's regiment, "which, to persons unaccustomed to such associations had a disagreeable, degrading effect." See Alexander Graydon, *Memoirs of His Own Time; with Reminiscences of the Men and Events of the Revolution*, ed. John Stockton Littell (1846; rpt. New York, 1969), 149. See also George Athan Billias, *General John Glover and His Marblehead Mariners* (New York, 1960), 69. In fact, Glover's men might have saved Washington's own life. At the September 15 battle at Kip's Bay, Washington was exposed on the field as soldiers fled before the British advance. He was saved, again, by Glover's Marblehead regiment, who reinforced the line. See Higginbotham, *War of American Independence*, 160. See also David Hackett Fischer, *Washington's Crossing* (New York, 2004), 81–114.

This announcement made Gaine one of the most notorious turncoats of the Revolution. His name would be synonymous with deceit and greed for the remainder of the war. When he returned to publishing the *New-York Journal* in Kingston, John Holt referred to his former competitor as "Lord and General Howe's" gazette. Because New York City was the central hub for American communications, the disruption of its newspapers—and, importantly, the reestablishment of Gaine as a sponsored British printer—damaged patriot information networks more than the loss of Boston in 1775–1776.[42]

The Howe brothers controlled the city and its communications, but they did not exert themselves enough to capture Washington, despite his repeated blunders and miscalculations. By early November, the only contingent of American troops on Manhattan Island was a garrison of 3,000 men in Fort Washington, a newly built fortification where the George Washington Bridge now spans the Hudson. Washington's chief engineer, Colonel Rufus Putnam, had laid out a pentagonal earthwork along the rugged cliffs more than two hundred feet above the river. Patriot confidence that the fort was impregnable dissolved on November 16, when Howe ordered 13,000 against it in a double assault. Americans faced German mercenaries in significant numbers at Fort Washington. Howe tasked General Wilhelm von Knyphausen's regiment of Hessians with attacking the fort's northern positions. The attackers, led by Colonel Johann Rall, charged through the woods and up the steep incline against rifle fire from Maryland and Virginia units. They took heavy losses but drove the Americans back after a few hours of fighting. It was the same along the southern defenses. Three hours after it started, the battle for Fort Washington ended when Colonel Rall accepted its surrender, along with a staggering amount of ammunition and 2,870 American soldiers.[43]

What might the bloodied, angry German mercenaries do to so many

42. For an exploration into who started the fire, see Benjamin L. Carp, "The Night the Yankees Burned Broadway: The New York City Fire of 1776," *Early American Studies,* IV (2006), 471–511. Gaine's first issue of his loyalist *New-York Gazette* was Nov. 11, 1776. "(Lord and General Howe's) New-York Gazette": *Pennsylvania Evening Post,* June 17, 1777; *New-York Journal,* July 13, 1777. For more on Gaine, see Sidney I. Pomerantz, "The Patriot Newspaper and the American Revolution," in Richard B. Morris, ed., *The Era of the American Revolution: Studies Inscribed to Evarts Boutell Greene* (New York, 1939), 306–308.

43. Ira D. Gruber, *The Howe Brothers and the American Revolution* (New York, 1972), 128–136.

"By the American Revolution You Are Now Free"

prisoners? Trumbull and several other patriot publicists had speculated wildly. According to one British observer in New York, "The Dread, which the Rebels have of these Hessians, is inconceivable: They almost run away at their Name." More stories during the fight for New York City deepened those worries. One delegate to Congress suspected that the "ungovernable Brutality" of "those Men monsters the Hessians," caused the fire in New York. The *Newport Mercury,* Solomon Southwick's newspaper that in five weeks would be silenced by a British invasion, published an eyewitness report of Hessians hanging women "up by the heels with their throats and mouths cut from ear to ear" the night of the blaze. On the battlefield they were no better, Pennsylvania delegate James Wilson alleged. The Hessians had "behaved with great Inhumanity" in New York: "They even knocked on the Head the Men that were lying wounded on the Field of Battle." To make matters worse, Wilson wrote, their countrymen in Pennsylvania were following their bad example, something the patriots had not considered. "The Germans, particularly in Berks County, are becoming totally unreasonable and ungovernable. They are jealous and violent to the last Degree." When not killing Americans, the Hessians were robbing them. Army officer Ebenezer Hazard wrote General Horatio Gates a letter that eventually found its way into nine newspapers as a "Gentleman at Harlem" to his "Friend" in Boston. Hazard informed Gates that the Hessians "plunder all indiscriminately, Tories as well as Whigs; if they see any thing they want, they seize it, and say, 'Rebel, good for Hesse man.'"[44]

44. Entry for Oct. 7, 1776, in Edward H. Tatum, Jr., ed., *The American Journal of Ambrose Serle, Secretary to Lord Howe, 1776–1778* (San Marino, Calif., 1940), 120; William Hooper to Robert R. Livingston, Philadelphia, Sept. 25, 1776, *LDC,* V, 238; *Newport Mercury,* Oct. 28, 1776; *Essex Journal,* Nov. 8, 1776; James Wilson to John Montgomery and Jasper Yates, Woodstock, N.J., Sept. 14, 1776, *LDC,* V, 170, 171. When the British took Newport on December 8, Southwick, who was a member of the Rhode Island Assembly in addition to printer of the *Mercury,* buried his press and types and barely made it out of town. The *Mercury* would be suspended for the three years that the British occupied the town, from December 2, 1776, until January 5, 1780. See Isaiah Thomas, *The History of Printing in America America: With a Biography of Printers and an Account of Newspapers,* ed. Marcus A. McCorison, 2d ed. (1810; rpt. New York, 1970), 316–321; Clarence S. Brigham, *History and Bibliography of American Newspapers, 1690–1820,* 2 vols. (Worcester, Mass., 1947), II, 997–998. For Hazard's letter, see Ebenezer Hazard to General Gates, Harlem Heights, N.Y., Oct. 11, 1776, 5 *Am. Archives,* II, 995–996. This appeared anonymously in *Independent Chronicle,* Oct. 24, 1776; *Continental Journal,* Oct. 24, 1776; *Essex Journal,* Oct. 25,

Now the German mercenaries had nearly three thousand helpless Americans at their disposal. The last time significant numbers of American soldiers had surrendered, at the Cedars four months earlier, they were left exposed to the Canadian elements. A week after independence, Congress had issued its final report indicting British military officers for allowing Indians to abuse American prisoners and promising that if "retaliation, [was] the sole means of stopping the progress of human butchery," they would do so until the British—and "foreigners or savages taken into his service"—"shall be taught to respect the violated rights of nations." Seventeen printers across North America had published this report in full over the weeks leading up to the New York campaign. The captured garrison at Fort Washington had to wonder what those foreigners would do. Were they really men monsters?[45]

"The Hessians . . . were extremely irritated at having lost a good many men in the attack," one British officer wrote in his diary, and they had killed some of the American riflemen after the surrender. Another remembered a British officer exclaiming, "Kill them, kill every man of them," shouts that

---

1776; *Massachusetts Spy*, Oct. 30, 1776; *Connecticut Gazette*, Nov. 1, 1776; *Newport Mercury*, Nov. 4, 1776; *Pennsylvania Evening Post*, Nov. 7, 1776; *Pennsylvania Packet*, Nov. 12, 1776; *Maryland Gazette*, Nov. 21, 1776; *Virginia Gazette* (Purdie), Nov. 22, 1776.

American soldiers were apparently taking similar liberties, though such stories did not find space in newspapers. Washington wrote Congress on Sept. 22, "Such a Spirit has gone forth in our Army that neither publick nor private Property is secure—Every hour brings the most distressing Complaints of Ravages of our own Troops who are become infinitely more formidable to the poor Farmers and inhabitants than the common Enemy" (GW to Hancock, New York, Sept. 22, 1776, *PGW: RW*, VI, 368–369). William Tudor concurred, writing to John Adams the following day, "Our Men are at present only Robbers, that they will soon be Murderers, unless some are hang'd, I have little Doubt" (Tudor to Adams, Harlem, Sept. 23, 1776, *PJA*, V, 36).

45. Cedars report, July 10, 1776, *JCC*, V, 533–539, esp. 538, 539; *Pennsylvania Evening Post*, July 25, 1776; *Pennsylvania Ledger*, July 27, 1776; *Pennsylvania Packet*, July 29, 1776; *Pennsylvania Journal*, July 31, 1776; *Maryland Journal*, July 31, 1776; *Constitutional Gazette*, July 31, 1776; *New-York Gazette*, Aug. 5, 1776; *Norwich Packet*, July 29–Aug. 5, 1776; *Connecticut Journal*, Aug. 7, 1776; *Continental Journal*, Aug. 8, 1776; *New-England Chronicle*, Aug. 8, 1776; *Connecticut Gazette*, Aug. 9, 1776; *Virginia Gazette* (Purdie), Aug. 9, 1776; *Virginia Gazette* (Dixon & Hunter), Aug. 10, 1776; *Boston Gazette*, Aug. 12, 1776; *Massachusetts Spy*, Aug. 14, 1776; *New Hampshire Gazette* (Exeter), Aug. 17, 1776.

"By the American Revolution You Are Now Free"

"unmanned" one captive. An ensign in a Pennsylvania regiment later wrote, "As soon as the enemy took possession of the fort the abuse and plunder commenced; side arms, watches, shoe-buckles, and even the clothes on our backs were wrested from us." Yet, though they were "threatened hanging as rebels," British and German officers did not treat them as insurrectionists who deserved no mercy. The Fort Washington prisoners were first quartered in a dangerous part of the burned-out city and later put on board the soon-to-be notorious transport ships anchored in the bay. At the Hessians' first opportunity to "compleat the works of death, desolation and tyranny," as the Declaration promised, they had shown restraint.[46]

3: WHAT HARM . . . AT TRENTON WAS DONE TO THE STANDARD OF HESSIAN?

Washington watched the November 16 debacle through his telescope from the Jersey side of the Hudson. With New York City in enemy hands, this was the moment that prompted several worried Morris County, New Jersey, in-habitants to subscribe to William Bradford's *Pennsylvania Journal*. They had to have reliable news. Washington had divided the remainder of his army into three parts and ordered them across the week before. Soon after, the Continental army started to run.

On November 22, Howe's British and German force, led by Cornwallis, began its sixty-mile chase of Washington's demoralized and shrinking army through the New Jersey countryside from the Hudson to the Delaware. Panic swept through Philadelphia that the British would march right into the city. This cascade was the worst phase of a difficult few weeks for the common cause.

Now began the "times that try men's souls," as Paine's now-legendary phrase had it. For the next two weeks, Washington retreated across New Jersey, from Hackensack to Newark, to Brunswick, to Princeton, to Trenton, to Pennsylvania, his force getting smaller and smaller as it went. When the soldiers rested at Brunswick, the calendar turned over to December, and some enlistments expired. Many went home, even with the enemy just hours away. Some units from Pennsylvania—including one of the German battal-

---

46. Allen French, ed., *Diary of Frederick Mackenzie* (Cambridge, Mass., 1930), I, 110–111; Alexander Graydon, *Memoirs*, 205 ("Kill them"), 207; "Isaac Van Horne Memoirs," August 1776–May 1778, in Dennis P. Ryan, ed., *A Salute to Courage: The American Revolution as Seen through the Wartime Writings of Officers of the Continental Army and Navy* (New York, 1979), 52 ("wrested from us").

ions—strengthened the army just as it arrived at the Delaware River, but even with reinforcement, only five thousand crossed the river with Washington on December 7.[47]

Howe and Cornwallis arrived in Trenton the following morning. News that British cavalry was less than a day's ride from Philadelphia threw the city into disarray. The following day, on December 9, patriot officers ordered the shops to remain closed and the patrolling militia to enforce a ten o'clock curfew. Most of the city's printing offices had already shuttered. Hall and Sellers closed their Market Street printing office after the November 27 issue. They would not resume publication of the *Pennsylvania Gazette* until February 5, 1777. Benjamin Towne tried to keep publishing his *Pennsylvania Evening Post* through the crisis, with intermittent success. William Bradford left the *Pennsylvania Journal* in the hands of his son Thomas and assumed his colonelcy in the now-active militia. Like the *Gazette,* the *Journal* would remain dormant from November 27 through the first weeks of 1777. John Dunlap also joined the defense of Philadelphia, serving as cornet for the Philadelphia troop of light horse. His *Pennsylvania Packet* missed less time, resuming publication on December 18.

Pennsylvania Ledger printer James Humphreys, Jr., was also on his way out of town, but not to join the Continental army. On November 16, as the committee of safety passed handbills throughout the city calling Philadelphians to arms, his rival Towne published a letter written by "A Tory" across the whole front page of the *Evening Post.* This article boldly accused Humphreys of being "a well-wisher to the enemies of his country, commonly called a *Tory.*" How did "A Tory" recognize a fellow traveler? He "pompously displayed large extracts from the *New-York* [*Gazette; and the Weekly*] *Mercury;* a paper published under the immediate influence of our inveterate enemies." Humphreys had exchanged stories from the pro-British version of Hugh Gaine's paper that was being published by Ambrose Serle, Admiral Howe's private secretary. For Towne and his contributor, this was a telltale sign of political allegiance. "A Tory"—who was obviously not really a loyalist—suggested that the Philadelphia committee of safety should take quick steps "in silencing a press whose weekly labors manifestly tend to dishearten our troops, to throw disgust on the friends of America, and hold up in false and glaring colours the characters and performances of those whose only errand is the total destruction of this country." Humphreys, jus-

47. Ward, *War of the Revolution,* I, 283–284; Fischer, *Washington's Crossing,* 125–136.

"By the American Revolution You Are Now Free"

tifiably concerned about what might happen to him at that tumultuous moment, put out one final issue on November 30, closed his shop, and fled to the countryside.[48]

For Congress, this was a particularly bad time for all this turbulence: the Ohio Indians were in town to meet with them. Just as they had tried to impress the delegation from the Six Nations earlier in the spring, now a group of Delaware and Shawnee Indians happened to be in town to witness this panic. They met with Congress on Thursday, Saturday, and again on that calamitous Monday as armed militia policed the city's streets. During the Saturday session, as boats from Philadelphia scrambled upriver to ferry the Continental army to safety, the delegates were preoccupied with business just as pressing: maintaining good relations with these Indians, factions among whom were already growing openly hostile to American interests in the Pennsylvania backcountry. "We . . . are extremely pleased to see you," they began an address; "we think that you must be fully convinced that your safety, as nations, depends on preserving peace and friendship with the white people of this island." Whether the Shawnees and Delawares were really "fully convinced" of that two days later, as they watched the city "all in hurry and confusion" and Congress itself decamp for Baltimore, is doubtful. The patriots had labored since the spring of 1775 to show strength whenever Indians were in observance. This was not good.[49]

At the same time, anxious polemicists and political leaders picked up their pens to beg the public to defend the common cause. Above all, they called on Americans to save themselves from occupation, especially at the

48. William Ellery to Nicholas Cooke, Philadelphia, Nov. 16, 1776, *LDC*, V, 495; *Pennsylvania Evening Post*, Nov. 16, 1776; Thomas, *History of Printing in America*, 398. Thomas offers one more wrinkle to this story: Towne had borrowed the paper on which he was printing the *Pennsylvania Evening Post* from Humphreys and had not repaid him. The paper that led to his self-banishment was his own. Since both papers began in January 1775, there had been a rivalry between them, and it is more than plausible Towne used this opportunity of chaos in the city to eliminate the competition. See also Dwight L. Teeter, "Benjamin Towne: Precarious Career of a Persistent Printer," *PMHB*, LXXXIX (1965), 316–330, esp. 320–321.

49. Christopher Marshall, Dec. 9, 1776, in William Duane, ed., *Extracts from the Diaries of Christopher Marshall, 1774–1781* (1877; rpt. New York, 1969), 107. The journals of Congress note the Shawnee and Delaware delegations were introduced to Congress on Dec. 5, 7, and 9, 1776. See *JCC*, VI, 1006, 1010–1011, 1013. See also "Benjamin Rush's Notes on Proceedings in Congress," [Dec. 5?], 1776, *LDC*, V, 577–578.

hands of the Hessians. An essay by "Epaminondas," published in the *Pennsylvania Evening Post,* made this clear. Under the guise of the heroic Greek who led Thebes out of Spartan tyranny, the writer exclaimed that if the cause failed, they would be "a hissing amongst the nations, and the despised of the world. He is an *American,* he dare not be free, will be a proverb translated into every language." "Step forth like men," this alleged voice from the ancient world cried, "you must know, you must feel, that your cause is good." A more proximate hero, "Hampden," also shook his finger at Pennsylvanians: "What apology shall we make to our brethren in Massachusetts Bay, Virginia, and South-Carolina, who have driven the royal banditti from their coasts, if we suffer them to get possession of the VITALS of the continent?"[50]

On December 10, the day after dismissing the Ohio Indians and two days before they voted to relocate to Baltimore, Congress issued "a few words of exhortation" in this "important crisis" to rouse the people "to an immediate and spirited exertion." Although they admitted that the people were "not unacquainted with the history of the rise and progress of this war," they rehearsed the well-established argument yet again, offering a condensed version of the Declaration's principal grievances. And, yet again, Congress used proxies as the ultimate provocation: "To crown the whole, they have waged war with us in the most cruel and unrelenting manner, employing not only the force of the British nation, but hiring foreign mercenaries, who, without feeling, indulge themselves in rapine and bloodshed." Just as they feared would be the case with "unlicensed strangers," as Epaminondas called them, Congress proclaimed that the Hessians had indeed shown "inhuman treatment" to American soldiers "who have unhappily fallen into their hands."[51]

On Thursday, December 12, after taking steps to publish this address, Congress left for Baltimore. Twenty miles north, someone at Washington's headquarters in Bucks County, Pennsylvania, composed a handbill that provided details to corroborate Congress's official accusations of Hessian barbarity. "The Progress of *British* and *Hessian* Troops through NEW JERSEY, has been attended with such scenes of Desolation and Outrage, as would

50. *Pennsylvania Evening Post,* Nov. 30, 1776; *Pennsylvania Packet,* Nov. 26, 1776.

51. *Pennsylvania Evening Post,* Nov. 30, 1776; "The Representatives of the United States of America in Congress Assembled, to the People in General, and Particularly the Inhabitants of Pennsylvania and the Adjacent States," Philadelphia, Dec. 10, 1776, *JCC,* VI, 1018–1020, esp. 1018–1019. This address would be published in *Pennsylvania Packet,* Dec. 18, 1776, and *Pennsylvania Evening Post,* Dec. 19, 1776.

"By the American Revolution You Are Now Free"

disgrace the most barbarous Nations," the handbill began. The notice detailed instances of particular savagery, including the story of William Smith, a farmer from Woodbridge, New Jersey. Smith allegedly heard "the cries of his daughter, rushed into the room, and found a Hessian Officer attempting to ravish her, and in an agony of rage and resentment, he instantly killed him; but the Officer's party soon came upon him, and now he lays mortally wounded at his ruined, plundered dwelling." This report, which came from Washington's camp and therefore carried an official imprimatur, chronicled other atrocities and ended with the warning, "If these scenes of desolation, ruin, and distress, do not rouse and animate every man of spirit to revenge their much injured countrymen and countrywomen, all Virtue, Honour and Courage must have left this Country, and we deserve all that we shall meet with."[52]

It is clear that Hessian and British troops did do a great deal of plundering in New York and New Jersey. British officers complained loudly about indiscriminate attacks on private property. "The circumstance of plunder is the only thing I believe gives trouble or uneasiness to General Howe with respect to the foreign troops," a British official wrote back to Lord George Germain. "Even in their own country," the Hessian troops "could never be restrained from the crime of marauding," and they were "unfortunately led to believe . . . that they were to come to America to establish their private fortunes and hitherto they have certainly acted with that principle." "The Hessians destroy all the fruits of the Earth without regard to Loyalists or Rebels," British army officer Stephen Kemble wrote in his journal. In early November, Kemble elaborated on the Hessians' pillaging "unmercifully," adding, "no wonder . . . the Country People refuse to join us."[53]

Patriot military and political leaders also expressed shock about the mercenaries' behavior in their private correspondence. Across the line from Kemble, Nathanael Greene shared the same opinion about all the marauding. British and Hessian troops "plunder without distinction: Whig and Tory

52. "The Progress of the British and Hessian Troops through New Jersey" ([Philadelphia], 1776), *Early American Imprints*, 15037. For more on the political context of rape in the Revolution, see Sharon Block, *Rape and Sexual Power in Early America* (Chapel Hill, N.C., 2006), 230–237.

53. Sir George Osborn to Lord George Germain, New York, Oct. 29, 1776, in Davies, ed., *Docs. of the Am. Rev.*, XII, 242; Oct. 3, 1776, "Journals of Lieut.-Col. Stephen Kemble," *Collections of the New-York Historical Society: For the Year 1883*, XVI (New York, 1883), 91 ("destroy all the fruits"), 96 ("refuse to join us").

all fare alike," Greene wrote in early December. Two weeks later, in a letter home to his wife, Greene blamed the "wicked, villainous, and oppressive" tories, who were really at the root of Hessian evil. "They lead the relentless foreigners to the houses of their neighbors and strip the poor women and children of everything they have to eat or wear . . . the brutes often [then] ravish the mothers and daughters, and compel the fathers and sons to behold their brutality; many have fallen sacrifices in this way." "To the disgrace of a Civilised Nation," a Virginia officer wrote Jefferson, they "Ravish the fair Sex, from the Age of Ten to Seventy." Samuel Adams wrote home about what he had heard, once Congress reconvened in Baltimore. Even to his wife, Samuel channeled the Declaration: "We are told that such savage Tragedies have been acted by them without Respect to Age or Sex as have equaled the most barbarous Ages and Nations of the World." A New Hampshire delegate to Congress lumped the Hessians in with other proxies, concluding that this was "what is to be expected from those worse then savages."[54]

A few days after Congress left Philadelphia and the Bucks County report documenting Hessian atrocities began to circulate, Thomas Paine took a short manuscript he had been working on over to the Second Street printing shop of Melchior Styner and Charles Cist. Paine had been with the army throughout the retreat; as they fell back from Newark, he began to write in a "passion of patriotism" under the "Common Sense" pseudonym. Since most newspaper printers had suspended their operations, Paine gave it to Styner and Cist "gratis" for them to publish as a pamphlet as long as they

54. Nathanael Greene to Nicholas Cooke of Rhode Island, Trenton, Dec. 4, 1776, *PNG*, I, 362, Nathanael Greene to Catherine Greene, Coryells Ferry, Pa., Dec. 16, 1776, 368; Adam Stephen to TJ, Camp on Delaware, [c. Dec. 20], 1776, *PTJ*, I, 659; Samuel Adams to Elizabeth Adams, Baltimore, Dec. 19, 1776, *LDC*, V, 616–617, esp. 617, William Whipple to Josiah Bartlett, Baltimore, Dec. 23, 1776, 652. Modern historians have either wholly or partially defended the Hessians from accusations that they were depraved, arguing instead that all participants in the Revolutionary War plundered and that it was a well-established practice in Europe. At the time, this hardly mattered. What did prove crucial was how patriot publicists seized upon this issue and exaggerated it to the point of hyperbole. Rodney Atwood shields the German mercenaries from blame in his *Hessians: Mercenaries from Hessen-Kasssel in the American Revolution* (Cambridge, 1980), 171–183. Fischer is more moderate. He suggests the Hessian plundering was indeed part of eighteenth-century warfare, but the scale of what happened in New Jersey at the end of the year was especially severe (*Washington's Crossing*, 177–181, 510).

"By the American Revolution You Are Now Free"

could "confine . . . the price [to] two coppers," he later recalled. Styner and Cist, printers of several significant political tracts and the original publishers of John Leacock's *Fall of British Tyranny*, brought out the first copies of *The American Crisis, Number I* on December 19.[55]

Although the opening lines of Paine's *Crisis* have become part of the mythological idiom of the Revolution, one sentence buried deep in the fourth paragraph provides a better key to understanding the "times that try men's souls" than the images conjured by "summer soldier" or "sunshine patriot." First admitting it is "surprising to see how rapidly a panic will sometimes run through a country," Paine turns the tables: "Yet panics, in some cases, have their uses; they produce as much good as hurt." Paine argued that Britain's overwhelming military success over the past few months had helped solve one of the most difficult problems patriots had faced ever since Lexington: the exposure of "secret traitors." The December crisis, if Americans did not "shrink from the service of his country," would be a beneficial event, "sift out the hidden thoughts of man, and hold them up in public to the world. Many a disguised Tory has lately shewn his head, that shall penitentially solemnize with curses the day on which Howe arrived upon the Delaware."[56]

The issue of secret loyalists had preoccupied patriot leaders for the past two years. Several allegedly trustworthy men had conspired to provide crucial information to the British, like Benjamin Church. More prominent citi-

---

55. According to Isaiah Thomas, Styner (sometimes Steiner) and Cist had published a newspaper in German at the beginning of the Revolutionary War, but it was discontinued in April 1776. They then took on book and job work in German and English. See Thomas, *History of Printing in America*, 404–405. See also Willi Paul Adams, "The Colonial German-Language Press and the American Revolution," in Bernard Bailyn and John B. Hench, eds., *The Press and the American Revolution* (Worcester, Mass., 1980), 151–228. For Paine's remarks, see Thomas Paine to HL, Philadelphia, Jan. 14, 1779, in Philip S. Foner, ed., *The Complete Writings of Thomas Paine*, 2 vols. (New York, 1945), II, 1164. Most books have stated that the Bradfords printed *The American Crisis* on Dec. 19 in the *Pennsylvania Journal*. They did not: the paper was suspended at that date. Paine's work was printed as a pamphlet first, then published in newspapers over the next few weeks. A second pamphlet printing appeared on December 23. This error of first printing in the *Journal* was most recently repeated in Fischer, *Washington's Crossing*, 140. See Eric Foner, ed., *Thomas Paine: Collected Writings . . .* (New York, 1995), 855.

56. [Paine], *The American Crisis, Number I*, Dec. 19, 1776, in Foner, ed., *Paine: Writings*, 91–92.

zens had turned their coats lately, including New York printer Hugh Gaine, former Congressman Joseph Galloway, and, as the rumor went at that hour, Pennsylvania delegate John Dickinson. Patriots had persistently tried to mark tories by associating them with other proxies, especially Indians and African Americans. The *Pennsylvania Evening Post* had recently offered another example of this campaign. Towne inserted "A Card" announcing, "Lord Dunmore presents his best compliments to his dear friends the Negroes and Tories of Pennsylvania and Delaware counties, and hopes they will not forsake the cause of our gracious King." Dunmore proposed "to raise three regiments of black and white *loyal Tories* to be officered by Negroes and whites, for the service of his Hanoverian Highness." Towne's satire was part of an established theme of conflating loyalists with "mercenaries," "slaves," and "savages." A few days later, Ebenezer Watson's *Connecticut Courant* published news of "a surprising and instructive scene" in Massachusetts. A man named Billings, "a noted tory," had a "bastard negro child born in his house."

> The stupid ass, to insult the distress of this country, express his utter contempt of its sacred rights and if possible to render himself more vile and infamous in the view of the people, named the child, George Washington. The child, though healthy and well over night, was dead in the morning;—and soon after two of the poor wretch's children the only tender branches of his family, were lodged in the silent grave. A solemn lecture to those who sport with the sacred cause of LIBERTY.

That these two articles conflating blacks with tories appeared the same week in November was a coincidence, but a revealing one. Patriot publishers endeavored to identify and thereby ostracize loyalists by associating them with people they deemed inferior. For Paine, the December crisis offered answers for the crucial question of, "What is a Tory?" "Good God! What is he? . . . Every Tory is a coward; for servile, slavish, self-interested fear is the foundation of Toryism; and a man under such influence, though he may be cruel, never can be brave."[57]

Even more than the specter of loyalist uprisings, the topic that really

57. Fischer, *Washington's Crossing,* 137; [Paine,] *American Crisis, Number I,* in Foner, ed., *Paine: Writings,* 94; "A Card," Red Hook, N.J., Sept. 8, 1776, *Pennsylvania Evening Post,* Nov. 2, 1776. "Bastard negro child": *Connecticut Courant,* Nov. 4, 1776; *Massachusetts Spy,* Nov. 13, 1776; *Essex Journal,* Nov. 15, 1776.

tried men's souls in New Jersey that December was Hessian plundering. Here was another opportunity that the panic offered. Though hampered by the loss of printing presses in New York (permanently), Newport (nearly permanently), and Philadelphia (temporarily), patriot leaders worked assiduously to spread the news of Hessian "barbarity" and to stoke American anger about the possibility of, in Paine's words, "our homes turned into barracks and baudy-houses for Hessians." In the hopes of rallying American arms to the Delaware, they embraced fears about Hessian depredations, seized upon a few instances of violence, and crafted a narrative that painted all German mercenaries as plunderers and rapists.[58]

Paine's *American Crisis* might have been the most eloquent production of the December crisis, but it was only one of many efforts to encourage military resistance. Most representations involved the Hessians. Patriots tried to scare Americans into enlisting by invoking the menace of a German occupation or shame them into fighting by challenging American masculinity and calling into question men's ability to protect their vulnerable families against a horde of German violators. The official handbill from Washington's Bucks County headquarters circulated throughout the Pennsylvania countryside before being published in the *Pennsylvania Packet* on December 18. In all, twelve newspapers—only two fewer than the total that would publish Paine's *American Crisis*—featured this account of Hessian ravage and rape. The Pennsylvania Council of Safety sponsored another collection of rape allegations and arranged for its publication in the *Packet* and *Evening Post*. Another widely exchanged, impassioned report listed a number of British and Hessian attacks "against Liberty, Virtue, and the Arts and Sciences" that "outraged the Feelings of Humanity," including the "wanton destruction" of New York City's "curious" water works, the "elegant" Trenton public library, and the "grand Orrery made by the celebrated Rittenhouse, which was placed at the College at Princeton." The final wrecked item, Dr. David Rittenhouse's model of the celestial bodies, was "a piece of mechanism which the most untutored savage, staying the Hand of Violence, would have beheld with Wonder, Reverence, and Delight!" *"How are the mighty fallen,"* read the italicized final comment, which first appeared in Mary Goddard's *Maryland Journal, and the Baltimore Advertiser.* Tories might be the same as savages, but these Hessians were worse! Eight printers hoped their readers would concur. By the end of December, the saturation of these subsidized

58. [Paine], *American Crisis, Number I,* in Foner, ed., *Paine: Writings,* 99.

images reached as far as Fredericksburg, Virginia, where diarist Dr. Robert Honyman, an avid follower of the news, noted on the last day of the year, "An account is published by authority of the devastations committed by the British Army in their march through New Jersey, mentioning particularly several instances of rapes, plundering, & massacre and in pathetic terms exhorting the people to rise and prevent the people of this state from suffering the like."[59]

Now more than ever, the patriots needed powerful, compelling rhetoric to save the Revolution. "There are cases which cannot be overdone by language, and this is one," Paine explained in *The American Crisis*. They needed representations to match the situation. At the moment of their greatest emergency, patriot publicists seized upon the scores of rumors and stories that were flying around army camps and agitated city streets about the behavior of these "unlicensed strangers"; the patriots documented the tales and circulated them as widely as they could, as quickly as they could. This is not to say that British, German, and American soldiers did not abuse persons and property in occupied New Jersey. They did, and in larger numbers

59. Dec. 31, 1776, entry in Robert Honyman Diary, 1776–1782, no. 8417, University of Virginia Library, Charlottesville, 98. Twelve is a substantial number, considering nearly all the papers in both New York and Philadelphia were out of commission at this time. See *Maryland Journal*, Dec. 18, 1776; *Pennsylvania Packet*, Dec. 18, 1776; *Virginia Gazette* (Purdie), Dec. 27, 1776; *Connecticut Courant*, Dec. 30, 1776; *Connecticut Journal*, Jan. 1, 1777; *Independent Chronicle*, Jan. 2, 1777; *Massachusetts Spy*, Jan. 2, 1777; *Connecticut Gazette*, Jan. 3, 1777; *Providence Gazette*, Jan. 4, 1777; *Freeman's Journal* (Portsmouth), Jan. 7, 1777; *Essex Journal*, Jan. 9, 1777; *New Hampshire Gazette* (Exeter), Jan. 14, 1777. The first newspaper installment of the *American Crisis* was published in *Pennsylvania Packet*, Dec. 27, 1776; *Pennsylvania Evening Post*, Dec. 31, 1776; *Maryland Gazette*, Jan. 2, 1777; *Connecticut Courant*, Jan. 6, 1777; *Virginia Gazette* (Dixon & Hunter), Jan. 10, 1777; *Virginia Gazette* (Purdie), Jan. 10, 1777; *Boston Gazette*, Jan. 13, 1777; *Continental Journal*, Jan. 16, 1777; *Essex Journal*, Jan. 16, 1777; *Connecticut Gazette*, Jan. 17, 1777; *Freeman's Journal* (Portsmouth), Jan. 28, 1777; *South-Carolina and American General Gazette*, Jan. 30, 1777; *New Hampshire Gazette* (Exeter), Feb. 4, 1777; *Gazette, of the State of South-Carolina*, Apr. 28, 1777. Rape allegations: *Pennsylvania Packet*, Dec. 27, 1776; *Pennsylvania Evening Post*, Dec. 28, 1776. "How are the mighty fallen": *Maryland Journal*, Dec. 30, 1776; *Virginia Gazette* (Purdie), Jan. 10, 1777; *Connecticut Courant*, Jan. 20, 1777; *Continental Journal*, Jan. 23, 1777; *Independent Chronicle*, Jan. 23, 1777; *Massachusetts Spy*, Jan. 23, 1777; *Connecticut Gazette*, Jan. 24, 1777; *Freeman's Journal* (Portsmouth), Jan. 28, 1777; *New Hampshire Gazette* (Exeter), Jan. 28, 1777.

than any civilians had yet experienced in the war. But if those instances of violence were at a higher magnitude, so, too, was the amplification of those events by desperate patriot publicists. As they had done since the war began, patriot leaders cultivated and propagated repellent images of proxy enemies to mobilize resistance.

* * *

It worked—at least, well enough to give Washington enough strength to execute his daring Christmas crossing of the Delaware and surprise the Hessian garrison at Trenton. A combination of factors kept the army in existence throughout the middle weeks of December: Washington's entreaties to his men; genuine belief in the cause; broad cultural conceptions of masculinity and honor; the challenging rhetoric of essayists like Thomas Paine; anger at British and German success, military discipline, rumors of what was happening in New Jersey; and a hatred of the enemy invaders sharpened by circulated news reports. "Intreat, exhort and use every exertion, to induce the people to act for their own preservation. Strain every Nerve for carrying on the necessary Works," Washington wrote to General Israel Putnam, the commanding officer in Philadelphia. "Strain every Nerve" for patriot leaders from the national, provincial, and local levels meant collecting testimony, drafting addresses, sending them to printers, and arranging for proclamations to be read to the troops. The inordinate amount of effort they spent on these projects suggests how fruitful they believed those enterprises might be.[60]

Still, Washington was not sanguine about the future. Although 2,000 militia from Philadelphia bolstered his force, they were only short-term volunteers; at the end of the year, the enlistments for all but 1,400 of his men were up. A British patrol had captured General Charles Lee, one of his best tacticians. Worst of all, if things remained the same and "every nerve is not straind to recruit the New Army . . . I think the game is pretty near up." He knew his only option was to do something to "raise the spirits of the People, which are quite sunk by our late misfortunes," he had written to Connecticut governor Jonathan Trumbull. He needed a "lucky blow in this Quarter." So he secretly began planning an attack on the Hessian garrison at Trenton. As

60. GW to Major General Israel Putnam, Headquarters at "Keiths," Dec. 21, 1776, *PGW: RW*, VII, 405; [Paine], *American Crisis, Number I*, in Foner, ed., *Paine: Writings*, 91–99, esp. 97.

Washington informed his aide Joseph Reed: "Christmas day at Night, one hour before day is the time is fixed upon for our Attempt on Trenton. For heaven's sake keep this to yourself."[61]

There is no reason to explain what occurred after nightfall on December 25; that story is a staple of America's founding mythology. Iconic portraits of Washington and his Continentals bravely crossing the ice-choked Delaware render the scene. Legend instructs what happened next: the surprise attack on Trenton, the capture of the entire Hessian garrison, the Revolution rescued. Plentiful accounts imagine Washington's relief after agonizing days planning the raid, scrambling for provisions, and stealthily preparing his defeated troops for battle. It is true, ever since he first crossed the river on December 7, the totality of his correspondence dealt with writing and receiving communiqués about the problems of keeping the army intact, whether that meant morale or provisions. He received letters that "Tories are Joyning the Enemy and Insulting and Disarming the Whigs" in New York, worries about the "Safety of the Common cause," and intelligence concerning "Malitious Active" tories who "spirited the Negroes against us." In replies, he recalled the rolling snowball metaphor used previously in reference to Dunmore. Letters flooded in and out of Washington's quarters about flour, blankets, and clothing. These issues comprise 160 consecutive pages of the *Papers of George Washington*.[62]

On Christmas Eve, then, we expect Washington to have been consumed in the logistics of the most important day of his military career, only hours away. It seems natural for Washington to sit down to write—perhaps in anticipation—about "a piece of News to tell you which I hope you will Attend to." This correspondence, though, was not to Congress or a family member or another army officer. He was writing letters to Indians. "Our Enemy the King of Great Britain endeavoured to Stir up all the Indians from Canada

61. GW to Samuel Washington, Camp near the Falls at Trenton, Dec. 18, 1776, *PGW: RW,* VII, 370, GW to Jonathan Trumbull, Sr., Bucks County, Pa., Dec. 14, 1776, 340, GW to Colonel Joseph Reed, Camp above Trenton Falls, Dec. 23, 1776, 423.

62. Major General William Heath to GW, Haverstraw, N.Y., Dec. 11, 1776, ibid., 298 ("Insulting and Disarming"), Brigadier General Alexander MacDougall to GW, Chatham, N.J., Dec. 19, 1776, 378 ("Safety of the Common cause"), Colonel David Chambers to GW, Amwell, N.J., Dec. 16, 1776, 350 ("spirited the Negroes"), GW to John Hancock, Camp above Trenton Falls, Dec. 20, 1776, 382 ("like a Snowball"). Flour: "Orders to Carpenter Wharton," Bucks County, Dec. 20, 1776, 391. Blankets and clothing: GW to Pennsylvania Council of Safety, Headquarters, Bucks County, Dec. 22, 1776, 413.

"By the American Revolution You Are Now Free"

to South Carolina Against Us," he wrote in two letters to the St. Johns and Passamaquoddy Indians from his Bucks County headquarters on December 24. "The Cherokees and the Southern Tribes were foolish enough to listen to them, and to take up the Hatchet Against us," he informed these northern New England tribes. "Upon this our Warriours went into their Country, burnt their Houses, destroyed their Corn, and Oblidged them to sue for peace and give Hostages for their future Good Behaviour. Now Brothers never lett the King's Wicked Councellors turn your Hearts Against Me and your Bretheren of this Country."[63]

These dispatches—the first on any topic outside the immediate "crisis" Washington had addressed for the whole month of December—should not surprise, actually. The battle orders Washington issued the following day were meant to preserve the common cause and defend American liberty. So were these letters to the Maine frontier. As Washington prepared to make war on one group of the king's proxies in Trenton, he worked to convince another group not to be so foolish—or else. As had been the case ever since Lexington Green, concerns about whom the British might convince to aid in crushing the rebellion infused how patriots interpreted, justified, and conducted the conflict. Washington's taking time to write letters to Indians hundreds of miles away on the eve of the battle of Trenton was, by now, a routine experience.

The next night, with almost no casualties, Washington and 2,400 Continental troops, ferried again by Glover's Marblehead regiment of black and white mariners, traversed the Delaware and overwhelmed the exhausted garrison at Trenton that had been harassed by New Jersey insurgents for the past three days. Colonel Johann Rall, the hero of Fort Washington, was killed, along with twenty-two others, trying to mount a defense. When Washington's men returned to Pennsylvania, they brought 918 Hessian prisoners with them, marching band and all.

This stunning turn of events redeemed the times that tried men's souls. Two weeks later, English diarist Nicholas Cresswell noted bitterly how the Trenton news affected public opinion in northern Virginia, two hundred miles removed. "The minds of the people are much altered," he wrote on January 7. "A few days ago they had given up the cause for lost. Their late successes have turned the scale and now they are all liberty mad again." Cresswell concluded with a refrain that surely resounded in many loyal-

63. GW to the Chiefs of the Passamaquoddy Indians, Bucks County, Dec. 24, 1776, ibid., 433–434.

ist households during those first weeks of 1777: "Confound the turn coat scoundrels and the cowardly Hessians together."[64]

Cresswell had it right: the Hessians were indeed "cowardly." At least, this was how Americans began to talk about them as soon as word spread of the Christmas surprise. Trenton completely—and permanently—transformed American fears about the German mercenaries. With Washington's mastery of the Hessians at Trenton, the Germans ceased to exist as a proxy enemy.

On December 29, three delegates to Congress who remained in Philadelphia reported to their colleagues that they had "the pleasure to see the Hessian Prisoners paraded" through the city. Gauging the crowd's reaction, they concluded that "most people seemed very angry they shou'd ever think of running away from such a Set of Vagabonds." No more would English observers revel in Americans' running at the sound of the Hessians' very name. That was an artifact of 1776, buried at Trenton. Mary Goddard put it this way:

> On the Hessian standards, taken at Trenton, were engraved these words:—NESCIT PERICULA, *a fearlessness of danger,* which was not displayed in the battle where the standards were surrendered to the American arms, and which hath drawn on the timid Hessian, and his vaunting motto, the following EPIGRAM:
>
> *The man who submits, without striking a blow,*
> *May be said, in a sense,* no danger to know:
> *I pray then, what harm, by the humble submission*
> *At Trenton was done to the standard of Hessian?*

Instantly forgotten were the reports of how Rall and his Hessian brigades had embarrassed American arms on Long Island, driven them out of New York, and marched with little trouble across New Jersey; now the Germans were pathetic, "timid" weaklings. Beginning with the news of Washington's smashing victories at Trenton and then Princeton, patriot newspapers promoted a new emotion for the Hessians: sympathy.[65]

64. Lincoln Macveagh, [ed.], *The Journal of Nicholas Cresswell, 1774–1777* (New York, 1924), 179–180.

65. "Executive Committee [George Clymer, Robert Morris, George Walton] to John Hancock," Philadelphia, Dec. 30, 1776, *LDC,* V, 700; *Maryland Journal,* Jan. 8, 1777; *Continental Journal,* Jan. 30, 1777; *New Hampshire Gazette* (Exeter), Feb. 4, 1777; *South-Carolina and American General Gazette,* Feb. 6, 1777; *Essex Journal,* Feb. 6, 1777; *Norwich Packet,* Feb. 10, 1777; *Connecticut Journal,* February 12, 1777.

Figure 9. *Engraving of Hessian prisoners marching through Philadelphia. By David Chodowiecki. 1783. This appeared in a German history of the Revolution, published in Leipzig, depicting a crowd of Philadelphians (including a person of African descent) watching the Hessians captured at Trenton march through the city on their way to prison. Courtesy of the Library of Congress.*

The Philadelphia papers offered a different interpretation of the parade of Hessian prisoners. Not only did Americans have nothing to fear from these soldiers; they might be fellow victims of British tyranny. "The wretched condition of these unhappy men, most of whom, if not all, were dragged from their wives and families by a despotic and avaricious prince," said a commentator in the *Evening Post* and *Packet*, "must sensibly affect every generous mind with the dreadful effects of arbitrary power." A few months later, Benjamin Edes's *Boston Gazette* concurred, arguing that the erstwhile fearsome mercenaries were dupes of a "knavish and arbitrary prince"; "His subjects privately call him The Soul Seller." The Hessians "were far from being volunteers—they were forc'd into the service; and many of them imprison'd before they embark'd . . . These Germans will soon make good settlers in America." Along the same lines, Samuel Loudon's revived *New York Packet* reported that the two tyrants, George III and the Landgrave of Hesse, were colluding to send "as many American Tories as may be necessary to replace the Hessians who may be killed or taken prisoners by the Americans." Loudon reported in a separate article that the Hessian prisoners "express great joy at being released from their late masters, and were greatly surprised to find themselves treated with clemency and dignity." According to Loudon, many had offered to enlist with the Continental army and "in general declare, that they will never again draw the sword against us; and that if the Germans in General Howe's army knew how well they were treated they would all desert." The *New York Packet* and seven other printers substantiated this claim with a report two weeks later that a Hessian major and his staff did, in fact, defect.[66]

The general orders Washington issued on January 1, 1777, expressed his desire that his troops display "humanity and tenderness to women and children" so as to "distinguish brave Americans, contending for liberty, from infamous mercenary ravagers, *whether* British or Hessians." Washington's "whether" captured the subtle but powerful rhetorical shift. Before, when the patriots publicized stories about plunder, rape, and destruction in New York and New Jersey, they emphasized the German mercenaries. Now, with nearly one thousand Hessians harmless in American custody, patriot leaders began to accentuate British crimes alongside—or instead of—German ones. This occurred in private, too. "If the Hessians are the smallest plunderers," Richard Henry Lee wrote on January 2, "what are the British?" A few days later, Samuel Adams also participated in this growing gulf, writing to his cousin John that the people of New Jersey had been "treated with

66. "Despotic and avaricious Prince": *Pennsylvania Evening Post*, Dec. 31, 1776; *Pennsylvania Packet*, Jan. 4, 1777; *Connecticut Courant*, Jan. 20, 1777; *Independent Chronicle*, Jan. 23, 1777; *Massachusetts Spy*, Jan. 23, 1777; *Essex Journal*, Jan. 30, 1777. "Soul Seller": *Boston Gazette*, July 7, 1777; *Pennsylvania Journal*, July 23, 1777; *Maryland Journal*, July 29, 1777; *Maryland Gazette*, July 31, 1777; *Virginia Gazette* (Dixon & Hunter), Aug. 15, 1777. "Replace the Hessians": *New York Packet*, Jan. 23, 1777; *Connecticut Gazette*, Jan. 31, 1777; *Connecticut Courant*, Feb. 3, 1777; *Boston Gazette*, Feb. 10, 1777; *Pennsylvania Journal*, Feb. 19, 1777; *Virginia Gazette* (Dixon & Hunter), Feb. 28, 1777. "How well they were treated": *New York Packet*, Jan. 23, 1777; *Connecticut Journal*, Jan. 30, 1777; *Connecticut Gazette*, Jan. 31, 1777; *Norwich Packet*, Feb. 3, 1777; *Independent Chronicle*, Feb. 6, 1777; *Freeman's Journal* (Portsmouth), Feb. 11, 1777; *New Hampshire Gazette* (Exeter), Feb. 11, 1777.

"By the American Revolution You Are Now Free"

savage Barbarity by the Hessians, but, I believe, more so by Britains [*sic*]" who attacked the inhabitants "without Regard to Sex or Age." Twenty days before, Sam applied that phrase to the Hessians only. What a difference three weeks made.[67]

Early in the new year, Congress would form a committee to "enquire into the conduct of the British and Hessian officers, with regard to the treatment by them shewn to the prisoners in their possession." Washington, in gathering evidence for this committee, wrote "in favor of the Hessians," stating, "Our people who have been prisoners generally agree that they rec[eive]d much kinder treatment from them than from the British Officers and Soldiers."[68]

When the committee completed its inquiry into "the conduct of the enemy" several weeks later, it underscored the Hessians' redemption. According to its final, official report, Congress divided its investigation into four categories: "wanton and oppressive devastation of the country," "inhuman treatment" of prisoners, "savage butchery" of wounded or surrendered men, and finally the "lust and brutality of the soldiers in abusing of women." Most Americans who had read or heard a newspaper between the landing of the Hessian transport ships in July and the engagements in New Jersey six months later would have testified that the Germans were at the root of those four evils. Patriot publicists had been almost unanimous in forwarding that representation. Yet when Congress elaborated on those points, it was the "whole tract of the British army" that had committed these crimes—a vague description that covered up more than it explained. They qualified the only explicit reference to Germans in the report, corroborating Washington's sentiment that "foreigners more than the English" often "expressed sympathy" with captured Americans. In the main, they preferred to label British officers and soldiers—not the German mercenaries—

67. General orders, Trenton, Jan. 1, 1777, *PGW: RW*, VII, 499 (emphasis added). An anonymous source calling himself a "LOVER OF HUMANITY" sent these orders to Dunlap, who printed them in the Jan. 14, 1777, issue of his *Pennsylvania Packet*. "Smallest plunderers": Richard Henry Lee to John Page, Baltimore, Jan. 2, 1777, *LDC*, VI, 22. "Sex or Age": Samuel Adams to JA, Baltimore, Jan. 9, 1777, 64. Another delegate, plainly not afraid of the Hessians anymore, wrote that same day to his brother wondering whether he could use "a few Hessians . . . as settlers" on his New Hampshire farm (William Whipple to Joseph Whipple, Baltimore, Jan. 9, 1777, *LDC*, VI, 78).

68. Jan. 18, 1777, *JCC*, VII, 49; GW to Samuel Chase, Morristown, N.J., Feb. 5, 1777, *PGW: RW*, VIII, 247.

as "barbarous ravagers." When this report, complete with a lengthy appendix providing documentation that supported their indictments, appeared in several newspapers by Congress's order, it contributed to the collective, popular amnesia about the Hessians that the patriot leadership cultivated in early 1777. John Adams sent a copy of the report as published in the *Pennsylvania Evening Post* to Abigail, to give her "some Idea of the Humanity of the present Race of Brittons." "My Barber," he wrote, "whom I quote as often as ever I did any Authority, says 'he has read Histories of Cruelty; and he has read Romances of Cruelty: But the Cruelty of the British exceeds all that he has ever read.'" Neither the Congressman nor his barber noticed the cruelty of the former men monsters.[69]

No longer a threatening proxy enemy, from Trenton forward, the Hessians all but disappeared; patriot public discourse now featured them in circumstances that supported this new, friendly image, reporting on performances by the captured Hessian marching band or publishing part of a soldier's "entertaining journal." At Trenton, something was indeed "done to the standard of Hessian." From 1777 onward, patriot printers happily chronicled accounts of German disaffection behind enemy lines, of their desertion, and of the two armies' sometimes violent refusal to serve together. Patriots still decried the "mercenary" as the opposite of a liberty-loving, virtuous American, but the conflation of that trope with "German" almost entirely ended after the Christmas raid.[70]

Perhaps the most telling example of how radically the image of the Hessians had changed circulated throughout the nation next April. A story from Woodbridge—the same town where Richard Smith and his daughter

69. Apr. 18, 1777, *JCC*, VII, 276, 278; JA to Abigail Adams, Apr. 27, 1777, *LDC*, VI, 661; *Pennsylvania Evening Post*, Apr. 24, 26, 29, May 3, 10, 1777; *Pennsylvania Packet*, Apr. 29, 1777; *Pennsylvania Journal*, Apr. 30, 1777; *Connecticut Journal*, May 14, 1777; *Connecticut Gazette*, May 23, 30, June 6, 1777; *New Hampshire Gazette* (Exeter), May 27, 1777; *Freeman's Journal* (Portsmouth), June 21, 28, July 5, 1777. In July, Congress would have it published as a pamphlet and ordered 4,000 copies in English and 2,000 in German to be "struck off and distributed through the several States" (July 19, 1777, *JCC*, VIII, 565).

70. In the *Pennsylvania Evening Post,* Benjamin Towne published "part of a Hessian [soldier's] journal found at Trenton," adding a comment that it was a shame the attack "disturbed . . . his literary labors" and the war "deprive[d] the world of the remainder of this entertaining journal." See *Pennsylvania Evening Post,* July 26, 1777; *Continental Journal,* Aug. 21, 1777; *Boston Gazette,* Aug. 25, 1777.

"By the American Revolution You Are Now Free"

had only a few months earlier fallen victim to Hessian rapists—now contained quite a different message:

> A young woman, passing an evacuated house in Woodbridge, saw, thro' the window, a drunken Hessian soldier, who had straggled from his party; there being no men within less than a mile of the town, she went home, dressed herself in man's apparel, and armed with an old firelock, returned to the house, entered it, and took the Hessian prisoner, whom she soon stripped of his arms, and was leading off, when she fell in with the patrole guard . . . to whom she delivered her prisoner.

Within a few short months, the abuser of New Jersey had become an unmanned, pathetic subject. Now everyone was taking Hessians prisoner with ease.[71]

The "fall" of the Hessians after Trenton, from monsters to pitiable victims, was significant. Several mitigating circumstances made the Germans' portrayal as foes problematic. The presence of tens of thousands of people in America who shared their culture and language (and whom the patriots urgently needed to support the cause) was primary, but also, because they were Europeans and mostly Christians, they did not present the depth of cultural antipathy that blacks or Indians did. Further, the trope of "mercenary" was shallower than that of "slave" or "savage"; their capacity for loyalty or principle was not denied—it was simply up for purchase. Nevertheless, at the moment of independence, they were lumped into the same category of proxy with African Americans and Indians. It was the story of their alleged ineptitude at Trenton, a narrative patriot publicists broadcast with enthusiasm, that opened the door for their redemption. For the remainder of the war, patriot printers and political leaders all but stopped depicting the Hessians as terrifying, formidable soldiers. They were portrayed as equal victims of tyrannical monarchs who could—and would—come over to the common cause. Stories told and, later, not told were key to the rehabilitation of the German mercenaries.

The disappearance of the men monsters underscores the contrivance of the common cause argument. It was selective, emphasizing stories of

71. *Pennsylvania Journal,* Apr. 2, 1777; *Maryland Gazette,* Apr. 10, 1777; *Connecticut Journal,* Apr. 16, 1777; *Virginia Gazette* (Dixon & Hunter), Apr. 18, 1777; *Norwich Packet,* Apr. 21, 1777; *Continental Journal,* Apr. 21, 1777; *Freeman's Journal* (Portsmouth), Apr. 26, 1777.

Dunmore's deluded proxies instead of lauding Colonel Glover's heroic black fishermen. And it was creative, blurring the lines between real runaways and Major Cudjo. Patriot publicists selected certain representations they thought would best animate the populace and cast—concealed, forgot, reinterpreted—others away. The ways in which patriot communications leaders molded and shaped the cause were a powerful reason why the Revolution survived 1776. As the ruins of Cherokee country testified, the continued success of the common cause argument was increasingly consequential.

4: THE DANGEROUS AMBROSE SERLE

The Revolution's survival more than dismayed those who supported the crown throughout North America. Chief among the disappointed was Ambrose Serle. Lord William Howe's secretary, Serle had arrived with the fleet a few days after Congress approved independence. He was, therefore, not an ordinary observer of the events of 1776. But he was an incisive one. Serle's journal reveals the prevalence of the issues of print and proxies to both combatants in the early phase of the Revolutionary War.

Had the patriots known what Serle was writing in his journal and doing on the streets of Manhattan, they would have been very concerned about his ideas' gaining traction among the British leadership in New York. Serle, unlike nearly all his colleagues, understood the need for propagating the British side of the Revolutionary argument. His journal was a vent for his frustration at the patriots' misleading, hypocritical, and deceptive tendencies in their publications. "A more impudent, false and atrocious Proclamation was never fabricated by the Hands of Man," he asserted about the Declaration. "An American News Paper was put into my Hands, full of Bitterness and Malignancy," he wrote on July 16. "The following Sentence may serve for a specimen. 'Be assured, the Sun, moon and Stars shall fall, the Ocean cease to roll, and all nature change its Course, before a few English, Scotch and German *Slaves* shall conquer this vast Country.'" Serle was probably holding the June 24 issue of the *Newport Mercury*, a patriot paper that he argued contained "several other Paragraphs . . . equally full of Nonsense, Madness and Fury." Through their manipulations in the press, he noted a few days later, "Their Leaders seem resolved to run all Lengths, and to draw the poor miserable People after them." Two weeks after that, he wrote about a Philadelphia paper that "never was more Insolence or more Falsehood comprized in so narrow a Compass before. Perhaps the Editor or his Mas-

"By the American Revolution You Are Now Free"

ters think . . . that 'it is right to lie for one's Country,' and that what they suppose a good End will sanctify any Means." Other patriot publications, especially *Common Sense,* drew Serle's ire, too. "Read over Adams's Pamphlet," he wrote on July 20, repeating the common misattribution of *Common Sense.* "A most flagitious Performance, replete with Sophistry, Impudence and Falshood; but unhappily calculated to work upon the Fury of the Times, and to induce the full avowal of the Spirit of Independence in the warm and inconsiderate."[72]

By the time he had been in New York two weeks, Serle had identified one of Britain's Achilles' heels in America: they were not taking steps to contradict patriot arguments and narratives. The Americans were afflicted, he confessed to the former American secretary of state, Lord Dartmouth. "The Madness of this People" was "inexpressible." Buoyed also by sympathetic English radicals, this "Madness" really stemmed from Americans' being "excited by their own Publications." Those publications drove the colonists to exhibit "a Barbarity unparalleled except among the Savages."[73]

Infuriated by the "daring Hypocrisy of these Men," he began to lobby for permission to counter the patriots' print campaign. Thanks to Serle, for the first time since James Rivington had fled New York, British publicists engaged the common cause argument in print. No matter how impressive the military buildup on Staten Island appeared that summer, they were losing the war for words, and someone needed to respond.[74]

It was the newspaper printers—or their "Masters," like "Adams"—who were not only holding that high ground but also bringing the public along with them. "Among other Engines, which have raised the present Commotions," Serle wrote to Dartmouth, "none has had a more extensive or

72. Entries for July 13, 16, 20, 25, 31, 1776, in Tatum, ed., *American Journal of Ambrose Serle,* 31 ("impudent, false"), 36 ("Nonsense, Madness and Fury"), 39 ("Spirit of Independence"), 45 ("poor miserable People"), 51 ("sanctify any Means"). Serle also copied this passage from the newspaper into his July 25 letter to Lord Dartmouth. See Ambrose Serle to the Earl of Dartmouth, New York, July 25, 1776, in [Benjamin Franklin Stevens], ed., *B. F. Stevens's Facsimiles of Manuscripts in European Archives Relating to America, 1773–1783; With Descriptions, Editorial Notes, Collations, References and Translations,* 25 vols. ([1889–1895]; rpt. Wilmington, Del., 1970), XXIV, no. 2040.

73. Serle to Dartmouth, New York Harbor, July 25, 1776, in [Stevens], ed., *Facsimiles,* XXIV, no. 2040, [4]–5.

74. July 13, 1776, in Tatum, ed., *American Journal of Ambrose Serle,* 31.

stronger Influence than the Newspapers of the respective Colonies. One is astonished to see with what Avidity they are sought after, and how implicitly they are believed, by the great Bulk of the People." Congress was well aware of the power of the press and had early on secured "this Advantage entirely to themselves, and of preventing all Publications, which might either expose or refute the Policy of their Measures." "A free Press, however teeming with heterogeneous Matters, would at least have retarded their great Design," Serle suggested. "Government may find it expedient, in the Sum of things, to employ this popular Engine; and it if be impossible to restrain the Publication of Falshood, it will be its Interest to give Power and Facility to the Circulation of Truth." By the time he wrote this penetrating letter to the American secretary of state, Serle had already convinced his superiors in New York to take such steps to reverse the patriots' "advantage."[75]

On September 16, Serle rambled around Manhattan in the evening, stopping in at Hugh Gaine's printing office on Hanover Square to buy some newspapers. Three days later, he again haunted printers' shops, this time nosing around Rivington's abandoned store to "look at some of his Books." A week later, he decided to stop being just a customer. He noted in his diary on September 26 that he took another walk in the city and afterward "called upon Govr. Tryon and Gaine the Printer, to settle the Publication of a News paper, which is to be accomplished on Monday next." Starting on September 30, under the cover of Hugh Gaine's name, Serle brought out his own version of the *New-York Gazette; and the Weekly Mercury,* even though the former proprietor had fled to Newark, New Jersey, and was then briefly publishing there. For the next six weeks, two different issues of the *Gazette* circulated around the battle lines: Gaine's Newark paper, published on Fridays, and Serle's paper, published out of Gaine's Hanover Square shop on Mondays. Serle published accounts of the "savage burning" of New York by "New England Incendiaries," a "villainous deed" that was a "lasting Monument of [the patriots'] inveterate malice." In Serle's hands, the Hessians "longed for nothing so much as to join their military Friends upon the field of Honor." From Newark, Gaine included patriot articles, publishing reports of "our people," fighting against the "King's troops" and New Jersey's recent act "to punish traitors and disaffected persons."[76]

75. Serle to Dartmouth, New York, Nov. 26, 1776, in [Stevens], ed., *Facsimiles,* XXIV, no. 2046.

76. Sept. 18, 26, 1776, in Tatum, ed., *American Journal of Ambrose Serle,* 110, 114 ("look at some of his Books"); *New-York Gazette,* Oct. 7, 28, 1776. Serle continued

"By the American Revolution You Are Now Free"

Perhaps Gaine meant the New Jersey act as ironic, for the morning before it appeared, he declared himself to be just such a person by returning to his Hanover Square shop to take over Serle's operation. Starting on November 11, Serle got his wish: a permanent, active royalist printer in New York City. Although his peers in the patriot press would excoriate Gaine for his apostasy for years to come, it was surely a relief to Serle that he did not have to continue supervising the production of a weekly paper. Now, he wrote two weeks later to Dartmouth, if the administration could only approve the "Expense of allowing Salaries (if needful) to some able Superintendents of the Press in different Colonies," the investment would pay great dividends, "considering the almost incredible Influence those fugitive Publications have upon the People." Something had to be done to neutralize the belief of the "poor simple Country People" in the "wicked and artful Stories [that] had been circulated among them to rouze their Fears and to induce them to take up Arms," he vented in his journal that November. A Gaine in every capital, Serle hoped, would bring the conflict to a quick end.[77]

Serle returned to his duties with Lord Howe but continued to manage the press by both watching over the political sections of Gaine's *Gazette* and contributing articles to it. In February 1777, he began conveying to Gaine a series of essays under the pseudonym "Integer." Gaine published Serle's Integer essays throughout the spring of 1777, whereby Howe's secretary took, as the subject of his scorn, a proclamation issued the previous December by the New York Assembly. Its author, John Jay, reiterated many points from the Declaration of Independence in an effort to rouse support during those critical hours, decrying that "the mercenaries of Germany [were] transported near four thousand miles, to plunder your houses, to ravish your wives and daughters, to strip your infant children, to expose whole families naked," and the crown "excite[d] the savages of the wilderness to murder our inhabitants." Over five weeks that spring, Serle set about dismantling the assembly's arguments with his own "ironical animadversions,"

Gaine's name on the masthead for the first few New York issues, removing it to say just "Printed at the Bible and Crown in Hanover Square," on Oct. 14, 1776. See Brigham, *History and Bibliography of American Newspapers,* I, 639–640.

77. Serle to Dartmouth, New York, Nov. 26, 1776, in [Stevens], ed., *Facsimiles,* XXIV, no. 2046. On November 1, 1776, Serle wrote, "Gaine, the Printer of the New York Gazette, escaped from Newark this Morning, and arrived in Town" (Tatum, ed., *American Journal of Ambrose Serle,* 134–135, Nov. 4, 1776, 136 ["wicked and artful Stories"]).

an effort that, he would later note, had been "particularly mortifying to the Rebels, who cannot stand Irony and Banter." Indeed, he reveled in the "great Spleen" both "Rebel News papers" and "the Author of the *Crisis*" directed at the *Gazette*. This "gives me some Proof" that Gaine's paper "has had a good Effect," he boasted in his diary. "My Labor and Superintendence of it have not been thrown away."[78]

But, as important as the politics of print were to Serle, his journal contained far more than just his efforts to make Americans doubt their newspapers. Almost immediately after disembarking on Staten Island, Serle chronicled encounters with people the patriots had spent a year lambasting as "domestic insurrectionists," "merciless savages," and "foreign mercenaries." Not only a document that underscores the centrality of print in the Revolution, Serle's journal reveals the ubiquity of the "proxies" in the everyday context of the Revolutionary War.

"A poor Black deserted to us early this Morning," Serle observed ten days after his arrival on Staten Island. "Three or four Whites had agreed to come off with him; but, staying beyond the Time agreed on, the poor Fellow ventured down alone." This New Yorker wanted no part of an independent America in July 1776. Several weeks later, Serle commented about the makeup of the army his employer had just defeated on Long Island. "Their army is the strangest that ever was collected: Old men of 60, Boys of 14, and Blacks of all ages, and ragged for the most part, compose the motley Crew, who are to give the Law to G. Britain and tyrannize over His Majesty's Subjects in America." Finally, in November, during one of Serle's walks around the city, he "fell in with a poor Negro Man, with whom I had a pleasing Con-

78. "An Address of the Convention of the Representatives of the State of New-York to Their Constituents," Fishkill, Dec. 23, 1776, 5 *Am. Archives*, III, 1382–1388, esp. 1384; Feb. 18, Mar. 4, Apr. 28, 1777, in Tatum, ed., *American Journal of Ambrose Serle*, 190 ("ironical animadversions"), 195 ("particularly mortifying"), 219 ("a good Effect"). See also Executive Committee to John Hancock, Philadelphia, Jan. 14, 1777, in *LDC*, VI, 95–96, Francis Lightfoot Lee to Landon Carter, Baltimore, Jan. 14, 1777, 100–101, William Whipple to John Langdon, Baltimore, Jan. 15, 1777, 111; Jan. 16, 1777, *JCC*, VII, 42. For Serle's comments as "Integer," see *New-York Gazette*, Mar. 3, 10, 24, 31, Apr. 7, 1777. For an example of Serle's continued involvement in the *Gazette*, see his Dec. 9, 1776, entry: "Very busy, all Day, in assorting intercepted Letters from Washington etc., and writing Remarks upon them praeparatory to their Publication" (156).

"By the American Revolution You Are Now Free"

versation." Serle confessed he "did not expect to find half his Sense or Sensibility in any of his Complexion. He was a [Christ]ian indeed!"[79]

Serle also had intimate contact, on several occasions, with Indians visiting the Howes' headquarters. Two days after reporting the lone desertion of a determined black man, Serle related the news, "an Indian informed one of our Scouts . . . that most of his People were ready and only waited for a Signal to join the King's Forces." On August 5, several leading British officials dined with Howe and his secretary, including Governor Tryon, Guy Johnson, and two Indian chiefs. Just as he had been pleasantly surprised by his talk with an African American on a Manhattan street, Serle was "much pleased with the Behavior and Conversation of the Indians, who both spoke English, and one of them, extremely well." That Indian was Joseph Brant. Serle was struck by Brant's "remarkably easy" demeanor and the "Air of Gravity" that made his "Discourse . . . the more engaging." Serle was only the latest to be impressed with the Mohawk chief. Brant and Johnson had just returned from England, where Londoners treated Brant as a celebrity. Copies of the July *London Magazine* probably had not reached New York before Howe's dinner, but if they had, Serle would have read James Boswell's description of Brant as "gentle" and "quiet" and lacking the "ferocious dignity of a savage leader"—certainly not how American writers would soon describe him. After another dinner conversation with Guy Johnson in November, Serle concluded that the Indians' "Character is certainly very complex, and in some respects very contradictory."[80]

Howe's secretary had similar things to say about the thousands of German mercenaries who supported the British army in New York. Mostly, he was less than charitable about the actions of the Hessians. After the Long Island rout, Serle was unable "to express the Devastations" those soldiers "have made upon the Houses and Country Seats of some of the Rebels." "Sad Complaints are made of the Hessians, who plunder all men, Friends

79. July 22, Sept. 2, Nov. 19, 1776, in Tatum, ed., *American Journal of Ambrose Serle*, 40 ("poor Black"), 88 ("army is the strangest"), 144 ("fell in with a poor Negro Man").

80. July 24, Aug. 5, Nov. 27, 1776, ibid., 44 ("waited for a Signal"), 55 ("much pleased"), 147 ("Character is certainly very complex"); James Boswell, "An Account of the Chief of the Mohack Indians, Who Lately Visited England (with an Exact Likeness)," *London Magazine* (1776), 339. See also Julie Flavell, *When London Was Capital of America* (New Haven, Conn., 2010), 183.

of Government as well as Foes, indiscriminately," he noted in September. And it was Serle who wrote, "The Dread, which the Rebels have of these Hessians, is inconceivable. They almost run away at their Name." At the same time, he allowed for more dimensions in regard to the Germans: "It was pleasing to hear the Hessians singing Psalms . . . with great Solemnity," while, "to our Shame," British soldiers and sailors spent their time "in Imprecations or Idleness."[81]

Serle's diary entries highlight the power of print at work in the Revolution. Serle and his opponents grasped the political consequences of the printed word in 1776. They understood that winning the war of words across as wide a readership as possible was as significant as victory on a battlefield. Both were trying to galvanize support for their side in this burgeoning conflict, either by exploiting or soothing the provincial jealousies that plagued the newly independent United States. The patriots still had a significant advantage in this part of the war, but the British—both in their targeting of major American cities and their emerging efforts to counter patriot representations—had cut into their capability to project those images. Serle, for one, recognized the gap between patriot representations and conversations with real people. Yet those print conventions were significant. The terms by which people became wartime representations in service of these military ends, however, would have more than just political importance. They would affect the lives of both the Indians and African Americans he sympathized with.

* * *

On October 15, as the Revolution in his quarter looked brightest, South Carolina Chief Justice William Henry Drayton gave a speech that pronounced, "Carolinians! Heretofore you were bound. By the American Revolution you are now free." Drayton was right: the Revolution did change the calculus of bondage and dependence in North America. Whether it made Carolinians or other Americans "free" was a complicated issue. Three hundred miles to the west, Dragging Canoe surely did not wish to be included in Drayton's pronouncement. He would deny that siding with the common cause could secure his way of life. But what about other Cherokees, or the Stockbridge, or the Ohio Indians who visited Congress to seek accommo-

81. Sept. 1, 17, Oct. 7, 1776, in Tatum, ed., *American Journal of Ambrose Serle*, 56–57 ("Hessians singing Psalms"), 86 ("Devastations"), 108 ("Sad Complaints"), 120 ("Dread").

dation with the patriots? They might have reluctantly backed such a notion. But they were given little choice. The sweeping statements made by Drayton and his colleagues refrained from subtlety or nuance that might have included friendly Indians. Instead, they were all lumped together as "merciless Indian savages." At the dinner table, Serle hardly found Joseph Brant a savage. At the printer's table, though, he, too, was not opposed to referring to his enemies' "savage barbarity."[82]

The hundreds of sickly runaway slaves who stood on the east side of Gwynn's Island in July hoping for deliverance did not see the patriot cause as a pathway to freedom. They rejected the Declaration of Independence, just as the groups of fugitives who had tried to flag down British cruisers from Sullivan's Island or individuals paddling to Staten Island wanted to get far away from the Revolution. But what about the "motley crew" in the ranks of the Continental army that Adams worried about and Serle laughed at—men like the free black sailors in Glover's Marblehead regiment, who twice saved the Revolution, first by ferrying their routed comrades off Long Island and then across the Delaware to victory at Trenton? They were no domestic insurrectionists, but they were represented as such in the patriot newspapers and congressional pronouncements Serle so despised.

Actually, they were not represented at all. The common cause argument made the British seem foreign by damning *their* actions as "savage," "brutal," or "monstrous." It was the king who was "totally unworthy." The behavior—the free will—of blacks, Indians, or German soldiers themselves was immaterial; patriots preferred to depict them using standard images of "slave," "savage," "mercenary." That portrayal left very little room for gradations or candid second thoughts like those found throughout Serle's diary. Patriot publicists did not say explicitly that blacks or Indians could not be proper patriots because of their race, but they did propagate dozens and dozens of stories of African Americans' and Indians' acting—or being acted upon—in ways that opposed Americans' republican conceptions of liberty and virtue. Actions on the ground and a lack of deep, preconceived antipathies helped the Hessians escape permanent ascription as the tyrant's proxies. But when those Revolutionary representations mixed with long-standing cultural prejudices about the inferiority of Indians and blacks, it poured American conceptions about who they were at the founding—and who they were not—into new, durable, national vessels.

82. "Judge [William Henry] Drayton's Charge to Grand Jury of Charleston," Oct. 15, 1776, 5 *Am. Archives,* II, 1047–1058, esp. 1047.

## CHAPTER 5

"It Is the Cause of Heaven against Hell"

TO THE CARLISLE COMMISSION, 1777–1778

"I take the Liberty to inclose you *The Impartial Chronicle,*" New Jersey governor William Livingston wrote to Washington on February 15, 1777. It was Livingston's turn to compose an enemies list, this one expanded for the new year. His enclosure to Washington was a mock newspaper, a satire "in ridicule of Gain's lying Gazetter" that Livingston hoped would give the commander "a little Diversion in a Leisure moment." He also sent a copy of *The Impartial Chronicle* to printer John Dunlap, who published it in his *Pennsylvania Packet* three days later.[1]

Taking up six entire columns of print in the *Packet,* the *Impartial Chronicle* focused on several "reports" from London sources divulging all the disparate forces the crown was considering recruiting for the next campaign. Livingston, playing on the narrative of the king's recruitment of proxy enemies, joked about the array of forces that George III welcomed from other European tyrants to help end his colonial troubles. The king of Denmark "has actually stipulated with his Majesty, to furnish him . . . with 4000 Laplanders, who are to be employed in winter," whereas "the Emperor of Persia, on the earnest solicitation of the Court of London, is to send next summer into America 3500 Korazan Archers"—and, because "the rebels avail themselves of woods and forests whenever they can," the crown had already recruited "7000 Ax-men, to cut down all the forests from Georgia to Ticon-

---

1. William Livingston to GW, Haddonfield, N.J., Feb. 15, 1777, *PGW: RW,* VIII, 344, published in *Pennsylvania Packet,* Feb. 18, 1777; *Continental Journal,* Mar. 13, 1777; *Freeman's Journal* (Portsmouth), Mar. 22, 1777; *Norwich Packet,* Mar. 24, 1777; *Massachusetts Spy,* Mar. 27, 1777. An annotated version of *The Impartial Chronicle,* [c. Feb. 15, 1777], is in Carl E. Prince et al., eds., *The Papers of William Livingston,* 5 vols. (Trenton, N.J., 1979–1988), I, 226–239, esp. 227.

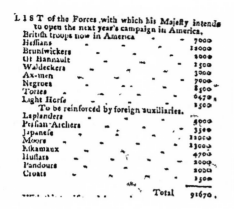

L I S T of the Forces with which his Majesty intends to open the next year's campaign in America.

British troops now in America . . . 7000
Hessians 13000
Brunswickers . . . 4000
Ut Hannault . . . 1500
Waldeckers . . . 3000
Ax-men . . . 7000
Negroes . . . 8500
Tories . . . 6470
Light Horse . . . 1500

To be reinforced by foreign auxiliaries.

Laplanders . . . 8000
Persian-Archers . . . 3500
Japanese . . . 12000
Moors . . . 13000
Mikamaux . . . 4700
Musfars . . . 2000
Pandours . . . 2000
Croats . . . 1500

Total 91670.

Figure 10. *"List of the Forces with which his Majesty intends to open the next year's campaign in America,"* part of New Jersey governor William Livingston's production The Impartial Chronicle. *From* Pennsylvania Packet, *February 18, 1777.*

deroga." "It is whispered at the court end of the town," another "item" from London informed,

> that the Emperor of Japan intends to lend his Majesty 12,000 of his most veteran troops, who . . . are to be landed on California; and after having desolated the western frontiers of the Continent, with the assistance of as many of the savages residing between the South Sea and the river Ohio as can be procured for that purpose, they are to form a junction with the British troops at New-York. The Emperor, it is said, is confident of being more successful in procuring those tribes of Indians to follow his standard Administration hath hitherto been on the part of Britain.

Livingston added that the ministry also intended "to employ 13,000 Moors from the coast of Barbara to act from Augustine as far north as New-Jersey; and 4700 Eskimaux from Hudson's Bay, to act from New-Hampshire to the most southern limits of the province of New-York." In case the reader missed all the previous paragraphs, at the end of all the "news," Livingston compiled a neat "List of the Forces with which his Majesty intends to open the next year's campaign in America." This list—reminiscent of the catalog John Adams assembled for Abigail the previous spring in response to her "remember the ladies" plea—blurred the line between real threats and fictional ones, with the crown enlisting thousands of Persian archers, Eskimos, and Laplanders to join British, Hessian, and Negro troops to quell the rebellion.

Livingston's inventory again underscores many of the themes the patriots had forwarded for nearly two years. The allegation that the Japanese emperor might succeed in convincing the Indians to be loyal to him and join forces with his 12,000 men because of their shared ancestry seems ridiculous. But Livingston's list struck a chord with American readers who had been able to compile real lists of proxy enemies since the outbreak of war. Readers of the satire, published in the *Pennsylvania Packet, Continental Journal, Freeman's Journal, Norwich Packet,* and *Massachusetts Spy,* could rest assured that all of *this* news was false, however. Of course, the *Impartial Chronicle* contained no reliable information: it came from the printing shop of "Hugo Lucre," a less-than-subtle reference to Hugh Gaine.[2]

Patriot leaders and publicists continued to write up lists of enemies. Although the magnitude of the danger posed by those opponents was in flux at that moment, Livingston's list illuminates how compelling such representations remained in early 1777. They believed these sentiments still had rhetorical—and political—power. It is an article of faith among historians of the American Revolution that public interest in the war effort flagged after independence, that Washington's Christmas raids might have been merely a fleeting morale boost. From what was once a towering height, the war's popularity fell in a slow, continual descent. But, though it is true that during the first seasons of the conflict "all kinds of military exercises, uniforms, and threats aimed at the British enjoyed a wide vogue among Americans," the so-called "rage militaire" was never an organic expression of natural patriotism. Passion to defend their rights and avenge bloodshed flowed freely for many Americans during 1775–1776, but patriot authorities did their best to guide that emotion into productive channels.[3]

One of the main reasons American patriotism began at such an artifi-

2. *Impartial Chronicle,* in Prince et al., eds., *Papers of William Livingston,* I, 227–229. Livingston's faux colophon was one of the sharpest parts of the satire. It read: "Printed and Sold by HUGO LUCRE, under the inspection and by permission of martial authority, in New-York, in Gasconading Square opposite to Rhodomontado Alley, at the sign of The Crown against the Bible, where all persons may be supplied with False Intelligence for hard money, and with Truth upon no terms whatsoever" (238). "Rhodomontado Alley" was a play on the word "rodomontade," which the *Oxford English Dictionary* defined as boastful or bragging language. So "Lucre's" shop was across from Braggart's Alley on Gasconading Square.

Washington wrote back to Livingston on February 22, thanking him for the "most poignant Satire, it afforded me real pleasure" and also commenting, "If *Lucre* has a spark of Modesty remaining, he must blush at being so vastly outdone in his *Ruling Passion*" (GW to Livingston, Feb. 22, 1777, *PGW: RW,* VIII, 414).

3. "Rage militaire": Charles Royster, *A Revolutionary People at War: The Continental Army and American Character, 1775–1783* (Chapel Hill, N.C., 1979), 25.

"It Is the Cause of Heaven against Hell"

cial height was because British officials in North America, lacking adequate means to make their writ run, turned to emergency measures to end the rebellion as cheaply and quickly as possible. From their perspective, those efforts—which included emancipation proclamations for slaves, the recruitment of trained foreign soldiers, and applications for Indian support across the backcountry—made sense. From the perspective of African Americans, Indians, or poor German men, these invitations, whether rumored or real, provided a unique opportunity to alter their future.

Colonists, though, were outraged that imperial officials would consider unleashing these forces on their families and property. Seen in this light, Dunmore, Carleton, Martin, Stuart, and their many collaborators provided patriot leaders with an expedient mechanism for stoking popular rage. All they had to do was broadcast those shocking plots, conspiracies, and schemes as widely as possible. This was the story of the war's first two years for thousands of people throughout the continent. With help from patriot publicists, the irregular start to the Revolutionary War, full more of rumors and half-truths about potential intrigue than actual battles, sustained the rage militaire. It was not a natural, spontaneous response but a managed phenomenon.

With the unloading of the invasion fleet on Staten Island in July 1776, the conflict entered a new phase. For the next few years—with the noteworthy exception of the northwestern frontier—the war would become an eighteenth-century competition between one professional army and another trying to become so. Although that conflict would take place throughout the countryside of the mid-Atlantic, the British focused on capturing American cities. British strategists embraced the port cities of America to anchor their land and sea forces. In hindsight, this policy would turn out to be misguided; British officers learned it did not matter that they held New York or Philadelphia or Charleston when they could not pacify the hinterland.[4]

But, starting in the fall of 1776, the ease with which British troops controlled many American cities did have a significant effect on patriot communication networks, a development that deeply enervated public morale. The British occupation of New York City, the North American hub of the Atlantic packet system, forced patriot printers to suspend operations for long periods, if not permanently. Those who had the financial security to relocate their presses often had to so do away from main post roads, moves that jeop-

4. Benjamin L. Carp, *Rebels Rising: Cities and the American Revolution* (New York, 2007), 214–216.

ardized their supplies of paper, ink, and news. This disruption, along with the short occupation of Philadelphia in 1777–1778 and the longer loss of Newport and Charleston, diminished the patriots' ability to get their narratives to continental audiences. Some British officials and prominent loyalists compounded that reduced capacity by following Ambrose Serle's lead and amplifying their own messages. Royalist printers trailed the British army and started their own papers in newly occupied cities to counteract the patriot argument. Beginning in 1777 and for the remainder of the war, the patriots lost their print monopoly.

This, too, had an effect on the rage militaire. The long decline in popular support for the Revolution was not wholly attributable to war weariness or a precocious American public giving up on its own war for independence. The stories that the patriots had relied on since Lexington to animate the public were not as domineering or unopposed in the coming years as they had been in 1775 and 1776. That is not to say that Livingston and his colleagues stopped telling those stories or that representations of blacks and, especially, Indians acting as the king's proxies lost their resonance among those who did hear them. Patriot publicists remained dedicated to maintaining this crucial part of the common cause narrative. Whenever hints emerged that British officials might again be "tampering" with slaves or "exciting" Indians, patriot publicists were sure to seize upon those stories and propagate them as widely as possible. They hoped that managing American outrage over the proxies would still be an effective technique to keep the cause alive—until outside help could be secured. Help, after all, was one of the chief purposes of both declaring independence and the Declaration of Independence. In the Declaration's final lines, Congress listed all the powers the new United States claimed, including contracting alliances and establishing commerce. If Congress could actually convince one of Britain's rivals to recognize those powers, the Revolution might be saved.

This chapter traces the eighteen months between the Trenton triumph and the almost simultaneous actions of ratifying the French alliance and rejecting the Carlisle Commission's potentially disastrous peace offerings in June 1778. It was only at that point, with allies assured and the gravest threat to the union—separate peace negotiations—spurned, that the common cause began to appear safe. Many macro and micro factors converged to get the patriots across that goal line in 1777 and 1778, including military skill on several battlefields, diplomatic triangulation by the French monarchy, and unwillingness on the part of British leaders to coordinate their strategy, not to mention individual agency, luck, and weather conditions.

"It Is the Cause of Heaven against Hell"

One vector that cannot be overlooked in holding the cause together, however, is the important role patriot publicists played in reminding Americans of the reasons they must continue to despise and resist the British and their assistants despite increasingly disrupted communications networks. The common cause reached a watershed in the summer of 1778 when the Carlisle commissioners, armed with an array of conciliatory proposals that could have spelled disaster for the patriots, left in defeat. That diplomatic achievement—perhaps the greatest test of unity—was as composed as the rage militaire. It was the product of strategy, to be sure, but also of stories.

1: "GIVING STRETCH": JOHN BURGOYNE AND JANE MCCREA

There was no consensus among patriot military and political leaders about where the Howes would open the 1777 campaign. In fact, there was confusion on all sides about how and where to proceed in the spring. The British government had not discussed strategy for the upcoming campaign as late as February, when the news of Trenton and Princeton reached London. Howe proposed moving north up the Hudson River—if the crown sent him reinforcements. Lord George Germain, the new American secretary of state, balked at the need to send more troops to Howe and began exploring an alternative plan proposed by General John Burgoyne.[5]

Burgoyne suggested a fresh incursion from Canada. He believed he could act independently of the force in New York; all he would need was a detachment, under the command of Lieutenant Colonel Barry St. Leger, to drive east from Fort Oswego down the Mohawk River and meet him in Albany, isolating New England. Burgoyne's bravado convinced the king. Soon, the general was en route across the Atlantic with a joint British and German force.[6]

For his part, Howe demurred, frustrating patriot leaders like John Adams, who wished he would march directly on Philadelphia. "Nothing would unite and determine Pensilvania so effectually" as a few houses afire, he wrote to Abigail. But Howe waited until June before he ordered his men back to their transport ships, sailed into the Chesapeake Bay, disembarked in Maryland, and drove toward Philadelphia from the south. After he had captured the

5. Ira D. Gruber, *The Howe Brothers and the American Revolution* (New York, 1972), 189.

6. Robert Middlekauff, *The Glorious Cause: The American Revolution, 1763–1789*, rev. ed. (1982; rpt. New York, 2005), 373–377; Piers Mackesy, *The War for America, 1775–1783* (Cambridge, Mass., 1964), 109–118; Gruber, *Howe Brothers*, 199–201.

city, he promised to send support toward the Hudson and Burgoyne. Howe was convinced Philadelphia was the key: taking the principal American city, dispersing the rebel leadership, and removing a significant portion of fertile farmland and trade, he believed, would rally loyalist support and render the patriots incapable of continuing the war. Meanwhile, Burgoyne and seven thousand British and German troops, with a covering body of Indians and loyalists, set off from Montreal.[7]

As he began what he believed would be a triumphant expedition guaranteeing his fame throughout the British Empire, Burgoyne issued a bombastic declaration addressed to the deluded inhabitants of New England. Nicknamed "Gentleman Johnny," Burgoyne fancied himself a poet and playwright as well as commander. His propensity for showmanship and theatricality had already made Burgoyne a favorite target of patriot publicists, who made fun of him as a dandified poet. In their hands, this proclamation would be his masterpiece. It called upon the multitudes "suffering" under patriot rule to declare their freedom from "the compleatest System of Tyranny that ever GOD, in his Displeasure suffered for a Time to be exercised over a froward and stubborn Generation." According to Burgoyne, the "Persecution and Torture" undertaken by patriot authorities "without Distinction of Age or Sex" was "unprecedented in the Inquisitions of the Romish Church," but he was there to accomplish the "glorious Task of redeeming [his] Countrymen from Dungeons." Yet, he cautioned, the "domestic, the industrious, the infirm, and even the timid" people within reach of his arms had better recognize their deliverer. If they did not abandon the "present unnatural Rebellion" or "remain quietly at their Houses," he would be forced to take drastic measures. "I have but to give Stretch to the Indian Forces under my Direction, and they amount to Thousands, to overtake the hardened Enemies of Great-Britain and America; I consider them the same wherever they may lurk." Once it got into patriot newspapers, this last statement would come back to haunt Gentleman Johnny.[8]

7. JA to Abigail Adams, Apr. 28, 1777, *LDC*, VI, 667; Christopher Ward, *The War of the Revolution*, ed. John Richard Alden (New York, 1952), I, 328–333; Gruber, *Howe Brothers*, 230–240.

8. Andrew Jackson O'Shaughnessy, *The Men Who Lost America: British Leadership, the American Revolution, and the Fate of the Empire* (New Haven, Conn., 2013), 123–164, esp. 124–125, 146; Burgoyne's Proclamation, in John Rhodehamel, ed., *The American Revolution: Writings from the War of Independence* (New York, 2001), 303–305. A few days after issuing his fateful proclamation, Burgoyne conveyed a somewhat different mes-

"It Is the Cause of Heaven against Hell"

There were many statements that raised eyebrows in Burgoyne's proclamation, easily one of the most notorious British publications of the Revolution. Certainly the phrase "but to give Stretch" was at the head of the list. But who were the "Thousands" of Indians over whom Burgoyne claimed dominion? They included Indians from all across Canada, including Abenakis, Ottawas, Algonquians, Oswegatchies, Nipissings, and Caughnawagas. Of even more concern to patriot leaders was the question of whether the Iroquois of upper New York would join the British invasion. Even as late as the previous summer, many in the Six Nations had underscored their desire to stay out of the conflict at a treaty conference at German Flats. Patriots knew, from the amount of attention they paid to treating with the Iroquois, that if these pledges of neutrality in the northern backcountry evaporated, it could prove disastrous to the cause.[9]

A subtle transformation had occurred in many Indian villages along the Canadian frontier. One of the main actors driving this change was the Mohawk chief who had so impressed James Boswell and Ambrose Serle: Joseph Brant.

In November 1776, Joseph Brant began his stealthy, arduous journey to Iroquoia. He had fought with distinction in the battle of Long Island

---

sage to a council of allied Indians. "You are free," he told them, to "go forth in might of your valour and your cause;—strike at the common enemies of Great-Britain and America." But he did not yet give full "stretch": "I positively forbid bloodshed, when you are not opposed in arms. Aged men, women, children, and prisoners must be held sacred from the knife or hatchet, even in actual conflict." This nuance disappeared as the expedition reached central New York in midsummer. See "Substance of the Speech of Lieutenant-General Burgoyne to the Indians, in Congress, at the Camp upon the River Bouquet, June 21, 1777; and Their Answer, Translated," in John Burgoyne, *A State of the Expedition from Canada, as Laid before the House of Commons . . .* , 2d ed. (1780; rpt. New York, 1969), appendix, xxi–xxiv, esp. xxii, xxiii.

9. Colin G. Calloway, *The American Revolution in Indian Country: Crisis and Diversity in Native American Communities* (Cambridge, 1995), 72; Robert S. Allen, *His Majesty's Indian Allies: British Indian Policy in the Defence of Canada, 1774–1815* (Toronto, 1992), 51–52; Paul Lawrence Stevens, "His Majesty's 'Savage Allies': British Policy and the Northern Indians during the Revolutionary War; the Carleton Years, 1774–1778" (Ph.D. diss., University at Buffalo, 1984), 1013–1016; "General Schuyler to the President of Congress," German Flats, Aug. 8, 1776, "General Schuyler's Congerence with the Indians of the Six Nations, 1776," German Flats, Aug. 8–10, 12–13, 1776, 5 *Am. Archives*, I, 856–857, 1035–1049; Barbara Graymont, *The Iroquois in the American Revolution* (Syracuse, N.Y., 1972), 107–108.

and was excited to tell as many Indians as possible about that victory and the others he expected would follow. Brant wanted the western Iroquois to break all promises of neutrality and enter the war for the king. At first, the traditionalist chiefs of the western tribes dismissed appeals from the likes of Brant, whose imperial connections were stronger than confederation ones. The Oneidas and Tuscaroras remained cold to him. By the spring of 1777, Brant had moved back southeast to the Susquehanna River near the Pennsylvania border to organize a small military unit. At that same moment, British Indian agent Guy Johnson boasted to Lord Germain that the Six Nations were "all determined, as they expressed it 'to Act as one Man.'" Whether or not Johnson was right, the patriots knew British success could tip the balance in this fluid situation. As Philip Schuyler, commander of the northern American army, put it, if the British captured Fort Ticonderoga, he believed "the Indians to a Man would join them."[10]

* * *

Burgoyne's forces approached that very place just as Johnson wrote and the United States cheered the anniversary of independence. Newspapers paid special attention to one particular performance in Philadelphia that first Fourth of July. "A Hessian band of music which were taken at Princeton performed very delightfully" for the assembled delegates of Congress. "The pleasure being not a little heightened by the reflection that they were hired by the British Court for purposes very different from those to which

10. Alan Taylor, *The Divided Ground: Indians, Settlers, and the Northern Borderland of the American Revolution* (New York, 2006), 89–90; Guy Johnson to Lord George Germain, New York, July 7, 1777, in E. B. O'Callaghan, ed., *Documents relative to the Colonial History of the State of New-York; Procured in Holland, England, and France* (Albany, N.Y., 1857), VIII, 713; Schuyler to GW, Albany, Mar. 25, 1777, *PGW: RW*, VIII, 632. For the patriots' attempt at counteracting Brant's efforts by welcoming Indians to visit them at Congress and holding another conference at Easton, Pennsylvania, see Pennsylvania Council of Safety to GW, Philadelphia, Jan. 16, 1777, *PGW: RW*, VIII, 86. For Washington's reply that he was "glad" they were coming and that "the proper steps will be taken to secure their interest," see GW to Pennsylvania Council of Safety, Morristown, N.J., Jan. 20, 1777, ibid., 118; Executive Committee to Hancock, Philadelphia, Jan. 17, 1777, *LDC*, VI, 117–118; see also Jan. 24, 1777, *JCC*, VII, 62–63; Col. John Bull to the Pennsylvania Council of Safety, Norriton and Easton, Jan. 26, 28, 31, 1777, in Samuel Hazard, ed., *Pennsylvania Archives Selected and Arranged from Original Documents in the Office of the Secretary of the Commonwealth . . .*, V, *Commending 1776*, 1st Ser. (Philadelphia, 1853), 201, 203, 208.

"It Is the Cause of Heaven against Hell"

they were applied," one delegate remarked. On the western shores of Lake Champlain, however, the besieged garrison of Ticonderoga was less merry. The fortress, built by the French in 1755, had been attacked, blown up, and rebuilt since the Seven Years' War. It had been securely in patriot hands since Ethan Allen and his Green Mountain Boys had surprised the commandant at the war's outset. "Tye," as some writers referred to it, was more than a strategically significant post; it held great symbolic import in the minds of many North Americans, whether former colonists or Indians. Losing it without much of a fight, in other words, would be a big deal.[11]

Although it would not preserve him from withering criticism and court-martial, there was little the fort's commander, General Arthur St. Clair, could do. He did not have enough men, ammunition, food, or clothing to hold out against Burgoyne's vastly superior force. Looking up at British cannon on the high ground and seeing an unwinnable battle, St. Clair chose to evacuate the night after America's first anniversary of independence.[12]

Because of what would eventually happen to Burgoyne and his army, Ticonderoga's easy capitulation was largely forgotten by the autumn and largely ignored ever after. But that July, many Americans paid great attention to the developments on Lake Champlain. In York, Maine, loyalist Jonathan Sayward documented in his journal that he heard "Ticonderoga is taken by the King's troops," but he had not read it in the newspapers because "no papers are printed or came abroad for political reasons." Sayward surmised that patriot publicists had censored this terrible news.[13]

Stephen Peabody, a Congregationalist minister in Atkinson, New Hamp-

11. Thomas Burke to Richard Caswell, Philadelphia, July 5, 1777, *LDC*, VII, 295–296. The performance by the Hessian band captured a great deal of attention in American newspapers. See *Pennsylvania Journal*, July 4, 1777; *Pennsylvania Packet*, July 8, 1777; *Pennsylvania Gazette*, July 9, 1777; *Dunlap's Maryland Gazette*, July 15, 1777; *Virginia Gazette* (Dixon & Hunter), July 18, 1777; *Virginia Gazette* (Purdie), July 18, 1777; *New-York Journal*, July 21, 1777; *Norwich Packet*, July 21, 1777; *Independent Chronicle*, July 24, 1777; *Freeman's Journal* (Portsmouth), Aug. 2, 1777; *Providence Gazette*, Aug. 2, 1777; *South-Carolina and American General Gazette*, Aug. 7, 1777. Several months later, Philadelphia merchant and diarist Christopher Marshall noted that the band played in Lancaster nightly, earning "Fifteen Pounds for each night's attendance" (Mar. 6, 1778, in William Duane, ed., *Extracts from the Diary of Christopher Marshall, 1774–1781* [1877; rpt. New York, 1969], 170).

12. Ward, *War of the Revolution*, I, 408.

13. June 12, 1777, in Jonathan Sayward Diaries, 1760–1799, XVIII, 418, MSS, octavo vols., S, AAS.

shire (just over the border from Haverhill, Massachusetts), was forty miles away from Sayward geographically and 180 degrees politically. Peabody's diary testifies to the "indignation and astonishment" patriots experienced after hearing of Ticonderoga's fall. It illustrates the vicarious, personal relationship Americans had with the events of war via their newspapers. Moreover, it offers another glimpse of patriot communication webs, providing a different snapshot of the engagement between urban print shops and hinterland customers thirsty for news. The Bradfords' subscription book, interrogated above, exemplifies how men like Peter Withington and William Carheart, distributors of the *Pennsylvania Journal,* were essential to making "the cause" common. Peabody's diary offers more proof of the vitality of those webs, depicting the schemes consumers devised to remain connected to the news of war, now in its third summer. The rage militaire might have been over, but the desire for information was undiminished, at least for this thirty-six-year-old New Hampshire minister. On July 1, 1777, he noted, "Hear that Ticonderoga is befell." For the next two months, in what is among the best sources of reader response during the Revolutionary War, Peabody dedicated many pages of his diary to documenting news of the fort's evacuation, the aftermath of that disaster, and Burgoyne's progress in New York.[14]

"Benjamin Little called here tonight and brought the paper," Peabody wrote ten days later, "and an account that our Forts at the Lake are all given up." The next day, Saturday, a militia colonel "sent me letters from the Army and a newspaper." Although he read about Howe's movement to Staten Island in that paper, Peabody could rely on no other intelligence concerning Ticonderoga. By the next Wednesday, informed either by another print account or someone in the community, he confessed, "All the bad news we have heard is true. . . . I am amazed and astonished." Corroboration of the worst, however, did not satisfy Peabody's desire for more information. Two days later, he "expected Mr. Dole to have gone to Haverhill and got the paper, but he did not come so I sent Oliver up to know the reason of his not coming, and whether he intends to go." Since it was Peabody's "turn to get the Papers," he needed someone to ride down to collect the weekly print. The next day, a neighbor sent the newspapers up to Atkinson, but "like a blockhead carry'd them by." On Sunday, his cousin Colonel Nathaniel Peabody called, bringing another newspaper that Stephen perused. "I read

14. July 1, 1777, in Stephen Peabody Diaries, 1767–1814, MSS, misc. boxes, P, AAS.

"It Is the Cause of Heaven against Hell"

Gill's paper but there is nihil new there," he remarked on Tuesday, July 22. Late in the afternoon on Friday, "the post came in and brought the papers. I looked into them there a little and find nihil very particular only in it pretty full of severe Queries about how that Fort came to be given up and the General officers are much alarmed. I read the papers and sent them to their owners."[15]

Every weekend in August, Peabody continued to describe his quest to get the newspapers, or dispatch someone down to Haverhill to collect them, or wonder anxiously where his were. In eighteenth-century parlance, he was a *quidnunc,* an obsessive pursuer of news, especially about Ticonderoga. As surely lots of other Americans did, Peabody followed Burgoyne's progress as closely as he could more than 150 miles away. Often the reverend related his frustration that there was "very little news" in those papers, but whether he meant there was nothing in them or nothing *good* in them is not known. Indeed, during those summer months, there was little positive news for patriot readers like Stephen Peabody. Perhaps Sayward's accusation that patriot publicists were censoring bad news was not off-base, after all.[16]

Peabody's frustration was understandable. Nor was he was the only one. Accounts varied wildly about the state of American troops at Ticonderoga. Some reports from "officers of distinction" offered rosy pictures of men well supplied and in good spirits. When this projection of military strength proved wrong, some patriots hurried to send printers essays under the

15. July 11, 12, 16, 18, 19, 22, 25, 1777, ibid. The "queries" Peabody mentions are probably the list of questions first printed in Benjamin Edes's *Boston Gazette* on July 21, 1777. Since those questions would not be exchanged in the *Freeman's Journal* in nearby Portsmouth, New Hampshire, until the following day, this means, first, that Peabody was more connected with Boston papers than those closer by, and second, that he was reading more than one, having noted earlier that week he had read John Gill's *Continental Journal.* See *Boston Gazette,* July 21, 1777. He was hardly the only one paying attention to Burgoyne's invasion. Dr. Samuel Adams, a physician from Dorchester, Massachusetts, also noted in his diary on July 12, "Read, wrote, and heard news of our Army's retreat from Ticonderoga" (diary, Samuel Adams Papers, 1758–1819, MSS, NYPL).

16. Peabody's engagement with newspapers appears in the following entries: Aug. 2, 3, 8, 15, 22, 30, 1777 (Stephen Peabody Diaries, MSS, misc. boxes, P). For an explanation of the term and usage of "quidnunc," see Uriel Heyd, *Reading Newspapers: Press and Public in Eighteenth-Century Britain and America* (Oxford, 2012), 94–98, 195–230.

names "Probus" or "Marcus Brutus," pleading for unity and demanding to know why they had been so misled. An item addressed to Ebenezer Watson, publisher of the *Connecticut Courant,* stated Ticonderoga's fall "was entirely unexpected" and "a subject of general surprise and astonishment." "The public are impatient to know the reasons" why the fort was abandoned and "are amazed, that in the latest accounts from Ticonderoga . . . there were no intimations of the weakness of the garrison, or that speedy reinforcements were necessary to maintain it." "Justus" in the Philadelphia and Boston papers summed up the nervous atmosphere: "The mind of the public, at this time, is like that of a man slumbering under the oppression of an uneasy dream; they feel something wrong, without directly knowing what it is, or where it lies."[17]

As for the army's response to the loss, patriot military officers—whose printed letters were really the public's source of this wrong news—scapegoated unfit men in their units. Schuyler, St. Clair's commanding officer and the man still in charge of the northern army, told Congress he had too many "Boys, Negroes and aged Men" to fight the British effectively. Samuel Adams lambasted this excuse but still queried Continental army recruiting officer William Heath about its veracity. Heath responded with the same, standard line he had used in previous years when questioned about unfit soldiers: it was "more than probabl that there were some men advanced in life, and some Lads, and a number of Negroes (the latter were generally able Bodied but for my own I must confess I am never pleased to see them mix'd with white men)." Though this exchange remained out of the public view, it came at the same time as other letters traveled from Boston to Philadelphia about a bill then before the Massachusetts Assembly—spurred to action by an African American freedom petition—to end slavery in the commonwealth, a measure that that body postponed in order to consult the Continental Congress. James Warren worried in a June 22 letter to John Adams, "If passed into An Act it should have A Bad Effect

17. "Officers of distinction": *Continental Journal,* July 24, 1777; *Boston Gazette,* July 28, 1777. "Probus": *Continental Journal,* Aug. 7, 1777. "Marcus Brutus": *Independent Chronicle,* July 17, 24, 1777. *Freeman's Journal* (Portsmouth) featured both articles on the front and back pages of the July 26, 1777, issue. "No intimations of the weakness": *Connecticut Courant,* Aug. 4, 1777; *Connecticut Journal,* Aug. 6, 1777. "A Card": *Pennsylvania Evening Post,* July 24, 1777; *Boston Gazette,* Aug. 18, 1777; *Continental Journal,* Aug. 21, 1777.

"It Is the Cause of Heaven against Hell"

on the Union of the Colonies." Adams agreed. The day after St. Clair abandoned Ticonderoga, John wrote, "The Bill for freeing the Negroes, I hope will sleep for a Time. We have Causes enough of Jealousy, Discord and Division, and this Bill will certainly add to the Number." Given the alarm that would grip Massachusetts as soon as word spread of "Tye's" fall, these Massachusetts patriots were not anxious to push for emancipation. Heath's confession of repugnance in seeing African Americans serving in the ranks next to white men further explains their hesitation. They understood the ramifications of such an act for the common cause and were more than willing to table it indefinitely. For enslaved African Americans in Massachusetts, however, this wartime choice of unity over principles would affect their lives for several years, long after the threat from Burgoyne's army had dissipated.[18]

Public condemnation for Ticonderoga's fall, meanwhile, fell upon St. Clair. The unfortunate general now found himself besieged by patriot printers rather than British cannon. Few of the newspapers delivered to Reverend Peabody's house—or the ones he borrowed, or the ones that passed by on their way to other New England customers—were kind to the forty-year-old Scottish general that season. Fighting back, St. Clair lectured one of his sharpest critics, *Boston Gazette* publisher Benjamin Edes: "Liberty of the press is a priviledge that a free people . . . ought to guard with the most watchful jealousy." He explained, "There are many substantial reasons why the affairs of Ticonderoga are not, at present, proper materials for a newspaper." St. Clair warned Edes and the Boston printers to be careful not to diminish the republican "virtue without which Liberty cannot long subsist" by "stabbing in the dark." This was the most significant gap yet between patriot political or military leaders and publicists. Never before had there been such an open display of internal dissent among patriot ranks, a development in which Jonathan Sayward and other loyalists surely reveled. Naturally, both royalist newspapers exchanged St. Clair's upbraiding of the Boston printers.[19]

18. Samuel Adams to Roger Sherman, Philadelphia, Aug. 11, 1777, *LDC*, VII, 452, Samuel Adams to William Heath, Philadelphia, Aug. 13, 1777, 473–474, JA to James Warren, Philadelphia, July 7, 1777, 308; Heath to Samuel Adams, Aug. 27, 1777, in Samuel Adams Papers, MSS, NYPL; Warren to JA, Boston, June 22, 1777, *PJA*, V, 229–232, esp. 231; Benjamin Quarles, *The Negro in the American Revolution* (Chapel Hill, N.C., 1961), 47.

19. Arthur St. Clair to Benjamin Edes, Camp at Stillwater, N.Y., Aug. 6, 1777,

Despite this damaging public quarrel, St. Clair at least acted honorably by refusing to pass blame onto his superior, Philip Schuyler. He decided to broadcast his absolution of Schuyler. With his reputation in tatters in the Boston papers, he was quite attuned to the power of print in the Revolution and used that avenue to back Schuyler. St. Clair arranged for New York patriot John Jay to defend him in John Holt's *New-York Journal.* Jay, too, was very concerned that the public was panicking and lashing out at patriot officers in part because people were not getting enough information. "We could wish that your Letters might contain Paragraphs for the Public," Jay wrote to fellow patriot Gouverneur Morris on July 21, just as the New England papers bristled with demands for inquiries. "The People suspect the worst because we say Nothing. Their Curiosity must be constantly gratified, or they will be uneasy." Jay imagined thousands of Reverend Peabodys clamoring for any news about Burgoyne's invasion and, just the same, lots of critics like Sayward mistrusting patriot accounts. Patriot leaders knew they had to battle accusations of deception as much as British arms. The Revolution had deepened the public's reliance on print, a commodity that was becoming harder to come by as the British continued to strike against cities and disperse printers. Jay's publisher of choice, John Holt, had only revived the *New-York Journal* the day after St. Clair ordered Ticonderoga evacuated.[20]

It is no small wonder that just two days before Jay wrote this revealing letter, in the middle of all the uproar, Washington asked Congress to purchase "A small travelling Press to follow Head Quarters." Washington believed this to be an indispensable weapon of war.

It would enable us to give speedy and exact information of any Military transactions that take place *with proper comments upon them;* and thereby frustrate the pernicious tendency of falshood and misrepresentation,

---

in Arthur St. Clair Papers, MSS, 356, Ohio Historical Society, Columbus, in *Boston Gazette,* Aug. 25, 1777; *Independent Chronicle,* Aug. 29, 1777. Loyalist reports: *Newport Gazette,* Aug. 21, 1777; *New-York Gazette,* Sept. 1, 1777.

20. Arthur St. Clair to John Jay, Moses Creek, July 25, 1777, in Richard B. Morris, ed., *John Jay,* I, *The Making of a Revolutionary: Unpublished Papers, 1745–1780* (New York, 1975), I, 429, John Jay to Gouverneur Morris, Kingston, July 21, 1777, I, 423, and see also Jay's letter to Schuyler, Kingston, July 26–28, 1777, I, 429–430; *New-York Journal,* July 28, 1777; *Connecticut Journal,* Aug. 6, 1777; *Continental Journal,* Aug. 7, 1777; *Boston Gazette,* Aug. 11, 1777; *Providence Gazette,* Aug. 16, 1777. "Marcus Brutus" continued the dispute by rebutting St. Clair's accusations in *Independent Chronicle,* Aug. 29, 1777.

"It Is the Cause of Heaven against Hell"

which, in my opinion of whatever complexion they may be, are in the main detrimental to our cause. If the People had a channel of intelligence, that from its usual authenticity they could look up to with confidence, they might often be preserved from that despondency, which they are apt to fall into from the exaggerated pictures our Enemies and their Emissaries among us commonly draw of any misfortunes we meet with, and from that diffidence of truths favorable to us which they must naturally feel from the frequent deception they are exposed to, by the extravagant colourings our friends often give to our successes. . . . An ingenious Man to accompany this Press and be employed wholly in writing for it might render it singularly beneficial.

Jay, Washington, and many of their colleagues understood the power the press had in this conflict. They knew that political leaders and publicists had to stay unified as well; public print feuds could be very dangerous. Worse, British measures to broadcast their own stories were becoming an increasing concern by the middle of 1777. Congress agreed that being able to shape public opinion—to not only provide "exact" information but have the ability to make "proper comments"—was indeed "singularly beneficial." On August 5, they resolved that a "travelling Press . . . appears to be necessary" and ordered the quartermaster general to contract a printer complete with "Types, and other Implements for Printing, and with a suitable Number of Journeymen" to accompany the main Continental Army." It would take more than a year to organize, but the fruit of this order would be setting up former army officer Shepard Kollock with a press in a shop in Chatham, just six miles down the road from Washington's headquarters in Morristown. Soon the *New-Jersey Journal,* sponsored by the Continental army and the New Jersey state legislature, would pour the right information into the nearby American camp.[21]

Patriot military and political leaders across the mid-Atlantic reached similar conclusions about two interrelated necessities—the need to reinforce unity and the need for a tightened grasp on the press—late in the summer of 1777, after the fall of Ticonderoga and just days before a young woman named Jane McCrea would meet an unfortunate end outside Fort Edward, New York. Her death could not have been better arranged; the story of

21. GW to Continental Congress Committee to Inquire into the State of the Army, Camp at the Clove, July 19, 1777, *PGW: RW,* X, 332–338, esp. 335 (emphasis added); Aug. 5, 1777, *JCC,* VIII, 609, 613.

Jane's murder engendered the most extensive and most orchestrated campaign the patriots had yet undertaken to propagate the common cause by damning the king's proxies.

* * *

Jane McCrea, an orphaned daughter of a Presbyterian minister, was living with her brother John near Fort Edward, an outpost built during the Seven Years' War near present-day Glens Falls. In her early twenties, and reputedly a great beauty with a striking head of hair, McCrea was engaged to David Jones, a loyalist officer assisting Burgoyne's pursuing army, which was rapidly approaching the Hudson. On July 26, a small number of Indians intercepted McCrea as she left her house and killed her. According to one British officer, the "melancholy catastrophe of the unfortunate Miss McCrea . . . affected the general and the whole army with the sincerest regret and concern for her untimely fate." Their opponents would respond to the news of her murder with different emotions.[22]

That McCrea was dead was the only fact that anyone could agree on in subsequent weeks, months, and years. Countless historical investigations, pieces of art, romantic tales, and poems would debate the details about who actually killed her, where the murder took place, how she was killed, whether she was actually dispatched in her wedding gown, and what the effects and meanings of her death were. But this last question—what the death of this single young woman meant to the Revolution—was too important to wait for posterity's judgment. Seeing an enormous opportunity to denigrate their enemies and bolster American spirits at a critical moment in a critical campaign, patriot publicists moved quickly to broadcast the story as widely as possible.[23]

22. "William Digby: Journal, July 24–October 13, 1777," in Rhodehamel, ed., *American Revolution: Writings from the War of Independence*, 306. The facts of what actually happened to McCrea have become so muddied that they cannot be reconstructed with any certitude. The color of McCrea's hair is just one example of the confusion. According to one scholar in the early twentieth century, "Here the conscientious historian pauses appalled, for we find that hair called all the shades there are, from raven black down through the browns, the auburns, the reds, and the blondes" (James Austin Holden, "Influence of Death of Jane McCrea on Burgoyne Campaign," New York State Historical Association, *Proceedings*, XII [New York, 1913], 249–310, esp. 260).

23. For an impressive fifteen-page bibliography that lists all the retellings of the

"It Is the Cause of Heaven against Hell"

Word spread about McCrea's death rapidly. The story first rippled through the camp at Fort Edward. One Massachusetts officer from Reverend Peabody's hometown noted in his journal, "A woman was taken out of the cellar and carried off by the Enemy about a mile and barbarously treated then killed and skulped." A letter, written on the very day she was killed, appeared in print the following week and from there dashed across the American mainland. The Indians "took a young woman, Janey M'Crea by name, out of a house at Fort Edward, carried her about half a mile into the bushes, and there killed and scalped her in cold blood," this first article reported. A host of other articles from nearby correspondents would also appear throughout patriot newspapers, condemning the Indians and their British sponsors. One account conflated the two: "This brutal scene was transacted by four Indians, under cover of three hundred British regulars, drawn up at a small distance." Another letter borrowed from the Declaration: "The barbarous savages, having received full liberty from the more barbarous Britain, to murder and scalp all before them, without regard to age or sex." According to this correspondent, McCrea's death was just the beginning. "Three little girls a few days ago, picking berries; two were killed and scalped, the other wounded and made her escape," asserted this letter from a gentleman in Albany. Still more letters appeared, relating that women "who choose to remain behind the army and enjoy Burgoyne's proffered protection" were nonetheless "scalped and mangled in a shocking manner."[24]

Jane McCrea story in the eighteenth and nineteenth centuries alone, see Holden, "Influence of Death of McCrea," NYSHA, *Proceedings,* XII (1913), 295–309.

24. July 27, 1777, Benjamin Farnum diary, MSS, S–394, Massachusetts Historical Society, Boston. "Janey M'Crea": *New York Packet,* July 31, 1777; *New-York Journal,* Aug. 4, 1777; *Pennsylvania Packet,* Aug. 5, 1777; *Pennsylvania Evening Post,* Aug. 5, 1777; *Pennsylvania Gazette,* Aug. 6, 1777; *Pennsylvania Journal,* Aug. 6, 1777; *Connecticut Journal,* Aug. 6, 1777; *Independent Chronicle,* Aug. 7, 1777; *Connecticut Gazette,* Aug. 8, 1777; *Providence Gazette,* Aug. 9, 1777; *Boston Gazette,* Aug. 11, 1777; *Norwich Packet,* Aug. 11, 1777; *Dunlap's Maryland Gazette,* Aug. 12, 1777; *Virginia Gazette* (Purdie), Aug. 13, 1777; *Maryland Gazette,* Aug. 14, 1777; *Virginia Gazette* (Dixon & Hunter), Aug. 22, 1777; *North-Carolina Gazette,* Sept. 5, 1777; *South-Carolina and American General Gazette,* Sept. 11, 1777. Hugh Gaine published this first notice on Aug. 11, 1777, but there was no further commentary (except Burgoyne's proclamation, which he had a different view about than the patriots) in his *New-York Gazette.*

Printers ran multiple reports of Indian aggression that mentioned McCrea. Often

The *Connecticut Courant* received a letter from an "officer of distinction" in the Continental army at Peekskill, who passionately called on the American people to rise up against such an unnatural enemy: "Hear, Oh Heavens! And give ear, Oh America! and be aroused as a strong lion at the infernal ferocity of our enemies, who, devil like, delight in the most barbarous acts of cruelty, sport themselves in inflicting the most excruciating miseries on their fellow-creatures, and have an insatiable thirst for human blood, without discrimination for friend or foe."[25]

When Burgoyne actually took steps to restrain his Indian allies, John Holt had his doubts, printing this sarcastic screed in his *New-York Journal:*

> We are credibly informed that *Burgoyne,* the chief and director of the King of Great-Britain's band of thieves, robbers, cut-throats, scalpers, and murderers of every denomination, now infesting the northern and western frontiers, of several of the United States, has not only discontinued the reward he had offered given to the Savage *Tories, Indians, Britons, Hessians, Brunswickers, Waldeckers,* and other profligate scum of the human race, now in his service, for the scalps they

these reports appeared in different newspapers than the above article, which added to the story's coverage. See an August 4 letter from Albany in *New York Packet,* Aug. 7, 1777; *Pennsylvania Packet,* Aug. 12, 1777; *Connecticut Journal,* Aug. 13, 1777; *Pennsylvania Journal,* Aug. 13, 1777; *Continental Journal,* Aug. 14, 1777; *Massachusetts Spy,* Aug. 14, 1777; *Maryland Journal,* Aug. 19, 1777; *Maryland Gazette,* Aug. 21, 1777; *South Carolina and American General Gazette,* Sept. 25, 1777. Also, a letter from Saratoga dated Aug. 1–2 appeared in *Independent Chronicle,* Aug. 14, 1777; *Continental Journal,* Aug. 14, 1777; *Freeman's Journal* (Portsmouth), Aug. 16, 1777. A third letter, "Extract of a Letter from a Gentleman at Head-Quarters, Moses Creek, Dated July 28," also mentioning McCrea, appeared in *Continental Journal,* Aug. 7, 1777; *Boston Gazette,* Aug. 11, 1777; *Connecticut Journal,* Aug. 13, 1777; *Connecticut Gazette,* Aug. 15, 1777; *Providence Gazette,* Aug. 16, 1777. "This brutal scene": *Pennsylvania Evening Post,* Aug. 12, 1777; *Pennsylvania Gazette,* Aug. 13, 1777; *Maryland Journal,* Aug. 19, 1777; *Dunlap's Maryland Gazette,* Aug. 19, 1777; *Maryland Gazette,* Aug. 21, 1777; *Virginia Gazette* (Dixon & Hunter), Aug. 29, 1777; *Norwich Packet,* Sept. 1, 1777. "Picking berries": *Independent Chronicle,* Aug. 14, 1777; *Freeman's Journal* (Portsmouth), Aug. 16, 1777; *Connecticut Gazette,* Aug. 22, 1777, *New-York Gazette,* Sept. 1, 1777. "Scalped and mangled": *Boston Gazette,* Aug. 11, 1777; *Connecticut Journal,* Aug. 13, 1777; *Massachusetts Spy,* Aug. 14, 1777; *Connecticut Gazette,* Aug. 15, 1777.

25. *Connecticut Courant,* Aug. 11, 1777. This also was reprinted in *Independent Chronicle,* Aug. 14, 1777; *Freeman's Journal* (Portsmouth), Aug. 16, 1777; and *Pennsylvania Journal,* Aug. 20, 1777.

"It Is the Cause of Heaven against Hell"

brought him from the murdered, and half murdered inhabitants, but has also strictly prohibited, for the future, under a severe penalty, the practice of *scalping*.

Ten other printers endorsed Holt's venomous outburst and exchanged it in their own papers.[26]

As the murder of McCrea and other innocent young women became the central story of North America, newspapers supplemented the reports from Fort Edward with documentation of Burgoyne's cruelty, especially his "pompous Proclamation," as John Dunlap called it. The patriot leadership had procured a copy of Burgoyne's proclamation as early as July 9, but now, with such plain evidence of what he meant by "give stretch to the Indians," printers published it with zeal.[27]

Soon enough, parodies of the "pompous Proclamation" appeared. With Benjamin Franklin abroad, New Jersey governor William Livingston was putting himself forward as America's chief satirist in 1777. Writing under the pseudonym "A New-Jersey Man," Livingston published a lengthy poem that culminated with the following lines:

26. "We are credibly informed": *New-York Journal*, Sept. 1, 1777; *New York Packet*, Sept. 4, 1777; *Connecticut Courant*, Sept. 8, 1777; *Pennsylvania Evening Post*, Sept. 9, 1777; *Pennsylvania Gazette*, Sept. 10, 1777; *Independent Chronicle*, Sept. 11, 1777; *Massachusetts Spy*, Sept. 11, 1777; *Continental Journal*, Sept. 11, 1777; *Providence Gazette*, Sept. 13, 1777; *Boston Gazette*, Sept. 15, 1777; *Virginia Gazette* (Purdie), Sept. 26, 1777.

27. Schuyler sent a copy to GW in his July 9, 1777, report. See Schuyler to GW, Fort Edward, N.Y., July 9, 1777, *PGW: RW*, X, 234. Burgoyne's proclamation: *Providence Gazette*, Aug. 16, 1777; *New-York Gazette*, Aug. 18, 1777; *Pennsylvania Evening Post*, Aug. 21, 1777; *Maryland Journal*, Aug. 26, 1777; *Pennsylvania Packet*, Aug. 26, 1777; *Pennsylvania Gazette*, Aug. 27, 1777; *New-York Journal*, Sept. 1, 1777; *Maryland Gazette*, Sept. 4, 1777; *Continental Journal*, Sept. 11, 1777; *Connecticut Gazette*, Sept. 12, 1777; *Norwich Packet*, Sept. 15, 1777; *Freeman's Journal* (Portsmouth), Sept. 20, 1777. The *Gazette, of the State of South-Carolina* printed an annotated version of the proclamation, instructing its readers where to look for lies and translating its most officious parts into language the Revolutionaries could properly revile (see Sept. 23, 1777). In his first issue of his *New-Jersey Gazette* (Dec. 5, 1777), Isaac Collins opened his publication with Burgoyne's July 21 proclamation and the articles of capitulation at Saratoga. For an angry response to the proclamation that threatened the life of the "sublime Lieutenant-General," see *Pennsylvania Packet*, Aug. 26, 1777; *Dunlap's Maryland Gazette*, Sept. 2, 1777; *Connecticut Gazette*, Sept. 12, 1777; *Connecticut Courant*, Sept. 15, 1777; *Massachusetts Spy*, Sept. 18, 1777; *South Carolina and American General Gazette*, Oct. 2, 1777.

I will let loose the dogs of Hell,
Ten thousand Indians, who shall yell,
And foam and tear, and grin and roar,
And drench their maukesins in gore;
To these I'll give full scope and play,
From *Ticonderoga* to *Florida;*
They'll scalp your heads, and kick your shins,
And rip your guts, and flea your skins,
And of your ears be nimble croppers,
And make your thumbs, tobacco-stoppers.

"I swear by George and by St. Paul," Livingston ended the 171-line poem, "I will exterminate you all." This is an almost perfect encapsulation of the wartime common cause argument: a patriot political leader using a pseudonym to craft an image of British agents sponsoring Indian proxies to commit murder, which would then be exchanged in newspapers from Pennsylvania to Massachusetts. It was pieces like these that furthered the exclusionary nature of the cause in the war's third year.[28]

With Livingston setting aside his work as governor to pen these representations, it is hardly a surprise that the chief military commander opposing Burgoyne on the field would do the same. The most important article to appear in the wake of the McCrea incident, however, was the one that was most often reprinted.

28. See also "Parody on Burgoyne's Proclamation," Aug. 26, 1777, in Prince et al., eds., *Papers of William Livingston,* II, 41–47. Livingston's parody appeared in the *Pennsylvania Packet,* Aug. 26, 1777; *New-York Journal,* Sept. 8, 1777; *Norwich Packet,* Sept. 15, 1777; *Independent Chronicle,* Sept. 18, 1777. Given that McCrea's fate seemed an embodiment of Burgoyne's threat to "give Stretch," many interpreted his proclamation through that lens. "Burgoyne's manifesto," one patriot soldier wrote in his diary, "excites universal indignation and contempt. . . . It was not long indeed before some innocent persons were made victims of savage barbarity, by means of the tomahawk and scalping knife, in the hands of the barbarians under his command." "Among the first of these victims was Miss Jenny McCrea," he went on, "who was murdered in a manner extremely shocking to the feelings of humanity" (Sept. 2, 1777, in James Thacher, *A Military Journal during the American Revolutionary War, from 1775 to 1783 . . . ,* 2d ed. [1823; Boston, 1827], 95). When Ethan Allen published his captivity narrative in 1779, he would include the entire proclamation "as a specimen of their arrogancy" (Allen, *A Narrative of Colonel Ethan Allen's Captivity: Containting His Voyages and Travels* [1779; rpt. Mineola, N.Y., 2013], 112–116, esp. 112).

No matter how much John Jay or Arthur St. Clair tried to save him, Ticonderoga's capitulation brought down Philip Schuyler. On August 4, after Schuyler had retreated one too many times, Horatio Gates replaced him as commander of the northern army. Gates would soon be forever linked with John Burgoyne as his conqueror at Saratoga, but a few weeks before that battle, the two exchanged letters on the topic of Indian incitement. Gates condemned Burgoyne for hiring "the Savages of America to scalp Europeans, and the descendents of Europeans," an act that would not "be believed in Europe, until authenticated facts shall, in every Gazette, convince mankind of the truth of the horrid tale." To back up his charge, Gates threw McCrea in Burgoyne's face: "Miss McCrea, a young lady lovely to the sight, of virtuous character, and amiable disposition, engaged to be married to an officer in your army, was . . . taken out of a house . . . carried into the woods, and there scalped and mangled in the most shocking manner." McCrea's "miserable fate," he added, "was particularly aggravated by her being dressed to receive her promised husband, but met her murderer, employed by you."[29]

Gates's public, official, signed accusations elevated the McCrea story to a new level. Not hiding behind conventions or pseudonyms, commanding generals were now openly fighting a war of words over McCrea and her Indian assailants. Gates's sentimental depiction of the murdered bride ironically made Jane a martyr for the Revolution; although a tory, she, too, was a victim of the ruthless British and their savage allies. No one was safe from America's enemies. Gates's interpretation offered American readers a powerful illustration of the differences between heroic, humane Americans and their barbarous foes. Although Burgoyne vigorously denied the charge, sympathetic printers by the droves recognized the power of this narrative and reprinted Gates's accusation.[30]

29. Middlekauff, *Glorious Cause*, 383. For his part, Burgoyne disagreed, arguing that McCrea's "fall wanted not the tragic display [Gates had] laboured to give it" (*Pennsylvania Evening Post*, Sept. 16, 1777).

30. In all, seventeen newspapers reprinted the Gates-Burgoyne exchange. Because the British had just burned Kingston, New York, and were on the verge of occupying Philadelphia, only nineteen American papers were active at that time, meaning that nearly 90 percent published the correspondence. See *Boston Gazette*, Sept. 15, 1777; *Pennsylvania Evening Post*, Sept. 16, 1777; *Continental Journal*, Sept. 18, 1777; *Massachusetts Spy*, Sept. 18, 1777; *Independent Chronicle*, Sept. 18, Oct. 2, 1777; *Connecticut Gazette*, Sept. 19, 1777; *Providence Gazette*, Sept. 20, 1777; *Freeman's Journal* (Portsmouth), Sept. 20, 1777; *Norwich Packet*, Sept. 22, 29, 1777; *Maryland Jour-*

The story of Jane McCrea was not an isolated episode known only by a few settlers in the neighborhood; her name was published from Charleston to Boston and all points in between. Patriot printers carried out the orders of military and political leaders to broadcast these images to the public. When Henry Laurens wrote home about the "menace" of Burgoyne's "extraordinary proclamation" giving "Stretch to his Savage friends," he also informed his correspondent, "If any thing above mentioned will be acceptable to Mr. [*South-Carolina and American General Gazette* printer John] Wells please to give it him or to Mr. [*Gazette, of the State of South-Carolina* printer Peter] Timothy if his Gazette is to come first out." But, unlike Gates, Laurens still wanted to hide his direct involvement in spreading stories about Britain's "Glory of Murdering many helpless Innocent Men, Women and Children," reminding the recipient, "I need not Say I dont wish to appear as a News Correspondent." The Charleston printers and all of their peers found these representations acceptable. With the widespread publication of the Gates-Burgoyne letters, at some point from August to October 1777, *every* active newspaper in America published the name of Jane McCrea, putting her story in the same exclusive category as Lexington and independence. Not since the start of the war had an event garnered such complete, detailed coverage. Although the patriots were losing their grip on print, the saturation of the Mc-Crea story remained remarkable. For Americans during the Revolutionary War, the fate of Jane McCrea was far more than another tragic tale from the New York frontier, as evidenced by the ubiquity of her image in the decades that followed. As its patriot sponsors Gates, Livingston, and other "officers of distinction" knew well, this story's intersection with preconceived ideas about "savagery," "barbarism," and the king's proxies made it compelling reading throughout the new nation.[31]

The collision of those prejudices with these new war stories was evident in a play published at that passionate moment. After graduating from Princeton in 1771, *Pennsylvania Journal* subscriber Hugh Henry Brackenridge served as a schoolmaster in Somerset County, Maryland, with his fel-

---

nal, Sept. 23, 1777; *Dunlap's Maryland Gazette,* Sept. 23, 1777; *Virginia Gazette* (Dixon & Hunter), Oct. 3, 1777; *New-York Gazette,* Oct. 6, 1777; *Connecticut Courant,* Oct. 7, 1777; *Connecticut Journal,* Oct. 15, 1777; *Gazette, of the State of South-Carolina,* Oct. 21, 1777; *South-Carolina and American General Gazette,* Oct. 23, 1777. Gaine's readers likely took Burgoyne's side in the exchange, of course.

31. HL to John Lewis Gervais, Aug. 17, 1777, *LDC,* VII, 495.

"It Is the Cause of Heaven against Hell"

low classmate and poet Philip Freneau as his assistant. In 1775, Bracken-ridge wrote a political play called *The Battle of Bunkers-Hill* for his students to perform. And, sometime in 1777, before he would leave the school to join Washington's army as a chaplain, he wrote another for them entitled *The Death of General Montgomery*. "It is my request," Brackenridge wrote in the preface to *General Montgomery*, "that the following Dramatic Composition may be considered only as a school piece." Since its subject was "not love" but the "great themes of patriotic virtue, bravery, and heroism," it was "intended for the private entertainment of Gentlemen of taste, and martial enterprize" and not the stage. Brackenridge was thinking first of molding young minds to the contemporary standards of sensibility, fellow feeling, and patriotism. He meant his "school piece" to impart lessons of glorious resistance to the enemy—and their despicable proxies.[32]

As a good divinity student, the twenty-nine-year-old Brackenridge fash-ioned his play as a sermon, taking as his text Philip Schuyler's widely re-printed letter of December 22, 1775, which documented Colonel Johnson inviting the Indians to "feast on a Bostonian, and drink his blood." In the published version, Brackenridge inserted Schuyler's letter in a long, itali-cized footnote, after Richard Montgomery says to Benedict Arnold in the play's opening lines,

Who late, at Montreal, with symbol dire,
Did call, the Savages, to taste of blood,
Life-warm, and streaming, from the bullock slain,
And with a fell language, told it was the blood,
Of a Bostonian, made the sacrament?
At this, the Hell-hounds with infernal gust,
To the snuff'd wind, held up, their blood stained-mouths,
And fill'd with howlings, the adjacent hills.

To which Arnold responds:

---

32. [Hugh Henry Brackenridge], *The Death of General Montgomery, in Storming the City of Quebec: A Tragedy . . .* (Norwich, Conn., 1777), rpt. in Norman Philbrick, ed., *Trumpets Sounding: Propaganda Plays of the American Revolution* (New York, 1972), 223–254, esp. 224. For background on this part of Brackenridge's life, see Daniel Marder, *Hugh Henry Brackenridge* (New York, 1967), 28–31. For an analysis of Brackenridge's early Revolution plays, see Jason Shaffer, *Performing Patriotism: National Identity in the Colonial and Revolutionary American Theater* (Philadelphia, 2007), 152–165, esp. 153.

Who, with dire artifice, of story feign'd,
Wrought up the Savage, to such a pitch of rage.
But, as for us, let indignation fire
Each patriot bosom, to resent the thought,
And turn to them, the meaning and the curse,
Of this dire cantico, at Montreal.

Brackenridge returned to the theme of British agents' encouraging of Indians to drink American blood four times throughout the play. Brackenridge wanted his students to recognize the gulf between tyranny and heroic sacrifice in defense of liberty. They were not to act as one of the king's "slave-born renegades." "Slavery, slavery dire, Cowards the spirit, and unmans the soul," Brackenridge lectured in Montgomery's voice.[33]

Others far from Brackenridge's classroom would have an opportunity to read *The Death of General Montgomery* in 1777. Thomas Paine's publisher Robert Bell and *Norwich Packet* printer John Trumbull advertised it for sale in the summer of 1777. Though expensive at "two-thirds of a dollar" (it was bound together with other literary pieces), *The Death of General Montgomery* also sold in Providence and, according to a chaplain in the French Army in 1781, Harvard students performed it along with John Leacock's *Fall of British Tyranny* and Brackenridge's other play, *Battle of Bunkers-Hill.* But the immediate timing of the New England publication of Brackenridge's play could not have been better calibrated.[34]

Again—as with James Warren's worries about the effects Massachusetts's antislavery bill might have on unity in the middle of Burgoyne's invasion— context mattered. Trumbull advertised *The Death of General Montgomery* in the July 14, 1777, issue of his *Norwich Packet*—fewer than two weeks before Jane McCrea's untimely death. Just as Leacock's play had blurred the lines

33. At the end of Schuyler's letter, Brackenridge surmised (wrongly) that Carleton must have gotten the idea from Aeschylus's *The Seven against Thebes*, where the chiefs slaughtered a bull and washed their hands in the blood, cited in [Brackenridge], *Death of General Montgomery*, in Philbrick, ed., *Trumpets Sounding*, 254, 227 ("Who late, at Montreal"), 228 ("Who, with dire artifice"), 242 ("Slavery, slavery dire"). The letter comes up in act 2, scene 2 (234), act 3, scene 3 (238), act 4, scene 2 (240), and act 5, scene 5 (251).

34. Charles Evans, ed., *American Bibliography* (Chicago, 1905), V, 22; Claude C. Robin, *New Travels through North America: In a Series of Letters* (1784; New York, 1969), 17. Robert Bell had published it a bit earlier, advertising in the May 20, 1777, *Pennsylvania Packet*. See also Philbrick, ed., *Trumpets Sounding*, 9.

"It Is the Cause of Heaven against Hell"

between fiction and reality in the case of Major Cudjo, Brackenridge resurrected the exaggerated, grotesque imagery of Indians "feasting on a Bostonian" at precisely the moment that American readers would be inundated with just such representations from Fort Edward. All readers in Connecticut or Rhode Island had to do was substitute Burgoyne for Carleton to make the play a document of the present, not the past. The themes that patriot publicists had circulated for two years—of evil Englishmen and their terrifying assistants abandoning their humanity to destroy liberty in America—were immediate and fresh again in the commentary on Burgoyne's proclamation, in Brackenridge's patriotic play, and, of course, throughout the ever-present McCrea story.[35]

Whether these events—or the outrage generated by reportage of them—actually rallied the New England populace to defend against Burgoyne at the Hudson River has been a topic of speculation for generations. It is true that, as one historian put it, the news of McCrea's death "spread like wildfire" and "stimulated week-kneed communities to send reinforcements, even to Schuyler, whom the New Englanders disliked." McCrea's death did not completely explain this resurgence of militia strength, just as the news of Hessian plundering did not wholly revitalize New Jersey's will to resist occupation in the days before Trenton. The news of terrible Indian violence and Burgoyne's approval and support of such behavior did convince frightened, wavering farmers that the British offered little protection. Indeed, it could have been the phrase "without distinction of age or sex" that encouraged men to muster. One young Massachusetts soldier described his engagement with "hell hounds," including a desperate flight through the woods, "for I thought of the bounty Burgoyne offered upon scalps."[36]

In the end, however, the important issue is not whether the propagation of the McCrea story mobilized people and compelled them to rush to the

35. *Norwich Packet,* July 14, 1777. Interestingly, Isaiah Thomas's *Massachusetts Spy* had run a dialogue between Guy Carleton and a group of tories on Mar. 13, 1777, two weeks before printing Livingston's *Impartial Chronicle.* In this dialogue, Major Cudjo from "Lord Kidnapper's fleet" returned, speaking in dialect and still starving, but in command of a group of tories who were the blacks' "fellow crew" (*Massachusetts Spy,* Mar. 13, 1777). Hartford bookbinder Nathaniel Patten advertised having copies of the play for sale a year later. See *Connecticut Courant,* Aug. 4, 1778.

36. Holden, "Influence of Death of Jane McCrea," *Proceedings of the NYSHA,* XII (1913), 249–310, esp. 286; Isaac Glynne Journal, 1775–1781, MSS, misc. boxes, G, AAS, 5.

northern army; that is impossible to prove. What is fascinating about the outpouring of print about McCrea, Burgoyne, and unleashed "savages" in the late summer is that it illuminates how patriot publicists thought these stories might produce such a mobilization. Washington was explicit about how defending against proxy enemies might motivate the New England militia. A week before McCrea's death, he had written to the recruiting generals in western Massachusetts and New Hampshire, imploring them to "repel an Enemy from your Borders who not content with hiring Mercenaries to lay waste your Country, have now brought Savages with the avowed and express intent of adding murder to desolation." Once those murders became reality, Horatio Gates was quick to capitalize on tragedy. John Adams pined for William Howe to galvanize public opinion by torching some houses, but McCrea's murder was even more perfect. These patriot generals believed fear, outrage, and prejudice would animate the populace and bring them to the defense of New York.[37]

* * *

In reality, far more than the response to Jane McCrea, it was the outcomes of clashes several miles away from Burgoyne's headquarters that would dash his dreams of imperial glory. On Jane McCrea's last full day of life, Lieutenant Colonel Barry St. Leger and 875 British, Hessian, and Canadian troops arrived at Fort Oswego, where they met Joseph Brant and a like number of Senecas and Mohawks. The next morning, they started for Fort Stanwix, a post built in 1758 to guard the "Great Carrying Place," the valuable portage between the Mohawk River and Lake Ontario. St. Leger believed only a few dozen men were at the fort. Having had advance warning that St. Leger was in motion, militia leader Nicholas Herkimer sent out a proclamation calling for all able hands. Since this was Tryon County, the seat of loyalism in New York, it was no sure thing that Herkimer would raise enough men to defend Stanwix. He was fortunate: about 800 did turn out, and on August 4, Herkimer marched to rescue the Stanwix garrison. Two days later, St. Leger ambushed Herkimer's force, with 60 Oneida Indian scouts in the van, near the village of Oriskany, six miles from the fort. Surrounded in a ravine, Herkimer's men fought a desperate hand-to-hand battle. One Seneca warrior, Blacksnake, later recalled the horrors of the fight: "There I have Seen the most Dead Bodies all it over that I never Did see, and never will again.

37. GW to Brigadier Generals of Militia of Western Massachusetts and New Hampshire, Headquarters at the Clove, July 18, 1777, *PGW: RW*, X, 318.

"It Is the Cause of Heaven against Hell"

I thought at that time the Blood Shed a Stream Running Down on the Desending ground."[38]

Although both would, neither side could claim victory. On the American side, Herkimer was mortally wounded, and the militia was unable to relieve Fort Stanwix; on the other side, St. Leger's crippling losses at Oriskany forced him to retreat back to Canada. Although patriots in Tryon rejoiced at having rebuffed a British invasion, Oriskany's importance lay elsewhere. As one delegate to Congress wrote, Oriskany was the first time Americans gave "General Burgoyne's Savage Allies a Check. . . . and we hope a more effectual one will Soon to be given to the head Savage Burgoyne himself." St. Leger's defeat isolated Burgoyne and contributed to the eventual surrender of his army.[39]

More important, the battle touched off a civil war among the Six Nations. A few days after Oriskany, Philip Schuyler reported, "The Oneidas Tuscaroras and such part of the Onandagas as are here have taken the Hatchet about fifty or Sixty will Join our Army to day." The dissension Joseph Brant had been sowing in Iroquoia, encouraging his kinsmen to abandon neutrality and fight for the British, was blossoming into a bitter internecine conflict. With Mohawks fighting Oneidas, Oriskany smashed the Great Peace, the cornerstone of the Six Nations' confederacy. For the remainder of the war, the Six Nations remained a divided people. The tribes listed by Schuyler continued to support the Americans, whereas Brant kept the Mohawks, Cayugas, and Senecas allied to the British.[40]

One correspondent to Samuel Loudon's *New York Packet* described the threatening approach of St. Leger using familiar images. Finding that Brant's Indians had already ambushed a party outside Fort Stanwix, he ar-

38. Thomas S. Abler, ed., *Chainbreaker: The Revolutionary War Memoirs of Governor Blacksnake, as Told to Benjamin Williams* (Lincoln, Neb., 1989), 128. For more on Oriskany, see Graymont, *Iroquois in the American Revolution,* 134–143; Joseph T. Glatthaar and James Kirby Martin, *Forgotten Allies: The Oneida Indians and the American Revolution* (New York, 2006), 149–169; Ward, *War of the Revolution,* II, 477–491, esp. 481, 484; and Gavin K. Watt, *Rebellion in the Mohawk Valley: The St. Leger Expedition of 1777* (Toronto, 2002).

39. HL to Elias Ball, Aug. 17, 1777, *LDC,* VII, 493. He elaborated on his calling Burgoyne a "Savage": "Who can forbear calling him Savage when he boasts of Sending them to Murder Innocent Women and Children, which they have done to a shocking extent and even to many who had taken Shelter under his proclamation."

40. Philip Schuyler to John Jay, Albany, Aug. 17, 1777, in Morris, ed., *John Jay,* I, 436.

gued that this was just "another specimen of the tender mercies of the King of Britain, in his hiring the Savages to murder us." The dominant news story from the northern frontier in August was undoubtedly Jane McCrea, but patriot newspapers also featured letters from the Mohawk Valley. There, too, girls were getting "shot, scalped and tomahawked" by the "mercenaries of Britain" while innocently gathering raspberries. Following Washington's orders, Marinus Willet, the commander inside Stanwix, boasted that American troops would never act like that. In a narrative sent to busy *New-York Journal* printer John Holt via Connecticut governor Jonathan Trumbull, Willet reported that he "was happy in preventing the men from scalping even the Indians" in a clash outside the fort, "being desirous, if possible, to teach even the Savages humanity."[41]

Yet amid these reports, a new narrative emerged. A few weeks later, reports of Indian assistance at Oriskany seemingly cut against the grain. American newspaper coverage of Oriskany was the first opportunity patriot publicists took to promote "good" Indians assisting the Revolution. The coverage of Oriskany offered a counterbalance to the demonization of Bur-

---

41. "Another specimen": *New York Packet*, July 10, 1777; *Pennsylvania Gazette*, July 16, 1777; *Pennsylvania Journal*, July 16, 1777; *Connecticut Journal*, July 16, 1777; *Virginia Gazette* (Dixon & Hunter), July 25, 1777. "Shot, scalped and tomahawked": *New York Packet*, Aug. 7, 1777; *Connecticut Courant*, Aug. 11, 1777; *Pennsylvania Packet*, Aug. 12, 1777; *Pennsylvania Journal*, Aug. 13, 1777; *Continental Journal*, Aug. 14, 1777; *Massachusetts Spy*, Aug. 14, 1777; *Providence Gazette*, Aug. 16, 1777; *Maryland Journal*, Aug. 19, 1777; *South-Carolina and American General Gazette*, Sept. 11, 1777. Willet's narrative appeared in ten papers, originating with John Holt's *New-York Journal*. Holt prefaced the article with a note from Trumbull: "I send you Lieut. Col. Marinus Willet's narration of occurrences at Fort Stanwix . . . it was drawn up by himself and left with me, with his desire that it may be communicated to the public thro' the Channel of your Paper. The narration must afford much pleasure to the Public—at the same time that it reflects great honour upon the gallant defenders of that important post." See *New-York Journal*, Aug. 18, 1777; *Maryland Journal*, Aug. 26, 1777; *Connecticut Journal*, Aug. 27, 1777; *Pennsylvania Gazette*, Aug. 28, 1777; *Connecticut Gazette*, Aug. 29, 1777; *Massachusetts Spy*, Aug. 29, 1777; *Freeman's Journal* (Portsmouth), Aug. 30, 1777; *Boston Gazette*, Sept. 1, 1777; *Continental Journal*, Sept. 4, 1777; *South-Carolina and American General Gazette*, Oct. 2, 1777. Another self-congratulatory letter from the New York frontier boasting that American commanders "humanely discount scalping" appeared in four papers that October. See *New-York Journal*, Oct. 6, 1777; *Massachusetts Spy*, Oct. 16, 1777; *Norwich Packet*, Oct. 20, 1777; *Connecticut Journal*, Oct. 22, 1777; *Independent Chronicle* Oct. 23, 1777.

"It Is the Cause of Heaven against Hell"

goyne's Indians one hundred miles to the east. One week after printing Willet's narrative—and one week before calling all Indians "profligate scum of the earth"—Holt published an anecdote that singled out the actions at Oriskany of "a friendly Indian, with his wife and son, who distinguished themselves remarkably on the occasion." "The Indian killed nine of the enemy," the article marveled, "when having received a ball through his wrist that disabled him from using his gun, he then fought with his tomahawk. His son killed two, and his wife on horseback, fought by his side, with pistols, during the whole action, which lasted six hours." Hardly a merciless savage—at least, not to Americans—the Indian, whose real name was Thawengarakwen, or Han Yerry Doxtader, was an Oneida leader who served the patriots with distinction not only at Oriskany but also at Saratoga later that year. Tellingly, however, in that terrible season when poet-politicians decried how Burgoyne's "dogs of Hell" would "rip your guts and [flay] your skins," only one other patriot paper found space for this "good" Indian. Holt's venom reached far more readers than his praise.[42]

With St. Leger's retreat, Burgoyne's invasion was in trouble. Then, in mid-August, Burgoyne sent a detachment of seven hundred men to procure supplies, especially horses. A group of New Hampshire militia twice its size, led by Colonel John Stark, engaged and routed them near Bennington, in the Vermont district. When Burgoyne sent reinforcements, Stark's militia beat them, too. In all, Burgoyne lost nine hundred men—nearly 15 percent—at Bennington, including four hundred more Hessian prisoners of war. Immediately, both the Continental Congress and Connecticut governor Trumbull ordered handbills printed up announcing Stark's victories, supplementing the newspaper coverage that the Boston papers generated, and offering yet another opportunity for people far away to connect to the events on the Hudson and Mohawk Rivers through ink.[43]

42. *New-York Journal*, Aug. 25, 1777; *Independent Chronicle*, Sept. 11, 1777; James Kirby Martin, "Forgotten Heroes of the Revolution: Han Yerry and Tyona Doxtader of the Oneida Indian Nation," in Alfred F. Young, Gary B. Nash, and Ray Raphael, eds., *Revolutionary Founders: Rebels, Radicals, and Reformers in the Making of the Nation* (New York, 2011), 199–211.

43. Mackesy, *War for America*, 134; Ward, *War of the Revolution*, I, 417–431. Official information about the Bennington victory entered the print discourse through several channels. One of the Bennington handbills originated as a letter from General Benjamin Lincoln to Schuyler, Aug. 18, 1777, American Revolution Collection, MSS, Connecticut Historical Society, Hartford. Four days after Lincoln penned it in Bennington, the letter had traveled from Albany to Philadelphia and had been

After Oriskany and Bennington, Burgoyne's campaign was all but doomed. At once, Gentleman Johnny had lost a good deal of men, learned that St. Leger was not going to meet him in Albany, and found his Indian allies beginning to desert him en masse after he ordered them to stop plundering and taking scalps. Despite mounting evidence of failure, he refused to regroup, instead deciding to press on to Albany.[44]

* * *

A week after Burgoyne determined he would winter on the Hudson after all, Howe's fleet finally landed at Head of Elk, Maryland, having taken six weeks to make a frustrating voyage from New York Harbor, around the Capes of Virginia, and up the Chesapeake Bay. Disembarking on August 25, Howe was convinced he still had time to take Philadelphia with little difficulty, disrupt the patriot command, and then rush north to support Burgoyne.[45]

Yet the length of the frustrating journey—over six hot summer weeks—

---

printed. Hancock forwarded a printed version to Washington (Hancock to GW, Philadelphia, Aug. 22, 1777, *LDC,* VII, 527). Washington wrote back on September 3 that he had received the handbills and that "they shall be distributed among the Soldiery, and I doubt not but they will answer the good End which is intended by them. Every piece of favorable News circulated in this manner thro' the Camp will certainly inspirit the Troops" (GW to Continental Congress Intelligence Committee, Wilmington, Sept. 3, 1777, *PGW: RW,* XI, 134). Lincoln's letter was published in English in *Pennsylvania Evening Post,* Aug. 23, 1777, 439; *Connecticut Journal,* Sept. 2, 1777; and in German in *Der Wöchentliche philadelphische Staatsbot* (Philadelphia), Aug. 27, 1777. The German print, interestingly, cut the number of Hessians captured in half, from 398 to 198. Richard Henry Lee sent a copy to Jefferson (Philadelphia, Aug. 25, 1777, *LDC,* VII, 550–552), and Washington sent one to Patrick Henry (Oct. 3, 1777, *PGW: RW,* XI, 383). Lincoln also sent a letter on August 18 to the Massachusetts Council providing many of the same details. That letter was published in *Boston Gazette,* Aug. 25, 1777; *Continental Journal,* Aug. 28, 1777; *Independent Chronicle,* Aug. 29, 1777; and *Providence Gazette,* Aug. 30, 1777. Major General Israel Putnam described details about the battle to Washington that he read from a "Connecticut Acct Which the Gov has order'd printed in Hand Bills." See Putnam to GW, Peekskill, Aug. 22, 1777, *PGW: RW,* XI, 47. New England diarists Stephen Peabody and Jonathan Sayward both mention seeing a copy of one of these handbills. See Stephen Peabody Diary and Jonathan Sayward Diary, MSS, AAS.

44. Ward, *War of the Revolution,* II, 501.

45. J. A. Robinson, "British Invade the Chesapeake, 1777," in Ernest McNeill Eller, ed., *Chesapeake Bay in the American Revolution* (Centreville, Md., 1981), 341–377.

"It Is the Cause of Heaven against Hell"

left his men unable to fight immediately after landing. It was early September before Howe's 17,000 troops began to march toward battle, where Washington moved to intercept them. On September 11, the two armies collided at Brandywine Creek in Pennsylvania. At day's end, Howe had the momentous victory that had eluded him for months. The Continental army, smashed but still intact, retreated back toward Chester. A week later, Philadelphians began to panic again that their city was about to be occupied.

This time, they had a chance to get the most precious items out. Five days after Washington's defeat at Brandywine, John Adams noted in his diary, "No Newspaper this Morning. Mr. Dunlap has moved or packed up his Types." Not inclined to leave such important decisions to the printers themselves, the next day Congress ordered Major General Armstrong to "cause all the printing presses and types in this city and Germantown, forthwith to be removed to secure places in the country." This had to be done, Massachusetts delegate James Lovell wrote home to a colleague, but at a cost: "You will be affected by not receiving News papers from hence. The failure of them makes a general melancholy impression. We took early care to remove types as a valuable article. . . . Let the people know that the Papers are not stopped by Congress to 'conceal bad news' as Tories used to propagate last winter." As Lovell and the other delegates fled Philadelphia, they were sure to take their most valuable accessory—the *Pennsylvania Gazette*—with them to York, though to the frustration of many it would take three full months for the paper to return.[46]

Two days after Lovell broke the bad news that a major node of the patriot communication network was about to be disrupted, British troops began occupying Philadelphia. Despite efforts by Washington to dislodge him, Howe would hold the city until the following June.

The news was better to the north. Between the battle of Brandywine and Howe's march into Philadelphia, Gates had fought his first significant battle against Burgoyne at Freeman's Farm, just south of the village of Saratoga. The Americans inflicted crippling wounds to Burgoyne's force at what would be the first of two battles at Bemis Heights (or Freeman's Farm). Washington had sent Colonel Daniel Morgan's Virginia rifle company to Gates a month earlier, specifically to fight "the Savage part of Genl Burgoyn's Force, which from every account spreads a General alarm among the Inhabitants and affects the Winds of the militia not a little." Gates was very grateful to receive

46. "John Adams's Diary," Sept. 16, 1777, *LDC*, VII, 668; James Lovell to Robert Treat Paine, Philadelphia, Sept. 24, 1777, VIII, 15; Sept. 18, 1777, *JCC*, VIII, 754.

Morgan's unit, if nothing else, to stop the "Panic Struck by the Indians" in his forces, adding that he wished "the bloody Hatchet he has so barbarously used, should find its Way into" Burgoyne's head. Since most of Burgoyne's Indians had left as the prospect of victory diminished, Morgan's rifle corps was instrumental in supporting Arnold's lines in the very heavy fighting of September 19.[47]

In fact, there were probably more Indians fighting alongside Morgan's corps than against them. Late in the evening of September 19, the news of that day's battle at Freeman's Farm reached headquarters at Albany. Patriot officers begged Indian leaders, which included Oriskany hero Han Yerry Doxtader, if they would go and support Gates at Saratoga. By the next evening, more than 150 Oneidas and Tuscaroras arrived at the American camp to act as scouts and intercept messages.[48]

In this instance, Doxtader and his fellow Iroquois had backed a winner. Burgoyne's army was in danger. The September 19 battle had decimated his most valuable units. After Bennington, he could not replace those men. There were too many disabled soldiers to retreat back to Canada. By early October, Burgoyne was stuck—and he knew it. His colleagues tried to rescue him. From Manhattan, General Henry Clinton ordered the Royal Navy to penetrate patriot defenses on the Hudson to attempt to reach Burgoyne, an expedition that resulted in the sacking of the town of Kingston (also called Esopus) on October 16 and the silencing, yet again, of John Holt's *New-York Journal.* In July, Holt's paper had resurfaced in Kingston only after he had fled New York City the previous September. Now he would have to relocate again; it would be another eight months before he would produce another *Journal,* this time in Poughkeepsie.

By the time Clinton's men had, in Washington's words, burned "Mills, Gentlemens Seats, and the Villages near the Water" in Kingston, it was all but over for Burgoyne. On October 7, he sent his men to scout out a way to gain the high ground, but once he did, Gates grasped the initiative and sent Morgan and Arnold against Burgoyne's flank. Burgoyne withdrew his beaten army that night to the high ground at Saratoga, but a few days later, Gates cut him off. Unable to cross the Hudson, Gentleman Johnny had to ask for terms of surrender. On October 17, as Kingston was still smolder-

---

47. GW to Hancock, Neshamini Camp, Aug. 17, 1777, *PGW: RW,* X, 649; Gates to GW, Aug. 22, 1777, XI, 38; and see Don Higginbotham, *Daniel Morgan: Revolutionary Rifleman* (Chapel Hill, N.C., 1961), 61–64.

48. Graymont, *Iroquois in the American Revolution,* 149–150.

"It Is the Cause of Heaven against Hell"

ing, 5,800 British and German soldiers grounded their arms and went into American custody. Although the two sides agreed that Burgoyne's men would march to Boston and then return to England, Congress disregarded this provision of the surrender agreement, worried that they would fight again. Burgoyne's army would indeed complete their southern march, but as prisoners who would be housed in barracks constructed in western Virginia for the war's duration. Upon hearing the news, Henry Laurens, who in a week would become the next president of Congress, exulted that if he had published "such a Braggadocio proclamation" as Burgoyne had, "and of following it with such daring menaces and unmanly acts of murder upon Women and Children as we have been witnesses of, I should have Surrendered my Self to a Pistol Ball in preference to becoming the prisoner of those people whom I had reviled by the Epithet of Rebels and every ignominious term."[49]

Burgoyne's surrender was the best news of the war thus far. An express reached the Continental camp on Saturday, October 18, with an inaccurate report that Burgoyne had surrendered four days earlier. Upon hearing the (premature) news, the soldiers celebrated by firing a *feu de joie,* and Washington allegedly "stood silent for some small time." By Monday evening, the inhabitants of York, Congress's temporary home, were preparing the town for illumination, parades, maneuvers, and "many patriotic healths." Can-

---

49. GW to Landon Carter, Philadelphia Co., Oct. 27, 1777, *PGW: RW,* XII, 25–27, esp. 27; Middlekauff, *Glorious Cause,* 391; HL to Marquis de Lafayette, Oct. 23, 1777, *LDC,* VIII, 165. The patriots did not want to publicize this decision countermanding the Saratoga convention, but it entered the print networks nonetheless. Major General William Heath reported to Washington from Boston that Congress "meant not to publish [them] here," but "a Printer, some how, availed himself" of their January 8 resolves to retain Burgoyne's army as prisoners "and very imprudently published it in his paper, from which the others have taken it." Heath did not mention the printer by name, but John Gill was the first to publish it in the Feb. 12, 1778, number of his *Continental Journal.* See William Heath to GW, Boston, Feb. 20, 1778, *PGW: RW,* XIII, 608. The editors of the *PGW: RW* inaccurately noted it was the *Boston Gazette* to break this news on February 16, but Edes's paper was the second to feature it. See Heath to GW, Feb. 20, 1778, *PGW: RW,* XIII, 608–609, esp. 609n. Four other New England papers and four loyalist ones exchanged it: see *New-England Chronicle,* Feb. 19, 1778; *Massachusetts Spy,* Feb. 19, 1778; *Providence Gazette,* Feb. 21, 1778; *Connecticut Journal,* Mar. 4, 1778; *New-York Gazette,* Mar. 9, 1778; *Royal Gazette* (New York), Mar. 7, 1778; *Royal Pennsylvania Gazette,* Mar. 17, 1778; *Pennsylvania Ledger,* Apr. 1, 1778. For the original resolutions, see Jan. 28, 1778, *JCC,* X, 29–35.

nons boomed salutes in Boston Harbor on October 23. Cambridge, Massachusetts, had a similar illumination "in high taste and elegance," according to the *Independent Chronicle*.[50]

For many towns south of New England that did not have the luxury of hosting the Continental Congress, however, the news of Saratoga would not be as readily forthcoming. The war's greatest dispatch occurred at a moment when the patriots' communication network was at its weakest point yet without New York City and Philadelphia. Although the surrender terms agreed to by Burgoyne "caused the loudest Acclamations of Joy, from as numerous and respectable a Body of Men, as ever were assembled on any Occasion" when they were proclaimed at the Massachusetts State House, they appeared in only seven patriot newspapers. Worse, the geographic coverage was slight, with five of the seven being papers in either Boston or Williamsburg, Virginia. Other details about Saratoga, including exact numbers of captured men and arms, ran in an additional three prints. Those numbers were not much greater than the number of loyalist newspapers that reported the surrender terms in November.[51]

This frustrated Congress. In the midst of celebration, delegates complained that they had no mechanism to forward the news except by less-reliable horse and voice. During the same weekend that news from Saratoga reached York, several patriots vented their anger with the general communications problems caused by the loss of two major cities. James Lovell refused to write anything "secret or confidential" because "one express has in all probability been lately taken by the enemy," and he worried anything he wrote "should find its way to Gaine's Gazette." Henry Laurens wrote to his friend and *South-Carolina and American General Gazette* printer John Wells, Jr., that he would do his best to forward a Boston paper and Holt's *Journal*

50. Oct. 20, 21, 1777, in Duane, ed., *Diary of Christopher Marshall*, 137 ("stood silent"), 138 ("many patriotic healths"). "High taste and elegance": *Connecticut Journal*, Nov. 5, 1777.

51. Report of the Massachusetts State House in *Independent Chronicle*, Oct. 30, 1777. Articles of Convention: *Independent Chronicle*, Oct. 23, 1777; *Continental Journal*, Oct. 23, 1777; *Connecticut Courant*, Oct. 28, 1777; *Massachusetts Spy*, Oct. 30, 1777; *Providence Gazette*, Nov. 1, 1777; *Virginia Gazette* (Dixon & Hunter), Nov. 7, 1777; *Virginia Gazette* (Purdie), Nov. 7, 1777. Saratoga details: *Boston Gazette*, Oct. 27, 1777; *Connecticut Gazette*, Oct. 31, 1777; *Norwich Packet*, Nov. 3, 1777. Saratoga surrender in loyalist papers: *Pennsylvania Ledger*, Nov. 5, 1777; *Pennsylvania Evening Post*, Nov. 8, 1777; *Rivington's New York Loyal Gazette*, Nov. 8, 1777; *New-York Gazette*, Nov. 10, 1777.

down to Charleston. "The want of a Press [in York] obliges us to furnish manuscript accounts of military events," Richard Henry Lee contended, "and this is attended with great difficulty amidst the pressure of much business." North Carolinian Cornelius Harnett related, "We have the Post at last Established here, but no Press, which prevents my sending you any News papers. I hope we shall not be long without this Necessary method of Conveying intelligence." To make matters worse, because Benjamin Towne had decided to turn his coat and keep publishing the *Pennsylvania Evening Post* in occupied Philadelphia, the British were able to produce their own stories of what had happened along the Hudson. Samuel Adams wrote that Howe had "published a Hand bill in Philadelphia setting forth that Burgoyne has gained a complete Victory having taken Gates and all his Army Prisoners." Although Adams shrugged off this lie with a perfunctory "It needs no comment," he, of all people, knew this was a problem. The patriots had won their greatest victory, but, outside New England, they had a difficult time telling the American public about it.[52]

That is not to say Americans were unaware of Burgoyne's surrender or that they were not thrilled—or devastated—by the news. At the edges, it seems that nothing had changed; when South Carolina governor John Rutledge reported that the "glorious News" had reached Charleston on November 6, that was the same amount of days (twenty) it had taken reports of Lexington to reach the Deep South. Baltimore and Williamsburg also found out with a timeliness that had not diminished. But the fact remains that the most "Necessary method of Conveying intelligence" had decreased by nearly 40 percent since the opening of the war.[53]

At the time of Burgoyne's surrender, New England still enjoyed the most coverage. Ten of the twenty-two active patriot presses were there: four newspapers in Massachusetts, four in Connecticut, and one each in New Hampshire and Rhode Island. Outside New England, the war had caused problems. Samuel Loudon was still publishing his *New York Packet* in Fishkill, but the British had knocked out the *Newport Mercury*, the *Constitutional Gazette*,

52. Lovell to William Whipple, York, Pa., Oct. 21, 1777, *LDC*, VIII, 158, HL to John Wells, York, Oct. 20, 1777, 151–152, Richard Henry Lee to George Wythe, Oct. 19, 1777, 146, Cornelius Harnett to William Wilkinson, Oct. 23, 1777, 165, Samuel Adams to James Warren, Oct. 26, 1777, 189.

53. John Rutledge to HL, Charleston, Nov. 7, 1777, *PHL*, XII, 36. Reports of the surrender appeared in both *Virginia Gazette*s on Oct. 31, 1777, and in *Maryland Journal*, Nov. 4, 1777.

and Holt's *New-York Journal* twice. Philadelphia prints were in shambles at that moment of triumph. Hall and Sellers had their types for the *Pennsylvania Gazette* in York with Congress, but they would not get fully supplied until the end of the year. Bradford's *Pennsylvania Journal* was also out of commission; Dunlap's *Pennsylvania Packet* would reopen in Lancaster in the end of November 1777. For many people in the mid-Atlantic states, the last pro-patriot news stories they would receive for several months were about Jane McCrea. In the South at that moment, there were still two papers active in Maryland, Virginia, and South Carolina, as well as one in North Carolina, but the Annapolis *Maryland Gazette* would soon go under in December, and a fire in Charleston in late January would force Peter Timothy's paper to suspend operations for six months. Charleston printer John Wells, Jr., had just sent two hundred dollars to relieve the financial pains of his "Brother Type" John Holt when his own house burned. New patriot organs would be on the way, most notably two new prints in New Jersey established and subsidized by the Continental army, but as of late October 1777, the number of patriot newspapers circulating through North America was at an all-time low for the Revolution.[54]

At the same time, there were more royalist newspapers than ever before. In addition to Hugh Gaine's high-profile *New-York Gazette; and the Weekly Mercury,* there was another British paper in Manhattan in 1777, the Robertson brothers' *Royal American Gazette.* When the Royal Navy landed at Newport, Rhode Island, John Howe started a loyalist newspaper there, the *Newport Gazette.* Joining the turncoat Benjamin Towne in British-occupied Philadelphia would be James Humphreys, Jr., who returned from exile to restart his *Pennsylvania Ledger.* Royalist papers were multiplying. The day after Burgoyne surrendered, James Rivington put out the first issue of his revived paper, now entitled *Rivington's New York Loyal Gazette.* In the spring, one Robertson brother, James, came down to Philadelphia to start the *Royal Pennsylvania Gazette.* In all, at this point in the war, there were seven loyalist papers emanating from the primary communication hubs of North America. This development could be very troubling for the future of the common cause.[55]

---

54. Wells sent this money to Henry Laurens for him to forward to Holt. See John Wells, Jr., to HL, Charleston, Nov. 28, 1777, *PHL*, XII, 107; HL to James Duane, York, Apr. 7–8, 1778, *LDC*, IX, 384. For the printing situation after the fire in Charleston, see Wells to HL, Charleston, Apr. 20, 1778, *PHL*, XIII, 162–163.

55. Rivington would soon alter the name of his paper again. In December 1777, he renamed it the *Royal Gazette.*

"It Is the Cause of Heaven against Hell"

In other words, an alliance with a European power, most preferably France, was more vital than ever before. Even though they had just staved off a serious invasion and captured an entire army, the patriots had lost both of their most important urban areas and their almost complete monopoly on information. It was becoming increasingly difficult for patriot publicists to propagate their side of the argument despite the mounting evidence that they believed clinched their case. The extent to which they were able to do this at all was by no means total either across the continent or across village squares. This is plain from both the relatively meager subscription numbers of newspapers and the large numbers of people who considered themselves disaffected. Nor was it the exclusive domain of newspapers or even print; patriot arguments could still be made orally, whether in sermons or conversations in private parlors, public taverns, and militia musters. Whatever depth the common cause argument had, there is no mistaking it was shallower in 1777 than it had been in 1775. What effect this new vulnerability might have on the huge numbers of disaffected Americans, on future recruits for the Continental army, and on the popular acceptance of new state governments was troubling. Because of the deprived troops' suffering, narrators often associate the Revolution's nadir with the harsh winter at Valley Forge, a cantonment that would begin a few weeks after the news of Saratoga. The lack of food, supplies, ammunition, and money was indeed critical. But another major problem facing the patriot leadership was their growing inability to broadcast the messages, images, and representations that had been at the core of the common cause argument since Lexington. They needed France.

2: FRANCE AND THE CARLISLE COMMISSION:
TURNING POINTS AND CLOSING ROADS

The Atlantic packet boat that would carry letters about Burgoyne's surrender to the American commissioners in Paris suddenly came to the attention of overjoyed patriots in Boston. The day after celebrating the news, the Massachusetts Board of War—not waiting for the Continental Congress to issue an official brief—decided "to inform" Benjamin Franklin "of events since the happy days of Trenton and Princeton." "The gazettes will give you details" of Saratoga, they argued, but the real reason for writing was to relate their "surprise" at France and Spain's insistence on staying neutral "when they could obtain a large share of our commerce and humble Great Britain." They entrusted Jonathan Loring Austin, the thirty-year-old son of a Massachusetts Council member, to carry this letter and the "Account" of "the Important Conquest" to Franklin. Samuel Cooper, one of Franklin's longtime correspondents, also rushed to his writing table with the news. "We have a running Vessel that sails to Morrow for France with the glorious Tale," Cooper wrote to John Adams. "The Honor it will do our Arms must be of substantial Service to our Cause." Hurrying to catch the "running Vessel," Cooper wrote Franklin "to congratulate you upon the most important and glorious success" of Gates's army. Cooper's letter reached the same conclusions as many patriots after the news of Saratoga: now more than ever, France or Spain needed to "exert themselves in the most efficacious Manner."[56]

Austin delivered his packet to Franklin in the first week of December. Franklin interpreted this significant development in familiar terms: in a letter to a member of the British opposition completed a few days after Austin reached Paris, Franklin still saw Britain's embrace of proxy fighters as the biggest roadblock to reconciliation. The British government

> has given us by her numberless Barbarities, in the Prosecution of the War, and in the Treatment of Prisoners, (by her Malice in bribing Slaves, to murder their Masters, and Savages to Massacre the Families of Farmers, with her Baseness in rewarding the unfaithfulness of Servants, and debauching the Virtue of honest Seamen, entrusted with our Property,) so deep an Impression of her Depravity, that we never again can trust her in the Management of our Affairs, and Interests.

Franklin's opinion had not changed since he had left Philadelphia: the king's use of slaves, Indians, and foreign mercenaries forced America to find new friends.[57]

For decades, diplomatic historians have battled with the legend that the Saratoga victory instantly convinced the French government to enter the American war. The French foreign minister, Charles Gravier, comte de Ver-

---

56. Massachusetts Board of War to BF, Boston, Oct. 24, 1777, *PBF*, XXV, 99, Benjamin Austin to BF, Boston, Oct. 25, 1777, 102. John Langdon, the speaker of the New Hampshire legislature, also wrote Franklin with the news, complete with his personal observations of the Saratoga battlefield. See Langdon to the American Commissioners, Portsmouth, N.H., Oct. 29, 1777, *PBF*, XXV, 121; Samuel Cooper to JA, Boston, Oct. 24, 1777, *PJA*, V, 321–322; Samuel Cooper to BF, Oct. 25, 1777, *PBF*, XXV, 103–111, esp. 104, 110.

57. Jonathan R. Dull, *A Diplomatic History of the American Revolution* (New Haven, Conn., 1985), 88; BF to David Hartley, Passy, Oct. 14–Dec. 11, 1777, *PBF*, XXV, 65.

"It Is the Cause of Heaven against Hell"

gennes, had already determined that the best time to make a final decision either for or against entering the conflict would be early in 1778. The French Navy had recently undertaken a program of rearmament and resupply, and that process would be completed by the spring. Before Burgoyne reached Saratoga, Vergennes had sent signals to officials in the French West Indies that war with Britain could be imminent. Vergennes had already set a deadline when the news of Burgoyne's surrender arrived. That news, however, did tip the scales toward the United States. The wily French minister then began negotiating on the Americans' behalf in December, lobbying both Louis XVI and Spanish ambassadors that they should go to war. His appeals worked with the French king but not the Spanish, yet. In early January, Louis XVI gave permission for Vergennes to work out an alliance with the United States.[58]

While Austin's vessel plied the freezing Atlantic waters with triumphant news, a ship from Montreal was also on the ocean, headed for London with the same (albeit less sanguine) message. Late in the evening on December 2, word of Saratoga reached the British administration. Burgoyne's failure forced several developments in British politics and policy, including calls for Lord North to step down as prime minister. Germain reconsidered military strategy for the coming campaign, having Howe return to New York and relying strictly on cheaper coastal occupations and the naval blockade.[59]

At high levels in the government, conversations began to revolve around the question of negotiating with the Americans. William Eden, a member of the Board of Trade and one of North's advisers, convinced the prime minister to send a commission to America to negotiate an end to the war. Starting in February 1778, just as the French crown acceded to a "Treaty of Amity and Commerce" with the United States, North took Eden's plan to Parliament for approval. The Carlisle Peace Commission, as it would be-

58. See Richard W. Van Alstyne, *Empire and Independence: The International History of the American Revolution* (New York, 1965), 133, 136; Dull, *Diplomatic History of the American Revolution*, 89, 91; Leonard J. Sadosky, *Revolutionary Negotiations: Indians, Empires, and Diplomats in the Founding of America* (Charlottesville, Va., 2009), 101. Vergennes especially wanted the Spanish to join as a coalition, twisting their arms by worrying aloud about the possibilities that the British might be willing to concede independence and perhaps work with the Americans to attack Bourbon holdings in the Caribbean.

59. Charles R. Ritcheson, *British Politics and the American Revolution* (Norman, Okla., 1954), 234.

come known, stood to challenge any agreement between the United States and France.[60]

* * *

British policymakers were not the only ones to realize that Saratoga was a turning point. In Philadelphia, loyalist Joseph Galloway recognized Burgoyne's surrender would initiate a host of strategic conversations, and he wanted to chime in. The former patriot leader–turned–outspoken tory wrote to Lord Dartmouth in January 1778, offering intelligence on the "Present State of America." Galloway tabulated the number of "Souls and fighting Men in America" that the British government could rely on, "distinguishing the Number of Whites and Blacks . . . supposing the Blacks, as they really are, in favor of Government." Galloway begged the crown to make use of the "800,000 Negroes," who he said "may be all deemed so many Intestine Enemies, being all Slaves and desirous of Freedom, and woud, was an opportunity offerd them, take up Arms against their Masters." Five weeks later, Galloway elaborated on his opinion that the British should redouble their military efforts in the upcoming campaign. The southern regions, he argued, could not send help. Virginia's slaves, "who are ever ready, upon the least Encouragement, to take up Arms against their Masters, forbid their sending many, were they to be had. . . . The Carolinas are too distant," and "the Numbers of their Negroes place them in the same Situation with the internal parts of Virginia." Given such a dismal portrait, Galloway lobbied for more—not less—military action in 1778. One-sided though Galloway's assessment was, his focus on the role slaves might play in the future joined a crescendo of voices in the British Cabinet that believed the best way to proceed was to relocate the conflict to a more advantageous location. Galloway's pleas to expand military operations would not be heard in the months that followed Burgoyne's surrender, but the arguments he made helped shape what would emerge as the "southern strategy."[61]

Just one week before Galloway, sitting in occupied Philadelphia, counted up all the slaves who could potentially assist the British army, twenty miles to the north, Colonel John Laurens reached a similar conclusion. Laurens

60. Ibid., 261.
61. [Joseph Galloway] to the Earl of Dartmouth, Philadelphia, Jan. 23, Mar. 4, 1778, [Galloway], "Present State of America," January 1778, both in Benjamin F. Stevens, ed., *Facsimiles of Manuscripts in European Archives Relating to America, 1773–1783* (1889–1895; Wilmington, Del., 1970), nos. 2078, [3], 2079, [1], 2090, [6].

"It Is the Cause of Heaven against Hell"

wrote his father from Valley Forge with a plan "to augment the Continental Forces from an untried Source." John asked Henry, the sitting president of Congress, to "cede me a number of your able bodied men Slaves, instead of leaving me a fortune," and he would turn them into "gallant Soldiers." The twenty-three-year-old aide to Washington hoped this would be more than just a personal decision: "If I could obtain authority for the purpose I would have a Corps of such men trained, uniformly clad, equip'd and ready in every respect to act at the opening of the next Campaign." Laurens knew he would incur popular criticism for leading such a unit, but he was convinced it was "essential Service to my Country." If the Revolution was to survive, the patriots needed to transcend "the Ridicule that may be thrown on the Colour." The problem was, the two men whose permission he needed to proceed with his own southern strategy — Henry Laurens and George Washington — had been instrumental in publicizing that ridicule.[62]

At first, Henry tried to put his son off. "More time will be required for me to consider the propriety of your scheme," his father scolded, "than you seem to have taken for concerting the project." Over the next few days, the president cautiously dropped a few hints of his son's plan to his colleagues. "Hitherto," he wrote John, "I have not heard one person approbate the Idea." He returned a list of questions for his son to reflect on, including, "Have you considered that your kind intentions towards your Negroes would be deemed by them the highest cruelty, and that to escape from it they would flee into the Woods"?[63]

62. John Laurens to HL, Valley Forge, Pa., Jan. 14, 1778, *PHL*, XII, 305–306. Laurens's attempts to create a black regiment in South Carolina have been well documented. See Quarles, *Negro in American Revolution*, 60–67; Pete Maslowski, "National Policy toward the Use of Black Troops in the Revolution," *South Carolina Historical Magazine*, LXXIII (1972), 1–17; Henry Wiencek, *An Imperfect God: George Washington, His Slaves, and the Creation of America* (New York, 2003), 220–228; Douglas R. Egerton, *Death or Liberty: African Americans and Revolutionary America* (New York, 2009), 80–85; and especially Gregory D. Massey, "The Limits of Antislavery Thought in the Revolutionary Lower South: John Laurens and Henry Laurens," *Journal of Southern History*, LXIII (1997), 495–530; Massey, *John Laurens and the American Revolution* (Columbia, S.C., 2000). For a general overview of the problem of arming slaves in the late eighteenth-century Atlantic, see Philip D. Morgan and Andrew Jackson O'Shaughnessy, "Arming Slaves in the American Revolution," in Christopher Leslie Brown and Morgan, eds., *Arming Slaves: From Classical Times to the Modern Age* (New Haven, Conn., 2006), 180–208.

63. HL to John Laurens, York, Jan. 22, 28, 1778, *LDC*, VIII, 636, 678.

John was not cowed by his father's disapproval, responding that he still believed "this trampled people have so much human left in them, as to be capable of aspiring to the rights of men by noble exertions." He remained certain that "a well chosen body of 5000 black men properly officer'd to act as light Troops . . . might give us decisive Success in the next campaign." John also hinted that his commander was in favor of the general outline of his plan but objected to its being regressive, punishing small slaveholders more than large. Henry, complaining, "Your whole mind is enveloped in the Cloud of that project," still resisted his son's entreaties. "The more I think of and the more I have consulted on your scheme, the less I approve of it." He accused his son of venal ambition—just wanting to command any regiment—an insinuation that upset John greatly. Throwing up his hands, Henry finally suggested that John go to South Carolina to sell his plan but warned him to "proceed warily in opposing the opinions of whole Nations— lest *without effecting any good,* you become a byeword, and be so transmitted, to Your Children's Children."[64]

Henry was very concerned about the damage John's plan would have for his public reputation. In one last plea, he told John that if he went forward with his "scheme . . . you would not have heard the last jeer till the end of your life." "I wish for an hours serious conversation with you on these points." Henry's apprehension is illuminating. Why was he so concerned about what this would do to his son's name? After all, John was merely exploring every option to keep the Continental army going and trying to be consistent with patriot claims of natural rights. Nor was he the only one making such a suggestion. In the middle of the heated correspondence between father and son, the Rhode Island Council of War was creating an African American regiment, a unit that had Washington's tacit approval. Back in August 1777, moreover, a broadside printed in Philadelphia and written by "Antibiastes" entitled *Observations on the Slaves and the Indented Servants, Inlisted in the Army, and in the Navy of the United States* appeared, calling on patriots to embrace emancipation—to "blot out the reproach which that neglect has justly rendered us liable to." Antibiastes, repeating Jefferson's (and Henry Laurens's) arguments that the king foisted the slave trade upon innocent Americans, requested the immediate freedom of all African Americans who took up arms for the Revolution. Two newspapers in Boston and Baltimore picked up *Observations* and exchanged it in their papers in October.

64. John Laurens to HL, Valley Forge, Pa., Feb. 2, 15, 1778, *PHL,* XII, 391, 446– 447; HL to John Laurens, York, Feb. 6, 1778, *LDC,* IX, 38–39.

"It Is the Cause of Heaven against Hell"

If a few people were discussing this as an option, why was the president of Congress so sure raising a black regiment would destroy his son?[65]

Antibiastes listed the reasons why blacks were "unjustly degraded" in the public's eye: their lack of education, their bondage, and "national prejudices and attachments." A year later, as John Laurens continued to lobby for his project, he used the same phrase, "deep rooted national prejudices." Jefferson would invoke that very construction in his *Notes on the State of Virginia* in a few years to sketch the reasons why emancipation was so difficult. But there was more to the patriots' putting arms in the hands of emancipated African Americans than just inherited colonial prejudice. Those roots had gotten deeper in the last two years as patriot publicists had excoriated British agents for "instigating" slaves to resist.[66]

Lord Dunmore's name was infamous throughout America. Early in the summer of 1778, a few New England newspapers reported that, "for his eminent services," the former Virginia governor had earned a £2,000 annual pension, "which probably is to come out of the Fund expected to arise from the Sale of runaway and kidnapped Negroes from Virginia." When the Rhode Island government debated in 1778 whether to recruit a black regiment, a petition signed by six of the governor's deputies protested the inconsistency of such a move. They did not want to "retort upon us the same kind of ridicule we so liberally bestowed upon them on account of Dunmore's regiment of blacks; or possibly might suggest to them the idea of employing black regiments against us." The memories of other southern governors, especially Josiah Martin and Sir William Campbell, were not far behind.[67]

65. HL to John Laurens, York, Mar. 1, 1778, *LDC,* IX, 193; Rhode Island Council of War to GW, Providence, Jan. 19, 1778, *PGW: RW,* XIII, 284, Nicholas Cooke to GW, Providence, Feb. 23, 1778, 646; Nathanael Greene to Christopher Greene, Valley Forge, Jan. 5, 1778, *PNG,* II, 248. For more, see Lorenzo J. Greene, "Some Observations on the Black Regiment of Rhode Island in the American Revolution," *Journal of Negro History,* XXXVII (1952), 142–172. "Antibiastes," *Observations on the Slaves and the Indented Servants, Inlisted in the Army, and in the Navy of the United States* (Philadelphia, 1777), *Early American Imprints,* 15239, in *Maryland Journal,* Oct. 7, 1777; *Boston Gazette,* Oct. 13, 1777.

66. "Antibiastes," *Observations,* esp. [1]; John Laurens to HL, Middlebrook, N.J., Feb. 17, 1779, *PHL,* XV, 60; Thomas Jefferson, *Notes on the State of Virginia,* ed. William Peden (1954; rpt. Chapel Hill, N.C., 1982), 138.

67. "For his eminent services": *Connecticut Gazette,* June 5, 1778; *New-Hampshire Gazette,* June 16, 1778; "Protest against Enlisting Slaves to Serve in the Army," in John Russell Bartlett, ed., *Records of the State of Rhode Island and Providence Plantations*

Patriot printers, supplied with information by political and military leaders, had loudly broadcast stories about British "tampering" on slave plantations since the summer of 1775. Some patriots had, like John Laurens, tried to bring rhetoric and reality more into line on the issue of slavery and freedom, but they had been stymied in the name of unity and the common cause. So far, the military necessity had not convinced patriot leaders to subsidize a controversial project such as Laurens's black regiment. Although that need would develop in the future, at this point, Henry Laurens expressed the same hope that John Adams had the last time the divisive issue of emancipation arose: "I hope [it] will sleep for a Time." The elder Laurens had often expressed a personal agony about slavery, but he had participated in the dissemination of images that conflated blacks and the British as America's enemy. That campaign had drowned out alternatives; it is significant that only two newspapers picked up Antibiastes's call for Americans to prove they were truly "VIRTUOUS PEOPLE." Three papers (including one that published *Observations*) exchanged a report in the middle of the Laurens's family disagreement about how "90 runaway negroes (including men, women, and children) were shipped off in a transport, fitted out by Captain Onslow of the British ship of war *St. Albans* for the West Indies, there to be sold for the benefit of his august masters." The common cause was on the verge of achieving its most important goal in the spring of 1778. One part of its success had been the depth and breadth of the drive to malign people who viewed slaves as potential allies. Henry did not want his son to be tarred with a similar brush. Any attempt by patriots to initiate this type of southern strategy would have to wait for the military situation to deteriorate to the point of complete collapse.[68]

---

in New England, VIII, *1776 to 1779* (Providence, R.I., 1863), 361. Whereas the act establishing the black regiment argued that "history affords us frequent precedents of the wisest, the freest, and bravest nations having liberated their slaves, and enlisted them as soldiers to fight in defence of their country," the deputies countered with the claim that Rhode Island's purchasing of "a band of slaves to be employed in the defense of the rights and liberties of our country . . . is wholly inconsistent with those principles of liberty and constitutional government, for which we are so ardently contending" (357, 361). See "Proceedings of the General Assembly, Held for the State of Rhode Island and Providence Plantations . . . ," in Bartlett, ed., *Records of R.I.,* VIII, 359, 361.

68. "Antibiastes," *Observations,* [2]. "90 runaway negroes": *Virginia Gazette* (Dixon & Hunter), Mar. 13, 1778; *Maryland Journal,* Mar. 24, 1778; *North-Carolina Gazette,* Apr. 3, 1778.

"It Is the Cause of Heaven against Hell"

* * *

At nearly the same moment that Henry did his best to convince his son to reconsider his plan, Massachusetts's men gathered in town meetings to debate the merits of a new state constitution. Whereas the other twelve states had agreed to a new frame of government, Massachusetts had been unable to solve procedural questions throughout 1776 and 1777. Finally, in February 1778, the House of Representatives and General Court, acting in joint session, produced a draft and sent it out to the towns for their approval. All that spring, they convened in their locales and transcribed their opinions. The towns rejected this draft in overwhelming numbers; totaling up all 177 surviving returns, the vote to refuse this constitution garnered nearly 85 percent of the whole.[69]

Historians have suggested several reasons why the Massachusetts drafters had failed so utterly. Reading the complaints given in the thick archive of town returns, they note the fifth article as especially noisome to ordinary folk in Massachusetts. If approved, Article 5 would have established economic and racial requirements for the franchise. All men except "negroes, mulattoes, or Indians" could vote for representatives, whereas only those with taxable property worth £60 were eligible to elect senators or governors and lieutenant governors.[70]

69. Willi Paul Adams, *The First American Constitutions: Republican Ideology and the Making of the State Constitutions in the Revolutionary Era,* trans. Rita Kimber and Robert Kimber (1980; Lanham, Md., 2001), 61–95. For the proposed constitution and the returns from the towns in 1778, see Robert J. Taylor, ed., *Massachusetts: Colony to Commonwealth: Documents on the Formation of the Constitution, 1775–1780* (Chapel Hill, N.C., 1961), 50–89; Oscar Handlin and Rita Handlin, *Popular Sources of Political Authority: Documents on the Massachusetts Constitution of 1780* (Cambridge, Mass., 1966), 190–382.

70. See Elisha P. Douglass, *Rebels and Democrats: The Struggle for Equal Political Rights and Majority Rule during the American Revolution* (Chapel Hill, N.C., 1955), 187–213; Gordon S. Wood, *The Creation of the American Republic, 1776–1787* (Chapel Hill, N.C., 1969), 339–341; Stephen E. Patterson, *Political Parties in Revolutionary Massachusetts* (Madison, Wis., 1973), 171–196; Adams, *First American Constitutions,* trans. Kimber and Kimber, 83–90; Marc W. Kruman, *Between Authority and Liberty: State Constitution Making in Revolutionary America* (Chapel Hill, N.C., 1997), 15–16, 30–34, 37–39; Gary B. Nash, *The Unknown American Revolution: The Unruly Birth of Democracy and the Struggle to Create America* (New York, 2005), 290, 296–297; Johann N. Neem, *Creating a Nation of Joiners: Democracy and Civil Society in Early National Massachusetts* (Cambridge, Mass., 2008), 35–36.

That several towns did not want to erect a "political color bar" is a sign for some historians that the patriots' universalist rhetoric had reached a high level of saturation by the spring of 1778—evidence that the elder Laurens was worrying too much. Some in Massachusetts had literally taken the Revolution to be about defending the "rights of man." But before we agree with the statement that "a good many whites" objected to the Massachusetts constitution "on the basis that blacks were excluded from voting," we must take a closer look at the town returns.[71]

Of 177 towns, a total of 21 disagreed with Article 5. Of these, 9 listed racial inequality as a reason for rejecting the proposed constitution. Several of these 9 towns, which were located either in the Maine district or the western counties of Worcester and Hampshire, provided eloquent defenses of natural, universal rights. For example, Georgetown, Maine, objected if "a Man being born in Afraca, India or ancient American or even being much Sun burnt deprived him of having a Vote for Representative." The inhabitants of Upton argued, "All Nations are made of one blood." Disfranchising blacks "manifestly add to the already acumulated Load of guilt lying upon the Land in supporting the slave trade," stated residents in the Worcester County town of Sutton. In another echo of Jefferson's accusation and displacement in the Declaration's rough draft, the men of Sutton proclaimed that Africans were "cruelly brought from their native Land, and sold here like Beasts and yet now by this constitution, if by any good Providence they or any of their Posterity, obtain their Freedom and a handsome estate yet they must be excluded the Privileges of Men!" This would only bring about "more Wrath upon us." Even more insulting was to "deprive the original Natives of the Land" of these same political rights.[72]

As laudatory as these articulate protestations might be, they must be kept in context. A similar number of town returns that listed problems with Article 5 had trouble only with the property restrictions and did not mention race at all. Five percent of the towns protested for racial equality. This meager number is also reflected in the individual votes against the suffrage requirements. When the entire plebiscite is considered, those who vocally protested the racial restrictions can be reliably determined at 539, or only 4 percent of 12,310 voters. Although patriot leaders in Massachusetts did drop the provision in the next iteration of the state constitution, it is diffi-

71. Nash, *Unknown American Revolution,* 297; Egerton, *Death or Liberty,* 104.

72. Handlin and Handlin, *Popular Sources of Political Authority,* 277 ("Afraca, India"), 263 ("one blood"), 231 ("cruelly brought").

"It Is the Cause of Heaven against Hell"

cult to credit the argument that Article 5 "sparked such a storm of protest" that chastened legislators never would have dreamed of raising it again.[73]

Its presence in the first place should be considered, as well as the overwhelming number of towns that did not take exception to the racial restrictions. In an essay in the *Continental Journal*, William Gordon explored the reasoning behind why Massachusetts's leaders limited the suffrage. He detested the restriction: "The complexion of the fifth article is blacker than that of any African; and if not alter'd will be an everlasting reproach upon the present inhabitants." "It hath been argued," the patriot minister related, "that were negroes admitted to vote, the Southern States would be offended." Gordon's contempt is illuminating. For the framers of Massachusetts's first constitution, worries about union trumped universal rights. Like Henry Laurens, George Washington, and John Adams, they were more anxious about how people outside New England would react than they were about following through natural rights arguments for their own inhabitants.[74]

Newburyport was one of the towns that voted unanimously against the constitution. In June, all 218 of Newburyport's representatives rejected it. If they disagreed with Article 5, though, they did not say so. In fact, some of them had already participated in a larger meeting composed of all the towns in Essex County to distill their thoughts on the constitution. That April meeting produced the *Essex Result*, a lengthy critique written by conservative Newburyport lawyer Theophilus Parsons. Later published as a pamphlet by printer John Mycall, the *Essex Result* had no qualms about the restrictions listed in Article 5. Parsons argued that slaves could not be entrusted with a

73. The nine towns who listed race as a problem in Article 5 were Blandford, Boothbay, Charlemont, Georgetown, Hardwick, Spencer, Sutton, Upton, and Westminster. Three of these (Boothbay, Spencer, and Westminster) did not list how many town inhabitants voted. The remaining six towns totaled 539 votes. Seven towns took issue with the £60 requirement: Chesterfield, Lenox, Mendon, New Salem, Pelham, Shelburne, and Williamston. Two of these (Mendon and Pelham) did not list number of voters. The remaining five towns totaled 389 votes. An additional four towns (Belcherton, Beverly, Monson, and Scarborough) also listed Article 5 as objectionable but did not list either economic or racial reasons why they disagreed with it. In these four towns, 269 men voted, for a total of 1,197 identifiable voters against Article 5. Of these 1,197, 45 percent listed race as a factor for rejection. For all of these town returns, see Handlin and Handlin, *Popular Sources of Political Authority*, 202–323. "Sparked such a storm": Kruman, *Between Authority and Liberty*, 106.

74. *Continental Journal*, Apr. 9, 1778.

franchise because they had "no wills." He snorted, "Are slaves members of a free government? We feel the absurdity, and would to God, the situation of America and the tempers of it's inhabitants were such, that the slave-holder could not be found in the land." He left unstated the question of where Indians or free blacks fitted into his imagined political community.[75]

Many of Parsons's Newburyport neighbors agreed, or at least did not oppose the *Essex Result.* One can imagine their remembering a sermon delivered as an evening lecture at the First Presbyterian Church a few months earlier. Reverend Abraham Keteltas was a thoroughgoing patriot. Having relocated to Long Island in the wake of a religious dispute, in 1776 Keteltas served as a delegate to the New York Provincial Congress from his new home in Jamaica, Queen's County. When William Howe made Jamaica the epicenter of his Long Island campaign, Keteltas fled to New England. One Sunday evening in October 1777, just a few days before Burgoyne's surrender, he delivered "God Arising and Pleading His People's Cause" in Newburyport.[76]

Keteltas contended America was engaged in "God's own cause." He implored his audience—whether in the church pews that evening or later when, "by particular desire," printer John Mycall turned this sermon into a thirty-two-page pamphlet—to carry on with the crusade. "It is a glorious cause: It is the cause of truth, against error and falshood; the cause of righteousness against iniquity; the cause of the oppressed against the oppressor; . . . it is the cause of heaven against hell. . . . It is the cause, for which heroes have fought, patriots bled, prophets, apostles, martyrs, confessors, and righteous men have died." As evidence that the common cause was a holy war, Keteltas exhorted a long list of war crimes, which, naturally, featured the king's proxies. "Our negroes, who have been nourished and brought up by us, and the savages of the wilderness, for whose temporal

75. Handlin and Handlin, *Popular Sources of Political Authority,* 320 (Newburyport rejection, June 15, 1778), 324–365 (*Essex Result, 1778*), 341 ("are slaves members"). For more on the *Essex Result,* especially its argument for an upper house being derived from propertied, wealthy men, see Wood, *Creation of the American Republic,* 217–218, 426, 431.

76. Abraham Keteltas, *God Arising and Pleading His People's Cause; or, The American War in Favor of Liberty, against the Measures and Arms of Great Britain, Shewn to Be the Cause of God* . . . (Newburyport, [Mass.], 1777), *Early American Imprints,* 15378, rpt. in Ellis Sandoz, ed., *Political Sermons of the American Founding Era, 1730–1805,* 2d ed. (1991; rpt. Indianapolis, 1998), I, 579–605.

"It Is the Cause of Heaven against Hell"

and eternal welfare we have labored, have been instigated to mangle, scalp, and murder us." "See our unnatural foes," he continued, "exulting over the ruins they have made, soliciting foreign aid, and hiring at an expensive rate, German mercenaries, to butcher their own best friends, and 'till cruelly and unjustly invaded and slain, their most affectionate children. Hear the shrieks of ravished women, the cries of helpless orphans, and the groans of murdered patriots."[77]

Inhabitants of Newburyport might have recalled hearing or reading Keteltas's impassioned sermon when they perused Article 5 of the proposed Massachusetts constitution. Even if they did not think of their local lecture, it would have been impossible to miss the additional rhetoric over the past three years stating that Britain, blacks, and Indians were all "unnatural foes." Newburyport voted against this constitution, but, like the other Essex towns, they did not do so because it barred blacks and Indians from participating. That nine towns did—and penned elegant statements defending racial equality—illuminates the Janus nature of the common cause. The universalist rhetoric emphasized by patriot leadership before Lexington and the exclusionary tactics amplified afterward were engaged in their own combat. Here, again, lay the tension between the "American Revolution" and the "Revolutionary War." Though it did not eventually become part of the Massachusetts constitution adopted two years later, the racial restrictions in the abortive draft illustrate the influence of the common cause's dual nature on political structures in 1778.

In some northern and western Massachusetts towns, the Revolution meant that all men, regardless of color, deserved the right to participate in their government. As William Gordon argued, "Will any be so hardy as to fly in the face of all the declarations through the Continent, and assert, that the negroes are made to be, and are fit for nothing but slaves?" This inclusive vision helped shape military policy, too. In the spring of 1778, just as some of these Worcester County towns protested the disfranchisement of free blacks, Massachusetts reversed policy to allow recruiters to include African Americans in their state regiments. This policy change ratified what was already in practice: as observers in Bethlehem, Pennsylvania, noticed, at least one New England company was "composed of whites, blacks and a

77. Keteltas, *God Arising and Pleading His People's Cause,* in Sandoz, ed., *Political Sermons,* I, 595 ("God's own Cause"), 599 ("instigated to mangle, scalp"), 601 ("groans of murdered patriots"), 603 ("cause of heaven against hell"). The title page of *God Arising* stated it was printed "by particular desire."

few Stockbridge Indians." In rhetoric and reality, many endorsed the idea that the common cause applied to all. John Laurens certainly thought a limited form of emancipation and recruitment could apply to his home state, as well.[78]

Had Galloway's suggestions gained full purchase among Britain's policymakers, however, patriot publicists like Abraham Keteltas, Hugh Henry Brackenridge, and William Livingston—or Horatio Gates, Samuel Adams, and George Washington—would have had far more ammunition to make the other side of the case. Fighting God's "cause" meant opposing and excluding those who aided tyranny.

These two sides of the common cause appeal collided in 1778. Opportunities for inclusion, although they never vanished, became less and less plausible and never materialized. True, careful readers of patriot papers saw exceptions, including images of "good" Indians. But they had to be paying considerable attention: images of Indians "drench[ing] their maukesins in gore" reached far more people, far more often than representations of pro-American natives. Stories told and not told began to coalesce into policies of exclusion. Roads not taken began to loom ever larger in the new republic.

* * *

In fact, the consideration of at least some Indians as full-fledged members of the United States began to evaporate around this time. Even as Burgoyne and Brant made their pitch for Indians to aid the British in the north, patriot leaders started to worry about a new source stirring up trouble in the Ohio Valley: the British lieutenant governor at Detroit, Henry Hamilton. Copies of a proclamation Hamilton wrote to convince settlers and Indians to remain loyal to the crown began to circulate in the backcountry. According to the commander at Fort Pitt, Indians would leave copies of Hamilton's proclamation "on or near the bodies of the People they murder, Good encouragement." Hamilton, patriot leaders in western Pennsylvania reported, "has been straining every Nerve to excite the Indians to take up the Hatchet

---

78. *Continental Journal,* Apr. 9, 1778. Outside New England, the New Jersey legislature cited the Declaration in their protest of the provision in the Articles of Confederation that calculated the number of recruits each state had to contribute based strictly on white inhabitants. See June 25, 1778, *JCC,* XI, 649; Quarles, *Negro in the American Revolution,* 54; Mar. 18, 1778, in John W. Jordan, ed., "Bethlehem during the Revolution: Extracts from the Diaries in the Moravian Archives at Bethlehem, Pennsylvania," *PMHB,* XIII (1889), 80.

"It Is the Cause of Heaven against Hell"

against the Americans." Starting in the fall of 1777, Hamilton would join Stuart, Johnson, Carleton, and Burgoyne as a prime patriot target of hatred and outrage. Soon he would be better known by a visceral patriot nickname: the Hair-Buyer.[79]

On November 20, Congress, having received intelligence about Hamilton's "instigation" of the Indians "to this barbarous and murderous war," ordered commissioners to repair to Fort Pitt to "[check] the progress of the enemy" and work with its commandant, General Edward Hand, to devise a plan "of carrying the war into the enemy's country." They implored the commissioners to "cultivate the friendship of the Shawanese and Delawares, and prevent our people from committing any outrages against them." What they did not know, however, was that just such a terrible event had already occurred.[80]

Tensions were very high; parties of Indians and settlers were indeed engaged in small-scale combat. In response, "murder gradually and inexorably became the dominant American Indian policy." A few days before Congress tried to put a "Speedy Stop" to the violence on the western frontier, another Virginia militiaman died in a clash with Indians. His friends, believing the perpetrators were Shawnees, rushed to Fort Randolph—where suspicious patriots had already detained Shawnee leader Cornstalk—and shot him and his son. Along with the Delaware leaders Captain White Eyes, John Killbuck, and Captain Pipe, Cornstalk was one of the patriots' most important friends in the Ohio Valley, leading pro-American factions of Delawares and Shawnees. The day before Cornstalk's death, Edward Hand wrote his wife with high hopes that "the prosperity of our affairs to the Northward will have a happy influence on the Western Indians." Two weeks later, Hand lamented to a friend, "If we had anything to expect from that Nation it is now vanished."[81]

79. Brigadier General Edward Hand to GW, Fort Pitt, Sept. 15, 1777, *PGW: RW*, XI, 238–239, esp. 239n; Indian Commissioners to Congress, Aug. 31, 1776, in George Morgan Letterbook, I, 28, MSS, Carnegie Library, Pittsburgh.

80. Nov. 20, 1777, *JCC*, IX, 942–945, esp. 942, 943.

81. Richard White, *The Middle Ground: Indians, Empires, and Republics in the Great Lakes Region, 1650–1815* (Cambridge, 1991), 384; Cornelius Harnett to William Wilkinson, York, Nov. 20, 1777, *LDC*, VIII, 292; Randolph C. Downes, *Council Fires on the Upper Ohio: A Narrative of Indian Affairs in the Upper Ohio Valley until 1795* (Pittsburgh, 1940), 206–207; Edward Hand to [Catherine] Hand, Fort Pitt, Nov. 9, 1777, in Reuben Gold Thwaites and Louise Phelps Kellogg, eds., *Frontier Defense on the Upper Ohio, 1777–1778* (Madison, Wis., 1912), 156; Hand to Jasper Yeates, Fort Pitt, Nov.

Patriot authorities voiced some outrage about this tragic event. Virginia governor Patrick Henry issued a proclamation in the spring of 1778 demanding justice for this "barbarous and atrocious murder" that had inflicted a "deep wound . . . to the honor and faith of this country" and offering a reward for the capture of the perpetrators. But, on the whole, patriot printers kept it quiet. Except for the publication of Henry's proclamation in one issue of Purdie's *Virginia Gazette,* the news about Virginia frontiersmen executing one of America's most reliable Indian allies did not appear in a single patriot newspaper, not even to distance themselves from such behavior. Every loyalist newspaper, on the other hand, described the "assassination . . . and other acts of the rebels' perfidy and cruelty" with great detail. To make the contrast more stark, news of this "treacherous piece of cruelty" appeared in both loyalist prints in occupied Philadelphia, all three in New York City, and in Newport. Outside western Pennsylvania or Virginia, it is probable this distressing news escaped the notice of most Americans sympathetic to the Revolution. Again, this is not to suggest conspiracy or direct censorship on the part of patriot political or military leaders, but the lack of any coverage in patriot papers on this important event is striking. Previous bad news, such as the Benjamin Church affair in 1775, had left a few visible traces of print as evidence. The murder of Cornstalk disappeared completely.[82]

24, 1777, in Edward Hand Papers, Thomas Addis Emmet Collection, NYPL. For more on how the murders of all of the patriots' best allies on the Ohio frontier shaped Indian relations, see Gregory Evans Dowd, *A Spirited Resistance: The North American Indian Struggle for Unity, 1745–1815* (Baltimore, 1992), 75–78.

82. *Virginia Gazette* (Purdie), Apr. 3, 1778; *Royal American Gazette,* June 2, 1778. Loyalist newspapers featured stories about Cornstalk's death in three accounts in February, May, and June 1778. First account: *Pennsylvania Evening Post,* Feb. 12, 1778; *Royal New York Gazette,* Feb. 13, 1778; *Pennsylvania Ledger,* Feb. 14, 1778; *Royal Gazette,* Feb. 14, 1778; *Newport Gazette,* Mar. 5, 1778. Second account: *Royal New York Gazette,* Apr. 30, 1778; *Royal Gazette,* May 2, 1778; *Pennsylvania Evening Post,* May 11, 1778. Third account, a long letter from Fredericksburg, Virginia: *Pennsylvania Evening Post,* May 20, 1778; *Pennsylvania Ledger,* May 20, 1778; *New-York Gazette,* June 1, 1778; *Royal New York Gazette,* June 2, 1778; *Royal Gazette,* June 3, 1778. Gaine's *New-York Gazette* published another letter from London that mentioned Cornstalk on Aug. 24, 1778. Virginia physician Robert Honyman did hear of it, noting in his diary about the murder — and mistakenly counting another key patriot ally, Captain White Eyes, among the dead — on January 6, 1778. See Robert Honyman Diary, 1776–1782, no. 8417, 198–199, University of Virginia Library, Charlottesville.

In fact, even the existence of these patriot allies barely found its way to patriot newspapers. One of the loyalist accounts about Cornstalk's murder also mentioned the name of Captain Pipe in passing. This, other than his participation at the 1776 Treaty at Pittsburgh and a later description of him in a 1782 narrative about Indians torturing Colonel William Crawford, was the only time printers ever composed Pipe's name in type. The same was true of John Killbuck. Readers might have remembered Killbuck's name from its association with John Connolly's infamous plot in the fall of 1775. Connolly's letters, with Dunmore's introduction, were addressed to Shawnee and Delaware leaders, Killbuck and White Eyes among them. Since then, however, he would turn up only once in a 1779 speech John Dunlap (and no others) printed in his *Packet* and again in 1781, when a Continental officer commended him for his assistance. White Eyes's name appeared only in Connolly's letters. When he, too, died suddenly, late in 1778—again, probably at the hands of frontier militia—patriot authorities at Fort Pitt tried to cover it up by blaming smallpox. Back east, patriot newspapers never mentioned the loss of another key Indian ally. This does not mean that no one at all knew about Cornstalk's murder or the presence of White Eyes, but it is significant that the identities of the patriots' most critical Indian friends were almost nonexistent in their most vital conveyance of information.[83]

A similar silence governed coverage of the Stockbridge Indians' partici-

83. Daniel Brodhead to [Benjamin Edes], Philadelphia, May 23, 1781, *Pennsylvania Packet*, Oct. 21, 1779. Brodhead to Congress: *Pennsylvania Packet,* June 5, 1781; *Pennsylvania Journal,* June 6, 1781; *Boston Gazette,* June 25, 1781; *Massachusetts Spy,* July 5, 1781; *New-Jersey Journal,* July 13, 1781. White Eyes died mysteriously while guiding American troops through Ohio in November 1778. Since relations with the Delawares were so fragile, patriot authorities at Fort Pitt spread the smallpox rumor to cover up another murder of a friend. One of the soldiers during the campaign remembered decades later that the Delaware chief had "taken with the Small-pox, and was sent to Pittsburg where he soon died." Indian Commissioner George Morgan, who was responsible for helping White Eyes's son, Killbuck's son, and Killbuck's half-brother attend Princeton on a subsidy provided by Congress, told a different story. In 1784, he confessed that White Eyes was "treacherously put to Death, at a moment of his greatest Exertions to serve the United States, in whose Service he held the commission of a Colonel." See "Recollections of Stephen Burkam," in Louise P. Kellogg, ed., *Frontier Advance on the Upper Ohio, 1778–1779* (Madison, Wis., 1916), 157; George Morgan to Congress, May 12, 1784, item 163, folios 365–367, in *Papers of the Continental Congress, 1774–1789,* National Archives Microfilm Publication M247, reel 180. For Connolly's affair, see Chapter 2, above.

pation in the Continental army. The Stockbridge, too, had earned attention in patriot papers back in the summer of 1775, when they tried to convince the Six Nations to stay neutral and ignore British entreaties. Since then, the Stockbridge had often crossed Washington's mind, but they had largely dropped from public sight.[84]

Late in the summer of 1778, a party of at least fifty Stockbridge attached to the Continental army encountered a British and Hessian ambush near Kingsbridge, New York. According to one British officer on the scene, the bloody, confused skirmish "very soon put a period to the existence of 37 Indians," including their chief, Abraham Nimham, and his son. These were significant casualties for any skirmish during the Revolutionary War, and this one decimated the Stockbridge. Such a catastrophe ought to earn notice in newspapers, not least in New England. Yet no letters appeared detailing the deaths of Nimham and the other Stockbridge in Westchester County. Loyalist papers in Manhattan boasted of their victory, but no laments over their losses appeared in patriot organs.[85]

Of course, they were there: hundreds of Indians fought for the Revolution. Eyewitnesses who saw the Continental army noticed the Stockbridge. One patriot soldier later in the war described Washington's "motley crew" that included "a number of Indian chiefs of the Stockbridge, Oneidas, and several of the Nontians, of no home." A few weeks before he helped kill dozens of them in that terrible August encounter, a Hessian officer com-

84. See John Hancock to GW, Philadelphia, Aug. 2–[6?], 1776, *PGW: RW*, V, 547; Aug. 2, 1776, *JCC*, V, 627–628. See also Chapter 2, above. Two newspapers had documented their participation with American troops near Fort Edward and Fort Ann, just after Ticonderoga's surrender in the summer of 1777. See *Continental Journal*, Aug. 21, 1777; *Pennsylvania Evening Post*, Sept. 2, 1777. For more on the Stockbridge participation, see Charles Patrick Neimeyer, *America Goes to War: A Social History of the Continental Army* (New York, 1996), 97–98.

85. Thomas F. DeVoe, "The Massacre of the Stockbridge Indians, 1778," *Magazine of American History*, V (1880), 187–195, esp. 193; Brigadier General Charles Scott to GW, Aug. 31, 1778, *PGW: RW*, XVI, 447–449; Aug. 31, 1779, in Johann Ewald, *Diary of the American War: A Hessian Journal*, ed. and trans. Joseph P. Tustin (New Haven, Conn., 1979), 144–145; John Graves Simcoe, *Simcoe's Military Journal: A History of the Operations of a Partisan Corps, Called the Queen's Rangers, Commanded by Lt. Col. J. G. Simcoe, during the War of the American Revolution* (1844; rpt. New York, 1968), 83–86. Death of Nimham: *Royal New York Gazette*, Sept. 3, 1778; *Royal Gazette*, Sept. 5, 1778; *New-York Gazette*, Sept. 7, 1778.

fü Indianer hm der Hockbridge Horde.

Figure 11. *Sketch of a Stockbridge Indian. By Johann Ewald (a Hessian officer).*
Although many Indians supported the common cause, patriot publicists minimized their
service throughout the war but instead broadcast countless stories of Indians fighting
with the British. Courtesy of Joseph Tustin papers, Special Collections, Harvey
Andruss Library, Bloomsburg University of Pennsylvania.

mented on seeing several "handsome and well-built" Stockbridge in the Continental army. But Americans far from army camps would have a difficult time knowing Indians were present and sacrificing themselves for the common cause. Many of the patriots' closest allies in the Revolution went unheralded and unnoticed in patriot papers. This blanket of silence is too complete to be coincidental.[86]

Reports detailing "merciless savages" were sure to find space in patriot newspapers. Compared to the permeation of images of hostile, British-allied Indians, however, accounts featuring the participation of "good" Indians left faint, fleeting impressions. The killers of Jane McCrea engulfed Abraham Nimham, Cornstalk, and Captain Pipe in American newspapers. This stark contrast in representation began to have policy consequences by the middle years of the Revolutionary War.

Following Saratoga, patriot leaders started to explore how much political capital the victory had earned them in Iroquoia. In December 1777, Congress sent provocative speeches to the Six Nations. Their aggressive, rhetorical questions reflected the confidence patriots projected after Burgoyne's surrender. "Why have you listened to the voice of our enemies?" they demanded. "Why have you suffered Sir John Johnson and Butler to mislead you? why have you assisted General St. Leger and his warriors from the other side of the great water . . . Is this a suitable return for our love and kindness?" "Did you suspect, that we were too weak or too cowardly to defend our country . . . what has been gained by this unprovoked treachery?" Not finished with their scolding, Congress continued the onslaught: "Much are you to blame, and greatly have you wronged us." They then boasted about their Indian friends in the western and southern frontiers and warned the Iroquois not to continue their hostility lest they suffer the same fate as the Cherokees, who, "like some of you, were prevailed upon to strike our people. We carried the war into their country and fought them." After all these threats, Congress reanimated a latent theme that they had rarely mentioned since 1775. They tried to convince the Six Nations that they were all brothers. The British were here only to "kill and destroy our inhabitants, to lay waste our houses and farms." "Let us, who are born on the same great

86. Enos Reeves journal, Sept. 13, 1780, Enos Reeves Papers, 1780–1782, MSS, William R. Perkins Library, Duke University, Durham, N.C.; May 19–22, in Ewald, *Diary of the American War,* ed. and trans. Tustin, 130. For more on the Stockbridge experience during the American Revolution, see Calloway, *American Revolution in Indian Country,* 85–107.

continent, love one another. Our interest is the same, and we ought to be one people, always ready to assist and to serve each other."[87]

This rhetoric of reconciliation, however, stood little chance of impressing many Indians in New York, especially because it followed a threatening, belittling harangue—and because British officials at Niagara held competing conferences that did not feign friendship or chastise but instead lavished gifts and food. But there was more to the irrelevance of this conciliatory rhetoric than the simple fact that most of the Six Nations were paying far more attention to the presents Major John Butler was handing out at Niagara. Patriot political leaders proved they were not committed to treating the Iroquois as the equals of Americans in the final revisions and debates of the Articles of Confederation.[88]

In mid-November 1777—as the news of Saratoga was still on the high seas and Indians on the northern and western frontiers were calculating their options—Congress took up the issue of finalizing the Articles of Confederation. They had postponed discussion since July 1776, after both the contingencies of war and problems with John Dickinson's draft stymied the process. As Benjamin Franklin's first proposal for confederation had in 1775, Dickinson's draft included a formal diplomatic relationship with Indian nations. The fourteenth article of Dickinson's version read, "No Colony or Colonies shall engage in any War *(with any Nations of Indians)* without the Consent of the Union, unless such Colony or Colonies be actually invaded by Enemies." But the editing committee for the Articles excised the most important words—*"any Nations of Indians"*—and left this provision vague and open to any enemy. This deletion was significant. It "creat[ed] a silence on Indian nations" at the continental level but still allowed states to retain full powers to make war on Indians. By removing the special status Dickinson had reserved for Indians, Congress turned the page on inherited ways of negotiating with native peoples. Whereas backcountry dealings had previously been nebulous, complex interactions between two seemingly equal parties, Congress now drew a formal line by not drawing one at all: individual states could deal with their frontiers as they wished; no central, executive power could restrain them. They moved forward with the assumption that relations would be predicated on antagonism rather than alliances. When, a few days later, Congress ordered General Hand at Fort Pitt to "carry

87. Dec. 3, 1777, *JCC*, IX, 995, 997, 998.

88. Graymont, *Iroquois in the American Revolution,* 161; Stevens, "His Majesty's 'Savage' Allies," 1477–1480.

the war" into the Ohio Valley, they were being consistent. Negotiating with people constantly portrayed as the king's friends would be a greater threat to unity than war. In other words, the removal of Indians from the Articles was a codification of the ubiquitous war stories about "merciless savages" acting as British proxies—almost without exception—that had circulated for more than two years.[89]

Congress finalized the frame of confederation amid the inescapable coverage of Jane McCrea's death and Burgoyne's proclamation on one hand and a lack of news about the murder of friendly Indians like Cornstalk on the other. Such a milieu did not open the way back to the alternate path that Dickinson's plan represented. Instead, Congress continued to move away from that road when they accepted the Articles as revised and sent them out to the states for ratification. When they tried to convince the Iroquois that they were "one people" with the United States, Congress was being disingenuous; they had already taken formal, political steps to prevent that from happening in the near future. Because Congress claimed they had faced the "difficulty of combining in one general system the various sentiments and interests of a continent divided into so many sovereign and independent communities," they chose to engender a spirit of common cause with each other rather than with Indians. That impulse was derived from political, military, and diplomatic necessity, but it was also reinforced by rhetoric, representation, and discourse about the unsuitability of all Indians—including the Oneidas, Tuscaroras, and Stockbridge, as well as Cornstalk's Shawnees and Killbuck's Delawares—to become fellow patriots.[90]

Later in 1778—after the war they authorized Hand to initiate had gone terribly—a group of friendly Delaware Indians, including White Eyes, Killbuck, and Pipe, attended another peace conference at Fort Pitt. This time, with military necessity pressing even harder, the commissioners sent by the Continental Congress reached a remarkable accord with the Delawares. Of the six articles agreed upon at Fort Pitt, the final provision was an arresting departure from previous promises that had been extended to earn Indian

89. Franklin, "Proposed Articles of Confederation" [c. July 21, 1775], *PBF*, XXII, 122–123; "Josiah Bartlett's and John Dickinson's Draft Articles of Confederation," [June 17–July 1, 1776], *LDC*, IV, 233–255, esp. 239. For background, see Jack N. Rakove, *The Beginnings of National Politics: An Interpretative History of the Continental Congress* (New York, 1979), 135–162. "Creating a silence": Sadosky, *Revolutionary Negotiations*, 87.

90. Nov. 17, 1777, *JCC*, IX, 933.

loyalty. To counteract growing concerns about British intrigues in the Ohio Valley, patriot leaders at Fort Pitt made a stunning offer to the Delawares: statehood.[91]

The commissioners invited them "to join the present confederation, and to form a state whereof the Delaware nation shall be the head, and have a representation in Congress." Though they admitted that this was not "to be considered as conclusive until it meets with the approbation of Congress," Article 6 was, potentially, a significant, alternative path. The Articles of Confederation had removed stipulations that treated Indian nations as diplomatic peers, but here was a new way to make a place for them in the new republic. Here was a path to treat the Indians as citizens. If it was a good-faith offer, it was a new way of reimagining Indian relations.[92]

But it would be a chimera. Patriot leaders outside Fort Pitt did not share the commissioners' inclusive vision. When the treaty reached Congress a few weeks later, it was assigned to a committee and never heard from again. Moreover, that such a crucial group of Ohio Indians had come to amicable terms with the United States would seem a very portentous—and newsworthy—event. Apparently, patriot publicists disagreed, too. The Delaware treaty conference left no traces in patriot newspapers. For all that American readers far from the backcountry knew, it had never happened. Alas, like the place of Indians in the Articles, the offer of statehood floated at Fort Pitt remained a road not taken. Unheralded, the "good" Indians all but disap-

---

91. For the text of the treaty, see "Treaty with the Delawares, 1778," Sept. 17, 1778, in Charles J. Kappler, comp. and ed., *Indian Affairs: Laws and Treaties*, II, *Treaties* (Washington, D.C., 1904), 3–5, esp. 5; proceedings and speeches during the September conference in "Treaty at Fort Pitt," Sept. 12–19, 1778, in Kellogg, ed., *Frontier Advance on the Upper Ohio*, 138–145.

92. Kappler, comp. and ed., *Indian Affairs*, II, 5. For historians' interpretations on the Fort Pitt treaty, especially the question of statehood for the Delaware, see Annie H. Abel, "Proposals for an Indian State, 1778–1878," *Annual Report of the American Historical Association for the Year 1907* (Washington, D.C., 1908), I, 89–104; Downes, *Council Fires*, 21–217; Max Savelle, *George Morgan: Colony Builder* (New York, 1932), 157–166; White, *Middle Ground*, 382–383; Dowd, *A Spirited Resistance*, 68–73; Nash, *Unknown American Revolution*, 376–377. Dowd's judgment on the issue of potential statehood is accurate, if caustic. "It is inconceivable," he argues, "that such a proposal was accepted, in good faith . . . but it certainly illustrates the lengths American agents were willing to run and the lies they were willing to spin in order to achieve Delaware neutrality" (Dowd, *A Spirited Resistance*, 72).

peared, as did the possibility for a position in the new republic that recognized their service in the Revolution.[93]

* * *

In February 1778, Parliament opened lots of roads, approving two bills of conciliation and drafting instructions for commissioners to go to America and settle the rebellion. They chose the earl of Carlisle, former West Florida governor William Johnstone, and William Eden as commissioners, with the renowned Scottish philosopher Dr. Adam Ferguson serving as official secretary. The chief British commanders in America, William and Richard Howe and Henry Clinton, were to join the commission once they arrived in Pennsylvania.[94]

Although they failed to accomplish any of their goals, it is valuable to pause and reflect on how the Carlisle Commission might have altered the American Revolution and the early history of the United States. Carlisle, Eden, and Johnstone were empowered to grant the patriots an amazing number of concessions: parliamentary supremacy would be revoked; Congress would be treated as a legal body (perhaps permanently); all offensive legislation passed since 1763 would be suspended; all standing troops in America would be removed, leaving defense to some version of the Continental army; no charter would ever be changed again; an American Bank would be established to help sink war debts; only Americans would serve as colonial officials or customs agents; and full pardon, amnesty, and indemnity would be available to all who participated in the rebellion. Parliament would regulate only imperial trade, but even then, not without American consent. The only item missing from this list was independence. Thus far, recognition of American independence had consistently been the sine qua non for any negotiation by patriot leaders. This was no guarantee, however, that the extensive catalog of British compromises would not appeal to the American public. Given that it would bring an end to the lengthening war, patriot leaders might not be able to hold back a wave of support for these deals, even if it meant sacrificing the Declaration of Independence. Perhaps the public would support the peace offerings in return for dissolving any developing relations with France. Or, worse, one or more states might break away from the union and negotiate a separate settlement. What might hap-

93. Oct. 6, 1778, *JCC*, XII, 986.

94. For more on the British response to Saratoga, see O'Shaughnessy, *The Men Who Lost America*, 61–65.

"It Is the Cause of Heaven against Hell"

pen to the union if enough people in one or more states greeted the commissioners as saviors, as lamps guiding the way out of the darkness of Revolutionary violence?[95]

The Carlisle Commission posed a sizable threat to the common cause. Patriot leaders had three powerful weapons at their disposal that could neutralize any popular support the commission might garner: outrage over the conduct of the war, control (though reduced) of communication networks throughout North America, and a ratified, legal treaty with France in hand by the time the commissioners landed. They would need all of these tools to defend independence from the best offer the American people were going to get from King George.

As Carlisle, Eden, and Johnstone prepared to cross the Atlantic, patriot leaders anxiously awaited word from France. They heard about North's conciliatory measures first, as loyalist newspapers in New York and Philadelphia began printing them in April 1778. Congress took several steps to defuse the threat of British conciliation, including drafting rebuttals that explained why Americans must reject North's proposals, passing a resolution that offered pardons to any "deluded and wicked" persons who might have aided the crown, and, finally, reviving dormant plans to bribe foreign mercenaries to desert British arms.[96]

---

95. Ritcheson, *British Politics and the American Revolution*, 268–270; Sadosky, *Revolutionary Negotiations*, 107.

96. For the loyalists printings of the conciliatory bills, see *Pennsylvania Evening Post*, Apr. 15, 20, 27, May 4, 1778; *Pennsylvania Ledger*, Apr. 18, 22, May 9, 13, 20, 1778; *Royal Pennsylvania Gazette*, Apr. 21, 24, May 1, 8, 19, 22, 1778; *New-York Gazette*, Apr. 27, May 4, 1778. Loyalist papers also printed transcripts of North's Feb. 17 speech in the House of Commons, for which, see *Pennsylvania Evening Post*, Apr. 17, 1778; *Royal Pennsylvania Gazette*, Apr. 17, 1778; *Royal Gazette* (New York), Apr. 18, 1778; *Pennsylvania Ledger*, Apr. 18, 1778. Patriot papers publishing the bills: *Pennsylvania Gazette*, Apr. 24, 1778; *Norwich Packet*, Apr. 27, 1778; *Continental Journal*, Apr. 30, 1778; *Independent Chronicle*, Apr. 30, 1778; *Virginia Gazette* (Clarkson & Davis), May 1, 1778; *Boston Gazette*, May 4, 1778; *Exeter Journal*, May 5, 1778; *Freeman's Journal* (Portsmouth), May 5, 1778; *Virginia Gazette* (Dixon & Hunter), May 8, 1778. North's conciliation speech: *Pennsylvania Packet*, Apr. 22, 1778; *Boston Gazette*, Apr. 27, 1778; *Connecticut Courant*, Apr. 28, 1778; *Connecticut Journal*, Apr. 29, 1778; *Massachusetts Spy*, Apr. 30, 1778; *Providence Gazette*, May 2, 1778; *Virginia Gazette* (Dixon & Hunter), May 8, 1778; *Exeter Journal*, May 12, 1778; *New-Jersey Gazette*, May 20, 1778. Resolution of pardon: Apr. 22, 23, 29, 1778, *JCC*, X, 379, 381–382, 405–410, printed in *Pennsylvania Gazette*, Apr. 24, 1778; *New-Jersey Gazette*, May 6, 1778; *Continental Journal*, May 7,

In a new address to the German mercenaries, they offered any defector something they would never grant to domestic insurrectionists or merciless savages: "Large and fertile tracts of country invite and will amply reward your industry." As one delegate put it, the mercenaries would "become resident as industrious and peaceable Subjects in a Country they cannot conquer." Congress hoped that the thousands of Hessians had heard about how well their captured comrades had been treated—"We have treated them more like citizens than prisoners of war"—and announced, "We now address you as part of the great family of mankind, whose freedom and happiness we most earnestly wish to promote and establish." The rhetorical posture of this post-Trenton offer suggests again how far the former men monsters had been redeemed. Pennsylvania printer Francis Bailey was to translate and publish a thousand copies of this new invitation immediately, an effort Congress deemed so secret they demanded the printer return the manuscript and all impressions so that "a single Copy" would not "get abroad." By early May, Bailey had completed this project, and the German translations were on their way to Washington at Valley Forge for him to find the "earliest and best Means of circulating the Papers among the German Troops."[97]

But the most significant step Congress took to neutralize British efforts of conciliation was to ratify the Treaty of Amity and Commerce with France. The treaty arrived in York on Saturday, May 2. Word of the momentous news inside the express rider's portmanteau apparently preceded the progress of his horse. Henry Laurens wrote the day before, "We hourly expect confirmatory accounts" of the French treaty. This news, Laurens believed, was sure to dismay the patriots' enemies: "This I hope will operate to good effect [on] the Savages of all Colours who are at this time attempting to ravage and distress us a little more in front and rear." For Laurens, a ratified, official alliance with France would not only dissuade less committed Americans from listening to British offers—it would depress the spirits of their potential friends.[98]

Unanimously, Congress accepted the treaty's articles whole and made

1778; _Independent Chronicle_, May 7, 1778; _Virginia Gazette_ (Clarkson & Davis), May 8, 1778; _Virginia Gazette_ (Dixon & Hunter), May 8, 1778; _Providence Gazette_, May 9, 1778; _Exeter Journal_, May 12, 1778; _Connecticut Courant_, May 12, 1778; _Connecticut Journal_, May 13, 1778; _Massachusetts Spy_, May 14, 1778.

97. Apr. 29, 1778, _JCC_, X, 406, 408; Richard Peters to GW, York, May 6, 1778, _PGW: RW_, XV, 66; HL to Francis Bailey, Apr. 30, 1778, _LDC_, IX, 547–548.

98. HL to George Galphin, May 1, 1778, _LDC_, IX, 553.

arrangements for them to be published "speedily." Within two days, a few "conspicuous" articles were already in print. Over the next several weeks, readers of twelve patriot prints perused the full provisions of the ratified treaty.[99]

Three days after Congress approved the treaty, the army "celebrated the new alliance with as much splendor as the short notice would allow." The strangeness that was America's embrace of Catholic France—celebrating what generations of colonists had regarded as a touchstone of political tyranny, religious slavery, and imperial rivalry—began in that instant. "The greatness of mind and policy of Louis XVI were extol'd," John Laurens reported from Valley Forge, "and his long life tosted with as much sincerity as that of the British King used to be in former times." Though hardly unique, this revolution of opinion about France was the most extreme example of minds changed because of the Revolution. "His Most Christian Majesty" had saved the common cause, and now "triumph beamed in every countenance." In Boston, Reverend Samuel Cooper "implor'd the Blessing of Heaven on the King of France and his Dominions" from the pulpit of the Brattle Street Church. He admitted this was "a new Thing in more Senses than one, and struck the whole Congregation with an agreable Surprize, who most cordially joyn'd in that Act of Devotion." The necessities of union had transformed public sentiment about the loathed Catholic French monarchy—or so patriot leaders bragged. Though they toasted Louis's birthday in Philadelphia and Baltimore that summer, many Americans did not instantly surrender their anti-Catholic prejudices. Nevertheless, as one historian put it, "By 1779 it was worse in New England eyes to be a Tory than a papist."[100]

99. HL to Richard Caswell, May 5, [1778], ibid., 602. "Conspicuous" treaty articles: *Pennsylvania Gazette,* May 4, 1778; *Pennsylvania Packet,* May 6, 1778; *New-Jersey Gazette,* May 13, 1778; *Virginia Gazette* (Dixon & Hunter), May 15, 1778; *Boston Gazette,* May 18, 1778 (supplement); *Connecticut Courant,* May 19, 1778; *Connecticut Journal,* May 20, 1778; *Massachusetts Spy,* May 28, 1778. Two royalist papers in Philadelphia also printed this early notice of the treaty (*Royal Pennsylvania Gazette,* May 12, 1778; *Pennsylvania Ledger,* May 13, 1778). Full treaty with France: *Pennsylvania Gazette,* May 9, 1778; *Pennsylvania Packet,* May 13, June 10, 1778; *Connecticut Courant,* May 19, 1778; *Independent Chronicle,* May 21, 1778; *Continental Journal,* May 21, 1778; *Providence Gazette,* May 23, 1778; *Boston Gazette,* May 25, 1778; *Norwich Packet,* May 25, 1778; *New-Jersey Gazette,* May 27, 1778; *Connecticut Journal,* May 27, 1778; *New York Packet,* May 28, 1778; *Connecticut Gazette,* May 29, 1778; *Exeter Journal,* June 2, 1778.

100. John Laurens to HL, Valley Forge, May 7, 1778, *PHL,* XIII, 264–265;

Finally, on Friday, Congress ended that propitious week with an address. It was the most emotional, impassioned statement yet issued by the Continental Congress, comparable only to Jefferson's rough draft of the Declaration. "Three years have now passed away, since the commencement of the present war," the delegates began, "a war without parallel in the annals of mankind." They again underscored the central front in the war: "On one side, we behold fraud and violence laboring in the service of despotism; on the other, virtue and fortitude supporting and establishing the rights of human nature." The righteous were "dragged into this arduous conflict" against their will. They then—again—described the terrible "rapine and devastation" their enemies inflicted on peaceful Americans, including driving women and children from their homes, and the "cool murder of men." But, of course, the coup de grâce was their employment of proxies:

> Nay, determined to dissolve the closest bonds of society, they have stimulated servants to slay their masters in the peaceful hour of domestic security. And as if all this were insufficient to slake their thirst of blood, the blood of brothers, of unoffending brothers, they have excited the Indians against us; and a general, who calls himself a Christian, a follower of the merciful Jesus, hath dared to proclaim to all the world, his intention of letting loose against us whole hosts of savages,

---

William Heath to JA, Boston, May 14, 1778, *PJA*, VI, 115; Samuel Cooper to BF, Boston, May 13, 1778, *PBF*, XXV, 443. Cooper wrote again the next day, telling Franklin, "You cannot conceive what Joy the Treaties with France have diffus'd among all true Americans, nor the chagrine they have given to the few interested and slavish Partizans of Britain among us" (Cooper to BF, Boston, May 14, 1778, *PBF*, XXVI, 453). "Tory than a papist": Francis D. Cogliano, *No King, No Popery: Anti-Catholicism in Revolutionary New England* (Westport, Conn., 1996), 84. For celebrations in Philadelphia, see *Pennsylvania Packet*, Aug. 25, 1778; *Connecticut Courant*, Sept. 8, 1778. For Baltimore, see *Dunlap's Maryland Gazette*, Sept. 1, 1778. For more on centrality of anti-Catholicism in colonial British America, see Carla Gardina Pestana, *Protestant Empire: Religion and the Making of the British Atlantic World* (Philadelphia, 2009); Owen Stanwood, *The Empire Reformed: English America in the Age of the Glorious Revolution* (Philadelphia, 2011). For more on how Americans interacted with French forces, see T. Cole Jones, "'Displaying the Ensigns of Harmony': The French Army at Newport, Rhode Island, 1780–1781," *New England Quarterly*, LXXXV (2012), 430–467. For British and loyalist reactions to the French alliance, see Brad Jones's forthcoming study, *Identity Crisis: Popular Patriotism in the Revolutionary British Atlantic*.

"It Is the Cause of Heaven against Hell"

whose rule of warfare is promiscuous carnage, who rejoice to murder the infant smiling in its mother's arms, to inflict on their prisoners the most excruciating torments, and exhibit scenes of horror from which nature recoils.

This venting of emotion recalled but significantly elaborated on the Declaration, making the language of that document look terse. To be sure, there was much more to say about Britain's Indian allies in the twenty-two months since independence, and Congress did not waste a chance to remind Americans of Burgoyne's proclamation.[101]

This established argument had grounding in the present and the past. Although they hardly needed more ammunition, it is likely that copies of the May 6 issue of John Dunlap's *Pennsylvania Packet* had traveled the two dozen miles from Lancaster to York as the delegates were preparing this address. In Wednesday's paper, they could read a new account from Carlisle, Pennsylvania, that "31 Tories lately formed the horrid design of joining the Savages in murdering and scalping their neighbours. . . . A few Indians met them: The banditti endeavoured to parley with them, and open their plan." But luckily, a "party of volunters," men Congress would deem "vindicators of liberty" in their address on Friday, went "in pursuit of these unnatural wretches, . . . proceeded towards the Ohio in search of any other whites who might have like designs." This was exactly what patriot polemicists had conjured: the line separating "us" from "them" embodied and in action.[102]

In Congress's address to the American public on the French alliance, just as in the Declaration, the engagement of slaves and Indians stood at the apex of their justification for continued resistance. When they turned to the prospect of conciliation, the delegates continued to feature the relationship between the crown and proxy fighters to discredit North's plan for peace. If the British were serious about negotiating a settlement, "why do they meanly court every little tyrant of Europe to sell them his unhappy slaves? Why do they continue to embitter the minds of the savages against you? Surely this is not the way to conciliate the affections of America. Be not, therefore, deceived." If they trusted the British, Congress warned ominously, Americans would "be exposed to every species of barbarity." If they

101. "Address of the Congress to the Inhabitants of the United States of America," May 8, 1778, *JCC*, XI, 474–481, esp. 474, 475, 476–477.
102. *Pennsylvania Packet*, May 6, 1778; "Address of the Congress," May 8, 1778, *JCC*, XI, 475.

resisted, the "sweets of a free commerce with every part of the earth will soon reimburse you for all the losses you have sustained."[103]

Far more than any previous statement, this singular address appealed to the passions of the American public. Saying nothing about abstract political topics likes taxation or consent, it focused on war crimes and called on the public to rekindle dying martial embers: "Arise, then! to your tents, and gird you for the battle! It is time to turn the headlong current of vengeance upon the head of the destroyer!" To compound this embrace of emotionality, Congress wanted this address to have a more direct impact on American hearts than what might arise from just reading it in patriot newspaper columns. They appended a recommendation to the end of the speech that the "ministers of the gospel of all denominations" read this address "immediately after divine service."[104]

At the triumphant moment of the French alliance, in other words, the climactic grievances of the Declaration overshadowed all other reasons for continuing the Revolution. Americans were to resist for no other motive than to punish the British for provoking slaves and Indians to violence. Foreign mercenaries were no longer a serious threat (only the king's dealings with other tyrant princes were now considered criminal), but British involvement with domestic insurrectionists and merciless savages remained reason enough to ignore all olive branches and soldier on, according to the Continental Congress. This address was a supplement to the ratified treaty with France. It was meant to be an exhortation that complemented the great news that the United States now had a powerful ally in Europe. This impassioned primer of war crimes would, it was hoped, stoke the public's outrage toward the British, overwhelm any lingering misgivings about embracing their old Catholic enemy, and defuse all talk of reconciliation and negotiation. Whether it actually did accomplish such a rekindling in American hearts as they walked out of their local churches, meeting houses, taverns, or coffeehouses is difficult to gauge. That these were the terms by which patriot publicists continued to frame the conflict is significant, nonetheless.

When the Carlisle commissioners arrived in Philadelphia a month later, therefore, not only had the details of their mission preceded them but patriot leaders had been working steadily to counteract their efforts while they

103. "Address of the Congress," May 8, 1778, *JCC*, XI, 478, 481.

104. Ibid.; *Pennsylvania Gazette*, May 16, 1778; *Connecticut Courant*, May 26, 1778; *New-Jersey Gazette*, May 27, 1778; *Continental Journal*, May 28, 1778; *Independent Chronicle*, May 28, 1778; *Boston Gazette*, June 1, 1778; *Massachusetts Spy*, June 4, 1778.

"It Is the Cause of Heaven against Hell"

were still on the ocean. Eden, Carlisle, and Johnstone would soon find that any prospects for their success were slight.

There was still some hope. France had not yet declared war on Britain, and perhaps enough political leaders either at national or state level could be persuaded to renounce the month-old alliance. On June 9, the commissioners dispatched their secretary, Adam Ferguson, to Valley Forge in the hopes that Washington would grant him a passport through American lines to begin communicating with Congress at York. Washington initially rejected the overture and dashed off a note to President Laurens for further instructions.[105]

Washington's inquiry of how to proceed engendered a vociferous debate in Congress the next day. Immediately, the delegates scribbled a circular letter to the surrounding states, notifying them of the commissioners' intentions and reciting yet again the themes of the May 9 address: "Indian irruptions and burning houses, in the moment of dispersing propositions for Peace, evince the insidious designs of the Enemy and demonstrate the necessity of wisdom in Council; of strength and vigour in the field." They then debated what to do about Dr. Ferguson. As had been the case at several key moments during the war, issues involving proxy fighters intruded on their minds. While Washington struggled with the protocol of Ferguson's request, an express rider was making his way from Albany with news of "parties of Savages and Tories" menacing the northern frontiers. This was Joseph Brant and Captain Walter Butler—two men who were about to become household names in America—and, the Indian agents reported, "the country is greatly alarmed and distressed." Congress's journal for June 11 shows that pages of resolutions and significant policy decisions concerning the apparent "commencement of an Indian war" followed the reading of Ferguson's passport request and Washington's inquiry. Intelligence from Albany and Pittsburgh led them to believe that "the Senecas, Cayugas, Mingoes, and Wiandots in general, a majority of the Onondagas, and a few of the Ottawas, Chippawas, Shawanese, and Delawares, acting contrary to the voice of their nations, amounting, in the whole, to about 1,600 warriors, ex-

---

105. General Henry Clinton to GW, Philadelphia, June 9, 1778, *PGW: RW*, XV, 358, GW to Clinton, [Valley Forge], June 9, 1778, 359, GW to HL, Valley Forge, June 9, 1778, 368, William Eden to GW, Philadelphia, June 9, 1778, 363; Carlisle Commission to HL, Philadelphia, June 9, 1778, *PHL*, XIII, 424–427. That hostilities had not yet broken out between France and Britain might have complicated matters; see John Laurens to HL, Valley Forge, June 7, 1778, *PHL*, XIII, 416–418.

clusive of several tories" were about to attack, having been "industriously in-stigated . . . by principal officers in the service of the king of Great Britain." They decided to authorize three thousand men to undertake an expedition against Detroit and the man who was becoming the most notorious instiga-tor, Colonel Henry Hamilton.[106]

Just as they had done at several other critical moments during the Revo-lution, patriot leaders dealt with Britain and its proxy allies simultaneously. These problems were indivisible. The Carlisle commissioners were unaware that their efforts were being further enervated by another set of actors, Indi-ans from Lake Ontario to the Ohio River. Henry Laurens summarized the situation aptly, from his perspective: "The Indians Northward and Westward have taken their Lesson from the Savages at Philadelphia, New-York and R[hode] Island. In the very Act of negociating for Peace they are burning, murdering, and Scalping." British officials, regular army soldiers, Indians, "savage Tories": these were all the foreign enemies of the United States.[107]

Stymied by Washington's refusal to grant Dr. Ferguson a passport, the commissioners decided to send a packet of letters for Washington to for-ward to Congress. This packet, which contained private letters written to individual delegates from George Johnstone and other English correspon-dents, as well as the official terms of the commissioners' peace offering, was sealed with a "fond picture of a mother caressing her Children," a device "no doubt, projected for the occasion." It reached Congress on Saturday, June 13. As Samuel Adams put it, writing to James Warren in Boston, "By the in-closed News Paper you will see that the Scene begins to open."[108]

Laurens broke open the seals and began reading the commissioners' statement. When he reached the second page, New York delegate Gouver-neur Morris, incredulous, stood and shouted for him to stop. The commis-sioners had made an unflattering reference to America's new ally, describ-ing France's interest in the conflict as an "Insidious interposition of a Power,

106. Henry Laurens to the States, June 10, 1778, *LDC*, X, 67–68, esp. 67; Com-missioners of Indian Affairs to GW, Albany, June 9, 1778, *PGW: RW*, XV, 359–362, esp. 360. See also John Wentworth to John Langdon, York, June 10, 1778, *LDC*, X, 70. Approval for Detroit expedition: June 11, 1778, *JCC*, XI, 587, 588.

107. HL to Rawlins Lowndes, June 12, [1778], *LDC*, X, 79–80, Wentworth to Langdon, York, June 10, 1778, 69–70, esp. 70.

108. John Laurens to HL, Valley Forge, June 11, 1778, *PHL*, XIII, 443, HL to Horatio Gates, York, June 13, 1778, 451; Samuel Adams to James Warren, York, June 13, 1778, *LDC*, X, 84–86, esp. 85.

"It Is the Cause of Heaven against Hell"

which has from the first Settlement of these Colonies been Actuated with Enmity to us both." This was meant to convince patriots to back out of the treaty, but Morris, among others, viewed it as an insult to the king of France. Congress resolved for Laurens to halt, reseal the documents, and adjourn for the weekend.[109]

When Congress reconvened on Monday, they began to explore an unprecedented step that exposed their concerns about how the commissioners might win over lukewarm or disaffected Americans. They assigned three men—William Henry Drayton, Samuel Adams, and Richard Henry Lee—to a committee "to prepare a resolution for preventing any correspondence with the enemy." This charge should give pause. The delegates were apparently troubled by the private correspondence Johnstone and his colleagues were holding with patriot political and military leaders, and they wanted to find a mechanism to interrupt those conversations. But entrance into this area would have meant a considerable enlargement of executive power. What would it mean if they resolved to prevent correspondence—and how did Congress propose to enact such a policy?[110]

The following day, Lee, Adams, and Drayton issued their report. Drayton, the Charleston jurist who was famous in South Carolina for his stirring addresses against the crown, wrote that because "many letters . . . have been lately received from England, through the conveyance of the enemy, and some of them, which have been under the inspection of members of Congress, are found to contain ideas insidiously calculated to divide and delude the good people of these states," they recommended "to the legislative and executive authorities of the several states, to exercise the utmost care and vigilance, and take the most effectual measures to put a stop to so dangerous and criminal a correspondence." They further suggested Washington and his commanders "in each and every military department be . . . hereby directed to carry the measures" out to their "most effectual execution."[111]

This was a decisive move. Drayton, Lee, and Adams were among the patriot leaders' most astute manipulators of public opinion. They had become experts in the cultivation and propagation of managed information. They understood that to achieve real success in substantiating their argument,

109. Carlisle Commission to HL, Philadelphia, June 9, 1778, *PHL*, XIII, 424–427, esp. 425–426; June 13, 1778, *JCC*, XI, 605–606; "Charles Thomson's Notes [on Carlisle Commission]," [June 16, 1778], *LDC*, X, 111–112.

110. June 16, 1778, *JCC*, XI, 608.

111. June 17, 1778, ibid., 613–616, esp. 616.

patriots not only had to spread their own stories and images but also hush all opposing interpretations. Leaders in many locales acted on this principle throughout the first years of war, using carrots (the prospect of lucrative government printing contracts) and sticks (raiding shops, burning pamphlets, threatening publicists with violence). This proposal, however, was the most sweeping effort yet to silence their opposition. In effect, "Drayton's proposals for restricting written communication within the United States knew no limits." If approved, this resolution—which produced little controversy or debate—could lead to military officers and state officials having the right to intercept post riders and examine private correspondence. The resolution to defuse the Carlisle Commission by criminalizing their ability to communicate with American elites and opinion makers was deemed a worthy, legitimate act.[112]

112. "Drayton's proposals": Sadosky, *Revolutionary Negotiations,* 112. This interpretation has influenced my thinking on the importance of the Carlisle Commission as a turning point of the Revolution, for which, see 109–118. The proposed resolution to interdict the mail was not as significant an abridgment of rights in the 1770s as it would seem to modern readers. Although the postal law Congress passed in July 1775 did not stipulate whether any officials could open the mail, William Goddard's proposed plan for reorganizing a "Constitutional Post Office" did state that postmasters could inspect letters, but they remained "under oath for the faithful discharge of the trust reposed in them." See July 26, 1775, *JCC,* II, 208–209; [William Goddard], *The Plan for Establishing a New American Post-Office* (Boston, 1774), *Early American Imprints,* 42609. Committees of correspondence in several locales, including New York City, had already usurped the power to not only inspect but "endorse" letters. It was not until the 1792 Postal Act that postal officers were strictly prohibited from opening letters. The apotheosis of the sacred mailbag—a cultural imperative that has become the familiar, modern standard in the United States—was a mid-nineteenth-century invention that scholars argue was caused by the onset of a commercial economy and new expectations of bourgeois privacy. See Leonard D. White, *The Federalists: A Study in Administrative History, 1789–1801* (New York, 1948), 187–193; Richard R. John, *Spreading the News: The American Postal System from Franklin to Morse* (Cambridge, Mass., 1995), 42; Millette Shamir, *Inexpressible Privacy: The Interior Life of Antebellum American Literature* (Philadelphia, 2006), 157–162; David M. Henkin, *The Postal Age: The Emergence of Modern Communications in Nineteenth-Century America* (Chicago, 2006), 99; Konstantin Dierks, *In My Power: Letter Writing and Communications in Early America* (Philadelphia, 2009), 203–205, 275. For their part, the British began intercepting correspondence from America in the summer of 1775, an abuse that Julie M. Flavell also sees as "proverbial," since crown officials could do this with or without a warrant, and had been doing so since 1711 (Flavell, "Govern-

In his explanation of this step to Washington, Laurens confessed, "The Idea of opening other people's Letter's is exceedingly abhorrent to me, but I think Congress have a power over Letters equal at least to that which necessity obliges them sometimes to exercise over persons." Whether or not they could wield that power over the sovereign states, moreover, was quite doubtful, especially since the Articles of Confederation had not been ratified. Because the union was not yet confederated, the specter of a state or multiple states possibly breaking away and negotiating a separate peace was not beyond the realm of possibility. Congress made an earnest recommendation that states be allowed to violate the privacy of their citizens for the purposes of protecting national security. It was not assured that everyone would agree this policy was necessary, especially since it mandated that Continental army troops were to be its enforcers. This step highlights the peculiar position of the common cause when confronted by William Eden's peace commission.[113]

Congress returned the resealed packet of letters to the commissioners, informing them that the only way Congress would treat with them would be via an "explicit acknowledgement" of independence or a wholesale military withdrawal. Eden, Carlisle, and Johnstone were not authorized to discuss either issue. Although it would turn out to be the moment of the union's greatest strength, patriot leaders could not know that at the time. The rejection of the Carlisle Commission might have produced a serious popular backlash, had a majority of Americans known what the commissioners were offering. The concessions were extensive and potentially enticing. In order to prevent them from gaining popularity, Drayton, Adams, and Lee and their colleagues endorsed drastic action to neutralize all communication with the commissioners.[114]

Patriot leaders, of course, did more than just try to isolate and discredit the commission. They also took the rhetorical offensive to remind Americans again why they should rally around the common cause. Drayton wrote a lengthy address (that he actually signed with his initials) for the *Pennsylvania Gazette* attacking Johnstone, who had previously been one of America's

ment Interception of Letters from America and the Quest for Colonial Opinion in 1775," *WMQ*, 3d Ser., LVIII [2001], 403–430, esp. 406).

113. HL to GW, York, June 18, 1778, *LDC*, X, 131.

114. HL to the Carlisle Commission, York, June 17, 1778, *LDC*, X, 123–124, esp. 124. They were, of course, printed extensively in the active loyalist papers in New York and Newport.

earliest and most eloquent supporters in Parliament. "Is he now come to our shore to invite us to surrender to the justice and mercy of our most un-just and vengeful enemies?" he queried. "Enemies who gave *stretch* to their savage allies, to murder our old and unarmed farmers, and their helpless women and children: Enemies who have plundered our country, burned our towns, and armed son against father, servant against master, and brother against brother, in order to subject us?" Five newspapers, including John Holt's *New-York Journal* recently revived in Poughkeepsie, exchanged Dray-ton's fiery speech, which concluded with the claim, "Our resolution is fixed, nor do we fear 'the horrors and devastations of war,' with which, . . . you threaten us." Drayton would write several more missives aimed at the Car-lisle commissioners throughout the summer and fall.[115]

Gouverneur Morris joined his colleague in writing polemical essays, though his were under the pseudonym "An American." Morris lectured the commissioners, "You have injured us too much. We might, on this occasion, give you some late instances of singular barbarity, committed as well by the forces of his Britannic Majesty, as by those of his generous and faithful allies, the Senecas, Onondagas, and Tuscaroras. But we will not offend a courtly ear by the recital of those disgusting scenes." As he had in previous install-ments, Thomas Paine asked in the sixth *American Crisis* what "sort of men" the commissioners supposed Americans to be, if they thought that Ameri-cans could forgive "an undeclared war let loose upon them, and Indians and Negroes invited to the slaughter." Another writer in the *North-Carolina Gazette* rhetorically asked the earl of Carlisle if his offers of peace stemmed from a benevolent sensibility. "What! Is it benevolent then to ransack Ger-many, to drain the jails of Britain, to let loose the rebellious Scot, our faith-less domestics, and savage tribes of Indians, to spread ruin and desolation through the whole continent of America?"[116]

115. During the debate over the Coercive Acts, Johnstone predicted in Parlia-ment that their harsh measures would produce a "general Confederacy" in America, for which see House of Commons, "On the Question, That This Bill Do Pass," Mar. 25, 1774, 4 *Am. Archives*, I, 49–57, esp. 54; *Boston News-Letter*, May 19, 1774; *Providence Gazette*, May 21, 1774. See also T. H. Breen, *American Insurgents, American Patri-ots: The Revolution of the People* (New York, 2010), 68. Drayton address: *Pennsylvania Gazette*, June 20, 1778; *Providence Gazette*, July 4, 1778; *Independent Chronicle*, July 9, 1778; *Pennsylvania Packet*, July 9, 1778; *New-York Journal*, July 13, 1778; *Exeter Journal*, July 14, 1778.

116. Gouvernor Morris to the Carlisle Commissioners, [June 20, 1778], *LDC*,

By the end of June, the Carlisle Commission was effectively finished. The chances of its success had never been assured; it was vexed from the start by squabbling among its military and civilian members. The British army's evacuation of Philadelphia and return to New York City, which began the day after Congress sent word they would not meet with the commissioners, further crippled their efforts. But the most significant factor that destroyed any peace initiative in 1778 was Congress's campaign against the commissioners. For several weeks before the earl of Carlisle arrived in Pennsylvania, they worked to discredit North's conciliatory bills by casting aspersions on them in patriot newspapers. They quickly ratified the treaty with France as an insurance policy against British peace offers. And when the commissioners did approach them with terms, they kept the ambassadors at bay and prevented as many Americans as possible from discovering just how generous those terms truly were. Eden, Carlisle, and Johnstone left Philadelphia in defeat, traveling to Manhattan, where they would continue to appeal to the American public through manifestos, public pronouncements, and advertisements in the New York royalist press—all to little avail. Morris, Drayton, and their colleagues continued to retaliate with their own fiery, defiant essays. Early in October, Johnstone went home. It was all over.[117]

X, 155–162, esp. 156, 161. His essay was published in *Pennsylvania Gazette*, June 15, 1778; *Pennsylvania Packet*, July 4, 1778; *Continental Journal*, July 9, 1778; *Pennsylvania Evening Post*, July 14, 1778; *New-Jersey Gazette*, July 15, 1778; *North-Carolina Gazette*, July 17, 1778; *New-Hampshire Gazette*, July 21, 1778; *South-Carolina and American General Gazette*, July 23, 1778. For Paine, see *The Crisis, Number VI*, Oct. 20, 1778, in Eric Foner, ed., *Thomas Paine: Collected Writings . . .* (New York, 1995), 185. In *The American Crisis, Number III* (Philadelphia, 1777), he accused Britain of being "never better pleased than when at war—that hath filled India with carnage and famine—Africa with slavery—and tampered with Indians and Negroes to cut the throats of the freemen of America" (Foner, ed., *Paine: Writings,* 137). "Ransack Germany": *Virginia Gazette* (Purdie), Oct. 30, 1778; *Virginia Gazette* (Dixon & Hunter), Oct. 30, 1778; *North-Carolina Gazette*, Nov. 20, 1778.

117. One of the final patriot statements against the Carlisle Commission was a 122-page pamphlet published in early 1779 by Gouverneur Morris, entitled *Observations on the American Revolution.* This document swore that Americans would seek vengeance against their British enemies for the unnatural war they had prosecuted. British "subjects and adherents may easily be found in any part of the earth," Morris threatened, "and the dreaded scalping-knife itself may, in the hands of our riflemen, spread horror through their island." See [Morris], *Observations on the American Revolution: Published According to a Resolution of Congress, by Their Committee . . .* (Philadelphia,

The rejection of the Carlisle Commission secured the common cause. Now the United States had, as one body, formed a political, military, and commercial alliance with France. It had officially entered the international states system. And, as a singular body, it had also rejected the best offer of reconciliation the British were ever going to tender. None from the "sovereign and independent communities" approached the commissioners with plans to negotiate a separate settlement. That it is difficult to imagine a development whereby any of the thirteen states took steps to reenter the British Empire in 1778 is a testament to the narrative and interpretative strength of the common cause.

The patriots accomplished this act of resistance in spite of growing problems with public support for the war, antipathy toward patriot recruiting officers and state conscription plans, diminishing supplies, and a looming financial crisis. Fragile as it was, the patriot coalition was still intact at the start of the war's third summer. One of the main goals of the common cause had been achieved: they had survived long enough to gain European assistance.

Accomplishing this goal also meant closing down possibilities for African Americans and Indians. Even though they were less able to dominate information networks in 1777 and 1778, patriot leaders still set great store in the power of print to cordon off friends from enemies. Defining the common cause as opposing the king's savages had produced real consequences for hostile and friendly Indians alike. The amplification of Burgoyne's claim of "giving stretch" to the Indians and the subsequent furor over Jane McCrea narrowed the patriots' vision, precluding their ability to imagine Indians as full participants in the fledgling republic. The managers of the common cause appeal treated all Indians as merciless savages, even the numerous groups who fought and died for them. The stories patriot publicists broadcast—from generals' letters to satires, to official proclamations, to plays, to general orders, to poems—blocked policymakers (often the same individuals) from pursuing political or diplomatic agendas that opened the door for friendly Indians to enjoy citizenship. African Americans, free and enslaved, suffered a similar foreclosure. The ghosts of Dunmore and numerous other British agents who encouraged domestic insurrectionists continued to haunt patriots' political imaginations in 1777 and 1778. Patriot leaders dismissed repeated emancipation schemes, even those proposed by their

---

1779), 121–122, esp. 121, *Early American Imprints*, 16625. For more on this text, see Sadosky, *Revolutionary Negotiations*, 90–91.

"It Is the Cause of Heaven against Hell"

own officers, as unwise because they threatened union. Excluding African Americans from the political community, as the 1778 Massachusetts state constitution proposed, fitted better with the common cause appeal. Even when exclusion led to protests that such prejudices violated the other side of the cause—namely, that the Revolution was a fight for natural rights—those claims gained little popular support.

The redemption of the German mercenaries and, even more strangely, the wholesale reversal of opinion about the French underscore the power—and contrivance—of the common cause appeal. Inversion was possible. Because the patriots emphasized some stories but not others, not only did the previously hated French become the Revolution's saviors but the German mercenaries, men who were sent to America for the specific purpose of crushing the rebellion, became sympathetic fellow victims of monarchical tyranny. This did not occur for African Americans or Indians. When patriot publicists loudly denounced Indians' slaying of Jane McCrea but not Virginians' slaying of Cornstalk, when they did not substantiate how many blacks served in the Continental army but exchanged stories about dozens of slaves running to the British, they rescinded any opportunity for the sort of redemption enjoyed by the French and Germans. Moreover, when those stories became codified in the Articles of Confederation, the Massachusetts state constitution, or Congress's proclamation announcing the French alliance, they became foundational to the new republic. Spurning Great Britain's best offer of reconciliation meant that the common cause would continue. This invited further opportunities to prove that African Americans and Indians did not deserve to be part of the newly recognized United States.

Interlude

FRANKLIN AND LAFAYETTE'S
"LITTLE BOOK"

After the Carlisle commissioners failed to convince many Americans to abandon their new alliance with France, the common cause entered a new phase of relative security. France's recognition of the United States brought a declaration of war from England, enlarging the war into a conflict that could be fought far outside North America, in Europe and throughout the Atlantic. When the war pivoted from a colonial rebellion to a conventional conflict between European powers, it naturally meant that the crown would shift its strategy. Now they had to guard against a French invasion across the Channel and protect their holdings in the Caribbean and in Asia. The priority of conquering the United States slipped.

This more solid footing for the patriots in the summer of 1778 was also the product of unceasing efforts to propagate certain stories and representations about themselves and their enemies to the American public. One of the key ingredients that kept the cause intact for three years was the patriots' ability to illustrate and broadcast the depth of British "barbarities."

In fact, during the previous year, patriot leaders in Congress had ordered Benjamin Franklin to do exactly that. In 1779, Franklin began to work on what would seem an odd assignment for the United States' ambassador to France. Congress had ordered him to contract an artist to create thirty-five engravings for a child's schoolbook. Enlisting the help of the marquis de Lafayette, who had just returned to Paris after serving in America throughout 1777 and 1778, Franklin developed a literal illustration of British cruelties since Lexington. As the ambassador would later explain to a British official, Congress had tasked him with producing a book "to impress the minds of Children and Posterity with a deep sense of your bloody and insatiable

Malice and Wickedness." Congress was asking Franklin to assemble an official catalog of American suffering. Franklin was to become the Revolution's John Foxe; he would arrange the creation of a *Book of Martyrs* for the new republic.[1]

Children's books were a new, expanding market in late-eighteenth-century Anglo-America. After 1750, publishers increasingly produced books of various length and quality in several genres, including romantic tales, advice and courtesy manuals, fables, religious instruction, and nursery rhymes. Franklin and Lafayette's book would blur many of these lines. Far from the religious base of most of its competitors, the unabashed political message of their project contained elements of these genres: romantic "derring-do" on the part of heroic patriots, moralizing national fables complete with monsters, and clear advice on how children should remember America's enemies as they grew up. Had it materialized, their schoolbook would have been a unique contribution to American education.[2]

Franklin and Lafayette drafted twenty-six descriptions of proposed illustrations. Far more than just a general list of ideas, the document is a working précis that details exactly what they wished a French engraver to depict. The first eighteen are in Franklin's hand, Lafayette added six of his own, and Franklin then came up with the final two.[3]

Franklin's list started with fire. The first seven pictures would depict the towns of Charlestown, Falmouth, Norfolk, and others ablaze and the inhabitants exposed. After two more pictures about the mistreatment of prisoners, Franklin began a run of prints that centered on British proxies. The tenth illustration was to depict the following:

> Dunmore's hiring the Negroes to murder their Master's Families.
> A large House
> Blacks arm'd with Guns and Hangers
> Master and his Sons on the Ground dead,
> Wife and Daughters lifted up in the Arms of the Negroes as they are
>   carrying off.

1. BF to David Hartley, Passy, Feb. 2, 1780, *PBF*, XXXI, 436–439, esp. 439. The original order from Congress is not in the *Journals of the Continental Congress*.

2. E. Jennifer Monaghan, *Learning to Read and Write in Colonial America* (Amherst, Mass., 2005), 302–332.

3. "Franklin and Lafayette's List of Prints to Illustrate British Cruelties," *PBF*, XXIX, 590–593.

The next portrayed a similar scene, also meant to terrify. The engraver was to show "Savages killing and scalping the Frontier Farmers and their Families, Women and Children, English Officers mix'd with the savages and giving them Orders and encouraging them." Prints 13, 14, and 15 further developed this theme of British pleasure at the sight of American scalps. Print 13 focused on East Florida governor Patrick Tonyn sitting at a table, receiving "Scalps of the Georgia People." Print 14 shifted the action to Niagara, where the commander received "in like Manner the Scalps of the Wioming Families." Finally, it was the king's turn: print 15 was to depict the secretary at war presenting George III with an "Acct. of Scalps. which he receives very graciously."[4]

Lafayette continued this bloody theme. His first contribution to the list of illustrations recaptured one of the more infamous images of 1775: General Philip Schuyler's report to Congress that the British had asked the Indians to "feast on a Bostonian and drink his blood." The horrific imagery that this singular letter brought to mind was a totem for patriot publicists, especially Hugh Henry Brackenridge, who had dramatized the scene in his 1777 play *The Death of General Montgomery*. Lafayette and Franklin wanted a Parisian artist to get this representation just right. Lafayette instructed the engraver to show prisoners being "Roasted for a great festival where the Canadian indians are eating American flesh, Colonel Buttler, an english officer Setting at table." Lafayette added other images involving proxy activity. Illustration 19 was another shocking domestic scene: "British officers who being prisoners on parole are well Receiv'd in the Best American families, and take that opportunity of corrupting Negroes and Engaging them to desert from the house, to Robb, and even to Murder they Masters."[5]

The list of prints is a fascinating document of patriot efforts to mobilize the population for battle. Nearly all of the proposed illustrations revolve around three topics: the cannonading of towns, British mistreatment of prisoners, and blacks and Indians destroying American households and familial bliss. Congress wanted Americans to remember British crimes, and these were the impressions Franklin and Lafayette decided best captured the Revolutionary experience thus far. Lafayette opined to his partner that they "Could indeed make out an immense Book upon so Rich a matter" as British cruelties. That they both believed British instigation of blacks and Indians was essential to understanding the conflict—and retaining its

4. "Franklin and Lafayette's List," *PBF*, XXIX, 591–592.
5. Ibid., 592.

salience—is significant, as is the absence of any mention of German mercenaries. Franklin and Lafayette meant to transform domestic insurrectionists
and merciless savages into indelible pictures that would instruct future generations about who tried to destroy liberty at the founding.[6]

Franklin apparently worked on the schoolbook prints over the next year,
and Lafayette periodically checked in on the progress of "our little Book."
In December 1779, Franklin hired an engraver and had at least one image
created by April 1780. A few months later, he sent a copy of the materials
to one of his regular correspondents, Reverend Samuel Cooper in Boston.
Cooper acknowledged receipt in a September 1780 letter to Franklin. "I received . . . the Caracaturas you were so kind as to send me," he wrote. "They
afford a striking Picture of Barbarity, and I have disposed of them in such a
Manner as to do Good." It is unclear what Cooper's avenue of dispensation
was. Franklin expected something to happen on the American end, writing
to London merchant William Hodgson, "A Book is preparing in America
containing a great Number of Authenticated Accounts of such Barbarities
. . . Engravings are intended to be made of each Transaction, proper to be
printed in the Book." As he did with many of his English correspondents,
Franklin chastised Hodgson on behalf of his country: "You may judge what
Impression this is likely to make in the Minds of Children, and what Effect
it may have on Posterity, with regard to any future Union or even Good Will
between the two Nations if the printing it is not prevented."[7]

Yet Franklin's anticipation that his project was about to shape the next
generation of American feelings toward Britain would soon evaporate.
After Cooper got the précis of the "little book," the trail ends abruptly,
even though the two coeditors continued to correspond about it through
the following winter. What came of their project is unknown. Cooper was
certainly not a hostile recipient of this manuscript; nor would Congress—
who sponsored this project in the first place—seek to censor it. Given the
patriots' financial straits by the fall of 1780, it is probable that there were no
available funds to subsidize a child's textbook. That the "little book" project

6. Lafayette to BF, Paris, May 19, 1779, in Stanley J. Idzerda, ed., *Lafayette in
the Age of the American Revolution: Selected Letters and Papers, 1776–1790*, 5 vols. (Ithaca,
N.Y., 1977–1983), II, 265.

7. Lafayette to BF, Le Havre, July 12, 1779, in Idzerda, ed., *Lafayette in Age of
the American Revolution*, II, 292; Samuel Cooper to BF, Boston, Sept. 8, 1780, *PBF*,
XXXIII, 262–264, esp. 264, BF to William Hodgson, June 19, 1780, 556–557, esp.
557.

was all for naught must have frustrated Franklin, who had high hopes for it. He envisioned these illustrations, "expressing every abominable Circumstance of [British] Cruelty and Inhumanity," to adorn the first coinage of the United States.[8]

Franklin and Lafayette's schoolbook, complete with lavish and shocking illustrations, never made it into America's classrooms, nor did the images find their way into American pockets and purses. Conversations about keeping American hearts and minds focused on British atrocities, however, hardly ceased.

Cooper perhaps mentioned the schoolbook in a letter to Franklin's colleague in Amsterdam, John Adams. Adams responded by encouraging Cooper on the power of propagation, frustrated that patriot leaders had not embraced it fully enough. Adams could not understand why they were not doing more to stoke American hatred of their enemy. "I know not the Reason," he wrote to Cooper, "but our Countrymen never appeared to me to have considered Seriously what it was to commit Hostilities against Great Britain. They seem to think the English still their Friends."[9]

Adams counseled Cooper on the excellent methods the Dutch used to foster national hatred for the French. The Dutch published "little Books containing short and Simple narrations, adapted to the Capacities of the common People of the Devastations, Cruelties and Brutalities of the french Armies . . . intermixed with little Prints representing many of the most detestible of those Scaenes." He added that these books, published a century before, when Louis XIV invaded the Dutch Republic, "were read by every body, and they contributed to excite a universal Hatred and Horror of that nation which runs through every Vein to this day." While the English were portraying Americans in a "light equally odious," Adams complained that the patriots "seem to be afraid to represent the British Conduct towards

8. In December 1780, Franklin asked his coeditor to keep sending him "authenticated Accounts of the Enemies Barbarity that are necessary for our Little Book" (BF to Lafayette, Passy, Dec. 9, 1780, *PBF*, XXXIV, 142–143). In February 1781, Lafayette responded that he did not know "if our little Book has yet made its Appearance — But am of Opinion that the first Volume Might go on with Such ornaments as you Have got, and as the Enemy are Working very fast on [that] Hellish trade, I shall furnish you With further Materials." See Lafayette to BF, New Windsor, N.Y., Feb. 1, 1781, in Idzerda, ed., *Lafayette in Age of the American Revolution*, III, 306; BF to Edward Bridgen, Passy, Oct. 2, 1779, *PBF*, XXX, 429–431, esp. 430.

9. JA to Samuel Cooper, Amsterdam, Dec. 9, 1780, *PJA*, X, 400–401, esp. 401.

Franklin and Lafayette's "Little Book"

them, lest it should alienate the Affections of the People." He was incensed that patriot leaders did not take greater steps to vilify the British. "They will find themselves the Dupes of their own good Nature and unsuspicious Temper," he lamented to Cooper. After all, the crown "have found means and had the Art to inspire even the Populace with a Hatred of Us, as bitter as that of the common Soldiers who are employed to butcher Us in America."[10]

When Cooper's letter arrived, Adams was employing his own art in Amsterdam to inspire bitterness. In the second of his twenty-six published letters in October 1780 that explained the Revolution to the Dutch, Adams indicted the British for their use of proxies. Responding to the question of whether Americans hated the British, Adams responded that they certainly should:

> burning their Towns—butchering their People—deliberately starving Prisoners, ravishing their Women—exciting Hosts of Indians to butcher and scalp them and purchasing Germans to destroy them, and hiring Negro servants to murder their Masters . . . All these Horrors, the English have practised in every Part of America from Boston to Savanna.

Adams must have taken some solace in hearing the details of an American "little book," but he wanted his colleagues to do much more, especially concerning the king's proxies.[11]

The efforts of Franklin and Adams to shape opinion about the lengthening war, and their view that their colleagues across the Atlantic should redouble their efforts to cultivate American hatred, are instructive. Adams

10. JA to Cooper, Dec. 9, 1780, ibid., 401. Among the most popular of the books Adams referred to were Romeyn de Hooghe, *Mirror of the French Tyranny* (Amsterdam, 1673) and Abraham Wicquevort, *De Fransch Tyrannie* (Amsterdam, 1674). These books also focused on foreign troops' terrorizing Dutch women, destroying familial peace and happiness, and massacring innocents. The books themselves were elaborations of works published in the late sixteenth century against the Spanish during the Dutch Revolt. In the 1670s, Dutch artists simply replaced Spanish tyrants with French ones. For more on these books and their influence, see Simon Schama, *The Embarrassment of Riches: An Interpretation of Dutch Culture in the Golden Age* (New York, 1987), 51–53, 275–283. For background on Louis's 1672 invasion, see Jonathan Israel, *The Dutch Republic: Its Rise, Greatness, and Fall, 1477–1806* (Oxford, 1995), 796–806.

11. JA to Hendrik Colkoen, Amsterdam, Oct. 5, 1780, *PJA*, X, 203–208, esp. 204.

and Franklin, of course, had been among the vanguard in justifying and amplifying the common cause for the public in the war's first years. When they went to Europe to negotiate for alliances and aid, they continued these activities. Both contributed correspondence and original articles to the *Affairs de l'Angleterre et de l'Amerique*, a Paris organ dedicated to news from America and sponsored by the French government. But Adams and Franklin were veterans of the rage militaire. Franklin had left America in the fall of 1776, Adams in the first weeks of 1778. Franklin did not witness the steady decline in popular support for the Revolution, and Adams's last days in Congress were the halcyon ones after Burgoyne's surrender, when any smoldering embers of the rage were briefly rekindled. When the envoys boarded ship for France, they severed the everyday experience of reading newspapers and discussing events at or near the moment. Their attitudes and expectations in 1779 and 1780 about the need to promote the common cause, therefore, were relics of 1776. They did not understand that the appeal to American patriotism had shifted in the later years of the war.[12]

The illustrations for Franklin and Lafayette's schoolbook—and Adams's desire that the patriots subsidize similar projects—are significant for another reason. They both signal an attitude that hatred toward the British and their proxies needed to be made permanent. Adams worried that if Americans did not despise the English for generations to come, the Revolution would fail. Franklin's little book was meant to make a fleeting rage engendered in wartime a permanent fixture in American education. They believed that if American children were to become good republican citizens, they needed to loathe the British crown—and remember the actions of those the British had sponsored.

Although the schoolbook did not materialize, other efforts that sought to codify war stories into enduring narratives of the founding were successful. Like Franklin and Lafayette's projected artwork, they, too, involved crafting narratives that fleshed out the final grievance in the Declaration of Independence. In the last years of the Revolutionary War, old and new stories that posited Indians and African Americans as enemies of the Revolution

12. Peter M. Ascoli, "American Propaganda in the French Language Press during the American Revolution," *La Révolution Américaine et L'Europe: Actes du colloque international, 21–25 février 1978, Paris-Toulouse* (Paris, 1979), 291–305; James H. Hutson, "Letters from a Distinguished American: The American Revolution in Foreign Newspapers," *Quarterly Journal of the Library of Congress*, XXXIV (1977), 292–305.

not only continued to circulate throughout North America, but they also began to have major consequences for people's lives.

The chapters that follow document the profundity of the discourse about proxies that continued long after the securing of the French alliance. Even without a didactic primer to teach America's children how to hate, for the remainder of the war, and for decades after, patriot political and communications leaders continued to justify the Revolution in terms of defending the cause of liberty from tyrants and their assistants. Popular support for the war did flag to dangerous levels by 1780. The reasons for this have most often been attributed to fiscal disasters, but the loss of the patriots' communications monopoly—especially in the South—mattered, too. Nevertheless, from all the ink and effort they dedicated to it, patriots still kept faith that the common cause appeal would deliver them. For the remainder of the Revolutionary War, during the months that Franklin and Lafayette labored on their little book, African Americans and, especially after 1778, Indians would feel the effects of that double-faced rhetoric.

CHAPTER 6

"A Striking Picture of Barbarity"

WYOMING TO THE DISASTER AT SAVANNAH,

1778–1779

What sort of men or christians must you suppose the Americans to be,
who after seeing their most humble petitions insultingly rejected; the most grievous
laws passed to distress them in every quarter; an undeclared war let loose upon them,
and Indians and Negroes invited to the slaughter . . . Ought we ever after to be
considered as a part of the human race? Or ought we not rather to be blotted from
the society of mankind and become a spectacle of misery to the world?[1]

Thomas Paine

On Thursday, July 2, 1778, Congress reconvened in Philadelphia after nearly ten months' exile in York. Since they lacked a quorum, the only business they accomplished was to draft an announcement for John Dunlap's *Pennsylvania Packet* concerning how the city should observe the second anniversary of independence, calling on Philadelphians not to break the windows of those who did not illuminate their houses because of an assumption that this signified a lack of support. There just were not enough candles to go around. The city was still in chaos after the British army's withdrawal. Philadelphia's patriot printers, also resettling into their old shops, capitalized on the disorder by publishing a (wrong) rumor that fifteen hundred Hessians had refused to accompany the British out of the city, thus contributing to an image of reticent German mercenaries refusing to fight against American liberty. In reality, about one hundred African Americans did accompany the British army out of town and bondage, though this escaped the printers' notice.[2]

1. [Thomas Paine], *The Crisis, Number VI,* Philadelphia, Oct. 20, 1778, in Eric Foner, ed., *Thomas Paine: Collected Writings . . .* (New York, 1995), 181–190, esp. 185–186.

2. *Pennsylvania Packet,* July 4, 1778. For the tumult Philadelphia's previous Fourth

In New London, the *Connecticut Gazette* commemorated the second Fourth of July with a poem entitled "A Short Reflection on the Anniversary of American Independence." "Hail joyful Day!" began the ninety-five-line poem, which focused, not on praising America's "illustrious Characters!" but on detailing British crimes. In this, their chief transgression was the instigating of Indians: "The British Court in this important Strife, / Employ the Tomahawk and Scalping Knife." According to this Connecticut poet, British involvement in this "employment" had corrupted them. Now, "to shew they are determined to prevail," they

> Instruct their Soldiery to Practices,
> 'Till now unknown to other Savages; . . .
> They ravish his dear Wife before his Eyes;
> They hold the Mother in indecent Plight,
> And force her Virgin Daughters in her Sight,
> And then to shew they Novelty prefer
> Before the Daughter's Eyes they ravish her;
> Their Indian Allies Shock'd at British Wars,
> Retire among the gentler Wolves and Bears,
> These brutal Actions they with Shame disown,
> Britain, such Glory must be thine alone.

------

of July celebration produced, which featured many windows broken in Quaker houses, see David Waldstreicher, *In the Midst of Perpetual Fetes: The Making of American Nationalism, 1776–1820* (Chapel Hill, N.C., 1997), 39. On Hessians' not going along, see *Pennsylvania Packet*, July 4, 1778; *Virginia Gazette* (Dixon & Hunter), July 17, 1778. Another report had recently circulated that "scarce one day passes" without a Hessian coming to American lines, and a third letter stated that 150 more Germans had deserted "in a body." See *New-Jersey Gazette*, Mar. 18, 1778; *Connecticut Journal*, Apr. 1, 1778; *Independent Chronicle*, Apr. 2, 1778; *Connecticut Gazette*, Apr. 3, 1778; *Providence Gazette*, Apr. 4, 1778; *Exeter Journal*, Apr. 7, 1778; *Continental Journal*, Apr. 9, 1778. "150 of the enemy (Germans)": *New-York Journal*, May 18, 1778; *Connecticut Journal*, May 27, 1778; *Connecticut Courant*, June 2, 1778; *Connecticut Gazette*, June 5, 1778. All of these accounts were erroneous; according to British army personnel records, only 219 Hessian enlisted soldiers deserted from Jan. 1, 1778, to the battle of Monmouth on June 24, 1778. See Piers Mackesy, *The War for America, 1775–1783* (Cambridge, Mass., 1964), 215n. African Americans following the British army out of Philadelphia in Gary B. Nash, *Forging Freedom: The Formation of Philadelphia's Black Community* (Cambridge, Mass., 1988), 47–49.

This "short reflection" celebrated American independence by denigrating the British for their savage ways—far worse than real Indians, who, in turn, were repulsed by *their* barbarity. Patriot publicists who crafted the common cause argument had long portrayed Indians and African Americans as passive proxies of cruel British agents; less guilty, perhaps, but not welcome as republican citizens just the same. Here, again, on the nation's second anniversary, a patriot publicist invoked Britain's lapse into savagery, complete with Indian referents to gauge the fall, in order to define Americans as a distinct, superior people.[3]

On that eve of Independence Day, as people in southeastern Connecticut settled down with their weekly paper, or sat around in New London taverns or coffeehouses perhaps discussing the meaning of this piece, such an episode of "savage" violence involving British agents and their Indian allies was happening 250 miles to their west—and possibly involving their kin. Consumers of the *Gazette* and many other patriot papers would soon recognize that event as the "Wyoming Massacre." It was how many more Americans would remember the second Fourth of July.

Together with the rejection of the Carlisle commissioners, the Wyoming Massacre began a new phase of the common cause. Over the next eighteen months, as the British adjusted their strategy and began to consider taking the war to the Deep South, the participation of African Americans and Indians in the Revolutionary War grew. The narrative of Indian proxies reached unprecedented levels as patriot publicists screamed about the evil behavior of villains such as Henry "the Hair-Buyer" Hamilton, Joseph Brant, and Walter Butler, spread rumors about the terrible things these men did at Wyoming and Cherry Valley, and gave Franklin and Lafayette more images for their schoolbook. At the same time, patriots found new heroes in George Rogers Clark and John Sullivan and vociferously praised their intrepid efforts to exact revenge against the king's agents and Indian allies. As Georgia became another important theater of war, the participation of African Americans there became another central topic heralded by patriot publicists. Stories of blacks aiding the British appeared whenever the patriots were able to get stories from the Deep South, a place where their communication networks—already declining in effectiveness—were weakest.

That the patriots continued to amplify these particular images, stories, and representations shows how vital the images were to a war effort that

3. *Connecticut Gazette,* July 3, 1778.

"A Striking Picture of Barbarity"

was rapidly disintegrating as financial distress and popular disorder threatened to engulf the enterprise. This narrative continued to undermine other possibilities, including emancipation schemes to draft blacks into the Continental army or plans to abolish slavery outright. It also enervated efforts to build strong alliances with Indians across the backcountry. The wartime common cause appeal, spurred on by new events, new actors, and new contexts, began to exert a powerful influence on American policy during the middle years of the conflict, exacerbating further the tensions between the promises of the American Revolution and the realities of the Revolutionary War.

1: *"THE HATCHET"*: WYOMING AND CHERRY VALLEY, GEORGE ROGERS CLARK AND JOHN SULLIVAN

On June 30, 1778, a body of 110 British rangers and loyalists under Major John Butler and 465 mostly Seneca and Cayuga Indians, led by Seneca chief Sayenqueraghta, approached Wyoming, Pennsylvania. The Wyoming Valley had long been a troubled region; for a decade before the Revolution, settlers from Connecticut and Pennsylvania had battled one another for claim to the Susquehanna River valley. Butler's men found the forewarned settlers secure in fortified stockades. Several hundred militiamen and sixty Continental soldiers gathered in Forty Fort, the main stockade protecting the Wyoming settlement.

The militia was under the command of Colonel Nathan Dennison, the Continentals under Colonel Zebulon Butler. The Connecticut-born Butler wanted to be defensive and wait to see what the British and Indian force would do, but many settlers were worried about the devastation the frustrated enemy might unleash on their vulnerable farms. They lobbied to fight. Butler acquiesced.[4]

In the afternoon on July 3, Zebulon Butler's 60 regulars and nearly 400 militiamen marched out of the fort—and into an ambush. In a scene reminiscent of Oriskany, the British and Indians surrounded and fell upon the Wyoming militia in gruesome, close fashion. The militiamen fled in a rout; Indians pursued, catching and scalping many, some in the Susquehanna River. Fewer than 60 survived. British major John Butler would later report that 227 scalps and 5 prisoners were taken that day, whereas he lost 3 men and had 8 wounded. Zebulon Butler and a handful of men slipped

4. Max M. Mintz, *Seeds of Empire: The American Revolutionary Conquest of the Iroquois* (New York, 1999), 59–61.

away. Dennison made it back to Forty Fort, where the families of the slain militiamen were hiding. He negotiated its surrender to John Butler. The British commander promised the Wyoming families their bodies and property would be secure, but he apparently lost control. His Indian and loyalist forces took their revenge, but not on the Wyoming inhabitants themselves. They destroyed the surrounding forts, burned a thousand dwellings, and drove off a like number of livestock before heading back to New York. Reporting back to his superiors, Butler was satisfied that "not a single person has been hurt of the inhabitants but such as were in arms." This was not how Americans would remember the afternoon of July 3, 1778.[5]

The story of the Wyoming Massacre that Americans learned from their newspapers differed from Butler's report. Newspapers in New York and Pennsylvania first published news of Wyoming on July 16. Samuel Loudon's *New York Packet* told the bare facts of losses inflicted by the "infamous Butler." Loudon did not offer much more than numbers of those "scalped and butchered by these inhuman allies of Britain." In Philadelphia, the *Pennsylvania Evening Post* related a "melancholy account of a large body in Indians, Tories, and some British troops . . . committing the most horrid murders on defenceless farmers, women and children." Even without all the facts in, the ever-opportunistic Benjamin Towne did not hesitate to comment on the irony of this attack while the Carlisle Commission pleaded for peace:

> Thus, while our defenceless wives and children are cut off by merciless savages . . . is the *humane* king of Britain offering his idle and delusive proposition of *peace!*—Let this fresh act of his cruelty and wickedness stimulate every good man to support, with redoubled vigor, that IN-DEPENDENCE which nature, necessity, and reason have dictated to us.

Towne—or some other patriot influence in newly reoccupied Philadelphia—seized upon Wyoming as another argument to delegitimize the Car-

5. Christopher Ward, *The War of the Revolution*, ed., John Richard Alden (New York, 1952), II, 629–632; Barbara Graymont, *The Iroquois in the American Revolution* (Syracuse, N.Y., 1972), 167–171; Major John Butler to Lieut.-Colonel Mason Bolton, Lackawanna, July 8, 1778, in K. G. Davies, ed., *Documents of the American Revolution, 1770–1783*, Colonial Office Series, XV, *Transcripts, 1778* (Dublin, 1976), 165–166, esp. 166. When interviewed in the nineteenth century, Blacksnake, a Seneca warrior present at Wyoming, did not recall that people had been burned in the houses. See Thomas S. Abler, ed., *Chainbreaker: The Revolutionary War Memoirs of Governor Blacksnake, as Told to Benjamin Williams* (Lincoln, Neb., 1989), 135–137.

lisle Commission and support the common cause. Several other papers picked up on this interpretation. Other readers would make the connection by coincidence: several papers published Gouverneur Morris's address against the commission, ridiculing the king's "generous and faithful allies, the Senecas, Onandagas and Tuscaroras" in the same issues that exchanged accounts of the devastation at Wyoming.[6]

When more details began to emerge about what had happened at Wyoming, they were still far from accurate. A Connecticut settler, Solomon Avery, gave a deposition about the battle to several patriot sources, one ending up in the hands of *Connecticut Gazette* printer Timothy Green. He ran Avery's account in the July 17 issue. That story began the first sketches of what would become the Wyoming Massacre, a legend that had little relationship to the actual combat along the Susquehanna. Avery had not really witnessed the aftermath of the battle. Apparently, he had fled due east the afternoon of July 3. Five days later, he was in northwest New Jersey, where he ran into patriot leader John Cleve Symmes and told him a story. Avery was vague in his deposition to Symmes, claiming that "when he was on the Mountain to the east of the Settlement he saw the Settlement all on fire, this deponent further saith that of 5,000 souls he supposes 2,000 have perished in the Carnage." This supposition was wrong. Avery gave a second deposition a week later; this one appeared first in the *Connecticut Gazette* and then in twelve other newspapers. Although less catastrophic than the first, it was just as damaging to popular understanding of what happened at Wyoming. Avery stated that the inhabitants were "making their Escape naked through the Wilderness." "Of about Five Thousand Inhabitants," he concluded, "one Half are killed and taken by the Enemy Prisoners, and the other Half fleeing away naked and distressed." To be sure, there was a massive flight away from the Susquehanna; many inhabitants abandoned frontier settlements in

6. "Inhuman allies": *New York Packet,* July 16, 1778; *Connecticut Journal,* July 22, 1778; *New-Jersey Gazette,* July 22, 1778; *Maryland Journal,* July 28, 1778; *North-Carolina Gazette,* Aug. 14, 1778. "Melancholy account": *Pennsylvania Evening Post,* July 16, 1778; *Dunlap's Maryland Gazette,* July 28, 1778; *New-York Journal,* Aug. 3, 1778; *Connecticut Journal,* Aug. 5, 1778; *Norwich Packet,* Aug. 10, 1778; *South-Carolina and American General Gazette,* Aug. 13, 1778; *North-Carolina Gazette,* Aug. 28, 1778. "Generous and Faithful Allies": *Pennsylvania Evening Post,* July 14, 1778, esp. 234–237, 235. Morris's address (see Chapter 5, above) first appeared in mid-June in Pennsylvania papers but was exchanged throughout New England and the South in mid-July, just as the news of Wyoming appeared.

Northumberland County for security in southeastern Pennsylvania. But to assert that thousands perished in the fighting, or that the entire settlement fled through the woods stark naked, was hyperbole.[7]

Avery's accounts were just the beginning of misinformation about Wyoming. Three days after his report appeared, *New-York Journal* printer John Holt would publish the most significant and influential account of the attack. This description, taking up five whole columns of print, would live on for decades in the American imagination.

John Butler would not have objected to Holt's depiction of the July 3 battle. His description of the rout itself was not extremely partisan or negligent. What Holt alleged happened the following day, however, became one of the most enduring atrocity stories of the Revolution, rivaling that of Jane McCrea's murder. This version of the "massacre" was far worse than Avery's. Holt's fiction of what happened at Forty Fort became reality for many Americans: he created a legend. When Franklin instructed his Parisian engraver to portray the Niagara commander receiving "the Scalps of the Wioming Families," he was one of thousands who believed Butler had actually butchered the inhabitants of Forty Fort.

According to Holt, when Colonel Dennison went to ask John Butler on what terms he would accept a surrender of Forty Fort, the answer was ominous: *"The Hatchet."* From there, the *New-York Journal* account was a series of episodes depicting Indians forcing inhabitants into their houses and setting the buildings on fire, of details about "desolation and horror almost beyond description, parallel or credibility," and of instances where the remaining soldiers were tortured. A tour de force of death and destruction, the story ended with the hope that this would be "the concluding scene of the tragedy acted by the British tyrant and his murderous, diabolical emissaries." Despite being full of wild inaccuracies, Holt's account quickly became the standard tale of the Wyoming Massacre. Nearly every active American paper

7. Deposition of Solomon Avery of Norwich, Conn., July 8, 1778, quoted in John Cleve Symmes to GW, Sussex Court House, July 8, 1778, *PGW: RW*, XVI, 40–41, esp. 40n. Avery account: *Connecticut Gazette*, July 17, 1778; *Connecticut Courant*, July 21, 1778; *Continental Journal*, July 23, 1778; *Independent Chronicle*, July 23, 1778; *Massachusetts Spy*, July 23, 1778; *Providence Gazette*, July 25, 1778; *Boston Gazette*, July 27, 1778; *Independent Ledger*, July 27, 1778; *New-Hampshire Gazette*, July 28, 1778; *Exeter Journal*, July 28, 1778; *Pennsylvania Evening Post*, July 30, 1778; *Pennsylvania Packet*, July 30, 1778; *New-Jersey Gazette*, Aug. 5, 1778.

exchanged Holt's lengthy report in full. Ten papers published both Avery's deposition and Holt's story.[8]

In Congress, Connecticut delegate Roger Sherman lamented, "The account given in a Poughkeepsie paper is said to be much beyond the truth." There was little Sherman could do; much like the McCrea story, the horrific news of the "massacre" became a national story. New York physician Dr. Samuel Adams wrote his wife that any news he had, "I trust you have in the Boston papers. The unparalleled barbarity and worse than diabolical behavior of the Tories and Savages at Wyoming on Susquehanna, you will no doubt have account of." In Virginia, diarist Robert Honyman recorded seeing a "circumstantial account" of Wyoming, which told of men being "put to death by cruel torments—the women and children they shut up in the houses, then set fire to them the burnt them altogether." Nearly fifty years later, James Thacher, a Continental army surgeon, published his journal from the war. His military diary—which also included many details about Jane Mc-Crea—recited Holt's account exactly, including Butler's alleged reply of *"the Hatchet,"* without correction. What Thacher labeled "one of the most dreadful instances of perfidious savage cruelty that can perhaps be found on the records of history" never happened as many believed it did. Yet Butler's "hatchet" would inform reactions to British-Indian relations for decades.[9]

8. *New-York Journal,* July 20, 1778. J. Hector St. John de Crèvecoeur's narrative of the "massacre" also corroborates Butler's report. "Happily," he wrote in an unpublished manuscript, "these fierce people, satisfied with the death of those who had opposed them in arms, treated the defenceless ones, the women and children, with a degree of humanity almost hitherto unparalleled." See Crèvecoeur, "On the Susquehanna; The Wyoming Massacre," *Letters from an American Farmer and Sketches of Eighteenth-Century America* (New York, 1981), 353–390, esp. 380–390, esp. 386. Holt's "diabolical emissaries" account exchanged in *Connecticut Courant,* July 28, 1778; *Connecticut Journal,* July 29, 1778; *Massachusetts Spy,* July 30, 1778; *Pennsylvania Packet,* July 30, 1778; *Pennsylvania Evening Post,* July 30, 1778; *Independent Chronicle,* July 30, 1778; *Providence Gazette,* Aug. 1, 1778; *Independent Ledger,* Aug. 3, 1778; *Norwich Packet,* Aug. 3, 1778; *Boston Gazette,* Aug. 3, 1778; *Dunlap's Maryland Gazette,* Aug. 4, 1778; *Maryland Journal,* Aug. 4, 1778; *New-Hampshire Gazette,* Aug. 5, 1778; *Continental Journal,* Aug. 6, 1778; *Connecticut Gazette,* Aug. 7, 1778; *North-Carolina Gazette,* Sept. 4, 1778.

9. Roger Sherman to Jonathan Trumbull, Sr., Philadelphia, Aug. 10, 1778, *LDC,* X, 417; Dr. Samuel Adams to Sally Preston Adams, Aug. 5, 1776, item 29 in Sol Feinstone Collection of the American Revolution, American Philosophical Society,

The shocking, wrong details that Holt published mattered both at the time and for subsequent generations. It contributed to a rising cry for vengeance. The representation of the Wyoming Massacre would produce far more bloodshed than the attack itself. As Massachusetts delegate James Lovell ominously wrote to Abigail Adams, the Indians "must be eradicated Root and Branch as soon as ever we get a little Relaxation from the War on the Sea Coasts." The patriots believed brutal incursions were the only way to secure the frontier if diplomacy failed. Force was the only way they could prevent Indians from acting on the false promises of their British sponsors; this impulse had previously animated New England's 1775 invasion of Canada. So, too, with Carolina and Virginia's joint expedition against Alexander Cameron and the Cherokees in 1776. Lovell's wish would be granted soon enough.[10]

* * *

Patriot leaders hardly needed to recall the expeditions of 1775 and 1776 to be reminded of the most effective way of dealing with British-sponsored Indians. At almost the same instant that Wyoming fell, Virginia militia leader George Rogers Clark seized the formerly French frontier settlement of Kaskaskia, the first success in a campaign that would earn him the nickname "Conqueror of the Illinois."

Nearly a year earlier, Clark had begun lobbying Virginia governor Patrick Henry for permission to take the war west. Scouts informed Clark that Kaskaskia, a vulnerable outpost on the Mississippi River, was a center for British agents to "influence as many Indians as possible to invade the Colonies." He begged Henry to approve an expedition to capture it. Clark hoped to conquer more territory for the United States, open the Ohio River, and neutral-

---

Philadelphia; Aug. 26, 1778, entry in Robert Honyman Diary, 1776–1782, no. 8417, University of Virginia Library, Charlottesville, 270; James Thacher, *A Military Journal during the American Revolutionary War, from 1775 to 1783* . . . , 2d ed. (1823; Boston, 1827), 140, 142. To his credit, Holt did retract some—but by no means all—of the mistakes in his August 10, 1778, issue. But this more sober, secondary account, in which some people testified that they were indeed still alive, only appeared in one-third as many papers as the first. See *New-York Journal*, Aug. 10, 1778; *Pennsylvania Evening Post*, Aug. 18, 1778; *Massachusetts Spy*, Aug. 20, 1778; *Connecticut Gazette*, Aug. 21, 1778; *Maryland Journal*, Sept. 1, 1778.

10. James Lovell to Abigail Adams, July 9, 1778, *LDC*, X, 247. For more, see Fred Anderson and Andrew Cayton, *The Dominion of War: Empire and Liberty in North America, 1500–2000* (New York, 2005), 168–170.

"A Striking Picture of Barbarity"

ize British power over Indians in the trans-Appalachian west, especially that of Henry Hamilton, the British lieutenant governor at Detroit.[11]

Patriot authorities in Virginia and the Continental Congress had already tried to take steps against the notorious Hamilton, but as yet they had met with failure. Clark promised that his venture would be a cheap affair. Henry consulted three trusted patriot leaders, Thomas Jefferson, George Wythe, and George Mason, before giving final approval early in 1778. Henry issued the twenty-six-year-old Clark secret instructions approving the mission and informing the commander, "If the white Inhabitants at that post and the neighbourhood will give undoubted Evidence of their attachment to this State . . . Let them be treated as fellow Citizens and their persons and property duly secured." Clark must act with the "Humanity that has hitherly distinguished Americans"; Henry recited the standard line of the heroic side of the common cause when he gave strict orders that Clark conduct a civilized campaign. But this was more than just making sure Clark's actions reflected the cause well. Henry had a specific person in mind whom he did not want Clark to emulate: the Hair-Buyer.[12]

Rumors of Indians' delivering their scalps to the lieutenant governor converged to earn Hamilton the nickname of Hair-Buyer in patriot circles by 1778. Whether this was an accurate characterization was another matter. Colonial governments had embraced scalp bounties during emergencies, most notably Pennsylvania during the Seven Years' War. Nor were Americans innocent of the practice after independence: the state of Pennsylvania would reinstitute this reward in 1780. Irony did nothing to slow patriot publicists who sought to attach such visceral and charged accusations to their enemies. In their lights, the Hair-Buyer was a disreputable instigator of British proxies.[13]

11. George Rogers Clark to [Patrick Henry], 1777, in James Alton James, ed., *George Rogers Clark Papers, 1771–1781*, Collections of the Illinois State Historical Library, VIII (Springfield, Ill., 1912), 30–32, esp. 31.

12. Randolph C. Downes, *Council Fires on the Upper Ohio: A Narrative of Indian Affairs in the Upper Ohio Valley until 1795* (Pittsburgh, 1940), 211; "Introduction," "Secret Instructions to Clark," Williamsburg, Jan. 2, 1778, in James, ed., *Clark Papers*, VIII, xii–clxvii, esp. lix (Henry's consultation), and 34–35.

13. John D. Barnhart, ed., *Henry Hamilton and George Rogers Clark in the American Revolution; With the Unpublished Journal of Lieut. Gov. Henry Hamilton* (Crawfordsville, Ind., 1951), 21–36; Bernard W. Sheehan, "'The Famous Hair Buyer General': Henry Hamilton, George Rogers Clark, and the American Indian," *Indiana Magazine of History*, LXXIX (1983), 1–28.

Without firing a shot, Clark's puny, starving force of fewer than 200 militiamen took fifteen minutes to capture Kaskaskia on July 4, 1778, the day of the Wyoming Massacre. Clark brought with him news of the French alliance; this helped sway the Illinois inhabitants to his side without any struggle. After taking the town, he quickly turned his attention to Vincennes, another former French settlement 180 miles away on the Wabash. Two weeks later, just as Holt's *New-York Journal* began twisting the truth about Wyoming, a French priest and physician sent by Clark from Kaskaskia arrived at that outpost armed only with a proclamation in French. Clark notified the inhabitants of Vincennes that Virginia had sent him so that he could cripple Hamilton's ability to "excite" the Indians "to assassinate the inhabitants of the frontiers of the United States of America." "The murders and assassinations of women and children and the depredations and ravages, which have been committed, cry for vengeance with a loud voice." He offered the traders at Vincennes the opportunity to swear allegiance to Virginia peaceably, and in turn he would "treat them as citizens of the Republic of Virginia." On July 20, 183 men "renounce[d] all fidelity to George the Third" and took oaths of allegiance to the United States.[14]

This success did not mean Clark was free from danger. Worried about the threat from Detroit, he opened negotiations with neighboring Indians to sway their allegiances, too. By early August, Hamilton knew about Clark's surprising victories in the Illinois country. It would take a few months for the lieutenant governor to gather a force to move against Vincennes. It would take even longer for news about Clark's success in Illinois to reach newspapers back east.[15]

Meanwhile, in mid-July, as Americans began to read about what John Butler had allegedly done in Wyoming, he pulled back from the Susquehanna. He moved most of his Indian and loyalist force toward Niagara but sent a small portion to reinforce Joseph Brant's body of men in Oquaga.

14. Ward, *War of the Revolution*, II, 855; Jay Gitlin, *The Bourgeois Frontier: French Towns, French Traders, and American Expansion* (New Haven, Conn., 2010), 37–38; Clark to the Inhabitants of Vincennes, July [13?], 1778, "Oath of Inhabitants of Vincennes," July 20, 1778, in James, ed., *Clark Papers*, VIII, 50–53, esp. 51–52 ("treat them as citizens"), 56–59, esp. 56.

15. Clark to the Chief of the Winnebagos, Aug. 22, 1778, and "Clark's Proclamation to the Fox Indians," Aug. 28, 1778, in James, ed., *Clark Papers*, VIII, 65, 66. See the account in Patrick Griffin, *American Leviathan: Empire, Nation, and Revolutionary Frontier* (New York, 2007), 143–144.

"A Striking Picture of Barbarity"

Despite persistent accusations (which would live on for half a century) that he was one of the perpetrators at Wyoming, Brant was more than 100 miles upriver when Zebulon Butler's men marched out of Forty Fort. On July 18, he drove farther north, attacking two towns in Tryon County, New York, near Otsego Lake, killing eight men and burning dozens of houses. As one published letter from "A Gentleman in Albany" put it regarding these raids, "These insults will not pass unrevenged."[16]

In September, Brant led a force against the German Flats, a village on the Mohawk River. As one patriot officer later described it in a few newspapers, the Flats settlement was a "fine, fertile country, consisting perhaps of near an hundred houses." Patriot scouts ran into Brant's body of 300 loyalists and 152 Indians as it approached the settlement, and one was able to warn the inhabitants, who fled into two stone forts. With nearly all the settlers protected, Brant's men laid waste to the surrounding farms, burning all those hundred barns and houses and either seizing or driving off 700 horses, cattle, and sheep.[17]

The next month, a patriot force, including a detachment of Daniel Morgan's rifle company, retaliated against Brant's headquarters on the Susquehanna while he was scouting to the south. They torched Oquaga, what the American commander called "the finest Indian Town I ever saw." They be-

16. Graymont, *Iroquois in the American Revolution*, 174; Colin G. Calloway, *The American Revolution in Indian Country: Crisis and Diversity in Native American Communities* (Cambridge, 1995), 124–126; "Colonel Jacob Klock's Description of Their Recent Depredations on Otsego Lake," Conajohary, N.Y., Jun. 22, 1778, in Hugh Hastings et al., eds., *Public Papers of George Clinton: First Governor of New York, 1777–1795, 1801–1804* (Albany, N.Y., 1899–1914), III, 475–476. "Unrevenged": *Connecticut Courant*, Aug. 25, 1778; *New-York Journal*, Aug. 31, 1778; *Pennsylvania Evening Post*, Sept. 2, 1778; *Continental Journal*, Sept. 3, 1778; *Exeter Journal*, Oct. 13, 1778.

17. Joseph T. Glatthaar and James Kirby Martin, *Forgotten Allies: The Oneida Indians and the American Revolution* (New York, 2006), 89. "Fine, fertile country": *Connecticut Courant*, Sept. 29, 1778; *Continental Journal*, Oct. 1, 1778; *Independent Chronicle*, Oct. 1, 1778; *New-Hampshire Gazette*, Oct. 6, 1778. Brant raid account: *New-York Journal*, Sept. 28, 1778; *Boston Gazette*, Oct. 12, 1778; *Connecticut Courant*, Oct. 13, 1778; *Maryland Journal*, Oct. 13, 1778; *Massachusetts Spy*, Oct. 15, 1778; *Boston Evening Post* (White & Adams), Oct. 17, 1778; *Virginia Gazette* (Purdie), Oct. 23, 1778. These numbers were confirmed in a letter from Colonel Ichabod Alden that appeared in *New York Packet*, Sept. 24, 1778; *Pennsylvania Packet*, Sept. 29, 1778; *New-Jersey Gazette*, Sept. 30, 1778; *Pennsylvania Evening Post*, Sept. 30, 1778; *Connecticut Gazette*, Oct. 2, 1778; *Boston Gazette*, Oct. 5, 1778; *South-Carolina and American General Gazette*, Oct. 29, 1778.

lieved that if they indeed destroyed this nest, then the Mohawk Valley would be safe from Brant and his "bad people" for at least the remainder of the year. This was a miscalculation.[18]

In fact, as it would turn out, this would be a double error, for it was not only Joseph Brant that New York settlers should have feared in the last weeks of 1778. The inhabitants of Cherry Valley, a village fifty miles west of Albany, had long worried about their vulnerability. Back in February, they had petitioned New York governor George Clinton for a unit of rangers to protect them. They were anxious that "Brant and his warriors are preparing to pay us a Visit," and they were sure they were about to "fall a pray [*sic*] to their Savage Barbarities."[19]

In early November, a force of 300 Indians, 150 loyalists, and 50 British regulars under the command of Captain Walter Butler—not Joseph Brant—were indeed on their way to that unfortunate place. Walter, Colonel John Butler's son, had little military experience; he was only in charge because his father's rheumatism had flared up. Inexperience was only one of Walter's problems. He compounded it by exhibiting disdain for Brant. Butler's open mistreatment of the Mohawk leader poisoned relations with everyone. Many of the loyalists in Brant's party refused to serve under the haughty captain. Nor did the Indian allies under Butler's command, Cayugas and Senecas under Cornplanter, appreciate this behavior. When these tensions mixed with the increasing brutality exhibited by all parties, conditions were favorable for an ugly incident.[20]

Early in the morning of November 11, Butler's men came upon the house of Robert Wells, on the outskirts of Cherry Valley. Inside the compound

18. Entry for Oct. 8, 1778, "Extracts from Lt. Col. [William] Butler's Journal," in Hastings et al., eds., *Public Papers of George Clinton*, IV, 223–228, esp. 225–226. Washington sent a copy of Butler's journal to Congress, who then ordered it published. See GW to HL, Camp near Fredericksburg, Oct. 22, 1778, *PGW: RW*, XVII, 520–525; Oct. 28, 1778, *JCC*, XII, 1070.

19. "Cherry Valley Petitions for Rangers under Competent Officers to Guard the State's Frontiers," Feb. 23, 1778, in Hastings et al., eds., *Public Papers of George Clinton*, II, 821–823, esp. 821.

20. Another factor was the incompetence of American commander Colonel Ichabod Alden. General Edward Hand had visited Cherry Valley less than a week before the attack and advised Alden to have the populace make arrangements to move inside the fort. Alden disagreed, allowed the farmers to remain outside, and even quartered his officers outside the stockade. This added to the tragedy at Cherry Valley. See Mintz, *Seeds of Empire*, 72.

"A Striking Picture of Barbarity"

were Colonel Ichabod Alden and the officers in command of the village's defenses. A detachment of Butler's rangers cut the house off while the main body prepared to assault the fort where most of the inhabitants took shelter. According to Isaac Glynne, an eighteen-year-old Continental inside the main stockade, Alden broke out of the house and tried to reach his men. "Just behind him appeared to be an acre of Indians in close pursuit," Glynne observed. They "knocked him down and scalped him, then pushed on towards the Fort. They were painted in all colors, and looked like so many devils." Five of Alden's junior officers died in the Wells house, along with all the others inside.[21]

Not everyone supported the attack on the fort, for most of the Indians then spread out to wreak havoc on the settlement. In Glynne's words, "The Indians burned everything they could lay their hands on, and killed everything, men, women, children, cattle, hogs, dogs, cats, and even the fowl, and did all the mischief they could invent." Some of those murdered were loyalists who did not seek the shelter of the fort because they believed they had nothing to fear from Butler's men. Brant arrived to try to restrain the violence. Some of the people in the settlement were his friends, including the unfortunate Wells family. In all, sixteen soldiers and thirty-two civilians died in the carnage. Most of the latter were women and children. The only building left standing when Butler's men withdrew was the fort itself.[22]

This attack was one of the most extreme of the Revolutionary War. Indians on either side of the conflict had not taken life in this manner before. Why? What produced a real massacre at Cherry Valley? Walter Butler, surely looking to externalize blame, pointed to several causes for why the Indians were "exasperated." The first was immediate. In the aftermath of the bloodshed, Butler left a letter for Philip Schuyler with the forty captives he de-

21. Isaac Glynne Journal, 1775–1781, 9, MSS, miscellaneous boxes, G, AAS.

22. Glynne Journal, 10, MSS, misc. boxes, G. Primary sources on the Cherry Valley incident include several reports by patriot military officers to George Clinton, for which see General Edward Hand to George Clinton, Schenectady, Nov. 15, 1778, General Abraham Ten Broeck to General Hand, Albany, Nov. 12, 1778, and Major Daniel Whiting to General Hand, Fort Alden, Cherry Valley, Nov. 12, 1778, all in Hastings et al., eds., *Public Papers of George Clinton*, IV, 284–287; and Blacksnake's memory as later related to Lyman Draper, for which see Abler, ed., *Chainbreaker*, 103–105. See also Glatthaar and Martin, *Forgotten Allies*, 231; Graymont, *Iroquois in the American Revolution*, 186–191; Mintz, *Seeds of Empire*, 72–73; Gary B. Nash, *The Unknown American Revolution: The Unruly Birth of Democracy and the Struggle to Create America* (New York, 2005), 256–257; and Ward, *War of the Revolution*, II, 634–635.

cided to release in the woods outside the still-burning village. In it, he swore he had done "every thing in my power to restrain the Indians . . . but they were to[o] much enraged by the late destruction" of Oquaga.[23]

Butler provided different explanations for Cherry Valley in his official report a few days later. In that, he first blamed Nathan Dennison. The militia colonel who surrendered Forty Fort at Wyoming had sworn he would not take up arms again. He broke this parole just a few weeks later, when he assisted Colonel Thomas Hartley's Pennsylvania regiment that soon came to protect the lower Susquehanna Valley. Butler explained to his superiors that his Indian allies were "more incensed at finding the colonel and those men who had there laid down their arms soon after marching into their country intending to destroy their villages." They did not want to "fight the enemy twice."[24]

Butler then provided perhaps the most interesting reason the Iroquois seemed out of control at Cherry Valley. "The death of the women and children upon this occasion may I believe be truly ascribed to the rebels having falsely accused the Indians of cruelty at Wyoming," the young captain explained. "This has much exasperated them . . . and they declared they would no more be falsely accused . . . meaning that they would not in future give quarter." If Butler accurately related this justification from his allies, it was a fascinating admission. According to the Senecas and Cayugas, patriot publicity contributed to this bloodshed. The misinformation patriot newspapers spread about Wyoming were not evanescent stories that perished with the next issue. They had a real effect, not only on American attitudes about their enemies but also apparently for the Iroquois. The false accusations about Forty Fort in part produced Cherry Valley. Although it would be too going far to suggest that John Holt and his fellow printers had blood on their hands for what they produced about the Wyoming Massacre, those publications did have consequences. When printers ignored "good" Indians but publicized the actions of "British Savages" as loudly as they could, they contributed to the murderous atmosphere of the American Revolution.[25]

23. *Independent Chronicle*, Dec. 24, 1778; *Independent Ledger*, Dec. 28, 1778; *Maryland Journal*, Jan. 19, 1779.

24. Captain Walter Butler to Lt. Col. Mason Bolton, Unadilla, Nov. 17, 1778, in Davies, ed., *Docs. of the Am. Rev.*, XV, 261–263, esp. 262.

25. Butler to Bolton, Nov. 17, 1778, ibid., XV, 261–263, esp. 262. See also Gregory T. Knouff, *The Soldiers' Revolution: Pennsylvanians in Arms and the Forging of Early American Identity* (University Park, Pa., 2004), 168–170.

At bottom, this explanation exposes the circular, tangible nature of these war stories. Events on the northern frontier contributed to the wartime discourse about Britain and its proxies, which, in turn, affected future events. Words printed and exchanged altered the experience of war for thousands of Indians and settlers in the Mohawk Valley. Historians struggle to find conclusive proof of how words affect human action. Butler's explanation of Cherry Valley offers evidence of a very direct readers' response, even though the Iroquois were not supposed to be Holt's audience. They responded all the same.

Of course, the coverage of the Cherry Valley incident only aggravated matters. The most widely exchanged account was a gruesome description full of what one historian has labeled the "anti-Indian sublime." Written by an officer who allegedly watched the "inhuman barbarities" from the fort, the article—exchanged in eleven papers—described how one man's "head was cut off, his skull bone cut out with the scalp." An infant was "scalp't and arm cut off," a pregnant woman's belly was "rip't up," and "the clergyman's wife's leg and arm cut off." "Many of the inhabitants and soldiers shut out from the fort, lay all night in the rain with children, which suffered very much," the officer lamented. Holt's *New-York Journal* soon produced a list of the twenty-two families who had lost loved ones, along with a catalog of destroyed property. Sounding a note reminiscent of the McCrea narrative, Holt mentioned that "a great part of the sufferers, both killed and prisoners, were people much suspected of tory principles, and greatly depended on protection from Brant and Butler, who conducted this bloody and inhuman business." This account, which seven other papers exchanged, concluded with the remark that many of the "horrid miscreants, were inhabitants of Cherry-Valley, and some whose parents were living there." This accusation was among the greatest charge patriot publicists could hurl at their enemy: British "instigation" unleashed terror that killed indiscriminately. First Jane McCrea, the butchered fiancée of a loyalist militia officer, and now innocent families of those friendly to the crown in Cherry Valley.[26]

26. "Anti-Indian sublime": Peter Silver, *Our Savage Neighbors: How Indian War Transformed Early America* (New York, 2008), xx. "Inhuman barbarities": *Continental Journal*, Dec. 3, 1778; *Boston Gazette*, Dec. 7, 1778; *Exeter Journal*, Dec. 8, 1778; *Massachusetts Spy*, Dec. 10, 1778; *Connecticut Gazette*, Dec. 18, 1778; *Pennsylvania Packet*, Dec. 19, 1778; *Connecticut Courant*, Dec. 22, 1778; *Connecticut Journal*, Dec. 23, 1778; *Maryland Gazette*, Dec. 29, 1778; *New-Jersey Gazette*, Dec. 31, 1778; *Norwich Packet*, Jan. 11, 1779. "Horrid miscreants": *New-York Journal*, Dec. 14, 1778; *Continental Journal*, Dec.

Calls to extirpate the merciless savages grew louder than ever. "I am perfectly convinced," Washington wrote to Congress upon hearing the news, "that the only certain way of preventing Indian ravages is to carry the war vigorously into their own country." Sadly, he admitted, the "late season" made that impracticable at the moment. As early as the first week of 1779, Nathanael Greene advised Washington that one of his major tasks for the upcoming campaign should be "to scourge the Indians." This ought to be done by sending a "considerable bodys of men . . . into their Country by different routes and at a season when their Corn is about half grown." Planning would soon begin apace for just such an expedition against the Iroquois.[27]

At the moment news of Cherry Valley began to circulate in the papers, accounts of George Rogers Clark's accomplishments in the remote Illinois country finally began to appear. Patriot publicists who encouraged aggressive war against loyalists and Indians held Clark's campaign up as a shining example of what should be done on the northern frontier. Though Clark's conquest of Kaskaskia and Vincennes had occurred months before, the coincidence that it appeared just weeks before the violence on the New York frontier added to its reception in eastern papers. A cursory line noting little more than Clark's taking "possession of . . . western posts between the rivers Ohio and Mississippi" appeared in the Williamsburg papers in mid-October. Patriot printers, desperate for some good information from any frontier, grasped onto this morsel of news. Fifteen papers—an impressive number, given that the total number of active prints had dropped to twenty-four by late 1778—picked up this bare paragraph, some running it a second time in the new year.[28]

31, 1778; *Independent Chronicle,* Dec. 31, 1778; *Providence Gazette,* Jan. 2, 1779; *Boston Gazette,* Jan. 4, 1779; *Pennsylvania Evening Post,* Jan. 7, 1779; *Pennsylvania Packet,* Jan. 7, 1779; *New-Jersey Gazette,* Jan. 13, 1779.

It is curious how Holt came upon this list of victims. An identical one is found in the papers of New York governor George Clinton, again underscoring the close connections between patriot leaders and printers. For the list in Clinton's papers, see "A Memorandum of the Popell Killed Wounded and Taken Prisener, and the Buildings Consumed at Chery Valy, the 11 Nov'r 1778 . . . ," in Hastings et al., eds., *Public Papers of George Clinton,* IV, 410–411.

27. GW to HL, Headquarters, Fredericksburg, N.Y., Nov. 16, 1778, *PGW: RW,* XVIII, 169; Nathanael Greene to GW, Philadelphia, Jan. 5, 1779, *PNG,* III, 144–145.

28. *Virginia Gazette* (Dixon & Hunter), Oct. 9, 1778; *Virginia Gazette* (Purdie), Oct. 16, 1778; *Maryland Journal,* Oct. 27, 1778; *Pennsylvania Evening Post,* Oct. 30, 1778; *Pennsylvania Packet,* Nov. 3, 1778; *North-Carolina Gazette,* Nov. 7, 1778; *New-Jersey*

Then, on November 20, Dixon and Hunter published a more lengthy account in their *Virginia Gazette,* the first reference to Clark by what would become his new sobriquet, Conqueror of the Illinois. This version exuded praise for Clark, boasting that his expedition "will put a finishing stroke to the British interest" in the west "and secure to us the friendship of all the Indian nations." Indeed, the anonymous writer continued, the "savages . . . [had already] began to suspect the boasted strength of the British Worthless" and had "slacken[ed] in their readiness to serve them." Before, the Indians considered Americans "no more to be dreaded than flies," but lately those "very harmless flies" had turned into "wasps and hornets, and sting the Great King's men most severely." Though the people of the Mohawk Valley would surely take issue with this interpretation, Americans weary of reading bloody accounts of butchered families probably welcomed this bravado, as papers throughout New England and the mid-Atlantic exchanged it.[29]

Soon, a letter from Captain Joseph Bowman, one of Clark's officers at Kaskaskia, would find its way into the hands of *Maryland Journal* printer Mary Katherine Goddard in Baltimore. Bowman provided firsthand details of the journey to the Mississippi and the overwhelming success of their mission. He, too, boasted of long-term sovereignty over the Ohio Indians: "Ere will it be long, I flatter myself we shall put a stop to the career of those blood-thirsty savages, who glory in shedding the blood of the innocent." Seven more papers reprinted this letter—really, the only primary document from the now-six-month-old campaign—from Goddard.[30]

Gazette, Nov. 11, 1778; *Independent Chronicle,* Nov. 19, 1778; *Providence Gazette,* Nov. 21, 1778; *Boston Gazette,* Nov. 23, 1778; *Independent Ledger,* Nov. 23 1778, Jan. 4, 1779; *Connecticut Courant,* Nov. 24, 1778; *Exeter Journal,* Nov. 24, 1778, Jan. 12, 1779; *Connecticut Gazette,* Nov. 27, 1778, Jan. 1, 1779; *Continental Journal,* Jan. 7, 1779; *New-York Journal,* Jan. 11, 1779; *New-Hampshire Gazette,* Jan. 12, 1779.

29. *Virginia Gazette* (Dixon & Hunter), Nov. 20, 1778; *Pennsylvania Evening Post,* Dec. 9, 1778; *Pennsylvania Packet,* Dec. 12, 1778; *Connecticut Gazette,* Jan. 1, 1779; *Massachusetts Spy,* Jan. 7, 1779; *New-York Journal,* Jan. 11, 1779; *Independent Ledger,* Jan. 11, 1779; *Exeter Journal,* Jan. 12, 1779; *Continental Journal,* Jan. 14, 1779; *Boston Gazette,* Jan. 18, 1779; *New-Hampshire Gazette,* Jan. 19, 1779. No copy of the November 20, 1778, *Virginia Gazette* (Dixon & Hunter) is extant. I have surmised from the exchanged headlines that this article originated in Williamsburg on November 20. Given that date of publication, it has to be Dixon & Hunter's paper.

30. *Maryland Journal,* Dec. 29, 1778; *Pennsylvania Evening Post,* Jan. 7, 1779; *Pennsylvania Packet,* Jan. 12, 1779; *New-Jersey Gazette,* Jan. 20, 1779; *Boston Evening Post* (White & Adams), Jan. 24, 1779; *Independent Ledger,* Jan. 25, 1779; *Connecticut Gazette,*

In late November, as this news began to circulate through patriot networks, the Virginia House of Delegates passed a resolution honoring Clark and his officers "for their extraordinary resolution and perseverance in so hazardous an enterprise." Thanks to his bravery, "great advantages may accrue to the common cause of America, as well as to this commonwealth in particular." The assembly's resolution made formal what the newspaper articles asserted through inference: that Clark's western strike against British instigators and Indian savages was the utmost expression of American patriotism.[31]

The confluence in early December of the news of Clark's summer campaign and the recent violence at Cherry Valley provided another example of how the events of the Revolutionary War kept the common cause discourse alive. In this case, the lag in news from Illinois might suggest an ineffective communication network, but its late appearance in December actually helped the patriots deflect attention away from failures in New York. In the December 19 issue of John Dunlap's *Pennsylvania Packet,* the text of the Virginia Assembly's formal congratulations of Clark appeared on the very same page as the report of Iroquois warriors ripping Cherry Valley farmers to pieces. When readers' eyes reached the bottom of the column whereby Virginia leaders expressed their gratitude for a successful expedition to protect frontier farmers, at the top of the next, they found a glaring need for just such a campaign along the Mohawk. The internal logic of the printed page suggested strongly that the common cause needed another Clark in New York.[32]

As newspapers back east sang his praises, Clark was engaged in a desperate struggle to hold on to his conquests in the Illinois country. Henry Hamilton quickly realized the potential of even this tiny force of American rangers and in October marched south from Detroit with 175 men to stop

---

Jan. 29, 1779; *New-York Journal,* Feb. 1, 1779; *Providence Gazette,* Feb. 6, 1779; *Connecticut Courant,* Feb. 16, 1779.

31. *Virginia Gazette* (Dixon & Hunter), Dec. 4, 1778.

32. Trish Loughran has argued that significant time lags in newspaper reporting are evidence of how weak, unreliable, and inefficient print networks were during the Revolutionary period. This seems an anachronistic analysis that does not consider the expectations of readers. Extralocal news was rarely timely in the eighteenth century; this does not mean that readers discounted dated news. Delays sometimes meant that context had changed, especially during wartime. Lags sometimes worked to the benefit of patriot publicists. See Trish Loughran, *The Republic in Print: Print Culture in the Age of U.S. Nation Building, 1770–1870* (New York, 2007), 11–12.

"A Striking Picture of Barbarity"

them. By the time he reached Vincennes, he had gathered more than three hundred additional Indian allies. On December 17, Hamilton retook the Wabash town without a fight. The impassable rivers convinced him that he should not continue to Kaskaskia, believing he would be safe for the winter. It took a month for the news to reach Clark, who was almost two hundred miles away on the Mississippi. He sent a letter back to Patrick Henry informing him that the "Famous Hair Buyer General" had captured Vincennes, and immediately made arrangements to march. Clark decided he needed to move against Vincennes before Hamilton could reinforce the town's defenses or rally Indian support to his side. Indeed, Hamilton wrote Canadian governor Frederick Haldimand that he expected numbers of Ottawas, Chippewas, Hurons, Shawnees, Delaware, and Wabash to fight for the crown in the coming spring.[33]

Two weeks after hearing the news, Clark set off for an arduous winter march to the Wabash with his own 175 men, half of them French volunteers. Overnight on February 23, they reached Hamilton's stockade and dug trenches a few hundred yards in front of its main gate. After they exchanged fire the next morning, Clark demanded the lieutenant governor's unconditional surrender. Hamilton refused, and the shooting continued. When Clark sent a flag several hours later, he backed up his threat that they would not receive quarter by executing five Indians right outside the fort. Hamilton described this grisly scene in his journal. Clark's men had apprehended those unfortunate five with American scalps and, under a flag of truce, brought them into the "street opposite the Fort Gate," where they "were butcherd in succession."[34]

Hamilton did not witness the execution but believed Clark had personally conducted it. "He had just come from his Indian tryumph all bloody and sweating," Hamilton related, describing his subsequent meeting with the young Virginian. Clark "seated himself on the edge of one of the batteaus, that had some rainwater in it, and while he washed his hands and face

33. Barnhart, ed., *Hamilton and Clark*, 60; Clark to Patrick Henry, "Kaskaskias," [Ill.], Feb. 3, 1779, in James, ed., *Clark Papers*, VIII, 97; Lieut.-Governor Henry Hamilton to General Frederick Haldimand, Vincennes, Jan. 24, 1779, in Davies, ed., *Docs. of the Am. Rev.*, XVII, 50.

34. Barnhart, ed., *Hamilton and Clark*, 73, 75, 182–183. For a diary documenting the challenges they faced on this winter march, especially the threat of starvation and freezing, see "Journal of Joseph Bowman," Jan. 29–Mar. 20, 1779, in James, ed., *Clark Papers*, VIII, 155–164.

still reeking from the human sacrifice in which he had acted as chief priest, he told me with great exultation how he had been employed." When Clark later wrote about this incident, he minimized his involvement, though without any expression of regret. In his journal, he described how "my people were so enraged" when they had first encountered the scalp-bearing Indians, and "they killed" them in front of the fort.[35]

This disavowal should not surprise. Patrick Henry had explicitly instructed Clark to avoid just such a terrible scene. Holding the moral high ground, or, at least, projecting it, was an essential part of the common cause appeal. That argument depended on British agents like Hamilton to be the sole perpetrators of heinous acts. Clark's becoming a sacrificial priest reversed the formula. It was the Hair-Buyer himself who wrote, "The Blood of the victims was still visible for days afterwards, a testimony of the courage and Humanity of Colonel Clarke." The sneer that accompanied "Humanity" in these instances was a hallmark of patriot publicists. Now those representations were inverted. Had Hamilton succeeded at Vincennes and captured the Conqueror of the Illinois, the British would have achieved an important strategic victory. Not only would they have strengthened their relationship with Indians throughout the Ohio Valley; they could have reaped a publicity harvest in hauling Clark to Detroit and broadcasting his actions to the world. Instead, that is exactly what happened to Henry Hamilton. He and his seventy-nine men surrendered to Clark later that day, February 24, 1779. Two weeks later, a guard escorted the lieutenant governor and twenty-six in his party east to Williamsburg for trial, parading him through the places where his proxies had wreaked destruction, including Kentucky and Fort Pitt. It would be the middle of June before they arrived at the capital.[36]

35. Feb. 23, 1779, Hamilton journal, in Barnhart, ed., *Hamilton and Clark*, 183; "Journal of George Rogers Clark," in James, ed., *Clark Papers*, VIII, 164–168, esp. 167. When Clark wrote his memoir of this expedition more than a decade later, he further minimized it, excising any details of how the Indians were ritually killed in front of the fort during a truce. See Clark to John Brown, 1791, in James, ed., *Clark Papers*, VIII, 288. For the theatricality of this incident, see Griffin, *American Leviathan*, 144; Sheehan, "The Famous Hair Buyer General," *Indiana Magazine of History*, LXXIX (1983), 1–28, esp. 20; and especially Richard White, *The Middle Ground: Indians, Empires, and Republics in the Great Lakes Region, 1650–1815* (Cambridge, 1991), 375–378.

36. Feb. 23, 1779, Hamilton journal, in Barnhart, ed., *Hamilton and Clark*, 183; Griffin, *American Leviathan*, 145.

"A Striking Picture of Barbarity"

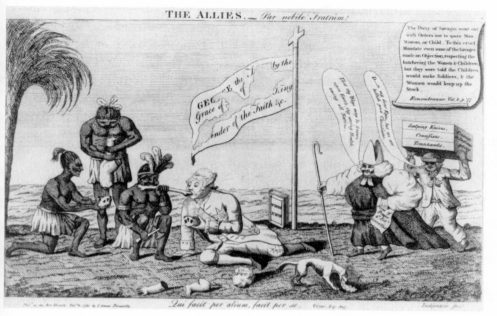

Figure 12. *"The Allies ~ Par nobile Fratrium!" [a noble pair of brothers]. 1780.*
In this British satire, King George, his standard in tatters, shares a bone with his
cannibal friends, a terrible feast that even the dog cannot stomach. Meanwhile, a sailor
brings ashore boxes full of scalping knives, crucifixes, and tomahawks. The Latin phrase
at the bottom translates as "he who acts through another, acts himself," a sentiment
Jefferson certainly endorsed. Courtesy of the Library of Congress.

When they did, Thomas Jefferson, now the governor of Virginia, initiated
proceedings to prosecute Hamilton as a criminal. It was the actions of the
Hair-Buyer, not the "chief priest" of Vincennes, that Americans would read
myriad details about that summer. Once he reached Williamsburg, the lieutenant governor was made to answer for his crimes. Hamilton's trial, itself
created by patriot propaganda, further underscored the need to eliminate
connections between Indians and British agents and stressed that military
invasion, à la Clark's intrepid campaign, was the best way to sever those ties.

The new Virginia governor certainly believed the stories about the Hair-
Buyer. Writing to Theodorick Bland, Jefferson effused, "The indiscriminate
murther of men, Women and children with the usual circumstances of barbarity practised by the Indian savages, was the particular task of Governor
Hamilton's employment." For the sake of their suffering compatriots, Jeffer-

son and his council agreed that Virginia had to "furnish a contemplation rather pleasing to the generous Soldier" and respect his "honourable bravery . . . discriminated from the cruel and cowardly warfare of the savage, whose object in war is to extinguish human nature."[37]

A few weeks later, Jefferson further justified his beliefs to Hamilton's successor at Detroit. "Those who act together in war are answerable for each other," he claimed in very revealing, self-referential language, concluding,

> No distinction can be made between principal and ally by those against whom the war is waged. He who employs another to do a deed, makes the Deed his own. If he calls in the hand of the assassin, or murderer, himself becomes the assassin or murderer. The known rule of warfare of the Indian Savages is an indiscriminate butchery of men, women, and children. These savages, under this well-known Character, are employed by the British Nation as allies in the war against the Americans. Governor Hamilton undertakes to be the conductor of the war. . . . Governor Hamilton then is himself the butcher of Men, Women, and Children.

Having blamed King George personally for these abominations in the Declaration, now Jefferson had the chance to prosecute the next best thing. He and his council backed up the conviction that Hamilton should suffer for his crimes. Not only was the impulse to imprison Hamilton animated by patriot propagation of the anti-Indian sublime—the language the Virginia council used in their sentence was straight from the Declaration, too: "They find that Governour Hamilton has executed the task of inciting the Indians to perpetrate their accustomed cruelties on the citizens of these states, without distinction of age, sex, or condition." The order continued to list the atrocities Hamilton had committed, from prisoner abuse to, of course, his encouragement of Indians to scalp and torture Americans. Jefferson arranged for *Virginia Gazette* printers Dixon and Nicolson to create a broadsheet of the council's resolutions. He then sent a copy to Congress with an accompanying note that "I thought it my duty to lay it before Congress as early as possible, with the reasons supporting it; nothing doubting but it will meet with their approbation; its justice seems to have been confirmed by the general sense of the people here." Americans outside Virginia were also interested in Hamilton's fate. Patriot newspapers up and down the continent exchanged news of his capture and the articles of his surrender to Clark.

37. TJ to Theodorick Bland, Williamsburg, Va., June 8, 1779, *PTJ*, II, 286–287.

"A Striking Picture of Barbarity"

Printers published reports of his appearance in Williamsburg, Jefferson's letters to Congress announcing his sentence, and the council resolves.[38]

This high level of public interest in Hamilton limited the options available to Congress. Prisoner abuse was one of the most controversial issues of the Revolution. From the Cedars in 1776 to the notorious prison ship *Jersey*—currently stinking at anchor in the marshes off Long Island and rapidly taking the lives of American prisoners—patriot leaders screeched about British treatment of their combatants. This made them highly aware of how they, themselves, cared for prisoners of war. Both sides regularly exchanged high-ranking officers shortly after capture. Even though the British

38. "Order of Virginia Council of State Placing Henry Hamilton and Others in Irons," June 16, 1779, TJ to Governor of Detroit, Williamsburg, Va., July 22, 1779, in H. R. McIlwaine, ed., *Official Letters of the Governors of the State of Virginia*, 3 vols. (Richmond, Va., 1926–1929), II, 29–33, esp. 31; "Order of Virginia Council of State Placing Henry Hamilton and Others in Irons," June 16, 1779, *PJM*, I, 288–292, esp. 288; TJ to John Jay, Williamsburg, Va., Jun. 19, 1779, *PTJ*, III, 4–6, esp. 4–5. The council relied heavily on the testimony of John Dodge, a Connecticut trader who was imprisoned at Detroit at the outbreak of war, escaped in 1779, and immediately wrote a narrative of his captivity, which Philadelphia printer Thomas Bradford published. It appeared in: *Continental Journal*, Dec. 30, 1779, Jan. 6, 13, 1780; *Connecticut Gazette*, Feb. 2, 9, 16, 1780; *Pennsylvania Journal*, Feb. 3, 1780. For Bradford's version, see John Dodge, *A Narrative of the Capture and Treatment of John Dodge, by the English at Detroit* (Philadelphia, 1779), *Early American Imprints*, 16262. Salem printer Ezekiel Russell's second edition (Salem, Mass., 1780), is also catalogued as no. 16765. Council resolutions broadsheet: *In Council, June 16, 1779* (Williamsburg, Va., [1779]), *Early American Imprints*, 16657. Robert Honyman of Hanover County noted in his diary, "When being convicted of great cruelties and especially barbarous usage of prisoners while in power, it was thought proper to retaliate in some measure, therefore [Hamilton] and two of his associates were put in irons and confined in a dungeon; where they still remain" (entry for Aug. 16, 1779, Honyman Diary, 362). Hamilton capture and surrender articles: *Virginia Gazette* (Dixon & Nicolson), June 5, 1779; *Pennsylvania Evening Post*, June 19, 1779; *Pennsylvania Packet*, June 22, 1779; *Pennsylvania Journal*, June 23, 1779; *New-York Journal*, July 5, 1779; *Connecticut Courant*, July 6, 1779; *Continental Journal*, July 8, 1779; *American Journal*, July 8, 1779; *Independent Chronicle*, July 8, 1779; *Boston Evening Post* (White & Adams), July 10, 1779; *Maryland Journal*, July 15, 1779; *Massachusetts Spy*, July 15, 1779; *Boston Gazette*, Aug. 23, 1779; *United States Magazine*, I (June 1779), 288. Hamilton's arrival in Williamsburg: *Virginia Gazette* (Dixon & Nicolson), June 19, 1779; *Maryland Gazette*, June 25, 1779; *Connecticut Courant*, July 13, 1779; *Massachusetts Spy*, July 15, 1779; *Providence Gazette*, July 17, 1779; *Connecticut Gazette*, July 21, 1779.

demanded his release, Governor Hamilton stayed in irons through the summer without any internal controversy. He was too dangerous and his actions too severe. As one might expect, two of the men the patriots decided to hold in closest confinement during the Revolution were John Connolly and Henry Hamilton—both infamous for trying to incite merciless savages.[39]

The man who neutralized this threat had executed a fantastic plan. Clark offered a solution to chronic insecurity on the northern frontier: attack the enemy, draw out its British sponsors, and punish the proxies for their treacherous behavior. In doing so, Clark made himself into a particularly attractive patriot hero. Clark and other frontier partisans like him, especially Daniel Boone, became a kind of super-American, conflating Indian hating and patriotic ardor for the common cause. By killing Britons and Indians, by protecting the homeland, and by securing enormous tracts of land for the new nation, Clark was an exemplary American. If only his success could be replicated along the Mohawk River.[40]

* * *

Discussions for an expedition against Iroquoia began one month after the attack on Wyoming. On August 3, 1778, Washington wrote Congress that it was too late to "march to the Seneca settlements." He advised any plan "for subduing the unfriendly indians ought to be deferred till a moment

39. British general William Phillips appealed to Jefferson not to hold Hamilton in close confinement, citing that "justice, humanity and honour" would be a better remedy to "those charges of blood and cruelty" rather than reciprocal treatment (William Phillips to TJ, "Colonel Carters House," July 5, 1779, *PTJ*, III, 25–28, esp. 26). Hamilton was incarcerated in Williamsburg until granted parole on Sept. 29, 1779. See "Advice of Council respecting Henry Hamilton and Others," Sept. 29, 1779, *PTJ*, III, 94–95. Connolly, on the other hand, languished in a Philadelphia prison from December 1775 until October 1780. For more on prisoners of war during the Revolution, see Edwin G. Burrows, *Forgotten Patriots: The Untold Story of American Prisoners during the Revolutionary War* (New York, 2010); Caroline Cox, *A Proper Sense of Honor: Service and Sacrifice in George Washington's Army* (Chapel Hill, N.C., 2004), 199–236; Ken Miller, *Dangerous Guests: Enemy Captives and Revolutionary Communities during the War for Independence* (Ithaca, N.Y., 2014).

40. Eric Hinderaker has explained how the Revolution inverted the concept of individual initiative on the Ohio frontier. The Revolutionary War shifted values toward celebrating expansion and fighting Indians as defining, patriotic American endeavors. See *Elusive Empires: Constructing Colonialism in the Ohio Valley, 1673–1800* (Cambridge, 1997), 185–225.

"A Striking Picture of Barbarity"

of greater leisure," and, if he had his druthers, he would advise attacking Canada to "strike at once at the root." Attacking Iroquoia would "only lop off a few branches, which would soon spread out anew nourished and sustained by the remaining trunk." Washington believed the British instigators should be the real target. While patriots contemplated how to react, Brant and Butler continued to lay waste to settlements all along the New York frontier.[41]

After Cherry Valley, an expedition could not be postponed. On January 5, Nathanael Greene began writing a formal strategic proposal for attacking the Iroquois. Greene's plan called for a multi-pronged attack with "considerable bodys of men," one marching from Fort Pitt, a second from the Wyoming Valley, and a third driving up the Mohawk River. This initial plan resembled the three-headed force commanded by John Sullivan, James Clinton, and Daniel Brodhead that would demolish upper New York later that summer. Congress gave approval in late February for the army to "take effectual measures" for the "chastisement of the savages."[42]

In May, Washington confessed to a correspondent his anguish over hearing "The cries of the distressed—of the fatherless and the Widows" that "come to me from all quarters." But the secret orders he issued to General John Sullivan that very month revealed little sympathy for human suffering. The instructions Washington gave Sullivan initiated a new phase of violent retribution between the United States and Indians across the northern frontier.[43]

Sullivan's mission was to cut the king off from his proxies and thereby bring peace to the entire northern frontier. If he achieved his objective, Washington would hear no more cries from distressed New Yorkers or Penn-

41. GW to Board of War, Headquarters, White Plains, Aug. 3, 1778, *PGW: RW*, XVI, 226–230, esp. 228–229. The "secret journals" of the Continental Congress show that they had developed a plan of attack to reach into New York as early as October 1778. Two thousand men were to be in Wyoming by May 1, so as to march out against Fort Niagara no later than June 1. See "Secret Journals of Congress," Charles Thomson Papers, 1774–1811, book 6, MSS, HSP.

42. Nathanael Greene to GW, Philadelphia, Jan. 5, 1779, *PNG*, III, 144–145. For the military's wrangling over strategy and logistics that preceded the 1779 Indian campaign, see Mintz, *Seeds of Empire*, 78–85; Joseph R. Fischer, *A Well-Executed Failure: The Sullivan Campaign against the Iroquois, July–September 1779* (Columbia, S.C., 1997), 102–128. Congress's approval for the campaign: Feb. 25, 1779, *JCC*, XIII, 252.

43. GW to John Armstrong, Middlebrook, May 18, 1779, *PGW: RW*, XX, 517–519, esp. 517.

sylvanians. Except, Sullivan was to accomplish this—officially—by attacking the Iroquois way of life. Sounding frightfully like a merciless savage himself, Washington's orders to Sullivan were unambiguous:

> The expedition you are appointed to command is to be directed against the hostile tribes of the six nations of Indians, with their associates and adherents. The immediate objects are the total destruction and devastation of their settlements and the capture of as many prisoners of every age and sex as possible. It will be essential to ruin their crops now in the ground and prevent their planting more.

Sullivan had 2,300 men at his disposal, General James Clinton was in support with another 1,400, and General Daniel Brodhead was to bring 600 up the Alleghany River from Fort Pitt. Together, they were to burn Iroquoia to the ground.[44]

Logistics somewhat dampened the fires of revenge. It took weeks for the men assigned to Sullivan's force to gather at Wyoming. Several units that arrived in late June had to wait more than a month for the coordination of food and boats. Officers passed the time by exploring the nearby ruins of the devastated Wyoming settlement.[45]

Philadelphia physician Ebenezer Elmer noted in his diary, "The Flats are exceeding fertile and the settlements increasing fast before the devastation which the inhumane and merciless savages made in their excursion hither in July last under the command of the infamous *Butler*. By them the Male inhabitants were all slain, habitations destroyed and the country laid desolate." Lieutenant Colonel Adam Hubley, commander of the 11th Pennsylvania Regiment, arrived late, but, upon inquiring about the swath of destroyed houses, was "informed by an industrious set of inhabitants though poor yet happy with their situation until that horrid moment when the British tyrant let loose upon them his Emissaries the Savages of the wood, who not only destroyed and laid waste those cottages but in cool blood massacred and cut off the inhabitants not even sparing the gray locks or helpless infant." "The distressed *widows* and *orphan* children at this place are real objects of

---

44. "Gen. Washington's Instructions to Gen. Sullivan, May 31, 1779," in Otis G. Hammond, ed., *Letters and Papers of Major-General John Sullivan, Continental Army*, III, *1771–1777* (Concord, N.H., 1939), 48–53, esp. 48–49. For a charged account that indicts Washington for this "genocide," see Barbara Alice Mann, *George Washington's War on Native America* (Westport, Conn., 2005), 51–110, esp. 52.

45. Ward, *War of the Revolution*, II, 638–645; Mintz, *Seeds of Empire*, 94–102.

"A Striking Picture of Barbarity"

pity and charity, some of them being quite naked and destitute," one officer wrote from Wyoming in a letter that would emerge in several newspapers.[46]

George Reid, a Continental army officer from Massachusetts, toured the surrounding countryside the afternoon before the massacre's anniversary. After viewing "bones scattered on the ground for near two miles and several skulls being brought in at different times that had been scalped and inhumanely mangled with the hatchet," he concluded, "This place may with propriety be called Golgotha." For Reid and other officers, what they had heard about Wyoming and what they saw of the ruins alike corroborated Jefferson's description of merciless savages. Soon they would begin an official campaign to take revenge against the nation's enemies.[47]

Before they did, Reid and Sullivan's other officers celebrated Independence Day. That the anniversary of the Wyoming Massacre almost coincided with the Fourth was not lost on his men. After toasting Congress, the French alliance, and George Washington, the staff officers turned to the task at hand: the tenth toast proclaimed, "Civilization or Death to all American Savages!" Whether the men leading a gathering invasion force into Iroquoia really considered this an option is debatable. One hundred miles to the west, their commander did not see much of one. Washington sat down on the third anniversary of independence to update Franklin's partner in the "little book," the marquis de Lafayette. Also invoking biblical imagery, he sneered, "I trust [Sullivan] will destroy their Settlements and extirpate them from the Country which more than probably will be effected by their flight as it is not a difficult matter for them to take up their Beds and Walk."[48]

46. June 23, 1779, in Ebenezer Elmer Commonplace Book, 1779–1781, HSP, Adam Hubley journal, July 31, 1779, item no. 62 of the Peter Force Collection, series 7E, LoC. In case future readers might misunderstand, Hubley later clarified Indians as "savages (emissaries employed by the British King)" (Aug. 18, 1779). "Distressed widows": New-Jersey Gazette, June 23, 1779; New-Jersey Journal, June 29, 1779; New-York Journal, July 12, 1779; Independent Chronicle, July 15, 1779; Independent Ledger, July 19, 1779; New-Hampshire Gazette, July 20, 1779; Connecticut Gazette, July 21, 1779; Massachusetts Spy, July 22, 1779; Royal Gazette, July 7, 1779; Connecticut Courant, July 27, 1779; Dresden Mercury, Aug. 3, 1779.

47. July 2–3, 1779, George Reid journal, Massachusetts Historical Society, Boston.

48. July 4, 1779, Reid journal; GW to Lafayette, New Windsor, July 4, 1779, in John C. Fitzpatrick, ed., The Writings of George Washington: From the Original Manuscript Sources, 1745–1799, 39 vols. (Washington, D.C., 1931–1944), XV, 369–370, esp. 370. Another observer of this party was Major James Norris; see "Journal of Major James

The Iroquois—Oneidas, Tuscaroras, and some Onondagas aside—had scorned the offers patriots had made in previous warnings to stay neutral. Now they would pay with their livelihoods, if not their lives. As Washington's chilling orders made clear, Sullivan's task was not only to seek out and defeat Indian warriors. It was to prevent their society from being able to wage war at all. As the army moved into Indian country, many diaries marveled at the bountiful fields full of pumpkins, corn, beans, squash, and potatoes they came across late that summer. They then expressed the same amazement at the size of the bonfires produced after American soldiers piled up all those crops and torched them.[49]

Sullivan's men left Wyoming on July 31 and followed the Susquehanna northwest to Tioga, just over the New York border. Sullivan began to reveal the punitive nature of his mission by having his men burn Chemung, a deserted town of thirty houses and a chapel. A week later, he approached Newtown (near modern Elmira, New York), where Butler and Brant decided to make their stand against the invaders. Butler's 180 Rangers and Brant's 500 Indians, already outnumbered 5 to 1, changed their minds quickly when American troops surrounded them on three sides. The battle of Newtown was the principal engagement of the entire campaign. In all, 12 Indians died, whereas 3 Continental soldiers were killed and nearly 40 more wounded. Butler and Brant's withdrawal left the entire countryside open to Sullivan's men.

Over the next week, they burned Catherine's Town, Appletown, Kindaia, Kanadaseaga (the principal settlement of the Senecas), Honeoye, Kanagha, and Genesee. Hundreds of houses and thousands of acres of ripening crops went up in smoke before Sullivan's men returned to the Susquehanna in early September. As one soldier wrote, the troops had "chearfully submitted" to the hardships of campaigning because they were to a man "anxious

Norris," July 4, 1779, in Frederick Cook, ed., *Journals of the Military Expedition of Major General John Sullivan: Against the Six Nations of Indians in 1779; With Records of Centennial Celebrations* (Auburn, N.Y., 1887), 225–227. "Take up your pallet and walk": John 5:8 (Revised Standard Edition).

49. There were an unusual number of journals kept by participants of Sullivan's expedition, which underscores the notion that they knew even the rank and file understood that they were accomplishing something historic and decisive on behalf of the Revolution. See especially Adam Hubley's journal. In the nineteenth century, Cook compiled the various accounts in one large volume (*Military Expedition of Major General John Sullivan*). See also Philip C. Mead, "Melancholy Landscapes: Writing Warfare in the American Revolution" (Ph.D. diss., Harvard University, 2012).

to extirpate those Hell-Hounds from off the face of the Earth." In all, fewer than fifty American soldiers died of illness or wounds. "General Sullivan has compleated the entire destruction of the Country of the Six Nations," Washington exulted to Lafayette when it was all over. "These unexpected and severe strokes, has disconcerted, humbled, and distressed the Indians exceedingly, and will, I am perswaded, be productive of great good; as they are undeniable proofs to them that Great Britain cannot protect them, and that it is in our power to chastise them whenever their hostile conduct deserves it."[50]

Sullivan did his own boasting even before he returned to the Susquehanna. He summarized his triumphs in a report to Congress, detailing fruit trees, houses, fields of corn, and the forty towns his men destroyed. "The quantity of Corn destroyed at a moderate computation must amount to 160,000 bushels, with a vast quantity of vegitables of every kind." "Except one Town . . . about 50 miles from Chinesee [Genesee]," he wrote, "there is not a single Town left in the Country" of the Six Nations. Sullivan implemented his superiors' vision of Indian destruction through starvation. The reason they went all the way to Genesee, "the grand capital of the Indian country," was that "Indians of all nations had been planting there this spring; that all the rangers and some British had been employed in assisting them, in order to raise sufficient supplies to support them while destroying our frontiers." That food was war matériel; the consequences for women and children of destroying it were not considered. "The corn was collected and burned in houses and kilns, that the enemy might not reap the least advantage from it, which method we have persued in every other place." Sullivan apologized only for the length of the letter, not the grim repercussions for thousands of people in New York, "as I thought particular and circumstantial detail of facts, would not be disagreeable." He was right: patriot leaders were thrilled with his success.[51]

Upon their safe return at Easton, an army chaplain named Israel Evans

50. "An American Soldier" to Dr. Stagg, Tioga, N.Y., Sept. 6, 1779, in Alexander C. Flick, ed., "New Sources on the Sullivan-Clinton Campaign in 1779," *Quarterly Journal of the New York State Historical Association*, X (1929), 310; GW to Lafayette, West Point, Oct. 20, 1779, in Fitzpatrick, ed., *Writings of Washington*, XVI, 491–494, esp. 492–493.

51. John Sullivan to John Jay, "Teaoga," Sept. 30, 1779, in Hammond, ed., *Papers of General Sullivan*, III, 123–137, esp. 134 ("not a single Town left"), 128–129 ("grand capital"), 131 ("corn was collected"), 136 ("would not be disagreeable").

delivered a sermon congratulating the officers and soldiers for their brave execution of God's will in Iroquoia. Soon turned into a pamphlet by *Pennsylvania Journal* printer Thomas Bradford and freely distributed through the ranks, Evans's sermon reminded the conquerors of the reasons for their recent destruction. "When the tyrant of Britain," he declaimed,

> sent his emissaries to raise the savages of the wilderness to war, and to provoke them to break their faith with the United States of America; then our defenceless frontiers became the seat of savage fury, and hundreds of our countrymen bled, and hundreds of them suffered more than the tender ear can hear related, or the compassionate heart can endure. Then the expectations of our enemies were high and joyful, that half our country would fall by the hands of tories and savages, . . . And indeed the prospect was full of horror to every compassionate friend of his country and mankind, and called, mercifully called, for the aid of an army, to save so large a part of the United States.

Thankfully, there were Americans "equal to the arduous and dangerous task." These brave soldiers "defeated the savage army and conquered those barbarians who had long been the dread of our frontiers," ensuring a wonderful future: "Methinks I see the rich lands from the Teaoga river to the banks of the Seneca and Cayuga lakes, and from thence to the most fruitful of lands on the [G]enesses to the great lakes Ontario, Erie, and Huron . . . all these lands inhabited by the independent Citizens of America." The soldiers learned through this circulated pamphlet—sponsored by their top commanders—that the mission they had just completed was, in fact, an imperial conquest: "I congratulate posterity on this addition of immense wealth and extensive territory to the United States." This land was for "American citizens, not their enemies."[52]

Congress soon passed their own commendation, formally thanking Sullivan "and the brave officers and soldiers under his command, for effectually

52. Israel Evans, *A Discourse Delivered at Easton, on the 17th of October, 1779, to the Officers and Soldiers of the Western Army: After Their Return from an Expedition against the Five Nations of Hostile Indians* (Philadelphia, 1779), 17–18 ("tyrant of Britain"), 19 ("arduous and dangerous task"), 21–22 ("Methinks I see"), 22 ("American citizens, not their enemies"), *Early American Imprints,* 16266. This interpretation corresponds with Wayne E. Lee's contrast in how patriots approached war with Indians and Europeans in *Barbarians and Brothers: Anglo-American Warfare, 1500–1865* (New York, 2011), esp. 171–231.

"A Striking Picture of Barbarity"

executing the important expedition against such of the Indian nations as, encouraged by the councils and conducted by the officers of his Britannic majesty, [who] had perfidiously waged an unprovoked and cruel war against these United States." Soon, they also provided for another day of thanksgiving so Americans could honor God for protecting "those who went out into the wilderness against the savage tribes."[53]

Proud as they were of his actions, Congress wasted no time in passing Sullivan's letters over to Philadelphia printers for publication. Patriot editors, though, hardly waited for congressional approval to inform their readers about actions on the New York frontier. The first report predicting the violence of that summer appeared weeks before Sullivan arrived at Wyoming. A Boston paper published a letter from Albany that displayed a rare sophistication in portraying Indians. It detailed—apparently without irony—how American forces "had it in contemplation to surprize" the Onondagas, "as part of them are avowed enemies to us, and have actually committed hostilities upon our frontiers, while the other part, under the mark of friendship, have been treating with us at Albany." Eleven papers picked up on this early news of a foray into Indian country. A few other references to friendly Indians appeared around the edges of the Sullivan expedition, especially as men gathered to march. Many patriot printers exchanged two reports about pro-American Indians joining Sullivan's expedition, one describing how "four Indians, of the Stockbridge Tribe" led other friendly Indians, and the other mentioning "a considerable number of Oneida, Tuscorora and Stockbridge" preparing at Wyoming. Here again, however, those mentions of friendly assistance were juxtaposed against and appeared two lines underneath the good news of Pennsylvania frontier families "undisturbed by the Savages," thanks to the "spirited and successful enterprizes of the gallant Col. Clarke."[54]

53. Commendation of Sullivan: Oct. 14, 1779, *JCC*, XV, 1170. The inhabitants of Northampton County, Pennsylvania, also sent an address thanking Sullivan for "Exertions you have made to secure our happiness." See "Address of Inhabitants of Northampton County, Pennsylvania," in Hammond, ed., *Papers of General Sullivan*, III, 167–168, esp. 168; also printed in *Pennsylvania Packet*, Oct. 19, 1779; *New-Jersey Gazette*, Oct. 20, 1779. Day of thanksgiving: Oct. 20, 1779, *JCC*, XV, 1192; *Pennsylvania Gazette*, Nov. 3, 1779.

54. *Continental Journal*, May 7, 1779; *American Journal*, May 7, 1779; *Independent Chronicle*, May 7, 1779; *Providence Gazette*, May 8, 1779; *Boston Gazette*, May 10, 1779; *Massachusetts Spy*, May 13, 1779. "Four Indians, of the Stockbridge": *Pennsylvania Packet*, June 24, 1779; *Pennsylvania Evening Post*, June 26, 1779; *Maryland*

Back on July 4, 1779, the same day he mocked the Iroquois for being uncivilized nomads in his letter to Lafayette, Washington had issued a commendation lauding a group of thirty-three Stockbridge for their "bravery and attachment to the United States." When Sullivan returned from his expedition, he, too, thanked his Indian allies for their help, sending a formal speech of appreciation to the Oneidas, which Congress ordered printed. Five editors obeyed. Though significant, these instances of recognizing the help of good Indians gained much less public attention than stories of Sullivan taking revenge on the king's proxies. Once Iroquois towns began to burn, representations of hostile Indians paying the price for siding with the enemy all but silenced any mention of Indians allied to the United States. For the rest of the war, the word "Stockbridge" would not appear again in patriot newspapers. Here were more stories not told, but, unlike the case of the Hessians, the refusal of patriot leaders to broadcast the valuable assistance of their Indian allies underscored policies of universal exclusion.[55]

The whisperlike presentation of good Indians was not a function of chance. The hand of patriot political leaders guided certain stories, and not others, into printers' shops. New York governor George Clinton wrote to General James Clinton in frustration with *Journal* printer John Holt because he had already "parted with all his Papers containing the Acc't of the Anandago [Onondaga] Expedition, which however was not so perfect as the one which was drawn up and sent to him to publish." The governor's

---

Journal, July 6, 1779; *New-York Journal,* July 12, 1779; *Independent Chronicle,* July 15, 1779; *American Journal,* July 15, 1779; *Providence Gazette,* July 17, 1779; *Virginia Gazette* (Dixon & Nicolson), July 17, 1779; *New-Hampshire Gazette,* July 20, 1779; *Gazette, of the State of South-Carolina,* Aug. 4, 1779. "Considerable number of Oneida, Tuscorora and Stockbridge" to join Sullivan: *New-Jersey Journal,* June 29, 1779; *New-York Gazette,* July 5, 1779; *Royal Gazette,* July 7, 1779; *New-York Journal,* July 12, 1779; *Independent Chronicle,* July 15, 1779; *Independent Ledger,* July 19, 1779; *New-Hampshire Gazette,* July 20, 1779; *Connecticut Gazette,* July 21, 1779; *Massachusetts Spy,* July 22, 1779; *Connecticut Courant,* July 27, 1779; *Dresden Mercury,* Aug. 3, 1779. The attribution that Clark was the reason for frontier calm was the paragraph above the "four Indians, of the Stockbridge" mention. Printers exchanged them together. See *Pennsylvania Packet,* June 24, 1779.

55. GW to Solomon Hendricks, New Windsor, July 4, 1779, in Fitzpatrick, ed., *Writings of Washington,* XV, 368. Appreciation of Oneidas: *Pennsylvania Packet,* Oct. 14, 1779; *New-Jersey Gazette,* Oct. 27, Nov. 3, 1779; *Connecticut Gazette,* Nov. 3, 1779; *Norwich Packet,* Nov. 9, 16, 1779; *Massachusetts Spy,* Nov. 18, 1779; *Independent Chronicle,* Nov. 18, 1779.

"A Striking Picture of Barbarity"

anger reveals the tension in this informal relationship but also serves as a reminder that patriot political leaders considered newspapers essential and supplied them accordingly.[56]

In early September, the first report circulated about Sullivan's penetration into Iroquois country, informing readers that he had burned the town of Chemung and that his magazine in Sunbury was "perfectly secure." The following week, Samuel Loudon published an "authentic account" from Sullivan in his *New York Packet,* a letter that featured in several other northern papers. Reporting that Clinton's contingent had joined him, Sullivan praised the "distinguished gallantry" of his troops as they were "employed in desolating the settlement" at Newtown, "which was one of the largest and richest in the Indian country." The next week featured more news from Indian country. John Holt in Poughkeepsie wrote with satisfaction that Sullivan's troops were "remarkably healthy" and in "high spirits" and that they had accepted half rations in order to "complete the business they are upon." Ten more printers copied a letter from officer in the expedition that dispassionately listed the names of towns left in "great heaps of ruin" and the kinds of vegetables they spoiled. Eleven New England printers devoured Samuel Loudon's judgment that the operation was "crowned with compleat success."[57]

56. [George Clinton] to Brigadier General James Clinton, Poughkeepsie, N.Y., May 16, 1779, in Hastings et al., eds., *Public Papers of George Clinton,* IV, 829–831, esp. 831.

57. "Perfectly secure": *Connecticut Courant,* Aug. 31, 1779; *Norwich Packet,* Aug. 31, 1779; *Connecticut Gazette,* Sept. 1, 1779; *Continental Journal,* Sept. 2, 1779; *Independent Chronicle,* Sept. 2, 1779; *American Journal,* Sept. 2, 1779; *Providence Gazette,* Sept. 4, 1779; *Virginia Gazette* (Dixon & Nicolson), Sept. 4, 1779; *New-Hampshire Gazette,* Sept. 7, 1779. "Distinguished gallantry": *New York Packet,* Sept. 9, 1779; *New-York Journal,* Sept. 13, 1779; *Connecticut Courant,* Sept. 14, 1779; *Connecticut Gazette,* Sept. 15, 1779; *Connecticut Journal,* Sept. 15, 1779; *Independent Chronicle,* Sept. 16, 1779; *Massachusetts Spy,* Sept. 16, 1779; *American Journal,* Sept. 16, 1779; *Providence Gazette,* Sept. 18, 1779; *Boston Gazette,* Sept. 20, 1779; *New-Hampshire Gazette,* Sept. 21, 1779. "Complete the business": *New-York Journal,* Sept. 20, 1779; *Connecticut Courant,* Sept. 28, 1779; *Connecticut Journal,* Sept. 29, 1779; *Pennsylvania Evening Post,* Sept. 29, 1779; *Pennsylvania Journal,* Sept. 29, 1779; *American Journal,* Sept. 30, 1779; *Pennsylvania Packet,* Sept. 30, 1779; *Continental Journal,* Sept. 30, 1779; *Massachusetts Spy,* Sept. 30, 1779; *Providence Gazette,* Oct. 2, 1779; *Boston Gazette,* Oct. 4, 1779; *New-Hampshire Gazette,* Oct. 5, 1779. The officer claimed they destroyed "a large country of corn, pumpkins, cymblines, cucumbers, water-melons, peaches and apples." See *New-*

After Sullivan's men had completed their mission, Americans through-out the nation read his final report to Congress. Even though it required anywhere from four to six entire columns of print, thirteen patriot printers found space to run it all. In fact, John Holt explained to his readers, "The long continued severity of the weather, having for many weeks past, pre-vented our receiving any intelligence by the post, we are obliged to enter-tain our reader with matters, which for want of room, were omitted at the proper time." This included Sullivan's report, "which we doubt not will be exceptable [*sic*] to our readers." Probably to Governor Clinton's satisfac-tion, Holt printed this account on January 24—albeit without acknowledg-ing how the same terrible winter weather that kept post riders away might be affecting the victims of Sullivan's expedition.[58]

One historian of the Revolutionary War has claimed, "The newspapers of the war years contained comparatively little discussion of the war through much of 1778, all of 1779, and the early months of 1780." The amount of coverage of the northern frontier and, especially, of Sullivan's expedition undermines this analysis. Patriot papers from August to October followed Sullivan, Clinton, and Brodhead closely. Most papers had some update each week that autumn. Letters from officers describing destroyed towns and fields appeared frequently. Consistent runs exist for twenty-two of the twenty-six patriot papers active during the fall of 1779. Printers of those twenty-two organs published an average of 7.8 articles describing Sullivan's men attack-ing hostile Indians in New York. In Philadelphia and Boston, where papers

Jersey Gazette, Sept. 29, 1779; *Pennsylvania Gazette*, Sept. 29, 1779; *Connecticut Courant*, Oct. 5, 1779; *Norwich Packet*, Oct. 5, 1779; *Independent Ledger*, Oct. 11, 1779; *New-Jersey Journal*, Oct. 11, 1779; *Connecticut Gazette*, Oct. 13, 1779; *Connecticut Journal*, Oct. 13, 1779; *Massachusetts Spy*, Oct. 14, 1779; *American Journal*, Oct. 14, 1779; *Providence Gazette*, Oct. 16, 1779. Most exchanged the "crowned with compleat success" account within a single week, unusually rapid for that era: *New York Packet*, Oct. 21, 1779; *New-York Journal*, Oct. 25, 1779; *Connecticut Courant*, Oct. 26, 1779; *Norwich Packet*, Oct. 26, 1779; *Connecticut Gazette*, Oct. 27, 1779; *Connecticut Journal*, Oct. 27, 1779; *Independent Chronicle*, Oct. 28, 1779; *American Journal*, Oct. 28, 1779; *Massachusetts Spy*, Oct. 28, 1779; *Boston Gazette*, Nov. 1, 1779; *New-Hampshire Gazette*, Nov. 2, 1779.

58. Sullivan report to Congress: *Pennsylvania Packet*, Oct. 9, 1779; *Pennsylvania Gazette*, Oct. 13, 1779; *New-Jersey Gazette*, Oct. 13, 1779; *Maryland Journal*, Oct. 19, 1779; *Maryland Gazette*, Oct. 22, 1779; *Connecticut Courant*, Oct. 26, 1779; *New-Jersey Journal*, Oct. 26, 1779; *Norwich Packet*, Nov. 2, 1779; *Independent Chronicle*, Nov. 11, 1779; *Continental Journal*, Nov. 12, 1779; *New-Hampshire Gazette*, Dec. 7, 1779; *New-York Journal*, Jan. 24, 1780. "Severity of the weather": *New-York Journal*, Jan. 24, 1780.

"A Striking Picture of Barbarity"

assumed a niche, some printed only a few notices—*Pennsylvania Evening Post* (4) and *Independent Ledger* (3)—but competitors exchanged more than a dozen—*Pennsylvania Packet* (15) and *Independent Chronicle* (13). Most detailed Sullivan's joining forces with Clinton and his victory at Newtown; against this onslaught, accounts of "good" Indians stood little chance. Just like Butler and Brant on the battlefield at Newtown, representations of Oneidas and "whig" Onondagas were outnumbered and surrounded.[59]

That these accounts of hostile Indians ran alongside news from Virginia about Henry Hamilton in that season only compounded the imagery of Indians as America's enemies. "We hear that Gen. Sullivan's army . . . having laid waste the Indian country to a great extent," one account went, "we hope, will prove a salutary check to those barbarian allies of Britain." The Iroquois "are taught by severe experience," stated another, "the power of the American empire, which must secure our frontiers from future molestation." The attention patriot printers gave Sullivan's expedition—and the detachment with which they related its devastation—illustrates the support Americans had for such an operation. Vicarious observers as far away as Virginia and Rhode Island followed the army's advance closely, copying down newspaper accounts in their diaries.[60]

59. "Comparatively little discussion": Charles Royster, *A Revolutionary People at War: The Continental Army and American Character, 1775–1783* (Chapel Hill, N.C., 1979), 284. Issues are either no longer available or are unreadable for *Pennsylvania Journal; Virginia Gazette* (Clarkson & Davis); *Gazette, of the State of South-Carolina;* and *Charlestown Gazette* in the fall of 1779. *Connecticut Courant:* 4; *Connecticut Gazette:* 8; *Connecticut Journal:* 7; *Norwich Packet:* 9; *Maryland Gazette:* 5; *Maryland Journal:* 5; *Boston Gazette:* 7; *Continental Journal:* 6; *Independent Chronicle:* 13; *Independent Ledger:* 3; *Massachusetts Spy:* 9; *New-Hampshire Gazette:* 12; *New-Jersey Gazette:* 11; *New-Jersey Journal:* 6; *New York Packet:* 6; *New-York Journal:* 13; *Pennsylvania Evening Post:* 4; *Pennsylvania Gazette:* 6; *Pennsylvania Packet:* 15; *American Journal:* 8; *Providence Gazette:* 7; *Virginia Gazette* (Dixon & Nicolson): 4.

60. "Barbarian allies of Britain": *New York Packet,* Oct. 14, 1779; *Norwich Packet,* Oct. 19, 1779; *Connecticut Journal,* Oct. 20, 1779; *Massachusetts Spy,* Oct. 21, 1779; *Independent Chronicle,* Oct. 28, 1779. "Future molestation": *Virginia Gazette* (Dixon & Nicolson), Oct. 30, 1779. In his journal, Virginian Robert Honyman described how Sullivan "penetrated into their country, which had before been inaccessible and destroyed their corn and burnt their towns. He destroyed about 40 towns of different magnitudes and an incredible quantity of Corn and fruit trees." See Dec. 20, 1779, Honyman Diary, 369–370. On October 29, Ezra Stiles copied Loudon's October 21 "crowned with compleat success" article verbatim in his journal. See Franklin Bow-

Moreover, the official, "authentic" accounts from Sullivan and his officers provided evidence for commentary featured on the front page. John Dunlap's *Pennsylvania Packet*, for example, published several pieces during Sullivan's campaign that called forth American patriotism either by referencing the proxies or celebrating patriot virtue. As Sullivan ascended the Susquehanna, Dunlap printed an essay by "A Whig," which once again linked loyalism with proxy violence.

Who prevailed on the savages of the wilderness to join the standard of the enemy? the Tories. Who have assisted the Indians in taking the scalp from the aged matron, the blooming fair one, the helpless infant, and the dying hero? the Tories. Who advised, and who assisted in burning your towns, ravaging your country, and violating the chastity of your women? . . . Who propagate lies among us to discourage the Whigs? the Tories.

If any of the "Freemen of America" were still unconvinced, "Leonidas" insisted, "Let him see the aged father of a family shot down by his fire-side. . . . Let him listen to the cries of the wilderness, and see whole counties laid waste by Indian savages, excited to war by British emissaries."[61]

---

ditch Dexter, ed., *The Literary Diary of Ezra Stiles, D.D., LL.D.: President of Yale College,* II, *March 14, 1776–December 31, 1781* (New York, 1901), II, 384. A week later, he detailed the "3 Western Expeditions . . . carrying War into the Bowels of the Indian Countries from North to South," including, again, exact numbers of corn and houses destroyed by Sullivan, as well as emerging facts about Daniel Brodhead's Allegheny campaign and the efforts of South Carolina general Williamson against the Chickamauga Cherokees (Nov. 8, 1779, II, 387). Two articles exchanged from Charleston appeared in a few northern papers about Williamson's expedition against the Cherokees. One described how Deputy Indian Superintendent Alexander Cameron had prevailed on the Cherokees to fight, but they had been "severely chastised" by Williamson. That appeared in *Pennsylvania Packet,* Oct. 26, 1779; *Pennsylvania Gazette,* Oct. 27, 1779; *Maryland Gazette,* Nov. 5, 1779; *Connecticut Courant,* Nov. 9, 1779; *Connecticut Gazette,* Nov. 10, 1779; *Boston Evening Post* (White & Adams), Nov. 13, 1779; *Independent Ledger,* Nov. 15, 1779; *Massachusetts Spy,* Nov. 15, 1779. A second account claimed Cameron "with great difficulty escaped," and Williamson—like Sullivan— had burned seven Cherokee towns in revenge. See *Pennsylvania Evening Post,* Oct. 26, 1779; *New-York Journal,* Nov. 8, 1779; *Norwich Packet,* Nov. 9, 1779; *Connecticut Journal,* Nov. 10, 1779. As he had before, Stiles probably got this account from the Green brothers' New Haven *Connecticut Journal.*

61. *Pennsylvania Packet,* Aug. 5, Aug. 24, 1779. The latter issue also documented

"A Striking Picture of Barbarity"

Finally, on September 9 and 11, sandwiched between letters Dunlap exchanged from Sullivan in issues before and after, he published a "EULOGIUM of the Brave Men who have fallen in the contest with Great Britain," Hugh Henry Brackenridge's speech from Independence Day. Brackenridge, now the editor of a new Philadelphia periodical, the *United States Magazine,* argued that the "Angel of America shall write, with his diamond point, the names of those" who had died fighting for the common cause and listed all the engagements in which noble men had sacrificed their lives for freedom. But Brackenridge, as ever, was sharply attuned to raising American awareness about British proxies. He continued his catalog of American heroes to include

> the names of those who have fought in other States, resisting the
> Briton unequalled in cruelty; the mercenary of Hesse, of Brunswick,
> of Waldeck, of Anspach, horrid in his inroad; the Savage, (so called
> from his uncultivated state) armed with his hatchet, and his knife, and
> fierce in his incursions on the western country; the treason-fraught
> American leagued in the thoughts of hostility with the foreign enemy.

These enemies, including a rare mention of German mercenaries, must be destroyed to honor those sacred men, according to Brackenridge. *Packet* readers could be sure that very punishment inflicted on both Indians and loyalists was already under way in New York, as proof continued to appear in the middle pages of Dunlap's paper over the next several weeks. In the *Packet,* as well as in other staunch patriot papers, commentary on page one matched the news inside, whether about burning Iroquois towns or accusations against the Hair-Buyer. Though support for the Revolution continued to flag in the fall of 1779, the fact that patriot publicists repeated these same arguments illustrates that they, as well as their political informants, thought these representations resonated with the public. They remained convinced this was still the best way to animate and motivate support for the war.[62]

Philadelphia's celebration of Louis XVI's birthday. On September 4, Dunlap also published a poem on how Louis XVI was a far better monarch than George III. See *Pennsylvania Packet,* Sept. 4, 1779.

62. *Pennsylvania Packet,* Sept. 9, 11, 1779. Brackenridge published this, too, in his *United States Magazine,* which also featured a report of Sullivan's burning Chemung just a few pages after this eulogy. See Brackenridge, "An Eulogium," and John Jay, letter, Philadelphia, Aug. 28, [1779], *United States Magazine,* I (1779), [343]–352,

The common cause narrative had an undeniable influence on the patriots' new policy of revenge. One Congressman wrote to Horatio Gates that he hoped "destroying their Towns, and taking a Number of *old Men, Women and Children* may strike an awe upon Their Minds and secure us against future Depredations, and Barbarities upon Our Inhabitants." Seeing themselves in a position of strength, on November 27, Congress ordered the northern Indian commissioners to inform the Iroquois that the United States was "disposed to peace" under a few conditions—including their acceptance of defeat and, especially, their willingness to "expel all British agents and emissaries." Flush with the reported success of the expeditions, the delegates to Congress and the American public were convinced that they had appropriately chastised the Six Nations for their foolishness in taking up the king's hatchet. The *Providence Gazette* reported that the "several Tribes of Indians which had been driven from their Towns by General Sullivan . . . were in a starving Situation." "Thus," the letter concluded, "by the spirited Exertions and Perseverance of this brave and active Officer, under every Difficulty, and the happy Success of the Expedition, our Frontiers are entirely secured against the Incursions of a perfidious savage Enemy."[63]

The actual success of the 1779 operations was still in doubt, however. Winter would be the litmus test, as the weather seemingly took sides, as well. The winter of 1779 and 1780 was harrowing; some in New York could not remember a colder one. The suffering at the British posts of Niagara and Oswego was appalling. More than three thousand Indians made claims for blankets and food at Niagara alone. Those that survived remained firm. In the spring of 1780, the Senecas, Cayugas, and Mohawks renewed their alliance with the British and continued to attack the New York frontier. They especially targeted their former allies, the Oneidas, Tuscaroras, and some Onondagas—Indians who had not been so "good" to them—continuing the Iroquois civil war. Patriots who thought they had severed the tie between the king and his merciless savages quickly found their hopes dashed. In Feb-

---

366. For coverage of Henry Hamilton, see *Pennsylvania Packet*, June 22, 29, July 3, Oct. 21, 1779.

63. Henry Marchant to Horatio Gates, Philadelphia, Aug. 24, 1779, *LDC*, XIII, 409. Orders to northern commissioners: Nov. 27, 1779, *JCC*, XV, 1320–1321; Philip Schuyler to George Clinton, Philadelphia, Nov. 29, 1779, *LDC*, XIV, 234–237. "Perfidious savage Enemy": *Providence Gazette*, Dec. 18, 1779; *Independent Chronicle*, Dec. 23, 1779; *Independent Ledger*, Dec. 27, 1779; *Massachusetts Spy*, Dec. 30, 1779; *Connecticut Courant*, Jan. 11, 1780; *Pennsylvania Packet*, Jan. 27, 1780.

ruary 1780, *Norwich Packet* printer John Trumbull broke the news to readers all over New England that "BUTLER and BRANT had formed an expedition to bring the Indians to ravage and plunder the defenceless settlements in those parts, in order (say they) to retaliate for injuries received from General Sullivan." As much as Washington had hoped that Sullivan's campaign would end the distress for frontier farmers in New York and Pennsylvania, the worst was yet to come.[64]

On both the northern and western frontiers, the interplay between words and war created a degenerating cycle of violence in 1778 and 1779. When patriots explained these incidents to the public, they did so in terms of British attempts to animate the most brutal characteristics of Indians and their loyalist mimics. At the heart of their interpretations lay an unspoken but indelible divide separating American heroes and faithful sufferers from evil British agents and their savage proxy destroyers. True Americans marched with John Sullivan and George Rogers Clark; treacherous ones acted like Joseph Brant. Everything filtered through this lens, from stories bemoaning the suffering of innocents at Wyoming and Cherry Valley to those heaping praise onto Clark and his intrepid rangers and hurling accusations at the "Famous Hair Buying General" Hamilton. These hyperbolic misrepresentations organized what were, in fact, messy, fluid situations on all frontiers, but they did so with even more tragic results.[65]

Caught in this totalizing, Manichean interpretation were real people. It is not an exaggeration to suggest that the five Indians at Vincennes and the Wells family died the way they did because of those misrepresentations. The common cause contributed to their deaths and those of many others. Printed accounts depicting a "massacre" of innocent women and children at Wyoming ranged from the misleading to the patently false. They fitted a now-three-year-old script. Those testimonies, aimed at garnering sympathy among American readers, led to real murder in Cherry Valley. Moreover,

---

64. Calloway, *American Revolution in Indian Country*, 136; Fischer, *Well-Executed Failure*, 193; Graymont, *Iroquois in the American Revolution*, 223–258. "BUTLER and BRANT": *Norwich Packet*, Feb. 8, 1780; *Independent Chronicle*, Feb. 24, 1780; *American Journal*, Feb. 24, 1780; *Providence Gazette*, Feb. 26, 1780; *Boston Gazette*, Feb. 28, 1780; *Independent Ledger*, Feb. 28, 1780; *Connecticut Journal*, Mar. 15, 1780; *New-York Journal*, Mar. 20, 1780. Mary Jemison, a Seneca captive, remembered it as the worst winter she had ever known. See James E. Seaver, *A Narrative of the Life of Mrs. Mary Jemison*, ed. June Namias (Norman, Okla., 1992), 105.

65. *Connecticut Gazette*, July 3, 1778.

because the patriots' appeal conflated American patriotism with killing the king's Indian allies, it legitimated and even celebrated violence on the frontier and gave popular support to Sullivan's brutal expedition. Sullivan and Clark were far from the only commanders motivated to kill Indians because they thought it helped the cause. Their actions aided the Revolution and were deemed righteous; America's savage enemies brought this vengeance upon themselves. A vicious circle ensnared the frontier: events produced stories that shaped policy that, in turn, produced even ghastlier events. Stories—printed or not printed, truthful or fallacious—were essential to deepening the continued cycles of violence.

2: SOUTHERN STRATEGIES

On November 27, 1778, just as the terrible news of Cherry Valley and the astounding news of Clark's victories circulated through patriot papers, three thousand British regulars, Hessian troops, and New York loyalists under the command of Lieutenant Colonel Archibald Campbell pulled up anchor in New York City. Their destination was Savannah, Georgia, to begin Britain's new plan to take the war south. This was the flowering of the "southern strategy" that British planners had long contemplated. For years, American loyalists in England had been telling the British cabinet about the weakness of the Revolution in the South; most people in the Carolinas and Georgia were either still openly the king's friends or, they claimed, the victims of wicked patriot tyrants who forced them to accept a false obedience. The British could use the great numbers of slaves and Indians there to terrify the patriots, wreck social and economic structures, and supplement their own forces. In many ways, the South was "the soft underbelly of the rebellion."[66]

There was one other factor that a southern strategy offered the British, though few commented on it at the time. By taking the conflict south, the

66. Paul H. Smith, *Loyalists and Redcoats: A Study in British Revolutionary Policy* (Chapel Hill, N.C., 1964), 79–99; Ira D. Gruber, "Britain's Southern Strategy," in W. Robert Higgins, ed., *The Revolutionary War in the South: Power, Conflict, and Leadership; Essays in Honor of John Richard Alden* (Durham, N.C., 1979), 205–238; John Shy, "British Strategy for Pacifying the Southern Colonies, 1778–1781," in Shy, *A People Numerous and Armed: Reflections on the Military Struggle for American Independence*, rev. ed. (1976; Ann Arbor, Mich., 1990), 193–212; Mackesy, *War for America*, 154–159; Jim Piecuch, *Three Peoples, One King: Loyalists, Indians, and Slaves in the Revolutionary South, 1775–1782* (Columbia, S.C., 2008), 125–132. "Soft underbelly": Mackesy, *War for America*, 159.

"A Striking Picture of Barbarity"

British army also would lead it away from patriot communication networks. War in South Carolina and Georgia would be ostensibly out of sight for most Americans, since newspaper coverage was so thin south of Baltimore. When Campbell's forces landed at Tybee Island on December 23, 1778, and began what would be an easy assault on Savannah, there were twenty-seven patriot newspapers active throughout the continent. That capacity had diminished by 23 percent since 1775 as a result of economic disruptions, military destruction, and shortages in supplies.

In New England, there were still fourteen printers producing weekly papers—half of the patriots' output. Four remained stable in Connecticut, as did six in Massachusetts through 1779. New Hampshire started 1779 with papers in both Portsmouth and Exeter, but Zechariah Fowle would close his Exeter shop in May. In Rhode Island, two patriot papers emanated from Providence, though they competed throughout most of the year with a loyalist paper, John Howe's *Newport Gazette*.[67]

Outside New England, that competition between patriot and loyalist organs increased. John Holt had relocated his *New-York Journal* for the second time in Poughkeepsie, where he would complain loudly for the remainder of the war that he was too far removed from a steady flow of both information and supplies. Samuel Loudon continued to publish his *New York Packet* in Fishkill. In New York City, however, three tory papers—Gaine's *New-York Gazette*, Rivington's *Royal Gazette*, and the Robertsons' *Royal American Gazette*—would be joined by a fourth in the fall, the *New-York Mercury*. With their publication dates spread throughout the week, New Yorkers, whether loyalist refugees, runaway slaves, or British personnel, had access to a newspaper every day, much to the pleasure of Ambrose Serle, to be sure. In New Jersey, George Washington fulfilled his long-standing goal to establish a newspaper for the Continental army. In February 1779, a former lieutenant, Shepard Kollock, began to publish the *New-Jersey Journal* in Chatham, six miles from his major subscription base, the army's winter encampment in Morristown. Kollock joined Isaac Collins's *New-Jersey Gazette* as a second amplifier of patriot news between New York and Philadelphia. In the American capital, the three exiled papers, the *Pennsylvania Packet, Pennsylvania Gazette,* and *Pennsylvania Journal,* had returned by the beginning of 1779. Benjamin Towne turned his coat back again when the British left Philadelphia, and

67. Connecticut: *Connecticut Courant, Connecticut Journal, Connecticut Gazette, Norwich Packet.* Massachusetts: *Boston Evening-Post, Boston Gazette, Continental Journal, Independent Chronicle, Independent Ledger, Massachusetts Spy.*

he maintained the demanding three-day-a-week publication schedule of his *Pennsylvania Evening Post.* The other two loyalist printers that published during the British occupation closed and went with the army to New York.[68]

South of Pennsylvania, the patriots' ability to propagate stories and images was less effective. In Baltimore, Mary Katherine Goddard took on a partner, Eleazer Oswald, to help continue putting out the *Maryland Journal* every Tuesday, but James Hayes, who had taken over production of *Dunlap's Maryland Gazette* in the fall of 1778, closed his shop on January 5, 1779. Soon, Frederick and Samuel Green would revive their father's dormant Annapolis paper, and it would carry through the end of the war for a second patriot organ in Maryland. Williamsburg continued to produce two versions of the *Virginia Gazette* in 1779, even with Alexander Purdie's death and William Hunter's decision to join the British. Nephews and new partners would keep these two vital southern papers in existence with little turbulence through the year. When James Davis stopped publishing his Newbern paper in November 1778, North Carolina was left without a reliable way to relate public information. South Carolina's newspapers had a difficult year after a significant fire in January 1778 silenced most for the first half of the year or more. At the start of 1779, though, three had returned to production: the *Charlestown Gazette, Gazette, of the State of South-Carolina,* and *South-Carolina and American General Gazette.* The last, edited by Henry Laurens's friend John Wells, Jr., would cease production late in the year. In Savannah, disaffected printer James Johnston—who had published the *Georgia Gazette* from 1763 to early 1776—revived his print. The title reflected the city's new occupants as of January 1779: the *Royal Georgia Gazette.*

In sum, the patriots could count on twenty-eight newspapers to broadcast their messages at the start of 1779, but that number was in flux throughout the year. Two more papers started while four closed, leaving twenty-six

68. Philip Davidson, *Propaganda and the American Revolution, 1763–1783* (Chapel Hill, N.C., 1940), 399. A few students have suggested that Washington allowed Kollock to resign strictly to start a paper. See Sidney I. Pomerantz, "The Patriot Newspaper and the American Revolution," in Richard B. Morris, ed., *The Era of the American Revolution: Studies Inscribed to Evarts Boutell Greene* (New York, 1939), 327. As Rollo G. Silver has pointed out, Kollock must have had some official approval: in 1780, the army commissary in Morristown furnished him with paper and papermaking materials (Silver, "Aprons Instead of Uniforms: The Practice of Printing, 1776–1787," *Proceedings of the American Antiquarian Society,* LXXXVII [1977], 111–194, esp. 143). See also John R. Anderson, *Shepard Kollock, Editor for Freedom: The Story of the New-Jersey Journal in Chatham, 1779–1783* (Chatham, N.J., 1975).

by year's end, and half of those north of New York. The British, on the other hand, started the year with four papers in Newport and Manhattan. The *Newport Gazette* ceased, but two new tory papers opened over the course of 1779. The ratio was still five to one, but 1779 saw a further slippage of the patriots' control over information throughout North America.

The southern strategy would continue this trend. The farther the British got away from New England, the less the patriots would be able to manage public information. South of Philadelphia, there were only six patriot papers in early 1779. If the British took Charleston, that number would be cut in half, decimating patriot ability to propagate images about the enemy and limiting how frequently intelligence about political and military events made it into northern patriot networks. A southern campaign would surely see British officers taking advantage of African American and Indian assistance, but if patriot publicists were unaware of those developments or were unable to shape American readers' perception about them, one of the bulwarks supporting the common cause would be greatly weakened.

The future of the emerging southern strategy depended on Archibald Campbell's success in this first foray. Campbell's expedition was a test case to see whether loyalism—of all complexions—in Georgia really was strong enough to merit carrying the war to the Deep South. If Britain's strategy depended on Campbell, the Scottish colonel found himself dependent on Quamino (or Quash) Dolly. One of Governor James Wright's slaves, Dolly volunteered to lead Campbell's men into the swamps and behind American lines.[69]

Campbell's men caught 1,200 Continental troops—led by the 1775 hero of Fort Johnston, North Carolina's Robert Howe—and 600 hundred Georgia militiamen by surprise. Nearly 100 Americans died fleeing the fighting, and another 450 were captured, whereas the British suffered 13 casualties. Howe and the rest of his shattered force retreated into South Carolina; Campbell entered Savannah unopposed on January 1, 1779. As per the plan, General Augustine Prevost, commander at Saint Augustine, also marched from Florida to support the Georgia incursion. Prevost took the town of Sunbury, thirty miles south of Savannah, two weeks later. Thanks to Dolly—and endemic rumors that the Creek Indians were preparing for a

69. Archibald Campbell, *Journal of an Expedition against the Rebels of Georgia in North America under the Orders of Archibald Campbell, Esq., Lt. Col. of His Majesty's 71st Regiment, 1778*, ed. Colin Campbell (Darien, Ga., 1981), 22–26; Ward, *War of the Revolution*, II, 680; Piecuch, *Three Peoples, One King*, 133.

full-scale assault—the first campaign in the South since 1776 was a smashing triumph. Campbell boasted that he was the first "to take a stripe and star from the rebel flag of Congress."[70]

News of Georgia's easy capitulation did not, of course, leave significant traces in patriot newspapers. Starting in late January, a few letters from Charleston relating that the enemy had taken possession of Georgia and "gave loose to their savage dispositions" began to appear, but no account was widely exchanged. Loyalist papers in New York published Prevost and Campbell's reports to British commander-in-chief Sir Henry Clinton, and several patriot printers copied them—adding the usual warning that they originated in Rivington's "Lying Gazette."[71]

A few reports did appear that better reflected what the British invasion meant to Quamino Dolly and hundreds of slaves in Georgia. Collins's *New-Jersey Gazette* published a vague account that said "numbers of negroes" had been "taken off" Georgia plantations. A South Carolina planter complained that forty-seven of his slaves were "taken . . . and carried to Georgia." The *Massachusetts Spy* published a letter from a correspondent in Providence stat-

70. Kenneth Coleman, *The American Revolution in Georgia, 1763–1789* (Athens, Ga., 1958), 117; Clyde R. Ferguson, "Carolina and Georgia Patriot and Loyalist Militia in Action, 1778–1783," in Jeffrey J. Crow and Larry E. Tise, eds., *The Southern Experience in the American Revolution* (Chapel Hill, N.C., 1978), 174–199, esp. 177–178; [Governor] James Houstoun to HL, Savannah, Ga., Nov. 25, 1778, *PHL*, XIV, 534–536; "Genl. Griffith Rutherford to Gov. Caswell," Nov. 15, 1778, in Walter Clark, ed., *The State Records of North Carolina* (Raleigh, N.C., 1896), XIII, 282–283, esp. 283; Lieut. Col. Archibald Campbell to the Earl of Carlisle, Savannah, Jan. 18, 1779, in [Benjamin Franklin Stevens], ed., *B. F. Stevens's Facsimiles of Manuscripts in European Archives Relating to America, 1773–1783: With Descriptions, Editorial Notes, Collations, References and Translations*, 25 vols. (1889–1895; rpt. Wilmington, Del., 1970), I, no. 113.

71. "Savage dispositions": *Pennsylvania Packet*, Jan. 28, 1779. Campbell to Clinton: *Pennsylvania Evening Post*, Feb. 17, 20, 1779; *Connecticut Courant*, Feb. 23, 1779; *Norwich Packet*, Mar. 1, 1779; *Continental Journal*, Mar. 4, 1779; *Independent Chronicle*, Mar. 4, 1779. Prevost letter to Clinton: *Royal Gazette* (New York), Feb. 4, 1779; *New-York Gazette*, Feb. 8, 1779; *Connecticut Courant*, Feb. 23, 1779; *Norwich Packet*, Mar. 1, 1779; *Independent Chronicle*, Mar. 4, 1779; *Exeter Journal*, Mar. 9, 1779. Several papers included Prevost's claim that he had "a large number of Indians" join him, but he denied that he would employ them unless necessary. See *Pennsylvania Evening Post*, Feb. 2, 1779; *New-Jersey Gazette*, Feb. 3, 1779; *Boston Gazette*, Feb. 15, 1779; *New-York Gazette*, Feb. 15, 1779; *Independent Chronicle*, Feb. 18, 1779; *Providence Gazette*, Feb. 20, 1779; *Exeter Journal*, Feb. 23, 1779.

ing that the British were indeed using "every artifice to bring over negroes over to them, and murder their masters." A few weeks later, the *Spy* exchanged a letter from a Baltimore paper that suggested "1500 negroes had joined the enemy." Though Savannah's fall did not generate a huge wave of news, one of the most widely exchanged letters came from South Carolina general Andrew Williamson, who wrote in February that "Numbers of Negroes have gone with" British forces, but he had some details: "Upwards of 200 of Mr. Galphing's (although such an indulgent master) have followed the example and gone."[72]

In public and private, patriot rhetoric began to match reality. The British occupation offered new opportunities for Georgia slaves, and they were leaving the plantations. South Carolina patriot Oliver Hart summed it up: "Negroes are a very precarious Tenure, anywhere near the Environs of Georgia." Their flight from slavery was unprecedented in North America; never in the eighteenth century had so high a percentage of the enslaved population run away en masse like what was happening on the roads around Savannah.[73]

As slaves flocked to British lines, patriot military and political leaders far from Savannah suddenly began to reconsider previous positions about recruiting blacks. In Philadelphia, Henry Laurens was unsurprised at the news of Georgia's capitulation. The numbers of slaves and Indians he figured

---

72. "Taken off": *New-Jersey Gazette,* Mar. 31, 1779; *Continental Journal,* Apr. 1, 1779; *American Journal,* Apr. 1, 1779. "Carried to Georgia": *Gazette, of the State of South-Carolina,* Apr. 14, 1779. "Every artifice": *Massachusetts Spy,* Feb. 11, 1779. "1500 negroes": *Massachusetts Spy,* Mar. 4, 1779. "Mr. Galphing's": *Pennsylvania Packet,* Mar. 18, 1779; *Pennsylvania Evening Post,* Mar. 19, 1779; *New-Jersey Gazette,* Mar. 24, 1779; *Boston Gazette,* Apr. 5, 1779; *Independent Ledger,* Apr. 5, 1779; *Norwich Packet,* Apr. 5, 1779; *Royal Gazette* (New York), Apr. 7, 1779; *American Journal,* Apr. 8 1779; *Massachusetts Spy,* Apr. 8, 1779; *Providence Gazette,* Apr. 10, 1779. Another of Williamson's letters also circulated describing how one of John Stuart's "indefatigable Deputies" was encouraging Indians to commit "indiscriminate destruction of defenceless men, women and children." See *Gazette, of the State of South-Carolina,* Apr. 7, 1779; *Virginia Gazette* (Dixon & Nicolson), May 1, 1779; *Massachusetts Spy,* May 27, 1779; *American Journal,* May 27, 1779. Isaac Collins appended a comment about the potential "deluge of blood by the British King's Indian allies" in the May 19, 1779, issue of his *New-Jersey Gazette.*

73. Oliver Hart to Joseph Hart, Feb. 16, 1779, 1st Ser., folder 2, Oliver Hart Papers, South Caroliniana Library, Columbia, S.C.; Sylvia R. Frey, *Water from the Rock: Black Resistance in a Revolutionary Age* (Princeton, N.J., 1991), 86–87.

would supplement the British were daunting. Laurens expected they would employ and arm at least 800 slaves. He also figured a number greater than four times that many would simply run away. At least 4,000 slaves—nearly one-third of all Georgia's slaves—had abandoned or would abandon their plantations, Laurens believed. Making matters worse, he estimated, 1,000 Creeks, 1,000 Choctaws, and 1,500 Cherokees would also "make War when they can." All told, when "beset by Britons, Indians, Negroes and Tories, on all sides in her bosom," he doubted South Carolina could muster more than 7,000 troops. Laurens's portrayal of this crisis convinced at least some of his colleagues in Congress. A Maryland delegate, John Henry, worried that "the greatest source of Danger" in Georgia "is the accession of strength they will probably receive from the black Inhabitants. Arms, we have some reason to believe, ha[ve] been sent into that Country, for such purposes; and in my own opinion, if they are resolved to prosecute the Measure, and to break through every tie of honor and Humanity, they will gain considerable Strength." New Hampshire delegate William Whipple wrote home in complete agreement with his southern colleagues. The British "will geather Great strength" in the Deep South, Whipple believed, "as there are many Disaffected, besides the opportunity they will have of arming the Negros." If accurate, this approximation was indeed frightening—and it required a drastic response.[74]

* * *

In mid-February, John Laurens reinvigorated his scheme for South Carolina to form black regiments. John wrote his father that either outside assistance "or the adoption of my black [regiment] project alone can save" South Carolina. He implored his father to "embrace the salutary measure which I propose," adding that if Henry did convince Congress to save South Carolina, he would "have the glory of triumphing over deep rooted national prejudices, in favor of your Country and humanity at large." What seemed a radical solution the previous year won patriot adherents in the wake of Georgia's fall.[75]

In March, a committee of Congress led by Henry drafted a report suggesting that South Carolina and Georgia create a number of black battal-

74. "Henry Laurens' Notes on a Georgia Campaign," Jan. 20, 1779, *LDC*, XI, 494–495, John Henry to Thomas Johnson, Philadelphia, Jan. 30, 1779, 537–539, esp. 538, William Whipple to Joseph Whipple, Philadelphia, [Feb.] 2, 1779, XII, 9.

75. John Laurens to HL, Middlebrook, N.J., Feb. 17, 1779, *PHL*, XV, 59–60.

ions. These battalions would not serve north of Virginia and would be commanded by white officers. At the end of service, every slave who "shall well and faithfully Serve as a Soldier" and "return his arms" would be emancipated.[76]

Even before Congress voted on this report, Laurens again queried Washington whether his thoughts had changed about his son's plan. Actually, Henry did not ask the commander; he simply stated, "Had we Arms for 3,000, such black Men as I could select in Carolina I should have no doubt of success in driving the British out of Georgia and subduing East Florida before the end of July." Laurens enclosed a copy of the letter from General Andrew Williamson that detailed hundreds of blacks going over to the British as evidence to support his rather brash lecturing of Washington on military matters. Washington's response surely disappointed the Laurenses: "The policy of our arming Slaves is in my opinion a moot point." "Should we begin to form Battalions of them," he wrote to Henry, "I have not the smallest doubt (if the war is to be prosecuted) of their following us in it, and justifying the measure upon our own ground. The upshot then must be who can Arm fastest—and where are our Arms?" Washington, perhaps feeling a bit prickly at the presumptions of father and son on this subject, concluded his letter with a disingenuous swipe: "But as this is a subject that has never employed much of my thoughts, these are no more than the first crude Ideas that have struck me upon the occasion." Thus ended one of Washington's most mendacious letters. Of course Washington had spent time considering the question of black troops; since his assumption of command over the Continental army, this issue had often recurred. There was a significant paper trail of letters to recruiting officers and congressional committees on the question of recruiting or reenlisting free blacks. A year earlier, he had even supported Rhode Island's formation of a regiment of emancipated slaves, free blacks, and Indians.[77]

76. "Thomas Burke's Draft Committee Report," *LDC*, XII, 243.

77. HL to GW, Philadelphia, Mar. 16, 1779, *PGW: RW*, XIX, 503, GW to HL, Middlebrook, Mar. 20, 1779, 542–543, esp. 542; Henry Wiencek, *An Imperfect God: George Washington, His Slaves, and the Creation of America* (New York, 2003), 227. Laurens enclosed Andrew Williamson's letter to John Lewis Gervais in this letter to Washington. Two days later, it appeared in the *Pennsylvania Packet*. Given the timing and the fact that Gervais was one of Laurens's most frequent correspondents, it is reasonable to assume that Laurens also gave John Dunlap this letter, which printers of nine other newspapers then exchanged. Washington gave tacit approval to Briga-

Moreover, if Washington could not remember referring to Dunmore's proclamation and other British recruitment efforts as dangerous snowballs, it would be a surprising lacuna in his memory. In addition to his involvement with black soldiers who volunteered to fight under his command, Washington's duplicitous confession that he had never considered the issue of arming slaves includes forgetting all the proclamations, statements, addresses, and forwarded items about British "instigation" that he and other patriot leaders had sponsored since the war began. After all, just a few days after authorities in Rhode Island asked him whether he opposed their creation of a black regiment, Washington again reminded members of Congress that "the enemy have set every engine at work, against us, and have actually called savages and even our own slaves to their assistance." And, just a few weeks before Georgia fell, he again invoked the specter of Britain's "Hessian, Indian, and Negro Allies" in a private letter. Washington's claim of amnesia on this subject was simply not credible.[78]

Alexander Hamilton also exhibited a parallel lapse in his letter supporting John's project. Hamilton, then serving alongside John Laurens as Washington's aide, wrote to John Jay in support of his friend. A longtime correspondent of Hamilton's, Jay had replaced Henry Laurens as president of Congress in December. Hamilton's letter, personally delivered by the younger Laurens, implored Jay that "an expedient" of forming black battalions in South Carolina "is the most rational, that can be adopted, and promises very important advantages." Hamilton denied that blacks were "too stupid to make soldiers," arguing instead, "Their natural faculties are probably as good as ours," and their "habit of subordination" would make them better soldiers "than our White inhabitants." This view of black soldiers' potential concurred with John Laurens's assessment.[79]

---

dier General James Varnum's request for black troops by forwarding his letter to Rhode Island Governor Nicholas Cooke. See Varnum to GW, Jan. 2, 1778, *PGW: RW*, XIII, 125, GW to Nicholas Cooke, Jan. 2, 1778, 114, Rhode Island Council of War to GW, Providence, R.I., Jan. 19, 1778, 284. See also Pete Maslowski, "National Policy towards the Use of Black Troops in the Revolution," *South Carolina Historical Magazine*, LXXIII (1972), 1–17; Philip D. Morgan and Andrew Jackson O'Shaughnessy, "Arming Slaves in the American Revolution," in Christopher Leslie Brown and Morgan, eds., *Arming Slaves: From Classical Times to the Modern Era* (New Haven, Conn., 2006), 180–208, esp. 193.

78. GW to Continental Congress Camp Committee, *PGW: RW*, XIII, 402, GW to Andrew Lewis, Fredericksburg, N.Y., Oct. 15, 1778, XVII, 388–390, esp. 389.

79. Alexander Hamilton to John Jay, in Harold C. Syrett, ed., *Papers of Alexan-*

But then Hamilton's perception suddenly failed him. "I foresee," he continued, "that this project will have to combat much opposition from prejudice and self-interest. The contempt we have been taught to entertain for the blacks, makes us fancy many things that are founded neither in reason nor experience." The passive construction of these sentences is telling. Hamilton blamed colonial history for engendering prejudice between blacks and whites—which is undeniable—but in doing so, he elided his own role, and that of the Laurenses, Washington, and their patriot colleagues, not only from perpetuating those stereotypes but from making them a central part of the common cause appeal. Patriot political leaders and publicists had been among the greatest teachers of contempt for African American resistance since Lexington. By broadcasting the susceptibility of blacks to the sinister appeals of British officers, they had deepened those "national prejudices" and made them crucial to the founding of the United States. Hamilton admitted as much in his next sentence to Jay, again returning to the ubiquitous theme of British "instigation": "But it should be considered, that if we do not make use of them in this way, the enemy probably will." That statement had been at the heart of the way patriots explained the conflict for nearly four years, and it had ramifications.[80]

Like many of his colleagues, Hamilton would have preferred to end slavery; with John Laurens, his belief that forming black units would "secure their fidelity, animate their courage," and open "a door to their emancipation" was genuine. A fellow Congressman also gushed that it would "lay a foundation for the Abolition of Slavery in America." But because political and military leaders had justified the war by arguing the British and their black proxies were the Revolution's collective enemy, the very thrust of the cause undermined their own antislavery desires. Unity trumped natural rights.[81]

Even as the emergency in Georgia convinced Congress to endorse black battalions as a viable policy, the question of British instigation was never far away from the minds of patriot leaders. Congress's recommendation to South Carolina and Georgia was predicated on the basis that they recruit "from among the Negroes which would not only be formidable to the

---

der Hamilton, II, 1779–1781 (New York, 1961), 17–19, esp. 17 ("most rational"), 18 ("habit of subordination").

80. Ibid., II, 18.

81. Ibid.; William Whipple to Josiah Bartlett, Philadelphia, Apr. 27, 1779, LDC, XII, 398–399, esp. 398.

Enemy by their Numbers, and the disciplin which they would very readily admit of, but would also lessen the danger to the Inhabitants from revolts, and desertions by detaching the most Enterprising and vigorous Men from amongst the Negroes." Abolition was never the core issue. The issue was as it had been since the summer of 1775: the safety of the union. Fear of losing the South, not principle, underlay this change of heart. No matter how much some patriot leaders might have privately detested slavery, because they had put the union above all else, they had strengthened it by giving public air to stories that slaves were potential foes of the cause. Though they had difficulty recognizing their complicity, Washington's idealistic young aides had tragically—but effectively—participated in the perpetuation of slavery.[82]

The strength of the prejudices from which Hamilton tried to distance himself was clear when Laurens arrived in South Carolina armed with Congress's recommendation. Because these battalions were meant to be raised and to operate in the Deep South only, Congress adopted this as a suggestion, not as a binding resolution. It was up to the legislatures of Georgia and South Carolina whether they wanted to "take measures immediately for raising three thousand able bodied negroes." Once Congress approved his plan on March 29, John Laurens set off to convince South Carolina to back his endeavor.[83]

Despite all the public statements expressing shock of British tampering on southern plantations, Charlestonians acted as if they knew nothing of real slave unrest, given the surprise they showed that March when the tolling bells of St. Michael's Church broke the silence of a spring night in the city. With the enemy a few dozen miles away and slavery dissolving all around them, it was a tense time in Charleston, reminiscent of the summer of 1775, when that fear had cost Thomas Jeremiah his life. Authorities discovered a "Negro Man" in the steeple "pretending to be fast asleep, and apparently drunk," but that did not convince many Charlestonians that it was not "intended as a Signal for the Perpetration of some diabolical Plan—it may be for burning the Town—or Perhaps something worse." It was only a few weeks after this scare that Laurens rode into town with his plan to put

82. "Thomas Burke's Draft Committee Report," *LDC*, XII, 244.

83. Mar. 29, 1779, *JCC*, XIII, 384–390, esp. 387. See also Gregory D. Massey, "The Limits of Antislavery Thought in the Revolutionary Lower South: John Laurens and Henry Laurens," *Journal of Southern History*, LXIII (1997), 495–530; Benjamin Quarles, *The Negro in the American Revolution* (Chapel Hill, N.C., 1961), 60–64.

"A Striking Picture of Barbarity"

guns in those suspicious slaves' hands, a plan that had the endorsement of the Continental Congress. South Carolina patriots needed help—but not this.[84]

Then, British forces under Prevost suddenly threatened to overwhelm William Moultrie's defenses at Purrysburg, South Carolina. If they defeated Moultrie, they were free to march directly into Charleston. While Laurens hurried to Purrysburg to aid Moultrie, patriot authorities in South Carolina panicked. They granted Governor John Rutledge dictatorial powers to maintain patriot authority in the face of this invasion. The moment could not be more auspicious for Laurens: if ever the Deep South could overcome its prejudices and fill the significant gaps in its regiments with able-bodied slaves, it would be now. From May 11 to the middle of June, Charleston was under siege. Prevost demanded its surrender. In the middle of the crisis, Laurens pressured Governor Rutledge to present his plan to his council. Rutledge knew it would be instantly rejected, and it was. In fact, some South Carolina patriots began to reconsider whether this union was worth fighting for at all. Five of the eight members of Rutledge's executive council recommended they pull South Carolina out of the war and declare the state a neutral party, a stipulation Prevost rejected. When a large military force commanded by General Benjamin Lincoln arrived to save Charleston, the British withdrew, and the city remained in patriot hands.[85]

Patriot papers, however, put a different spin on the desperate situation in Charleston. Maine loyalist Jonathan Sayward lamented in his diary on June 26 that New England prints related how "the King's army at Charlestown in Carolina is 553 killed and about 1200 taken, and now they hear . . . General

84. Oliver Hart diary, Mar. 4, 1779, series 2, folder 10, Oliver Hart Papers, South Caroliniana Library; Piecuch, *Three Peoples, One King*, 161.

85. John W. Gordon, *South Carolina and the American Revolution: A Battlefield History* (Columbia, S.C., 2003), 65–66; Ward, *War of the Revolution*, II, 684–687; Hugh F. Rankin, *The North Carolina Continentals* (Chapel Hill, N.C., 1971), 199; John Rutledge to John Laurens, May 26, 1779, HL and John Laurens papers, 1732–1811, LoC. For more Laurens's presentation of his project to South Carolina patriots, see Quarles, *Negro in the American Revolution*, 63–64; Gregory D. Massey, *John Laurens and the American Revolution* (Columbia, S.C., 2000), 140–144; Douglas R. Egerton, *Death or Liberty: African Americans and Revolutionary America* (New York, 2009), 83–84; Jack Rakove, *Revolutionaries: A New History of the Invention of America* (New York, 2010), 234–236; William Moultrie, *Memoirs of the American Revolution* ([1802]; New York, 1968), I, 427–434; James Haw, "A Broken Compact: Insecurity, Union, and the Proposed Surrender of Charleston, 1779," *South Carolina Historical Magazine*, XCVI (1995), 30–53.

Prevost is taken." A few weeks later Sayward—always keenly suspicious of news stories—wrote, "I suppose that most all we have had in the newspapers for three weeks past concerning the King's troops in Charlestown is false" but was inserted "to answer political purposes."[86]

As readers throughout North America learned (mostly false) facts about the crisis that gripped South Carolina, they also heard of another British incursion in the South. On May 10, just as Prevost approached Charleston, a flotilla of thirty ships under the command of Sir George Collier brought General Edward Mathew and 1,800 British infantrymen to Portsmouth, Virginia. Together, Collier and Mathew pillaged the Virginia tidewater for a week. They dismantled the fortifications at Portsmouth, engaged and sank vessels in the Chesapeake, burned the town of Suffolk to the ground, and brought off at least 500 slaves. The damage was extensive. Patriot printers were short on details but forwarded their indignation nonetheless, exchanging exultant loyalist accounts or publishing letters from Virginia and Maryland militia leaders that described the "many ravages and depredations, such as plundering, and burning" the British inflicted.[87]

86. Entry for June 26, 1779, Jonathan Sayward Diaries, 1760–1799, XX, 483, MSS, octavo vols., S, AAS. The account Sayward refers to was wildly inaccurate, boasting of Moultrie's smashing of all British forces. It had a strange publication history. Apparently a patriot participant or eyewitness in Charleston corresponded with someone in Baltimore. That person (or someone else who saw the account) then wrote to a delegate to Congress with the news. Extracts of the original letter appeared as a handbill in Baltimore and also printed in *Maryland Journal,* June 9, 1779; *New-Jersey Gazette,* June 16, 1779; *Connecticut Journal,* June 23, 1779; *Continental Journal,* June 24, 1779. The letter to Philadelphia was then published with many of the same errors in *Pennsylvania Packet,* June 8, 1779; *New-Jersey Gazette,* June 9, 1779; *Connecticut Courant,* June 22, 1779; *Norwich Packet,* June 22, 1779; *Massachusetts Spy,* June 24, 1779. It is probable that Sayward saw one of the two accounts in the *Spy* or *Continental Journal.*

87. Robert Fallaw and Marion West Stoer, "The Old Dominion under Fire: The Chesapeake Invasions, 1779–1781," in Ernest McNeill Eller, ed., *Chesapeake Bay in the American Revolution* (Centreville, Md., 1981), 432–474, esp. 443–452; John E. Selby, *The Revolution in Virginia, 1775–1783* (Williamsburg, Va., 1988), 204–206; Michael A. McDonnell, *The Politics of War: Race, Class, and Conflict in Revolutionary Virginia* (Chapel Hill, N.C., 2007), 343–344; "Return of Persons Who Came off from Virginia with General Matthew in the Fleet the 24 May 1779," British Headquarters (Sir Guy Carleton) Papers (Washington, D.C., 1957), microfilm reel 28, item no. 10325. Loyalist accounts: Robertson's *Royal American Gazette,* May 20, 1779; *Royal*

Virginians' perception of how many slaves went with the British was far higher than American readers could have surmised from the meager news coverage. Edmund Pendleton estimated the British "stole" 1,500 blacks and practiced a "Second Act of Iniquity upon this race of men" by selling them to the West Indies. Hanover County physician and diarist Dr. Robert Honyman estimated the number of blacks taken at 1,000. This important perception of the British gathering up Virginia's slaves by the thousands would grow in the months to come.[88]

In the last days of May, both Virginia and South Carolina faced incursions that humiliated their leaders. South Carolina patriots in Rutledge's inner circle were so frustrated that Congress and the Continental army were unwilling to rush men to their aid that they entertained leaving a union that seemed of little benefit to them. Abandoning the Revolution, though, was apparently preferential to John Laurens's plan to arm slaves, for they never seriously considered it, during or after the siege. Not even imminent occupation could induce them to contemplate black enlistment. In fact, if Christopher Gadsden's reaction was representative, the nerve of Congress to even make a recommendation further jeopardized the common cause for South Carolinians. "We are much disgusted here at the Congress recommending us to arm our Slaves," he wrote to Samuel Adams; "it was received with great resentment, as a very dangerous and impolitic Step." South Caro-

---

Gazette (New York), May 22, 1779; *New-York Gazette,* May 24, 1779. Five patriot papers exchanged Rivington's account: *Connecticut Gazette,* May 27, 1779; *American Journal,* June 3, 1779; *Massachusetts Spy,* June 3, 10, 1779; *Providence Gazette,* June 5, 1779; *Boston Gazette,* June 7, 1779. Even though Rivington's report dominated the coverage of the Collier-Mathew raid, he still felt compelled to state on June 5 "as the Rebel Accounts from the South respecting the late Expedition to Virginia . . . are atrociously interlarded with falsehood," so he published Collier's journal "as a real state of the whole affair" (*Royal Gazette,* June 5, 1779). "Many ravages": *Virginia Gazette* (Dixon & Nicolson), May 15, 1779; *Connecticut Courant,* June 8, 1779; *Massachusetts Spy,* June 10, 1779; *Providence Gazette,* June 12, 1779. See another exchanged letter from Baltimore that generally described the "cruel and wanton outrages on defenceless neighbours and countrymen" in *Pennsylvania Evening Post,* May 25, 1779; *Pennsylvania Gazette,* May 26, 1779; *New-Jersey Gazette,* May 26, 1779; *Connecticut Journal,* June 9, 1779; *American Journal,* June 10, 1779; *Norwich Packet,* June 15, 1779.

88. Edmund Pendleton to William Woodford, Edmundsbury, Va., June 21, 1779, in David John Mays, ed., *The Letters and Papers of Edmund Pendleton, 1734–1803,* 2 vols. (Charlottesville, Va., 1967), I, 290–292, esp. 290–291.

lina patriots were incredulous that their northern colleagues would suggest such a move.[89]

Undaunted, John Laurens continued to forward his project. When the legislature met later that summer, he introduced his plan as an amendment to an older defense bill. Despite its real chance of saving South Carolina from future invasions, Laurens's amendment went down in flames. "The measure for embodying the negroes had about twelve votes," patriot David Ramsay related. "It was received with horror by the planters, who figured to themselves terrible consequences."[90]

Several months earlier, John Adams had wished emancipation to "sleep for a Time." His fear was coming true that any move toward emancipation, no matter how much it might preserve patriot authority, would aggravate "Jealousy, Discord and Division." That such a proposal came from the state's favorite son mattered not at all. John Laurens continued to try, but it was no use. South Carolinians, it seemed, preferred to abandon the Revolution before they freed slaves. Arming resistant slaves was suicide. His father, trying to console his disappointed son, later wrote, "I learn your black Air Castle is blown up, with contemptuous huzzas."[91]

As significant as slave resistance was to defeating Laurens's "black Air Castle," there was another key element to understanding why it never stood a chance. Just as it narrowed any alternative policies that could make

89. "Account of Operations in S.C., May 1779," 37/45b/1–22, microfilm roll no. 45/146, Henry Laurens papers, 1747–1860 (37), SCHS; Haw, "Broken Compact," *South Carolina Historical Magazine*, XCVI (1995), 30–53, esp. 49–50; Christopher Gadsden to Samuel Adams, Charleston, July 6, 1779, in Richard Walsh, ed., *The Writings of Christopher Gadsden, 1746–1805* (Columbia, S.C., 1966), 165–166, esp. 166.

90. David Ramsay to William Henry Drayton, Charleston, S.C., Sept. 1, 1779, in R. W. Gibbes, ed., *Documentary History of the American Revolution: Consisting of Letters and Papers Relating to the Contest for Liberty, Chiefly in South Carolina . . .* , II, *1776–1782* (New York, 1857), 121. Ramsay was deeply concerned that "The patriotism of many people [in Charleston] is *vox et præterea nihil*" (a sound and nothing more).

91. JA to James Warren, Philadelphia, July 7, 1777, *LDC*, VII, 308. Actually, John Laurens's sponsorship of the black battalions plan diminished his reputation in South Carolina, at least in the short term. He wrote to Alexander Hamilton that summer that he was "doing daily penance here, and making successless harangues, I shall execrate my Stars—and be out of humour with the world." See John Laurens to Alexander Hamilton, Charleston, S.C., July 14, 1779, in Syrett, ed., *Papers of Alexander Hamilton*, II, 102–104, esp. 103; HL to John Laurens, Philadelphia, Sept. 27, 1779, *PHL*, XV, 177.

"A Striking Picture of Barbarity"

strong, steadfast alliances with friendly Indians, so the common cause argument had eliminated any possibility of recruiting slaves to fight for American liberty. Even more than it would have in 1774, a suggestion of arming, then emancipating, slaves seemed much more than simply the chimerical notions of an idealistic twenty-four-year-old. Laurens's project was more serious than just an air castle, and the alarmed reaction of South Carolina patriots reflected this new context. Now the idea of embracing domestic insurrectionists cut across the grain of the Revolution itself. It was more than terrifying; it was treasonous.

The threat of occupation—and the shocking emancipatory suggestions put forward by their supposed comrades—made South Carolinians angry with their fellow patriots. In Virginia, too, invasion did not produce a new wave of support for the cause. Laurens learned the same lesson in Charleston: imminent defeat and humiliation engendered division rather than unity. As one Virginia delegate wrote Jefferson in late May, "Our great concerns wear a very gloomy aspect."[92]

* * *

One month later, Sir Henry Clinton issued a proclamation from his headquarters in Philipsburg, New York, aimed at bringing more proxies over to the king's side. "Whereas the Enemy have adopted the practice of enrolling Negroes among their troops," Clinton ordered that any blacks captured in American service would be sold into bondage, whereas those who ran to the British would be given "full security to follow within these lines, any occupation which [they] shall think proper." If the British were going to develop a southern strategy in the future, Clinton's Philipsburg Proclamation would be a crucial policy maneuver that promised to bolster their own power. For patriot publicists, it was another opportunity: the British had issued another emancipation proclamation.[93]

The Philipsburg Proclamation instantly recalled memories of Lord Dunmore. Over the past four years, the notorious Lord Kidnapper had never really disappeared. In 1778, the *Connecticut Gazette* published rumors from London that Dunmore had received a £2,000 pension for his activities in Virginia. Just two months before Clinton's proclamation, New Jersey gov-

92. William Fleming to TJ, Philadelphia, May 22, 1779, *PTJ*, II, 267. McDonnell makes a similar point about Virginia in *Politics of War*, 345.

93. Sir Henry Clinton proclamation, June 30, 1779, in British Headquarters (Sir Guy Carleton) Papers, reel 9, item no. 2094.

ernor William Livingston sent Congress an intercepted copy of the earl of Dartmouth's 1775 response to Dunmore in which he first raised the possibility of Indian and slave assistance. Livingston contended this stale letter was nothing of the sort. It was "convincing proof of what has been so often denied by our enemies, that the British court endeavoured to procure both our domestic slaves, and the savages of the wilderness to destroy us." Congress thereupon ordered American printers to publish Livingston's assessment. Brackenridge's *United States Magazine* and five other newspapers reproduced the short letter. Meanwhile, in France that same season, Franklin and Lafayette sought out a Parisian engraver to illustrate the effects of Dunmore's proclamation in their "little book." "Kidnapper" and "Cudjo" cast a long shadow over the entire war for independence.[94]

94. There is some disagreement about the impact of the Philipsburg Proclamation. Quarles contended that it "aroused no general outcry in America," and since it was "not shocking or even new . . . [it] had no propaganda value for home-front consumption, nor could it be exploited for any effect upon public opinion in the capital cities of continental Europe" (*Negro in the American Revolution,* 114). Frey, on the other hand, argues it did "raise the specter of emancipation. In so doing it inspirited instead of intimidated white rebels, embittered instead of demoralized them" (Frey, *Water from the Rock,* 114). Thelma Wills Foote has sided with Frey, arguing that Clinton's announcement promised security for slaves who ran to British lines, a policy that "dramatically transformed the circumstances of runaway slaves" (Thelma Wills Foote, *Black and White Manhattan: The History of Racial Formation in Colonial New York City* [New York, 2004], 214–216, esp. 215). For other interpretations that maximize the importance of the Philipsburg Proclamations, see Cassandra Pybus, *Epic Journeys of Freedom: Runaway Slaves of the American Revolution and Their Global Quest for Liberty* (Boston, 2006), 40; Simon Schama, *Rough Crossings: Britain, the Slaves, and the American Revolution* (New York, 2006), 100; Egerton, *Death or Liberty,* 84. These historians have rightly stressed how important Philipsburg was for African Americans. I contend that Philipsburg was important to patriot leaders, too, because it gave them proof to continue accusing the British of interfering with slavery and rekindled the embers of outrage associated with Dunmore. Dunmore pension: *Connecticut Gazette,* June 5, 1778; *New-Hampshire Gazette,* June 16, 1778. It is probable Livingston gave a copy of Dartmouth's letter to Isaac Collins before he sent it to Congress: Collins published it in his *New-Jersey Gazette,* on Apr. 23, 1779, the same date of Livingston's letter to Congress. See Livingston to John Jay, Esq., President of Congress, Trenton, Apr. 23, 1779, in *The Remembrancer; or, Impartial Repository of Public Events,* part 2 (London, 1779), 278. See also *United States Magazine,* I (1779), 191; *Pennsylvania Packet,* Apr. 27, 1779; *Pennsylvania Gazette,* Apr. 28, 1779; *Independent Chronicle,* May 13, 1779; *Norwich Packet,* May 18, 1779; *Exeter Journal,* May 18, 1779.

"A Striking Picture of Barbarity"

Although not on the same scale as Dunmore's initial offer of freedom, Clinton's proclamation did engender some public outcry in patriot circles. In July, Continental army officer–turned-printer Shepard Kollock published a sonnet in his *New-Jersey Journal* about Clinton that concluded with an epithet reminiscent of Virginia snarls against the "Negro-Thief":

A proclamation oft of late he sends
To thieves and rogues, who only are his friends;
Those he invites; all colours he attacks,
But deference pays to *Ethiopean blacks.*

Later in 1779, an essayist criticized Clinton across a wide front, including the accusation, "You have even dishonored your few former acquirements in the disgrace of publishing negro proclamations."[95]

Clinton meant this announcement to aid British forces as they deployed in the southern provinces. Patriot publicists did their best to keep the people abreast of developments in the South, though news was difficult to procure, given the weakness of communication networks there. In the summer of 1779, ten patriot newspapers published an account documenting how British forces marched "along the sea coast, and plundered the richest settlements." "There are individuals," the correspondent lamented, "who have lost from 3 to 400 negroes. . . . They have made no distinction between whig and tory; and the very persons to whom they gave protection, have notwithstanding been plundered." Another Philadelphia paper published a letter from Charleston that put all the various proxies into one terrible array against liberty: they were "a large body of the most infamous banditti and horse thieves that perhaps ever were collected together any where . . . a corps of Indians, with Negro and white savages disguised like them, and about fifteen hundred of the most savage disaffected poor people seduced from the back settlements" of the Carolinas.[96]

95. *New-Jersey Journal*, July 20, 1779; *Boston Evening Post* (White & Adams), Aug. 7, 1779; *Independent Ledger*, Aug. 9, 1779; Oct. 26, 1779, *Boston Evening Post* (White & Adams), Nov. 13, 1779; *New York Packet*, Nov. 18, 1779; *Connecticut Courant*, Nov. 23, 1779; *Pennsylvania Packet*, Dec. 21, 1779.

96. When printers exchanged this article, they attributed it to a Philadelphia paper of either Aug. 21 or 26. Saturday, August 21, could either be Dunlap's *Packet* or Towne's *Evening Post*, whereas Thursday, August 26, could only be the *Packet*. This article does not appear in the extant issues of any of these, leaving the conclusion that either a supplement has been lost or somewhere the exchangers made an error.

bound to the Weſt-Indies, and ſome ſmaller veſſels.

April 26. The enemy ſent a party up the North River, with an intention to ſurprize a detachment of the Americans. They however miſſed their aim, but ſet fire to High Sheriff Van Breenk's houſe, and to an outhouſe of Col. Hendrickſon's, which were conſumed. They alſo ſet fire to and plundered ſeveral other houſes, and carried off with them Juſtice Covenhoven and ſon, and ſome others, with ſome horſes and cattle. The militia by this time aſſembled under Col. Holmes, who drove them to their boats; they had one killed, and another taken priſoner.

Trenton, April 23, 1779.
" Sir,

" Thinking that the incloſed letter, which lately fell into my hands, may perhaps be of ſome uſe to Congreſs, as a moſt convincing proof of what has been ſo often denied by our enemies, that the Britiſh court endeavoured to procure both our domeſtic ſlaves and the ſavages of the wilderneſs to deſtroy us, and that at ſo early a period of the conteſt as the year 1775, I do myſelf the honour to tranſmit it to Congreſs, and am, with great eſteem, Sir,
Your Excellency's moſt
obedient humble ſervant,
WILLIAM LIVINGSTON."
His Excellency John Jay, *Eſq.*
Preſident of Congreſs.

Whitehall, 2d *Auguſt,* 1775.
" My Lord,

" The hope you held out to us in your letter of the 1ſt of May, that with a ſupply of arms and ammunition, you ſhould be able to collect from amongſt Indians, negroes, and other perſons, a force ſufficient, if not to ſubdue rebellion, at leaſt to defend government, was very encouraging; but I find by your letters delivered to me by Lieut. Collins, that you have been obliged by the violence of the times, menaced by one branch of the legiſlature, and abandoned by the other, to yield up all the powers of government, and to retire yourſelf on board the Fowey. I have the King's commands to ſend you his leave to return to England, which, together with this letter, and a commiſſion to Mr. Corbin to adminiſter government during your abſence, will be delivered to you by Capt. Atkins of his Majeſty's ſhip Acteon, who goes convoy to the Maria ſtore-ſhip.

At the ſame time it is left to your Lordſhip's diſcretion to uſe this leave of abſence or not, as you ſhall ſee occaſion; for, relying on your firmneſs, I have ſtill a hope that with the ſupply of arms now ſent to you, and with the aſſiſtance of a greater naval force, the King's government may yet be maintained; and ſhould this happily be the caſe, it will not be neceſſary that Mr. Corbin ſhould be informed of his Majeſty's intention in his favour. I am, my Lord,
Your Lordſhip's moſt
obedient humble ſervant,
DARTMOUTH."
Earl of Dunmore.

Publiſhed by order of Congreſs,
CHARLES THOMSON, *Sec.*
Philadelphia,

Figure 13. *Lord Dartmouth's letter to Dunmore, August 21, 1775. From* United States Magazine, *I (1779), 191. In the spring of 1779, New Jersey governor William Livingston (himself an experienced patriot satirist) received a copy of this 1775 letter from Britain's former secretary of state to the then–Virginia royal governor. Livingston forwarded the four-year-old letter to Congress, who ordered it published. Hugh Henry Brackenridge, another creative patriot publicist, was then-editor of the short-lived* United States Magazine. *He followed Congress's order in the April issue.*

The most significant scene involving British forces and African Americans in the last months of 1779, however, was in Savannah. On September 8, as several Indian towns still smoldered in Iroquoia, the French fleet, commanded by the comte d'Estaing, appeared off the coast of Savannah, surprising British and patriot leaders alike. D'Estaing had left the North American coast a year earlier to operate in the West Indies; when Prevost's capture of Charleston seemed imminent, South Carolina governor John Rutledge sent messengers to beg d'Estaing to sail to his rescue. If the American union was uninterested in helping, perhaps the French alliance could save Carolina. Not knowing the fate of those messages, patriot leaders were caught unaware by d'Estaing's sudden arrival off Savannah.

Since British pilots had spotted the approach of "strange ships in the offing," Prevost had a few days' warning to repair the city's wrecked defenses. He convinced the royal Georgia government to enlist several hundred slaves from neighboring plantations to rebuild walls facing the Atlantic and a series of earthworks protecting the city from any attack by land. In addition to drafting blacks to aid in the city's defenses, Prevost also armed a few hundred more. In short, nearly 3,000 British, loyalist, and African American men furiously prepared Savannah for a combined French-American siege. On September 12, d'Estaing ordered his 3,500 soldiers to disembark. Worried about having his ships destroyed by hurricanes or the British fleet, the French admiral did not want to linger in Georgia and sent word to Benjamin Lincoln for his 1,100 Continentals and Carolina militia troops to join him as soon as possible. When they arrived four days later, d'Estaing sent a flag to the British garrison calling for their surrender, boldly threatening Prevost that he alone would be responsible for the destruction that would ensue if

---

Since it appeared in both the *Pennsylvania Journal* and *New-Jersey Gazette* on Sept. 1, neither of those could be the original source. See *Pennsylvania Journal*, Sept. 1, 1779; *New-Jersey Gazette*, Sept. 1, 1779; *Connecticut Courant*, Sept. 7, 1779; *New-York Journal*, Sept. 13, 1779; *Norwich Packet*, Sept. 14, 1779; *Connecticut Journal*, Sept. 15, 1779; *American Journal*, Sept. 16, 1779; *Massachusetts Spy*, Sept. 16, 1779; *Boston Gazette*, Sept. 20, 1779; *New-Hampshire Gazette*, Oct. 12, 1779. The August 25 issue of the *Pennsylvania Gazette* had an alternative account of this news from South Carolina, also describing how the British "never had the pleasure of ravaging so opulent a country before, and the havoc they have made is not to be described. . . . The furniture which they could not carry off they wantonly broke, burnt and destroyed; they have however taken with them some thousands of Negroes, with a great quantity of plate, jewels, and all kinds of treasure" (*Pennsylvania Gazette*, Aug. 25, 1779). "Banditti and horse thieves": *Pennsylvania Evening Post*, Aug. 16, 1779.

he declined. Prevost, having recently received a much-needed reinforcement of 800 men who had waded through the swamps to get there, did just that.[97]

Rains precluded the impatient d'Estaing from beginning the siege for two weeks, a devastating delay. Finally, on October 3, nearly three dozen French naval guns began bombarding the now fully entrenched, multiracial British garrison. D'Estaing had already stayed three weeks longer in Georgia than he had planned. After six days of shelling, d'Estaing decided his only course of action was to storm the city. In the middle of the night on October 9, French and American forces (themselves multiracial, with free black troops from Saint-Domingue among d'Estaing's ranks) organized into assault columns. Starting late and not well organized, the attack was a disaster, though men on all sides fought bravely. D'Estaing was wounded twice, while 800 men—one-fifth of the combined French and American force—were also casualties. The British lines held at all points with approximately 150 lost. The violence of October 9 ended d'Estaing's desire to continue the siege. To Lincoln's dismay, d'Estaing quickly returned to his ships and left the Americans vulnerable. Small-scale fighting continued. One British officer recounted in his journal "our Armed Negroes skirmishing with the Rebels the whole afternoon" of October 16, and two days later he again wrote, "The armed negroes brought in two Rebel Dragoons, and eight Troop Horses, and killed two rebels." That was the rear guard of patriot forces, for Lincoln had marched back into South Carolina. D'Estaing was headed back to France. The siege of Savannah was an utter failure.[98]

97. Francis Rush Clarke, journal, Sept. 4, 1779, Sol Feinstone Collection of the American Revolution, American Philosophical Society, Philadelphia, no. 2338; Lilla M. Hawes, ed., *Collections of the Georgia Historical Society*, X, *The Proceedings and Minutes of the Governor and Council of Georgia* . . . (Savannah, Ga., 1952), 49–51; Ward, *War of the Revolution*, II, 688–691; David B. Mattern, *Benjamin Lincoln and the American Revolution* (Columbia, S.C., 1995), 80–84; Piecuch, *Three Peoples, One King*, 168–169. D'Estaing also had several hundred black troops with him from Saint-Domingue, and, like Gage in Boston at the start of the war, Prevost blamed his opponent for initiating the practice of including blacks as a justification for his use of Georgia slaves. See Alexander A. Lawrence, *Storm over Savannah: The Story of Count d'Estaing and the Siege of the Town in 1779* (Athens, Ga., 1951), 64–65, 81–82.

98. Francis Rush Clarke journal, Oct. 16, 18, 1779, in Feinstone Collection, American Philosophical Society. The account printed in Rivington's *Royal Gazette* corroborated this skirmishing between armed slaves and patriots on October 16. See *Royal Gazette*, Dec. 11, 1779; *Independent Ledger*, Jan. 10, 1780. For a larger context

"A Striking Picture of Barbarity"

In the days that followed, several inhabitants of Savannah petitioned British authorities to disarm those slaves, neutralize their "great Insolence," and prevent acts of "great Outrages and plunder in and about the Town." If the government did not act quickly, "dreadful Evils" might occur, a consequence that was surely "obvious to every Person of Thought and Property." Even though the number of armed blacks in Savannah was miniscule compared to the several thousand British regulars and loyalist partisans who defended the city, the participation of armed slaves in the siege loomed large not only for those inside Savannah but for Americans far to the north.[99]

Patriot publicists could not find much to say about the disaster in Georgia. The most widely exchanged notice about the Savannah defeat was that Britain's arming of slaves caused it. After Lincoln and d'Estaing retreated, Charleston printer Peter Timothy listed three rationalizations to explain the failure. The first two attributed some causation to blacks who either were armed as part of the garrison or among the "2000" the commander employed "night and day incessantly engaged in adding to the strength and number of the works." "Two thousand" was an embellishment: there were fewer than half that number in total aiding British military forces and only two hundred actually in arms. But this was one of the most important pieces of information Americans learned about the siege.

Eleven newspapers recopied Timothy's pointed rationalizations, a significant number for this late in the war. It was the most widespread account of the engagement. The only other well-circulated story, appearing in four papers, referred to the number of enemy troops inside Savannah as three thousand, "exclusive of negroes and other rubbage, which General Prevost seduced to join him." This report probably originated with Henry Laurens, for he related nearly the exact same information to Washington (complete with the spelling error) just two days before.[100]

---

of how war in the Deep South shaped notions of slavery and freedom, see Jane G. Landers, *Atlantic Creoles in the Age of Revolutions* (Cambridge, Mass., 2010), 15–54.

99. "Petition of Sundry Inhabitants of Savannah, and Parish of Christ Church," Oct. 25, 1779, in Hawes, ed., *Colls. of the Ga. Hist. Soc.*, X, 53–54, esp. 53. South Carolina planter Philip Porcher reported the loss of 228 slaves "taken by the British" after the siege in November. See Philip Porcher papers, MSS, South Caroliniana Library.

100. *Gazette, of the State of South-Carolina*, Oct. 20, 1779; *Pennsylvania Gazette*, Nov. 24, 1779; *Maryland Gazette*, Nov. 26, 1779; *New-Jersey Gazette*, Dec. 8, 1779; *Connecticut Courant*, Dec. 14, 1779; *New-York Journal*, Dec. 20, 1779; *Norwich Packet*, Dec. 21, 1779; *American Journal*, Dec. 23, 1779; *Connecticut Journal*, Dec. 29, 1779; *Massachusetts Spy*, Dec. 30, 1779; *Boston Evening Post* (White & Adams), Jan. 1, 1780; *Newport Mercury*,

South Carolina patriots, anxious about their precarious situation and frustrated with the unwillingness of their colleagues to send help, posted letters that were not well received in the north. Since South Carolina had rejected Congress's suggestion to recruit their own black units, some patriot political leaders had little sympathy for their vulnerability. "The State of Sth. Cara. have *thought* we neglected them," Massachusetts delegate James Lovell wrote in November, but "we *know* they neglected themselves. They will not *draught* to fill up their Battalions, they will not raise *black Regiments*. . . . They have not been neglected by *us here* but their Neighbours have not regarded our Recommendations." Lovell blamed South Carolina's troubles on their intolerance. He closed this contentious letter with a warning to its recipient, Horatio Gates: "You must not give this to [the] Printer." Lovell's attitude — and his reticence to have it published — reflects the attitudes of many patriot leaders by the end of 1779. Lovell probably did not know that a majority of Rutledge's council had advised the governor to surrender in May, but he was hardly sanguine about South Carolina's dedication to the Revolution. Lovell was concerned about the signs of erosion weakening the cause, but neither did he want to see those concerns substantiated in print, especially when it came to slavery. Best to keep the threat of disunity a secret between patriot leaders.[101]

As it turned out, these threats were only beginning at the end of 1779. As that year drew to a close, a large fleet carrying Sir Henry Clinton and a huge invasion force of 8,000 men left Sandy Hook, New Jersey, en route to Charleston, South Carolina. Once he heard the news of d'Estaing's abandonment of Savannah, Clinton decided to press the southern strategy. Thanks in large part to the participation of slaves, Indians, and loyalists in Georgia over the last year, Clinton had decided to take the entire war to them. The next few years of war would feature the increasing involvement of British proxies.

While patriot military action against the king's Indian allies seemed to consolidate the common cause along the New York–Pennsylvania frontier

---

Jan. 5, 1780. "Exclusive of negroes": *Pennsylvania Packet,* Oct. 26, 1779; *Pennsylvania Gazette,* Oct. 27, 1779; *Connecticut Journal,* Nov. 10, 1779; *Independent Chronicle,* Nov. 11, 1779; *Boston Evening Post* (White & Adams), Nov. 13, 1779. See also HL to GW, Philadelphia, Oct. 24, 1779, *LDC,* XIV, 105–107.

101. James Lovell to Horatio Gates, Philadelphia, Nov. 11, 1779, *LDC,* XIV, 178–180, esp. 179.

"A Striking Picture of Barbarity"

in 1779, the issue of African American involvement pulled at the seams of the American union in the Deep South. Patriot leaders did not announce those tensions, but with the combined influence of increasing numbers of African Americans in the Continental army and pressing difficulty to meet recruitment quotas, they privately believed that drafting blacks would help save the war. What Lovell and his colleagues did not comprehend was that their public justifications for war impeded any quiet embrace of black soldiers in their armies. It was more than inherited colonial prejudices that prevented most Americans from accepting plans to emancipate and enlist African Americans. It was the common cause argument itself that compounded those obstacles.

* * *

Even far away from states with majority slave populations, the common cause argument complicated any drives to make liberty apply to African Americans. In the summer of 1778, Quaker abolitionist Samuel Allinson wrote to New Jersey governor William Livingston asking him to throw his authority behind a manumission bill. Livingston replied that his personal sentiments were wholly in line with Allinson's. Slavery was "utterly inconsistent" with humanity, and "Americns who have almost idolizd liberty" should find it "peculiarly odious and disgraceful." He had indeed sent a message "to lay the foundation for their Manumission" in the last session. But, the governor and author of several pieces of patriot "proxy" rhetoric confessed, the legislature, "thinkg us in rather too critical a Situation to enter on the consideration of it," asked him "in a private way to withdraw the Message." War and the union took precedent over principle, Livingston admitted. In his response, Livingston thanked Allinson for sending a pamphlet written by Anthony Benezet entitled *Serious Considerations on Several Important Subjects,* which included pacifism, temperance, and abolition. This was the latest essay to come from Benezet's pen—but it had been three long years since his last comment against slavery. Since the war began, only a pamphlet by Samuel Hopkins had appeared calling for abolition. The public outcry to end slavery, so loud in 1774, had all but vanished. In the meantime, Kidnapper and Cudjo had dominated news columns. That hiatus mattered. Quaker activists had not pressed issues that may have seemed to undermine the war effort, especially abolition. As a result, in late 1778, when Quakers pressured the Pennsylvania legislature to pass a gradual abolition bill, they had to compete with the darker connotations of the common cause. Patriot claims for freedom should have been a gust of wind filling abolitionist sails; in many places, they were not.[102]

In March 1779, the bill came up for a second reading in the Pennsylvania Assembly after an initial tabling. A few Philadelphia newspapers called attention to it, simply mentioning that it was on the legislature's docket. A proposed preamble also appeared in a Philadelphia and Boston paper. Another reading in November brought a greater spotlight in print, but the timing of this third appearance shows the discursive context in which abolition operated during the Revolutionary War.[103]

In the intervening months between readings, not only had Clinton issued his proclamation from Philipsburg, but incidents of black unrest had gripped New Jersey. In June, the *New-Jersey Journal* reported, "It was discovered that the negroes had it in contemplation to rise and murder the inhabitants of Elizabeth-Town." A few weeks later, patriot publicists began to document the participation of blacks in the plundering raids that wracked the state. The most notable of these groups was led by "Colonel Tye." Tye, who was rumored to have been Major Cudjo himself, formerly belonged to Monmouth County slaveholder John Corlies and had been known by the name of Titus. Corlies advertised for the twenty-one-year-old, six-foot-tall Titus in the *Pennsylvania Gazette* only a few days after Dunmore's proclamation was known in the mid-Atlantic, and many believed that Tye had joined the "Ethiopian Regiment." At the battle of Monmouth in June 1778, he gained attention, capturing a patriot officer and carrying him back to New York City. Former New Jersey governor William Franklin rewarded this bravery with a commission in a loyalist military unit. Franklin sponsored loyalist raids from "Refugeetown" on Sandy Hook, beginning in 1779. The main target was Tye's former home of Monmouth County. On July 15, Tye led a force

102. William Livingston to Samuel Allinson, Morristown, July 25, 1778, in Roger Bruns, ed., *Am I Not a Man and a Brother: The Antislavery Crusade of Revolutionary America, 1688–1788* (New York, 1977), 442; [Anthony Benezet], *Serious Considerations on Several Important Subjects* . . . (Philadelphia, 1778), *Early American Imprints*, 15737.

103. Pa. Abolition Bill: *Pennsylvania Packet*, Mar. 4, 1779; *Independent Chronicle*, Mar. 18, 1779; *New-Hampshire Gazette*, Mar. 23, 1779; *Massachusetts Spy*, Mar. 25, 1779. Dunlap's *Packet* also printed proposed amendments to the bill forwarded by "A Citizen" on Mar. 13, 1779. White & Adams's *Boston Evening Post* published a proposed preamble on Mar. 27, 1779, saying it was exchanged from a Philadelphia paper that has not survived, surely the *Pennsylvania Journal*. For a greater background, see Gary B. Nash and Jean R. Soderlund, *Emancipation by Degrees: Emancipation in Pennsylvania and Its Aftermath* (New York, 1991), 101–105.

"A Striking Picture of Barbarity"

of fifty black and white partisans on a raid near Shrewsbury, New Jersey, where they made off with one hundred horses and cows and two patriot hostages. Tye's guerrilla band would wreak havoc on New Jersey patriots—and he would achieve significant notoriety far away from Monmouth County in patriot newspaper columns that impugned his actions as the result of sinister British machinations.[104]

Unrest both at home and throughout North America: this was the context into which Pennsylvania patriots debated a gradual emancipation bill. *Pennsylvania Gazette* printers Hall and Sellers published information about the bill in the November 24 issue, reporting only "eight votes against the Bill." But that same issue—six *paragraphs* above it, in the same column of print—contained the reasons the siege of Savannah failed. The main one, of course, was slaves fighting with America's enemies. A month later, John Dunlap printed the text of the proposed abolition bill in his *Packet*. Here again, this information followed on the heels of countervailing representations of African Americans working with the enemy. Just two days before, Dunlap exchanged a criticism of Clinton's Philipsburg Proclamation that accused its author of the "disgrace of publishing Negro proclamations." Even those organs that supported efforts to abolish slavery did so at the same time they forwarded images that cut across the grain of antislavery.[105]

104. *New-Jersey Journal*, June 22, 1779; *New-York Journal*, July 5, 1779; *Continental Journal*, July 8, 1779; *Independent Chronicle*, July 8, 1779; *Massachusetts Spy*, July 8, 1779. Advertisement for Titus: *Pennsylvania Gazette*, Nov. 22, 1775. Colonel Tye is a favorite topic of Revolutionary War historians. See Sidney Kaplan and Emma Nogrady Kaplan, *The Black Presence in the Era of the American Revolution*, rev. ed. (1973; rpt. Amherst, Mass., 1989), 81; Graham Russell Hodges, *Slavery and Freedom in the Rural North: African Americans in Monmouth County, New Jersey, 1665–1865* (Madison, Wis., 1997), 96–104, esp. 97; Nash, *Unknown American Revolution*, 231–232; Schama, *Rough Crossings*, 111, 114–116; Joyce Lee Malcolm, *Peter's War: A New England Slave Boy and the American Revolution* (New Haven, Conn., 2009), 177–180; Harry M. Ward, *Between the Lines: Banditti of the American Revolution* (Westport, Conn., 2002), 62–64. Egerton's survey of African American experiences during the Revolution wove his chapter on war experiences around Tye's "transformation"; see *Death or Liberty*, 65–92, esp. 67.

105. *Pennsylvania Gazette*, Nov. 24, 1779. For others who exchanged the information about the abolition bill's third reading, see *Pennsylvania Packet*, Nov. 23, 1779; *New-Jersey Gazette*, Nov. 24, 1779; *Connecticut Journal*, Dec. 8, 1779. "Disgrace of publishing": *Pennsylvania Packet*, Dec. 21, 23, 1779. In New Hampshire, at that same moment, nineteen slaves invoked natural rights, the language of sensibility, and even America's "cause" to petition for freedom, but the legislature denied it too, claim-

* * *

War and the demands of union exacerbated the friction between patriot rhetoric and reality. To be sure, as John Laurens, Alexander Hamilton, James Lovell, and Samuel Allinson argued, abolition fitted snugly with the narrative of the American Revolution: that the common cause was one of universal liberty and self-determination. At the same time, those efforts defied the critical narrative of the Revolutionary War: that the common cause was defending liberty-loving Americans from the king's treacherous proxies. African Americans found themselves caught between these two competing concepts.

Since the middle of 1778, endemic Indian and loyalist violence across a wide arc from the upper Hudson to the lower Ohio had dominated patriot attention. The economy and boldness of George Rogers Clark inspired those who received accounts of terrible suffering and bloodshed on frontier farms. Patriot military and political leaders adopted an aggressive policy of invasion to sever ties between Indians and their British sponsors either at Niagara or Detroit. The triple expedition commanded by Sullivan, Clinton, and Brodhead was the culmination of this policy.

Patriot rhetoric influenced the parameters of this punitive, scorched-earth campaign. Wild, inaccurate stories about the Wyoming Massacre ratcheted up the bloodshed on both sides, producing, to an extent, the destruction of Cherry Valley. Patriot newspapers propagated images that described all Indians as "British Savages," passive proxies of evil men like Henry "the Hair-Buyer" Hamilton. The thousands of acres of farmland in Iroquoia devastated by American soldiers stemmed in no small part from decisions made by patriot printers and those who supplied them with information.

This, too, had a significant effect for thousands of people in the backcountry. Images of "bad" Indians aiding the British all but drowned out notices of friendly groups, like the Stockbridge, Delawares, and Oneidas, who supported the common cause. "Good" Indians found their situation increasingly untenable by the war's fourth year. The Delawares continued to listen to American promises but still suffered at the hands of vigilante

---

ing, "The House is not ripe for a determination in this matter." See "State of New Hampshire: To the Honorable, the Council and House of Representatives . . . ," Portsmouth, Nov. 12, 1779, and New Hampshire House of Representatives Journal, Exeter, June 9, 1780, quoted in Isaac W. Hammond, "Slavery in New Hampshire," *Magazine of American History*, XXI (1889), 63–64.

"A Striking Picture of Barbarity"

murderers, and the Oneidas' choice to back the United States spurred civil war in Iroquoia. The celebration of friendly Indians paled in comparison to the applause reserved for Sullivan and Clark's conquests. This construction contributed to emerging ideas that taking land away from America's enemies, such as the supporters of Joseph Brant and Walter Butler, was an act of patriotism. The Stockbridge, Oneidas, and Tuscaroras, despite the blood they spilled for the cause, did not escape such exclusionary concepts.

It had been eighteen months since the ratification of the French alliance, the rejection of the Carlisle Commission, and any compromise for peace. Patriot publicists had broadcast the well-cultivated common cause argument enough to achieve a great victory: it had held the infant American states together long enough and well enough to secure essential European assistance. Since that turning point, the war had entered a new phase. Public support for the now-four-year-old war began to wane to dangerous levels for several reasons. In addition to war fatigue, most states experienced severe financial distress, which brought with it the specter of high taxes and rapidly depreciating currency. Those economic straits meant soldiers could not be paid monthly wages, and that, in turn, bred discontent with patriot leaders and threatened army recruiting. From the perspective of elites, social pressure being exerted by people with more radical ideas of democracy or equality only worsened this crisis. As one Continental army officer put it, "The people of America seem to have lost sight entirely of the noble principle which animated them at the commencement of [the war]. That patriotic ardor which then inspired each breast, — that glorious, I had almost said godlike, enthusiasm, — has given place to avarice, and every rascally practice which tends to the gratification of that most sordid and most disgraceful passion."[106]

In the face of these exponential troubles, patriot publicists continued to believe the most effective way to inspire and motivate the American public was to keep stoking anger and outrage over British involvement with proxies, whether blacks, Indians, or German mercenaries. By 1778 and 1779, the latter had just about run its course; newspaper mentions of German soldiers acting against the Revolution had become all but invisible by this time. Their participation in Georgia went unnoticed. If they captured any attention in print, it was to detail Hessian soldiers deserting British lines

106. Samuel Shaw to his parents, New Windsor, Conn., June 28, 1779, in Josiah Quincy, ed., *The Journals of Major Samuel Shaw, the First American Consul at Canton: With a Life of the Author* (Boston, 1847), 58–60, esp. 58.

in favor of American liberty. A letter from one distressed local leader to Massachusetts patriot leader Timothy Pickering typified American attitudes at the end of 1779. On Christmas Eve, Samuel Phillips found himself "at a loss" after hearing that Congress had decided to move a number of German prisoners of war out of Massachusetts. "We have always supposed that the Community would be much benefited by the final continuance among us of those Brunswickers, who are well behaved and we thought Congress was in the same opinion," he wrote from Boston. Many of these Germans "are very useful Mechanics, of whom have married among us, had children, taken the oath of allegiance, paid taxes, and are very useful Members of Society." Phillips then pled his own case to Pickering, one of the most instrumental men in alerting the American people about the approach of the "men monsters" back in 1776. He claimed there was "one in particular I don't know how I could replace, for by his ingenuity and attention he has so recommended himself that after working in my Powder Mill about 9 or 10 months I have committed the care of it to him, and know not how I could supply his place." In this case, at least, the soldiers Captain Lee saw crossing the ocean to put down the rebellion were now anything but proxy enemies of the Revolution. Instead, they were reliable operators of Massachusetts gunpowder mills. These German mercenaries, Phillips argued, were American citizens.[107]

For African Americans and Indians, those attitudes were quite different. The final years of the 1770s witnessed unprecedented involvement with the war from both slaves and Indians, as well as more discussion of that engagement among patriot leaders. Leaders in the Continental army and Congress wrangled over the question raised by John Laurens whether to embrace emancipation to bolster recruitment for patriot military forces. As British developed a new southern strategy, the common cause seemingly approached a crossroads: either slavery or independence. For most southerners, there was no choice. They believed even limited emancipation threatened not only their economic future but also their personal safety. That nondecision had been, in part, influenced by patriot rhetoric since 1775. Supporting the Revolution, as patriot publicists defined it, meant fighting the king's still-dangerous assistants, Indians and African Americans—everywhere.

107. Samuel Phillips to Timothy Pickering, Boston, Dec. 24, 1779, in Timothy Pickering Papers, MHS, microfilm, reel 27, 317–318.

"A Striking Picture of Barbarity"

## CHAPTER 7

"This Class of Britain's Heroes"

FROM THE FALL OF CHARLESTON TO YORKTOWN

"A newspaper in South Carolina in the present State of their Affairs
would be equal to two regiments."
Benjamin Rush to Nathanael Greene, Sept. 4, 1781

When the news began to circulate about Benedict Arnold's defection to the enemy in the fall of 1780, the patriots' stalwart printer John Holt responded with a poem to inform his readers how to think about the apostate. The poet insisted Arnold's first name should from now on be *"maledicted,"* or, perhaps "Britain's *Benediction,"* for

> Such blessings, she with lib'ral Hand
> Confers on this devoted land;
> For instance, let us only mention
> Some proofs of her benign intention:
> The *slaves* she sent us o'er the deep
> She bribes to cut our throats in sleep;
> To take our lives and scalps away, ⎱
> The savage *Indians* keep in pay, ⎬
> And *tories,* worse by half than they, ⎰
> Then in this class of Britain's Heroes,
> The *tories,* savage *Indians, negroes,*
> Recorded *Arnold'*s name shall stand,
> While freedom's blessings crown our land.

Though by October 1780 they hardly needed to be associated, the bracket helped readers connect loyalists, Indians, and African Americans as a panoply of America's enemies. The members of this "Class of Britain's Heroes" had been solidly established at the heart of patriot representations for more than five years before Arnold's betrayal. The traitor had chosen that "Class";

A RNOLD, thy name, as heretofore,
   Shall now be Benedict no more ;
Since, inſtigated by the Devil,
Thy ways are turn'd from good to evil.
'Tis fit we brand thee with a name,
To ſuit thy infamy and ſhame ;
A nd ſince 6t treaſon thou'rt convicted,
Thy name ſhould now be maledicted ;
Unleſs, by way of contradiction,
We ſtyle thee BRITAIN's Benediction,
Such bleſſings, ſhe with lib'ral hand,
Confers on this devoted land ;
For inſtance, let us only mention,
Some proofs of her benign intention :
The ſlaves ſhe ſent us o'er the deep,
She bribes to cut our throats in ſleep ;
To take our lives and ſcalps away,   ⎫
The ſavage Indians keep in pay,   ⎬
And tories, worſe by half than they.   ⎭
Then in this claſs of Britain's Heroes,
The tories, ſavage Indians, negroes,
Recorde'd Arnold's name ſhall ſtand,
While freedom's bleſſings crown our land ;
And odious ♦ the blackeſt crimes,
Arnold ſhall ſtink to lateſt times.

Figure 14. "This Class of Britain's Heroes."
From Independent Ledger (Boston), Oct. 23,
1780. In this poem, Benedict Arnold is bracketed
together with "tories, savage Indians, [and]
negroes" as a special "class of Britain's heroes."

he was now first among those terrible proxies. All of them together had rejected the blessings of freedom.[1]

Arnold's treachery was perhaps the lowest point of the Revolutionary
War for the patriots. His negotiation with Major John André came on the
heels of the worst military losses the patriots had yet suffered. The fall of
Charleston in May 1780 had cost the patriots dearly in prestige and public confidence. South of Virginia, British fortunes were in the ascendant.
The patriot war effort dragged everywhere. When Arnold decided to turn
his coat not long after, he believed he was abandoning a foundering ship.[2]

In spite of all these disasters, the patriots still clung to images of British
proxies as mirror opposites of heroic American freedom fighters. In what
would be the war's final years, patriot publicists continued to broadcast

1. *New-York Journal*, Oct. 9, 1780. The poem was also published in: *Maryland
Journal*, Oct. 17, 1780; *Pennsylvania Evening Post*, Oct. 17, 1780; *Independent Ledger*,
Oct. 23, 1780; *Pennsylvania Packet*, Oct. 24, 1780; *New-Jersey Journal*, Oct. 25, 1780;
Massachusetts Spy, Oct. 26, 1780; *Continental Journal*, Oct. 26, 1780.

2. For more on Arnold's treachery and the patriot reaction, see Charles Royster, *A Revolutionary People at War: The Continental Army and American Character, 1775–
1783* (Chapel Hill, N.C., 1979), 282–294; Sarah Knott, *Sensibility and the American
Revolution* (Chapel Hill, N.C., 2009), 170–184.

stories about African Americans and Indians acting on behalf of the crown as a way to distinguish between friends and enemies and mobilize support for the common cause. Although their communication networks were at their weakest and most limited after 1780, whenever patriot publicists had opportunity to amplify stories involving African Americans or Indians fighting for the king, they did so as noisily as they could, engulfing nearly all counterexamples of blacks and Indians aiding the cause. At the same time, the silence that had veiled nearly all depictions of hostile German mercenaries since early 1777 also held—they were not included in "Britain's Heroes"—even though thousands of Hessians fought for Clinton and Cornwallis in the Deep South.

From the siege of Charleston in the spring of 1780 to the final evacuation of New York City at the end of 1783, patriot political leaders, military officials, and publicists deviated little from the well-established narratives that underpinned the common cause. The positive side of that appeal centered on a celebration of America's struggle against tyranny. According to patriot publicists like John Holt's poet, real Americans rushed to defend "Freedom's Blessings." On the other hand, the poet also highlighted the negative connotations that were just as vital to the common cause appeal: choosing not to defend America's blessing showed one to be an enemy of the new republic.

The last years of war witnessed unprecedented movement for African Americans, shocking violence on the northern and western frontiers, and internecine conflict in the Carolinas. Patriot publicists interpreted these events a particular way, turning them into a discourse that reinforced the common cause. That discourse provided a powerful argument for shaping policy once major hostilities ended at Yorktown, including how patriot political leaders on the state and national levels would deal with frontier expansion and the reinforcement of the slave system after the war. The full impact of the patriots' war stories began to materialize after the Treaty of Paris.

1: LOSING CHARLESTON

In the same letter describing how John Laurens's plan to raise black regiments was "received with horror by the planters," David Ramsay also sketched out what the city of Charleston meant to the common cause in the South. Charleston was the *"vinculum* that binds three States to the authority of Congress," he wrote to William Henry Drayton in early September 1779. "If the enemy posses themselves of this town, there will be no living for honest whigs" in the Deep South. On February 12, 1780, the fleet transporting Sir Henry Clinton and 8,000 British and German soldiers landed south of Charleston. That calamity had arrived.[3]

Over the next few weeks, Clinton's troops made preparations for a lengthy siege. American commander Benjamin Lincoln begged South Carolina authorities to reconsider their refusal to enlist African Americans. As soon as scouts sighted the British fleet, Lincoln began pressing Governor John Rutledge, requesting "that our deficiencies may be in part supplied by arming some Blacks, agreeable to the repeated recommendations of Congress." "Circumstances were very different" when the South Carolina Assembly had rejected that measure before; now the recruitment of African Americans was "an absolute necessary" move. For the next month and a half, he sent a biweekly missive calling on Rutledge to arm slaves and thereby save the capital. He tried threats. He wrote the governor on February 14, reminding Rutledge that it was his responsibility to protect the 1,200 Continental troops inside the city, and, if the 2,000 militia or a "like number of blacks" did not turn out to man the lines, he would be forced to march the Continentals out to prevent capture. No avail. On February 28, he took a more humble tack, acknowledging that "nothing could persuade me to urge a measure so opposite as this, has hitherto appeared to the general sentiment of the people," but he held that arming slaves was "unavoidably necessary if we mean to hold the town." Finally, just as British batteries opened the siege, Lincoln gave it one last try: "Give me leave to add once more that I think the measure of raising the black Corps a necessary one, and that I have great reason to believe if permission is given for it, that many men would soon be obtained." None of Lincoln's tactics gained a sympathetic audience.[4]

Meanwhile, six hundred miles to the north, the Pennsylvania legislature debated the merits of a bill for gradual emancipation. This bill proposed that all children of slave mothers would be required to serve until their

3. David Ramsay to William Henry Drayton, Charleston, S.C., Sept. 1, 1779, in R. W. Gibbes, ed., *Documentary History of the American Revolution: Consisting of Letters and Papers Relating to the Contest for Liberty . . .* , II, *1776–1782* (New York, 1857), 121.

4. Benjamin Lincoln to Governor John Rutledge, Charleston, Jan. 30, 1780, Benjamin Lincoln Letterbook, BPL, I, 177 ("repeated recommendations"), Feb. 14, 1780, I, 206 ("like number of blacks"), Feb. 28, 1780, II, 10 ("nothing could persuade me"), Mar. 13, 1780, II, 17 ("give me leave"). For more on Lincoln's predicament and his belief that black troops were his only safety, see David B. Mattern, *Benjamin Lincoln and the American Revolution* (Columbia, S.C., 1995), 90–94.

twenty-eighth birthday, upon which they would be emancipated. Its proponents, principally Philadelphia merchant George Bryan, appealed to the morality and patriotism of Pennsylvania representatives, quoting the natural rights phrases in the 1776 state constitution back to them. But there was another side to that patriotism as amplified by patriot leaders throughout the Revolution. Just as Bryan or Anthony Benezet or other advocates for abolition could invoke the opening paragraphs of the Declaration of Independence, opponents of the measure could also point to that document's ultimate grievance as a reason to keep slavery. A petition signed by twenty-three dissenting members of the legislature argued that even this moderate, gradual abolition was imprudent. The first reason was that it imperiled the union. "The pernicious consequences which such a measure may draw on any state or states in the union," they contended, "tend to weaken that body." If that was not enough, Britain's apparent southern strategy further worried more than one-third of the Pennsylvania Assembly. "Since the seat of war is likely to be transferred to the southward," they protested,

> and to all appearance the force of that country may be called out, when the white inhabitants will be obliged to leave their families, and all that is near and dear to them, at the mercy of a superior force of slaves, which may from the sound of freedom, that may go forth from this law, (perhaps unattended with every circumstance) lead the negroes of these states, to a demand of an immediate and intire freedom, or to other disorders that may end in the greatest cruelties, which an ignorant, and perhaps desperate people, stimulated by the enemies of their masters, can be capable of committing.

Luckily for the children of the 7,000 slaves in Pennsylvania, these concerns about how emancipation might imperil the fragile union did not carry sufficient weight to defeat the measure. It passed 34–21 on March 1, 1780, just as South Carolina patriots rebuffed Lincoln's pleas to include African Americans as part of Charleston's defense.[5]

Couched in the rhetoric of sensibility, the act announced, "We find our hearts enlarged with kindness and benevolence towards men of all condi-

5. Gary B. Nash and Jean R. Soderlund, *Freedom by Degrees: Emancipation in Pennsylvania and Its Aftermath* (New York, 1991), 100–101, 104–105; *Journals of the House of Representatives of the Commonwealth of Pennsylvania: Beginning the Twenty-Eighth Day of November, 1776, and Ending the Second Day of October, 1781* . . . (Philadelphia, 1782), 436, *Early American Imprints,* 17658.

tions and nations." Yet, the loopholes that existed in this new law made it less than the natural rights achievement its sponsors boasted of. Importantly, the law did not address what political, economic, and social standing freed people would have in Pennsylvania after emancipation. Even though there would be no freedom in Pennsylvania until 1808, since the act applied only to children born after March 1, 1780, the bloc of legislators who opposed the bill worried it could induce violence on southern plantations. Because British agents and officers were already there to "stimulate" southern slaves, there was no predicting how grave the consequences might prove.[6]

Bryan and his allies justified gradual abolition by calling upon the positive imagery of the common cause appeal; they believed the central ideology of the Revolution meant liberty should extend to ever-widening circles. But their opponents could make an equally valid counterclaim. The concerns voiced by those who voted against the bill were also based in how the patriots represented the Revolution. Patriot publicists and leaders had forwarded union its own ideological construct that competed with abstract conceptions of liberty, self-determination, or consent. Worries that emancipation in Pennsylvania might embolden resistant blacks to the south were not irrational; anything that might imperil the fragile compact (especially since the Articles of Confederation, adopted by Congress in November 1777, had not yet been ratified) had to be treated carefully. Two weeks later, a long letter from Henry Clinton—intercepted by patriot privateers on its way to England—appeared, in which the British commander assured Secretary of State George Germain that he would do his best to cultivate black support if Germain needed it. This letter first found its way to *New York Packet* printer Samuel Loudon's hand, and soon half the patriot printers exchanged it in full. Just one month after they raised questions about how emancipation might affect other Americans, those who voted against the

6. "We find our hearts enlarged": *Pennsylvania Packet,* Mar. 4, 1780. Nash and Soderlund criticized the moderate, lukewarm provisions of the 1780 law. They pointed out that if a slave woman gave birth on February 28, 1780, that child would die in slavery. If that newborn was a woman who bore children until her fortieth year, then that last child, born in 1820, would still have to serve twenty-eight years. Thanks to the loopholes, there were still traces of slavery in Pennsylvania in 1848. "If the 1780 law was a death sentence for slavery" in Pennsylvania, they argued, "it was a sentence with a two-generation grace period" (Nash and Soderlund, *Freedom by Degrees,* 111). See also Arthur Zilversmit, *The First Emancipation: The Abolition of Slavery in the North* (Chicago, 1967), 124–137; Douglas R. Egerton, *Death or Liberty: African Americans and Revolutionary America* (New York, 2009), 99–101.

"This Class of Britain's Heroes"

bill could hold up Clinton's report to suggest how real and immediate the issue of African American involvement was for both sides in this increasingly southern conflict.[7]

The publication of Clinton's letter underpinned another hazard that the southern strategy raised for the patriots. When Loudon published it, he provided a short introduction establishing its provenance. He also provided a revealing admission: "As the letter contains, in particular, a state of our Southern affairs, of which we have been almost totally in the dark for some time past, we flatter ourselves we shall gratify the curiosity of our readers by its publication." Even before Clinton's troops began to invest the city, their mere presence closed up all the patriots' print shops in Charleston. John Wells, Jr., had suspended his *South-Carolina and American General Gazette* the previous December, whereas the imminent assault convinced Peter Timothy that the February 9 issue of his paper *Gazette, of the State of South-Carolina* should be his last. Timothy stayed in Charleston during the siege, was taken prisoner, and drowned at sea on his way to captivity in Saint Augustine. The silence that now engulfed the South was problematic; from this point through the British evacuation three years later, no patriot printers produced or exchanged stories about the war's central theater. South of Virginia, where the fighting was, American readers would indeed be largely "in the dark" from the spring of 1780 until Yorktown. There was no newspaper in North Carolina after 1778, and even the reliable *Virginia Gazette*s experienced some turbulence in 1781 when multiple British invasions overwhelmed the state.[8]

7. *New York Packet,* Mar. 30, 1780; *Pennsylvania Packet,* Apr. 8, 1780; *Connecticut Courant,* Apr. 11, 1780; *New-Jersey Gazette,* Apr. 12, 1780; *Pennsylvania Journal,* Apr. 12, 1780; *Connecticut Gazette,* Apr. 14, 1780; *Independent Chronicle,* Apr. 20, 1780; *Massachusetts Spy,* Apr. 20, 1780; *Continental Journal,* Apr. 20, 1780; *Boston Gazette,* Apr. 24, 1780; *Independent Ledger,* Apr. 24, 1780; *New-Hampshire Gazette,* Apr. 29, 1780. One loyalist paper also printed it: *Royal Gazette,* Apr. 22, 1780.

8. "We flatter ourselves": *New York Packet,* Mar. 30, 1780; *Pennsylvania Packet,* Apr. 8, 1780; Clarence S. Brigham, *History and Bibliography of American Newspapers, 1690–1820,* 2 vols. (Worcester, Mass., 1947), II, 1033, 1036. John Dixon and Thomas Nicolson published their *Virginia Gazette* in Williamsburg until April 1780, when they followed the government in their relocation to Richmond. They restarted their paper in Richmond in May 1780 and continued it until May 19, 1781, when British invasion closed their shop until December. At that time, Nicolson began publishing again with William Prentis as his new partner. John Clarkson inherited the other *Virginia Gazette* from his uncle Alexander Purdie when he died in August 1779. Clarkson

On the other hand, loyalist printers started publishing in the Deep South soon after the British arrived. James Johnston started the *Royal Georgia Gazette* a few weeks after Savannah fell back into British hands in 1779. The itinerant James Robertson, who had gone to Philadelphia to produce the *Royal Pennsylvania Gazette* during William Howe's occupation of the city in 1777, now joined Clinton's fleet bound for South Carolina. Soon his *Royal South-Carolina Gazette* would appear in Charleston, accompanied on the masthead by Donald MacDonald and a man well known to southern patriots: the infamous Alexander Cameron. John Wells, Jr., had been Henry Laurens's close correspondent and a previously reliable patriot printer; he even participated at the siege of Savannah. But with Clinton's invasion, he valued his property over his politics and eventually transformed his *American General Gazette* into the *Royal Gazette*.[9]

This was a significant setback for the common cause. Newspapers had helped organize the very messy Revolution. Printed stories mitigated the ugliness of war by providing evidence that justified violent action, explaining away retributive violence perpetrated by patriot vigilantes, or—best of all—allowing patriot leaders to distance themselves (and the cause) from bad behavior. None of that existed in the lower South once Clinton began the siege of Charleston.

Starting in the spring of 1780, the Carolinas would see the most severe internecine conflict yet. They saw unprecedented amounts of "Hanging, House Burning, Plundering, and other Cruelties and Acts of Barbarity," as Rutledge put it. There are multiple reasons why violence in the South was so terrible. African American resistance forced both British and patriot leaders to consider them constantly in policy decisions. As one historian

---

took Augustine Davis as his partner. Clarkson and Davis published their *Gazette* in Williamsburg until December 1780. In December 1781, a new imprint, *The Virginia Gazette, or, the American Advertiser,* began publishing in Richmond under the editorship of James Hayes. It continued until 1786. See Brigham, *History and Bibliography of American Newspapers,* II, 1145, 1150, 1162, 1163.

9. After 1781, John Wells operated the *Royal Gazette* with his brother and in the name of his exiled loyalist father, Robert Wells. Robertson, MacDonald, and Cameron managed the *Royal South-Carolina Gazette* for more than a year, until Robertson took over sole proprietorship sometime in 1781. He operated the paper alone until the British evacuation of Charleston in September 1782. See Brigham, *History and Bibliography of American Newspapers,* II, 1035–1036; Isaiah Thomas, *The History of Printing in America: With a Biography of Printers and an Account of Newspapers,* ed. Marcus A. McCorison, 2d ed. (1810; rpt. New York, 1970), 577–578.

"This Class of Britain's Heroes"

has put it, "The American Revolution in the South was a war about slavery, if not a war over slavery." Yet this was not the only triangle that produced shocking violence after 1780 in the South. Cherokees, Creeks, Choctaws, and other southern Indians also found themselves between the two combatants; both sides jockeyed for their loyalty, as well. But by far the worst fighting was between patriots and tories. Scholars have investigated many avenues to discover why the South—especially the Carolina backcountry— devolved into such chaos from 1780–1783. They have pointed to deeper structural forces, especially class tensions or ethnic relations, and more contingent influences, including familial ties, neighborhood rivalries, and ambition, to explain the trauma. According to some, a culture of violence, stoked by Indian wars and pre-Revolutionary disorder in both Carolinas, fed the fires of vengeance; by 1780, any attempts at restraint had been consumed by the flames.[10]

One factor that has not yet been interrogated is how the absence of print might have contributed to the chaos. Patriot leaders had long put their

10. John Rutledge to SC Delegates to Congress, Salisbury, N.C., Nov. 20, 1780, no. 51–140, fiche 1, in John Rutledge Papers, SCHS. "War over slavery": Sylvia R. Frey, *Water from the Rock: Black Resistance in a Revolutionary Age* (Princeton, N.J., 1991), 45. For analysis of the Revolution's violence in the South, see James H. O'Donnell III, *Southern Indians in the American Revolution* (Knoxville, Tenn., 1973); Edward J. Cashin, *The King's Ranger: Thomas Brown and the American Revolution on the Southern Frontier* (Athens, Ga., 1989); Jim Piecuch, *Three Peoples, One King: Loyalists, Indians, and Slaves in the Revolutionary South, 1775–1782* (Columbia, S.C., 2008), esp. 204–213, 258– 265; Ronald Hoffman, "The 'Disaffected' in the Revolutionary South," in Alfred F. Young, ed., *The American Revolution: Explorations in the History of American Radicalism* (Dekalb, Ill., 1976), 273–316; Clyde R. Ferguson, "Carolina and Georgia Patriot and Loyalist Militia in Action, 1778–1783," in Jeffrey J. Crow and Larry E. Tise, eds., *The Southern Experience in the American Revolution* (Chapel Hill, N.C., 1978), 174–199; A. Roger Ekirch, "Whig Authority and Public Order in Backcountry North Carolina, 1776–1783," Jeffrey J. Crow, "Liberty Men and Loyalists: Disorder and Disaffection in the North Carolina Backcountry," Emory G. Evans, "Trouble in the Backcountry: Disaffection in Southwest Virginia during the American Revolution," all in Ronald Hoffman, Thad W. Tate, and Peter J. Albert, eds., *An Uncivil War: The Southern Backcountry during the American Revolution* (Charlottesville, Va., 1985), 99–124, 125–178, 179–212; Rachel N. Klein, *Unification of a Slave State: The Rise of the Planter Class in the South Carolina Backcountry, 1760–1808* (Chapel Hill, N.C., 1990), 78–108, esp. 107– 108; Wayne E. Lee, *Crowds and Soldiers in Revolutionary North Carolina: The Culture of Violence in Riot and War* (Gainesville, Fla., 2001), 176–211.

faith in print to appeal to the "disaffected." In the South, however, this avenue was closed once Clinton's sappers dug their siege lines outside Charleston. In New Jersey or New York, Samuel Loudon or Shepard Kollock could publish accounts that justified the harsh measures patriot authorities were "forced" to adopt to combat loyalism. In the Carolinas after 1780, this was not possible. Whether small-scale assaults on individuals or atrocities on groups of suspected loyalists, violence committed in the patriots' name only embittered and alienated the public at large. There was little patriot leaders could do to recover loyalties or make amends for retributive violence enacted by their own militia forces in the Carolina backcountry. The cycle simply continued. As Nathanael Greene would write late in 1780, "The Whigs and Tories pursue one another with the most relent[less] Fury killing and destroying each other wherever they meet." The depredations "so corrupted the Principles of the People that they think nothing but plundering one another."[11]

Six months later, he thought he had found an antidote: "Nothing will contribute more to the recovery of these Southern States than a proper channel to convey intelligence to the people; for want of which they are kept

11. Nathanael Greene to General Robert Howe, Camp on the Pedee, Dec. 29, 1780, *PNG*, VII, 17–18, esp. 17. In the neutral zone surrounding New York City, too, patriot printers competed with Manhattan loyalist papers in a marketplace of ideas. This perhaps contributed to the nearly even split between loyalties in these areas. For more on the social, political, economic, and military factors that also helped clarify allegiances in the New York and New Jersey counties near Manhattan, see Jonathan Clark, "The Problem of Allegiance in Revolutionary Poughkeepsie," in David D. Hall, John M. Murrin, and Thad W. Tate eds., *Saints and Revolutionaries: Essays on Early American History* (New York, 1984), 285–317; Joseph S. Tiedemann, "Patriots by Default: Queens County, New York and the British Army, 1776–1783," *WMQ*, 3d Ser., XLIII (1986), 35–63; John Shy, "Armed Loyalism: The Case of the Lower Hudson Valley," in Shy, *A People Numerous and Armed: Reflections on the Military Struggle for American Independence*, rev. ed. (1976; rpt. Ann Arbor, Mich., 1990), 181–192; Sung Bok-Kim, "The Limits of Politicization in the American Revolution: The Experience of Westchester County, New York," *JAH*, LXXX (1993), 164–188; Harry M. Ward, *Between the Lines: Banditti of the American Revolution* (Westport, Conn., 2002), 51–68; Joseph S. Tiedemann and Eugene R. Fingerhut, eds., *The Other New York: The American Revolution beyond New York City, 1763–1787* (Albany, N.Y., 2005); Michael S. Adelberg, "An Evenly Balanced County: The Scope and Severity of Civil Warfare in Revolutionary Monmouth County, New Jersey," *Journal of Military History*, LXXIII (2009), 9–47.

in ignorance and subject to every British imposition." "If," Greene wrote to a prospective printer, "you will remove your press to Charlotte or Salisbury [North Carolina] and open the business of printing I think you will render an essential service to your Country and you may depend upon my giving you every possible encouragement so as to render it beneficial to your interest." Word of Greene's request eventually reached Philadelphia, for in September, Benjamin Rush informed the southern commander, "I hear that you have written for a parson and a printing press, both material engines in moving the world. A newspaper in South Carolina in the present State of their Affairs would be equal to two regiments." He added, with a penetrating comparison, given the internecine state of affairs by late 1781, "Cardinal De Ritz remarks that in the civil wars of France that party that wrote *most* and wrote *best* always prevailed."[12]

There was yet another important consequence to the severance of print networks south of the James River. The silencing of patriot newspapers in Charleston also meant that northern states could no longer benefit from hearing southern theater war updates to the degree they were accustomed. In July, a New Jersey delegate wrote John Jay, then in Madrid negotiating with the Spanish court, that he would probably learn of the war's progress in South Carolina "in the European Papers before it reaches you from this City: our Intelligence being over-land, is tedious in it's Passage." One of Thomas Jefferson's correspondents in Paris, Philip Mazzei, heard about the fall of Charleston before the Virginia governor did. Since he had it from a London paper, Mazzei assumed Jefferson had the news long before. It took

12. Nathanael Greene to Thomas Walters, Headquarters near Orangeburg S.C., July 10, 1781, *PNG*, VIII, 514–515, Benjamin Rush to Greene, Philadelphia, [Sept.] 4, 1781, IX, 323. Jean François Paul de Gondi, Cardinal de Retz (1613–1679), was a leader of the Fronde, the 1648–1653 civil wars in France. Retz's leadership stemmed from his involvement in the publication of mazarinades, polemical pamphlets published mostly in Paris by the thousands attacking the French minister Jules Mazarin. Howard G. Brown, in his forthcoming book *Violence and the Self: Personal Suffering and Collective Trauma from the French Wars of Religion to the Paris Commune,* writes that the "polemical nature of so many of these pamphlets suggests that contemporaries believed that waging a war of words could actually alter opinions in significant ways." In Retz, Rush indeed identified a kindred spirit. Rush was likely referencing *Memoires,* Retz's reflections on the Fronde and his role in it, which was first published in 1717. For more, see J. M. H. Salmon, *Cardinal de Retz: Anatomy of a Conspirator* (London, 1969). Sincere thanks to my colleague Howard Brown for his assistance and for sharing material.

less time for the news to cross the Atlantic, be placed on a printer's table in London, get stuffed in a mailbag for shipment across the English Channel, and make its way to Paris than it did to be published two states away. Jefferson himself confessed, "Our information from the Southward has been at all times defective, but lamentab[ly] so on the late occasion." This state of affairs would not improve. Given how dire the military situation in Carolina would get by the fall of 1780, this incapacity was perhaps a silver lining. But, for the most part, the patriots' ability to keep their constituents informed of the war's progress in the South was diminished considerably. This, too, contributed to war weariness and a loss of "spirit."[13]

This is not to suggest that newspapers should be viewed as the signal reason why public support for the war had flagged almost to fatal levels by the fall of 1780. Since so many patriots acknowledged their significance in earlier years of the imperial crisis and war, it should also hold that their absence from 1780 to 1783 had consequences. By the time Benedict Arnold plotted to betray West Point, panic had set in among patriot publicists about the total evaporation of American patriotism. It is more than a coincidence that the fall of 1780 was also the moment when patriot print networks reached their nadir. From a high of thirty-five prints operating in the summer of 1775, by the time of Arnold's defection, that number had decreased by nearly a third. Only twenty-five prints remained active, and of that, more than a dozen were in New England and eight more were concentrated in New York, Pennsylvania, and New Jersey. Only four papers continued south of Philadelphia by the fall of 1780. The war had taken its toll on printers, either because of military occupation or financial dislocations. They faced substantial disruptions in supplies of materials, customers, or information—or all three—because of the war.[14]

13. William Churchill Houston to John Jay, Philadelphia, July 10, 1780, *LDC*, XV, 419–421, esp. 419. For similar sentiment about the poor progress of news, see William Churchill Houston to JA, Philadelphia, July 11, 1780, *LDC*, XV, 429–432; Philip Mazzei to TJ, Paris, June 22, 1780, *PTJ*, III, 458–460, esp. 458, TJ to Samuel Huntington, Richmond, Va., June 9, 1780, 426. Congress ordered Governor Jefferson to use public monies to hire more post riders to carry news from Cape Henry to Philadelphia, with which he complied. See TJ to Thomas Sim Lee, Richmond, Va., June 14, 1780, *PTJ*, III, 444–446.

14. Connecticut: *Connecticut Courant, Connecticut Gazette, Connecticut Journal, Norwich Packet*. Maryland: *Maryland Gazette, Maryland Journal*. Massachusetts: *Boston Gazette, Continental Journal, Independent Chronicle, Independent Ledger, Massachusetts Spy*. New Hampshire: *New-Hampshire Gazette*. New Jersey: *New-Jersey Gazette, New-Jersey*

"This Class of Britain's Heroes"

* * *

The silencing of southern networks began when Clinton's fourteen thousand troops began laying siege to the city of Charleston. By May 1, British cannon lobbed shells into the city. Though casualties were relatively light, starvation mounted. On May 12, the crown regained control of the largest city south of Philadelphia and took more than five thousand American troops prisoner.[15]

It took nearly three weeks for the news to reach loyalist printer James Rivington in New York City. On May 31, he published letters from Clinton and other British officers documenting the city's capitulation. Since updates were not forthcoming from South Carolina, a few patriot printers exchanged this news from Rivington, although prefaced with a warning. In Philadelphia, Congress did not have any reliable news concerning Charleston, either. A full month after General Benjamin Lincoln surrendered, the delegates complained that they were "unaccountably Tantalized with the News of Charlestown." Corroboration, in the form of an officer dispatched personally by Lincoln, finally reached Congress on June 14. Soon, the official articles of capitulation that placed the city in the enemy's hands began surfacing in patriot newspapers.[16]

Journal. New York: *New-York Journal, New York Packet.* Pennsylvania: *Pennsylvania Evening Post, Pennsylvania Gazette, Pennsylvania Journal, Pennsylvania Packet.* Rhode Island: *Newport Mercury* (restarted by Solomon Southwick on Jan. 10, 1780), *Providence Journal, American Journal.* Virginia: *Virginia Gazette* (Dixon & Nicolson), *Virginia Gazette* (Clarkson & Davis). Loyalist papers: *New-York Gazette, New-York Mercury, Royal Gazette* (Rivington), *Royal American Gazette* (Robertsons), *Royal Georgia Gazette, Royal South-Carolina Gazette.*

15. For military histories of the siege of Charleston, see Carl P. Borick, *A Gallant Defense: The Siege of Charleston, 1780* (Columbia, S.C., 2003); John Ferling, *Almost a Miracle: The American Victory in the War of Independence* (Oxford, 2007), 415–427; Mattern, *Benjamin Lincoln and the American Revolution,* 88–109; Robert Middlekauff, *The Glorious Cause: The American Revolution, 1763–1789,* 2d ed. (1982; rpt. New York, 2005), 444–455; John S. Pancake, *This Destructive War: The British Campaign in the Carolinas, 1780–1782* (University, Ala., 1985), 56–72; Christopher Ward, *The War of the Revolution,* ed. John Richard Alden (New York, 1952), II, 695–703.

16. Benjamin Huntington to Nathaniel Shaw, Philadelphia, June 12, 1780, *LDC,* XV, 302. Letters from British officers: *Royal Gazette,* May 31, 1780. He published the official articles of capitulation on June 7. Hugh Gaine exchanged them in the June 10, 1780, issue of *New-York Gazette.* Exchanged from Rivington: *Massachusetts Spy,* June 15, 1780; *Connecticut Gazette,* June 16, 1780. Philadelphian George Nelson wrote

This came as a shock. Just a week or two before the news of Charleston's surrender, several northern papers had boasted of Lincoln's intransigence, publishing a report that he had rejected any discussion of giving up the city. During the siege, New England papers had reprinted other instances of defiance from Charleston, including a proclamation issued by Governor John Rutledge banning any activity that might aid the enemy, especially "persuading negroes to desert from their owners and join the enemy." Another account had it that eleven spies had been executed in Charleston for "inticing Negroes to set fire to the town." As far as readers removed from the Carolina siege lines were concerned, all was going well. Suddenly, however, the scene changed. Lincoln's surrender "is a fatal Blow indeed to that Country," James Lovell wrote to Abigail Adams, "as well as injurious to the common Intrest of the Union." A New York delegate used a phrase better associated with the founding of Lovell's Massachusetts: "I fear, that, unless We strain every Nerve, we shall become a Bye-word among the Nations."[17]

What would the British do now that they controlled the largest city in the Deep South? Surely they would honor Clinton's Philipsburg Proclamation, but, worse, would they follow Dunmore's example and actually arm slaves? Patriot publicists did not know, but the British were indeed planning this.

------

in his diary on June 8 that "an account came to town published in the Baltimore paper that Charlestown was safe the 18th May at 4:00 PM" (George Nelson diary, 1780–1792, MSS, HSP). Articles of capitulation: *Virginia Gazette* (Dixon & Nicolson), June 7, 1780; *Pennsylvania Gazette,* June 14, 1780; *Massachusetts Spy,* June 15, 22, 1780; *Pennsylvania Packet,* June 17, 1780; *Connecticut Gazette,* June 16, 1780; *Boston Gazette,* June 19, 26, 1780; *Maryland Journal,* June 20, 1780; *American Journal,* June 21, 1780; *Independent Chronicle,* June 22, 29, 1780; *Continental Journal,* June 22, 29, 1780; *Providence Gazette,* June 24, 1780; *Newport Mercury,* June 24, 1780; *Independent Ledger,* June 26, 1780; *New-Jersey Gazette,* June 28, 1780; *Connecticut Journal,* June 29, 1780; *New-Hampshire Gazette,* July 1, 1780; *Connecticut Courant,* June 6, 1780. Issue no. 352 (June 29) of the *Norwich Packet* is not extant; this very possibly could have carried the articles of capitulation.

17. James Lovell to Abigail Adams, June 13, 1780, *LDC,* XV, 314–315, John Morin Scott to Ezra L'Hommedieu, Philadelphia, June 6, 1780, 270–274, esp. 270. Lincoln rejection of surrender: *Maryland Journal,* May 16, 1780; *Pennsylvania Evening Post,* May 20, 1780; *Norwich Packet,* June 1, 1780; *Connecticut Gazette,* June 2, 1780; *Providence Gazette,* June 3, 1780; *Independent Ledger,* June 5, 1780; *American Journal,* June 7, 1780; *Continental Journal,* June 8, 1780. "Persuading negroes": *Continental Journal,* Apr. 27, 1780; *Massachusetts Spy,* May 4, 1780. "Inticing Negroes": *Independent Chronicle,* Apr. 27, 1780; *Connecticut Journal,* May 4, 1780.

Cyphers, written in French and cut into strips, which have survived in Henry Clinton's papers, reveal a conversation between British intelligence officers George Beckwith and the ill-fated John André suggesting that they raise "a black [regiment] of 6,000 men and another, to begin the campaign next month. . . . It will be better if you raise a black corps with promises of their liberty and some land after their good services. Make blacks sergeants and corporals." This action, Beckwith believed, would ensure the real objective: "Establish your power in all your towns." Although the British did not follow this plan with any alacrity, the threat that they might was ubiquitous for the duration of the war. It lent credence to the wartime common cause argument. The patriot accusation that the British contemplated and sometimes implemented these strategies, as well as the eighteenth-century prejudices about how Americans interpreted them, both grew from fertile soil.[18]

Thomas Paine and other publicists flew to their desks to try to lift patriot spirits at this critical moment. Paine, now the clerk of the Pennsylvania Assembly, composed the ninth installment of the *American Crisis* in the wake of Charleston's fall. For the next few weeks, anonymous essayists joined Paine, inundating the front pages of newspapers, begging for a renewal of American patriotism. This efflorescence of opinion had not been seen since the months leading up to independence. This was an emergency. In addition to the dozen papers that exchanged Paine's *Crisis*, readers perused articles written by "[The Ghost of] Gen. Montgomery," "A Citizen," "A Soldier," "Americanus," and addressed to "the Young Men of Massachusetts," "My Dear Countrymen," "the People of Maryland, Virginia, North and South Carolina." In some fashion, each of these implored Americans to renew their dedication to the Revolution. "Unite as one man, to crush that nest of villains," "An American" pleaded.[19]

18. Henry Clinton Papers, CCXXXIV, 10, CL.

19. [Paine], *The Crisis, Number IX*, Philadelphia, June 9, 1780, in Eric Foner, ed., *Thomas Paine: Collected Writings* . . . (New York, 1995), 230–234, esp. 230; *Pennsylvania Packet*, June 10, 13, 1780; *Pennsylvania Gazette*, June 14, 1780; *New-Jersey Gazette*, June 21, 1780; *Connecticut Courant*, June 27, 1780; *Independent Chronicle*, June 29, 1780; *Continental Journal*, June 29, 1780; *Connecticut Gazette*, June 30, 1780; *Providence Gazette*, July 1, 1780; *American Journal*, July 5, 1780; *Massachusetts Spy*, July 6, 1780; *Norwich Packet*, July 6, 1780; *New-Hampshire Gazette*, July 8, 1780. "[Ghost of] Gen. Montgomery": *Pennsylvania Gazette*, July 5, 1780; *Pennsylvania Packet*, Nov. 4, 1780. "A Citizen": *New-Jersey Journal*, July 12, 1780; *Pennsylvania Gazette*, July 19, 1780. "A Soldier": *Continental Journal*, July 13, 1780; *Independent Chronicle*, July 13, 1780; *Massachusetts Spy*, June 22, July 22, 1780. "Americanus": *Massachusetts Spy*, June 15,

Then, just in time to have a positive effect on the otherwise spiraling discourse, another incident captured the public's attention. Hannah Ogden Caldwell lived in Connecticut Farms, a village near Elizabethtown, New Jersey, with her husband, an outspoken patriot leader and Presbyterian minister, and their nine children. On June 7, a British and Hessian force led by General Wilhelm von Knyphausen skirmished with a group of Jersey militia, and in the melee a British soldier fired through the window of the Caldwell house, instantly killing Hannah as she huddled with her children. Within a week, the news of Caldwell's death had already appeared in several New Jersey and Pennsylvania papers. Such accounts joined the news of the loss of Charleston that June. Samuel Loudon offered his own abridgement of the story in his *New York Packet,* claiming, "The recent horrid examples . . . of their cruelty, particularly in the murder of Mrs. Caldwell, a Clergyman's wife, have only served to rouze the inhabitants of these States, and heighten our indignation." Several New England papers exchanged Loudon's take on the incident. A few others included multiple accounts of Caldwell's murder, copying articles from a combination of New York, New Jersey, and Pennsylvania papers.[20]

1780; "To the Young Men of Massachusetts": *Continental Journal,* June 22, 1780; "My Dear Countrymen": *Connecticut Courant,* June 20, 1780; "To the People of Maryland, Virginia, North and South Carolina": *Maryland Journal,* June 13, 1780; *Pennsylvania Packet,* June 17, 1780.

20. Ward, *War of the Revolution,* II, 621; Adrian C. Leiby, *The Revolutionary War in the Hackensack Valley: The Jersey Dutch and the Neutral Ground,* rev. ed. (1962; rpt. New Brunswick, N.J., 1992), 227. Three different sources describing the Connecticut Farms account appeared: *Pennsylvania Packet,* June 13, 1780; *Pennsylvania Gazette,* June 14, 1780; *New-Jersey Gazette,* June 14, 1780. Unknown correspondent: *New-Jersey Journal,* June 14, 1780. Delaware patriot leader Thomas McKean heard in Philadelphia on June 12 that "they shot her sitting in her own room with nine little children of her own standing round her begging for mercy" (Thomas McKean to William Atlee, Philadelphia, June 12, 1780, *LDC,* XV, 304–305). Quaker diarist George Nelson also noted the British "shot the Reverend Mr. Caldwell's wife in her house in a most barbarous and cruel manner" on June 13 (Nelson diary, HSP). "Recent horrid examples": *New York Packet,* June 15, 1780. From *New York Packet: Continental Journal,* June 22, 1780, *Independent Chronicle,* June 22, 1780, *Connecticut Gazette,* June 23, 1780, *Providence Gazette,* June 24, 1780. From *Pennsylvania Packet: American Journal,* July 5, 1780. From *New-Jersey Gazette: Connecticut Journal,* June 22, 1780, *Massachusetts Spy,* June 29, 1780. The *Norwich Packet* published accounts from both the *New York Packet* and *New-Jersey Gazette* in the June 22, 1780, issue, while the *Independent Chronicle* pub-

Hannah Caldwell's death offered a powerful opportunity that patriot publicists desperately needed in June 1780 to remind readers of their enemies. Her story contained several long-established elements that made it easy to magnify and exploit. Though the perpetrator was a British soldier, the men were under Knyphausen's command—whom one writer referred to as "the hireling of Hesse"—and that reminded some of Paine's "trying times" when Hessians terrorized Jersey women. For a brief moment, the loathing of Hessians—which had been absent since early in 1777—resurfaced. In a scathing essay addressed to Knyphausen, "A Citizen" held up Caldwell's martyred death "as to shew Americans in what detestation they are to hold the name of *Hessian, Briton,* and *Tory.*"[21]

The discourse (however dormant) representing Hessians as America's enemies was not the story's only thread involving proxies. A "Friend" of Hannah offered an epitaph for her tomb that referred to the "merciless barbarity" of the British army. That loaded phrase invoked other British allies. According to another commentator, "The brutality to some women at Connecticut Farms would make even Savages blush." Descriptions of cruelty led many patriot scribes to speculate that Caldwell's murderers acted like Indians. From there, it was a short step to conflate Hannah with Jane McCrea. A month after the incident, several essays appeared that commented on British brutality as exemplified in the June 7 attack, and several of them recalled the famous bride-to-be slain three years earlier. A "Lady" published her sentiments in the *New-Jersey Gazette,* imploring readers to remember "the tragical death of Miss M'Crea, torn from her house, murdered and scalped by a band of savages hired and set on by British emissaries," as well as the "melancholy fate of Mrs. Caldwell, put to death in her own house in the late incursion of the enemy." These terrible events must induce "brave men to reflect" on their defense of the "rights and liberties of their country" and protect "the best and most glorious of all causes." *Virginia Gazette* printers Dixon and Nicolson appended a note comparing the "unhappy fate" of McCrea and Caldwell after publishing "Sentiments of an American Woman" from the *Pennsylvania Gazette.* They admired that "the ladies of that state have shown their gratitude by ample donations to those brave men who are

---

lished its own take on the Caldwell murder alongside the *Pennsylvania Packet* letter in the June 29, 1780, issue, one week after already exchanging Loudon's extraction.

21. "Hireling of Hesse": *New-Jersey Journal,* June 14, 1780. "A Citizen": *New-Jersey Journal,* July 12, 1780. Also reprinted in *Pennsylvania Gazette,* July 19, 1780; *Pennsylvania Packet,* July 25, 1780.

shielding us from the sword of the one, and the scalping knife of the other."
After James Rivington scoffed at the patriots' propagation of the Caldwells'
innocence—he referred to Hannah's husband as "the *very Reverend and Holy
Priest* James Caldwell; Retailer of *Sedition* on Sundays; and *Ammunition, Shoes,*
and *Boots* the Week Days"—four papers devoted an entire page to establishing the "truth" via a well-established method of publishing depositions
taken from six witnesses. James Caldwell sponsored these statements himself, and they included his opinion about the calamity that had befallen his
family. He, too, compared his wife to Jane McCrea—only worse. The crimes
against his household could not "be laid to the charge of Indians, whose
native fierceness, unrestrained by discipline, led them beyond the will of
the commanding officers." His wife's death, instead, "was a violation of every
tender feeling . . . unprovoked, deliberate, and not so much as frowned
upon by those in command."[22]

At the same time that distressing news arrived from South Carolina about

22. "Merciless barbarity": *New-Jersey Journal,* Sept. 13, 1780; *Pennsylvania Journal,*
Oct. 11, 1780. "Savages blush": *New-Jersey Journal,* June 14, 1780. "Sentiments": *New-
Jersey Gazette,* July 12, 1780. *"Very Reverend": Royal Gazette,* June 17, 1780. "Laid to the
charge of Indians": *New-Jersey Journal,* Sept. 6, 1780; *Pennsylvania Journal,* Oct. 4,
1780; *Independent Chronicle,* Oct. 12, 1780; *Connecticut Gazette,* Oct. 24, 1780. James
Thacher, whose journal helped keep the legend of Jane McCrea alive when it was
published in 1827, also noted Hannah's murder. See Thacher, *A Military Journal during the American Revolutionary War, from 1775 to 1783; Describing Interesting Events and
Transactions of this Period . . . ,* 2d ed. (1823; Boston, 1827), 194. "Anti-Brittanus," an
item published in two patriot papers, proclaimed "Unhappy M'Crea, and thou still
more unfortunate Caldwell, tell us what kind of monsters they are who have thus inhumanely dipt their hands in your innocent blood.—They call themselves Britons.—
Curst forever be the name!" (*Pennsylvania Packet,* June 24, 1780; *Independent Ledger,*
July 17, 1780). "Unhappy fate": *Virginia Gazette* (Dixon & Nicolson), Aug. 9, 1780.
Rivington republished a letter from Washington to Congress back in February that
mentioned Caldwell's assistance in securing boots for the Continental army as proof
of the minister's political involvement in the war. That letter had already surfaced in
patriot papers: *Pennsylvania Packet,* Jan. 22, 25, 1780, *Pennsylvania Evening Post,* Jan.
23, 1780, *Virginia Gazette* (Dixon & Nicolson), Feb. 12, 1780. Rivington ran this letter a second time on July 1 under the title *"BOOTS! BOOTS for the GENERAL!"* (*Royal
Gazette,* July 1, 1780). He also battled patriot representations of the Caldwell incident
by publishing letters from British officers and loyalist leaders who claimed that "the
manner in which the rebels aggravate this unfortunate affair, in their publications, is
of a piece with their uniform conduct, plausible, but fallacious" (*Royal Gazette,* June
21, 1780, Aug. 5, 1780).

"This Class of Britain's Heroes"

the loss of an entire army—and perhaps all the southern provinces—patriot publicists deflected that blow by amplifying the deaths of innocent individuals. Highlighting the suffering of a few sympathetic victims better explained the conflict. In this case, it was the tragedy of a New Jersey mother of nine; a few weeks earlier, ten printers had also highlighted the plight of a Pennsylvania farmer named Asa Upton, killed by Indians on the Susquehanna River. Later, several papers detailed a brutal attack on New York militia colonel Joannis Jensen's household. Even more printers—nearly two-thirds—quickly exchanged an account of a family of four in Stone Arabia, New York, fighting heroically for six hours against a party of sixty Indians and loyalists. The fate of Upton, Jensen, and other families, often depicted hiding in their own houses-turned-stockades, forwarded certain images that patriot publicists cultivated. It was no accident that these stories dominated the already limited space available inside patriot newspapers.[23]

These individuals, though long forgotten, were critical to advancing the common cause. Patriot publicists seized upon and broadcast these incidents, packaging them—to the frustration of James Rivington and other loyalist publishers—in ways that would manage their readers' "tender feelings" and, hopefully, animate their indignation and outrage to take action against their enemies. Many of those same newspaper readers who learned of Caldwell's death that summer also read Thomas Paine's contention that "the war on the part of America, has been a war of natural feeling." "Every passion, but that of dispair, has been called to a tour of duty," Paine claimed. As they had since 1775, Paine and his colleagues again tried to manage those passions by describing British actions in terms of savages and merce-

23. Upton: *New-York Journal*, Apr. 17, 1780; *Connecticut Courant*, Apr. 25, 1780; *Continental Journal*, Apr. 27, 1780; *Connecticut Journal*, Apr. 27, 1780; *Independent Chronicle*, Apr. 27, 1780; *Connecticut Gazette*, Apr. 28, 1780; *New-Jersey Gazette*, May 3, 1780; *American Journal*, May 3, 1780; *Norwich Packet*, May 4, 1780; *Pennsylvania Evening Post*, May 5, 1780. Jensen: *New York Packet*, Sept. 21, 1780; *Pennsylvania Packet*, Sept. 26, 1780; *Pennsylvania Journal*, Sept. 27, 1780; *Pennsylvania Gazette*, Sept. 27, 1780; *New-Jersey Journal*, Sept. 27, 1780; *Connecticut Journal*, Sept. 28, 1780; *Independent Chronicle*, Oct. 5, 1780. Stone Arabia: *New York Packet*, Sept. 14, 1780; *New-York Journal*, Sept. 18, 1780; *Connecticut Courant*, Sept. 19, 1780; *Pennsylvania Journal*, Sept. 20, 1780; *Pennsylvania Gazette*, Sept. 20, 1780; *New-Jersey Gazette*, Sept. 20, 1780; *Connecticut Journal*, Sept. 21, 1780; *Independent Chronicle*, Sept. 21, 1780; *Massachusetts Spy*, Sept. 21, 1780; *New-Hampshire Gazette*, Sept. 23, 1780; *Pennsylvania Packet*, Sept. 23, 1780; *Independent Ledger*, Sept. 25, 1780; *American Journal*, Sept. 27, 1780; *Connecticut Gazette*, Sept. 29, 1780; *Providence Gazette*, Sept. 30, 1780; *Boston Gazette*, Oct. 2, 1780.

By His EXCELLENCY

Joſeph Reed, Eſq. *Preſident*,

And the SUPREME EXECUTIVE COUNCIL, *of the Commonwealth of* Pennſylvania.

A PROCLAMATION.

WHEREAS the Savages in Alliance with the King of *Great-Britain*, have attacked ſeveral of the Frontier Counties, and, according to the Cuſtom of barbarous Nations, have cruelly murdered divers of the defercelefs Inhabitants of this State: A N D W H E R E A S it has been found, by Experience, that the moſt effectual Mode of making War upon and repelling the Savage Tribes has been by Parties, confiſting of ſmall Numbers of vigorous, active Volunteers, making ſudden irruptions into their Country, and ſurpriſing them in their Marches: W H E R E F O R E, for the Encouragement of thoſe who may be difpoſed to chaſtiſe the Infolence and Cruelty of thoſe Barbarians, and revenge the Loſs of their Friends and Relations, W E H A V E thought fit, and do hereby offer a Reward of THREE THOUSAND DOLLARS for every *Indian* Priſoner, or Tory acting in Arms with them, and a Reward of TWO THOUSAND AND FIVE HUNDRED DOLLARS for every *Indian* Scalp, to be paid on an Order of the Preſident or Vice-Preſident in Council, to be granted on Certificate ſigned by the Lieutenant, or any two Sub-Lieutenants of the County, in Conjunction with any two Freeholders, of the Service performed. Such Reward to be in Lieu of all other Rewards or Emoluments to be claimed from the State.

> *G I V E N, by Order of the Council, under the Hand of His Excellency* J O S E P H R E E D, *Eſquire, Preſident, and the Seal of the State, at* Philadelphia, *this Twenty-ſecond Day of* April, *in the Year of our Lord One Thouſand Seven Hundred and Eighty.*

JOSEPH REED, PRESIDENT.

Atteſt. T. M A T L A C K, *Secretary.*

GOD Save the PEOPLE

Figure 15. *Pennsylvania scalp bounty, broadside. 1780. By the war's fifth year, patriot leaders in Pennsylvania endorsed vigilantism as a way to combat the "Savages in Alliance with the King of Great Britain," offering a bounty of $3,000 for every Indian or tory taken in arms and $2,500 for each dead native's scalp. This grisly proclamation was an example of how the common cause rhetoric of seeing Indians as proxies of the enemy shaped patriot policy. Historical Society of Pennsylvania*

naries. As McCrea's had been three years earlier, Caldwell's murder offered a perfect chance to underscore this interpretation.[24]

There was a coincidence that had nothing to do with the Caldwell episode but became part of the coverage from New Jersey that June anyway. It, too, showcased patriot representations that the British instigation of proxies, this time blacks, proved their desire to strip Americans of their liberty. While printers exchanged letters and essays instructing readers how to understand the attack on Hannah Caldwell, several of them also included accounts of an attack thirty miles southeast of Elizabethtown. A letter from Monmouth County, printed in the same issue of the *New-Jersey Gazette* that informed of Caldwell—the next column over, actually—described how "Ty, with a party of about twenty blacks and whites . . . carried off" two prisoners and four horses, and spiked a few patriot cannon. Although stories of Ty had surfaced a year earlier, *Gazette* printer Isaac Collins clarified the matter for puzzled readers: "The above-mentioned Ty is a negroe, who bears the title of Colonel, and commands a motley crew at Sandy-Hook." Collins's explanation gave a face to readers who might remember a harrowing report in his *Gazette* (and ten other patriot papers) just two months earlier of a March 30 attack on Shrewsbury, in which a Mr. Russell was killed but his grandson survived despite having "five balls shot through him." Now they had a name for the head of these "banditti": Colonel Tye.[25]

The raid Collins described was actually one of a series of incursions during the second week of June. Starting the day after Caldwell was slain, Tye and his men initiated several attacks on Monmouth County while Knyphausen kept the majority of the Jersey patriot forces busy up in Essex. Four papers exchanged the news of Tye's attacks from the *New-Jersey Gazette;* two in Connecticut included it when they exchanged the news of the Connecticut Farms incident. This news was concerning, too, since Tye's raids encouraged other African Americans to take action. Collins published a letter from Bergen County the next week that stated, "Twenty-nine negroes of both

24. [Paine], *The Crisis, IX,* in Foner, ed., *Paine: Writings,* 230–324, esp. 230.

25. "Ty": *New-Jersey Gazette,* June 14, 1780; *Pennsylvania Evening Post,* June 16, 1780; *Pennsylvania Packet,* June 17, 1780; *Connecticut Journal,* June 22, 1780; *Norwich Packet,* June 22, 1780. Russell attack: *New-Jersey Gazette,* Apr. 12, 1780; *Pennsylvania Evening Post,* Apr. 15, 1780; *Pennsylvania Packet,* Apr. 15, 1780; *New-Jersey Journal,* Apr. 19, 1780; *New-York Journal,* Apr. 24, 1780; *Connecticut Journal,* Apr. 27, 1780; *Independent Ledger,* May 1, 1780; *Boston Gazette,* May 1, 1780; *American Journal,* May 3, 1780; *Massachusetts Spy,* May 4, 1780; *Providence Gazette,* May 6, 1780.

sexes have deserted within two weeks past; upwards of twenty went off in one company." Colonel Tye led a more daring raid on June 21. According to the letter published in Collins's *Gazette,* "A party of the enemy, consisting of Ty with 30 blacks, 36 Queen's Rangers, and 30 refugee tories" plundered the houses of local militia officers, took eight men captive, and brought them back to New York. Papers in Philadelphia and Providence also circulated this account.[26]

When "A Citizen" took up his pen for the *New-Jersey Journal* in early August to remind readers, "Rise then together to extirpate those wretches root and branch from this continent" (wretches who "fired upon us out of the windows" in Elizabethtown), it made sense that he also included mention of the "high demands of *Clinton's* proclamations." In South Carolina, the Philipsburg Proclamation was "sufficient to draw the pale ghosts from the graves of their former fears, resolved to check the tyrant, or deliver themselves by an honourable death in arms." He hoped New Jersey—faced with similar threats—would be duly inspired. "Let affection strengthened by sufferings; fears, roused by dangers; . . . unite and invigorate the grand struggle, that we may soon be in full liberty and peace, each enjoy all that is contained in the character of A CITIZEN." Hannah Caldwell's death, together with the news of Tye's simultaneous raids, gave patriot publicists another excellent opportunity to portray British as embodiments of evil. The king's emissaries—whether of African, German, Indian, or English descent—were, to use the words of "A Citizen," fearsome, dangerous men who inflicted suffering. Americans, rather, must let affection "unite and invigorate" them to carry on the campaign to "full liberty and peace."[27]

Patriot publicists focused attention on events in New Jersey and upstate New York in part because news from the main theater of action was not forthcoming, and also because that news was so distressing. After Charles-

26. David Forman to William Livingston, June 9, 1780, in Carl E. Prince et al., eds., *The Papers of William Livingston,* III, *January 1779–June 1780* (New Brunswick, N.J., 1986), 423. See also Graham Russell Hodges, *Slavery and Freedom in the Rural North: African Americans in Monmouth County, New Jersey, 1665–1865* (Madison, Wis., 1997), 100. Exchanges of Tye attacks: *Pennsylvania Evening Post,* June 16, 1780; *Pennsylvania Packet,* June 17, 1780; *Norwich Packet,* June 22, 1780; *Connecticut Journal,* June 22, 1780. "Twenty-nine negroes": *New-Jersey Gazette,* June 21, 1780; *Pennsylvania Evening Post,* June 23, 1780. "Party of the enemy": *New-Jersey Gazette,* June 28, 1780; *Pennsylvania Evening Post,* June 30, 1780; *American Journal,* July 26, 1780.

27. *New-Jersey Journal,* Aug. 2, 1780.

"This Class of Britain's Heroes"

ton fell, detachments of the Continental army and South Carolina patriot units fought three more significant battles, including one at the Waxhaws on May 29. There, men under the command of brash British cavalry officer Banastre Tarleton caught up with a retreating force of 350 Continentals under Colonel Abraham Buford after chasing them for more than 150 miles. Though the details were very confused, Tarleton's cavalry rode into Buford's lines and struck down many men as they attempted to surrender, creating an epithet in patriot circles known as "Tarleton's quarter." Despite the fact that there were important themes to highlight in these multiplying conflicts, just the bare details emerged in the northern press. There was good news to exploit: at the Waxhaws, Tarleton's cutting down of unarmed men was a ready-made atrocity story. Yet, when compared to the number of stories and the depth of circularity concerning the New York frontier, even the most dedicated readers would not know much about the burgeoning civil war in the Carolinas.[28]

A story about the Waxhaws, mentioning just "Tarliton who massacred col. Buford's party after they begged quarter," appeared only in the *Virginia Gazette, Pennsylvania Gazette,* and *New-Jersey Gazette.* Several papers picked up a single sentence about Waxhaws from the *Royal South-Carolina Gazette:* "Intelligence was received that a signal victory had been obtained by Col. Tarleton over the REBELS." *Virginia Gazette* printers Dixon and Nicolson published a few more details about the "massacre," including the "Terms of capitulation" Tarleton offered Buford and an elegy to Captain Adam Wallace, one of those victims "whose bravery merits universal applause." Neither of these circulated in more than five northern papers, however. In contrast, sixteen printers exchanged news of the Stone Arabia family's six-hour siege. Although infamous to southerners—who kept it alive through conversations at army encampments, militia musters, and other politicized social gatherings—most people far removed from the Carolina piedmont read only a handful of words about "Tarleton's quarter," if anything at all. Despite sizeable encounters—there were more than 2,500 men at a clash at Ramsour's Mill on June 20—the only news came in the form of three letters that mentioned these patriot victories. These letters circulated through several papers, but they did not offer nearly the depth of details that repeated

28. John W. Gordon, *South Carolina and the American Revolution: A Battlefield History* (Columbia, S.C., 2003), 86–87, esp. 86; Ward, *War of the Revolution,* II, 705–706, esp. 706; Don Higginbotham, *War of American Independence: Military Attitudes, Policies, and Practice, 1763–1789* (1971; rpt. Boston, 1983), 361.

accounts of much smaller skirmishes between settlers and Indians in Tryon County, New York, or between patriot militia and Tye's partisans in Monmouth County, New Jersey, did.[29]

Neither censorship nor weakened communication networks are to blame for this discrepancy. It is difficult to deny that richer descriptions of less consequential clashes involving escaped slaves and hostile Indians appeared in the press, whereas considerable battles between white Carolinians did not earn much space in newspaper columns—even when they described patriot victories. Here again, through the selectivity of the "exchanges," is an illustration of the contrivance of the common cause appeal.

If patriot printers spilled little ink describing military victories in South Carolina, they did not do much better describing the rout at Camden, Horatio Gates's humiliating defeat in August 1780, in which his men panicked and fled with hardly a shot. Early reports had Cornwallis killed and the Carolina militia having "greatly distinguished themselves." Gates's letters describing the "unhappy affair" emerged in September, wherein he confessed his "deepest distress and anxiety of mind" at two thousand militia running "like a torrent." The disaster at Camden was the lowest point of the war since the November flight across New Jersey in 1776. In a single sentence, one Congressman described it as "melancholy," "distressing," "ruinous," and "destructive."[30]

---

29. "Tarliton who massacred col. Buford's party": *Virginia Gazette* (Dixon & Nicolson), July 5, 1780; *Pennsylvania Gazette*, July 19, 1780; *Pennsylvania Evening Post*, July 21, 1780; *New-Jersey Gazette*, July 26, 1780. "REBELS": *Royal South-Carolina Gazette*, June 8, 1780; *Boston Gazette*, June 26, 1780; *American Journal*, June 28, 1780; *Connecticut Gazette*, June 30, 1780; *Providence Gazette*, July 1, 1780; *Massachusetts Spy*, July 6, 1780; *Connecticut Journal*, July 6, 1780; *Continental Journal*, July 6, 1780. Tarleton's terms of surrender: *Virginia Gazette* (Dixon & Nicolson), July 5, 1780; *Pennsylvania Evening Post*, July 7, 1780; *Norwich Packet*, July 13, 1780; *Massachusetts Spy*, Aug. 3, 1780; *Boston Gazette*, Aug. 28, 1780. Wallace elegy: *Virginia Gazette* (Dixon & Nicolson), July 12, 1780; *Pennsylvania Evening Post*, July 21, 1780; *New-Jersey Gazette*, July 26, 1780; *American Journal*, Aug. 16, 1780. John Shy has argued persuasively that the militia was the most effective engine of political education, especially in the South, late in the war. See "The Military Conflict Considered as a Revolutionary War," in Shy, *A People Numerous and Armed*, 213–244.

30. John Henry to Thomas Sim Lee, Philadelphia, Sept. 2, 1780, *LDC*, XVI, 9–10, esp. 9. "Greatly distinguished themselves": *Maryland Journal*, Aug. 29, 1780; *Pennsylvania Gazette*, Sept. 6, 1780; *Providence Gazette*, Sept. 16, 1780; *Boston Gazette*, Sept. 18, 1780; *Independent Ledger*, Sept. 18, 1780; *Connecticut Courant*, Sept. 19, 1780; *Connecti-*

Gates's letters were in northern papers just as three patriot sentries detained a suspicious man near Tarrytown, New York, who turned out to be John André, the British adjutant general tasked with bringing Benedict Arnold back to the king. Arnold's "infernal and traiterous" attempt to betray West Point in exchange for a British command further exacerbated that "anxiety of mind." The Revolution was in jeopardy: near financial collapse, military failure, a distressed communications network, and a diminished ability to project its side of the argument. Emotions ran high. Arnold's former colleagues lashed out at his character. Crowds in Philadelphia twice paraded an effigy of the former Saratoga hero around the city.[31]

Patriot publicists did their best to turn the shocking news of Arnold to their advantage. As they had with Dr. John Connolly's plot in 1775, they pointed to the discovery of Arnold's treachery as evidence of providence shielding the United States. Paine argued that it showed the "declining power of the enemy." And, as narrated at the beginning of this chapter, several printers sought to destroy his reputation by conflating him with tories, slaves, and Indians as a single "class of British heroes."[32]

But both the plot itself and the impassioned reaction to it—a year later, Shepard Kollock would remark in his *New-Jersey Journal,* "The streets of

cut *Journal,* Sept. 21, 1780; *Continental Journal,* Sept. 21, 1780; *Independent Chronicle,* Sept. 21, 1780; *Massachusetts Spy,* Sept. 21, 1780; *Norwich Packet,* Sept. 21, 1780; *New-Hampshire Gazette,* Sept. 23, 1780. Gates to Congress, August 20: *Pennsylvania Packet,* Sept. 12, 1780; *Pennsylvania Gazette,* Sept. 13, 1780; *New-Jersey Gazette,* Sept. 13, 1780; *Boston Gazette,* Sept. 25, 1780; *Independent Ledger,* Sept. 25, 1780; *Connecticut Courant,* Sept. 26, 1780; *American Journal,* Sept. 27, 1780; *Continental Journal,* Sept. 28, 1780; *Connecticut Journal,* Sept. 28, 1780; *Norwich Packet,* Oct. 3, 1780; *Connecticut Gazette,* Oct. 6, 1780. Gates to Congress (including his letter to GW and list of officers dead, wounded, and missing), August 30: *Pennsylvania Packet,* Sept. 12, 1780; *New-Jersey Gazette,* Sept. 13, 1780; *Independent Ledger,* Sept. 25, 1780; *American Journal,* Sept. 27, 1780; *Independent Chronicle,* Sept. 28, 1780; *Continental Journal,* Sept. 28, 1780; *Providence Gazette,* Sept. 30, 1780; *Norwich Packet,* Oct. 3, 1780; *Massachusetts Spy,* Oct. 5, 1780; *Connecticut Gazette,* Oct. 6, 1780.

31. William Churchill Houston to William Livingston, Philadelphia, Sept. 27, 1780, *LDC,* XVI, 114–116, esp. 114; Royster, *Revolutionary People at War,* 288–292; Knott, *Sensibility and the American Revolution,* 155–157; Benjamin H. Irvin, *Clothed in Robes of Sovereignty: The Continental Congress and the People out of Doors* (New York, 2011), 251–253.

32. [Paine], *The Crisis Extraordinary* (Oct. 4, 1780), in Foner, ed., *Paine: Writings,* 235–252, esp. 252. See Arnold poem above, fn. 1.

every city and village in the United States, for many months, rung with the crimes of General Arnold"—revealed how far patriot fortunes had fallen by October 1780. Not only had the southern army collapsed, but daring raids continued to terrify people on the coasts of New Jersey and the frontiers of New York. Despite a premium of space for domestic news at that moment, as it was the height of the Arnold affair, newspapers from Virginia to Massachusetts carried a story of Tye's most ambitious—and final—expedition that October. His attempt to capture a patriot militia officer named Joshua Huddy, an infamous figure to British loyalists who had several times harassed Staten Island, had ended in disaster. Tye and a group of seventy-two men surrounded Huddy's house in the middle of the night to take him by surprise. According to the printed account, "On their entering the house, when they found that none but himself had defended it, and their brave Negro Tye (one of Lord Dunmore's crew) wounded, it was with the greatest difficulty he was prevented from being murdered."[33]

33. "Rung with the crimes": *New-Jersey Journal*, Nov. 21, 1781. See also Royster, *Revolutionary People at War*, 290–294. "Brave Negro Tye": *Pennsylvania Packet*, Oct. 3, 1780; *Maryland Gazette*, Oct. 13, 1780; *Virginia Gazette* (Clarkson & Davis), Oct. 21, 1780; *Independent Ledger*, Oct. 23, 1780; *Providence Gazette*, Oct. 25, 1780. In the spring of 1782, a body of tory partisans initiated another round of raids down the Jersey coast in Monmouth County. One report circulated about a "party of refugees, consisting of blacks and whites" who captured more than a dozen people in the swamps until being chased out by patriot militia; the story ran in a dozen papers that February (*Pennsylvania Gazette*, Feb. 13, 1782). A few weeks later, this body of 120 men took their revenge on Huddy, taking him prisoner and transporting him back to New York. Three weeks after his capture, loyalist leaders in New York got permission to carry Huddy back to New Jersey and hang him from a tree until astonished passersby cut him down. This incident led to one of the most important sideshows of 1782, for it touched off a cycle of retribution and retaliation that soon involved Washington, Tom Paine, Congress, an unfortunate nineteen-year-old British captain, and, eventually, Marie Antoinette.

The details related in patriot newspapers about Huddy's execution, however, are relevant here. Just as the fictional Major Cudjo continued to redound through patriot prints over several years, so the name of Colonel Tye endured—even though he was real, if two years dead. Ridding New Jersey of Tye was the achievement outraged patriots held up as the cornerstone of Huddy's heroism. Huddy was, according to a correspondent to the *New-Jersey Gazette*, "one of the bravest of men" because he killed "the famous negro *Tye*, justly much more to be feared and respected, as an enemy, than any of this brethren of the fairer complexion." Huddy became a touchstone for patriot fury. The anger expressed by New Jersey patriots, and amplified by publicists,

"This Class of Britain's Heroes"

At that same time, reports circulated about the "motley allies of Great-Britain"—men under Joseph Brant and John Johnson—who had destroyed Canajoharie (in August) and Schoharie (in October), villages on the Mohawk one hundred miles northwest of West Point, killing many women and children. One correspondent, echoing Wyoming, described for readers in ten papers "scenes which I beheld are not to be equalled by any thing I ever saw" as he observed the damage caused by "his Brittanic Majesty's savage Allies" at Canajoharie.[34]

------

was particularly concentrated because of Huddy's credentials as a killer of British proxies. If men proved themselves effective against those who took up the king's standard—especially outstanding enemies who were "feared and respected"—they were seen as essential to the common cause. His association with armed blacks raiding and plundering the Jersey coast initiated the firestorm that eventually became an international issue. For references to Huddy as Tye's killer: *New-Jersey Gazette*, Apr. 24, 1782; *Pennsylvania Journal*, May 1, 1782; *Pennsylvania Packet*, May 2, 1782; *Maryland Journal*, May 7, 1782; *Independent Ledger*, May 13, 1782; *Massachusetts Spy*, May 16, 1782; *Connecticut Journal*, May 16, 1782; *Connecticut Gazette*, May 17, 1782; *Providence Gazette*, May 18, 1782; *Boston Evening-Post*, May 25, 1782; *Salem Gazette*, May 30, 1782. For more on the Huddy episode, see Maya Jasanoff, *Liberty's Exiles: American Loyalists in the Revolutionary World* (New York, 2012), 64–65; Edwin G. Burrows, *Forgotten Patriots: The Untold Story of American Prisoners during the Revolutionary War* (New York, 2008), 180–183; Knott, *Sensibility and the American Revolution*, 184–188; Harry M. Ward, *Between the Lines: Banditti of the American Revolution* (Westport, Conn., 2002), 63–67; L. Kinvin Wroth, "Vengeance: The Court-Martial of Captain Richard Lippincott, 1782," in Howard H. Peckham, ed., *Sources of American Independence: Selected Manuscripts from the Collections of the William L. Clements Library*, 2 vols. (Chicago, 1978), II, 499–612.

34. "Motley allies": *New York Packet*, Aug. 17, 1780; *Independent Chronicle*, Aug. 24, 1780; *New-Hampshire Gazette*, Aug. 26, 1780; *Providence Gazette*, Aug. 26, 1780; *Pennsylvania Packet*, Sept. 12, 1780. Another account listing the damage at Canajoharie in *New York Packet*, Sept. 7, 1780; *New-York Journal*, Sept. 11, 1780; *Pennsylvania Packet*, Sept. 12, 1780; *Connecticut Courant*, Sept. 12, 1780; *New-Jersey Gazette*, Sept. 13, 1780; *Independent Chronicle*, Sept. 14, 1780; *Continental Journal*, Sept. 14, 1780; *Boston Gazette*, Sept. 18, 1780; *New-Jersey Journal*, Sept. 20, 1780. "His Brittanic Majesty's savage Allies": *Pennsylvania Gazette*, Sept. 20, 1780; *Pennsylvania Packet*, Sept. 23, 1780; *New-Jersey Gazette*, Sept. 27, 1780; *New-Jersey Journal*, Oct. 4, 1780; *Independent Ledger*, Oct. 9, 1780; *American Journal*, Oct. 14, 1780; *Continental Journal*, Oct. 19, 1780; *New-Hampshire Gazette*, Oct. 21, 1780; *Norwich Packet*, Oct. 24, 1780; *Independent Chronicle*, Oct. 26, 1780. Worse, news of violence in the Kentucky settlements also competed with reports about Arnold, Tye, and Brant. Multiple reports detailing 600–700 Indi-

In the fall of 1780, there was little for patriot printers to relate that reflected well on the common cause. Even when they did have positive information from the southern theater, it was often sparse. Failure on several fronts seemed to be the theme of 1780. Small wonder Benedict Arnold deserted what many American readers must have agreed was a collapsing concern. Yet patriot publicists continued to emphasize the role proxies played in the war to try to stanch this increasingly critical ebb of patriotic fervor. They highlighted the work of men like Tye and Brant. So committed to telling stories of British "instigation" when visceral stories were not readily at hand, patriot publicists made some up.

For example, Hall and Sellers printed a shipping invoice in a late November issue of their *Pennsylvania Gazette* that contained some shocking cargo. A "correspondent from the eastward" forwarded to the Philadelphia printers a catalog of "Military Stores shipped by order of John Jenkins, His Majesty's Secretary at War," found on board a captured vessel bound for Quebec. Listed on the invoice were eighteen chests containing 219 muskets and bayonets, 2,190 tomahawks, 3,829 scalping knives, and 1,600 daggers. Accompanying these weapons was a letter from Jenkins to the governor of Canada, but, alas, it was written in cipher. Since "the contents could not be known," this "correspondent" related, "we may easily suppose it to have been to the following purpose." What ensued can only be understood as a fictional interpretation of what such a letter might contain. "Nothing is more near his Majesty's wish, than to take proper methods to put an end to the rebellion," Jenkins wrote. He then instructed the governor that Brant and Johnson's forces needed them most, adding, "It is to be wished they would embarrass your Excellency or themselves with no prisoners, but to put to

----

ans, on orders from Detroit, had broken up settlements and taken several hundred people captive near Licking Creek in Kentucky. Letter from Pittsburgh, Aug. 4: *Pennsylvania Journal*, Aug. 23, 1780; *New-Jersey Journal*, Aug. 30, 1780; *Connecticut Journal*, Aug. 31, 1780; *Connecticut Courant*, Sept. 5, 1780; *Boston Gazette*, Sept. 11, 1780; *American Journal*, Sept. 13, 1780; *Independent Chronicle*, Sept. 14, 1780; *Providence Gazette*, Sept. 16, 1780; *Independent Ledger*, Sept. 18, 1780. Letter from Fort Pitt, Aug. 18: *Pennsylvania Packet*, Sept. 12, 1780; *Pennsylvania Gazette*, Sept. 13, 1780; *Pennsylvania Journal*, Sept. 13, 1780; *New-Jersey Gazette*, Sept. 20, 1780; *Independent Chronicle*, Sept. 28, 1780; *Connecticut Journal*, Sept. 28, 1780; *Providence Gazette*, Sept. 30, 1780; *Norwich Packet*, Oct. 3, 1780; *Connecticut Gazette*, Oct. 6, 1780. Letter from Pittsburgh, 1 September: *Pennsylvania Packet*, Oct. 7, 1780; *New-York Journal*, Oct. 16, 1780; *Maryland Journal*, Oct. 17, 1780; *Maryland Gazette*, Oct. 20, 1780; *Connecticut Courant*, Oct. 24, 1780; *Connecticut Journal*, Oct. 26, 1780; *Connecticut Gazette*, Oct. 31, 1780.

death all without exception. It would be well also to enjoin it on them to put to death with their usual ways of torture, by burning with lighted matches stuck in the body, coals on the head, etc. in order to strike a greater dread on the minds of the rebels." This extraordinary article was a fabrication; not only did the Massachusetts "correspondent" admit that they only surmised what was written in Jenkins's letter, but since it touched every American fear about Indian captivity, warfare, and torture, it was too perfect to have been written by the real secretary at war, who was actually named Charles Jenkinson. A year and a half later, when Benjamin Franklin concocted his own hoax about what he imagined Indians did with those weapons, perhaps he had this shocking "Invoice"—which had appeared in *his* paper—in mind.[35]

However much "truth" there was in this "Invoice," it was symptomatic of patriot publicists' framing of the conflict. This "proof" matched public statements issued by official bodies that reminded Pennsylvanians about "the devastation of our frontiers, the cries of women and children flying in distress before inhuman Savages, and unoffending infants butchered in the presence of their captured parents point to the field." Diligent readers of the *Gazette* had no difficulty putting these two items together; the official address issued by the Pennsylvania Supreme Executive Council decried the horrific violence on the state's frontiers, and the captured, discovered "Invoice" laid bare exactly who was putting those weapons in the enemy's hands. Both were productions—performances that played on terror and fear—but together, they made a convincing argument to maintain the common cause. Even with the war going badly at the end of 1780, with communication networks all but cut off south of Virginia, with generals and enlisted men deserting the army, the theme of describing the Revolution as a desperate fight against multiple agents of tyranny was so deeply embedded that it was nearly automatic by the end of the war's fifth year. The patriot effort to propagate the common cause by defining it as a war against the king and his black and Indian proxies endured.[36]

2: THE ROAD TO YORKTOWN

In the spring of 1780, publishers of both New Jersey newspapers, the *New-Jersey Gazette* and *New-Jersey Journal*, printed Pennsylvania's recently adopted bill of gradual abolition in full. A few months later, just after Colonel Tye's band laid siege to Joshua Huddy's house, three petitions calling for a simi-

35. *Pennsylvania Gazette*, Nov. 22, 1780.
36. Ibid., Aug. 9, 1780.

lar gradual plan were introduced to the New Jersey Assembly, which immediately tabled them. With the petitions postponed, writers submitted several essays for publication to both papers. Throughout the fall and winter of 1780 and 1781, readers were confronted with lively arguments for and against the abolition of slavery in their state. Both sides found room inside the larger common cause argument to justify their claims to strengthen or demolish slavery.

Leading antislavery advocate and Quaker John Cooper published an essay under his own name in former Friend Isaac Collins's paper, stating that Americans must follow the ideals of the Declaration of Independence or else "our words must rise up in judgment against us." But, "Eliobo" countered, where should free blacks go? Emancipated slaves resettled outside New Jersey would immediately revert to savagery, and—"*O horrida bella*"— they would join forces with other proxies. If "200,000 Negroes" joined Indians, they would "sweep our land by outsallies of murder and rapine. Then will the shrieks of murdered children, and the lamentations of assassinated friends . . . force conviction upon us of the evils we have brought upon ourselves, our friends and country." Full of charged language and acrimony, both sides in this newspaper debate drew from the common cause argument. Essays under pseudonyms like "A Whig," "A Lover of True Justice," "A Friend to Justice," and "Impartial" argued for what they thought the Revolution was about: the meaning of equality, property rights, human nature, and, not insignificantly, the threat emancipated slaves posed to the public. On this final point, writers against emancipation forwarded the examples of Tye and other black partisans as compelling evidence for postponing any talk of emancipation until after the war. Their arguments won: the cause of abolition in New Jersey, as it would in New York, had to wait until long after the emergencies of the Revolutionary War had ended.[37]

37. Cooper: *New-Jersey Gazette*, Sept. 20, 1780; *Pennsylvania Gazette*, Oct. 4, 1780. "Eliobo": *New-Jersey Journal*, Dec. 20, 1780. Interestingly, "Eumenes" (Reverend Jacob Green) countered this accusation with a different yet powerful claim that American slaveholders were the real "enemies to what Congress say in their declaration of independency" and are more "liable to be made tools of by our British enemies" (*New-Jersey Journal*, Jan. 10, 1781). For a full discussion of this newspaper debate, see: Zilversmit, *First Emancipation*, 141–146. "A Whig": *New-Jersey Gazette*, Oct. 4, 1780. "A Friend to Justice": *New-Jersey Gazette*, Nov. 8, 1780. "Eliobo": *New-Jersey Journal*, Nov. 29, Dec. 7, 1780. "Eliobo Secundus" (Reverend Jacob Green): *New-Jersey Journal*, Jan. 10, 31, 1781. "Impartial": *New-Jersey Gazette*, Jan. 10, 1781. "Marcus Aurelius": *New-*

"This Class of Britain's Heroes"

To the south, British invasions of the Chesapeake at the end of 1780 gave even more evidence that Americans should treat emancipated slaves as suspicious. As New Jersey writers waged a newspaper war over slavery, in October, General Alexander Leslie and 2,200 troops reprised Sir George Collier and General Edward Mathew's 1779 Chesapeake raid, landing at Portsmouth, Virginia. For several weeks, Leslie's forces ransacked the nearby estates and prepared to march toward Cornwallis's force in North Carolina. Virginia governor Thomas Jefferson believed Leslie's goal was to reach the thousands of British and German prisoners from Burgoyne's army held at Charlottesville. He ordered them moved farther north to Fort Frederick but soon decided to leave the Germans alone, since "From them we have no apprehensions of desertion to the enemy."[38]

Patriot newspapers published accounts of Leslie's invasion, focusing on the commander's willingness to welcome runaway slaves. The *Maryland Journal* reported attackers on the Eastern Shore had "taken off about 300 Negroes." A few papers reported a party of British soldiers' attacking Nathaniel Burwell's house in Isle of Wight County. "Being piloted there by

---

Jersey Journal, Feb. 7, 28, 1781. "A Lover of True Justice": *New-Jersey Gazette,* Feb. 14, 1781. "Homo Sum": *New-Jersey Gazette,* Mar. 21, 1781. "E": *New-Jersey Gazette,* Mar. 14, 1781. "Truth et Justice": *New-Jersey Gazette,* Apr. 11, 1781. A parallel debate in Bradford's *Pennsylvania Journal* also raged during early 1781, as opponents to the emancipation bill began to make their voices known in public. The first statement, made in the January 31 and February 21 issues, was a strong proslavery argument cherishing classical slavery and the biblical allowance for keeping prisoners as bondsmen. He concluded, "Our present circumstances seem to render [abolition] highly imprudent, if not impracticable, on diverse accounts, to enter upon so difficult an affair" (*Pennsylvania Journal,* Feb. 21, 1781 [continuation of a Jan. 31, 1781, essay]). "Liberalis" responded in the Apr. 4, 1781, issue that, by such logic, Americans should have enslaved "country lads, sons of the husbandmen of *Cassel* and *Hanau,* compelled, on that occasion, to enter the regiments and embark for this country. Would it be justifiable to enslave these hessians when they fall into our hands, forced, in this manner, by despotic power, to bear arms?" (*Pennsylvania Journal,* Apr. 4, 1781). Note the pastoral, positive discourse this writer employed to describe the Hessians. This was not his point, but it still employs this rhetoric ("country lads," "sons of husbandmen") and illustrates the way many Americans viewed the German mercenaries by 1781. For more, see Nash and Soderlund, *Freedom by Degrees,* 111–113.

38. John E. Selby, *The Revolution in Virginia, 1775–1783* (Williamsburg, Va., 1988), 220–225; TJ to Thomas Sim Lee, Richmond, Va., Oct. 26, 1780, in *PTJ,* IV, 70–71, TJ to Horatio Gates, Richmond, Va., Nov. 10, 1780, 108–109, esp. 109.

one of his own Negroes," the raiders plundered Burwell's watch "out of his pocket, took all his plate . . . and carried off nine of his Negroes."[39]

Leslie had never intended to stay in Virginia, nor did he have the shipping to carry off all the African Americans who wished to go with him. Nonetheless, his mid-November departure from Portsmouth surprised patriot publicists. A widely circulated letter reported that this development was even more shocking because "the negroes [were] not admitted on board" the evacuating ships. Virginia patriots were not the only ones caught off-guard, for, this writer concluded, "whole legions of negroes on these plains seemed distressed." Patriot leader Edmund Pendleton could hardly believe it, either, writing to James Madison that there was "something Mysterious in their leaving their Slaves on shore," worried that they had "designs of further Hostility" in mind.[40]

This puzzle would be solved just a few weeks later, when, in the last days of that unfortunate year, a second invasion fleet under the command of British general Benedict Arnold entered the Virginia capes. Arnold would stay longer than the previous two raiders, and his range of destruction would also be more widespread. As with much of the commentary surrounding Leslie's hit-and-run raid, newspaper coverage of Arnold's invasion focused on how African Americans responded to yet another British incursion.

Within a week of his arrival in the Chesapeake, Arnold landed troops at the Byrd plantation at Westover on the James River, thirty miles southeast of Richmond. They marched into the capital with little resistance. As one of Governor Jefferson's slaves later remembered, "In ten minutes not a white man was to be seen." They set fire to warehouses and public buildings—a conflagration that consumed one of the two printing presses in the town—and took many slaves, including several of Jefferson's. Arnold's men then re-

39. "Taken off about 300": *Maryland Journal*, Oct. 24, 1780; *Independent Ledger*, Nov. 20, 1780. Burwell raid: *Virginia Gazette* (Clarkson & Davis), Nov. 22, 1780; *Maryland Journal*, Nov. 14, 1780; *Pennsylvania Journal*, Nov. 22, 1780; *Pennsylvania Gazette*, Nov. 22, 1780; *Pennsylvania Evening Post*, Nov. 25, 1780.

40. Edmund Pendleton to James Madison, Virginia, Nov. 27, 1780, *PJM*, II, 208–209, esp. 208. "Distressed": *Virginia Gazette* (Dixon & Nicolson), Nov. 18, 1780; *Maryland Journal*, Nov. 28, 1780; *Pennsylvania Packet*, Nov. 28, 1780; *Pennsylvania Journal*, Nov. 29, 1780; *New-Jersey Gazette*, Dec. 6, 1780; *Connecticut Courant*, Dec. 12, 1780; *Connecticut Journal*, Dec. 14, 1780; *Continental Journal*, Dec. 14, 1780; *Independent Chronicle*, Dec. 14, 1780; *Massachusetts Spy*, Dec. 14, 1780; *American Journal*, Dec. 16, 1780; *Boston Gazette*, Dec. 18, 1780; *Independent Ledger*, Dec. 18, 1780; *New-Hampshire Gazette*, Dec. 18, 1780; *Providence Gazette*, Dec. 20, 1780.

"This Class of Britain's Heroes"

turned to Westover and continued to pillage the nearby estates. According to a contemporary, "The damage sustained by individuals on this occasion is inconceivable, especially in Negroes; the infatuation of these poor creatures was amazing: they flocked to the Enemy from all quarters, even from very remote parts."[41]

News of Arnold's expedition further revealed the weakness of patriot communication networks by 1781. Two weeks into his invasion, patriot leaders in Philadelphia were still skeptical of the information, writing, "We have for several days had reports in town of the appearance of the enemy in James River," but since Baltimore printers had gotten things wrong so often before with "fictitious tales," "no more confidence is now put in a story from Baltimore." Soon, published letters from Virginia appeared, corroborating the news of Arnold's invasion. Nearly all of them explicitly described the reactions of African Americans. Letters from Petersburg that detailed the infamous traitor burning estates on the James River and carrying off slaves appeared in several northern papers. Jefferson's official description to Washington of how the "parricide Arnold" devastated Richmond circulated anonymously in several more. Later reports documented Arnold's "receiving run away negroes," noted his "triumphant" return to New York City with this bounty, and took joy in guessing that the man they publicly declared a savage and slave would be "driven to the old trade of . . . *soul driving*."[42]

41. Isaac, "Memoirs of a Monticello Slave as Dictated to Charles Campbell by Isaac," in James A. Bear, Jr., ed., *Jefferson at Monticello: Memoirs of a Monticello Slave as Dictated to Charles Campbell by Isaac . . .* (Charlottesville, Va., 1967), 7; Michael A. McDonnell, *The Politics of War: Race, Class, and Conflict in Revolutionary Virginia* (Chapel Hill, N.C., 2007), 398–434; Michael Kranish, *Flight from Monticello: Thomas Jefferson at War* (Oxford, 2010), 157–223; Harry M. Ward and Harold E. Greer, Jr., *Richmond during the Revolution, 1775–1783* (Charlottesville, Va., 1977), 80–81; Cassandra Pybus, *Epic Journeys of Freedom: Runaway Slaves of the American Revolution and Their Global Quest for Liberty* (Boston, 2006), 44–45; Robert Honyman, May 11, 1781, in Richard K. MacMaster, ed., "News of the Yorktown Campaign: The Journal of Dr. Robert Honyman, April 17–November 25, 1781," *VMHB*, LXXIX (1971), 387–426, esp. 394. When he recollected several decades later, Isaac Jefferson, one of the slaves taken by Arnold's forces, said that nine of Jefferson's slaves went, too. Pybus disputes this and other high estimates of how many slaves Jefferson and other Virginians claimed in her "Jefferson's Faulty Math: The Question of Slave Defections in the American Revolution," *WMQ*, 3d Ser., LXII (2005), 243–264.

42. Ralph Izard to Richard Henry Lee, Philadelphia, Jan. 16, 1781, MSS, Lee

Leslie and Arnold's invasions posed a significant threat to Virginia's faltering defenses—and Cornwallis was still in North Carolina. The psychological harm these British expeditions inflicted far outweighed actual property damage. The assembly considered collecting a body of slaves from the general public and awarding one to each white volunteer, a redistribution of wealth that reveals the depth of the state's crisis. Virginians who wanted to be rid of slavery, like Quaker Robert Pleasants, hoped this would be the emergency that would bring about emancipation, though Pleasants worried the "plundering parties, with the assistance if not by the instigation of the Negroes" would complicate matters.[43]

In Maryland, the situation was hardly better. A Royal Navy squadron also menaced the upper Chesapeake in the spring of 1781. They went up the Potomac to Alexandria, all the while accepting large numbers of slaves, including seventeen of George Washington's. In May, the Maryland Assembly discussed raising a black regiment of 750 troops drawn from the state's

---

Family Papers, 1638–1867, section 108, folder 5, VHS. Petersburg: *Maryland Journal,* Jan. 23, 1781; *New York Packet,* Feb. 8, 1781; *Connecticut Courant,* Feb. 13, 1781; *Connecticut Journal,* Feb. 15, 1781; *Connecticut Gazette,* Feb. 16, 1781; *Providence Gazette,* Feb. 17, 1781; *American Journal,* Feb. 17, 1781; *Pennsylvania Packet,* Feb. 27, 1781. "Parricide Arnold": *Virginia Gazette* (Dixon & Nicolson), Jan. 13, 1781; *Pennsylvania Evening Post,* Jan. 25, 1781; *Connecticut Journal,* Feb. 8, 1781; *Independent Chronicle,* Feb. 8, 1781; *Providence Gazette,* Feb. 10, 1781; *American Journal,* Feb. 10, 1781; *Norwich Packet,* Feb. 13, 1781. The original is in TJ to GW, Richmond, Va., Jan. 10, 1781, *PTJ,* IV, 333–335. Arnold's "receiving" slaves: *Maryland Gazette,* Mar. 22, 1781; *Pennsylvania Evening Post,* Mar. 26, 1781; *Pennsylvania Journal,* Mar. 28, 1781; *Pennsylvania Gazette,* Mar. 28, 1781; *Connecticut Courant,* Apr. 10, 1781; *Connecticut Journal,* Apr. 12, 1781; *Norwich Packet,* Apr. 12, 1781; *American Journal,* Apr. 14, 1781; *Newport Mercury,* Apr. 14, 1781; *Providence Gazette,* Apr. 14, 1781; *Independent Ledger,* Apr. 16, 1781. Arnold the "soul-driver" in NYC: *Pennsylvania Packet,* June 19, 1781; *Freeman's Journal* (Philadelphia), June 20, 1781; *New-Jersey Gazette,* June 27, 1781; *New York Packet,* June 28, 1781; *Connecticut Courant,* July 3, 1781; *Connecticut Journal,* July 5, 1781; *Continental Journal,* July 5, 1781; *Independent Chronicle,* July 5, 1781; *Norwich Packet,* July 5, 1781; *Connecticut Gazette,* July 6, 1781; *Newport Mercury,* July 7, 1781; *American Journal,* July 7, 1781; *Providence Gazette,* July 7, 1781; *Vermont Gazette, or, Green-Mountain Post-Boy* (Westminster), July 9, 1781. "Soul-driver" is an eighteenth-century term for a slave trader.

43. McDonnell, *Politics of War,* 400; L. Scott Philyaw, "A Slave for Every Soldier: The Strange History of Virginia's Forgotten Recruitment Act of 1 January 1781," *VMHB,* CIX (2001), 367–386; Robert Pleasants to Samuel Pleasants, Curles, February 1781, in Robert Pleasants Letterbook, 1771–1781, MSS, Swem.

"This Class of Britain's Heroes"

largest slaveholders. But, again, even in these moments of extreme emergency in the Chesapeake, patriot policymakers were unable to overcome their prejudices.[44]

April brought a new commander and reinforcement to Portsmouth. General William Phillips, who had been one of Burgoyne's officers captured by Arnold at Saratoga, now relieved his former foe. Together, Phillips, Arnold, and their 4,500 British and German troops wreaked havoc on tidewater Virginia. In late April, they occupied Williamsburg and again drove up the James to threaten Richmond, forcing the governor, council, and assembly to flee to Charlottesville. More important, their success convinced Cornwallis to bring his 7,000 men out of the Carolinas to join forces. In mid-May, Cornwallis sent the 500 slaves that were attached to his army to Edenton, and crossed into Virginia. By the end of the month, all British forces had linked up at Petersburg, though neither Phillips (who died of fever on May 15) nor Arnold (who was sent back to New York) would see Cornwallis take command. For patriot military leaders, Cornwallis's abandoning a "Country he had been two years fighting" seemed inexplicable. "And for what? The Question is easily Answered," Virginia general George Weedon opined: "To steal Negroes and burn a few [hogsheads of] Tobacco."[45]

From early June through the rest of summer, Virginia planters wrote about the chaos this huge British army inflicted on their plantations. They summarized in private correspondence: "Negroes gone to the Enemy numerous . . . Tories appear with as confident smiles." Another guessed that the British had "carried off with them many thousand negroes—the uncer-

44. Frey, *Water from the Rock*, 160–161; John Skinker to TJ, Boyd's Hole, Md., Apr. 11, 1781, *PTJ*, V, 406–407, George Weedon to TJ, Fredericksburg, Va., Apr. 21, 1781, 529–530. Maryland's considering a black regiment: Benjamin Quarles, *The Negro in the American Revolution* (Chapel Hill, N.C., 1961), 56–57; Charles Carroll of Carrollton to Charles Carroll of Annapolis, June 4, 1781, in Ronald Hoffman, Sally D. Mason, and Eleanor S. Darcy, eds., *Dear Papa, Dear Charley: The Peregrinations of a Revolutionary Aristocrat, as Told by Charles Carroll of Carrollton and His Father, Charles Carroll of Annapolis . . .* , 3 vols. (Chapel Hill, N.C., 2001), III, 1442–1445. Maryland delegate to Congress Daniel of St. Thomas Jenifer argued, "Drafting [of] Blacks is a serious Question . . . those not drafted will be miserable, and probably will fly to the Enemy" (Daniel of St. Thomas Jenifer to John Hall, Philadelphia, June 11, 1781, *LDC*, XVII, 309).

45. General Jethro Sumner to Nathanael Greene, Williamsboro, N.C., May 18, 1781, *PNG*, VIII, 284, George Weedon to Greene, Fredericksburg, July 27, 1781, IX, 91.

tainty of that property is so great that I shall defer binding the boys till the enemy leaves us." "The great scene of action" was Virginia, one delegate to Congress urged Washington, worrying about the low ebb of patriotism in the Old Dominion. Richard Henry Lee was even more concerned. "Every thing [is] in the greatest possible confusion," and Virginia's patriots were "dispersed, unarmed, and [in an] unadvised condition; without government . . . render[ing] them an easy prey" to Cornwallis.[46]

Lee, too, begged for Washington to march to the rescue. But, in a postscript, he offered a different prescription. "By the Delegates who have returned from Charlottesville it is supposed that the last remaining press in this Country has been taken by the Enemy." The British invasion of Richmond had silenced Dixon and Nicolson's *Virginia Gazette;* there would not be another Richmond paper until the last weeks of 1781. "I reckon the want of a press here a most essential injury to our Cause and Country," Lee submitted. "Should the commander in chief come here . . . he will find himself much distressed for want of a press thro' which to communicate his desires to the People." More than the lack of soldiers volunteering to fight, Lee emphasized that "every nerve . . . be strain'd to get a press" into Virginia, "the People being now destitute of information and left a prey to Tory lies and bad influences." Lee, who had been at the confluence of patriot policymaking and communication since the war began, believed the vacuum of patriot print contributed to the lack of militia turnout. That Lee made this plea just a month before southern commander Nathanael Greene also schemed to get a patriot press for the Carolinas reinforces patriot leaders' view of types as an essential weapon of war. In the South, Greene and Lee knew, they were losing this part of the war, too; even Virginia, where they had maintained solid organs in Richmond and Williamsburg, was now lost for patriot propagation.[47]

The first week of June, Cornwallis sent detachments under John Simcoe

46. William Withers to St. George Tucker, May 20, 1781, reel 3, Francis [Randolph] Tucker to Theodorick Bland, June 4, 1781, reel 3, both in Tucker-Coleman Papers, Swem; Joseph Jones to GW, Philadelphia, June 20, 1781, *LDC*, XVII, 336–338, esp. 338; Richard Henry Lee to the Virginia Delegates in Congress, Chantilly, June 12, 1781, *PTJ*, VI, 90–93, esp. 91.

47. Richard Henry Lee to the Virginia Delegates in Congress, Chantilly, June 12, 1781, *PTJ*, VI, 90–93, esp. 92; Harry M. Ward and Harold E. Greer, Jr., *Richmond during the Revolution, 1775–1783* (Charlottesville, Va., 1977), 53–54, 80–83.

and Banastre Tarleton in several directions to disrupt patriot networks, the latter almost capturing the governor at Monticello. Several American units were not far away, though. Lafayette's troops, including Anthony Wayne's 750 Pennsylvanians, three brigades of Virginia militia, and a new unit of freshly recruited Virginia Continentals, totaling 4,500 men, pushed Cornwallis to the east. Soon Lafayette had Cornwallis pinned against the Chesapeake Bay. "If he catches his Lordship, and his Negro stealing myrmidons," Richard Henry Lee said of Lafayette, "he shall be my Magnus Apollo."[48]

Hearing of Lafayette's efforts, and then news that the French fleet under Admiral François Joseph Paul de Grasse was also sailing to the bay, Washington ordered the main body of the Continental army to march south as stealthily as possible, with the French Army under the comte de Rochambeau not far behind. De Grasse's victory over the British navy left the French in command of the Chesapeake and Cornwallis without a route of escape. A few weeks later, Washington, Rochambeau, and 16,000 troops arrived in Williamsburg, having completed a 450-mile march in five weeks.[49]

With the British trapped "handsomely in a pudding bag," as one American officer put it, the siege of Yorktown lasted from October 6 to October 19, when Cornwallis surrendered and the band played "The World Turned Upside Down." The details of this famous encounter do not need to be retold here. To read patriot newspapers as the Continental army marched into tidewater Virginia, however, one would not get the sense that many public opinion leaders grasped the significance of what was about to occur.[50]

Again, the "everydayness" of the Revolution mattered then, and matters now, to understanding this experience. Just as it is unexpected that Washington took time to write letters to Indians on the eve of the 1776 Christmas attack on Trenton—or, to take a more proximate example, that Governor Jefferson would distract himself by drafting a speech to convince a representative of the Kaskaskia Indians to reject British offers just days after being chased from Richmond and while Tarleton galloped toward Monticello—so

48. Ward, *War of the Revolution*, II, 847; Kranish, *Flight from Monticello*, 283–293; Richard Henry Lee to Nathanael Greene, Chantilly, Sept. 3, 1781, *PNG*, IX, 288.

49. Middlekauff, *Glorious Cause*, 582–584.

50. George Weedon to Nathanael Greene, Fredericksburg, Va., Sept. 5, 1781, in Henry Steele Commager and Richard B. Morris, eds., *The Spirit of 'Seventy-Six: The Story of the American Revolution as Told by Participants*, 2 vols. (Indianapolis, 1958), II, 1218.

the news columns of patriot papers from August to October 1781 contain a surprise.[51]

Although historians might assume American attention would concentrate on Cornwallis and Virginia in the weeks before Yorktown, the exchange system actually brought to prominence the fate of a small number of individuals on the New York frontier. On August 13, just as the French Army under General Rochambeau joined Washington in White Plains, New York, John Holt published a harrowing account about a "sculking Party from Canada" in his newly revived *New-York Journal.* This "Party" consisted of two British regulars and six men acting just like Indians, who attacked the house of John James Bleecker, Esq., a magistrate of a village twenty-five miles north of Albany. Though surely of great consequence for Bleecker, in the face of what was about to unfold in the Chesapeake, this would seem a nonevent. Modern readers might expect notice of Washington and Rochambeau's sudden move to the south—especially since the combined French and American force marched through New Jersey, Pennsylvania, and Maryland, where patriots maintained active newspapers—with the prospect of ensnaring another British army in the offing. Yet it was news of assaults on families like the Bleeckers that garnered far more space in patriot newspapers at that moment.[52]

Further, in mid-September, half of the patriot printers circulated a letter from a gentleman in Albany that related a "most extraordinary piece of bravery, that should be told to the world," performed by "his *Most Sacred Majesty's* savage subjects." These enemies had entered the house of the Feitz family, near Schoharie, and killed a man and his wife, "both of them at least 70 years of age, his son's wife and 5 children—his son being a Captain of the militia, was kept alive to be an eye and ear-witness to the horrid cruelties perpetrated on his dear relatives." "Surely Heaven will be avenged on such a people as this!" the correspondent exclaimed. The account of the Feitz family is intriguing not only because it invokes an increasingly popular term—"His Majesty's Savage Subjects"—but also because of the speed of

51. "Speech to Jean Baptiste Ducoigne," Charlottesville, Va., June 1781, *PTJ,* VI, 60–64.

52. *New-York Journal,* Aug. 13, 20, 1781; *Connecticut Courant,* Aug. 21, 1781; *Connecticut Gazette,* Aug. 24, 1781; Providence Gazette, Aug. 25, 1781; *Independent Ledger,* Aug. 27, 1781; *Pennsylvania Packet,* Aug. 28, 1781; *Pennsylvania Gazette,* Aug. 29, 1781; *Pennsylvania Journal,* Aug. 29, 1781; *New-Jersey Gazette,* Aug. 29, 1781; *Connecticut Journal,* Aug. 30, 1781; *New-Jersey Journal,* Sept. 5, 1781; *Massachusetts Spy,* Sept. 6, 1781.

its circulation: ten papers recopied this story within one week. In all, fourteen papers exchanged this terrible anecdote. As it had throughout the war, the frontier loomed large in newspaper columns, even as Washington's men began the siege of Yorktown. Patriot printers focused equally on the late October engagements between Colonel Marinus Willet's rangers and Major John Ross's British-Indian force on the scorched earth near Stone Arabia, New York, as they did on stories emerging from the Chesapeake.[53]

53. Feitz: *New York Packet*, Sept. 13, 1781; *New-York Journal*, Sept. 17, 1781; *Connecticut Courant*, Sept. 18, 1781; *Pennsylvania Packet*, Sept. 18, 1781; *New-Jersey Journal*, Sept. 19, 1781; *Pennsylvania Gazette*, Sept. 19, 1781; *Pennsylvania Journal*, Sept. 19, 1781; *Massachusetts Spy*, Sept. 20, 1781; *Norwich Packet*, Sept. 20, 1781; *Connecticut Journal*, Sept. 20, 1781; *Newport Mercury*, Sept. 22, 1781; *Pennsylvania Evening Post*, Sept. 24, 1781; *Independent Ledger*, Oct. 1, 1781. On October 24 and 26, 1781, Willet and Ross had two battles, the second of which took the life of Captain Walter Butler. Samuel Loudon reprinted accounts of them in the Nov. 1 and 8, 1781, issues of his *New York Packet*, the former of which also contained news of the "GLORIOUS VICTORY" at Yorktown. Even though Willet's engagements occurred a week after Cornwallis's surrender, it was faster to get information from the Hudson into the patriot communication network than from Virginia, and these stories competed for space with actual details from Yorktown.

First battle: *New York Packet*, Nov. 1, 1781; *Pennsylvania Gazette*, Nov. 7, 1781; *Norwich Packet*, Nov. 8, 1781; *Connecticut Journal*, Nov. 8, 1781; *Independent Chronicle*, Nov. 8, 1781; *Pennsylvania Packet*, Nov. 8, 1781; *Connecticut Gazette*, Nov. 9, 1781; *Boston Evening-Post*, Nov. 10, 1781; *Newport Mercury*, Nov. 10, 1781; *Providence Gazette*, Nov. 10, 1781; *Pennsylvania Journal*, Nov. 10, 1781; *Boston Gazette*, Nov. 12, 1781; *Pennsylvania Evening Post*, Nov. 12, 1781; *Salem Gazette*, Nov. 15, 1781; *Norwich Packet*, Nov. 15, 1781; *Providence Gazette*, Nov. 17, 1781; *New-Hampshire Gazette*, Nov. 17, 1781; *Independent Ledger*, Nov. 19, 1781.

Second Willet-Ross battle: *New York Packet*, Nov. 8, 1781; *New-Jersey Journal*, Nov. 14, 1781; *New-Jersey Gazette*, Nov. 14, 1781; *Continental Journal*, Nov. 15, 1781; *Connecticut Journal*, Nov. 15, 1781; *Independent Chronicle*, Nov. 15, 1781; *Salem Gazette*, Nov. 15, 1781; *Massachusetts Spy*, Nov. 15, 1781; *Norwich Packet*, Nov. 15, 1781; *Connecticut Gazette*, Nov. 16, 1781; *Providence Gazette*, Nov. 17, 1781; *New-Hampshire Gazette*, Nov. 17, 1781; *Independent Ledger*, Nov. 19, 1781; *Boston Gazette*, Nov. 19, 1781; *Maryland Journal*, Nov. 20, 1781. Lord Stirling (William Alexander) forwarded Willet's narrative of these battles one week later, which was then published in eleven more papers: Marinus Willet to Stirling, Fort Rensselaer, Nov. 2, 1781, *Pennsylvania Packet*, Nov. 15 and 17, 1781; *Pennsylvania Journal*, Nov. 17, 1781; *Pennsylvania Evening Post*, Nov. 17, 1781; *Pennsylvania Gazette*, Nov. 21, 1781; *New-Jersey Gazette*, Nov. 21, 1781; *New-Jersey Journal*, Nov. 28, 1781; *Independent Chronicle*, Nov. 29, 1781; *Salem Gazette*, Nov. 29,

The substantial coverage patriot newspapers gave Indians and their British instigators while Washington and Rochambeau trapped Cornwallis illustrates not only the continued power of the frontier and the interpretative freight those stories carried but also the importance of paying attention to the small print, the stories on the inside of the weekly newspapers. For readers throughout New England and the mid-Atlantic, the stories of John Bleecker and the Feitz family underscored British crimes as much as Cornwallis's invasion did. Focusing on the power of seemingly insignificant images recovers a discourse that was self-evident in 1781 but has been forgotten since. Another example of those insignificant images came in the form of a passing sentence that Dr. John Connolly had been captured during the siege. Readers did not need reminding who that person was, and nearly 80 percent of patriot printers exchanged a letter from an army officer without any explanation. It simply stated, "Lieut. Col. John Conolly was taken near York-Town by two militia men, and is paroled to Hanover in Virginia."[54]

————

1781; *New-York Journal*, Dec. 3, 1781; *Connecticut Journal*, Dec. 12, 1781; *Norwich Packet*, Dec. 12, 1781.

54. *Freeman's Journal* (Philadelphia), Oct. 8, 1781; *Pennsylvania Evening Post*, Oct. 8, 1781; *Pennsylvania Packet*, Oct. 9, 1781; *Pennsylvania Gazette*, Oct. 10, 1781; *Pennsylvania Journal*, Oct. 10, 1781; *New-Jersey Journal*, Oct. 10, 1781; *New-Jersey Gazette*, Oct. 10, 1781; *Connecticut Courant*, Oct. 16, 1781; *Connecticut Journal*, Oct. 18, 1781; *Massachusetts Spy*, Oct. 18, 1781; *Independent Chronicle*, Oct. 18, 1781; *Salem Gazette*, Oct. 18, 1781; *Connecticut Gazette*, Oct. 19, 1781; *Boston Evening-Post*, Oct. 20, 1781; *Providence Gazette*, Oct. 20, 1781; *Newport Mercury*, Oct. 20, 1781; *New-Hampshire Gazette*, Oct. 20, 1781; *New-York Journal*, Oct. 22, 1781; *Independent Ledger*, Oct. 22, 1781. Connolly had been held in a Philadelphia prison from his arrest in December 1775 through a prisoner exchange in October 1780, the longest term of incarceration among all conspirators. Connolly went to New York City to negotiate a new command and, just as Thomas Gage had done in 1775, Sir Henry Clinton sent him back to Virginia to gain Cornwallis's permission to join John Johnson in encouraging Indian attacks across the frontier. He was captured, as St. George Tucker noted in his Yorktown diary, on September 24 by "2 or 3 York county men, who met with him as he was taking an airing on the Hampton road" (St. George Tucker, Yorktown journal, Oct. 15, 1781, 5, Tucker-Coleman Papers, Swem). Another Yorktown diarist, Captain Benjamin Bartholomew of the Pennsylvania Continentals, also noted his capture in his journal; see Benjamin Bartholomew Diary, Sept. 24, 1781, 64, MSS, VHS. For Connolly's efforts to revive his old plot, see Connolly to Cornwallis, 1781, Cornwallis Papers, 1614–1854, 30/11/5, folio 11–16, National Archives. For British discussion of Con-

"This Class of Britain's Heroes"

Just as historians blithely pass over terse sentences like these about John Connolly, John James Bleecker, or the Feitz family, so, too, was there another powerful, forgotten—or perhaps misplaced—story that emerged from the Yorktown siege. As readers of patriot newspapers knew well, there was more to the story at Yorktown than the accuracy of American and French cannonballs or the maneuvers of British redcoats. A tragedy lay inside this stunning victory, a fact better understood by contemporaries than the generations that followed.

Newspaper articles emanating from Yorktown consistently and pointedly described the presence, treatment, and future of what one patriot officer described as a "vast Concourse of runaway Negroes" that accompanied Cornwallis's army. In a strange circularity, those thousands of hopeful runaways ended the Revolutionary War in Virginia in a similar place and situation as many of their peers began it. They also faced many of the same accusations and epithets that were hurled in 1775. And, tragically, many hundreds of them would experience suffering along the York similar to that endured by hundreds of other Virginia slaves on Gwynn's Island six years before and two dozen miles away.[55]

In early August, a letter from Hampton, Virginia, enjoyed wide coverage in more than half of active patriot papers. Reporting that Cornwallis's forces had crossed the James River on their way to Yorktown, the correspondent noted, "Our negroes flock fast to them, and ease the soldiery of the labourer's work." "Many persons in Virginia, with large fortunes," he added, "are totally ruined. The inhabitants in our county have not, as yet, suffered much (only in the loss of some negroes) but I fear the time of our distress is drawing near." Soon, when Cornwallis's men began digging trenches at

nolly's revived plot, see Gen. Frederick Haldimand to Gen. Sir Henry Clinton, Quebec, Sept. 29, 1781, in K. G. Davies, ed., *Documents of the American Revolution, 1770– 1783*, Colonial Office Series, XX, *Transcripts, 1781* (Dublin, 1972–1981), 233–236. For patriot knowledge of Connolly's revived plot, see GW to the President of Congress, New Windsor, Apr. 25, 1781, in John C. Fitzpatrick, ed., *The Writings of George Washington: From the Original Manuscript Sources, 1745–1799*, 39 vols. (Washington, D.C., 1931–1944), XXI, 503–504; William Grayson to George Weedon, Philadelphia, May 1, 1781, Allyn Kellogg Ford Collection of Historical Manuscripts, microfilm, reel 2, fol. 620, Minnesota Historical Society, Saint Paul.

55. Josiah Parker to Marquis de Lafayette, Portsmouth, Aug. 19, 1781, in Stanley J. Idzerda, ed., *Lafayette in the Age of the American Revolution: Selected Letters and Papers, 1776–1790*, IV, *April 1, 1781–December 23, 1781* (Ithaca, N.Y., 1981), 334–336, esp. 334.

Yorktown, reports noting black assistance circulated. Another account from Baltimore claimed Cornwallis's 5,000 men were erecting strong works at Yorktown "in which they were aided by the labours of 3000 Negroes." A few weeks later, a letter from Philadelphia described the exact makeup of Cornwallis's force. This one, long paragraph with blunt sentences became the standard account and was exchanged by nearly all patriot papers: "1000 armed negroes" were among Cornwallis's force. Apparently, blacks at Yorktown were doing more than digging.[56]

How Cornwallis treated these black refugees became another topic of debate. As they had in 1775 when they suggested Dunmore's proclamation would lead to much greater suffering for enslaved people, patriots broadcast stories of immense hardship among the African Americans taking refuge in Cornwallis's lines. Philadelphia papers reported that the general had restricted blacks in his lines to rations of horseflesh. News that smallpox was prevalent among the runaways recalled five-year-old rumors of Dunmore's wantonly spreading disease. Indeed, smallpox had been a problem for the British in Virginia since midsummer. One planter described to his wife the distress in Williamsburg: "The Enemy having eat them out of House and Home and carried off almost every negro in the place, to that they

---

56. "Distress is drawing near": *Maryland Journal*, Aug. 14, 1781; *Pennsylvania Gazette*, Aug. 22, 1781; *Pennsylvania Packet*, Aug. 23, 1781; *New-Jersey Journal*, Aug. 29, 1781; *Connecticut Courant*, Sept. 4, 1781; *Connecticut Journal*, Sept. 6, 1781; *Independent Chronicle*, Sept. 6, 1781; *New York Packet*, Sept. 6, 1781; *Massachusetts Spy*, Sept. 6, 1781; *Connecticut Gazette*, Sept. 7, 1781; *Newport Mercury*, Sept. 8, 1781; *Providence Gazette*, Sept. 8, 1781; *Independent Ledger*, Sept. 10, 1781; *Norwich Packet*, Sept. 13, 1781. "Aided by the labours": *Maryland Journal*, Aug. 21, 1781; *Pennsylvania Evening Post*, Aug. 27, 1781; *Pennsylvania Packet*, Aug. 28, 1781; *Freeman's Journal* (Philadelphia), Aug. 29, 1781; *New-Jersey Journal*, Sept. 5, 1781. Edmund Pendleton referred to Cornwallis's diggers as a "swarm of Negroes busily employed in intrenching and Fortifying" (Pendleton to James Madison, Virginia, Sept. 10, 1781, in David John Mays, ed., *The Letters and Papers of Edmund Pendleton, 1734–1803*, 2 vols. [Charlottesville, Va., 1967], I, 371). "1000 armed negroes": *Freeman's Journal* (Philadelphia), Oct. 8, 1781; *Pennsylvania Evening Post*, Oct. 8, 1781; *Pennsylvania Packet*, Oct. 9, 1781; *Pennsylvania Gazette*, Oct. 10, 1781; *Pennsylvania Journal*, Oct. 10, 1781; *New-Jersey Journal*, Oct. 10, 1781; *New-Jersey Gazette*, Oct. 10, 1781; *Connecticut Courant*, Oct. 16, 1781; *Connecticut Journal*, Oct. 18, 1781; *Independent Chronicle*, Oct. 18, 1781; *Salem Gazette*, Oct. 18, 1781; *Connecticut Gazette*, Oct. 19, 1781; *Boston Evening-Post*, Oct. 20, 1781; *Providence Gazette*, Oct. 20, 1781; *Newport Mercury*, Oct. 20, 1781; *New-Hampshire Gazette*, Oct. 20, 1781; *New-York Journal*, Oct. 22, 1781; *Independent Ledger*, Oct. 22, 1781.

have added the Small Pox which is so universally dispersed there, that not a House in Town is clear of it." In late June, a soldier in Lafayette's army wrote in his diary about "some villany" he observed:

> Within these days past, I have marched by 18 or 20 Negroes that lay dead by the way-side, putrifying with the *small pox.* How such a thing came about, appears to be thus: The Negroes here being much disaffected (arising from their harsh treatment), flock'd in great numbers to Cornwallis, as soon as he came into these parts. This artful general takes a number of them (several hundreds) inoculates them, and just as they are all growing sick, he sends them out into the country where our troops had to pass and repass.

This soldier, a Connecticut blacksmith named Josiah Atkins, attributed guilt to both Virginia slaveowners and British officers. This dual judgment reflects the doubleness of the common cause argument as a whole. Atkins, who had just enlisted in April, was critical of Washington's slaveholding when he passed close by Mount Vernon three weeks earlier. "Alas! That persons who pretend to stand for the *rights of mankind* for the *liberties of society,* can delight in oppression, and that even of the worst kind!" he noted. Yet, now he had witnessed even more sinister behavior in the enemy—"Cornwallisean cruelty. . . . Which is another piece of his conduct that wants a name." He was not comfortable with the hypocritical distance between natural rights and slavery, but Cornwallis's conduct was an evil of a different order.[57]

57. Horseflesh: *Pennsylvania Evening Post,* Sept. 17, 1781; *Pennsylvania Packet,* Sept. 18, 1781; *New-York Journal,* Oct. 1, 1781; *Connecticut Courant,* Oct. 2, 1781. Christopher Marshall noted blacks' being forced to eat horseflesh in his diary on September 19, 1781 (William Duane, ed., *Extracts from the Diary of Christopher Marshall, 1774–1781* [1877; rpt. New York, 1969], 283). Smallpox: Philip Ranlet, "The British, Slaves, and Smallpox in Revolutionary Virginia," *Journal of Negro History,* LXXXIV (1999), 217–226; Elizabeth A. Fenn, *Pox Americana: The Great Smallpox Epidemic of 1775–82* (New York, 2001), 129–133; Christopher Johnston to Susanna (Stith) Johnston, Richmond, July 16, 1781, Miscellaneous Collection, MSS 2 J6507a1, VHS; Steven E. Kagle, ed., *The Diary of Josiah Atkins* (New York, 1975), 32–33 ("lay dead by the way-side), 24–25 ("alas!"), 33 ("Cornwallisean cruelty"). One Hessian officer might have agreed with Atkins's indictment of Cornwallis. "I would just as soon forget to record a cruel happening," he wrote in his journal on October 16. "On the same day of the enemy assault, we drove back to the enemy all our black friends, whom we had taken along to despoil the countryside. We had used them to good advantage and set them free, and now, with fear and trembling, they had to face the reward of their cruel

Other American soldiers also observed this tragedy. General Edward Hand paid particular attention. He wrote a friend from the siege lines that the British "sent out upwards of 2000 Negroes including Women and Children." A few days later, he lamented to the same correspondent, "Almost every thicket affords you the disagreeable prospect of a wretched Negro's carcass brought to the earth by disease and famine — the poor deluded creatures were either so much afraid of the displeasure of their owners that they voluntarily starved to death or were by disease unable to seek sustenance." The day before, St. George Tucker had made a similar notation in his journal, writing that "An immense number of Negroes have died, in the most Miserable manner in York." According to a French officer, "These miserable creatures could be found in every corner, either dead or dying. No one took the trouble to bury them, so you can imagine the infection this must have engendered." One Continental soldier wrote sympathetically, "We saw in the woods herds of Negroes which Lord Cornwallis (after he had inveigled them from their proprietors), in love and pity to them, had turned [them] adrift, with no other recompense for their confidence in his humanity than the smallpox for their bounty and starvation and death for their wages." As in the other accounts, he observed they were "scattered about in every direction, dead and dying."[58]

Printers dedicated a significant amount of coverage to this element of the Yorktown engagement. While the three-week siege raged, many publicists printed accounts that eschewed the considered nuance of Josiah Atkins's judgment and instead placed the blame for this tragedy entirely on Cornwal-

---

masters." See Johann Ewald, *Diary of the American War: A Hessian Journal,* ed. and trans. Joseph P. Tustin (New Haven, Conn., 1979), 335–336.

58. Edward Hand to Dr. Jasper Yeates, Camp before York, Oct. 1, 12, 1781, in Edward Hand Papers, Thomas Addis Emmett Collection, NYPL; Edward M. Riley, ed., "St. George Tucker's Journal of the Siege of Yorktown, 1781," *WMQ,* 3d Ser., V (1948), 375–395, esp. 387; "Journal of Jean-François-Louis, Comte de Clermont-Crèvecœur," in Howard C. Rice, Jr., and Anne S. K. Brown, eds. and trans., *The American Campaigns of Rochambeau's Army, 1780, 1781, 1782, 1783,* 2 vols. (Princeton, N.J., 1972), I, 62–64, esp. 64; Joseph Plumb Martin, *Private Yankee Doodle: Being a Narrative of Some of the Adventures, Dangers and Sufferings of a Revolutionary War Soldier* (Boston, 1962), 241. Dr. Robert Honyman also described hundreds of Negroes turned out in a "most deplorable condition" on October 9, 1781 (MacMaster, ed., "News of the Yorktown Campaign," *VMHB,* LXXIX [1971], 420). French officer quoted in Richard M. Ketchum, *Victory at Yorktown: The Campaign That Won the Revolution* (New York, 2004), 246.

"This Class of Britain's Heroes"

lis's shoulders. Eliding the reasons why the runaways were in his lines in the first place, patriot publicists indicted the general. Several papers reported that Cornwallis had "banished 300 negroes from the garrison" and that the "Negroes have the small-pox raging amongst them violently." This focus on connecting Cornwallis and black refugees would continue for months after the news of his surrender washed over North America.[59]

The morning following Cornwallis's October 19 surrender, Washington dispatched one of his staff, Tench Tilghman, to carry documentation of the great news to Congress. He reached Philadelphia in the middle of the night on Monday, October 22. Tilghman's arrival created such a disturbance in the city that a night watchman—who was German—turned up at Congress president Thomas McKean's house to check on the ruckus. McKean and Tilghman told the watch the news, and he then went about his rounds announcing (as several newspapers would later have it) in a thick German accent, "Basht dree o'—glock, und Gorn—wal—lis isht da—ken!" The first knowledge of the surrender at Yorktown was a verbal announcement made, significantly, by a German friendly to the common cause.[60]

Over the next two days, between street activities that "nearly approached madness" celebrating the news, workers in the city's print shops labored to get this story out. Both the *Pennsylvania Journal* and *Freeman's Journal* were Wednesday publishers, and both employed seldom-used enormous fonts on their front pages to make the still-fresh announcement. *"LAUS DEO!"*

59. "Banished 300 negroes": *Freeman's Journal* (Philadelphia), Sept. 29, 1781 (supplement). "Small-pox raging": *New York Packet,* Sept. 27, 1781; *Massachusetts Spy,* Oct. 4, 1781; *Norwich Packet,* Oct. 4, 1781; *New-Hampshire Gazette,* Oct. 6, 1781; *New York Packet,* Sept. 27, 1781; *Independent Chronicle,* Oct. 4, 1781; *Connecticut Journal,* Oct. 4, 1781; *Continental Journal,* Oct. 4, 1781. On November 7, Francis Bailey's *Freeman's Journal* printed a lengthy Philip Freneau poem entitled "On the Fall of General Earl Cornwallis," which included the following lines:

> Your courage slacken'd as the foe drew nigh—
> Ungrateful wretch, to yield your *favourite band*
> To chains and prisons in a hostile land;
> To the wide world your *Negro friends* to cast,
> And leave your *Tories* to be hang'd at last!

Freeman's Journal (Philadelphia), Nov. 7, 1781; *Boston Gazette,* Dec. 24, 1781.

60. *Freeman's Journal* (Philadelphia), Oct. 24, 1781; *Salem Gazette,* Nov. 8, 1781; *Boston Gazette,* Nov. 12, 1781; *Independent Ledger,* Nov. 12, 1781; *Continental Journal,* Nov. 15, 1781; *Providence Gazette,* Nov. 17, 1781; *Massachusetts Spy,* Nov. 22, 1781.

Francis Bailey's new paper, the *Freeman's Journal,* pronounced across the front page of its October 24 issue. The same day those headlines swept through Philadelphia, a boat arrived in Newport from Virginia that had carried the news to New England. Newspapers in Rhode Island published this maritime report on October 27, and within a couple of days, all of the northern papers had it from this source.[61]

Throughout early November, newspapers carried official letters written by Washington and Lafayette; they included returns of soldiers and stores captured, and, especially, documented celebrations of the news not only in Boston and Philadelphia but also in villages such as New Castle, Pennsylvania, Paxton, Massachusetts, and Newburgh, New York. Inhabitants of the latter "enliven[ed] the entertainment" by hanging and burning Benedict Arnold in effigy again, whereas others expressed their joy via fireworks, illuminations, toasts, and cannon salutes.[62]

But another narrative that emerged in the weeks following the news of

61. Major John Clark, Jr,. to Nathanael Greene, Philadelphia, Oct. 25, 1781, *PNG,* IX, 487; *Pennsylvania Journal,* Oct. 24, 1781; *Freeman's Journal* (Philadelphia), Oct. 24, 1781. DeGrasse's letter to Maryland governor Thomas Sim Lee beat Tilghman to Philadelphia, as well, as *Pennsylvania Evening Post* publisher Benjamin Towne reported in his October 22 issue. Compositors in Bailey's shop were working so hastily that they got their facts wrong—Cornwallis had not been taken on 17th (which would have been the fourth anniversary of Burgoyne's surrender!) but rather on the 19th, and Washington had not captured 5,000 troops but nearly 7,000. Virginia news to Newport: *Newport Mercury,* Oct. 27, 1781; *Providence Gazette,* Oct. 27, 1781; *Boston Gazette,* Oct. 29, 1781; *Continental Journal,* Nov. 1, 1781; *Salem Gazette,* Nov. 1, 1781; *Independent Gazette,* Nov. 1, 1781; *Massachusetts Spy,* Nov. 1, 1781; *Connecticut Gazette,* Nov. 2, 1781; *Boston Evening-Post,* Nov. 3, 1781; *New-Hampshire Gazette,* Nov. 3, 1781.

62. For celebrations in Philadelphia, see *Pennsylvania Evening Post,* Nov. 3, 1781; for Boston, see *Boston Gazette,* Nov. 5, 1781; *Continental Journal,* Nov. 8, 1781; *Independent Chronicle,* Nov. 8, 1781; *Salem Gazette,* Nov. 8, 1781; *Providence Gazette,* Nov. 10, 1781; *New-Hampshire Gazette,* Nov. 10, 1781; *Independent Ledger,* Nov. 12, 1781; *Pennsylvania Gazette,* Nov. 14, 1781; *Newport Mercury,* Nov. 17, 1781. For New Castle, Pennsylvania, see *Pennsylvania Packet,* Nov. 1, 1781; *Providence Gazette,* Nov. 17, 1781. For Paxton, Massachusetts, see *Massachusetts Spy,* Dec. 14, 1781. For Newburgh, New York, see *New York Packet,* Nov. 1, 1781; *Connecticut Courant,* Nov. 6, 1781; *Pennsylvania Gazette,* Nov. 7, 1781; *Connecticut Journal,* Nov. 8, 1781; *Independent Chronicle,* Nov. 8, 1781; *Pennsylvania Packet,* Nov. 8, 1781; *Providence Gazette,* Nov. 10, 1781; *Newport Mercury,* Nov. 10, 1781; *New-Hampshire Gazette,* Nov. 10, 1781; *Boston Gazette,* Nov. 12, 1781.

"This Class of Britain's Heroes"

Cornwallis's surrender was about what had happened to African Americans along the York River. Throughout November and December, several items appeared and circulated in many different locales, each approaching the issue of how Cornwallis had treated African American refugees, especially about smallpox.

After the surrender, "An American Soldier" wrote in the *Maryland Gazette,* "Your lot, my Lord, is really severe, but it is what you have richly merited! Your inhumane treatment to the wretched slaves who fled to you for freedom and protection, is more than sufficient to entitle you to the heaviest calamity." The essayist added a footnote in case Americans had not heard about the slaves' suffering at Yorktown: "Out of the upwards of 2000 slaves who joined Lord Cornwallis's army, upwards of 1500 have perished from disease and famine."[63]

Cornwallis's behavior must "inspire every feeling bosom with horror and resentment," not only for his abuse of the runaways but for another crime: purposely spreading smallpox to white Virginians. "Lord Cornwallis's attempt to spread the small-pox among the inhabitants in the vicinity of York, has been reduced to a certainty, and must render him contemptible in the eyes of every civilized nation, it being a practice as inconsistent with the law of nations and war, as repugnant to humanity." The "certainty" to which An American Soldier referred was probably based on a story that also circulated in the wake of the surrender. This story, which began with Samuel Loudon's *New York Packet* and enjoyed wide coverage, was exchanged under the title "An Anecdote of Lord Cornwallis." Dredging up old memories of Dunmore's barreling up the bodies of diseased runaways, the "Anecdote" claimed that while marching through Brunswick, North Carolina, in May, Cornwallis "ordered great numbers of [blacks] to be innoculated [*sic*] for the small-pox, under his immediate inspection, and sent into all parts of the country round about, by which the infection was communicated throughout Virginia, and killed hundreds of innocent men, women, and children." "This," the writer concluded, "is fact." Josiah Atkins, for one, could testify that he was telling the truth.[64]

63. *Maryland Gazette,* Oct. 25, Nov. 1, 1781; *Pennsylvania Gazette,* Nov. 14, 1781; *New York Packet,* Nov. 22, 1781; *Continental Journal,* Nov. 29, 1781; *Salem Gazette,* Dec. 6, 1781.

64. "Horror and resentment": *Maryland Gazette,* Oct. 25, Nov. 1, 1781. Philip Ranlet has argued these accusations of germ warfare were without merit. Although Alexander Leslie did suggest to Cornwallis in June 1781 that he "distribute" 700

When they were not excoriating Cornwallis for mistreating blacks or trying to wage germ warfare, publicists were lampooning the general by linking him to blacks—healthy or diseased. Just as they had with Burgoyne and Indians, and Dunmore with "Major Cudjo," patriot publicists conflated Cornwallis and slaves.

In fact, more than at any other time during the war, blacks seemingly had something to say after Yorktown. For the first time, publicists began to ventriloquize patriot arguments through black voices. The *Pennsylvania Journal* asked what Cornwallis would hear if he were to "attempt to take a ride into any of those parts of Virginia thro' which he has marched." Bradford imagined the "medley of salutations" sung to Cornwallis: "You murdered my father in cool blood," "You starved my husband," "You burnt my house," and "You stole my negroes." But white Virginians were not the only ones with complaints. Bradford had a black man say: "You tole my wife, poor Hagar—I find him now." Another anecdote that circulated late in 1781 described an encounter between a slave and Cornwallis in Virginia. The general, sounding a familiar note, ordered the black man be shipped to the West Indies, which exasperated the African American:

> Cuffee being whiggishly disposed, and having a kind master, was much affected by the order, and upon leaving the room addressed his Lordship in the following broken language: "Dam you Englishmen—you bring me to dis country, and now God gives me good massa, you send me to de devil in West-Indies—Where your broder Arnold? He take my wife—I wish he no sleep wid him—O! poor negro—poor negro."

---

blacks with smallpox "about the Rebell Plantations," it is not apparent that Cornwallis planned to start an epidemic. This mattered little to Revolutionary publicists. See Ranlet, "Smallpox in Revolutionary Virginia," *Journal of Negro History,* LXXXIV (1999), 218, 224; Fenn, *Pox Americana,* 132; Leslie to Cornwallis, July 1, 1781, Cornwallis Papers, 30/11/6, reel 6, folio 280–281. "Ordered great numbers": *New York Packet,* Nov. 15, 1781; *New-Hampshire Gazette,* Nov. 17, 1781; *Pennsylvania Packet,* Nov. 20, 1781; *Pennsylvania Journal,* Nov. 21, 1781; *Independent Chronicle,* Nov. 29, Dec. 27, 1781; *Continental Journal,* Nov. 29, 1781; *Salem Gazette,* Nov. 29, 1781; *Newport Mercury,* Dec. 1, 1781; *Connecticut Gazette,* Dec. 7, 1781. The anonymous writer in the *Packet* concluded his "Anecdote" with a familiar invocation of American superiority: "By shewing mercy to the *unfortunate,* demonstrate to the world that you are the *brave,* the *generous, true-born* sons of LIBERTY."

To this speech, Cornwallis was "affected to laugh . . . and ordered him immediately out of his sight," the story concluded.[65]

This invention was ostensibly the first time in print that an African American argued on behalf of the patriot cause during the Revolution. Others had argued for them, but their voices had been heretofore largely silent. Patriot publicists had told many stories over the war years that reflected their disposition; account after account of slaves' being passively "carried off" illustrated not only African Americans' rejection of slavery but also slaveholders' inability to comprehend their slaves' ability to make such a choice. For the most part, however, patriot leaders told stories that fused blacks and Britons together as one enemy. They tried to shape this image by constantly putting the two in similar situations and conversations. Before Yorktown, blacks conversing with British officers in dialect had been used in print to complete the transaction.[66]

Suddenly, though, the voices of "whiggish" or "continental" blacks began to appear in print. With indications pointing toward a new phase in the war after Cornwallis's surrender, perhaps Americans now felt safe to celebrate "good" blacks in print. But even this exception underscores the general representation forwarded for half a decade by patriot leaders. The inclusion of the descriptors "honest," "continental," and "Black Whig" suggest that these were not the way most readers thought about African Americans throughout the war years. While French and American troops battled Cornwallis at York, Philadelphia printers Bradford and Hall published a sermon

65. "Medley of salutations": *Pennsylvania Journal*, Oct. 31, 1781; *Freeman's Journal* (Philadelphia), Nov. 7, 1781; *New-Jersey Journal*, Nov. 7, 1781; *Newport Mercury*, Nov. 17, 1781; *Providence Gazette*, Nov. 24, 1781; *Boston Evening-Post*, Nov. 24, 1781; *Independent Ledger*, Nov. 26, 1781; *Boston Gazette*, Nov. 26, 1781; *Salem Gazette*, Nov. 29, 1781; *Norwich Packet*, Nov. 29, 1781; *Connecticut Gazette*, Dec. 7, 1781. "Affected to laugh": *Pennsylvania Journal*, Sept. 1, 1781; *Newport Mercury*, Sept. 22, 1781; *Providence Gazette*, Oct. 6, 1781; *Boston Gazette*, Oct. 9, 1781; *New-Hampshire Gazette*, Nov. 17, 1781; *Virginia Gazette* (Nicolson & Prentis), Jan. 5, 1782.

66. There is one exception. In March 1781, the *Boston Gazette* and the *New-Hampshire Gazette* printed a "Dialogue between Cuffe and Toney about State Affairs." The loyalist Toney debated with Cuffe, who had just returned to Boston from serving in the Continental Army. Cuffe argued many standard patriot arguments: that the British made them slaves, that capturing all the major cities would not end the rebellion, and that the British really wanted to sell them to the West Indies for profits. See *Boston Gazette*, Mar. 12, 1781; *New-Hampshire Gazette*, Mar. 26, 1781.

on the conflict between Britain and America written by "A Black Whig," a piece that restated all the principal arguments of the common cause. "Fear not ye brave sons of Columbia, though some of your brethren the citizens of America have by treachery deserted you and your cause for avaricious purposes, they with their accomplices will never be able to hinder the republican American establishment," wrote this "Black Whig," who, an ostensibly white sponsor wrote in the preface, "has taken the liberty of a citizen, though unacquainted with learned phrases and grammatical questions, to offer this to every son of freedom."[67]

A few publicists now used blacks to make fun of their former sponsors. As it was after Saratoga, even the euphoric afterglow of Cornwallis's surrender revolved around images of British proxies. "A specimen of African humour" documented a conversation on the street between two blacks after news of Cornwallis's defeat. "O! how do Cuffee? You hear about *Corn*wallis?" "No. What about *Corn*wallis?" "Why, General Washington shell off the *Corn*, now he *Cob*wallis." At the same time, a "Bon Mot of an honest Continental Negro" appeared in Massachusetts and circulated through several other papers. "The day on which the American troops at North River fired a *feu de joye* for the capture of Lord Cornwallis's army," the story went, "a scouting party . . . met another party sent out as a relief." "A Negro belonging to the first, call to one in the latter, sa[ying] *Cuffee, whas all dhat firing we hear to-day?* The other replied—*O, my dear soul, nossing tall, only General Burgone had a broder born to-day.*" Here, finally, patriot publicists forwarded a "Continental Negro" to combat Major Cudjo.[68]

67. "A Black Whig," *Sermon, on the Present Situation of the Affairs of America and Great-Britain; Written by a Black, and Printed at the Request of Several Persons of Distinguished Characters* (Philadelphia, 1781), [4], 11, *Early American Imprints*, 12557.

68. "*Cob*wallis": *Independent Chronicle*, Feb. 21, 1782; *New-Hampshire Gazette*, Feb. 23, 1782; *Connecticut Courant*, Feb. 26, 1782; *Massachusetts Spy*, Feb. 28, 1782; *New-Jersey Gazette*, Mar. 6, 1782; *Connecticut Journal*, Mar. 7, 1782. A sergeant in a Massachusetts regiment at Yorktown transcribed a very similar conversation between two African American patriot soldiers the day after the surrender: "Two negroes came near where I was standing, and one said, 'Wot you stop shooting for?' Someone answered, 'We have taken Cornwallis.' The second negro, not hearing the reply, asked his brother blackey, 'Wot they say?' The other replied, 'Who, dey say dey take Cornwallis.' 'No, you dum fool, no Cornwallis, for Washington has picked all de corn off the cob'" (Isaac Glynne Journal, 1775–1781, 21, MSS, AAS). "Scouting party": *Salem Gazette*, Dec. 20, 1781; *New-Hampshire Gazette*, Dec. 22, 1781; *Independent Ledger*, Dec. 24, 1781; *Connecticut Gazette*, Dec. 28, 1781; *Providence Gazette*, Dec. 29, 1781; *Connecti-*

"This Class of Britain's Heroes"

Earlier, while British soldiers lay siege to Charleston, Paul Cuffe, a twenty-one-year-old free African American, argued in a petition to the Massachusetts General Court that "many of our colour (as is well known) have cheerfully entered the field of battle in the defence of the common cause." Cuffe was certainly right that thousands of African Americans participated in the Revolutionary War, but whether that was indeed "well known" was another matter. When a French officer sketched the different types of Continental troops he saw in the American line, he included an African American, a soldier of the Rhode Island regiment. Like the Stockbridge, these black patriots were more than present, but the knowledge of their service was reserved only for eyewitnesses, not faraway readers. African Americans' participation was impossible to deny in person, but the primary conveyance of information, newspapers, did not elaborate for their readers about the various colors of Continental soldiers; only those who saw them marching past understood how integrated Washington's forces truly were. Those who monitored the war's progress via print would have been hard-pressed to assent to Cuffe's statement that blacks supported the common cause.[69]

The presence of black units in the enemy's ranks, on the other hand, was well documented. Patriot newspapers provided mounds of evidence that reified the image of domestic insurrectionists. From Governors Dunmore and Martin through Cornwallis's invasion, they provided reports of slaves by the hundreds and thousands running off their plantations—or, in a construction that more adequately reflected their views, being "stolen" from their masters—and detailed scores of blacks aiding the British army. Despite long-standing publishing standards that mandated an "official silence" about slave insurrections, patriots still published British-incited insurrection scares and celebrated their own ingenuity when they prevented them. In order to indict their enemies and mobilize popular support for the war, they exploited stereotypes, playing with the distance between fictional and actual men. In so doing, they gave those prejudices a new, patriotic salience. By December 1781, after years of such propagation, if those same publicists

cut Journal, Jan. 3, 1782; Pennsylvania Journal, Jan. 5, 1782; Pennsylvania Packet, Jan. 8, 1782; Virginia Gazette (Hayes), Jan. 19, 1782.

69. "Petition of Paul Cuffe and Other Blacks, February 10, 1780," in Roger Bruns, ed., Am I Not a Man and Brother: The Antislavery Crusade of Revolutionary America, 1688–1788 (New York, 1977), 454–456, esp. 454; Charles Patrick Neimeyer, America Goes to War: A Social History of the Continental Army (New York, 1996), 86.

Figure 16. *Sketch of Continental soldiers in Yorktown Campaign. By Jean Baptiste Antoine de Verger. C. 1781. The African American soldier on the far left is a member of the First Rhode Island Regiment, which had several companies of free black soldiers in the Continental Line and saw action at the Yorktown siege. As with Ewald's sketch of the Stockbridge Indian above, artists who witnessed the Continental army documented how diverse the ranks were. But they were the only ones. Unless Americans watched the army march by, they had scarcely any idea that there were hundreds of African American and Indian soldiers serving under Washington's command. Even though the Continental army would be the most integrated army the United States would field until the Vietnam War, most Americans had little knowledge of their service in fighting for the common cause.*
Courtesy of Anne S. K. Brown Military Collection, Brown University Library.

now wanted to put positive words in the mouths of African Americans, they would have to resort to disclaimers, signaling to their readers that these sentiments came from a very unexpected source—an "honest Continental negro."[70]

The context had changed since 1775, but it had not been inverted. Early in 1782, several papers dedicated an entire page to reprint all the provisions of a 1739 treaty negotiated between the English and Jamaican maroon

70. "Official silence": Patricia Bradley, *Slavery, Propaganda, and the American Revolution* (Jackson, Miss., 1998), 133.

"This Class of Britain's Heroes"

slaves. It was first published by Francis Bailey (and picked up by four others) as a rebuttal to British claims that they would not negotiate with America because it would "hurt the pride of the nation to yield to those whom she once called her liege subjects." If the British had allowed themselves to treat with runaway slaves, then they must acknowledge independence. "Americans are . . . *white men*," after all. The Jamaican signer of the 1739 treaty? Captain Cudjoe.[71]

While some printers exchanged that piece, others published another Freneau poem that rendered a "petition" by Lord Dunmore begging forgiveness from the Virginia legislature. It included the following lines:

I missed it some how in comparing my notes,
Or six years ago I had joined with your votes;
Not aided the negroes in cutting your throats.

And Thomas Paine, under his nom de guerre of "Common Sense," returned to the central theme of the Revolution by accusing the king of having "stirred up the Indians on one side, and the Negroes on the other, and invoked every aid of Hell in his behalf." Six years on, the ripples of the Janus-faced narrative of the common cause were still moving along the surface—and still crashing into one another. Attitudes toward blacks' serving in the Continental army had changed over the course of the war, but little was said publicly about that shift. The trope that dominated the discourse at the end of 1781 was still the "Spirit of '76," and that excluded African Americans. Stories had changed somewhat in the public arena too, but not much; in fact, they had receded from the heady days of 1774, when cries for universal freedom were loudest.[72]

71. Cudjoe treaty: *Freeman's Journal* (Philadelphia), Jan. 2, 1782; *Independent Chronicle,* Jan. 31, 1782; *Pennsylvania Journal,* Feb. 13, 1782; *New-Jersey Journal,* Feb. 13, 1783; *Connecticut Gazette,* Apr. 19, 1782.

72. Dunmore "petition": *Freeman's Journal* (Philadelphia), Feb. 13, 1782; *New-Jersey Journal,* Feb. 20, 1782; *Virginia Gazette* (Nicolson & Prentis), Mar. 2, 1782; *Boston Evening-Post,* Mar. 9, 1782; *Massachusetts Spy,* May 2, 1782; "Lord Dunmore's Petition to the Legislature of Virginia" (1782), in Fred Lewis Pattee, ed., *The Poems of Philip Freneau: Poet of the American Revolution,* 3 vols. (Princeton, N.J., 1902–1907), II, 114–116, esp. 115. Paine: *Common Sense, on the King of England's Speech,* Feb. 19, 28, 1782, in Foner, ed., *Paine: Writings,* 287–295, esp. 287, published in: *Pennsylvania Packet,* Feb. 19, 28, Mar. 7, 1782; *Pennsylvania Gazette,* Feb. 20, 27, 1782; *Freeman's Journal* (Philadelphia), Feb. 27, 1782; *Independent Ledger,* Mar. 11, 25, 1782; *Continental Journal,* Mar.

Figure 17. *"Old Cudjoe Making Peace." From R[obert] C. Dallas,* The History
of the Maroons . . . , *2 vols. (London, 1803). Captain Cudjoe was a famous figure in
the eighteenth-century Atlantic, having led the Jamaica maroons to a negotiated peace with
the British crown in 1739. Not only did patriot publicists play with this character in their
representations throughout the war, but, in early 1782, several patriot printers published the
text of Cudjoe's forty-year-old treaty, ridiculing the British for having to release another group
of people they tried to enslave. Courtesy of the John Carter Brown Library at Brown University.*

Tellingly, the most outspoken critic of the slave trade, Anthony Benezet, was all but silent during the Revolutionary War, publishing only one pamphlet in 1778 on several subjects (just one of which was the slave trade). In 1781, his pen returned to life, republishing the slave trade sections of the 1778 pamphlet and writing a new piece, *Short Observations on Slavery*, breaking a deafening silence that had held for six years. The last of these sections of the pamphlet began by quoting the universal phrases of the Declaration and sought to "assist in eradicating the deep rooted prejudice which an education amongst Slaves has planted in many minds." The war years, while Benezet was quiet, had compounded his difficulties in setting American minds straight about abolition. Between 1774 and 1781, he published only twelve pages criticizing slavery; the dictates of union and the common cause muzzled his campaign to get Americans to feel for the "flowing eyes, the heaving brest, or the bleeding sides and tortured limbs of your fellow-creatures." For six crucial years, the leading voice of American abolitionism had censored himself.[73]

Blacks found themselves caught between attitudes that had been roughly, unevenly transformed. The nexus between private values and public discourse was a complex one. This was part of the context in which Quok Walker and Elizabeth Freeman entered Massachusetts's courthouses to secure their freedom late in 1781. One historian has stressed that the force of public opinion convinced the commonwealth's jurists to find on behalf of African American plaintiffs. This interpretation is half right, if a direct

---

14, Apr. 4, 1782; *Norwich Packet*, Mar. 14, 1782; *Massachusetts Spy*, Mar. 16, 1782; *Providence Gazette*, Mar. 16, 30, 1782; *Boston Evening-Post*, Mar. 23, 1782; *Newport Mercury*, Mar. 23, Apr. 6, 1782.

73. [Anthony Benezet], *Serious Considerations on Several Important Subjects . . .* (Philadelphia, 1778), *Early American Imprints*, 15737. This forty-eight-page pamphlet covered religion and war, temperance, and slavery. Benezet dedicated thirteen pages to antislavery, provocatively arguing that slaveowners "partake of the same cup of distress" that the Paxton Boys had inflicted upon Indians in 1763 (29). See [Benezet], *Short Observations on Slavery: Introductory to Some Extracts from the Writing of the Abbe Raynal, on That Important Subject* ([Philadelphia, 1781]), 7 ("planted in many minds"), *Early American Imprints*, 17096; [Benezet], *Notes on the Slave Trade* ([Philadelphia, 1781]), 5 ("flowing eyes"), *Early American Imprints*, 17095. The former was Benezet's introduction to a few extracts by the Abbé Raynal criticizing slavery.

The only exception to this silence is Stephen Hopkins, *A Dialogue Concerning the Slavery of the Africans: Shewing It to Be the Duty and Interest of the American Colonies to Emancipate . . .* (Norwich, Conn., 1776), *Early American Imprints*, 14804.

line is drawn between the ideals espoused by the positive side of the common cause—enshrined in the 1780 Massachusetts constitution as "All men are born free and equal"—and the Walker and Freeman cases that brought slavery to a judicial end in the Bay State. But that leaves out much of the story. Thanks to years of patriot cultivation, fear, outrage, and suspicion about black sympathy for the enemy was also part of public opinion, as were worries that abolition might have a deleterious effect on union. In fact, those very concerns reared again in Pennsylvania during appeals to Walker's case, as proslavery legislators tried (unsuccessfully) to amend their gradual emancipation law to protect the property of southern slaveowners who fled north from British invasions.[74]

As much as devotion to Revolutionary ideals might have been the wedge

74. *The Constitution of the State of Massachusetts, Adopted 1780: With the Amendments Annexed* (Boston, 1822), 5; T. H. Breen, "Making History: The Force of Public Opinion and the Last Years of Slavery in Revolutionary Massachusetts," in Ronald Hoffman, Mechal Sobel, and Fredrika J. Teute, eds., *Through a Glass Darkly: Reflections on Personal Identity in Early America* (Chapel Hill, N.C., 1997), 67–95, esp. 94. Breen argues that public opinion was behind abolition in Massachusetts in 1781, but the preponderance of his evidence for this rests on attitudes expressed in the 1760s, not during the Revolutionary War itself. To be sure, there were multiple locales in Massachusetts where antislavery was an expected outcome of the Revolution, but not everywhere. In the months leading up to Lexington, this commanded far greater assent, even outside New England. But the way the patriots argued for the common cause contributed to a slippage; 1774 would be a high-water mark for public discussion of abolition, especially in legislatures, for the 1770s and early 1780s. Breen further admits that anxiety over violence and criminality was one of the triggers that "provoked doubt—a defensive reaction—among whites already uneasy about slavery" in the years before the Revolutionary War (74). I would argue that, in part because of patriot publicists deploying those worries to serve political ends, similar concerns would have been further entrenched because of the experience and stories of war. For more on the Walker and Freeman (or Mum Bet) cases, see William O'Brien, "Did the Jennison Case Outlaw Slavery in Massachusetts?" *WMQ*, 3d Ser., XVII (1960), 219–241, Arthur Zilversmit, "Quok Walker, Mumbet, and the Abolition of Slavery in Massachusetts," XXV (1968), 614–624; A. Leon Higginbotham, Jr., *In the Matter of Color: Race and the American Legal Process: The Colonial Period* (New York, 1978), 91–98; Joanne Pope Melish, *Disowning Slavery: Gradual Emancipation and "Race" in New England, 1780–1860* (Ithaca, N.Y., 1998), 64–65; Emily Blanck, "Seventeen Eighty-Three: The Turning Point in the Law of Slavery and Freedom in Massachusetts," *New England Quarterly*, LXXV (2002), 24–51; Egerton, *Death or Liberty*, 93–121; Zilversmit, *First Emancipation*, 136.

Walker, Freeman, their sponsors in the African American community, and their legal counselors employed to begin the process of ending slavery in Massachusetts, that strategy did not then translate into blacks' being included in the commonwealth. The ways patriot leaders had played on stereotypes to solidify union narrowed the ability of those creative politicians to envision the opaque concept of citizenship as including African Americans. Even in Massachusetts, the preamble of that state's new 1780 constitution defined the "body politic" as a "voluntary association of individuals: it is a social compact, by which the whole people covenants with each citizen, and each citizen with the whole people." Walker, Freeman, and the dozens of others that earned their freedom—like Paul Cuffe—were not considered part of this body. Instead, they occupied a liminal zone between persons and citizens, an amorphous status that closely resembled proxies.

CHAPTER 8

"The Substance Is Truth"

AFTER YORKTOWN, 1782–1783

Only in hindsight did it become apparent that Yorktown meant the end of the Revolutionary War. Although some suspected that the capture of Cornwallis's army would convince the crown to negotiate a settlement, the patriots could not be sure that future campaigns would not be necessary. As 1782 began, many Americans believed that more riders like Tench Tilghman would be required before the Revolution was secured. They were right. The war was not over when Tilghman began his trek north with news of Cornwallis's surrender. In fact, in some locales, 1782 would be the bloodiest year of the war.

The year after Yorktown witnessed some of the most significant consequences of patriot rhetoric, with the Ohio Valley descending into terrible violence. At the same time, the issue of recovering African American runaways crowded both British and American leaders' agendas as the war wound to a conclusion. Stories that magnified how many slaves the British had "taken" complicated negotiations over the peace treaty in Paris and across the lines between armies in America about what to do regarding the thousands who sought freedom in British-occupied Savannah, Charleston, and New York City. The common cause appeal did not dissipate once Cornwallis surrendered. Just the opposite: with the war all but won, what those stories meant in terms of belonging to the new republic was beginning to emerge.

1: "SCALPS OF UNHAPPY COUNTRY FOLKS":
RHETORIC AND REVENGE IN THE BACKCOUNTRY

In many patriot newspapers, notices of seemingly innocuous occurrences that eventually led to the central event that would wash the Ohio Valley in blood in 1782—the massacre at Gnadenhutten—shared space alongside

[534]

post-Yorktown enthusiasm. While printers exchanged squibs about Cornwallis's mistreatment of blacks, a letter from Fort Pitt explained how, the previous August, a force of British-allied Wyandot Indians had ordered three congregations of Moravian Delaware Indians to leave the Muskingum Valley in eastern Ohio. Angry Wyandot leaders believed the Christianized Delawares were aiding the Americans. The Wyandots had sacked the Delawares' farms and given an ultimatum: relocate or face destruction. The Delaware Indians abandoned Gnadenhutten, Salem, and Schoenbrunn in mid-September; meanwhile, the Wyandots used the Muskingum region as a base from which to launch further attacks on American settlements near Fort Pitt. Yet, because the Delawares had not prepared for their sudden ejection, many returned over the winter to recoup lost crops and supplies.[1]

When Pennsylvanians heard about Delawares back in the Muskingum vicinity, they misinterpreted this as betrayal: their alleged friends were seemingly now supporting the hostile Wyandots. A Wyandot raid that claimed the life of a settler's wife and three children that February convinced some Pennsylvania militiamen to take matters into their own hands. The impulse that had animated the Paxton Boys' vigilantism against the supposedly friendly Conestoga Indians nearly two decades earlier now reappeared. This seeming treachery, mixed with frustration at Fort Pitt commander Daniel Brodhead, who tried to restrain violence and cultivate friendship with the Delawares, led a group of two hundred Washington County militiamen, commanded by David Williamson, to set out for the Muskingum River to find the Moravians, who they suspected harbored Wyandot raiders.[2]

1. *Pennsylvania Packet,* Dec. 22, 1781; *New-Jersey Gazette,* Jan. 2, 1782; *Connecticut Courant,* Jan. 8, 1782; *Norwich Packet,* Jan. 10, 1782; *Boston Evening-Post,* Jan. 12, 1782; *Providence Gazette,* Jan. 12, 1782; *Boston Gazette,* Jan. 14, 1782; *Independent Ledger,* Jan. 14, 1782; *Connecticut Journal,* Jan. 17, 1782; *Salem Gazette,* Jan. 17, 1782; *Connecticut Gazette,* Jan. 18, 1782; Earl P. Olmstead, *Blackcoats among the Delaware: David Zeisberger on the Ohio Frontier* (Kent, Oh., 1991), 36–39; Rob Harper, "Looking the Other Way: The Gnadenhutten Massacre and the Contextual Interpretation of Violence," *WMQ,* 3d Ser., LXIV (2007), 621–644. A second notice of the Wyandots' ultimatum, though not the November 4 letter from Fort Pitt, also appeared in *Freeman's Journal,* Dec. 26, 1781; *Pennsylvania Evening Post,* Dec. 28, 1781; *Independent Chronicle,* Jan. 17, 1782; *New-Hampshire Gazette,* Jan. 19, 1782.

2. Randolph C. Downes, *Council Fires on the Upper Ohio: A Narrative of Indian Affairs in the Upper Ohio Valley until 1795* (Pittsburgh, 1940), 272. For Brodhead's diplomatic efforts as a contributing factor to Gnadenhutten, see Leonard Sadosky, "Rethinking the Gnadenhutten Massacre: The Contest for Power in the Public World of

Williamson's men arrived on the outskirts of Gnadenhutten and Salem on March 7, 1782. They found the villages unprotected and rounded up the inhabitants. The men from both settlements were led to one "slaughter-house," the women and children to another. That evening, the Pennsylvanians called a "Council" to decide the inhabitants' fates. A few disagreed, but the majority decided to execute the Indians instead of transporting them to Fort Pitt and the unreliable Brodhead. According to the testimonies of a few lucky escapees, the Indians prayed and sang in preparation for their deaths. Early the next morning, the militiamen bludgeoned more than ninety on the head with coopers' mallets, scalped the corpses, extensively plundered the houses, set them on fire, and left.[3]

This bloodbath was a manifestation of Indian-hating that had been simmering on the Pennsylvania frontier since the middle of the eighteenth century. But it was more than that. After hearing report after report about the king's proxies attacking their neighbors, after experiencing repeated raids by British-incited Indians firsthand, and after celebrating the Declaration of Independence and its denunciation of merciless savages, Williamson's militia saw themselves as staunch defenders of the Revolution. The massacre at Gnadenhutten was, for the perpetrators, a patriotic act of defense.[4]

---

the Revolutionary Pennsylvania Frontier," in David C. Skaggs and Larry L. Nelson, eds., *The Sixty Years' War for the Great Lakes, 1754–1814* (East Lansing, Mich., 2001), 187–213; and Peter Silver, *Our Savage Neighbors: How Indian War Transformed Early America* (New York, 2008), 267.

3. Frederick Lineback, "Relation of What Frederick Lineback Was Told by Two of His Neighbours, Living near Delaware River above Easton, Who Were Jus[t] Returned from the Monaungahela" (April 1782), in Samuel Hazard, ed., *Pennsylvania Archives . . .* , IX, *Commencing 1781* (Philadelphia, 1854), 524–525. For more on the massacre, see Silver, *Our Savage Neighbors*, 265–274; Gregory T. Knouff, *The Soldiers' Revolution: Pennsylvanians in Arms and the Forging of Early American Identity* (University Park, Pa., 2004), 155–158; Richard White, *The Middle Ground: Indians, Empires, and Republics in the Great Lakes Region, 1650–1815* (Cambridge, 1991), 389–390; Downes, *Council Fires on the Upper Ohio*, 272; Thomas P. Slaughter, *The Whiskey Rebellion: Frontier Epilogue to the American Revolution* (New York, 1986), 75–78; Patrick Griffin, *American Leviathan: Empire, Nation, and Revolutionary Frontier* (New York, 2007), 167–175; Gregory Evans Dowd, *A Spirited Resistance: The North American Indian Struggle for Unity, 1745–1815* (Baltimore, 1992), 85–88.

4. For more on how the Seven Years' War transformed attitudes between Indians and colonists, especially on the mid-Atlantic frontier, see Silver, *Our Savage Neighbors;* Jane T. Merritt, *At the Crossroads: Indians and Empires on a Mid-Atlantic Frontier,*

Given the cruelty displayed along the Muskingum, it would make sense that patriot publicists would excoriate the western Pennsylvanians for their actions. They had, after all, promoted incessantly the idea that Americans waged war with humanity and justice. Some printers did. But many more Americans read in their papers about the Wyandot attack on the Moravian towns than they did about the acts carried out by Williamson's militia. Patriot printers exchanged the former account widely because it fitted with the common cause narrative, even after Yorktown.[5]

When accounts of the massacre did appear in patriot newspapers that April, they were accompanied by justifications of the militia's actions. Four newspaper accounts surfaced describing the Gnadenhutten massacre. One vague account, first published in the *Maryland Journal* and exchanged five times, simply stated, "Advice had been received of fifty savages having been lately put to the sword at the Moravian Town." The second account circulated in a total of thirteen papers, starting with all the Philadelphia prints. It was a lengthy item (taking up more than one column of print), related by a "gentleman who arrived here last Saturday from Washington county." Three paragraphs long, it began, not with grisly details of coopers' mallets, but instead the specifics about the Wyandots' February attack on two settler families. The latter raids "so greatly alarmed the people and but too plainly evinced [the Indians'] determination to harass the frontiers . . . they therefore came to a determination to extirpate the aggressors." Then the source provided full details of the massacre, including his opinion that forty of the victims were "warriors," and the Moravian Indians in general had been "most severe and ill-natured" to him. He imparted no moral judgment on the attackers whatsoever and concluded, "It is hoped they will succeed in their expedition and hereby secure themselves from future encroaches of the savages." A majority of this account was a justification that explained away the reason the Pennsylvanians "killed and scalped upwards of ninety" Delawares. A third account that mentioned Williamson's act appeared only in Bradford's *Pennsylvania Journal*. It, too, charged that the Indians' "innate

_____

1700–1763 (Chapel Hill, N.C., 2003), 169–197; James H. Merrell, *Into the American Woods: Negotiators on the Pennsylvania Frontier* (New York, 1999), 225–252; Fred Anderson and Andrew Cayton, *The Dominion of War: Empire and Liberty in North America, 1500–2000* (New York, 2005), 118–144; Gregory Evans Dowd, *War under Heaven: Pontiac, The Indian Nations, and the British Empire* (Baltimore, 2002); Colin G. Calloway, *The Scratch of a Pen: 1763 and the Transformation of North America* (New York, 2006), 47–91.

5. See footnote 1, above.

barbarity instigated [the militia] to the cruel massacre of the harmless unarmed Indians."[6]

The final account about the incident at Gnadenhutten concerned Virginia's investigation of the "late massacre . . . which we have every reason
to fear has been a very unjustifiable aggression." But in this instance, too,
when other printers exchanged this from James Hayes's *Virginia Gazette*,
they copied the sentences that preceded it, which stated, "Reports from
our north-western frontier mention, some very daring inroads of the Indians, who it is said, have cut off several families settled upon the branches of
the Monongahela," and "Colonel [William] Crawford, with a considerable
number of men, have, we hear, set out in pursuit of their parties." Like the
murder of Cornstalk and other Indian allies throughout the war, the din of
reports in favor of taking swift action against British-allied Indians drowned
out protests of Gnadenhutten. No one brought charges against Williamson
or any of his men.[7]

This does not mean that patriot leaders agreed with the murder of ninety
innocent people, but their inaction was revealing. Congress received testimony about the event and encouraged authorities in Pennsylvania and Virginia to investigate (without any follow-up), but their journal left no trace
of a debate, nor did any delegates discuss it in their private correspondence.
Even the editors of the modern letterpress edition of the delegates' letters
admitted, "The silence of the journals on this matter is . . . puzzling." A few
years after the incident, George Grieve noted in his translation of Chastel-

6. "Put to the sword": *Maryland Journal*, Apr. 9, 1782; *Pennsylvania Packet*, Apr.
16, 1782; *Pennsylvania Journal*, Apr. 20, 1782; *Virginia Gazette* (Hayes), Apr. 20, 1782;
New-Jersey Journal, Apr. 24, 1782; *Salem Gazette*, May 2, 1782; *Newport Mercury*, May 4,
1782. "Future encroaches": *Pennsylvania Packet*, Apr. 16, 1782; *Pennsylvania Evening
Post*, Apr. 16, 1782; *Pennsylvania Journal*, Apr. 17, 1782; *Pennsylvania Gazette*, Apr. 17,
1782; *New-Jersey Journal*, Apr. 24, 1782; *Connecticut Courant*, Apr. 30, 1782; *Continental Journal*, May 2, 1782; *Connecticut Journal*, May 2, 1782; *Salem Gazette*, May 2, 1782;
Boston Evening-Post, May 4, 1782; *Providence Gazette*, May 4, 1782; *Independent Ledger*,
May 6, 1782, *Connecticut Gazette*, May 10, 1782. "Innate barbarity": *Pennsylvania Journal*, May 18, 1782.

7. *Virginia Gazette* (Hayes), June 1, 1782; *Pennsylvania Packet*, June 11, 1782;
Pennsylvania Gazette, June 12, 1782; *Pennsylvania Journal*, June 12, 1782; *Massachusetts
Gazette*, June 25, 1782; *Connecticut Courant*, June 25, 1782; *Norwich Packet*, June 27,
1782; *Connecticut Gazette*, June 28, 1782; *Boston Evening-Post*, June 29, 1782; *Newport
Mercury*, June 29, 1782; *Massachusetts Spy*, June 6, 1782; *Connecticut Journal*, June 4,
1782; *Boston Gazette*, Sept. 9, 1782.

"The Substance Is Truth"

lux's *Travels in North America* that he "was in Philadelphia when the news arrived, and it is but justice to say, that horror was painted on every countenance, and every mind was at work to devise expedients for avenging this atrocious murder." But neither Congress nor Pennsylvania nor Virginia acted. Why? According to Grieve, there were several reasons. The frontiersmen were "armed, distant from the seat of government, the only safeguard and protection of the frontiers, and from their own savage nature, alone fit to cope with the dreadful enemy brought into action by the British." In the end, though they were reluctant to say so, the patriots needed men like David Williamson—or George Rogers Clark or Daniel Boone. Or, at least, they had argued as much since 1775.[8]

Patriot publicity helped create a milieu that made conditions ripe for atrocity. By connecting Indians to British sponsors, they provided villainous scapegoats, whether "Hair-Buyer" Hamilton, Guy Carleton, John Stuart, or the recently escaped John Connolly. When reality did not provide salacious enough stories, the invented ones served, like the false invoice of "John Jenkins" sending weapons for scalps in 1780.[9]

Benjamin Franklin, always paying close attention, only made things worse. In the spring of 1782, nearly 4,000 miles away in Passy, France, Franklin was hard at work composing type on his own printing press to produce a second, more famous entry in this burgeoning "invoice" genre. Incensed that British prints were floating ideas about "reconciliation" after Yorktown, Franklin did not want Americans to forget the atrocities the British had inflicted on them and start compromising now. On April 22, just seven weeks after the massacre, he produced a one-sheet "Supplement to the Boston *Independent Chronicle*," featuring extracts of two letters, one from the New York frontier and a second attributed to renowned American naval officer John Paul Jones.[10]

8. Charles Thomson to William Moore, Apr. 9, 1782, *LDC*, XVIII, 448–449, esp. editors' note, 448n; [François Jean], marquis de Chastellux, *Travels in North America in the Years 1780, 1781 and 1782*, ed. Howard C. Rice, Jr., 2 vols. (Chapel Hill, N.C., 1963), II, 599n.

9. Notice of Connolly breaking his parole (again) was contemporaneous with Gnadenhutten. See *Virginia Gazette* (Hayes), Mar. 23, 1782.

10. Franklin, "Supplement to the Boston Independent Chronicle," Passy, France, 1782, *PBF*, XXXVII, 184–196. For more, see Carla Mulford, "Benjamin Franklin's Savage Eloquence: Hoaxes from the Press at Passy, 1782," *Proceedings of the American Philosophical Society*, N.S., CLII (2008), 490–530.

The first, supposedly originating in Albany, reported American forces' discovering eight large packages containing "SCALPS of our unhappy Country-folks, taken in the three last years by the Senneka Indians from the Inhabitants of New York, New Jersey, Pennsylvania, and Virginia, and sent by them as a present to Colonel Haldimand, Governor of Canada, in order to be by him transmitted to England." "Captain Gerrish," the letter's alleged author, then described in graphic detail the contents of each package. In this "invoice," British clerk "James Crauford" had totaled them up, divided them into categories separating young boys, girls, infants, women, "Congress soldiers," and farmers, and explained that the markings gave clues as to how the 743 people had died. The women's scalps, for example, were decorated with a "short Club or Cassetete, to shew they were knocked down dead, or had their Brains beat out." If that short club resembled a cooper's mallet, "Crauford" did not stipulate. As with the fake "Jenkins" invoice, Franklin also fabricated a note from the Seneca chiefs to the king "that he may regard them and be refreshed, and that he may see our faithfulness in destroying his Enemies, and be convinced that his Presents have not been made to ungrateful people." Franklin ended this gruesome scene with Boston's reaction to receiving these packages: "Thousands of People are flocking to see them this Morning, and all Mouths are full of Execrations."[11]

The second letter Franklin concocted for his hoax was a letter from John Paul Jones to the British ambassador to the Netherlands, Joseph York. "Jones" took issue with York's referring to him as a pirate and responded with his justifications for war. Reminding York of his "whig Principles," Franklin had Jones recite a familiar list of grievances against the king, substituting Jefferson's "he has" with "if":

If he wages war against them: . . .
If he hires foreign mercenaries to help him in their destruction:
If he engages savages to murder their defenseless farmers, women,
    and children . . .
If he excites domestic insurrections among their servants, and
    encourages servants to murder their masters: ——
Does not so atrocious a conduct towards his subjects dissolve their
    allegiance?

11. Franklin, "Supplement to the Boston Independent Chronicle," Passy, France, 1782, *PBF*, XXXVII, 187–188 ("Invoice"), 189 ("Seneca chiefs"), 190 ("Boston's reaction").

"The Substance Is Truth"

By reprinting the climactic grievances of the Declaration, Franklin sought to reignite American passion and foster resistance to British offers of reconciliation. He believed reminding Americans about the proxies was the most time-tested and effective way to accomplish that task.[12]

Franklin sent copies of his "Supplement" to his American and French colleagues, cleverly "doubting" the form but insisting, "The substance is truth." As he surely expected, the fake paper found its way into several British prints a few months later, and it eventually appeared in eight American papers in December 1782 through January 1783. Franklin wanted to stop the idea of compromise in its tracks. He knew the best way to do so was via his printing table. As he said in a letter to Richard Price just as his hoax began to circulate through print networks, "By the press we can speak to nations." Because of newspapers, he boasted, political leaders could not only "strike while the iron is hot" but also stoke fires by "continually striking." With Franklin in the vanguard, patriot publicists had embraced this feature of newspapers to manage public opinion about friends and enemies; the "Supplement" was simply an extension, if a hyperbolic one, of this now-seven-year-old campaign.[13]

Of course, Franklin did not approve of what Williamson's militia had done at Gnadenhutten. It would be shocking if Franklin now endorsed such vigilantism after everything he had published in the wake of the Paxton Boys massacres. Twenty years earlier he referred to the "unhappy Perpetrators of [the] horrid Wickedness" committed against the "poor defenceless Creatures." "All good People everywhere detest your Actions," he had stated. But then, in 1764, Franklin had been a loyal subject of the crown. The "Supplement" was another manifestation of the transformations the Revolution had effected in Franklin, his colleagues, and thousands of Americans. Not only had the exigencies of war and independence forced

12. Ibid., 184–196, esp. 190, 193.

13. BF to JA, Passy, France, Apr. 22, 1782, ibid., 196–197, esp. 197, BF to John Jay, Passy, Apr. 24, 1782, 205–207, esp. 206–207, BF to Dumas, Passy, May 3, 1782, 268–269, esp. 268, BF to [Richard Price], Passy, June 13, 1782, 472–473. Hoax published in *Public Advertiser* (London), Sept. 27, 1782; *Parker's General Advertiser and Morning Intelligencer*, June 29, 1782; *The Remembrancer; or Impartial Repository of Public Events*, part 2 (1782), 135–136; *New-Jersey Gazette*, Dec. 18, 1782; *Pennsylvania Packet*, Dec. 26, 1782; *Connecticut Courant*, Jan. 14, 1783; *New York Packet*, Jan. 16, 1783; *Providence Gazette*, Jan. 18, 1783; *Massachusetts Spy*, Jan. 23, 1783; *Continental Journal*, Jan. 23, 1783; *New-York Gazetteer*, Jan. 27, 1783.

Americans to embrace the hated French, which they had done with seeming alacrity, but they also had to reconsider many of their previous conceptions. The colonial rebellion–turned–independence movement had revolutionized America and Americans. According to patriot publicists from Thomas Paine on down, they had changed.[14]

Not all colonial sentiments would be overturned, however. The Revolution actually reinforced and reified some of their darker notions, especially about the propensity of certain people to embrace savage violence instead of civilizing sensibility or fellow feeling. For the most part, Indians and African Americans had not changed, in public discourse, at least. Colonists had always been uneasy about Indian attacks and slave uprisings. That some Indians and enslaved Africans had seemingly sided with the tyrant king confirmed their worst fears. This allegation, underscoring their agency, proved that those groups were incapable of being trusted with "liberty" or "freedom." Even the Hessians, once they arrived in America, had recognized the justice of the common cause and stopped being an accessory in destroying it. Representations of African Americans and Indians by patriot publicists left little room for similar transformations. They were, and remained, simply vessels of the king.

14. [Benjamin Franklin], *A Narrative of the Late Massacres, in Lancaster County, of a Number of Indians, Friends of This Province, by Persons Unknown; with Some Observations on the Same* (Philadelphia, 1764), 6 ("poor defenceless Creatures"), 27 ("unhappy Perpetrators"), 28 ("All good People"), *Early American Imprints,* 9667. For Franklin and the Paxton Boys, see Alden T. Vaughan, "Frontier Banditti and the Indians: The Paxton Boys' Legacy, 1763–75," in Vaughan, *Roots of American Racism: Essays on the Colonial Experience* (New York, 1995), 82–102; Alison G. Olson, "The Pamphlet War over the Paxton Boys," *PMHB,* CXXIII (1999), 31–55; Kevin Kenny, *Peaceable Kingdom Lost: The Paxton Boys and the Destruction of William Penn's Holy Experiment* (New York, 2009), 182–192. The extravagant balls to celebrate the birth of the Dauphin that were being planned from Philadelphia to West Point just as Franklin crafted his hoax testify to that metamorphosis. Philadelphia's celebration of the Dauphin's birth was documented in exquisite detail by Benjamin Rush; see Rush to "a lady," Philadelphia, July 16, 1782, in "The French Fête in Philadelphia in Honor of the Dauphin's Birthday, 1782," *PMHB,* XXI (1897), 257–262. For West Point's event, see *New York Packet,* June 6, 20, 1782; *Pennsylvania Evening Post,* June 10, 1782; *Pennsylvania Packet,* June 11, 1782; *New-Jersey Gazette,* June 12, 1782; *Freeman's Journal,* June 12, 1782; *Connecticut Journal,* June 13, 1782; *Massachusetts Spy,* June 13, 20, 1782; *Boston Evening-Post,* June 15, 29, 1782; *Providence Gazette,* June 15, 22, 1782; *Independent Ledger,* June 17, 1782; *Maryland Journal,* June 18, 1782; *Salem Gazette,* June 20, 1782; *New-Hampshire Gazette,* June 22, 1782.

"The Substance Is Truth"

Franklin's reaction to the news of Gnadenhutten illustrates this situation yet again. Once he heard of the massacre, Franklin responded as he had repeatedly since the new context of 1775—with a frenzied attack on King George. "It is he who has furnished the Savages with hatchets and Scalping Knives," he wrote to English merchant James Hutton in June, "and engages them to fall upon our defenceless Farmers, and murder them with their Wives and Children, paying for their Scalps, of which the Account kept already amounts as I have heard to near *two Thousand*." "Perhaps," he argued, "the People of the Frontier exasperated by the Cruelties of the Indians have . . . been induced to kill all Indians that fall into their hands without distinction, so that even these horrid Murders of our poor Moravians may be laid to his Charge." "Horrid Murders" and "poor Moravians," yes, but as in most of the other descriptions of Gnadenhutten, Franklin held that the Indians, having infected themselves by allying with tyranny, had brought this tragedy on themselves. Williamson's bloodlust was really the king's fault.[15]

Indeed, the Declaration of Independence suggested as much. Its arguments were just as valid in 1782 as they had been in 1776, as Franklin's transposition of the document's grievances into John Paul Jones's words elucidates. By now, thanks to "continual striking," it had become a call for action on the frontier. Although Williamson's militia had certainly displayed an "undistinguished destruction of all ages, sexes, and conditions" on the Muskingum, neither Franklin in Passy nor his colleagues across the Atlantic acted on that hypocrisy. They maintained that the king and his merciless savages were the real villains of this episode, without much distinction between friendly or enemy Indians and blacks. The common cause discourse convinced Williamson and his men that they were only acting in the best interests of the United States. In the new context of revolutionized America, Williamson and his men were patriots.[16]

15. BF to James Hutton, Passy, July 7, 1782, *PBF*, XXXVII, 586–588, esp. 587. Hutton disagreed. See his reply: Hutton to BF, July 23, 1782, ibid., 666–667.

16. Of course this was not total: in July, fourteen newspapers reported Washington's surprise visit to the frontier forts along the Mohawk River, where he was welcomed not only by the "ringing of bells, firing of cannon, and every other possible demonstration of felicity" but by "one hundred warriors of the Oneidas and Tuscaroras, completely armed and painted for war." But these exceptions hardly dented the general impression of Indians as enemies; indeed, just a few lines below was yet another story about "small parties" readying at Oswego to "harass our frontiers." See *New York Packet*, July 11, 1782; *Connecticut Courant*, July 16, 1782; *Freeman's Journal*, July

Needless to say, Indians in the Ohio Valley did not share this interpretation. They looked to avenge Gnadenhutten. The remainder of 1782 would witness carnage across the entire backcountry. On the same day that Williamson's men performed their executions, Washington ordered William Irvine to relieve Daniel Brodhead at Fort Pitt and continue to carry the war into the Ohio Valley. Irvine sent another force of militia—including some who had been at Gnadenhutten—under the command of Colonel William Crawford to discover the base of hostile Wyandot, Shawnee, and Delaware Indians.[17]

Meanwhile, reports filled eastern newspapers of "British sable-headed allies" conducting raids in central Pennsylvania. These "savage allies" of the "Royal Brute of England," in one well-circulated story, had captured a settler's wife and four children while he was away. More violence to homes and household was reported from the Minisink region of New York. A letter in Hayes's Richmond newspaper documented that a band of Creeks was marching against southern settlements with "the noted [Alexander] Cameron at their head . . . with British colors flying in the centre." Fewer than two months later, Hayes eased readers' minds, as new accounts from the southern frontier were "more favorable," but "our accounts from the frontiers of this State afford a gloomy aspect; scarcely one of the counties along the Alleghany, that has not had some of its inhabitants massacred by the Savages; and the inhabitants of the two outer counties, Monongahela and Greenbrier, are all in forts." Thirteen other papers picked up this bad news. In other words, even though British arms were encamped harmlessly in New York, Savannah, and Charleston, the Revolutionary War continued to rage throughout the backcountry. Blood continued to spill long after Cornwallis's surrender.[18]

17, 1782; *New-Jersey Journal*, July 17, 1782; *Pennsylvania Gazette*, July 17, 1782; *Continental Journal*, July 18, 1782; *Massachusetts Spy*, July 18, 1782; *Connecticut Journal*, July 18, 1782; *Providence Gazette*, July 20, 1782; *Boston Evening-Post*, July 20, 1782; *Newport Mercury*, July 20, 1782; *Boston Gazette*, July 22, 1782; *Independent Ledger*, July 22, 1782; *Salem Gazette*, July 25, 1782.

17. "Instructions to Brigadier General William Irvine," Headquarters, Philadelphia, Mar. 8, 1782, in John C. Fitzpatrick, ed., *The Writings of George Washington: From the Original Manuscript Sources, 1745–1799*, 39 vols. (Washington, D.C., 1931–1944), XXIV, 48–49.

18. "British sable-headed allies": *Independent Gazetteer*, May 25, 1782; *Pennsylvania Evening Post*, May 27, 1782; *New-Jersey Gazette*, June 5, 1782; *Maryland Gazette*, June 6,

Gnadenhutten was primarily the reason why. Ohio Indians were furious at what had happened along the Muskingum. On June 4, William Crawford ran directly into this rage near Lake Erie at Sandusky. He skirmished with a larger force of Shawnees but was able to hold on until British reinforcements arrived from Detroit. That night, Crawford beat a retreat, but the orderly march turned into a rout. Wounded, Crawford eluded capture for two days. When taken, he would pay the price for Gnadenhutten. Two men, John Slover and Dr. John Knight, witnessed what happened next. Their narratives kept Crawford's name alive for much longer than he would be.[19]

1782; *Salem Gazette,* June 20, 1782; *New-Hampshire Gazette,* June 22, 1782. "Wife and four children": *New York Packet,* Apr. 25, 1782; *Connecticut Courant,* Apr. 30, 1782; *Pennsylvania Journal,* May 1, 1782; *Connecticut Journal,* May 2, 1782; *Norwich Packet,* May 2, 1782; *Massachusetts Spy,* May 2, 1782; *New-Jersey Journal,* May 2, 1782; *Connecticut Gazette,* May 3, 1782; *Pennsylvania Packet,* May 4, 1782; *Boston Evening-Post,* May 4, 1782; *Independent Ledger,* May 6, 1782; *Boston Gazette,* May 13, 1782. Minisink: *New-Jersey Journal,* Apr. 17, 1782; *Pennsylvania Evening Post,* Apr. 22, 1782; *Pennsylvania Gazette,* Apr. 24, 1782; *Pennsylvania Journal,* Apr. 24, 1782; *Freeman's Journal,* Apr. 24, 1782; *Independent Gazetteer,* Apr. 27, 1782; *Maryland Journal,* Apr. 30, 1782; *New-Jersey Gazette,* May 1, 1782; *Maryland Gazette,* May 2, 1782; *Massachusetts Spy,* May 2, 1782; *Connecticut Journal,* May 2, 1782; *Independent Ledger,* May 6, 1782. "Noted Cameron": *Virginia Gazette* (Hayes), Mar. 16, 1782; *Pennsylvania Evening Post,* Mar. 25, 1782; *Connecticut Courant,* Apr. 9, 1782; *Connecticut Journal,* Apr. 11, 1782; *Independent Chronicle,* Apr. 11, 1782; *Newport Mercury,* Apr. 13, 1782. "Gloomy prospect": *Virginia Gazette* (Hayes), May 11, 1782; *Maryland Journal,* May 21, 1782; *Pennsylvania Gazette,* May 22, 1782; *Freeman's Journal,* May 22, 1782; *Connecticut Courant,* June 4, 1782; *Norwich Packet,* June 6, 1782; *Connecticut Journal,* June 6, 1782; *Salem Gazette,* June 6, 1782; *Independent Chronicle,* June 6, 1782; *Connecticut Gazette,* June 7, 1782; *Boston Evening-Post,* June 8, 1782; *Newport Mercury,* June 8, 1782; *New-Hampshire Gazette,* June 8, 1782; *Providence Gazette,* June 8, 1782.

19. Downes, *Council Fires on the Upper Ohio,* 274; Griffin, *American Leviathan,* 168–169; Larry L. Nelson, *A Man of Distinction among Them: Alexander McKee and the Ohio Country Frontier, 1754–1799* (Kent, Oh., 1999), 124–125. That detachment from Detroit corroborated a story currently in eastern newspapers that the British were indeed continuing the war via Detroit. See: *Virginia Gazette* (Hayes), Apr. 27, 1782; *Pennsylvania Packet,* May 7, 1782; *Pennsylvania Journal,* May 8, 1782; *Pennsylvania Gazette,* May 8, 1782; *Maryland Gazette,* May 9, 1782; *Pennsylvania Evening Post,* May 10, 1782; *Providence Gazette,* May 18, 1782; *Connecticut Courant,* May 21, 1782; *Connecticut Journal,* May 23, 1782; *Massachusetts Spy,* May 23, 1782; *Norwich Packet,* May 23, 1782; *Boston Evening-Post,* May 25, 1782; *Boston Gazette,* May 27, 1782. For the British version of the Sandusky battle, see Lt. John Tierney to Major A. S. De Peyster, Upper

Once Knight made it back to Fort Pitt after three weeks in the woods, he related the story of the colonel's brutal treatment at the hands of the Delaware Indians who had lost kin at Gnadenhutten. Knight's story appeared in eighteen patriot newspapers. According to the doctor, the grieving Delawares "first tied [Crawford] to a long post . . . then cut out his ears, after that blew squibs of powder on the different parts of his body; then the squaws etc. procured hickory brands and darted against such parts as they thought might most affect him." After an hour of this ordeal, "The colonel leaned upon his knee and elbow for rest, when a squaw took a shovel of hot embers and threw upon his back to put him again in motion." When Crawford begged loyalist trader and interpreter Simon Girty to shoot him, Girty laughed, saying, "Examples must take place, the Moravian towns were destroyed, and inhabitants murdered by our militia." A British officer on the scene related that Crawford told Girty he would "communicate something of consequence" if "his life could be spared," but Girty refused, and Crawford "died like a hero."[20]

Sandusky, June 7, [1782], in Davies, ed., *Documents of the American Revolution*, XXI, 86–87. Two waves of published stories documented the Sandusky encounter. The first, begun by the *Freeman's Journal*, stated that Crawford's force had been attacked and that he was missing. For that, see *Freeman's Journal*, July 3, 1782; *Pennsylvania Packet*, July 4, 1782; *Pennsylvania Evening Post*, July 5, 1782; *Pennsylvania Journal*, July 6, 1782; *Maryland Journal*, July 16, 1782; *Connecticut Courant*, July 16, 1782; *Massachusetts Gazette*, July 16, 1782; *Pennsylvania Gazette*, July 17, 1782; *Connecticut Journal*, July 18, 1782; *Providence Gazette*, July 20, 1782; *Virginia Gazette* (Hayes), July 20, 1782; *Boston Gazette*, July 22, 1782; *New-Jersey Gazette*, July 24, 1782; *New-Jersey Journal*, July 24, 1782; *Maryland Gazette*, Aug. 1, 1782; *Independent Ledger*, Aug. 5, 1782; *Boston Evening-Post*, Aug. 10, 1782. The second documented Crawford's torture, for which, see below.

20. Captain William Caldwell to Major A. S. DePeyster, Sandusky, June 13, 1782, in Frederick Haldimand: Unpublished Papers and Correspondence, 1758–1784, reel 43, item no. 21762, 80, British Library, London. There were two different accounts of Crawford's torture. The first, published by Thomas Bradford in the July 24, 1782, issue of his *Pennsylvania Journal*, was misdated by the type compositor as an April 6 letter from Fort Pitt. The actual date was more likely July 6. The second account was dated Westmoreland County, July 16, and it first appeared in Eleazer Oswald's new Philadelphia paper, the *Independent Gazetteer*, on July 27. Both correspondents received their information from John Knight. From Bradford: *Pennsylvania Journal*, July 24, 27, 1782; *Pennsylvania Packet*, July 27, 1782; *Virginia Gazette* (Hayes), Aug. 3, 1782; *Boston Gazette*, Aug. 12, 1782; *Connecticut Courant*, Aug. 13,

"The Substance Is Truth"

Patriot leaders were unwilling to connect Crawford's suffering to William-son's brutality in public. Some among them did acknowledge it privately. Edmund Pendleton lamented to James Madison that Crawford's torture was revenge for the "poor Moravians" but admitted, "Resentment for this will take place in our back people, and perhaps continue for years a scene of mutual bloodshed." In Congress, Rhode Island delegate David Howell said he rejected further expeditions against Indians "as believing that the Massa-creing of the Moravian Indians lead on to the outrages suffered by our Fron-tiers." Washington related to Fort Pitt commander William Irvine that he was "particularly affected with the disastrous fate of Col. Crawford," though it should have been "expected . . . especially under the present Exasperation of their Minds for the treatment given their Moravian friends." Virginia gov-ernor Benjamin Harrison hoped Crawford's torture "will prove a warning in future to the people in the backcountry to abstain from such horrid acts of cruelty as they were guilty of to the Moravian Indians."[21]

But what was understood in private conversation did not find its way to the printed pages. None of these leaders was willing to share his let-

1782; *Salem Gazette*, Aug. 15, 1782; *Massachusetts Spy*, Aug. 15, 1782; *Connecticut Jour-nal*, Aug. 15, 1782; *Norwich Packet*, Aug. 22, 1782; *Connecticut Gazette*, Aug. 23, 1782. From Oswald: *Independent Gazetteer*, July 27, 1782; *Pennsylvania Gazette*, July 31, 1782; *New-Jersey Journal*, Aug. 7, 1782; *Independent Ledger*, Aug. 19, 1782; *Continental Jour-nal*, Sept. 5, 1782. The *Maryland Journal* and the *Massachusetts Gazette* in Springfield each printed both accounts, one after the other. See *Maryland Journal*, Aug. 6, 1782; *Massachusetts Gazette*, Aug. 13, 1782. It is possible Major William Croghan—nephew to the well-connected trader, speculator, and Indian agent George Croghan—was Bradford's source. He was at Fort Pitt when Knight returned, and his July 6 letter to William Davies is not an identical copy, but it limns very close to Bradford's account. See William Croghan to William Davies, Fort Pitt, July 6, 1782, in James Alton James, ed., *George Rogers Clark Papers, 1781–1784,* in *Collections of the Illinois State Historical Library,* XIX (Springfield, Ill., 1926), 71–73.

21. Edmund Pendleton to James Madison, Virginia, Aug. 12, 1782, *PJM*, V, 44–45, esp. 44; David Howell to Moses Brown, Philadelphia, Nov. 6, 1782, *LDC*, XIX, 357; GW to William Irvine, Headquarters, Aug. 6, 1782, in Fitzpatrick, ed., *Writings of Washington*, XXIV, 474; Gov. Benjamin Harrison to Col. John Evans, Council Cham-ber, Aug. 13, 1782, in H. R. McIlwaine, ed., *Official Letters of the Governors of the State of Virginia*, 3 vols. (Richmond, Va., 1926–1929), III, 293. The British certainly con-nected what happened at Muskingum to Sandusky. See Canadian Governor-General Sir Frederick Haldimand's Letter to Sir Guy Carleton, Quebec, July 13, 1782, item no. 21806, Haldimand papers, microfilm, reel 72, frames 4–6, British Library.

ters with a printer. Only Eleazer Oswald connected Gnadenhutten and Sandusky in print. John Holt's former apprentice and son-in-law, Oswald served as a lieutenant colonel in the Continental artillery but left military service to become Mary Goddard's partner in the *Maryland Journal, and the Baltimore Advertiser* in 1779. In April 1782, he began publishing the *Independent Gazetteer* in Philadelphia. When he related the story of Crawford's torture, Oswald added an editorial comment: *"Query.* Should not the Ringleaders of the Party, who murdered the Moravians, be brought to an Account for their Conduct, as is doubtless is the Cause of the Distresses brought on by this unhappy Country?" It was the only public acknowledgment that someone other than ferocious Indians or their evil British sponsors had contributed to Crawford's ordeal. It is telling that only two of the six printers who exchanged the story included Oswald's query in their paper.[22]

Even after Sandusky, there was little variation on the common cause theme that the British and their proxies were really behind all the suffering on the frontier. While the early narrative of Crawford's torture circulated through American newspapers, sixteen published another letter from a militia officer at Fort Rensselaer in war-torn Canojaharie, New York, which related that

> Murder is become so common that it is hardly taken account of. Two days ago a very aged man and his wife were killed and scalped back of fort Paris, as they were pulling flax. . . . These are the tender mercies of the mild and amiable British, and are performed under the direction of a very humane and generous Carleton; and under the administration of the tender hearted, affectionate, sympathetic Burke, Barr[é], Fox, and the rest of their associates, whose breasts have often shuddered at the barbarities of the savage British and tories, with their Indian allies.

Nearly a dozen more published a letter from a "whig gentleman of good information" in England, who informed readers, "Not less than the sum of £215,000 sterling has been expended in presents for the American Indians. Six workmen are constantly employed at Birmingham, . . . wholly in making tomahawks, scalping knives, and a sort of short muskets for the use of the same copper coloured gentry."[23]

22. *Independent Gazetteer,* July 27, 1782; *Massachusetts Gazette,* Aug. 13, 1782; *Salem Gazette,* Aug. 29, 1782.

23. "Murder is become so common": *New York Packet,* Aug. 8, 1782; *Pennsylvania*

"The Substance Is Truth"

The printers' campaign to highlight the real villains did little to soothe pain for people in the backcountry. After Crawford's failure at Sandusky, the frontier was, as one historian put it, "wide open." Seneca leader Kayashuta burned Hanna's Town, the seat of Westmoreland County, Pennsylvania, and threatened to sack Wheeling. "For two weeks" late that summer, "the inhabitants were in such consternation, that a total evacuation of the country was to be dreaded," Hayes's *Virginia Gazette* and nineteen other papers reported.[24]

Then, on August 12, British Indian agent Alexander McKee and Simon Girty led a large force of Shawnee, Delaware, and Wyandot Indians across the Ohio into Kentucky, first besieging the stockade at Bryant's Station, about five miles from Lexington. After two days they withdrew north, pursued by Colonel John Todd, Daniel Boone, his son Israel, and 179 other Kentuck-

---

Packet, Aug. 13, 1782; *Connecticut Courant*, Aug. 13, 1782; *Massachusetts Gazette*, Aug. 13, 1782; *Pennsylvania Gazette*, Aug. 14, 1782; *New-Jersey Journal*, Aug. 14, 1782; *Independent Chronicle*, Aug. 15, 1782; *Connecticut Journal*, Aug. 15, 1782; *Salem Gazette*, Aug. 15, 1782; *Massachusetts Spy*, Aug. 15, 1782; *Connecticut Gazette*, Aug. 16, 1782; *Independent Gazetteer*, Aug. 17, 1782; *Pennsylvania Journal*, Aug. 17, 1782; *Providence Gazette*, Aug. 17, 1782; *New-Hampshire Gazette*, Aug. 17, 1782; *Boston Gazette*, Aug. 19, 1782. Note that Babcock and Haswell printed this letter in the same issue of their Springfield paper as Oswald's query. "Copper coloured gentry": *Freeman's Journal* (Philadelphia), Sept. 18, 1782; *Connecticut Courant*, Oct. 1, 1782; *Massachusetts Gazette*, Oct. 1, 1782; *Continental Journal*, Oct. 3, 1782; *Connecticut Journal*, Oct. 3, 1782; *Independent Chronicle*, Oct. 3, 1782; *Massachusetts Spy*, Oct. 3, 1782; *Salem Gazette*, Oct. 3, 1782; *Connecticut Gazette*, Oct. 4, 1782; *Newport Mercury*, Oct. 5, 1782; *Pennsylvania Journal*, Oct. 16, 1782. This paragraph is a good illustration of the circularity (and inefficiencies) of the exchange system. Even though it first appeared in Oswald's paper in Philadelphia, Bradford did not pick it up for nearly a month when he copied it from the *Massachusetts Spy*, who got it from the *Independent Gazetteer*. This article, then, went from Philadelphia to New England and back.

24. Downes, *Council Fires on the Upper Ohio*, 274; *Virginia Gazette* (Hayes), Sept. 21, 1782; *Pennsylvania Packet*, Oct. 1, 1782; *Pennsylvania Gazette*, Oct. 2, 1782; *Pennsylvania Journal*, Oct. 2, 1782; *New York Packet*, Oct. 10, 1782; *Maryland Gazette*, Oct. 10, 1782; *Connecticut Courant*, Oct. 15, 1782; *Independent Chronicle*, Oct. 17, 1782; *Massachusetts Spy*, Oct. 17, 1782; *Salem Gazette*, Oct. 17, 1782; *Connecticut Gazette*, Oct. 18, 1782; *New-Hampshire Gazette*, Oct. 19, 1782; *Independent Ledger*, Oct. 21, 1782; *Boston Gazette*, Oct. 21, 1782; *New-Jersey Gazette*, Oct. 30, 1782. A second letter from Fort Pitt giving details about Hanna's Town and Wheeling's being "cut off" appeared in: *Virginia Gazette* (Nicolson & Prentis), Aug. 17, 1782; *Pennsylvania Packet*, Aug. 27, 1782; *New-York Gazetteer*, Sept. 9, 1782; *Boston Gazette*, Sept. 9, 1782; *Salem Gazette*, Sept. 12, 1782.

ians. At the Blue Licks, along the Licking River, they ran right into an ambush. At day's end on August 19, half were dead, including Israel Boone and John Todd, and more taken captive. Three separate reports from Kentucky documenting the defeat at Blue Licks appeared, each detailing what happened after the shooting stopped: "After scalping and mangling their bodies, the Indians retired"; "the Indians spared none, but mangled and disfigured them to such a degree, that when Col Logan came to the place of action many of them could not be distinguished who they were"; "the usual scene of torturing the wounded and prisoners followed the defeat." George Rogers Clark massed as many Kentuckians as he could to retaliate. In November, more than one thousand crossed into Ohio, but, in Clark's words, they found "all attempts to bring" a significant number of Indians or British soldiers "to a general action fruitless." The "Conqueror of the Illinois" torched the Shawnee town of Chillicothe but did little other damage. Clark's anticlimactic expedition, of which readers across the mid-Atlantic and New England learned right around the same time that Franklin's "Supplement" hoax made it across the Atlantic and into their local papers, ended what would later be known in the Ohio Valley as the "year of blood."[25]

25. John Grenier, *The First Way of War: American War Making on the Frontier, 1607–1814* (Cambridge, 2005), 161–162; Nelson, *A Man of Distinction among Them*, 127–129; Jack M. Sosin, *The Revolutionary Frontier, 1763–1783* (New York, 1967), 140; White, *Middle Ground*, 407; John Mack Faragher, *Daniel Boone: The Life and Legend of an American Pioneer* (New York, 1992), 217–224. "Scalping and mangling": *Virginia Gazette* (Hayes), Oct. 5, 1782; *Pennsylvania Packet*, Oct. 15, 1782; *Maryland Journal*, Oct. 15, 1782; *Pennsylvania Gazette*, Oct. 16, 1782; *Freeman's Journal* (Philadelphia), Oct. 16, 1782; *Pennsylvania Evening Post*, Oct. 18, 1782; *New-Jersey Journal*, Oct. 23, 1782; *Independent Ledger*, Nov. 4, 1782. "Spared none": *Virginia Gazette* (Hayes), Oct. 12, 1782; *Pennsylvania Packet*, Oct. 22, 1782; *Independent Gazetteer*, Oct. 22, 1782; *Pennsylvania Gazette*, Oct. 23, 1782; *Freeman's Journal* (Philadelphia), Oct. 23, 1782; *Pennsylvania Journal*, Oct. 24, 1782; *New-Jersey Journal*, Oct. 30, 1782; *Providence Gazette*, Nov. 9, 1782; *Boston Gazette*, Nov. 11, 1782; *Salem Gazette*, Nov. 14, 1782; *Connecticut Journal*, Nov. 14, 1782; *New-Hampshire Gazette*, Nov. 16, 1782. "Usual scene": *Freeman's Journal* (Philadelphia), Oct. 30, 1782; *Pennsylvania Packet*, Oct. 31, 1782; *Pennsylvania Journal*, Nov. 2, 1782; *New-Jersey Gazette*, Nov. 6, 1782; *New-Jersey Journal*, Nov. 6, 1782; *Connecticut Journal*, Nov. 14, 1782; *Newport Mercury*, Nov. 16, 1782; *Connecticut Courant*, Nov. 19, 1782; *Massachusetts Spy*, Nov. 21, 1782; *Providence Gazette*, Nov. 23, 1782. "Fruitless": *Virginia Gazette* (Hayes), Dec. 28, 1782; *Pennsylvania Packet*, Jan. 7, 1783; *Maryland Journal*, Jan. 7, 1783; *Freeman's Journal* (Philadelphia), Jan. 8, 1783; *Pennsylvania Journal*, Jan. 8, 1783; *Pennsylvania Gazette*, Jan. 8, 1783; *New-Jersey Gazette*, Jan.

The events of that year, as represented in patriot newspapers, provided more evidence that action was needed to sever the alliance between Britain and Indians throughout the backcountry. Stories of frontier violence dominated the interior pages of American newspapers throughout 1782. With little exception, those stories depicted Indians as barbarians who, instigated by British agents, would never cease raiding the United States. According to patriot publicists, those merciless savages carried on the war, though both constructions embedded in that statement—that all Indians were enemies of the common cause and that they continued to pursue war without justification—were false. Soon, after the crown abandoned them in the Treaty of Paris, thousands of Indians throughout North America would have to deal with the consequences of those representations.

2: PEACE, EVACUATION, AND THE RUNAWAY PROBLEM

Even though the armies had left the Yorktown battlefield, the devastation to Virginia's slave plantations wrought by the war lingered for months after Cornwallis's surrender. Planters placed more than sixty notices in the two Richmond *Virginia Gazette*s throughout 1782 that specifically mentioned slaves who were attached to the British army. The long histories some provided are a revealing snapshot of what the war had done to slavery in Virginia. One master was searching for former *Virginia Gazette* printer Alexander Purdie's slave, taken by Tarleton in Charlottesville. Another was still looking for his bondsman who had run away to Gwynn's Island in 1776. One fascinating example of the upheavals the war had caused is evident in a notice filed by Francis Watkins in Prince Edward County, Virginia. Watkins informed fellow *Virginia Gazette* subscribers that he had "possession" of Ned, a "likely" African American in his early twenties. Ned had belonged to a Maryland attorney living at the Head of Elk, but when Howe's army came by that place in 1777, he went along to Philadelphia, where he was sold to a British officer who subsequently "carried him to the siege of Charlestown." Ned was with his new military master in Charleston for nearly a year until he "found means to escape to General Greene's camp" and tried to go "to the

15, 1783; *Connecticut Courant*, Jan. 21, 1783; *Connecticut Journal*, Jan. 23, 1783; *Providence Gazette*, Jan. 25, 1783; *Boston Gazette*, Jan. 27, 1783; *Independent Ledger*, Jan. 27, 1783; *Independent Chronicle*, Jan. 30, 1783; *Connecticut Gazette*, Jan. 31, 1783; *Newport Mercury*, Feb. 1, 1783; *New-Hampshire Gazette*, Feb. 15, 1783. For more on Clark's 1782 expedition, see James, "Introduction," and chaps. 5–6 in James, ed., *Clark Papers*, XIX, lii–lxii, 110–182.

northward." Watkins believed that he was trying to "return to" his former master at the Head of Elk but by July 1782 had ended up in Prince Edward County. Ned's extraordinary journey was not unlike many attempts thousands of other African Americans made to turn the war to their advantage. Historians have increasingly paid attention to these strategies, especially analyzing the adventures of those who documented their attempts as published narratives after the war, but for every Boston King or Thomas Peters or David George or even Ned, there were thousands who, though untraceable in the historical record, made similar calculations to maximize the opportunity war suddenly presented when it came near.[26]

26. William Hooper, a patriot leader in North Carolina, offered a fascinating portrait of the complicated, varied interaction between the British military and slaves on southern plantations. A few months after Yorktown, Hooper wrote to his friend and colleague James Iredell about a black servant, John, "to whom I was partial." "Everything was attempted to attach him to the service of the British." John was "offered clothes, money, freedom—everything that could captivate a youthful mind. He pretended to acquiesce, and affected a perfect satisfaction at this change of situation; but in the evening . . . he stole through the British sentries, and, without a pass . . . followed Mrs. Hooper seventy miles on foot, and overtook her, to the great joy of himself and my family." In his master's eyes, John was the perfect, loyal slave. But there was more. "His sister, Lavinia," Hooper added, "pursued a different conduct. She went on board the fleet after the evacuation of the town, and much against her will was forced ashore by some of my friends, and returned to me." Publicists on both sides of the war used euphemisms, most often invoking some intonation of theft or thievery, to describe what was going on between the British army and slaves. Occasionally it is possible to peek underneath that heavy rhetorical cover to see experiences as varied as John's and Livonia's. There were thousands of variations to their stories (William Hooper to James Iredell, Wilmington, Feb. 17, 1782, in Don Higginbotham, ed., *The Papers of James Iredell* [Raleigh, N.C., 1976], II, 327–331, esp. 329). Runaway to Gwynn's Island: *Virginia Gazette* (Hayes), Jan. 26, 1782. Purdie's former slave: *Virginia Gazette* (Hayes), July 20, 1782. Ned: *Virginia Gazette* (Nicolson & Prentis), Aug. 17, 1782. See Cassandra Pybus, *Epic Journeys of Freedom: Runaway Slaves of the American Revolution and Their Global Quest for Liberty* (Boston, 2006); Simon Schama, *Rough Crossings: Britain, the Slaves and the American Revolution* (New York, 2006); Gary B. Nash, "Thomas Peters: Millwright and Deliverer," in David G. Sweet and Nash, eds., *Struggle and Survival in Colonial America* (Berkeley, Calif., 1981), 69–85. The narratives published by King and George are collected in "An Account of the Life of Mr. David George, from Sierra Leone in Africa, Given by Himself in a Conversation with Brother Rippon of London and Brother Pearce of Birmingham" (London, 1793–1797); "Memoirs of the Life of Boston King, a Black Preacher;

This was the Revolution in the east in 1782. While patriot leaders focused their attention on the three still-occupied cities of New York City, Charleston, and Savannah and their surrounding hinterlands, patriot newspapers continued to document disorder all around. Nearly a year after Yorktown, a Richmond paper reported that a "gang of robbers" had broken into "several houses in Fluvanna [County], plundered sundry of the inhabitants, and set fire to, and wholly destroyed a small magazine of powder." According to the correspondent, this "corps of banditti" was "composed of runaway blacks, headed, it is thought, by some white emissaries of the enemy." Closer to the Chesapeake, another Virginian complained at the same time, "We are daily and nightly exposed to the Robberies of the Privateers . . . this banditti are composed mostly of Negroes, there not being four whites in twenty."[27]

In the areas surrounding the three occupied cities, the story was similar. After Yorktown, Washington returned the main body of the Continental army to the Hudson highlands near New York City for the winter. Nathanael Greene also repositioned his forces in the Deep South to put pressure on British forces, camping at a place called Round O, between occupied Savannah and Charleston. As soon as Greene settled in there, rumors began flying around camp that Clinton had sent a large reinforcement to Charleston. Further, word had it that the British were making another "attempt . . . to Arm the Negroes and some are now in service." Greene panicked. He ordered his officers to "pay particular attention" to slaves in their areas because they accounted for how "the enemy get all their best intelligence."[28]

Greene also instantly decided what needed to be done to shore up his weak army. "The natural strength of this country in point of numbers, ap-

---

Written by Himself, during his Residence at Kingswood-School" (London, 1798), in Vincent Carretta, ed., *Unchained Voices: An Anthology of Black Authors in the English-Speaking World of the Eighteenth Century*, expanded ed. (1996; Lexington, Ky., 2004), 333–368.

27. "Corps of banditti": *Virginia Gazette* (Nicolson & Prentis), Aug. 24, 1782; *Pennsylvania Gazette*, Sept. 4, 1782; *Pennsylvania Packet*, Sept. 5, 1782; *Pennsylvania Evening Post*, Sept. 6, 1782; *Massachusetts Gazette*, Sept. 17, 1782. "Daily and nightly exposed": *Maryland Journal*, Sept. 17, 1782; *Pennsylvania Packet*, Sept. 24, 1782.

28. Governor Nathan Brownson of Georgia to Nathanael Greene, Augusta, Dec. 1, 1781, *PNG*, IX, 644–646, Greene to Colonel Otho H. Williams, Mr. Warring's Plantation, 7 Miles from Dorchester, S.C., Dec. 2, 1781, 649–651, esp. 650, Greene to Col. Henry Lee, Jr., Headquarters, Mrs. Branford's Plantation, S.C., Dec. 7, 1781, X, 13, Greene to Thomas McKean, President of the Continental Congress, Headquarters, Round O, [S.C.], Dec. 9, 1781, 18.

pears to me to consist much more in the blacks, than the whites. Could they be incorporated, and employed for its defense it would afford you double security," he wrote to South Carolina governor John Rutledge on December 9. "That they would make good Soldiers I have not the least doubt . . . the sooner it is adopted the better," he added. John Laurens, seeing the prospects of his pet "black levy plan" revive, also insisted the Carolina government "should not lose a moment" in adopting it. Greene needed no goading; he continued to write to the governors of South Carolina and Georgia, begging them to adopt his plan. He was sure the British had already enrolled "3,000 for the defence of Charleston," and more were to come since "Lord Sandwich declared in Parliament that the Ministry would avail themselves of everything that God and Nation had put in their power to crush this rebellion."[29]

No matter how loudly the southern commander insisted that he needed black troops, neither legislature in Georgia or South Carolina took the matter seriously. In his new capacity as elected assemblyman, John Laurens did get the chance to bring this to the floor in South Carolina, but he was defeated soundly again. Edward Rutledge, the governor's younger brother, recounted the proceedings. "We have had another hard Battle on the Subject of arming the Blacks," he wrote to Arthur Middleton in early February. "Laurens, Ramsey, Ferguson, and one or two more pushed the matter as far is it could well go." He asserted, "About 12 or 15 were for it and about 100 against it—I now hope it will rest forever and a day." One of Middleton's other correspondents, Aedanus Burke, also breathed a sigh of relief when Laurens's "favorite scheme" was again defeated. But he offered another angle on what really lay behind Greene's support:

> The northern people I have observed, regard the condition in which we hold our slaves in a light different from us. I am much deceived, indeed, if they do not secretly *wish* for a general Emancipation, if the present struggle was over—A very sensible men whom you well know in Philadelphia once mentioned to me, that our Country would be a fine one, if our whites and blacks inter-married—the breed would be a hardy excellent race, he said, fit to bear our climate.

29. Greene to John Rutledge of South Carolina, Round O, Dec. 9, 1781, ibid., X, 22, John Laurens to Nathanael Greene, Col. Lee's Quarters, [S.C.], Dec. 28, 1781, 130–131, esp. 130, Greene to John Rutledge of South Carolina, Headquarters, [Skirving's, S.C.], Jan. 21, 1782, 228–230, esp. 229, Greene to Governor John Martin of Georgia, [Pon Pon, S.C., Feb. 2, 1782], 304–305.

"The Substance Is Truth"

Burke suspected the common cause might have dangerous results. After the "present struggle" ended, what might northerners like Greene propose? Since the war had obviously nationalized the sentiments of South Carolinians like John Laurens, what was next? Georgia's assembly was wiser, from Rutledge and Burke's point of view. They did not even consider the plan.[30]

Greene blamed the failure of his proposal to raise black regiments to save the South on a combination of private self-interest and "imagenary evils," or, as he reported to Washington, southerners' "apprehension of the consequences." For Greene, Laurens, Ramsey, and a few other patriots, those so-called evil consequences far outweighed the almost assured collapse of Greene's army if the British decided to continue the war in the Carolinas.[31]

For the majority of others, however, those evils were hardly "imaginary." The British had extended limited offers of freedom, and, more important, many thousands of African Americans had responded to them. Although Greene was misinformed, his wild speculations that thousands of uniformed, armed African Americans were marching through Charleston's streets suggests popular belief. Even though patriot leaders overestimated the numbers, there were black soldiers out in the Carolina pine barrens in 1782. Charleston garrison commander Alexander Leslie had indeed organized about seven hundred (not three thousand) African Americans into a cavalry unit called the Black Dragoons that periodically skirmished with patriot forces. Although there were many others attached to British auxiliary units, including a unit of Black Pioneers that included one of George Washington's runaway slaves, Harry Washington, these fugitive slaves–turned–cavalry soldiers were the main group drawing patriots' attention outside Charleston. Since the war had become a collection of skirmishes and pitched battles between handfuls of men—just such a small engagement took John Laurens's life on August 27—the Black Dragoons were distinctive.[32]

30. [Aedanus] Burke to Arthur Middleton, Jacksonborough, [S.C.], Jan. 25–Feb. 5, 1782, and [Edward Rutledge to Middleton], Jacksonborough, Feb. 8, 1782, in "Correspondence of Hon. Arthur Middleton," *South Carolina Historical and Genealogical Magazine*, XXVI (1925), 183–213, esp. 194, XXVII, nos. 1–3 (Jan. Apr., July, 1926), 1–29, 51–80, 107–155, esp. 4; Governor John Martin of Georgia to Greene, Augusta, Mar. 15, 1782, *PNG*, X, 506–508, esp. 508n.

31. Greene to John Martin, *PNG*, X, 304, Greene to GW, Headquarters, Pon Pon, Mar. 9, 1782, 472.

32. Sylvia R. Frey, *Water from the Rock: Black Resistance in a Revolutionary Age* (Princeton, N.J., 1991), 138; Jim Piecuch, *Three Peoples, One King: Loyalists, Indians, and Slaves in the Revolutionary South, 1775–1782* (Columbia, S.C.), 316–319. For Harry Washington,

They certainly loomed large in the popular imagination. A letter from South Carolina appeared late in May suggesting that the British had tried to disarm "their black regiment, for there happened some misunderstanding between the black and red soldiers at the lines, and an action immediately commenced." Later in the year, a story about how twelve black British dragoons ambushed patriot militia under the "Swamp Fox," General Francis Marion, appeared in more than ten northern newspapers. "It seems that the enemy court even the assistance of the negroes in the southern states," the Carolina correspondent related. Some of them "are incorporated with the British regiments, as being desperate, are often very mischievous in plundering." Another letter sent to Arthur Middleton, this time a report from Charles Cotesworth Pinckney, concurred with this comment, adding, "The black dragoons, which Leslie has armed, are daily committing the most horrible depredations and murders on the defenceless parts of our Country." It may have surprised Aedanus Burke to learn that northern soldiers also viewed the black dragoon unit with a similar mixture of contempt and pity, including one New York officer who thought the "poor unhappy blacks who, to the disgrace of human nature, are subject to every species of oppression while we are contending for the rights and liberties of mankind." Proxies of tyranny, indeed.[33]

---

see Pybus, *Epic Journeys of Freedom*, 40, 42. The number of African Americans serving with the British army in the Deep South in 1782 was probably about one-third of what Greene thought. They served the British military in many capacities. George Wray, commissary of the Royal Regiment of Artillery in Charleston, listed 219 African American males and 53 women attached to his unit in his returns for this period. See "Muster Rolls, Journal of Stores, Expense Book, Charleston, 1780–83," George Wray Papers, CL. James Moncrieff, a British military engineer, wrote to Henry Clinton in March 1782 asking what he should do about the Black Pioneers, which, as Clinton knew too well, was a unit made up of a "number of slaves who have attached themselves to the Engineer Department." He did not list how many slaves there were but asked Clinton to consider formally "embodying a Brigade of Negroes" (Moncrieff to Henry Clinton, Charleston, Mar. 13, 1782, James Moncrieff papers, CL).

33. Lewis Morris to Jacob Morris, Camp, "Round O," S.C., Dec. 10, 1781, in "Letters to General Lewis Morris," *Collections of the New-York Historical Society: For the Year 1875* (New York, 1876), 496; [Col. Charles Cotesworth Pinckney to Arthur Middleton], Ashley River, Aug. 13, 1782, in "Correspondence of Middleton," *South Carolina Historical and Genealogical Magazine*, XXVII (1926), 65. "Immediately commenced": *Independent Gazetteer*, May 11, 1782; *New-Jersey Journal*, May 15, 1782; *Pennsylvania Packet*, May 16, 1782; *Norwich Packet*, May 30, 1782; *Massachusetts Spy*, May 29, 1782;

African Americans helped the British military around the occupied cities, whether in reality or as ghosts that haunted patriot imaginations. In the Deep South, however, their main job was not to plunder or terrify white planters. Instead, it was to round up Hessian deserters. As Greene begged for sources of effective men to shore up his deteriorating force, he had one thing in his favor. The Germans in Charleston and Savannah did not want to fight under any circumstances. Patriot general Anthony Wayne, one of the most seasoned Continental army commanders ordered south in 1782 to sever British ties with Creeks and Cherokees, reported from Ebenezer, Georgia, that the enemy at Savannah "have filled the swamps round their works with tories, Indians, and armed Negroes, to prevent desertions, notwithstanding which a Number of Hessians f[ou]nd the way out, and the Defection of that Corps is so great, that they are not trusted to mount guard but in the Center of the Town." The British were apparently using some proxies to police the infidelity of others. In November, a patrol of black troops killed two Hessian deserters outside Charleston; British authorities ordered the corpses laid underneath the gallows where they dealt with other deserters.[34]

Patriot leaders kept Americans apprised of major German disaffection by feeding their correspondence to northern printers throughout 1782. In May, a letter from Augusta, Georgia, stated with confidence, "We may expect a total desertion of the Germans" in Savannah "whenever a suitable opportunity offers." Wayne or someone in his Ebenezer headquarters underscored this news by posting a letter to a Philadelphia paper (and then

---

Boston Gazette, June 3, 1782; *Salem Gazette,* June 6, 1782; *Providence Gazette,* June 8, 1782. In a few papers that story appeared either alongside or right around another report from Charleston giving details about an "Ethiopian Ball" lately thrown by the British in Charleston, whereby female slaves accompanied army officers. The "tyrants danced with the slaves 'till four o'clock in the morning. Thus you see to what a state of shame and perfidy the officers of that once great nation (Britain) has arrived to." See *New-Hampshire Gazette,* Apr. 27, 1782; *Pennsylvania Packet,* May 21, 25, 1782; *Massachusetts Spy,* May 23, 1782; *Boston Gazette,* June 3, 1782. "Mischievous in plundering": *Independent Gazetteer,* Nov. 30, 1782; *Pennsylvania Journal,* Nov. 30, 1782; *New York Packet,* Dec. 12, 1782; *Virginia Gazette* (Hayes), Dec. 14, 1782; *Connecticut Courant,* Dec. 17, 1782; *Massachusetts Gazette,* Dec. 17, 1782; *Connecticut Journal,* Dec. 19, 1782; *Independent Chronicle,* Dec. 19, 1782; *Providence Gazette,* Dec. 21, 1782; *Boston Gazette,* Dec. 23, 1782; *Salem Gazette,* Dec. 26, 1782.

34. General Anthony Wayne to Nathanael Greene, Ebenezer, Ga., Mar. 11, 1782, *PNG,* X, 485–486; Rodney Atwood, *The Hessians: Mercenaries from Hessen-Kessel in the American Revolution* (Cambridge, 1980), 196.

nine others) celebrating that "the Hessians are not trusted on the advanced guards." Many northern readers understood why: Georgia's patriot government had offered every Hessian deserter "200 acres of land, one milch cow, and two breeding swine: this has so effectually answered the purpose, that they come off in great numbers," as one published letter from a South Carolina officer related in July. This was not simply a discontented group in Savannah. Stories of Hessians' not being trusted outside Charleston, along with rampant desertion at the camp at Staten Island, also appeared throughout American prints in 1782. Alexander Leslie threw up his hands in the spring: "When the Hessian troops are sent to outposts Desertion takes place." Because they had formed "too many connections" in America and also because "the Enemy has taken every care to encourage desertion as much as in their power, this together with the assistance of their Friends within our walls enables them to seduce the foreigners from the encouragement given them."[35]

Congress sought to capitalize on this news of Hessian alienation with the

35. Alexander Leslie to Henry Clinton, Mar. 12, 1782, in British Headquarters (Sir Guy Carleton) Papers (Washington, D.C., 1957), reel XIV, no. 4222. "Total desertion of the Germans": *Freeman's Journal* (Philadelphia), May 8, 1782; *Continental Journal*, May 23, 1782; *Norwich Packet*, May 23, 1782; *Boston Evening-Post*, May 25, 1782; *Providence Gazette*, May 25, 1782; *Boston Gazette*, May 27, 1782. "Not trusted": *Pennsylvania Packet*, June 4, 1782; *Independent Gazetteer*, June 8, 1782; *New-Jersey Journal*, June 12, 1782; *Newport Mercury*, June 15, 1782; *Providence Gazette*, June 15, 1782; *Norwich Packet*, June 20, 1782; *Independent Chronicle*, June 20, 1782; *Connecticut Journal*, June 20, 1782; *Salem Gazette*, June 20, 1782; *Boston Evening-Post*, June 22, 1782; *New-Hampshire Gazette*, June 22, 1782. "200 acres of land": *Pennsylvania Packet*, July 13, 1782; *New-Jersey Gazette*, July 24, 1782; *Connecticut Courant*, July 30, 1782; *Massachusetts Spy*, Aug. 1, 1782; *Newport Mercury*, Aug. 3, 1782; *Independent Chronicle*, Aug. 4, 1782; *Boston Gazette*, Aug. 5, 1782. The officer's letter claimed that Georgia governor John Martin issued this proclamation, but back in February, Anthony Wayne wrote in a draft letter to Nathanael Greene that he had "found means to deliver a number of Proclamation[s] wrote in German among the Hessians offering Land Cows, etc. to all Deserters." See Wayne to Greene, Ebenezer, Feb. 28, 1782, *PNG*, X, 425n. South Carolina: *Independent Gazetteer*, June 8, 1782; *New-Jersey Journal*, June 12, 1782; *Providence Gazette*, June 15, 1782; *Massachusetts Gazette*, June 18, 1782; *Independent Chronicle*, June 20, 1782; *Boston Evening-Post*, June 22, 1782; *New-Jersey Gazette*, July 24, 1782. Staten Island: *Connecticut Courant*, July 9, 1782; *Norwich Packet*, July 11, 1782; *Providence Gazette*, July 13, 1782; *Virginia Gazette* (Hayes), July 13, 1782; *Boston Evening-Post*, July 13, 1782; *Newport Mercury*, July 13, 1782.

"The Substance Is Truth"

British by passing a controversial policy. Faced with a three-headed problem of bankruptcy, recruitment failures, and the "considerable number of German prisoners . . . [who] have expressed an earnest desire to . . . become citizens," delegates reached for a solution to all issues. In May, they passed a resolution that arranged for captured Germans to become naturalized citizens if they enlisted in the Continental army, paid an eighty-dollar fee, or otherwise offset the cost by becoming an indentured servant for three years. Although Washington endorsed the move, it was not without criticism: notes from a speech prepared by South Carolina delegate Arthur Middleton outline his strident objections that it was "against the rules of war," showed "political failure," and revealed a "sign of weakness in that we cannot or will not fill up our Armies from our own people." German officers reacted to this plan with horror. One general wrote that their situation was as bad "as if we had been captured by Turks." The plan to allow them to buy their way out of captivity was "a thunder-clap in our ears," he went on, "and it was an act of cruelty to force us to forward our decision upon the matter in writing the very next day." Although it did not materialize into an effective policy, Congress's report illustrates how differently patriot leaders—reflecting public opinion at large—viewed the German mercenaries. They claimed "a considerable proportion" of the Hessians and their countrymen were "involuntarily hired" and had a "view of eventually becoming Citizens." That image of the Hessians as fellow victims of monarchical tyranny had developed into a stable representation since 1777. Now Congress and Washington trusted them enough to enroll them in the Continental army and offered another opportunity to belong to the United States, an invitation not extended to the other proxies tasked to hunt their colleagues down in southern swamps.[36]

* * *

Nine months after Yorktown, Americans got some news from England that the war might indeed be over. Late in February 1782, Parliament passed a

36. Plan for Germans to become citizens: [May 15], Jun. 5, 1782, *JCC*, XXII, 275, 316–317; "Report on German Prisoners of War," *PJM*, IV, 318–321, esp. 320; GW to Secretary of War, Headquarters, Newburgh, Apr. 27, 1782, in Fitzpatrick, ed., *Writings of Washington*, XXIV, 175–177; "Arthur Middleton's Notes for a Speech in Congress," *LDC*, XVIII, 518–519, esp. 518; Anton Heinrich von Lossberg to Baron de Borck, Aug. 10, 1782, *Lidgerwood Collection of Hessian Transcripts of the American Revolution, 1776–1783*, Morristown National Historical Park, Morristown, New Jersey (Boston, 1989), band V, fiche 341, frame 33–36.

resolution that informed the king he should cease using force to subjugate America; a week later, they issued a second resolve that labeled anyone who made or even advised war in North America an "enemy to his country." Transcripts of these resolutions reached American newspapers in early May. Despite this desist order, patriot leaders were positive the conflict would continue. In the backcountry, attacks from Lake Erie to Kentucky persisted even as British authorities in Canada tried to stop Joseph Brant and his allies from attacking northern New York. They hoped the new military commander, Sir Guy Carleton, sent to relieve Henry Clinton as commander of Britain's forces in America, would bring an end to the bloodshed.[37]

Within a few weeks, Carleton sent word to Alexander Leslie in Charleston that he was to remove troops from Savannah, occupied since the first days of 1779. The order stunned Georgia's royal governor, Sir James Wright. He believed that if Carleton could send him five hundred more troops, he could permanently keep Georgia in the British Empire. Wright could count on the support of many Choctaw and Creek Indians, the latter of which battled with patriot troops in May just as Leslie passed on the order to evacuate Georgia. That not-insignificant attempt to make "a Junction" between British forces and "their Savage Allies" resulted in the death of a man Anthony Wayne acknowledged as "our great enemy and principle Warrior of the Creek Nation," Emistisiguo. "Every path leading to their Nation [was] shut up and Bloody," Wayne boasted to Washington, and the Choctaws and Creeks now "express the greatest dissatisfaction at the deception of the British by whom high sounding promises and the Intrigues of their Agents, they were precipitated into this war."[38]

37. Barbara Graymont, *The Iroquois in the American Revolution* (Syracuse, N.Y., 1972), 255; Alan Taylor, *The Divided Ground: Indians, Settlers, and the Northern Borderland of the American Revolution* (New York, 2006), 105–106; Piers Mackesy, *The War for America, 1775–1783* (Cambridge, Mass., 1964), 466–468; Richard B. Morris, *The Peacemakers: The Great Powers and American Independence* (New York, 1965), 253–254; Samuel Flagg Bemis, *The Diplomacy of the American Revolution* (1935; rpt. Bloomington, Ind., 1957), 190–193. Parliament's resolutions exchanged in: *Pennsylvania Packet*, May 9, 1782; *Independent Gazetteer*, May 11, 1782; *New-Jersey Gazette*, May 15, 1782; *Connecticut Journal*, May 16, 1782; *Independent Chronicle*, May 16, 1782; *Maryland Gazette*, May 16, 1782; *Massachusetts Spy*, May 16, 1782; *Salem Gazette*, May 16, 1782; *Boston Evening-Post*, May 18, 1782; *Independent Ledger*, May 20, 1782; *Connecticut Courant*, May 21, 1782.

38. General Anthony Wayne to Nathanael Greene, Sharon, [Ga.], June 24, 1782, *PNG*, XI, 365, Wayne to Greene, Ebenezer, May 7, 1782, 169. Wright's efforts to keep

The governor's protests did not impress Carleton. By the end of May, he pressed on, ordering transport ships from New York to remove all loyal personnel from Savannah. The flotilla arrived in early July. All the British and German soldiers, along with more than 3,000 loyalists and 3,500 slaves, awaited embarkation on Tybee Island, the site of a gruesome patriot raid on runaway slaves seven years earlier. The soldiers were bound for New York, the loyalists and African Americans for either East Florida or Jamaica, allegedly. On July 20, six ships carrying ten white families and 1,568 slaves left for Jamaica. Two more ships laden with 580 loyalists and 768 slaves left for Saint Augustine on July 22. The remaining transports carried nearly 2,000 British and German troops to New York two days later, leaving more than 5,000 loyalists and slaves to fend for themselves. Many of them went to Saint Augustine either overland or by small vessel down the coast. East Florida Governor Patrick Tonyn reported in October that the settlement of Saint Augustine had increased by more than 50 percent since "the refugees from Georgia . . . about 1500 whites and 1000 Negroes" arrived. British authorities figured another 1,600 went to Jamaica. Tonyn wrote a few months later that there was another group of immigrants flowing into Saint Augustine: "a considerable influx of transient people from Georgia and Carolina to recover their property in Negroes." In total, an estimated 3,100 loyalists and 3,500 slaves left Georgia.[39]

British in Georgia are in Eldon Jones, "The British Withdrawal from the South, 1781–1785," in W. Robert Higgins, ed., *The Revolutionary War in the South: Power, Conflict, and Leadership; Essays in Honor of John Richard Alden* (Durham, N.C., 1979), 259–285, esp. 266–267; Patrick J. Furlong, "Civilian-Military Conflict and the Restoration of the Royal Province of Georgia, 1778–1782," *Journal of Southern History*, XXXVIII (1972), 415–442, esp. 440–442. Creeks and death of Emistisiguo: James H. O'Donnell III, *Southern Indians in the American Revolution* (Knoxville, Tenn., 1973), 123; Edward J. Cashin, "But Brothers It Is Our Land We Are Talking About: Winners and Losers in the Georgia Backcountry," in Ronald Hoffman, Thad W. Tate, and Peter J. Albert, eds., *An Uncivil War: The Southern Backcountry during the American Revolution* (Charlottesville, Va., 1985), 240–275, esp. 271–272; Edward J. Cashin, *The King's Ranger: Thomas Brown and the American Revolution on the Southern Frontier* (Athens, Ga., 1989), 147–158.

39. Jones, "British Withdrawal," in Higgins, ed., *Rev. War in the South*, 268; Benjamin Quarles, *The Negro in the American Revolution* (Chapel Hill, N.C., 1961), 162; Kenneth Coleman, *The American Revolution in Georgia, 1763–1789* (Athens, Ga., 1958), 145–146; Gov. Patrick Tonyn to Sir Guy Carleton, St. Augustine, Oct. 11, 1782, in British Headquarters Series (Carleton Papers), reel 18, no. 5850; Tonyn to Thomas

This was not what most Americans learned about the evacuation of Savannah. Late in August, Philadelphia newspapers exchanged a report from a royal paper in Charleston that "5,000" slaves boarded Royal Navy transports out of Savannah. Sixteen patriot papers took it from there. This report formed the baseline of common understanding of the Savannah evacuation—and the numbers were grossly exaggerated. "According to some accounts," this correspondent concluded, the "5,000" slaves that left "were at least three-fourths, and to others, seven-eighths of all the slaves in the province of Georgia." This was the dominant account covering the Savannah evacuation. Only one other item, a single sentence describing how a privateer captured one of the Savannah transports headed to Jamaica with "250 negro slaves on board," surfaced in five patriot papers.[40]

If readers believed the report, they would be convinced that Georgia resembled New England after such a thorough loss of slaves. After all, this report stated baldly that the British "took" a huge majority of Georgia's slaves away, all at once, in July 1782. Georgia patriot leader James Jackson was sure that more than 5,000 left in 1782, a belief that he would call upon eight years later when, as a member of the United States House of Representatives, he berated antislavery advocates for trying to limit the slave trade.[41]

Townshend, St. Augustine, May 15, [1783], in Davies, ed., *Documents of the American Revolution*, XXI, 166–169, esp. 168. By December 1782, a return from East Florida showed that 782 whites from Georgia and 1,383 from South Carolina had arrived there, along with 1,659 blacks from Georgia and 1,681 from South Carolina, totaling 2,165 white men, women, and children and 3,340 black men, women, and children. See Carleton Papers, reel 18, no. 6159.

40. "About 5000 are negroes": *Royal Gazette* (New York), Aug. 28, 1782; *Pennsylvania Journal*, Aug. 31, 1782; *Independent Gazetteer*, Aug. 31, 1782; *Pennsylvania Packet*, Sept. 3, 1782; *Pennsylvania Gazette*, Sept. 4, 1782; *New-Jersey Gazette*, Sept. 4, 1782; *Freeman's Journal* (Philadelphia), Sept. 4, 1782; *Newport Mercury*, Sept. 7, 1782; *Maryland Journal*, Sept. 10, 1782; *New York Packet*, Sept. 12, 1782; *Maryland Gazette*, Sept. 12, 1782; *Virginia Gazette* (Hayes), Sept. 14, 1782; *Independent Chronicle*, Sept. 19, 1782; *Connecticut Courant*, Sept. 24, 1782; *Salem Gazette*, Sept. 26, 1782; *New-Hampshire Gazette*, Sept. 28, 1782; *Independent Ledger*, Sept. 30, 1782. "250 negro slaves on board": *Freeman's Journal* (Philadelphia), July 31, 1782; *New-Jersey Journal*, Aug. 7, 1782; *Connecticut Journal*, Aug. 15, 1782; *Newport Mercury*, Aug. 17, 1782; *Pennsylvania Journal*, Aug. 28, 1782.

41. In 1773, the slave population in Georgia was about 15,000, making the loss at the evacuation at Savannah approximately one-fifth, though there were significant wartime losses before 1782. See Coleman, *American Revolution in Georgia*, 145–

Perception mattered for more than just James Jackson. When it came to the future controversy over paying prewar debts owed to British merchants, southerners would seek political support to argue that the "theft" of their valuable slave property would suffice as payment enough. Because public opinion held that southerners had indeed suffered catastrophic losses, patriot leaders across America supported this rejoinder for a decade after 1783. Of course, for the thousands of African Americans who took advantage of this opportunity and left—or the tens of thousands more who tried to manage, as best they could, the "mobile hole in the fabric of slave society" that the British army specifically and the war generally produced—the reality of war and political upheaval was, in the short term, far more instrumental to their lives than public opinion. Soon, however, the thousands who chose neutrality would learn that patriot perceptions of British "tampering" on the plantations would affect their lives nearly as much as the emancipation proclamation British commander Henry Clinton had issued from Philipsburg, New York, back in 1779.[42]

As black and white refugees from Georgia navigated their new situations in Florida and Jamaica, Benjamin Franklin, John Jay, and John Adams discussed a peace treaty with British envoys Richard Oswald and Thomas Gren-

---

146. One scholar believes that the total loss of Georgia's slave population over the course of the war did indeed approach this high number. She argues that if all wartime dislocation is aggregated—including willing African Americans rallying to the Philipsburg Proclamation, blacks actually taken against their will by military units, runaways into the backcountry or to maroon communities or to Florida, deaths, and slaves coerced by loyalist masters—then it is reasonable to assume that "perhaps as much as two-thirds of Georgia's prewar black population" was gone. But this contemporary report did not include such nuance (Frey, *Water from the Rock*, 174).

42. Cassandra Pybus has argued that the aggregate number of slaves who successfully ran to the British was far lower than contemporaries believed then and historians have judged since. Although it is valuable to ascertain just how many blacks left the South, the long-term power of this inflated assessment would become perhaps even more significant, because it became a crucial foreign policy issue for the infant republic, and it was how southern slaveowners justified the use of repressive, brutal means to reassert their power on the plantations. Perception of the numbers of slaves defecting to the British was just as important as the actual numbers who fled. See "Jefferson's Faulty Math: The Question of Slave Defections in the American Revolution," *WMQ*, 3d Ser., LXII (2005), 243–264. "Mobile hole": Robert Olwell, *Masters, Slaves, and Subjects: The Culture of Power in the South Carolina Low Country, 1740–1790* (Ithaca, N.Y., 1998), 246.

ville in Paris. The British negotiators insisted that the treaty include two provisions: one, that American borrowers had to guarantee prewar debts to British merchants, and, two, that the United States must compensate loyalists for their losses of property. Over the next several months, the delegations haggled with each other over an assortment of issues, including the western boundary and fishing rights. One issue that did not complicate the talks was what to do about the people living in the trans-Appalachians. Despite so many pledges to the contrary, at the treaty table, Britain abandoned all responsibilities to its Indian allies.[43]

In November 1782, the two parties began to come to an agreement. At the last minute, the fourth American negotiator, Henry Laurens, arrived. The last years of the Revolution had been arduous for the former Continental Congress president. Early in 1780, after that body elected him to serve as ambassador to the Netherlands, the Royal Navy captured his ship off the coast of Newfoundland, charged him with treason, and clapped him in the Tower of London. While his friends and business partners, especially his former associate in the African slave trade, Richard Oswald, lobbied for his release, Laurens's health declined in confinement. Nominated to serve on the peace delegation, the ill Laurens was reluctant after more than a year's incarceration, particularly after having just heard news of his slain son John, but he did go to Paris.

The South Carolina leader made one important contribution to the proceedings: a provision that stemmed from his relationship with slave trader–turned-diplomat Oswald. Laurens suggested the treaty stipulate that upon evacuating the United States, the British should not carry any slaves away, no matter what promises they had made. Though Laurens's colleagues did not anticipate it and accepted the provision without controversy, what became the seventh article of the Treaty of Paris had enormous consequences for people in many parts of the globe. Article 7 would demand the British evacuate all American positions without "carrying away any Negroes or other Property." In exchange, the American delegation agreed not to raise any "lawful impediments" blocking the collection of all "bona fide debts heretofore contracted."[44]

43. Jonathan R. Dull, *A Diplomatic History of the American Revolution* (New Haven, Conn., 1985), 144–145; Bemis, *Diplomacy of the American Revolution*, 206–214.

44. For the international implications of the Treaty of Paris for African Americans, see Pybus, *Epic Journeys of Freedom;* Maya Jasanoff, *Liberty's Exiles: American Loyalists in the Revolutionary World* (New York, 2012); Eliga Gould, *Among the Powers of the*

Laurens had been Oswald's agent for importing slaves into South Carolina, earning 10 percent commissions on humans sold into bondage; Oswald endorsed this friendship by posting the £50,000 bail to secure his former agent's release from the Tower. Although Laurens—especially after his lengthy discussions with John about the merits of freeing and arming African Americans—had reservations about holding men in bondage, for the former slave traders, article 7 was primarily a property issue.[45]

* * *

On November 30, apart from the French and in violation of the 1778 alliance, all parties signed preliminary articles of peace. It would take several weeks for this news to cross the Atlantic. By the time the treaty reached America, the British had already broken article 7 in Charleston.[46]

Patriot leaders rightly viewed the evacuation of Savannah as a "prelude" to the more significant development of removing British forces from Charleston. In the months following the withdrawal from Georgia, while negotiations progressed in Paris, Alexander Leslie debated how to please everyone in the imminent Charleston evacuation. African Americans were, again, at the center of the controversy.[47]

Within a few days of the last transports' leaving Tybee Island, Leslie revealed his plans to depart Charleston, too. From that announcement in early August through the final sailing of the British fleet out of Charleston Harbor on December 14, all parties—loyalist refugees, British officers, Carolina slaveowners, patriot leaders, and slaves themselves—turned to Leslie for solutions to the intractable "property" problem. Carleton instructed Leslie "to prevent the carrying away any Negroes or other property of the Ameri-

---

Earth: The American Revolution and the Making of a New World Empire (Cambridge, Mass., 2012), 150–153. The text of the preliminary peace treaty is reprinted in "Preliminary Terms of Peace between Britain and the United States, November 30, 1782," in Dull, *Diplomatic History of the American Revolution,* 170–174, esp. 172–173.

45. Bemis, *Diplomacy of the American Revolution,* 194; Esmond Wright, "The British Objectives, 1780–1783: 'If Not Dominion Then Trade,'" in Ronald Hoffman and Peter J. Albert, eds., *Peace and the Peacemakers: The Treaty of 1783* (Charlottesville, Va., 1986), 13–29, esp. 14–15. For more on Oswald and his involvement in the slave trade, see David Hancock, *Citizens of the World: London Merchants and the Integration of the British Atlantic Community, 1735–1785* (Cambridge, 1995), 162, 177.

46. Leonard J. Sadosky, *Revolutionary Negotiations: Indians, Empires, and Diplomats in the Founding of America* (Charlottesville, Va., 2009), 117.

47. John Hanson to Philip Thomas, Philadelphia, Aug. 14, 1782, *LDC,* XIX, 64.

can inhabitants." However, Carleton insisted, any blacks "who had been declared free previous to my arrival" would not be returned, since he "had no right to deprive them of that liberty I found them possessed of." As a way to sort through the contradictions, Carleton had Leslie register all refugees, black and white, who wanted to leave with the army. More than seven thousand blacks responded, not including the slaves of patriot masters living on sequestered estates or those working directly for the army. Leslie concurred with Carleton's sympathy for black refugees; he, too, could not "in justice" allow them to "be abandoned to the merciless resentment of their former masters." This put Leslie in a difficult position. After more than two years in Carolina, fugitive slaves worked as servants throughout the British officer corps. Discerning between recent arrivals and those who had sought protection under the Philipsburg Proclamation was not an easy task, especially since some of his colleagues insisted on disregarding orders.[48]

Moreover, as it became clear that the British intended to leave Charleston, patriot political leaders became more adamant that they not leave with their valuable bonded property. South Carolina governor John Mathews was the first to warn that if the British did indeed remove thousands of slaves belonging to patriot masters, the patriots would retaliate by not honoring any debts owed to British merchants. Although the treaty had not yet been finalized in Paris, what Mathews threatened would soon be a tactic often employed by Americans in the coming decade: to use "stolen" slaves against unpaid American debts.

Mathews's threat worked. Leslie agreed on October 10 to form a commission to oversee all applications to remove African Americans from Charleston. Leslie promised to return all those who had not either been promised their freedom or had assisted the British army and "rendered themselves obnoxious" to their former masters. Both of those exceptions, patriot leaders

48. Guy Carleton to GW, New York, May 12, 1782, in Davies, ed., *Docs. of the Am. Rev.*, XXI, 165–166. Carleton orders to Alexander Leslie in British Headquarters Series (Carleton Papers), reel 28, no. 10316; Leslie to Carleton, Aug. 10, 1782, in Leslie Letterbook, box 78, item 15628, Thomas Addis Emmet Collection, NYPL. Leslie had to intervene when a superior officer loaded slaves on board ships along with two regiments leaving Charleston. See Leslie to Major General Charles O'Hara, Charleston, May 3, 1782, in Leslie Letterbook, box 78, item 15539. On August 13, Leslie underscored his orders "strictly forbid[ding] al Officers and others attempting to secret or carry out of this district any Negro that does not belong to them." See "Great Britain—Army—Orders, 1782, Aug. 13," SCHS.

"The Substance Is Truth"

and aggrieved Carolina planters complained, left enormous loopholes for both slaves and British officials to exploit. Their protests doomed the commission. After it imploded, no further agreement could be arranged. From the middle of October through the final evacuation on December 14, patriots had no supervision over how many African Americans sailed away from South Carolina. Patriot units continued to skirmish with Black Dragoons searching for provisions throughout November, as transports took loyalists and slaves in all directions.[49]

Exactly how many slaves went with the British at the end of 1782 is impossible to discern. Five days after the British occupation ended, Nathanael Greene surmised, "They took with them . . . between 5 and 6,000 Negroes, the greater part of which they had once promised to deliver up." This matches one British return of December 13 totaling 5,327 blacks leaving the city in the final evacuation, nearly all of those going to either Jamaica or East Florida. Both the Black Dragoons and Harry Washington's Black Pioneers departed in the final evacuation, headed to New York City. Other patriot leaders varied widely in their estimates. From Congress, South Carolina delegate Ralph Izard thought the British would take 12,000 slaves (including 170 of his), whereas several of his colleagues put the total between 6,000 and 7,000.[50]

49. Henry Lee, *Memoirs of the War in the Southern Department of the United States,* rev. ed. (1869; rpt. New York, 1969), 566–567, esp. 566; Colonel Thaddeus Kosciuszko to Nathanael Greene, [Ashley Ferry, S.C.], [Nov.] 5, 1782, *PNG,* XII, 150, Kosciuszko to Greene, [Ashley Ferry, S.C.], Nov. 14, [1782], 181. On the commission's fourth day of existence, the American representatives found 136 slaves whom they claimed as their property hidden away on a British ship already cleared to sail to Saint Augustine. Mathews canceled the commission, claiming Leslie acted in bad faith. Leslie, naturally, had a different take, writing to Carleton, "All my good intentions of assisting the Loyalists in returning the Enemy their Negroes, have proved abortive from the behavior of Mr. Matthews, the Rebel Governor and General Green[e], insulting the outposts at the very time I was acting with the utmost moderation and forbearance." See Leslie to Carleton, Charleston, Nov. 18, 1782, LXIX, 203–206, Earl of Shelburne (William Petty) Papers, CL; see also Frey, *Water from the Rock,* 178.

50. Nathanael Greene to Robert R. Livingston, Dec. 19, 1782, Papers of the Continental Congress, M247, reel 175, item 155, II, 599, National Archives; "Return of People Embarked from South Carolina and Georgia, Charleston, 13 December 1782," Massachusetts Historical Society, *Proceedings,* 2d Ser., III (Boston, 1887), 95; Quarles, *Negro in the American Revolution,* 167; Ralph Izard to Alice Izard, Philadelphia, Oct. 7, 1782, *LDC,* XIX, 231, Oliver Wolcott to Oliver Wolcott, Jr., Philadel-

Historians' estimates have varied even more widely. Modern students generally see Greene's estimate as too low, reflecting only the final transportations out in mid-December and not including how many the British army secreted out during the last months of 1782. Recent scholarship holds that the number between 6,000 and as many as 12,000 African Americans left South Carolina, or between 8 and 16 percent of the total prewar slave population.[51]

Just as historians remain unsure of how many thousands left, neither did contemporaries have a clear picture of the bustle in Charleston Harbor. Oddly, the American public knew less about the evacuation from Charleston—a larger and more significant withdrawal—than Savannah five months earlier. The only real published announcement came in the form of another December 19 dispatch from Nathanael Greene to Congress. This one did not provide numbers, but rather, since it was obviously calculated for public consumption, effused about Charleston's liberation. Greene exulted, "The People are once more free, and I hope will manifest their gratitude by a vigorous exertion in support of the common Cause." "The struggle and conflict has been long and severe," not only because "the Enemy had upwards of 18,000 regular Troops" in South Carolina but also because "several thousands Militias and Negroes employed for the reduction of the Southern States" had supplemented their forces. Victory over such an enemy should "merit the approbation of Congress," he hoped. Congress ordered Greene's letter published and sent it over to the *Packet* office, as usual. Seventeen other printers followed the command and exchanged the good news. Other than this letter, little surfaced describing what former governor and now South Carolina delegate to Congress John Rutledge termed an "Event, greatly interesting to the United States, particularly fortunate for South Carolina."[52]

phia, Jan. 15, 1783, 586, Elias Boudinot to Lewis Pintard, Philadelphia, Jan. 16, 1783, 589, William Floyd to George Clinton, Philadelphia, Jan. 16, 1783, 590.

51. "Charleston 6,000 . . . [but might be] a bit low": Quarles, *Negro in the American Revolution,* 172. "Between 6,000 and 10,000": Schama, *Rough Crossings,* 135. "Between seven thousand and eight thousand": Egerton, *Death or Liberty,* 200. "Between 7,000 and 8,000": Pybus, *Epic Journeys of Freedom,* 60. "A reasoned guess of about 10,000": Frey, *Water from the Rock,* 174. "At least 10,000 and perhaps even 12,000": Gary B. Nash, *The Forgotten Fifth: African Americans in the Age of Revolution* (Cambridge, Mass., 2006), 43. "10,000 to 12,000": Ira Berlin, *Many Thousands Gone: The First Two Centuries of Slavery in North America* (Cambridge, Mass., 1998), 303.

52. John Rutledge to Nathanael Greene, Philadelphia, Jan. 24, 1783, *LDC,* XIX,

Much of the other printed news surrounding the evacuation revolved around John Mathews's threat to cancel all debts because the British carried away so many slaves. Three separate accounts appearing over three consecutive months discussed this strategy openly. Another story that earned wide circulation concerned the British practice of allowing "the Ethiopians" to "man the lines and defend the town" after evacuation. Just as in the more documented case of the Savannah withdrawal, the main narrative of the Charleston evacuation focused on African Americans. The tiny amount of information available to most newspaper readers far from Carolina still kept blacks at the center of the story. Some projected sympathy for the so-called latest victims of British tyranny, the "poor, unfortunate Negroes," as one of Francis Marion's correspondents put it, who "will be carried from hence, into a thousand times (if possible) worse Bondage, than they experienced here." Whether this was true remained to be seen: the future would certainly not be bright and clear for most. The next months and years would be trying ones for refugee free blacks (estimated to be 15 percent of the total evacuees leaving Charleston) going to East Florida and New York, and little improved for slaves of loyalist masters headed to the West Indies.[53]

612; Nathanael Greene to Elias Boudinot, President of the Continental Congress, Headquarters, S.C., Dec. 19, 1782, *PNG*, XII, 301–304, esp. 303, published in: *Pennsylvania Packet*, Jan. 16, 1783; *Independent Gazetteer*, Jan. 18, 1783; *Pennsylvania Gazette*, Jan. 22, 1783; *New-Jersey Gazette*, Jan. 22, 1783; *Freeman's Journal* (Philadelphia), Jan. 22, 1783; *New-Jersey Journal*, Jan. 22, 1783; *Independent Ledger*, Jan. 27, 1783; *Salem Gazette*, Jan. 30, 1783; *Continental Journal*, Jan. 30, 1783; *Independent Chronicle*, Jan. 30, 1783; *Boston Evening-Post*, Feb. 1, 1783; *Boston Gazette*, Feb. 3, 1783; *New-York Gazetteer*, Feb. 3, 1783; *Connecticut Courant*, Feb. 5, 1783; *Massachusetts Spy*, Feb. 6, 1783; *Connecticut Gazette*, Feb. 7, 1783; *Providence Gazette*, Feb. 8, 1783; *Newport Mercury*, Feb. 8, 1783.

53. *Pennsylvania Packet*, Dec. 10, 1782; *Pennsylvania Journal*, Dec. 11, 1782; *Maryland Journal*, Dec. 17, 1782; *New-Jersey Gazette*, Dec. 18, 1782; *Maryland Gazette*, Dec. 19, 1782; *New-York Gazetteer*, Dec. 23, 1782; *Connecticut Courant*, Dec. 24, 1782; *Salem Gazette*, Dec. 26, 1782; *Independent Chronicle*, Dec. 26, 1782; *Massachusetts Spy*, Dec. 26, 1782; *Connecticut Gazette*, Dec. 27, 1782; *Boston Evening-Post*, Dec. 28, 1782; *Providence Gazette*, Dec. 28, 1782; *New-Hampshire Gazette*, Dec. 28, 1782; *Independent Ledger*, Dec. 30, 1782. Shepard Kollock published a summary of this letter in *New-Jersey Journal*, Dec. 18, 1782, and the *Independent Chronicle* exchanged it on Jan. 2, 1783. See also *Freeman's Journal* (Philadelphia), Jan. 8, 1783; *Maryland Journal*, Jan. 14, 1782; *Virginia Gazette* (Hayes), Jan. 25, 1783; and another item in *Boston Gazette*, Feb. 3, 1783; *Independent Gazetteer*, Feb. 18, 1783. "Man the lines": *Pennsylvania Packet*, Sept.

* * *

"Sir Guy Carleton is almost idolized by everybody in this place," loyalist Rebecca Shoemaker wrote to her daughters from New York City on April 13, 1783. Few outside Manhattan would agree. Even if they did not remember the visceral stories about Carleton's friends asking Indians to "feast on a Bostonian," his decisions in supervising the evacuations caused resentment throughout America. Compare Shoemaker's encomium to the bitterness expressed by a Maryland resident in a letter to the Philadelphia papers about how vessels manned by tories and runaway blacks continued to plunder estates on the Chesapeake. "Thus while the British ministry and Sir Guy Carleton hold out the idea of a speedy peace," he spat, "they suffer the scum of America to burn, plunder, and destroy the habitations and effects of the peaceable citizens of the United States." Even after the securing of peace, Carleton threw in his lot with that "scum" by disregarding article 7, a decision that would stoke this resentment further.[54]

The text of the preliminary peace treaty arrived at the end of March 1783, just before recriminations from Pennsylvania settlers in the Wyoming Valley and at Fort Pitt lambasting Congress for not sending assistance to help with continued attacks began to circulate. "Indians are worse this spring than ever," one account cried, while a second chastised Congress's inaction, asking, "Are these savages to reign forever?" Patriot leaders leaned on the king's cease and desist order to bring the war to a close on the frontier without their having to exert the political capital they did not possess, a development they were happy to publicize—though it did not turn out to be easy or immediate.[55]

10, 1782; *Freeman's Journal* (Philadelphia), Sept. 11, 1782; *New-Jersey Gazette*, Sept. 18, 1782; *Newport Mercury*, Sept. 21, 1782; *New-York Gazetteer*, Sept. 23, 1782; *Connecticut Courant*, Sept. 24, 1782; *Norwich Packet*, Sept. 26, 1782; *Connecticut Journal*, Sept. 26, 1782; *Massachusetts Spy*, Sept. 26, 1782; *Salem Gazette*, Sept. 26, 1782; *Providence Gazette*, Sept. 28, 1782; *Boston Gazette*, Sept. 30, 1782. "97" (secret correspondent) to Francis Marion, Wando, South Carolina, Nov. 4, 1782, in Peter Force Collection, MSS, 19,061, series 7E, reel 16, Peter Horry Collection, 1777–1809, book 5, LoC.

54. Rebecca Shoemaker to her daughters, New York City, Apr. 13, 1783, in Rebecca Shoemaker Papers, 1780–1786, MSS, HSP. "Scum of America": *Pennsylvania Packet*, Mar. 22, 1783; *Independent Gazetteer*, Mar. 22, 1783.

55. Letter from Fort Pitt with a list of places under continued attacks: *Freeman's Journal* (Philadelphia), Apr. 23, 1783; *Maryland Journal*, Apr. 29, 1783; *Newport Mercury*, May 10, 1783; *Independent Ledger*, May 12, 1783; *Salem Gazette*, May 16, 1783;

The other sticking point of peace, the matter of formerly enslaved African Americans awaiting escape in New York City, would not be resolved simply, either. A few weeks later, Congress instructed Washington to "enter into the necessary preparatory arrangements relative to the 7th Article of the said Treaty with the Commanders in Chief of the British land and naval forces in America," especially "for obtaining the delivery of all negroes and other property of the inhabitants of the United States in the possession of the British forces." On May 6, they met in Orangetown, New Jersey, to discuss the interpretation of the peace treaty in regard to runaway slaves.[56]

For his part, Carleton was surprised about article 7 and expressed disgust in letters back to London that Oswald had capitulated on this point unnecessarily—but, as he had advised Leslie several months earlier, he had begun registering the thousands of blacks inside his lines in case remuneration might be decided upon at a later date. That 157-page document containing nearly three thousand names would become known as the "Book of Negroes." Because entry in the ledger—and the certificates Carleton issued each claimant—was tangible proof of freedom, backed by bureaucratic process and official imprimaturs, the book was (and remains) a central artifact for black loyalists who eventually relocated to Nova Scotia.

Slaveholders who flocked into New York in search of their lost investments spurred Carleton to take this step, in spite of his orders. Boston King, a fugitive slave from South Carolina who had come with the Black Pioneers from Charleston, described the "inexpressible anguish and terror" at seeing "our old masters coming from Virginia, North-Carolina, and other parts . . . seizing upon their slaves on the streets of New-York, or even dragging them out of their beds." Carleton's papers reflect Virginians inundating the com-

Connecticut Gazette, May 23, 1783. "Indians are worse this spring": *Freeman's Journal* (Philadelphia), June 18, 1783; *Pennsylvania Evening Post*, June 19, 1783; *Pennsylvania Packet*, June 19, 1783; *Pennsylvania Journal*, June 21, 1783; *New-Jersey Gazette*, June 25, 1783; *New-Jersey Journal*, June 25, 1783; *Connecticut Journal*, July 2, 1783; *Virginia Gazette* (Hayes), July 5, 1783; *Independent Chronicle*, July 10, 1783. "Are these savages to reign forever?" *Independent Gazetteer*, Apr. 19, 1783; *Pennsylvania Packet*, Apr. 26, 1783; *Connecticut Journal*, May 1, 1783; *Providence Gazette*, May 3, 1783; *Connecticut Courant*, May 6, 1783; *New-Jersey Gazette*, May 7, 1783; *Maryland Gazette*, May 8, 1783. "King of Great Britain doubtless has directed them to desist": *Pennsylvania Journal*, Apr. 23, 1783; *Connecticut Courant*, May 6, 1783; *Massachusetts Spy*, May 8, 1783; *Newport Mercury*, May 10, 1783; *Boston Gazette*, May 12, 1783; *Salem Gazette*, May 16, 1783.

56. Apr. 15, 1783, *JCC*, XXIV, 242–243.

mander for permission to collect runaway slaves even before he had met Washington to discuss this issue.[57]

Although King remembered masters scouring New York streets, Carleton refused to sanction any patriot efforts to reenslave African Americans behind his lines. He believed the British government had pledged itself to any blacks who took shelter with the army as a result of declarations issued by his predecessors. Article 7 was irrelevant if blacks had responded to Dunmore's or Clinton's proclamation. As he told Washington in their meeting, "It could not have been the intention" of his government to be complicit in a "dishonorable violation of the public Faith pledged to the Negroes" and actually aid them in "delivering them up, some possibly to Execution . . . [or] severe Punishment." According to a loyalist observer, Washington "affected to be startled" when Carleton admitted that he had already permitted "a Number of Negroes" to accompany several thousand loyalists who had sailed to Nova Scotia. Washington believed Carleton's behavior was "a Departure both from the Letter and Spirit of the Articles of Peace," but it mattered little. The British commander would not return any blacks who had reached him before November 30, 1782; he deemed them exempt from article 7. "I have discovered enough . . . in the course of the conversation," Washington confessed to new Virginia governor and fellow sufferer of lost slaves Benjamin Harrison, "to convince me that the Slaves which have absconded from their Masters will never be restored to them." As Leslie had attempted as a compromise in Charleston, Carleton did allow a commission to investigate the cases of any runaways who had come to New York since December, but, in keeping with Leslie's experience, it, too, broke down quickly. Carleton's principled stance made him the most revered man in America, one New Yorker observed; "even what they call his breach of the peace, his sending away those Negroes who came in under the sanction of proclamations, is not looked upon as the least bright part of his character."[58]

57. Boston King, "Memoirs," in Carretta, ed., *Unchained Voices,* 356; Benjamin Harrison to Carleton, Richmond, Apr. 13, 1783, Carleton Papers, reel 21, no. 7448, "Petition of Sundry Inhabitants of Virginia to Carleton, Apr. 28, 1783," reel 28, no. 10098, "Book of Negroes," reel 29, no. 10427.

58. "Substance of a Conference between General Washington and Sir Guy Carleton," Orangetown, [N.Y.], May 6, 1783, in Fitzpatrick, ed., *Writings of Washington,* XXVI, 402–406, esp. 403–404; William H. W. Sabine, ed., *Historical Memoirs of William Smith* (New York, 1971), II, 586; GW to Governor Benjamin Harrison, Tappan, [N.Y.], May 6, 1783, in Fitzpatrick, ed., *Writings of Washington,* XXVI, 401–402,

News of Carleton's "breach" found its way into American newspapers soon after Washington's frustrating meeting with him at Orangeburg. Carleton did not reveal how many African Americans he had already allowed to leave for Nova Scotia, but two weeks later, Shepard Kollock (connected as he was to Continental army staff) had details. He reported in his *New-Jersey Journal,* "The British and their adherents, so habituated to perfidy, find it difficult to forego it; in the last Nova Scotia fleet, they sent off upwards of 700 Negroes, belonging to the good people of these states." Farther south, Harrison or someone close to him informed *Virginia Gazette* printer James Hayes of what Washington learned, as Hayes printed news on May 31 that Carleton "has positively refused to give up the Negroes in his possession." Boston's *Independent Chronicle* took it a step further, reminding readers that many of those slaves were "wantonly pilfered by Arnold and his nefarious banditti."[59]

The alleged plight of Jacob Duryee, a slaveholder from Dutchess County, New York, symbolized that "perfidy" but also patriot publicists' twisting stories to support the common cause. According to the report that appeared in several patriot papers, Duryee had come down the Hudson in a sloop "and carried with him a Negro man, who was to assist in navigating the vessel." When Duryee had completed his business in Manhattan and wanted to return home, "the Negro refused to return." With the master of the boat's assistance, Duryee tied him up, carted him to his ship, and left. "They had not sailed far," the printed account stated,

> before they were boarded by a barge, with a Negro Colonel and a company of Hessian soldiers, who treated Duryee and the Master with great insolence, obliged the sloop to go back to New York, seized her,

---

esp. 401; [T? S?] Michaels to Major Bernwith, New York, Oct. 4, 1783, in Carleton Papers, reel 25, no. 9294; Thelma Wills Foote, *Black and White Manhattan: The History of Racial Formation in Colonial New York City* (New York, 2004), 222.

59. "Habituated to perfidy": *New-Jersey Journal,* May 21, 1783; *Pennsylvania Packet,* May 27, 1783; *Maryland Gazette,* June 5, 1783; *Salem Gazette,* June 5, 1783; *Independent Chronicle,* June 5, 1783; *Virginia Gazette* (Hayes), June 7, 1783; *Providence Gazette,* June 7, 1783; *New-Hampshire Gazette,* June 7, 1783. "Positively refused": *Virginia Gazette* (Hayes), May 31, 1783. Hayes also had an account the next week corroborating Carleton's stance in a letter from a "person lately from New York." See *Virginia Gazette* (Hayes), June 7, 1783. "Pilfered by Arnold": *Independent Chronicle,* Aug. 21, 1783.

released the Negro, put the Master and Duryee in the provost, where they are to remain, it is said, till tried by a court martial.

The correspondent related that the affair "occasions great speculation and emotion," but which part—the seizure itself, the "Negro Colonel," the Hessian accomplices, or the British protection of black rights—was most distressing, he did not say. "What are we to think of the late abominable treatment of Mr. Jacob Duryee?" a contributor to Eleazer Oswald's Philadelphia paper opined two weeks later. "Sir Guy's proclamations have rather insulted our understandings, than restored our property and possessions, which he was bound to give up by the treaty."[60]

Of course, the real story about Jacob Duryee and his slave, Frank Griffin, was more complicated than patriot printers represented. Most of the printed story was utterly false. The exchanged account did not let on that Duryee had left Griffin in New York to look after his Manhattan townhouse when the British first invaded in 1776; that Griffin had married a free black woman named Dinah; that it was Griffin who had volunteered to return to Duryee if he could bring his family; that Griffin had made the proper arrangements with British authorities to leave, and only then changed his mind, angering his master; or, most significant, that in Carleton's eyes, Frank Griffin was a free man. These details emerged in Duryee's trial, but American readers were not privy to them. By then, the misleading, if not fabricated, story of Duryee's "ordeal" had been published in Pennsylvania, Massachusetts, New Hampshire, Vermont, and Connecticut. Just as patriot publicists massaged and amplified the stories surrounding Jane McCrea or Hannah Caldwell to serve political purposes, so did Jacob Duryee find welcome space in their columns. It is likely those printers did not know how wildly inaccurate their presentation of Duryee's case was, but neither did any express doubt about its veracity or follow up with a more accurate version. His narrative of suffering and embarrassment at the hands of his own slave backed by British tyranny fitted a mold long cast by patriot publicists. One of his Poughkeepsie neighbors completed Duryee's victimhood. In a fiery broadside published in August, the author, disguised as "Brutus," invoked Duryee as just another casualty of the "many thousand negroes, the

60. Duryee: *Independent Gazetteer,* July 19, 1783; *Pennsylvania Packet,* July 22, 1783; *Connecticut Gazette,* Aug. 1, 1783; *Boston Evening-Post,* Aug. 9, 1783; *Salem Gazette,* Aug. 14, 1783; *New-Hampshire Gazette,* Aug. 16, 1783; *Vermont Journal* (Westminster), Sept. 11, 1783. "Sir Guy's proclamations": *Independent Gazetteer,* Aug. 2, 1783; *Freeman's Journal* (Philadelphia), Aug. 6, 1783.

"The Substance Is Truth"

property of citizens of this state [who] have already been carried off" by the enemy.[61]

∗ ∗ ∗

The British finally completed their evacuation of New York City on November 25. For the first time in eight years, Washington and eight hundred American soldiers marched into Manhattan. It had been that long since New Yorkers had seen pandemonium like this: that week witnessed the frantic completion of an evacuation that totaled the movement of fifty thousand people. Twenty thousand soldiers (including six thousand German mercenaries and thirty thousand civilians (including three thousand emancipated African Americans) boarded transports bound either across the ocean or north to already-frozen Nova Scotia. "The shores were crowded with people who threw their hats in the air, screaming and boisterous with joy," one Hessian officer observed from the deck of a transport. Late that afternoon, they weighed anchor, and by the next morning the last British units, together with those Germans who wanted to, "lost sight of the coast of America."[62]

Back in Manhattan, Washington feted his officers at Fraunces Tavern, and the city prepared for a weeklong celebration. There was much to cheer: Carleton's evacuation came less than a week after details of the definitive peace treaty arrived. Providence had ordained the common cause. As if they needed more proof that a higher power was on their side, just four days

---

61. Jacob Duryee trial, July 11, 1783, Records of British War Office, 71/155, Public Records Office; Judith L. Van Buskirk, *Generous Enemies: Patriots and Loyalists in Revolutionary New York* (Philadelphia, 2002), 174–175; Pybus, *Epic Journeys of Freedom*, 25, 62–63. Frank Griffin did not witness what happened to his former masters' name; three weeks after the trial, his family sailed for Nova Scotia. See: "Book of Negroes," Carleton Papers, reel 29, no. 10427. On July 31, 1781, the *Clinton* left for Port Roseway carrying 184 African Americans, including Frances Griffin, age forty-five, formerly of "John Duryea"; Dinah Griffin, age twenty-three, who presented a certificate from her late masters showing she had purchased her freedom; and their one-year-old daughter. Frances's entry is on page 80, Dinah's on page 76. For "Brutus's" comments, see his *To All Adherents to the British Government and Followers of the British Army Commonly Called Tories, Who Are at Present within the City and County of New-York* ([New York, 1783]), *Early American Imprints*, 44464. Albany printers Morton and Borner originally published the broadside on August 15, 1783. It also appeared in *New-York Gazetteer*, Oct. 27, 1783; *Independent Gazetteer*, Nov. 1, 1783.

62. Ewald, *Diary of the American War*, ed. and trans. Tustin, 360.

after the evacuation, an earthquake shook Americans out of their beds from Pennsylvania to New Hampshire, and, in Rhode Island's capital, "the wind being high, the beacon erected in this town at the commencement of the war, was blown down." *Providence Gazette* printer John Carter, inserting himself in the miracle, made the connection: "What renders this circumstance remarkable is that it happened a few hours after the Definitive Treaty of Peace had been published here."[63]

The loyalists who remained in North America hoped these were not portents of political disasters yet to come. The same day Washington appeared before Congress in Annapolis to announce his retirement "from the great theatre of action," the *Pennsylvania Packet* published a "card" warning tories they should absolutely be watchful of the weather: "The *Whigs* take the liberty to prognosticate that the calm which the enemies of *Columbia* at present enjoy, will 'ere long, be succeeded by a bitter and *neck-breaking* hurricane." One circulated report concerned a visit three men made to James Rivington's print shop on New Year's Eve. Colonel John Lamb, Colonel Marinus Willet, and the printer's old foe Isaac Sears "waited on" Rivington to ensure he did not revel in being allowed to remain. The officers "forbid [his] prosecution of any farther business in the city." "The whigs are just rousing from their lethargy," the New York correspondent related, "and are determined to extirpate all obnoxious characters from this city. . . . to the joy of every whig in the United States, Jemmy Rivington's political existence terminated last Wednesday, the 31st ultimo. Take warning, ye anti-republicans! Behold the fate of your patron!"[64]

63. Earthquake: *Connecticut Courant,* Dec. 2, 9, 16, 1783; *New York Morning Post,* Dec. 2, 1783; *Pennsylvania Packet,* Dec. 2, 12, 23, 1783; *Freeman's Journal* (Philadelphia), Dec. 3, 17, 1783; *Norwich Packet,* Dec. 4, 18, 1783; *Salem Gazette,* Dec. 4, 12, 18, 1783; *Independent Gazette* (New York), Dec. 6, 1783; *Providence Gazette,* Dec. 6, 13, 20, 1783; *Political Intelligencer* (New Brunswick, N.J.), Dec. 9, 23, 1783; *Massachusetts Spy,* Dec. 10, 1783; *Vermont Gazette* (Bennington), Dec. 11, 1783; *Connecticut Gazette,* Dec. 12, 19, 1783; *Continental Journal,* Dec. 12, 1783; *Independent Gazetteer,* Dec. 13 20, 1783; *New-Hampshire Gazette,* Dec. 13, 1783; *Boston Gazette,* Dec. 15, 22, 1783; *New York Packet,* Dec. 15, 1783; *Connecticut Journal,* Dec. 17, 1783; *South-Carolina Gazette,* Dec. 18, 1783; *Independent Chronicle,* Dec. 18, 1783; *South Carolina Weekly Gazette,* Dec. 19, 1783; *New-Jersey Gazette,* Dec. 23, 1783; *Vermont Journal* (Windsor), Dec. 25, 1783. Providence beacon: *Providence Gazette,* Dec. 6, 1783; *Boston Gazette,* Dec. 15, 1783; *Pennsylvania Evening Post,* Dec. 20, 1783; *Pennsylvania Packet,* Dec. 23, 1783; *Freeman's Journal* (Philadelphia), Dec. 24, 1783.

64. "Address to Congress on Resigning His Commission," [Annapolis, Md.], Dec.

Though he had little love for Rivington, this was precisely the action and rhetoric Alexander Hamilton hoped to neutralize. Writing as the heroic Athenian citizen "Phocion," Hamilton rejected all talk of banishing former loyalists or stripping them of their political rights. He invoked the positive side of the common cause, arguing the "spirit of Whiggism is generous, humane, beneficent, and just." Do not vote for men who wish to attack the tories, he contended—perhaps including his former colleagues Lamb, Willet, and Sears—for they only wanted "revenge, cruelty, persecution, and perfidy," traits resembling British tyranny. The "Phocion" letters (of which there were two, the second appearing in April) saw Hamilton develop his theories of citizenship, especially his belief that with the Declaration of Independence all free people in North America stopped being British subjects and automatically—unless they specifically divested themselves—became American citizens. According to the young American colonel, there was nothing New York or any other state could do about restricting or rescinding the privileges of former tories; they could not be deemed aliens or traitors and prosecuted. Taking such steps "is to enact civil war," he warned. Restraint and tolerance were the best medicine to incorporate all political disagreement.[65]

Even though "Phocion" appeared as pamphlets in major northern cities and in a few southern newspapers, Hamilton's view of citizenship was not universally accepted. But, for the most part, Hamilton's words had their desired effect. He admitted in his second incarnation as Phocion of the pamphlet's "favorable reception," and the "progress of the sentiments advocated

23, 1783, in Fitzpatrick, ed., *Writings of Washington*, XXVII, 285; "A Card," New York, Dec. 10, 1783, *Pennsylvania Packet*, Dec. 23, 1783; *Political Intelligencer*, Dec. 23, 1783; *Freeman's Journal* (Philadelphia), Dec. 24, 1783. "Rousing from their lethargy": *Political Intelligencer*, Jan. 6, 1784; *New-Jersey Gazette*, Jan. 13, 1784; *Pennsylvania Packet*, Jan. 15, 1784; *Independent Gazetteer*, Jan. 17, 1784; *Connecticut Journal*, Jan. 21, 1784; *Newport Mercury*, Jan. 24, 1784; *American Herald* (Boston), Jan. 26, 1784; *Boston Gazette*, Jan. 26, 1784; *Independent Ledger*, Jan. 26, 1784; *Continental Journal*, Jan. 29, 1784; *Salem Gazette*, Jan. 29, 1784; *New-Hampshire Gazette*, Jan. 31, 1784. For Rivington's intimidation, see Ruma Chopra, *Unnatural Rebellion: Loyalists in New York City during the Revolution* (Charlottesville, Va., 2011), 221.

65. *A Letter from Phocion to the Considerate Citizens of New York*, New York, Jan. 1–27, 1784, in Harold C. Syrett, ed., *The Papers of Alexander Hamilton*, III, *1782–1786* (New York, 1962), 483–497, esp. 484. The *Second Letter from Phocion* (New York, 1784) is in Syrett, ed., *Papers of Alexander Hamilton*, III, 530–558, esp. 556, and see 533 on how independence was the trigger to American citizenship.

by him." Throughout the United States, by the spring of 1784, former tories who chose to stay would not find their necks broken, suffer legal persecution, or have to worry that their property would be seized. Even prominent ones like Gaine and Rivington would be left alone. This cannot be attributed solely to Alexander Hamilton, of course.[66]

There were multiple reasons the streets of New York City did not run with tory blood. In addition to the liberal, public stance taken by Hamilton and his colleagues, sheer war exhaustion after eight long years, a desire to embrace the future and not dwell on the past, and the limited method by which the British fought the war in southern New York all contributed to the speed with which New Yorkers moved on from the difficult experience of occupation. Moreover, this swiftness also lends itself to the suggestion that the ideological divisions separating patriots from loyalists were never as wide as they might have seemed from the perspective of Rivington's or Loudon's newspaper. Other personal considerations, primarily kin and neighborly connections, trumped politics and helped keep the peace after evacuation. Hamilton's effort to build bridges to the former tories was an easy one: the old spans had never been destroyed.[67]

The almost instantaneous reintegration of the loyalists is, at first glance, a very surprising development, one that provided grist for future commentators looking to prove the superiority of the American experience over other

66. Pamphlets: [Hamilton], *A Letter from Phocion to the Considerate Citizens of New-York, on the Politics of the Day* (New York: Samuel Loudon, 1784), (Boston: T. and J. Fleet, 1784), (Philadelphia: Robert Bell, 1784), *Early American Imprints*, 18508, 18511, 8514; [Hamilton], *A Second Letter from Phocion to the Considerate Citizens of New-York; Containing Remarks on Mentor's Reply* (New York: Samuel Loudon, 1784) and (Newport: Solomon Southwick, 1784), *Early American Imprints*, 18516, 18513; Hamilton, *Second Letter from Phocion*, in Syrett, ed., *Papers of Alexander Hamilton*, III, 530–531. "Phocion's Letters" were advertised in *Freeman's Journal* (Philadelphia), Feb. 11, 1784; *Boston Gazette*, Mar. 1, 1784; *United States Chronicle: Political, Commercial, and Historical* (Providence), Apr. 8, 1784. Newspapers: *Virginia Journal and Alexandria Advertiser*, Mar. 25, Apr. 1, 1784; *South-Carolina Gazette and Public Advertiser*, Apr. 28, May 5, 1784. "Pedigree": *New-York Journal, and State Gazette*, Mar. 25, Apr. 1, 24, 1784; *Independent Gazetteer*, Apr. 24, 1784. "Numerous train": *Salem Gazette*, Apr. 27, 1784; *Vermont Journal* (Windsor), May 19, 1784.

67. This paragraph summarizes the central argument of Van Buskirk, *Generous Enemies*, 192–195. For a new study on the important issue of reintegration, see Brett Palfreyman, "Peace Process: The Reintegration of the Loyalists in Post-Revolutionary America" (Ph.D. diss., Binghamton University, 2014).

"The Substance Is Truth"

modern revolutions. But by 1784, Americans were no strangers to abrupt transformations; the Revolution forced the public to accept the strangest of candidates as dear friends. If they could celebrate frontier banditti or the king of France as saviors of the common cause or quietly employ Hessian soldiers at their gunpowder mills, what was so shocking about James Rivington continuing to live undisturbed in New York?

If, at war's end, it seemed that loyalties were more permeable on the ground than in print, it does not follow to cast doubt back on the efficacy of the patriots' propagation campaign to cordon off "friends" from "enemies" as a whole. The case of the loyalists was always a peculiar one. Lacking characteristics that would aid in differentiation, such as language, culture, appearance, or physical space, patriot publicists struggled throughout the war to "mark" tories. With African Americans, Indians, and German auxiliaries, they had these elements at their disposal. Patriot publicists found much more success in tapping into established prejudices about "savages," "slaves," and "mercenaries" to represent those groups as the king's proxies.

The tories, however, had been slippery from the outset. Worse, the diminished capacity of patriot print networks from 1780 to 1783 compounded their difficulties in representing loyalists. This was especially the case in the South after the fall of Charleston. Patriot leaders understood the correlation between the lack of a newspaper giving their side of the Revolutionary argument in the Carolinas and the desperate, internecine conflict that raged throughout the South.

As much as they could, patriot leaders magnified stories that conflated loyalists and traitors such as Benedict Arnold behaving like, with, or on behalf of African Americans and Indians. These groups were with Colonel Tye in New Jersey, and they continued to wreak havoc with Joseph Brant in the Mohawk Valley. As the poem went, the British bribed slaves to kill their masters and paid Indians to scalp innocent settlers, and then there were the *"Tories,* worse by half than they." But these images did not fasten to the loyalists in any lasting way. This, too, helped maintain bridges between patriots and loyalists.[68]

On the eighth anniversary of the battle of Lexington, an exuberant Thomas Paine published the final installment of the *American Crisis.* "'The times that try men's souls' are over—and the greatest and compleatest revolution the world ever knew is gloriously and happily accomplished," he wrote in triumph. Looking out from "the eminence we now stand on, and

68. Poem on Benedict Arnold: *New-York Journal,* Oct. 9, 1780.

the vast prospect before us," he reminded Americans to hold the union—"that great palladium of our liberty and safety"—sacred. The American union defeated the mightiest military power on earth, according to Paine. Patriots had reached this prospect by surviving the tumult of war, but also by deploying words, images, and stories more effectively than their opponents. For the sake of unity, patriot political and communications leaders had substantiated narratives that many of them reviled in private. They did not expect these stories to last past the end of the war. They did not know they were crafting what one political theorist calls an "ethically constitutive" narrative, a founding story that would live on for decades in the American imagination. The common cause appeal, built with equal parts hope and fear, would continue to have cultural power in the new republic. Some, like Paine, celebrated this achievement, but for thousands of other people, it would be a haunting. Decades after the Treaty of Paris, the shadow cast by representations of merciless savages and domestic insurrectionists would continue to appeal to those who wanted to counter the claims of universal human rights declared during the Revolution. Hardly disposed of as old news, the darker side of the common cause would continue to exert an effect on who was allowed to be a citizen of the United States.[69]

69. *The Last Crisis, Number XIII*, Philadelphia, Apr. 19, 1783, in Eric Foner, ed., *Thomas Paine: Collected Writings . . .* (New York, 1995), 348, 352; Rogers M. Smith, *Stories of Peoplehood: The Politics and Morals of Political Membership* (Cambridge, 2003), 64–70, 94–95.

"The Substance Is Truth"

CHAPTER 9

"New Provocations"

THE POLITICAL AND CULTURAL CONSEQUENCES

OF REVOLUTIONARY WAR STORIES

The principle of government being radically changed by the revolution,
the political character of the people was also changed from subjects
to citizens. The difference is immense.

David Ramsay, 1789

From its inception through the end of the war, the entire common cause appeal was only an expedient to mobilize resistance and galvanize the union. The patriots boasted of its being a universal call for "inalienable rights," but, once military exigencies made the imperative of union irresistible, this appeal transformed. When the "American Revolution" became the "Revolutionary War," the common cause quickly became an alloy, an invocation that mixed together self-evident, natural rights and colonial fears and prejudices. "Liberty" might have been the base metal, but the "cause" gained its durability when hardened with ubiquitous images and representations that marked resistant slaves and hostile Indians as enemies of the Revolution. Once fused together, those atoms—the "founding story" that sustained the war effort for more than three thousand days—were difficult to disentangle.

Most of the political, military, and communication leaders who broadcast stories about the king's proxies were bothered by slavery and hoped it would soon pass away. The list of patriot leaders who believed themselves at least mild opponents of slavery was extensive and growing. So many of the men featured in this study—Benjamin Rush, John Jay, Alexander Hamilton, John Adams, Benjamin Franklin, Henry Laurens, George Washington, Nathanael Greene, Patrick Henry, St. George Tucker, Hugh Henry Brackenridge, Thomas Paine, Philip Freneau, Benjamin Lincoln, William Livingston, Thomas Jefferson—stated either privately or publicly that they were against the institution of slavery. They congratulated themselves for legislative and judicial movements against slavery throughout the nation, which they regarded as evidence that the Revolution would remake the world. They pointed to New England, where Vermont abolished slavery in its 1777 state constitution, court cases in Massachusetts had ended the institution in many people's minds in 1783, and the Connecticut Assembly passed a gradual emancipation bill in 1784. They looked to the mid-Atlantic: the preamble to Pennsylvania's 1780 gradual abolition law declared slavery "highly detrimental to morality, industry, and the arts," and similar plans were on the docket in New Jersey and New York. And they even looked to the upper South, where patriot opponents of slavery took heart as Quakers successfully pressured the Virginia Assembly in 1782 to ease the restrictions on personal manumission, and the numbers of free blacks in the Chesapeake swelled to a "sizable minority."[1]

Yet, south of Virginia, the postwar years saw a further entrenchment and expansion of slavery. The roots of what some interpret as the patriots' hypocrisy or a failure of leadership were embedded in the common cause argument itself. No matter how much they wanted to dismantle the institution of slavery, those same men helped make the conditions to perpetuate it. The particular ways they argued for American independence meant that the republic they created would be a slaveholder's one.[2]

1. [David Ramsay], *A Dissertation on the Manner of Acquiring the Character and Privileges of a Citizen of the United States* (1789), [3], *Early American Imprints*, 22088; William O'Brien, "Did the Jennison Case Outlaw Slavery in Massachusetts?" *WMQ*, 3d Ser., XVII (1960), 219–241; Benjamin Quarles, *The Negro in the American Revolution* (Chapel Hill, N.C., 1961), 32–50; State of Pennsylvania, An Act for the Gradual Abolition of Slavery (1780), quoted in Arthur Zilversmit, *The First Emancipation: The Abolition of Slavery in the North* (Chicago, 1967), 35, and see also 109–138; T. H. Breen, "Making History: The Force of Public Opinion and the Last Years of Slavery in Revolutionary Massachusetts," in Ronald Hoffman, Mechal Sobel, and Fredrika J. Teute, eds., *Through a Glass Darkly: Reflections on Personal Identity in Early America* (Chapel Hill, N.C., 1997), 67–95; Margot Minardi, *Making Slavery History: Abolition and the Politics of Memory in Massachusetts* (New York, 2010), 13–42. "Sizable minority": Ira Berlin, *Slaves without Masters: The Free Negro in the Antebellum South* (New York, 1974), 16.

2. Duncan J. MacLeod, *Slavery, Race, and the American Revolution* (London, 1974); David Brion Davis, "American Slavery and the American Revolution," in Ira Berlin and Ronald Hoffman, eds., *Slavery and Freedom in the Age of the American Revolution*

Over the eight years of war, references to the king's proxies were a vital, vibrant part of the patriots' mobilization. They argued that playing upon colonial outrage and prejudice—the keystone of this darker side of the common cause—was something the tyranny of their enemies forced upon them. Some of them insisted such illiberal notions should be cast aside once the union was secure, thus fulfilling the promise of Revolutionary ideals. But that would not be the case.

The common cause appeal, in all its elements, had consequences for many people in the postwar republic. The discomfort about the longevity of this campaign is evident in a terse, underappreciated phrase in one of the most studied sections of a book written by one of those "founders" caught between the rhetoric and reality of slavery.

Early in the summer of 1781, while British troops ravaged the Virginia countryside, Thomas Jefferson sought an outlet for his frustration. The middle months of that turbulent year had been trying for the patriot leader. In June, during the last days of his ignominious term as governor, British cavalry under Banastre Tarleton nearly captured him at Monticello. They did carry away valuable pieces of his property, including, as Jefferson would calculate it, several humans. A few weeks later, while he formulated a response to public criticism about his alleged cowardice, Jefferson broke his wrist falling from a horse and was confined to his Bedford County estate for several weeks. It was during this convalescence that he began to write *Notes on the State of Virginia*.[3]

In the fourteenth query of *Notes*, Jefferson described Virginians' plan to revise the state's common-law heritage to reflect their new republican regime. This included a gradual abolition bill that would free all slaves over the age of twenty-one but order them "colonized to such place as the cir-

---

(Charlottesville, Va., 1983), 262–280; Barbara Jeanne Fields, "Slavery, Race, and Ideology in the United States of America," *New Left Review*, 1st Ser., no. 181 (May–June 1990), 95–118; William Freehling, "The Founding Fathers, Conditional Antislavery, and the Nonradicalism of the American Revolution," in Freehling, *The Reintegration of American History: Slavery and the Civil War* (New York, 1994), 12–33; Gary B. Nash, *The Forgotten Fifth: African Americans in the Age of Revolution* (Cambridge, Mass., 2006), 69–122, esp. 90–92.

3. Dumas Malone, *Jefferson the Virginian*, vol. I of *Jefferson and His Time* (Boston, 1948), 373–377; Michael Kranish, *Flight from Monticello: Thomas Jefferson at War* (New York, 2010), 294–301.

cumstances of the time should render most proper." In answering his own rhetorical question of why Virginia would not choose to "retain and incorporate" free blacks instead of ordering them to leave, Jefferson began a long digression about black inferiority.[4]

Of all Jefferson's voluminous writings, a particular passage in this section has become one of the most often quoted: his list of all the reasons emancipation would be disastrous. "Deep rooted prejudices entertained by the whites; ten thousand recollections, by the blacks, of the injuries they have sustained; *new provocations;* the real distinctions which nature has made; and many other circumstances, will divide us into parties, and produce convulsions which will probably never end but in the extermination of the one or the other race." Scholars have dissected and analyzed almost all of these charged phrases, except the two words "new provocations."[5]

What did Jefferson mean by "new provocations"? We can only speculate, but reports about the scores of slaves (including his own) running to the British army—which Governor Jefferson had received only weeks before he began writing *Notes*—might have crossed his mind. If not current events, his pantry of Revolutionary memories would be quite stocked.

For many Americans, Jefferson included, those two vague words held a great deal within them. Packed inside "new provocations" were hundreds of individual actions (slaves' stealing boats to reach ships commanded by Dunmore, Mathews, or Howe, instant decisions about whether to follow soldiers

4. Thomas Jefferson, *Notes on the State of Virginia,* ed. William Peden (1954; rpt. Chapel Hill, N.C., 1982), 138.

5. Ibid., 138 (emphasis added). For example, Eva Sheppard Wolf includes this paragraph in a chapter epigraph, using ellipses to excise "new provocations." See Jefferson, *Notes on the State of Virginia* (1785), quoted in Wolf, *Race and Liberty in the New Nation: Emancipation in Virginia from the Revolution to Nat Turner's Rebellion* (Baton Rouge, La., 2006), 85. For analyses of Jefferson's take on slavery leading to potential race war in "Query XIV," see Winthrop D. Jordan, *White over Black: American Attitudes toward the Negro, 1550–1812* (Chapel Hill, N.C., 1968), 430–436; David Brion Davis, *The Problem of Slavery in the Age of Revolution, 1770–1823* (Ithaca, N.Y., 1975), 166–183; John Chester Miller, *The Wolf by the Ears: Thomas Jefferson and Slavery* (New York, 1977), 38–45; Garry Wills, *Inventing America: Jefferson's Declaration of Independence* (Garden City, N.Y., 1978), 302; Peter S. Onuf, *Jefferson's Empire: The Language of American Nationhood* (Charlottesville, Va., 2000),147–188; Ari Helo and Peter S. Onuf, "Jefferson, Morality, and the Problem of Slavery," *WMQ,* 3d Ser., LX (2003), 583–614; and Douglas R. Egerton, *Death or Liberty: African Americans and Revolutionary America* (New York, 2009), 225–228.

commanded by Cornwallis, Arnold, or Clinton) and other methods of improving their situations (African Americans filing petitions for freedom in New England courts or shouldering arms in the ranks with the promise that military service would translate into republican membership). "New provocations" also contained gallons of ink, column after column of newspaper stories introducing readers to places like Sullivan's Island, Gwynn's Island, and Fort Johnston and people like Colonel Tye. There were printed renderings of characters like Lord Kidnapper and Major Cudjo who danced along the line between fiction and fact. And there were official broadsides sent from Congress, like the Declaration of Independence, that excoriated the actions of "domestic insurrectionists." Like the English official in Achebe's *Things Fall Apart*, who was certain he could boil Igbo society down to a single paragraph, Jefferson condensed African Americans' Revolutionary experience—the largest slave rebellion until the Civil War—into two words. No matter what details Jefferson invoked by "new provocations," his point was clear: the Revolutionary War had further deepened "deep rooted prejudices" and added to the "ten thousand recollections" for both blacks and whites. Jefferson's gloss suggests that patriot leaders wanted to forget the ugly business of propagating war stories. His statements might have been on the leading edge of American racial ideology, but many American readers would have assented to the "new provocations" spurred by the Revolutionary War.[6]

When it came to describing Indians in Query VI of *Notes*, Jefferson again showed signs of deliberate forgetting. He made no mention of his or his colleagues' rhetoric of "merciless savages" or their "known rule of warfare." Instead, Jefferson offered his Enlightenment audience an argument that Indians deserved respect, not loathing. "Eloquence in council, bravery and address in war, become the foundations of all consequence with them," he wrote in admiration. He included the famous 1774 speech "Logan's Lament" as proof of Indian expression and even laid the blame for frontier violence at the feet of grasping white frontiersmen, such as those who had killed Cornstalk in 1777.[7]

6. Chinua Achebe, *Things Fall Apart* (1959; rpt. New York, 1994), 209; Bruce Dain, *A Hideous Monster of the Mind: American Race Theory in the Early Republic* (Cambridge, Mass., 2002), 26–39.

7. Jefferson, "Query VI: Productions Mineral, Vegetable, and Animal," in Jefferson, *Notes*, ed. Peden, 26–72, esp. 62. See also Anthony F. C. Wallace, *Jefferson and the Indians: The Tragic Fate of the First Americans* (Cambridge, Mass., 1999), esp. 1–21.

This, in contrast to his statements on black inferiority, was an arresting departure. Jefferson and some of his colleagues did want to pursue a different diplomatic path on the frontier after the war, to confer "the Blessings of Civilization" on the Indians instead of following the European imperial example of pitting groups against each other. According to Jefferson and other former patriots, including Henry Knox and Timothy Pickering, Indians could be "cured" of their savagery through exposure to American ideas of education, husbandry, gender conventions, Christianity, and trade goods. The postwar west could be an "empire of liberty" for all.[8]

This may at first seem like backtracking by Jefferson. *Notes* was, rather, a book past its time, an artifact of the early 1770s. In his analysis of Indian "civilization," Jefferson signaled that he was out of step with how the Revolution shifted the discourse away from conceptions of inclusion on the frontier. Had the American public looked over Governor Jefferson's shoulder as he composed Query VI in the summer of 1781, they would have been perplexed. Was he trying to erase all the stories of the past six years? "New provocations" certainly applied to backcountry as well as plantations, they knew. Soon, when the news of the slaughter at Gnadenhutten trickled out of the Ohio Valley, whom, they might wonder, did Jefferson really blame? From the *Notes*, readers might conclude he believed it was David Williamson's fault, but that was a position in conflict with Jefferson's own efforts in propagating the common cause and begging those same frontiersmen to fight Indians as an expression of their patriotism. During the war, he had labored to convince Americans that the Indians had brought violence down upon themselves for their willingness to listen to treacherous British officials. His laudatory defense of Indian men as "affectionate to [their] children" and "indulgent in the extreme" stands in stark contrast to his own

8. Eric Hinderaker, *Elusive Empires: Constructing Colonialism in the Ohio Valley, 1673–1800* (Cambridge, 1997), 225–236; Patrick Griffin, *American Leviathan: Empire, Nation, and Revolutionary Frontier* (New York, 2007), 183–211, 259, esp. 259; Peter S. Onuf, *Jefferson's Empire: The Language of American Nationhood* (Charlottesville, Va., 2000), 18–52; James H. Merrell, "Declarations of Independence: Indian-White Relations in the New Nation," in Jack P. Greene, ed., *The American Revolution: Its Character and Limits* (New York, 1987), 197–223, esp. 204–205; Robert F. Berkhofer, Jr., *The White Man's Indian: Images of the American Indian from Columbus to the Present* (New York, 1978), 134–144; David Andrew Nichols, *Red Gentlemen and White Savages: Indians, Federalists, and the Search for Order on the American Frontier* (Charlottesville, Va., 2008), esp. 204.

"New Provocations"

words in the Declaration, denouncing all Indians as wanting the "undistinguished destruction of all ages, sexes and conditions." Tragic as it was, Gnadenhutten arose from that culture of justified, martial resistance to the Revolution's enemies—or, at least, that was how Jefferson and his colleagues had defined it ever since independence. Now, however, from the perspective of Query VI, it was as if the Revolution had never happened. As much as Jefferson might have wished to return to those days when the "great object of desire" was to abolish slavery or to forget all the turmoil in the backcountry, the rhetoric of the war years would not allow such an easy revision. It would prove impossible to abridge those experiences into two words, or, worse, to forget them altogether.[9]

But it is not enough to suggest Jefferson's *Notes* was merely behind the times. Doing so elides the direct role the author himself had played in that transformation. Jefferson and his fellow patriot publicists had chosen union over inclusion. They not only conjured but fetishized union as the Revolution's only security. The particular way they argued for unity—by highlighting stories of unfaithful Indians and African Americans—blocked off the very avenues Jefferson now sought to pursue. Jefferson and some of his patriot colleagues might not have wanted them to, but war stories marking African Americans and Indians as enemies of the United States persisted long after 1783. During the conflict, these images complemented and reinforced an ideology that projected the patriots as defenders of universal, natural rights. Now those foundational stories about African Americans and Indians—but not Hessians—competed with a heroic rendering of the Revolution and gave credence to those who wanted to exclude certain former proxies from a notion of inclusion in the new United States. With the emergency of war passed, the tensions inherent in the common cause became apparent by the mid-1780s. The memory of words they had written in anger and desperation during the Revolutionary War stymied efforts Jefferson and his colleagues sponsored to extend the natural rights rhetoric of the common cause to everyone (under certain conditions). "New provocations" blunted the universal appeal of the American Revolution. Their efforts to "strain every Nerve," as many patriot political leaders and polemicists phrased what was needed in desperate moments, had consequences.

9. Jefferson, *Notes*, ed. Peden, 26, 60. Of course he intended *Notes* for a very different audience than the Declaration; indeed, he worried that his political standing might be jeopardized if the book escaped the small audience of intellectuals that he had written it for. See William Peden's introduction on xvii.

The necessity of union and the exigencies of explaining the Revolutionary War would haunt the founders—and the United States—long after Yorktown for three reasons. First, the common cause appeal carried on in myriad texts that Americans circulated throughout the postwar years, including early histories of the Revolution, epic poems, travelogues, novels, and captivity narratives. Through this repetition came cultural codification. Second, the continued political wrangling over the Treaty of Paris (which included thousands of *real* African Americans and Indians) and the crisis of the mid-1780s sustained the political imperative to encourage frontier settlers and slaveholders to maintain their allegiance to the union, keeping the practical impulse that had always animated the cause appeal alive for decades after the war ended. Finally, the most significant reason the common cause mattered after 1783 was the decision to turn away from subjecthood and embrace a radically different conception of political belonging, the as-yet opaque theory of citizenship. Because, as petitioners from a Virginia county stated at war's end, "admission to citizenship is a matter of favour, and not of right," the community decided who belonged to the republic and who did not. Instead of all being universal subjects of the king, in which only the monarch could make legal distinctions, American citizenship suggested that "the people" defined the boundaries of who was a "citizen," who was an "alien," and who lurked in between.[10]

Just as they had been during the war, these postwar codification processes were circular, each drawing from new events (or new texts or new arguments), which, in turn, shaped the discourse, which then influenced political policy. By the end of the eighteenth century, however, the common cause's founding narrative exerted increasing weight, closing off many opportunities for free and enslaved African Americans and Indians to escape the stigma that they had made critical—treasonous—decisions during the test of the American Revolution.

1: THE CULTURAL CODIFICATIONS OF WAR STORIES

In the summer of 1775, former Yale tutor and lawyer John Trumbull wrote *M'Fingal*, an enormously popular poem that described the comic encounter

10. Caroline County, Va. petition: *Pennsylvania Journal,* Nov. 8, 1783; *Royal Gazette,* Nov. 15, 1783; James H. Kettner, *The Development of American Citizenship, 1608–1870* (Chapel Hill, N.C., 1978); Douglas Bradburn, *The Citizenship Revolution: Politics and the Creation of the American Union, 1774–1804* (Charlottesville, Va., 2009).

at a New England town meeting between a whig, "Honorius," and a tory, "Squire M'Fingal." With the assistance of his law mentor John Adams (who was the model for Honorius), Trumbull published the first canto of *M'Fingal* in Philadelphia that first Revolutionary winter, only a few days removed from the appearance of *Common Sense*. Reflecting the pervasive stories about blacks' and Indians' being "instigated" by the British throughout the "rage militaire" of 1775–1776, Trumbull lingered over the proxy image for more than fifty lines in the poem's first iteration. He accused Britain of sending a "duplicate of Guys" to rain destruction on the backcountry:

> Has she not set at work all engines
> To spirit up the native Indians,
> Send on your backs the tawney band,
> With each an hatchet in his hand,
> T' amuse themselves with scalping knives,
> And butcher children and your wives;
> And paid them for your scalps at sale
> More than your heads would fetch by tale . . .
> On this brave work to raise allies,
> She sent her duplicate of Guys,
> To drive at different parts at once on,
> Her stout Guy Carlton and Guy Johnson.

Trumbull then pivoted from threats out west to those down south, turning General Thomas Gage into Dunmore.

> And has she not essay'd her notes
> To rouse your slaves to cut your throats;
> Sent o'er ambassadors with guineas,
> To bribe your blacks in Carolinas?
> And has not Gage, her missionary,
> Turn'd many an Afric to a Tory;
> Made the New-England Bishop's see grow,
> By many a new-converted negro?
> As friends to government, when he
> Your slaves at Boston late set free,
> Enlisted them in black parade,
> Emboss'd with regimental red;
> While flared the epaulette, like flambeau,

On Captain Cuff and Ensign Sambo:
And were they not accounted then
Among his very bravest men?[11]

Key elements of the common cause argument, as it developed early on in the war, are evident in this passage, including reference to the well-known "notes" that British agents (Sir William Draper and Dr. Samuel Johnson) had published calling for the crown to free and arm slaves if war broke out in America. His referring to the "friends to government" as "slaves" marching alongside blacks in the "black parade," moreover, conflated tories with African Americans, a repeated device used by patriot publicists to denigrate the slippery loyalists.

In the later years of the Revolution, Trumbull settled in the relative calm of Hartford, opened a law practice, and, encouraged by supportive literary friends, revised his epic. By 1782, Trumbull had doubled it in length and added two more cantos. In the postwar period, it enjoyed an even greater popularity.[12]

More than a thousand lines long, one of those new cantos, entitled "The Vision," was Squire M'Fingal's Miltonian nightmare of the Revolutionary War. "The Vision" ranged across time and space retelling war stories. Of course, the proxies played recurring and prominent roles in the tory's tortured dream. Hessians appear as pathetic intruders and pitiful sights:

Rush rude these uninvited guests;
Nor aught avails the captured crew
Their martial whiskers' grisly hue!

11. Kenneth Silverman, *A Cultural History of the American Revolution: Painting, Music, Literature, and the Theatre in the Colonies and the United States from the Treaty of Paris to the Inauguration of George Washington, 1763–1789* (New York, 1976), 296–299. John Trumbull published *M'Fingal: A Modern Epic Poem; Canto First; or the Town Meeting* (Philadelphia, 1775), at the beginning of the Revolution but continued to revise it until it reached its most complete form in 1820. See John Trumbull, *M'Fingal: A Modern Epic Poem* (1776–1820), in *The Poetical Works of John Trumbull . . .* , 2 vols. (Hartford, Conn.,1820), esp. 50–52. For more on Trumbull, see Christopher Grasso, *A Speaking Aristocracy: Transforming Public Discourse in Eighteenth-Century Connecticut* (Chapel Hill, N.C., 1999), 285–326; Robert A. Ferguson, *Law and Letters in American Culture* (Cambridge, Mass., 1984), 100–111. This John Trumbull was not the printer of the *Norwich Packet.*

12. Grasso, *Speaking Aristocracy*, 324.

From "Del'ware's icy roar," M'Fingal's vision shifts south to "See plund'ring Dunmore's negro band / Fly headlong from Virginia's strand." The body of the verse, though, lampooned British generals. Burgoyne's activities on the New York frontier certainly could not pass without comment, including a biting reference to Jane McCrea:

> This, this is he—the famed Burgoyne!
> Who pawn'd his honor and commission,
> To coax the patriots to submission,
> By songs and balls secure allegiance,
> And dance the ladies to obedience.

Worst of all, however, was Cornwallis and his "mighty band."

> Nor yet this hero's glories bright
> Blaze only in the fields of fight.
> Not Howe's humanity more deserving
> In gifts of hanging and starving;
> Not Arnold plunders more tobacco
> Or steals more negroes for Jamaica.

Along with the Revolutionary poetry of Philip Freneau, *M'Fingal* brought stories about the proxies out of the daily digest of war news and legitimized them as literary subjects.[13]

Sadly, Trumbull learned the difficult economic lesson that the printers' system of exchanges applied to more than just battlefield reports. Pirated editions of *M'Fingal* flooded the print market. The problems of Trumbull's purse aside, the reception of *M'Fingal* illustrates the proxy stories' continuation long after the war. In the early 1790s, Mathew Carey's renowned peri-

---

13. Trumbull, *M'Fingal*, in *Poetical Works of John Trumbull*, 121, 130, 137, 139–142, 159–160. Trumbull's reference might have been too clever by half. In an 1820 collection of his poetry, he added a note to clarify "dance the ladies to obedience": "Such were Burgoyne's declarations, when he was setting out to command in America. This pleasant mode of warfare not meeting with the expected success at Boston, he appears to have changed his plan in his northern expedition; in which the Indians received compensation for American scalps, without distinction of gender. He denied however his personal agency in these transactions. See the correspondence between him and General Gates, occasioned by the murder and scalping of Miss McCrea" (Trumbull, *M'Fingal*, in *Poetical Works of John Trumbull*, I, 139).

odical *American Museum* reprinted the 1782 edition in full, further cementing the poem as a major work of the Revolutionary era.[14]

One of Trumbull's peers in American letters was Hugh Henry Brackenridge. As detailed above, throughout the war Brackenridge had written plays, sermons, and poetry that reinforced the common cause, often by invoking proxy enemies. In 1779, he edited the *United States Magazine,* the only active periodical during the Revolutionary War. The *Magazine* printed more than literary items. As editor, Brackenridge published state constitutions, letters from Congress, and, in the final issue, an essay he wrote entitled "Thoughts upon the Enfranchisement of the Negroes." Protesting that America's retention of slavery "casts a shade upon the face of this country," the author wrote that slaves should be enfranchised—but not in the United States. "Shall they be set immediately at liberty amongst ourselves? No; for my part I am for the plan to colonize them. . . . Thus would I have these black people led out by some generous mind, and colonized, perhaps beyond the Ohio, or the Misissippi river, in that country forfeited by the native Indians, in consequence of their hostilities against us." This anticipated Jefferson's rhetorical question in Query XIV by two years. Neither advocate of abolition could envision an independent America that included free blacks as citizens.[15]

By war's end, Brackenridge had moved west to Pittsburgh. When two survivors of Colonel William Crawford's ill-fated 1782 expedition to Sandusky, Dr. Knight and John Slover, stumbled back to Fort Pitt, Brackenridge was there to receive their gruesome tales. The following summer, he arranged for the publication of their narratives. Actually, he had them in his possession for a while before presenting them to the public. As Brackenridge explained in a preface that introduced the powerful stories, upon hearing that Guy Carleton had issued orders from New York that the Indians "desist from their incursions, [which] gave reason to hope there would be an end to their barbarities," he kept them to himself. "But," he lamented, "as they still continue their murders on our frontiers, these narratives may be

14. On January 7, 1783, the *Connecticut Courant* published a bitter complaint from Trumbull that "among more than thirty different impressions, one only, at any subsequent time, was published with the permission, or even the knowledge, of the writer" (*Connecticut Courant,* Jan. 27, 1783). See also Cathy N. Davidson, *Revolution and the Word: The Rise of the Novel in America* (New York, 1986), 33–36.

15. Brackenridge, "Thoughts upon the Enfranchisement of the Negroes," *United States Magazine,* I (1779), 487–488.

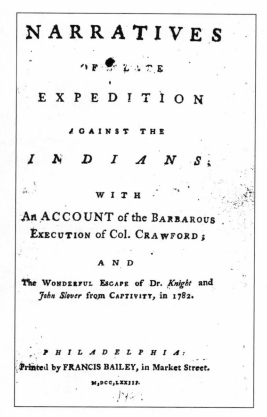

Figure 18. *Title page,* Narratives *of a Late Expedition against the Indians . . . (Philadelphia, 1783), broadside. Hugh Henry Brackenridge documented Knight and Slover's tales of Colonel William Crawford's torture at Sandusky in 1782 and sent them to Philadelphia printer Francis Bailey. Brackenridge wrote in the preface that he hoped they would again illustrate for Americans "the sufferings of some of her citizens by the hands of the Indian allies of Britain." University of Pittsburgh.*

serviceable to induce our governments to take some effectual steps to chastise and repress them; as from hence they will see that the nature of an Indian is fierce and cruel, and that an extirpation of them would be useful to the world, and honourable to those who can effect it." Just like Franklin thousands of miles away, Brackenridge saw it as his patriotic duty to urge the American public to remain steadfast against their enemies—by reminding them of Indian atrocities.[16]

Brackenridge, like Franklin, had been consistent throughout the Revo-

16. *Narratives of a Late Expedition against the Indians; with An Account of the Barbarous Execution of Col. Crawford . . .* (Philadelphia, 1783), [4], *Early American Imprints,* 17993. Either in excerpt or serial form, the narratives also appeared in several newspapers. See *Freeman's Journal* (Philadelphia), Apr. 30, May 7, 14, 21, 28, 1783; *Boston Evening-Post,* May 24, 31, 1783; *Massachusetts Spy,* Oct. 2, 1783; *Connecticut Gazette,* Oct. 17, 24, 1783; *Connecticut Courant,* Nov. 11, 1783; *Connecticut Journal,* Nov. 19, 26, 1783.

lution. Just as he had with the fictionalization of Schuyler's letter in *Death of General Montgomery* (1777), Brackenridge's sponsorship of the Slover and Knight narratives—complete with a plea to exterminate the Indians—deepened the imprint of Crawford's ordeal in American culture. By the early 1790s, someone had apparently set Slover and Knight's narratives to music. The lyrics of "A Song, Called Crawford's Defeat by the Indians" appeared as a broadsheet in 1791.[17]

Of the postwar anti-Indian reflections, however, the publication of a slim volume by John Filson was by far the most influential, since it forwarded "the first nationally viable statement of a myth of the frontier." Filson had been one of the nearly three thousand American soldiers captured by German mercenaries—then considered "men monsters"—at Fort Washington, in November 1776. By war's end, after working as a schoolteacher and a surveyor in Pennsylvania, he set off for Lexington, Kentucky, to try his luck on the new frontier. Soon, he found an opportunity by offering a different kind of survey, a book entitled *The Discovery, Settlement and Present State of Kentucke,* published in 1784. This was a settler's guide, introducing prospective migrants to the region's nature, people, and early history. The most important part of Filson's book was its appendix, a thirty-three-page supplement entitled "The Adventures of Col. Daniel Boon." Two-thirds of those pages, though, did more than just sketch the outlines of a frontier hero; they breathed life into Kentucky's Revolutionary War. Filson's book brought some untold stories of the Revolution to light, but it also retold some familiar stories from Boone's perspective. Throughout Boone's narrative, Indians appear as British proxies whose "savage minds were inflamed to mischief" by British Indian agents Simon Girty and Alexander McKee, men who had worked with Henry "Hair-Buyer" Hamilton and Guy Johnson.[18]

17. *A Song, Called Crawford's Defeat by the Indians; On the Fourth Day of June, 1782,* Early American Imprints, 49382.

18. "First nationally viable": Richard Slotkin, *Regeneration through Violence: The Mythology of the American Frontier, 1600–1860* (Middletown, Conn., 1973), 269; John Filson, *The Discovery, Settlement and Present State of Kentucke; and An Essay towards the Topography and Natural History of That Important Country* (1784; rpt. Bowie, Md., 1996), 49–82, esp. 75. For two studies that have tried to separate fact from myth surrounding Boone, see John Mack Faragher, *Daniel Boone: The Life and Legend of an American Pioneer* (New York, 1992); Michael A. Lofaro, *Daniel Boone: An American Life* (Lexington, Ky., 2003).

In Boone's narrative, natives act the part of merciless savages perfectly. Boone documents their treachery in battle and "savage treatment" of the "tender women, and helpless children, [who] fell victims to their cruelty." The heroic frontiersman, however, stands above the fray. He is the opposite of the British instigators and Indian proxies. As presented by Filson, Boone possesses what the Indians cannot: civic responsibility, restraint, and humanity in war. He is the archetypal American citizen: exposure to the wilderness only heightens his sensibilities and patriotism. The Indians, on the other hand, exhibit none of these traits. Quite the opposite: during the critical test of the Revolution, they prove susceptible to British intrigue and are especially cruel in war.[19]

Another commentary on the war that featured images of the proxies came from a foreign source. One of the top commanding officers in the French Army, the marquis de Chastellux, collected notes on the places he went and the stories he heard in the United States from 1780–1782. What would become known as *Travels in North America* was published in a few pieces during the mid-1780s, translated into English in 1787, and well known in America by the end of the decade.

Several of Chastellux's conversations during his journey illustrated the persistence of popular memory about war stories of the king's proxies. At a tavern in New York, he met a survivor of the Wyoming Massacre more than four years after the attack. The young woman's "eyes filled with tears in relating her misfortune," remembering how she watched her brother murdered "almost before her eyes," and she recalled her fifty-mile flight from danger, her feet "raw and bleeding." As Chastellux traveled up the Hudson through upstate New York, the house of "the unfortunate Miss McCrea, who was killed by the Indians, was pointed out to me." These happenstances gave Chastellux the perfect opportunity to delve into well-worn war stories. "If the Whigs were superstitious, they would attribute this event to divine vengeance," he noted, implying that McCrea deserved her fate when, rejecting the good political sentiments her parents "had inspired in her," she fell prey to loyalist David Jones, "who triumphed over both her scruples and her patriotism." Chastellux linked her political and sexual virtue and found both wanting.[20]

19. Filson, *Kentucke*, 72.

20. [François Jean], marquis de Chastellux, *Travels in North America in the Years 1780, 1781 and 1782*, ed. Howard Rice, Jr., rev. ed., 2 vols. (Chapel Hill, N.C., 1963), I, 214–215, II, 512–513.

Chastellux ended his discussion of McCrea with a comment that "a death so cruel and unforeseen would furnish a most pathetic subject for a drama or an elegy." His countryman, author and colonial officer Michel-René Hilliard-d'Auberteuil, took up the task. Hilliard followed two histories on the Revolution written in the early 1780s with a short novel about America's "first folk heroine," published in Brussels in 1784. Hilliard drenched his version of the incident outside Fort Edward in stock conventions of late-eighteenth-century sentimental fiction. His retelling of the McCrea story featured heaving breasts, rolling tears, and fathers clashing with innocent daughters over corrupt suitors. Hilliard added a new character, however: "Kiashuta," a tragic Indian hero who tries to protect Jane and then, when he fails, tracks down and dispatches her murderers, and laments how Europeans are right to call them savages. The McCrea episode offered Hilliard the opportunity to combine two of the more popular literary genres of the reading public in western Europe: sentimental fiction best associated with Samuel Richardson and the image of the "Noble Savage" as conjured by, among others, Rousseau, Voltaire, Díderot, and Raynal.[21]

21. Ibid., I, 215; Michel René Hilliard-d'Auberteuil, *Miss McCrea (1784): A Novel of the American Revolution; A Facsimile Reproduction,* trans. Eric LaGuardia (Gainesville, Fla., 1958), 58–59, 61–62. Since the first part of Chastellux's *Travels* (in which the McCrea passages appear) had been both passed around Paris in manuscript form and printed in 1783, it is probable that Hilliard had seen his comment on McCrea. The complete edition of Chastellux's *Travels* was printed in Paris in 1786, and in England in 1787. There was not an edition published in the United States until 1827, though imported copies of the translated versions published in Britain were common in Philadelphia and New York by 1788. For the publication history of Chastellux, see I, 25–39. Hilliard: Jay Fliegelman, *Prodigals and Pilgrims: The American Revolution against Patriarchal Authority, 1750–1800* (Cambridge, 1982), 138; June Namias, *White Captives: Gender and Ethnicity on the American Frontier* (Chapel Hill, N.C., 1993), 121–124. The real Seneca leader Kayashuta led the 1782 attack on Hanna's Town. See Colin G. Calloway, *The American Revolution in Indian Country: Crisis and Diversity in Native American Communities* (Cambridge, 1995), 29–30; Barbara Graymont, *The Iroquois in the American Revolution* (Syracuse, N.Y., 1972), 80, 94.

For discussions of the Enlightenment image of "Noble Savage," see Berkhofer, *White Man's Indian,* 72–80; Roy Harvey Pearce, *Savagism and Civilization: A Study of the Indian and the American Mind* (Berkeley, Calif., 1988), 136–150; Erik Hinderaker, "The 'Four Indian Kings' and the Imaginative Construction of the First British Empire," *WMQ,* 3d Ser., LIII (1996), 487–526. For a penetrating analysis that questions

In the early 1780s, Benjamin Franklin, Philip Freneau, and Thomas Jefferson extolled the virtues of the noble savage, too—but their complicated involvement in framing the original context for McCrea's death cannot be forgotten. Hilliard's portrayal of Indians in his sentimental novelette left plenty of space for the alternative image of Indians as forwarded by those patriot publicists who first exploited her death: merciless savages incited to horrible violence by evil British agents. Jane's captors in Hilliard's story vied for the privilege of controlling her based on "how many rebels [they] had massacred in carrying out the orders of the great king." This was what had made the story so attractive to patriot publicists originally, and it was this politically charged sentiment that made McCrea an international celebrity. After the war, the texts that those former patriot leaders generated lauding America's noble savages sat uncomfortably next to other manufactures of recent vintage. Those productions offered a very different image of Indians as a collective. War stories about what happened at Fort Edward, Wyoming, and Oriskany, which Chastellux heard firsthand and Hilliard surely learned from the publications generated by France's ally, competed with Enlightenment ideals of primitive innocence.[22]

McCrea's story enjoyed significant longevity after 1777 and far outside upstate New York. Painters would soon cement the "merciless savage" rep-

---

how these tropes developed from sixteenth- and seventeenth-century accounts, see Gordon M. Sayre, *Les Sauvages Américains: Representations of Native Americans in French and English Colonial Literature* (Chapel Hill, N.C., 1997).

22. Hilliard-d'Auberteuil, *Miss McCrea*, 60. Franklin: "Remarks concerning the Savages of North-America" (Passy, 1783), in J. A. Leo Lemay, ed., *Benjamin Franklin: Writings; Boston and London, 1722–1726* . . . (New York, 1987), 969–974. Freneau: "The Prophecy of King Tammany" (1782), "The Dying Indian: Tomo-Chequi" (1784), "The Death Song of a Cherokee Indian" (1787), in Fred Lewis Pattee, ed., *The Poems of Philip Freneau: Poet of the American Revolution*, 3 vols. (Princeton, N.J., 1902–1907), II, 187–189, 243–245, 313–314; "Query VI," in Jefferson, *Notes*, ed. Peden, 26–72, esp. 58–64. Joel Barlow's epic poem *The Vision of Columbus* (1787) also featured images of "noble" and "merciless" savages simultaneously. See Barlow, *The Vision of Columbus: A Poem in Nine Books* (Hartford, 1787), 152–154. In this iteration of his poem, Barlow employed this fearsome language for the Seven Years' War. When he revised and expanded the poem years later (eventually known as the *Columbiad*), he would add specific stories about Indian violence during the Revolution, for which see Conclusion, below. For more, see Danielle E. Conger, "Toward a Native American Nationalism: Joel Barlow's *The Vision of Columbus*," *New England Quarterly*, LXXII (1999), 558–576.

resentation in the romantic iconography of the Revolution. Painter John Trumbull first planned to have McCrea join Dr. Joseph Warren and Richard Montgomery as a third installment in his series of Revolutionary martyrs, making preliminary sketches of a study in the 1780s. Although Jane would have to wait two more decades, once John Vanderlyn completed his visceral painting in 1804, her beatification was complete. So, too, was the erasure of "Kiashuta" and of Indians behaving as anything but bloodthirsty murderers enthralled by British tyranny.[23]

* * *

In addition to poems, travelogues, novels, and captivity narratives, the first histories of the Revolution also transferred war stories about the proxies into something more durable. The first historians of the Revolution were all former patriots with varying involvement in the war. Their projects did not stray from that inner circle: they enlisted other former patriots to send documents and check their facts, and begged still other leaders to sponsor their books.

The first history focused specifically on the Revolution was David Ramsay's *History of the Revolution of South-Carolina,* published in 1785. Threats from proxies were a central, recurring theme for Ramsay, a Pennsylvania-born physician who had relocated to Charleston, become Henry Laurens's son-in-law, and served in both the South Carolina Assembly and the Continental Congress. He confirmed, for example, General Charles Lee's allegation that the British had coordinated the 1776 Cherokee War to begin in concert with Peter Parker's assault on Sullivan's Island. In a very revealing passage that went to the heart of why patriot leaders amplified British connections to Indian hostility, Ramsay argued the British design to "massacre the defenceless frontier settlers" had

> increased [Carolina's] opposition to Great-Britain. Several who called themselves tories in 1775 became active whigs in 1776, and cheerfully took up arms in the first instance against Indians, and the second against Great-Britain, as the instigator of their barbarous devastations. Before this event some well-meaning people could not see the justice or propriety of contending with their formerly protecting

23. For more on the McCrea myth in the nineteenth and twentieth centuries, see Jeremy Engels and Greg Goodale, "'Our Battle Cry Will Be: Remember Jenny McCrea!' A Précis on the Rhetoric of Revenge," *American Quarterly,* LXI (2009), 93–112.

parent-state; but Indian cruelties, excited by royal artifices, soon extinguished all their predilection for the country of their forefathers.

The effectiveness of these representations—the political capital they gave patriot leaders—were why, as British Indian Superintendent John Stuart snorted from his exile in Saint Augustine, these were "Words in the mouth of every Child" in 1776.[24]

Ramsay also documented South Carolina's conflict with its slaves. Estimating that South Carolina had lost a total of 25,000 slaves during the course of the war, he described the repeated coastal raids that "contributed very little to the advancement of the royal cause, but it added much to the wealth of the officers . . . of the British army." During one such incursion, "the hapless Africans, allured with hopes of freedom, forsook their owners, and repaired in great numbers to the royal army. . . . All subordination being destroyed, they became insolent and rapacious, and in some instances exceeded the British in their plunderings and devastations." Ramsay's history let readers in on some tragic scenes they had not read about in their local papers, especially his description of runaway slaves so terrified to return to their owners that they would "fasten themselves to the sides of the boats. To prevent this dangerous practice, the fingers of some of them were chopped off, and soldiers were posted with cutlasses and bayonets to oblige them to keep at proper distances." Hundreds died in the woods, their bodies "devoured by beasts and birds." Patriot publicists nearly always referred to enslaved Africans as inanimate objects; it was British agents that acted. They were the ones who "tampered," "instigated," and "stole" slaves from southern plantations. Yet, as Ramsay revealed in this glimpse into the desperation that pervaded these encounters, enslaved people were the ones doing the running, the risking, and the dying to get away from American masters.[25]

24. David Ramsay, *A History of the Revolution of South-Carolina: From a British Province to an Independent State*, 2 vols. (Trenton, N.J., 1785), I, 160; John Richard Alden, "John Stuart Accuses William Bull," *WMQ*, 3d Ser., II (1945), 320. For a general study of the first histories of the Revolution, see Arthur Shaffer, *The Politics of History: Writing the History of the American Revolution, 1783–1815* (Chicago, 1975); Lester H. Cohen, *The Revolutionary Histories: Contemporary Narratives of the American Revolution* (Ithaca, N.Y., 1980); and Eileen Ka-May Cheng, *The Plain and Noble Garb of Truth: Nationalism and Impartiality in American Historical Writing, 1784–1860* (Athens, Ga., 2008), esp. 208–254.

25. Ramsay, *History of the Revolution of South-Carolina*, II, 31 ("contributed very little"), 31–32 ("hapless Africans"), 33 ("devoured").

After completing his history of South Carolina, Ramsay turned his attention to writing a chronicle of the nation's experience as a whole. In 1788, he stood for election to the first Federal Congress but lost to William Loughton Smith because his neighbors saw him as too friendly to abolition. He had voted with John Laurens in 1782 for South Carolina to form black regiments, after all. Soon after this political setback, he brought out *The History of the American Revolution,* completed in late 1787 but withheld until 1789 to include the ratification of the Constitution. In his second foray into history, Ramsay sharpened his analytical edge and made some penetrating arguments. Of the multiple patriot histories that would appear in the postwar years, his was "the least celebratory and most skeptical."[26]

Ramsay often exposed the patriot propagation campaign. It was in an appendix of this book that Ramsay made his famous statement, "In establishing American independence, the pen and the press had merit equal to that of the sword." He admitted that the project "to rouse and unite the inhabitants, and to persuade them to patience for several years . . . was a work of difficulty." He then let readers have a peek onto the shop floor. He discussed, for example, Johnson's alleged invitation to "feast on a Bostonian" in December 1775. Although it "meant no more than to partake of a roasted ox and a pipe of wine, at a public entertainment," Ramsay observed, "The colonial patriots, affected to understand it in its literal sense. It furnished in their mode of explication, a convenient handle for operating on the passions of the people." His discussion of the "universal horror" of McCrea's murder was equally frank. With the help of the press, he argued that the patriots had used the incident as an "Occasion . . . to inflame the populace, and to blacken the royal cause. The cruelties of the Indians, and the cause in which they were engaged, were associated together, and presented in one view to the alarmed inhabitants." "Their cruel mode of warfare," Ramsay noted, "by putting to death as well the smiling infant and the defenceless female, as the resisting armed man, excited an universal spirit of resistance." For Ramsay,

26. Ramsay wrote a friend that he lost because he was "a northward man" and was "represented as favoring the abolition of slavery. Such is the temper of our people here that it is unpopular to be unfriendly to the farther importation of slaves." See Ramsay to John Eliot, Charleston, Nov. 26, 1788, in Robert L. Brunhouse, ed., "David Ramsay, 1749–1815, Selections from His Writings," *Transactions of the American Philosophical Society,* N.S., LV (1965), 1–250, esp. 123. For more, see Karen O'Brien, "David Ramsay and the Delayed Americanization of American History," *Early American Literature,* XXIX (1994), 1–18, esp. 2.

"New Provocations"

the news of McCrea's death functioned as the stories about Hessian rapes had during the "December crisis": they forced many who "remained peaceably at their homes" to choose between "the dangers of a manly resistance, with those of a passive inaction." He did not include these analyses to portray patriot leaders as false manipulators, nor did he aim at full disclosure (which is apparent since the name of patriot-turned-informant Benjamin Church does not appear in his six-hundred-page chronicle). Ramsay's revelations did suggest, however, that patriot publicists realized the potential that stories about the proxies held for generating popular support.[27]

Ramsay followed convention regarding the events in Virginia at the time of Dunmore's Proclamation by resorting to the passive voice in discussing resistant African Americans. After Dunmore fled to his ship, he related, a "predatory war" ensued along the coasts of Virginia in which "Negroes were carried off—plantations ravaged—and houses burnt." Ramsay downplayed the impact of Dunmore's emancipation notice, suggesting that because the governor had first threatened to "enfranchise the negroes, and arm them against their masters" back in May but had not done so, when he did offer freedom, "the negroes had in great measure ceased to believe, and the inhabitants to fear. It excited less surprize, and produced less effect, than if it had been more immediate and unexpected." In the end, "The injury done the royal cause by the bare proposal of the scheme, far outweighed any advantage that resulted from it." After discussing Connolly's plot and capture, Ramsay offered what he thought were the real effects of Dunmore's machinations:

> The various projects which were devised and put in operation against them, pointed out the increasing necessity of union, while the havock made on their coasts—the proffer of freedom to their slaves, and the encouragement proposed to Indians for making war on their frontier inhabitants, quickened their resentment against Great-Britain.

Ramsay did not mention how patriot publicists amplified these "projects" to ensure that the American public drew the lesson that that the union was indeed necessary.[28]

Ramsay returned to the subject of runaway slaves and British instigation regarding the aftermath of Charleston's fall, about which he had firsthand

27. David Ramsay, *The History of the American Revolution*, ed. Lester H. Cohen, 2 vols. ([1789]; rpt. Indianapolis, 1990), esp. I, 213, II, 370–371, 633–634.

28. Ibid., I, 229, 232, 233, 236.

knowledge. Perhaps it was this knowledge that made him eschew the canard of passivity in describing slave resistance. "The mischievous effects of slavery, in facilitating the conquest of the country, now became apparent," he wrote of the enslaved people who flocked to Cornwallis's standard. "As the slaves had no interest at stake, the subjugation of the State was a matter of no consequence to them. Instead of aiding in its defence, they by a variety of means threw the weight of their little influence into the opposite scale." Ramsay granted African Americans an active role yet at the same time misrepresented how much "influence" he believed they truly had. If so little, his support for Nathanael Greene's proposal in the South Carolina Assembly to enlist thousands of them as the only way to maintain an effective army in the Deep South after Yorktown made even less sense.[29]

Finally, Ramsay dedicated a lengthy chapter to Indian affairs. Despite patriot efforts to keep Indians neutral in 1775 and 1776, he argued, John Stuart, "in concert with the King's governors, and other royal servants," worked to convince Indians and tories to attack the backcountry. This led to a terrible "storm of Indian and tory vengeance [that] burst with particular violence on Wyoming." Ramsay's description of the Wyoming attack was accurate and, surprisingly, devoid of the "massacre" hyperbole that John Holt and fellow patriot publicists had broadcast in the weeks afterward. He continued to detail Butler's raid on Cherry Valley and Clark's expedition against Henry Hamilton, summarizing that across the frontier, "sometimes cruelty were inflicted and retorted, with infinite variety of scenes of horror and disgust. The selfish passions of human nature unrestrained by social ties, broke over all bounds of decency or humanity." "The savages encouraged by British presents and agents," Ramsay concluded, "extended their depredations and murders far and near."[30]

In the face of these crimes, Ramsay excused Sullivan's men for their destructive mood: "The Americans were so full of resentment against the Indians, for the many outrages they had suffered from them . . . that the officers and soldiers cheerfully agreed to remain till they had fully completed the destruction" of Iroquoia. A few pages after his celebration of Sullivan's expedition, Ramsay described the "barbarous and unprovoked massacre of some civilised Indians" at Gnadenhutten. His interpretation of this tragedy praised the Moravian Indians as "harmless, inoffensive people" and referred

29. Ibid., II, 496.
30. Ibid., II, 464, 466–467, 470–471.

to the perpetrators as men "infinitely more deserving of the name of Savages than those whom they inhumanely murdered." Ramsay's analysis, because it sometimes sympathized with Indians caught up in a gruesome war, was conflicted. He could not condone what David Williamson's men had done at Gnadenhutten, of course, but his harsh words about Indian depredations and praise of patriotic Americans who battled them did so nonetheless.[31]

Ramsay meant his *History of the American Revolution* to stand as a final expression of the common cause. The experience of war had brought colonists together in unprecedented ways. "Local prejudices abated. By frequent collision asperities were worn off, and a foundation was laid for the establishment of a nation, out of discordant materials," he wrote, just two pages before confessing the publicists' "work of difficulty." War encouraged the "great body of the people" to embrace "such practices and sentiments as were favourable to union." Yet, Ramsay contended, the violence necessary to defeat Britain was also America's undoing. "War never fails to injure the morals of the people engaged in it," he bemoaned, and the Revolutionary War "had an unhappy influence of this kind." The problems of the 1780s all stemmed from the experience of war, in Ramsay's opinion. Collectively, America's "moral character is inferior to what it formerly was." The "cause" had evaporated. "In 1775 there was more patroitism [*sic*] in a village than is now in the 13 states," he sighed in a 1786 letter to Benjamin Rush.[32]

Ramsay saw history as an antidote to this moral backsliding. He hoped his work, along with others', would rekindle the fires of unity. "Enthusiastic as I am for the Unity of our republic I wish for every thing that tends to unite us as one people who know esteem and love each other," he wrote to fellow historian and founder of the Massachusetts Historical Society Jeremy Belknap. Remembering the spirit—and stories—of '76 had the potential of healing the divisions that had arisen in the 1780s. Since they made up a significant

31. Ibid., II, 472, 474–475. Ramsay's conclusion to this chapter reveals his resignation about who was to blame for the endemic violence: "Each was made a scourge to the other, and the unavoidable calamities of war were rendered doubly distressing, by the dispersion of families, the breaking up of settlements, and an addition of savage cruelties to the most extensive devastation of those things, which conduce to the comfort of human life." See ibid., II, 475.

32. Ramsay, *History of the American Revolution*, ed. Cohen, II, 631, 634, 637–638; Ramsay to Benjamin Rush, New York, Feb. 11, 1786, in Brunhouse, ed., "Ramsay Writings," *Transactions of Am. Phil. Soc.*, N.S., LV (1965), 98.

part of the fabric of the common cause, it was logical then that Ramsay featured several proxy stories from the war in his nationalist narrative.[33]

Unfortunately, not nearly as many consumers agreed with him. Ramsay had significant publication problems with both his histories. Far fewer copies of his South Carolina history sold than he expected; as with Trumbull, pirated copies ate into his royalties. Aggregate book sales were not the only barometer of influence, however. Soon, Georgia Congressman James Jackson would meticulously comb through Ramsay's South Carolina book, making extensive notes when the text corroborated his own experience.[34]

Ramsay's *History of the American Revolution* reached the public through other outlets. The editors of the *Columbian Magazine,* the "most ambitious periodical yet published in America," serialized large sections of it from March 1789 to November 1792. "America has produced a Ramsay," commented a student at the University of North Carolina a few decades later, "the Tacitus of this western hemisphere to transmit to posterity in the unpolished language of truth, the spirit of liberty which actuated the first founders of our republic." This exclamation, written by a young James K. Polk in 1817, reflected the aegis of objectivity that many others had long bestowed upon Ramsay. The proxy stories Ramsay featured—complete with semi-confessions of manipulation by patriot publicists—also shared this honor. Those war stories, which patriot publicists often crafted in frantic, anxious settings, were now further reified by their reaffirmation in detached volumes penned by deliberate historians.[35]

33. Ramsay to Jeremy Belknap, Charleston, Mar. 11, 1795, in Brunhouse, ed., "Ramsay Writings," *Transactions of Am. Phil. Soc.,* N.S., LV (1965), 139–140. For more on Ramsay's nationalism, see Shaffer, *Politics of History,* 42–48; O'Brien, "David Ramsay and the Delayed Americanization of American History," *Early American Literature,* XXIX (1994), 1–18.

34. Ramsay to John Eliot, Charleston, Apr. 12, 1793, in Brunhouse, ed., "Ramsay Writings," *Transactions of Am. Phil. Soc.,* N.S., LV (1965), 135–136, and see also Robert L. Brunhouse, "David Ramsay's Publication Problems, 1784–1808," *Papers of the Bibliographic Society of America,* XXXIX (1945), 51–67; Shaffer, *Politics of History,* 161; Lilla M. Hawes, ed., *Collections of the Georgia Historical Society,* XI, *The Papers of James Jackson, 1781–1798* (Savannah, Ga., 1955), 8–27.

35. "Most ambitious periodical": Silverman, *Cultural History of the American Revolution,* 487. Polk quoted in Charles G. Sellers, Jr., "The American Revolution: Southern Founders of a National Tradition," in Arthur S. Link and Rembert W. Patrick, eds., *Writing Southern History: Essays in Historiography in Honor of Fletcher M. Green* ([Baton Rouge, La.], 1965), 42.

Because he wanted to include the drafting and ratification of the Constitution in his history, Ramsay's was not the first history of the Revolution published. Massachusetts minister William Gordon's *History of the Rise, Progress, and Establishment, of the Independence of the United States of America* appeared several months beforehand, published in London in 1788. Gordon, a longtime correspondent of Franklin, Adams, and Washington, had a similar research method to Ramsay's. Like his competitor, Gordon canvassed patriot leaders for information throughout the postwar decade. It was in response to one of Gordon's queries, for instance, that Jefferson estimated Virginia at having lost 30,000 slaves in 1781 alone.[36]

Gordon's work reached many of the same conclusions as Ramsay, and featured many familiar British villains, from John Stuart and John Connolly to Henry Hamilton and, of course, Lord Dunmore. His conclusions about the press coverage of Jane McCrea were eerily similar to Ramsay's, stating, "The murder of Miss McRea exasperated the Americans; and from that and other cruelties occasion was taken to blacken the royal party and army." Gordon maintained, "The people detested that army which accepted of such Indian aid, and loudly reprobated that government which could call in such auxiliaries. Gen. Gates was not deficient in aggravating, by several publications, the excesses which had taken place; and with no small advantage to his own military operations."[37]

There were some variations. He placed more emphasis than Ramsay on the transformation of the Hessians. Gordon's text followed the familiar trajectory of commentary about the German mercenaries: they entered the narrative as ferocious plunderers and rapists and then, as a consequence of

36. TJ to William Gordon, Paris, July 16, 1788, *PTJ*, XIII, 362–365. In 1775, John Adams described Gordon in his diary as "an eternal Talker, and somewhat vain, and not accurate nor judicious. Very zealous in the Cause, and a well meaning Man, but incautious, and not sufficiently tender of the Character of our Province, upon which at this Time much depends." "Fond of being thought a Man of Influence . . . He is a good Man, but wants a Guide" ("John Adams' Diary," Sept. 16, 1775, *LDC*, II, 18). For an example of Ramsay's inquiries to patriot leaders, see Ramsay to JA, Charleston, Sept. 20, 1787, in Brunhouse, ed., "Ramsay Writings," *Transactions of Am. Phil. Soc.*, N.S., LV (1965), 114. For a recent reconsideration of this information, see Cassandra Pybus, "Jefferson's Faulty Math: The Question of Slave Defections in the American Revolution," *WMQ*, 3d Ser., LXII (2005), 243–264.

37. William Gordon, *The History of the Rise, Progress, and Establishment, of the Independence of the United States of America: Including an Account of the Late War . . .* , 3 vols. (New York, 1789), II, 261.

Trenton, Gordon concluded, "The Hessians will be no longer terrible." His account erroneously left Dunmore's runaways "to shift for themselves" on the shore after the Norfolk fire, an abandonment that did not happen. He did not mention Guy Johnson's call on Indians to "feast on a Bostonian" but included a detailed examination of Benjamin Church's "perfidy." Ramsay did not recall the 1776 debacle at the Cedars, but Gordon recounted that many American soldiers "were sacrificed to Indian fury." The Massachusetts patriot reinforced the myth of the Wyoming Massacre. He reified John Holt's creation of *"the hatchet"* as Colonel John Butler's response to the question of what terms he would accept surrender. He repeated Holt's accusations that Indians and tories locked many inhabitants "promiscuously in the houses and barracks; which having set on fire, they enjoyed the savage pleasure of beholding the whole consumed in one general blaze." These details were patently false, generated by patriot publicists.[38]

Gordon's description of Indians, however, differed in many ways from the standard narratives. He included more documentation of friendly tribes than Ramsay, inserting Oneida and Stockbridge messages of support into the text, and later mentioned that a "few" of the Six Nations "were friendly to the Americans." His take on the destructiveness of Sullivan's expedition was especially notable. Whereas Ramsay believed—as most commentators at the time did—that the scorched-earth tactics Sullivan's men employed in 1779 were justified, Gordon was critical of this method. According to Gordon, "Several officers thought it a degradation of the army to be employed in destroying apple and peach trees, when the very Indians in their excursions spared them, and wished the general to retract his orders for it." Upon returning to Pennsylvania, Gordon related that Sullivan then issued a "pompous account of his military peregrination," which "made him the

38. Ibid., II, 168, 409, III, 79, 402. Back in 1776, Gordon wrote to Horatio Gates with a "scheme" of how to scare the German mercenaries into submission. Since "the *Germans* have no business to interfere in our contest with *Great Britain*," Gordon began, "Let us, by way of retaliation, employ five hundred or a thousand *Indians* against them. The very appearance of such dark and painted enemies will go near to terrify them." Gordon did not mean actual Indians, just "those that can best imitate the war-whoop, etc., of the *Indians*." He argued that these men should be kept sequestered even from American soldiers to maintain the integrity of the surprise. The faux savages should be deployed at the front, ready "to fall upon the foreigners instantly" as they disembarked in New York. "Were I present, and in the military," Gordon would certainly "be a volunteer in turning *Indian*" (William Gordon to General [Horatio] Gates, Roxbury, June 23, 1776, 4 *Am. Archives*, VI, 1041–1042).

laugh of the officers in the army." Moreover, when it came to Gnadenhutten, Gordon contended that "a disposition to misrepresent and blacken the Indians, in order to justify, or palliate the practice of cruel measures toward them" contributed to the "barbarity of the whites." Gordon quoted a sentence from the lengthy *Pennsylvania Packet* report that emphasized how Williamson's men had taken horses, furs, and skins with them after the attack. Although the thrust of that article was far less damning than Gordon let on, he concluded, "It was for the sake of the plunder that the Indians were killed." Gordon, like Jefferson, sounds as if he wants to revise—and excise—at least some of the darker sides of the common cause appeal. Indeed, much of his excoriation of both Sullivan and the Gnadenhutten assailants appeals to modern sensibilities. However, that portrayal did not fit with the larger public memory of those events. Those legends also fed on representations like Gordon's repetition of "the hatchet" myth at Wyoming.[39]

Another Massachusetts minister, Jedidiah Morse, published a *History of America* in 1790, the second half of which concerned the American Revolution. Morse's history was much shorter than either Ramsay's or Gordon's, with only 110 pages dedicated to the war. Yet Morse found room to relate several proxy stories. Like Gordon, for example, Morse described the turn of opinion against the German mercenaries after Trenton. Washington's victory "tended greatly to lessen the apprehensions which the provincials had of the Hessians," in agreement with the way patriot publicists had managed opinion about the Germans ever since 1776.[40]

Morse's short history skipped over many stories, though, especially in reference to the war on the frontier. He made no mention of Jane McCrea, Wyoming, Cherry Valley, or Gnadenhutten but did include Burgoyne's proclamation, where he claimed he would "give Stretch" to the Indians. If he largely ignored the backcountry, it was not because he disagreed with the common cause's emphasis on proxies. In fact, Morse focused more on African Americans than any of his historian colleagues. He was the only postwar narrator to connect slave insurrections to the 1775 so-called Gunpowder Incident in Williamsburg. In fact, readers of Morse's history learned how integral slaves were to the origins of the Revolution in Virginia. "As Virginia contained a great number of slaves," Morse wrote, "it was necessary that a

39. Gordon, *History*, III, 19, 21–22, 330, 332.

40. [Jedidiah Morse], *The History of America, in Two Books, Containing: I. A General History of America; II. A Concise History of the Late Revolution* (Philadelphia, 1790), 186, *Early American Imprints*, 22682.

militia should be kept constantly on foot to keep them in awe." When Dunmore dissolved the Virginia Assembly, the militia law expired as well, "and the people, after complaining of the danger they were in from the negroes, formed a convention, which enacted that each county should raise a quota for the defence of the province." Morse later documented the "numbers of black slaves" that ran to Dunmore and outlined the "scheme of the utmost magnitude and importance" wherein Connolly was "into a league with the Ohio Indians." Because the other southern governors "proceeded to regulate their internal concerns in the same manner," he argued, "by the end of the year 1775, Britain beheld the whole of America united against her in the most determined opposition." And, in describing the effects of British invasion in South Carolina in 1779, Morse wrote, "Negroes were seduced or forced from their masters, . . . and the most infamous violations of every law of honour and honesty were openly penetrated. Individuals thus accumulated wealth, but the reputation of the British arms incurred an everlasting stigma."[41]

Many Americans were becoming familiar with Morse just as the *History of America* appeared, with editions of his massive *American Geography* (1789) selling through several print runs. Morse's history, with the second half a chronicle of "the rise and establishment of the AMERICAN REPUBLIC, which has given a new face to the western world," acted as a patriotic companion to the popular geographic survey and further secured the place of the proxy war stories for post-Revolutionary readers.[42]

Finally, Mercy Otis Warren began writing what would be her 1,298-page *History of the Rise, Progress, and Termination of the American Revolution: Interspersed with Biographical, Political, and Moral Observations* in 1775. As James Otis's sister, James Warren's wife, Abigail Adams's confidant, and John Adams's correspondent, Mercy was in many ways the epicenter of Boston's patriot movement. She intended her history as a family chronicle, but over the course of several years she decided to prepare it for publication. Mercy was, moreover, as important a contributor to the common cause propagation campaign as Ramsay or Gordon, having contributed several politi-

41. Ibid., 160, 162–164, 213–214.

42. [Morse], *History of America*, 113, *Early American Imprints*, 22682. For analysis of Morse and his book *The American Geography; A View of the Present Situation of the United States of America* (Elizabethtown, N.J., 1789), see Kariann Akemi Yakota, *Unbecoming British: How Revolutionary America Became a Postcolonial Nation* (New York, 2011), 42–50.

"New Provocations"

cal satires to Boston newspapers during the imperial crisis. She had completed her manuscript at nearly the same moment that Gordon, Morse, and Ramsay finished theirs. Warren, though, put hers in a desk drawer in her Plymouth home, where it remained until publication in 1805.[43]

Warren's history forwarded many of the proxy stories found in the other histories written in the 1780s. She, too, included Johnson's "feast on a *Bostonian*" invitation, stating—just as Congress said in 1775—"These transactions were considered as incontestable proof, that the administration was determined to employ as their allies, the fierce and numerous *hordes* of the wilderness, to subdue and butcher the Americans." She also included more detail about southern governors Josiah Martin and William Campbell early in the war. Whereas Morse made an oblique reference to how those officials "regulated their internal concerns," Warren was specific: "With the same spirit and cruel policy that instigated Lord Dunmore, they carried on their negotiations with the Indians, and encouraged the insurrections of the negroes, until all harmony and confidence were totally destroyed between themselves and the people." After 1775, however, Warren showed no interest in discussing slaves or slavery until inserting article 7 of the Treaty of Paris concerning the removal of blacks during the British evacuation. She did not mention Colonel Tye's raids in New Jersey, the participation of armed blacks during the Savannah siege, or the presence of thousands of African American refugees at Yorktown. In Warren's narrative, they disappeared.[44]

Her interpretation of the Hessian redemption after Trenton paralleled the contemporary newspaper coverage in 1776. When discussing the initial British agreements with the German princes, she scolded British leaders

43. Mercy Otis Warren, *History of the Rise, Progress, and Termination of the American Revolution: Interspersed with Biographical, Political, and Moral Observations,* ed. Lester H. Cohen, 2 vols. (Indianapolis, Ind., 1994); Rosemarie Zagarri, *A Woman's Dilemma: Mercy Otis Warren and the American Revolution* (Wheeling, Ill., 1995), 58–77, 140–150.

44. Warren, *History of the American Revolution,* ed. Cohen, I, 112, 138, II, 632. Since she collected materials for her history during the war itself, the tendency to feature those reports that gripped the public's attention at the moment found significant space in her final manuscript. For example, she was the only historian to keep alive the rumor that ran around Boston in the tense days before the 1770 "massacre" that the "continual bickerings" between English soldiers and the inhabitants had "carried so far" as to include their encouragement of "the African slaves to murder their masters, with the promise of impunity" (I, 52). For more on the real incident that led to this rumor, see Hiller B. Zobel, *The Boston Massacre* (New York, 1970), 102.

for their "unworthy submission" in introducing "barbarous strangers" to assist in the reduction of the rebellion. The American public had "viewed the Hessians as a most terrific enemy," she argued, but upon hearing that they "yield[ed] themselves prisoners to the shreds of an American army," their "despair" evaporated. By 1781, the transformation of those strangers was complete when she depicted them as victims: "Feudal vassals of despotic lords, the mere *automatons* of German princes, who held them as their heredity property." In all these early histories, the Hessians vanished after Trenton. Except for a few spare mentions of their presence in patriot victories at Bennington and Red Bank, it was almost as if the Hessians went home after their Christmas humiliation.[45]

On the other hand, Warren had much to say about the participation of British-allied Indians throughout the war. The tangle of legends that instantly cropped up surrounding Jane McCrea was evident in her manuscript. She depicted Jane in her "bridal habiliments" and mistakenly referred to Jane's father as a "zealous loyalist." Nor was Warren immune to invoking sentimentality in describing Jane's "bleeding corpse left in the woods, to excite the tear of every beholder." She, too, included Holt's myth that John Butler, "with all the *sang-froid* of the savage," informed Nathan Dennison that *"the hatchet"* was the single term of surrender at Wyoming. She followed this two paragraphs later with the comment, "It is true the Illinois, and other distant warlike tribes, were at the instigation of governor Hamilton, the British commander at Detroit, generally assisting in the measures perpetrated under Butler and Brandt, nearer the frontiers; and perhaps the law of retaliation, may, in some measure, justify the depredations of Clark." But then, like Gordon, she turned around to condemn Sullivan's expedition, especially his assault on the "gardens, orchards, corn-fields, and fruit trees." She stated that Sullivan was far too "proud of this war upon nature," and it "cannot be justified."[46]

This led to a moving, three-page digression on the tragic history of violence between Indians and Europeans in America since contact. Warren rejected any claims that Indians "cannot be civilized" as "absurd and unfounded." She said, "Nature has been equal in its operations" for all humans and called for Americans to "use the most strenuous efforts to instruct [Indians] in arts, manufactures, morals, and religion, instead of aiming at

45. Warren, *History of the American Revolution*, ed. Cohen, I, 155, 189, II, 474.
46. Ibid., I, 233–324, 280–282.

their extermination." But then, a qualification. "It is true," she admitted, that during the Revolution

> few of the tribes of the wilderness appeared to be contented with their own native inheritance. They were every where stimulated by the British government to hostility, and most of the inhabitants of the wilderness seemed to be in array against their former colonies. This created a necessity in congress, to act offensively against the rude and barbarous nations.

She disagreed strongly with this policy to "spread slaughter and bloodshed among innocent and unoffending tribes" but could not deny the linkage between stories about Jane McCrea or *"the hatchet"*—stories she helped propagate—and calls for vengeful, punitive operations. On the following page, she quoted an observation made by her son Winslow "that the white savages were generally more savage than the copper colored; and that nine times out of ten, the settlers on the borders were the aggressors." When they finally appeared in print, Warren's and her son's views complemented then-President Jefferson's, but Winslow would not live to see his words published in his mother's history. He died fighting British-armed Indians in 1791.[47]

The impetus to continue battling Indians—and their British sponsors—arose in part from war stories crafted to compel allegiance and union. Warren, Gordon, and Jefferson each argued for "civilizing" missions on the frontier, but their presentations appeared alongside convincing evidence of Indians' acting as English proxies. A similar discursive tension unsettled calls by Brackenridge, Ramsay, and others for abolition. The proxy stories proved more durable than the newspapers that carried them. Fearsome war stories involving Hessians or even loyalists had all but disappeared. By the mid-1780s, Americans only heard the name "Hessian" in reference to devastating insects. On the other hand, Americans still heard about Carleton, Dunmore, Connolly, McCrea, Brant, Wyoming, Cedars, Cherry Valley, and Gwynn's Island. Even after the Revolution, the representations readers associated with those people and places lived on.[48]

47. Ibid., I, 284–286, esp. 285, 286 (Winslow Warren quoted).

48. Philip J. Pauly, "Fighting the Hessian Fly: American and British Responses to Insect Invasion, 1776–1789," *Environmental History,* VII (2002), 485–507. Shaffer discusses the newspaper and magazine serialization of Gordon and Ramsay's work. He shows that the *Farmer's Almanac* of 1793 recommended Ramsay's history as one of three books "worthy of the perusal of every American." See *Politics of History,* 162.

Via all these mediums—history, poetry, captivity narratives, novels, travelogues, and essays—writers in the postwar decade incorporated war stories into their portrayals of the Revolution. They pulled reports of insurrections, plundering, rape, and murder out of the everyday war news and made them a central component of the romance of the Revolution. What was intended as evanescent—a crystallization of American outrage to spur immediate military action—became a permanent fixture of the Revolution. They helped solidify both sides of the dual-faceted common cause appeal as a compelling "ethically constitutive story" for the American people. Texts that appeared in the 1780s deepened and developed the negative images of that founding narrative. Filson and Trumbull took images that originally appeared in perishable, disposable mediums like sermons, newspapers, and broadsides and transformed them into something permanent. Generations of American schoolchildren would learn about merciless savages, domestic insurrectionists, and British instigators as they recited *M'Fingal* or read Daniel Boone's adventures with wonder. The historians made some attempt to distance themselves from the heat of these moments, but their narratives nevertheless illustrated the strains inherent in the common cause appeal from its inception. The continued retelling of proxy stories—"new provocations"—exerted further influence over policy after the war, in part because those images provided ample evidence, dripping with American patriotism, for the opponents of abolition and fair dealing with Indian tribes.[49]

2: THE POLITICAL CODIFICATIONS OF WAR STORIES

Reading the resolutions of legislative bodies, including Congress, in the early 1780s often belies this stress on the war stories' pervasiveness. These resolutions outlined policies that reflected the more positive aspects of the common cause argument. Take, for example, the instructions Congress issued to Indian commissioners in their October 15, 1783, session. Congressional delegates acknowledged that even though Indians in the northern and western districts "could not be restrained from acts of hostility and wanton devastation" and were "determined to join their arms to those of

49. Rogers M. Smith, *Stories of Peoplehood: The Politics and Morals of Political Membership* (Cambridge, 2003), 64–70, 94–95. For a powerful examination of how the initial manifestations of an American national identity coalesced in the post-Revolutionary years in opposition to African Americans and native peoples, see Carroll Smith-Rosenberg, *This Violent Empire: The Birth of an American National Identity* (Chapel Hill, N.C., 2010).

"New Provocations"

Great Britain," the victorious patriots were "disposed to be kind to them." Congress maintained they would take the high road, a pose they had repeatedly struck since 1775. They would, "from motives of compassion draw a veil over what is passed."[50]

Central to this liberality, they suggested, was the establishment of a boundary line "separating and dividing the settlements of the citizens from the Indian villages and hunting grounds, and thereby extinguishing as far as possible all occasion for future animosities, disquiet, and contention." When the three appointed commissioners, Richard Butler, Arthur Lee, and Oliver Wolcott, convened treaty conferences, first with the Iroquois at Fort Stanwix (1784) and later with the Delawares and Wyandots at Fort McIntosh (1785) and Shawnees at Fort Finney (1786), they presented this spirit of liberality—a totem of American claims of superiority in their sacred cause— with proposals of just such boundary lines. It appeared that Congress might assume the role of referee on the frontier.[51]

But then things broke down. The political stakes at these conferences were significant for all parties; not only did land rights for future generations of Indians hang in the balance, but as several states were putting forward claims of sovereignty over those acres, the nature of the union itself was in question. Congress's desire to extend "compassion" was an early victim. Soon the commissioners, irritated by defiant Indian claims that they were not aggressors and remained a "free and independent nation," promulgated what became known as a "conquest theory." They deemed the Iroquois a "subdued people . . . overcome in a war which you entered with us, not only without provocation, but in violation of most sacred obligations." "You joined the British King against us, and followed his fortunes," they informed a delegation of the Shawnees at Fort Finney; "we have overcome him, he has cast you off, and given us your country; and Congress, in bounty and mercy, offer you country and peace." According to the commissioners, all Indians had to accept that they had been defeated in war, recognize United States sovereignty over all their lands, and trust Congress to consider their interests in future policy.[52]

50. Oct. 15, 1783, *JCC*, XXV, 680–695, esp. 685–686.

51. Ibid., 684.

52. Speech of U.S. Commissioners to Sachems and Warriors, Fort Stanwix, Oct. 20, 1784, "Proceedings of the United States and the Six Nations at Fort Stanwix," and entry for Jan. 30, 1786, "Excerpts from the Journal of General Richard Butler at the Treaty of Fort Finney," in Colin G. Calloway, ed., *Early American Indian Docu-*

It should not surprise that they rejected these premises, because all parties understood that this projection of power announced by Butler, Lee, and Wolcott was nothing but an illusion. Charles Thomson, the secretary of Congress throughout the war, was not the only one to recognize in late 1783 that many states were forgetting "the motto, *Join or die,* which was at the beginning of this contest" so universal; Indians throughout the north and west were besieged by a panoply of representatives—from various states, private companies, and the confederation government—to agree to terms. To call the union fragile in the immediate postwar years drastically understates the problem. After Spain closed the Mississippi River to foreign commerce in 1784, disgruntled backcountry settlers considered the Spanish Empire as more advantageous than the ineffective American republic. Indian leaders understood the weaknesses of the confederation perhaps best of all.[53]

The inability for the United States to demand enforcement of the Treaty of Paris was even more evidence of this impotency. Here, too, the king's proxies played a central role. Article 4 of the treaty demanded that American borrowers of British credit would have to repay their debts, but the American riposte to this was that British "theft" of slave property was payment enough to cover these deficits. They argued that when the British violated article 7 by taking thousands of runaway slaves, those actions nullified American responsibilities in article 4. In response, the British decided to interpret broadly the stipulation that they remove all troops with "all convenient speed" by refusing to evacuate nine western posts across a wide arc from Lake Champlain through the Great Lakes. With British troops remaining at all the outposts, Americans blamed for their troubles on the frontier—Oswego, Niagara, Sandusky, and Detroit—the connection between the king and his Indian proxies (caused in part by the issue of black proxies)

------

ments: *Treaties and Laws, 1607–1789,* XVIII, *Revolution and Confederation* (Bethesda, Md., 1994), 323–324, 346. For more United States representatives espousing this "conquest theory," see XVIII, 393–401, 412–414, 423–424. For more on these postwar treaties and "conquest theory," see Leonard J. Sadosky, *Revolutionary Negotiations: Indians, Empires, and Diplomats in the Founding of America* (Charlottesville, Va., 2009), 127–140, esp. 138; Nichols, *Red Gentlemen and White Savages,* 19–36; J. David Lehman, "The End of the Iroquois Mystique: The Oneida Land Cession Treaties of the 1780s," *WMQ,* 3d Ser., XLVII (1990), 523–547.

53. Charles Thomson to Hannah Thomson, Oct. 17, 1783, *LDC,* XXI, 72–74, esp. 73; Andrew R. L. Cayton, "Radicals in the 'Western World': The Federalist Conquest of Trans-Appalachian North America" in Doron Ben-Atar and Barbara B. Oberg, eds., *Federalists Reconsidered* (Charlottesville, Va., 1998), 77–96, esp. 81.

persisted. Violence continued in the Ohio Valley, and Americans continued to point fingers at "tampering" British commanders.[54]

Thus the legacy of the Treaty of Paris was a cycle of disobedience fueled by the king's not-so-former proxies. Maryland attorney John Francis Mercer penned an incendiary pamphlet in 1789 excoriating the British for their impertinence in demanding that Americans repay the debt. Incredulous, Mercer reminded his readers of British perfidy during the war:

> Who prosecuted this cruel war—desolated and plundered our country with a barbarity unknown to civilized men?—The British!
>
> Who employed negro slaves to cut the throats of their masters, and the savage Indians to murder our people, not sparing helpless women and children?—The British!

He repeatedly invoked the proxies in the forty-four-page pamphlet to castigate the British for calling the Americans deadbeats. Mercer insisted that the entire reason for the large American debt "arose from the negroes they sold us.—And here we may remark, that we had made repeated attempts to check this disgraceful and pernicious traffic, which were all baffled on the other side of the water." Mercer ventriloquized Jefferson's rough draft of the Declaration, concluding that the British had compounded their tyranny by "rous[ing] the unhappy wretches to cut their masters throats, by a promise of freedom." Mercer's passion illustrates not only the outrage concerning these issues that still obviously festered among former patriots but also a deep sense of frustration by the end of the 1780s. The controversy over the debt and western posts provided yet another instance of the weaknesses in the Articles of Confederation. That those groups were the chief beneficiaries of this diplomatic and political impotency served as proof for many Americans that the republic needed reform, while Indian leaders continued to depend on British material and political support to bolster their confidence in resisting the United States. Because of constitutional vulnerability,

54. Treaty of Paris, article 7, quoted in Arnett G. Lindsay, "Diplomatic Relations between the United States and Great Britain Bearing on the Return of Negro Slaves, 1783–1828," *Journal of Negro History,* V (1920), 391–419, esp. 395n; Charles R. Ritcheson, *Aftermath of Revolution: British Policy toward the United States, 1783–1795* (1969; rpt. New York, 1971), 70–86; Colin G. Calloway, *Crown and Calumet: British-Indian Relations, 1783–1815* (Norman, Okla., 1987), 3–76; Timothy D. Willig, *Restoring the Chain of Friendship: British Policy and the Indians of the Great Lakes, 1783–1815* (Lincoln, Neb., 2008), esp. 220.

Mercer stated, "Councils of Indians have been held under [British] countenance and direction, within our territory."[55]

A second reason the nature of boundary disputes transformed over the Revolutionary decade was the common cause argument. Congress and their appointed commissioners reassured Indians that they wanted to prevent settlers from encroaching on native lands, but, aside from their inability to execute such restraint, the method by which they had justified and promoted the patriot cause had compromised those pledges long before 1784. Desperate to retain the loyalty of frontier settlers, patriot publicists had embraced them as the Revolution's secret weapon against professional grenadiers, especially early on in the war. The lauded riflemen had come to the rescue in Canada and Virginia in 1775, at Saratoga in 1777, at Vincennes in 1778, at King's Mountain in 1780, and at Cowpens in 1781. Patriot publicists had turned frontiersmen from white savages who destabilized the backcountry into heroic Americans and quintessential republican citizens, a flip second only to the astounding conversion of the French from papist devils to saviors.

Born out of military necessity, this metamorphosis—especially as it was in the process of being culturally codified by John Filson's account of Daniel Boone—complicated policy during the war. It shielded the murderers of Cornstalk, White Eyes, and eight dozen Moravian Delawares from prosecution. Patriot leaders condemned these tragedies and called for investigations but never followed up. Public opinion, as cultivated by those same leaders, canceled those inquiries before they began. George Rogers Clark's execution of Indians in front of the fort at Vincennes was not a crime but rather an intrepid act by the "conqueror of the Illinois." William Crawford's ordeal incited far more outrage than the bloody event on the Muskingum that sparked it.

After the war, some patriot leaders privately returned to their prewar criticism of "white savages," but they had thrown in their lot with these settlers. Because patriot publicists had chosen to herald a natural rights ide-

55. John Francis Mercer, *Introductory Discourse to an Argument in Support of the Payments Made of British Debts into the Treasury of Maryland during the Late War* (Annapolis, Md., 1789), 22, 32–33, 40. Mercer returned yet another time to the issue of runaway slaves and British sponsorship, discussing the British ministry's decision to be "more honourable to keep their faith with their old black, than their new white friends— that the promise of a British general, to give freedom to other peoples negroes, was a more sacred thing than a public and solemn treaty between two nations" (39).

"New Provocations"

ology as the essence of the common cause's positive side, frontier settlers put in a convincing claim that they embodied the Revolution: they animated the self-determinative impulse that prized consent and freedom from restraint. Settling the frontier—and continuing to battle British-allied Indians—was an emblem of American patriotism. In addition, thanks to British and Spanish desires to maintain a presence in the North American interior, eastern Americans continued to depend upon the loyalty of backcountry settlers to keep order. In other words, when Congress suggested a boundary line separating "the settlements of the citizens from the Indian villages and hunting grounds," this should have made any Indian anxious. One side of the line held the rights and privileges of being an American citizen, and the other did not. Even though some in Congress and other leaders—like Henry Knox or Timothy Pickering—saw encroaching settlers as the real threat to peace, those governing bodies could never approach objectivity. They had to choose a side.[56]

In 1786, Ethan Allen—who knew about boundary disputes—helped write an address to the greater Pennsylvania public informing them of what the inhabitants of the long-suffering Wyoming Valley expected after being "exposed to the relentless fury, savage barbarity, and devastation of the common enemy."

> In these scenes of horror, and complicated woe, we were your frontier. Our blood answered for yours. Our hazard and unparalleled distress purchased your safety. We stood between you and the tomahawk and scalping-knife, and diverted the inhuman strokes from you. But alas! what returns have we had from your government? The widows and orphans, of those who fell in the common cause of America, particularly in your defence, have been plundered, despoiled of their goods, and driven from their habitations, and legal possessions . . . and the whole treated nearly as inhumanly, as by the common enemy.

56. See the letters Timothy Pickering read and received in the late 1780s and early 1790s, such as Paine Wingate to Pickering, New York, Aug. 18, 1788, in Timothy Pickering Papers, microfilm, reel XIX, 140, Pickering to Samuel Hodgdon, Wilkes-Barre, Pa., Feb. 28, 1791, reel XXXV, 109–110, Massachusetts Historical Society, Boston. Generally, see Nichols, *Red Gentlemen and White Savages.* Settling the frontier as a badge of American patriotism: Hinderaker, *Elusive Empires,* 185–186. Imperial competition in backcountry: Nichols, *Red Gentlemen and White Savages,* 15. "Settlements of the citizens": Calloway, ed., *Revolution and Confederation,* 291.

The inhabitants of Wyoming believed they had earned the blessings of good government with their blood. The settlers from Connecticut felt betrayed by both Congress and Pennsylvania for their refusal to recognize this patriotic service and their legal claims to land on the Susquehanna. Governments, Allen argued on their behalf, were created "to secure the lives, liberty and property of the subjects." "But when government and law are degenerated in the administration," he warned, "and subverted to answer to the over-bearing, unjust and monopolizing purposes of cruel men, or to dispossess and ruin a large settlement of industrious yeomanry (the supporters of the world of mankind) in such cases the oppressed have a just and natural right to make a bold and manly resistance." This was a serious challenge, not only because it constituted yet another threat to the union and domestic peace in the fragile Confederation years but because it was steeped in the idea that "Our blood answered for yours." Political leaders could extrapolate out that settlers across the trans-Appalachian frontier might all put in similar claims that the United States government owed their desires greater credence than the desires of the British-allied Indians. The war had given the settlers this political capital, and they intended it to be honored at full value—or else. And, because nearly all the state constitutions drafted during the 1780s had recast the apportionment of their legislatures to incorporate western settlement, newly elected representatives from the backcountry had even greater opportunity to craft policies that reflected these postwar expectations.[57]

Indians stood little chance against this construction of settlers-as–patriotic heroes. The postwar history of the staunchest American allies, the Oneida, Tuscarora, and Stockbridge Indians, testify to this point. At war's end, George Washington issued the Stockbridge a certificate attesting to their fidelity during the war. Washington recommended that, because they had "fought and bled by our side," no one should "molest . . . in any manner" these "friends and *subjects to* the United States of America." This parchment declaration had little effect. While large numbers of Stockbridge men were away serving in the Continental army, their communities at home had indeed been molested. Encroachments on their land forced them to petition Congress in 1782 for relief, to no avail. Not long after receiving Washing-

57. Ethan Allen, John Franklin, and John Jenkins, *An Address from the Inhabitants of Wyoming and Others, Contiguously Situated on the Waters of the River Susquehannah . . .* (Hudson, N.Y., 1786), *Early American Imprints*, 20164; Jackson Turner Main, "Government by the People: The American Revolution and the Democratization of the Legislatures," *WMQ*, 3d Ser., XXIII (1966), 391–407.

ton's blessing, many Stockbridge accepted a tract of land from their fellow "good" Indians, the Oneidas, and left Massachusetts for "New Stockbridge" in central New York.[58]

Their sponsors fared little better. Commissioners Butler, Lee, and Wolcott singled the friendly Oneidas and Tuscaroras out at the Fort Stanwix conference, and the second article of the treaty stipulated that these allies "shall be secured in the possession of the lands on which they are settled," but, again, American authorities did not enforce this provision. Soon, speculators from New York, Massachusetts, and private land companies descended on the Oneidas, lobbying them to sell prime real estate. Petitions from Oneida, Tuscarora, and Stockbridge Indians kept flooding into Congress for years demanding compensation for their losses.[59]

The common cause caught these northern Indians in a double bind. First, the overwhelming message that they were potential British proxies had created a narrative that all Indians supported the crown, a fiction that fueled wholesale evictions after the war. At the same time, a parallel representation developed during the war that celebrated the beneficiaries of that dispossession. Implicit in the common cause was a critical interpretation: when the test came in 1775, Indians failed to comprehend the principles of liberty, whereas their frontier rivals rallied around republican values and died to defend inalienable rights. They had confirmed long-standing suspicions that they could not be trusted with citizenship. Washington's reference to the Stockbridge as "subjects *to* the United States" and Congress's description of frontier people as "citizens" reveals a critical fault line, an evolving legal divide that grew out of the common cause. That codification

58. "Certificate to the Muhhekunnuk [Stockbridge Mohicans] Indians," Headquarters, July 8, 1783, in John C. Fitzpatrick, ed., *The Writings of George Washington: From the Original Manuscript Sources, 1745–1799*, 39 vols. (Washington, D.C., 1931–1944), XXVII, 53 (emphasis added); Calloway, *American Revolution in Indian Country*, 100–107; David J. Silverman, *Red Brethren: The Brothertown and Stockbridge Indians and the Problem of Race in Early America* (Ithaca, N.Y., 2010), 125–148.

59. See, for example, Sept. 14, 1785, *JCC*, XXIX, 705–706. The Oneidas would eventually get partial compensation from the U.S. government in 1794: $5,000 for individual claims, $1,000 to rebuild a church, and monies to build a new saw and gristmill. See Joseph T. Glatthaar and James Kirby Martin, *Forgotten Allies: The Oneida Indians and the American Revolution* (New York, 2006), 299, 310; Minutes of the Treaty of Fort Stanwix Negotiations, Oct. 20, 1784, in *Olden Time*, II (1848), 423–427, esp. 425. For speculators, see Lehman, "End of Iroquois Mystique," *WMQ*, 3d Ser., XLVII (1990), 536–541.

was the result of an embrace of frontier settlers and squatters as equal republican citizens who had "purchased" the safety of easterners—no matter how cruelly they did so—and a denial of a similar status for the notorious "merciless savages." Caught in a Revolutionary whipsaw, soon all Indians, even friendly ones, would find themselves cordoned off from Americans.[60]

* * *

African Americans in the immediate postwar period faced similar challenges posed by the legacies of the common cause argument. On the one hand, the natural rights justification that undergirded part of the cause problematized slavery to such a degree that it made abolition imaginable and possible. Antislavery advocates, with Quakers and evangelicals in the vanguard, drew upon Revolutionary rhetoric after the war to clinch a moral case that slavery was incompatible with a republic based on consent and personal liberty. "Juvenis" made this assertion in a 1785 pamphlet aimed at Virginians, stating that the "declarations of our Congress, and the Constitutions of the different States" all claimed that all men had natural rights and therefore "the Negroes are rightfully entitled to their liberty." "The memory of those who have fallen in our cause, who have bled in the support of our honor and our rights," he implored, "requires that we should be vigilant . . . of the ransom which they have given for our Liberty."[61]

Scholars have long highlighted this consequence of Revolutionary ideas, famously referring to a "contagion of liberty" that rippled out from patriot pamphlets, evolving from constitutional debates about sovereignty into a thoroughgoing critique of slaveholding. Suddenly, they argue, Revolutionary rhetoric "led to a *perception* of the problem" of slavery as never before. For them, Juvenis was one of a rising chorus of voices connecting inalien-

60. For a similar interpretation, see Colin G. Calloway, "The Continuing Revolution in Indian Country," in Frederick E. Hoxie, Ronald Hoffman, and Peter J. Albert, eds., *Native Americans and the Early Republic* (Charlottesville, Va., 1999), 3–33. Of the few Indian groups that supported the patriot cause, only the Catawbas in North Carolina were able (through very arduous work) to use that fidelity as a useful totem to protect most of their interests in the long term. That they were a small tribe without extensive land also contributed to their success. See James H. Merrell, *The Indians' New World: Catawbas and Their Neighbors from European Contact through the Era of Removal* (Chapel Hill, N.C., 1989), 216–218.

61. "Juvenis," *Observations on the Slavery of the Negroes, in the Southern States: Particularly Intended for the Citizens of Virginia* (New York, 1785), 7–8, 22, *Early American Imprints*, 44751.

able rights to abolition. It is impossible to deny the connections between a discourse of natural rights trumpeted by patriot publicists and a wave of abolition in the last quarter of the eighteenth century. When this discourse matched up with other practical interests—whether religious impulses, economic opportunities, or political considerations—antislavery schemes found some success in the postwar period. Yet scholars have recalculated the energy of that antislavery wave, downgrading it from a tsunami of radical change to a heavy surf. A large contingent of historians has shown that the pace of freedom for slaves from New England through the Upper South was far from quick and that emancipation did not translate into acceptance in early republic communities.[62]

62. The original statement of a "contagion of liberty" is in Bernard Bailyn, *The Ideological Origins of the American Revolution* (Cambridge, Mass., 1967), 230–246. "*Perception* of the problem": Davis, *Problem of Slavery in the Age of Revolution*, 285. Jordan also referred to the Revolution as a "great awakening" in colonial awareness of slavery as a problem; see *White over Black*, 269–311, esp. 310–311. See also Zilversmit, *First Emancipation;* William W. Freehling, "The Founding Fathers and Slavery," *American Historical Review*, LXXVII (1972), 81–93. Steve Pincus's forthcoming book on the Declaration of Independence seeks to reinvigorate this antislavery interpretation of the founding fathers. Christopher Leslie Brown has recently traced the influence of Revolutionary ideology on British abolitionism in Brown, *Moral Capital: Foundations of British Abolitionism* (Chapel Hill, N.C., 2006), 228–258. For an emphasis on how ideas alone accomplished little outside a nexus of practical self-interest, see Matthew Mason, "Necessary but Not Sufficient: Revolutionary Ideology and Antislavery Action in the Early Republic," in John Craig Hammond and Matthew Mason, eds., *Contesting Slavery: The Politics of Bondage and Freedom in the New American Nation* (Charlottesville, Va., 2011), 11–31. The leader of this criticism of an "awakening" or "contagion" has been Gary B. Nash. See his multiple treatments, including *Forging Freedom: The Formation of Philadelphia's Black Community, 1720–1840* (Cambridge, Mass., 1988); *Race and Revolution* (Madison, Wis., 1990); Nash and Jean R. Soderlund, *Freedom by Degrees: Emancipation in Pennsylvania and Its Aftermath* (New York, 1991); *The Forgotten Fifth: African Americans in the Age of Revolution* (Cambridge, Mass., 2006). See also Joanne Pope Melish, *Disowning Slavery: Gradual Emancipation and "Race" in New England, 1780–1860* (Ithaca, N.Y., 1998); John Wood Sweet, *Bodies Politic: Negotiating Race in the American North, 1730–1830* (Baltimore, 2003); Graham Russell Hodges, *Root and Branch: African Americans in New York and East Jersey, 1613–1863* (Chapel Hill, N.C., 1999); Shane White, *Somewhat More Independent: The End of Slavery in New York City, 1770–1810* (Athens, Ga., 1991); David N. Gellman, *Emancipating New York: The Politics of Slavery and Freedom, 1777–1827* (Baton Rouge, La., 2006); Wolf, *Race and Liberty in the New Nation.*

Here, too, the common cause argument provided a script that opponents of abolition could use to formulate a counterclaim based just as much on Revolutionary patriotism. As with Indians, former patriot leaders—no matter what they believed privately about slavery—had to tread lightly, in part because they had predicated the union on supporting the interests of slaveholders since 1775. Champions of abolition and manumission plans had to fend off consistent challenges to their vision that were also steeped in Revolutionary rhetoric.

The power of the common cause to restrict antislavery was most evident in two cases from the mid-1780s: first, in the failure of gradual abolition in New York and, second, in the backlash against the enlarged Virginia manumission law of 1782. In both instances, opponents of abolition charged antislavery advocates with sympathizing with America's enemies. They turned Quaker and evangelical lobbyists into British instigators and, occasionally, explicitly invoked the ghosts of Dunmore, Clinton, and Cornwallis.

Four months after the British evacuated Manhattan, the city's authorities revisited laws regulating the behavior of enslaved African Americans. For eight years, New York City had been a central site for African Americans to seek British protection and escape slavery. Now municipal leaders passed rules about illumination—no burials at night, slaves must carry lanterns—and commercial access, trying to reestablish control of the city's two thousand slaves. The next year, in January 1785, the lower house of the state assembly introduced a gradual emancipation bill that also reflected the complex Revolutionary legacy about blacks and citizenship rights. It called for emancipation after a further twenty-five years of service for men and twenty-two for women. Amendments soon imperiled the bill, however, as some in the lower house sought to curtail rights for people who would eventually be freed. These amendments called for miscegenation to be illegal and free blacks to be barred from the franchise, from serving as witnesses or jurors in court, and from holding office. The upper chamber balked at most of these restrictions, forcing the lower house to rescind them. It was all for naught: the Council of Revision vetoed the bill as contradictory. Despite having passed in Connecticut, Rhode Island, and Pennsylvania, gradual abolition would have to wait until the late 1790s to become law in New York.[63]

Just as the moment passed in early 1785, two articles in Samuel Loudon's

63. Gellman, *Emancipating New York*, 45–46.

New York Packet again highlighted the discursive boundaries that simultaneously allowed for and undermined abolition just after the Revolution. A few days after one essayist chastised New Yorkers for not following through on the Revolution's claims to universal human rights, an "American" reminded readers of Jefferson's "new provocations." "We have already experienced their fidelity in the late contest," this writer argued, "when they fought against us by whole regiments." Lambasting Quakers for assisting slaves when they did not support the cause during the war, "American" also snorted about a "General Quacco" and "Col. Mingo," both "seated in our Senate and Assembly." It is a wonder he did not invoke Major Cudjo in this excoriation. Just so, five days earlier, Loudon had printed a "Letter from Cuffee to the Printer" in pidgin dialect. "Cuffee" declared, "Me wante be freemen, Legislaterman too." Clearly this was not the speech of someone to be entrusted with citizenship rights. The common cause appeal supported both sides of the law, allowing for abolition and restricting African Americans from enjoying secure rights as citizens. It buttressed both sides of this newspaper commentary. Although state legislators did take steps to stem the slave trade and allow for private manumissions in New York, abolition was not yet to be. The memories of the war were too fresh.[64]

Those memories were even more recent in Virginia when, just eight months after Yorktown, the legislature passed a manumission law allowing individuals to free adult slaves as they chose. In 1778, a slave named George had petitioned the assembly that his master had freed him in his will. George, supported by his former master's descendants, asked the legislature to reconsider the 1723 statute that made the bequest illegal. A subcommittee drafted a bill that allowed private manumission under certain conditions, especially that freed people had to leave Virginia within six months. Although it did not become law, this bill began the process that, after four years of sustained Quaker pressure, would allow Virginia slaveholders to manumit if they chose to do so. The 1782 law stipulated that slaves had to be adults (women over eighteen, men over twenty-one), and if they were infirm, their former masters had to provide financial support. This law did not require freed African Americans to leave Virginia, but neither did it make them citizens: they had to keep written proof on them at all times to prove their status, and if they failed to pay taxes, their labor could be confiscated until debts were paid. White Virginians would not have to suffer either of

64. Ibid., 48–55; *New York Packet,* Mar. 31, Apr. 4, 1785.

these stipulations. Over the next few decades, about ten thousand slaves did find freedom in Virginia but remained of unequal status.[65]

That the legislature took this step in June 1782, as the back pages of the *Virginia Gazette*s continued to be filled with advertisements for slaves who had run away to Cornwallis or were still at large, did not please many Virginians. Over the next couple of years, antimanumission petitions began to flood into Richmond asking the assembly to rescind this liberality. "Many Evils have Arisen" from the manumission law, argued petitions from Hanover and Henrico Counties with more than 250 signatures in November 1784. "Your Petitioners have room to believe A Great number of slaves taken by The British army are now passing in this Country as Freemen," and the only way to "prevent their becoming more General" was to repeal the law. The pamphlet written by Juvenis in the middle of this backlash stated that this was the risk of not following through on ideals of natural rights. That the Revolutionary War had witnessed the largest slave rebellion in North American history was still a raw memory. "The Negroes will always in time of war, prove injurious to the country wherein they live; for being naturally inimical to those who are their oppressors, they will avail themselves of every opportunity which may offer, of liberating themselves from their oppression." As Virginians had recently learned, "The Country or State which possesses a considerable number of slaves, is incapable of defending itself against invasions from abroad; and whenever attacked, will unavoidably become an easy conquest to its invaders." But others disagreed that abolition was the way to defuse future conflict.[66]

In 1785, as gradual abolition fell apart in New York, Quakers continued to pressure the Virginia legislature to enlarge private manumission into a general emancipation. More petitions from Virginia's southside arrived in Richmond. A longer document sent by Amelia, Mecklenberg, and Pittsylvania Counties invoked the common cause to a great degree. It contended that the Quaker attempt at dismantling slavery was against the Revolution itself. "We," the petitioners asserted, "established a Constitution and

65. Wolf, *Race and Liberty in the New Nation*, 29–34; Alan Taylor, *The Internal Enemy: Slavery and War in Virginia, 1772–1832* (New York, 2013), 39–42.

66. "To the Honourable the General Assembly, the Remonstrance and Petition of the Free Inhabitants of Amelia County," Nov. 16, 1784, in Fredrika Teute Schmidt and Barbara Ripel Wilhelm, "Early Proslavery Petitions in Virginia," *WMQ*, 3d Ser., XXX (1973), 133–146, esp. 138; "Juvenis," *Observations on Slavery in the Southern States*, 20, *Early American Imprints*, 44751.

Form of Government of our own" and "risked our Lives and Fortunes, and waded through Seas of Blood" to secure it. "Our Attempt was crowned with Success," but now these Quakers—"Enemies of our Country, Tools of the British Administration"—wanted to destroy all they had achieved. This plea, drenched in the imagery of the cause, begged the assembly to reject these attempts by unpacking what Jefferson tried to contain in the sanitized phrase "new provocations": "The Horrors of all the Rapes, Murders, and Outrages, which a vast Multitude of unprincipled, unpropertied, revengeful, and remorseless Banditti are capable of perpetrating" would bring "sure and final Ruin to this now flourishing free and happy Country." The impulse of maintaining, even deepening, slavery that undergirded these petitions won the day. The manumission law, as conservative as it was, would be as far as Virginians would go in the aftermath of the Revolution. The war had armed Quakers and antislavery advocates with natural rights rhetoric, but it had scared others.[67]

As much as Juvenis and his opponents thought about what slaves might do in Virginia's future wars, African Americans also remembered the lesson of resistance during the continental upheaval of the Revolutionary War. With gradual abolition succeeding in some northern states but failing in others—and all places denying full citizenship rights—they kept alive the memories of heroes in different ways. Not long after the war's end, an African American festival in Windsor, Connecticut, centered on the figure of "General Ti," about whom a number of black troops in ranks paraded in accordance with the day's topsy-turvy ceremony. Since it was so close to Colonel Tye (Titus), the African American partisan who had earned notoriety for conducting daring raids in New Jersey, that particular name "suggested to the slaves that they too had a military tradition and reminded them of compatriots who, in an attempt to become free, had sided with the enemies of the Windsor slaves' Yankee masters."[68]

More than anyone else, African Americans experienced the double-ness

67. "To the Honourable the General Assembly of Virginia," in Schmidt and Wilhelm, "Early Proslavery Petitions," *WMQ*, 3d Ser., XXX (1973), 139–140. This same language is found in a Lunenberg County petition (141) and one from Halifax County (146). Lunenberg petitioners added, "Such a Scheme indeed consists very well with the principles and Designs of a *Bute* or a *North*, whose Finger is sufficiently visible in it" (141).

68. Shane White, "'It Was a Proud Day': African Americans, Festivals, and Parades in the North, 1741–1834," *JAH*, LXXXI (1994), 13–50, esp. 29.

of the common cause. In the decade after Yorktown, the cause simultaneously provided grounds for, on the one hand, gradual abolition, personal manumission, and amelioration in material conditions—but, on the other, a strengthening of slaveholding, the reopening of the African slave trade, and a deeper embedding of slavery into the political, constitutional, and economic structure of the new republic.

3: "THE DIFFERENCE IS IMMENSE": WAR STORIES AND CITIZENSHIP IN THE NEW NATION

In February 1790, the first United States Congress took up the task of giving life to one of its constitutionally enumerated powers: establishing a uniform rule of naturalization. The issue of adding new members to the republic was a critical and controversial one. It also went to the heart of the developing notion of what it meant to be an American citizen.[69]

David Ramsay, before he finished his *History,* weighed in on this issue. He had lost election to the first House of Representatives to William Loughton Smith, a native of South Carolina who spent the war years studying law at London and Geneva. Smith returned to Charleston in 1783, opened a law practice, and served in the state assembly. Ramsay believed his absence during the Revolution made him ineligible for election to the Federal Congress: Smith did not meet the standard of being seven years a citizen as per the new Constitution. To mediate the impression that this was simply a case of sour grapes, Ramsay elaborated on his theory in an eight-page pamphlet, *A Dissertation on the Manner of Acquiring the Character and Privileges of a Citizen of the United States,* published in 1789.

"The principle of government," Ramsay contended, "radically changed" with the Revolution because the nature of "the people was also changed from subjects to citizens. The difference is immense." Subjects "look up to a master," whereas citizens "possess in their own right original sovereignty." This did not address the problem of Smith's qualifications, though. Ramsay then developed a level of difference between Americans: that of citizens from inhabitants. Inhabitants did not have full voting rights and "many other privileges" that citizens enjoyed. He described five situations by which inhabitants could become citizens: being an original party to the Declara-

---

69. Some of the material in this section appeared earlier in my essay Robert G. Parkinson, "'Manifest Signs of Passion': The First Federal Congress, Antislavery, and the Legacies of the Revolutionary War," in Hammond and Mason, eds., *Contesting Slavery,* 49–68.

"New Provocations"

tion of Independence, taking an oath of fidelity, coming of age and tacitly accepting rights (if a minor), birth, or adoption. That Smith had done none of these (and was therefore ineligible) was Ramsay's main objective in *A Dissertation*. His pamphlet, however, held more importance as a snapshot of what some political leaders believed citizenship meant at the outset of the "more perfect union," what those rights entailed, who could claim them, and the process by which they might be obtained.[70]

What Ramsay categorized as "inhabitant"—a resident of a particular place with some rights, but not fully a vested member—English common law called "denizen." The concept of "denizen" was distinct from "subject," "alien," or "citizen" in early modern English law. Denization was part of the royal prerogative and a way to incorporate somewhat suspicious aliens into the body politic, but since full naturalization (permanently making aliens subjects) was a parliamentary power, this status was conditional and unstable. Denizens were "halfway members" in arenas beyond just the political sphere: they could purchase but not own or deed property, and they continued to pay the same duties as aliens. At bottom, the main issue at stake was the perception of loyalty. Aliens were dangerous; they had to prove their worthiness and attachment to the sovereign over many years in order to earn status as a naturalized subject, according to English law. This exhibition of proof was one of the areas the Americans did not revolutionize.[71]

Ramsay's argument that Smith was not an alien, but neither a citizen, and therefore held some economic and political rights but not a full share of the people's sovereignty, is revealing. His concept of "inhabitant" (or "denizen") illustrates the spectrum of belonging that the former patriots comprehended in the postwar years. Hardly a Manichaean construction that only allowed for "us" and "them," the opaque, evolving concept of citizenship in the first years of the republic allowed for several gradations. Because the loyalties of several groups had been in question before and after Ramsay's magical moment of independence, the stories of the Revolutionary War

70. Ramsay, *Dissertation*, [3], *Early American Imprints*, 22088. Bradburn has argued that Ramsay overestimated the truly revolutionary nature of this break, in large part because patriot leaders did not jettison all of English common law and put the American republic on a wholly new legal footing based on natural law, but instead only republicanized those parts of the common law heritage that they disagreed with. See *Citizenship Revolution*, 42–54.

71. Kettner, *Development of American Citizenship*, 29–34, esp. 29; Bradburn, *Citizenship Revolution*, 238.

were an ethereal presence in the halls of the new Congress as they decided who could become a naturalized United States citizen, who could not, and who would occupy a shifting, liminal middle ground. Whether some of those people deemed dangerous groups—Indians, African Americans, or German mercenaries—had proved themselves worthy of naturalization was up for debate late in that winter of 1790.

The assumptions that framed that debate are indicative. Members of the House of Representatives spent a good deal of time discussing the details about how some people could obtain rights, but not others. They discussed how to keep standards for citizenship high, so that the status of American membership equaled that of the Roman republic. They discussed appropriate residency requirements, the ideal type of person they wanted to emigrate to America, stipulations for purchasing land, barriers for officeholding, and the constitutional issue of whether the general government could dictate these issues to the states. They debated the possibilities of a multitier vesting process, whereby candidates would earn more rights the longer they were in America. And they worried about exercising great care in this because future generations not "active in rearing up the present government" might not share their "laudable vanity" and exert every effort to protect the republican experiment.[72]

What they did not question, however, was the key phrase that led the eventual Naturalization Act of 1790: "that any Alien being a free white person" would be eligible to become an American citizen. The words "free" and "white" were the foundation of America's first naturalization law. Those were the only people deemed worthy to enjoy the full fruits of citizenship. They were the only people who—reliably—were "person[s] of good character." The French qualified; in fact, one Congressman pointed out that even Frenchmen, "brought up under an absolute monarchy, evinced their love of liberty in the late arduous struggle." "Many of them are now worthy citizens, who esteem and venerate the principles of our revolution." Former German mercenaries qualified, too.[73]

The contours of that inclusion—"free white person"—had roots in the experience of war and union going back to 1775; it reflects how Americans conceptualized the panoply of enemies not wearing red coats they opposed for nearly fifteen years.

---

72. *DHFFC,* XII, 162. For the extensive debate, see 45–175. See also Marilyn C. Baseler, *'Asylum for Mankind': America, 1607–1800* (Ithaca, N.Y., 1998), 255–260.

73. *DHFFC,* VI, 1516 ("Person[s] of good character"), XII, 167 ("worthy citizens").

Patriot publicists had tried unsuccessfully to generate a sustained hatred for the king's supporters in their communities. There were flashpoints of rage, but as much as Thomas Paine, Samuel Adams, and their colleagues had tried to answer the question of "What is a tory?" (often by conflating them with Indians and African Americans), they had failed to fix a durable image to the loyalists. That failure was a great benefit to postwar peace and part of the reason why the reintegration of most loyalists occurred without significant bloodshed. In the Naturalization Act debates, some members of the House offered an amendment that would prevent "alien enemies" from eligibility, perhaps a nod toward the specter of former loyalists who might yet want to return to the United States—but, befitting the hesitancy of many American leaders regarding the loyalists, the Senate rejected the exception.[74]

The steep decline in how patriot publicists identified the German mercenaries as fearsome enemies also paved the way for their acceptance as American citizens. Scholars estimate that more than three thousand soldiers from Hesse-Cassel, Hanover, Waldeck, and Anspach remained after the war. Singling them out as unfit was not only impractical—it was impolitic: it would not be wise to alienate the largest demographic of European immigrants in America, whether they wanted to assimilate or not. Benjamin Rush had recently published a paean to the Pennsylvania Germans, asserting that the state was "so much indebted" to German immigrants for its "prosperity and reputation" and that legislators should "learn from the history of your German fellow citizens that [they] possess an inexhaustible treasure in the bosom of the State, in their manners and arts." "Invite them to share in the power and offices of government," Rush lectured in the conclusion of his 1789 pamphlet. The final Naturalization Act reflected this embrace: it would be issued under the signature of Frederick Augustus Muhlenberg, the first Speaker of the House of Representatives and brother of former Continental army brigadier general John Muhlenberg.[75]

74. Ibid., VI, 1520–1521, XII, 529.

75. Benjamin Rush, *An Account of the Manners of the German Inhabitants of Pennsylvania, Written 1789,* ed. I. Daniel Rupp (Philadelphia, 1875), 1–2, 5, 60–61. For mercenaries staying in America, see Rodney Atwood, *The Hessians: Mercenaries from Hessen-Kassel in the American Revolution* (Cambridge, 1980), 256. For resistance by Pennsylvania Germans to collapse their ethnic identity into an "American one," see Steven M. Nolt, *Foreigners in Their Own Land: Pennsylvania Germans in the Early Republic* (University Park, Pa., 2002).

For a few months in 1776, as detailed above, that redemption seemed impossible. Patriot publicists had depicted the Hessian troops as terrifying marauders who posed even more danger to American liberty than British redcoats. They were men monsters set on destroying the Revolution and perhaps even setting up manors for themselves, complete with new American serfs. Then, just as the French and frontier white savages were instantly transformed, so, too, were the Germans: after Trenton, that fear evaporated, turning into sympathy for these poor soldiers. Patriot publicists represented them as fellow victims of tyrannous European monarchs. By 1790, the only bad feelings that surfaced about the German mercenaries revolved around the Hessian fly. Ever since 1777, the former monsters increasingly appeared as worthy members of society. That former Hessian corporal and violinist Philip Phile (Pfeil) not only stayed in America but later composed "The President's March"—which choruses of girls *in Trenton* had just a few months back sung to President Washington on his journey to inauguration in New York—captures perfectly the scope of the German mercenaries' redemption.[76]

Who did not qualify in the "free white" construction is, of course, apparent. The Naturalization Act did not address the chances for free, nonwhite people who already met the residency requirements to become citizens. Alternative paths during the Revolution that might have led to Indian citizenship, most significantly the provision in a 1778 treaty with the Delawares to consider statehood, had not been followed. Moreover, in the postwar period, most Americans who shaped Indian policy debated whether tribes were independent, foreign nations that merited diplomatic relations or conquered, domestic groups bound by either state or national sovereign law. The notion that they might be individuals whose allegiance was based on personal choice was dimly perceived in the eighteenth century. At bottom, Indians suffered from the interpretation that they had, as a whole, fought against the United States and therefore would not want to join it.[77]

76. Former patriot publicist Francis Hopkinson attached lyrics to Phile's tune in 1798 and it became better known as "Hail Columbia," the unofficial American national anthem until 1931. See: Silverman, *Cultural History of the American Revolution,* 375, 605–606, 674.

77. Kettner, *Development of American Citizenship,* 288–300; Rogers M. Smith, *Civic Ideals: Conflicting Visions of Citizenship in U.S. History* (New Haven, Conn., 1998), 106–110. Destroying tribal identity and turning Indians into individual farmers was, however, one of the goals of some reformers who thought this was critical to "civilizing"

What the Naturalization Act meant for African Americans was even more vague than the language concerning "other persons" in the Constitution. David Ramsay had eliminated African Americans—enslaved and free—right off the top in his *Dissertation*. "Negroes are inhabitants, but not citizens," he declared. The 1790 act codified Ramsay's blanket judgment, denying access for the thousands of blacks freed during the Revolution. This exclusion meant free blacks would permanently occupy a liminal space between citizens and aliens, a concept that matched up with patriot leaders' rendering of them as the king's passive proxies. Many states did not ban free blacks from the franchise explicitly, but that did not necessarily translate into full participation on election day. Like denizens, those "other privileges," especially economic opportunities, would be restricted. That many free blacks were at risk of capture and reenslavement lays bare the divide between their precarious existence and the rights enjoyed by "American citizens."[78]

Citizenship for slaves was, of course, unthinkable, but what freedom meant for the African Americans freed in New England and the mid-Atlantic states was just as difficult for many in the United States to imagine. During the war, Hugh Henry Brackenridge had called for resettlement, and in the 1780s, more writers forwarded plans for emancipation, only with wholesale removal. Jefferson had endorsed this in *Notes,* suggesting the wrongs of the colonial past and "new provocations" had poisoned the chances of peace and community. As fellow Virginia planter Fernandino Fairfax opined in Matthew Carey's *American Museum* in 1790, "It would never do to allow them *all* the privileges of citizens" because they would form a "separate interest from the rest of the community." For Fairfax and Jefferson, emancipated slaves could never be loyal; they would be perpetual threats to the safety of the union. As they had been throughout the Revolution, according to the myth created by patriot publicists, African Americans were untrustworthy and susceptible to the whispers of tyrants. The construction that they were aliens—proxies—forever nagged.[79]

---

them. See especially Bernard W. Sheehan, *Seeds of Extinction: Jeffersonian Philanthropy and the American Indian* (Chapel Hill, N.C., 1973).

78. Ramsay, *Dissertation,* [3], *Early American Imprints,* 22088; Smith, *Civic Ideals,* 105–106, 332; Berlin, *Slaves without Masters,* 58–66.

79. Ferdinando Fairfax, "Plan for Liberating the Negroes within the United States," Richmond, Va., Mar. 6, 1790, *American Museum,* VIII (1790), 285–287, esp. 285. For more, see Bradburn, *Citizenship Revolution,* 257–258; Nicholas Guyatt, "'The Outskirts of Our Happiness': Race and the Lure of Colonization in the Early Re-

Fairfax wrote this on March 6, 1790, just two weeks after New York newspapers had published the House debate over naturalization and sent the bill to the Senate. What occurred later that month, just as the upper house approved the bill, underscores how some Americans—many of them former patriot leaders—drew upon memories of the Revolutionary War to sharpen their evolving conceptions of citizenship.

All discussion in the Senate ended, the Naturalization Bill was ready for President Washington's signature on Monday, March 22, 1790. That afternoon, Pennsylvania Senator William Maclay wondered what the racket emanating from the House of Representatives was about. Upon entering their chamber, he recorded the scene with wide eyes:

> The house have certainly greatly debased their dignity. Using base invective indecorous language 3 or 4 up at a time. manifest signs of passion. the most disorderly Wandering, in their Speeches, telling Stories, private anecdotes etc etc. I know not What may come of it. but there seems a General discontent among the Members. and many of them do not Hesitate to declare, that the Union Must fall to pieces, at the rate we go on.

It seems the important question of who was eligible to join the new nation produced more than a little excitement in Congress that season. The ruckus in the House was a debate over three petitions that demanded the Federal government close the twenty-year window mandated by the Constitution allowing the international slave trade to continue to the United States.[80]

Several factors contributed to harm relations that March. First, the House, unsure of the prudence of reopening this compromise, repeatedly postponed debate. The petitions' sponsors, two Quaker-led delegations

---

public," *JAH*, XCV (2009), 986–1011; Paul J. Polgar, "'To Raise Them to an Equal Participation': Early National Abolitionism, Gradual Emancipation, and the Promise of African American Citizenship," *JER*, XXXI (2011), 229–258.

80. *DHFFC*, IX, 226. The 1790 petition episode is covered in David Waldstreicher, *Runaway America: Benjamin Franklin, Slavery, and the American Revolution* (New York, 2004), 235–239; Howard A. Ohline, "Slavery, Economics, and Congressional Politics, 1790," *Journal of Southern History*, XLVI (1980), 335–360; William C. diGiacomantonio, "'For the Gratification of a Volunteering Society': Antislavery and Pressure Group Politics in the First Federal Congress," *JER*, XV (1995), 169–197; Richard S. Newman, *The Transformation of American Abolitionism: Fighting Slavery in the Early Republic* (Chapel Hill, N.C., 2002), 39–49.

from New York and Pennsylvania, continued to sit in the gallery as constant reminders. What was to the Quakers a faithful expression of resolve to "shew ourselves and to remind them we are waiting upon them" was taken as an ominous sign by southern members: they were "Like evil spirits hovering over our heads in the gallery." Further complicating matters, one of the petitions came under the signature of the president of the Pennsylvania Abolition Society, Benjamin Franklin. It was exceedingly difficult to ignore that particular imprimatur, as the Quakers well knew. Finally, the question of what exactly the petitioners wanted clouded the discussions. Each petition attacked the slave trade—the "gross national iniquity of trafficking in the persons of fellow-men"—but the one from Franklin went further. The Pennsylvania Abolition Society petition implored Congress "to countenance the Restoration of liberty to those unhappy men, who alone, in this land of Freedom, are degraded into perpetual Bondage, and who, amidst the general Joy of surrounding Freemen, are groaning in Servile Subjection, that you will devise means for removing this Inconsistency from the Character of the American People." It was unclear to many men in the House whether the Quakers were calling for a halt to the slave trade or wanted Congress to endorse full emancipation.[81]

The debate quickly got bitter, personal, and (to use Maclay's word) passionate. Southerners, led by Georgian James Jackson and South Carolinians Aedanus Burke and, ironically, William Loughton Smith, wondered aloud whether the eighty-four-year-old Franklin was in full possession of his faculties. As he was a member of the convention that drafted the document, one suggested Franklin "ought to have known the Constitution better." It was "astonishing," Ramsay's nemesis William Loughton Smith observed, "to see Dr. Franklin taking the lead in a business which looked so much like a persecution of the southern inhabitants." Before the shouting was over, a Delaware representative summarized, the debate "produced some rather acrimonious animadversions upon the conduct of that venerable philosopher and statesman Dr. Franklin."[82]

81. John Pemberton to James Pemberton, Mar. 2, 1790, Pennsylvania Abolition Society Papers, series 2, HSP. "Evil spirits": *DHFFC*, XII, 719; "Memorial of the Philadelphia Yearly Meeting, October 1789," Feb. 11, 1790, ibid., VIII, 322–323, esp. 322, "Memorial of the Pennsylvania Abolition Society, 15 February 1790," 324–326, esp. 326.

82. *DHFFC*, XII, 302 ("ought to have known"), 813 ("persecution"), XII, 825 ("venerable philosopher"). One New York newspaper suggested that the animosity

Franklin had his defenders, but he was far from the sole target. Quakers seated in the gallery exhibited an impressive modicum of restraint, listening to accusations like that of Aedanus Burke, who suggested that they "and the schemes they are now agitating, put me in mind of Milton's Lucifer." This rather shocking statement of Burke's came at the end of a long indictment that painted all Quakers as traitors during the Revolution, as several Virginians had done five years earlier in their proslavery petitions.[83]

Pennsylvania representative Thomas Scott, for one, was taken aback by the southerners' arguments. "An advocate for slavery, in its fullest latitude, at this age of the world, and on the floor of the American Congress too, is, with me, *a phenomenon in politics;* yet such advocates have appeared, and many arguments have been advanced on that head, to all which I will answer only by calling upon this committee, and upon every person who has heard them, *to believe them if they can!* With me they defy, yea, mock all belief." But Burke's more subtle tack was not a *"phenomenon."* Burke appealed to the still-fresh memories of the Revolutionary War as a more effective way of impugning the petitions' sponsors. He and other southerners turned over and over to Quaker loyalism during the conflict with Britain. "Who are these same Quakers?" Burke asked. "Are they not the very men, who, a few short years ago were the avowed friends and supporters of the most abject slavery?" "These are they," he continued, "who submitted to the degradation of acting in the base treacherous character of spies to the enemy, for no other purpose but to rivet the shackles of slavery on their country." "They, in the needful hour, were the enemies of America, but now assume another mask, that of enemies to slavery." Virginia representative John Brown stated that he hoped that his colleagues would not "gratify people who never had been friendly to the independence of America." James Jackson stressed that these anti-Quaker attitudes were not limited to the halls of Congress: "Public opinion has declared them, throughout America, to have been enemies to our cause and constitution: Gordon's history declares it; and all others who have written, and have mentioned that society." Another deepened this accusation: "In time of war they would not defend their country from the enemy, and in time of peace they were interfering in the concerns of others,

---

was reminiscent of a terrible moment from Franklin's past: "Franklin, with the whole body of Quakers, have received such abuse, as would make even a Wedderbourn blush!" See *New-York Daily Advertiser,* Mar. 23, 1790; *Federal Gazette* (Philadelphia), Mar. 26, 1790.

83. *DHFFC,* XII, 749.

"New Provocations"

and doing every thing in their power to excite the slaves in the southern states to insurrection."[84]

Here was the key connection. The southerners' line of attack was significant. They invoked, not the American Revolution, but the Revolutionary War as proof to maintain the republic's commitment to slavery. What made the recent terrible memories of the Revolution so significant was that former tories were now taking on many of the aspects of their British enemy: namely, exciting "tumults, seditions, and insurrections" throughout the South. Emancipation, Burke testified, would bring the "greatest cruelty" to the Africans; "Of this we have had experience in South Carolina in 1780." He reminded his colleagues that Lord Cornwallis, "A very intimate old friend of the Quakers," had issued a proclamation giving freedom "to all the Africans who should join his army. After plundering the country, they crowded to him from all quarters, but the invitation in a short time proved one of the greatest calamities to them. Thousands perished miserably by hunger and disease, exhibiting a melancholy example, to shew, how totally incapable *he* is of making a proper use of his new gained liberty, who has been brought up in the habits of slavery." The British had already attempted these "cruel" emancipation schemes during the war, and now, the southern Congressmen argued, Quakers were following right in their footsteps.[85]

Benjamin Franklin's prominent signature on the petition did not deter Burke and his colleagues from smearing Quakers as British sympathizers. The aged Franklin would, as one would expect, take umbrage with Congressmen questioning his sanity and attacking the company he had chosen to keep. He would eventually fire back in a typical Franklinian fashion. But when he did so, he should have castigated himself, as well. After all, as detailed above, Franklin was the most creative publicist of the proxy image, trying to insert it throughout Revolutionary iconography from American coinage to children's books, and a main supplier of Burke's catalog of Revolutionary images.

In fact, Franklin's contribution to the project of using the proxies to define America's enemies did not end with Yorktown. As a lead negotiator at

84. Ibid., 819–820 *("phenomenon in politics")*, 748 ("a few short years ago"), 754 ("in time of war"), 762 ("gratify people"), 800 ("Gordon's history"). Jackson is referring to Gordon's *History of the Rise, Progress, and Establishment, of the Independence of the United States of America.*

85. *DHFFC,* XII, 648 ("tumults, seditions, and insurrections"), 747 ("intimate old friend of the Quakers").

the Paris peace conference, Franklin participated in the contentious negotiations over what became article 4, the British demand that Americans
repay all debts. When the British refused to return runaway slaves, stayed
in the nine western posts, and then howled that the Americans needed to
honor their debts, he unleashed his anger in a sharp rebuttal entitled "The
Retort Courteous" (1786).

Franklin skewered these demands by invoking war stories about British
"tampering." He went all the way back to 1775 to remind everyone that the
British had already seized plenty of American property: "An order arrives
from England, advised by one of their most celebrated *moralists,* Dr. Johnson, in his *Taxation no Tyranny,* to excite [the] slaves to rise, cut the throats
of their purchasers, and resort to the British army, where they should be rewarded with freedom. This was done, and the planters were thus deprived
of near thirty thousand of their working people." As Americans who had
read their newspapers during the war already knew, this was only the beginning. Later on in the war, Franklin reminded his readers, the "ingenious
and humane" British had "inoculated some of the negroes they took as prisoners . . . and then let them escape, or sent them, covered with the pock,
to mix with and spread the distemper among the others of their colour, as
well as among the white country people; which occasioned a great mortality
of both." He concluded that Britain "chose to keep faith rather with its old
black, than its new white friends; a circumstance demonstrating clear as
daylight, that, in making a present peace, they meditated a future war, and
hoped, that, though the promised manumission of slaves had not been effectual in the *last,* in the *next* it might be more successful." For fifteen years,
Franklin had worked arduously to connect British tyranny and black resistance. When Aedanus Burke invoked these images in 1790, he had Franklin
to thank for their discursive resonance.[86]

Benjamin Franklin did not like slavery. Although some scholars suggest
that his "antislavery credentials have been greatly exaggerated," it is still safe
to say that Franklin did not wish to see the institution strengthened in the
new nation. Nor did he see blacks as inhuman forms of property, as was testified by his insistence, during the 1776 Articles debate over counting slaves
in apportionment formulas, that "Sheep will never make any Insurrections."
His personal opinions about slavery, however, have to be understood in tan-
dem with the political campaign to substantiate a common cause. The "Po-

86. Benjamin Franklin, "The Retort Courteous" (1786), in Lemay, ed., *Franklin:
Writings,* 1126–1128.

litical Creed of Americans," argued the 1790 antislavery petition that bore Franklin's name, dictated that the new nation begin curtailing the institution of slavery. For more than a decade, Franklin had been instrumental in the development of that "Political Creed." Franklin and his fellow patriots had continually portrayed themselves and all sympathetic Americans as liberal, sensitive men of the Enlightenment. They were men of action who had recognized British tyranny and resisted it with masculine valor. This was the "spirit" that animated patriots.[87]

Yet that spirit had another manifestation, one that carried significant implications for identifying who was a valued part of "the American people." The notion of a common cause also contained an inherent condemnation of the actions taken by both the king's agents and those who were susceptible to their lies. In the public discourse of the Revolutionary War, African Americans fitted this description. No matter how many actually supported, fought for, and died to secure American independence, as in the fiction condemning all Indians as "merciless savages," blacks were simply "domestic insurrectionists," passive tools of the king. The prejudicial notion that some men were naturally slaves had been part of western culture as far back as Aristotle, but the Revolutionary War gave such ideas a new republican grounding. Nearly without exception, newspapers throughout the Revolution offered images of blacks either embracing the king or joining his troops without a fight. According to patriot publicists, they were amenable to tyranny. When the conflation of Britain and black intersected with colonial racial prejudices and fears about slave rebellions—just as it did with fears of horrific Indian violence—it dampened the universalist, inclusive potential of the patriots' natural rights rhetoric. Quakers, lacking much of this baggage, could recover from being tarred as tories, but blacks could not. African Americans, slave and free, would suffer deep wounds from the specific ways patriots reacted to and shaped the public's perception of the war. One early-twenty-first-century historian has shown how nineteenth-century civic texts put forward narratives that simultaneously showed "white Americans choosing to risk their lives to fight for their liberty" and slaves who "refused to risk their lives fighting for their own freedom." They chose to render

87. Franklin, "Petition from the Pennsylvania Abolition Society to Congress," in Nash, *Race and Revolution*, 144–145, esp. 145; Waldstreicher, *Runaway America*, xii. For more on the patriots' "spirit" and concepts of sentimentality in the eighteenth century, see Nicole Eustace, *Passion Is the Gale: Emotion, Power, and the Coming of the American Revolution* (Chapel Hill, N.C., 2008), 397.

themselves "incapable of citizenship." That vital construction did not wait for Parson Weems, though. Franklin, Jefferson, and many of their patriot colleagues first crafted it at the founding moment itself.[88]

The arguments made by Aedanus Burke and other southerners in the first Federal Congress were not a "phenomenon." When Georgia representative James Jackson claimed that Quaker efforts "would excite tumults, seditions, and insurrections," he, too, carried forward what the patriots had loudly proclaimed was the basis of so-called British tyranny from 1775 on. Recalling these war memories produced the "base invective, indecorous language," and "manifest signs of passion" that Maclay recorded in his diary.[89]

Franklin, only five weeks away from death, refused to ignore the sullying of his name on the floor of Congress. He fought back with satire, publishing an essay that was a dazzling act of ventriloquism: he repeated South Carolina's arguments in the voice of an imaginary African Muslim slaveholder. Noting that southern speeches "put me in mind of a similar one made about one hundred years since, by Sidi Mehemet Ibrahim," he then quoted the "speech," which decimated the proslavery arguments made by Smith, Jackson, and their colleagues. "Let us then hear no more of this detestable proposition, the manumission of christian slaves," Franklin mocked as Ibrahim, "the adoption of which would, by deprecating our lands and houses, and thereby depriving so many good citizens of their properties, create universal discontent, and provoke insurrections, to the endangering of government, and producing general confusion."[90]

This clever inversion would be Franklin's last bagatelle and as such has been held up as proof of his antislavery convictions. No matter how brilliant, though, this satire flew in the face of many of the images Franklin had helped publicize over the past fifteen years. As much as Franklin and the other so-called "founding fathers" might have wished slavery away, by the end of the eighteenth century, it was increasingly secure. To be sure, the Revolutionaries provided a linguistic template that African American activists and abolitionists would use to expose American hypocrisy to that same "candid world" the Declaration of Independence had addressed. At the same time, Franklin and dozens of other patriot publicists had also

88. François Furstenberg, *In the Name of the Father: Washington's Legacy, Slavery, and the Making of a Nation* (New York, 2006), 22.

89. *DHFFC*, IX, 225–226, esp. 226, XII, 819–820, esp. 820.

90. *Federal Gazette* (Philadelphia), Mar. 25, 1790.

"New Provocations"

buried, deep in the political structure of the new republic, the notion that certain groups were not fit for inclusion. Patriot political and communication leaders constructed this argument to achieve a wholly different goal: to maintain unity and stand up to the world's greatest military. All the polemics that played on fear did more than just mobilize Americans to defeat the British, though. They also armed slaveholders with a new rhetorical weapon with which they could defend slavery: attack any abolitionists as pro-British enemies of the Revolution. That device would become a staple of American politics for more than a generation.

Yet there was even more damage. The values intrinsic to the common cause appeal—sharpened by the experience of war—helped reify what would, over a few years, harden into racial difference in the new nation. It gave racial prejudice a whole new valence, a cornerstone in the American republican edifice. Given the "passion" that resounded through the House in 1790, the conception of blacks and their defenders as threats to the republic was obviously neither hegemonic nor consensual, but it was nevertheless an inherent, if buried, part of the American founding. It cannot be denied that, as one Congressman stated that March, the "language of America in the day of distress" featured concepts of equality and universal rights. But American unity was also achieved by showing how the people who "seduced," "excited," and "instigated" passive slaves were truly enemies of independence. War images further entrenched and grounded colonial stereotypes about black inferiority and their natural incapability of acting as full-fledged republican citizens.[91]

When the new Federal government debated the future of America's connection to the international slave trade and set about making rules about who could become a citizen, these old war stories mattered. The Naturalization Act of 1790 stipulated that a "person of good character" who would "support the Constitution of the United States" could become an American citizen. After all the proclamations, newspaper reports, children's books of atrocities, peace treaties, and declarations of independence—kept alive by poems, histories, novels, captivity narratives, and travelogues—that connected "black," "Indian," and "enemy," Congress did not need to include the words "free" and "white" when defining who constituted "we the people." Those words were well understood. Even the thousands of free blacks created by liberalized manumission statutes, gradual emancipation schemes,

91. *DHFFC,* XII, 815.

or military service would find themselves at best in the indeterminate position of permanent denizens in the United States. They joined Indians, even the ones who received certificates of commendation from George Washington himself, as outsiders inside the American republic. As that man exchanged eight years of commanding the Continental army for eight years as the President of the United States, these stories continued to resound.

CONCLUSION

By the rude bridge that arched the flood,
Their flag to April's breeze unfurled,
Here once the embattled farmers stood,
And fired the shot heard round the world. . . .

Spirit, that made those heroes dare
To die, or leave their children free,
Bid Time and Nature gently spare
The shaft we raise to them and thee.
Ralph Waldo Emerson
Hymn: Sung at the Completion of the Concord Monument

"You have in a common cause fought and triumphed together," George Washington pleaded in his last farewell address. "The independence and liberty you possess are the work of joint councils, and joint efforts; of common dangers, sufferings, and successes." President Washington's desperation illustrates how the appeal for Americans to put away their differences and hold tightly to the union—the "Palladium of your political safety and prosperity," as he called it—remained relevant two decades after the Declaration. Some things had changed: by 1796, when Washington worried about "batteries of internal and external enemies," he meant bitter partisans who threatened to undermine Americans' "cordial, habitual and immoveable attachment" to union, not hostile Indians, resistant slaves, and fearsome foreign mercenaries. Yet, even if President Washington would have placed party rivals at the head of the list of dangers to the common cause, it did not mean that the "batteries" he had faced as General Washington had dissipated entirely.[1]

1. Ralph Waldo Emerson, "Hymn: Sung at the Completion of the Concord Monument," Apr. 19, 1836, in John Hollander, ed., *American Poetry: The Nineteenth Century*, 2 vols. (New York, 1993), I, 318–319; Washington, "Farewell Address," Sept. 19, 1796, in John Rhodehamel, ed., *George Washington: Writings* (New York, 1997), 964–965.

In part, this was owing to the continuation of those external enemies. At the end of Washington's first presidential term, the massive insurrection in Haiti coupled with the outbreak of war across Europe magnified the importance of these older concerns. The early 1790s military disasters that plagued the United States Army in their prolonged fight against hostile Ohio Valley Indians could be blamed on Britain's continued interference across the Great Lakes. Worries about a contagion of insurrection emanating from Haiti also challenged many Americans to reconsider their slaves and reconceptualize slavery in that decade. Washington's other admonition in the farewell address—to avoid getting entangled in Europe's wars—was therefore an illusion in what would turn out to be an age of revolution. As the infant republic's leaders navigated that tempestuous decade, the problems of outsiders' instigating, tampering, or agitating Indians and slaves continued to press in ever-evolving contexts.[2]

In other words, both sides of the common cause appeal as first crafted in 1775 remained a vital force in the United States for the remainder of the eighteenth century. What Washington feared as a threat to the Constitution in 1796—the promise and safety of unity as the only haven against an array of devious enemies both within and without—was only the latest rehashing of those well-established Revolutionary themes.

So, too, the memory of those people and events from the Revolutionary War remained, though diminished and boiled down. The partisanship that Washington lamented, fueled in part by those external revolutions in France and Haiti, politicized for Americans many stories about their own revolution in the 1790s. What had been, in the 1780s, consensual celebrations of Revolutionary heroes or battles were, a decade later, scenes of political discord as both Federalists and Republicans tried to prove they were the true inheritors of the common cause, and conflated "nation" with their views of what should be remembered about the Revolution and who should participate in that commemoration. Federalists chose to valorize heroes; Republicans asserted the Revolution was, instead, a people's war. This hothouse atmosphere bred suffocation and stasis: gravesites left unattended, bills to raise monuments abandoned on the tables of state legislatures,

2. Wiley Sword, *President Washington's Indian War: The Struggle for the Old Northwest, 1790–1795* (Norman, Okla., 1985), 11–22; Timothy D. Willig, *Restoring the Chain of Friendship: British Policy and the Indians of the Great Lakes, 1783–1815* (Lincoln, Neb., 2008), 11–58; Ashli White, *Encountering Revolution: Haiti and the Making of the Early Republic* (Baltimore, 2010), 124–165.

heroes fading into obscurity. By the first years of the nineteenth century, it seems, the only venue safe enough to remind Americans of their Revolutionary past were the bare facts found along the bottom of calendars in household almanacs recalling past glory: "Hessians taken at Trenton," or "Independence declared."[3]

Except on the frontier. Just as they had for more than two decades, war stories about British instigation of Indians remained a topic well worth discussing in the early nineteenth century. For Americans in the backcountry, this meant, just as it had since the 1770s, howling about and plotting to sever British sponsorship of native resistance. Indiana territory governor William Henry Harrison was among the converted. As the Shawnee Prophet Tenskwatawa and his brother Tecumseh began to gain spiritual, political, and military strength in the region starting in 1806, Harrison wrote back to his superiors in Washington complaining that the British were behind their defiance. He was convinced the Prophet's increasing power "was produced by British intrigue and influence in anticipation of war between them and the United States." Other American officials on the frontier corroborated Harrison's case.[4]

3. Sarah J. Purcell, *Sealed with Blood: War, Sacrifice, and Memory in Revolutionary America* (Philadelphia, 2002), 92–132; David Waldstreicher, *In the Midst of Perpetual Fetes: The Making of American Nationalism, 1776–1820* (Chapel Hill, N.C., 1997), 108–173. For a small sample of almanacs, see Abraham Shoemaker, *Carey's Franklin Almanac, for the Year 1804; Being Bissextile or Leap Year* (Trenton, N.J., 1803), Shoemaker, *Weems's Washington Almanack, for the Year 1804; Being Bissextile or Leap Year* (Philadelphia, [1803?]), Robert Stubbs, *The Ohio Almanac, for the Year of Our Lord, 1807: Being the Third after Bissextile or Leap Year* (Cincinnati, Oh., [1806]), J. Sharp, *The Georgia and South-Carolina Republican Almanac, for the Year of Our Lord, 1809 . . .* (Augusta, Ga., [1808]), all in *Early American Imprints: Series II: Shaw-Shoemaker, 1801–1819*, nos. 3930, 5568, 11063, 50853. Alfred F. Young referred to this memory as "tamed" in Young, *The Shoemaker and the Tea Party: Memory and the American Revolution* (Boston, 1999), 94, 108–120, 140, esp. 94, 140. See also Robert E. Cray, "Major John André and the Three Captors: Class Dynamics and Revolutionary Memory Wars in the Early Republic, 1780–1831," *JER*, XVII (1997), 371–397, esp. 384–385.

4. William Henry Harrison to Secretary of War, Vincennes, Aug. 13, 1807, in Logan Esarey, ed., *Indiana Historical Collections*, VII, *Governor's Messages and Letters: Messages and Letters of William Henry Harrison*, I (Indianapolis, 1922), 229, Harrison to Secretary of War William Eustis, Vincennes, July 5, 1809, 349; James W. Stevens to James Madison, Batavia, N.Y., Mar. 2, 1809, in Robert A. Rutland et al., eds., *The Papers of James Madison: Presidential Series*, 8 vols. to date (Charlottesville, Va., 1984–),

Another power broker in the west, Andrew Jackson, had the same opinion about the dangers of British influence among southern Indians. "There can remain no doubt," he wrote to President Jefferson in 1808, that there were "agents of a foreign nation; exciting the creeks, to hostilities against the United States." "These horrid scenes bring fresh to our recollection, the influence, during the revolutionary war," Jackson continued. "That raised the scalping knife, and Tomhawk, against our defenceless weoman and children—I have but little doubt but the present savage cruelty is excited from the same source." By 1810, Jackson and Harrison were certain that Indians, from the Gulf of Mexico to the Great Lakes, were only a threat to American security because of their British sponsors. Three weeks after Harrison claimed a sweeping victory at Tippecanoe over Indian forces led by Tenskwatawa on November 7, 1811, Jackson sent congratulations to his colleague: "The blood of our murdered Countrymen must be revenged—That banditti, ought to be swept from the face of the earth—I do hope that government will see that it is necessary to act efficiently, and that this hostile band, which must be excited to war, by the secret agents of great Britain, must be destroyed." The premise behind, intent conveyed, and even language employed in this letter were far from the rash or hurried impressions that first came to Jackson as he rushed to congratulate Harrison upon hearing of Tippecanoe. They were, rather, as old as the republic itself: Jefferson had written the same letter about the people Jackson would come to know well, the Cherokees, in the summer of 1776. The toasts that went up in celebration of Harrison's "triumph" at Tippecanoe reflected Jackson's (and Jefferson's) demarcation separating heroes from villains on the frontier: "hisses" for "The British agents at Vincennes" and "An everlasting cheer" for the "brave sons of Kentucky" who defeated them—and their proxies.[5]

———

I, 6–10, esp. 6–8. For a new interpretation of this power struggle on the western frontier, see Adam Jortner, *The Gods of Prophetstown: The Battle of Tippecanoe and the Holy War for the American Frontier* (New York, 2012).

5. Andrew Jackson to TJ, Apr. 20, 1808, in Sam B. Smith et al., eds., *The Papers of Andrew Jackson*, 9 vols. to date (Knoxville, Tenn., 1980–), II, 191–193, Jackson to William Henry Harrison, Hermitage, Nov. 28, 1811, II, 270. Jefferson himself reprised his own angry 1776 letter, which called for the extirpation of the Cherokees, in an 1813 letter to Alexander Humboldt, explaining that

the interested and unprincipled policy of England has defeated all our labors for the salvation of these unfortunate people. They have seduced the greater part of the tribes within our neighborhood, to take up the hatchet against us,

Conclusion

Nor were Jackson and Harrison's convictions that the British lay behind all Indian resistance merely misapplications or misremembrances of history, for the same stories involving what merciless savages did in the Revolutionary War stayed with the American public during the years of Tenskwatawa and Tecumseh's rise to power. Many people, places, and events from the Revolution had disappeared or become controversial since the 1780s, but memories involving Britain and their "savage allies" had not.

Artists and writers maintained these connections. Mercy Otis Warren's history finally left her desk drawer and found space in bookshops in 1805. Joel Barlow, the "Connecticut Wit" who then became one of President Jefferson's most important diplomats, found time to enlarge his successful 1787 poem, *The Vision of Columbus*, into *The Columbiad*, published in 1807. His expansion added several books on the history of the American Revolution and featured the murder of "Lucinda," Barlow's pseudonym for Jane McCrea, by Britain's "kindred cannibals" who "scour the waste" around the battlefield "for undistinguish'd prey." After the Mohawks who dispatch the fair Lucinda present their prizes—"scalps by British gold are paid"—Barlow chastised her real murderers: "Are these thy trophies, Carleton! these swords / Thy hand unsheath'd and gave the savage hordes"?[6]

Barlow imagined the *Columbiad* would become a national epic, America's *Aeneid*. Barlow's friends, especially Robert Fulton, arranged for a lavish publication, featuring several illustrations. Barlow asked several artists, including John Vanderlyn, to submit sketches. Vanderlyn, an aspiring painter who was just learning to walk when the unfortunate McCrea died near his upstate New York home, submitted a draft. Although Barlow commissioned another artist, Robert Smirke, to complete the eleven illustrations for the

---

and the cruel massacres they have committed on the women and children of our frontiers taken by surprise, will oblige us now to pursue them to extermination, or drive them to new seats beyond our reach.

Jefferson to Baron Alexander von Humboldt, Montpelier, Dec. 6, 1813, in Andrew A. Lipscomb and Albert Ellery Bergh, eds., *The Writings of Thomas Jefferson: Library Edition* . . . (Washington, D.C., 1903–1907), XIV, 20–25, esp. 23; "Toasts," Dec. 27, 1811, "Messages and Letters of Harrison," in Esarey, ed., *Governors Messages and Letters*, I, 681.

6. James Woodress, *A Yankee's Odyssey: The Life of Joel Barlow* (Philadelphia, 1958), 245–249; Joel Barlow, *The Columbiad: A Poem* (London, 1809), x, book 6, 206–207, lines 644, 660 ("Lucinda"), 204, lines 608–609 ("kindred cannibals"), 207, line 671 ("British gold"), 208, lines 685–686 ("trophies, Carleton").

Columbiad, Vanderlyn would carry on with the project, developing it into an icon of early American painting, *The Murder of Jane McCrea,* which Fulton bought and donated to the New York Academy of Fine Arts. Together, poet Barlow and artists Smirke and Vanderlyn revitalized and deepened the legend of the McCrea story for the new century.[7]

Just a few months after Barlow's expensive book appeared, publishers brought out an American edition of *Gertrude of Wyoming; or, The Pennsylvanian Cottage,* a lengthy production by the Scottish poet Thomas Campbell. Born a year before the events at Wyoming, Campbell explained that he had read a number of accounts of the 1778 attack as background for what would become one of the most popular poems of its time. His artistic license kept with what many Americans believed happened along the Susquehanna, including who was to blame. The chief villain of the romantic epic is Mohawk leader Joseph Brant, whom Campbell turns into "the monster":

With all his howling desolating band; —
These eyes have seen their blade, and burning pine
Awake at once, and silence half your land.
Red is the cup they drink; but not with wine:
Awake, and watch to-night! or see no morning shine!

Part of Campbell's license was his invention of a "good" Indian, an Oneida, whose family was also destroyed by "the monster Brandt" and who saves the beautiful heroine Gertrude. Though in reality Brant was nowhere near Wyoming on July 3, 1778 (and *his* family took such umbrage at Campbell's aspersions that his son John Brant threatened legal action against the poet), the popularity of the poem, along with the savageness displayed by "the monster," fitted precisely with Americans' conceptions of Indian hostility. Booksellers across the Eastern Seaboard advertised Campbell's romantic rendering of frontier domestic bliss torn asunder just as real tensions were again about to spill over into actual bloodshed on the western frontier.[8]

7. Samuel Y. Edgerton, Jr., "The Murder of Jane McCrea: The Tragedy of an American *Tableau d'Histoire," Art Bulletin,* XLVII (1965), 481–492, esp. 481–483.

8. Thomas Campbell, *Gertrude of Wyoming: A Pennsylvanian Tale; and Other Poems* (New York, 1809), 61, *Early American Imprints, Series II: Shaw-Shoemaker, 1801–1819,* 17145; Peter Silver, "Indians Abroad," *WMQ,* 3d Ser., LXVII (2010), 145–154, esp. 146–147. For a sample of newspapers advertising Campbell's poem, see *Commercial Advertiser* (New York), June 23, 1809; *Columbian Centinel* (Boston), Aug. 12, 1809; *Alex-*

Figure 19. *"The Death of Jane McCrea." By John Vanderlyn. 1804.*
Born in Kingston, New York, just as the Revolutionary War started, Vanderlyn grew
up with the story of McCrea's death. His painting kept ideas about British-sponsored
"merciless savages" murdering vulnerable white women at the heart of the romance
surrounding the Revolution in the early years of the nineteenth century. Courtesy
of the Wadsworth Atheneum Museum of Art, Hartford, Connecticut.

"Wyoming" had never really left the American vernacular since the Revolution, but its resonance grew as tensions with Britain increased. Over this period, newspaper articles continued to highlight the connections between Britain and Indians, and the famous "massacres" of the Revolution were repeatedly invoked. Writers and speakers begged audiences not to forget about the king's original proxies. In 1808, a July Fourth oration in Lexington, Kentucky, reprinted the Declaration of Independence in full—including putting the final grievance about "merciless savages" entirely in italics—with the added commentary: "The same Indian savages are stirred up to tomahawk our farmers—the same attacks are made on our liberties by that mad man, which this declaration so justly designates by the title of a TYRANT." The following year, a Massachusetts orator celebrated the Fourth by reminding Americans that "the savages of the wilderness had become the allies of our more savage invaders, and the horrors of Wyoming and Cherry-Valley exhibited the concentrated ferocity of combined barbarians." Several months before New York's publishers brought out Campbell's paean to the peaceful Pennsylvania cottagers, one of that city's newspapers lectured its readers that the "conduct of the *British,* or as they have been aptly termed the *Brutish,* throughout the contest was totally unworthy of a civilized people. Remember the massacre at Wyoming."⁹

Republican anger at Federalist refusals to blame the British for frontier violence resulted in accusations that they were just like the tories of old. In the fall of 1809, one printer featured the warnings of an "Old Whig of '76": "I remembered the time when some of the noisiest of these fellows, or their fathers, were arrayed in arms against us, when they were united with the English, Hessians and Indians, in the work of murder, conflagration and ruin." "How can I forget the capture of Wyoming in 1778, when man, woman and child were indiscriminately burnt together by the combined crew?" Frontier newspapers, naturally, were in the vanguard to lambast those who "forgot" the Revolution. The *Reporter,* the local paper in Washington, Pennsylvania (where some of the descendants of the Gnadenhutten murderers surely still

andria Gazette (Va.), Nov. 11, 1809; Orange County Patriot; or, the Spirit of '76 (Goshen, N.Y.), Jan. 21, 1812.

9. "TYRANT": "American Independence," *The Reporter* (Lexington, Ky.), July 2, 1808. "Combined barbarians": *Old Colony Gazette* (New Bedford, Mass.), Aug. 4, 1809; *Columbian Phenix* (Providence, R.I.), Aug. 12, 1809; *Eastern Argus* (Portland, Maine), Aug. 24, 1809. "Remember the massacre": "Paragraph Second," *Public Advertiser* (New York), Aug. 13, 1808.

resided), kept alive the terrible legend of the "Wyoming Massacre" by reprinting the decidedly false but most widely circulated account of the event, first produced by *New-York Journal* printer John Holt and still intact after thirty years—complete with the accusation that the simple response of *"the hatchet"* was the reply given to offers of surrender, and subsequently "all perished all together in the flames." This relic of the Revolution was as vital in 1809 as it was when Holt first created it in 1778. The *Carthage Gazette,* with its offices not far from Andrew Jackson's home in Tennessee, also preserved Holt's aged fabrication.[10]

* * *

"In reviewing the conduct of Great Britain towards the United States, our attention is necessarily drawn to the warfare just renewed by the Savages, on one of our extensive frontiers," President James Madison wrote in his June 1, 1812, message to Congress asking for war. Then, following convention, he invoked the Declaration: "a warfare which is known to spare neither age nor sex, and to be distinguished by features peculiarly shocking to humanity." Not just Madison thought this was a proper cause for war against Britain. Groups from all over the United States sent their approval of the first declaration of war in the republic's history, citing the "Yell of the Savage . . . Tis Britains deed; more cruel than the Savage foe, she excites them to murder our defenceless women and children" as an appropriate casus belli. Former President Jefferson also sent in his approval, writing from Monticello that an anticipated invasion of Canada would save "our women and children forever from the tomahawk and scalping knife, by removing those who excite them."[11]

10. "How can I forget": *Bee* (Hudson, N.Y.), Sept. 19, 1809. *"The hatchet"*: *Reporter* (Washington, Pa.), May 22, 1809; *Carthage Gazette* (Tenn.), May 31, 1809.

11. James Madison to Congress, Washington, D.C., June 1, 1812, in Rutland et al., eds., *Papers of James Madison: Presidential Series,* IV, 432–439, esp. 436, "From the Citizens of Darlington District, South Carolina," July 18, 1812, V, 48–49, "From the Republican Delegates from Towns in Hampshire, Franklin, and Hampden Counties, Massachusetts," July 24, 1812, 72, 77, "From the Citizens of Fayette County, Kentucky," Aug. 15, 1812, 162, "From the Republican Citizens of Worcester County, Maryland," Sept. 8, 1812, 292, Thomas Henderson to James Madison, Mecklenburg Co., N.C., Sept. 10, 1812, 296, "From the Republican Citizens of York County, District of Maine," Sept. 10, 1812, 301, "From the Delegates of Hillsborough County, New Hampshire," Sept. 15, 1812, 319, "From the Tennessee General Assembly," [ca. Oct. 17, 1812], 400, "From the Pennsylvania General Assembly," Dec. 16, 1812, 512;

The War of 1812 would indeed see a repeat of the connection between British armed forces and proxies from the Revolutionary War, both Indians and African Americans. Although much of the rhetoric espoused by those who wanted war emphasized British instigation on the frontier, concerns about what emancipatory actions the British might promote in another conflict began to emerge with the actual onset of war. During the tense years of 1807 to 1812, insurrection scares had gripped the South, Virginia especially. Late in 1808, another series of conspiracies stretched up the James from Norfolk to Albemarle, just as it had in April 1775. Scholars have traced an increase in slave rebellions beginning in 1810 and lasting throughout the war, with scares in North Carolina, Kentucky, and Virginia. In 1811, the "largest slave rebellion in the history of the United States" took place on the sugar plantations near New Orleans, with hundreds of slaves taking advantage of another "Disturbance"—again, just as they had in 1775.[12]

This might have given some political leaders pause in reflection of what war with Britain had meant before. But two of the most prominent voices for and against war each rejected—for his own purposes—a memory of the Revolution that gave credit to the tens of thousands of slaves who escaped John Randolph's Virginia and John C. Calhoun's South Carolina. When Randolph broke with his party and joined the opposition, begging not to go to war in part because he was now terrified of the consequences of slave revolt, he blamed the Haitians entirely: "During the war of the Revolution, so fixed were [the slaves'] habits of subordination, that when the whole southern country was overrun by the enemy, who invited them to desert, no fear was ever entertained of an insurrection of the slaves." But now, after the unfortunate "progress of society, within the last twenty years," Randolph was sure this time would be different. Calhoun agreed with Randolph's memory of "our Revolution," saying, "No attempts were made by that portion of our population," but he laughed off the effects of the French or Haitians on "our

---

TJ to JA, Monticello, June 11, 1812, in Lipscomb and Bergh, eds., *Writings of Jefferson,* XIII, 161. Jefferson wrote nearly the exact same sentiments in a letter to John Adams five days later. See TJ to JA, Monticello, June 11, 1812, in Lester J. Cappon, ed., *The Adams-Jefferson Letters: The Complete Correspondence between Thomas Jefferson and Abigail and John Adams,* II, *1812–1826* (Chapel Hill, N.C., 1957), 308.

12. Herbert Aptheker, *American Negro Slave Revolts* (New York, 1943), 243; Adam Rothman, *Slave Country: American Expansion and the Origins of the Deep South* (Cambridge, Mass., 2005), 106–117, esp. 106. See also Alan Taylor, *The Internal Enemy: Slavery and War in Virginia, 1772–1832* (New York, 2013).

ignorant blacks." "I dare say more than one half of them never heard of the French Revolution," Calhoun scoffed.[13]

To be sure, the thousands of slaves who responded to Dunmore's and Clinton's emancipation proclamations, the thousands more who followed Cornwallis's army through the South, and the thousands more who boarded ships bound for Nova Scotia did not compare to the fearsome tales that emerged from Haiti, but Randolph's and Calhoun's confident retellings of the Revolution were highly inaccurate. Nor was it the way everyone remembered that war. A few months after Calhoun's arguments for war won the day, worried citizens from Greene County, Georgia, implored the Madison administration to invade Florida immediately. Their concerns undermined both Calhoun's memories and his bravado about "ignorant blacks." They begged Madison to deny the enemy the "power, to stir up against us, the merciless and unrelenting Savages, immediately bordering upon us; and from a history of the revolutionary war, have we not much to fear from her seductive overtures to our black population, exciting them to abandon their owners, and perhaps to rise up in rebellion against them?" Maybe the Georgians had heard the swirling rumors that had swept across the Gulf Coast that the British might bring black troops from the Caribbean to initiate a slave insurrection if war was declared. Randolph feared that while the War Hawks might busy themselves with plans to invade Canada, southerners would be "shuddering for our own safety at home." But no matter how Calhoun and Randolph blithely comforted themselves, this, too, had happened before, in Massachusetts as well as Virginia and South Carolina—and more than a decade before the Haitian Revolution.[14]

In May 1813, a British fleet under the command of Admiral George Cock-

13. Mr. Randolph, Speech before House of Representatives, Dec. 10, 1811, in *The Debates and Proceedings in the Congress of the United States . . .* , I, *Annals of Congress,* 12th Congress, Session 1 (Washington D.C., 1853), 450–452, esp. 452; Calhoun, "Speech on the Report of the Foreign Relations Committee," Dec. 12, 1811, in Robert L. Meriwether et al., eds., *The Papers of John C. Calhoun,* 28 vols. (Columbia, S.C., 1959–2003), I, 81. For more on how the tumult of the Age of Revolution affected American conceptions of slaveholding, see Ashli White, *Encountering Revolution: Haiti and the Making of the Early Republic* (Baltimore, 2010).

14. "From the Citizens of Greene County, Georgia," Aug. 13, 1812, in Rutland et al., eds., *Papers of James Madison: Presidential Series,* V, 154–155; Frank Lawrence Owsley, Jr., *Struggle for the Gulf Borderlands: The Creek War and the Battle of New Orleans, 1812–1815* (Gainesville, Fla., 1981), 18; Mr. Randolph, Speech before House, Dec. 10, 1811, in *Annals of Congress,* I, 451.

burn sailed into the Chesapeake Bay, and, for slaveholders in the tidewater, history did repeat itself. The British presence in the Chesapeake began another prolonged cycle of depredatory raids, as had happened almost constantly from 1775 to 1783. For nearby slaves, it meant another possibility of escape. Although the British commanders had strict instructions not to incite slave revolts, they were allowed to shelter and protect runaways. The man they sent to conduct these raids, Colonel Sir Thomas Sydney Beckwith, was exactly the kind of man the Georgians feared. He had led the free black First West Indian Regiment, and British authorities believed this experience might produce better effects than Dunmore had achieved in 1776.[15]

Or, at least, that was the connection Americans began to make once they learned of Cockburn and Beckwith's activities in Maryland and Virginia. "A considerable number of negroes belonging to Princess Ann County, have at different times eloped from their owners and gone on board the British men of war," reported the *Daily National Intelligencer* in May 1813. "One would have thought from the treatment which the fathers of these deluded wretches met with, by deserting to the British last war, that they would have been deterred from such a course," opined the Norfolk correspondent, "but it seems they have forgot how the great Lord Dunmore enticed the Princess Ann negroes away from their masters, with fine promises, and afterwards shipped them off to Jamaica." Just as in 1775, Virginians could not understand this behavior. Since they "fare better than a great many poor white families," why would these "unfortunate beings" choose to follow "the foul example of Lord Dunmore"?[16]

Reports that were nearly identical to those in the Revolution appeared with just the names changed. American papers again excoriated Royal Navy captains for their "pitiful and dishonorable . . . species of warfare," of raiding, burning, and stealing property, which caused their character and name "to descend to oblivion, coupled with that of the infamous Dunmore." Reports that ships had taken slaves on board and that "a great many

---

15. Frank A. Cassell, "Slaves of the Chesapeake Bay Area and the War of 1812," *Journal of Negro History*, LVII (1972), 144–155; Anthony Iacarrino, "Virginia and the National Contest over Slavery in the Early Republic, 1780–1833" (Ph.D. diss., University of California, Los Angeles, 1999), 138–140; Gene Allen Smith, *The Slaves' Gamble: Choosing Sides in the War of 1812* (New York, 2013), 85–114; Taylor, *Internal Enemy*, 245–274.

16. *Daily National Intelligencer*, May 12, 1813; also in *Universal Gazette* (Washington, D.C.), May 14, 1813.

others have eloped," as well as concerns that the "enemy holds a secret correspondence with the negroes on the shore," again flew out of print shops and over post roads in the nineteenth century as they had in the late eighteenth. Headlines blared: "The Dunmore and Cornwallis, alias the Negro and Sheep Stealing System, revived." A few papers even resurrected primary sources, including a letter from John Page to William Woodford (the bane of Dunmore's campaign, who had fought the governor with pen and sword), dated November 28, 1775, so as to instruct Americans in 1813 how to conduct operations against British predators. Dunmore's ghost stalked the Virginia tidewater once more. A year later, when Vice Admiral Alexander Cochrane issued a proclamation that offered "due encouragement" to *anyone* who wished to "withdraw" from the United States, the specter was more than just a figment of printers' imaginations. As they had in the Revolution, hundreds of slaves throughout the Chesapeake sought the protection of the royal standard.[17]

The outpouring of thirty-year-old hatred for Dunmore was not the only connection American printers made tying the present war to the last. At the same time that the printers reintroduced their readers to Lord Dunmore, a concoction from Benjamin Franklin's long-dormant printing press was still present in the cultural bloodstream. The fall 1812 campaign in the west had ended in disaster. British forces captured Detroit, Mackinaw, and Dearborn. Then, in January 1813, along the River Raisin, British and Indian forces wiped out nearly half of the Americans in arms. After the battle, a group of Wyandot Indians, rumored to be drunk, plundered those who had suffered severe wounds and set fire to their shelters. Dozens of Kentuckians died in what would become a rallying call for the remainder of the war: "Remember the Raisin!" The River Raisin then took rank alongside older massacre places at Wyoming and Cherry Valley. Newspaper publishers remem-

17. "Secret correspondence": *Norfolk Herald,* Sept. 3, 1813; *Daily National Intelligencer* (Washington, D.C.), Sept. 7, 1813; *Columbian* (New York), Sept. 10, 1813; *Palladium of Liberty* (Morristown, N.J.), Sept. 16, 1813. Dunmore and Cornwallis: *Columbian* (New York), May 15, 1813; *Independent Chronicle,* May 20, 1813; *New-Hampshire Gazette,* May 25, 1813; *Investigator* (Charleston), June 3, 1813. This article informed readers that the "vile wretch" Dunmore "succeeded" with "many of those deluded beings." Page to Woodford: *Argus* (Albany), June 18, 1813; *Rhode-Island Republican* (Newport), July 1, 1813; Alexander Cochrane, "A Proclamation," Apr. 2, 1814, in Michael J. Crawford, ed., *The Naval War of 1812: A Documentary History,* III, *1814–1815* (Washington, D.C., 2002), 60.

bered the Raisin by resurrecting the "Supplement to the Boston *Independent Chronicle"* from 1782. That spring, in order to illustrate the long roots of the River Raisin massacre, seventeen newspapers reintroduced Franklin's hoax to their readers. Captain Gerrish's lurid account of bags of scalps being sent to King George for his "refreshment" again hummed along the exchange network. Franklin had intended his creation to stir up feeling in 1782; it did, both then and three decades later. Ironically, in another strange circularity that should hardly surprise, it was the actual *Independent Chronicle* that, the summer before, first published a letter that would become "proof" of official British instigation under the headline "Savage Allies of England." Just as it had since 1775, when it came to the emotional issue of the king's proxies, the line between fact and fiction—between hoax and proof—was impossible to discern.[18]

In short, as long as the United States viewed itself as the avowed enemy of Great Britain, the dual nature of the common cause appeal continued to shape how Americans conceived of themselves and their polity. Unlike the other facts Jefferson submitted to a candid world in 1776 to justify American independence, in private and in public, the language of the Declaration's final grievance endured. Madison had all but plagiarized it in his 1812 war message. Toward the end of "Mr. Madison's War," newspaper publishers related another military defeat, the fall of Fort Niagara, by evoking

18. Donald R. Hickey, *The War of 1812: A Forgotten Conflict* (Urbana, Ill., 1989), 85–86; Alan Taylor, *The Civil War of 1812: American Citizens, British Subjects, Irish Rebels, and Indian Allies* (New York, 2010), 210–214, esp. 213; J. C. A. Stagg, *The War of 1812: Conflict for a Continent* (Cambridge, 2012), 68–69. Franklin hoax: *Columbian Register* (New Haven), Mar. 23, 1813; *Richmond Enquirer*, Mar. 26, 1813; *City Gazette* (Charleston, S.C.), Mar. 27, 1813; *Investigator* (Charleston, S.C.), Mar. 29, 1813; *Carolina Gazette* (Charleston, S.C.), Apr. 3, 1813; *National Advocate* (Washington, D.C.), Apr. 9, 1813; *Columbian* (New York), Apr. 16, 1813; *Bee* (Hudson, N.Y.), Apr. 20, 1813; *New-Hampshire Patriot* (Concord), Apr. 27, 1813; *Ontario Messenger* (Canandaigua, N.Y.), Apr. 27, 1813; *Long-Island Star* (Brooklyn), Apr. 28, 1813; *Washingtonian* (Windsor, Vt.), May 3, 1813; *Lexington Reporter* (Ky.), May 8, 1813; *Baltimore Patriot*, Aug. 28, 1813; *Daily National Intelligencer* (Washington, D.C.), Sept. 10, 1813; *Federal Republican* (Washington, D.C.), Sept. 17, 1813; *Universal Gazette* (Washington, D.C.), Sept. 17, 1813. "The Savage Allies of England": *Independent Chronicle*, August 17, 1812; *Essex Register* (Salem, Mass.), Aug. 19, 1812; *National Aegis* (Worcester, Mass.), Sept. 2, 1812. A follow-up to this exposé, entitled "Savage Allies—Confirmed," appeared a few weeks later. See *Independent Chronicle*, Sept. 28, 1812; *Native American* (Norwich, Conn.), Oct. 7, 1812; *Sun* (Pittsfield, Mass.), Oct. 8, 1812.

Figure 20. *"A Scene on the Frontiers as Practiced by the Humane British and Their Worthy Allies." By William Charles. 1812. The connection between the British and Indians was a constant theme of the early American republic for decades after the Revolution. Courtesy of the Library of Congress.*

the "hideous yells of the merciless savages"; a few months later, Andrew Jackson received a letter from Governor William Claiborne expressing concerns that "Louisiana has at this moment much to apprehend from Domestic Insurrection" because "the Enemy has been intriguing with *our slaves.*" By 1814, the resonance—and political power—behind these phrases was nearly forty years old; they were cornerstones of the American founding itself.[19]

The common cause remained a litmus test for how Americans should react in the face of British tyranny. By the War of 1812, it had taken on a partisan bent, but, at bottom, it remained another version of what one scholar termed—in a slightly different context—an "unthinking decision": for de-

19. *Cabinet* (Schenectady, N.Y.), Jan. 5, 1814; *Salem Gazette* (Mass.), Jan. 11, 1814; *Long-Island Star* (Brooklyn, N.Y.), Jan. 12, 1814; *Reporter* (Brattleboro, Vt.), Jan. 15, 1814; William Charles Cole Claiborne to Andrew Jackson, New Orleans, Sept. 20, 1814, in Smith et al., eds., *Papers of Andrew Jackson,* III, 143.

cades, political and publicity leaders crafted and broadcast a narrative construction that assumed that certain groups were incapable of perceiving the difference between "liberty" and "tyranny." Although men of European ancestry, whether loyalist or Hessian (or Federalist), could be redeemed, with little nuance or careful consideration, American political leaders and publicists represented all Indians and African Americans as unfeeling, irrational, foolish proxies—passive, malleable assassins whose autonomic services were readily available to the evil whispers, empty promises, and venal gifts extended by even more corrupt agents of King George. This defined what constituted the opposite of a citizen of the American republic from 1776 to 1815 and beyond.[20]

"Amicus Patria," a contributor to a Pennsylvania newspaper, captured the persistence of the appeal. As smoke still hung in the air over Washington, D.C., after the British invaded and burned the city in August 1814, he queried his readers, "Were you to submit to Britain, would not the ashes of those heroes who fell in the revolution be troubled"? Channeling Thomas Paine and the Second Continental Congress, the writer pleaded with words that fit as precisely in 1814 as they had when first formulated at the beginning of the Revolutionary War:

> Can the formidable appearance of Britain intimidate Americans? Or can the savage yell, or the secret whispering of slaves cause them to tremble? . . . Your resources are great; . . . That your cause is just, needs not an argument, for it is so plain, that it is not possible that a free man, in America, with common rationality, can be so blinded as not to see; nor so case hardened as not to sympathise with his fellow citizens, who are toiling in British bottoms, while their families are left to struggle with the ills of fortune, without a guide.

This was the crux of the common cause, still intact and powerful four decades after its original creation. With such a panoply of enemies against them, no rational or sympathetic free citizen could choose the wrong side; it was self-evident. Whoever did was not worthy of the responsibilities of citizenship. Amicus Patria then detailed further scenes to "rouse" readers "to action," including British plundering—with the substantial assistance of African Americans—of the town of Hampton, Virginia (again), and, of course, a generic impression of "savage allies who imbrue their hands

20. Winthrop D. Jordan, *White over Black: American Attitudes toward the Negro, 1550–1812* (Chapel Hill, N.C., 1968), 44–98.

in the blood of smiling infants." "These are the atrocious acts of Britain, and justly merit your hottest displeasure," he concluded, offering one final plea for the present generation to seize the legacy left them by the heroic Revolutionaries:

> Rouse then to energetic measures . . . join heart and hand, as a band of brothers; grasp your swords, and buckle on your helmets, rally round the standard of liberty, always bearing in mind that a glorious death should be sought in preference to an ignominious life, and remember your Fathers, and your affectionate chief, GEORGE WASHINGTON.

These qualities represented a set of values that, in the absence of a clear definition of the boundaries of American citizenship, were what people who belonged to the republic should adhere to.[21]

Some of the people who challenged this representation found themselves on precarious ground in those years. But not all of them. Loyalists of European descent—whether supporters of the king in the 1770s or opponents of "Mr. Madison's War" in the 1810s—did not have to endure persistent trouble getting their property claims or personal rights defended in the early republic. In part, this was because American efforts to castigate and smear them as traitors failed; the marks were not indelible. During the Revolution, the stories told, or not told, about loyalists and former German mercenaries mitigated these effects. Although patriots tried to conflate loyalists with other proxy enemies, the tories proved too slippery. The loyalist problem was too vast, too prevalent, and too local for newspapers to make a lasting impression. Thus, their assimilation into the American republic, complete with the extension of full citizenship rights, followed after the peace in 1783 with surprising speed. Amicus Patria offers one answer why. He, like those who formulated the appeal before him, presented a choice: the pleas to his audience to remember past wrongs, recall past heroism, and select a right behavior implies that such a transformation was possible. Further, it implies not only action, the essential ingredient in a virtuous republican citizen, but reaction: the ability to reconsider and alter one's behavior. People might fail an initial test but still have the capacity for redemption.[22]

In the inside pages of newspapers, starting with Lexington and Concord,

21. *True American* (Bedford, Pa.), Sept. 7, 1814. For an account of the attack on Hampton with black assistance, see *Richmond Enquirer*, July 16, 1813.

22. Judith L. Van Buskirk, *Generous Enemies: Patriots and Loyalists in Revolutionary New York* (Philadelphia, 2002).

American political and publicity leaders never extended the same choice to Indians and African Americans. With very little exception, patriots depicted them as mindless followers susceptible to base offers and bloodthirsty revenge. Unlike other groups—and with plenty of evidence to the contrary—the patriots' war stories closed off any possibilities for natives and African Americans to escape this stigma. They were founding traitors: simply, merciless savages and domestic insurrectionists. Eighteenth-century colonists had long suspected these groups of being incapable of handling their particular conceptions of liberty, and, when the test came, they failed. There would be little chance for reconsideration.

Even the thousands of African Americans and Indians whose support of the United States should have provided them protection against such slurs struggled to translate that fidelity into security, whether in property or personal rights. The most reliable friends of the United States, the Oneida, Stockbridge, and Tuscarora Indians, suffered tremendous losses of their homelands almost as soon as the Revolution ended. Although these three groups would be partially compensated for being Americans' "faithful friends," their dispossession continued with little hesitation. One Oneida leader, known to the Americans as Good Peter, lamented in 1792 that, at war's end, he "did not then expect" that his nation's loyalty to the so-called common cause would result in their being "reduced to our present situation." Highlighting one of the central elements of the rights of citizenship that were denied to even the loyal Oneidas, Good Peter remarked, "If we understand what is meant by a person's being free and independent," then their inability to dispose of their property as they chose meant "we are not really freemen." Down in North Carolina, for decades the Catawba also did their best to remind the South Carolina government of their devotion during the Revolution.[23]

23. "Treaty with the Oneida, etc., 1794," Dec. 2, 1794, in Charles J. Kappler, comp. and ed., *Indian Affairs: Laws and Treaties* (Washington, D.C., 1904), II, 37–39; Karim M. Tiro, *The People of the Standing Stone: The Oneida Nation from the Revolution through the Era of Removal* (Amherst, Mass., 2011), 65–95; David J. Silverman, *Red Brethren: The Brothertown and Stockbridge Indians and the Problem of Race in Early America* (Ithaca, N.Y., 2010), 125–148. Good Peter interview with Timothy Pickering, April 1792, in Timothy Pickering Papers, microfilm, reel LX, 121–122, Massachusetts Historical Society, Boston. See also Alan Taylor, *The Divided Ground: Indians, Settlers, and the Northern Borderland of the American Revolution* (New York, 2006), 406–407; James H. Merrell, *The Indians' New World: Catawbas and Their Neighbors from European Contact through the Era of Removal* (Chapel Hill, N.C., 1989), 218–225.

That the United States "conveniently forgot the contributions and sacrifices" of these Indians in subsequent decades is accurate but misses a larger point: patriot leaders offered a construction of the United States that was in opposition to Indians, without distinction between hostile or allied groups, at the founding itself. This image was crafted in 1775, and Indians began feeling its effects immediately, not only in the grasping, unethical years that swirled around a disappointed Good Peter in the 1790s.[24]

Yet, in 1813, when the American union was again at its breaking point, the United States once more called on the Oneidas for help. They responded to President Madison with reminder of their previous sacrifices: "We fought. We bled. We conquered by the side of our American Brethren, and our bones with thiers [*sic*] whiten the fields where British tyranny yielded to the prowess of the American Arms. We are the same people still." Themselves forgetting, the Oneidas fought against their fellow Iroquois again, as they did at Oriskany in 1777. And, when the war ended, with the remaining scraps of Oneida land directly in the center of where surveyors plotted the Erie Canal, their services were all for naught, as New Yorkers soon negotiated with the remaining Oneidas and Stockbridge for their removal to Wisconsin. The repeated decision to join forces with the United States did not secure Oneida claims, despite their many attempts to remind American leaders of their fidelity. Other Indian groups, such as Black Hoof and his Shawnee followers who broke with Tecumseh in the 1810s, also found themselves up against an enemy they could not defeat: a narrative construction that conflated them all as merciless savages in league with their dreaded enemy. This representation denied even the men who marched alongside American soldiers in 1776 and 1813 all the multivalent notions of citizenship in the new republic, as Good Peter and many others understood them.[25]

Free and enslaved African Americans also suffered from the persistent effects of the common cause appeal. It hardly needs stating that the Revolution fundamentally changed slavery in North America. Previous generations

24. Silverman, *Red Brethren*, 120–121, esp. 120.

25. Chiefs of the Oneida Nation to James Madison, "Oneida," Sept. 11, 1813, in Rutland et al., eds., *Papers of James Madison: Presidential Series*, VI, 615; Carl Benn, *The Iroquois in the War of 1812* (Toronto, 1998); Silverman, *Red Brethren*, 164–183; Tiro, *People of the Standing Stone*, 125–126, 129–150; R. David Edmunds, "'A Watchful Safeguard to Our Habitations': Black Hoof and the Loyal Shawnees," in Frederick E. Hoxie, Ronald Hoffman, and Peter J. Albert, eds., *Native Americans and the Early Republic* (Charlottesville, Va., 1999), 162–199.

of historians have suggested the alteration came from the "first emancipation"—the wave of antislavery sparked by the language of universal human
rights embedded in the patriots' explanations of their protest—which culminated in gradual abolition in most northern states. Scholars have revised
this image, not only putting more stress on the gradualness of those efforts
in the North and mid-Atlantic states but also to highlight how the patriots'
commitment to property as a competing Revolutionary value further entrenched slavery in the Deep South even before cotton. At the same time,
as one classic account put it, the Revolution virtually created the status of
"free black" in the South. But this, too, did not translate into the extension of citizenship rights, which meant much more than just the franchise.
The notion that manumitted African Americans could not become part of
the body politic or remain inside the republic accompanied many emancipation schemes long before colonization rose to prominence in the early
nineteenth century. Free blacks were "in a legal status between slave and
unfettered citizen, and were thus excluded from cultural inclusion" in the
conception of the American citizenry. The way the patriots connected African Americans to their enemies helped foster this liminal space, whereby
free African Americans enjoyed some rights on a local or state level—and
even then, those were conditional and revocable—but never something that
transcended provincial boundaries after the Revolution. That representation mitigated the possibilities of inclusion.[26]

26. See, for example, Arthur Zilversmit, *The First Emancipation: The Abolition of
Slavery in the North* (Chicago, 1967). This interpretation may be experiencing a re-
vival, for which see Paul Polgar, "Standard Bearers of Liberty and Equality: Reinter-
preting the Origins of American Abolitionism" (Ph.D. diss., City University of New
York, 2013). James Oakes has pointed out the competition inherent in the dual
Revolutionary ideals of protecting property and extending natural rights in John
Craig Hammond and Matthew Mason, eds., *Contesting Slavery: The Politics of Bondage
and Freedom in the New American Nation* (Charlottesville, Va., 2011), 291–303. See Ira
Berlin, *Slaves without Masters: The Free Negro in the Antebellum South* (New York, 1974),
15. "In a legal status between": see Douglas Bradburn, *The Citizenship Revolution: Politics and the Creation of the American Union, 1774–1804* (Charlottesville, Va., 2009), 235–
271, esp. 238. For some of the recent studies that emphasize the gradualness of
antislavery efforts in the early republic, see Joanne Pope Melish, *Disowning Slavery:
Gradual Emancipation and "Race" in New England, 1780–1860* (Ithaca, N.Y., 1998);
David N. Gellman, *Emancipating New York: The Politics of Slavery and Freedom, 1777–
1827* (Baton Rouge, La., 2006); and John Wood Sweet, *Bodies Politic: Negotiating Race*

Conclusion

The tragedy was that tens of thousands of African Americans and Indians had seen the Revolutionary War as an opportunity. They risked their lives, were separated from their families, suffered, and died in efforts to improve their situations—but they lost. They did not take the "right" action. For many of them, April was indeed the cruelest month: the war that began on Lexington Green initiated an evolution, a deepening of exclusion in America. While white men celebrated their success in determining their own futures, in securing liberty for their posterity, in establishing a political system based on popular sovereignty, and in defending their inalienable rights to the pursuit of happiness, blacks and Indians were seen as alien, unfit to fully belong as members of the new republic. This was a revolutionary change.

The decades after 1815 witnessed a deepening commitment to excluding all but free whites from membership in the American body politic. The way this story has been told depicts the end of the War of 1812 as the turning of a new page in American history. With Britain prevented from interference in American affairs, expansion, with race at its core, became the central theme. New states added to the union in the late 1810s made whiteness an explicit requirement for citizenship. Organizations proposing schemes to send (or banish) free African Americans to colonies outside the United States gained popularity. A commitment to remove all remaining Indians across the Mississippi River also won an increasing number of supporters in some of those new state houses and in Washington. A deepening notion of innate, biological racial inferiority, backed by the Bible and mainstream

---

in the American North, 1730–1830 (Baltimore, 2003). Even the most egalitarian thinkers and writers of the age acknowledged that prejudice threatened their ideas of racial harmony. See Melvin Patrick Ely's discussion of St. George Tucker and Richard Randolph in "Richard and Judith Randolph, St. George Tucker, George Wythe, Syphax Brown, and Hercules White: Racial Equality and the Snares of Prejudice," in Alfred F. Young, Gary B. Nash, and Ray Raphael, eds., *Revolutionary Founders: Rebels, Radicals, and Reformers in the Making of the Nation* (New York, 2011), 323–336; Phillip Hamilton, "Revolutionary Principles and Family Loyalties: Slavery's Transformation in the St. George Tucker Household of Early National Virginia," *WMQ*, 3d Ser., LV (1998), 531–576. For Jefferson's thoughts on the place of emancipated slaves in the republic, see Peter S. Onuf, *Jefferson's Empire: The Language of American Nationhood* (Charlottesville, Va., 2000), 147–188; Richard Newman, "'Good Communications Corrects Bad Manners': The Banneker-Jefferson Dialogue and the Project of White Uplift," in Hammond and Mason, eds., *Contesting Slavery*, 69–93.

science, justified these exclusions. By the 1830s, the now-much-extended republic was strictly a nation for whites.[27]

This is most often narrated as a declension story, a hardening of racial attitudes marked by the emergence of new racial hierarchies espoused not just by Americans but by Europeans across the globe in the nineteenth century—in a word, the disintegration of the promise of universalism that marked the Age of Revolution. But those ideals also did the opposite, deepening an intellectual commitment to finding new hierarchies of difference. The Enlightenment had transformed from a celebration of universal human reason into a particularist worship of the capacity of some individuals as the only truly autonomous selves. The social equality espoused by revolutions in America, France, and Haiti also produced a backlash, giving rise to new ideologies of difference, neutralizing this wave. Intellectual arguments of innate differences of race and gender grew in the early nineteenth century, giving seemingly scientific proof that only white men were capable of being entrusted with full citizenship rights. The chance for real equality was lost, the promise of the American Revolution spurned.[28]

But this was not an opportunity lost or corner turned, for it was never there in the first place. Eighteen-fifteen did not mark the beginning of a

27. Roxann Wheeler, *The Complexion of Race: Categories of Difference in Eighteenth-Century British Culture* (Philadelphia, 2000); Bruce Dain, *A Hideous Monster of the Mind: American Race Theory in the Early Republic* (Cambridge, Mass., 2002); Stephen R. Haynes, *Noah's Curse: The Biblical Justification for American Slavery* (New York, 2002). For more on how white, propertied men in the early republic developed an American identity apart from using the British or memories of the Revolutionary War as negative referents, but just as marked by racial exclusivity, see Carroll Smith-Rosenberg, *This Violent Empire: The Birth of an American National Identity* (Chapel Hill, N.C., 2010).

28. Barbara Jeanne Fields, "Slavery, Race and Ideology in the United States of America," *New Left Review*, 1st Ser., no. 181 (May–June 1990), 95–118; Alexander Saxton, *The Rise and Fall of the White Republic: Class Politics and Mass Culture in Nineteenth-Century America* (London, 1990); David Roediger, *The Wages of Whiteness: Race and the Making of the American Working Class* (New York, 1991); Eric Lott, *Love and Theft: Blackface Minstrelsy and the American Working Class* (New York, 1993); Theodore W. Allen, *The Invention of the White Race*, 2 vols. (London, 1997); Noel Ignatiev, *How the Irish Became White* (New York, 1995); Melish, *Disowning Slavery;* Michael A. Morrison and James Brewer Stewart, eds., *Race and the Early Republic: Racial Consciousness and Nation-Building in the Early Republic* (Lanham, Md., 2002); Lynn Hunt, *Inventing Human Rights: A History* (New York, 2008).

Conclusion

new age. After all, as Robert Ambrister and Alexander Arbuthnot found out in 1818, Andrew Jackson and others still suspected the British of inciting Indians and African Americans to take up arms against the United States. Just after Jackson invaded Florida and captured the "Negro Fort," a stockade near the Gulf manned by runaway slaves and hostile Indians armed by the crown, he arrested the men he deemed responsible. Ambrister and Arbuthnot were two British civilians that Jackson believed were "authorised Agents of Great Britain" who had attempted "to excite the Negroes and Indians in East Florida to war against the U States." He tried and hanged "these Two unprincipled villains" to "convince the Government of Great Britain as well as her subjects that certain, if slow retribution awaits those uncristian wretches who by false promises delude and excite a Indian tribe to all the horrid deeds of savage war." For Jackson, the final charge of the Declaration of Independence *still* resonated. The Revolution was far from over; Ambrister and Arbuthnot were merely paying for the crimes originally charged against John Stuart and Alexander Cameron nearly a half century before. Nor was the specter of British interference diminished after 1815, for British interest in—and American fears of British interest in—central North America were uppermost on policymakers' minds until 1870.[29]

The real problem with the interpretation that posits the years after 1790 as a gradual squandering of the ideas of the Revolution is that it assumes natural rights encapsulated those ideas. Although historians have complicated this heroic narrative of the American Revolution, no one as yet has grasped the totality of the consequences of unity in 1775. Patriot leaders had a momentous task of narration in the days after Lexington. Not only did they have to convince a majority of colonists that their cultural cousins were

29. Andrew Jackson to John Caldwell Calhoun, Fort Gadsden, May 5, 1818, in Smith et al., eds., *Papers of Andrew Jackson*, IV, 197–200, esp. 199. See also Smith, *Slaves' Gamble*, 178–183. For more on Jackson's court-martial and execution of Ambrister and Arbuthnot, see J. Leitch Wright, Jr., *Creeks and Seminoles: The Destruction and Regeneration of the Muscogulge People* (Lincoln, Neb., 1986), 205–212; Robert V. Remini, *Andrew Jackson and His Indian Wars* (New York, 2001), 143–163; Andrew Burstein, *The Passions of Andrew Jackson* (New York, 2003), 134–135; and Eliga Gould, *Among the Powers of the Earth: The American Revolution and the Making of a New World Empire* (Cambridge, Mass., 2012), 179–190. For continued Anglophobia, see Sam W. Haynes, *Unfinished Revolution: The Early American Republic in a British World* (Charlottesville, Va., 2010); Jeremy Black, *Fighting for America: The Struggle for Mastery in North America, 1519–1871* (Bloomington, Ind., 2011); Kariann Akemi Yokota, *Unbecoming British: How Revolutionary America Became a Postcolonial Nation* (New York, 2011).

now their mortal enemies; they had to make such an appeal using arguments that all could agree on. Jealousies, rivalries, and even violent controversies alienated the colonies in the early 1770s. Border conflicts, religious disputes, and concerns about slavery drove them apart. The colonies were just as poised to attack one another as to join together on the eve of war. The near impossibility of getting the colonies to agree to oppose Great Britain with one voice meant compromises on the most divisive issues on the one hand, and creative storytelling on the other. The representation that they constructed, almost immediately as the war began in 1775, was a Janus-faced creation. It was a call to arms for all rational, virtuous, right-thinking, moral colonists to recognize tyranny and fight for freedom, for themselves and for their posterity. At the same time, however, in order to highlight the depravity of their enemies, they dredged up colonists' deepest fears about what slaves, savages, and mercenaries, "instigated," "tampered with," or "excited" by evil agents of the king, might do to their loved ones.

The common cause appeal evolved from the first months of the conflict as those agents, from Indian superintendents to royal governors to military officers, explored the possibilities of gaining Indian and slave assistance to put down the rebellion as quickly and as inexpensively as possible. That thousands of Indians and African Americans did respond to their calls gave all the more credence to the accusation that British representatives were scheming with them. For slaves, the possibility of freedom raised by hailing a Royal Navy ship, responding to a governor's emancipation proclamation, or falling in behind a British army unit marching nearby turned the Revolutionary War into the largest insurrection up to the Civil War. For Indians, the chance to trade military assistance for the protection of land or hunting rights or commercial opportunities convinced most to respond to the king's call to take up the hatchet. Although the Revolutionary War would become a civil war in Iroquoia in 1777, most Indians believed the British offered the greatest chance to improve their postwar situations.

For patriot political and publicity leaders, these actions, taken by dozens of British agents and thousands of Indians and African Americans, also provided a golden opportunity. The patriots worked assiduously to make this the foundation of why colonists should support resistance and, eventually, independence. The common cause appeal was, then, the merging of both these interpretations: it simultaneously valorized white citizen soldiers for defending freedom and castigated those who opposed it. This added to, deepened, and gave a new republican valence to long-standing colonial prejudices about the incapacity of Indians and African Americans to grasp

Conclusion

these concepts of liberty. Through hundreds of stories told and retold, published and republished, in weekly patriot newspapers, the first construction of what it meant to be an American meant the diametric opposite of merciless savages or domestic insurrectionists.

The opening paragraphs of the Declaration did not encapsulate the ideals of the Revolution. True, they were touchstones for some, but the final grievance also reverberated throughout the first decades of the early republic. It defined the boundaries of the Revolution and gave some grounding to very inchoate categories, especially the uncharted territory of citizenship. Although some Americans might not have been comfortable with the notion, the common cause narrative reinforced the conflation of "white" and "citizen." The architects of that narrative, especially Jefferson, Adams, and Franklin, might have had mixed feelings about such a conflation, but they did much of the crucial labor to establish it. They did so not because of racism but because of political expediency. The cement of union was catastrophically thin; one of its only effective coagulants was a set of powerful stories about scapegoats. Though thousands of Indians and African Americans did support the patriot side, they were never part of the common cause appeal. Because that narrative lived at the heart of the republic it helped create for decades to come, it continued to prevent their inclusion as Americans. The refusal to extend to African Americans and Indians the benefits of emerging concepts of liberal subjectivity in the form of citizenship had ghastly consequences, for it legitimated and excused the destruction of vast numbers of human beings.

* * *

Fifty years on, the Revolutionary War was becoming a fleeting memory. On the fiftieth anniversary of the battle, the residents of Concord, Massachusetts, asked the newly elected Congressman from Dorchester, Edward Everett, to give an opening address for their fundraising campaign to build a monument. Everett recounted the heroism of Paul Revere and rhapsodized about the alarm bells, the beating drums, and the citizens rushing to their muskets. The nineteenth of April was "one of those great days, one of those elemental occasions in the world's affairs, when the people rise, and act for themselves." "It was the people, in their first capacity, as citizens and as freemen, starting from their beds at midnight, from their firesides, and from their fields, to take their own cause into their own hands," the thirty-one-year-old Congressman cheered. "Such a spectacle is the height of the moral sublime; when the want of every thing is fully made up by the spirit of the cause." Their opponents were a "mercenary army," full of desperate, depraved men, a "fearful, ravenous, irrational monster of prey," but the Americans were made up of "the yeomanry of the country [who] rose as a man, and set their lives on this dear stake of liberty." "Bravely they dared; patiently, aye more than patiently,—heroically, piously, they suffered; largely, richly, may they enjoy." Eleven years later, when the granite monument was completed, it was Ralph Waldo Emerson's turn to interpret the opening battle of the American Revolution. Emerson reprised Everett's hagiography but turned it into a national hymn that famously solemnized the "embattled farmers," for they embraced a "Spirit, that made those heroes dare" who thusly left their "children free."[30]

As we have seen, the night of Paul Revere's ride was more complicated than an organic upwelling of patriotic fervor or a defense of a hopeful future carried by the promises of "April's breeze." Even in Middlesex County, Massachusetts, as those minutemen reported to Lexington Green and the Concord Bridge, there were men of Indian and African ancestry shouldering muskets. Families back home in Natick and Framingham worried that this "Disturbance" might not mean the "shot heard round the world"—an intrepid war of freedom and liberation—but, instead, signaled a slave uprising, a terrifying and wholly unwelcome fight for liberty. That meaning, mostly lost to us, was how many other colonists far from Massachusetts interpreted the news of the Concord fight as well.

Yet, by the time Everett and Emerson commemorated those who stood there defending their liberty, all those nonwhite faces had evaporated, vanished in a mythology of American patriotism that coded heroic freedom fighters as unquestionably white men. Just a few months after Emerson's valorization of the "embattled farmers," a New York City newspaper reported the arrest of an "old colored man" by the city watchman for being in the "uniform of a revolutionary soldier." The watchman assumed the man was "an old fool, madman, or mountebank," but, to everyone's surprise, he recounted his actions in the Revolutionary War. He really had been a member of the Continental army. By the 1830s, many other African American veterans of the Revolution had to overcome significant obstacles in proving their

30. Purcell, *Sealed with Blood*, 204; Edward Everett, *An Oration Delivered at Concord, April the Nineteenth, 1825* (Boston, 1825), esp. 42–43, 47, 52; Emerson, "Hymn," Apr. 19, 1836, in Hollander, ed., *American Poetry*, I, 318–319. For more on how the memory of the Revolution changed in the 1830s, see Young, *Shoemaker and the Tea Party*, 143–179.

Figure 21. *Concord Monument and Old North Bridge. C. 1900.*
Courtesy of the Library of Congress.

service to be awarded a pension. In 1855, William Cooper Nell, a son of one of those African American veterans, published *Colored Patriots of the American Revolution,* restoring those tales of blacks who aided the common cause. The mere title of the book came as a shock; as far as American mythology went, patriots could not possibly be colored.[31]

Perhaps this effacement was what the artist Johannes Oertel noticed in his 1852 rendering of New Yorkers pulling down the king's statue on the

31. Emerson, "Hymn," Apr. 19, 1836, in Hollander, ed., *American Poetry,* I, 318–319, esp. 318; *Atkinson's Saturday Evening Post,* Oct. 8, 1836, 2; Keith Tony Beutler, "The Memory Revolution in America and Memory of the American Revolution, 1790–1840" (Ph.D. diss., Washington University in St. Louis, 2005), 72–73; Judith L. Van Buskirk, "Claiming Their Due: African Americans in the Revolutionary War and Its Aftermath," in John Resch and Walter Sargent, eds., *War and Society in the American Revolution: Mobilization and Home Fronts* (Dekalb, Ill., 2007), 132–160; W[illia]m C[ooper] Nell, *Colored Patriots of the American Revolution; with Sketches of Several Distinguished Colored Persons . . .* (Boston, 1855).

Figure 22. *"Pulling Down the Statue of King George III." By Johannes Adam Oertel. 1852. Courtesy of New-York Historical Society.*

Bowling Green upon first hearing independence declared. Oertel had recently come to the United States from Bavaria in 1848. His envisioning of the event on Bowling Green featured the proxies—as outsiders. An Indian in stereotypical headdress stands with a native woman and her infant off to the extreme left, looking back at the toppling monarch but clearly exiting the scene, and, in front of the statue, a young African American is being pinned to the ground by two freshly minted American boys. Whether or not Oertel was criticizing this depiction of a republic for whites only, it was a penetrating analysis nonetheless. The German painter captured an almost photographic likeness of the Declaration's real consequences.[32]

32. Little is ascertainable about Oertel's politics in the early 1850s. For a study that is admittedly rife with speculation, especially concerning whether his emigration had any relation to the 1848 revolution in Germany, see Arthur S. Marks, "The

The difficulty African Americans and Indians faced in establishing that they, too, had fought at the founding was not only a function of Edward Everett and Ralph Waldo Emerson, or of the consequences of the French and Haitian Revolutions, or of post-Enlightenment discourses on scientific racism, or of the exclusionary ideologies of racial consensus that under-pinned the "equality" of Jacksonian democracy. Free African Americans and Indians had to fight against the common cause to prove they were pa-triots—not trespassers as in Oertel's scene. For decades after the war's end, they still had to insist that they had actually been there. Even those who had been sympathetic to ending slavery in America, like St. George Tucker, by the nineteenth century argued Virginians had no reason to "give freedom to those very people whom we have been compelled from imperious circum-stances to retain, generally, in the same state of bondage that they were in at the revolution, in which they had no concern, agency, or interest." But the construction that they did not deserve the rights of American citizens was not a postwar product. It stemmed from actions taken at the founding itself. It grew from decisions men like Jefferson, Adams, Franklin, and Washington made to solidify the almost fatal fragility of the common cause. Those men, at the creation, developed a myth about who was and was not a part of the Revolutionary movement; about who had an interest and who did not. They told stories that Everett and Emerson were just the latest to retell. The Con-cord eulogists were elaborating a myth that was created before they were born. The stories that brought the king's statue down brought it down upon African Americans, like the boy at the pedestal's base, and the shockwaves pushed the natives clear out of the frame of the founding.[33]

It was the inner pages of those now-moldy columns, which Nathaniel Hawthorne's narrator marveled at in his short story "Old News" (written at the same time as Emerson's Concord Hymn), that established this founding paradigm. In those columns, patriot publicists crafted a particular argu-ment for who was a part of the common cause. They, too, sculpted a kind of granite base. When their ideas found new contexts because of subsequent

---

Statue of King George III in New York and the Iconology of Regicide," *American Art Journal*, XIII, no. 3 (Summer 1981), 78–82.

33. St. George Tucker ruling in *Wright v. Hudgins* (1806), in William Waller Hening and William Munford, *Reports of Cases argued and Determined in the Supreme Court of Appeals of Virginia*, 4 vols. (Philadelphia, 1808), I, 141. See also Eva Sheppard Wolf, *Race and Liberty in the New Nation: Emancipation in Virginia from the Revolution to Nat Turner's Rebellion* (Baton Rouge, La., 2006), 149; Taylor, *Internal Enemy*, 108.

revolutions in France and Haiti, or when intellectuals developed ideas about scientific racism, Americans fastened those concepts to an already sturdy floor.

The details, therefore, matter. The development of the double-faced common cause appeal, and its staying power long after Yorktown, is another example of what one scholar termed the "deep contingency" of history. "Deep contingency" is the interplay of large structural forces—including social conditions, ideological hierarchies, economic factors, political systems, and cultural norms—with epiphenomenal surface events, such as personality traits, accident, or coincidence. It is a way to approach the past that takes both climate and weather into consideration.[34]

Our understanding of why war between Britain and the American colonies began on April 19, 1775, was just such a phenomenon. The preceding sentence does not have to read that way; it very easily might read, "Our understanding of why a rebellion began in Massachusetts in the spring of 1775 that elements of the British Army quelled, and that led to the arrests and executions of a few men and pardons for the rest, was just such a phenomenon." There were deep forces and surface contingencies at work that explain why the beginning of the American Revolution did not resemble other provincial colonial uprisings.

Nothing about the Revolution was inevitable. It was not inevitable that it occurred at all, let alone that the rebellion would then proceed on the basis of self-evident claims that all men were created equal. Moreover, it was far from probable that the mainland colonies would become one independent polity that eschewed monarchy and would instead embrace a republic based on universal rights of citizens.

That it became a truly continental effort, with the participation of all the mainland colonies, is marvelous. Such an enterprise depended on innumerable decisions made by millions of people throughout North America. Edward Everett believed that the people's rising on April 19 was an "elemental occasion," a chemical reaction that freely occurred in nature. Perhaps. But, even if Everett was right, the actions taken by thousands of people outside Middlesex County, Massachusetts, were even more critical to Everett's interpretation and his own occasion of dedicating a monument to remember those who had fallen fifty years before.

34. Edward L. Ayers, "What Caused the Civil War?" in Ayers, *What Caused the Civil War? Reflections on the South and Southern History* (New York, 2005), 131–144, esp. 134–135.

Those thousands of people included colonial political and military leaders who believed their interests would best be served by taking an active role in the revolt against Britain. They included the tens of thousands of "disaffected" colonists who, for countless reasons, were not convinced that the patriots were right and made decisions to stay out of the conflict or to manage their participation in it. They included British officials and agents on both sides of the Atlantic who crafted plans and made policy decisions to crush the rebellion or limit its scope. They included the tens of thousands of British soldiers who traveled across the ocean to enact those policies. They included the tens of thousands of loyalists who agreed with the crown and participated in some fashion over the course of the long war. They included the tens of thousands of colonists who were convinced neither side was right and stayed neutral. They included the tens of thousands of soldiers from various German states who became mercenaries to participate in a foreign war for private gain. They included the tens of thousands of enslaved African Americans who saw the conflict as a way to improve their situations, either by running toward British authorities or by trying to renegotiate their lives among familiar surroundings. They included the tens of thousands of Indians across the backcountry who also saw the conflict as a way to alter their relationships with the various power brokers in North America, by fighting for the king, aiding the patriots, or trying to remain quiet altogether.

All these people reacted as they did because of deep currents: the history of slavery in colonial America; nearly two centuries' experience of disease, dispossession, and conflict between Indians and colonists; the political language of liberty, consent, and representation inherited from the English past; social mobility in America; gender conventions of masculinity; the constitutional structures of the British Empire; religious traditions and confessional hierarchies; geopolitical imperatives in the Western Hemisphere. Their reactions to the outbreak of war were also owing to surface tensions, such as family preferences, personal beliefs, economic opportunities, birth order, personal slights, ambition, age, and whim. All of these waves collided and drove forward events known as the Revolutionary War.

Yet all those decisions were not created equal. They needed narratives. Because the American Revolution was, at its core, a massive argument, the propagation of effective stories that cordoned off friends from enemies was an essential factor of the conflict. How successfully either side encoded contingent events as scripts that broadcast images of heroes or villains would offer the advantage in political mobilization. As Ambrose Serle lamented, the British ignored the patriots' recognition of this facet of war to their peril. What helped make the patriots' cause common, durable, and, ultimately successful, was the way it was packaged and delivered. Not only was the American Revolution far from inevitable—neither was there any assurance that the political community it produced would be reserved almost exclusively for whites.

That this became so during the Revolution and especially after was also the product of its own combination of deep and surface forces. The deep currents that shaped patriot narratives included the discourse of cultural stereotypes about Africans and Indians, tropes about civility and savagery, Enlightenment notions of individual freedom and slavish behavior, political expectations about participation and belonging to a community, a social commitment to literacy and texts, the economic prosperity that fostered an embrace of print culture, and cultural mores about sensibility, fellow feeling, and refinement. Surface phenomena were also critical to making the cause common; after all, there were other profound cultural references from the colonial past that did not resonate in the context of the Revolution, especially the hatred of the French and antipopery that most Americans' grandparents assumed was a staple of their Protestant, English identity. The stories they chose to tell—or not tell—mattered.

The contingent reactions of patriot leaders in army camps and in political meetings to shape what the public knew about the war, the everyday labor done by printers like John Holt, William Bradford, and Isaiah Thomas in selecting exchanges, the work of type compositors and apprentices to create the interior pages of weekly newspapers that bore those stories, the delivery brokers like Peter Withington who distributed them throughout the countryside, and riders like William Carheart who battled elements and bad roads to complete the cycle—these were the people who made the common cause. They selected, amplified, and broadcast certain images they thought were essential to shore up the fragility of union. Their everyday work put the names John Connolly, Jane McCrea, Henry "the Hair-Buyer" Hamilton, Colonel Tye, and Major Cudjo before a wide segment of the American people. They were essential in why a Long Island crowd reacted to the reading of the Declaration of Independence by blackening the king's face, stuffing his coat with feathers, and setting him on fire. In important ways, patriot printers and their helpers were accessories to the hanging of Robert Ambrister and Alexander Arbuthnot forty years later.

They were the ones who defined what the Revolution meant for many Americans. We have overlooked so many of those decisions and so many of those names, but they were critical to the founding of the United States. We have cast them aside as unimportant—as perishable as the newspapers they delivered—but because of the narratives they helped to establish, they in turn created some of their own deep currents of race, nation, citizenship, and belonging in American history long after 1776.

Those forces converged to craft America's founding myth. When the war was won, the so-called founding fathers wanted the "candid world" to believe that only the first paragraphs of the Declaration—with the lofty sentiments of self-evident truths and universal rights—animated the colonists' fight for liberty. In a stupendous feat of prestidigitation, they projected an interpretation that the cause was indeed an "elemental" uprising of "embattled farmers," as Everett and Emerson proclaimed half a century later, standing reverently at the Concord Bridge.

But the common cause is not all they said it was. The founders wanted Americans to remember only a certain segment of the fight for independence: the heroic, the liberating, and the creative. In so doing, they distorted our understanding of the Revolution, for the cause also rested on representations they propagated over and over again, delineating merciless savages and domestic insurrectionists as America's enemies and thereby disqualifying them from pursuing happiness inside the new American republic. What Adams, Jefferson, Franklin, and Washington wanted Americans to forget was that the appeal was also a campaign stamped by the vicious, the confining, and the destructive.

This bifurcation still frames how modern Americans interpret the Revolution. For a long time, historians have divided over who and what drove the American Revolution: ideas or interests, elites in assembly houses or people outside those doors, top-down or bottom-up. The fault line of Revolution scholarship is deep and seems fixed. But that is because it really runs back to the 1770s. It is a result of the stories told at the moment of Revolution and long after. The inability to integrate the role African Americans and Indians played in the political history of the Revolution, the propensity for rendering the lives of Indians and the enslaved without weaving them into the national narrative—these are also consequences of the common cause itself. They are indivisible parts of the same founding story.

A Note on Newspapers during the Revolutionary War[1]

As of April 19, 1775, there were thirty-seven active newspapers in the colonies. When Cornwallis surrendered on October 19, 1781, there were thirty-five. Of those thirty-seven papers that printed the news of Lexington and Concord, only twenty made it through the war, and very few of those were able to continue publishing a paper each week. This number would ebb and flow. Seventeen prewar prints would expire during the fighting, whereas eighteen new ventures were started but did not survive the duration. The mean number for active newspapers between 1775 and 1783 is thirty-five.[2]

The average paper was fifteen years old, and its proprietor was an average age of 39.2 years when the war began. The top patriot printers were no younger than their leading loyalist opponents, though. The loudest voices on both sides (James Rivington, Benjamin Edes, Hugh Gaine, William Bradford, John Holt) were older than most of their colleagues.[3]

BOSTON

In April 1775, there were five newspapers publishing weekly in Boston. Two of them espoused the patriot cause, royal patronage subsidized two others, and one tried to remain open to both sides.

Every Monday since 1755, copies of Edes and Gill's *Boston Gazette, and*

---

1. I have analyzed the role of printers and the press in the Revolution generally in "Print, the Press, and the American Revolution," in Jon Butler and Christopher Grasso, eds., *Oxford Research Encyclopedia of American History* (Oxford, 2015), reproduced by permission of Oxford University Press, http://americanhistory.oxfordre .com.

2. This includes the *Boston Evening-Post,* which lasted less than a week after the battle. Clarence S. Brigham, *History and Bibliography of American Newspapers, 1690–1820,* 2 vols. (Worcester, Mass., 1947), is an invaluable source for pinpointing the confusing changes and upheaval of the press during the Revolutionary War. Much of the following information is drawn from Brigham. See also Edward Connery Lathem, ed., *Chronological Tables of American Newspapers, 1690–1850: Being a Tabular Guide to Holdings of Newspapers Published in America through the Year 1820* (Barre, Mass., 1972), 9–13.

3. The average age of the top four patriot publishers in 1775 (Edes, Thomas, Holt, Bradford) was 44.75 years. The average age of the top four loyalist publishers in 1775 (Rivington, Humphreys, Johnston, Gaine) was 43.75 years.

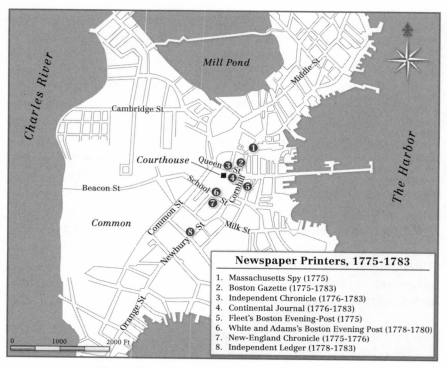

Map 4. *Newspaper print shops in Boston, 1775–1783*

Newspaper Printers, 1775-1783

1. Massachusetts Spy (1775)
2. Boston Gazette (1775-1783)
3. Independent Chronicle (1776-1783)
4. Continental Journal (1776-1783)
5. Fleet's Boston Evening-Post (1775)
6. White and Adams's Boston Evening Post (1778-1780)
7. New-England Chronicle (1775-1776)
8. Independent Ledger (1778-1783)

Country Journal flowed out of their shop on Queen Street. Their pages were often filled with sundry items "cooked up" by the Adamses, James Otis, Benjamin Church, and other leading patriot scribblers. Forty-three when the war started, Benjamin Edes was a member of the innermost circle of Boston radicals. His résumé was difficult to match: a member of the Loyal Nine, the Sons of Liberty, and the North End Caucus. Recent scholarship has him breaking open crates of East India tea on December 16, 1773, along with Nathaniel Willis, then still an apprentice but soon to be editor of the propatriot Boston paper *Independent Chronicle*. John Gill, too, was forty-three in 1775. Unlike his partner, however, while Edes was upstairs in the *Gazette* offices hosting political meetings, Gill preferred to stay downstairs by the press, working on next Monday's issue.[4]

Interested readers of the *Gazette* might have been familiar with the col-

4. Benjamin L. Carp, *Defiance of the Patriots: The Boston Tea Party and the Making of America* (New Haven, Conn., 2010), 133, 236, 239.

umns of the other staunch patriot organ in town, Isaiah Thomas's *Massachusetts Spy,* emanating every Saturday from his Dock Square shop just a few doors up the street from Edes and Gill's. At sixteen, Isaiah Thomas—following in Franklin's footsteps—had run away from his apprenticeship to printer Zechariah Fowle, fleeing Boston not south to Philadelphia but north to Nova Scotia, beginning a short itinerancy that took him to England, New Hampshire, and the Carolinas. In 1770, Thomas, now twenty-one, returned to Boston, started the *Spy,* and quickly developed the paper into a second megaphone for radicals in Boston. Within a year, Thomas had proved himself a worthy colleague to the elder *Gazette* printers. By the start of war, Edes and Gill's *Gazette* and Thomas's *Spy* were the two leading patriot papers in mainland North America.

Their opponents were not far away. A few streets removed from the patriot printing shops, Nathaniel Mills and John Hicks had taken over the *Massachusetts Gazette, and the Boston Post-Boy and Advertiser* (founded in 1757) from Green and Russell in 1773. As Isaiah Thomas would later remember, Mills and Hicks, "having received patronage and encouragement from the officers of the crown," operated the *Post-Boy* "with renewed spirit." Every Monday, Mills and Hicks's *Post-Boy* battled Edes and Gill's *Gazette* for public opinion in the city. This rivalry must have exacerbated the apparent political tension in the Hicks family, for the printer's father was an active patriot, allegedly aiding Edes and his colleagues in destroying the tea. One of the six men shot by retreating British troops in Cambridge late in the afternoon on April 19, 1775, was John Hicks, Sr. "Notwithstanding the sacrifice of his father on the altar of liberty," as Thomas later put it, the junior Hicks continued to publish for the king throughout the war, and later in New York.[5]

Mills and Hicks's *Post-Boy* was in league with the other pro-government paper in Boston, the *Massachusetts Gazette; and the Boston Weekly News-Letter.* In the care of the Draper family for four decades, this title was the oldest newspaper in the colonies, founded by Bartholomew Green in 1704. Richard Draper had established its tory credentials during his management that dated from 1762, becoming official printer to the governor and council over that period. Just before he died in 1774, Richard brought on a partner, John

5. Isaiah Thomas, *The History of Printing in America: With a Biography of Printers and an Account of Newspapers,* ed. Marcus A. McCorison, 2d ed. (1810; rpt. New York, 1970), 173–174, 263; David Hackett Fischer, *Paul Revere's Ride* (New York, 1994), 320; Arthur B. Tourtellot, *Lexington and Concord: The Beginning of the War of the American Revolution* (1959; rpt. New York, 1963), 198–199.

Boyle; together with Richard's widow, Margaret Draper, Boyle continued to turn out the *News-Letter* every Thursday until the British evacuated the city in March 1776.

The unfortunate Fleet brothers, Thomas and John, labored to maintain a middle ground. They tried to remain faithful to their father's values, from whom they had inherited the *Boston Evening-Post* in 1758. The elder Fleet had established his paper in 1733 with the announcement that his columns were open to anyone "to write anything of a political Nature, that tends to enlighten and serve the public." In the tense 1760s, they tried to publish from both sides, including fiery essays by Boston radical Dr. Thomas Young as well as pro-administration articles. By 1775, this strategy was untenable. The *Boston Evening-Post* suffered from its moderation; its appearance every Monday morning alongside the two extremist papers heightened this contrast. The Fleets abandoned their father's project after the war began; the *Evening-Post*'s last number was dated April 24, 1775.[6]

Their paper was not the only casualty. The outbreak of war would prove chaotic for Boston's presses, too. Only Draper and Boyle's paper remained active in the same location. Mills and Hicks's *Post-Boy* did not survive the beginning of hostilities, either. Isaiah Thomas, finding the "Liberty of the Press in [Boston] daily declining" and worried about their "*Military Masters,*" had asked patriot leaders in Lexington whether it was "proper . . . for me to remove my Printing Office," a move they deemed "*highly requisite,*" to be undertaken "*immediately.*" Thomas got out of Boston "the day of the battle and left everything any tools excepted behind me," he later related, and caught up to his packed-up press in Worcester a few days later. Starting on May 3, and aided by John Hancock's efforts to secure him a paper supply at public expense, the *Spy*—now dubbed the *Massachusetts Spy Or, American Oracle of Liberty*—returned to broadcasting patriot stories after a month's absence. Edes and Gill had more difficulty. War induced them to dissolve their two-decade-long partnership. On June 5, Edes resumed the *Gazette* in Watertown, just west of the thousands of militia then gathering in Cambridge. John Gill remained in Boston throughout what would be an eleven-month siege. It would be a few more months still before he returned to publishing, bringing out his own paper, the *Continental Journal*, starting on May

6. Quoted in Stephen Botein, "'Meer Mechanics' and an Open Press: The Business and Political Strategies of Colonial American Printers," *Perspectives in American History,* IX (1975), 181.

30, 1776. The strong pro-patriot content of Gill's new paper showed that his time away from the press had not diminished his political ardor.[7]

In 1778, Edward Draper and John Folsom started another Boston paper, the *Independent Ledger*. For much of the war, Boston boasted six prints. When one closed, another, like James White and Thomas Adams's *Boston Evening Post* (which ran from October 1778 to March 1780), opened.

MASSACHUSETTS

A similar scene of disruption and dislocation caused by the outbreak of war occurred outside Boston for other Massachusetts printers, too. Samuel Hall had sold the *Newport Mercury* in 1768 and moved to Salem, where he and his brother Ebenezer Hall started the *Essex Gazette*. Two weeks after Lexington, the Halls decided they could better aid the cause they supported (and surely take advantage of the changing economics of wartime Massachusetts) by relocating their press to the camp at Cambridge. Ten days after they closed up shop in Salem, the *New-England Chronicle* appeared (in 1776, it would be in Boston under the management of Edward Powars and Nathaniel Willis and renamed *Independent Chronicle*). This move surely disappointed many Salemites hungry for news. The port town had enjoyed two newspapers in the months leading up to war, after Ezekiel Russell founded the *Salem Gazette* in the summer of 1774. Like his brother Joseph, partner in the *Boston Post-Boy*,

---

7. Isaiah Thomas to Daniel Hopkins, Worcester, Oct. 2, 1775, box 1, folder 3, Isaiah Thomas Papers, MSS, AAS. Thomas appealed to Hopkins, a member of the Massachusetts legislature, for some relief for his losses in this move. His complaints reveal the connections between printers and political activity at the war's start:

> As none of the Boston Printers then published a paper or were like to do it myself excepted, I was desired by many Gentlemen both in the Congress, the different Committees, and the Army to forward mine to them; and several who I imagined knew my circumstances told me I should send a number to the Congress and to the headquarters:—I immediately established a Post to the army to bring me intelligence, and carry my Papers to the Hon. Congress and the Army—As matters were then in much disorder, together with my residing at such a distance, added to the desire I ever have had of doing my Country *all the service in my power,* I did what my Superiors bade, without ever inquiring *Who was to reward me?*

John Hancock to Joseph Warren, Worcester, Apr. 26, 1775, box 1, folder 3, Thomas Papers, AAS.

Russell was a loyalist. Russell's paper did not survive the news of Lexington, either, closing permanently after the April 21 issue.

The communication vacuum in northern New England left by the removal of presses from Salem was probably to the benefit of Ezra Lunt and Henry-Walter Tinges, printers of the *Essex Journal* in Newburyport, Massachusetts. This, too, was a newspaper of recent vintage, established by Tinges and Isaiah Thomas just a few days before the tea went into Boston Harbor. Though Thomas sold his share to Lunt after only six months, the association with the *Spy* printer suggests the political affiliation of this paper. The *Essex Journal* would continue through the war's first year, though paper scarcity and turnover in management brought it down by the end of 1776.

NEW HAMPSHIRE

The *Journal's* only competition outside of Boston was to the north in Portsmouth, New Hampshire, where Daniel Fowle had brought out the *New Hampshire Gazette* on Fridays since 1756. Fowle, born in 1715, had taken his nephew Robert on as a partner in 1764, but the imperial crisis divided their loyalties. Robert, more in line with the strongly loyalist Portsmouth, broke with his uncle in 1774. He left for Exeter, New Hampshire, where he would eventually start a paper but rapidly ran afoul of patriot authorities there in 1776. New Hampshire authorities suspected Fowle of counterfeiting and printing items against independence. The *Gazette* ceased publication on January 9, 1776. A few months later, Benjamin Dearborn picked up printing in Portsmouth with the *Freeman's Journal,* which operated until 1778, when Robert's uncle Daniel Fowle took over and changed the name of the print back to the *New-Hampshire Gazette.*[8]

RHODE ISLAND

In Rhode Island, there were two active papers at the start of war, both dedicated to the "cause." The *Providence Gazette,* which William Goddard struggled to get off the ground in the 1760s (even enlisting his mother, Sarah, for help), was now in the hands of Benjamin Franklin's former apprentice John Carter. Carter, a thirty-year-old Philadelphia native, revealed himself a partisan in 1772 with the *Gaspée* affair, taking a leading position in the *Gazette* informing colonists of the commission to bring the perpetra-

8. For a time in the middle of the war, Daniel and his brother Zechariah had been simultaneously printing newspapers in both Portsmouth and Exeter. For a detailed explanation see Brigham, *History and Bibliography of Am. Newspapers,* I, 471–473.

tors of the attack to England for trial. In Newport, Solomon Southwick had purchased types and equipment from Samuel Hall in 1768 and continued the *Newport Mercury,* founded by Ben Franklin's brother James a decade earlier. Southwick, born in 1731, was not brought up a printer but rather the son of a fisherman and a failed merchant. The *Mercury* was a strong patriot paper, and as a result, Southwick became a target. He barely escaped capture when the British occupied Newport in 1776, driving him to bury his press and types and flee to Attleborough, Massachusetts. He tried to keep active by printing on a borrowed press in the interim, but the *Newport Mercury* would lie dormant for four years until January 1780, when Henry Barber carried on.[9]

CONNECTICUT

Connecticut, conversely, was the land of steady print habits. The same four papers that contained the news of Lexington would also publish the text of the Treaty of Paris in 1783. Members of the Green family operated three of Connecticut's four papers. In New London, Timothy Green started the *Connecticut Gazette* in 1763 at the age of twenty-six. With little turbulence, he brought out that paper every Friday for nearly thirty years. The following year, his younger brother Thomas founded the *Connecticut Courant* in Hartford, a paper he would operate for four years. In 1767, Thomas Green made Ebenezer Watson managing partner of the *Courant* and went to New Haven, where he and another brother, Samuel, born in 1743, founded the *Connecticut Journal.* Though untrained as a printer, Watson kept the *Courant* afloat until his death in 1777 at age thirty-three, after which his widow and a new partner maintained the business. Isaiah Thomas would later praise the political leanings and conduct of the *Courant,* saying that after the occupation of New York had dispersed many northern printers, the *Courant* "became of much consequence; its circulation rapidly increased; and, for some time, the number of copies weekly was equal to, if not greater, than that of any other paper then printed on the continent." The fourth Connecticut paper, the *Norwich Packet,* was founded late in 1773. It had three partners: twenty-three-year-old John Trumbull, born in Charlestown, Massachusetts, and two brothers from Scotland, Alexander and James Robertson. The Robertsons had first tried publishing in New York City without success, and then, through the financial assistance of Indian Superintendent Sir William

9. Arthur M. Schlesinger, *Prelude to Independence: The Newspaper War on Britain, 1764–1776* (New York, 1957), 154.

Johnson, started the first newspaper in frontier Albany in 1771. It, too, was short-lived. Though the *Norwich Packet* would be a reliably patriot paper, the Robertsons would become important printers for the king once the British invasion fleet landed at Staten Island in 1776. The Robertsons would eventually become itinerant printers following the British army to Philadelphia and Charleston, turning out loyalist papers as they went. Trumbull, a staunch patriot, was left to operate the *Packet* alone, which he did for more than a quarter century.[10]

NEW YORK CITY

New York City was the hub of information in late-eighteenth-century America. In fair weather, the mails moved regularly: a post from Albany arrived every Tuesday afternoon; riders arrived from Boston Wednesday and Saturday evenings; three posts from Philadelphia arrived the mornings of Monday, Wednesday, and Friday; and a packet boat sailed for London the first Wednesday of every month. This activity made life much easier for Hugh Gaine, James Rivington, and John Holt, the three newspaper publishers active in 1775.

In 1766, when, with the aid of the local Sons of Liberty, the *New-York Journal* first appeared, John Holt was starting over for the third time. Born in Virginia in 1721, Holt had initially tried his hand at business, rising through ranks as a merchant, a career that culminated in his being elected mayor of Williamsburg at the age of thirty-two. But all was apparently not well, for at the end of his political term, he changed trades, taking up the craft of his wife's family instead and joining forces with printer James Parker to found the first newspaper in Connecticut. Parker, a publishing entrepreneur with ventures across the mid-Atlantic, had bought John Peter Zenger's press from his defunct Manhattan shop and shipped it up to New Haven. For the rest of the 1750s, Holt and Parker turned out papers in Connecticut, but in 1760, they closed up there and went to New York City, making room for the Green family to corner the market on Connecticut printing. Holt continued with Parker in New York City, leasing his shop and producing Parker's *New York Gazette; or, the Weekly Post-Boy* with diminishing returns. The imperial controversy—especially the Stamp Act crisis—radicalized the Virginian; his patriot connections in the city induced him to bring out his

10. Thomas, *History of Printing in America*, 308; Schlesinger, *Prelude to Independence*, 165.

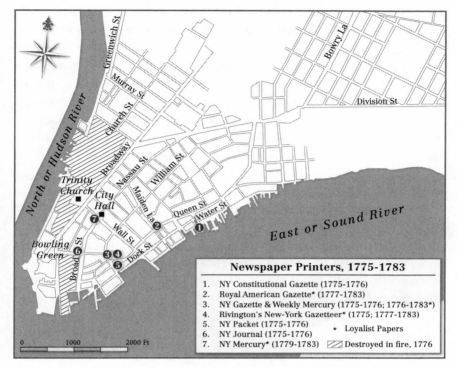

Map 5. *Newspaper print shops in New York City, 1775–1783*

own paper, and subscribers began to receive the *New-York Journal,* one of the most vital and rabid patriot papers, every Thursday from his shop on Beaver Street, two blocks south of Wall Street.

It was less than a four-hundred-yard walk east from Holt's shop to Hanover Square. So named for the British dynasty, Hanover Square was, appropriately, also the location of Holt's competitors, Hugh Gaine and James Rivington, soon famous throughout the continent as the two most notorious loyalist printers in America. Gaine, born in Ireland and trained there as a printer, had come to America in the 1740s, where he, too, worked with James Parker in his *Post-Boy* shop. About the time Holt stood for office in Williamsburg, Gaine began his own paper, initially titled the *New-York Mercury* (in 1768 he would change it to *New-York Gazette; and the Weekly Mercury*). Like the Fleets' print in Boston, Gaine's paper was a moderate one during the imperial crisis, even tilting toward the patriots in the early 1770s. But, as Thomas would later opine, since Gaine's "political creed, it seems, was to join the strongest party," he would throw his lot in with the British in 1776, a decision much derided and commented on during the Revolution.[11]

Gaine had to share Hanover Square with an English bookseller who would become an even greater lightning rod for patriot vitriol. Like Holt, James Rivington had fled economic disaster to reinvent himself far away. Rivington had incurred high debts brought on by profligacy in England, and his creditors initiated a suit of bankruptcy against him. In 1760, he fled, first to Philadelphia, where he briefly opened an unsuccessful bookshop. Two years later, he came to lower Wall Street to try again. In the spring of 1773, at the age of forty-nine, he introduced *Rivington's New-York Gazetteer; or the Connecticut, New-Jersey, Hudson's River, and Quebec Weekly Advertiser*. The elaborate title suggests the wide reach Rivington imagined his paper would achieve. His egotism was not wholly misplaced: the *Gazetteer* would indeed quickly become one of the most preeminent and admired papers in America. Every Thursday, Rivington's *Gazetteer* battled Holt's *Journal* for political attention in New York—and "the King's Printer" seemed to have the upper hand.

Whatever combat Rivington and his opponents thought they were engaged in during their heated debates in 1773 and 1774 ended abruptly with the news of real war. Only a few days after accounts of Lexington reached New York, patriot authorities placed him under arrest. The king's printer had the displeasure of appealing to the Continental Congress for pardon and signing the Association in order to be free to return to his press. Allegedly chastened, the printer surely held his nose as he included several pro-patriot items over the next several months. But the damage was done. In November 1775, a group of patriots finally made good on their repeated threats, invading his Hanover Square shop, carrying off the press, and forcing him to seek the protection of the Royal Navy.

Before this, while Rivington was attempting to reform his image, a new paper appeared in the city: John Anderson's *Constitutional Gazette*. Anderson's shop, on Beekman's Slip near Golden Hill, produced a smaller sheet on Wednesdays and Saturdays. Soon after Rivington's exile, another new patriot paper, the *New York Packet*, published by Samuel Loudon, also appeared on Thursdays. These two were very strong patriot papers, joining Holt's *Journal*. By the end of 1775, New York City—never the strongest bastion of grassroots support for the patriots—boasted several partisan newspapers nonetheless.

11. Thomas, *History of Printing in America,* 472; Ruma Chopra, "Printer Hugh Gaine Crosses and Re-Crosses the Hudson," *New York History,* XC (2009), 271–285.

The British invasion in September 1776, however, changed everything. Anderson closed permanently, Loudon went to Fishkill, New York, Holt took his types to Kingston, New York (also known as Esopus), and Gaine fled for a few weeks to Newark, New Jersey. While Gaine was in New Jersey, the British army, lacking a paper, commissioned Ambrose Serle to start his own "engine." Gaine, who had been printing a paper in New York since 1752, decided after a few weeks that the British market would better serve his financial interests, and he returned to the city on November 11, 1776, to take over Serle's nascent operation. Gaine's decision to turn his coat infuriated the patriots, and his name would be synonymous with deceit and greed for the remainder of the war.

In occupied New York, loyalist papers flourished. Rivington also returned in 1777 and reestablished his print triweekly, which he would later rename the *Royal Gazette*. The Robertson brothers from Norwich also began a biweekly *Royal American Gazette* that year, and when William Lewis started the *New-York Mercury* in September 1779, New York had a combination daily newspaper.[12]

Meanwhile, the dispersed patriot papers had a more difficult time beyond the city. Outside the main avenues of communication, Loudon still maintained publication of the *New York Packet* from Fishkill throughout the war. Holt published the *New-York Journal* in Kingston from July to October 1777, when disaster struck again as the British sacked the town. In May 1778, he resurfaced in even more remote Poughkeepsie, New York, where he struggled to maintain his connections with Governor George Clinton and keep the *Journal* in circulation.[13]

12. Rivington had various names for his paper during the war: Rivington's *New-York Gazetteer* (1773–1775), Rivington's *New-York Gazette* (1777), Rivington's *New-York Loyal Gazette* (1777), *Royal Gazette* (1777–1783), and back to Rivington's *New-York Gazette, and Universal Advertiser* (1783). James Robertson acted as traveling printer for the British army. During the occupation of Philadelphia, he started a *Royal Pennsylvania Gazette* there, and when the army took Charleston in 1780, he went along, establishing a *Royal South-Carolina Gazette* there with two other partners, Alexander Cameron and Donald MacDonald.

13. In all, Holt had three gaps: two from war (August 1776–July 1777 and October 1777–May 1778), and a third from paper scarcity (November 1780–July 1781). He discontinued in January 1782 until the peace.

At the outbreak of war, Philadelphia sustained six newspapers in English. One, Story & Humphreys's *Pennsylvania Mercury,* had just put out its first number that month, debuting in the city on April 7. Sadly, this print would not last the year, though not because of political reasons: a fire destroyed the shop on New Year's Eve, and the printers could not continue. Before this calamity, however, for most of 1775, Philadelphians had the luxury of at least one fresh newspaper every day except Sunday.[14]

The city's newspapers were staples of Philadelphia society. The most renowned of these was, of course, the *Pennsylvania Gazette,* founded by Samuel Keimer in 1728 and soon assumed by Benjamin Franklin. David Hall, a Scot-

---

14. This study focuses on newspapers published in English in mainland North America. In 1775, there were two Pennsylvania newspapers printed in German. Heinrich Miller had brought out *Der Wöchentliche Philadelphische Staatsbot,* twice weekly from his shop on Race Street in Philadelphia since 1762. More than seventy when the war broke out, Miller supported the patriots. During the imperial crisis, he translated speeches by James Otis and exchanged reports from Holt's *New-York Journal.* His paper was the first American newspaper to announce the existence of the Declaration of Independence on July 5, 1776. Miller continued to publish in Philadelphia until the British occupation in 1777. In Germantown, Christopher Sauer, Jr., had changed the name of his father's *Pensylvanische Berichte* (started in 1746) to the *Germantowner Zeitung.* Sauer (sometimes spelled Saur or Sower) published this paper biweekly through the early 1770s, but only a few issues are extant. Age fifty-four when the war started, Sauer remained uncommitted. Because his son (Christopher III) entered the city to publish a loyalist paper when the British occupation displaced Miller's paper, the elder Sauer's political affiliations are often portrayed as loyalist, too. Indeed, the Pennsylvania government thought so, including both father and son on a list of seventy-five traitors in May 1778, and confiscated his estate a few weeks later. Christopher Sauer III left Philadelphia with the British army.

See: Thomas, *History of Printing in America,* 387–389, 405–408, 446–447; and, especially, Willi Paul Adams, "The Colonial German-Language Press and the American Revolution," in Bernard Bailyn and John B. Hench, eds., *The Press and the American Revolution* (Worcester, Mass., 1980), 151–228.

Monday: *Pennsylvania Packet*
Tuesday: *Pennsylvania Evening Post*
Wednesday: *Pennsylvania Journal, Pennsylvania Gazette*
Thursday: *Pennsylvania Evening Post*
Friday: *Story & Humphreys' Pennsylvania Mercury*
Saturday: *Pennsylvania Evening Post, Pennsylvania Ledger*

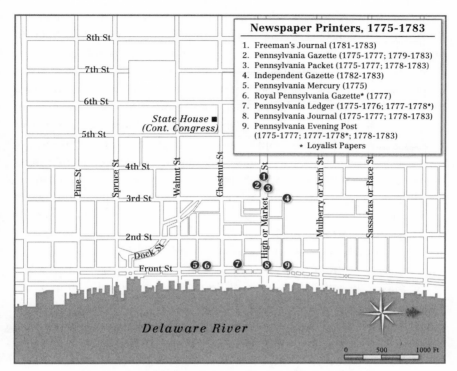

Map 6. *Newspaper print shops in Philadelphia, 1775–1783*

tish printer who came to America at eighteen, had continued Franklin's three-decade management of the *Gazette* in 1765. By that date, Hall boasted, the *Gazette* "spreads more generally than all the other Papers put together on the Continent." When Hall died in 1772, an English bookseller that had relocated to Philadelphia, William Sellers, stepped in and helped his sons, William and David, Jr., keep the paper going. Hall and Sellers's *Gazette* continued to emanate from Franklin's "Newest Printing Shop" on Market Street every Wednesday throughout the start of the Revolution. Close by was John Dunlap's operation, the *Pennsylvania Packet, or the General Advertiser.* Dunlap, born in 1747 in Northern Ireland, came to Philadelphia to join his book-publishing uncle, William Dunlap. He founded the *Packet* in November 1771; it would soon become a very reliable patriot paper, earning the respect and patronage of local resistance organizations, including the Continental Congress.[15]

15. David Hall to BF, Philadelphia, Sep. 6, 1765, *PBF,* XII, 258.

A short walk down Market Street toward the Delaware River wharves was the other central district of print communication in Philadelphia. On Front Street, very proximate to incoming ships carrying mail, newspapers, and information, were the shops of William Bradford, Benjamin Towne, and James Humphreys, Jr. Thanks to longevity, Bradford had the prime location: his shop, at the southwest corner of Front and Market, had been turning out the *Weekly Advertiser, or Pennsylvania Journal* at that location since 1754. Most Philadelphians were more familiar with the establishment next door, the London Coffee House, which Bradford also operated in an effort to supplement a meager printer's income. He continued to seek out more revenue, diversifying further by opening a marine insurance office in 1762. More than many printers, Bradford had established himself as a well-respected member of Philadelphia's political community, in part because of his myriad business ventures. During the Seven Years' War, Bradford had served as captain of one of the city's militia companies. Both Bradford and his coffeehouse played an active role in Philadelphia's resistance to the Stamp Act, a position that made him a long-standing enemy of Benjamin Franklin. Colonel Bradford, as he was known during the Revolution, would don his uniform again in the 1770s. During the war, his son Thomas Bradford (whom he took as a partner in 1766) occasionally kept the *Journal* before the public while the elder Bradford—fifty-six when the war began—served the cause in different capacities.[16]

Benjamin Towne, who had shown himself as an opportunist during the war, took advantage of Bradford's prime location and also set up shop near the London Coffee House. His *Pennsylvania Evening Post* was nevertheless singular in one respect: it was published three times a week. Starting late in January 1775, Towne brought out a paper of small stature (quarto rather than the typical folio, with two columns rather than three on a page) every Tuesday, Thursday, and Saturday evening. After the Revolution, the *Pennsylvania Evening Post* would become the first daily newspaper in America, but given the political storms that would engulf its printer during the war, this was hardly assured. Towne would run competitors out of town, turn his coat

16. Edmund S. Morgan and Helen M. Morgan, *The Stamp Act Crisis: Prologue to Revolution* (1953; rpt. Chapel Hill, N.C., 1995), 189, 260–261, 265; Gary B. Nash, *The Urban Crucible: Social Change, Political Consciousness, and the Origins of the American Revolution* (Cambridge, Mass., 1979), 305–306; David Waldstreicher, *Runaway America: Benjamin Franklin, Slavery and the American Revolution* (New York, 2004), 166.

more than once to shield himself from the war's turbulent winds, and yet escape harm at the hands of angry Philadelphia crowds.[17]

Towne's principal enemy in 1776 was James Humphreys, Jr. Perhaps his anger stemmed from the fact that Humphreys, a former Bradford apprentice, brought out the first issue of *The Pennsylvania Ledger: or the Virginia, Maryland, Pennsylvania, & New-Jersey Weekly Advertiser* the same week that Towne's paper debuted. Perhaps it was just proximity. Humphreys's shop was half a block down Front Street from Towne, in the Black Horse Alley shop where Bradford first published the *Journal* in 1742. That paper was five years old when Humphreys was born in Philadelphia. His father sent him to the College of Philadelphia to study medicine, but he disliked it and went to work for Bradford instead. With this schooling, Humphreys was not a typical printer's apprentice; some time after leaving the *Journal,* he worked as a clerk in the court of chancery in Philadelphia. Such a position required swearing an oath to the king, an act Humphreys apparently took seriously. When the war began, just a few months after he had started printing the *Ledger,* he refused to offer support to the patriots and was accused of being a tory. Towne did his best to cultivate this opinion by publishing several pieces impugning him. Late in 1776, Humphreys suspended the *Ledger* and fled to the countryside, returning only when British forces occupied Philadelphia in 1777.

It is possible that Towne sharpened his sense of opportunism working in the late 1760s as William Goddard's journeyman (and unhappily for a year as his partner) in his *Pennsylvania Chronicle, and Universal Advertiser.* Goddard had learned the printer's craft from John Holt in New York. In the 1760s, he struggled to establish his own imprint in Providence; during the Stamp Act crisis, he intermittently produced a *Providence Gazette* but lacked enough subscribers to keep it before the public regularly. In 1767, two leading Philadelphians, Joseph Galloway and Thomas Wharton, staked him to start a politically moderate paper to counter what they saw as the city's radical papers, the *Journal* and *Gazette.* Soon he brought out the *Pennsylvania Chronicle.* The *Chronicle*'s appearance in 1767 did indeed spark much comment from the publishers of those papers. Both Bradford and Hall attacked their new competitor in their columns, initiating a vicious exchange that was surely the talk of the town in the summer of 1767. Goddard, who replaced

17. Dwight L. Teeter, "Benjamin Towne: The Precarious Career of a Persistent Printer," *PMHB,* LXXXIX (1965), 316–330.

Towne's place in his shop with both future New Jersey newspaper printers Shepard Kollock and Isaac Collins, would seemingly have the upper hand in this heated rivalry when he began publication of Dickinson's famous series "Letters from a Farmer in Pennsylvania" at year's end. But this success convinced others that the new Philadelphia printer was rather unbrotherly— namely, his loyalist financial backers, who were surprised to find Dickinson's "exposé" on the pages of the paper they sponsored. They soon dissolved their partnership.[18]

Early on in the war, there was some turbulence in the Philadelphia print community. In December 1775, a fire ended the *Mercury.* The following November, Towne's political acts drove Humphreys out of town. Just as he fled, it appeared that the British might sweep into Philadelphia and all papers suspended publication except Towne's *Evening Post.* After the invasion scare dissipated with Washington's victories at Trenton and Princeton, Philadelphia papers resumed operations. The following fall, though, Howe's successful expedition against Philadelphia scattered printers and delegates alike across Pennsylvania. With the occupation, Bradford suspended his *Journal,* Hall and Sellers followed Congress to York and published there, and Dunlap took the *Packet* to nearby Lancaster for a period of months. Towne, on the other hand, stayed put, deciding to turn his coat and print a loyalist paper. Humphreys returned to Philadelphia and restarted the *Ledger* during the nine-month occupation. James Robertson came down from New York to produce a *Royal Pennsylvania Gazette* from March to May 1778. When the British left Philadelphia in May, Humphreys closed the *Ledger* and went along. Apparently attached to the city no matter the political climate, Towne turned his coat back again toward the Revolution and kept his paper alive. The *Gazette* and *Journal* returned from the countryside after the British evacuated, although Thomas Bradford took over production from his aging father, who had reprised his role as printer-turned-officer when the British occupied Philadelphia. Later in the war, two volatile prints appeared in Philadelphia, Francis Bailey's *Freeman's Journal* and Eleazer Oswald's *Independent Gazetteer,* which were each attached to political factions surrounding the Pennsylvania constitution. Bailey had previously published the *United States Magazine* in Philadelphia, which was edited by Hugh Henry Brackenridge and featured the poetry of Philip Freneau.

18. John Dickinson, "For the Pennsylvania Chronicle: Letters from a Farmer in Pennsylvania to the Inhabitants of the British Colonies," quoted in Ward L. Miner, *William Goddard, Newspaperman* (Durham, N.C., 1962), 73–75, 79, 82, 86–110.

NEW JERSEY

The presence of the British army in New York City also meant that New Jersey would be an active theater of violence from 1776 onward. In December 1777, Governor William Livingston sponsored a former Quaker, Isaac Collins, to begin the *New-Jersey Gazette* in Burlington. The state of New Jersey partly fronted Collins money to begin publication. A few months later, Collins relocated the *Gazette* to Trenton, where he would maintain publication until July 1783. Shepard Kollock, a former Continental army lieutenant, started a second newspaper, the *New-Jersey Journal,* in Chatham in February 1779. George Washington wanted his troops to have a newspaper while they were in winter quarters in nearby Morristown. Since a large number of Kollock's subscribers were soldiers, this paper contained a high quotient of war news until the end of hostilities.[19]

BALTIMORE

William Goddard's belligerence led to a combination of financial difficulties and obstacles in obtaining information, for making an enemy out of the city's postmaster (William Bradford) translated into being unable to receive timely news. By 1773, the environment in Philadelphia was too poisonous, and the itinerant began to consider the print opportunities in the growing town of Baltimore, where there were no Galloways, Bradfords, Halls, or Townes. In August 1773, he began publishing the *Maryland Journal, and the Baltimore Advertiser,* beginning a hectic six-month period when he published papers in both places, a project impossible without the essential aid of his sister Mary Katherine Goddard.

19. Philip Davidson, *Propaganda and the American Revolution, 1763–1783* (Chapel Hill, N.C., 1941), 399. A few students have suggested that Washington allowed Kollock to resign strictly to start a paper. See: Sidney I. Pomerantz, "The Patriot Newspaper and the American Revolution," in Richard B. Morris, ed., *The Era of the American Revolution: Studies Inscribed to Evarts Boutell Greene* (New York, 1939), 305–331, esp. 327. As Rollo G. Silver has pointed out, Kollock must have had some official approval: in 1780 the Army commissary in Morristown furnished him with paper and paper-making materials. Silver, "Aprons Instead of Uniforms: The Practice of Printing, 1776–1787," *Proceedings of the American Antiquarian Society,* LXXXVII (1977), 111–194, esp. 143. See also John R. Anderson, *Shepard Kollock, Editor for Freedom: The Story of the New-Jersey Journal in Chatham, 1779–1783* (Chatham, N.J., 1975); and Richard F. Hixson, *Isaac Collins: A Quaker Printer in 18th Century America* (New Brunswick, N.J., 1968).

Early in 1774, he discontinued the *Chronicle* and focused on his new Baltimore paper. But the frustration of being at William Bradford's mercy for exchanged news still stung, and soon he was off on his quest to develop a new postal system, placing Mary Katherine at the helm of the *Maryland Journal*. After a year, she finally received credit for her labor, as "M. K. Goddard" replaced "William" as printer on the colophon.[20]

But all was not well in Baltimore. Just as Mary's name appeared, the Goddard's monopoly in town ended when *Pennsylvania Packet* printer John Dunlap, following William's example, sent James Hayes, Jr., to manage a branch office, and *Dunlap's Maryland Gazette; or, the Baltimore General Advertiser* began to appear on Tuesdays. With Dunlap and Goddard supervising the publication of news in Baltimore, the patriot side of the imperial argument reigned in the growing commercial town. It is little wonder that when British arms induced the Continental Congress to flee Philadelphia in the last days of 1776, they followed the same roads that these print entrepreneurs had, and set up their own temporary shop in Baltimore.

In 1779, Mary Katherine Goddard took on Eleazer Oswald as a partner, which lasted for two years before he left for Philadelphia to begin his own paper, the *Independent Gazetteer.*

ANNAPOLIS

The other active Maryland newspaper was in Annapolis. Jonas Green, scion of the publishing family and former Franklin apprentice, had established the *Maryland Gazette* there in 1745, taking William Rind on as a partner in the mid-1750s. The *Maryland Gazette* had been one of the more partisan prints in the Stamp Act protests, upon which time Rind left the *Gazette* and went to Williamsburg. Green did not break the law and continue the *Gazette* at that moment per se, but rather he brought out a publication entitled *The Apparition of the Maryland Gazette, Which Is Not Dead but Sleepeth.* Green died in 1767, and production fell to his wife, Anne Catherine, who operated the *Gazette* with her son William until his death in 1770. The intrepid widow kept on until her death in March 1775, whereby the paper continued into the Revolution produced by her sons Frederick and Samuel Green. Under Anne's management by the outbreak of war, the *Gazette* had become "an organ of the Anne Arundel committee of correspondence," as one scholar

---

20. Miner, *William Goddard, Newspaperman,* 114–115.

put it. "Resolutions and proceedings of local, provincial, and continental assemblies filled their pages."[21]

WILLIAMSBURG

Confusion reigns about Revolutionary newspapers in eighteenth-century Virginia because they all shared the same name. In April 1775, there were four *Virginia Gazettes,* three in Williamsburg and one in Norfolk.

William Parks established the first in 1735. In the mid-1760s, it was in the care of William Hunter, John Holt's brother-in-law, until his death in 1761, whereby he legally entrusted the press to his infant son William, Jr. Until William could inherit, Joseph Royle was to operate as a printer regent until the boy came of age, but he also died. When John Dixon married Royle's widow, he, along with recent Scots arrival Alexander Purdie, took over operation of this imprint. From 1766 to 1775, this was a Purdie and Dixon production, until, just before the Revolution, Hunter, Jr., took his place at the press, and then Dixon and Hunter's *Gazette* published through the war. Although this was a solidly patriot paper, the partnership between Dixon and Hunter was apparently not politically compatible. Dixon was an officer in the Williamsburg militia and later mayor of the town. But when the British army invaded Virginia in 1779, Hunter accompanied them. Dixon then took on a new partner, Thomas Nicolson, and continued operations until April 1780.

In 1765, William Rind left Maryland to start the second *Virginia Gazette* in Williamsburg. When Rind died in 1773, his wife Clementina maintained the press for more than a year until she transferred operation of this shop to John Pinkney, just before dying herself. The vexation of this shop did not end there: Pinkney, too, passed in February 1776, and this iteration of the *Virginia Gazette* closed permanently.

Alexander Purdie had set off on his own just before the Revolutionary War began. With Dixon now teamed with the young Hunter, Purdie brought out his own *Virginia Gazette* starting in March 1775, until his death four years later in April 1779, when his nephew John Clarkson and one of Purdie's apprentices Augustine Davis continued the press until December 1780.

For the war's first few seasons, though, Virginians enjoyed three fresh papers at the end of each week, with Pinkney bringing out his edition on Thursdays, Purdie on Fridays, and Dixon and Hunter on Saturdays. All

---

21. Thomas, *History of Printing in America,* 542; David C. Skaggs, "Editorial Policies of the *Maryland Gazette,* 1765–1783," *Maryland Historical Magazine,* LIX (1964), 348.

three of these were patriot papers. British invasions in later years wreaked havoc on the Williamsburg presses. Clarkson and Davis's *Gazette* folded, and Dixon and Nicolson transferred their operation to the safety of Richmond, where they would print until May 1781. Cornwallis's surrender allowed the submerged press to resurface, and two new versions of the *Virginia Gazette* appeared in Richmond at the end of 1781: one by Nicolson and William Prentis, and a second by James Hayes.

NORFOLK

Just as the news of the Coercive Acts reached America in the summer of 1774, a fourth newspaper appeared in Virginia, the *Virginia Gazette, or the Norfolk Intelligencer*. First run by William Duncan, within a few months publication fell to the well-connected John Hunter Holt, nephew of the two printers reflected in his surname. Early on in the war, his partisanship in supporting the "cause" made him so obnoxious to Virginia royal governor Lord Dunmore that Dunmore confiscated Holt's press and took it on board his warship late in 1775, bringing a swift end to newspapers in Norfolk.

NORTH CAROLINA

At midcentury, James Davis began printing in North Carolina, having received some support from the colonial government in Newbern. Davis, also the postmaster, struggled. He started the *North-Carolina Gazette* in 1751, but little information about this particular print has survived. Issues ranging over several years are not extant; whether they ever existed is not known. Appearing again in 1768, the *Gazette* was available to Carolina readers for a year before a hurricane destroyed Davis's shop. Bearing the motto "semper pro libertate, et bono publico," it returned before the Revolution, with nine issues intact from 1775, none in 1776, and then a fair run from July 1777 to the end of 1778, when it was discontinued permanently. The intermittence of the surviving issues suggests the slight footprint the *Gazette* left behind.

In the mid-1760s, a second North Carolina newspaper also struggled to gain support. Interested elite in Wilmington had invited Philadelphia printer Andrew Steuart to start a print there in 1764; his *North-Carolina Gazette and Weekly Post Boy* briefly appeared before Steuart upset his benefactors by opening and publishing some private correspondence without permission. Sadly, Steuart drowned in 1769, and Adam Boyd, an English immigrant not trained as a printer, purchased his press and soon brought out the *Cape-Fear Mercury* on Fridays through the early 1770s. It, too, had difficulty with regular publication. On January 30, 1775, the Wilmington

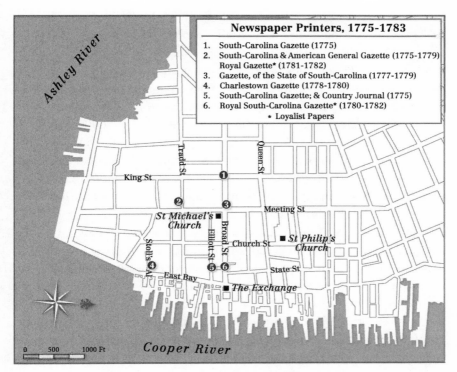

Map 7. *Newspaper print shops in Charleston, 1775–1783*

committee of safety voted to encourage the "laid aside" *Mercury,* which re-appeared through most of that year; but soon, Boyd "exchanged the press for the pulpit," according to Isaiah Thomas. Like Davis's paper, only a few issues of the *Mercury* remain. Though they were slight, both North Carolina papers were patriot prints.[22]

CHARLESTON

For the most part, southerners had to rely on Charleston for news. The first newspaper in the Lowcountry capital was the *South-Carolina Gazette,* started in 1734 by French Huguenot refugee Lewis Timothée. Timothée, who angli-cized his surname to Timothy, had worked on the *Pennsylvania Gazette* and was the first librarian for Franklin's Library Company before being sent to Charleston to manage the *South-Carolina Gazette.* Lewis died in 1738, and

22. Thomas, *History of Printing of America,* 563; "Proceedings of the Safety Com-mittee at Wilmington," Jan. 30, 1775, in William L. Saunders, ed., *The Colonial Records of North Carolina,* 10 vols. (Raleigh, N.C., 1886–1890), IX, 1118.

his wife Elizabeth carried on for a year until his teenage son Peter Timothy took over production. The *Gazette* was a large print, sometimes four columns across, but irregular, both in day of publication and with periodic hiatus in production. As Thomas notes, although it was supposed to appear on Mondays, rarely was this actually the case, since mail and ships into the port were not reliable in the mid-eighteenth century. For three decades, Peter sent out the *Gazette* from his shop on the corner of Broad and King Streets, a somewhat remote location four blocks back from the water's edge. The Stamp Act caused another interruption in Timothy's *Gazette,* this time lasting until June 1766. "My natural eyes being almost worn out," he claimed in 1772, he "declined the Printing business" and attempted to put the *Gazette* into new hands. This lasted fewer than two years; by the end of 1773, he was back at the press. At the end of 1775, with the fifty-year-old Timothy having experienced significant problems with management over the previous few years, he closed up his shop. Sixteen months later, he would reemerge with a new paper, this one announcing the change that had occurred during his absence: *The Gazette, of the State of South-Carolina.* Timothy's Revolution would be eventful and ultimately tragic. He remained in the city throughout the 1780 siege, was taken as a prisoner of war, and drowned during his transportation to Saint Augustine, Florida. Though he was elderly, the loss of Timothy was a blow to the cause. As he boasted to Franklin in a 1777 letter, the *Gazette* printer rivaled Benjamin Edes for his centrality to the patriot movement in Charleston:

> I was both a Member of and Secretary to the Congresses, General Committee, Charles-Town Committee; Chairman, (and did all the Business) of the Committee of Observation and Inspection, in such a Manner as too many well remember; and also Secretary to the Councils of Safety, who, while they existed, sat Day and Night, without a single Day's Intermission—continually in Motion from Congress to Committee, from Committee to Council, from Council to Inspection, and so on.

Even if this listing of "the Labour I underwent in these Employments" was mostly hyperbolic puffery, one still wonders how the *Gazette* appeared in Charleston at all during the mid-1770s.[23]

The loss of the busy Timothy at sea was, unfortunately, an all-too-familiar

23. Thomas, *History of Printing in America,* 580; Peter Timothy to BF, Charleston, S.C., Aug. 24, 1772, *PBF,* XIX, 283, Timothy to BF, [Charleston, S.C.], June 12, 1777, XXIV, 155.

theme for Charleston printers during the Revolution. His brother-in-law, Charles Crouch, opened a print shop on Elliot Street, just down from the Exchange, and in December 1765 began to turn out the *South-Carolina Gazette; And Country Journal.* The timing of Crouch's paper gives a hint as to his politics: according to Thomas, "The general opposition of the colonies to the Stamp Act induced the public to patronize this Gazette." Crouch had just passed his 500th issue of publication in the spring of 1775 when he, too, boarded a doomed ship bound for New York, and the forty-year-old, solidly patriot printer perished. His wife, Mary, briefly attempted to keep the *Country Journal* before the public, but by August it ceased. When the British laid siege to the city in 1780, Mary shipped her husband's old press up to the safety of Salem, Massachusetts, and tried her hand at publishing again, but this venture also lasted only a few months.[24]

The third paper active in Charleston in April 1775 was the *South-Carolina and American General Gazette,* published by Robert Wells and his son John. The title of the *American General Gazette* belied the politics of its founder: the senior Wells was an ardent supporter of the crown. Born in Scotland and trained there as a printer, Robert Wells came to Charleston in the 1750s, established what would become an extensive bookshop in the city, and in 1758 started his newspaper. He also held civil positions in Charleston, including being one of the city's principal auctioneers, an enterprise that involved the sale of many humans. Wells himself owned several slaves whom he employed as pressmen in his shop at the corner of Bay and Tradd Street. In Robert's hands, the *American General Gazette* was the most reliably progovernment paper in Charleston during the imperial crisis. When his son John returned in the first days of 1775 from his apprenticeship in an Edinburgh printing shop, politics may have strained their relationship. John Wells, twenty-five when the war began, did not fully share his father's loyalty to the king. For five months they published together, but the news of bloodshed in Massachusetts broke Robert's confidence in his adopted country. In May, he boarded ship back to Britain, leaving his son John sole publisher, and the paper drifted toward the patriots. John did more than print during the war: he was a member in one of Charleston's military companies that participated in the 1779 American-French siege of Savannah. He even added "Jr." to his name to distance himself from his loyalist father.[25]

24. Thomas, *History of Printing in America,* 582.

25. Ibid., 570. Timothy also employed slaves at his press. See Timothy to BF, Charleston, S.C., June 14, 1754, *PBF,* V, 343.

But John's dedication to the cause had its limits. When Charleston fell in 1780, he put personal interest over political ideal and began publishing the *Royal Gazette*. He claimed to British commissioners after the war that his actions in support of the "rebel cause" were because of duress. After the war, this decision forced him to take his press to Nassau and found the *Bahama Gazette*. With the occupation of Charleston, New York printer James Robertson arrived with Cornwallis and, along with two partners, Alexander Cameron and Donald MacDonald, established the *Royal South-Carolina Gazette* in June 1780. Both of these royalist papers ran throughout the British occupation.[26]

GEORGIA

Early in the 1760s, the colonial government in Savannah offered to subsidize a printer to come and publish the laws. James Johnston, a twenty-five-year-old printer trained in Scotland, responded, founding the *Georgia Gazette* in 1763. Johnston initially continued the *Gazette* after the Stamp Act went into effect, arguing that no stamped paper had yet arrived in the province, but the governor convinced him to suspend it late in November; it then stayed dormant for seven months. This episode revealed Johnston as a supporter of the crown, but not an absolute one. As the imperial crisis deepened, Johnston's *Gazette* tacked toward the government, but—like most of the printers who would later declare themselves as loyalists by producing royal newspapers behind British lines—his columns were not wholly off-limits to patriot writers despite public reputation.

Johnston discontinued the paper in February 1776 only to revive it as the *Royal Georgia Gazette* in January 1779 after the British occupied the city. He maintained that paper until the British evacuated in 1782 but was able to stay in Savannah when his name was placed on a list of those loyalists who were allowed to remain if they paid a fine. In January 1783, he established the *Gazette of the State of Georgia*.[27]

26. *American Loyalist Transcripts*, LVII, 351; Christopher Gould, "Robert Wells, Colonial Charleston Printer," *South Carolina Historical Magazine*, LXXIX (1978), 23–49, esp. 31.

27. Schlesinger, *Prelude to Independence*, 78; Brigham, *History and Bibliography of American Newspapers*, I, 131–132. Johnston's relationship with Georgia is explored in detail in William David Sloan and Julie Hedgepeth Williams, *The Early American Press, 1690–1783* (Westport, Conn., 1994), 190–191.

Table 1: Publication Schedule

Monday	Tuesday	Wednesday	Thursday	Friday	Saturday
Boston Gazette*	Essex Gazette*	Massachusetts Spy*	Boston News-Letter+	Salem Gazette*	Providence Gazette*
Boston Evening-Post+	Pennsylvania Evening Post*	Essex Journal*	Pennsylvania Evening Post*	Connecticut Gazette*	Pennsylvania Evening Post*
Boston Post-Boy+	Dunlap's Maryland Gazette* (starting 5/75)	Pennsylvania Gazette*	Norwich Packet*	Connecticut Journal*	Pennsylvania Ledger+
Newport Mercury*		Pennsylvania Journal*	New-York Journal*	New-Hampshire Gazette*	Virginia Gazette (Dixon & Hunter)*
Connecticut Courant*		Georgia Gazette+	Rivington's NY Gazetteer+	Pennsylvania Mercury*	Constitutional Gazette (starting 8/75)*
New-York Gazette*+		Constitutional Gazette (starting 8/75)*	Maryland Gazette*	Virginia Gazette (Purdie)*	
Pennsylvania Packet*			Maryland Journal*	Cape-Fear Mercury*	
South-Carolina Gazette*			Virginia Gazette (Pinkney)*	North-Carolina Gazette*	
			Virginia Gazette (Norfolk)*	South-Carolina and American General Gazette+	

* = patriot paper   + = loyalist paper

Table 2: Newspaper Publication during the Revolutionary War

	1775	1776	1777
Connecticut			
Connecticut Courant (Hartford)	X	X	X
Connecticut Journal (New Haven)	X	X	X
Connecticut Gazette (New London)	X	X	X
Norwich Packet	X	X	X
Georgia			
Georgia Gazette (Savannah)	X	End 2/7	
Royal Georgia Gazette (Savannah)*			
Maryland			
Maryland Gazette (Annapolis)	X	X	End 12/25
Dunlap's MD Gazette (Baltimore)	Start 5/2	X	X
Maryland Gazette (Baltimore)			
Maryland Journal (Baltimore)	X	X	X
Massachusetts			
Boston Evening Post (White & Adams)			
Boston Evening-Post (Powars)			
Continental Journal (Boston)		Start 5/30	X
Boston Gazette	X	X	X
Independent Chronicle (Boston)		Start 9/19	X
Independent Ledger (Boston)			
New-England Chronicle (Boston)	Start 5/12	End 9/12	
Essex Journal (Newburyport)	X	X	End 2/13
Salem Gazette (Salem)			
Mass. Gazette (Springfield)			
Massachusetts Spy (Worcester)	X	X	X
New Hampshire			
Dresden Mercury (Hanover)			
Exeter Journal			
New Hampshire Gazette (Exeter)		Start 6/1	End 7/15
Freeman's Journal (Portsmouth)		Start 5/25	X
New-Hampshire Gazette (Portsmouth)	X	End 1/9	
New Jersey			
New-Jersey Journal (Chatham)			
New-Jersey Gazette (Trenton)			
New York			
NY Gazette (NYC)*	X	X	X
NY Jrnl (NYC/Kingston/Pghkpse)	X	X	End 10/13
New York Packet (NYC/Fishkill)		X	X
New-York Mercury (NYC)*			
Rivington's Gazt/Royal Gazt (NYC)*	Stop 11/23		Start 12/13
Royal American Gazette (NYC)*			Start 1/16
NY Gazetteer (Albany)			
North Carolina			
North-Carolina Gazette (Newbern)	X	X	X
Cape-Fear Mercury (Wilmington)	Stop 9/1		

1778	1779	1780	1781	1782	1783
X	X	X	X	X	X
X	X	X	X	X	X
X	X	X	X	X	X
X	X	X	X	X	X
	Start 2/11	X	X	End 6/6	
	Resume 4/30	X	X	X	X
End 9/8					
Start 9/15	End 1/5				
X	X	X	X	X	X
Start 10/17	X	End 5/11			
			Start 10/20	X	X
X	X	X	X	X	X
X	X	X	X	X	X
X	X	X	X	X	X
Start 6/15	X	X	X	X	X
			Start 10/18	X	X
				Start 5/14	X
X	X	X	X	X	X
	5/4 to 9/27				
Start 2/24	End 5/25				
End 6/9					
Resume 6/16	X	X	X	X	X
	Start 2/16	X	X	X	X
Start 3/4	X	X	X	X	X
X	X	X	X	X	X
Resume 5/11	X	End 11/6	Resume 7/30	X	
X	X	X	X	X	X
	Start 9/10	X	X	X	X
X	X	X	X	X	X
X	X	X	X	X	X
				Start 6/3	X

Stop 11/30

Table 2: Continued

	1775	1776	1777
Pennsylvania			
Penna Evening Post (Philadelphia)	X	X	X
Penna Gazette (Phila/York/Phila)	X	X	To York 12/20
Penna Journal (Philadelphia)	X	X	Stop 9/17
Penna Ledger (Philadelphia)*	X	End 11/30	Start 10/10
Penna Mercury (Philadelphia)	End 12/22		
Penna Packet (Phila/Lancaster)	X	X	X
Freeman's Journal (Philadelphia)			
Independent Gazetteer (Philadelphia)			
Royal Penna Gazette (Philadelphia)*			
Rhode Island			
Newport Gazette			Start 1/16
Newport Mercury	X	Stop 12/2	
American Journal (Providence)			
Providence Gazette	X	X	X
South Carolina			
Charleston Gazette			
Charlestown Gazette			
Gazette of State of SC (Charleston)			Start 4/9
South-Carolina and American General Gazette (Charleston)	X	X	X
South-Carolina Gazette	Stop 12/11		
South-Carolina Gazette, & Country Journal (Charleston)	Stop 8/1		
Royal SC Gazette*			
Royal Gazette*			
Virginia			
Virginia Gazette, or Norfolk Intellig.	Stop 9/20		
Virginia Gazette (Dixon & Hunter)	X	X	X
Virginia Gazette (Dixon & Nicolson)			
Va Gaz (Nicolson & Prentis) Richmd			
Virginia Gazette (Pinkney)	X	End 2/3	
Virginia Gazette (Purdie)	X	X	X
Virginia Gazette (Clarkson & Davis)			
Virginia Gazette (Hayes) Richmond			

Sources: Clarence S. Brigham, *History and Bibliography of American Newspapers, 1690–1820* (Worcester, Mass., 1947), and Charles Lathem, ed., *Chronological Tables of American Newspapers* (Barre, Mass., 1972), 9–17.
Key: * denotes loyalist newspapers

1778	1779	1780	1781	1782	1783
X	X	X	X	X	X
York	Phila 1/5	X	X	X	X
Start 12/30	X	X	X	X	X
End 5/23					
X	X	X	X	X	X
			Start 4/25	X	X
				Start 4/13	X
3/3 to 5/24					
X	Stop 10/6				
		Start 1/10	X	X	X
	Start 3/18	X	Stop 8/29		
X	X	X	X	X	X
Start Aug	X	End 1/18			
Start 8/?	X	End 1/18			
Suspended	X				
1/6 to 6/24					
X	Stop 12/17				X
		Start 7/6	X	End 9/12	
			Start 3/3	End 9/28	
Stop 12/4					
	Start 2/12	X	End 5/19		
			Start 12/29	X	X
X	End 4/12				
	Start 4/19	End 12/9			
			Start 12/22	X	X

Pennsylvania Journal Subscription Books

BOOK 1: 1766–1773

Table 1: *Journal* Customers in Philadelphia and Environs, 1766–1773[1]

Papers in Philadelphia	Existing customers	Added 1766	Added 1767	Added 1768	Added 1769	Added 1770	Added 1771	Added 1772	Added 1773	Total Jan. 1774
Downtown	43	66	10	11	10	6	18	15	28	207
Uptown	64	43	5	5	4	17	8	6	10	162
"Small Round"	31	29	5	1	4	3	6	—	1	80
Singles left in shop	58	4	2	2	3	5	7	4	10	95
Papers left at Mr. Hall's shop	1	—	—	1	2	1	—	2	—	7
Total	197	142	22	20	23	32	39	27	49	551

1. These tables reflect an inference for the first column, the category of "existing customers." For 722 of the 1,703 names in the 1774 customer list, there are no dates attached. Given current understanding of circulation numbers for the mid-1760s, it makes sense that these dateless names were subscribed to the *Journal* in a previous account book, before this one began in 1766. See "List of Customers for Pennsylvania Journal Taken January 1774," Bradford Family Papers (collection 1676), series 2, box 9, folder 1, HSP.

Table 2: *Journal* Customers in Rural Philadelphia, 1766–1773

Papers to rural Pennsylvania	Existing customers	Added 1766	Added 1767	Added 1768	Added 1769	Added 1770	Added 1771	Added 1772	Added 1773	Total Jan. 1774
Nottingham	18	1	2	3	3	6	1	—	—	34
Easton	6	3	1	—	—	1	—	1	4	16
Reading	5	1	3	—	—	—	1	—	—	10
Readye (Reedy) Island	5	4	—	—	—	—	—	—	1	10
Penn's Neck	—	2	—	—	—	—	—	—	—	2
Lancaster	23	12	1	2	2	3	4	—	—	47
Left on Lancaster Road	11	—	—	—	—	1	2	2	1	17
Lewiston	7	1	1	3	—	2	—	—	2	16
Colchester	2	—	—	—	5	—	1	—	—	8
Bristol	7	2	1	1	—	—	2	—	—	13
Newtown (Bucks County)	3	—	—	2	—	—	—	—	—	5
Timber Creek	1	—	—	—	1	—	—	—	—	2
Papers left at Mr. Clinghan's	1	—	—	—	—	—	2	—	3	6
Country—singles (left in shop)	30	17	2	6	4	—	1	—	—	60
Total	119	43	11	17	15	13	14	3	11	246

Table 3: *Journal* Customers in New Jersey and Delaware, 1766–1773

Papers to New Jersey & Delaware	Existing customers	Added 1766	Added 1767	Added 1768	Added 1769	Added 1770	Added 1771	Added 1772	Added 1773	Total Jan. 1774
Amboy, NJ	—	1	—	—	—	—	—	—	—	1
Elizabethtown, NJ	11	1	—	1	—	—	1	2	1	17
Woodbridge, NJ	2	1	—	1	—	—	—	—	—	4
Brunswick, NJ	4	4	1	1	—	—	2	—	—	12
Trenton, NJ	42	25	1	1	2	1	5	2	2	81
Burlington, NJ	9	11	—	2	1	—	—	2	2	27
Princeton, NJ	13	3	—	5	4	7	3	2	5	42
Andover, NJ	58	—	—	—	17	7	4	1	—	87
Cohansey, NJ	11	11	2	6	2	6	5	7	2	52
Salem, NJ	16	1	1	—	—	3	—	3	—	24
Bordentown, NJ	4	4	1	—	1	—	2	1	1	14
Mount Holly, NJ	5	1	1	—	—	—	2	—	—	9
Newark, NJ	17	—	—	—	—	—	—	—	—	17
Maidenhead, NJ	1	—	—	—	—	—	—	—	—	1
Norrington, NJ (left in shop)	—	1	—	—	—	—	—	—	—	1
Eversham, NJ (left in shop)	—	3	—	1	—	—	—	—	—	4
Cape May, NJ (left in shop)	—	2	—	—	2	—	—	1	—	5
New Castle, DE[1]	26	15	16	14	32	2	22	14	7	148
Lewiston, DE	7	1	1	3	—	2	—	—	2	16
Christiana Bridge, DE	4	—	1	—	1	—	—	—	—	6
Total	230	85	25	35	62	28	46	35	22	568

1. The Bradfords list this town as "Newtown," but given the people and places under this category this must be New Castle, Delaware.

Table 4: *Journal* Customers in Chesapeake Bay Region, 1766–1773

Papers to Chesapeake	Existing customers	Added 1766	Added 1767	Added 1768	Added 1769	Added 1770	Added 1771	Added 1772	Added 1773	Total Jan. 1774
Baltimore, MD	29	23	6	8	2	5	7	4	—	84
Susquehanna Ferry, MD	—	3	1	—	—	—	—	—	—	4
Joppa, MD	4	4	—	—	—	—	—	—	—	8
Head of Elk, MD	2	1	—	—	1	—	—	—	—	4
Annapolis, MD	3	6	1	4	—	2	2	—	—	18
Charlestown, MD	4	6	3	—	1	—	1	1	—	16
Upper Marlboro, MD	2	2	—	3	1	1	—	—	—	9
Bladensburgh, MD	—	2	—	—	—	—	1	—	—	3
Frederick, MD (Frederick County)	10	—	—	—	—	—	—	—	—	10
Bushtown (Harford County, MD)	13	4	1	—	—	2	—	—	—	20
Alexandria, VA	—	—	—	1	—	1	1	—	—	3
Williamsburg, VA	2	1	—	—	—	2	1	1	—	7
Fredericksburg, VA	—	2	—	—	—	—	—	1	—	3
Total	69	54	12	16	5	13	13	7	—	189

Appendix B

Table 5: *Journal* Customers outside Mid-Atlantic Region, 1766–1773

Papers outside Mid-Atlantic	Existing customers	Added 1766	Added 1767	Added 1768	Added 1769	Added 1770	Added 1771	Added 1772	Added 1773	Total Jan. 1774
New York City	16	6	1	1	2	1	5	4	3	39
Boston	17	1	1	1	1	1	1	—	—	23
Albany	5	1	—	—	1	—	—	—	—	7
Connecticut	5	—	—	—	—	—	—	—	—	5
Newport, RI	7	—	—	—	—	—	—	—	—	7
Wilmington, NC	4	—	—	—	—	—	—	—	—	4
South Carolina	20	—	—	—	—	—	—	—	—	20
Georgia	1	—	—	—	1	—	—	—	—	2
Antigua	4	—	—	—	—	—	—	—	—	4
Barbados	8	—	1	—	—	—	—	—	—	9
St. Kitts	6	—	—	—	—	—	—	—	—	6
St. Eustatius	1	—	—	—	—	—	—	—	—	1
Jamaica	9	—	—	—	—	—	—	—	—	9
Lisbon	1	—	—	—	—	—	—	—	—	1
Edinburgh	1	—	—	—	—	—	—	—	—	1
Glasgow	1	—	—	—	—	—	—	—	—	1
Cork	1	—	—	—	—	—	—	—	—	1
Dublin	1	—	—	—	—	—	—	—	—	1
Grenada	2	—	—	—	—	—	—	—	—	2
Dominica	1	—	—	—	—	—	—	—	—	1
London	2	—	—	—	—	—	—	—	—	2
Halifax	3	—	—	—	—	—	—	—	—	3
Total	116	8	3	2	5	2	6	4	3	149

Table 6: *Journal* Customers, 1766–1773

Location	Existing customers	Added 1766	Added 1767	Added 1768	Added 1769	Added 1770	Added 1771	Added 1772	Added 1773	Total Jan. 1774	% total
Philadelphia	197	142	22	20	23	32	39	27	49	551	32.35
Pennsylvania	119	43	11	17	15	13	14	3	11	246	14.44
NJ/DE	230	85	25	35	62	28	46	35	22	568	33.36
Chesapeake	69	54	12	16	5	13	13	7	—	189	11.10
Outside Mid-Atlantic	116	8	3	2	5	2	6	4	3	149	8.75
Total	731	332	73	90	110	88	118	76	85	1703	100

Table 7: *Journal* Customers in Central New Jersey, 1775–1777[1]

Central New Jersey	Existing customers	Added 1775	Subtracted 1775	Added 1776	Subtracted 1776	Added 1777	Subtracted 1777	Subtracted misc.	Total 1777
Burlington	11	5	2	4	—	—	—	2	16
Gloucester	—	1	—	—	—	—	—	—	1
Springfield	7	—	—	—	4			1	2
Bordentown	11	4	—	9	2	—	3	4	15
Hightstown	—	—	—	1	1	—	—	—	—
Haddonsfield	5	2	1	3	1	—	—	1	7
Total	34	12	3	17	8	—	3	8	41

1. List of subscribers, *Pennsylvania Journal*, 1775, in Bradford Family Papers (collection 1676), series 2, box 9, folder 2, HSP.

Table 8: *Journal* Customers in Outskirts of Philadelphia, 1775–1777

Philadelphia outskirts	Existing customers	Added 1775	Subtracted 1775	Added 1776	Subtracted 1776	Added 1777	Subtracted 1777	Subtracted misc.	Total 1777
Papers left in shop	22	9	1	25	8	9	—	12	44
Germantown	5	6	—	1	—	2	—	2	11
Total	27	15	1	26	8	11	—	14	55

Table 9: *Journal* Customers in Berks and Chester Counties, Pennsylvania, 1775–1777

Berks/Chester County	Existing customers	Added 1775	Subtracted 1775	Added 1776	Subtracted 1776	Added 1777	Subtracted 1777	Subtracted misc.	Total 1777
Pottstown	1	—	—	11	—	—	—	—	12
Reading	5	—	—	11	3	—	—	—	13
West Nottingham	9	—	—	9	—	—	—	—	18
East Nottingham	5	—	—	1	—	—	—	—	6
Fogg's Manor	7	—	—	—	3	—	—	—	4
New London	4	—	—	—	—	—	—	—	4
Chester	8	—	—	1	—	—	—	—	9
Crossroads	7	—	—	2	—	—	—	—	9
Octararo	3	—	—	2	—	—	—	—	5
New Munster	3	—	—	—	—	—	—	—	3
Newark	1	3	—	—	—	—	—	—	4
New Garden	5	—	—	—	—	—	—	—	5
Norrisville (Cecil County, MD)	4	—	—	5	—	1	—	—	10
Reading Furnace	—	—	—	4	—	—	2	—	2
Total	62	3	—	46	6	1	2	—	104

Appendix B

Table 10: *Journal* Customers on Northumberland County Frontier, 1775–1777

Northumberland frontier	Existing customers	Added 1775	Subtracted 1775	Added 1776	Subtracted 1776	Added 1777	Subtracted 1777	Subtracted misc.	Total 1777
Fort Augusta~	1	—	—	—	—	—	—	—	1
Sunbury~	2	1	—	—	—	—	—	—	3
Northumberland County~	3	2	—	1	—	—	—	—	6
Paxton & Juniata+	2	19	—	13	3	—	1	1	29
Upper Paxton+	3	1	—	—	—	—	—	—	4
Juniata+	13	1	—	—	1	—	—	—	13
Northumberland County (@ Sign of the Garden of Eden)+	—	5	—	—	1	—	—	—	4
Carlisle+	—	45	1	37	3	—	—	—	78
Chambersburg+	—	6	—	—	—	—	—	—	6
Big Spring+	—	3	—	10	—	—	—	—	13
Left at Tobias Hendrick's (Conestoga)+	—	9	—	2	—	—	—	4	7
Shippensburg+	—	3	—	6	—	—	2	—	7
Cumberland County#	—	8	2	1	—	—	—	—	7
Derry∧	—	7	—	1	1	—	—	—	4
Total	24	107	3	71	9	—	3	5	182

~ = under the heading "Single papers to the care of Peter Withington, Reading, Lancaster, Wednesday."

+ = "Delivered by William Carheart; papers to Peter Withington's house in Reading for distribution."

= "Care of Jonathan Hoge, Esq., Cumberland County, via Lancaster, Wednesday."

∧ = "To be sent in Middletown Packet, not to be ty'd up with Carheart's but to go loose, via Lancaster, Wednesday."

Table 11: *Journal* Customers along Delaware River, 1775–1777

Delaware River	Existing customers	Added 1775	Subtracted 1775	Added 1776	Subtracted 1776	Added 1777	Subtracted 1777	Subtracted misc.	Total 1777
Woodberry, NJ	6	7	—	3	2	—	—	—	14
Salem, NJ	7	4	—	8	1	6	—	2	22
Neshiminy Creek (Bucks Cty)	—	6	—	3	—	—	—	—	9
Easton	5	8	—	20	3	—	—	—	30
Fort Penn	4	—	—	1	—	—	—	—	5
Total	22	25	—	35	6	6	—	2	80

Table 12: *Journal* Customers in Delaware Bay, 1775–1777

Delaware Bay	Existing customers	Added 1775	Subtracted 1775	Added 1776	Subtracted 1776	Added 1777	Subtracted 1777	Subtracted misc.	Total 1777
Lewiston, DE	2	1	—	—	—	2	—	—	5
Broad Kill, DE	3	2	—	2	—	—	—	1	6
Bridgetown, DE	1	7	—	4	—	—	—	—	12
Piles Grove, NJ	1	—	—	3	—	—	—	—	4
Dover, DE	1	2	—	—	—	—	—	—	3
Wilmington, DE	15	5	—	2	—	—	—	—	22
New Castle, DE	4	3	—	—	—	3	—	—	10
Total	27	20	—	11	—	5	—	1	62

Table 13: *Journal* Customers in Northern Colonies and New England, 1775–1777

Northern/ New England	Existing customers	Added 1775	Subtracted 1775	Added 1776	Subtracted 1776	Added 1777	Subtracted 1777	Subtracted misc.	Total 1777
New York City	24	5	1	7	1	—	—	8	26
Albany	—	—	—	7	—	—	—	—	7
Newark, NJ	4	2	—	12	—	2	1	5	14
Connecticut	8	—	—	3	—	—	—	—	11
Rhode Island	5	—	—	—	—	—	—	—	5
Boston	1	10	—	—	—	—	—	—	11
Cambridge, MA	5	16	—	8	1	—	—	6	22
Fort Ticonderoga	—	—	—	4	4	—	—	—	—
Headquarters	—	7	—	4	—	—	—	3	8
Total	47	40	1	45	6	2	1	22	104

Appendix B

Table 14: *Journal* Customers in North and Central New Jersey and Pennsylvania, 1775–1777

North central NJ/PA	Existing customers	Added 1775	Subtracted 1775	Added 1776	Subtracted 1776	Added 1777	Subtracted 1777	Subtracted misc.	Total 1777
Elizabethtown, NJ	5	1	—	7	—	—	—	3	10
Brunswick, NJ	10	—	—	6	—	—	—	1	15
Maidenhead, NJ	1	—	—	2	—	—	—	1	2
Bristol, PA	6	—	—	4	—	4	—	2	12
Trenton, NJ	32	22	—	6	3	—	1	2	54
Trenton Ferry, NJ	2	1	—	—	—	—	—	1	2
Woodbridge, NJ	2	—	—	1	—	—	—	1	2
Princeton, NJ	16	4	2	5	4	—	—	2	17
Andover, NJ	37	18	1	12	5	—	1	12	48
Morris County, NJ	—	—	—	23	—	2	—	—	25
Total	111	46	3	66	12	6	2	25	187

Table 15: *Journal* Customers along Lancaster Road, 1775–1777

Lancaster Road	Existing customers	Added 1775	Subtracted 1775	Added 1776	Subtracted 1776	Added 1777	Subtracted 1777	Subtracted misc.	Total 1777
Left at White Horse Tavern	10	8	—	11	—	5	1	3	30
Anderson's Ferry (Hallam, PA)	—	—	—	—	—	1	—	—	1
Papers left to care of William Clingan	4	9	—	—	1	1	—	3	10
Left at Mariner's Compass (East Caln, PA)	—	3	—	—	—	—	—	—	3
Left at Sign of Bull's Head	5	13	—	17	—	2	5	—	32
Papers left with William Bribanes (Salisbury Township)	—	2	—	—	—	—	—	—	2
Lancaster Post	—	—	—	—	—	1	—	—	1
Colerain Township	—	—	—	—	—	2	—	—	2
Lancaster	6	5	—	25	2	19	—	3	50
York	3	30	—	19	4	16	1	6	57
Middletown	—	52	—	5	2	—	—	1	54
Total	28	122	—	77	9	47	7	16	242

Table 16: *Journal* Customers on Delmarva Peninsula, Eastern Shore of Maryland and Virginia, 1775–1777

Eastern Shore	Existing customers	Added 1775	Subtracted 1775	Added 1776	Subtracted 1776	Added 1777	Subtracted 1777	Subtracted misc.	Total 177
Salisbury, MD	3	1	—	—	—	—	—	—	4
Accomack, VA	11	1	—	—	—	—	—	—	12
Somerset County, MD	3	3	—	1	—	—	—	—	7
Northampton County, VA	—	6	—	—	—	—	—	—	6
Upper Marlboro, MD	6	1	—	1	1	—	—	—	7
Wye Mills, MD	7[1]	—	—	—	—	—	—	—	7
Queenstown, MD	2	15	—	—	—	2	—	—	19
Tolbert County Courthouse, MD	40[2]	—	—	—	—	—	—	—	40
Dorchester County, MD	15	1	—	1	—	—	—	5	12
Warwick, MD	98[3]	—	—	—	—	—	—	—	98
Total	185	28	—	3	1	2	—	5	212

1. The Bradfords do not note when these customers at Wye Mills, Md., began taking the *Journal*. The only notation is "Papers left at Jacob Gibson's at Wye Mills, 7." This is part of the book that lacks much detail, for which see Table 18.

2. The Bradfords do not note when these customers at Tolbert County Courthouse, Md., began taking the *Journal*. The only notation is "Papers left at Tolbert Courthouse, 40." This is part of the book that lacks much detail, for which see Table 18.

3. The Bradfords do not note when these customers at Warwick, Md., began taking the *Journal*. The only notation is "Papers left at Warwick to the Care of Ferdinand Carson, 98." This is part of the book that lacks much detail, for which see Table 18.

Table 17: *Journal* Customers in Tidewater Maryland/Virginia and South Carolina, 1775–1777

Tidewater MD/VA & SC	Existing customers	Added 1775	Subtracted 1775	Added 1776	Subtracted 1776	Added 1777	Subtracted 1777	Subtracted misc.	Total 1777
Princess Anne, VA	9	2	—	2	—	—	—	—	13
Urbanna, VA	—	1	—	—	—	—	—	—	1
Bladensburgh, MD	3	—	—	—	—	—	—	—	3
Alexandria, VA	3	2	—	—	2	—	—	—	3
Williamsburg, VA	5	6	1	3	—		1	3	9
Levy Groom's Virginia Post Rider	1	—	—	—	—	—	—	—	1
Fredericksburg, VA	3	—	—	8	—	3	—	—	14
Georgetown, MD	8	1	—	—	—	1	—	—	10
Fredericktown, MD (Cecil County)	—	4	—	1	—	—	—	—	5
Annapolis, MD	13	—	—	1	—	—	—	—	14
Baltimore, MD	45	2	—	8	2	—	—	4	49
Frederick, MD (Frederick County)	9	—	—	1	2	—	—	—	8
Winchester, VA	4	—	—	1	—	11	—	—	16
Charleston, SC	4	—	—	4	—	—	—	—	8
Total	107	18	1	29	6	15	1	7	154

Table 18: Issues of *Journal* Left at Unspecified Public Houses and Private Homes

Notation in subscription book	# of papers
Papers left at the Red Lion	17
Papers left at William Carson's Tavern	10
Papers left on the Road	6
Left at the Cross Roads	10
Papers left at William Downes	28
Papers left at William Stuart's	29
Papers left at Robert Emory, Newtown	58
Papers left at Robinson's Tavern	7
Papers left with Emanuel Kent	9
Papers left at John Rouse's	23
Papers left at George Hansen's Tavern	25
Papers left at Clinton's Tavern	6
Total	228

Table 19: *Journal* Customers in Wyoming Valley, 1775–1777

Wyoming Valley	Existing customers	Added 1775	Subtracted 1775	Added 1776	Subtracted 1776	Added 1777	Subtracted 1777	Subtracted misc.	Total 1777
Kingston	—	—	—	28	—	5	—	6	27
Pittstown	—	—	—	6	—	—	—	—	6
Plymouth	—	—	—	10	—	—	—	—	10
Total	—	—	—	44	—	5	—	6	43

Table 20: *Journal* Customers, 1775–1777

Totals	Existing customers	Added 1775	Subtracted 1775	Added 1776	Subtracted 1776	Added 1777	Subtracted 1777	Subtracted misc.	Total 1777
Central NJ	34	12	3	17	8	—	3	8	41
Philadelphia outskirts	27	15	1	26	8	11	—	14	56
Berks & Chester County	62	3	—	46	6	1	2	—	104
Northumberland	24	107	3	71	9	—	3	5	182
Delaware River	22	25	—	35	6	6	—	2	80
Delaware Bay	27	20	—	11	—	5	—	1	62
Northern/ New England	47	40	1	45	6	2	1	22	104
North Central NJ/PA	111	46	3	66	12	6	2	25	187
Lancaster Road	28	122	—	77	9	47	7	16	242
Delmarva Peninsula	185	28	—	3	1	2	—	5	212
Tidewater MD/VA & SC	107	18	1	29	6	15	1	7	154
Unspecified locations	228[1]	—	—	—	—	—	—	—	228
Wyoming Valley	—	—	—	44	—	5	—	6	43
Philadelphia from 1774 book[2]	546[3]	?	9	?	8	—	—	24	505
Total	1448	436	21	470	79	100	19	135	2200

1. Given that there are no dates or places assigned to these numbers, it cannot be ascertained when the Bradfords began sending these issues to these locations. I have added them as "existing customers" as a default. If, for example, the papers "left at the Red Lion" were at the same "Red Lion" on the Lancaster Road mentioned in the 1774 book, then at least some of these papers date from before 1774.

2. This is an educated guess that the Bradfords continued to use their city list from the 1774 book. Given that the 1775 list does not account for city customers (whereas the previous book had meticulous detail for downtown, uptown, and suburban subscribers) and that they continued to strike off people through the end of 1776, long after the start of the new book, it is my hypothesis that this part of the older book remained active. What cannot be proved is when people added to the lists after January 1774, for there are no dates or issue numbers provided for then.

3. This number represents the 551 carried over from the January 1774 list, minus 5 names that, the Bradfords note, stopped their subscription at some point during 1774.

Contents of *Pennsylvania Journal*, 1775

Table 1: Opinion Items on Front Page

Essay/feature/opinion pieces	#
American opinion on political issues	19
British opinion on political issues	18
Government documents	14
Opinion by or about loyalists	10
Documents on war	8
On religion	2
On slave trade	1
On manufacturing	1
Total	73

Table 2: Number, Type of Advertisements

Advertisements	#
Runaway servants	163
Runaway slaves	20
Land for sale	117
Other items/people for sale	101
Legal notices	27
Print for sale	71
Ship advertisements	28
Merchant/store advertisements	166
Marriage/family notices	8
Newspaper proposals	4
Other notices (items wanted, for hire, lost and found, animals)	195
Total	900

Table 3: Origination of News Items in *Journal,* 1775

Type of item	#	%
News originating in Philadelphia	266	30.82
News from London	129	14.95
News from NYC	105	12.16
News from other American sources	91	10.54
News from Boston	80	9.27
Local Philadelphia city news	56	6.5
News from Williamsburg	48	5.56
News from Europe	47	5.45
News from Newport	33	3.82
News from Canada/other British Empire	8	.93
Total	863	99.97

863 news items / 67 issues = 12.88 news items per issue in 1775.

Table 4: Issues of *Journal* in 1775 with London News; Number of Items Per Issue

# *of articles*	*1 article*	*2 articles*	*3 articles*	*4 articles*	*5 articles*	*6 articles*	*7 articles*	*8 articles*	*9 articles*
# of issues	6	9	7	5	5	3	1	—	2

Table 5: Issues of *Journal* in 1775 with New York City News; Number of Items per Issue

# *of articles*	*1 article*	*2 articles*	*3 articles*	*4 articles*	*5 articles*	*6 articles*
# of issues	29	12	8	1	4	1

Table 6: Issues of *Journal* in 1775 with Boston News; Number of Items per Issue

# *of articles*	*1 article*	*2 articles*	*3 articles*	*4 articles*
# of issues	21	12	11	2

Table 7: Issues of *Journal* in 1775 with Williamsburg
News; Number of Items per Issue

# of articles	*1 article*	*2 articles*	*3 articles*	*4 articles*
# of issues	17	5	6	1

Table 8: Number of
News Stories from Other
Sources in *Journal*, 1775

Other sources of news	#
Charleston, SC	15
Providence, RI	10
Worcester, MA	10
Newbern, NC	9
Savannah, GA	8
New London, CT	6
Annapolis, MD	6
Baltimore, MD	5
Portsmouth, NH	4
Hartford, CT	4
New Haven, CT	3
Norfolk, VA	3
Norwich, CT	2
Fairfield, CT	2
Perth Amboy, NJ	1
Newburyport, MA	1
Salem, MA	1
Wilmington, NC	1
Total	91

Table 9: Issues of *Journal* in 1775 with Other American News; Number of Items per Issue

# of articles	*I article*	*2 articles*	*3 articles*	*4 articles*	*5 articles*	*6 articles*
# of issues	25	10	6	5	—	—

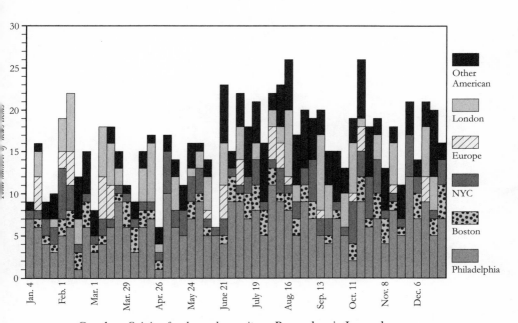

Graph 1. *Origin of exchanged news items,* Pennsylvania Journal, *1775.*

Drawn by Rebecca Wrenn

INDEX

455–456, 555, 625; and petition for freedom in Massachusetts, 336–337; as British proxies, 451, 542, 615; "good," imagined conversations of, 524–526; representations of, in postwar literature, 589–591; in postwar period, 620–625; on Tye, 625; and citizenship, 631; and colonization, 631, 661; and free blacks, 660. *See also* Laurens, John; Slave insurrections; Slavery

Albany committee of safety, 93
Alden, Ichabod, 420n, 421
Algonquian Indians, 331
Allen, Edward, 85
Allen, Ethan, 91, 101, 333, 344n, 617–618
Allinson, Samuel, 471
Ambrister, Robert, 663
"American," 623
"American, An" (Gouverneur Morris), 396
American Museum (Carey), 591–592, 631
"American Soldier, An," 523
American unity: as presumed unlikely, 1–4, 24, 663–665; and Constitutional Post Office, 33; and Lexington and Concord, 98; and British use of proxies, 98–99, 101–102; and African Americans as allies, 100–102; and Indians as allies, 100–102; and newspapers' exchange system, 110; contingency of, 261–263, 670; versus inclusion, 587
"Americanus," 491
Amherst, Jeffrey, 219
"Amicus Patria," 656–657
Anderson, John, 121, 177n, 207, 282–283, 293, 684. *See also Constitutional Gazette* (NYC)
André, John: and Benedict Arnold, 478, 501; on plan to arm African Americans, 491; capture of, 501
"Answer to the Declaration of the Congress" (Lind), 254n
"Anti-Brittanus," 494n
Apparition of the Maryland Gazette, Which Is Not Dead but Sleepeth, 692
Arbuthnot, Alexander, 663
"Armatus," 249–250
Armstrong, John, 355
Arnold, Benedict: and battle at Cedars, 236–237; fictional portrayal of, 347–348; and battle at Freeman's Farm, 355–356; at Saratoga, 356–357; association of, with proxies, 477, 501; as traitor, 477–478, 501–502; hanging of, in effigy, 501, 522; burning of Richmond by, 508; and runaway slaves, 508–509; in Chesa-

peake, 508–510; raid of Virginia by, 511; in *M'Fingal,* 591
Article 7 (Treaty of Paris): and debt repayment to British merchants, 563, 614–615; Congress on, 571; and evacuation of New York City, 571–572; and Washington, 571–572; and Dunmore's proclamation, 572; and Philipsburg Proclamation, 572; in early histories of the Revolution, 609
Articles of Confederation, 284–286, 374n, 381–382, 615–616
Ashe, John, 196–205, 208
Atakullakulla (Little Carpenter), 270
Atkins, Josiah, 519, 523
Attucks, Crispus, 79
Austin, Jonathan Loring, 361–362
Avery, Solomon, 413–414

Bahama Gazette, 698
Bailey, Francis, 386, 690; and *Freeman's Journal,* 521–522, 680, 690
Bancroft, George, 88–89
Barber, Henry, 681
Barrington, William, 98–99
Bartholomew, Benjamin, 516n
Bartlett, Josiah, 220–221, 239
Beckwith, George, 491
Beckwith, Sir Thomas Sydney, 652
Bedel, Timothy, 236–237
Belknap, Jeremy, 603
Bell, Robert, 192, 194–195, 223n, 348
Bemis Heights (battle), 355–356
Benezet, Anthony, 481; *Serious Considerations on Several Important Subjects,* 471; *Short Observations on Slavery,* 531
Bennington (battle), 353
Bernard, Francis, 16
Black Dragoons, 555–556, 567
Black Hoof, 659
Black Pioneers, 555, 567, 571
Blacksnake, 350–351, 412
Bleecker, John James, 514, 516–517
Bonham, Absolom (*Pennsylvania Journal* distributor), 57
Boone, Daniel, 432, 539, 549–550; in Filson's *Discovery, Settlement, and Present State of Kentucke,* 594–595
Boone, Israel, 549–550
Boston committee of correspondence, 27–28, 30
Boston committee of safety: on Lexington and Concord, 81
Boston Evening-Post (Fleet), 678, 683
Boston Evening Post (White & Adams), 679

Carleton, Sir Guy: and patriots' response to negotiations with Indians, 97; and British use of Indians as allies, 98, 102, 539, 548, 592; fictional portrayal of, 283, 347–349; as commander of British forces, 560; and removal of troops from Georgia, 560; and evacuation from Georgia, 560–563; and evacuation from Charleston, 565–568; and article 7 of Treaty of Paris, 570–575; and "Book of Negroes," 571; and Washington, 572; in *M'Fingal*, 589; in early histories of the Revolution, 609

Carlisle, Frederick Howard, fifth earl of. *See* Carlisle Peace Commission

Carlisle Peace Commission: creation of, by Parliament, 363–364; on independence, 384; and concessions for peace, 384–385; and patriot need for French alliance, 386; commissioners of, 391–392; and "Drayton's proposal," 393–395; and lack of newspaper coverage on concessions, 395; failure of, 395, 397–398; and British use of proxies, 396; and Wyoming Massacre, 412–413

Carmichael, Alexander (*Pennsylvania Journal* distributor), 60

Carroll, Charles, Sr., 57

Carter, John, 40, 680–681. *See also Providence Gazette*

Carter, Landon, 224, 246, 283

Carthage Gazette, 649

Caswell, Richard, 196–198, 201–203, 205

Catawba Indians: as British allies, 103; as patriot allies, 113–114, 658; and land encroachment, 620n

Caughnawaga Indians, 92–93, 236, 331

Cayuga Indians, 351, 391, 411, 420, 422, 446. *See also* Six Nations

Cedars (battle), 235–237; newspaper reports of, 237–238, 241; Continental Congress on, 238–240, 243; and treatment of prisoners, 296; in early histories of Revolution, 606

Charleston (S.C.), siege of: and print shops, 483, 698; and occupation by British, 489; and African Americans, 490; newspapers on, 490–491, 494–495; and Philipsburg Proclamation, 490; and Dunmore's proclamation, 490–491

Charleston Committee of Intelligence, 86n

Charleston committee of safety, 85–87, 105

Charleston council of safety, 162n

Charlotte County (Va.) committee, 227–228

Chase, Samuel, 57, 284–286

Chastellux, François Jean, marquis de, *Travels in North America*, 538–539, 595

Cherokee Indians: during Seven Years' War, 5; as British allies, 102–103, 105, 113, 117–118, 231n, 243–244, 453–454, 557; and Drayton, 118; and request for gunpowder, 118; willingness of, to support patriots, 118; representation of, as proxies, 130, 183, 269, 309, 322–323, 644; attack on southern backcountry by, 269–272, 485, 598; and patriot invasion, 273–276, 380, 416; and Andrew Williamson, 444n

Cherry Valley (NY), 420–423, 426, 648

Choctaw Indians, 454, 485, 560

Christian, William, 272

Church, Benjamin, 27–28, 135–141, 169, 184, 303, 376, 601, 606, 676

Cist, Charles, 302–303

"Citizen, A," 491, 493, 498

Citizenship: versus subjecthood, 626; versus "denizen," 627; gradations of, 627; and African Americans, 628, 631; and Indians, 628; and German mercenaries, 628–630; and Naturalization Act (1790), 628–632, 639; virtues of, 657; and whiteness, 661–662

Claiborne, William, 655

Clark, George Rogers: western campaign of, 416–418, 426, 550; and Henry Hamilton, 417, 426–428; capture of Kaskaskia by, 418; and Vincennes, 418, 427–428; newspaper accounts of, 424; and Cherry Valley, 426; legacy of, 432; and Iroquoia, 447–448; in early histories of the Revolution, 610; expedition of, 616

Clarkson, John: and *Virginia Gazette* (Purdie), 483n; and *Virginia Gazette* (Clarkson & Davis), 693–694

Clingan, William (*Pennsylvania Journal* distributor), 54

Clinton, George, 420, 440–441, 685

Clinton, James, 433–434

Clinton, Sir Henry: travels of, to North Carolina, 202; and Burgoyne, 356; and Philipsburg Proclamation, 463–465, 472, 563, 563n, 566; and Charleston, 470, 480; on African American support, 482; and Connolly, 516n; replacement of, by Carleton, 560

Cochrane, Alexander, 653

Cockburn, George, 651–652

Coercive Acts, 1, 30, 252, 396n, 694

Collet, John, 109–110, 128, 143n, 144, 160n, 172, 183, 286

slave insurrection, 83–85; and African Americans, 142, 148–149, 162, 244–245; and Indians, 142; retreat of, to Royal Navy, 142, 153, 163, 279–280; and runaway slaves, 142–143, 153, 277–283, 367; and use of Indians as proxies, 149–153, 162; and black regiment, 229–230, 245–249, 283; at Gwynn's Island, 245–246, 276–277; and smallpox epidemic, 245–246, 277–280; in *Fall of British Tyranny*, 280–283; in *M'Fingal*, 591; legacy of, in War of 1812, 651–654. *See also* Dunmore's proclamation

Dunmore's proclamation: response to, 55, 154–159, 165, 167–176, 228; and runaway slaves, 143–144, 153–154, 246; and newspaper coverage, 155–159, 195, 228, 230; and patriot suggestion of doing same, 171–172

Duryee, Jacob, 573–575

Early histories of the Revolution, 598–612
East India Company, 1
Eden, Robert, 82
Eden, William, 363. *See also* Carlisle Peace Commission
Edes, Benjamin, 16, 33, 36, 38, 675–676, 678, 696. *See also* Boston Gazette
"Eliobo," 506
Elmer, Ebenezer, 434
Emerson, Ralph Waldo, 25, 641, 666, 669, 673
Emistisiguo, 560
"Epaminondas," 300
Erie Canal, 659
Essex Gazette, 679
Essex Journal, 680
Essex Result (Parsons), 371–372
Estaing, Charles Hector Théodat, comte de, 467–470
"Eumenes" (Jacob Green), 506n
Evans, Israel, 437–438
Everett, Edward, 665–666, 669–670, 673
Exchanges (news-gathering method), 15–16, 68, 76–77; and creation of American unity, 110, 344; and preference for stories of British proxies, 500, 502–505; circularity of, 549n

Fairfax, Fernandino, 631–632
Fall of British Tyranny, The (Leacock), 280–283, 348–349
Faucitt, William, 215
Federalists, 642, 648
Feitz family, 514–516

Ferguson, Adam, 384. *See also* Carlisle Peace Commission
Finlay, Hugh, 34–36, 61, 70, 75
Fitch, Jabez, 140
Fithian, Philip Vickers, 154
Fleet, John, 678
Fleet, Thomas, 678
Fletchall, Thomas, 112–115, 117n
Folsom, John, 679
Foreign mercenaries: atrocities of, 20–21, 287–288; alleged British use of, 130n, 187. *See also* German mercenaries
Fort Johnston, 108–109, 143n, 144, 451, 585
Fort Pitt treaty, 382–383
Fort Ticonderoga, 52, 91, 98, 197, 256, 332–337, 339
Fort Washington (battle), 294–295
Foster, George, 236–237
Fowle, Daniel, 680
Fowle, Robert, 680
Fowle, Zechariah, 449, 677, 680n
Francis, Jacob, 173n
Franklin, Benjamin: on newspapers' importance, 11; and use of black propaganda, 18; and Constitutional Post Office, 33; on open press, 36; and government contracts, 37; on perceptions of printers, 37; apprentices of, 40, 680, 692; and Albany Plan, 68; on American unity, 98; and "Declaration of the Causes and Necessity of Taking up Arms," 123, 126; on British use of proxies, 126, 179–180, 286, 362, 401–403; on outbreak of war, 179; on German mercenaries, 229; and abolitionism, 236, 581–582, 636–639; on Articles of Confederation, 236, 636; and Declaration of Independence, 241–242, 665; on Cherokee attacks in southern backcountry, 269; on Continental Congress's addresses to German mercenaries, 291; and need for foreign alliance, 361; as ambassador to France, 400, 406; and children's book of wartime atrocities, 400–407, 464; on imagined Indian brutality, 505; and "Supplement to Boston *Independent Chronicle*" hoax, 505, 539–542, 550, 653–654; on Indians, 539–542; on Paxton Boys, 541; on Gnadenhutten, 543; and Treaty of Paris, 563–564; as president of Pennsylvania Abolition Society, 633–635; and "Retort Courteous," 635–637; as Sidi Mehemet Ibrahim, 638; and *Pennsylvania Gazette*, 686; and William Bradford, 688; and Stamp Act, 688; and Library Company, 695

Green, Anne Catherine, 692–693. *See also Maryland Gazette*

Green, Bartholomew, 677–678

Green, Frederick, 450, 692. *See also Maryland Gazette*

Green, John, 40

Green, Jonas, 40, 57, 692. *See also Maryland Gazette*

Green, Samuel, 450, 681, 692; and *Connecticut Journal*, 245n, 681. *See also Maryland Gazette*

Green, Thomas, 681; and *Connecticut Journal*, 245n, 681. *See also Connecticut Courant*

Green, Timothy, 681. *See also Connecticut Gazette*

Green, William, 192, 692

Greene, Nathanael: and *Pennsylvania Journal* subscription, 52; on "Declaration of the Causes and Necessity of Taking up Arms," 128n; on Continental army's desertions, 166; on British and German troops' plundering, 301–302; on war with Indians, 424, 433; on importance of press, 486–487, 512; on violence in South, 486–487; on African American troops, creation of, 553–555, 602; on evacuation of Charleston, 567–568; and abolitionism, 581–582

Greenleaf, Joseph, 208n

Green Mountain Boys, 91, 333

Grenville, Thomas, 563–565

Grieve, George, 538–539

Griffin, Frank, 573–575

Haitian Revolution, 642, 650–651, 662, 669–670

Haldimand, Frederick, 427

Hall, David, 686–687, 689. *See also Pennsylvania Gazette*

Hall, David, Jr., 687

Hall, Ebenezer, 679

Hall, Lyman, 225

Hall, Samuel, 40, 679, 681. *See also Pennsylvania Gazette*

Hall, William, 687

Hamilton, Alexander: on Sears's attack on Rivington's press, 178; and Jay, 456; and creation of African American troops, 456–458; and abolitionism, 457, 581–582; on British use of slaves, 457; on citizenship, 577–578; on loyalists and reintegration, 577–578; as "Phocion," 577–578

Hamilton, Henry: and instigation of Indians, 374–375, 392; representation of, as

proxy, 410, 445, 474, 539, 594, 672; and Clark, 417–418, 426–428; surrender of, 428; trial, 428–431; as prisoner, 431–432

"Hampden," 300

Hancock, John, 135, 141n, 175, 190n, 220, 240, 255, 296n, 354, 678

Hand, Edward, 375, 381–382, 420n, 520

Harnett, Cornelius, 197–205, 359

Harris, Joseph, 146, 162n, 183

Harrison, Benjamin, 547, 572–573

Harrison, William Henry, 643–645

Hart, Oliver, 113–119, 122, 453

Hartley, Thomas, 422

Hawthorne, Nathaniel, 11, 13–15, 669

Hayes, James, 692, 694; and *Dunlap's Maryland Gazette*, 450; and *Virginia Gazette, or, the American Advertiser,* 484n

Hazard, Ebenezer, 295

Heath, William, 336–337, 357n

Hector, Charles Théodat, comte d'Estaing, 467–470

Hendrick, Tobias, 50

Henry, John, 454

Henry, Patrick: and Virginia committee of correspondence, 29; on Bennington, 354n; on Cornstalk's murder, 376; and Clark, 416, 427–428; and abolitionism, 581–582

Henry, Samuel (*Pennsylvania Journal* distributor), 54

Herkimer, Nicholas, 350

Hessians. *See* German mercenaries

Hewes, Joseph, 133, 191, 227, 232

Hicks, John, 677

Hicks, John, Sr., 677

Hilliard-d'Auberteuil, Michel-René, 596–598

History of America (Morse), 607–608

Hodgson, William, 403

Holt, John, 675, 693; receives aid from Sons of Liberty, 38, 682; and relationship with John Hunter Holt, 39–40; and relationship with William Hunter, 39–40; and relationship with James Parker, 40, 682; on challenges of health, 74; on canceling of subscriptions, 74–75; on Gaine as turncoat, 294; and Oswald, 548; biographical information of, 682; relocations of, 685; and Goddard, 689. *See also New-York Journal*

Holt, John Hunter: and William Hunter, relationship with, 39; and John Holt, relationship with, 39–40; and confiscation of press, 147–149, 694. *See also Virginia Gazette, or the Norfolk Intelligencer*

Honyman, Robert: on plundering, 306;

on Cornstalk, 376n; on Wyoming Massacre, 415; on Henry Hamilton, 431n; on Sullivan's expedition, 443n; on southern strategy and slavery, 461; on Cornwallis and runaway slaves, 520n

Hooper, William, 55, 209n, 552n

Hopkins, Daniel, 679n

Hopkins, Stephen, 171–172, 471, 531n

Hopkinson, Francis, 630n

Horrower, John, 84

Houston, William Churchill, 46

Howe, John, 449

Howe, Richard, 286, 298, 319, 384

Howe, Robert, 56, 209n, 451

Howe, Sir William: pursues Continental army, 297–298; and Indians, 321; and Guy Johnson, 321; and Tryon, 321; and Germain, 329; and capture of Philadelphia, 329–330; and march to Philadelphia, 354–355; and occupation of Philadelphia, 355; in *M'Fingal*, 591

Howell, David, 547

Hubley, Adam, 434

Huddy, Joshua, 502, 505

Humphreys, James, Jr., 110, 138–139, 675, 688; as suspected loyalist, 41, 298–299, 689; follows British out of Philadelphia, 360; and William Bradford, 689; and Towne, 689; exile from and return to Philadelphia, 690. *See also Pennsylvania Ledger*

Hunter, William, 39–40, 693

Hunter, William, Jr., 694; as loyalist, 450, 693. *See also Virginia Gazette* (Dixon & Hunter)

Hutchings, Joseph, 153

Hutchinson, Thomas, 16, 67

Hutton, John (*Pennsylvania Journal* distributor), 51–52

"Impartial," 506

Impartial Chronicle, The (Livingston), 324–326

Independence: events leading up to, 187–189; and Moore's Creek Bridge, 203–205; and British use of foreign mercenaries, 223–229, 240, 247; and British use of Indians, 240, 247; and British use of slave insurrections, 247–249, 286, 300; and necessity to make foreign alliances, 328; and proxies, 389–390

Independent Chronicle, 443, 573, 676, 679

Independent Gazetteer, 548, 574, 690, 692

Independent Ledger, 443, 679

Indian attacks: fear of, 91–94, 96–97, 451–452; and British instigation, 104–106,

130–131, 134–135, 150–153, 548–549, 551; as false threat to patriots, 187; as patriot allies, 352–353; by British allies, on loyalists, 421

Indians: as patriot allies, 99–102, 265; as British proxies, 126, 286, 451, 542, 615; and Continental army, 234–235, 239–240, 291–292; at battle of the Cedars, 235–240; and exclusion, 271, 322–323, 382–384, 398–399, 587–588, 617, 619–620, 639–640, 657–659, 661–662, 665, 669–670, 673; military campaigns against, 275–276; and McCrea's death, 340–349; at Freeman's Farm, 355–356; "good," and lack of news coverage, 375–377, 474–475, 543, 606–607, 658–659; and Articles of Confederation, 381–382; and history of scalp bounties, 417; "civilizing" of, 586, 610–611; in *M'Fingal*, 589; representations of, in postwar literature, 589–598; in early histories of the Revolution, 610; and postwar frontier boundaries, 612–620, 643; and "conquest theory," 613; and postwar reliance on British, 614–616; and citizenship, 630; removal of, 661; at Lexington and Concord, 666. *See also* Brant, Joseph; *individual indigenous nations*

Inflation, 75, 475

"Integer" (Ambrose Serle), 319–320

Iroquois Indians. *See* Six Nations

Irvine, William, 544

Izard, Ralph, 567

Jackson, Andrew, 644–645, 655

Jackson, James, 562, 604, 633, 638

Jamaica, 528–529

Jasper, William, 267–269

Jay, John: and Hamilton, 178, 456; on Sears's attack on Rivington's press, 178n; on British use of proxies, 319; and news, 338, 487; on Schuyler, 338; and creation of African American troops, 456; and Treaty of Paris, 563; and abolitionism, 581–582

Jefferson, Isaac, 509n

Jefferson, Thomas: and abolitionism, 7, 253, 581–582; *Summary View of the Rights of British Americans*, 7, 66; and Virginia committee of correspondence, 29; "Declaration of the Causes and Necessity of Taking up Arms," 123–124; on Dunmore's proclamation, 154; on German mercenaries, 234; and Declaration of Independence, 234, 241–243, 246–247,

Lee, Francis Lightfoot, 55
Lee, John, 216–220, 224–226
Lee, Richard Henry: on communication networks, 26, 359; and Virginia committee of correspondence, 29; and *Pennsylvania Journal* subscription, 56–57; on threat of Indian attacks, 93–94; on raid of Holt's press, 148; on Dunmore, 154, 158, 159n, 174, 279; and independence, 225n, 241; and preamble to resolution on colonial government, 226–227; on Six Nations delegation to Congress, 231–232; on German mercenaries, 234, 312; and Charles Lee on slavery, 266n; "Drayton's proposal," 393–395; on Cornwallis, 512; on importance of press, 512
Leonard, Daniel ("Massachusettensis"), 27–28
"Leonidas," 444
Leslie, Alexander, 555; and runaway slaves, 507; Chesapeake raid, 507–508, 510; on smallpox, 523n; on German mercenaries, 558; and evacuation of Charleston, 560, 565–569, 571–572
Leslie, Samuel, 153
"Letters from a Farmer in Pennsylvania" (Dickinson), 690
Lewis, Andrew, 231n
Lewis, William, 685
Lexington and Concord (battles), 7, 25, 78–79; reaction to, in North America, 78–97; newspaper accounts of, 81–86
"Liberalis," 507n
Liberty Tree, 199n
Lillington, Alexander, 197, 205
Lincoln, Benjamin, 353n; and Charleston, 459, 489–490; and Savannah siege, 467–469; on African American troops, creation of, 480–481; and abolitionism, 581–582
Literacy rates, 58n
Livingston, Robert, 241–242, 581–582
Livingston, William: and day of fasting and thanksgiving, 211–212; address of, on German mercenaries, 234; *Impartial Chronicle*, 324–326, 328; on Burgoyne's proclamation, 343–344; "A New-Jersey Man," 343–344; and McCrea story, 346; on Dartmouth's correspondence with Dunmore, 464, 466; on abolitionism, 471, 581–582; sponsor of *New-Jersey Gazette* by, 691
London Coffee House, 37, 45, 70–71, 73, 688; description of, 63–65; as politi-
cal hub, 64; and news of independence, 255n. *See also* Bradford, William
Loudon, Samuel, 312, 351, 441, 482–483, 486, 684; and *The Deceiver Unmasked*, 205–206, 209; attack on print shop of, 206, 209–211; and restarting of paper in Fishkill, 293, 359, 449, 685. *See also New York Packet*
Louis XIV (king of France), 404
Louis XV (king of France), 5
Louis XVI (king of France), 363, 387
Lovell, James, 355, 474; on disruptions of communication networks, 358; on Indians, 416; on creation of black troops, 470–471; on fall of Charleston, 490
"Lover of True Justice, A," 506
Loyalists: in South Carolina backcountry, 112–116; in North Carolina backcountry, 133–135, 195; association of, with other proxies, 304, 579, 629, 657; newspaper publications of, 328, 339, 360, 376, 385, 395n, 484, 677–678, 682, 684–685, 686n, 690, 697–698; refugees of, from Georgia, 561–563; and reintegration, 576–579, 629, 657; versus other proxies, 579; and citizenship, 629
Lunt, Ezra, 680
Lyman, Simeon, 166–167

MacDonald, Donald, 685n; and battle at Moore's Creek Bridge, 196–197, 200–202; and *Royal South-Carolina Gazette*, 484, 698
Maclay, William, 632–633, 638
Madison, James, 508, 547; on fear of slave insurrections and publicity, 82, 146; and War of 1812, 649, 654, 657, 659
"Marcus Brutus," 336, 338n
Marion, Francis, 556, 559
Marshall, Christopher, 64, 202n, 333, 519n
Martin, Josiah: retreat of, to Fort Johnston, 108–109; and patriots' accusation of inciting slaves, 127–128, 143, 172, 183, 203, 286, 327, 367, 527; on loyalist support in North Carolina backcountry, 195–197, 200, 202; as "rebel," 208; in early histories of Revolution, 609
Martin, Laughlin, 95, 103
Maryland Assembly, 510–511
Maryland committee of safety, 152
Maryland emancipation, 531–533
Maryland Gazette, 692–693; on Dunmore and runaway slaves, 279–280; and end of run, 360; on Cornwallis and dying slaves, 523

Lexington and Concord, 78–82, 666; Indian involvement in, 79–80; plots of, uncovered, 79–80, 82–83, 106–108; fear of, following Lexington and Concord, 84–88, 103, 105–108; general fear of, 96–97, 172; British instigation of, 103–104, 108–110, 129–131; publication of, 140, 146, 527; as non-threatening to patriots, 187; in Declaration of Independence, 253–254, 258, 269, 540; Franklin critique of Articles and, 286, 636; as justification for exclusion, 286

Slavery: and advertisements, 13, 68; versus patriot claims of liberty, 99–100; and British use of slaves as proxies, 126, 286; and newspapers' printing of Dunmore's proclamation, 157–159; and runaway slaves, 162n, 170, 246, 267, 551–552, 584–585; and Articles of Confederation, 284–286, 636; and population numbers, 562n; and evacuation of Charleston, 565–569; entrenchment of, after Revolution, 582, 625, 660; and citizenship, 631; and slave trade, 632–633. *See also* Abolitionism; Slave insurrections

Slover, John, 545–549, 592–594

Smirke, Robert, 645–646

Smith, Richard, 165n, 314–315

Smith, William (N.J. farmer), 301

Smith, William (N.Y. loyalist), 207n

Smith, William Loughton, 600, 626–627, 633

Smyth, John, 160–161

"Soldier, A," 491

Sons of Liberty, 38, 176, 202, 280, 676, 682

South-Carolina and American General Gazette, 76, 274, 697; and fire, 360; and end of production, 450, 483; becomes *Royal Gazette*, 484; and use of slave labor, 697

South Carolina Assembly, 598; Sullivan's Island, commemoration of victory, 267; and creation of African American troops, 459, 480, 554, 602

South Carolina committee of safety, 170

South-Carolina Gazette, 40, 61, 695; and use of slave labor, 66, 697n; on slaves and Indians as British proxies, 94, 132; and interruption of production, 360; establishment of, 695–696; irregular production of, 696

South-Carolina Gazette, And Country Journal, 697

"Southern strategy": and communication networks, 448–451, 483, 487–488; and use of African Americans, 451; and use of Indians, 451; and slavery, 452–454, 460–461; in Charleston, 458–459; in Virginia, 460

Southwick, Solomon, 52, 681. *See also Newport Mercury*

Spain, 363

Spangler, Rudolph (*Pennsylvania Journal* distributor), 54

Squire, Matthew: and rumors of instigating slave insurrections, 143–146; and threatening of Holt, 144; and response about Harris, 146; and confiscation of Holt's press, 147–149

Stamp Act: politicization of newspapers by, 38, 61–62, 682, 689, 692, 696–698; and William Bradford, 688; and Franklin, 688

Stark, John, 353

St. Clair, Arthur, 256, 333, 337–338, 345

Steuart, Andrew, 694

Stiles, Ezra, 171; and *Common Sense*, 190n; on patriotism in Carolinas, 205; on Cherokee attacks in southern backcountry, 275; on Gwynn's Island, 280n; on Sullivan's expedition, 443n

Stirling, William Alexander, 280, 292

St. Leger, Barry: and Burgoyne's plan, 329; and Brant, 350; and battle of Oriskany, 350–352

St. Luke le Corne (Luc de la Corne), 92–93

Stockbridge Indians, 382; as patriot allies, 90, 322; and Continental army, 242–243, 289–290, 376–380; silence on, 377–378, 440, 528; as patriot allies, 439–440, 474–475, 606, 618, 658; and land encroachment, 618–619; removal of, to Wisconsin, 659

Stockton, Richard, 46

Stuart, Henry, 243, 270, 275–276

Stuart, John: on fear of slave insurrections, 85; and patriot response to negotiations with Indians, 97; and British use of Indians as allies, 102–103, 105, 127; exile of, to Saint Augustine, 113, 243; and rumors of British instigating Indian attacks, 117–118; confiscated letters of, published in newspapers, 127; on patriot newspapers, 184; on patriots' representation of Indians as British proxies, 599

Styner, Melchoir, 302–303

Sulley, Thomas (*Pennsylvania Journal* distributor), 52

Sullivan, John, 292, 410; attack on Iroquoia

by, 433–439, 447–448; and battle of Newtown, 436; on Indian allies, 440; in early histories of the Revolution, 606–607, 610

Sullivan's Island (S.C.): runaway camp on, 170, 267; building of fort on, 266–268; battle at, 267; role of, in slave trade, 267–268

Symmes, John Cleve, 413

Tarleton, Banastre, 499, 512–513, 551, 583

Tecumseh, 643–645

Temple, Josiah, 78–79

Tennent, William, 113–119

Tenskwatawa (Prophet), 643–645

Thacher, James, 415, 494n

Thomas, Isaiah: and *Essex Journal*, 40, 680; relocation of, to Worcester, 72, 678–679; on challenges of weather, 74; on N.C. Regulators, 208; *History of Printing in America*, 677, 681, 683, 691, 695–697; and printing of *Massachusetts Spy*, 677, 679n; and Hancock, 678; and patriot support, 678, 679n; on Gaine, 683–684. *See also Massachusetts Spy*

Thomas, Jonathan (*Pennsylvania Journal* distributor), 54

Thomson, Charles, 255, 614

Thornbrough, Edward, 162n

Tilghman, Tench, 521

Timothy, Elizabeth, 695–696

Timothy, Lewis, 695

Timothy, Peter, 469, 483; and *Gazette, of the State of South-Carolina*, 483, 696; biographical information of, 696; death of, 696; as patriot leader, 696. *See also South-Carolina Gazette*

Tinges, Henry-Walter, 680

Todd, John, 549–550

"To His Majesty George the Third" (Iredell), 254n

Tonyn, Patrick, 402, 561

"To the People of Ireland," 131

Towne, Benjamin, 40, 140, 181, 298; as loyalist, 359–360, 688–690; as patriot, 449, 688–690; and Goddard, 689; and Humphreys, 689–690. *See also Pennsylvania Evening Post*

Treaty of Amity and Commerce, 363; ratification of, 386–387; celebrations for, 387; and declaration of war on France, 400

Treaty of Paris, 563–565; and Indian allies, 564; British provisions of, 564; article 7 of, 564–565; and preliminary articles of

peace, 565, 570; news arrives of, 575–576; United States's inability to enforce, 614; article 4 of, 614–615

Trumbull, Benjamin, 280n

Trumbull, John (lawyer/poet), 604, 612. *See also M'Fingal* (Trumbull)

Trumbull, John (painter), 598

Trumbull, John (printer), 447, 681–682. *See also Norwich Packet*

Trumbull, Jonathan (governor of Connecticut), 307, 352–353

Trumbull, Joseph, 287

Tryon, William, 178, 183, 196, 209, 260n, 318, 321; and Regulators, 196, 208; hanging of, in effigy, 206–207, 210; as "rebel," 208; on need for crown newspaper, 293–294

Tucker, St. George, 669; on Connolly's capture, 516n; on Cornwallis and runaway slaves, 520; and abolitionism, 581–582

Tudor, William, 124–125, 190n, 296n

Tuscarora Indians, 332, 382, 396, 413, 436, 446; as patriot allies, 351, 439–440, 475, 543n, 658; at Saratoga, 356; and land encroachment, 618–619

Tye (former slave), 472–473; and raids on New Jersey, 497–498; and Philipsburg Proclamation, 498; and Huddy, 502

United States Magazine, 445, 464, 592, 690; on British use of proxies, 464; on African American citizenship, 592

Upton, Asa, 495

Vandeput, George, 178n

Vanderlyn, John, 598, 645–646

Varnum, James, 456n

Vergennes, Charles Gravier, comte de, 362–363

Vincennes, 418, 424, 427–429, 447, 616, 644

Virginia Assembly: on British raids and runaway slaves, 510; and manumissions, 582, 623–625; and African American citizenship, 623–624

Virginia committee of safety, 228n; on Dunmore's proclamation, 55; and Connolly's plans, 152

Virginia Convention, 142; on independence, 227–229; on Dunmore's proclamation, 228; on proxies, 233; and state constitution, 247

Virginia Gazette (Clarkson & Davis), 484n, 693–694

Virginia Gazette (Dixon & Hunter), 693; on

Dunmore's seizing of gunpowder, 83; on confiscation of Holt's press, 147; on Dunmore and smallpox epidemic, 246; on Clark, 425; relocation of, 483n

Virginia Gazette (Dixon & Nicolson), 493–494, 693; on Henry Hamilton, 430–431; relocation of, 483n; on battle of Waxhaws, 499–500; and end of production, 512

Virginia Gazette (Hayes), 484n, 694; on Gnadenhutten massacre, 538; on Indian raids in Pennsylvania frontier, 544, 549; and runaway slaves, 551–552; on Carleton's breach of Treaty of Paris, 573

Virginia Gazette (Nicolson & Prentis), 694; and runaway slaves, 551–552

Virginia Gazette (Pinkney), 693; on confiscation of Holt's press, 147; and direct addresses to slaves, 157; on Dunmore's proclamation, 157; on Connolly's plot, 161

Virginia Gazette (Purdie), 693; on Dunmore, 110, 156, 245n; on Squire, 145; on confiscation of Holt's press, 147; and "Minos," 156n; on Sears's attack on Rivington's press, 177n; on British use of proxies, 182–183; on Virginia Convention's stance for independence, 227; on threat by Cherokee and Creek Indians, 244; on Cherokee backcountry attacks, 272–273; on Cornstalk's murder, 376; and Clarkson, 483n

Virginia Gazette (Rind), 693

Virginia Gazette, or the Norfolk Intelligencer, 694; on British use of slave insurrections, 142–143; on British use of Indian attacks, 144; on Squire, 144; on Joseph Harris, 146

Virginia House of Delegates, 426

Walker, Quok, 531–533
Wallace, Adam, 499
Ward, Artemas, 217
Ward, Samuel, 137n, 168, 191
War of 1812: and British instigation of Indians, 649, 654–655; as compared to Revolutionary War, 650; and Philipsburg Proclamation, 651; and Dunmore's proclamation, 651–654; and runaway slaves, 652–653; and Cornwallis, 653; and slave insurrections, 654–655; and burning of Washington, D.C., 656

Warren, James, 99, 101, 124–125, 135, 138, 336–337
Warren, Joseph, 27–28, 66

Warren, Mercy Otis: on Church's arrest, 137n; *History of the Rise, Progress, and Termination of the American Revolution,* 608–611, 645
Warren, Winslow, 611
Washington, George, 24, 60, 269, 304, 553; and *Pennsylvania Journal* subscription, 52; assumption of command by, 110–111, 123; and narrative of Revolutionary War, 110–111; on Church's arrest, 137; and Connolly's plans, 149, 152, 160; on Dunmore's proclamation, 155, 159, 168–169, 174, 283; and army's professionalization, 164–165, 292; and desertions, 166–167; and African Americans in Continental army, 173–176; and Boston siege, 188, 197–198, 205; on *Common Sense,* 189; on German mercenaries, 217, 220, 288–289, 300–301, 305, 313; on George Merchant, 220; and relations with Indians, 231–232; on battle at Cedars, 237; on Indians in Continental army, 242–243, 289–290; general orders of, 264–265, 312; and raid on Trenton, 265, 308–310; on Stockbridge Indians, 289, 440, 618–619; on Congressional addresses to German mercenaries, 291; on battle at Long Island, 291–292; and occupation of New York City, 294; on Continental army's plundering, 296n; retreat of, from New York City, 297–298; on morale, 307–308; on Continental army numbers, 307–308; and crossing of the Delaware, 307–309; to Passamaquoddy Indians, 308–309; to St. John Indians, 308–309; on Cherokee attacks in southern backcountry, 309; on plundering, 312; and prisoners, 312, 352; and *Impartial Chronicle,* 324, 362n; and newspaper for Continental army, 338–339, 449, 691; on British use of proxies, 350, 352, 456; on battle of Bennington, 354n; and battle of Brandywine, 355; and Saratoga news, 357; on Carlisle Peace Commission, 391; on attacking Iroquoia, 424, 432–435, 437; on war with Indians, 424; on creation of black regiments, 455–456; and slaves gone to British, 510; and march to Virginia, 513–514; and Yorktown news, 521–522; and Indian allies, 543n; and visit to northern frontier, 543n; on Crawford, 547; and citizenship for German mercenaries, 559; and article 7 of Treaty of Paris, 571–572; and Carleton, 572–573; return of, to New

York City, 575; retirement of, 576; and abolitionism, 581–582; as president of United States, 630, 632, 640–641; farewell address of, 641–642. *See also* Sullivan, John
Washington, Harry, 555, 567
Washington, Lund, 152, 169
Washington, Martha, 64
Watkins, Francis, 551–552
Watson, Ebenezer, 681. *See also Connecticut Courant*
Waxhaws (battle), 499–500
Wayne, Anthony, 513, 557–558, 560
Weedon, George, 511
Wells, John, Jr., 76; and *Royal Gazette* (Charleston), 484, 698; *South-Carolina and American General Gazette* becomes *Royal Gazette*, 484; military service of, 697–698
Wells, Robert (Cherry Valley victim), 420–421, 447
Wells, Robert (printer), 484n; biographical information of, 697; and slavery, 697. *See also South-Carolina and American General Gazette*
Wharton, Thomas, 689
"Whig, A," 506
Whipple, William, 238–239, 454
White, James, 679
White Eyes, 365, 377, 382, 616
Willet, Marinus, 352, 515, 576
Williams, Jarrett, 273–275
Williamson, Andrew, 272, 444n; on Savannah and slavery, 453; on John Stuart and British use of Indians, 453n; on southern strategy and slavery, 455
Williamson, David, 535, 538–539, 543, 586, 603
Willis, Nathaniel, 676, 679. *See also Independent Chronicle*
Wilmington committee of safety, 109–110, 694

Wilson, James, 295
Witherspoon, John, 46, 286
Withington, Peter, 49–51, 60, 62–63, 73, 97, 221, 334, 672
Wöchentliche philandelische Staatsbot, Der, 354n, 686n
Wolcott, Oliver, 190n, 613–614, 619
Women: as printers, 41; subscribe to *Pennsylvania Journal,* 44; Abigail Adams on, 185; as proxy enemy, 185–186; as printers, 305, 678, 680–681, 691–693, 695–697; and exclusion, 662
Wood, James, 149–150
Woodford, William, 159, 163, 653
Wright, James, 451, 560
Wyandot Indians, 149, 391, 549–550; as British allies, 228, 535; and Delaware Indians, 535, 537; hostilities in frontier, 544; postwar negotiations with Congress, 613–614; and War of 1812, 653–654
Wyoming Massacre: and Wyoming Valley boundary disputes, 59, 132, 165n, 411; Zebulon Butler's account of, 411–412; newspaper accounts of, 412–413; Avery's account of, 413–414; and *"the hatchet"* myth, 414–415, 606–607, 610–611, 649; and British-Indian relations, 415–416; and Cherry Valley, 422; anniversary of, 434–435; in *Travels in North America,* 595; in early histories of the Revolution, 606, 610; in *Gertrude of Wyoming,* 646; legacy of, 648–649
Wythe, George, 240, 247; on German mercenaries, 234–235; on Clark, 417

York, Joseph, 540
Yorktown (siege): and Cornwallis's surrender, 513, 521; newspaper stories of, 513–526; and runaway slaves, 517–521
Young, Thomas, 208n, 678

Zenger, John Peter, 682